50TH EDITION

KOVELS'
Antiques &
Collectibles
PRICE GUIDE 2018

BLACK DOG
& LEVENTHAL
PUBLISHERS
NEW YORK

Cover design by Christopher Lin and Carlos Esparza

Front cover photographs, from left to right:
Clock, Nelson, George, Ball, brass, wood, 1949
Toy, cat, walking, tin, clockwork, Japan, 5 In.
Roseville, Peony, vase, yellow flowers, handles, 8 ¼ In.

Back cover photographs, top to bottom:
Bottle, flask, Washington & Taylor, yellow olive, c.1850, Qt.
Furniture, chair, Windsor, elm, plank seat, 1700s, 39 In.
Holt-Howard, cruet, Pixieware, Russian salad dressing, c.1959, 7 In.

Spine:
Jewelry, pin, sunburst, 24 diamonds, seed pearls, 1 ¼ in.

Authors' photographs © Kim Ponsky (top) and Alex Montes de Oca (bottom)

Black Dog & Leventhal Publishers
Hachette Book Group
1290 Avenue of the Americas
New York, NY 10104

www.hachettebookgroup.com
www.blackdogandleventhal.com

First Edition: September 2017

Black Dog & Leventhal Publishers is an imprint of Hachette Books, a division of Hachette Book Group.
The Black Dog & Leventhal Publishers name and logo are trademarks of Hachette Book Group, Inc.

The publisher is not responsible for websites (or their content) that are not owned by the publisher.
The Hachette Speakers Bureau provides a wide range of authors for speaking events.
To find out more, go to www.HachetteSpeakersBureau.com or call (866) 376-6591.

Print book interior design by Sheila Hart Design, Inc.

ISBN: 978-0-316-47194-7

Printed in the United States of America

WW
10 9 8 7 6 5 4 3 2 1

BOOKS BY RALPH AND TERRY KOVEL

American Country Furniture, 1780–1875

A Directory of American Silver, Pewter, and Silver Plate

Kovels' Advertising Collectibles Price List

Kovels' American Antiques 1750–1900

Kovels' American Art Pottery

Kovels' American Collectibles 1900–2000

Kovels' American Silver Marks, 1650 to the Present

Kovels' Antiques & Collectibles Fix-It Source Book

Kovels' Antiques & Collectibles Price Guide

Kovels' Bid, Buy, and Sell Online

Kovels' Book of Antique Labels

Kovels' Bottles Price List

Kovels' Collector's Guide to American Art Pottery

Kovels' Collector's Guide to Limited Editions

Kovels' Collectors' Source Book

Kovels' Depression Glass & Dinnerware Price List

Kovels' Dictionary of Marks— Pottery and Porcelain, 1650 to 1850

Kovels' Guide to Selling, Buying, and Fixing Your Antiques and Collectibles

Kovels' Guide to Selling Your Antiques & Collectibles

Kovels' Illustrated Price Guide to Royal Doulton

Kovels' Know Your Antiques

Kovels' Know Your Collectibles

Kovels' New Dictionary of Marks— Pottery and Porcelain, 1850 to the Present

Kovels' Organizer for Collectors

Kovels' Price Guide for Collector Plates, Figurines, Paperweights, and Other Limited Edition Items

Kovels' Quick Tips: 799 Helpful Hints on How to Care for Your Collectibles

Kovels' Yellow Pages: A Resource Guide for Collectors

The Label Made Me Buy It: From Aunt Jemima to Zonkers— The Best-Dressed Boxes, Bottles, and Cans from the Past

BOOKS BY TERRY KOVEL AND KIM KOVEL

Kovels' Antiques & Collectibles Price Guide

INTRODUCTION

It's really our 50th price book! And time has changed what we collect, prices we pay, what is "best," and what has dropped in price. This has been another year of the weak "collecting economy" that started in 2008. However, prices are a little better than last year, and record prices were set as bidders fought for the best of the best, especially the best of collectibles, art made after 1950, and sculpture and pottery made after 2000. (See page ix for a list of this year's record prices.) The changes in the way art and antiques are collected, thanks to the Internet, cell phones, tablets, computers, and other electronic ways to buy and sell have taken over the action. Some changes are caused by lifestyle and modern design. Older collectors (now over 60) wanted collections of as many different toys or plates as possible or a house furnished with only country furniture. A collection of good to excellent examples was the goal. Now a single perfect piece is the goal. There is interest in "design," and there are museum exhibits and collectors who display and explain modern sculptures, unfamiliar furniture, even teapots or corkscrews as good or bad "design." It's a hard term to define since everything is designed by someone. But it seems to include what today is considered to be great design in any category, including painting, sculpture, jewelry, kitchen tools, cars, packaging, advertising, clothing, and more. That has shifted some buyers' attention in the antiques and vintage collectors' world to great graphics, unique jewelry, unusual chairs and tables, glass, silver, pottery, and even medical devices. But the most apparent change of interest in the 2017 era is condition. This has made top price for many antiques, especially for refinished furniture, repainted mechanical banks, and the amount of original paint on other metal collectibles, as well as bottles, glass, and ceramics that have no chips, cracks, flaws, or repairs, no matter how old. And there is also interest in repaired pieces from the 1700s and early 1800s, like stapled export porcelain. "Go-withs" and "make-dos" are collecting categories. Buyers want broken goblet stems made into candleholders or damaged 18th-century porcelain teapots with silver spouts added as replacements. It may be just part of the way being "green" and recycling has influenced the concerns of collectors. We can brag that antiques collectors were the first serious recyclers.

Since 1953, the year we published our first book, the antiques world has gone from one or two antiques shows in a city per year to one almost every week. But with so many new online ways to buy and sell antiques—and the weak economy—many shows have been discontinued. Auctions of expensive antiques used to be held in New York, Chicago, and a few other large cities. Small towns had "farm auctions" held outside a farmhouse, or a local auctioneer who sold antiques, tractors, and tools in the barn. There were no malls, no Internet shops, sales, or auctions. Today many major cities have auction houses that run sales at their galleries with online access that reaches buyers in every country. And major auctions are also online from London, Paris, Hong Kong, and sometimes from the home of a special collection. Every day there are dozens of auctions you can watch and bid on from your computer or phone. And there are many online auction sites that advertise, list coming auctions, then handle the competing bids in real time. There are also timed auctions, usually for one type of collectible like bottles, that are online for a specified length of time, usually about two weeks.

Our first book, *Kovels' Dictionary of Marks: Pottery & Porcelain*, was one of just 60 titles about antiques announced that year. In 1969, there were about 200 new books. Now, few books about collectibles and antiques are published, but much old and new information is found on the Internet. Much of the information found in old books, company catalogs, and advertisements can be found online. Our previous years of newspaper columns and questions, newsletters, special reports, books of marks, and other writings are now on our website, Kovels.com. More can be found with an Internet search. Look for current Kovel columns in your local newspapers.

The economic problems that started in 2008 with the stock market crash and housing bust spread to other investments, including antiques and collectibles. There is still a saying that if you buy antiques, they go up in value every year and are a good investment. That is only half true. If you buy the right antiques and sell at the right time, they sell for higher prices than you paid, even when you factor in inflation. Consider this: Our first price book lists a Diamond Dyes cabinet for $50. In the early months of 2008, the same cabinet sold for $1,112 to $2,633. In 2012, two Diamond Dyes cabinets were listed, one at $540, the other $550—very low prices. In 2013, common Diamond Dyes cabinets were $407, $1,320, and $1,540. In 2014, the cabinet featuring Children with Balloons was $896, the Governess was $1,560, and Washer Woman was $720. In 2015, Evolution of Woman was $360; Maypole, $1,596; Children with Balloons, $2,400; and Blond Fairy, $1,112. Last year Children Skipping Rope was $617; Children with Balloons was $472; Governess, $531; Maypole, $531; Prism, $660; and Washer Woman with a blue background, $1,680. And in this book there are two cabinets: Evolution of Woman sold for $423 and Washer Woman with a blue background sold for $495. There are twelve original designs used on the tin fronts of these cabinets. The cabinets have been so popular there are now fake cabinets in a slightly smaller size and copies of the tin panel from the cabinet door are being sold as a vintage sign.

There seem to be more shows closing or joining other shows and there are many more auction bidders because of the added activities online. Almost every auction is online as well as on the phone and most also have a live group of bidders at the sale. But many auctions end up with unsold pieces. Even eBay is selling about one-third of the offered antiques.

It has become more difficult to sell vintage collections of figurines, small advertising items like tape measures, or glass shoes. Pressed glass is priced so low it is now a bargain and selling a bit better. Carnival glass rarities are hitting all-time highs while common pieces are difficult to sell. In 2012, prices leveled for things with international appeal, like Chinese porcelain and ivory. The best pieces are high priced, and common pieces are selling for the decorative value.

The endangered species laws for the sale of antique and new ivory have caused great confusion. New rules from the U.S. Fish and Wildlife Service went into effect July 6, 2016. They prohibit the importation of most African elephant ivory except for items made with ivory parts, such as musical instruments used in orchestras, items that are part of a traveling exhibition, a household move or inheritance (with special criteria), and ivory for law enforcement or scientific purposes. Also exempt are furniture, firearms, and other antiques that have less than seven ounces of ivory. "Bona fide" antiques (age proven by a professional appraisal or verifiable document) are exempt as well. But most African elephant ivory, including antique ivory, still can't be imported or sold across state lines. We tried to list the parts of the law that affect collectors, but we suggest you read the long and complicated regulations at https://10172-presscdn-0-75-pagely.netdna-ssl.com/wp-content/uploads/2016/06/final-rule-african-elephant-4d.pdf. Some ivory items, including antiques, have been seized and crushed because some feel allowing anything ivory to be sold suggests that ivory is valuable and living elephants are being killed for profit. Many other EPA laws forbid the sale of parts of endangered species, elephants (ivory), rhinoceros (horns), eagles (feathers), tigers and other cats (skins), and even some types of turtles (shells). There is also pressure to do what is politically correct and this may cause an unexpected legal problem even if it is an historic item. Sales of vintage Ku Klux Klan items, caricatures of African, Irish, Chinese, Indian, and Jewish people on postcards or joke figurines are criticized and result in bad publicity or removal from a sale. Beware of anything that mentions Muslims or their religion in a derogatory manner. Legal auctions of historic antique guns caused controversy and unpleasant publicity as the laws covering guns, ammunition, and even antique firearms are being argued by many government and protest groups.

From 2013 to 2015, Chinese bidding slowed down for all but top-quality pieces. From 2008 to 2016, Hummel, Royal Doulton figurines and character jugs, "country furniture" with peeling paint, and "brown furniture" like period Chippendale desks have gone way down in value. And by 2016 the auction houses led the way to accepting only higher-priced items. Sotheby's and Christie's won't sell antiques or art worth less than thousands of dollars in their important sales. Some advertising auctions want items over $500 or $1,000. Large advertising signs, enameled metal signs, die-cut cardboard advertising, auto-related pieces, even small oil cans and other small tins with great graphics are up but only if in very good to excellent condition. Rock 'n' roll and travel posters still sell well.

Unfortunately many items are repaired and restored before being sold and the only way to know this is to contact a person before the sale and ask. It is often not part of the catalog description. Malls and shops have been closing but many shows and shops seem to have better prices than they could get ten years ago. Collectors and dealers agree that "good stuff sells" and well-run shows, shops, and sales are doing "OK." Usable furniture in good condition and decorative "smalls" are selling for expected prices. And 1890s oak dining tables that were hard to sell are attracting more buyers because of the low prices. The "best" of every type of antique or collectible is in demand. Some auctions get prices that are close to retail. But easy-to-find antiques are at about one-third of retail because the Internet has revealed the large, worldwide supply. Art (including pictures) have totally flipped. Norman Rockwell, portraits, and Warhol pictures are selling for thousands of dollars. Rembrandt, Van Gogh, and Renoir have gone down from the multi-million dollar records.

There is still a problem with bids from China. Some bidders refused to honor their bids and instead asked for a price reduction—or just didn't pay for or pick up a purchase. Often the sale price is reported online at the time of the auction bid, but there is rarely a public announcement that the bid was not honored. Most auction houses selling expensive art and antiques now require a cash deposit before the sale that will be forfeited if a buyer does not honor a bid.

Kovels' Antiques & Collectibles Price Guide 2018 has current, reliable information, plus edited content. The book has 2,500 new color photographs, 760 categories, black and white pictures, plus 55 photographs in the center section report and the record price report, and 20,000 prices. You will also find more than 200 added facts of interest and tips about care and repair. Each photograph is shown with a caption that includes the description, price, and source. The book has color tabs and color-coded paragraphs that make it easy to find listings, and it uses a modern, readable typestyle. Paragraphs introduce separate price categories. They give history and descriptions that help identify an unknown piece. We make some changes in the paragraphs every year to indicate new owners, new distributors, or new information about production dates. This year we made updates to 25 paragraphs, many of which tell of the sale or closing of a company. All of the antiques and collectibles priced here were offered for sale during the past year, most of them in the United States. Other prices came from sales that accepted bids from all over the world. Almost all auction prices given include the buyer's premium, because that is part of what the buyer paid. Very few include local sales tax and the extra charges involving phone bids, online bids, credit cards, or shipping.

READ THIS FIRST

This is a book for the buyer and the seller. We check prices; visit shops, shows, and flea markets; read hundreds of publications and catalogs; check Internet sales, auctions, and other online services; and decide which antiques and collectibles are of most interest to most collectors in the United States. We concentrate on the average pieces in any category. Sometimes high-priced items are included so you can see that special rarities are very valuable. Prices of some items were very high because a major collection by a well-known collector of top-quality pieces were auctioned. Auction houses like to have huge sales of things that belonged to one well-known collector or expert. Many catalogs now feature the name and biography of the collector and advertise the auction with the collectors name in all the ads. This year there were major sales of collections of toys, banks, guns, art pottery and exceptional artists' personal collections. A few famous bottle collections were auctioned at online-only bottle auctions. Single collector auctions of dolls, Victorian glass, lamps with leaded glass shades, and Tiffany of all types were well advertised and prices were high.

Most of this book's listed pieces are less than $10,000. The lowest price is $1 for a Curious George PEZ candy container. The highest price is an Ohr vase, twisted body, ruffled rim, ribbon handles, feather glaze, stamped, 12 inches, $87,500. The largest, an architectural mantel, carved walnut, England, mid 1800s, 128 x 122 inches sold for $3,960. The smallest was an Akro Agate marble with corkscrew, blue, green, red, and yellow glass. It was ⅝ inches, made in the 1940s, and sold for $55.

Many unusual, unique, and weird things are included. This year, we list a trunk for transporting human blood, by Hollinger Corp., $393; an architectural marble water closet, by S. Wagner, $3,500; a souvenir statue of a Hawaiian Hubba hula girl, topless, wearing a string skirt, from the 1940s, $190; a medical prosthetic stump, boot, shoe leather, 1800s, $403; a bronze doorknocker penis shape, $1,952; and a bottle prototype of an Indian maiden, painted wood, 1865, $2,340.

Of major interest today, and getting the highest prices, are antique guns and ammunition, the best of modern furniture and modernist jewelry by artists like Art Smith or Bertoia. Early comic books in excellent condition are selling at high prices and the comics that are the first appearances of Batman, Superman, and other superheroes or first issues like Action No. 1 are selling for thousands of dollars. Original art for the covers of important comic books or magazines is selling as art, not collectibles. A Norman Rockwell study for a painting sold for over $1 million. Daniel Boone items are way down but Betty Boop collectibles are up in price. The biggest surprise is oil cans. Good graphics bring very high prices.

There are still bargains to be had, some that have been emerging as "collectibles" over the last ten years. Big is still "big." Groups of small figurines or sets of plates are very hard to sell. Large-scale accent pieces with colors and lines that blend in with modern furnishings—pieces like huge crocks, floor vases, centerpieces, bronze sculptures, large posters, and garden statuary—attract decorators as well as the owners of large homes. Blue and white, the colors favored in the 17th and 18th centuries, are back. Anything from clothes and glass to ceramics and furniture in the "newest style" between the 1950s and 2010 is hot. They are all going up in price and attracting new, younger buyers. Iron objects like bookends, doorstops, pots and pans, even snow eagles and carnival shooting targets are getting harder to find and sell quickly. But costume jewelry is the most popular item we see selling at shows and online. Prices for pieces marked with important makers' names can sell for as much as $1,500 to $2,500. Unmarked pieces of jewelry are bargains when compared to new store prices. A few very popular collectibles of the past, like Roseville and Rookwood pottery, Mexican silver jewelry, and almost any colored glass have come down in price for all but the largest and most important pieces.

The meltdown price of sterling silver the last few years made it profitable to destroy many pieces. Hundreds of coin silver items, especially spoons and no-name sterling silver serving dishes and flatware, disappeared in the meltdown craze. Sterling silver by well-known companies or designers like Tiffany, Gorham, and Liberty now get top dollar. And very modern unfamiliar shapes make tea services saleable at high prices. Ordinary traditional services are low priced. Almost all coin silver spoons and serving pieces that were not destroyed sell for a little less than melt-down price even if in perfect, useable condition.

Art as investment is the latest trend for millionaires and billionaires. Prices of very important art have been rising faster than most traditional investments like real estate or stocks and bonds. And the buyer has the added prestige of great taste and sophistication and bragging rights for owning a one-of-a-kind masterpiece. Highest price for a famous painting this year was a 1982 untitled painting by Jean-Michel Basquiat, a face in the shape of a skull, $110.5 million. Quality and works of recognized contemporary artists sell high—because collectors consider it an "investment" that will increase in value. Newly popular are works by contemporary studio potters that are made in non-traditional shapes. Teapots and vases are not made to be used, but are one-of-a-kind, large, and often colorful sculptures. Tiffany lamps have become so expensive there are now rising prices for all other leaded glass lamps like Handel, Pairpoint, Moe Bridges, and Pittsburgh. Fifties and after mixed metal furniture by Paul Evans is setting records. Wooden furniture by George Nakashima is popular and expensive. Authentic Western and American Indian items are steadily rising in price. Even some souvenirs made for tourists are wanted. There is more interest and rising prices for TV, radio, space exploration, and computer collectibles. Unique celebrity-related photographs, autographs, clothing, or belongings like baseballs or guitars can start bidding wars if the celebrity is still remembered by the bidders. Vintage watches by Rolex and Patek Philippe are in demand and prices are getting higher, especially for those made after 1926, when the first waterproof models were made. Many are bought to wear, not just to display. Additions to the auction sales that started less than ten years ago are designer purses by makers like Hermès or Chanel and special edition sneakers by Nike and other name brands. These are selling for hundreds to thousands of dollars and are not really collected but often are bought to use or to resell to make a profit.

Kovels' Antiques & Collectibles Price Guide prices have gotten younger over the past 50 years. Most items in our original book were made before 1860, so they were more than a century old. Today we list pieces made as recently as 2010, and there is great interest in furniture, glass, ceramics, and good design made since 1950.

The book is more than 500 pages long and crammed full of prices and photographs. We try to have a balanced format—not too many items that sell for over $5,000. We list a few very expensive pieces so you can realize that a great paperweight may cost $10,000 but an average one is only $25. Nearly all prices are from the American market for the American market. Only a few European sales are reported. We don't include prices we think result from "auction fever." We do list verified bargains.

There is an index and cross references. Use them often. It includes categories and much more. For example, there is a category for Celluloid. Most celluloid will be there, but a toy made of celluloid may be listed under Toy and also indexed under Celluloid. There are also cross-references in the listings and in the paragraphs. But some searching must be done. For example, Barbie dolls are in the Doll category; there is no Barbie category. And when you look at "doll, Barbie," you find a note that "Barbie" is under "doll, Mattel, Barbie" because Mattel makes Barbie dolls and most dolls are listed by maker.

All photographs and prices are new. Antiques and collectibles pictured are items that were offered for sale or sold for the amount listed in 2016–2017. Auction prices include the buyer's premium. Wherever we had extra space on a page, we filled it with tips about the care of collections and other useful information. Don't discard this book. Old Kovels' price guides can be used in the coming years as a reference source for price changes and for tax, estate, and appraisal information.

The prices in this book are reports of the general antiques market. As we said, every price in the book is new. We do not estimate or "update" prices. Prices are either realized prices from auctions or completed sales, a few are asking prices. We know that a buyer may have negotiated an asking price to a lower selling price, but we sometimes report asking prices. We do not pay dealers, collectors, or experts to estimate prices. If the price is from an auction, it includes the buyer's premium but prices do not include sales tax. If a price range is given, at least two identical items were offered for sale at different prices. Price ranges are found only in categories like Pressed Glass, where identical items can be identified. Some prices in *Kovels' Antiques & Collectibles Price Guide* may seem high and some low because of regional variations, but each price is one you could have paid for the object somewhere in the United States. Internet prices from sellers' ads or listings are avoided. Because so many non-collectors sell online but know little about the objects they are describing, there can be inaccuracies in descriptions. Sales from well-known Internet sites, shops, and sales, carefully edited, are included.

If you are selling your collection, do not expect to get retail value unless you are a dealer. Wholesale prices for antiques are 30 to 40 percent of retail prices. The antiques dealer must make a profit or go out of business. Internet auction prices are less predictable—because of an international audience and "auction fever," prices can be higher or lower than retail.

RECORD PRICES

Record prices for antiques and collectibles make news every year. We report those that relate to the entries in this book. We do not include record prices for works of art that are often seen in museums, like oil paintings, antique sculptures, or very recent work by modern artists unless the artist also worked in decorative arts. Our list is a snapshot of the collectors' market.

ADVERTISING

Gas sign: $85,400 for a Polly Gas sign, single-sided porcelain, neon skin only, diecut, two-pieces attached at center, 74 x 48 in. Sold July 23, 2017, by Morphy Auctions, Denver, Pennsylvania.

CLOCK & WATCHES

Automaton clock: $998,250 for an automaton musical clock made in England, tall pagoda shape on black wood block base, weighing 100 lbs., Roman hour numerals, plays two different tunes on a nest of eight bells, plays every two hours, 18th century, 50 in. tall. Fontaine's Auction Galleries, Pittsfield, Massachusetts.

GLASS

Lacy salt: $35,100 for a lacy period Lyre covered salt, opaque soft violet blue with subtle mottling, Boston & Sandwich Glass Co., 1830–1845, 2 x 3¼ in., extremely rare CD-4. Jeffrey S. Evans, Mt. Crawford, Virginia.

Lacy period Lyre covered salt: $35,100.

MISCELLANEOUS

Any firearm: $2,466,000 for a "Divine Gun," a musket made in China for the Qianlong emperor, elm wood curved stock and fore-stock, cast iron barrel, inlaid with gold, silver, and copper, separate cast iron muzzle, incised "Supreme Grade Number One," 5 ft. 9 ½ in. Sotheby's, London.

Apple-1 prototype computer: $815,000 for an Apple-1 Celebration Edition computer built by Steve Jobs and Steve Wozniak in 1976. Charitybuzz auction, New York. ("Celebration Edition" is different because it's manually soldered on a blank PC board rather than a green board.)

Campaign flag: $275,000 for an 1856 campaign flag for President James Buchanan with his portrait, stripes, stars circling a central star, 21 ½ x 15 in. Heritage Auctions, Dallas, Texas. Previous record: $95,600 set November 2009, for an 1860

President James Buchanan 1856 campaign flag: $275,000.
Roderick scrimshaw whale's tooth: $180,000.

John Breckinridge portrait flag, at Jeff R. Bridgman American Antiques, York County, Pennsylvania.

Carte-de-visite card, image of its type: $175,000 for an 1862 signed carte-de-visite of Abraham Lincoln seated at a table, taken by Mathew Brady in Washington, D.C., with an inscription on the back by John Hay, presidential secretary. Heritage Auctions, Dallas, Texas.

Disney animation cel: $59,750 for a Disney animation cel from the 1937 Walt Disney film *Snow White and the Seven Dwarfs*, the scene is the Evil Queen asking, "Mirror, mirror on the wall…who is the fairest one of all?" framed, matted, 15 x 12 in. Heritage Auctions, Beverly Hills, California.

Handbag: $379,261 for a Hermes Birkin 35 bag with matte white crocodile skin, strap loops, 18K gold buckles and 10 carats of diamonds, 35 x 25 x 18 in.. Christie's, Hong Kong.

M4 Enigma machine: $463,500 for the rarest of all Enigma machines, the M4 used by the German Navy during World War II, fully operational, dates from 1943. Bonhams, New York.

Mary Lincoln memorabilia: $100,000 for Mrs. Lincoln's jet black silk mourning dress ensemble. Heritage Auctions, Dallas, Texas.

Medal honoring Henry Clay: $346,000 for an 1852 medal honoring Secretary of State Henry Clay, struck by the U.S. Mint, 30 ounces, solid California gold, 3 ½-inch diameter. Heritage Auctions, Dallas, Texas.

Roderick scrimshaw whale's tooth: $180,000 for a scrimshawed whale's tooth by W.L. Roderick, titled "In Shore Whaling The Death," picturing a detailed whaling scene, inscribed "The Tooth of A Sperm Whale Captured March 30th 1855," signed W.L. Roderick, 8 ½ in. Eldred's Auction Gallery, East Dennis, Massachusetts.

PAINTINGS & PRINTS

Banksy print: $104,750 for the screen print "Girl with Balloon," by Banksy, 2004, signed and dated in black ink, numbered, certificate of authenticity, unframed, 25 ⅞ x 19 in. Forum Auctions, London, England.

Norman Rockwell study: $1,332,500 for the oil on photographic paper, Study for Triple Self Portrait, by Norman Rockwell, his first cover for Saturday Evening Post, published February 13, 1960, 11 ½ x 9 ¼ in. Heritage Auctions, Dallas, Texas.

Painting by Jean-Michel Basquiat/American artist at auction: $110,500,000 for the Jean-Michel Basquiat, "Untitled" painting of a face in the shape of a skull, 1982. Sotheby's, New York.

PAPER

Houdini poster: $114,000 for a Harry Houdini poster picturing Houdini performing his famous Water Torture Cell escape. Printed in London in 1912, 40 x 88 in. Potter & Potter, Chicago.

Original American comic art: $717,000 for the original cover by underground comic artist Robert Crumb, Fritz the Cat, ink on Bristol board, 11 x 12 ½ in. Heritage Auctions, Dallas, Texas.

POTTERY & PORCELAIN

Kentucky stoneware: $143,750 for a stoneware pitcher incised with cobalt blue bird-on-branch designs, applied and impressed decoration, stamped "E.H. Wood," and the date "1840," tooled collar, and ribbed strap handle, 3 gallon, 15 ½ in. Crocker Farm, Sparks, Maryland.

Ohr pottery: $87,500 for a George Ohr vase with ribbon handles, in-body twist and ruffled rim, raspberry, purple, green, and gunmetal pigeon feather glaze, stamped G.E. OHR Biloxi, Miss., incised, 1900, 11 ¾ x 6 ½ in. Rago, Lambertville, New Jersey.

Pablo Picasso form: $24,130 for bird-form pitcher known as "Pichet Anse Prise (pitcher with seized handle)," artist's proof for 1953 edition of 200, 7 ¾ x 10 ¾ x 4 ¾ in. Palm Beach Modern Auctions, West Palm Beach, Florida.

Wedgwood Portland vase: $147,000 for a Wedgwood Portland vase, first edition copy, numbered 22 in pencil, black body with applied white classical figures in relief, gray wash, England, 18th century, 2 ⅜ in. Skinner, Marlborough, Massachusetts.

SILVER & OTHER METALS

Civil War belt buckle: $52,275 for a Civil War era belt buckle, 2-piece officer's saber belt plate, embossed "CSA." Baldini Auction Co., Hermitage, Tennessee.

Whistling Jim doorstop: $22,420 for a Bradley & Hubbard "Whistling Jim" doorstop, Huckleberry Finn type boy, barefoot on green grass, 16 ¼ x 5 ½ in. Bertoia Auctions, Vineland, New Jersey.

SPORTS

Babe Ruth first baseball card as a Yankee: $115,626 for a black and white Babe Ruth American Carmel Co. card picturing Babe Ruth as a New York Yankee while still in his Boston uniform, 1921, E121, PSA 6 EX-MT. Memory Lane Inc., Tustin, California.

Honus Wagner T206 baseball card: $3,120,000 for a 1909–11 Honus Wagner T206 baseball card with white border, PSA EX 5, known as the "Jumbo Wagner." Goldin Auctions, Runnemede, New Jersey.

1909–11 Honus Wagner T206 baseball card: $3,120,000.

Joe DiMaggio 1938 Goudey baseball card: $288,000 for a Joe DiMaggio 1938 Goudey Gum Company rookie card. Heritage Auctions, Dallas, Texas.

Lou Gehrig 1925 Exhibit rookie card: $60,000 for Lou Gehrig's oversized Exhibit Supply Co. rookie card, PSA 3 (VG). Memory Lane Inc., Tustin, California.

Mickey Mantle game worn 1968 Yankees jersey: $486,000 for the 1968 Mickey Mantle game worn New York Yankees jersey attributed to 535th home run. Heritage Auctions, Dallas, Texas.

Mickey Mantle Topps rookie card: $660,000 for a 1952 Topps Mickey Mantle baseball card, No. 311, PSA NM-MT 8. Heritage Auctions, Dallas, Texas.

Ted Williams Triple Crown Season game used bat: $180,000 for the 1947 Ted Williams Triple Crown Season game used vault-marked bat, PSA/DNA GU 10, 35 inches long, 33.1 ounces. Heritage Auctions, Dallas, Texas.

TOYS, DOLLS, & BANKS

Chanticleer still bank: $15,600 for the Chanticleer still bank by A.C. Williams, cast iron, c.1910. RSL Auction Co., Whitehouse, New Jersey.

KOVELS OFFER EVEN MORE PRICE INFORMATION SOURCES

Website: Kovels.com

Kovels.com is the go-to source for antiques and collectibles information since 1996. Join the community of collectors at Kovesl.com for up-to-the minute information available 24/7. You can register for free. Access to more than 1,000,000 searchable prices, a database of pottery and porcelain marks, latest news. Collecting forums, and more. More premium features, including an online/tablet version of *Kovels on Antiques & Collectibles* newsletter, are available for a fee.

Newsletter: *Kovels on Antiques and Collectibles*

You already know this book is a great overall price guide for antiques and collectibles. Each entry is current, every photograph is new, and all prices are accurate. There is also another Kovel publication designed to keep you up-to-the-minute in the world of collecting. For over 40 years, *Kovels on Antiques & Collectibles*, our monthly newsletter, has kept collectors informed with up-to-the-minute reporting on the world of collecting. Things change quickly. Important sales produce new record prices. Fakes appear. And rarities are discovered. To keep up with developments, you can read *Kovels on Antiques & Collectibles*. Each newsletter is filled with color photographs (about 40 per issue), a dictionary of marks, fakes alerts, and answers to readers' questions. It reports prices, trends, auction results, Internet sales, and other news for collectors. *Kovels'* newsletter is available by subscription in two forms: a print edition that is mailed and a digital edition available as part of Kovels.com Premium online subscription. The digital edition gives you access to 10-plus years of past newsletters as well. See the back page of this book to order.

HOW TO USE THIS BOOK

There are a few rules for using this book. Each listing is arranged in the following manner: CATEGORY (such as silver), OBJECT (such as vase), DESCRIPTION (as much information as possible about size, age, color, and pattern). Some types of glass, pottery, and silver are exceptions to this rule. These are listed CATEGORY, PATTERN, OBJECT, DESCRIPTION, PRICE. All items are presumed to be in good condition and undamaged, unless otherwise noted. In most sections, if a maker's name is easily recognized (like Gustav Stickley) we include it near the beginning of the entry. If the maker is obscure, the name may be near the end.

- To save space, dollar amounts do not include dollar signs, commas, or cents at the end, so $1,234.00 is written 1234.

- You will find silver flatware in either Silver Flatware Plated or Silver Flatware Sterling. There is also a section for Silver Plate, which includes coffeepots, trays, and other plated hollowware. Most solid or sterling silver is listed by country, so look for Silver-American, Silver-Danish, Silver-English, etc. Silver jewelry is listed under Jewelry. Most pottery and porcelain is listed by factory name, such as Weller or Wedgwood; by item, such as Calendar Plate; in sections like Dinnerware or Kitchen; or in a special section, such as Pottery-Art, Pottery-Contemporary, Pottery-Midcentury, etc.

- Sometimes we make arbitrary decisions. Fishing has its own category, but hunting is part of the larger category called Sports. We have omitted most guns except toy guns. These are listed in the Toy category. It is not legal to sell weapons without a special license, so guns are not part of the general antiques market. Air guns, BB guns, rocket guns, and others are listed in the Toy section. Everything is listed according to the computer alphabetizing system.

- We made several editorial decisions. A butter dish is a "butter." A salt dish is called a "salt" to differentiate it from a saltshaker. It is always "sugar and creamer," never "creamer and sugar." Where one dimension is given, it is the height; or if the object is round, it's the diameter. The height of a picture is listed before width. Glass is clear unless a color is indicated.

- Some antiques terms, such as "Sheffield" or "Pratt," have two meanings. Read the paragraph headings to know the definition being used. All category headings are based on the vocabulary of the average person, and we use terms like "mud figures" even if not technically correct. Some categories are known by several names. Pressed glass is also called pattern glass or EAPG (Early American pattern glass). We use the name pressed glass because much of the information found in old books and articles use that name.

- This book does not include price listings for fine art paintings, antiquities, stamps, coins, or most types of books. Comic books are listed only in special categories like Superman, but original comic art and cels are listed in their own categories.

- Prices for items pictured can be found in the appropriate category. Look for the matching entry with the abbreviation "Illus." The color photograph will be nearby.

- Thanks to computers, the book is produced quickly. The last entries are added in June; the book is available in September. But human help finds prices and checks accuracy. We read everything at least five times, sometimes more. We edit more than 35,000 entries down to the 20,000 entries found here. We correct spelling, remove incorrect data, write category paragraphs, and decide on new categories. We proofread copy and prices many times, but there may be some misspelled words and other errors. Information in the paragraphs is updated each year and this year more than 25 updates and additions were made.

- Prices are reported from all parts of the United States, Canada, Europe, and Asia, converted to U.S. dollars at the time of the sale. The average rate of exchange in June 1, 2017, was $1 U.S. to about $1.34 Canadian, €0.89 (euro), and £0.77 (British pound). Prices are from auctions, shops, Internet sales, shows, and even some flea markets. Every price is checked for accuracy, but we are not responsible for errors. We cannot answer your letters asking for price information, or where to sell, but please write if you have any requests for categories to be included or any corrections to the paragraphs or prices. You may find the answers to your other questions at Kovels.com or in our newsletter, *Kovels' On Antiques & Collectibles.*

- When you see us at shows, auctions, house sales, and flea markets, please stop and say hello. Don't be surprised if we ask for your suggestions. You can write to us at P.O. Box 22192, Beachwood, OH 44122, or visit us on our website, Kovels.com.

TERRY KOVEL AND KIM KOVEL
July 2017

ACKNOWLEDGMENTS

In 1953 Ralph and I were lucky enough to have our first book, a dictionary of pottery and porcelain marks, accepted by a publisher. It led to a lifetime of writing about antiques and collectibles, 108 books, a syndicated newspaper column, television shows, and many articles, special reports, speeches, and a lifestyle filled with other antiques enthusiasts and friends. So this is a special thank you to Nat Wartels and Alan Mirken, who owned and ran Crown Publishing, hired us as authors, and became friends. They sold the business to Random House in 1988 which continued publishing our old books and new ones until they reorganized in 2008. J.P. Leventhal, owner of Black Dog and Leventhal Publishers, had worked for Crown Publishing and he agreed to publish the price book. In 2016 Black Dog joined Hachette Book Group and they have been our publishers ever since. Our proudest claim is that we have worked for only one publisher all these years; they just kept changing partners and names.

Thanks to the Hachette crew:

- J.P. Leventhal, who was with us from the start. It has been a successful, comfortable time and a great book each year.
- Lisa Tenaglia, who did all those almost-unseen things good editors do.
- Lilian Sun in production and Mike Olivo, managing editor, who understand the peculiarities of the book and find ways to solve problems.
- Mary Flower, Robin Perlow, and Cynthia Schuster Eakin, who once again searched the mountain of prices and pictures and did the proofreading and copyediting to find the large and small errors.
- Sheila Hart has put all the prices, photographs, paragraphs, and even the special center section's complicated timeline together to make everything look amazing for each of the last 11 *Kovels' Antiques & Collectibles Price Guide* editions.
- Janet Dodrill, who outlined each of the 2,500 color pictures and made sure they were the right color and shape.

But most of all we want to thank our staff:

- Gay Hunter, who has guided, pushed, and kept track of the minutia of the project for most years of the price books. She even spellchecks, keeps track of pictures and their codes, and insists we keep to deadlines.
- Lauren Rafferty, our photo editor, who actually could smile when we "lost" an entry or needed yet another special picture. She miraculously could find and fix them all.
- Cherrie Smrekar who typed almost every picture listing and helped in any way she could.
- Liz Lillis, our fact checker and proofreader, makes sure we put the quote marks in the right place and edits out grammar problems. She checks the spelling of foreign names. Liz is an expert researcher and catches many of our spelling and historic errors.
- Beverly Malone, Tina McBean, Renee McRitchie, Erika Risley, Katie McMenamin Sabo, and Kristen Stogsdill who recorded the prices and pictures and helped any place we needed them.
- Hamsy Mirre, who is in charge of marketing. She's the expert who makes sure everyone knows about out price book on the web, in social media, and in print.

And I want to say how lucky I am to have a chance to work with my daughter, Kim Kovel, who worries about technology, finance, advertising, business problems, and even writes and corrects parts of the book. We count on her to be our expert on the 1950s and newer collectibles now that the book is filled with younger items. I couldn't do it without her.

CONTRIBUTORS

The world of antiques and collectibles is filled with people who have answered our every request for help. Dealers, auction houses, and shops have given advice and opinions, supplied photographs and prices, and made suggestions for changes. Many thanks to all of them:

Photographs and information were furnished by: Accurate Auctions, Ahlers & Ogletree Auction Gallery, Alderfer Auction, Alex Cooper Auctioneers, Allard Auctions, American Antique Auctions, Anderson Americana, Antique Reader, AntiqueAdvertising.com, Auction Team Breker, Bertoia Auctions, Brown Tool Auctions, Brunk Auctions, Bunte Auction Service, Burchard Galleries, Burns Auction Service, Case Antiques, Copake Auction, Cottone Auctions, Cowan's Auctions, Crocker Farm, DuMouchelles, Early American History Auctions, Early Auction Co., Fairfield Auction, Fenton Art Glass Collectors of America, Fontaine's Auction Gallery, Forsythe's Auctions, Fox Auctions, Garth's Auctioneers & Appraisers, Glass Works Auctions, Hake's Americana, Heritage Auctions, Hess Auction Group, Hudson Valley Auctions, Humler & Nolan, Jackson's International Auctioneers, James D. Julia Auctioneers, Jeffrey S. Evans, John McInnis Auctioneers, Kamelot Auction House, Kaminski Auctions, Kimballs Auction & Estate Services, Leighton Galleries, Leland Little Auctions, Leonard Auction, Leslie Hindman Auctioneers, Los Angeles Modern Auctions, Martin Auction Co., MBA Seattle Auction House, McMasters Harris Auction Co., Milestone Auctions, Morphy Auctions,, Myers Auction Gallery, Neal Auctions, New Orleans Auction Galleries, Norman Heckler & Co., North American Auction Co., Pierre Berge & Associates, Pook & Pook, Potter & Potter, Rachel Davis Fine Arts, Rago Arts and Auction Center, Replacements Ltd., Richard D. Hatch & Associates, Rich Penn Auctions, Robert Edward Auctions, Roland Auctioneers & Valuers, RSL Auction, Ruby Lane, Saco River Auction Co., Selkirk Auctioneers & Appraisers, Showtime Auction Services, Skinner, Inc., Sotheby's, Strawser Auction Group, Susanin's Auctioneers & Appraisers, The Stein Auction Co., Theriault's, Thomaston Place Auction Galleries, Tias, Time & Again Auction Galleries, Tom Harris Auctions, Treadway Toomey Auctions, Treasureseeker Auctions, Turner Auctions + Appraisals, Weiss Auctions, Wiederseim Associates, Wickliff Auctioneers, William H. Bunch Auctions, Willis Henry Auctions, Wilton Gallery, Wm Morford Auction, Woody Auction, and Wright. The contact information for these people is at the back of this book on page 546.

To the others who knowingly or unknowingly contributed to this book, we say thank you: Aleph-Bet Books, Inc., Antique Bottle & Glass Collector, Antique Toy World, Auctions by Adkins, Apple Tree Auction Center, Aspire Auctions, Auction Gallery of Boca Raton, Auktionshaus Eppli, Billings Auction, Beer Cans & Brewery Collectibles (BCCA), Bonhams, Bottles & Extras, Bruneau & Co. Auctioneers, Butterfly Net, California Auctioneers & Appraisers, Chandler's International Auctions & Estate Sales, Charleston Estate Auctions, Charlton Hall Galleries, Christie's, Clars Auction Gallery, Concept Art Gallery, Crescent City Auction Gallery, CRN Auctions, Crown Jewels of the Wire, Daguerreian Society, Dallas Auction Gallery, Dirk Soulis Auctions, Don's Antiques, Doyle New York, Eagle Ridge Collectibles, Eldred's, Faganarms, Finney's Auction & Estate Services, Flannery's Estate Services, Florida Estate Sales, Fusco Auctions, Great Gatsby's Auction Gallery, Greenwich Auction, Grogan & Co., Hannam's Auctioneers, Hartzell's Auction Gallery, Hill House Wares, Homestead Auctions, J. James Auctioneers & Appraisers, Jaremos, Jasper52, John Moran Auctioneers, Kennedy's Auction Service, Mark Mattox Auctioneer & Real Estate Broker, Matthew Bullock Auctioneers, Michaan's Auctions, Mid-Hudson Auction Galleries, Northeast Auctions, O'Gallerie, Open-Wire Insulator Services, Perry's Auctioneers, Philip Weiss Auctions, Phoebus Auction Gallery, Pioneer Auction Gallery, Rex Stark – Americana, Robbins Nest, Saucon Valley Auction Co., Simpson Galleries, Stair Galleries, Stephenson's Auctioneers & Appraisers, Stoney Ridge Auction, Swann Auction Galleries, Toothpick Bulletin, Weschler & Son, Westport Auction, William J. Jenack Estate Appraisers & Auctioneers, Wooten & Wooten, and other sites.

A. WALTER made pate-de-verre glass under contract at the Daum glassworks from 1908 to 1914. He decorated pottery during his early years in his studio in Sevres, where he also developed his formula for pale, translucent pate-de-verre. He started his own firm in Nancy, France, in 1919. Pieces made before 1914 are signed *Daum, Nancy* with a cross. After 1919 the signature is *A. Walter Nancy.*

Bowl, Lid, Cicada, Yellow Orange, c.1920, 5¼ x 4½ In.	1250
Figurine, Bird, Blue, Brown Base, 4 x 3¾ In., Pair	937
Paperweight, 2 Nude Women, Erotica, c.1910, 3½ x 5 x 3¾ In.	7102
Paperweight, Frog, Sitting Up, Green With Orange Base, 3½ x 2¾ x 3¼ In.	1046
Paperweight, Moth, Red, Green, Yellow Wings, Mottled Green Base, Signed, 4⅜ In. .....*illus*	5333
Paperweight, Turkey, 3¾ x 2½ In.	1020
Paperweight, Turkey, Yellow, Chest Out, Wings Spread, 3¼ x 2½ In.	1046
Tray, Blue, Flowers, Moth, 2¾ x 6¾ In.	900
Vase, Goblet, Red Flowers, Green Arches, Shaded Green & Yellow, 6 In.	2133

ABC plates, or children's alphabet plates, were most popular from 1780 to 1860 but are still being made. The letters on the plate were meant as teaching aids for children learning to read. The plates were made of pottery, porcelain, metal, or glass. Mugs and other items were also made with alphabet decorations.

Bowl, Jack & Jill, Tumbling Down Hill, Lord Nelson Pottery, 1900s, 7 In.	15
Butter, Cover, Glass, Ribbed, 7 x 3 x 3 In.	59
Plate, Baby In Blanket, Moon, Pottery, c.1930, 6½ In.	32
Plate, Children, Beehive, Poem, Raised Rim, Porcelain, 8 In.	76
Plate, Clockface & Numbers, Embossed, Notched Rim, Glass, 1900s, 7 In.	55
Plate, Dog Head, Glass, 1940s, 6 In.	35
Plate, Hens, Chicks, Brick Wall, Water Pail, Glass, King, Son & Co., c.1880, 6 In.	55
Plate, Horse & Rider, The Walk, Porcelain, 1800s, 7⅞ In.	58
Plate, Marigold, Stork, Glass, 7⅝ In.	97
Plate, Mary Had A Little Lamb, Nursery Rhyme, Embossed, Tin, c.1885, 8 In.	75
Plate, Niagara, American Side, Raised Letters, Porcelain, 7 In.	85
Plate, Organ Grinder, 3 Children, Porcelain, 1800s, 6 In.	49
Plate, The New Pony, Pony, Children, Pottery, 1800s, 6¾ In.	67

ABINGDON POTTERY was established in 1908 by Raymond E. Bidwell as the Abingdon Sanitary Manufacturing Company. The company started making art pottery in 1934. The factory ceased production of art pottery in 1950.

Bowl, Scalloped, Scroll Handle, Blue, 14 In.	7
Flowerpot, LaFleur, Blue & Red Flower, Cream Ground, 4 x 4¾ In. ......*illus*	32
Planter, Yellow, Sprigs, Boat Shape, Reeded, Scroll Ends, c.1945, 4 x 9 In.	20
Vase, Cornucopia Shape, Pink, White Flower Design, Square Foot, 1940s, 5 In., Pair	65
Vase, Cornucopia Shape, White, Ribbed, Scalloped Rim, Leaf Shape Feet, 1940s, 5 In.	44

ADAMS china was made by William Adams and Sons of Staffordshire, England. The firm was founded in 1769 and became part of the Wedgwood Group in 1966. The name *Adams* appeared on various items through 1998. All types of tablewares and useful wares were made. Other pieces of Adams may be found listed under Flow Blue and Tea Leaf Ironstone.

Cup & Saucer, Red, Blue, Rose, 2 Piece	120
Cup, Little Gray Rabbit, Verse, Bunny With Basket, Flowers, Squared Handle	22
Pitcher, Rose, Blue, Wavy Spout, Flared Foot, c.1850, 6 x 6 In.	575
Plate, 3 Cows, Cobalt Blue, Flowers, Scalloped Rim, c.1850, 10 In.	99
Plate, Countryside, Cows, Couple, Cottage, Red Transfer, Scalloped Border, c.1900, 9 In.	25
Platter, Adams' Rose, Oval, Flower Border, Scalloped Rim, c.1830, 10 x 8 In.	107
Teapot, Adams' Rose, Black, Brown, Rainbow, Spatterware, 7 In.	111
Tureen, Damascus, Blue & White, Octagonal, Dome Lid, Knob Finial, 1800s, 6 x 9 In.	250
Tureen, Lily, Blue & White, Cutout Handles, Scalloped Rim & Undertray, Ladle, 6 x 8 In.	158
Vase, Lid, Dark Blue Jasper, Flower Borders, Classical Figures, c.1900, 10½ In.	615

A. Walter, Paperweight, Moth, Red, Green, Yellow Wings, Mottled Green Base, Signed, 4⅜ In.
$5,333

James D. Julia Auctioneers

Abingdon, Flowerpot, LaFleur, Blue & Red Flower, Cream Ground, 4 x 4¾ In.
$32

Ruby Lane

Collector Language
The hobby of collecting pre-paid telephone cards is called "fusilately."

Advertising, Bag, Wah Wah Tobacco, Cloth, Indian Image, Hancock Bros., 3¼ x 1¾ In.
$219

Wm Morford Auctions

ADVERTISING

Advertising, Banner, Waterman's Ideal Fountain Pen, Fabric, Fringe, Hanging, 43 x 26 In.
$333

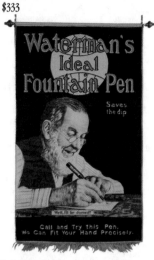

Rachel Davis Fine Arts

Advertising, Beaker, Root Beer, Hires Kid, Health & Cheer, Print Under Glaze, Mettlach, ¼ Liter
$66

The Stein Auction Company

Advertising, Bench, Bulletin, Painted Wood, 16 x 30 x 11 ½ In.
$531

Hess Auction Group

ADVERTISING containers and products sold in the old country store are now all collectibles. These stores, with crackers in a barrel and a potbellied stove, are a symbol of an earlier, less hectic time. Listed here are many advertising items. Other similar pieces may be found under the product name, such as Planters Peanuts. We have tried to list items in logical places, so enameled tin dishes will be found under Graniteware, auto-related items in the Auto category, paper items in the Paper category, etc. Store fixtures, cases, signs, and other items that have no advertising as part of the decoration are listed in the Store category. The early Dr Pepper logo included a period after "Dr," but it was dropped in 1950. We list all Dr Pepper items without a period so they alphabetize together. For more prices, go to kovels.com.

Ashtray, Goodrich Silvertown, Tires, Tire Rim, Glass Insert, Box, 1940, 6 In.	115
Ashtray, Goodrich Tires, Reverse Image Of Bus, Glass Insert, 1⅛ x 6⅜ In.	153
Ashtray, Kenton Hardware Co., Woman Spreading Skirt, Iron, 1920s, 6 x 7 In.	173
Ashtray, Royal Crown Cola, Pull Match, Bakelite Base, Metal Rod, c.1940s, 8 In.	158
Bag, Flour, Extra Graham, Cotton, Label, Train, Blue Print, Frame, c.1910, 19 x 13 In.	523
Bag, Wah Wah Tobacco, Cloth, Indian Image, Hancock Bros., 3¼ x 1¾ In. ....*illus*	219
Banner, Waterman's Ideal Fountain Pen, Fabric, Fringe, Hanging, 43 x 26 In. ....*illus*	333
Banner, Yardley's Old English Lavender, Woman, Basket, 1920s, 30 x 35 In.	175
Barrel, Diamond Queen, Chewing Tobacco, Paper Label, Lid, 1880s, 14 In.	92
Beaker, Root Beer, Hires Kid, Health & Cheer, Print Under Glaze, Mettlach, ¼ Liter .....*illus*	66
Bench, Bulletin, Painted Wood, 16 x 30 x 11 ½ In. ....*illus*	531
Bench, Home Furnishing Co., Wooden, Etched Seat & Back, 60 x 36 In.	1107
Bill Clip, Champion Spark Plugs, Die Cut, 2½ x 1¼ In.	142
Bill Clip, Hughes Buggy Co., Early Buggy Logo, 2¼ x 2¼ In.	94
Bin, A&P Coffee, Mixed Wood, Red Paint, Label, U.S.A., c.1910, 30 x 19 In.	344
Bin, Martin L. Hall & Co., Boston, Coffee, Blue With Stencil, Late 1800s, 17 x 18 x 14 In.	390
Bin, Plow Boy Tobacco, Faux Wood, Pouches, 10½ In.	1140
Bin, Wilbur Seed Meal, Wood, Slogans, 29 x 16 x 18 In.	2856
Bookrack, Classics Illustrated, 15 Cents, Wire, Paint, Tin Lithograph Plate, 1960s, 11 In.	311
Books may be included in the Paper category.	
Bottles are listed in the Bottle category.	
Bottle Openers are listed in the Bottle Opener category.	
Box, see also Box category.	
Box, A.J. Medlar, Crack, Cakes & Biscuits, Farm, Wood, 21½ In.	92
Box, Beck's Hunting Tobacco, Indian Hunting Buffalo, Wood, Slide Lid, 7 In.	345
Box, Cereal, Kellogg's Corn Flakes, Corbett, Space Cadet Cutouts, 1950s, 12 x 19 In., Pair	115
Box, Cereal, Kellogg's Pep, Superman Strip On Back, 1948, 8½ In. ....*illus*	670
Box, Cereal, Kellogg's Sugar Smacks, Star Trek's Mr. Spock, Badge, 1970, 8 x 12 In. ....*illus*	540
Box, Cereal, Nabisco Shredded Wheat, Televiewer Premium, c.1954, 3 x 4 x 7½ In. ....*illus*	326
Box, Cereal, Post Corn Crackos, Magic Monocle Premium, Flat, 1968, 12 x 16¾ In. ....*illus*	696
Box, Colburn's Laundry Bluing, Wood, 2½ x 11¾ x 11¾ In.	201
Box, Cycle Cigarettes, Man Riding Bike, Cardboard Pack, c.1883, 3 x 3 In.	207
Box, Display, Baking Powder, Pearce Duff Co., Wood, 3¾ x 14¼ x 6⅜ In.	708
Box, Display, Bixby's Ready Glue, Wood, Graphic Label, Lift Lid, 4 x 9 x 7 In.	661
Box, Display, Chewing Gum, Pinocchio, Cardboard, Tree Branch Nose, 6 x 8 In.	380
Box, Display, Ferry Seed Co., Flower Garden, Wood, Lift Lid, Label, 4 x 12 x 7 In.	184
Box, Display, Secret Agent 002, Grab Bags, 5 Cents, Cardboard, 1960s, 8 x 11 In.	174
Box, Edison Lamps Box, Edison Mazda Co., 6 Unused Lightbulbs, 7 x 8⅝ x 10¾ In.	1097
Box, Gum Card, American Beauties, 12 Pictures, 5 Cents Per Set, 1944, 8 x 10 In.	230
Box, Gum Card, Display, Rails & Sails, 5 Cents, Train & Ship, 4 x 9 In.	173
Box, Gum Card, Display, World On Wheels, 5 Cents, Auto Photos, c.1950, 6 x 8 In.	211
Box, Gum Card, Man On Moon, 10 Cents, 24 Packs, 99 Cards, c.1969, 4 x 8 In.	863
Box, Heinz, Baked Beans, Wood, 13 x 20 In.	61
Box, Humphrey's Veterinary Specifics, Hardwood, Full Paper Label, 5¼ x 9½ x 5¾ In.	94
Box, Oatmeal, Bunny Brand Rolled Oats, Bunny Logo, Yellow, Cylindrical, 7⅜ x 4¼ In.	575
Box, Oatmeal, Golden Valley Rolled Oats, Cardboard, Cylindrical, 3 Lb., 10 x 5 In.	633
Box, Oatmeal, Home Brand Oats, Griggs, Cooper & Co., Cylindrical, 9½ x 5⅜ In.	83
Box, Oatmeal, Honor Rolled Oats, George Washington, Cardboard, Cylindrical, 10 x 5 In.	431

Box, Oatmeal, Jack Sprat Oats, Cardboard, Jack Sprat Foods, Cylindrical, 9½ x 5⅜ In....	94
Box, Oatmeal, Jack Sprat Rolled Oats, Western Grocer Company, Cylindrical, 9⅝ x 5⅜ In.	115
Box, Oatmeal, Pathfinder Rolled Oats, Gen. J.C. Freemont, Cardboard, Cylindrical, 10 x 6 In...	690
Box, Oatmeal, Paw-Nee Oats, Indian With Arrow Logo, Yellow, Red, Cylindrical, 7 x 4 In.........	288
Box, Oatmeal, Polar Bear Rolled Oats, Polar Bear, Iceberg, Cardboard, Cylindrical, 10 x 6 In..	546
Box, Oatmeal, Puritan Rolled Oats, Hewett Grocery Co., Cylindrical, 7¼ x 4¼ In.	130
Box, Oatmeal, White Villa Rolled Oats, Country Home Scene, Cylindrical, 9½ x 5⅜ In...............	115
Box, Pedro Tobacco, Lunch Box Shape, Playing Cards, Yellow, Tin Lithograph, 4 x 8 In.	403
Box, Rinso Blue Detergent, Paladin Trading Card Offer, Richard Boone, 1959, 6 x 8 In.	820
Box, Toilet Soap, La Soubrette, 3½ x 16⅝ x 13½ In.	106
Box, Traveling Salesman's Sample, Dr. Munroe's Cherokee Indian Remedies, c.1870, 16 x 10 In.	1110
Box, Wells Fargo, 26 x 13 In.	234
Box, Wild West Soap, Cowboys, Lasso, Wooden, Paper Label, Flip Lid, 16 x 13 In.	546
Box, Winchester, Red Stenciling, Wood, 25½ In.	213
Box, Woodworth & Son Shaving Mug Soap, Display, Wood, Flip Lid, 3 x 12 In.	949
Box, Zebra Polishing Paste, Running Zebra Label, Wood, Flip Lid, 3 x 15 x 12 In.	690
Cabinet, Diamond Dyes, Governess, Children, Oak, 22½ x 29½ x 9¾ In. .... 531 to 1020	
Cabinet, Dr. Daniels' Veterinary Medicines, Oak, Tin Lithograph, 29 x 22 In.	2963
Cabinet, Dr. Daniels', Man, Wares, Embossed, Multicolor, 27 In...............................	3900
Cabinet, Humphrey's Specifics, Embossed Horse, 33 In..	4305
Cabinet, Humphrey's Specifics, List Of Animal Diseases, Animals, Grass, 27½ In................	2400
Cabinet, Niagara Search Lights, Wood, Glass Door, 1930s, 20 x 36 In.	555
Cabinet, Spool, Corticelli, Curved Glass Case, Inner Drawers, 21¼ In.	1920
Cabinet, Spool, J. & P. Coats', 4-Sided, 22½ In.	1140
Cabinet, Spool, J. & P. Coats', Best Six Cord, Walnut, 6 Drawers, 20 x 24 x 17 In..............*illus*	826
Calendars are listed in the Calendar category.	
Can, Cafe Extra Coffee, Indian Chief, Cardboard, Tin Lid & Base, Lb., 6 x 5 In.	374
Candy Dish, Hires Root Beer, Silver Plate, Lid, 10 In.	1750
Canisters, see introductory paragraph to Tins in this category.	
Cards are listed in the Card category.	
Case, Display, Bee Brand, Flavoring Extracts, Wood, Glass Door, Decal, 21 In.	338
Case, Display, Blewett's 38 Dollar Cigar, Wood, Copper Trim, Slant Lid, Bell, 8 x 10 In.	518
Catalog, Hoge Toys Catalog, Color Illustrations, c.1930s, 8½ x 11 In............................	242
Catalog, Imperial Wheels, American Bicycle Co., 1901	176
Change Receiver, see also Tip Tray in this category.	
Cigar Cutter, Crane Valve & Fittings Co., Valve Faucet, Embossed, Iron, 4 x 5 In.	546
Cigar Cutter, Lighter, Barnes Smith & Co., Oil Lamp, Amber Globe, 14½ In........................	3300
Clocks are listed in the Clock category.	
Cooler, Figural Bottle, Ice Cold Moxie, Brown & Yellow Paint, Display, 35 In.	2091
Dispenser, Brooke & Co., Ginger Beer, Pottery Jug, Wood Spout, 17 In.	185
Dispenser, Buckeye Root Beer, 5 Cents, Bulb, Round Foot, Pump, Ceramic, 17 In.	3383
Dispenser, Drink Howel's Orange Julep, Soda Fountain, Clear, Metal Cap, 13 In.	2091
Dispenser, Indian Rock Ginger Ale, 5 Cents, 2-Sided, Pump, c.1900, 15½ In.............*illus*	9440
Dispenser, Kitco Seat Cover, Toilet Tissue, 1 Cent, Enamel, White, Kirch-Trymbuss, 12 In.	275
Dispenser, Mission Brand Fruit Flavored Soda, Seminude Holding Logo, 7¼ x 3 In.	142
Dispenser, Root Beer, Rochester Root Beer, White Milk Glass, Red Lettering, 14 x 6 In.	1035
Display, Beech-Nut, Big League Chew, Tobacco, Cardboard, 1926, 60 In.	2160
Display, Bixby's Shu White, Figural, Woman, Cloth Dress, Cardboard, 30 x 9 In.	776
Display, Blue Coal, For Clean Healthful Heat, Fire, 6 Types Coal, Blue, 12 x 24 In.	71
Display, Boal's Rolls, Laxative, Drugstore, 6½ x 8 x 7 In.	403
Display, Booth's Gin, Hard Plastic, Red, Black, 1950s, 7 In....................................	127
Display, Bottle, Smile Soda, Orange, Bottle Cap, Pat. July 11, 1922, 18½ In....................	1720
Display, Bright Star Flashlights, Battery Shape, Red, Black, Star Finial, Base, 20 In.	523
Display, Centennial Parade Flags, Globe Stand, 87-Star Flags, c.1880, 10 In.	2520
Display, Chew-Smoke Mail Pouch, Child, Tray, 3-D, Tin, Die Cut, 16 x 22 In.............*illus*	968
Display, Cow, Standing On Cart, Bucket, Sneezy, Metal Plaque, 1900s, 18 x 24 In.	1680
Display, Cubbies, Wooden, Red, Green, 57 x 11 In.	438
Display, Elgin Watches, Woman, Wearing Watch, Wood, Art Deco, 16 x 17 In.	374
Display, Flexaire, Flexees Bras, Woman, Bra, Hat, Gloves, Plaster, 1930s, 12 In.	285

Advertising, Box, Cereal, Kellogg's Pep, Superman Strip On Back, 1948, 8½ In.
$670

Hake's Americana & Collectibles

Advertising, Box, Cereal, Kellogg's Sugar Smacks, Star Trek's Mr. Spock, Badge, 1970, 8 x 12 In.
$540

Hake's Americana & Collectibles

Advertising, Box, Cereal, Nabisco Shredded Wheat, Televiewer Premium, c.1954, 3 x 4 x 7½ In.
$326

Hake's Americana & Collectibles

Advertising, Box, Cereal, Post Corn Crackos, Magic Monocle Premium, Flat, 1968, 12 x 16¾ In.
$696

Hake's Americana & Collectibles

Advertising, Cabinet, Spool, J. & P. Coats', Best 6 Cord, Walnut, 6 Drawers, 20 x 24 x 17 In.
$826

Hess Auction Group

Advertising, Dispenser, Indian Rock Ginger Ale, 5 Cents, 2-Sided, Pump, c.1900, 15½ In.
$9,440

Hess Auction Group

Advertising, Display, Chew-Smoke Mail Pouch, Child, Tray, 3-D, Tin, Die Cut, 16 x 22 In.
$968

Rachel Davis Fine Arts

Advertising, Display, Kentucky Fried Chicken, Col. Sanders Head On Chicken, Nodder, 13 In.
$1,020

Milestone Auctions

Advertising, Display, Leg, Duribilknit Hosiery, John B. Flaherty, Composition, Stand, 33 In.
$348

Showtime Auction Services

Advertising, Display, My First Sweetheart, Sweetheart Soap, Baby In Bassinet, 33 x 22 In.
$928

Showtime Auction Services

> **TIP**
> *Remove old staples, rubber bands, paper clips, etc., from paper objects. They can stain the paper.*

Advertising, Display, Omega Corn Cure, Foot, Light-Up, 29 x 14 x 12 In.
$1,160

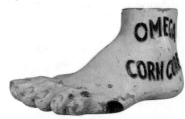

Showtime Auction Services

Advertising, Door Push, Magic Yeast, Enameled Porcelain, Grommet Holes, 6 x 3 In.
$1,380

Morphy Auctions

Display, Giles Brand Boot Protectors, 3 x 13 In.	104
Display, Heinz, Figural Pickle, 2-Sided, Stringholder, Wood, Paint, 3 x 16 In.	1150
Display, Ide Silver Collar, Wall Mount, Brass Trim, Iron Hook, 53 In.	1476
Display, Kate Latter's Candies, 6 Wax Street Vendor Figurines, 7 x 3 x 3 In.	5250
Display, Kentucky Fried Chicken, Col. Sanders Head On Chicken, Nodder, 13 In. ....*illus*	1020
Display, King Oscar Cigar, Broom Holder, 2 Brooms, Early 1900s, 33 ½ x 21 ½ x 22 In.	1020
Display, Leg, Duribilknit Hosiery, John B. Flaherty, Composition, Stand, 33 In. ....*illus*	348
Display, Life Savers, Mint, Product, 16 In.	3690
Display, Monarch Teenie Weenie Peanut Butter, Characters, 15 x 13 In.	863
Display, My First Sweetheart, Sweetheart Soap, Baby In Bassinet, 33 x 22 In. ....*illus*	928
Display, OCB Rolling Papers, 150 Leaves, 5 Cents, Cardboard, c.1910, 5 x 11 In.	196
Display, Occidental Flour, 7 Glass Display Domes Showing Wheat Samples, 9 x 14 In.	604
Display, Omega Corn Cure, Foot, Light-Up, 29 x 14 x 12 In. ....*illus*	1160
Display, Raleigh Cigarettes, Figural, Bust, Sir Raleigh, Papier-Mache, Paint, 15 In.	185
Display, Reliable Seeds, 23 ¼ In.	1200
Display, Satin Gloss Soap, Black Boy In Washtub, Chalkware, Base, 17 In.	523
Display, Squirt Soda, Soda Kid, Just Call Me Squirt, Figural, Plaster, 12 x 8 In.	345
Display, The Clinic Shoe, Footwear, Figural Nurse, Mid-Stride, 1960s, 21 In.	244
Display, Window, RCA, Radio, Radio Head Characters, Cardboard, 4 Piece	661
Dolls are listed in the Doll category.	
Door Push, Hamm's Beer, Theo. Hamm Brewing Co., Enamel, 15 x 4 In.	1590
Door Push, Jacob Ruppert Brewing Co., Beer Can, Green, Tin Lithograph, 11 x 3 In.	403
Door Push, Magic Yeast, Enameled Porcelain, Grommet Holes, 6 x 3 In. ....*illus*	1380
Door Push, Orange Crush, Come In, Drink Orange Crush, Bottle, Orange, Tin Lithograph, 12 In.	480
Door Push, Sunbeam Bread, Batter Whipped, Miss Sunbeam, Loaf Shape, Tin, 20 x 9 In.	300
Door Push, Sunbeam, Batter Whipped, Loaf Shape, Trademark Girl, 8 ½ x 26 In.	408
Drum, Cicero Minstrel Theatrical Supplies, Clown, Wood, c.1900, 29 x 29 In.	984
Envelope, Akron Tourist Tubes Condoms, 2 ⅜ x 9 In.	71
Fans are listed in the Fan category.	
Figure, Admiration Cigars, Indian Scout Carrying Cigar Box, 18 ¼ x 4 ½ x 8 In.	805
Figure, Bryant Pup, Reclining, Collar Marked Bryant, Papier-Mache, 1900s, 18 In.	738
Figure, Case, Agricultural Machinery, Eagle, Full Figure, Iron, Base, 8 x 3 In.	690
Figure, Hotpoint Appliances, Wood, Display Doll, Slotted Hands, 1918, 16 In.	506
Figure, Speedy Alka-Seltzer, Vinyl, Paint, 1960s, 8 In.	220
Fly Swatter, Bigelow Faultless Wire Fly Killer, Original Paper Wrapper, 15 ⅜ x 3 In.	189
Foam Scraper, Bartels Crown Beer, Syracuse, 1905, 1 x 8 ⅝ In.	295
Foam Scraper, Smile With Gesundheit, Neustadtl Brewing Co., Stroudsburg, Pa., 1 x 8 ⅞ In. .	71
Glass, Beer, Greenway Brewing Co., India Pale Ale, 3 ¾ x 2 ⅜ In.	401
Globe, Budweiser In Bottles, Eagle, A With Star, Paint, Transfer, 8 In. Diam. ....*illus*	1599
Gum Pack, Kis-Me, All 5 Foil Wrapped Square Gum Sticks, 1 ⅜ x 1 ¼ In.	35
Icebox, Salesman's Sample, Karder Refrigerator Co., Kleenkold, Wooden, 11 ⅝ x 9 x 5 In.	2990
Jar, Morris Supreme Peanut Butter, Ribbed Bottle, Red Metal Lid, c.1935	78
Jar, Walla-Walla Gum, Clear Glass, Embossed, Indian Chief, Square, Lid, 13 In.	1323
Jug, White Rose Rye Whiskey, Cobalt Blue Highlights, Late 1800s, 7 ½ In.	152
Keg, Hazard Gunpowder Co., Sea Shooting, Wood, Label, 13 x 10 In.	403
Knife, Hires Root Beer, German Made, 2-Sided, 2 ⅞ x ¾ x ¼ In.	106
Label, San Tox Cigars, Red Cross Nurse, Holding Box Of Cigars, Paper, c.1910	150
Label, Sunrise Chewing Tobacco, Lithograph, Man, Dog, Sunrise, 9 x 13 In.	489
Lamps are listed in the Lamp category.	
Letter Opener, Mountain States Telephone & Telegraph Co., Logo, Steel, Brass, 8 In.	85
Lunch Boxes are also listed in the Lunch Box category.	
Medal, Red Cross, Donor Award, Dr. Landsteiner Portrait, Bronze, 1939, 2 ¼ In.	20
Milk Bottle Opener, Broughton's Ice Cream, Metal	10
Milk Bottle, Berney-Bond Co., Salesman's Sample, Carrying Rack, Set Of 6, 3 ¾ x 3 x 2 In.	732
Milk Box, Borden's, Emblazoned In Red, Hinged, 13 x 11 x 11 ¾ In.	58

Advertising mirrors of all sizes are listed here. Pocket mirrors range in size from 1 ½ to 5 inches in diameter. Most of these mirrors were given away as advertising promotions and include the name of the company in the design.

Mirror, Barry's Tricopherous, Grows Thick Glossy & Beautiful Hair, Celluloid, 3 In..........*illus*	1438

Advertising, Globe, Budweiser In Bottles, Eagle, A With Star, Paint, Transfer, 8 In. Diam.
$1,599

Morphy Auctions

Advertising, Mirror, Barry's Tricopherous, Grows Thick Glossy & Beautiful Hair, Celluloid, 3 In.
$1,438

Wm Morford Auctions

Advertising, Pail, Oriole Tobacco, Paper Label, American Tobacco Co., Wood, 10 Lb.
$104

Wm Morford Auctions

Advertising, Print, Winchester, 2 Bear Dogs In Barn, H.R. Poore, Frame, 29 x 37 In.
$2,300

James D. Julia Auctioneers

Advertising, Sign, Bixby's Shoe Polish, Cutout Woman Holding Package, Fabric, Cardboard, 35 In.
$363

Rachel Davis Fine Arts

Advertising, Sign, Boston Garter, Fred Clarke & Frank Chance, Cardboard, 1912, 4 x 8¼ In.
$24,000

Robert Edward Auctions

Mirror, Berry Brothers, Toy Wagon, 4 Girls, Wagon, Dog, Multicolor, 2 In.	171
Mirror, Crown Lithia Water, Woman With Tray, Oval, Celluloid, Pocket, 3 x 2 In.	1610
Mirror, Good For 5 Cents At Bar, Woman, Gloves, Metamorphic, Nude, c.1910, 2 In.	196
Mirror, J.J. Kirwin, Saloon, Cartoon, Geezer Spying, Seminude Woman, Bath, 2 In.	187
Mirror, Liberty Fire Company, 53rd Anniversary, Celluloid, Pocket, 2¼ In.	118
Mirror, Logan Havana Cigars, 5 Cents, Black Boy, Goose, Celluloid, 2 In. Diam.	374
Mirror, Meet Me At George's Place, 2 Nude Women, c.1910, 2¼ In.	285
Mirror, Quaker Oats, Oats Box Image, Yellow, Celluloid, Pocket, 2⅛ In. Diam.	219
Mirror, Wizard Shoes, Devil Logo, Pocket, 1½ In.	130
Mirror, Woolsey's Marine Paint, Nude Siren Logo, Best Copper Paint, Pocket, 2¾ x 1¾ In.	212
Mug, Fred Krug Brewing Co., Stoneware, 2 x 1¾ In.	83
Mug, Hires Root Beer, Trademark Kid Holding Up Similar Mug, 5 x 2⅞ In.	248
Mug, Iroquois Brewing Co., Indian Chief, Stoneware, Gilt, Handle, Rolled Rim, 3 In.	230
Pails are also listed in the Lunch Box category.	
Pail, Armour's Veribest Peanut Butter, Tin, 3 x 3⅝ In.	83
Pail, Chase & Sanborn's Coffee, Milk Pail Shape, Tin Lithograph, 4 Lb., 10 x 7 In.	345
Pail, Coffee, Wak-Em Up, Andersen-Ryan Coffee Co., Indian Chief Logo, 5 x 4⅝ In.	1783
Pail, Drummond's Tobacco, Black Jockey, Wood, Wire Bail Handle, 6 x 7 In.	127
Pail, H.J. Heinz Mince Meat, Wood, Bail Handle, Paper Label, 1906, 10 In.	1265
Pail, Jackie Coogan Candy, Lithograph, Foss & Co., 3⅜ x 3¾ In.	142
Pail, MacLaren Peanut Butter, Mug Handle, Pry Lid, Tin, Canada, 2½ x 3⅝ In.	106
Pail, Ojibwa Chewing Tobacco, American Indian, Yellow, Red, Tin Lithograph, 6 x 6 In.	604
Pail, Oriole Tobacco, Paper Label, American Tobacco Co., Wood, 10 Lb. ....*illus*	104
Pail, Ox Heart Peanut Butter, Heart Shape Fruit, Yellow, Handle, Tin, 1930s, 4 In.	50
Pail, Peter Rabbit Peanut Butter, Characters At Table, Tin Lithograph, Lid, 4 x 3 In.	1064
Pail, Sweet Clover Tobacco, Buffington Tobacco, Wood, 12 x 13 In.	265
Pail, Tobacco, Board Of Trade, Power & Stuart, Toledo, Ohio, 9¾ x 12½ x 12¾ In.	115
Pail, Tobacco, Sweet Cuba, Spaulding & Merrick Co., Wood, Lithograph Label, 11 x 12 In.	253
Pail, Tobacco, Wooden, Senate, Barbe & Stout Co., Senators Debating, 12¼ x 12 In.	58
Pail, Toyland Peanut Butter, Pail, Pry-Lid, E.K. Pond Co., Tin, 4 x 3⅝ In.	201
Pin, Altoona Tyrone Speedway, Motorcycle Races, Admission, 1957, 1 In.	115
Pin, Cisco Kid, Radio Station & Mrs. Wagner's Pies, Portrait, 1950s, 3½ In.	633
Pin, Faust Coffee, Devil, Sentney Wholesale Grocery Co., c.1910, 1¼ In.	192
Pin, Hamilton, World's Best Watch, Steam Engine, Pocket Watch, c.1910, 2 In.	253
Pin, Jordan Marsh Co., Teddy Bear, Seated, Open Arms, 1900s, 1¼ In.	201
Pin, Meet Me At Woodman's, Santa Portrait, Bag Of Toys, 1920s, 1¼ In.	251
Pin, National Tractor Co., Cedar Rapids, Tractor Photo, 1900s, 1¼ In.	279
Pin, Teddy Bear Bread, Tin Lithograph, Figural, Roosevelt Teacher Bear, 1904, 2 In.	115
Pin, Walker's Soap, Is Good Soap, Red & Green Bird, 1¼ In. Diam.	127
Pin, Wonder Woman, Sensation Comics, Portrait, Yellow, Red, 1942, 1 In.	1380
Print, Winchester, 2 Bear Dogs In Barn, H.R. Poore, Frame, 29 x 37 In. ....*illus*	2300
Program, Ringling Bros., World's Greatest Shows, 40 Pgs., 1915, 7 x 10 In.	139
Ring, Captain Video, TV's 1st Space Show, Brass, Plastic Dome, Portrait, c.1950	383
Salt & Pepper Shakers are listed in the Salt & Pepper category.	
Scales are listed in the Scale category.	
Shoebox, Daniel Green Felt Shoe Co., Cat Images, Cat Felt Shoes, 8¼ x 5¼ x 2⅝ In.	307
Shoehorn, J. & T. Cousins Shoe Co. Hoserie, Woman's Crossed Legs, Celluloid, 3⅜ x 1⅜ In.	83
Sign, 7Up, Moe's Lunch, Red, 44 x 56 In.	819
Sign, 7Up, Open, Tin, Sidewalk, 2-Sided, Easel Style, Black, Red, 1950s, 33 x 21 In.	738
Sign, A.B. Wells Dentist, Wood Plank, Rectangular, Beveled Edge, 9 x 23 In.	177
Sign, Aetna Insurance Co., Reverse Painted, Gilt, Mt. Vesuvius, 1800s, 53 x 39 In.	1700
Sign, Albert C. Whitaker, General Store, Black & White, c.1900, 30 x 72 In.	1080
Sign, American Painted Horseshoe, W.L. Riley, 1800s, 32 x 32 x 1¾ In.	563
Sign, Andre, Orangeade, A. Cometti, Paris, Frame, 1930, 49 x 33 In.	600
Sign, Anheuser-Busch, Fine Beer, On Draught, Reverse Glass, Shaped, 12 x 6 In.	4920
Sign, Aurora, Frankenstein Model Kit, Figural, 2-Sided, Cardboard, 1963, 13 In.	538
Sign, Avery Medicine, Lactart Acid Of Milk, Milkmaid In Country Setting, 29¼ x 13 In.	575
Sign, Ball-Band Rubbers, Trademark, Red, White, Blue, Canvas, Tacked, c.1925, 10 x 60 In.	100
Sign, Bartels Beer, People At Table, Drinking, Tin Lithograph, Frame, 28 x 23 In.	4485
Sign, Beech-Nut Black Cough Drops, Cardboard, 11 x 21 In.	1438

Sign, Beech-Nut Gum, Cardstock, Die Cut, c.1929, 6½ x 5 In.	47
Sign, Beech-Nut Gum, Woman In Hat, Orange & Blue, Taste Tells, 16 x 44 In.	316
Sign, Beech-Nut Gum, Will Rogers, Cardboard, c.1929, 11⅛ x 21 In.	184
Sign, Beech-Nut Mints, Cardboard Lithograph, Easel Back, Man, Woman, Formal Wear, 26 x 17 In.	546
Sign, Big League Chewing Gum, Player Portraits, Babe Ruth, 1933, 14 x 12 In.	5400
Sign, Bin Topper, Aim Toothpaste, Superman Kites, Cardboard, 1976, 19 x 30 In.	146
Sign, Bin Topper, Oh Dawn Soap, Super Heroes, Cardboard, 1979, 20 x 20 In.	221
Sign, Bixby's Shoe Polish, Cutout Woman Holding Package, Fabric, Cardboard, 35 In. ...... *illus*	363
Sign, Bloomer Club Cigar, White Frame, Stencil, Mat, Glass, c.1890, 29 x 35 In.	125
Sign, Boiled Eggs, Beans, Pies, Tea & Coffee, Late 1800s, 47 x 11½ In.	4250
Sign, Boston Garter, Fred Clarke & Frank Chance, Cardboard, 1912, 4 x 8¼ In. ...... *illus*	24000
Sign, Bromo-Seltzer, Figural, Nurse, Die Cut Cardboard, Easel Back, 60 x 17 In.	1200
Sign, Buchanan The Tailor, 1-Board Panel, 1800s, 24½ x 81¾ In.	360
Sign, Buck Cigar, King Of The Range, Figural Buck, Die Cut, Embossed, 13 In.	523
Sign, C.W. Common, Black & White, 2-Sided, c.1900-20, 9¾ x 96 In.	270
Sign, Camel Cigarettes, R.J. Reynolds, Trainer & Lion, Paper Lithograph, 1930s, 10 x 21 In.	345
Sign, Campbells, Tomato Soup, Red, Enamel, Can Shape, 1920s, 13 x 24 In.	1650
Sign, Carnival, 3 Darts, Fallen Darts Not Returned, Wood, Arched, 9 x 24 In., Pair	708
Sign, Case Farm Equipment, Eagle, Globe, Die Cut, Enamel, J.I. Case Co., 80 x 33 In. ...... *illus*	11550
Sign, Cereal, Kellogg's Corn Flakes, Superman, Cardboard, 2-Sided, 1956, 13 x 34 In.	721
Sign, Champagne Joseph Perrier, Grapes, Champagne Bottle, J. Stall, c.1929, 62 x 46 In.	3120
Sign, Chester Whites, Thomas Hans, Livestock, Metal, 2-Sided, 36 x 40 In.	330
Sign, Chesterfield Cigarettes, Best For You, Ben Hogan, Golfer, 1951, 21 x 22 In.	371
Sign, Chesterfield Cigarettes, Fred Waring, Harry James, Paper Lithograph, 1940s, 11 x 21 In..	59
Sign, Clabber Girl, The Healthy Baking Powder, Tin, 2-Sided, 1912, 11¾ x 34 In.	100
Sign, Coleman Lamps & Lanterns, Tin, Cardboard, Lamp, Lantern, c.1918, 6 x 9 In.	604
Sign, Columbia Records, Art Hickman's Orchestra, Indian, Girl, Cardboard, 1920s, 17 x 11 In.	265
Sign, Columbian, Beer, Embossed, Tennessee Brewing Co. Logo, c.1900	380
Sign, Concord Dairy Inc., Red & Yellow, Enameled, 22 In. Diam.	1006
Sign, Coors, Illinois State Shape, Neon, 24 x 19 In.	70
Sign, Cottolene, Shortening, N.K. Fairbank Co., Child Scholar, Paper Litho, 29 x 14 In. ...... *illus*	690
Sign, Cream Separators, Vermont Farm Machine Co., 9¼ x 19⅝ In.	118
Sign, Creole Bookstore, Carved Bust Of Creole Woman, 18¾ x 24¼ x 3 In.	875
Sign, Curtiss Wright Flying School, Bi-Wing Plane, Cardboard, 23 x 13 In.	1783
Sign, DeLaval Cream Separators, Tin, Green Version, Gesso Frame, 29½ x 41 In. ...... *illus*	2900
Sign, DeLaval Dairy Farm, Tin Lithograph, Yellow, 11⅞ x 15¾ In.	224
Sign, Dr. D. Jayne's, Blood Purifier, Reverse Painted, Cherub, 13½ x 11½ In. ...... *illus*	1276
Sign, Dr. Daniels' Special Dog Medicines, Dogs Playing Poker, Paper, Frame, 13 x 17 in. ...... *illus*	160
Sign, Dr. Jayne's Blood Purifier, Glass, Child, Wings, Flower, Frame, 12 x 13 In.	1898
Sign, Dr. Scholl's Zino-Pads, Blue With White Lettering, Enamel, 7½ x 23⅞ In.	1495
Sign, Dr. W.F. Long, Physician & Surgeon, Shamrock, Berks Co., Pa., 16⅝ x 11¾ In.	248
Sign, Drink Grape Ola It's Real Grape, Embossed Tin, Grape Cluster, 20 x 14 In. ...... *illus*	203
Sign, Edison Phonographs, Records & Supplies, Wood, Paint, c.1915, 48 x 24 In.	1185
Sign, Effinger's Schlehen Brau, Tin Over Cardboard, Red, Cigar, 19¼ x 6¼ In.	1410
Sign, Elephant Brand Fertilizers, Elephant, Enamel, Embossed, 30 x 40 In.	440
Sign, Elliott Bros., Ready Mixed Paint, Barrels, Yellow, 2-Sided, c.1880, 22 x 51 In. ...... *illus*	5535
Sign, Enjoy Taystee Bread, Enamel, 1½ x 17 In.	271
Sign, Enterprise Mfg. Co., Uncle Sam, Men, Meat Choppers, Paper Litho, 15 x 17 In. ...... *illus*	546
Sign, Eveready Sold Here, India's Best Batteries, Enamel, 1930s, 18 x 12 In.	300
Sign, Eveready Columbia Dry Batteries, They Last Longer, Frame, 25 x 19 In.	489
Sign, F.W. Cook Famous Bottled Beer, Fortune-Teller, Frame, 23 x 19 In.	800
Sign, Fairy Soap, Little Sweethearts, Boy Giving Girl Flower, 1901, 23 x 31 In.	30
Sign, Father John's Medicine, Paper Over Tin, 41½ x 83 In.	234
Sign, Fisk Service Station, Boy Holding Candle & Tire, Blue & Yellow, Wood, 47 x 30 In.	4485
Sign, Frings 3 Bros Cigars, Hand Painted, Tin, Black, Red, Yellow, Frame, c.1910, 37 x 47 In. ...	175
Sign, G.S. Withers Marble & Granite Works, Scalloped Ends, Late 1800s, 18½ x 108 In.	180
Sign, Garage L.W. McConnaughey, Painted, 2-Board, Black, Green, White, c.1920, 24 In.	300
Sign, Gee-Whiz Chewing Gum, Cardboard, Frank Fleer & Co., Phila., 11 x 8 In. ...... *illus*	174
Sign, Geo. B. Deardorff & Son Hardware, Late 1800s, 11½ x 66½ In.	270
Sign, Ghirardelli's Cocoa, Pyrography, c.1900, 10½ x 22 In.	270

Advertising, Sign, Case Farm Equipment, Eagle, Globe, Die Cut, Enamel, J.I. Case Co., 80 x 33 In. $11,550

Rich Penn Auctions

Advertising, Sign, Cottolene, Shortening, N.K. Fairbank Co., Child Scholar, Paper Litho, 29 x 14 In. $690

Wm Morford Auctions

Advertising, Sign, DeLaval Cream Separators, Tin, Green Version, Gesso Frame, 29½ x 41 In. $2,900

Showtime Auction Services

Advertising, Sign, Dr. D. Jayne's, Blood Purifier, Reverse Painted, Cherub, 13 ½ x 11 ½ In.
$1,276

They Might Have Been Clara Rolls

Tootsie Roll candy was first made in 1896 in New York City by Leo Hirshfield. He named the candy for his daughter Clara, whose nickname was Tootsie.

Advertising, Sign, Dr. Daniels' Special Dog Medicines, Dogs Playing Poker, Paper, Frame, 13 x 17 In.
$160

Advertising, Sign, Drink Grape Ola It's Real Grape, Embossed Tin, Grape Cluster, 20 x 14 In.
$203

Sign, Grain Belt Beer, Cardboard, S, August Schell Brewing Co., 12 x 26¾ x 1¾ In.		153
Sign, Grape-Nuts, To School Well Fed, Tin Lithograph, Self-Framed, 20 x 30 In.	*illus*	1276
Sign, Greenback Smoking Tobacco, Frog, Cardboard, Die Cut, 11 In.	*illus*	230
Sign, H.W. Johns' Liquid Paints, Asbestos, Painted, 2-Sided, c.1900, 12 x 32 In.		480
Sign, Hamm's, Woman, Sandwich, Chips, Beer, Cardboard, 34 x 25 In.		610
Sign, Hawkes Oil & Vinegar Cruets, Frame, 11¾ x 7¾ In.		345
Sign, Hercules Gunpowder, Hercules, Nude, Tin Over Cardboard, String, 13 x 9 In.		460
Sign, Hershey's Baking Chocolate & Cocoa, Boy & Girl, Eating Cake, c.1934, 46 x 30 In.		403
Sign, Hollywood Picture Star Gum, Cardboard, Red, White, 6 x 8½ In.		209
Sign, Home Comfort, Wrought Steel Ranges & Furnaces, Factory Scene, 1890s, 4 x 5 In.		220
Sign, Horny Goat Brewing Co., 21 x 25 In.		53
Sign, Huntsman Rigen's Fine Ale, Fox Hunter On Horse, Wood, Mid 1900s, 35½ x 24 In.		510
Sign, Hussey Leaf Tobacco, Nude Woman, Paper Lithograph, Cardboard, 17 x 13 In.		2300
Sign, Huyler's Candy, Candy Box Shape With Ribbon, 2-Sided, Die Cut, 13¾ x 19¾ In.		219
Sign, I. Wharper Whiskey, Vitrolite Glass, Here's Happy Days, Frame, c.1909, 24 x 18 In.		2196
Sign, I.W. Harper Whiskey, Here's To Happy Days, Bernheim, 1909, 24 x 30 In.	*illus*	1160
Sign, International Stock Food, New Orleans Fire Department Endorsement, 1909, 16 x 22 In.		1800
Sign, Iroquois Brewing Co., N.Y., Paper Lithograph, Factory Scene, Frame, 34 x 41 In.	*illus*	5865
Sign, J.C. Lewis Jeweler, Pocket Watch Shape, Tin, 2-Sided, c.1900, 57 x 40 In.		2370
Sign, J.H. Glover, Veterinarian, Wood, 2-Sided, 15 x 28 In.		212
Sign, James H. Walker & Co. Wholesale Drygoods, Red Walnut Frame, Calendar, 1886, 24 x...		600
Sign, James Law, Ladies Boot & Shoe Maker, Tin, Sheet Iron, c.1880, 14 x 20 In.	*illus*	800
Sign, Jax Keg Beer, Authorized Dealer, DSP, Red, Yellow, Logo, 25½ In.		4920
Sign, John Collins Soda, Not Too Sweet, Bellboy, 6-Pack, Tin, 47 x 17 In.		615
Sign, John Franks Licensed To Retail Beer, c.1880, 25 x 37 In.		1800
Sign, John Jameson & Son Whiskey, Oil On Panel, Golfers, Frame, 33 x 48 In.		7703
Sign, John Phelan, Mug Of Beer, Wood, Weathered Paint, Concave Cut Edges, 42 x 61 In.		8610
Sign, Kansas Livery Stable, Horse, Buggy, Watercolor, Paper, c.1885, 14 x 19 In.		450
Sign, Keen Kutter Tools, Green, Red, Tin Lithograph, Embossed, 10 x 28 In.		242
Sign, Keil, Keys Made, Key Shape, 11 x 31 In.		234
Sign, Kerr's Spool Cotton, Thread, Girl & Dog, Paper, Cardboard, 20 x 15 In.		633
Sign, Kodak Film, Figural Film Box, Steel, Yellow, Red, 2-Sided, Iron Hanger, 21 In.		1476
Sign, Korry Krome, Leather Shoe Soles, Tin, Lithograph, 9⅜ x 19½ In.		307
Sign, Learn To Drink Moxie, Very Healthful, Woman Serving Glass, Die Cut, Wood, 42 In.		6600
Sign, Levi's, Neon, 17 x 7 In.		105
Sign, Lift Brand, 3 Star Bottling Works, Drink, It's Good For You, 24 x 12 In.		265
Sign, Lightning Rods, National Lightening Protection Co., Metal, 3 x 15⅜ In.		47
Sign, Limonade Brault, Philippe Henri Noyer, 1938, 63 x 46 In.		5750
Sign, Lord Calvert Coffee, Since 1842, Canvas, Hand Painted, 2-Sided, 18 x 36 In.		177
Sign, Mayo's Plug Tobacco, Rooster, Yellow Ground, Cloth, 30 x 18 In.		719
Sign, Mayo's Tobacco, Man Lighting Cigarette, Bag Of Posters, Paper, 23 x 14 In.		748
Sign, Mennen's Talcum, Tray, Child, Tin, Die Cut, Flange, 22 x 14 In.	*illus*	3190
Sign, Messenger Boy Tobacco & Cigars, 5 Cents, Cardboard, Figural, 24 In.		584
Sign, Miller Genuine Draft, Football Shape, Neon, 26 In.		177
Sign, Milwaukee Brewing Co., Kid, Huge Beer Bottle, Paper, Frame, 26 x 22 In.		1610
Sign, Morning Glory Ice Cream, Metal, Embossed, M.H. Co. Phila 1159, 30 x 42 In.	*illus*	130
Sign, Mrs. E.M. Farnsworth, Dress Maker, c.1880, 16½ x 43 In.		750
Sign, Nabisco, Boxes Of Products, Tin Lithograph, Serpentine Frame, 1905, 28 x 29 In.		917
Sign, Neuweiler's Cream Ale, Woman, Glass, Cardboard, Frame, 29 x 40 In.		840
Sign, New Bremen, Pine, Gold On Black, Weathered, Late 1800s, 14 x 76 In.		120
Sign, Nutwood Whiskey, Woman, Reclining, Ivory, Frame, c.1890, 29 x 23 In.		4305
Sign, Old Possum Hollow Whiskey, Nude In Woods, Round Tin Lithograph, 10 In.		1438
Sign, Orange Crush, Figural Bottle, Brown, Orange, Tin, Embossed, 1930s, 18 In.		1800
Sign, Original Budweiser, In Bottles, Eagle, Tin, Oval, Red, Yellow, Frame, 12 In.		1046
Sign, Pabst, Tin Over Cardboard, Yellow, Beer Can & Bottle, 14 x 17 In.		1059
Sign, Park & Pollard, Poultry Feeds, Lay Or Bust, Enamel, 7 x 20 In.		1265
Sign, Pay Car Scrap Tobacco, Tobacco Pack, Tin Lithograph, Embossed, 18 x 14 In.		345
Sign, Perma-Lac, Woman Holding Can, Shellac, Shield Shape, Self-Framed, 19 x 27 In.	*illus*	949
Sign, Petrole Hahn, Pour Les Cheveux, Lithograph, Frame, c.1900, 54 x 42 In.		246

Advertising, Sign, Elliott Bros., Ready Mixed Paint, Barrels, Yellow, 2-Sided, c.1880, 22 x 51 In.
$5,535

Skinner, Inc.

Advertising, Sign, Enterprise Mfg. Co., Uncle Sam, Men, Meat Choppers, Paper Litho, 15 x 17 In.
$546

Wm Morford Auctions

Advertising, Sign, Gee-Whiz Chewing Gum, Cardboard, Frank Fleer & Co., Phila., 11 x 8 In.
$174

Showtime Auction Services

Advertising, Sign, Grape-Nuts, To School Well Fed, Tin Lithograph, Self-Framed, 20 x 30 In.
$1,276

Showtime Auction Services

Advertising, Sign, Greenback Smoking Tobacco, Frog, Cardboard, Die Cut, 11 In.
$230

Rachel Davis Fine Arts

Advertising, Sign, I.W. Harper Whiskey, Here's To Happy Days, Bernheim, 1909, 24 x 30 In.
$1,160

Showtime Auction Services

Advertising, Sign, Iroquois Brewing Co., N.Y., Paper Lithograph, Factory Scene, Frame, 34 x 41 In.
$5,865

Wm Morford Auctions

Advertising, Sign, James Law, Ladies Boot & Shoe Maker, Tin, Sheet Iron, c.1880, 14 x 20 In.
$800

Skinner, Inc.

Advertising, Sign, Mennen's Talcum, Tray, Child, Tin, Die Cut, Flange, 22 x 14 In.
$3,190

Showtime Auction Services

Advertising, Sign, Morning Glory Ice Cream, Metal, Embossed, M.H. Co. Phila 1159, 30 x 42 In.
$130

Leonard Auction

Advertising, Sign, Perma-Lac, Woman Holding Can, Shellac, Shield Shape, Self-Framed, 19 x 27 In.
$949

Hake's Americana & Collectibles

Advertising, Sign, Polar Bear Tobacco, Always The Best, Polar Bear Pictured, Enamel
$600

Robert Edward Auctions

Advertising, Sign, Renk Dealer, Kernel Renk, Seed Dealer Mascot, Metal, Presco, 27 x 18 In.
$248

Rich Penn Auctions

Sign, Pharmacy, Chief Two Moon Bitter Oil, Die Cut, Cardboard, c.1888-1933, 40½ x 53 In. ...	150
Sign, Phelps, Shoe Shape, 66 x 43 In.	263
Sign, Piedmont Cigarettes, Virginia Tobacco Is Best, Enamel, Steel, c.1920, 46 x 30 In.	100
Sign, Pigeon Cove Inn, Carved Pigeon Head, Closed Beak, Pine, c.1810, 25 In.	9480
Sign, Polar Bear Tobacco, Always The Best, Polar Bear Pictured, Enamel..........*illus*	600
Sign, Pollard & Son Armourers, Crossed Cannons, Pine, Arched, 1900s, 42 x 36 In.	770
Sign, Poll-Parrot Shoes, Perched Parrot, Plastic, Paint, 1940s, 11 x 19 In.	139
Sign, Portland Taxi Co., Black & White Taxi, Cardboard Window Sign, 10½ x 14⅜ In.	177
Sign, Post Office, Blue & Gilt Lettering, Painted, Black Ground, 62 x 13 In.	5175
Sign, Poth's Beer, Yellow & Orange, Light-Up, Metal Frame With Chain, Round, 17¼ In.	6555
Sign, Public Telephone, 19 x 19 In.	35
Sign, Pullman Sleeping Cars, Chicago & Alton Railway, Frame, 29¼ x 11¾ In.	276
Sign, Rare Books, William Todd, Black, Gilt, Wood, Carved, c.1880, 21 x 23 In.	3250
Sign, Red Goose Shoes, For Boys For Girls, Sheet Steel, c.1925, 60 x 42 In.	100
Sign, Red Indian Tobacco, 5 Cents, Indian Chief, Bow, Arrow, Paper, 28 x 22 In.	2415
Sign, Renk Dealer, Kernel Renk, Seed Dealer Mascot, Metal, Presco, 27 x 18 In........*illus*	248
Sign, Roger Williams Brewing Corp., The Beer Of Good Cheer, Seal, Tin, 9½ x 14 In.	889
Sign, R-Pep Soda, Tin Lithograph, Soda Bottle Shape, 47¾ x 11½ In.	374
Sign, Safe-T Cones, Illinois Baking Co., Die Cut, Easel Back, 12⅝ x 7 In.	224
Sign, Safe-T Cones, Pinup Girl, Ice Cream Cone, Cardboard, Die Cut, Easel, 12 x 7 In.	225
Sign, Samoset Chocolates, Heavy Felt, Wooden Hanger, Indian In Canoe, 13½ x 11 In.	661
Sign, Sanitary Groceries, A.J. Eustice Dry Goods Stop & Shop, Late 1800s, 23 x 33½ In.	570
Sign, Schlitz Beer, Globe Logo, Reverse Glass, Oval, 45½ In.	3660
Sign, Sherwin-Williams Paints, Cover The Earth, Figural, Enamel, 35 x 18 In.	1380
Sign, Sherwin-Williams Paints, Enamel, For All Kinds Of Good Painting, 20⅜ x 12¾ In.	776
Sign, Squire's Arlington, Hams-Bacon-Sausage, Pig, Human Features, 24 x 20 In. .....*illus*	2128
Sign, Star Shoes, Die Cut Tin Lithograph, Race Car Driver, Wheels Fold Down, 2 x 8 In.	1955
Sign, Sterling Beer, Bottle, Bullet Shape, Reverse Glass, Wood, Light-Up, 13 In.	1046
Sign, Stetson Hats, Carl Moon, Photograph, Mat, Gilt Imprint, Frame, 12 x 15 In.........*illus*	984
Sign, Store, Store Display, Figural Scissors, Metal, Black Handles, c.1945, 36 In.	308
Sign, Store, Undertaker, White, Black, Gold Letters & Border, 2-Sided, 48 x 12 In.	1353
Sign, Store, Watch, Figural, Wood, Weathered Paint, 2-Sided, 29 x 21 In.	1046
Sign, Sugar Puff Waffles, Oh My But They Are Good, Early 1900s, 38¾ x 65½ In.	1440
Sign, Sunday World, Flying Witch, Black Cat & Broom, c.1900, 20 x 15 In.	661
Sign, Sunshine Premium Beer, Enamel, Sunshine Brewing Co., Reading, Pa., 8 x 16 In.	236
Sign, Sunshine Premium Beer, Plastic, Light-Up, 25½ x 6¼ In.	280
Sign, Sweet-Orr, Pants, Overalls, Shirts, Yellow, Blue, Enamel, 10 x 24 In.	776
Sign, The Golfers Arms, Golfer, Wood, Arch Top, Multicolor, 1950s, 40 x 27 In.	400
Sign, The Neighbor Co. Drygoods, Newcomerstown, Hand Painted, Woman, Tin, 36 x 12 In.	225
Sign, This Bud's For You, Budweiser, Neon, 14 x 21 In.	146
Sign, Time Supply, Jockey On Racehorse, Painted Wood, 2-Sided, 15 x 24 In.	148
Sign, Tolstoi Russian Cigarettes, Chromolithograph, 1900s, 22½ x 17½ In.	360
Sign, Turkey Red Cigarettes, Woman Holding Package, Red & Black, c.1910, 34 x 24 In.	840
Sign, Tydol, Red A, Wings, Round, 72 In.	2574
Sign, U.S. Cartridges & Black Shells, Standing, Growling Bear, Die Cut, 75 x 39 In.	7800
Sign, U.S. Standard Weights, She Did Not Care, She Watched Her Weight, Art Deco, 9 x 8 In.	1840
Sign, Valley Farms, Drink More Milk, Holstein Cow, Tin Lithograph, 12½ x 17 In.	118
Sign, Verifine Ice Cream, Metal, Embossed, Red Banner Accents, 41 x 49 In.	80
Sign, Waterloo Boy Tractor, Red, Yellow, Metal, Embossed, 11½ x 23 In.	2090
Sign, Wayne Dog Food, More Go Power Slogan, Dog Food Bag, 35½ x 28 In.	80
Sign, Welch Grape Juice, Drink A Bunch Of Grapes, Tin Lithograph, c.1929, 18 x 40¼ In.	1323
Sign, Welcome Soap, Real Cloth Dresses On Women, Gold Leaf Frame, 32 x 17 In..........*illus*	949
Sign, Western Union Telegraph, Blue & White, Oval Shape, Enamel, 2-Sided, 22 x 31¼ In.	661
Sign, Whale's Tale, Bait & Tackle, Whale Shape, 39 x 12 In.	380
Sign, Whipped Cream Caramels, 2 Children, Bath Bucket, Cardboard, 6 x 11 In.	316
Sign, Wiedemann's Fine Beers, Reverse Painted Glass, Donaldson, 1914, 27 x 19 In.........*illus*	3190
Sign, Wieland's Extra Pale Lager, Image Of Indian Girl, Round Tin Lithograph, 17¼ In.	2530
Sign, Wil Wite Swimwear, Turquoise, Girl Skiing On Wake Board, 41⅞ x 27⅝ In.	776
Sign, Winchester Loaded Shotgun Shells, American Lithograph NY, 25 x 33 In.........*illus*	6325

Sign, Wolverine Hybrids, Ear Of Corn, Michigan Hybrid, Metal, Embossed, 17 x 23 In.	495
Sign, Wood, Swan Hotel, 2-Sided, Barton On Humber, England, Wood, 34½ x 27½ In.	313
Sing, White Loaf Baking Powder, Tin Lithograph, Blue, Red, Embossed, 10 x 14 In.	489
Spinner, Gambling, Universal Cigars, Who Pays, Die Cut, 2¾ x 1⅜ In.	543
Stand, Old Gold Cigarettes, Figural Mae West, Cardboard, 1934, 17 x 30 In.	202
Standee, Had Your Squeeze Today?, Soda, Woman, Cardboard, 1940s, 16 x 20 In.	522
Standee, Kellogg's Pep, Boy It's Super, Superman & 3 Kids, 1947, 26 x 39 In.	3480
Standee, Pepsodent, Amos & Andy Figures, Cardboard, Easel Back, 1930, 62 In., Pair	557
Statue, Kub Kuebler, Beer, Polar Bear Holding Bottle, Chalkware, 9 In.	600
Stein, Budweiser, Glass, Etched, Cylindrical, Molded Bands, Loop Handle, 8 In.	3075
Stein, Kathreiner's Coffee Bag, Character, Enamel, ½ Liter	1140
Tap Handle, Grey Lady Ale Tap, Mermaid, 12 In.	61
Tap Handle, Six Rivers Raspberry Lambic, Nude Woman, Wrapped In Ribbon, 12 In.	208
Tap Knob, Horton Beer, Ball Shape, 2½ In.	406
Tap Knob, National Bohemian Beer, Chrome, Enameled Porcelain, 2½ x 1¾ In.	165

Thermometers are listed in the Thermometer category.

Advertising tin cans or canisters were first used commercially in the United States in 1819 and were called tins. Today the word *tin* is used by most collectors to describe many types of containers, including food tins, biscuit boxes, roly poly tobacco containers, gunpowder cans, talcum powder sprinkle-top cans, cigarette flat-fifty tins, and more. Beer Cans are listed in their own category. Things made of undecorated tin are listed under Tinware.

Tin, A&P Egg Nog, Ready To Serve, Cylindrical, Red, Blue, 1960s, 1 Qt., 7½ x 3 In.	55
Tin, Apache Trail Cigar, 5 Cent, Indian, Horse, Trail, Blue, 5¾ In.	1320 to 1920
Tin, Bagdad Short Cut Tobacco, 3¾ x 3¼ x 1⅛ In.	94
Tin, Biscuit, Chad Valley Bus, Passengers, Blue, Yellow, England, 12 In.	180
Tin, Biscuit, Chad Valley Double Decker Bus, Passengers, Green, Yellow, England, 10 In.	390
Tin, Biscuit, Normandie Ocean Liner, c.1920, France, 22½ In.	732
Tin, Biscuit, Railroad Engine, Engineers At Work, Red, England, c.1920, 12 In.	1586
Tin, Biscuit, Set Of 8 Books, Famous Titles, Multicolor, 6½ In.	396
Tin, Black Fox Cigars, Red, 5¼ In.	1140
Tin, Blackhawk's Blood & Body Tonic, Indian Chief Image, 4½ x 2¼ x 1¼ In.	106
Tin, Bunny Brand Paprika, Seated Rabbit, Tin, Paper Label, Oz., 3 x 2 In.	604
Tin, Campus Mixture Tobacco, Peach & Brown, Square Corner, Lithograph, 3 x 5 In.	920
Tin, Chef Cloves, Chef, Cardboard, Paper Label, Metal Lid & Base, 3 Oz., 4 In.	150
Tin, Cigar, Pippins, H. Traiser & Co., Boston, Red Fruit Graphics, 5½ x 3 x 3 In.	196
Tin, City Club, Red & Green, Man In Wicker Chair, Tobacco, 3⅝ x 2¾ x 1⅜ In.	201
Tin, Coburn & Co., Allspice, Red, Eggshell Blue, Square, c.1890, 6½ x 9½ In.	240
Tin, Coffee, Arrow Brand, Indian Pulling Bow & Arrow, Green & Orange, 5½ x 4¼ In.	1006
Tin, Coffee, Little Boy Blue, Lansing Wholesale Grocers, 2-Sided, 3½ x 5⅛ In.	189
Tin, Coffee, Wampum, Paper Label, American Indian Logo, 5⅞ x 4¼ In.	531
Tin, Davis Baking Powder, Pry Lid, Sample, 1⅝ x 2 In.	24
Tin, DeSoto Coffee, Explorer, Canoe, Indian Chiefs, Paper Label, Lb., 6 x 4 In.	345
Tin, Dr. Lesure's Veterinary, Blister Treatment, Product Directions, Round, 1 x 2⅛ In.	59
Tin, Drum Mixture, Drum Shape, Brown Bros Co., Tobacco, 2¼ x 3 In.	719
Tin, DuPont, Indian Rifle Gunpowder, Red, Oval, Metal Cap, 5 In.	308
Tin, English Walnut Tobacco, 4⅜ x 3 x 7⅞ In.	378
Tin, Ever-Well Spice, Mace, Everette & Treadwell Co., 2½ x 2¼ x 1¼ In.	106
Tin, First American Peas, Fame Canning Co., Indian Logo, 4½ x 3⅜ In.	83
Tin, Forest Giant, Scotten, Dillon Co., Detroit, 4 x 4 In.	283
Tin, Fra-Bac Mixture Tobacco, Black, Red, Tin Lithograph, Vertical, Pocket, 4 x 3 In.	1323
Tin, Full Dress Tobacco, Man In Tuxedo, Vertical, Sears, Pocket, 4 x 3 In.	1035
Tin, Genesco Condom, Black & Yellow Stripes, 1¾ x 1⅞ x ⅜ In.	130
Tin, Gevalia Coffee, Father, Christmas, Lantern, Walking Stick, Elves, c.1930, 5 x 9 In.	1005
Tin, Gobblers, The Latest Smoke, Turkey, Round, Tin Lithograph, 50 Count, 5 x 5 In.	661
Tin, Golf Club Brand Tumeric, Tin Top & Base, Cardboard, Golf Scene, 3 x 2 In.	184
Tin, Gordon's Cocoanut, Ginna & Co. Monkey Logo, 6 x 3⅝ x 2⅝ In.	71
Tin, Guards Cold Tablets, Whitehall Pharmacal Co., Hinged Lid, c.1944, 1¾ x 1⅜ In.	25
Tin, H&K Coffee, Vacuum Packed, Genie Tray, Key Wind, c.1928, 7½ x 6 In.	195
Tin, Hand Made Tobacco, Flake Cut, Woman's Hand, Tin Lithograph, Pocket, 4 x 4 In.	316

Advertising, Sign, Squire's Arlington, Hams-Bacon-Sausage, Pig, Human Features, 24 x 20 In.
$2,128

Wm Morford Auctions

Advertising, Sign, Stetson Hats, Carl Moon, Photograph, Mat, Gilt Imprint, Frame, 12 x 15 In.
$984

Cowan's Auctions

Advertising, Sign, Welcome Soap, Real Cloth Dresses On Women, Gold Leaf Frame, 32 x 17 In.
$949

Wm Morford Auctions

Advertising, Sign, Wiedemann's Fine Beers, Reverse Painted Glass, Donaldson, 1914, 27 x 19 In.
$3,190

Showtime Auction Services

Advertising, Sign, Winchester Loaded Shotgun Shells, American Lithograph NY, 25 x 33 In.
$6,325

James D. Julia Auctioneers

Tin, Hiawatha Tobacco, Hinged Lid, Indian Image, 4 Oz.	105
Tin, Indian Chief Canned Clams, Shaw & Ellis Co., 4¾ x 3 In.	94
Tin, Jipco Brand, Ground Ginger, Buffalo, Cardboard, Metal Top & Base, 4 x 2 In.	546
Tin, Kim-Bo Tobacco, 5 Cents, Gypsy Woman, Cardboard, Tin Lid & Base, 4 In.	127
Tin, Kipawa Cigars, Indian Image, Tobacco, 6⅜ x 4⅜ x 4⅜ In.	3795
Tin, Kopper Kettle Klub Cigars, Tin Lithograph, Kettle Image, 50 Ct., 5½ x 5 In.	288
Tin, Logan Brand, Sugar Corn, Indian Chief, 4½ x 3⅜ In.	106
Tin, Lucky Duck Cigars, 5 In.	976
Tin, Lucky Strike Tobacco, 4½ x 3 x ⅞ In.	307
Tin, Mambo Talk, Latin American Dancer, 5½ x 5 x 2 In.	177
Tin, Manoli Tobacco, Cigarettes, Gibson Girl, Box, c.1915, 3 x 4 In.	85
Tin, Maryland Club Mixture, Marburg Bros., Orange & Blue, 4 x 3⅜ x 1¼ In.	403
Tin, Masga Spar Varnish, Airplane, Speedboat, Black, Light Blue, Gal., 10 x 7 In.	138
Tin, Meteor Spice, Turmeric, Lebanon Wholesale Grocer's, Lebanon, Mo., 3 x 2 x 1 In.	35
Tin, Mohawk Tobacco, Indian Image, Lithograph, 2⅛ x 3⅜ x ⅞ In.	307
Tin, Molly Pitcher Cookies, Lithograph, Brown & Gold, Savory Baking Co., c.1930, 6 x 5 In.	90
Tin, N.V. Van Melle's, Toffee, Bird, Shaped, Slant Lid, Turquoise, Gold, 10 In.	369
Tin, Natoma Rose Talc, Indian Princess, Roses, Green, Conical, Lid, Finial, 5 x 3 In.	184
Tin, No-To-Bac, Sterling Remedy Co., Slaying Tobacco Habit, Set Of 3, 2⅜ x 3¾ x ⅝ In.	189
Tin, Oak Hill Spice, Country Estate, Tin Lithograph, Round, Oz., 3 x 1½ In.	70
Tin, On Time Chewing Gum, Clockfaces, Light Blue, Gilt Stencil, Handle, 2 x 8 In.	95
Tin, Our Own Black Cough Drops, E.J. Hoadley, Cylindrical, 1880s, 8½ In. *illus*	363
Tin, Popper's Ace Cigars, Bi-Wing Plane, Mint & Gold, Tin Lithograph, 10 Ct., 6 x 3 In.	1840
Tin, Puritan, Philip Morris, Pilgrim Logo, Tobacco, 4⅜ x 3⅞ In.	165
Tin, Red Indian Tobacco, Red, Black Letters, Indian Chief Logo, 4¼ x 7⅞ x 5⅜ In.	2530
Tin, Re-Joyce Ginger, 2 Girls Skipping, Holding Hands, Tin Lithograph, 2 Oz., 4 x 2 In.	518
Tin, Rose Bud Pure Spices, Thyme, Red Rose Bud, Stem, Tin Lithograph, 3 x 2 In.	105
Tin, Sailor Boy Cocoanut, Sailor Climbing Pole, Stepped Lid, Tin Lithograph, 9 x 8 In.	633
Tin, Silvertip's Popcorn, Indian Chief, White, Red, Blue, Tin Lithograph, 8 Oz., 5 x 3 In.	518
Tin, Sir Walter Raleigh Tobacco, Portrait, Red, Black, Tin Lithograph, 3 In. Diam.	431
Tin, Skookum Syrup, Indian Teepee, Maple, Symbols, Figural, 12 Oz., 6 x 4 In.	403
Tin, Smith's White Fruit Cake, Delicacy From Dixie, Woman, Round, 8 x 3 In.	20
Tin, Spice, Cloves, Manhattan Products Co., St. Louis, Mo., 3¼ x 2⅜ x 1¼ In.	142
Tin, Spice, Fiesta, Field & Start Co., Green & Yellow & Red, 3⅛ x 2¼ x 1¼ In.	71
Tin, Sunset Trail Cigar, Men Riding Horses, Roby Cigar Co., 5¼ In.	1375
Tin, Syrup, Log Cabin Brand, Towle Co., Log Cabin Shape, 4 x 3⅝ x 2½ In.	35
Tin, Three Feathers, Blue & Orange, Tobacco, 4⅛ x 3⅜ x 1¼ In.	177
Tin, Tiger Chewing Tobacco, Early 1900s, 11¾ In.	105
Tin, Tippecanoe Brand Vegetable Oil, Sugar Corn, Indian In Canoe, 5 x 4 In.	288
Tin, Totem Cigars, Totem Pole, Multicolor, Tin Lithograph, Rectangular, 25 Ct., 6 x 3 In.	460
Tin, Trout-Line, Burley Cut, Green, Red, Fly Fisherman Logo, Tobacco, 3¾ x 3½ In.	431
Tin, Turkey Brand Coffee, Turkey, Olive Green, 10½ In.	461
Tin, Turkey Coffee, 10⅝ x 5½ In.	401
Tin, Wagon Wheel Tobacco, Yellow, Brown, Tin Lithograph, Vertical, Pocket, 4 x 3 In.	431
Tin, Wapello Chief Pure Spices, Cinnamon, Indian Chief, Square, 8 Oz., 5 x 3 In.	690
Tin, White Bear Coffee, Polar Bear, Lithograph, Key Wind, Lb., 4 x 5 In.	280
Tin, White Horse, Indian On Horse, Reid Murdoch & Co., Chicago, 6 x 4¼ In.	484
Tin, Yankee Brand Cigarettes, Hinged Lid, Patriotic Images, 3⅛ x 4 x ⅜ In. *illus*	403
Tin, Zeno Chewing Gum, Lithograph, Dutch Images, 5¾ x 9½ x 2¼ In.	83

Advertising tip trays are decorated metal trays less than 5 inches in diameter. They were placed on the table or counter to hold either the bill or the coins that were left as a tip. Change receivers could be made of glass, plastic, or metal. They were kept on the counter near the cash register and held the money passed back and forth by the cashier. Related items may be listed in the Advertising category under Change Receiver.

Tip Tray, Bartels, Medieval Watchman, Round, 4¼ In.	189
Tip Tray, Black Label Whiskey, Tin Lithograph, Gallagher & Burton Co., Rye Whiskey, 4 In.	71
Tip Tray, Deutsche Kuche & Saloon, Syracuse, N.Y., Multicolor, 4¼ In.	201
Tip Tray, Jenney Aero, Gasoline, Tin Lithograph, 4⅛ In.	130

Tip Tray, National Brewing Co., Cowboy On Horse, Bottle, Tin Lithograph, 5 In. Diam.	489
Tip Tray, Pippins 5 Cent Cigar, Apple Shape, Red, Green, White, Tin Lithograph, 5 x 5 In.	431
Tip Tray, Ryan's Pure Beers, 1907, American Art Works, 4 1/4 In.	201
Tip Tray, Success Manure Spreader, Kemp & Burpee Co., 3 3/8 x 4 3/4 In.	224
Tip Tray, Taka-Cola, 5 Cents, Clock, Woman Holding Bottle, Tin Lithograph, 4 In. Diam.	196
Toothbrush Holder, Zodenta, 4 Toothbrush Slots, 4 1/2 x 1 3/4 x 3/8 In.	271
Toy, Maxwell Coffee, Plush Bear, Pours Coffee, Tin Lithograph, Box, 1960s, 10 In.	173
Tray, A.G. Van Nostrand, Bunker Hill Breweries, Round, 12 In. ....*illus*	1694
Tray, Beer, Esslinger's Ale, Bellhop, Holding Tray, American Can Co., 1940s, 12 In.	55
Tray, Bowler Brewing Co., Profile, Woman, Fur Shawl, Tin Lithograph, 13 In. Diam.	690
Tray, Drink Dr Pepper, 5 Cents, Dog, Oval, Tin Lithograph, Scallop Rim, c.1905, 2 x 3 In.	142
Tray, Drink Zipp's, Cherri-O, 5 Cents, Bird, Berries, Drinking Soda, 1920s, 12 In.	431
Tray, Falstaff Beer, Group, Outside, Castle, 1910, 22 In.	35
Tray, Findlay Market Liquor Store, Dutch Tavern Scene, Tin, 1900s, 17 1/4 x 12 1/4 In.	480
Tray, Haberle Brewing Co., Congress Beer, Syracuse, N.Y., Round, 12 In.	2415
Tray, Hudson County Consumers Brewing Co., Factory, Square, Gilt, 10 x 14 In.	2337
Tray, Orange-Julep Soda, Bathing Beauty, Shoreline, Tin Lithograph, c.1922, 13 x 10 In.	460
Tray, Tip, see Tip Trays in this category.	
Tray, Wright & Taylor Whiskey, Round, Image Of Old Charter Distillery, 12 In.	2645
Umbrella Holder, Hanson's Magic Corn Salve Sold Here, Late 1800s, 23 1/2 In.	900
Wagon Seat, Butter & Cream, Devonshire Cream To Order, England, Late 1800s, 6 x 36 In.	1320

AGATA glass was made by Joseph Locke of the New England Glass Company of Cambridge, Massachusetts, after 1885. A metallic stain was applied to New England Peachblow, which the company called Wild Rose, and the mottled design characteristic of agata appeared. There are a few known items made of opaque green with the mottled finish.

Pitcher, Pink To White, Oil Spot Glaze, Cylindrical, Reeded Handle, 8 In.	520
Toothpick Holder, Pink To White, Gold Mottled, 1880s, 2 1/2 x 2 In.	395
Tumbler, Pink To White, Gold & Blue Mottled, 1880s, 5 In.	517
Vase, Pink To White, Gold Splash, Oval, Dimpled, Inverted Ruffled Rim, 1920s, 6 In.	795

AKRO AGATE glass was founded in Akron, Ohio, in 1911 and moved to Clarksburg, West Virginia, in 1914. The company made marbles and toys. In the 1930s it began making other products, including vases, lamps, flowerpots, candlesticks, and children's dishes. Most of the glass is marked with a crow flying through the letter A. The company was sold to Clarksburg Glass Co. in 1951. Akro Agate marbles are listed in this book in the Marble category.

Cigarette Cup, Octagonal, Milky White, Red Swirls At Base, 1930s, 3 In.	29
Flowerpot, Orange, Marbleized, Darted, Flared Rim, c.1935, 7 In.	150
Match Holder, Oxblood, Marbleized, Octagonal, Marked, 1930s, 3 x 3 In.	203
Planter, Orange, Marbleized, Oval, Lobed, Shaped Rim, 1940s, 2 1/4 x 6 In.	37
Plate, Opaque Yellow, Paneled Pattern, Marked, Child's, 4 1/4 In. Diam.	26
Powder Jar, Jade Green, Round, Crimped, Beading, Lid, Reeded Finial, 2 1/2 x 4 In.	32
Teapot, Opaque Pink, Concentric Ring Design, Angular Handle, Lid, 1940s, 3 In.	47

ALABASTER is a very soft form of gypsum, a stone that resembles marble. It was often carved into vases or statues in Victorian times. There are alabaster carvings being made even today.

Bust, Beatrice, Pink Clothes, Italy, 1920, 10 1/4 In. ....*illus*	256
Bust, Child, Finger In Mouth, Italy, c.1900, 14 1/2 In.	944
Bust, Dante, 19th Century, 13 1/2 In.	413
Bust, Goethe, 14 In.	375
Bust, Head Turned, Laurel Garland, Square, 19 In.	343
Bust, Horse, Square, 7 1/4 In.	150
Bust, Plumed Hat, Lacy Collar, 27 In.	1000
Bust, Woman As Daphne, Garland, c.1900, 21 1/2 x 13 In.	386
Bust, Woman, Flowers, Tunic, 6 1/2 x 6 1/4 In.	171

Advertising, Tin, Our Own Black Cough Drops, E.J. Hoadley, Cylindrical, 1880s, 8 1/2 In.
$363

Rachel Davis Fine Arts

Advertising, Tin, Yankee Brand Cigarettes, Hinged Lid, Patriotic Images, 3 1/8 x 4 x 3/8 In.
$403

Wm Morford Auctions

Advertising, Tray, A.G. Van Nostrand, Bunker Hill Breweries, Round, 12 In.
$1,694

Rachel Davis Fine Arts

Alabaster, Bust, Beatrice, Pink Clothes, Italy, 1920, 10 1/4 In.
$256

Jackson's International Auctioneers & Appraisers

Alabaster, Bust, Young Woman,
Gold Color Around Shoulders, c.1890,
14 x 14 x 8 In.
$805

Cottone Auctions

Alabaster, Lamp, Figural, Romeo
Climbing Ladder, Juliet, Pedestal, 68 In.
$600

Woody Auction

Aluminum, Dish, Serving, Lid, Figural,
Turtle, Hammered, Geometric Line
Design, Glass Eyes, 1979, 6 x 23 In.
$448

Neal Auctions

Bust, Woman, Hooded Robe, 8 7/8 In.	131
Bust, Woman, Square Neck, Marked Meditazione, 9 1/4 x 9 1/4 In.	129
Bust, Young Man, Looking Up, Curls, 18 3/4 In.	625
Bust, Young Woman, Gold Color Around Shoulders, c.1890, 14 x 14 x 8 In. ....*illus*	805
Centerpiece, Fluted, Pedestal, 12 7/8 In.	25
Centerpiece, Rococo, 3 Swans, Support Round Bowl, Flowers, Vines, Italy, 23 x 24 3/4 In.	125
Cup, Translucent, Opaque Brown Streaks, Handle, Peach Branch Feet, Openwork, 2 In.	62
Figurine, Beggar Boy, Seated, Head Down, Italy, 1900-25, 17 1/2 x 6 In.	125
Figurine, Woman, Sitting On Panther, Egyptian Revival, c.1920, 10 x 16 1/4 In.	1000
Group, Angels, Embrace, Wings Up, 18 x 24 In.	562
Group, Wrestlers, 17 In.	625
Group, Young Boy, Young Girl, Kissing, 34 x 17 In.	2320
Lamp, Figural, Romeo Climbing Ladder, Juliet, Pedestal, 68 In. ....*illus*	600
Pedestal, Capital, 42 In.	343
Pedestal, Child, Seated, Barefoot, Italy, 27 1/2 In.	813
Pedestal, Dancing Putti, Fluted, Carved Leaves, Swags, Round Base, c.1900, 55 In.	5500
Pedestal, Metal Mount, 36 In.	375
Pedestal, Metal Mount, Green Band, Square Plinth, 40 In.	156
Pedestal, Square Capital, 30 In.	67
Sculpture, Foo Dog, 15 x 19 In., Pair	250
Sculpture, Nude Male, Carved, Standing, Head Turned To Side, Square Base, 23 In.	60
Sculpture, Robed Woman With Book, Alabaster Pedestal, 1800s, 66 x 13 In.	863
Sculpture, Water Carrier, Woman, Stepped Onyx Plinth Base, Continental, c.1925, 27 In.	750
Sculpture, Woman, Child, Sitting, Bench, 27 1/2 In.	1125
Sculpture, Woman, Seminude, Leaning, Antique Pedestal, 23 1/2 In.	1250
Urn, Fern Frond Handles, 31 x 30 In.	1250
Urn, Neoclassical, White, Square Wooden Stepped Base, 31 1/2 In., Pair	1188
Vase, Carved Elephants, Gilt Banding, Art Deco, 8 In.	200
Vase, Cornucopia, Hippocampi, Leafy Rim, Italy, 7 In., Pair	281
Vase, Lid, Squat, Veined, Italy, 12 In.	200

ALUMINUM was more expensive than gold or silver until the 1850s. Chemists learned how to refine bauxite to get aluminum. Jewelry and other small objects were made of the valuable metal until 1914, when an inexpensive smelting process was invented. The aluminum collected today dates from the 1930s through the 1950s. Hand-hammered pieces are the most popular.

Boot Sole, Cleats, Rivet Holes On Rim, Overland Shoe Co., Marked, c.1916, 10 In.	165
Dish, Serving, Lid, Figural, Turtle, Hammered, Geometric Line Design, Glass Eyes, 1979, 6 x 23 In. . *illus*	448
Lunch Pail, Miner's Bucket, Oval, Bail Handle, Lid, Tray Insert, 9 x 7 In., 3 Piece	105
Match Holder, Roosevelt, Bust, Relief Carved, Tray, Slant Lid, c.1905, 2 x 4 1/4 In.	200
Pitcher, Baluster, Wide Wavy Spout, Loop Handle, Wagner Ware, c.1910, 8 x 9 In.	135
Pitcher, Embossed Rose, Hammered, Curved Ribbed Handle, Ice Lip, c.1950, 8 In.	24
Planter, Cylindrical, Wheels, 18 x 19 In.	94
Sculpture, Horse Head, Wall Mount, 21 x 13 In.	236
Sculpture, Owl, Glass Eyes, Wood Base, Signed, C. Jere, 1969, 10 1/2 x 5 1/2 In. ....*illus*	1063
Tray, 3 Scalloped Tiers, Gold, Mauve & Fuchsia, Silvertone Pole, Loop Handle, 13 1/2 In.	45
Tray, Banana Leaf, Royal Hickman, 25 1/2 x 5 1/2 In.	50
Trinket Box, Plays Music, Enamel, Man Wooing Woman, Round, Windup, 1940s, 4 In.	55

AMBER, *see Jewelry category.*

AMBER GLASS is the name of any glassware with the proper yellow-brown shading. It was a popular color just after the Civil War and many pressed glass pieces were made of amber glass. Depression glass of the 1930s–1950s was also made in shades of amber. Other pieces may be found in the Depression Glass, Pressed Glass, and other glass categories. All types are being reproduced.

Bowl, Fruit, Pinecones, Yellow To Brown, Ring Foot, Wide Rim, 1932, 11 In. Diam.	355
Candy Dish, Embossed Grape Clusters, Pedestal Foot, Dome Lid, Finial, 7 x 4 In	50
Compote, Cut Glass, Square Foot, 8 1/2 In., Pair	468

Compote, Cut To Clear, Birds, Animals, Tower, 5 x 8 In.	12
Decanter, Raised Diamond Pattern, Bottle Shape, Spear Finial, 23 In.	325
Liqueur Set, 3 Bottles, Silver Rococo Fittings, Cupid Finials, Germany, 14 Piece...........*illus*	1250
Powder Box, Scrolling Vines, Pale Blue Paint, Squat, Dome Lid, c.1905, 3 x 4 In.	350
Vase, Crackled, Wide Mouth, Andries Dirk Copier, 8¾ x 9¾ In.	500

AMBERINA, a two-toned glassware, was originally made from 1883 to about 1900. It was patented by Joseph Locke of the New England Glass Company but was also made by other companies and is still being made. The glass shades from red to amber. Similar pieces of glass may be found in the Baccarat, Libbey, Plated Amberina, and other categories. Glass shaded from blue to amber is called *Blue Amberina* or *Bluerina*.

Butter, Cover, Coin Spot, Matching Tray, Ball Handles, 6½ x 7 In.	201
Butter, Cover, Pumpkin Shape, Silver Plated Dish, 4¾ In.	8050
Condiment, 2 Shakers & Mustard Pot, Wilcox & Co. Silver Plated Holder, 6 In.	374
Cruet, Coin Spot, Squat, Stick Neck, Loop Handle, Faceted Stopper, 1800s, 7 In.	102
Cruet, Rose To Amber, Optic Diamond, Reeded Handle, 7 In.	24
Cuspidor, Scalloped Rim, Mt. Washington, 2¾ x 5¼ In.	61
Pitcher, Diamond-Quilted, Cylindrical, Reeded Handle, 7 In.	58
Pitcher, Narrow, Dark, Optic Ribbed, Applied Handle, 9½ In.	345
Sculpture, Bull, Salviato & Co., c.1980, 14½ x 14 In.	413
Strawholder, Rippled, Cylinder, Rolled Rim, Ring Foot, Amber Lid, Ball Finial, 14 In.	1599
Sugar, Coin Spot, 2 Applied & Reeded Handles, 4¼ In. ....*illus*	316
Syrup, Coin Spot, Applied Clear Handle, 4½ x 4 In.	24
Toothpick Holder, Red To Amber, Cylindrical, Inward Trifold Rim, c.1885, 3 x 3 In.	450
Tumbler, Pear, Cranberry Shaded To Citrus, Applied Camphor Stem, 5 In.	20
Vase, Purple, 3-Footed, Mt. Washington, 5½ In.	37
Water Set, Bulbous Pitcher, 6 Tumblers, Coin Spot, Pitcher 8 In., Tumblers 3¾ In.	58

AMERICAN DINNERWARE, *see Dinnerware.*

AMERICAN ENCAUSTIC TILING COMPANY was founded in Zanesville, Ohio, in 1875. The company planned to make a variety of tiles to compete with the English tiles that were selling in the United States for use in fireplaces and other architectural designs. The first glazed tiles were made in 1880, embossed tiles in 1881, faience tiles in the 1920s. The firm closed in 1935 and reopened in 1937 as the Shawnee Pottery.

Dish, Figural Lion Edge, Green Glaze, Tan Speckles, c.1910, 3 x 5 In.	185
Dish, Inkwell, Pen Tray, Scrolling Edges, Blue Glaze, c.1920, 4 x 7 In.	40
Tile, Bats, Low Relief, Gold Glaze, 6 x 6 In. ....*illus*	246
Tile, Cowgirl, Bucking Bronco, Tan, Red, Blue Glaze, c.1935, 4 x 4 In.	130
Tile, Fleur-De-Lis, Amber Glaze, Green, Blue, Orange, c.1920, 6 x 6 In.	135
Tile, Grape Cluster, Embossed, Green Glaze, c.1900, 6 x 6 In.	75
Tile, Peacock On Branch, Olive Green Glaze, Oak Frame, c.1880, 12 x 6 In.	861

AMETHYST GLASS is any of the many glasswares made in the dark purple color of the gemstone amethyst. Included in this category are many pieces made in the nineteenth and twentieth centuries. Very dark pieces are called *black amethyst*.

Barber Bottle, Enamel & Bead Flowers, Swollen Neck, Metal Lid, c.1905, 8 In.	140
Basket, Amulet, Laura Donefer, 14¼ x 11 In. ....*illus*	498
Bowl, Flint, Folded Rim, Faint Rims, Mid 1800s, 6¼ x 9¾ In.	420
Decanter, Etched, Landscape, 10¼ x 3¾ In.	36
Lemonade Set, Pitcher, 5 Tumblers, Flowers, On Diagonal, Leaves, 6 Piece	72
Pokal, Gilt, Shepherd, Sheep, Horn, Frost, Egg Shape Finial, 10½ x 2⅞ In.	106
Salt, Blown, Footed, Salt Diamond Pattern, Early 1800s, 3 In.	540
Sugar, Black Amethyst, Square, Scallop Rim, Pedestal Foot, Handles, c.1934, 4 In.	22
Vase, Crocus, 3½ In.	48
Vase, Gilt, Applied Flowers, 4-Footed, 16 x 4 In.	141
Vase, Ribbed, Globular, Trumpet Neck, c.1925, 6 In.	300

A

Aluminum, Sculpture, Owl, Glass Eyes, Wood Base, Signed, C. Jere, 1969, 10½ x 5½ In.
$1,063

Rago Arts and Auction Center

Amber Glass, Liqueur Set, 3 Bottles, Silver Rococo Fittings, Cupid Finials, Germany, 14 Piece
$1,250

New Orleans Auction Galleries

Amberina, Sugar, Coin Spot, 2 Applied & Reeded Handles, 4¼ In.
$316

Early Auction Company

American Encaustic, Tile, Bats, Low Relief, Gold Glaze, 6 x 6 In.
$246

Skinner, Inc.

Amethyst Glass, Basket, Amulet, Laura Donefer, 14¼ x 11 In.
$498

Jeffrey S. Evans

Animal Trophy, Buffalo Head, Glass Eyes, c.1975, 27 In.
$900

Garth's Auctioneers & Appraisers

Animal Trophy, Sawfish Bill, Brass Mount, 1900s, 43¼ x 12 In., Pair
$1,250

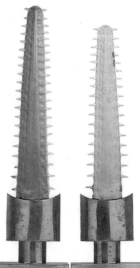

Rago Arts and Auction Center

AMPHORA *pieces are listed in the Teplitz category.*

ANDIRONS *and related fireplace items are included in the Fireplace category.*

ANIMAL TROPHIES, such as stuffed animals (taxidermy), rugs made of animal skins, and other similar collectibles made from animal, fish, or bird parts, are listed in this category. Collectors should be aware of the endangered species laws that make it illegal to buy and sell some of these items. Any eagle feathers, many types of pelts or rugs (such as leopard), ivory, rhinoceros horn, and many forms of tortoiseshell can be confiscated by the government. Related trophies may be found in the Fishing category. Ivory items may be found in the Scrimshaw or Ivory categories.

Big Horn Ram, Head Mount, 30 x 24 In.	480
Brown Bear Head, Late 1900s, 13½ In.	240
Buffalo Head, Glass Eyes, c.1975, 27 In. ....*illus*	900
Butterfly Fish, Skeleton Mount, Frame, 12 x 18 In.	930
Caribou, Shoulder Mount, Rack, 34 x 36 In.	406
Chimpanzee, Diorama, 12¼ x 14 In.	437
Deer Head, 26 x 15 In.	240
Duck Skeleton, Glass Cloche, 18½ In.	416
Elephant Foot, Trash Bin, Hinged Lid, 17 x 19 In.	335
Gazelle Head, 29 x 10 In.	944
Hippopotamus Head, Horn, 1971	1102
Horse Head, 23 x 16 In.	593
Pygmy Marmoset, Skeleton Mount, Intact Muscle, 4 In.	682
Sawfish Bill, Brass Mount, 1900s, 43¼ x 12 In., Pair ....*illus*	1250
Southern Cape Buffalo, Shoulder Mount, Angola, 1961	225
Wolverine, Full Body Mount, 19 x 33 In.	472

ANIMATION ART collectibles include cels that are painted drawings on celluloid needed to make animated cartoons shown in movie theaters or on TV. Hundreds of cels were made, then photographed in sequence to make a cartoon showing moving figures. Early examples made by the Walt Disney Studios are popular with collectors today. Original sketches used by the artists are also listed here. Modern animated cartoons are made using computer-generated pictures. Some of these are being produced as cels to be sold to collectors. Other cartoon art is listed in Comic Art and Disneyana.

Cel, Bambi, Thumper, Full Body, Tree Trunk, Mat, 1942, 13¼ x 15 In.	1012
Cel, Huckleberry Hound & Friends, Mat, Signed, c.1985, 15 x 17½ In.	261
Cel, Tom & Jerry, Filet Meow, Jerry & Goldfish, Mat, c.1966, 11 x 13 In.	115
Drawing, Gertie The Dinosaur, Rice Paper, Board, India Ink, c.1914, 12 x 14 In.	1910
Layout, Gigantic, Gorilla, Superman, Terror On The Midway, 1942, 14 x 17 In.	575

Anna Pottery **ANNA POTTERY** was started in Anna, Illinois, in 1859 by Cornwall and Wallace Kirkpatrick. They made many types of utilitarian wares, bricks, drain tiles, and giftware. The most collectible pieces made by the pottery are the pig-shaped bottles and jugs with special inscriptions, applied animals, and figures. The pottery closed in 1894.

Bottle, Pig, Albany Slip, St. Louis The Future Great, 1880, 6¼ In.	3321
Bottle, Pig, Incised Hooves & Face & Map, Albany Slip, Molded, c.1894, 6¼ In.	3300
Bottle, Pig, Incised Horace Greeley, Brown Slip Glaze, 1872, 8 In.	11500
Bottle, Pig, Incised, Cobalt Blue Highlights, Map, Landmarks, Salt Glaze, 1889, 7 In. ....*illus*	8400
Bottle, Pig, Railroad Map, A Little Good Old Bourbon, 7¼ In.	3075
Bottle, Pig, Reclining, Incised Railroad Map, Hole At Rear, 1880, 6 In.	3105
Bottle, Pig, Salt Glaze, With A Little Good Old Rye, c.1965, 8¼ In.	2091
Jug, Incised Harper's, Little Brown Jug, Snake Handle, 1883, 8¾ In.	9775
Jug, Little Brown Jug, Incised, 1884, 4 In.	210
Mug, Frog, Interior, Inscribed, Strap Handle, Flared Base, 1882, 3 In.	2875
Pipe, Indian Face, Headdress, Incised, Red Slip Glaze, 1873, 6 x 6 In.	12650

APPLE PEELERS *are listed in the Kitchen category under Peeler, Apple.*

ARABIA began producing ceramics in 1874. The pottery was established in Helsinki, Finland, by Rörstrand, a Swedish pottery that wanted to export porcelain, earthenware, and other pottery from Finland to Russia. Most of the early workers at Arabia were Swedish. Arabia started producing its own models of tiled stoves, vases, and tableware about 1900. Rörstrand sold its interest in Arabia in 1916. By the late 1930s, Arabia was the largest producer of porcelain in Europe. Most of its products were exported. A line of stoneware was introduced in the 1960s. Arabia worked in cooperation with Rörstrand from 1975 to 1977. Arabia was bought by Hackman Group in 1990 and Hackman was bought by Iittala Group in 2004. Arabia is now a brand owned by Iittala Group.

ARABIA FINLAND

Charger, Stylized Flowers, Glazed, B. Kaipainen, Finland, c.1950, 2 x 18½ In. ....*illus*	1375
Pitcher, Ivory Jug, Blue Smiling Cat, Loop Handle, c.1955, 6 In.	75
Pitcher, Stylized Hen, Blue & Black, Dots, White Ground, Marked, 6 x 8 In.	76
Plate, Cobalt Blue, Black, Flowerhead, Circle Designs, c.1960, 7½ In.	65
Platter, Anemone Flower Wreath, Cobalt Blue, Banded Rim, Oval, 14 In.	65
Salt & Pepper, Eskimo, Man & Woman, White, Red, Blue, Yellow, Bullet Shape, 2 In.	102
Sculpture, Woman, Glazed, B. Kaipainen, c.1950, 19 In. ....*illus*	1250
Sugar, Green Apples, White Ground, Flared Rim, Indented Circle Lid, 3 x 4 In.	57

ARCHITECTURAL antiques include a variety of collectibles, usually very large, that have been removed from buildings. Hardware, backbars, doors, paneling, and even old bathtubs are now wanted by collectors. Pieces of the Victorian, Art Nouveau, and Art Deco styles are in greatest demand.

Applique, Carved Walnut, Trailing Fruit, Mid 1900s, 19 x 8¾ In., Pair	1625
Applique, Wood, Gilt, Rococo Style, Roses, Italy, 1700s, 43 x 7¼ x 4 In., Pair...............	1875
Bathtub, Iron, Copper, Wood, Brass, Flower Design Legs, 1870, 24 x 74 In.	2500
Bracket, Angel Heads, Wooden, Gilt, Multicolor, 12 x 13 x 10¼ In., Pair.......................	875
Bracket, Ebony, Carved, Anglo-Ceylonese, c.1850, 21 x 17 x 6 In.	732
Bracket, Gilt, Carved, Bull's Head, America, 1800s, 12 x 11¾ x 7¾ In.	1098
Bracket, Gilt, Tapered, Leaves, Scroll, Grapes, Drop Finial, c.1965, 21 x 14 In., Pair	1250
Bracket, Giltwood, Pierced, Rocaille Work, Scrolling, Shells, 1900s, 15 In., Pair.......................	1187
Bracket, Plaster, Gilt, Rocaille, Flowers, 1900s, 13½ x 8½ x 6 In., Pair	937
Capital, Corinthian, Carved Oak, Leaves, 15 x 18½ In., Pair.......................................	688
Cartouche, Arched, Central Shell, Molded Edge, Zinc, c.1900, 23 x 42 In., Pair.............*illus*	332
Ceiling Medallion, Plaster, Irving & Casson, Round, Acanthus, 16¼ In.	120
Column, Parcel Gilt, Upswept Acanthus, Spiral, Winding Vines, Gilt Foot, 70 x 13 In., Pair.......	1071
Column, Solomonic, Spiral Design, Carved Giltwood, Paint, Grape Clusters, 51 In....................	330
Column, Wood, Turned, Painted, Twisted, Round, 39½ In., Pair...................................	125
Corbel, Pine, Figural, Heads, Multicolor, 14½ In.	1750
Corbel, Turned Wood, Gingerbread Style, Urns, Spheres, Scrolled Supports, 37¾ In., Pair.......	360
Corbel, Wood, Scrolled Acanthus, High Relief Flowers, 27 x 13½ In., Pair	476
Door Handle, Bronze, Penis Shape, After Carl Kauba, 12 x 4 In., Pair	593
Door Handle, Iron, Round, Circular Plates, Long Wavy Finials, Punched Date, 1787, 20 In.....	1230
Door Handle, Iron, Wood, Square Plate, Ring Knocker, Yellin, 1915, 13 x 13 In.	2500
Door Surround, Glass, Leaded, Stylized Flowers, Beveled Panels, Transom, 78¾ x 86¾ In.....	413
Door, Dancers, Red, Gold, 100 x 29 In., Pair	225
Door, Dog, Chrysanthemum, Wood, Multicolor, Japan, 65 x 25½ In., Pair	1000
Door, Fiberglass, Charlotte Perriand, 1960, 29 x 77 In.	3427
Door, Hidden, Bookshelf, Simulated Books, 79¼ x 47¼ In., Pair	5652
Door, Mahogany, Starburst, 61½ x 24 In.	200
Door, Painted Wood, Raised Panels, Blue & Brown, Mexico, 1950s, 32 x 76 In.	400
Door, Pine, 4 Panes, 84½ In.	125
Door, Pine, Arched, Panels, 2 Glass Panes, Gaudi, Bardes, 1910, 111 x 43 In., Pair...............	8125
Door, Pine, Iron Mount, 2 Panes, 74 x 33½ In.	125
Doorknocker, Abraham Lincoln, Profile, Text, Bronze, Round, 1915, 4 x 3 In.	300
Doorknocker, Brass, Eagle, Leaves, Flowers, Ribbons, 14 In., 4 Piece	595
Doorknocker, Bronze, 2 Putti, Heraldic Shield, 8½ In.	120

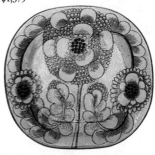

Architectural, Cartouche, Arched, Central Shell, Molded Edge, Zinc, c.1900, 23 x 42 In., Pair
$332

Leland Little Auctions

Architectural, Doorknocker, Ram's Head, Iron, Backplate With Grapevine, 1800s, 9 In.
$1,320

Brunk Auctions

Architectural, Doors, French Colonial, Iron Scrollwork, Pine, Paint, 11 x 43 In.
$184

Leland Little Auctions

Doorknocker, Bronze, Foo Dog, Be Rich & Lucky, 7½ x 5 In., Pair	359
Doorknocker, Bronze, Penis, Scrotum, 7 x 4¼ In.	1952
Doorknocker, Iron, Bird, Bird House Cottage, Yard, Trees, Oval, Multicolor, 4 In.	330
Doorknocker, Iron, Butterfly, Bouquet, Multicolor, 4 In.	420
Doorknocker, Iron, Castle, Clouds, Landscaping, Cream, Brown, Green, Oval, 4 In.	91
Doorknocker, Iron, Castle, Medieval Fortress, Woods, Judd Co., 4 In.	150
Doorknocker, Iron, Castle, Trees, Multicolor, Oval, 4 In.	150
Doorknocker, Iron, Rooster, Crowing, Black, Brown, Green, Oval, 4 In.	152
Doorknocker, Iron, Rose, Yellow, Variegated Green Leaves, Oval, 5 In.	420
Doorknocker, Ram's Head, Iron, Backplate With Grapevine, 1800s, 9 In. ....*illus*	1320
Doors, French Colonial, Iron Scrollwork, Pine, Paint, 11 x 43 In. ....*illus*	184
Downspout, Copper, Patinated, 1800s, 19 In.	135
Drain, Downspout, Sandstone, Carved, Square Border, 8 x 39 x 18 In.	767
Eagle, Earthenware, Late 1800s, 35 x 21½ x 27¼ In.	1952
Element, Carved, Draping, Wood, 48 x 26 In.	82
Element, Cast Stone, Face, 29 In.	138
Element, Cross, Medallion, 23½ x 10¼ In.	281
Element, Crown Molding, Figural, Male Head, 12 x 19 In.	1125
Element, Rococo, Oak, Curved Panel, Applied Decoration, 13½ x 35½ In.	70
Element, Stair Riser, Chicago Stock Exchange, Bronze, Louis Sullivan, 18 x 24 In.	750
Finial, Copper, Pyramid Form, Scalloped, Pointed Spire, Belted Ball Finial, 42 In.	984
Finial, Floral Designs, Layers Of White Paint, Zinc, Early 1900s, 53 x 22 x 22 In., Pair	540
Finial, Obelisk & Eagle, Spread Wings, Banner, Copper, Verdigris, c.1900, 75 In.	3555
Finial, Turned Wood, Gesso, Parcel Gilt, Flared Top, Acanthus, 21½ x 9½ In.	357
Fireplace Surround, Composition, Simulated Marble, 43½ x 48 In.	313
Fireplace Surround, Gilt Bronze, Gray Marble, Bead & Scroll, Fluted Legs, 43 x 77 In.	6710
Fireplace Surround, Louis XVI, Marble, White, Gray Veins, 45⅛ In.	1250
Fireplace Surround, Maple, Gray, Beveled, Serpentine, Fluted, Rocaille, Cabriole, 43 x 61 In.	2460
Fireplace Surround, Oak, Clock, Glass Cabinets, Belgium, Mid 1800s, 99 x 109 x 24 In.	4200
Fireplace, Wood, Marquetry, Mantel, Electric, Clock, Faux Logs, B. La Clair, 1967, 55 x 54 In. .	677
Flagpole Topper, Zinc, Anchor Shape, Molded Spear Tip, Base, c.1910, 17 x 6 In.	100
Font, Holy Water, Onyx, Enamel, Porcelain, Bronze, Art Nouveau, c.1900, 18¾ x 12 In.	1375
Foundation Peg, Carved, Granite, Deity Shape, Hands Together, Standing, 18 In.	246
Gate, Torch-Cut Bronze, Brass, Copper, 1960s, 96 x 21½ In.	625
Gate, Wrought Iron, Peaked, 44 x 46 In.	70
Gate, Wrought Iron, Stylized Peacock Feathers, 2 Doors, c.1900, 45 x 45 In.	360
Gate, Wrought Iron, Top Band, Curlicues, 48 x 45½ In.	70
Gate, Wrought Iron, Top Band, Stylized Flowers, 44 x 46 In.	175
Gate, Wrought Iron, White, 43 x 44 In.	93
Grille, Iron, Wrought & Gilt, 7 Medallions, Scroll Ends, c.1908, 54 x 17 In., Pair	1500
Iron, Decorative, Scroll & Fruit Form Crest, Samuel Yellin, Late 1800s, 7 x 15 In.	375
Lion's Head, Roaring, Terra-Cotta, 1910, 12½ x 17¾ In.	1416
Lion's Head, Roundel, c.1925, 13½ In. Diam.	150
Lock, Door, Iron, Peter Derr, Signed P.D. On Both Handles, Late 1800s, 3½ x 5⅜ In.	3186
Mail Box, Embossed, Pull Down, Letters, Door, Iron, Key, 1908, 20 x 13 In.	725
Mantel, Carved Sandstone, Eagle, Trees, Serpents, Urns, 1827, 68 x 74 In.	4500
Mantel, Faux, Onyx, Iron, 46½ x 52½ In.	354
Mantel, Federal, Pine, Reeded Molding, Carved, 3 Fans, Early 1800s, 55¼ x 66 In.	600
Mantel, Pine, George III, Columns, Medallions, 65½ x 100 In.	4750
Mantel, Purple Marble, Serpentine, Cartouche, Shells, 44½ x 66½ In.	4500
Mantel, Walnut, Carved, Boar's Head & Grapevines, Continental, 1800s, 100 x 124 x 29 In.	6120
Mantel, Walnut, Carved, Cornice, Crosses & Angels, England, Mid 1800s, 128 x 122 x 38 In.	3960
Mantel, Wood, Carved, Painted, Fans, Marbleized Columns, Md., c.1810, 63 x 84 In.	2460
Mantel, Wood, Paint, Stepped Crest, Block Columns, 1800s, 50 x 55 In.	207
Model, Victorian House, Cutwork Porch & Fence, c.1890, 24½ x 28 x 20½ In.	420
Ornament, Lion Head, Fluted Background, Stone, 24½ x 24¾ In.	297
Ornament, Wall, Gilt Composition, Ribbed Basket, Fruit, Bow, c.1950, 22 x 17 In.	593
Overmantel Mirror, Carved, Giltwood, Pierced Crest, c.1888, 83 x 69 In.	4514
Overmantel Mirror, Giltwood, Georgian, Wedgwood Plaque, 1800s, 58 x 66 In. ....*illus*	2091

Overmantel Mirror, Neoclassical, Giltwood, Carved, Divided, c.1810, 23 x 60 In. ....*illus*	750
Overmantel Mirror, William IV, Parcel Gilt, Oval, Carved Scrolls, c.1835, 45 x 50 In. ....*illus*	875
Paving Tile, Square, Painted, Rearing Horse & Circles, Tin Glazed, c.1600, 5 In.	800
Pediment, Eagle Landing, 1800s, 12 x 23 In.	160
Pediment, Flowers, Leaves, Paint, 12 ¼ x 36 ¼ In.	206
Pilaster Capital, Corinthian, Leaves, 16 ¼ x 5 ⅛ In., Pair	488
Plaque, Wood, Gilt, Carved Drums, Cannons, Flags, Early 1900s, 21 ½ x 21 ½ In., Pair	1500
Post, Renaissance, Oak, Mary, Jesus, 78 In.	2125
Roof Finial, Copper, Central Shaft, Gothic Design, Gold Leaf, c.1885, 62 x 12 In. ....*illus*	3933
Roof Finial, Dragon, Perched On Rooftop, Verdigris, Copper, c.1900, 36 x 29 In.	7110
Roof Finial, Tapered, Scalloped Collar, Square Foot, Zinc, 1800s, 38 In., Pair	905
Roof Ornament, Eagle, Spread Wings, Sphere, Copper, Gold Paint, c.1900, 22 x 32 In.	178
Roof Tile, Guardian, Riding Dragon, Waves, Sancai Glaze, Green, c.1880, 31 In.	1185
Roof Tile, Soldier, Riding Toad, Wood Stand, 12 x 11 ½ In.	531
Roof Tile, Warrior, On Dragon, Wood Base, Asian, 12 x 14 In.	218
Roof Tile, Warrior, Riding Tiger, Poles, Asian, 13 ⅜ x 14 In.	400
Roof Tile, Woman, Riding Chicken, Brown, c.1900, 13 In.	150
Screens are also listed in the Fireplace and Furniture categories.	
Sculpture, Elm, Carved Putti, Italy, Late 1800s, 28 In.	510
Staircase, Model, Spiral, Wood, Stained, Turned Balusters, 22 x 14 In. ....*illus*	406
Swag, Giltwood, Leaves, Grapes, c.1850-1900, 50 ½ In.	2250
Temple Door, Wood, High Relief Carving, Hindu, Persia, 1800s, 37 x 18 x 4 ½ In.	2000
Temple Lantern, Bronze, Roof Hanging, Tokugawa Hollyhock, Edo Period, 27 x 19 In.	2400
Wall Bracket, Blackamoor, Wood, Painted, Gilt Trim, Italy, c.1935, 13 x 12 In. ....*illus*	468
Wall Bracket, Carved, Rococo, Green & Gold, 1800s, 36 x 14 x 10 In.	2196
Wall Bracket, Spread Wing Eagle, Shelf, Gilt Gesso, 1800s, 23 x 30 In., Pair	4920
Wall Hanging, Gilt Wood, Gesso, Bouquet, Roses, Daffodils, Sunflowers, 40 ½ x 29 ½ In.	714
Wall Panel, Eagle, Carved, Gilded, Wings Outstretched, 1800s, 39 In.	1320
Wall Panel, Hardstone, Cloisonne Inlay, Flower Branches, 1900s, 38 x 29 In.	7110
Water Closet, Marble, Giltwood, Scroll & Flourish, S. Wagner, 23 x 32 In. ....*illus*	3500
Water Pump, French Provincial, Reeded Spout, Leaf Handle, Iron, 48 x 12 In.	200
Window, Grate, Repeating C-Scrolls Set In Circles, 1800s, 51 x 31 In.	161

AREQUIPA POTTERY was produced from 1911 to 1918 by the patients of the Arequipa Sanatorium in Marin County, north of San Francisco. The patients were trained by Frederick Hurten Rhead, who had worked at Roseville Pottery.

Bowl, Pansies, Carved, Squat, Pale Blue & Beige, Marked, 2 ½ x 4 ½ In.	561
Bowl, Pink, Sunken Rim, Squat, 2 x 5 In.	472
Vase, Carved Leaves, Green Matte Glaze, 5 ⅛ In. ....*illus*	1149
Vase, Carved Leaves, Green Matte Glaze, Blue, Brown, Smokestack, Marked, 5 In.	1121
Vase, Dark Green Glaze, Glossy, High Shoulders, 3 ¾ In. ....*illus*	250
Vase, Incised Decoration, Teal High Glaze, 3 ⅞ x 7 ¼ In.	259
Vase, Leaves, Squeezebag Decoration, Mauve Ground, F.H. Rhead, 1911-13 In. 7 ¼ In. ....*illus*	12160
Vase, Light Green High Glaze, Carved Flower Both Sides, 3 ⅜ In.	259
Vase, Light Green, Flower, 3 ⅜ In.	265
Vase, Mauve, Squeezebag, Leafy Band On Swollen Shoulder, 7 x 5 In.	11875
Vase, Molded Prunus Branches, Green, Oval, Shouldered, 5 x 3 ½ In.	1500
Vase, Sable Brown Glaze, Cylindrical, Paneled, c.1915, 8 In.	2247
Vase, Squeezebag, Stylized Mistletoe, Blue, Frederick H. Rhead, 1912, 3 x 3 In.	10000
Vase, Stick, Teal, Swirl, 8 ¾ In.	236
Vase, Student, Teal, 3 ⅞ In.	265
Vase, Stylized Mistletoe, Blue, Yellow, Round, Shouldered, 1912, 3 In.	10000

ARGY-ROUSSEAU, *see G. Argy-Rousseau category.*

ARITA is a port in Japan. Porcelain was made there from about 1616. Many types of decorations were used, including the popular Imari designs, which are listed under Imari in this book.

Bowl, Concentric Circle Bands, Flowers, Blue, White, Dutch East India Co., Japan, 15 ¾ In.	800
Bowl, Flared Rim, Round Foot, Blue, Multicolor, Gilt, Hill, Water, Buildings, Leaves, 7 x 3 In. ...	76

Architectural, Overmantel Mirror, Giltwood, Georgian, Wedgwood Plaque, 1800s, 58 x 66 In.
$2,091

Skinner, Inc.

Architectural, Overmantel Mirror, Neoclassical, Giltwood, Carved, Divided, c.1810, 23 x 60 In.
$750

Neal Auctions

Architectural, Overmantel Mirror, William IV, Parcel Gilt, Oval, Carved Scrolls, c.1835, 45 x 50 In.
$875

New Orleans Auction Galleries

Architectural, Roof Finial, Copper, Central Shaft, Gothic Design, Gold Leaf, c.1885, 62 x 12 In.
$3,933

James D. Julia Auctioneers

Architectural, Staircase, Model, Spiral, Wood, Stained, Turned Balusters, 22 x 14 In.
$406

New Orleans Auction Galleries

Architectural, Wall Bracket, Blackamoor, Wood, Painted, Gilt Trim, Italy, c.1935, 13 x 12 In.
$468

New Orleans Auction Galleries

Bowl, Flowers, Birds, Blue, White, Footed, Dutch East India Company, Japan, 15¾ In.	1200
Bowl, Flowers, Vines, 12 In.	120
Bowl, Gilt, People, Rockery, Court, Landscapes, 4 x 12¼ In. ....*illus*	310
Bowl, Leaf Wreath, Blue, White, Footed, Dutch East India Company, Japan, 10⅞ In.	250
Bowl, Rabbit, Peony, 8¾ In.	60
Bowl, Stand, Gilt, Blue, Rocky Landscape, Architectural Elements, 4 x 12¼ In.	297
Charger, Blue, White, Phoenix, Tree Branch, 16 In.	120
Charger, Fish, Flowers, Branches, Blue, White, 18 In.	68
Jardiniere, White, Flowers, Blue, Red, 12 In., Pair	12500
Platter, Bird On Flowering Branch, Cobalt Blue & White, Iron Red Rim, 13 In. Diam.	100
Sculpture, Hawk, Craggy Rock, Blue, White, 15 x 9 In.	472
Strainer, Birds, Trees, Flowers, Vase, Scroll Border, Blue & White, c.1680, 11 In. Diam.	943

 ART DECO, or Art Moderne, a style started at the Paris Exposition of 1925, is characterized by linear, geometric designs. All types of furniture and decorative arts, jewelry, book bindings, and even games were designed in this style. Additional items may be found in the Furniture category or in various glass and pottery categories, etc.

Dresser Jar, Blue Glass, Ribbed, Shell Pillars, Etched Brass Lid, Scroll Feet, 2 x 3½ In.	29
Figure, Dancer, Woman, Pleated Skirt, c.1990, 4½ x 4½ In.	200
Jewelry Box, Black Glass, Diamond Pattern, Hinged Lid, France, c.1930, 2¼ x 5 In.	244
Vase, Porcelain, Hand Painted, Green, Gilt Flowers, Birds, Tapered Oval, 1920, 15 In.	400

ART GLASS, *see Glass-Art category.*

 ART NOUVEAU is a style of design that was at its most popular from 1895 to 1905. Famous designers, including Rene Lalique and Emile Galle, produced furniture, glass, silver, metalwork, and buildings in the new style. Ladies with long flowing hair and elongated bodies were among the more easily recognized design elements. Copies of this style are being made today. Many modern pieces of jewelry can be found. Additional Art Nouveau pieces may be found in Furniture or in various glass categories.

Cigarette Box, Grouse Cock, Bronze, Cedar, 2½ x 4½ In.	150
Mirror, Desktop, Pewter, Orion, Germany, 1900s, 15 x 16 In.	1188
Mirror, Maiden Mask, Easel Back, Traces Of Gilding & Bronze Mask, 15 x 9½ In.	230
Sculpture, Butterfly Dancer, Gilt & Enameled Bronze, Louis Chalon, c.1900, 16½ x 6½ In.	9375
Scuttle, Copper, Embossed, Stylized Flower, Pod, Shaped Lid, c.1905, 19 x 14 In.	277
Vase, Glass, Silver Overlay, Flowers & Vine, c.1900, 13⅞ In.	1125
Vase, Green Matte Glaze, Flowers, Applied Twist Stems, Julius Dresser, 17½ x 9 In.	976
Vase, Lidded, Gilt Bronze, Nude Woman On Top, Maurice Bouval, c.1900, 6 x 5 In.	2000
Vase, Pheasant Shape, Gilt Highlights, Bohemia, 14⅛ x 7 In.	295
Vase, Portrait, Yellow, Black, Cup Shape Neck, 14¾ In.	200
Waste Basket, Wrought Iron, Rectangular, Square Cutouts, 17½ x 10½ In.	1000

ART POTTERY, *see Pottery-Art category.*

ARTS & CRAFTS was a design style popular in American decorative arts from 1894 to 1923. In the 1970s collectors began to rediscover Mission furniture, art pottery, metalwork, linens, and light fixtures from this period. The interest has continued. Today everything from this era is collectible, including jewelry, graphics, and silverware. Additional items may be found in the Furniture category and other categories.

Biscuit Box, Brass, Hammered Lid, Glass Insert, Conical Feet, Marked, 1900s, 6 In.	92
Box, Bronze, Cutout Twin Deer Silver Overlay, Lift Lid, Marked, 2 x 6 In.	177
Box, Copper & Enamel, Canister, Hinged Enameled Lid With Yellow Bird On Blue, 3½ In.	173
Box, Copper, Enamel Inset, Ivory Swans, Blue Water, Lift-Off Lid, 2½ x 7 In.	502
Box, Copper, Rectangular, Oval Enamel Overlay, 2 Peacocks On Lid, 1⅞ x 5¼ x 4 In.	3105
Candlestick, Copper, Hammered, Stick Stem, Lobed Dish Base, c.1915, 7 In., Pair	1046
Humidor, Oak, Hammered Copper, Helmet Form Cover, Pipe Stand Base, 9½ In.	180
Lamp, Green Octagonal Glass Shade, Metal Cutout Overlay, Column Stem, 17 In.	708
Lantern, Copper & Glass, Square, Roof Shape Top, Wire Grid, Socket, c.1920, 16 In.	431

Tray, Curved Copper Bowl, Scroll Handle, Encircling Antlers, 8½ x 21 In.	111
Vase, Pewter, Branches, Turquoise Enamel Hearts, Silver Foil, Footed, c.1920, 8 In.	708
Window, Prairie Style, Glasgow Roses, America, Early 1900s, 50¼ x 15½ x 1 In., 4 Piece	2625

AURENE *pieces are listed in the Steuben category.*

AUSTRIA *is a collecting term that covers pieces made by a wide variety of factories. They are listed in this book in categories such as Royal Dux or Porcelain.*

AUTO parts and accessories are collectors' items today. Gas pump globes and license plates are part of this specialty. Prices are determined by age, rarity, and condition. Collectors say "porcelain sign" for enameled iron or steel signs. Packaging related to automobiles may also be found in the Advertising category. Lalique hood ornaments may be listed in the Lalique category.

Cabinet, Edison Mazda Super Auto Lamps, Spare Lamps Save You Trouble, 16 x 7 x 7½ In.	690
Can, A.R.O. Thrift Motor Oil, Arrowhead, Green & White, Tin Lithograph, 1 Qt., 6 x 4 In.	1265
Can, Chieftain Motor Oil, Low Carbon Double Filtered, Red & Green, Indian Chief, 5 x 4 In.	1898
Can, Gold Medal Lubricant, Axle Grease, Pine Trees, Tin Litho, Handle, 10 Lb., 9 x 7 In.	604
Can, Good Rich Empire, Tin Lithograph, World Map, Canada, Qt.	305
Can, Mohawk Motor Oil, Pure Pennsylvania, Red With Indian Graphic, 5½ x 4 In.	1208
Can, Monamobile Oil, Tin Litho, Blue & White, Touring Car Image, 6¼ x 8½ x 5½ In.	546
Can, Motor Oil, Golden Penn, Yellow With Blue & Red, 5⅝ x 4 In.	518
Can, Motor Oil, Jayhawk Oils, Kent Oil, Jayhawk, White Blue Red & Yellow, 5⅝ x 4 In.	2990
Can, Motor Oil, Kochenderfe, Dependable Lubrication For Your Motor, 6½ x 8 x 3 In.	604
Can, Motor Oil, Palomino, Blue, Brown Horse Logo, 5⅝ x 4 In.	2990
Can, Motor Oil, Polarine For Fords, Standard Oil Co. Of Indiana, 7 x 8 x 3⅛ In.	242
Can, Motor Oil, Polly Prem, Black With Green Parrot Logo, 5½ x 4 In.	2415
Can, Motor Oil, Supreme Auto, Gulf Refining Co., Yellow, Blue Letters, 6 x 8½ x 5⅝ In.	345
Can, Motor Oil, Texaco 574 Oil, Green, Red Star Logo, 6½ x 3¾ In.	374
Can, Nichols Oil, Dependable Lubrication For Your Motor, Red Type On Gray, 11 x 8 x 3 In.	863
Can, Penn Convoy Motor Oil, Battleship, Red, White, Blue, Tin Litho, Sealed, Qt., 6 x 4 In.	460
Can, Purity Motor Oil, Nurse, White, Red, Black, Tin Lithograph, Sealed, Qt., 7 x 4 In.	978
Can, Tankard Ring Seal, Carbon's Natural Enemy, Dark Blue & Red, 5⅝ x 4 In.	4485
Can, Texaco Motor Oil Medium, Green, Black & Red, Texaco Logo, 11 x 8 x 3⅛ In.	546
Can, Texaco Oil, Green With Red Lettering, Tin Lithograph, 5½ x 3½ x 1⅞ In.	242
Can, Whiz Auto Top Dressing, Tin, Yellow & Blue, 1910 Packard Limo, 6 x 4⅝ x 2⅝ In.	1380
Can, Whiz Motor Oil, Car, Hand Soldered Tin Lithograph, Blue & Cream, Gal., 10 x 6 In.	1150
Can, Wilube Motor Oil, Seaplane, Cars, Trucks, Red, Black, Tin Lithograph, Qt., 6 x 4 In.	6440
Clock, Phillips 66, Red & White, 15 In.	819
Clock, Wall, Fram Filters Service Station, Light-Up, Double Bubble, Orange, 5 x 15½ In.	518
Clock, Wolf's Head Motor Oil & Lubes, Octagonal, 18 x 18 In.	861
Cup, Trop-Artic Auto Oil, Manhattan Oil Co., Graphic Motoring Image, 2¾ x 4 In.	2128
Display, Gulf Oil, Orange & Blue, Lubricates Polishes & Prevents Rusts, 12 x 10 x 4½ In.	4025
Display, Tire Gauge, Figural Tin Lithograph, Schrader Brand, Hinged Door, 14¾ x 6 In.	2875
Gas Pump Globe, Kendall OPE, White, Red, 14 In.	1140
Gas Pump Globe, Lion, Glass, White Border, Red & Black, Screw Base, 13½ In.	1353
Gas Pump Globe, O-Peak-O, White Mountain, 16½ In.	2700
Gas Pump Globe, Pale Filtered Galtrex Motor Oils, 16 In.	840
Gas Pump Globe, Red Crown Ethyl, White, 17 In.	450
Gas Pump Globe, Rock Island, Ethyl, Yellow, 13½ In.	1560
Gas Pump Globe, That Good Gulf Gasoline, Orange, White, 17½ In.	570
Headlight, Brass, Acetylene Gas, Made For Mitchel By Solar, Custom Stand, 1900s, 19 In.	406
Headlights & Grill, Ford, Old Red Paint, Early 1900s, 32 x 37 In.	180
Hood Ornament, Aviator, Chrome Plated, 1920s, 4 In.	540
Hood Ornament, Buick, Figural, Bust, Woman With Wings, Metal, Chrome Finish, 5 x 3 In.	604
Hood Ornament, Eagle, Wings Outstretched, 3½ In.	153
Hood Ornament, Heisman Football Player, Chrome Finish, 6½ x 6 x ½ In.	265
Hood Ornament, Lalique, Fish, Signed, 6 x 4 In.	495
Hood Ornament, Leaping Ram, Bronze, 5½ In.	738
Hood Ornament, Man, Motorcycle Rider, Nickel Plated Bronze, 3 In.	1045

Architectural, Water Closet, Marble, Giltwood, Scroll & Flourish, S. Wagner, 23 x 32 In.
$3,500

New Orleans Auction Galleries

Arequipa, Vase, Carved Leaves, Green Matte Glaze, 5⅛ In.
$1,149

Humler & Nolan

Arequipa, Vase, Dark Green Glaze, Glossy, High Shoulders, 3¾ In.
$250

Turner Auctions + Appraisals

Arequipa, Vase, Leaves, Squeezebag Decoration, Mauve Ground, F.H. Rhead, 1911-13, 7¼ In.
$12,160

Rago Arts and Auction Center

Arita, Bowl, Gilt, People, Rockery, Court, Landscapes, 4 x 12 1/4 In.
$310

Ahlers & Ogletree Auction Gallery

Auto, License Plate Topper, Reflector, Knox Glass Asso. Band Member, 4 In.
$40

Ruby Lane

Auto, Sign, Bulldog, Die Cut, Enamel, 28 x 38 In.
$6,600

Morphy Auctions

Auto, Sign, Liberty Gasoline, Statue of Liberty, Black, Orange, Die Cut, 30 x 48 In.
$5,700

Morphy Auctions

Hood Ornament, Man, Top Hat, Nickel Plated Bronze	584
Hood Ornament, Shivering Fairy, Nickel Plated Bronze, Marked F. Basin, 1926, 5 1/2 In.	246
Hood Ornament, Temperature Gauge, Art Deco, Boyce Moto-Meter Co., 5 3/4 x 6 1/2 x 3 In.	4600
Key Chain, 1933 Cadillac Auto On Front, 3 1/2 x 3 x 5/8 In.	165
Key Fob, 2-Sided, Cardboard, Kelly-Springfield Tires, 4 x 2 1/4 In.	142
License Plate Attachment, Capper's National, Early Auto Theft Protection, 3 1/8 x 3 1/8 In.	153
License Plate Attachment, Early Birds, 4 x 11 In.	354
License Plate Attachment, Miami Beach, Swordfish, Aluminum, 6 5/8 x 13 In.	106
License Plate Topper, Reflector, Knox Glass Asso. Band Member, 4 In. ....*illus*	40
Mirror, Dodge & Plymouth, Pinup Girl, Art Deco, Blue, Reverse Glass, 18 x 16 In.	288
Oil Cup, Trop-Artic Oil Co., Car, Hillside Landscape, Handle, Tin Lithograph, 3 x 4 In.	748
Picture, Gulf Oil, Station Attendant, Ellwood Flaherty, Frame, c.1949, 15 x 12 In.	150
Radiator, Packard, Brass, Converted To Display Shelf, 26 x 32 In.	900
Side Lamp, Square, Maxwell Model 20, Brass, 13 In., Pair	420
Side Light, Lantern, CM Hall, Model 115, Kerosene, Ball Handles, Brass, 14 In., Pair	540
Sign, AC Service, 2-Sided, Flange, 3 Chain-Hung Smaller Signs Beneath, 21 x 10 1/2 In.	2415
Sign, Air, Enamel, 3-Sided, White With Red Letters, Mounting Bracket, 17 3/4 In.	2070
Sign, American Corto Radiators, Girl Measuring Boy, Paper Lithograph, 29 3/4 x 19 1/2 In.	604
Sign, Bowser Gasolene, Jones & Gurley, Utica, N.Y., Embossed Tin Litho, 11 1/2 x 35 1/2 In.	690
Sign, Bulldog, Die Cut, Enamel, 28 x 38 In. ....*illus*	6600
Sign, Cadillac Crest, Multicolor, Round, 18 In.	1920
Sign, Champion Spark Plugs, Spark Plug, Metal, Thermometer, c.1930, 34 x 28 In.	660
Sign, Chevrolet, We Use Genuine Parts, Yellow & Blue & Orange, 2-Sided, 18 1/8 x 20 In.	1006
Sign, Esso Girl, Die Cut, Tin, Esso Oil Co., 15 3/4 x 6 3/4 In.	94
Sign, Flange, Purolator Oil Filters, Red & Black, Lithograph Die Cut, 2-Sided, 11 x 13 1/4 In.	2415
Sign, G & J Tires, Cardboard Die Cut Sign, Motoring Scene, 20 x 18 1/2 In.	1121
Sign, Gasoline, Fisk Tires, Auto Supplies, Enamel Flange, Red & Black, 18 x 24 In.	720
Sign, Goodyear Tires, Dark Blue, Yellow Type, Enamel, 2-Sided, 26 1/2 x 48 1/2 In.	776
Sign, Gulf Motor Oil, Sign Of The Orange Disc, 60 x 28 In.	960
Sign, Hood Tires, Dark Blue & Red, Arrow, Enamel, Frame, 20 x 62 In.	14950
Sign, Imperial Garage, Automobiles Supplies Repairs, Embossed, Tin Lithograph, 14 x 20 In.	2128
Sign, Liberty Gasoline, Statue Of Liberty, Black, Orange, Die Cut, 30 x 48 In. ....*illus*	5700
Sign, Mack Truck, Blue With Orange Script, Enamel, 3 5/8 x 13 1/4 In.	2243
Sign, Marathon Products, Runner, Green Border, Round, 2-Sided, 48 In.	3300
Sign, Metal, Racing Oil, 2-Sided, Quaker State, c.1960, 5 x 26 In.	288
Sign, Mobiloil A, Gargoyle Lubester, Make The Chart Your Guide, 10 7/8 x 8 3/4 In.	431
Sign, Nash, Authorized Service, Shield Shape, Fish Scale, Blue, Die Cut, 36 x 22 In.	250
Sign, Pennzoil, Enamel, Expert Lubrication, White Letters In Red Arrow, 7 1/4 x 27 In.	431
Sign, Republic Authorized Service, Green, Red, Yellow, 27 x 48 In.	1920
Sign, RPM Motor Oil, Mickey Mouse, Metal, Aqua Ground, 1939, 24 In. Diam.	3289
Sign, Socony Motor Oil, Enamel, Standard Oil, Red & Blue, 15 x 13 1/4 In.	661
Sign, Stop, 30 In.	35
Sign, Texaco Fire Chief Gasoline, Curved, Enamel, Red & White & Green, c.1940, 18 x 10 In.	805
Sign, Timken, Tapered, Roller Bearings, Authorized Sales For Service, Die Cut, 18 x 30 In.	1560
Sign, Vall-Oil, Tin Litho, Die Cut, Football Player Carrying Ball, Vall-Oil Jersey, 15 3/4 x 9 In.	130
Sign, Valvoline Diamond Jubilee, Tin Lithograph Display, Glitter Surface, 14 1/2 x 13 3/8 In.	523
Sign, Veedol Oil Co., Flying Yankee Train, Heavy Paper, 35 3/4 x 28 In.	378
Sign, Whiz Radiator Stop Leak, Die Cut, Cardboard, 4 1/4 x 13 1/2 In.	342
Speedometer, Jones, Trip, Distance, Brass, 50 MPH, Patent 1908, 6 In.	584
Speedometer, Stewart-Warner, Clock, Trip, Distance, 60 MPH, 10 In.	780
Spotlight, Brass & Copper, Acetylene Gas Lamp, Badge Brass Mfg. Co., c.1903, 15 In.	438
Street Light, Midcentury, Marbelite	136
Tail Light Assembly, Buick, 1955, 17 x 6 In.	276
Tail Light Assembly, Packard Clipper, 1956-58, 16 x 7 In.	338
Thermometer, Raybestos Auto Fan Belts, Blue & Red, 30 3/4 x 9 1/2 x 3/4 In.	978
Tin, Dust-Puff, Car Polish, Woman Polishing Car, Blue, 5 3/4 x 3 1/4 In.	130
Tin, Master Spark Plug, Original Plug Inside, 4 x 1 1/2 In.	106
Tin, Mat's Body Polish, Man Polishing Car, Top Handle, Spout, Tin Lithograph, 8 x 5 In.	161
Tin, Mazda Auto Lamps, Blue, 1920s, 3 1/2 x 1 1/2 In. ....*illus*	29
Tin, Viking Motor Oil, Can, Lithograph, Crimp Seam, 5 1/2 x 4 In.	118
Tin, Whiz Auto Cushion Dressing, Hand Soldered Tin Lithograph, 5 1/2 x 3 3/4 x 1 7/8 In.	1265

Wheel Lock, Iron, Brass Tag, Auto-Theft Signal System, 1914, 10 x 5 In. ....*illus*   175

AUTUMN LEAF pattern china was made for the Jewel Tea Company beginning in 1933. Hall China Company of East Liverpool, Ohio, Crooksville China Company of Crooksville, Ohio, Harker Potteries of Chester, West Virginia, and Paden City Pottery, Paden City, West Virginia, made dishes with this design. Autumn Leaf has remained popular and was made by Hall China Company until 1978. Some other pieces in the Autumn Leaf pattern are still being made. For more prices, go to kovels.com.

Bowl, 9 x 5 In.	23 to 24
Bowl, Cereal, 6 1/8 In.	10
Bowl, Nesting, 3 Piece	45
Coffee Set, Coffeepot, Sugar & Creamer, Cup & Saucer, 5 Piece	6
Coffeepot, 9 1/2 x 6 In. *illus*	55
Cookie Jar, Lid, Roll Handles, Roll Finial, 9 1/2 x 7 1/2 In. *illus*	23
Gravy Boat *illus*	48
Jug, Milk, c.1930s, 7 1/2 x 4 1/4 x 5 3/4 In.	22
Jug, Utility, 40 Oz.	28
Pie Baker, 9 3/4 In.	26
Plate, Dinner, 10 In.	32
Ramekin	15
Salt & Pepper, Ruffled	30
Soup, Dish, Rimmed, 8 1/2 In.	11
Sugar & Creamer, Ruffled	76

AZALEA dinnerware was made for Larkin Company customers from about 1915 to 1941. Larkin, the soap company, was in Buffalo, New York. The dishes were made by Noritake China Company of Japan. Each piece of the white china was decorated with pink azaleas.

Bowl, Dessert, 5 1/4 In., 3 Piece	10
Bowl, Grapefruit, 4 3/4 x 4 In.	57
Bowl, Grapefruit, c.1920, 3 1/2 x 4 5/8 In.	78
Butter, Cover, 3 x 6 1/2 In. *illus*	59
Condiment Set, Salt & Pepper, Tray, Jam Pot With Lid, Serving Spoon	22
Condiment Tray, Salt, Pepper & Jam Pot, Spoon, Tray With Handles, Gilt	65
Cup & Saucer, 12 Piece	20
Plate, Dinner, 10 In., 4 Piece	20
Plate, Salad, 7 5/8 In.	15
Relish, Divided, 4 Sections, Handles, 1930s, 9 In.	59
Sauceboat, Under Plate, 2 Piece	45
Serving Dish, Divided, 2 Handles, c.1934, 2 1/2 x 10 1/8 In.	65
Shaker, 1918, 2 3/8 In.	10
Sugar, Lid, Square Finial, Angular Handles, 3 In.	15
Teapot, Lid, 6 In.	225
Vase, 5 5/8 In.	30

BACCARAT glass was made in France by La Compagnie des Cristalleries de Baccarat, located 150 miles from Paris. The factory was started in 1765. The firm went bankrupt and began operating again about 1822. Cane and millefiori paperweights were made during the 1845 to 1880 period. The firm is still working near Paris making paperweights and glasswares.

Bowl, Square, Concave Panels, Shaped Rim, Clear, Marked, 1900s, 6 x 7 In.	150
Candelabrum, 2-Light, Bobeches, Pendants, Round Foot, 13 In., Pair	1750
Candlestick, Twist, c.1975, 6 1/2 In., Pair	125
Carafe, Marked, 8 1/4 x 8 In.	250
Champagne Flute, Cut Body, Acid Etched Ark, 8 1/2 x 1 7/8 In., 4 Piece	460
Crystal Ball, Metal Ring Base, Acid Etched Signature, 4 In.	418
Decanter, Stopper, 9 1/2 In., Pair	1000
Figurine, Falcon, Crystal, Marked, 10 1/2 x 16 In.	1120

Auto, Tin, Mazda Auto Lamps, Blue, 1920s, 3 1/2 x 1 1/2 In.
$29

Ruby Lane

Auto, Wheel Lock, Iron, Brass Tag, Auto-Theft Signal System, 1914, 10 x 5 In.
$175

Ruby Lane

Autumn Leaf, Coffeepot, 9 1/2 x 6 In.
$55

Ruby Lane

Autumn Leaf, Cookie Jar, Lid, Roll Handles, Roll Finial, 9 1/2 x 7 1/2 In.
$23

Martin Auction Co.

Road Maps
The first automobile road maps were printed in 1914.

Autumn Leaf, Gravy Boat
$48

Azalea, Butter, Cover, 3 x 6½ In.
$59

Ruby Lane

Baccarat, Vase, Frosted, Enameled, Blossoms, Leaves, Gold Trim, Signed, 5 x 6½ In.
$403

Early Auction Company

Badge, Scranton PA. School Of Practical Nursing, Mercedian, Oval, Blue Enamel, 1 x ¾ In.
$380

Ruby Lane

Paperweight, Canes, Animals, 1848, 3¾ In.	2640
Paperweight, Heart Shape Quadrants, Red, White, Blue, c.1973	265
Paperweight, Millefiori, Concentric, Yellow, Blue, Red, c.1973, 2½ In.	354
Paperweight, Salmon Pink Flower, Green Leaves, Star Cut, 2¾ In.	1800
Paperweight, Scramble, Pink, Cobalt Blue, Mustard, White, 2½ In.	265
Vase, Frosted, Enameled, Blossoms, Leaves, Gold Trim, Signed, 5 x 6½ In. ......*illus*	403
Vase, Green Over Frost, Snails, Engraved, Cameo, A. Houillon, Art Deco, 7 x 5 In.	546

BADGES have been used since before the Civil War. Collectors search for examples of all types, including law enforcement and company identification badges. Well-known prison or law enforcement badges are most desirable. Most are made of nickel or brass. Many recent reproductions have been made.

Commander's Cross, Hungarian Empire, 18K Gold, Guilloche, Crown, 3 x 2 In.	1652
Ottoman Military Order, Silver, Enamel, 7-Point Star Shape, 3¼ In.	469
Rank, Dangsang Mungwan, Cranes, Clouds, Waves, Blue Silk, Gold Thread, 9 x 8 In.	1230
Rank, Embroidered, Metallic Thread, Bird, Standing On 1 Leg, Frame, c.1910, 9 x 8 In.	237
Rockaway Steeple Chase Members, Silver, Rider, RSA, 1885, 1¼ In.	289
Salesman, Metal Uniform, Hook Fast Specialties Co., Cloisonne, 8 Piece, 8 x 11 In.	403
Scranton PA. School Of Practical Nursing, Mercedian, Oval, Blue Enamel, 1 x ¾ In. ...*illus*	380
Wells Fargo Security, Brass, Copper, Rolled Gold, Blue Enamel, Eagle, 3¼ x 2¼ In. ......*illus*	48

BANKS of metal have been made since 1868. There are still banks, mechanical banks, and registering banks (those that show the total money deposited on the face of the bank). Many old iron or tin banks have been reproduced since the 1950s in iron or plastic. Some old reproductions marked *Book of Knowledge, John Wright,* or *Capron* may be listed. Pottery, glass, and plastic banks are also listed here. Mickey Mouse and other Disneyana banks are listed in Disneyana. We have added the M numbers based on *The Penny Bank Book: Collecting Still Banks* by Andy and Susan Moore and the R numbers based on *Coin Banks by Banthrico* by James L. Redwine.

Atlas Car Batteries, Battery Shape, Tin, c.1950, 5½ x 3⅝ x 2 In.	24
Atlas Holding The World, Lock, Lead, 4¼ In.	240
Bank Building, City Bank With Teller, Cast Iron, Judd Mfg., M 1099, 5¼ In.	295
Bank Building, County Bank, Cast Iron, John Harper, M 1110, 4¼ In.	71
Bank Building, Fidelity Trust, Cast Iron, J. Barton Smith, 6½ x 5⅞ x 5⅜ In.	502
Bank Building, Fidelity Trust, Columns, Finials, Shaped Feet, Cast Iron, c.1890, 7 x 6 In.	71
Bank Building, Home Bank, Cast Iron, Judd Mfg., M 1019, 4 In.	142
Bank Building, Home Bank, Red, White & Blue Paint, Crack In Roof, 5 In. ......*illus*	472
Bank Building, Home Savings, Cast Iron, M 1126, 5¾ In. ......*illus*	118
Bank Building, Judd City, Arched Entry, Brick, Cast Iron, 5½ In.	62
Barrel Of Money, Nickel Plated, Cast Iron, Nicol & Co., Il., 1893, 4 In.	125
Baseball, Silver, On 3 Red Bats, American & National, 5½ x 3 In.	604
Boy Holding Football, Iron, 5 x 3½ x 3½ In.	661
Buffalo Sled Co., Toy Wagons, Wheel Shape, Auto-Coaster, Celluloid, Metal, 3 In.	633
Building, Caisse, Arched Window, Front Steps, Bell Tower, M 1156, 5¾ In.	37
Building, Independence Hall Tower, Cast Iron, Enterprise Mfg., Reproduction, 10 In.	59
Building, Independence Hall, Cast Iron, Painted, Enterprise Mfg., 8½ In.	165
Building, Multiplying, Cast Iron, J. & E. Stevens, 6½ In. ......*illus*	875
Building, Palace, Cast Iron, Gold Painted, Green, Embossed IB & Co., M 1116, c.1885, 7½ In.	850
Building, Tower, Cast Iron, John Harper, 9¼ In.	130
Car, Model T, Figural, Driver, Cast Iron, Black, Silver, Arcade, 4 x 7 In.	690
Chest, Empire Style, Paw Feet, Scoddle Ware, England, 5½ x 6¼ In. ......*illus*	59
Coats Safe & Lock Co., Cast Iron, Small Victorian Coats, Late 1800s, 29 x 19 In.	593
Crosley Radio, Iron, Green, 4½ x 4 x 2 In.	316
Dog Chasing Cat, Tin Chest, Lead, 3¼ In.	457
Ferdinand The Bull, Holding Fabric Flower, Painted Composition, c.1938, 5 In.	168
General Pershing, Cast Iron, Gold Paint, 8 In. ......*illus*	54
Happy Days, Barrel Shape, Tin, Chein, c.1950, 4 In.	50

Badge, Wells Fargo Security, Brass, Copper, Rolled Gold, Blue Enamel, Eagle, 3 ¼ x 2 ¼ In.
$48

Ruby Lane

Bank, Bank Building, Home Bank, Red, White & Blue Paint, Crack In Roof, 5 In.
$472

Bertoia Auctions

Bank, Bank Building, Home Savings, Cast Iron, M 1126, 5 ¾ In.
$118

Hess Auction Group

Bank, Building, Multiplying, Cast Iron, J. & E. Stevens, 6 ½ In.
$875

Morphy Auctions

Bank, Chest, Empire Style, Paw Feet, Scoddle Ware, England, 5 ½ x 6 ¼ In.
$59

Hess Auction Group

Bank, General Pershing, Cast Iron, Gold Paint, 8 In.
$54

The Stein Auction Company

Bank, Mechanical, Humpty Dumpty, Cast Iron, Shepard Hardware, 7 ½ In.
$983

Morphy Auctions

Bank, Mechanical, Kiltie, Lever, Deposits Coin In Pocket, John Harper & Co., Patented 1931
$384

Bertoia Auctions

Bank, Poor Weary Willie, Man, Motto, Tin, Germany, c.1915, 4 ¾ In.
$118

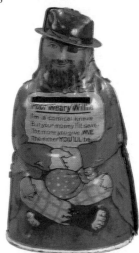

Bertoia Auctions

Barber, Pole, Turned Wood, Old Weathered Paint, 18th Century, 84 x 8 In.

$450

Cowan's Auctions

Barber, Pole, Turned Wood, Painted, Red, White, Blue, Acorn Finial Ends, 1800s, 69 In.

$708

Hess Auction Group

Barber, Pole, Turned Wood, Painted, Red, White, Blue, Cannonball Finial, 1800s, 31 In.

$767

Hess Auction Group

Hen On Nest, Iron, Original Paint Surface, Worn, 3 1/4 x 3 3/8 x 2 In.	604
Indian, Tomahawk, Fringe Pants, 6 In.	780
Japanese Woman, Playing Lute, Flowered Pillow Base, Cast Iron, Painted, 6 1/2 In.	24
Log Cabin, Black Man Playing Banjo, Black Girl Dancing, Tin Litho, Chein, 3 x 3 In.	403

 Mechanical banks were first made about 1870. Any bank with moving parts is considered mechanical. The metal banks made before World War I are the most desirable. Copies and new designs of mechanical banks have been made in metal or plastic since the 1920s. The condition of the paint on the old banks is important. Worn paint can lower a price by 90 percent.

Mechanical, American Indian Holding Fish & Frog, Cast Iron, c.1899, 6 x 9 3/4 In.	840
Mechanical, Bank Building, Arched Windows, Sloped Roof, J. & E. Stevens, 6 In.	240
Mechanical, Bank Building, Mansard Roof, Door, 1872, 4 3/8 In.	350
Mechanical, Cat & Mouse, Cast Iron, J & E. Stevens, c.1891, 11 1/2 In.	720
Mechanical, Child, Hiding, Mule, Cart, Man, Cast Iron, J. & E. Stevens, c.1888, 6 In.	800
Mechanical, Clown Face, Blue & Red Outfit, 7 1/2 In.	540
Mechanical, Darktown Battery, Black Baseball Players, J. & E. Stevens, 9 In.	5700
Mechanical, Dog On Turntable, H.L. Judd Manufacturing, c.1895, 4 3/4 In.	439
Mechanical, Dog, Howling, Red Base, Cast Iron, H.L. Judd, c.1880, 5 1/2 In.	550
Mechanical, Elephant, With 3 Stars, Black Paint With Gold, 9 In.	240
Mechanical, Frogs, Two, J. & E. Stevens, c.1882, 4 1/2 x 9 In.	780
Mechanical, Hall's Excelsior, Painted, Yellow & Red, Cast Iron, J. & E. Stevens, 5 In.	165
Mechanical, Humpty Dumpty, Cast Iron, Shepard Hardware, 7 1/2 In. ....*illus*	983
Mechanical, Humpty Dumpty, Shepard Hardware Co., c.1884, 7 1/2 In.	439
Mechanical, Independence Hall, Centennial, Cast Iron, 1876, 9 1/2 In.	240
Mechanical, Indian, Teepee, Fish, Frog, Cast Iron, J. & E. Stevens, c.1899, 6 In.	600
Mechanical, Jockey, J. & E. Stevens, c.1879, 10 In.	780
Mechanical, Kiltie, Lever, Deposits Coin In Pocket, John Harper & Co., Patented 1931......*illus*	384
Mechanical, Lion, Two Monkeys, Cast Iron, Kyser & Rex, Frankfurt, Pa., c.1853, 9 1/2 In.	819
Mechanical, Magician, Cast Iron, c.1901, 8 1/4 In.	1800
Mechanical, Mammy, Spoon, Baby, Cast Iron, Kyser & Rex, c.1880, 7 1/2 In.	1900
Mechanical, Monkey, Early Paint Surface, Original Key, 8 x 8 3/4 In.	180
Mechanical, Organ Grinder With Dancing Bear, Clockwork, c.1885, 5 1/2 In.	1800
Mechanical, Organ, Monkey With Paddle, Dog, Cat, Side Crank, Music, 1880, 7 1/2 In.	325 to 540
Mechanical, Owl, Stump, Turns Head, Glass Eyes, J. & E. Stevens, c.1888, 7 1/2 In.	242 to 420
Mechanical, Pig, Otto Von Bismarck, Black, White, Cast Iron, J. & E. Stevens, c.1883, 5 In.	1900
Mechanical, Punch & Judy, Puppet Show, Red, Yellow, Cast Iron, Shepard Hardware, 8 In.	1300
Mechanical, Saluting Sailor, Waves Arm, Tin Litho, Saalheimer & Strauss, c.1920, 6 In.	1180
Mechanical, Santa Claus At Chimney, Painted, 6 x 3 x 4 1/2 In.	604
Mechanical, Soldier, Firing Cannon, Tower, Cast Iron, J. & E. Stevens, 1892, 5 3/4 In.	700
Mechanical, Tammany, c.1885, 6 In.	180
Mechanical, Teddy, Bear, Rifle, Stump, Cast Iron, J. & E. Stevens, c.1907, 7 1/2 In.	900
Mechanical, The Munsters, Rocks, Hand Takes Coin, Plastic, Box, 1960s, 4 x 5 In.	144
Mechanical, Trick Pony, Shepard Hardware, 7 3/4 In.	420
Mechanical, Uncle Sam, Shepard Hardware, c.1886, 11 1/4 In.	1080
Mechanical, William Tell, J. & E. Stevens, c.1896, 6 3/4 x 10 1/4 In.	375 to 780
Merry-Go-Round, Nickel Plated, Animals, Reticulated Base, Grey Iron Casting Co., 5 In.	275
Oriental Boy, On Pillow, Painted, Hubley, M 186, 5 1/2 In.	12
Pig, Pottery, Earthenware, Green Mottled Glaze, Wales, 1919, 4 x 7 In.	1440
Pig, Sewer Tile, Standing, Missing Tail, Early 1900s, 7 1/2 x 12 1/2 In.	180
Poor Weary Willie, Man, Motto, Tin, Germany, c.1915, 4 3/4 In. ....*illus*	118
Radio, Templetone, Early Floor Radio, Kenton, 4 1/2 x 3 x 2 In.	288
Santa Claus, Hinged Lock Box, Images Of Santa, Tin Lithograph, 6 x 4 x 2 In.	142
Santa Claus, Spaghetti Trim, Red, White, Ceramic, Japan, c.1960, 6 1/2 In.	38
Seal On Rock, Arcade Manufacturing Co., M 732, c.1910, 3 1/2 In.	140
Space Man, Standing, Jetpack, Ray Gun, Coin Slot, Silver, Blue, Plaster, 1950s, 12 In.	173
Statue Of Liberty, Iron, Painted Silver & Gold, 9 3/4 x 3 1/2 x 3 1/2 In.	403
Turkey, Red Paint, Patina, Tail Feathers Up, Cast Iron, c.1910, 3 1/2 x 3 In.	162
U.S. Mail Box, Green, Gold, Cast Eagle, Kenton Hardware, c.1930s, 4 1/4 In.	35
U.S. Tank, World War I, Cast Iron, c.1919, 1 3/4 In.	100

BARBER collectibles range from the popular red and white striped pole that used to be found in front of every shop to the small scissors and tools of the trade. Barber chairs are wanted, especially the older models with elaborate iron trim.

Chair, Elephant, Saddle, Riser, 43 x 47 In.	693
Chair, Emil J. Paidar, White Enamel, Cast Iron, Felt Headrest, 47 ½ x 37 In.	354
Chair, White Enamel, Chrome, Cast Iron Frame, 46 ½ x 26 In.	383
Display Case, Clauss Cutlery Straight Razors, Wood, Decal, 30 Razors, 36 In.	3998
Pole, Electric, Blue, Red, White, 27 In.	438
Pole, Marvy, Electric, Wall, Cast Iron Mount, Chrome Caps, 27 x 8 In.	324
Pole, Metal, Chrome Caps, Wall, Rotating, Light-Up, Red, White, Blue, Striped, 32 In.	400
Pole, Milk Glass Globe, Electric, Cylindrical, Swirl Stripes, Red, White, Blue.	236
Pole, Porcelain, Stand-Up, Light-Up, Red, White, Blue, Striped, Crank, 85 In.	1476
Pole, Stand-Up, Red, White, 82 In.	497
Pole, Tin, Paint, Wood, Cylindrical, Spiral Stripes, Platform, 76 In.	266
Pole, Turned Wood, Old Weathered Paint, 18th Century, 84 x 8 In. *illus*	450
Pole, Turned Wood, Painted, Red, White, Blue, Acorn Finial Ends, 1800s, 69 In. *illus*	708
Pole, Turned Wood, Painted, Red, White, Blue, Cannonball Finial, 1800s, 31 In. *illus*	767
Pole, Turned Wood, Painted, Red, White, Blue, Wrought Iron Brackets, 49 In. *illus*	413
Pole, Turned Wood, Red, White, Blue, Square Base, Ball Finial, 77 ½ In. *illus*	510
Sign, Barber Shop, Black, White, Red, Geometric Stripes, Porcelain, Enamel, 24 In.	185
Sign, Fred's Barber Shop, 2-Sided, c.1910, 52 ½ x 16 ¼ In.	360

BAROMETERS are used to forecast the weather. Antique barometers with elaborate wooden cases and brass trim are the most desirable. Mercury column barometers are also popular with collectors. It is difficult to find someone to repair a broken one, so be sure your barometer is in working condition.

Aneroid, Carved Walnut, Beaux Arts, Ribbon Crest, c.1900, 39 x 12 In.	366
Aneroid, Oak, Grapes, Leaves, 1800s, 32 ½ x 14 In.	175
Aneroid, Thermometer, Iron, Guichard, Fruit Basket Finial, France, 25 x 12 In.	147
Banjo, Black Forest, Hunting Theme, 1900s, 49 In.	292
Banjo, Inlaid Mahogany, P.F. Bollenback, 40 ½ In.	375
Banjo, Mahogany, Broken Arch Pediment, Brass Finial, Shell Inlay, 40 x 10 In.	225
Banjo, Pine, Carved, Leaves, France, 1800s, 38 x 12 In.	100
Banjo, Thermometer, Hygrometer, Mahogany, Swan's Neck Crest, 45 x 12 In.	531
Clock, Gothic, Walnut, Winged Gargoyle, 1800s, 37 x 16 ½ In. *illus*	1950
James Pioty, Mahogany & Pine, Silvered Face, Boston Fecit, c.1810, 39 In.	750
Salon De Coricely, Oval, Ebonized, Carved, Gilt Ropes, Tassels, France, 35 In.	540
Short & Mason, Brass, Leather Case, 1948, 2 In.	58
Stick, Husbands & Clarke, Walnut, 40 x 3 ½ In. *illus*	593
Stick, Louis Philippe, Weather Tube, Thermometer, Signed Pedraglio, c.1825, 37 ½ x 4 In. *illus*	640
Stick, Ship, Mahogany & Brass, 1900s, 37 x 13 In.	1625
Stick, Ship, Walnut Case, Brass Gimbal, 37 In.	360
Stick, Wecchio Salisbury, Mahogany, Line Inlay, Finial Crest, 1800s, 38 In.	420
Thermometer, Banjo, Mother-Of-Pearl, Rosewood, 46 x 46 In.	250
Thermometer, Clock, Weather Dial, Johnson, Rosewood, Brass Inlay, 51 In.	4800
Thermometer, Eiffel Tower, Metal Fretwork, France, 21 In.	940
Thermometer, F. Pradal & Co., Wheels, Mahogany, Chester, England, 39 In.	225
Thermometer, Giltwood, Carved, Lovebird Crest, Flowers, c.1810, 39 In.	1625
Thermometer, J.E. Ames, Carved Rosewood, Bath, Marked, c.1840, 43 In.	1220
Thermometer, Wheel, Rosewood, Mother-Of-Pearl Inlay, 38 ½ In.	225
Thermometer, Wood Case, Reeded Edge, Double Window, 38 x 4 In.	41
Tycos Model, Short & Mason, Brass, Monogram, 3 In.	58
Wheel, Aneroid, Thermometer, Black Forest, Leaves, Flowers, 18 x 9 ½ In.	476
Wheel, Banjo, Mahogany, Swan's Neck Pediment, Inlay, c.1815, 39 In., Pair	500
Wheel, Black Forest, Hunting Theme, 49 In.	292
Wheel, D. Fagiolo & Son, Rosewood, England, 1800s, 41 In.	360
Wheel, F. Amadio & Son, Flame Mahogany, Regency, England, 1800s, 38 In.	330
Wood, Empire, Gilt, Eglomise, Lyre Shape, France, 1800s, 34 x 17 ½ In.	1140

Barber, Pole, Turned Wood, Painted, Red, White, Blue, Wrought Iron Brackets, 49 In.
$413

B

Hess Auction Group

Barber, Pole, Turned Wood, Red, White, Blue, Square Base, Ball Finial, 77 ½ In.
$510

Cowan's Auctions

Barometer, Clock, Gothic, Walnut, Winged Gargoyle, 1800s, 37 x 16 ½ In.
$1,950

Ruby Lane

B

Barometer, Stick, Husbands & Clarke, Walnut, 40 x 3 ½ In.

$593

Barometer, Stick, Louis Philippe, Weather Tube, Thermometer, Signed Pedraglio, c.1825, 37 ½ x 4 In.

$640

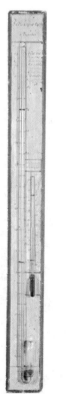

BASALT is a special type of ceramic invented by Josiah Wedgwood in the eighteenth century. It is a fine-grained, unglazed stoneware. Some pieces are listed in that section. The most common type is black, but many other colors were made. It was made by many factories. Some pieces are listed in the Wedgwood section.

Bowl, Globular, Footed, Relief Leaves & Flowers, Banding, 4 x 10 In.	106
Bust, Paul Bunyan, Collared Shirt, Long Hair, Waisted Socle, c.1850, 12 In.	400
Creamer, Scrolling Leaves, Gadrooned, Ribbed, Shaped Handle, 1800s, 4 In.	135
Vase, Roman Figures, Cherub, Huntress, Trumpet Shape, Pedestal, 1800s, 7 In.	110

BASEBALL *collectibles are in the Sports category, except for baseball cards, which are listed under Baseball in the Card category.*

BASKETS of all types are popular with collectors. American Indian, Japanese, African, Nantucket, Shaker, and many other kinds of baskets may be found in other sections. Of course, baskets are still being made, so a collector must learn to judge the age and style of a basket to determine its value. Also see Purse.

Bird Carrier, Splint, Woven, Gourd, Lid, Upright Handle, Braided Band, 1800s, 15 In.	550
Buttocks, Splint, Woven, Bentwood Handle, c.1885, 5 x 5 In.	120
Buttocks, Split Hickory, Bentwood Handle, 4 ¼ x 3 In.	98
Buttocks, Split Hickory, Half Eye Of God Binding, 7 ½ x 7 ½ In.	98
Cheese, Splint, Woven, Hexagonal, Round Rim, Side Handles, 1800s, 11 x 24 In.	750
Clam, Splint, Woven, Bucket Shape, Upright Handle, Wrapped Rim, 1800s, 16 In.	1600
Coil, Rye, Straw, Openwork, Green, Applied Arch Handle, Penn., 1800s, 17 x 19 In. ....*illus*	236
Ebony, Quillwork, Black, Rectangular, 4 ¼ x 7 ½ In.	175
Eel Trap, Splint, Woven, Angled, Center Opening, 1800s, 11 x 12 x 4 In.	600
Egg, Splint, Oak, Strap Handle, Green & Red Bands, Double Wrapped Rim, 8 x 9 In.	153
Egg, Wire, c.1900, 3 ½ x 10 In.	25
Flat Sided, Split Hickory, Green Paint, Bentwood Hickory Handle, 14 ½ In. ....*illus*	118
Fruit, Slatted, Handles, Blue Paint, c.1900, 28 x 19 In. ....*illus*	570
Gathering, Splint, Robin's-Egg Blue, Bent Ash Handles, c.1885, 10 x 30 In.	523
Hanging, 3 Tiers, Red Paint, Lollipop Hanger, 1800s, 24 x 12 ½ x 5 In.	1000
Ikebana, Bamboo, Handle, 22 ½ In.	180
Ikebana, Bamboo, Lizuka Rokansai, Japan, 11 x 13 x 12 In.	38000
Ikebana, Bamboo, Splint, Cylinder, 16 In.	144
Ikebana, Crescent Moon Shape, Splint, Bamboo, Wrapped Handle, 13 x 13 In.	270
Ikebana, Flower, Kosuge Kogetsw, Signed, 1980s, 17 x 5 x 5 In.	7500
Ikebana, Handle, Signed Hosai, 14 In.	150
Ikebana, Tea Jar Shape, Bamboo, Splint, Rootwood Handle, 14 ½ In.	420
Laundry, Splint, Woven, Bent Ash Handles, Iron Staples, Inscribed, 12 x 18 In.	492
Market, Splint, Woven, Oval, Bentwood Handle, God's-Eye Supports, 1800s, 10 x 15 In.	71
Nantucket, Lightship, Oval, Carved Swing Handle, A.D. Williams, 1922, 8 In.	711
Nantucket, Lightship, Swing Bentwood Handle, Brass Staves, Mitchell Ray, 7 ½ In. ....*illus*	633
Nantucket, Oval, Swing Handle, 14 x 12 ½ In.	1020
Nantucket, Oval, Swing Handle, Turned Hardwood Base, 4 ¼ x 8 In.	270
Nantucket, Swing Handle, Carving, Turned Wood Bottom, Signed, Asa Brown, 12 In. ....*illus*	489
Nantucket, Threaded Design, Swing Handle, Rolled Rim, Label, c.1885, 7 In.	960
Pigeon Carrier, Wicker, Top Door, Leather Strap Closure, c.1910, 13 x 23 In.	450
Q-Tip Shape, Lid, Applied Handles, 16 In.	96
Rye Straw, Cylindrical, Shouldered, Arched Handle, X-Supports, c.1900, 11 In.	140
Sewing, Rye Straw, Coiled, Wrapped Rim, Round, Open Handles, 1800s, 3 x 9 In.	20
Splint, Oak, Kidney Shape, Ribbing, Arched Handle, 6 ½ In.	82
Splint, Oak, Patina, Fixed Bail Handle, c.1915, 15 x 14 x 23 In.	330
Splint, Oak, Round, Tapered Sides, Late 1800s, 4 ½ In.	211
Splint, Open Weave, Square Base, Round Rim, Fixed Bail Handle, 1800s, 13 In.	150
Splint, Saucer Base, Cylindrical Pedestal, Upright Double Handle, c.1880, 19 In.	400
Splint, Woven, Green Paint, Braided Rim, Strap Swing Handle, c.1880, 7 x 10 In.	1700
Splint, Woven, Oak, Bentwood Handle, 15 In.	41
Splint, Woven, Painted Dots Design, Rectangular, Side Handles, c.1890, 5 x 11 In.	3250

Splint, Woven, Square, Lid, Handles, Painted Flowers & Hearts, c.1890, 7 x 12 In.		3250
Splint, Woven, Square, Upright Handle, Green & Red Leaves, c.1890, 6 x 5 In.		2300
Split Oak, Footed, c.1875, 7 ½ x 8 ¾ In.		420
Split Oak, God's Eye, 1800s, 12 ½ x 15 ½ In.		111
Storage, Splint, Oak, Woven, Rectangular, Wrapped Oval Rim, 1800s, 16 x 44 In.		384
Walnut, Birch, Coiled, Undulating, Signed, Kerry Vesper, 5 x 11 ½ In.		849

BATCHELDER products are made from California clay. Ernest Batchelder **BATCHELDER** established a tile studio in Pasadena, California, in 1909. He went into partnership **LOS ANGELES** with Frederick Brown in 1912 and the company became Batchelder and Brown. In 1920 he built a larger factory with a new partner. The Batchelder-Wilson Company made all types of architectural tiles, garden pots, and bookends. The plant closed in 1932. In 1936 Batchelder opened Batchelder Ceramics, also in Pasadena, and made bowls, vases, and earthenware pots. He retired in 1951 and died in 1957. Pieces are marked *Batchelder Pasadena* or *Batchelder Los Angeles*.

Tile, Arts & Crafts, Knight On Horseback, Relief, Terra-Cotta, Matte Glaze, 4 In.		70
Tile, Double Diamond, Cobalt, Terra-Cotta, 1909-12, 5 ½ x 8 In.	*illus*	49
Tile, Peacock, Tan & Gray Matte, Embossed, c.1920, 5 ¾ x 5 ¾ In.		160
Tile, Raised Scroll, Hexagonal, Brown, Blue Matte Glaze, Signed, 4 x 4 In.		147
Tile, Stylized Flower, Green, Buff, Black, Satin Glaze, Arched, Signed, 6 x 4 In.		165
Vase, Pale Green Glaze, Yellow Interior, Shaped Rectangle, 1920s, 5 x 8 In.		195

BATMAN and Robin are characters from a comic strip by Bob Kane that started in 1939. In 1966, the characters became part of a popular television series. There have been radio and movie serials that featured the pair. The first full-length movie was made in 1989.

Action Figure, Climber, Powerized Cable, Remco, Window Box, 1980, 9 In.		191
Action Figure, Robin, Posable, Polyester Outfit, Window Box, Mego, 1972, 8 In.		283
Bank, Plastic, Figural, Arms Crossed, c.1980, 7 ¼ In.		14
Batamaran, Boat, Cockpit, Batman Pilot, Hard Plastic, Battery, Box, 1966, 9 In.		759
Batcycle, With Sidecar, Black Plastic, Bat Symbol, On Card, 1973, 10 x 11 In.		387
Batmobile, Metal, Glossy Black, Red Bat Symbols, Gold Hubcaps, Box, 1966, 5 In.		115
Bookrack, Comics, Wire, Tin Litho Plates, Adventures Of Batman, 1966, 7 x 15 In.		1021
Cake Pan, Aluminum, Hands On Hips, Wilton, c.1985, 13 x 13 In.		16
Card, Gum, Black Bat, Art Fronts, Orange Text Backs, Box, 1966, Set Of 55		478
Card, Gum, Blue Bat, Color Images, Puzzle Piece Back, 1966, 3 x 4 In., Set Of 44		209
Coffee Table, Wood, Tile, Batman, Brenda White, Disney, 1991, 16 x 40 x 18 In.		3999
Comic Book, Batman, No. 157, Batwoman & Vicki Vale, DC Comics, 1963		202
Comic Book, Lex Luther Appears, No. 130, 1960		230
Comic Book, Origin Of Catwoman, No. 62, 1950		477
Cookie Jar, Batmobile, Porcelain, Warner Brothers, 1997, 14 x 8 x 7 In.		125
Doll, Plush, Cape, Belt, Chest Insignia, Ace Toy, 1989, 26 In.		55
Drawing, Batman In Spotlight, Pen & Ink On Board, Jack Burnley, 11 x 15 In.		543
Figure, Batgirl, Posable, Cape, Boots, Purse, Hairband, Blister Card, 1977, 8 In.	*illus*	278
Figure, Batman, Batmobile, Blue Rubber, National Periodicals Lawson Novelty, 3 In.		30
Figure, Batman, Posable, Plastic, Suit, Kresge, Blister Card, 1972, 8 In.	*illus*	1489
Figure, Catwoman, Posable, Plastic, Blue Suit, Blister Card, 1973, 8 In.		855
Figure, Joker, Posable, Suit, Shoes, Jacket, DC Comics, Blister Card, 1977, 8 In.		467
Figure, Robin, Resin, Clenched Fists, Warner Brothers, 1990s, 6 ½ In.		75
Game, Board, 50th Anniversary, University Games		20
Game, Board, Milton Bradley, 1966, 10 x 19 In.		40
Game, Board, TV Show, Playing Pieces, Marbles, Box, Japan, 1966, 9 x 16 In.		538
Glass, Batman, Hands On Waist, Pepsi-Cola, 1976, 6 In.		35
License Plate, Riddler, Embossed, Color, Header Card, c.1965, 6 x 11 In.		444
Lunch Box, Batman, Bat Signal, Knocking Out Bad Guy, 8 x 7 In.		213
Model Kit, Batman, No. 467-149, Instructions, Color Illustrated Box, 1964		474
Model Kit, Batskiboat, Unassembled, Ertl, 1992		15
Model Kit, The Penguin, Decals, Instruction Book, Aurora, Sealed Box, 1966		506

Basket, Coil, Rye, Straw, Openwork, Green, Applied Arch Handle, Penn., 1800s, 17 x 19 In.
$236

Hess Auction Group

Basket, Flat Sided, Split Hickory, Green Paint, Bentwood Hickory Handle, 14 ½ In.
$118

Forsythe's Auctions

Basket, Fruit, Slatted, Handles, Blue Paint, c.1900, 28 x 19 In.
$570

Garth's Auctioneers & Appraisers

TIP
Let your basket share the bathroom with you when you take a shower. The hot, moist air is good for the basket. Then let it dry.

Basket, Nantucket, Lightship, Swing Bentwood Handle, Brass Staves, Mitchell Ray, 7½ In.
$633

Myers Auction Gallery

Basket, Nantucket, Swing Handle, Carving, Turned Wood Bottom, Signed, Asa Brown, 12 In.
$489

Myers Auction Gallery

Batchelder, Tile, Double Diamond, Cobalt, Terra-Cotta, 1909-12, 5½ x 8 In.
$49

Leland Little Auctions

Batman, Figure, Batgirl, Posable, Cape, Boots, Purse, Hairband, Blister Card, 1977, 8 In.
$278

Hake's Americana & Collectibles

Ornament, Batman, Swings On Rope, Hallmark, Box, 1994	30
PEZ, Black Body, 1980s	11
Pinback, Bat Signal, Batman Club, Black On White, Red, 1960s, 2¼ In.	16
Pinback, Ron Riley's Batman Club, Chicago, Black, White, Red, 1960s, 2¼ In.	16
Playset, Batcave, Vinyl, Cardboard, Batpole, Computer, Box, 1974, 12 x 16 In.	169
Poster, Movie, The Batman, Ch. 15, Doom Of The Rising Sun, 1954, 27 x 41 In.	633
Puppet, Hand, Cloth Body, Vinyl Head, Header Card, Germany, 1966, 11 In.	886
Sip-A-Cup, Batman & Robin, Handle Doubles As Straw, Plastic, 1966, 8 x 10 In.	418
Toy, Batcopter, Plastic, Black, Yellow, Rotor, Free-Wheeling, Card, 1974, 6 x 13 In.	278
Toy, Batcycle, Sidecar, Blue Plastic, Free-Wheeling, Box, 1974, 6 x 11 In. ......*illus*	190
Toy, Batlab, Van, Bat Grappling Hook, Revolving Platform, Box, 1975, 8 x 14 In.	522
Toy, Batmobile, Black Plastic, Batman Driver, Blister Card, 1966, 4 x 8 In. ....*illus*	1725
Toy, Batmobile, Black Plastic, Decal, Free-Wheeling, Folded 1974, 9 x 14 In.	253
Toy, Batmobile, Red Lights, Sounds, Battery Operated, DC Comics, 1980s, 7 In.	24
Toy, Command Console, Plastic, Buttons, Screen, Light-Up, Box, 1977, 10 x 10 In.	196
Toy, Jokermobile, Plastic, Squirt Flower, Boxing-Glove Trap, Box, 1975, 8 x 14 In.	522
Toy, Lex-Soar 7, Assault Ship, Super Powers Series, Box, 1984, 8 x 9 In.	266
Toy, Tumbling Ladder, Plastic, Ladders, Base, Blocks, Card, 1966, 7 x 15 In.	949

 BATTERSEA enamels, which are enamels painted on copper, were made in the Battersea district of London from about 1750 to 1756. Many similar enamels are mistakenly called Battersea.

Matchbox, Port Scene, Ship, Castle, Heart Shape, Hinged, c.1750, 2 x 2 In.	455
Mirror Knob, Portrait, George Washington, Banner, Transfer, 3 In., Pair	1968
Needle Case, White, Enameled Flowers, Tubular, 1700s, 5 x 1 In.	464
Pillbox, Portrait, Woman, Plumed Hat, Enamel, Round, Lid, c.1755, 2 In. Diam.	345
Tieback, Drapery, Boy Playing Flute, Jaunty Hat, Church, c.1755, 2 x 2 In.	200

 BAUER pottery is a California-made ware. J.A. Bauer bought Paducah Pottery in Paducah, Kentucky, in 1885. He moved the pottery to Los Angeles, California, in 1909. The company made art pottery after 1912 and introduced dinnerware marked *Bauer* in 1930. The factory went out of business in 1962 and the molds were destroyed. Since 1998, a new company, Bauer Pottery Company of Los Angeles, has been making Bauer pottery using molds made from original Bauer pieces. The pottery is now made in Highland, California. Most pieces are marked "2000." Original pieces of Bauer pottery are listed here. See also the Russel Wright category.

Aladdin, Teapot, Lid, Cream Gloss, Ray Murray, 1940s, 11 In.	85
Bowl, Green, Marked 12 Bauer USA, 4½ x 4 In. ....*illus*	115
Coconut Grove, Vase, Cornucopia Shape, Cream, 1940s, 8 In.	70
La Linda, Cup & Saucer, Burgundy, Glossy	9
La Linda, Cup & Saucer, Yellow, Glossy	15
La Linda, Cup, Green, Glossy, 2½ In.	14
La Linda, Cup, Pink, Glossy	14
La Linda, Gravy Boat, Green, Glossy	55
La Linda, Salt & Pepper, Gray, Glossy	30
La Linda, Saucer, Brown, Glossy	8
Mission Modern, Creamer, Light Green	20
Monterey, Bowl, Turquoise, 13 In.	80
Monterey, Casserole, Lid, Speckled, Beige, 1½ Qt.	30
Monterey, Mug, 3 In.	5
Monterey, Pitcher, Turquoise, c.1939, 6 x 9 In.	40
Monterey, Teapot, Pink, Lid, 4 Cup	42
Ring, Chop Plate, Orange, 12½ In.	125
Ring, Cookie Jar, Lid, Barrel Shape, Orange, c.1960, 10 In.	100
Ring, Cup, Cobalt Blue, 3 In.	10
Ring, Pitcher, Orange, 5¾ In.	60
Teapot, Copper Glaze, Aladdin, 13 In. ....*illus*	65

BAVARIA is a region in Europe where many types of porcelain were made. In the nineteenth century, the mark often included the word *Bavaria*. After 1871, the words *Bavaria, Germany*, were used. Listed here are pieces that include the name *Bavaria* in some form, but major porcelain makers, such as Rosenthal, are listed in their own categories.

Basket, Cupid Shape Standard, Cornucopia, Pierced, Scrolled, Swags, c.1940, 22 x 10 In., Pair	708
Bonbon, Pink Roses, Shaped Border, Karen Lemmon, 10¼ In. ....*illus*	149
Lemonade Set, Pitcher, 6 Cups, Red Poppies, Gold Handles, 8¼ x 4 In., 7 Piece	47
Mug, Grapes, Vines, 5¾ x 4⅛ In.	12
Pitcher, Blackberries, Green, 6¼ In.	50
Plate, Black Knight, Gold, Flowers, 10½ In., 11 Piece	295
Plate, Concentric Gold Borders, Monogram, 11 In., 12 Piece	944
Plate, Fruit, Cobalt Shaped Rim, Blue & Yellow Ground, Off Center Fruit, 8 In., 12 Piece	88
Plate, Gold Encrusted Wide Rim, Laurel Leaves, Flowers, White Ground, 10¾ In., 11 Piece	944
Plate, Love Story, Fragonard, Green Border, 10 Scenes, 13 In.	61
Sugar & Creamer, Purple Band, Purple Bird, Green Handles, PM Moschendorf, 2 Piece	6
Vase, Birds, Pecking, Landscape, Green, Blue, Yellow, Black, 15¾ x 7½ In.	165
Vase, Yellow & Pink Roses, Gilt Handles, 16 In.	127
Vase, Yellow & Pink Roses, Pastel Green, Signed Ganzhorn, 1911, 11¾ In., Pair	59

BEADED BAGS *are included in the Purse category.*

BEATLES collectors search for any items picturing the four members of the famous music group or any of their recordings. Because these items are so new, the condition is very important and top prices are paid only for items in mint condition. The Beatles first appeared on American network television in 1964. The group disbanded in 1971. Ringo Starr and Paul McCartney are still performing. John Lennon died in 1980. George Harrison died in 2001.

Alarm Clock, Yellow Submarine, Metal, Brass, Group Image, 1968, 4 In.	345
Album Cover, Yesterday And Today, LP, Butcher Coats, Third State, 1966 ....*illus*	720
Album, Beatles At Hollywood Bowl, Ticket Stubs	65
Button, Portrait, I Love Ringo, Blue, Flasher, Pinback, 1960s, 2½ In.	48
Charm Bracelet, Goldtone, Brass, Links, Head Charms, 1964, 7 In.	49
Diary, Vinyl, Beatles On Stage, Photos, Scotland, 1965, 3 x 4 In.	145
Display Box, Gum Card, 6 Cents, Band Photos, Gum, Cardboard, 1964, 5 x 7 In.	475
Harmonica, Press Release, Instructions, Hohner, Photo Illustrated Box, 1964, 4 In.	190
Magazine, Beatles Are Back, N. Rockwell Style, MacFadden-Bartell, 1964, 72 Page	25
Necktie, Do You Want To Know A Secret, Couple, Stars, Silk, c.1990	30
Necktie, She's Leaving Home, Abstract, Silk, 1990s	35
Nodder, Ringo Starr, Plastic Body, Rubber Head, Drum, Remco, 1964, 4½ In.	77
Picture, Band Members, Suits & Ties, Lithograph, Canvas, Leo Jensen, 17 x 14 In.	30
Pin, Guitar Shape, Portrait, Paul McCartney, Plastic, 1960s, 4¼ In. ....*illus*	25
Postcard, Beatles, Seated, Jackets & Ties, 1960s	22
Postcard, Receiving Variety Club Awards, Great Britain, 1963	18
Poster, The Beatles, Hard Day's Night, 41 x 27 In.	375
Scarf, Portraits, Autographs, Music Notes, Tan, 1964, 22 x 22 In.	60
Suspenders, Clip, Help, Black, Teal, Purple, 1980s, One Size	36
Ticket Stub & Tour Book, Forest Hills Concert, 1964	1078
Ticket Stub, Baltimore Concert, Matinee, Section 17, Row J, 3 Dollars, 1964, 2 x 2 In.	223
Toy, Drum, Snare, Printed Portraits & Signatures, Mastro, c.1964, 14 x 7 In.	288
Tray, Portraits, Red, Blue, Star Border, Metal, Great Britain, 1964, 13 x 13 In.	64

BEEHIVE, Austria, or Beehive, Vienna, are terms used in English-speaking countries to refer to the many types of decorated porcelain bearing a mark that looks like a beehive. The mark is actually a shield, viewed upside down. It was first used in 1744 by the Royal Porcelain Manufactory of Vienna. The firm made what collectors call Royal Vienna porcelains until it closed in 1864. Many other German, Austrian, and Japanese factories have

Batman, Figure, Batman, Posable, Plastic, Suit, Kresge, Blister Card, 1972, 8 In.
$1,489

Hake's Americana & Collectibles

Batman, Toy, Batcycle, Sidecar, Blue Plastic, Free-Wheeling, Box, 1974, 6 x 11 In.
$190

Hake's Americana & Collectibles

Batman, Toy, Batmobile, Black Plastic, Batman Driver, Blister Card, 1966, 4 x 8 In.
$1,725

Hake's Americana & Collectibles

This is an edited listing of current prices. Visit Kovels.com to check thousands of prices from previous years and sign up for free information on trends, tips, reproductions, marks, and more.

Bauer, Bowl, Green, Marked 12 Bauer USA, 4½ x 4 In.
$115

Ruby Lane

Bauer, Teapot, Copper Glaze, Aladdin, 13 In.
$65

Ruby Lane

Bavaria, Bonbon, Pink Roses, Shaped Border, Karen Lemmon, 10¼ In.
$149

Ruby Lane

Beatles, Album Cover, Yesterday And Today, LP, Butcher Coats, Third State, 1966
$720

Robert Edward Auctions

reproduced Royal Vienna wares, complete with the original shield or beehive mark. This listing includes the expensive, original Royal Vienna porcelains and many other types of beehive porcelain. The Royal Vienna pieces include that name in the description.

Bowl, Egyptian Revival, 4 Caryatids, Round Base, 6 x 4½ In.	182
Bowl, Lid, White Ground, 2 Children, Flowers, c.1880, 11 In.	246
Cachepot, Cherubs, Bird, Courtyard, Brown, Gilt Rim, 9 In., Pair	4731
Compote, Musicians, Cobalt Blue, Cresting Handles, c.1910, 7½ x 10 x 5 In.	338
Figurine, Spaniel, Gray, White, Seated, Royal Vienna, 8 In.	100
Group, Hunter, 2 Hounds, Trumpet, Tree Base, Royal Vienna, c.1900, 10 x 12 In. ....*illus*	246
Plate, Man & Woman, With Infant, Stone Patio, Landscape, 9½ In.	406
Plate, Mythological Scene, Women, Baskets On Heads, Seaside, 9 In.	250
Plate, Portrait, 18th Century Woman, Gilt Border, Royal Vienna, 9¾ In., Pair ....*illus*	1375
Plate, Portrait, Woman In Hat, Gold, Blue, Gilt Border, 1800s, 11 x 8 In.	200
Plate, Portrait, Woman, Blue Eyes, Dark Hair, Cobalt Blue Rim, Gilt, 10 In.	208
Plate, Portrait, Woman, Brown Dress, Bare Shoulders, 9½ In.	875
Plate, Psyche, Wings, Butterfly, Pond, 9½ In.	500
Plate, Woman, Harp, Grasses, Gilt & Red Border, 9½ In.	344
Urn, Lid, Mythological Clotho, Cobalt Blue, Winged Handles, c.1910, 12½ In.	277
Urn, Lid, Women, Putti, Music, Cobalt Blue, Gilt, Handles, 13 In.	204
Urn, Milton's Visit With Galileo, Gilt, Royal Vienna, 20¼ In.	720
Urn, Woman Playing Lyre, Scrolls & Garland, Iridescent, Gilt, 1900, 14 In.	1750
Urn, Women In Courtyard, Cupid, Clouds, Blue, Gilt, Handles, Plinth, 13 x 6 In.	230
Vase, Austrian Bleu-Royale, Figural Scenes, Amphora, c.1885, 25 In.	1792
Vase, Cobalt Blue, Gold, Classical Women, Banding, 12 In.	625
Vase, Game Of Elves, When Roses Bloom, Fairies, Magenta, 12 x 7 In., Pair	413
Vase, Lid, Mercury Discovers Herse, Banding, Cartouche, 1800s, 13 x 5 In.	259
Vase, Stand, Cobalt Blue, Gilt Jewels, Lid, Gilt Finial, Paris & Helena, 19 In.	984
Vase, Woman With Violin, Cartouche, Maroon, Gilt, 16½ x 8 In.	2400

BEER BOTTLES *are listed in the Bottle category under Beer.*

BEER CANS are a twentieth-century idea. Beer was sold in kegs or returnable bottles until 1934. The first patent for a can was issued to the American Can Company in September of that year, and Gotfried Kruger Brewing Company, Newark, New Jersey, was the first to use the can. The cone-top can was first made in 1935, the aluminum pop-top in 1962. Collectors should look for cans in good condition, with no dents or rust. Serious collectors prefer cans that have been opened from the bottom.

Black Label, Carling, Flat Top, Black, Red, White	8
Boston Light Ale, Cone Top, Dot Design, Center Oval, Lighthouse, 5¼ In.	185
Budweiser Light, Flat Top, Blue, Red, Silver, St. Louis, 1981	77
Free State Beer, Cone Top, Red, Gold, Blue, 6 In.	246
Old Imperial, Rahr's Brewing Co., Cone Top, Red, Brown, c.1940	123
Rocky Mountain Beer, Cone Top, Red, Black, Silver, Anaconda Brewing, 5 x 2 In. ....*illus*	250
Schlitz, Flat Top, c.1949	8

BELL collectors collect all types of bells. Favorites include glass bells, figural bells, school bells, and cowbells. Bells have been made of porcelain, china, or metal through the centuries.

Brass, Ship, Great Lakes, Acorn Finial, Metal Stand, Stadacona, 1909, 18 In.	840
Bronze, Brass Buckle, Leather Strap, Spain, 18 In.	457
Bronze, Come Away Make No Delay, Cast, 1775, 14 In.	7800
Bronze, Copper, Hanging, 4 Bells, Paolo Soleri, 20 In.	236
Bronze, Copper, Hanging, 6 Bells, 3 Tiers, Graduated Sizes, Paolo Soleri, 28 In.	531
Bronze, Cowboy Artists Of America, 25th Anniversary, c.1990, 9 x 9 In.	480
Bronze, Iron Yoke, Hanger & Clapper, Inscribed G.W. Coffin Co., Cincinnati, 18 In. ....*illus*	738
Bronze, Overall Raised Design, Gilt Patina, Tibet, 12½ x 5 In.	7085
Bronze, San Diego, Spain, 9½ In.	3250
Custard Glass, Daisies, Fenton, Marked, 1970s, 6½ In.	12

Dinner, Charles Rohlfs, Carved R Cipher, Buffalo, N.Y., c.1902, 31 x 6 x 9 In.	5625
Iron, Hanging, House, Roof, Weathervane, 60 In.	406
Servant, Shell, Ormolu, Dove Finial, Thumb-Activated Clapper, 6½ In.	84
Service, Push, Bulldog Head, Bronze, Glass Eyes, Germany, 4½ In.	732
Service, Push Button, Round, 4 In.	72
Shrine, Bronze, Detailed Calligraphy, Japan, Early 1800s, 23 x 12 In.	1920
Silver, Cherub Finial, Gorham, 3¼ x 2¼ In.	94
Sleigh, 15 Graduated Brass Bells, Leather Belt ....*illus*	221
Sleigh, 25 Brass Bells, Leather Strap, 96 In.	225
Sleigh, 28 Brass Bells, Leather Strap, 72 x 1 In.	185
Stand, Jos Bernhard, 1868, 39 x 31 In.	492
Temple, Carved Teak Stand, 10 Graduated Bells, 81 x 29½ In. .... *illus*	246

BELLEEK china was made in Ireland, other European countries, and the United States. The glaze is creamy yellow and appears wet. The first Belleek was made in 1857. All pieces listed here are Irish Belleek. The mark changed through the years. The first mark, black, dates from 1863 to 1890. The second mark, black, dates from 1891 to 1926 and includes the words *Co. Fermanagh, Ireland.* The third mark, black, dates from 1926 to 1946 and has the words *Deanta in Eirinn.* The fourth mark, same as the third mark but green, dates from 1946 to 1955. The fifth mark (second green mark) dates from 1955 to 1965 and has an R in a circle added in the upper right. The sixth mark (third green mark) dates from 1965 to 1981 and the words *Co. Fermanagh* have been omitted. The seventh mark, gold, was used from 1981 to 1992 and omits the words *Deanta in Eirinn.* The eighth mark, used from 1993 to 1996, is similar to the second mark but is printed in blue. The ninth mark, blue, includes the words *Est. 1857,* and the words *Co. Fermanagh Ireland* are omitted. The tenth mark, black, is similar to the ninth mark but includes the words *Millennium 2000* and *Ireland.* It was used only in 2000. The eleventh mark, similar to the millennium mark but green, was introduced in 2001. The twelfth mark, black, is similar to the eleventh mark but has a banner above the mark with the words *Celebrating 150 Years.* It was used in 2007. The thirteenth trademark, used from 2008 to 2010, is similar to the twelfth but is brown and has no banner. The fourteenth mark, the Classic Belleek trademark, is similar to the twelfth but includes Belleek's website address. The Belleek Living trademark was introduced in 2010 and is used on items from that giftware line. The word *Belleek* is now used only on the pieces made in Ireland even though earlier pieces from other countries were sometimes marked *Belleek.* These early pieces are listed by manufacturer, such as Ceramic Art Co., Haviland, Lenox, Ott & Brewer, and Willets.

Basket, Heart Shape, Reticulated, Woven, Molded Flowers, c.1980, 6 x 6 In.	200
Biscuit Jar, Basket Weave, Shamrocks, Lid, Twig Handle, 4th Mark, Green, c.1946, 7 In.	145
Jug, Shamrock, Basket Weave, Twisted Handle, Marked, c.1960, 4½ In.	40
Pitcher, Figural, Young Girl, Marked, 4¾ x 2½ In.	36
Plate, Clover, Marked, 8 In., 6 Piece	60
Platter, Ribbed, Green Edge, Marked, 17½ x 14 In.	390
Teapot, Echinus, Pink Finial & Handles, Flowers, Marked, 5 In.	188
Teapot, Lid, Finial, Cream, Yellow, Bulbous, Ribbed, Coral Shape Handle, 1950s	240
Teapot, White, Yellow, Textured, Peaked Lid, Finial, 6th Mark, Green, c.1965, 8 x 8 In.	220
Tray, Thorn, 14½ In.	437
Trinket Box, Dome Lid, Pierced, Molded Roses, Twig Handles, c.1980, 4 x 5 In.	1850
Vase, Applied Pink Roses, Shamrocks, Molded, Ribbed, Crimped, 5th Mark, Green, 4 In.	325
Vase, Encrusted Flowers, Squat, Folds, Ripples, Pierced Ruffled Rim, c.1900, 4 In.	275
Vase, Ribbed Swirled Pattern, Applied Flowers, Shamrocks, Mark, c.1950, 4 In.	145
Vase, Ruffled, Applied Flowers, Leaves, 3½ x 4¼ In.	24

BENNINGTON ware was the product of two factories working in Bennington, Vermont. Both the Norton Company and Lyman Fenton & Company were out of business by 1896. The wares include brown and yellow mottled pottery, Parian, scroddled ware, stoneware, graniteware, yellowware, and Staffordshire-type vases. The name is also a generic term for mottled brownware of the type made in Bennington.

Bank, Figural, Hippo, Green Glaze, Mottled, Open Mouth, Top Slit, 9 x 5 In.	225
Coffeepot, Streaked Glaze, Brown, Cream, Flint Enamel, Helmet Lid, Marked, c.1850, 12 In. *illus*	420

Beatles, Pin, Guitar Shape, Portrait, Paul McCartney, Plastic, 1960s, 4¼ In.
$25

Ruby Lane

Beehive, Group, Hunter, 2 Hounds, Trumpet, Tree Base, Royal Vienna, c.1900, 10 x 12 In.
$246

Cowan's Auctions

Beehive, Plate, Portrait, 18th Century Woman, Gilt Border, Royal Vienna, 9¾ In., Pair
$1,375

New Orleans Auction Galleries

Beer Can, Rocky Mountain Beer, Cone Top, Red, Black, Silver, Anaconda Brewing, 5 x 2 In.
$250

North American Auction Co.

Bell, Bronze, Iron Yoke, Hanger & Clapper, Inscribed G.W. Coffin Co., Cincinnati, 18 In.
$738

Cowan's Auctions

Bell, Sleigh, 15 Graduated Brass Bells, Leather Belt
$221

Milestone Auctions

Cuspidor, Paneled, Molded Seashells, Rockingham Glaze, 1800s, 5 x 9 In.	150
Ewer, Pink, White, Grape Clusters, Vines, Twisted Vine Handles, 13 In., Pair	184
Jug, Brown, Flowers, Norton & Fenton, 2 Gal., 1845-47, 13 ¼ In.	720
Jug, Cobalt Blue, Bird In Tree, J. & E. Norton, c.1854, 11 In.	3500
Pitcher, Rockingham Glaze, Pond Lily, Lyman Fenton & Co., c.1854, 10 In.	439
Pitcher, Trailing Roses, Octagonal, Twig Handle, Ruffled Rim, 1800s, 10 In.	190

 BERLIN, a German porcelain factory, was started in 1751 by Wilhelm Kaspar Wegely. In 1763, the factory was taken over by Frederick the Great and became the Royal Berlin Porcelain Manufactory. It is still in operation today. Pieces have been marked in a variety of ways.

Bowl, Birds, Butterflies, Insects, Basket Weave Border, Gilt Rim, c.1900, 11 In.	277
Figurine, 2 Children Playing, Grecian Bust, Art Easel, 1913, 6 x 7 In.	526
Jar, Lid, Finial, Jester Masks, Flower Sprays, Putti, Gilt, Winged Handles, 1800s, 6 In.	250
Plaque, Laura, White Dress, Veil, Holding Wreath, Frame, c.1880, 16 x 10 In.	12081

 BESWICK started making pottery in Staffordshire, England, in 1894. The pottery became John Beswick Ltd. in 1936. The company became part of Royal Doulton Tableware, Ltd. in 1969. Production ceased in 2002, and the John Beswick brand was bought by Dartington Crystal in 2004. Figurines, vases, and other items are being made and use the name Beswick. Beatrix Potter figures were made from 1948 until 2002. They shouldn't be confused with Bunnykins, which were made by Royal Doulton.

Basket, Footed, Art Deco, Leaves, Majolica Style, 12 x 10 In.	399
Figurine, Bird, Blue, Spread Wings, No. 757-1, c.1900, 6 x 7 In.	139
Figurine, Bird, Bullfinch, Perched On Branch, No. 1042, 2 ½ In.	43
Figurine, Cat, Seated, No. 1031, c.1960, 4 ½ In.	30
Figurine, Dog, Bulldog, No. 1731, c.1960, 2 ½ In.	31
Figurine, Dog, Collie, No. 1814, c.1965, 3 ¼ In.	36
Figurine, Lamb, No. 937, c.1950, 2 ¼ In.	19
Figurine, Mrs. Tiggy Winkle, Holding Iron, Cap & Apron, BP 3A, 3 ½ In.	54
Sugar & Creamer, Pecksniff, No. 1129 & No. 1117, c.1967, 3 ½ In.	30
Teapot, Lid, Sairey Gamp, No. 691, 5 In.	58

 BETTY BOOP, the cartoon figure, first appeared on the screen in 1930. Her face was modeled after the famous singer Helen Kane and her body after Mae West. In 1935, a comic strip was started. Her dog's was named Bimbo. Although the Betty Boop cartoons ended by 1938, there was a revival of interest in the Betty Boop image in the 1980s and new pieces are being made.

Button, Betty On Stage, Curtains, White, Black & Yellow, 1930s, 1 ¼ In.	383
Clock, Betty, Sitting, Puckered Lips, Red Plastic, Neon, Round, 20 In.	250
Cookie Jar, Betty On Motorcycle, Black Boots & Jacket, 1990s, 13 x 13 In.	95
Cookie Jar, Cleobooptra, Sitting In Chair, 1997, 14 x 10 In.	150
Cookie Jar, Fruit Bowl Hat, Red Flowered Dress, c.1985, 12 In.	250
Doll, Celluloid, Movable Arms, Japan, 1920s, 9 In.	40
Doll, Composition, Fleischer American, 1930s, 11 ½ x 4 In. *illus*	595
Handkerchief, Betty In Red Dress, Hands On Hips, Cotton, 12 x 12 In.	55
Nodder, Celluloid, Japan, Prewar, Box, 7 In.	793
Statue, Carnival, Plaster, Paint, Beaded Red Dress, Rosy Cheeks, 1930s, 15 In.	576
Statue, Standing, Hands In Front, 35 In.	230
Stringholder, Bust, Chalkware, c.1940, 9 x 10 In.	560
Wrapper, Candy Bar, Red, Yellow, Glassine Paper, Garter, 1930s, 4 x 6 In.	127

BICYCLES were invented in 1839. The first manufactured bicycle was made in 1861. Special ladies' bicycles were made after 1874. The modern safety bicycle was not produced until 1885. Collectors search for all types of bicycles and tricycles. Bicycle-related items are also listed here.

AMX, Swift Hornet, Blue, Banana Seat, Tall Handlebars, 41 x 54 In.	90

Comet, High Wheel, Leather Seat Pad, Red & Gold Paint, U.S.A., c.1890, 55 In.	3600
Diamant, Steel, Wooden Mudguards, Rubber Tires, Leather Seat, France, 1930s	1485
Elliot Hickory, Double Dice, Columbia Pedals, Ram's Horn Handlebars, c.1893	3068
Firestone Pilot, Steel Frame, Bendix Rear Brake, Balloon Tires, Prewar ....*illus*	673
King Wheel Co., High Wheel, Ratchet Drive, c.1889, 50 In.	18720
Lantern, Badger Brass, Clamp, Acetylene Gas, 7 x 5 In.	180
National Cycle, Wooden Grips & Wheels, Men's, c.1885, 39 x 75 In.	720
Schwinn, Stingray, Grey Ghost, Steel Frame, Chrome, 1970s	2223
Tricycle, Buster Bike, Wooden, R.T. Co., 19 ½ x 22 In., Child's ....*illus*	30
Tricycle, Horse & Sulky, Wood, Maple Rails, Fabric Seat, c.1895, 24 x 31 In.	2223
Wood Bros., Boneshaker, 1870, 48 x 70 In.	10200

BING & GRONDAHL is a famous Danish factory making fine porcelains from 1853 to the present. Underglaze blue decoration was started in 1886. The annual Christmas plate series was introduced in 1895. Dinnerware, stoneware, and figurines are still being made today. The firm has used the initials *B & G* and a stylized castle as part of the mark since 1898. The company became part of Royal Copenhagen in 1987.

Bell, Christmas, 1982, Christmas Tree, 3 ¼ In.	20
Figurine, Brother & Sister, No. 1568, 5 x 5 In.	295
Figurine, Elephant, No. 1601, c.1958, 6 x 7 In.	600
Figurine, Girl, Petting Cat, Basket, No. 2249, 4 x 4 ¼ In. ....*illus*	125
Figurine, Hallo Again, No. 2387, c.1975, 7 ½ In.	135
Figurine, White Greyhound, No. 2079, 5 x 12 In.	295
Figurine, Who Is Calling, No. 2251, Child Holding Pot, c.1965, 6 In.	72
Group, Man Feeding 2 Dapple Gray Horses, 9 ¾ In.	500
Plaque, Porcelain, Classical Figures, Round, 11 ½ In., Pair	156
Plate, Christmas, 1924, Lighthouse In Danish Waters, 7 In.	32
Plate, Christmas, 1969, Arrival Of Christmas Guests, 7 In.	24
Plate, Christmas, 1970, The Royal Palace, 1895-1970, 7 In.	25
Sculpture, Man & Octopus, Jean Rene Gauguin, 1900s, 20 x 32 In.	3750
Vase, Sculpted Lizard, Glazed Stoneware, K. Kyhn, 1912, 7 x 3 In.	1125

BINOCULARS of all types are wanted by collectors. Those made in the eighteenth and nineteenth centuries are favored by serious collectors. The small, attractive binoculars called opera glasses are listed in their own category.

Chevalier Opticien, Brass Tubes, Black Enamel, Paris, 1860s	150
Colmont, Brass, Mother-Of-Pearl, France, 1800s, 3 ½ x 4 ¼ In.	256
Leica, Nickel Plated Brass, Wood Tripod, Pencil Tip Feet, c.1940, 54 x 26 In.	7500
LeMaire, Enameled Brass, Leather, Anti-Glare, Hard Case, France, c.1900, 9 In.	216
Ross Of London, Galilean, British Army Issue, Leather Case, c.1910	190

BIRDCAGES are collected for use as homes for pet birds and as decorative objects of folk art. Elaborate wooden cages of the past centuries can still be found. The brass or wicker cages of the 1930s are popular with bird owners.

Bamboo, Bird, Heart Shape Wings, Painted, Folk Art, Strawser, 11 x 6 In.	145
Brass, Cylindrical, Dome Top, Tray, 3 Bars, c.1890, 45 In.	3900
Cathedral, Victorian, Columns, Domed, 20 x 21 In.	1071
Ceramic, Blue, White, Delft, Signed, 19 ½ x 11 In.	125
Mahogany & Parcel Gilt, 41 In.	1250
Metal, 2-Peaked Roof, Black, 17 ½ In.	88
Pine, Hexagonal, 3 Tiers, Posts, Acorn Finials, c.1885, 37 x 26 In.	600
Pottery, Cylindrical, White, Gold Banding, Faience, 16 ¼ x 9 ¼ In.	62
Stand, Wood, Red Roof, 58 x 53 In.	1250
Wood, Peaked Roof, Lime Green, 13 x 13 In.	81
Wood, Rectangular Base, Dome Top, 1890s, 33 x 21 ¾ In. ....*illus*	995
Wood, Wire, Green Victorian House, Bay Windows, Rotates Out, 35 x 35 In.	615

Bell, Temple, Carved Teak Stand, 10 Graduated Bells, 81 x 29 ½ In. $246

Hudson Valley Auctions

Bennington, Coffeepot, Streaked Glaze, Brown, Cream, Flint Enamel, Helmet Lid, Marked, c.1850, 12 In. $420

Garth's Auctioneers & Appraisers

Betty Boop, Doll, Composition, Fleischer American, 1930s, 11 ½ x 4 In. $595

Ruby Lane

Bicycle, Firestone Pilot, Steel Frame, Bendix Rear Brake, Balloon Tires, Prewar
$673

Copake Auction

Bicycle, Tricycle, Buster Bike, Wooden, R.T. Co., 19½ x 22 In., Child's
$30

Hess Auction Group

Bing & Grondahl, Figurine, Girl, Petting Cat, Basket, No. 2249, 4 x 4¼ In.
$125

Ruby Lane

Birdcage, Wood, Rectangular Base, Dome Top, 1890s, 33 x 21¾ In.
$995

Ruby Lane

BISQUE is an unglazed baked porcelain. Finished bisque has a slightly sandy texture with a dull finish. Some of it may be decorated with various colors. Bisque gained favor during the late Victorian era, when thousands of bisque figurines were made. It is still being made. Additional bisque items may be listed under the factory name.

Bust, Empress Maria Theresa, Socle, Elias Hutter, 15 In.	313
Figurine, Allegorical, Woman, 17 In., Pair	2500
Figurine, Woman, Seated, Knees To Side, 7½ In.	88
Group, Eros On Pedestal, 1900s, 14 x 9 x 6 In.	625
Group, Goddess, Chariot, Horses, Cloud, 15 x 20 In.	200
Group, Louis XVI, Eros, Pan, Putto, Horn, Laurel Branches, 16 x 16 In.	350
Group, Women, Clipping Cupid's Wings, Oval Base, 10 In.	313

BLACK memorabilia has become an important area of collecting since the 1970s. The best material dates from past centuries, but many recent items are also of interest. F & F is the mark used on plastic made by Fiedler & Fiedler Mold & Die Works, Inc. in the 1930s and 1940s. Objects that picture a black person may also be listed in this book under Advertising, Sign; Bank; Bottle Opener; Cookie Jar; Doll; Salt & Pepper; Sheet Music; Toy; etc.

Carving, Wood, Black Man, Standing With Arm Up, Bowtie, Stump, c.1950, 77 In.	237
Cookie Jars are listed in the Cookie Jar category.	
Doorstop, Mammy, Iron, Hubley, 8¾ In. ....*illus*	184
Lamp, Mammy, Standing, Yellow & Blue Paint, Pottery, Electric, 1930s	225
Letter Opener, Bronze, Figural, Tattered Hat, 10½ In. ....*illus*	129
Pedestal, Blackamoor, Multicolor, Italy, c.1850, 40 x 15½ In.	812
Plaque, Wood, Gilt Draped Backplate, Extended Black Arm & Hand, 16 x 6 In., Pair	338
Poster, Original New Orleans Minstrels, John Stiles Comedian, 1857, 28 x 21 In. ....*illus*	610
Roly Poly, Clown, Yellow Diamond Shirt, Blue Hat, 13¼ In.	192
Roly Poly, Clown, Yellow Shirt, Blue Hat, Red Band, 9½ In.	247
Sculpture, Josephine Baker, Bakelite, 7¾ In.	187
Smoking Stand, Butler, Holding Tray, Cast Iron, Metal, Paint, 1920s, 32 In.	506
Spice Rack, 6 Jemimas, Red Rack, Shaped Spices, Labeled With Spice Names, 4 In., 7 Piece	144
Stand, Blackamoor, Painted Table Top, Gesso Fabric, c.1900, 37 In.	1230
Toys are listed in the Toy category.	
Whirligig, Black Figure Wearing Top Hat, Carved & Painted, 1800s, 29¼ In.	2000

BLENKO GLASS COMPANY is the 1930s successor to several glassworks founded by William John Blenko in Milton, West Virginia. In 1933, his son, William H. Blenko Sr., took charge. The company made tablewares and vases in classical shapes. In the late 1940s it hired talented designers and made innovative pieces. The company made a line of reproductions for Colonial Williamsburg. It is still in business and is best known today for its decorative wares and stained glass. All products are made to order.

Bookends, Elephant, Glass, Blue, 1950s, 7 x 6 In.	57
Decanter, Warm Honey, Conical, Tapered, Flared Lip, Stopper, c.1968, 34 In.	675
Lighter, Yellow To Tangerine, Metal Capsule, Oval, Flared Foot, c.1955, 11 In.	95
Vase, Olive Green, Bulbous, Tulip Top, Flared Rim, c.1955, 14 x 7 In.	395

BLOWN GLASS, *see Glass-Blown category.*

BLUE GLASS, *see Cobalt Blue category.*

BLUE ONION, *see Onion category.*

BLUE WILLOW, *see Willow category.*

BOCH FRERES factory was founded in 1841 in La Louviere in eastern Belgium. The wares resemble the work of Villeroy & Boch. The factory closed in 1985. M.R.L. Boch took over the production of tableware but went bankrupt in 1988. Le Hodey took over Boch Freres in 1989, using the name Royal Boch Manufacture S.A. It went bankrupt in 2009. A new managing director is now running the company.

Censer, Flowers, Turquoise, Cobalt Blue, Tan, Stepped Lid, 1920s, 7 x 10 In.	1750
Vase, Flowers, Medallions, Gray, Mottled Blue, Panels, Swollen, 1920s, 18 In.	1188
Vase, Gres Keramis, Flowers, Charles Catteau, 1920s, 18 x 9½ In.	1188
Vase, Gres Keramis, Stylized Flowers, Belgium, 1920s, 11 x 5¾ In.	813
Vase, Parrots, Green, Yellow, White Flowers, Blue Interior, Oval, 12 In., Pair	2000
Vase, Stoneware, Centennial, Brown, Beige, Charles Catteau, c.1941, 13 In.	4500

BOEHM is the collector's name for the porcelains of Edward Marshall Boehm. In 1953 the Osso China Company was reorganized as Edward Marshall Boehm, Inc. The company is still working in England and New Jersey. In the early days of the factory, dishes were made, but the elaborate and lifelike bird figurines are the best-known ware. Edward Marshall Boehm, the founder, died in 1969, but the firm has continued to design and produce porcelain. Today, the firm makes both limited and unlimited editions of figurines and plates.

Baby Bunting, 2 Robins, Blue, Gray, Nest, c.1965, 2 x 4 In.	165
Black-Capped Chickadee, Holly Leaves & Berries, c.1957, 9 In.	139
Canada Goose, Goslings, Marked, c.1953, 6 In., Pair	500
Catbird, Purple & White Hyacinths, 15 x 8 In.	1500
Creche, Mary, Joseph, Baby Jesus, Wise Men, Bisque, Box, c.1950, 11 In., 13 Piece	1220
Crested Flycatcher, Sweet Gum Branch, Leafy, 19 x 14 In.	2500
Eagle Of Freedom II, Perched On Rockery, Multicolor, 16 x 22½ In. ....*illus*	5000
Horse, Brown, Black Mane, Western Saddle, 17 In.	225
Horse, White, Boy, Walking, 8½ In.	1500
Hummingbird, Lily, Signed, c.1991	556
Orchard Oriole, Yellow Flowers, 11½ x 14½ In.	200
Peregrine Falcon, Perched, Spread Wings, Rockery, 21 x 20 In.	708
Pipilo, Mushrooms & Vegetation, 7¼ In.	351
Road Runner, Rockery, 13½ x 16 In.	472
Screech Owl, 10½ In.	148
Tern, Spread Wings, Rockery, 14 In.	188
Wood Thrush, Baby, Butterfly In Mouth, 5 x 4 In.	149

BONE DISHES were considered a necessary part of a table setting for the Victorian table. The crescent-shaped dish was kept at the edge of the dinner plate so the bones removed from the fish could be stored away from the uneaten food. Some bone dishes were made in more fanciful shapes and many resemble fish.

Blackberries, Gilt Trim, 6½ x 2¾ In.	59
Butterflies, Sprays, Scalloped Edge, Gold Trim, Porcelain, Japan, 6¾ In.	18
Flowers & Buds, Transfer, Burford Pottery	15
Pansies, Painted, c.1978, 6 In.	15
Lobed, Majolica, Italy, 9¼ x 5 In.	68

BOOKENDS have probably been used since books became inexpensive. Early libraries kept books in cupboards, not on open shelves. By the 1870s bookends appeared, especially homemade fret-carved wooden examples. Most bookends listed in this book date from the twentieth century. Bookends are also listed in other categories by manufacturer or material. All bookends listed here are pairs.

Chief Sitting Bull, Cast Bronze, 7 x 5 x 3 In.	500
Chinese Girl, Reading, Bronze, Onyx Base, Hester Mabel White, 6 x 6 In.	180
Dog, Boston Terrier, Studded Collar, Cast Iron, Bradley & Hubbard, c.1900, 5 In.	212
Eagle, Capturing Serpent, Carved Horn, Japan, 8½ In.	129
Fish, Faith, Bronze Finish, Enamel, Multicolor, c.1967, 5¼ In. ....*illus*	45
Head, Alabaster, Art Deco, c.1925, 8½ In.	1812
Hoofed Animal, Leaping, Green, Cast Metal, 6 In.	25
Horse, Nickel Plated, Style Of Russel Wright, 1930s, 5½ x 6½ In.	1342
Hurdler, Brass, Hammered, 6¾ In.	153
Musician, Horn, Short Hair, Silvered Bronze, 9¼ In.	207

Black, Doorstop, Mammy, Iron, Hubley, 8¾ In.
$184

Bertoia Auctions

Black, Letter Opener, Bronze, Figural, Tattered Hat, 10½ In.
$129

Richard D. Hatch & Associates

Black, Poster, Original New Orleans Minstrels, John Stiles Comedian, 1857, 28 x 21 In.
$610

Neal Auctions

Boehm, Eagle Of Freedom II, Perched On Rockery, Multicolor, 16 x 22½ In.
$5,000

Ruby Lane

Bookends, Fish, Faith, Bronze Finish, Enamel, Multicolor, c.1967, 5¼ In.
$45

Ruby Lane

Bottle, Bitters, Berkshire, Amann & Co., Cincinnati, O., Pig, Shaded Amber, 9 In.
$2,457

Norman Heckler & Company

TIP

If you want to clean a bottle that has a paper label, try to protect the label. Wrap the bottle tightly in thin plastic wrap. Seal the wrap with tape and rubber bands. Clean the inside carefully, using a mixture of water, automatic dishwasher detergent and slightly abrasive kitty litter. Fill the bottle part way and shake.

Petrified Wood, 8½ In.	138
Saddle, Book, Red, Mehl Lawson, 8½ x 8 In.	900
Scrolling Leaves, Bronze, Rococo Revival, Beveled Base, 11 x 7 In.	206
Sea Lion, Upright, Bronze, Green Marble Base, 1900s, 9 x 5¼ In.	150

 BOOKMARKS were originally made of parchment, cloth, or leather. Soon woven silk ribbon, thin cardboard, celluloid, wood, silver, tortoiseshell, and metals were used. Examples made before 1850 are scarce, but there are many to be found dating before 1920.

Silver Plate, Amethyst Glass, Figural Thistle, Tapered Blade, 1920s, 4 In.	150
Sterling Silver, Horse, Trotting, Dimensional, 3 In.	60
Wool, Cross-Stitch, Paper Punch, Beaded, Silk, Wreath, Verse, 1800s, 3 x 7 In.	125

BOSSONS **BOSSONS** character wall masks (heads), plaques, figurines, and other decorative pieces were made by W.H. Bossons, Limited, of Congleton, England. The company was founded in 1946 and closed in 1996. Dates shown are the date the item was introduced.

Figurine, Briar Rose Pelican, Brick Red, 1970s, 4 In.	135
Wall Mask, Harry Wheatcroft, Red Rose, c.1971, 6 x 4½ In.	500
Wall Mask, Sea Captain, Blue Eyes, 1950s, 5 x 4 In.	30
Wall Plaque, Warrior, Turban, Holding Spear, Oval, Gold, Green, 1950s, 17 x 11 In.	95

BOSTON & SANDWICH CO. *pieces may be found in the Sandwich Glass category.*

 BOTTLE collecting has become a major American hobby. There are several general categories of bottles, such as historic flasks, bitters, household, and figural. ABM means the bottle was made by an automatic bottle machine after 1903. Pyro is the shortened form of the word *pyroglaze*, an enameled lettering used on bottles after the mid-1930s. This form of decoration is also called ACL or applied color label. For more prices, go to kovels.com.

Allen's Soda Syrup, Red Tame Cherry, Label Under Glass, Cap, 11 x 3 In.	4600
Beer, Anheuser-Busch, Lager, Red, White, Blue, C. Conrad & Co., 11½ In.	150
Beer, Fesenmeier Centennial, West Virgina Glass, 10½ In.	10
Beer, Lorelei Kessler, Helena, Montana, Yellow & Red, Label, 11½ x 3 In.	30
Beer, W. Losey, New York, Brown Stout, Slug Plate, Blue Green, Blob Top, 7 In.	546
Bitters, American Life, P.E. Iler, Tiffin, Ohio, Cabin, Amber, Sloped Collar, 9 In.	8775
Bitters, Baker's Orange Grove, Semi-Cabin, Apricot Puce, 9½ In.	748
Bitters, Baker's Orange Grove, Semi-Cabin, Strawberry Puce, 9½ In.	1093
Bitters, Beggs Dandelion, Sioux City, Iowa, Amber, Square, Beveled Corners, 9 In.	380
Bitters, Berkshire, Amann & Co., Cincinnati, O., Pig, Shaded Amber, 9 In. ....*illus*	2457
Bitters, Berkshire, Amann & Co., Pig, Figural, Brown Glaze, Pottery, 8 In.	199
Bitters, Bissell's Tonic, Patented Jan. 21, 1868, Peoria, Ill., Yellow, Sloped Collar, 9 In.	819
Bitters, Bourbon Whiskey, Barrel, Strawberry Puce, Flattened Collar, 9½ In.	489
Bitters, Brown's Celebrated Indian Herb, Patented 1868, Citron, 12 In. ....*illus*	7605
Bitters, Brown's Celebrated Indian Herb, Patented 1868, Yellow Green, 12 In.	2300
Bitters, Brown's Celebrated Indian Herb, Patented Feb. 11, 1868, Amber, 12 In.	1035
Bitters, Caldwell's Herb, Great Tonic, Amber, 3-Sided, Sloped Collar, 12 In.	316
Bitters, Clotworthy's Oriental Tonic, Amber, Indented Panels, Sloped Collar, 10 In.	265
Bitters, Constitution, Put Up By B.M. & E.A.W. & Co., N.Y., Aqua, Gazebo, 8 In.	9775
Bitters, Dimmitt's, 50 Cts, Saint Louis, Amber, Strap Side Flask, ½ Pt.	1521
Bitters, Dr. Bell's Golden Tonic, School Bell, Amber, Mouth Ring, Pontil, 10 In. ....*illus*	12870
Bitters, Dr. Bishop's Wa-Hoo, New Haven, Conn., Semi-Cabin, Red Amber, 10 In.	489
Bitters, Dr. F.A. Sabine's Harvest, Yellow Amber, Square, Sloping Collar, 9 In.	410
Bitters, Drake's Plantation, Cabin, 6 Log, Ginger Ale, Sloping Collar, 10 In.	3738
Bitters, Drake's Plantation, Cabin, 6 Log, Strawberry Puce, 10 In.	460
Bitters, Drake's Plantation, Cabin, 6 Log, Yellow Amber, Sloping Collar, 10 In.	546
Bitters, Excelsior Herb, J.V. Mattison, Semi-Cabin, Amber, Flat Collar, 10 In.	1380
Bitters, Frank Miller & Co.'s Stomach, Amber, Arched Sides, Sloping Collar, 9 In.	920
Bitters, Greeley's Bourbon Whiskey, Barrel, Pink Puce, Flattened Collar, 9¼ In.	978
Bitters, Greeley's Bourbon, Barrel, Smoky Copper Puce, Flattened Collar, 9¼ In.	403

B

Bitters, Greeley's Bourbon, Barrel, Smoky Olive, Topaz Tone, Flat Collar, 9 In.	863
Bitters, H.P. Herb Wild Cherry, Tree, Cabin, Orange Amber, Tooled Lip, 9 In.	748
Bitters, Hall's, E.E. Hall, New Haven, Barrel, Amber, Foil Neck, 9 In.	1150
Bitters, Holtzermann's Patent Stomach, Cabin, Amber, Tapered Collar, Label, 10 In.	546
Bitters, Holtzermann's Patent Stomach, Cabin, Orange Amber, 9 1/4 In.	3738
Bitters, Holtzermann's Patent Stomach, Cabin, Red Amber, Label, 1880-95, 9 3/4 In. ....*illus*	518
Bitters, Jones Universal Stomach, Amber, Case, Sloping Collar, 10 In.	431
Bitters, Kelly's Old Cabin, Patented 1863, Cabin, Red Amber, Sloping Collar, 9 In.	2530
Bitters, Kelly's Old Cabin, Patented 1863, Cabin, Golden Yellow Amber, 9 In. ....*illus*	4888
Bitters, Keystone, Barrel, Deep Red Amber, Sloping Collar, 9 3/4 In.	546
Bitters, McKeever's Army, Drum Base, Cannonball Shoulders, Amber, 10 1/2 In.	3803
Bitters, Moffat, New York, Price $1, Phoenix, Yellow Chocolate Amber, 6 In.	1380
Bitters, National, Ear Of Corn, Golden Yellow, Topaz, Sloping Collar, 12 In. ....*illus*	878
Bitters, National, Ear Of Corn, Patent 1867, Strawberry Puce, Double Collar, 12 In.	978
Bitters, National, Ear Of Corn, Patent 1867, Yellow Olive, Double Collar, 12 In.	2530
Bitters, Old Cabin, Patented 1863, Amber, Applied Mouth, 9 In.	2365
Bitters, Old Sachem & Wigwam Tonic, Barrel, Copper Topaz, Flattened Collar, 9 In.	431
Bitters, Old Sachem & Wigwam Tonic, Barrel, Pink Puce, 9 1/4 In.	1265
Bitters, Old Sachem & Wigwam Tonic, Barrel, Yellow Amber, 9 In.	345
Bitters, Pineapple, J.C. & Co., Figural, Amber, Double Collar, 8 1/2 In.	690
Bitters, Pineapple, J.F.L., Capitol, Orange Amber, Double Collar, 9 In. ....*illus*	1287
Bitters, Pineapple, W & Co., Green, Applied Mouth, Pontil, 8 1/2 In.	4652
Bitters, Pineapple, W & Co., N.Y., Figural, Amber, Double Collar, 8 1/2 In.	920
Bitters, Professor Geo. J. Byrne, Great Universal Compound Stomach, Amber, 11 In.	3163
Bitters, Silver Overlay, Karl Kurz, Germany, 1904, 7 1/2 x 4 In.	236
Bitters, Simon's Centennial Trade Mark, Bust Of Washington, Aqua, 10 1/4 In.	1035
Bitters, Suffolk Bitters, Pig, Philbrook & Tucker, Boston, Yellow Amber, 9 7/8 In. ....*illus*	1638
Bitters, William Allen's Congress, Semi-Cabin, Blue Green, Sloping Collar, 10 In.	1955
Chippewa Indian Liniment, Indian Chief Image, Cork Sealed, 5 1/2 x 1 In.	83
Coca-Cola bottles are listed in the Coca-Cola category.	
Cologne, Bunker Hill Monument, Cobalt Blue, Flattened Lip, 11 3/4 In.	800
Cosmetic, Barker, Hair Dresser, Bd Way, N.Y., Aqua, Square, Rolled Lip, 4 In.	1150
Cosmetic, D. Batchelor Liquid Hair Dye No. 1, Green, Square, Double Collar, 5 In.	5463
Cosmetic, Diddell's Chemical Reproductor For The Hair, Clear, Flared Rim, 7 In.	690
Cosmetic, Dr. Tebbett's Physiological Hair Regenerator, Amethyst, Collar, 7 1/2 In.	403
Cosmetic, E.A. Ward's Vegetable Oil For The Hair, New York, Clear, 3 In.	431
Cosmetic, Hurd's Golden Gloss For The Hair, New York, Aqua, Double Collar, 6 In.	207
Cosmetic, Mrs. S.A. Allen's World's Hair Restorer, Amethyst, Flat Collar, 7 In.	345
Cosmetic, Professor Wood's, Hair Restorative, St Louis, Mo., Aqua, 9 In.	403
Decanter, Blown, 3-Piece Mold, Olive Amber, Sheared Mouth, Keene, New Hampshire, Pt.*illus*	585
Decanter, Cobalt Blue, Blown, Cut, Sprigs, Diapering, White Enamel, Gilt, 23 In., Pair	406
Decanter, Cut Glass, Fluted, Paneled, Disc Knops, Mushroom Stopper, 10 In., Pair	240
Decanter, Spirits, Red, Silver Overlay, Clasped Hands, 11 1/4 In.	534
Demijohn, Blown, Olive Green, 19 In.	120
Dresser, Tortoiseshell Lid, Silver Inlay, 1911, 3 1/4 x 2 In., Pair	175
Figural, Arab, Frosted & Clear, Painted, France, c.1915, 11 1/4 In.	80
Figural, Bear, Sitting, Black Amethyst, Boston & Sandwich, c.1852, 4 In.	160
Figural, Bust, Ferdinand DeLesseps, Frosted & Clear, c.1894, 10 In.	80
Figural, Column, Milk Glass, Metal Christopher Columbus Statue, 1893, 18 In.	210
Figural, Czar Nicholas, Alexandra, Milk Glass, Sheared Edge, c.1904, 13 In., Pair	250
Figural, Ear Of Corn, El Kahir Temple, Cedar Rapids, Ia., Milk Glass, 3 1/2 In.	275
Figural, Man In Moon, Milk Glass, Painted, Stopper, Spigot, c.1900, 9 In.	2100
Figural, Porcelain, Sailor, Schafer & Vater, 6 1/2 In.	50
Figural, Turtle On Rock, Head Is Stopper, Amber, Cologne, c.1900, 4 3/4 In.	350
Flask, Amber, Spiral Design, Folded Lip, c.1810, 7 1/4 x 5 1/2 In.	950
Flask, Bitter Witch, Embossed Horseshoe, Amber, Shouldered, Double Collar, 8 In.	575
Flask, Book, Impressed Spine, Departed Spirits G, Streak Glazed, 6 In.	189
Flask, Byron & Scott, Olive Green, Sheared Mouth, 1/2 Pt.	316
Flask, Chestnut, 24 Ribs, Swirled, Orange Amber, Flattened, 4 3/4 In.	497
Flask, Chestnut, 24 Ribs, Swirled, Red Amber, Sheared, Pontil, Zanesville, 5 In.	242

Bottle, Bitters, Brown's Celebrated
Indian Herb, Patented 1868, Citron,
12 In.
$7,605

Bottle, Bitters, Dr. Bell's Golden Tonic,
School Bell, Amber, Mouth Ring, Pontil,
10 In.
$12,870

Bottle, Bitters, Holtzermann's Patent Stomach, Cabin, Red Amber, Label, 1880-95, 9¾ In.
$518

Glass Works Auctions

Bottle, Bitters, Kelly's Old Cabin, Patented 1863, Cabin, Golden Yellow Amber, 9 In.
$4,888

Glass Works Auctions

Bottle, Bitters, National, Ear Of Corn, Golden Yellow, Topaz, Sloping Collar, 12 In.
$878

Norman Heckler & Company

Flask, Chestnut, Amber, Quilted, Oval, Stick Neck, c.1840, 4¾ In.	1125
Flask, Chestnut, Olive Green, String Rim, Pontil, Miniature, 2¼ In.	615
Flask, Corn For The World, Golden Amber, Iron Pontil, c.1870, Qt., 8½ In.	2760
Flask, Corn For The World, Medium Copper Puce, Double Collar, 1855-65, Qt. ....*illus*	1150
Flask, Cornucopia & Urn, Blue Green, Sheared, Pontil, Lancaster, N.Y., Pt.	1053
Flask, Cornucopia & Urn, Sapphire Blue, Sheared, Pontil, Pt.	10925
Flask, Cut Glass, Silver Mount, Hip, Finnigans Ltd., 5¾ In.	100
Flask, Double Eagle, Light Aqua, Vertical Ribs, Sheared Mouth, Pontil, Pt.	265
Flask, Double Eagle, Olive Amber, Sheared Mouth, Pontil, Stoddard, Qt.	2106
Flask, Eagle & Grapes, Shaded Amber, Ribbed Sides, Qt.	2300
Flask, Eagle & Ravenna, Golden Amber, Applied Ring Mouth, Pt.	690
Flask, Eagle & Ravenna, Yellow Amber, Olive Tone, Ring Mouth, Pt.	4888
Flask, Eagle & Willington, Olive Green, Double Collar, Pt.	374
Flask, Eagle, Flattened Oval, Swirled Ribbing, Amber, c.1840, 6¼ In.	875
Flask, Flora Temple & Horse, Teal, Ring Mouth, 8½ In.	1380
Flask, For Pike's Peak, Prospector, Light Blue Green, Ring Mouth, Pt.	1265
Flask, Franklin & Franklin, Green, Sheared Mouth, Pt.	5265
Flask, Horseman & Hound, Shaded Pink Puce, Sheared, Pontil, Pt.	1725
Flask, Hunter & Stag, Aqua, Strap Side, Pt.	690
Flask, Jackson & Flowers, Aqua, Horizontal Ribs On Sides, Sheared, Pontil, Pt.	3510
Flask, Jenny Lind & Glasshouse, Calabash, Sapphire Blue, Ribs, Collar, Qt.	4388
Flask, Kossuth & Tree, Calabash, Yellow Olive, Double Collar	1093
Flask, Masonic & Eagle, Blue Aqua, Sheared & Tooled, Pontil, Pt.	489
Flask, Masonic & Eagle, Farmer's Arms, Zanesville, Amber, c.1840, 6 In.	1200
Flask, Masonic & Eagle, Yellow Green, Sheared, Pontil, Pt.	1872
Flask, Murdock & Cassel, Deep Blue Aqua, Tooled Lip, Zanesville, Pt.	1610
Flask, Pitkin Type, 16 Broken Ribs, Swirled, Grass Green, Pontil, 6¼ In.	690
Flask, Pitkin Type, 31 Broken Ribs, Swirled, Olive Green, Sheared, Pontil, 6 In.	1035
Flask, Pitkin Type, 36 Ribs, Swirled To Right, Olive Green, Sheared Mouth, 5 In.	644
Flask, Pitkin Type, 36 Ribs, Swirled To Right, Olive, Sheared Mouth, Pontil, 7 In.	1404
Flask, Pitkin Type, Swirled Ribs, Flattened Oval, Green, Half Post, c.1830, 5½ In.	1920
Flask, Porcelain, White, Flowers, Gilt, Genie Bottle Shape, Gilt Stopper, 1775, 3 In.	557
Flask, Pumpkinseed, I Got My Fill At Jakes, Drunk Man, Dog, 1890-1900, 6½ In. .....*illus*	316
Flask, Scroll & BP & B, Aqua, Tooled Lip, Pontil, ½ Pt.	374
Flask, Sheets & Duffy, Kensington, Tombstone, Aqua, Ring Mouth, Qt.	374
Flask, Silver Overlay, Woman Golfer, Clubs, Balls & Bag, 5 In.	360
Flask, Silver, Round, Repousse, Masks, Mermaids, Wm. B. Kerr & Co., 5 x 5 In.	390
Flask, Spirits, Cobalt Blue, Hobnail, Sheared & Tooled, Pontil, 5¼ In.	546
Flask, Spring Garden & Anchor, Yellow Olive, Double Collar, ½ Pt.	4025
Flask, Strap Side, Grass Green, Double Collar, Pocket, ½ Pt.	115
Flask, Strap Side, Milk Glass, Double Collar, Pocket, Pt.	518
Flask, Success To The Railroad, Aqua, Sheared & Tooled, Pontil, Pt.	690
Flask, Success To The Railroad, Horse Pulling Cart, Olive Green, Pontil, Pt.	403
Flask, Sunburst, Keen In Oval, P & W, Olive Amber, Keene, New Hampshire, c.1825, Pt. .....*illus*	1638
Flask, Sunburst, Moss Green, Side Ribs, Sheared Mouth, Pontil, Pt.	7605
Flask, Sunburst, Olive Green, Horizontal Ribs On Sides, Pt.	748
Flask, Sunburst, Pale Apple Green, Sheared Mouth, Pontil, Pt.	748
Flask, Swirled Ribs, Olive Amber, Pear Shape, 5¼ In.	584
Flask, Taylor & Corn For The World, Green Aqua, Sheared Mouth, Pt.	633
Flask, Union, Clasped Hands & Cannon, Yellow, Amber & Olive Tones, Pt.	936
Flask, Washington & Eagle, Aqua, Sheared Mouth, Pontil, Pt.	219
Flask, Washington & Eagle, Blue Aqua, Sheared Mouth, Pt.	1840
Flask, Washington & Taylor Never Surrenders, Olive Green, Pt.	805
Flask, Washington & Taylor, Applied Ring Mouth, Green, c.1865, Qt.	1836
Flask, Washington & Taylor, Golden Amber, Double Collar, Qt.	633
Flask, Washington & Taylor, Golden Amber, Sheared Mouth, Pt.	6435
Flask, Washington & Taylor, Green, Flattened Oval, Pt., c.1830, 7¼ In.	688
Flask, Washington & Taylor, Yellow Olive, Open Pontil, Sheared Tooled Lip, c.1850, Qt. .....*illus*	863
Flask, Washington & Tree, Calabash, Cobalt Blue, Sloped Collar, Qt.	15210
Flask, Wheat Price, Bushy Haired Bust, Shaded Blue Green, Ribs, Pt.	15210

Flask, Whiskey, Deep Strawberry Puce, Double Collar, Qt.	207
Flask, Whiskey, Peach Puce, Double Collar, Qt.	184
Flask, Whiskey, Pink Puce, Double Collar, Pt.	460
Food, Blueberry Preserves, Amber, Cylindrical, Fluted Shoulder, Double Collar, 11 In.	495
Food, Catsup, T.G. Hawkes, Optic Design, Engraved, Swag, Pinched Waist, 1910, 8 In.	85
Food, Shriver's Oyster Ketchup, Baltimore, Olive Amber, Sloped Collar, 8 In.	4255
Fruit Jar, American NAGC, Green, Mason Zinc Lid, Milk Glass Insert, c.1885, Pt. ....*illus*	242
Fruit Jar, Automatic Sealer, Clayton, N.J., Patd. Sept. 15th 1885, Aqua, Wire Closure, Pt.	978
Fruit Jar, Ball, Script, Pat. Apld. For, Aqua, Pinched Neck, Tin Lid, Wire Closure, Pt.	805
Fruit Jar, Beehive, Aqua, Embossed Bees & Hive, Zinc Lid, c.1905, Qt.	265
Fruit Jar, Excelsior, Blue Green, Insert, Patd. Aug. 8th, 1865, Zinc Band, Qt. ....*illus*	518
Fruit Jar, Flaccus Bros, Steer's Head, Yellow Amber, 1885-1900, Pt. ....*illus*	403
Fruit Jar, Gilberds Improved Jar, Star, Aqua, Pat. July 31st, Oct. 13, 1885, Pt. ....*illus*	1955
Fruit Jar, Lafayette, Script, Clear, Cast Iron Lever Clamp, Pt.	518
Fruit Jar, Leader, Yellow Amber, Glass Lid, Wire Clamp, Pt. ....*illus*	863
Fruit Jar, Magic Fruit Jar, 5-Point Star, Aqua, Embossed Lid, Wire Clamp, Pt.	546
Fruit Jar, Mason's Pat. Nov. 30th 1858, Yellow Amber, Ground Lip, Zinc Lid, Qt.	253
Fruit Jar, Mason's Patent Nov. 30th 1858, Dupont, Aqua, Zinc Screw Lid, Qt.	460
Fruit Jar, Mason's Union, Shield, Cornflower Blue, Zinc Lid, ½ Gal.	1265
Fruit Jar, Mason's, Green, Pat. 1858, Embossed, Zinc Lid, 1880s, Qt.	250
Fruit Jar, Millville Improved, Cluster Of Grapes, Monogram, Aqua, Zinc Band, Pt.	184
Fruit Jar, Moore's Pat. Dec. 3rd 1861, Aqua, Gutta Percha Gasket, Iron Yoke, Pt.	316
Fruit Jar, Olive Amber, Cylindrical, Square Collar, 3-Piece Mold, 4 In.	2457
Fruit Jar, Protector, Aqua, 6 Indented Panels, Metal Lid, Wire Clamp, Pt.	403
Fruit Jar, Ruby Coffee, Amber, Label, Zinc Lid, A.G. Smalley & Co., c.1898, Qt., 7 In.	155
Fruit Jar, Safety, Yellow Amber, Embossed Glass Lid, Wire Clamp, Pt.	288
Fruit Jar, Trademark, Lightning, Putnam, Honey Amber, Bail & Lid, Bubbles, Qt.	105
Fruit Jar, Van Vliet Jar Of 1881, Aqua, Thumbscrew, Embossed, c.1865, Qt.	500
Household, Liquid Mirror Blacking, Olive Green, Cylindrical, Rolled Rim, Label, 6 In.	3218
Household, Pavar Polish, Polish That Varnishes, 1920s, 8½ x 1⅝ In.	94
Ink, Carlton, Umbrella, 8-Sided, Cornflower Blue, Applied Ring Mouth, 2¾ In.	184
Ink, Carter, Cathedral, Cobalt Blue, Rubber Seal, Labels, c.1920-35, 6¼ In. ....*illus*	575
Ink, Cross & Robinson's, American Writing Fluid, Aqua, Cylindrical, Master, 7 In.	1404
Ink, Estes, N.Y., Aqua, 8-Sided, Shouldered, Sloping Collar, Master, 4¼ In.	207
Ink, Estes, Umbrella, 8-Sided, Blue Aqua, Inverted Lip, 3 In.	489
Ink, Farley's, 8-Sided, Olive Amber, Sheared Mouth, Pontil Scar, Stoddard, c.1855, 1¾ In. ..*illus*	644
Ink, Farley's, Yellow Amber, 8-Sided, Sheared & Tooled, 1¾ In.	633
Ink, Fine Blacking, Made & Sold By J.L. Thompson, Yellow Olive, Master, 6 In.	1380
Ink, Gibb, Umbrella, 8-Sided, Blue Aqua, Sheared Mouth, 2¾ In.	403
Ink, Gross & Robinson, American Writing Fluid, Aqua, Flat Rim, Master, 5 In.	489
Ink, Harrison's Columbian, Cylindrical, Sapphire Blue, Inverted Rim, 2 In.	1404
Ink, Harrison's Columbian, Emerald Green, 8-Sided, 1¼ In.	1035
Ink, Harrison's Columbian, Sapphire Blue, 8-Sided, Rolled Lip, 1½ In.	1840
Ink, Hover, Philada., Green, Cylindrical, Flared Lip, Master, 4½ In.	230
Ink, Hover, Philada., Umbrella, Green, Inverted Lip, 2 In.	288
Ink, J. & I.E.M., Igloo, Amber, Paneled Base, Sheared & Ground, 1¾ In.	127
Ink, J. & I.E.M., Igloo, Emerald Green, Sheared & Ground Lip, 1¾ In.	403
Ink, James S Mason & Co., Umbrella, 8-Sided, Aqua, Inverted Lip, 2½ In.	288
Ink, Jones' Empire, N.Y., Emerald Green, 12-Sided, Iron Pontil, 1840-60, 5¾ In. ....*illus*	6325
Ink, Log Cabin, Clear, Ground Lip, Smooth Base, c.1885, 3 In.	1585
Ink, Logan & Thompson, Cone, Aqua, Red Ink, Inverted Lip, 2 In.	265
Ink, Pitkin Type, Ribs, Swirled Left, Cone, Yellow Olive, Pontil, c.1800, 1⅞ In. ....*illus*	2691
Ink, R.B. Snow, St. Louis, Umbrella, 12-Sided, Aqua, Rolled Lip, 2 In.	374
Ink, S. Fine, Black, Aqua, Cylindrical, Flared Lip, 3 In.	242
Ink, Shepard & Allen's Writing Fluid, Umbrella, 8-Sided, Amber, Label, 2¾ In.	690
Ink, Superior Black Ink, Umbrella, 8-Sided, Yellow, Amber, Label, 2¾ In.	253
Ink, Talcott's Improved Jet Black Writing Ink, Umbrella, 8-Sided, Teal, Label, 3 In.	345
Ink, Teakettle, 7-Sided, Alternating Vertical Ribs, Cobalt Blue, 2½ In.	460
Ink, Teakettle, 8-Sided, Amethyst, Brass Neck Ring, 2 In.	431
Ink, Teakettle, 8-Sided, Cobalt Blue, Brass Neck Ring, 2 In.	345

Bottle, Bitters, Pineapple, J.F.L., Capitol, Orange Amber, Double Collar, 9 In.
$1,287

Norman Heckler & Company

Bottle, Bitters, Suffolk Bitters, Pig, Philbrook & Tucker, Boston, Yellow Amber, 9⅞ In.
$1,638

Norman Heckler & Company

Bottle, Decanter, Blown, 3-Piece Mold, Olive Amber, Sheared Mouth, Keene, New Hampshire, Pt.
$585

Norman Heckler & Company

Bottle, Flask, Corn For The World,
Medium Copper Puce, Double Collar,
1855-65, Qt.
$1,150

Glass Works Auctions

Bottle, Flask, Pumpkinseed,
I Got My Fill At Jakes, Drunk Man, Dog,
1890-1900, 6 1/2 In.
$316

Glass Works Auctions

Bottle, Flask, Sunburst, Keen In Oval,
P & W, Olive Amber, Keene,
New Hampshire, c.1825, Pt.
$1,638

Norman Heckler & Company

Ink, Teakettle, 8-Sided, Emerald Green, Painted, Sheared Lip, 2 In.	316
Ink, Teakettle, 8-Sided, Milk Glass, Opalescent, Brass Neck Ring, 3 In.	286
Ink, Teakettle, Barrel Shape, Sapphire Blue, 2 1/4 In.	633
Ink, Teakettle, Vertical Flutes, Cobalt Blue Cut To Clear, Brass Hinged Cap, 2 In.	1035
Ink, Umbrella, 8-Sided, 7Up Green, 2 1/2 In.	230
Ink, Umbrella, 8-Sided, Apple Green, Inverted Lip, 2 1/4 In.	173
Ink, Umbrella, 8-Sided, Cobalt Blue, Inverted Lip, 2 1/2 In.	403 to 690
Ink, Umbrella, 8-Sided, Dark Pink Amethyst, Inverted Lip, 2 1/2 In.	633
Ink, Umbrella, 8-Sided, Emerald Green, Inverted Lip, 2 1/2 In.	1610
Ink, Umbrella, 8-Sided, Golden Yellow, Inverted Lip, 2 3/4 In.	546
Ink, Umbrella, 8-Sided, Medium Steel Blue, Inward Rolled Lip, c.1850, 2 3/8 In. ....*illus*	936
Ink, Umbrella, 8-Sided, Olive Yellow, Inverted Lip, 2 1/2 In.	2070
Ink, Umbrella, 8-Sided, Red Amber, Puce Tone, Sheared Lip, 2 1/4 In.	805
Ink, Umbrella, 8-Sided, Red Amber, Sheared Lip, 2 3/4 In.	242
Ink, Umbrella, 8-Sided, Topaz Puce, Inverted Lip, 3 1/2 In.	920
Ink, Warren's Congress, Olive Green, 8-Sided, Flared Lip, 2 3/4 In.	207
Ink, Writing Fluid, J.J. Butler, Cincinnati, Blue Aqua, Cylindrical, Rolled Lip, 3 In.	374
Medicine, American Medicinal Oil, Burkesville, Ky., Aqua, Sloped Collar, 6 In.	690
Medicine, American Oil, Cumberland River, Kentucky, Aqua, Rolled Lip, 7 In.	575
Medicine, Apothecary, Amethyst, Blown, Contents Labels, 11 1/2 In., Pair	437
Medicine, Apothecary, Blown Glass, Ground Glass Stopper, Canada, c.1825, 9 In.	90
Medicine, Apothecary, Cobalt Blue, Cylindrical, Banding, England, 13 In.	115
Medicine, Apothecary, Dark Green, Onion Shape, Banner Labels, 10 1/2 In., Pair	1062
Medicine, Apothecary, Ground Glass Stopper, Canada, c.1825, 8 3/4 In.	90
Medicine, Apothecary, Leech, Porcelain, Cobalt Blue, Handles, 9 1/4 In.	656
Medicine, Apothecary, Lid, Leech, White, Cylindrical, Knob Handle, 7 3/4 In.	2875
Medicine, Apothecary, Lid, Leeches, Creamware, Cylindrical, Bands, 9 1/4 In.	875
Medicine, Apothecary, Lid, Leeches, Stoneware, Knobs, Clamp, Germany, 12 In.	1093
Medicine, Apothecary, Lid, Porcelain, Shield, Branches, Transfer, Germany, 10 In.	218
Medicine, Apothecary, Syrup, Mythical Woman Handles, Blue, White, 12 In.	375
Medicine, Apothecary, Uranium Glass, Paneled, Concave Sides, Labels, 6 In.	1187
Medicine, B. Denton, Auburn, N.Y., Embossed Leaves, Blue, Double Collar, 7 In.	345
Medicine, Bigelow's Alterative, C.W. Bleecker Proprietor, Aqua, 5 3/4 In.	460
Medicine, Cream, Rawleighs, Mustard Compound, Label, Embossed, Clear, 1920s, 5 In.	135
Medicine, Delmonico's Syrup Pectoral, New York, Aqua, Indented Panels, 7 In.	288
Medicine, Dr. Baker's Compound, New York, Blue Aqua, Sloping Collar, 8 In.	633
Medicine, Dr. De Angelis, Syrup Of Salza, Aqua, Arches, Sloped Collar, 10 In.	1150
Medicine, Dr. H.W. Jackson, Druggist, Vegetable Syrup, Olive Amber, 6 In.	3218
Medicine, Dr. Ham's Aromatic Invigorating Spirit, N.Y., Aqua, Iron Pontil, c.1850, 8 1/2 In.*illus*	241
Medicine, Dr. Munn's Bronchitic Pulmonary Syrup, Phil., Aqua, Oval, 7 1/4 In.	1840
Medicine, Dr. S. Hart, Vegetable Extract, New York, Aqua, Tapered Collar, 8 In.	374
Medicine, Dr. Seymour's Balsam Of Wild Cherry, Aqua, 8-Sided, Sloped Collar, 7 In.	690
Medicine, Edward Finlay, M.D., Havana Crescentia, Tree, Aqua, Flattened Lip, 6 In.	690
Medicine, Garlegants Balsam Of Health, Aqua, Flared & Flattened Lip, 5 1/2 In.	1170
Medicine, Gibb's Bone Liniment, Yellow Olive, 6-Sided, Sloped Collar, Pontil, 6 In.	3218
Medicine, Gouley's Fountain Of Health, Embossed Fountain, Aqua, 9 3/4 In.	633
Medicine, H.H. Warner & Co., Tippecanoe, Embossed Canoe, Yellow Amber, 9 In.	230
Medicine, Hampton's V Tincture, Mortimer & Mowbray, Balto., Copper Puce, 6 In.	1265
Medicine, Hampton's V Tincture, Mortimer & Mowbray, Balto., Green, 6 1/2 In.	6325
Medicine, Horse, Figures, Peachbloom, Tubular, Rolled Rim, Chinese, 1800s, 5 In.	1353
Medicine, Lindsey's Blood Searcher, Hollidaysburg, Aqua, Arched Panels, 9 In.	863
Medicine, Loomis's Cream Liniment, Emerald Green, 6-Sided, Pinched Waist, 5 In.	690
Medicine, Marsh's Family Medicines, N.Y., Aqua, Oval, Sloped Collar, 6 1/2 In.	575
Medicine, Paul's Patent Columbian Oil, Yellow Green, Flared Rim, Pontil, 4 In.	2691
Medicine, Phelps's Arcanum, Worcester, Mass., Olive Amber, Round, Paneled, 8 In.	1150
Medicine, Rogers Rheumatic Liniment, Blue Aqua, Oval, Inverted Lip, 6 In.	1093
Medicine, S.S. Seely & Co., Morris, Otsego County, New York, Sapphire Blue, 5 In.	288
Medicine, Smelling Salts, Free-Blown, Figural, Seahorse Shape, Yellow Amber, c.1825, 3 In.*illus*	878
Medicine, Smelling Salts, Marbleized, Blue, Milk Glass, Threaded Cap, 3 In.....*illus*	293
Medicine, Smelling Salts, Seahorse, Swirled, Pink & Milk Glass, Rigaree, 3 In.....*illus*	644

Medicine, Smith's Green Mountain Renovator, East Georgia, Vt., Amber, 7 In.	5463
Medicine, Swaim's Panacea, Aqua, 8-Sided, Sloped Collar, 7½ In.	2185
Medicine, Swaim's Panacea, Philada., Aqua, Indented Panels, Sloped Collar, 8 In.	978
Medicine, Swaim's Panacea, Philada., Olive Green, Paneled, Sloped Collar, 8 In.	489
Medicine, Thompsonian Appetizer, JJ Vogt, Cleveland O, Portly Gentleman, Amber, 9 In.	936
Medicine, Tom's Russian Liniment, Aqua, Indented Panels, Sloped Collar, 4½ In.	546
Medicine, Tom's Russian Liniment, Olive, Indented Panels, Sloped Collar, 4½ In.	1265
Medicine, U.S.A. Hosp. Dept., Blue Aqua, Flattened Rim, 9 In.	431
Medicine, U.S.A. Hosp. Dept., Yellow Amber, Double Collar, 9¼ In.	690
Medicine, Vaughn's Vegetable Lithontriptic Mixture, Buffalo, Aqua, Arched Panels, 8 In.	316
Milk, Bentley & Sons, Farm Dairy, Cow, 10 Cents, c.1940, ¼ Pint, 4 In.	158
Mineral Water, A. Allen, Lumberton, N.J., Milford Glass Works, Sapphire Blue, 7 In.	633
Mineral Water, Akesion Spring, Owned By Sweet Springs, Mo., Orange Amber, Pt.	173
Mineral Water, Buffalo Lithia, Teal Blue, Embossed, Dome Shoulder, 1906, 11 In.	180
Mineral Water, Caledonia Spring, Wheelock, Vt., Amber To Yellow Amber, Qt.	805
Mineral Water, Clarke & White, New York, Deep Olive Green, High Shoulder, Qt.	431
Mineral Water, Congress & Empire Spring, Hotchkiss' Sons, Saratoga, Olive, ½ Pt.	173
Mineral Water, E. Roussels, Philada., Patent, Blue Green, Tapered Collar, 7 In.	518
Mineral Water, E. Roussels, Philada., Patent, Yellow Olive, 8¼ In.	2875
Mineral Water, Haskins' Spring Co., Script H, Shutesbury, Mass., Green, Pt.	2300
Mineral Water, Hessberg Bottling Co., Embossed, 1800s, 9 In.	225
Mineral Water, Highrock Congress Spring, 1767, Saratoga, N.Y., Red Amber, Qt.	431
Mineral Water, Highrock Congress Spring, Saratoga, N.Y., Yellow Amber, Pt.	1265
Mineral Water, Hopkins' Chalybeate, Baltimore, Grass Green, Sloped Collar, Pt.	242
Mineral Water, Improved, Patent, Emerald Green, Sloping Collar, 7 In.	3163
Mineral Water, J. Boardman, New York, B, Bottle Is Never Sold, Pink Puce, 7 In.	7605
Mineral Water, L. Schmitt, Columbia, Slug Plate, Sapphire Blue, 7 In.	690
Mineral Water, Levi Ender, B, Williamsport, Slug Plate, Sapphire Blue, Blob Top, 7 In.	1093
Mineral Water, Lynch & Clarke, New York, Yellow Olive, Sloped Collar, Qt.	2925
Mineral Water, M. Keeley, Chicago, Ill., Yellow Amber, Sloped Collar, Qt.	863
Mineral Water, Poland, H. Ricker & Son's, Seated Bearded Man, Amber, 11 In.	1053
Mineral Water, Union Lava Works, Conshohocken, Patd. 1852, Cobalt Blue, 7 In.	1035
Mineral Water, W.H. Buck, Talbot St., Norfolk, Va., Yellow Olive, 7¾ In.	7480
Mineral Water, Wm. H. Weaver, Belvidere, Slug Plate, Green, Blob Top, Pony, 7 In.	316
Mineral Water, Wm. H. Weaver, Hackettstown, Green, Squat, Double Collar, 7 In.	920
Nursing, Opaline Glass, Standing Bird, Feathers, Red, White, 4 x 5 In.	175
Nursing, Stylized Pineapple, Pewter Mounting & Nipple, 6¾ In.	312
Nursing, Tin, Cone Shape, Domed Lid, Hinge, Grooved Handle, 4 In.	137
Perfume Bottles are listed in the Perfume Bottle category.	
Pickle, Cathedral, 4-Sided, Aqua, Embossed, Cork Top, c.1865, 9 In.	175
Pickle, Cathedral, 6-Sided, Blue Aqua, Arched Panels, Outward Rolled Lip, 9 In.	316
Pickle, Cylindrical, Blue Green, 7 Recessed Panels, Outward Rolled Lip, 8 In.	761
Prototype, Go-With, Indian Maiden, Carved Wood, Painted, 1865, 12 In. ....illus	2340
Sarsaparilla, Bush's Smilax, Aqua, Indented Panels, Inverted Lip, 10 In.	345
Sarsaparilla, Dr. De Andries, E.M. Rusha, New Orleans, Amber, Columns, 10 In.	2185
Sarsaparilla, Dr. Townsend's, Albany, N.Y., Forest Green, Sloped Collar, 9½ In.	633
Sarsaparilla, Dr. Townsend's, Albany, N.Y., Olive Amber, Sloped Collar, 9¾ In.	460
Scent, Blown Glass, Ice Blue, Engraved, Flowering Vines, Victorian, c.1890, 7½ In.	109
Scent, Cut Glass, Diamond Pattern, Tapered, Brass Mount, Hinged, 2¼ x 1 In.	88
Scent, Flowers, Grapes, Yellow Iridescent, Stopper, 8 In.	75
Scent, Porcelain, Pear Shape, Molded, Gilt, Stopper, Du Paquier, c.1725, 3½ In.	6428
Scent, Portrait, Madame Pompadour, Gadroon, Leaves, Scrolls, c.1880, 5 In., Pair	178
Seal, CCA In Triangle, Onion, Dark Olive Green, String Lip, 6½ In.	4888
Seal, Class Of 1864, W, Shield, Cylinder, Olive Amber, Sloped Collar, Dyottville, 11 In.	546
Seal, DB, In Beaded Circle, Olive Green, Sheared, String Lip, Magnum, 11 x 5 In.	863
Seal, H. Littledale 1762, Bulbous, Dark Olive Green, String Rim, 14 x 10½ In.	7995
Seal, H.C., Hand, Beer, Olive Brown, Tapered Neck, Applied Lip, 10 In.	1107
Seal, HH 1785, Beer, Mallet Shape, Olive Brown, Applied Rim, Pontil, 9 x 4 In.	584
Seal, I Dot I, Onion Shape, Olive Green, Squat, Tapered Neck, String Lip, 6 In.	2875
Seal, IG, Onion Shape, Elongated Neck, Dark Blue, Pontil, 6½ x 5 In.	2706

Bottle, Flask, Washington & Taylor, Yellow Olive, Open Pontil, Sheared Tooled Lip, c.1850, Qt.
$863

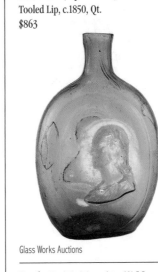

Glass Works Auctions

Bottle, Fruit Jar, American NAGC, Green, Mason Zinc Lid, Milk Glass Insert, c.1885, Pt.
$242

Glass Works Auctions

Bottle, Fruit Jar, Excelsior, Blue Green, Insert, Patd. Aug. 8th, 1865, Zinc Band, Qt.
$518

Glass Works Auctions

Bottle, Fruit Jar, Flaccus Bros, Steer's Head, Yellow Amber, 1885-1900, Pt. $403

Glass Works Auctions

Bottle, Fruit Jar, Gilberds Improved Jar, Star, Aqua, Pat. July 31st, Oct. 13, 1885, Pt. $1,955

Glass Works Auctions

Bottle, Fruit Jar, Leader, Yellow Amber, Glass Lid, Wire Clamp, Pt. $863

Glass Works Auctions

Seal, Jno. Amhurst 1730, Mallet, Olive Green, Sheared, Silver Cap, Ring Pull, 7 In.	748
Seal, John Tabor 1767, Cylinder, Olive Amber, Tapered Neck, String Lip, 10 In.	2300
Seal, Modtonham 1737, Onion Shape, Dark Olive Green, String Rim, 7 x 6 In.	4305
Seal, S Lee 1735, Wine, Yellow Olive, Sheared Mouth, String Rim, 8 x 5 In.	2808
Seal, Sir W. Strickland, Bart. 1809, Wine, Cylinder, Olive Amber, Double Collar, 11 In.	316
Seal, T-G 1801, Cylinder, Dark Olive Green, Applied Collar, Magnum, 10 In.	2185
Seal, VR, Flanking Inverted Anchor, Cylinder, Dark Olive, Short Neck, 10 In.	316
Seal, W Ludlow, Wine, Olive Green, Applied String Rim, Pontil, 11 ¾ In.	1170
Seal, Wm Shiles 1718, Onion Shape, Olive Green, Squat, String Lip, 6 ½ x 6 In.	1840
Seltzer, Gazogene, Wire Mesh, L. Gilles & Cie. Brevete, 17 x 6 ½ In., Pair.........*illus*	183
Snuff, Agate, Cream & Amber, Relief Carved, Bamboo Tree, Stopper, 2 x 2 In.	100
Snuff, Black Lacquer, Mother-Of-Pearl Inlay, Red Stone Stopper	200
Snuff, Cameo, Chalcedony, Peanut, c.1900, 2 ¼ In.	2500
Snuff, Cloisonne, Landscape, White Cranes, Mums & Lotus, 3 In.	238
Snuff, Glass, Crickets, Praying Mantis, Lion Mask Handles, Reverse Painted, 3 In.	687
Snuff, Glass, Figures, Bridge, Green Stone Stopper, 4 x 2 In.	150
Snuff, Glass, Overlay, 5 Colors, Cream Ground, Purple Stopper, c.1800, 2 ¼ In.	2000
Snuff, Glass, Overlay, Red, Bats, Clouds, Round Panel, Green Stopper, 2 ¼ In.	5000
Snuff, Glass, Overlay, Red, Crane, Bat, Bird, Deer, Green Stone Stopper, 3 x 1 ¼ In.	300
Snuff, Glass, Overlay, Red, Warrior, Landscape, Green Stone Stopper, 3 x 2 In.	325
Snuff, Glass, Table, People, Window, Reverse Painted, 2 ½ In., Pair	2000
Snuff, Glass, Yellow, Cranes, Rockwork, Waves, Lotus Leaf, Oval, 2 ¼ In.	1250
Snuff, Horses, Riders, Fortress, Mountain, Blue, White, Agate Stopper, 3 In.	241
Snuff, Jade, Celadon Green, Landscape, People, Silver Mount, Red Stopper, 3 In.	1625
Snuff, Jade, Coral & Turquoise Cabochons, Scrolled Wire, Stopper, 4 x 3 In.	250
Snuff, Jade, Eggplant, Butterfly, 2 ½ In.	3125
Snuff, Jade, Green, White, Russet, Bat & Peach, c.1900, 2 ¼ In.	1187
Snuff, Jade, Lavender, Green Highlights, Bulbous, Malachite Stopper, 1900s, 3 In.	356
Snuff, Jade, Pale Green, Carved, Bird, Tree Branch, Butterflies, Stopper, 2 ½ x 2 In.	478
Snuff, Jade, Russet, Arrows, Mountains, Waves, Dragon, Green Stopper, 2 In.	2500
Snuff, Jade, Russet, Pebble Shape, Butterflies, Branches, Leaves, Melons, 3 In.	6250
Snuff, Jade, White, Red Stone Stopper, 3 ¼ x 2 ¼ In.	325
Snuff, Jade, White, Seated Boy, Scroll, Lion Head, Ring Handles, Chinese, 2 In.	6875
Snuff, Jadeite, Moon Flask, Incised Birds, Flowers, Red Stopper, 2 In., Pair	10000
Snuff, Lapis, Pebble Shape, Face & Hand Of Buddha, Brass, Coral Stopper, 4 In.	123
Snuff, Magpie, Plum Flower, Blue Ground, Enamel, Green Stopper, 2 ¼ In.	2000
Snuff, Mother-Of-Pearl, Cranes, Flowers, Carved, Footed, Hardstone Stopper, 3 In.	135
Snuff, Peking Glass, Relief, Deer, Stork, Tree, Awabi Bats, 2 ½ x 2 In.	76
Snuff, Porcelain, Grasshopper, Butterfly, Flattened Circle, Oval Foot, Stopper, 3 In.	4305
Snuff, Quartz, Reticulated, Ring Handles, Green Stone Stopper, 2 ½ x 1 ½ In.	200
Snuff, Rock Crystal, Oval, Roosters, Handles, Coral Glass Stopper, 1800s, 3 In.	1845
Snuff, Rock Crystal, Reverse Painted, Figures, Calligraphy, Pink Stopper, 3 In., Pair	3125
Snuff, Smoky Crystal, Emperor Napoleon, Coin, Ornate Stopper, 2 ¼ In.	1875
Soda, Chuk-Ker, The Sporting Thing To Drink, Polo Player, ACL	30
Soda, Crystal Palace Premium, W. Eagle, New York, Blue Green, Blob Top, 7 In.	3218
Soda, G.D. Coggeshall, No. 421 Pearl St., New York, Olive Green, 10 Pin, 7 In.	7605
Soda, Haddock & Sons, Olive Yellow, Torpedo Shape, Applied Collar, c.1830, 6 ⅝ In.........*illus*	4095
Soda, J. Mulligan, Aqua, Blob Top, c.1880, 7 ½ In.	5
Soda, Knicker Bocker, C & M, Cobalt Blue, 10-Sided, Blob Top, 7 ½ In.	604
Soda, O-So Good, Rich In Dextrose, 10 Oz.	10
Soda, St. Louis, Aqua, Registered, Return This Bottle To Crone & Co., 11 x 3 ¼ In.	10
Soda, Triple XXX, Makes Thirst A Joy, Amber, Yellow & Red Label, c.1969, 10 Oz.	8
Soda, W. Cadd, Deer Bust Embossed, Blob Top, 7 In.	50
Stiegel Type, Striated, Amethyst, Fluted, Ogee Pattern, Pocket Flask, 5 In.	4973
Syrup, Jin Jer Pep, J. Hungerford Smith, Reverse Glass Label, 11 ¾ In.	1230
Target Ball, Allover Diamond Pattern, Midnight Blue, Long Neck, 1880-1900, 2 ⅜ In.......*illus*	1035
Target Ball, Amber, Raised 4-Point Stars, Sheared, 2 ¼ In.	2300
Target Ball, Amethyst, 3-Piece Mold, Sheared Lip, 2 ¼ In.	253
Target Ball, Bogardus, Diamond Pattern, Center Band, Yellow, c.1895, 2 ⅜ In. ....*illus*	748
Target Ball, Bogardus, Diamond, Center Band, Cobalt Blue, 2 ¾ In.	375

Bottle, Ink, Carter, Cathedral, Cobalt Blue, Rubber Seal, Labels, c.1920-35, 6 1/4 In.
$575

Bottle, Ink, Farley's, 8-Sided, Olive Amber, Sheared Mouth, Pontil Scar, Stoddard, c.1855, 1 3/4 In.
$644

Bottle, Ink, Jones' Empire, N.Y., Emerald Green, 12-Sided, Iron Pontil, 1840-60, 5 3/4 In.
$6,325

Bottle, Ink, Pitkin Type, Ribs, Swirled Left, Cone, Yellow Olive, Pontil, c.1800, 1 7/8 In.
$2,691

Bottle, Ink, Umbrella, 8-Sided, Medium Steel Blue, Inward Rolled Lip, c.1850, 2 3/8 In.
$936

Bottle, Medicine, Dr. Ham's Aromatic Invigorating Spirit, N.Y., Aqua, Iron Pontil, c.1850, 8 1/2 In.
$241

Bottle, Medicine, Smelling Salts, Free-Blown, Figural, Seahorse Shape, Yellow Amber, c.1825, 3 In.
$878

Bottle, Medicine, Smelling Salts, Marbleized, Blue, Milk Glass, Threaded Cap, 3 In.
$293

Bottle, Medicine, Smelling Salts, Seahorse, Swirled, Pink & Milk Glass, Rigaree, 3 In.
$644

Bottle, Prototype, Go-With, Indian Maiden, Carved Wood, Painted, 1865, 12 In.
$2,340

Norman Heckler & Company

Bottle, Seltzer, Gazogene, Wire Mesh, L. Gilles & Cie. Brevete, 17 x 6 ½ In., Pair
$183

Neal Auctions

Bottle, Soda, Haddock & Sons, Olive Yellow, Torpedo Shape, Applied Collar, c.1830, 6 ⅝ In.
$4,095

Norman Heckler & Company

Target Ball, Bogardus, Diamond, Center Band, Sapphire Blue, 2 ¾ In.	275
Target Ball, Bogardus, Patd. Apr.10th 1877, Diamond, Band, Cobalt Blue, 2 ¾ In.	431
Target Ball, Bogardus, Patd. Apr.10th 1877, Diamond, Golden Amber, 2 ¼ In.	374
Target Ball, Bogardus, Patd. Apr.10th 1877, Diamond, Olive, Pink Striations, 2 ¼ In.	978
Target Ball, C. Newman, Center Band, Diamond, Yellow Amber, Sheared, 2 ¼ In.	805
Target Ball, Cobalt Blue, Grid, Squares, Unembossed Center Band, 2 ¼ In.	219
Target Ball, Cobalt Blue, Horizontal Ribbing, Sheared Lip, 2 ¼ In.	316
Target Ball, Cornflower Blue, Sand, Pat. Aug. 13th 1878, Sheared, 2 ¼ In.	575
Target Ball, Dark Chocolate Amber, Horizontal Ribbing, Sheared Lip, 2 ¼ In.	253
Target Ball, E. Jones Gunmaker, Blackbourne, Lancs, Light Blue, Diamond, 2 ¼ In.	276
Target Ball, E.E. Eaton Guns & C., 53 State St. Chicago, Amber, Sheared, 2 ¼ In.	1840
Target Ball, For Hockey's Patent Trap, Apple Green, Band Of XS, Sheared, 2 ½ In.	920
Target Ball, Gurd & Son, 185 Dundas St., London, Ont., Band, Amber, 2 ¼ In.	518
Target Ball, Ira Paine's Filled, Pat. Apld For, Yellow Amber, Sheared Lip, 2 ¼ In.	460
Target Ball, Man Aiming Shotgun, Pink Amethyst, Diamond, Sheared, 2 ¼ In.	403
Target Ball, Man Aiming Shotgun, Sapphire Blue, Diamond, Sheared, 2 ¼ In.	489
Target Ball, N.B. Glass Works Perth, Cobalt Blue, Diamond, Sheared Lip, 2 ¼ In.	127
Target Ball, Topaz Puce, Diamond, Unembossed Center Band, Sheared, 2 ¼ In.	242
Target Ball, W.W. Greener, St. Mary's Works, London, Pink Amethyst, Diamond, 2 ¼ In.	748
Target Ball, Yellow Amber, 7 Horizontal Ribs, Sheared Lip, 2 ¼ In.	374
Utility, Forest Green, Cylindrical, Dip Mold, Rolled Rim, 8 ¼ In.	410
Utility, Sapphire Blue, Globular, Dip Mold, Blob Top, 10 In.	316
Whiskey, Ambrosial, Seal, B.M. & E.A.W. & Co., Amber, Chestnut Shape, Handle, 9 In.	196
Whiskey, Casper's, Made By Honest North Carolina People, Cobalt Blue, Fluted, Qt.	468
Whiskey, E.G. Booz's Old Cabin, Cottage, Amber, Sloped Collar On Chimney, 8 In.	1725
Whiskey, Griffith Hyatt & Co., Baltimore, Olive Yellow, Jug, Handle, Label, 7 In.	2645
Whiskey, Haltz & Freystedt Co., Amber, Jug Shape, Handle, Tooled Spout, 8 In.	207
Whiskey, J.F. Tobias & Co., Philad., Slug Plate, Amber, Vertical Ribs, Handle, 7 In.	1150
Whiskey, Mist Of The Morning, Barnett & Lumley, Barrel, Amber, Double Collar, 10 In.	374
Whiskey, Mohawk, Pure Rye, Indian Maiden, Yellow Amber, 1865, 12 ¼ In. ......*illus*	2925
Whiskey, Old Mill, Whitlock & Co., Seal, Yellow Amber, Bell Shape, Double Collar, 8 In.	920
Whiskey, Old Monongahela Rye, CH, Sheaf Of Grain, Slug Plate, Olive Amber, 9 In.	265
Whiskey, Old Wheat, S.M. & Co., Slug Plate, Yellow Amber, Globular, Sloped Collar, 11 In.	316
Whiskey, Perrine's Ginger, Raised Apple, Semi-Cabin, Amber, Rope Corners, 10 In.	316
Whiskey, R.B. Cutter, Louisville, Ky., Deep Tobacco Amber, Jug, Handle, 8 ¾ In.	316
Whiskey, R.B. Cutter, Louisville, Ky., Topaz Puce, Jug, Handle, Blob Top, 8 ¾ In.	345
Whiskey, SM & Co., NY, Seal, Amber To Yellow, Neck Ring, Scroll Handle, 9 In.	489
Whiskey, Star Whiskey, New York, W.B. Crowell, Slug Plate, Amber, Handle, 8 In.	1265
Whiskey, Wharton's 1850 Chestnut Grove, Red Amber, Ewer Shape, Handle, 10 In.	690
Wine, 1863 Madeira, Red Wax Seal	420
Wine, Black Glass, Deep Yellow Olive, 8-Sided, Long Neck, Ring Mouth, 10 In.	1112
Wine, Cylindrical, Tapered Neck, Olive Amber, String Lip, Double Magnum, 13 In.	460
Wine, Globular, Loop Handle, White & Blue, Tin Glaze, c.1649, 5 In.	4305
Wine, Globular, Olive Green, String Lip, Magnum, 11 x 3 ¾ In.	748
Wine, Globular, Yellow Olive Amber, String Lip, Dutch, Magnum, 11 ½ x 6 In.	546

BOTTLE CAPS for milk bottles are the printed cardboard caps used since the 1920s. Crown caps, used after 1892 on soda bottles, are also popular collectibles. Unusual mottoes, graphics, and caps from bottlers that are out of business bring the highest prices.

Crown, Corky, Soda, Clown, Red, White, Blue, Metal, Cork Lined, 1 ¼ In.	5
Crown, Nehi Monkey, Soda, Yellow, White, Metal, Cork Lined	10
Crown, Pluto Water, America's Physic, Soda, Devil, Red, White, Metal	20
Crown, Sun-Rise Root Beer, Soda, Brown, White, Metal Cork Lined	7

BOTTLE OPENERS are needed to open many bottles. As soon as the commercial bottle was invented, the opener to be used with the new types of closures became a necessity. Many types of bottle openers can be found, most dating from the twentieth century. Collectors prize advertising and comic openers.

4-Eyed Black Woman, Wall Mount, Cast Iron, 4 ¼ In.	37

7Up, White With Red Lettering, 6 x 2½ x 1⅜ In.	94
Black Face Crowley, Cast Iron, 4¼ In.	120
Butterfly, Enameled, Metal, Brass Color, 4½ x 2¼ In.	12
Corkscrew, Silver, Mermaid & Fish Shape, Box Set, 1938, 4 In.	955
Elephant, Big Ears, Cast, Brass, 3¼ In.	152
Face, 4 Eyes, Moustache, Iron, Wall Mount, 3½ In.	99
Golf Caddy, Nickel, Cast Iron, 6 In.	183
Man, Double Eyes, Open Mouth, 4 In.	58
Nude Woman, Fan, Art Nouveau, Cast Iron, 8½ In.	40
Sea Gull, White, Pier, Jamestown R.I., Iron, 3¼ x 2¾ In. .....*illus*	39
Silver King, Sale Orange Fizz	10
Waiter, Hands In Pockets, Clear & Frosted Glass, Amber Head, 14 In.	150
Waiter, Holding Tray, Shot Glasses, Milk Glass, Black Head, 14 In.	296
Woman, Double Eyes, Open Mouth, 4 In.	58

BOTTLE STOPPERS are made of glass, metal, plastic, and wood. Decorative and figural stoppers are used to replace the original cork stoppers and are collected today.

Ceramic, Dog, Head, Black & White, 1 Ear Flopped Down, Japan, 2½ In.	89
Wood, Kissing Couple, Heads Turn, Kiss, Push Lever, Anri, c.1950, 6 In.	20
Wood, Sailor, Head, Painted, Anri	119
Wood, Woman, Fly On Cheek, Red Flowers, Anri, 5 In.	249

BOXES of all kinds are collected. They were made of thin strips of inlaid wood, metal, tortoiseshell, embroidery, or other material. Additional boxes may be listed in other sections, such as Advertising, Battersea, Ivory, Shaker, Tinware, and various Porcelain categories. Tea Caddies are listed in their own category.

3 Sections, Yellow Grain Painted, Green Lids, Slide Lid, Lancaster, Pa., 1800s, 3 x 12 In...*illus*	71
14K Gold, Florentine, Malachite Tablet, Abstract Circles, Chinese, 1950s, 3 In.	2460
14K Gold, Paneled, Vases, Leaves & Scrolls, Rectangular, Russia, 3¼ In.	4920
18k Gold, Engraved, Threaded, Rococo Scrolls, Continental, 1900s, 2½ x 1½ In.	1500
Artist's, Rosewood, Compartments, Lift Lid, Red Felt, 1800s, 9½ In.	240
Ballot, Wood, Turned Handle, 2 Sections, Lift Lids, Metal Latches, Sloped, 3 x 9 In.	150
Bandbox, Wallpaper, Blue Ground, Squirrels, Horse On Lid, 1800s, 12 x 16 x 12 In.	1800
Bandbox, Wallpaper, Blue, Peach, Flowers, Oval, Lid, Newspaper Lined, c.1810, 6 x 10 In.	600
Bandbox, Wallpaper, Flocked, Cardboard, Flowers, Pink, Gold, Oval, Lid, c.1840, 4 x 9 In.	480
Bandbox, Wallpaper, Fruit Baskets, Swan Handles, Hanna Davis, 1800s, 11 x 15 x 11 In.	780
Bandbox, Wallpaper, House, Blue Ground, Lid, 11 x 15 In.	308
Bandbox, Wallpaper, Yellow, Brown, Flowers, Round, Pine Lid & Base, c.1855, 4 x 6 In.	189
Basswood, Pine, Poplar, Mid 1800s, 8½ x 22 In.	140
Bentwood, Leaf & Dot Design, Orange Ground, 2 x 5½ In.	3840
Bentwood, Oval, Houses, Trees, Animals, Lid, Scandinavian, 1849, 8 x 17 In.	1845
Bentwood, Painted, Green, Red & Yellow Flowers, Vines, 1800s, 11 x 18 x 15 In.	2706
Bible, Slate Green, Flower, Leaves, Snipe Hinges, New England, 8 x 22 In.	4800
Bible, Walnut, Inlaid, Vines & Lattice, Cartouche, Pierced Brass Corners, c.1700, 7 x 24 In.	687
Bible, William & Mary, Oyster Veneer, Marquetry Panels, c.1800, 6 x 23 x 18 In.	2400
Bird's-Eye Maple, Painted, Vines, Building, Amelia Spooner, Phila, 1826, 2 x 11 In.	5000
Bloodstone, 18K Gold, Carved Scarab Lid, Oval, Cartier, 1950s, 1½ In.	2214
Bone & Mother-Of-Pearl Inlay, Scrimshaw, Captain Spencer Pratt, c.1845, 6 x 12 In.	9840
Book, Carved, Gold Painted Edges, Slide Lid, 1800s, 8 x 2 x 5 In.	325
Bride's, Bentwood, Couple On Lid, Flowers, c.1810, 18½ x 12 x 8 In.	350
Bride's, Bentwood, Couple, Flower Bands, Continental, 8 x 19 In.	615
Bride's, Bentwood, Oval, Lid, Painted Flowers, Seams, Europe, c.1850, 5 x 10 In.	240
Bride's, Bentwood, Oval, Woman On Lid, c.1910, 6 x 18 In.	240
Bride's, Bentwood, Painted Flowers, Transfer Lid, Children, c.1810, 18 x 11 In...*illus*	118
Bride's, Bentwood, Painted, Flowers, Blue Ground, Continental, 1800s, 6 x 15 x 9 In.	400
Bride's, Bentwood, Painted, Red Wash, Blue & White Blossoms, c.1810, 4 x 12 In...*illus*	369
Bronze, Openwork, Zodiac, Red, Cedar Lining, Oscar Bach, c.1920, 4 x 7 In.	185

Bottle, Target Ball, Allover Diamond Pattern, Midnight Blue, Long Neck, 1880-1900, 2⅜ In.
$1,035

Glass Works Auctions

Bottle, Target Ball, Bogardus, Diamond Pattern, Center Band, Yellow, c.1895, 2⅜ In.
$748

Glass Works Auctions

Bottle, Whiskey, Mohawk, Pure Rye, Indian Maiden, Yellow Amber, 1865, 12¼ In.
$2,925

Norman Heckler & Company

Bottle Opener, Sea Gull, White, Pier, Jamestown R.I., Iron, 3 ¼ x 2 ¾ In. **$39**

Ruby Lane

Box, 3 Sections, Yellow Grain Painted, Green Lids, Slide Lid, Lancaster, Pa., 1800s, 3 x 12 In. **$71**

Hess Auction Group

Box, Bride's, Bentwood, Painted Flowers, Transfer Lid, Children, c.1810, 18 x 11 In. **$118**

Hess Auction Group

> **TIP**
>
> *If you return home at night and see a stranger outside your house, drive past your house and go to a neighbor's or call for help on your cell phone.*

Bronze, Raised Figures, Saints, Arched Panels, Gilt, Lift Lid, 2 ¾ x 6 In.	120
Candle, Paint, Gilt, Flowers, Urn, Slide Lid, Sloped Edge, Thumb Pull, 1793, 6 x 11 In.	1482
Candle, Pine, Red Graining, White Pin Stripes, Star, Slide Lid, c.1850, 5 x 12 In.	240
Candle, Poplar, Mahogany, Paint, Slide Lid, Beveled Edge, c.1850, 6 x 11 In.	250
Candle, Softwood, Grain Painted, Dovetailed, Fitted Interior, Slide Lid, 5 ½ x 11 In.	266
Candle, Walnut, Mixed Wood, Red Paint, Slide Lid, Chip Carved, c.1850, 6 x 14 In.	570
Candle, Walnut, Wallpaper Interior, Slide Lid, Early 1800s, 4 x 8 In.	351
Candle, Wood, Paint, Tulip Design, Molded Base, Slide Lid, c.1800, 3 x 9 In.	2700
Card, Tartan Print, Playing Cards Design, Wood, Hinged Lid, Tartanware, c.1880, 11 x 7 In.	1525
Carrier, Bentwood, Dovetailed, Upright Handle & Lid, Turned Knob, 1800s, 9 x 15 In.	480
Carved, Lion & Leaf, Slide Lid, Original Finish, Late 1800s, 12 x 16 x 11 In.	805
Casket, Needlework, Silk, Fitted Interior, Inkwells, Charles II, 1600s, 8 x 12 In. ....*illus*	9225
Casket, Table, Dome Lid, Inset Horn, Ivorine, Tooled Leather, 10 ¾ x 15 In.	375
Casket, Walnut, Carved, Black Forest, Roses & Grapevines, 1800s, 7 ½ x 12 x 8 In.	625
Cellarette, Mahogany, Oval, Gadroon Edge, William IV, c.1880, 18 x 37 x 22 In.	1250
Cigarette, 14K Gold, Most & Fogel, 1900s, 3 ½ x 3 In.	2125
Cigarette, Silver, Enamel, Yachting Scene, Engraved, Hon. Jacob Ruppert Jr., 1898	4000
Cigarette, Wood, Carved Flowers & Leaves, Hinged Dome Lid, Chinese, 4 x 5 In.	123
Coin, Brass, Owl Shape, 2 ½ In.	112
Comb, Paint, Parallel Bands, Convex Sides, Inscribed, Green, Red, Blue, Lid, 1 x 5 In.	1968
Comb, Wood, Tapered Back, Pocket, Hanging, 1700s, 7 x 6 In.	6000
Cutlery, Hepplewhite, Mahogany, Sloped Lid, Shell Inlay, c.1815, 15 x 9 In., Pair..............*illus*	3933
Cutlery, Mahogany, Banding, Georgian, c.1780, 19 x 7 ½ In.	98
Cutlery, Poplar, 2 Compartments, Cutout Handle, 1800s, 6 In.	351
Cutlery, Urn, Mahogany, Inlaid, Shield Escutcheon, Early 1800s, 22 x 10 In., Pair	832
Desk, Carved, Painted, Thistles, Geometric Shapes, Lock, c.1750, 6 x 11 x 8 In.	325
Desk, Oak, Carved, Blue Paint, Molded Lift Lid, Punched Design, 1600s, 11 x 20 In.	20000
Desk, Red, Black, Dovetailed, 36 x 27 In.	105
Desk, Rosewood, Brass, Jasperware Plaque, Drawer, 2 Inkwells, 9 ½ x 12 In.	125
Desk, Tabletop, Slant Front, Pine, Stain, Drawers, Cubbies, Butterfly Hinges, 17 x 24 In.	3075
Document, American, Vinegar Graining, Green Trim, Early 1800s, 7 ½ x 14 In.	240
Document, Basswood, Faux Maple Graining, Dovetailed, c.1850, 5 x 10 In.	375
Document, Bentwood, Red Paint, Lapped Seams, Late 1800s, 7 ½ x 12 In.	300
Document, Copper, Punched, Hex Sign, Hinged Lid, Ring Handles, c.1810, 4 x 9 In.	415
Document, Curly Maple, Poplar Base, Mid 1800s, 5 x 10 x 5 ½ In.	330
Document, Mahogany, Inlaid Star, Keyhole, Refinished, Late 1800s, 5 x 13 x 10 In.	180
Document, Pine, Grain Painted, Cream, Brown, Brass Bail Handle, c.1850, 5 x 12 In.	510
Document, Pine, Mahogany Veneer, Inlaid, Brass Handles, 6 ½ x 12 In.	270
Document, Pine, Paint, Sponge Graining, Dovetailed, Dome Lid, c.1850, 7 x 14 In.	480
Document, Pine, Pyrography, Tan, Gray Smudging, Flat Lid, c.1850, 5 x 12 In.	240
Document, Pine, Vinegar Sponged, Amber Feathering, c.1850, 4 x 10 In.	480
Document, Red, Brown, Seashell, Leaf, Sgraffito, 11 x 21 In.	480
Document, Relief Carved, Dovetailed, Brass Bail Handles, 9 ½ x 23 In.	108
Document, Seal, United States, Red, Black, Dome Lid, Hidden Drawer, c.1830, 6 In.	12600
Document, Shells, Ormolu Mounts, Brass Inlay, Pierced Coromandel, 12 x 19 In.	700
Document, Softwood, Pyrography, Paint, Dome Lid, Metal Latch, 1859, 8 x 18 In.	384
Document, Tin, Paint, Black, Yellow, Red, Flowers, Loop Handle, 1800s, 6 x 9 In.	3750
Document, Walnut, Inlaid Scroll, Flowers, Hinged Lid, Turned Feet, 6 x 16 In.	1422
Document, Walnut, Iron Locks, Baroque, Belgium, c.1700, 12 ½ x 20 ½ In.	600
Dresser, Beech, Painted, Portrait Busts, 3 ¼ x 9 In.	277
Dresser, Bronze, Gilt, Silvered, Putti Holding Trident, 13 ½ x 12 In.	2677
Dresser, Celluloid, Green, Textured, Shaped, Marked, Amerith, 1930s, 5 x 3 ½ In.	20
Dresser, Cloisonne, Red, Lotus, Carved Jade Medallion, 2 ¼ x 5 ½ In.	1428
Dresser, Cut Glass, Gilt Metal, Paw Feet, 6 x 8 ½ In.	714
Dresser, Gilt Metal, Jade Mount, Peonies, Dragon, 3 x 10 In.	2142
Dresser, Glass, Enamel, Flowers, Late 1800s, 6 x 8 In.	305
Dresser, Ivory, Round, Portrait, Woman, Veil, c.1880, 1 ½ x 3 ½ In.	200
Dresser, Leather, Scrolling Leaves, Gilt Bronze Border, Hinged Lid, 3 x 13 In.	208

Dresser, Malachite Glass, Nudes, Flowing Hair, Shallow Foot, 2 x 4 In.	94
Dresser, Opaline, Canted Corners, Twisted Bail Handles, Leaf Feet, Hinged Lid, 5 x 7 In.	714
Dresser, Poplar, Graining, Gilt Stencil, Acorns, Asian Scenes, Drawer, Lid, c.1835, 5 x 10 In.	180
Dresser, Silvered, Pierced, Mythological Creatures, Acanthus, Scrolls, 7 x 8 In.	1180
Dresser, Wood, Hand Painted, Flowers, Landscape, Line Border, Hinged Lid, 5 x 10 In.	90
Egg, Sterling Silver, Yellow Enamel, Fitted Case, 2 x 1½ In.	343
Figural, Dog Head, Glass Eyes, Collar, Loures Barbazan, Black Forest, c.1880, 7 In.	600
Glass, Gilt Metal Banding, France, c.1980, 3 x 9½ In.	813
Glove, Parquetry, 3 Octagons, 14 In.	238
Handkerchief, Walnut, Inlay, Brass Plaque, Velvet Lined, 3 x 7 In.	115
Hat, Black, Stylized Gold Flowers, Brass Mounts, Tassels, Footed, Japan, 16 x 17 In.	488
Hat, Latch, Louis Vuitton, 18 x 17 In.	1661
Hat, Leather, Holds Stovepipe Top Hat, Canvas Interior, Strap & Lock, Lid, Handle, c.1830	775
Hat, Tole, Officer's Dress Helmet, 13½ x 18 In., Pair.	593
Hat, Wallpaper, Blue, 1800s, 12½ x 15½ In.	258
Hat, Wallpaper, Brown, Yellow, Landscape, House, Fence, Oval, c.1835, 11 x 14 In.	2100
Hat, Wallpaper, Ship, House, 6 x 13¼ In.	180
Humidor, Brass, Carved Hardstone, Phoenix, Lotus, Lid, Scroll Feet, c.1910, 2 x 12 In.	83
Ironwood, Oval, Free-Form, Textured Bark, Lid, Doug Muscanell, c.1990, 5 In.	246
Jewelry, 4 Drawers, Red, Brass Pulls, Sow Back, Japan, 8 x 9 In.	100
Jewelry, Brass Veneer, 3 Drawers, Footed, 14 x 17 In.	156
Jewelry, Brass, Copper, Steel, Nails, Tiles, Richard Bitterman, 1960s, 6½ x 9½ In.	1220
Jewelry, Bronze, 4¾ x 9 In.	156
Jewelry, Bronze, Wreaths, Garlands, Musical Instruments, Horse Head, 6 x 9 In.	200
Jewelry, Burl, Embroidered Medallion, Bone Rim, 6-Sided, Lid, Austria, c.1910, 3 x 6 In.	78
Jewelry, Burlwood Veneer, Ogee Shape, Framed Mirror, 1800s, 7 x 12 x 8 In.	240
Jewelry, Casket, Gilt Metal, Egyptian Revival, Early 1900s, 9 x 13 x 9 In.	1750
Jewelry, Casket, Tortoiseshell, Gilt Brass, Fin De Siecle, Late 1800s, 4 x 12 x 9 In.	937
Jewelry, Ebonized, Brass Mounts & Inlay, Napoleon III, 8 x 15 In.	218
Jewelry, Gilt, Portraits, French Monarchs, Lid, Warrior Finial, A. Girous, 12 x 10 In.	6875
Jewelry, Mahogany, String Inlay, Hinged Lid, Brass Sphere Handles, 7½ x 15 In.	360
Jewelry, Marriage Coffer, Wood, Leather, Bronze, Studs, Lift Lid, c.1700, 15 x 10 In.	3350
Jewelry, Metal, Pietra Dura, Flowers, Beaded, Lift Lid, Finial, Footed, c.1880, 6 x 8 In.	2450
Jewelry, Pagoda Shape, Brown, 16 x 15½ In.	62
Jewelry, Pine, Red Paint, Gilt Lines & Scrolls, Nellie On Lid, c.1875, 4 x 11 In.	510
Jewelry, Porcelain Plaques, Woman & Child, River Bank, Bellflowers, 5 x 8 In.	750
Jewelry, Porcelain, Pink, Green, Yellow, Chinese, 2 x 4 In.	218
Jewelry, Rosewood, Beaded, Brass Inlay, 2 Doors, Music Box, Reuge, Swiss, 5 x 9 In.	531
Jewelry, Rosewood, Brass, Sarcophagus, Erhard & Sohne, 5 x 8 In.	732
Jewelry, Rosewood, Lacquer, Mother-Of-Pearl Inlay, Storks, Flowers, Hinged, 5 x 9 In.	112
Jewelry, Rosewood, Maple Interior, Velvet Tray, Tapered, Disc Feet, France, 12 x 8 In.	175
Jewelry, Rosewood, Pearl Inlay, 11 x 12½ In.	125
Jewelry, Rosewood, Silver Repousse Mounts, Hinged Lid, 1900s, 7 x 10 In.	240
Jewelry, Sarcophagus, Enamel, Gilt, Leaf Design, Strapwork, Dome Lid, 2½ x 4 In.	720
Jewelry, Silvered Metal, Enameled Cabochons, Byzantine Style, 4 x 6 In.	833
Jewelry, Walnut, Carved, House, Porch & Chimney, 10 x 13 In.	1000
Jewelry, Walnut, Carved, Relief Shield, Leaves, Nuts, Bombe Sides, Henri II, 9 x 17 In.	375
Jewelry, Wood, Inlay, Flowers, Interior Mirror, Flip Top, Shaped Feet, 1927, 8 x 12 In.	344
Jewelry, Wood, Leather, Silver, Putti, Clouds, 6 x 5 In.	183
Knife, Mahogany, Goblet Shape, Dome Lid, Square Base, George III, 24 In., Pair.	1000
Knife, Mahogany, Inlaid Knife & Fork Design, 1800s, 5½ x 16 x 8½ In.	3750
Knife, Mahogany, Satinwood, Inlay, 1800s, 17 x 9½ x 13½ In., Pair	1800
Knife, Mahogany, Serpentine Front, Shell Inlay, George III, 14 x 9 In., Pair	1250
Knife, Mahogany, Serpentine, Hinged, Star Inlay, Georgian, England, 14 x 9 In.	755
Knife, Mahogany, Serpentine, Shell Inlay, Hinged Lid, Georgian, 14 x 8 In., Pair.	2100
Knife, Mahogany, String Inlay, George III, 15 In., Pair	450
Knife, Mahogany, Urn, Carved, Tapered & Faceted, c.1900, 22 x 8½ In., Pair	562
Knife, Mahogany, Veneer, Urn, Serpentine, George III, c.1800, 14 x 9 x 10 In., Pair	875
Knife, Urn, Mahogany, Lift Lid, Pinecone Finial, Square Foot, George III, 26 In., Pair	1375

Box, Bride's, Bentwood, Painted, Red Wash, Blue & White Blossoms, c.1810, 4 x 12 In.
$369

Skinner, Inc.

Box, Casket, Needlework, Silk, Fitted Interior, Inkwells, Charles II, 1600s, 8 x 12 In.
$9,225

Cowan's Auctions

Think Before You Refinish
The original finish on an antique is considered part of the history of the piece and should be kept. If the original finish is removed, it can't be replaced and the value of the piece is lowered.

Box, Cutlery, Hepplewhite, Mahogany, Sloped Lid, Shell Inlay, c.1815, 15 x 9 In., Pair
$3,933

James D. Julia Auctioneers

Box, Salt, Mixed Wood, Hanging, Red Varnish, Lid, 11 In.
$118

Hess Auction Group

Box, Work, Tunbridge Ware, Inlaid Bands, Green, Brown, 6¾ x 10¼ In.
$255

Ruby Lane

> **TIP**
> Remove the handles
> from jalousie or
> casement windows
> to make them more
> burglarproof.

Boy Scout, Whistle, Metal, Acme, c.1915, 3¾ In.
$75

Ruby Lane

Knife, Urn, Mahogany, Octagonal, Hinged Lid, Acorn Finial, George III, 24 In., Pair	813
Knife, Urn, Mahogany, Turned Finial, Round Foot, George III, 22 In., Pair	625
Knife, Walnut, Serpentine, Inlaid Paterae, England, Early 1800s, 12 x 9 In.	150
Letter, Brass, Etched Florentine, 4 Inset Medallions, Slant Lid, 1800s, 5 x 7 In.	270
Letter, Mahogany, Parquetry, Inlay, 10 x 13 In.	50
Letter, Oak, 3 Letter Racks, Pen Tray, Hinged, Arts & Crafts, 10½ x 9 In.	206
Letter, Papier-Mache, Brown, Ferns, Slant Front, 11 x 12 In.	125
Letter, Wood, Hearts, Diamond, Stars, Hinged Lid, Lift Tray, Lock, Key, 1900s, 4 In.	250
Lock, Oak, Paint, Continental, 1800s, 10 x 22 In.	86
Lock, Softwood, Dovetailed, Iron Latch, Strap Hinges, Lift Lid, 1700s, 10 x 19 In.	118
Lock, Walnut, Iron Latch, Molded Panels, Scribed Design, Carved Feet, 1700s, 7 x 16 In.	118
Mahogany, Satinwood, Inlaid Geometric Shapes, 1800s, 5 x 12½ x 7 In.	500
Marquetry, Cherry, Rose & Kingwood, Hinged Lid, Geometric, Eng., 1800s, 2 x 6 In.	250
Money, Parquetry, Inlay, Money Slot, Side Slides Open, Ogee Feet, c.1835, 7 x 11 In.	812
Money, Wood, Paint, Molded, Eagle, Coin Slot, Ball Feet, c.1810, 5 x 6 In.	4750
Pantry, Bentwood, Original Red Paint, Late 1800s, Imperfections, 3 x 6½ In.	120
Pantry, Bentwood, Round, Old Paint Swirls, Lid, 3 x 6¾ In.	875
Pantry, Cranberry Red, Oval, Tacked Lap, 1800s, 2 x 6 In.	234
Pantry, Oak, Pine, Round, Red Paint, Lid, Mid 1800s, 5½ x 10½ In.	439
Pantry, Oval, Carved Heart & Tulip Design Sides, Lid, 1800s, 2½ x 5½ In.	1500
Pantry, Round, Carved, Stylized Tulip, JHS, Flower Border, Lid, 4 x 10 In.	2100
Pencil, Pine, Slide Lid, Rectangular, c.1920, 3½ x 8 In.	199
Pine, Blue, Red Border, Green, Yellow Swags, Paper Lined, Lid, 1828, 12 x 24 In.	2214
Pipe, Blue Paint, Scrolled Sides, Cutout Heart, Drawer, Lollipop Hanger, c.1750, 19 x 5 In.	2963
Pipe, Wood, Green Paint, Pocket, Drawer, Heart-Shape Hanger, c.1810, 18 x 6 In.	11000
Poplar, Yellow, Red Tulips, Star, Script & Squiggles, Brown Dome Lid, 6 x 8 In.	10455
Powder, Girl, Hat, Black Gloves, Book, Lenci, Torino, Italy, 8¾ x 5¾ In.	3750
Powder, Glass, Frosted, Yellow, Finial, 6 In.	38
Prayer, Relief Panels, Animals, Deities, Symbols, 18 x 54 In.	357
Puzzle, Heart, Blue Transfer, Flower, 1¼ x 2½ In., 5 Piece	359
Rosewood, Inlaid Pewter & Mother Of Pearl, England, Late 1800s, 4 x 10 x 7 In.	63
Salt, Hanging, Pine, Paint, Square Nails, Cube, Shaped Wall Mount, Beaded, c.1850, 7 In.	360
Salt, Mixed Wood, Carved, Slanted Lift Lid, Wooden Spoon, 7 x 6½ In.	129
Salt, Mixed Wood, Hanging, Red Varnish, Lid, 11 In. *illus*	118
Sarcophagus, Enameled, Cobalt Blue, Copper, France, 7½ In.	750
Storage, Chest, Wood, Paint, Flowers & Leaves, Flip Lid, Scroll Apron, 1800s, 9 x 12 In.	1062
Storage, Oval, Laced Fingers, Grain Paint, Lid, Spring Latch, c.1860, 6 x 12 In.	90
Storage, Pine, Grained, Brown, Amber, Fitted, Dovetailed, Lift Lid, Loop, 4 x 10 In.	330
Storage, Pine, Green Paint, Gold Lettering, Dovetailed, W.L.A. & Co., 1856, 8 x 16 In.	240
Storage, Pine, Sprigs, Fruit, Yellow, Hinged Lid, Brass Handle, c.1810, 9 x 15 In.	830
Storage, Pine, Sprigs, Monogram, Dome Lid, Hinged, Iron Lock, c.1850, 10 x 24 In.	237
Storage, Wood, 3 Drawers, Iron Holdings, Hinged Lid, Japan, 8 x 11 In.	153
Storage, Wood, Black Paint, Tin Hinges & Hasps, Dome Lid, 1800s, 10 x 19 In.	71
Storage, Wood, Grain Paint, Dovetailed, Shoe Feet, Beaded Hinged Lid, c.1860, 20 x 49 In.	180
Storage, Wood, Paint, Flowers, Leaves, Gilt, Hinged Dome Lid, c.1950, 5 x 10 In.	296
Storage, Wood, Red, Gold Vines, Deer, Sides Slide Open, Drawers, Handle, 6 x 13 In.	1481
Strong, Iron, Oak, England, 16 x 24 In.	500
Strong, Iron, Stuffed, 1800s, 31 x 24 In.	1058
Strong, Wood, Carved, Medallions, Hinges, Compartments, Velvet Lined, 7 x 20 In.	338
Table, Tunbridge Ware, Inlay, Cubes, 1800s, 7 x 15 In.	500
Tantalus, Book Stack Shape, 4 Books, 5½ x 9 In.	250
Tantalus, Gilt, 4 Decanters, 16 Glasses, France, Late 1800s, 11 x 14 x 11 In.	2750
Tantalus, Hinged, Tray, 16 Glasses, 4 Decanters, France, 1800s, 10 x 12 x 9 In.	2280
Tantalus, Mahogany, Gilt Bronze, Inlay, 4 Decanters, France, 1800s, 10 x 13 x 9 In.	500
Tantalus, Mahogany, Gilt Bronze, Mirror, France, Late 1800s, 11 x 13 x 11 In.	1250
Tantalus, Oak, 3 Cut Glass Decanters, 13½ x 13½ In.	625
Tantalus, Oak, Brass, Mirror, 3 Cut Glass Decanters, Stoppers, 13½ x 14½ In.	240
Tantalus, Rosewood, Ebonized, Brass Inlay, France, Late 1800s, 11 x 13 x 9 In.	687
Tantalus, Walnut, Molded, Faceted Bottles, Applied Silver Leaf, 18 x 14 In.	118

Trick, Wood, Paint, Cat Head Panels, Mouse Springs Out, Molded Slide Lid, 5 x 8 In.	413
Trinket, Birch, Chip Carved, Pinwheels, Heart, Slide Lid, 8 In.	1500
Trinket, Birch, Chip Carved, Pinwheels, Heart, Sliding Lid, Canada, 8 In.	1500
Trinket, Bronze, Horse's Head, Relief, Verdigris, Lift Lid, Wood Lined, c.1910, 3 x 6 In.	800
Trinket, Exotic Wood, Ball Finial, Lid, 5 x 5 In.	213
Trinket, Faience, Yellow, Red Leaves, Turquoise Band At Rim, Round, 3 x 6 In.	416
Trinket, Figural, Seated Man, Arms Up, Inlaid Shell Eyes, Lid, c.1885, 4 x 8 In.	185
Trinket, Flowerhead, Carved Flowering Branches, Lobed, Red, Black, 1900s, 10 In.	178
Trinket, Hardwood, Carved, Rectangular, Scalloped, Poem, Lid, c.1900, 5 x 4 In.	246
Trinket, Houses Of Parliament, Roundels, 2 Hinged Lids, London, 1800s, 3 x 7 In.	531
Trinket, Landscape, Roundel, Ring Border, Round, Dome Lid, c.1885, 2 x 4 In.	338
Trinket, Mixed Wood, Marquetry, Hexagonal, Hinged Lid, Star Design, 5 x 10 In.	60
Trinket, Persimmon, Brass, Copper, Enamel, Marie Zimmerman, c.1915, 5 x 4 In.	518
Trinket, Pine, Early Nails, Snipe Hinges, Canada, 5 In.	600
Trinket, Porcelain, Sevres Style, Cobalt Blue, Vignette, Shaped, 11 In.	688
Trinket, Silver Gilt, Filigree, Flowers, Fluting, Lapis Cabochons, Dome Lid, 3 x 8 In.	1375
Trinket, Wallpaper, Pale Blue, Yellow, Crescent Design, Round, Lid, c.1850, 2 x 2 In.	1600
Trinket, Wood, Chip Carved, Slide Lid, Tab Handle, Inscribed, c.1890, 1 x 3 In.	500
Trinket, Wood, Heart Shape, Black Paint, Carved, Lid, U.S.A., 1800s, 1 x 3 In.	2200
Trinket, Wood, Red, Brown, Yellow, Bands & Dots, Dome Lid, 1800s, 6 x 14 In.	8500
Valuables, Yellow Pine, Hinged Lid, Brass Handle, Mid 1800s, 6 x 13 In.	117
Vanity, Walnut, Rounded, Brass Swing Handle, Dome Lid, Satin Lined, 6 x 11 In.	180
Wagon, Wrought Iron Hardware, Slant Lid, Early 1800s, 15 x 36 In.	720
Wall, Curly Maple, Chip Carved Heart Crest, 8 x 12 ½ In.	720
Wall, Mahogany, Inlaid, Drawer, Early 1800s, 15 x 10 ½ In.	374
Wall, Mail, Wood, Red Paint, Shaped Back, Lollipop Hanger, 14 x 13 In.	3250
Wall, Pine, Scouring, Original Yellow Paint, Hanging, Late 1800s, 17 x 7 In.	600
Wall, Wood, Black, Drawer, Slant Lid, Shaped Hanger, Inscribed, 1760, 18 x 11 In.	3444
Wallpaper, Flowers, Blue, Round, Tacks, Lloyd Supple & Walton, Philadelphia, 2 In.	1968
Wallpaper, Flowers, Blue, White, Black, Newspaper Lined, Oval, Penn., 1826, 8 In.	615
Wallpaper, Leaves, Orange, Turquoise, Newspaper Lined, Oval, Penn., 1829, 4 x 9 In.	1046
Wallpaper, Poplar, Dome Lid, Mid 1800s, 3 ¼ x 7 In.	322
Wallpaper, Squares, Blue, Black, White, Newspaper Lined, Oval, Penn., 2 x 3 In.	400
Walnut, Carved, Ornate, Renaissance Revival, 1800s, 10 x 16 x 10 In.	384
Walnut, Open Dovetailed, Raised Sides, Drawer, Compartments, 4 x 7 x 5 In.	1680
Wood, 6-Board, Blue & Red Squiggles, Hinged Lid, Till, New England, 4 x 8 In.	30750
Wood, Carved, Hearts & Geometrics, Footed, Inscribed Lid, Anno, 1683, 4 x 7 In.	1046
Wood, Notched Sides, Elongated, Slide Lid, Heart Tab, 17th Century, 1 x 9 In.	2600
Wood, Poplar, Red & Yellow Paint, E. Fleming, Slide Lid, c.1850, 6 x 16 x 8 In.	625
Wood, Putty Paint, Blue, Dovetailed, Wire Hinged, Dome Lid, 7 x 18 In.	4920
Wood, Red Stain, House, Yard, Trees, Ferns, Shaped Panels, Lid, 7 x 14 In.	3321
Wood, Saffron, Lid, Lehnware, Painted, Salmon, Pomegranates, Strawberries, 5 In.	677
Work, Tunbridge Ware, Inlaid Bands, Green, Brown, 6¾ x 10¼ In. ....illus	255
Writing, Burl, Brass Inlay, Rounded Corners, 12 x 9 In.	250
Writing, Rosewood, Wedgwood Plaque, Brass Mount, Betjemann & Sons, 14 In.	375
Writing, Wood, Blue Painted Flowers, JBSDV, 1862, Drawer, Slant Lid, 10 x 9 In.	738

Bradley & Hubbard, Lamp, Wrought Iron, Pierced Brass Overlay Shade, Slag Glass, 73 In.
$875

New Orleans Auction Galleries

Bradley & Hubbard, Stationery Holder, Bronze, 2 Sections, Carry Handle, Openwork, 5 x 2 ½ In.
$50

Ruby Lane

BOY SCOUT collectibles include any material related to scouting, including patches, manuals, and uniforms. The Boy Scout movement in the United States started in 1910. The first Jamboree was held in 1937. Girl Scout items are listed under their own heading.

Bank, Figural, Scout, Knapsack, Cast Iron, Gold Wash, c.1910, 6 In.	95
Gum Wrapper, Some Boy Series, Goudey Gum Co., Wax Paper, 1933, 6 x 6 In.	253
Knife, Faux Wood, Spoon, Fork, Scissors, Corkscrew, Japan, 1950s	25
Patch, Mohegan Council B.S.A., Treasure Valley, Round, 1975, 3 In.	12
Pennant, Patrol 3, Troop 117, Pontiac Indian, Canvas, 2-Sided, 1940s, 40 x 40 In.	195
Ring, Sterling Silver, Cub Scout, Wolf Logo, Fleur-De-Lis, 1940s, Size 6	45
Tin, First Aid Kit, Official Scout Of America Kit, Green, Red, 1930s, 6 x 4 In.	42
Whistle, Metal, Acme, c.1915, 3¾ In. ....illus	75
Whistle, Nickel Plated Brass, Embossed, Cylindrical, c.1905, 3 In.	58

This is an edited listing of current prices. Visit **Kovels.com** to check thousands of prices from previous years and sign up for free information on trends, tips, reproductions, marks, and more.

Brass, Gong, Mallet, Wooden Handle, Concentric Lines, 1890-1910, 11 x 9 In. $145

Ruby Lane

Brass, Letter Box Receptacle, US Mail, Eagle & Shield POD Front, Cutler Mfg. Co., 21 x 36 In. $4,350

Showtime Auction Services

Bristol, Vase, Bird, Butterfly, Flowers, Branch, 11¾ In. $55

Ruby Lane

BRADLEY & HUBBARD is a name found on many metal objects. Walter Hubbard and his brother-in-law, Nathaniel Lyman Bradley, started making cast iron clocks, tables, frames, andirons, bookends, doorstops, lamps, chandeliers, sconces, and sewing birds in 1854 in Meriden, Connecticut. The company became Bradley & Hubbard Manufacturing Company in 1875. Charles Parker Company bought the firm in 1940. Bradley & Hubbard items may be found in other sections that include metal.

Lamp, Amber Slag Glass, Bronzed Metal, 18½ x 21 In.	2250
Lamp, Oil, Country Store, Hanging, Embossed, 28½ In.	312
Lamp, Oil, Cranberry Coin Spot Shade, 31 x 14 In.	625
Lamp, Panels, Reverse Painted, Metal Twisted Base, Dolphin Feet, 27 In.	948
Lamp, Slag Glass, Bronze, Leaves, 12½ In.	408
Lamp, Slag Glass, Palm Trees, Pineapple Finial, Art Deco, 30 In.	1947
Lamp, Slag Glass, Panels, Green, Yellow, Red, Bronze Base, 18 x 25 In.	2125
Lamp, Wrought Iron, Pierced Brass Overlay Shade, Slag Glass, 73 In. ....*illus*	875
Plaque, Courting Couple, Garden, Trees, Cast Iron, 15 x 9½ In.	75
Plaque, Man & Woman, Sitting Under Tree, Cast Iron, 9 x 7 In.	183
Plaque, Man, Reading, Woman Peeking, 9 x 7 In.	183
Plaque, Woman, Blue Dress, Carrying Tray, Iron, 19 x 12 In.	240
Plaque, Woman, Holding Dove, Dog, Mauve Dress, 18 x 12 In.	396
Stationery Holder, Bronze, 2 Sections, Carry Handle, Openwork, 5 x 2½ In. ....*illus*	50

BRASS has been used for decorative pieces and useful tablewares since ancient times. It is an alloy of copper, zinc, and other metals. Additional brass items may be found under Bell, Candlestick, Tool, or Trivet.

Bed Warmer, Pan, Rooster, Flowers, Pierced Lid, Iron Chamfered Handle, 1700s, 42 In.	375
Bed Warmer, Pierced & Engraved Lid, c.1800, 44½ In.	35
Bed Warmer, Pierced Pie Plate Warmer, Twisted Wooden Handle, 38 In.	146
Belt Buckle, Embossed Peach Blossoms, Coral, Lapis, Turquoise Cabochons, c.1905, 3 In.	205
Book Stand, Rectangular Back, Pierced Star & Geometrics, Adjustable Rest, 7 x 9 In.	246
Bowl, Hammered, Bands, Hayno Focken, Germany, 4 x 14¼ In.	396
Bowl, Hammered, Shallow, Hayno Focken, Germany, 1920s, 4 x 13 In.	671
Censer, Squat, Dome Lid, Lion Finial, Strap Handles, Champleve, Lotus Scroll, 10 In.	338
Cigarette Box, Repousse, Cossack, Monogrammed, Russia, 4 x 3⅛ In.	125
Cigarette Box, Royal Seal, Russia, 3¾ x 2⅞ In.	25
Figurine, Cat, Walking, Circles, 3 In.	25
Flag Holder, Eagle, Spread Wings, Tin Back, Hanging Loops, 1800s, 12 x 26 In.	540
Footman, Pierced, 1800s, 12¼ x 16 In.	150
Gong, Mallet, Wooden Handle, Concentric Lines, 1890-1910, 11 x 9 In. ....*illus*	145
Jardiniere, Hammered, Patina, Tapered, Thin Lip, 12½ x 10 In.	244
Jewelry Box, Gilt, Eglomise, Opaline, Stippled, Scroll, Ball Feet, c.1850, 7 x 10 In.	1750
Kettle, Round, Bail Handle, Copper Rim, Hudson Bay Company, 1800s, 10 x 19 In.	1230
Ladle, Wide Bowl, Rod Handle, Ring, Inset Initials & Hearts, c.1800, 17 In.	150
Lavabo, Putti, Flower Medallions, Leaf Spout, Cherub Mask, Wall Mount, 19 x 10 In.	354
Letter Box Receptacle, U.S. Mail, Eagle & Shield POD Front, Cutler Mfg. Co., 21 x 36 In. *illus*	4350
Lock, Railroad Switch, Heart Shape, Embossed, H.R.R., Marked, Patent 1878, 3 In.	175
Pedestal, Ebonized, Circular Top, 3 Carved Storks, Late 1800s, 38 x 15 In.	1062
Plaque, Pressed, Leaf Shape, Repousse, 17 In., Pair	138
Sconce, Wall, Baroque Style, Pierced, Tulip Shape Candleholders, 12 In., Pair	490
Scribe's Box, Quill Holder, Attached Inkwell, Calligraphy, Hinged, 1800s, 9 x 2 In.	425
Sculpture, Fifth Day, Selded, Max Finklestein, 1960, 33 x 38 In.	5000
Skimmer, Pierced Bowl, Openwork Heart Handle, Hook, 1800s, 21 x 6 In.	750
Spoon, Oval Bowl, Long Rod Handle, Flat Top, Ring Finial, 1800s, 35 In.	600
Tasting Ladle, Tapered, Beveled Wrought Iron Handle & Hook, 1800s, 9 In.	2360
Teakettle, Bail Handle, Gooseneck Spout, Dome Lid, Mushroom Finial, 1800s, 10 In.	213
Tieback, Enamel, Sacred To Friendship, Multicolor, 6 Piece	197
Tray, Cranes, Acid Etched, Carence Crafters, 5 x 9 In.	366
Tray, Metal Inlay, Syria, 21 x 17¾ In.	1250

Vase, Enamel, Gilt, Court Scene, Lion Mask Handles, Blue Interior, 9 In., Pair	937
Vase, Enamel, Molded, Geometric Design, Purple, Pink, Gold, c.1930, 12 x 9 In.	17500
Vase, Eye, Vines, Carl Deffner, c.1950, 13 ¼ x 4 ¼ In.	1772

BRASTOFF, *see Sascha Brastoff category.*

BREAD PLATE, *see various silver categories, porcelain factories, and pressed glass patterns.*

BRIDE'S BOWLS OR BASKETS were usually one-of-a-kind novelties made in American and European glass factories. They were especially popular about 1880 when the decorated basket was often given as a wedding gift. Cut glass baskets were popular after 1890. All bride's bowls lost favor about 1905. Bride's bowls and baskets may also be found in other glass sections. Check the index at the back of the book.

Cased Glass, Dark Green To Mint, Ruffled, Round Foot, 3 x 8 In.	24
Cased Glass, Pink, White, Tufts, Crimped, Blue & White Flowers, 9 x 10 In.	265
Cranberry Glass, Swirled, Crimped Rim, Metal Frame, 1800s, 4 x 9 In.	410
Glass, Aqua Opalescent, Raised Enamel Flowers, Ruffled Rim, 1800s, 4 x 12 In.	97
Glass, Fuchsia To Pink, Ruffled Crimped Edge, Flower Sprays, 12 x 12 In.	118
Glass, Orange, Yellow Enamel Flowers, Gilt, Crimped Rim, 1800s, 4 x 10 In.	225
Glass, Red Iridescent, Gilt Vines, Lobed, Ruffled Rim, Silver Plated Frame, c.1905	450
Milk Glass, Blue, Beehive, Ball Shape, Ruffled Rim, Upright Handle, c.1910, 10 In.	50
Spangled Glass, Cranberry, White, Silver Flecks, Ruffled Rim, c.1880, 3 x 10 In.	75

BRISTOL glass was made in Bristol, England, after the 1700s. The Bristol glass most often seen today is a Victorian, lightweight opaque glass that is often blue. Some of the glass was decorated with enamels.

Compote, Blue, Pink & Gold, Bluebird, Flowers, Cylinder Base, 1800s, 10 In.	110
Lamp, Oil, Blue, Flowers, Bird, Butterfly, Gilt, Conical, Stepped Foot, c.1900, 20 In.	395
Perfume Bottle, Blue, Bird, Flowers, Gilt, Footed, Crimped Stopper, 1800s, 11 In.	95
Vase, Bird, Butterfly, Flowers, Branch, 11 ¾ In. ....*illus*	55
Vase, Birds, Perched On Cherry Branch, Silver Moon, Bamboo Tree, Shaded Tan, 12 In., Pair .	593
Vase, Gilt, Blue, Cartouche, Woman, Child, Flute, 10 x 3 ½ In., Pair	61
Vase, Greek Key, Frosted Glass, 19th Century, 12 In. ....*illus*	30
Vase, Peach, Flowers, Bird, Gilt, Gourd, Out-Folding Rim, c.1890, 12 In.	165
Vase, Pink Satin Glass, Ruffled Mouth, Yellow Flowers, 12 In., Pair.	70
Vase, Ships, Flowers, Leaves, Ruffled Mouth, Light Green, c.1890, 10 ½ x 5 In.	36

BRITANNIA, *see Pewter category.*

BRONZE is an alloy of copper, tin, and other metals. It is used to make figurines, lamps, and other decorative objects. Bronze lamps are listed in the Lamp category. Pieces listed here date from the eighteenth, nineteenth, and twentieth centuries.

Ashtray, Seahorse Trio, Incised Lines, Round, Flat Edge, E.T. Hurley, 4 In.	649
Bas Relief, Flower With Branches, 8 x 6 ⅝ In.	1180
Bonbon, Pheasants, Rabbits, Foxes, Egg & Dart Scalloped Dishes, 19 x 10 In., Pair	3272
Buddha, Standing, Ayutthaya Style, Hands Raised, Thailand, 1800s, 32 x 40 In.	2250
Bust, Carpeaux, Jean-Baptiste, Genie De Las Danse, 17 ½ In.	2750
Bust, Dante Alighieri, Death Mask, Italy, c.1900, 15 x 18 x 8 ½ In.	625
Bust, Diana, Original Patina, c.1900, 27 x 15 x 8 In.	1500
Bust, Duke Of Wellington, Patina, Turned & Fluted Pedestal, c.1835, 12 x 4 In.	875
Bust, Homer, Original Patina, Continental, Early 1900s, 10 ¼ x 4 x 4 ½ In.	500
Bust, Pseudo Seneca, Villa Of The Papyri, Patina, Plinth Base, 1900s, 11 In.	875
Bust, Roux, Constant, The Gladiator, 22 In.	2242
Bust, Shakespeare, Wide High Collar, Flared Foot Pedestal, 11 In.	35
Cassoulet, Figural, Cherub Heads, 14 ½ In., Pair	875
Censer, Bulbous, Bat Handles, Openwork Lid, Tripod, Monkey Feet, 14 x 11 In.	2963
Censer, Globular, Squat, Pointed Feet, Pierced Dome Lid, 8 Petals, 3 In.	246

Bristol, Vase, Greek Key, Frosted Glass, 19th Century, 12 In.
$30

Leland Little Auctions

Bronze, Gong, Temple, Carved Rosewood, Dragons, Stand, Chinese, c.1890, 69 x 32 In.
$2,415

Cottone Auctions

Bronze, Jardiniere, Bird & Bamboo Design, Lobed, Japan, 1868-1912, 13 x 14 In.
$437

New Orleans Auction Galleries

BRONZE

Bronze, Plaque, World War I, Liberation, Figures, Classical Style, France, 12 In.
$225

Ruby Lane

Bronze, Sculpture, DeVries, A., Tres Jolie, Woman, Handstand, Marble Base, 32 In.
$1,046

Skinner, Inc.

Bronze, Sculpture, Bergman, Man & Camel, Cold Paint, Geschutzt, 2½ x 2½ In.
$375

Neal Auctions

Censer, Lacquer, Drum Shape, Pierced Handles, Splay Feet, Lid, Lion Finial, c.1885, 7 In.	800
Censer, Raised Cranes, Wind, Clouds, 3-Footed, 9½ In.	625
Censer, Round, 3 Figural Legs, Upswept Handles, Openwork Lid, Foo Dog, c.1910, 12 In.	415
Censer, Slanted Sides, Bracket Feet, Molded Gilt Flowers, Black Panel, 3 x 5 In.	5535
Censer, Squat, 3 Bulbous Legs, Ruyi, Gilt Splashes, Dome Wood Lid, 7 In.	3851
Centerpiece, Beaded Rim, Tapered Base, Acorn Finials, 14½ x 13½ In.	70
Centerpiece, Charles X, Dore, Reticulated Basket, Oval, Lion Paw Feet, 7 x 12 In.	1600
Centerpiece, French Renaissance, Dore, Pierced, Griffins, 6 Candle Arms, 22 x 20 In.	750
Centerpiece, Gilt, Putti With Wings, Laurel Swags, France, 1900s, 25 x 11 In., Pair	7187
Charger, Butterfly, Bird, Flower, Leaves, 17¾ In.	240
Column, Monumental Grand Tour, Cannon Shaft, Mars Top, Mid 1800s, 27 In.	2074
Cross, Micro Mosaic Panel, Dove, Flowers, Vatican, 14 x 8 In.	780
Dish, Chased Fish, Leaves, Tinned, Medallion, Undulating Rim, c.1900, 2 x 8 In.	123
Ewer, Bulbous, Reeded, Ear Handle, Mask, Turned Socle, 1800s, 17 In., Pair	492
Ewer, Cherub Sitting On Handle, 33½ In.	250
Garniture Set, Gilt, Marble, Lyre Clock, Sun, Medusa, 3-Light Candelabrum, c.1900, 3 Piece .	937
Garniture, 2-Light Candelabrum, Clock, Marble, 3 Piece	750
Gong, Temple, Carved Rosewood, Dragons, Stand, Chinese, c.1890, 69 x 32 In. ....*illus*	2415
Humidor, Neoclassical Style, Gilt Urns & Swags, Patinated, Tiffany, 2 x 5 In.	610
Incense Burner, Foo Dog Lid, Decoration, 14 In.	312
Jar, Flowering Plants, Relief, Swollen Top, Tapered, 5 Figural Feet, c.1900, 14 In.	119
Jardiniere, Bird & Bamboo Design, Lobed, Japan, 1868-1912, 13 x 14 In. ....*illus*	437
Jardiniere, Gilt, Figures, At Well, Drinking, Jug, France, 20½ In.	1500
Jardiniere, Laurel Swags, Circular, Paw Footed Bases, 1900s, 31 x 18 In., Pair	1500
Mortar & Pestle, Raised Designs, 5½ In., 2 Piece	188
Plaque, Art Deco, Security, Armor, Silvered, 14 x 12½ In.	2074
Plaque, World War I, Liberation, Figures, Classical Style, France, 12 In. ....*illus*	225
Pocket Watch Holder, Coiled Snake, Art Nouveau, 5½ x 4 In.	1250
Pot, Bulbous, Ring Handles At Mouth, Incised Bands, Flowers, India, 14 In.	308
Scepter, Ruyi, Dragons, Clouds, Relief, Treasures Handle, Banding, 1900s, 13 In.	554
Scroll Holder, Foo Dogs, Silvered, 2 x 4 In., Pair	188
Scroll Weight, Gilt, Reclining Dog, Crossed Paws, Head Raised, 3 In.	1304
Sculpture, Abduction, Ape, Nude Woman In Arm, Gilt, Base, c.1930, 15 In.	13819
Sculpture, Acrobats, 2 Women, Nude, Trapeze & Stand, U.S.A., 1900s, 25½ In.	600
Sculpture, After The Bath, Nude Woman, Towel, Ivory, Marble Base, c.1900, 11 In.	861
Sculpture, Alexander The Great, Horse, Italy, c.1900, 19 x 19 x 11 In.	1000
Sculpture, Amalthea & Jupiter's Goat, 16½ In.	1375
Sculpture, Arabian Horse, Rider, Leg Curled Up, Stepped Base, c.1800, 29 In.	1476
Sculpture, Arabian Rug Dealer, Cold Paint, Brown, Tan, Marked, 7 x 7 In.	345
Sculpture, Ariadne, Nude, Drape, Seated On Panther, Base, c.1800, 30½ In.	5535
Sculpture, Art Deco, Archer, Boy, Kneeling, Bow, Greek, Stone Base, c.1930, 15 x 15 In.	500
Sculpture, Ballerina, Green Tutu, Arm Raised, Stepped Marble Base, 1980, 24 In.	687
Sculpture, Barbedienne, Robed Man, Children, c.1875, 36 In.	6250
Sculpture, Barbedienne, Woman, Children, Nursing, Charite, France, 31½ In.	2750
Sculpture, Bear, Walking, Open Mouth, Cold Paint, Austria, c.1890, 8 In.	1000
Sculpture, Becquerel, Andre-Vincent, Bird, Wheat Sheaf, 9½ x 12 In.	750
Sculpture, Beeler, Joe, Great Plains Buffalo, 15 x 17½ In.	1875
Sculpture, Bergman, Franz, Girl, Goats, Cold Paint, Austria, Early 1900s, 4 In.	554
Sculpture, Bergman, Franz, Man Selling Oranges, Cold Paint, 11 In.	2000
Sculpture, Bergman, Franz, Man Selling Slave, Woman, Cold Paint, 7 x 9 In.	1250
Sculpture, Bergman, Franz, The Rug Seller, Cold Paint, 1875, 7 In.	625
Sculpture, Bergman, Man & Camel, Cold Paint, Geschutzt, 2½ x 2½ In. ....*illus*	375
Sculpture, Bird Of Prey, Songbirds, 15½ In.	2500
Sculpture, Bodhisattva, Seated On Foo Dog, Lotus Throne, c.1885, 9 x 6 In.	2460
Sculpture, Boisseau E., Man, Crouching Woman, Incised, France, 28 In.	2500
Sculpture, Boudin, Eleanor, Buffalo, 1929, 8½ x 12 In.	350
Sculpture, Bouret, Eutrope, Boy Singing, Playing Flute, 18 In.	813
Sculpture, Braslow, Paul, Lilith, Abstract Woman, Multicolor, 40 x 14 In.	480

Sculpture, Buddha, Maitreya, Standing, Arched Body, Lotus Base, 1800s, 11 In.	248
Sculpture, Buddha, Seated, Pierced Throne, Tibet, Early 1900s, 15 In.	1080
Sculpture, Buddha, Seated, Smile Of Compassion, Lotus, Gilt, Cloisonne, 13 In.	236
Sculpture, Buddha, Standing, Hand Raised, Mudra, Robe, Wood Base, 1800s, 25 In.	1185
Sculpture, Bust, Zeus, Polished, France, Late 1800s, 19 x 11 In.	875
Sculpture, Cambos, Jean Jules, Fauneuse, Staff, 32 x 11 In.	900
Sculpture, Carp, Head Up, Gilded Mouth Open, Japan, 5 ½ In., Pair	175
Sculpture, Cavanaugh, John, The Traveler, 14 ¾ In.	1560
Sculpture, Cerracchio, Enrico, Well-Dressed Man, Cigar, Cane, 22 ½ x 7 In.	1440
Sculpture, Dali, S., Christ Of St. John Of The Cross, 14 x 4 ½ In.	2360
Sculpture, Daltchev, Lubomir, Job, On Knees, Supplicant, 1975, 15 x 7 ½ In.	1180
Sculpture, Dancer, On Toes, Original Patina, 1900s, 27 x 7 x 20 In.	812
Sculpture, Dancing Girl, Priestess, Grapes, Leg Bent, Marble Base, c.1925, 22 In.	5159
Sculpture, Dancing Woman, Seminude, On 1 Foot, Silvered, Onyx Base, c.1925, 16 In.	4053
Sculpture, DeVries, A., Tres Jolie, Woman, Handstand, Marble Base, 32 In. ....illus	1046
Sculpture, Diana, Goddess, Seminude, Seated, Bow, Marble Base, c.1910, 28 In.	3132
Sculpture, Dog Playing With Ball, Gilt, Oval Marble Base, 7 ½ In.	240
Sculpture, Dog, Pointer, On The Scent, France, Early 1900s, 11 x 24 x 7 In.	1750
Sculpture, Dog, Whippet, Seated, Paws Crossed, Ebonized Base, 1900s, 16 x 10 In.	687
Sculpture, Donkey, Marked Geschutzt, c.1900, 8 ½ x 11 ½ In.	1440
Sculpture, Dragon King, Holding Tablet, Robe, Fish Scale Design, Gilt, 7 ½ In.	185
Sculpture, Duchoiselle, Allegory Of Fishing, Silvered, Signed, 12 In.	1625
Sculpture, Dumiage, Henry, Classical Women, Dancing, Gilt, 1800s, 14 x 7 In.	300
Sculpture, Eagle & Dragon, Raptor, Perched On Rocks, Fierce Look, c.1900, 23 In.	533
Sculpture, Eagle Slayer, Man, Arm Raised, Seminude, Drape, Plinth, 1861, 24 In.	2750
Sculpture, Eagle, Standing On One Leg, Wood Base, 7 ¾ x 5 In.	106
Sculpture, Egyptian Dancer, Marble Base, Signed, Claire J. Roberte Colinet, 16 In.	1800
Sculpture, Elder, Seated On Water Buffalo, Loose Robes, 1800s, 13 x 14 In.	1185
Sculpture, Elephant, Walking, Trunk Raised, Cast, Signed, c.1910, 17 x 15 In.	660
Sculpture, Eros, Bow, Torch, Continental, c.1900, 17 ½ x 12 ½ In.	1534
Sculpture, Erte, La Danseuse, Cold Paint, c.1985, 13 In.	1875
Sculpture, Erte, Rue De Lapaix, Cold Paint, c.1987, 14 In.	1875
Sculpture, Fairley, Paul, Cello Player, Mounted, Stone Base, Artcast, 17 x 13 In...............illus	5264
Sculpture, Flautist & Piper, Original Patina, France, 1900s, 11 ½ x 4 x 7 In., Pair	187
Sculpture, Franklin, Gilbert, Cone Sections, Hemisphere, Abstract, c.1975, 30 In.	2460
Sculpture, Gautier, Jacques Louis, Mephistopheles, 30 In.	2000
Sculpture, Girl, Nude, Tambourine, Posed On 1 Foot, Onyx Base, c.1925, 9 In.	4974
Sculpture, Girl, Seated, 4-Legged Chair, Dress, Hair Bow, 15 In.	208
Sculpture, Graham, R., MOCA Torso, Woman, Textured Cylinder Base, 11 x 5 In.	2700
Sculpture, Graziosi, Giuseppe, Cow, 14 In.	5312
Sculpture, Greek Warrior, Continental, 1900s, 14 x 16 x 5 ½ In.	625
Sculpture, Hafner, Charles, Peter Pan, Round Base, 59 x 24 ½ In.	3000
Sculpture, Hermes The Messenger, Marble Base, c.1920, 26 In.	600
Sculpture, Hiolin, Louis Auguste, Running Man, Pointing, Dog, 22 In.	3000
Sculpture, Horse, Canter, White, 14 In.	344
Sculpture, Horse, Colt, Stopping Suddenly, 12 In.	250
Sculpture, Horse, Prancing, White Mane, Forelocks, 14 In.	313
Sculpture, Horse, Side-Glancing, Cheval Libre, Reeded Base, Signed, c.1910, 16 x 19 In........illus	2500
Sculpture, Horse, Walking, Biting Bridle, Saddle, 12 ½ In.	150
Sculpture, Iguana, Gecko, Orchids, Stone Base, 11 x 4 ½ In.	2242
Sculpture, Jackson, Harry, Sacajawea III, Study For A Monument, 38 ½ In.	11250
Sculpture, Jambhala, Riding Dragon, Lotus Throne, Mongoose, Gilt, 1900s, 8 In.	1046
Sculpture, Jenkins, Frank Lynn, Huntress, Bow & Arrow, Brown, 1921, 12 In.	1875
Sculpture, Kauba, Carl, Sioux Chief, Headdress, Weapon, 18 ½ In.	2250
Sculpture, Kieff, Antonio, Concerto, Spherical, Marble Base, 1976, 14 In.	5000
Sculpture, Kitten Orchestra, Cold Paint, Austria, 4 In.	1187
Sculpture, Kubera, God Of Wealth, Gilt, Sino Tibetan, 11 ¼ In.	1200
Sculpture, Kurukulla, 6 Heads, 4 Arms, Dancing Pose, Lotus Stand, c.1800, 5 In.	2337

Bronze, Sculpture, Fairley, Paul, Cello Player, Mounted, Stone Base, Artcast, 17 x 13 In.
$5,264

James D. Julia Auctioneers

Bronze, Sculpture, Horse, Side-Glancing, Cheval Libre, Reeded Base, Signed, c.1910, 16 x 19 In.
$2,500

New Orleans Auction Galleries

Bronze, Sculpture, Little Girl In Basket, Turtle, Nephrite Base, Gilt, France, 3 x 4 ½ In.
$560

Ruby Lane

BRONZE

Bronze, Sculpture, MacDonald, Richard, Showtime II, Performer, Marble Base, 20 In.
$5,700

Garth's Auctioneers & Appraisers

Bronze, Sculpture, Mene, Pierre Jules, Wild Horse On Rocks, Signed, 24 x 18 In.
$570

Garth's Auctioneers & Appraisers

Bronze, Sculpture, Morise, Marie, Napoleon On Horseback, Green Marble Base, 24 x 26 In.
$3,328

James D. Julia Auctioneers

Sculpture, La Nuit, Woman With Wings, Swirling Scarf, Marble Base, c.1900, 37 In.	7001
Sculpture, Larche, Raoul Francois, Woman, Flowing Drapery, 13 x 7 In.	8500
Sculpture, Lavergne, Adolphe, Boy, Lantern, 20 ½ In.	737
Sculpture, Lion & Vulture, Oval Wood Base, Signed, Italy, 1921, 12 x 21 In.	523
Sculpture, Lion, Lionne Marchant, France, 1900s, 10 x 28 In.	1500
Sculpture, Little Girl In Basket, Turtle, Nephrite Base, Gilt, France, 3 x 4 ½ In. ...*illus*	560
Sculpture, Lizard, K., Shepherd Boy, Original Patina, Signed, 13 x 18 x 11 In.	1140
Sculpture, MacDonald, Richard, Showtime II, Performer, Marble Base, 20 In. ...*illus*	5700
Sculpture, Mader, Walter, Mother & Pup, Retrievers, 10 x 16 In.	2540
Sculpture, Mars, Black Marble Base, 1900s, 11 x 6 ½ x 4 In.	1000
Sculpture, Matto, Dancers, 3 Maidens, Garland, Gilt, Marble Base, c.1925, 18 In.	2211
Sculpture, Mene, Pierre Jules, Wild Horse On Rocks, Signed, 24 x 18 In. ...*illus*	570
Sculpture, Mestovic, Ivan, Mother With Child, Signed, 27 x 6 ½ In.	1600
Sculpture, Money Tree, 3 Stacked Figures, Holding Branches, Wood Stand, 8 In.	923
Sculpture, Morise, Marie, Napoleon On Horseback, Green Marble Base, 24 x 26 In. ...*illus*	3328
Sculpture, Narcissus, Chiurazzi Napoli, Italy, Late 1800s, 24 x 12 x 10 In.	812
Sculpture, Panther, Prowling, Wooden Base, Art Deco, Marked, c.1925, 20 In.	1842
Sculpture, Parakeet, Hoop Swing, Chain Suspension, Geschutzt Mark, 11 In.	2800
Sculpture, Puzzle, Torero, Muguel Berrocal, Italy, 1970s, 11 x 8 In.	2500
Sculpture, Radicevich, Lilana, Tumbling Nude, Backbend, Wood Base, 10 x 12 In.	354
Sculpture, Ram, Kudu, Loet Vanderveen, Signed, Holland, 1900s, 11 x 14 x 9 In.	687
Sculpture, Ram, Lying Down, Santi, Signed, Continental, 1980, 14 x 18 x 9 In.	875
Sculpture, Ready To Fly, Nude Girl, On Toes, Arms Spread, Geometric Base, 9 x 5 In.	236
Sculpture, Rearing Horse, Original Patina, Early 1900s, 18 x 20 x 8 In.	1000
Sculpture, Reclining Woman, Naturalistic Base, 5 x 17 In.	225
Sculpture, Red Squirrel, Nose To Ground, Raised Tail, 14 In.	300
Sculpture, Reno, Jim, On The War Path, 28 In.	1875
Sculpture, Roman Gladiator, Sword, Shield, France, c.1870, 35 x 15 In.	2000
Sculpture, Rooster, Tail Up, Parcel Gilt, Paint, Wood Base, c.1860, 5 x 4 In.	1625
Sculpture, Ruffier, Noel, The Daydreamer, Woman, Lute, 31 x 9 ½ In.	1000
Sculpture, Running Demon, Full Flight, Tablet, Dragon Skin, Japan, 13 In.	2000
Sculpture, Samurai, Bow & Arrow, Signed, 10 x 8 In.	1830
Sculpture, Satyress, Holding Grapes, Putti, Incised, Base, c.1800, 14 In.	400
Sculpture, Shadakshari Lokeshvara, Nepal, 1900s, 14 In.	562
Sculpture, Sighieri, Enzo, Woman, Standing, Bird Aloft, Marble Base, 12 x 3 In.	579
Sculpture, Sweet Dreams Little Guy, Seated Boy, 13 x 8 In.	165
Sculpture, Sykes, Charles, Spirit Of Ecstasy, Marble, 1900s, 23 In.	1482
Sculpture, Taureau Et Ours, France, 1900s, 9 ½ x 16 x 7 ½ In.	937
Sculpture, Tibetan God, Gilded, Late 1800s, 7 ½ x 6 ½ In.	2645
Sculpture, Tiger, Mouth Open, Extended Tail, Belly Signed, Japan, c.1890, 19 In. ...*illus*	2723
Sculpture, Turtle Family, Mother & 6 Crawling Baby Turtles, Japan, 12 x 9 In.	1192
Sculpture, Ullmann, Theodore, Dancer, Ivory, 1925, 10 In.	2625
Sculpture, Vaishravana, Chief King, Standing On Rocks, Chinese, 1700s, 10 In.	360
Sculpture, Vienna, Bear Holding Umbrella, Jeweled Lantern, Gilt, c.1900, 6 In. ...*illus*	281
Sculpture, Walsh, Edward, Reclining Woman, Marble Base, 7 x 18 In.	246
Sculpture, Warrior Woman, On Horse, Helmet & Cape, Cold Paint, 1984, 17 In.	2250
Sculpture, Warrior, Holding Spear, Shield, Feathers, Shaped Base, Signed, 44 in. ...*illus*	2400
Sculpture, Water Buffalo, Reclining, Boy With Flute, Seated On Back, c.1910, 15 In.	660
Sculpture, Wisdom, Woman & Eagle, Cold Paint, After Erte, 1988, 16 In.	1375
Sculpture, Woman, Crouching, Seminude, Drape, Marble Base, c.1935, 10 In.	1107
Sculpture, Woman, Harp, Standing, Draped Gown, Signed, c.1900, 17 In.	360
Sculpture, Woman, Holding Basket Of Roses, Draped Gown, Round Base, 19 In.	130
Sculpture, Woman, Nude, Balancing Spheres, Standing On 1 Leg, Gilt, c.1925, 22 In.	4422
Sculpture, Woman, Nude, Ivory Playing Pipes, Marble Base, 1898, 15 In.	2118
Sculpture, Woman, Nude, Le Chagrin, A. Bartholome, France, c.1893, 16 x 5 In.	937
Sculpture, Woman, Nude, Long Hair, Leaning Against Rock, Base, c.1900, 33 In.	1046
Sculpture, Woman, Standing, Draped In Cloak, Square Base, France, 1900s, 10 In.	450
Sculpture, Woman, Walking Dogs, Plum Dress, Hounds, 19 x 25 In.	472

Seal, Dragon, Coiled Tail, Rectangular Base, 3 x 3 In.	365
Seal, Gilt, Dragon, Clutching Pearl, Chinese, 7 x 7 In.	488
Seal, Venus De Milo, c.1875, 3 1/4 In.	63
Shrine, Jina, Seated, Deities, Carved, Tiers, Metal Inlay, Swastika, India, 8 In.	431
Tazza, Classical Woman, Nude, Grape Leaves, Orchid, 4-Footed, 17 x 12 In.	531
Tazza, Gilt & Silvered, Dolphins & Putti, France, Late 1800s, 13 x 13 In.	1500
Tray, Intertwining Vines, Ruffles, Handle, 6 x 9 In.	37
Tray, Lion & Lioness, Bas Relief, Austria, 4 x 12 In.	150
Tray, Parcel Gilt, Demon, Japan, 6 3/4 x 9 In.	250
Umbrella Stand, Birds & Flowers, Japan, Late 1800s, 23 x 9 In.	687
Urn, Angel Decor, 2 Handles, 1900s, 24 1/2 x 25 x 13 1/2 In.	343
Urn, Classical Masks, Red Variegated Marble, Paw Feet, Late 1800s, 28 In.	1586
Urn, Empire, Gilt, Brown Paint, Square Foot, 9 In., Pair	500
Urn, Flower Swags, Beaded, Ram's-Head Handles, Lid, Marble, c.1915, 19 In., Pair	937
Urn, Green Marble, Tendril Handles, c.1900, 13 In., Pair	598
Urn, Lid, Neoclassical, Gilt, Marble, Satyr Masks, Serpent Handle, 22 x 11 In.	2500
Urn, Masks, Swags, Lion's Head, Cupid Handles, Lid, Finial, Gilt, Marble, 32 In.	937
Urn, Renaissance, Lion Handles, Pierced, Torches, 30 x 14 In.	4000
Vase, Amphora, Figural Sphinx Supports, Ring Handles, Paw Feet, 26 In., Pair	1875
Vase, Applied Grape Clusters, Leaves, Japan, 9 1/2 In.	94
Vase, Barbedienne, F., Grand Tour, Warwick, Inscribed, Fondeur, Marble Base, 7 In.	704
Vase, Flowers, Green, Blue, Yellow, Trumpet, Double Handle, Chinese, 12 In.	468
Vase, Gilt, Nautilus Shell, Cherub, Seminude Support, France, 1800s, 14 x 9 In. *illus*	2070
Vase, Kann, Leon, Daffodils, Ruffled Rim, c.1910, 12 In., Pair	1562
Vase, Lid, Lozenge Shape, Taotie Mask Band, Dragons, Chinese, 11 In., Pair *illus*	492
Vase, Lotus Blossom, Lizard, 9 3/4 In., Pair	400
Vase, Masks, Symbols, Gourd Shape, Pierced Dragon Handles, Lotus Foot, 8 x 6 In.	1990
Vase, Mixed Metal, Relief Flowers, Genie Bottle, Petal Rim, Japan, c.1910, 13 In.	554
Vase, Scholar, Bird, Mythological Creature, Clouds, 15 x 8 In.	472
Vase, Wide Lip, Cylindrical Body, Ikebana Usubata, Japan, 1700s, 11 1/2 In.	600
Water Dropper, Man, Reclining, Reading Book, Patina, 5 x 6 1/2 In.	135

BROWNIES were first drawn in 1883 by Palmer Cox. They are characterized by large round eyes, downturned mouths, and skinny legs. Toys, books, dinnerware, and other objects were made with the Brownies as part of the design.

Andiron, Black, Seated On Boot Jack Bench End, 8 x 19 1/2 In., Pair	369
Banner, Strike Up The Band, R. John Wright, 17 x 13 In.	240
Dish, The Gym, Gymnastics, Green Scroll Loop Handle, c.1906, 6 In. Diam.	50
Toy, Stand-Up Figure, Lithograph & Wood, Paint, Stepped Base, 1800s, 8 In.	80
Utensil Set, Fork, Spoon, Knife, Metal, Embossed Wavy Handles, Child's, c.1900	75

BRUSH-MCCOY, *see Brush category and related pieces in McCoy category.*

BRUSH POTTERY was started in 1925. George Brush first worked in 1901 in Zanesville, Ohio. He started his own pottery in 1907, but it burned to the ground soon after. In 1909 he became manager of the J.W. McCoy Pottery. In 1911, Brush and J.W. McCoy formed the Brush-McCoy Pottery Co. After a series of name changes, the company became The Brush Pottery in 1925. It closed in 1982. Old Brush was marked with impressed letters or a palette-shaped mark. Reproduction pieces are being made. They are marked in raised letters or with a raised mark. Collectors favor the figural cookie jars made by this company. Because there was a company named Brush-McCoy, there is great confusion between Brush and Nelson McCoy pieces. Most collectors today refer to Brush pottery as Brush-McCoy. See McCoy category for more information.

Cookie Jar, Donkey With Cart, Tan & Orange Glaze, Glossy, 1960s, 8 x 7 In.	250
Jardiniere, Calla Lily, Mauve, Green, High Gloss Glaze, Tapered, c.1930, 8 x 9 In.	180
Jardiniere, McCoy Green Matte, Greek Key, White Enamel, 8 1/2 x 10 In.	81
Vase, Jeweled, Shapes, Beaded, Spherical, Trumpet Neck, c.1920, 8 1/2 In.	175
Vase, Zuni, Indian Symbols, Swastikas, 4 In.	150

Bronze, Sculpture, Tiger, Mouth Open, Extended Tail, Belly Signed, Japan, c.1890, 19 In.
$2,723

James D. Julia Auctioneers

Bronze, Sculpture, Vienna, Bear Holding Umbrella, Jeweled Lantern, Gilt, c.1900, 6 In.
$281

New Orleans Auction Galleries

Bronze, Sculpture, Warrior, Holding Spear, Shield, Feathers, Shaped Base, Signed, 44 in.
$2,400

Cowan's Auctions

Bronze, Vase, Gilt, Nautilus Shell, Cherub, Seminude Support, France, 1800s, 14 x 9 In.
$2,070

Cottone Auctions

Bronze, Vase, Lid, Lozenge Shape, Taotie Mask Band, Dragons, Chinese, 11 In., Pair
$492

Skinner, Inc.

Buck Rogers, Toy, Spaceship, Windup, Multicolor, Louis Marx & Co., 1927, 12 In.
$1,095

Ruby Lane

BUCK ROGERS was the first American science fiction comic strip. It started in 1929 and continued until 1967. Buck has also appeared in comic books, movies, and, in the 1980s, a television series. Any memorabilia connected with the character Buck Rogers is collectible.

Book, Whitman No. 1409, The Fiend Of Space, Hardcover, P. Nowlan, 1940	765
Club Membership Kit, Card, Premium List, Button, Buck Portrait, c.1937	696
Drawing, Buck, 25th Century, Pencil, Calkins, Signed, c.1953, 11 x 15 In.	209
Lunch Box, Metal, Embossed, Action Scenes, Plastic Thermos, Aladdin, 1979, 7 In.	115
Ring, Repeller Ray, Supreme Inner Circle, Buck In Rocket, Goldtone, 1936	1139
Ring, Sylvania TV, Brass, Plastic Glowing Light Bulb, Adjustable, c.1953	288
Toy, Laboratory, Canisters, Chemicals, Glass Tubes, Box, 1937, 8 x 12 In.	481
Toy, Ray Gun, Sonic, Plastic, Black, Red, Flashlight, Buzzer, Box, 1952, 6 x 9 In.	323
Toy, Rocket, Police Patrol, Tail Fin, Figure, Gun, Tin Lithograph, Marx, 12 In.	793
Toy, Rocket Ship, Tin Lithograph, Sounds, Key Wind, Box, 1934, 12 In.	1225
Toy, Spaceship, Windup, Multicolor, Louis Marx & Co., 1927, 12 In. ....*illus*	1095
Toy, Telescope, Hard Plastic, Gear Focus, 25-Mile View, Box, 1953, 9 In.	196

BUFFALO POTTERY was made in Buffalo, New York, after 1902. The company was established by the Larkin Company, famous manufacturers of soap. The wares are marked with a picture of a buffalo and the date of manufacture. Deldare ware is the most famous pottery made at the factory. It has either a khaki-colored or green background with hand-painted transfer designs.

Basin, Chrysanthemum, Green & Ivory, c.1910, 17 In.	127
Bowl, Vegetable, Willow, Cobalt Blue & White, Dome Lid, 1911, 6 x 9 In.	165
Dish, Serving, Vienna, Blue & White, Lid, Handles, c.1910, 8 x 11 In.	110
Gravy Boat, Blue & White, Gilt, Underplate, 8 In.	149
Pitcher, Countryside, Farmer's Wife, 1908, 6 In.	140
Pitcher, Milk, Roosevelt Bears, 1907, 8 In.	181
Plate, Chesapeake & Ohio Railroad, Geo. Washington, 1732 Bi-Centennial 1932, 11 In.....*illus*	936
Plate, Thunderbird, Fred Harvey, Marked, Colorido Ware, 1930, 9¾ In.....*illus*	1989
Platter, Blue & White, Transfer, c.1910, 12 In.	175
Tureen, Forget-Me-Nots, Dome Lid, Handles, 1900s	110

BUFFALO POTTERY DELDARE

Bowl, Nut, Squirrels, Acorns, Flowers, Squat, 1911, 4 x 8 In.	1805
Bowl, Ye Village Tavern, Men At Table, Emerald, c.1910, 4 x 9 In.	200
Calendar Plate, Vignettes, Children, Signed, W. Foster, 1910, 9 In.	201
Chamber Pot, Cairo Pattern, Pink, Yellow Roses, Gilt, c.1915, 9 x 10 In.	60
Charger, An Evening At Ye Lion Inn, 1908, 13¾ In. ....*illus*	375
Charger, The Landing, Ducks, Stream, Gold, Emerald, 1911, 12 In.	236
Drink Set, Pitcher, Cups, Fallowfield Hunt, c.1909, 7 Piece	446
Jardiniere, Ye Lion Inn, Signed, W. Foster, 9⅛ In. ....*illus*	1053
Mug, Fallowfield Hunt, Loop Handle, Green, c.1905, 5 x 4 In.	100
Pitcher, African Violets, Gilt, Ruffled Rim, C-Handle, c.1905, 11 x 9 In.	85
Pitcher, Pilgrims, Scroll Handle, Wavy Spout, Emerald, c.1908, 9 In.	62
Plate, Flower-Like Geometric Medallion, Emerald, Willow, 8⅜ In. ....*illus*	222
Plate, Teddy Roosevelt Bears, Vignettes, Scalloped, 1906, 10 In. Diam.	250
Relish, Ye Olden Times, Oval, Handles, Khaki, c.1908, 12 x 7 In.	185
Teapot Trivet, Breaking Cover, Round, Khaki, c.1908, 1 x 7 In.	125

BURMESE GLASS was developed by Frederick Shirley at the Mt. Washington Glass Works in New Bedford, Massachusetts, in 1885. It is a two-toned glass, shading from peach to yellow. Some pieces have a pattern mold design. A few Burmese pieces were decorated with pictures or applied glass flowers of colored Burmese glass. Other factories made similar glass also called Burmese. Related items may be listed in the Fenton category, the Gundersen category, and under Webb Burmese.

Bowl, Bulbous, Ruffled Rim, 3 Reeded Splay Feet, 6 x 8 In.	199

B

Cruet, Ribbed Body, Applied Handle, Satin Finish, Matching Stopper, 7 In.	230
Lamp, Fairy Dome, Ruffled Insert, 3½-In. Dome, 4 x 5 In.	431
Pitcher, Hobnail, Shaded, Applied Handle, Satin Finish, 5½ In.	201
Spooner, Amber To Yellow, Fluted, Scalloped, Mt. Washington, 4½ x 3¼ In.	86
Vase, Applied Blossom Branch, Applied Reeded Feet, Dip Rim, 8 x 8 In.	230
Vase, Gourd, Stick, Amber To Yellow, Mt. Washington, 8¼ x 3½ In.	86
Vase, Hobnail, Bulbous, Stick Neck, Out-Turned Crimped Rim, 1950s, 11 In.	150
Vase, Yellow To Peach, Gloss Glaze, Beaker, Scalloped Rim, 1800s, 6 In.	249
Vase, Yellow, Peach Roses, Globular, Stick Neck, Folded, Ruffled Rim, 8 In.	190
Whimsy Ball, Amber To Yellow, Mt. Washington, 4¼ x 2¾ In.	36

BUSTER BROWN, the comic strip, first appeared in color in 1902. Buster and his dog, Tige, remained a popular comic and soon became even more famous as the emblem for a shoe company, a textile firm, and other companies. The strip was discontinued in 1920. Buster Brown sponsored a radio show from 1943 to 1955 and a TV show from 1950 to 1956. The Buster Brown characters are still used by Brown Shoe Company, Buster Brown Apparel, Inc., and Gateway Hosiery.

Bank, Cast Iron, Buster, Tige, Horse, Horseshoe, Black & Gold, c.1905, 5 In.	200
Bowl, Porcelain, Hat Shape, Buster & Tige, Pink, White, Red, Blue, c.1908, 5 In.	80
Button, Buster Brown Shoes, Buster & Tige, c.1910, 1½ In. ....*illus*	127
Button, Morton's Buster Brown Bread, Hughie Jennings, Detroit Tigers, 1909, 1¼ In. ......*illus*	960
Mirror, Pocket, Buster Brown Shoes, Buster, Shoe, Tige, c.1910, 2 In.	256

BUTTER CHIPS, or butter pats, were small individual dishes for butter. They were the height of fashion from 1880 to 1910. Earlier as well as later examples are known.

Baltimore & Ohio Railroad Centenary, Train, Horse, 3 In.	30
Boston & Albany Railroad, Berkshire, 3¼ In.	156
Dresden Hopfen, Alfred Meakin, 1880s	10
English Rose, Cream, Pink, Green, Shaped Gilt Rim, 1902, 3 In., Pair	20
Erica Pattern, Red Flowers, J.E. Heath, England, 3¼ In.	19
Flow Blue, Gold Rim, 3⅛ In., 5 Piece	20
Flower Spray, Scalloped Rim, Gilt Trim, Germany, 3½ In.	17
Flowers, Insects, Black Transfer, Ashworth Brothers, Square, c.1880, 4 x 4 In.	40
Flowers, Pink, Blue, Majolica, Eureka Pottery Co., Fan Shape, 4 In.	85
Geranium Leaf Shape, Yellow, Green, Majolica, Griffen, Smith & Hill, c.1860, 2¾ In.	100
Gold Flower Garland, Gold Trim, Scalloped, Porcelain, 3 In.	12
Majolica, Geranium Leaf, Green, Yellow, Etruscan, 3 In., 6 Piece	132
Majolica, Shell & Seaweed, Green, Yellow, Etruscan, 4 In., 6 Piece	300
Morning Glory, Raised Pentagon Center, Blue Blossoms, c.1898, 3 In., Pair	35
Olympia, Oceanliner Logo, Blue, A.J. Wilkinson, Royal Staffordshire, 2⅞ In. ....*illus*	34
Rocky Shoreline, Sea, Brown Aesthetic Transfer, G.W. Turner, England, c.1880, 3 In.	50
Sairey Gamp Entertains Betsy Prig, Dickens, Sandlandware, England, 3¼ In.	8
Ship, Gold Trim, Rippled Edge, 3 In., 6 Piece	29
Silver, Gilt, Squared Well, Schultz & Fisher, 2¾ In., 6 Piece	72
Silver, Repousse, Partial Chased, Kirk, 3⅛ In., 6 Piece	216
Silver, Shaped, 3 In., 6 Piece	84
Silver, Starburst, J.E. Caldwell Co., 3⅛ In., 7 Piece	132
Spongeware, Blue, Folk Images, Stoneware, 3¼ In., 11 Piece	6

BUTTER MOLDS *are listed in the Kitchen category under Mold, Butter.*

BUTTON collecting has been popular since the nineteenth century. Buttons have been used on clothing throughout the centuries, and there are millions of styles. Gold, silver, or precious stones were used for the best buttons, but most were made of natural materials, like bone or shell, or from inexpensive metals. Only a few types favored by collectors are listed for comparison.

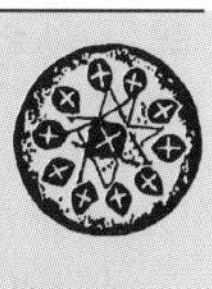

Buffalo Pottery, Plate, Chesapeake & Ohio Railroad, Geo. Washington, 1732 Bi-Centennial 1932, 11 In.
$936

Jeffrey S. Evans

Buffalo Pottery, Plate, Thunderbird, Fred Harvey, Marked, Colorido Ware, 1930, 9¾ In.
$1,989

Jeffrey S. Evans

Buffalo Pottery Deldare, Charger, An Evening At Ye Lion Inn, 1908, 13¾ In.
$375

Ruby Lane

Buffalo Pottery Deldare, Jardiniere, Ye Lion Inn, Signed, W. Foster, 9⅛ In.
$1,053

Jeffrey S. Evans

Buffalo Pottery Deldare, Plate, Flower-Like Geometric Medallion, Emerald, Willow, 8³/₈ In.
$222

Jeffrey S. Evans

TIP
Small collectibles can be used as window-shade pulls.

Buster Brown, Button, Buster Brown Shoes, Buster & Tige, c.1910, 1½ In.
$127

Hake's Americana & Collectibles

Buster Brown, Button, Morton's Buster Brown Bread, Hughie Jennings, Detroit Tigers, 1909, 1¼ In.
$960

Robert Edward Auctions

Bakelite, Green, Scalloped Edge, 2 Center Holes, 1 In. Diam.	4
Bakelite, Green, Triangular, 1½ In.	3
Brass, Cherub, Drummer, 1800s, 1 In.	65
Brass, Embossed, Steam Train, Railroad, 1st Railway, Netherlands, c.1890, 1 In.	75
Glass, Coralene, Red, Yellow & Blue Beaded Flowers, Petal Center, 1940s, ¾ In.	35
Glass, Pierced, Red Ground, Blue & Yellow Flowers, Reeded Edge, 1930s, ½ In.	23
Glass, White, Multicolored Beads, 1940s, ¾ In.	34
Lucite Cabochon, Pearlized, Goldtone, Fleur-De-Lis Border, c.1900, 1 In.	65
Plastic, Anchor, 4-Hole, Blue, ¾ In.	2
Plastic, Pearl Finish, Heart Shape, c.1930, 1½ x 1¼ In.	39
Porcelain, Violets, Leaves, Gilt Rim, Marked, Meissen, 1700s, ¹³/₁₆ In.	175
USSR Army, Brass Color, Star Crest, ¹³/₁₆ In.	8

BUTTONHOOKS have been a popular collectible in England for many years and are now gaining the attention of American collectors. The buttonhooks were made to help fasten the many buttons of the old-fashioned high-button shoes and other items of apparel.

Gold On Metal, Folding, Scrolling Flowers, 1800s, 1½ In.	78
Metal, Open Loop Handle, Beaded Design, c.1908, 5 In.	16
Mother-Of-Pearl, Reeded & Shaped, 1920s, 4 In.	12
Sterling Silver, Twist Design, Scroll, Finial, 1899, 7 In.	40

Genuine Bybee

BYBEE POTTERY of Bybee, Kentucky, was started by Webster Cornelison. The company claims it started in 1809, although sales records were not kept until 1845. The pottery is still operated by members of the sixth generation of the Cornelison family. The handmade stoneware pottery is sold at the factory. Various marks were used, including the name *Bybee*, the name *Cornelison*, or the initials *BB*. Not all pieces are marked. A mark shaped like the state of Kentucky with the words *Genuine Bybee* and similar marks were also used by a different company, Bybee Pottery Company of Lexington, Kentucky. It was a distributor of various pottery lines from 1922 to 1929.

Bean Pot, Black Gloss Glaze, Flecks, Domed, Loop Handle, Lid, 1940s, 6 x 6 In.	100
Bean Pot, Handles, Lid, Berry Red Glaze, Glossy, 4 In.	52
Bowl, Beige, Blue Band, Flower Sprig, 1900s, 2 x 4 In.	45
Bowl, Cobalt Blue Satin Glaze, Squat, Wide Rim, 1920s, 3 x 8 In.	90
Relish, White, Blue Splotches, 4 Scalloped Bowls, Square Top Handle, 2 x 8 In.	85
Vase, Cattails, Celadon Green Glaze, Rust, 3 Handles, Swollen Collar, 1927, 7 In.	345
Vase, Green Matte Glaze, Twin Handles, Impressed, 6½ In. ....*illus*	184

CALENDARS made to hang on the wall or to be displayed on a desk top have been popular since the last quarter of the nineteenth century. Many were printed with advertising as part of the artwork and were given away as premiums. Calendars with guns, gunpowder, or Coca-Cola advertising are most prized.

1889, Clausen & Son Brewing Co., NYC, Coach, People, Fancy Dress, 20 x 28 In.	2250
1897, Winchester, Man Aiming Gun, Horse, Trail, 35 x 22 In.	4200
1899, Trifold, Violets, Women, Shaped Edge, 10½ x 8 In.	45
1899, Winchester, 2 Hunters, Black Bear, Snipe Shooting, 35 x 21 In.	4800
1900, Winchester, Hunters Lying In Snow, Quail Hunting, 35 x 21 In.	3900
1903, Indian Maidens, Syracuse Herald, Die Cut Carboard Fan, 10 x 17 In.	431
1905, Chicago & Alton Railway, Gypsy Girl, Cardboard, 15 x 10 In.	184
1905, Deering Harvesters, Boy Holding Basket, Puppies, Tear Sheet, 20 x 13 In.	690
1907, A.O. Schramm Grocery & Produce, Die Cut, December, Frame, 14 x 8 In. ....*illus*	493
1907, Golden Memories, Dutch Children, Pressed Cardboard, Frame, 10 x 10 In.	24
1910, Crown Dandruff Cure, Woman, Crown, Die Cut, Cardboard, 20 x 15 In.	1006
1918, Bristol Fishing Rods, Couple Fishing, Canoe, 41 x 26 In.	2440
1923, Southwestern Barber Supply, Indian Princess, Water's Edge, 13 x 7 In.	75
1925, Edison Mazda, Dream Light, Girl, Swing, Forest, Parrish, Full Pad, 22 x 12 In.	127
1926, Edison Mazda, Enchantment, Parrish, Frame, Full Pad, 16 x 28 In.	596

1927, Edison Mazda, Reveries, Women, Garden Pool, Parrish, Full Pad, 19 x 9 In.	690
1927, General Electric, National Mazda Brand Lamps, 20 x 9 In.	177
1927, Pompeian Brand Beauty Products, Rolf Armstrong, Litho, Roll, 26 x 7 In.	59
1929, Edison Mazda Lamps, Golden Hours, Trees, Parrish, 19 x 8 In.	403
1930, Cardboard Mat, Setting Sun, Mountain, 15 x 6 In.	75
1930, Edison Mazda, Ecstasy, Parrish, Full Pad, Frame, 19 x 39 In.	1810
1931, Edison Mazda Lamps, Waterfalls, Maxfield Parrish, 19 x 8 In.	661
1932, Johannes Bros. Co., Art Deco Glamour Girl & Parrot, 23 x 17 In.	59
1938, Economy Radiator Works, Seated Woman, Dress, Parrot, 21 x 46 In.	150
1939, Nehi Royal Crown Cola, Woman, Rowing Boat, Full Pad, 28 x 16 In.	308
1941, Maas & Steffen Inc., Furs, Beaver, Habitat, Metal Strip, 26 x 14 In.	738
1941, Motor Freight, McVicker Bros., Michigan, Desktop, 4 x 6 In.	189
1944, Kuebler Beer-Ale, Woman Holding Glass, Wood Frame, 24 x 34 In.	277
1945, Tongg's Hawaiian, Ukulele, Brown Basket Weave, 12 x 9 In.	26
1952, Wayne's Welding, Marilyn Monroe, Nude, Full Pad, 8 In. ....*illus*	272
1979, Jarvis Auction Mart, Woman, Perfect Bait, Bikini, Fishing Tackle, 14 x 9 In.	25

CALENDAR PLATES were popular in the United States as advertising giveaways from 1906 to 1929. Since then, a few plates have been made every year. A calendar and the name of a store, a picture of flowers, a girl, or a scene were featured on the plate.

1909, Golf, Women, Holly Leaves, Berries, Schwarzburg, 12 In. ....*illus*	240
1909, Lavender Rose, Silver Scrolling Flower Vines, 9 In.	27
1909, Victorian Woman, Hat, Scarf, Flower Border, Scalloped Rim, 9 In.	147
1910, Cherubs, Bell, Flowers, Shaped Rim, 8 ½ In.	38
1910, Girl, Horse, Red Jacket, Gold Rim, Detroit White Lead Works, 6 ¼ In. ....*illus*	24
1914, Shamrock Wreath, Flowers, Gilt, Cartouche & Swag Border, 9 In.	19
1917, Purple Violets, Basket, Gilt Scroll Border, Scalloped Rim, 7 In.	21
1969, Green, Coupe, Currier & Ives, 10 In.	30
1973, Personified Sun, White, 10 In.	18
1975, Zodiac, White, Green, Gold, 10 ¼ In.	9
1980, Home Of The Free, Lincoln Memorial, Close Up Portrait, 9 In.	5
1984, Zodiac, Farmhouse, Livestock, Brown, Alfred Meakin	26
1984, Zodiac, House, Red, Alfred Meakin	28
1987, Four Seasons, Multicolor, Avon	15

CAMARK POTTERY started out as Camden Art Tile and Pottery Company in Camden, Arkansas. Jack Carnes founded the firm in 1926 in association with John Lessell, Stephen Sebaugh, and the Camden Chamber of Commerce. Many types of glazes and wares were made. The company was bought by Mary Daniel in the early 1960s. Production ended in 1983.

Bowl, Brown Matte, Yellow, Flower Shape, Flared Petal Rim, 1930s, 4 x 12 In.	56
Pitcher, Pink Matte, Basket Weave Pattern, Angled Handle, 1940s, 6 In.	48
Vase, Peach, Green Drip, Lobed, Inverted Scallop Rim, Ring Foot, c.1930, 8 In.	95
Vase, Sage Green, Red Drip, Ring Pattern, Barrel Shape, Folded Rim, 1920s, 5 In.	85

CAMBRIDGE GLASS COMPANY was founded in 1901 in Cambridge, Ohio. The company closed in 1954, reopened briefly, and closed again in 1958. The firm made all types of glass. Its early wares included heavy pressed glass with the mark *Near Cut.* Later wares included Crown Tuscan, etched stemware, and clear and colored glass. The firm used a *C* in a triangle mark after 1920.

Alpine, Ice Bucket, Hammered Metal Handle	42
Amethyst Pinch, Tumbler, 2 Oz.	9
Candy Jar, Lid, Rose Du Barry, Peach-Blo, Acid Etched, Silver Leaf Bands, Knob, 6 In. ....*illus*	115
Caprice, Cruet, Moonlight Blue, Stopper, c.1945, 6 x 3 In.	175
Caprice, Goblet, Blue Stem, 7 ¾ In.	34
Caprice, Iced Tea, Footed	14
Caprice, Iced Tea, Stem, c.1936-58, 6 ¼ In.	17
Cleo, Candlestick, Emerald Green, 4 In., Pair	28
Cleo, Dish, Mayonnaise, Footed, Light Blue, 3 ½ x 7 In.	50

Butter Chip, Olympia, Oceanliner Logo, Blue, A.J. Wilkinson, Royal Staffordshire, 2 ⅞ In.
$34

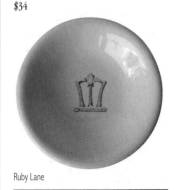

Ruby Lane

Bybee Pottery, Vase, Green Matte Glaze, Twin Handles, Impressed, 6 ½ In.
$184

Humler & Nolan

Calendar Paper, 1907, A.O. Schramm Grocery & Produce, Die Cut, December, Frame, 14 x 8 In.
$493

Showtime Auction Services

TIP
Try to keep your paper collectibles out of the light. If you frame and display some pieces, keep them on the dark side of the room, away from sunlight and direct lamp light.

Calendar Paper, 1952, Wayne's Welding, Marilyn Monroe, Nude, Full Pad, 8 In.
$272

Calendar Plate, 1909, Golf, Women, Holly Leaves, Berries, Schwarzburg, 12 In.
$240

Calendar Plate, 1910, Girl, Horse, Red Jacket, Gold Rim, Detroit White Lead Works, 6 ¼ In.
$24

Cleo, Plate, Blue, 7 In.	15
Cleo, Plate, Pink, 8 ½ In.	15
Croesus, Goblet, Oblong, c.1946, 8 ½ In.	49
Decagon, Bowl, Centerpiece, Green, 16 ¼ In.	185
Etch Green, Compote, 10 ¾ In.	33
Portia, Relish, 5 Sections	40
Pristine, Cornucopia, Moonlight Blue, c.1940, 8 In.	40
Rose Point, Creamer	20
Rose Point, Cruet, Stopper, c.1940, 6 In.	95
Rose Point, Pitcher, c.1945, 76 Oz., 9 ½ In.	195
Tally-Ho, Vase, Cobalt Blue, Footed, c.1932, 12 In.	375
Topaz, Plate, Vaseline, 8-Sided, 8 In.	11
Vase, Ebony, Apple Blossom, c.1935, 12 x 5 ½ In. ....*illus*	425

CAMBRIDGE POTTERY was made in Cambridge, Ohio, from about 1895 until World War I. The factory made brown-glazed decorated artwares with a variety of marks, including an acorn, the name *Cambridge,* the name *Oakwood,* and the name *Terrhea.*

Bowl, Incised Linear Design, Green, Loop Handles, c.1906, 2 x 6 In.	289
Pitcher, Leaf & Berry, Green Matte, Bulbous, Wavy Rim, c.1915, 7 x 10 In.	203
Planter, Palm Leaves, Green, Orange, Brown Glaze, c.1900, 5 x 4 In.	155
Vase, Bamboo Leaves, Green Matte Glaze, Beaker, Reticulated, c.1915, 9 In.	643

CAMEO GLASS was made in much the same manner as a cameo in jewelry. Parts of the top layer of glass were cut away to reveal a different colored glass beneath. The most famous cameo glass was made during the nineteenth century. Signed cameo glass pieces by famous makers are listed under the glasswork's name, such as Daum, Galle, Legras, Mt. Joye, Webb, and more. Others, signed or unsigned, are listed here.

Bowl, Art Nouveau, Yellow, Purple Flowers, Signed Charder, France, 6 x 7 In.	281
Perfume Lamp, Red Butterflies, Frost To Blue, Iron Mount, c.1920, 7 In.	2250
Salt, Canary Yellow, Acorn, Triangular Rim Band, c.1880, 1 ½ In.	1521
Vase, Amber, Purple, Acid Etched, Tapered Mouth, Signed, De Vianne, 8 In.	182
Vase, Apricot, Beetle, Butterfly, Bulbous Base, Conical Mouth, c.1885, 12 In.	2457
Vase, Art Deco, Orange, White, Acid Etched, 19 In.	437
Vase, Blue Cased, Pine Trees, Lake, Mountains, Lamartine, France, 7 ¾ x 5 In. ....*illus*	889
Vase, Canary Yellow, Flowers, Bees, Elongated Neck, Signed, c.1890, 14 In.	1872
Vase, Celebration Of Life Force, Carved, Overlay, Palm Trees, Sun, 10 x 10 In.	1044
Vase, Citron Yellow, Brown, Grapes On Vine, Gourd Shape, Ring Foot, 8 In.	295
Vase, Citron, White Flowers, Bulbous, Pinched Neck, Swollen Rim, c.1910, 6 In.	461
Vase, Cranberry Matte Glaze, Palms, Bees, Flowers, Bottle Shape, c.1910, 19 In.	2706
Vase, Enamel, 4-Sided, Green Meadow, Birch Trees & Pink Sky, 11 In.	920
Vase, Frosted Glass, Burgundy, Grapes, Vines, Leaves, 10 x 4 In.	135
Vase, Frosted, Pink, Green, Morning Glories, Arsal, 16 x 7 In.	375
Vase, Green Tulips Against Peach & Lavender, Signed, Arsal, 6 ¼ In.	403
Vase, Lake, Boats, Trees, Overlay, Andre Delatte, c.1921, 10 In.	3750
Vase, Landscape, Bridge & Birds, Amber, Pink & Olive, Arsal, 12 x 6 In.	546
Vase, Landscape, Sailboat, 3 Colors, France, Late 1800s, 2 ½ In.	293
Vase, Lemon, Red Peony Blooms, Signed, 1990s, 5 In.	380
Vase, Orange Sky, Dark Green, Vitrified Outer Layer, France, c.1910, 11 x 4 In.	1875
Vase, Pink Flowers, Leaves, Maroon Swirl, Icicle Trim, Bergun & Schverer, 5 In........*illus*	4740
Vase, Poppies & Butterflies, Yellow, Red, A. Reyen, 1890s, 11 x 7 In.	2250
Vase, Purple Leaf, Wisteria, Pink To White, Flared, Round Foot, 7 x 4 In.	177
Vase, Red Poppies & Butterflies, Yellow, France, A. Reyen, 1890s, 11 x 6 In.	2250
Vase, Serpent, Garden Of Eden, Green, Amber, Plum, Frosted, Domed Foot, 17 In.	160
Vase, Tangled Leaves & Vines, Red & Orange, Carved, Swollen, Bottle, 15 In.	2950
Vase, White Polar Bears, Ice Flow, Dark Red Ground, Waves, 4 x 4 In.	3437
Vase, Yellow, Bearded Iris, Ginko, c.1885, 11 ¾ In.	2250

CAMPAIGN *memorabilia are listed in the Political category.*

CAMPBELL KIDS were first used as part of an advertisement for the Campbell Soup Company in 1904. The kids were created by Grace Drayton, a popular illustrator of the day. The kids were used in magazine and newspaper ads until about 1951. They were presented again in 1966; and in 1983, they were redesigned with a slimmer, more contemporary appearance.

Bank, Still, Cast Iron, A.C. Williams & Co., 4¼ In.	50
Doll, Boy, Rubber, Side-Glancing Eyes, Rosy Cheeks, 1950s, 12 In.	244
Doll, Girl, Blond, Molded Hair, Kilt, Rubber, 10 In. ....*illus*	40
Doorstop, Cast Iron, Painted, 10 In.	15
Oven Mitt, Characters, Green, Quilted, Tag, 1950s	36
Sandwich Holder, Mini, 5½ x 4½ In.	10
Spoon Rest, Red, White, c.1955, 4 In., Pair ....*illus*	20
Spoon, Silver, Boy, Girl, 6 In., Pair	10

CANDELABRUM refers to a candleholder with more than one arm to hold many candles; a candlestick is designed to hold one candle. The eccentricity of the English language makes the plural of candelabrum into candelabra.

2-Light, Amethyst Glass, Etched Grapes, Crystal Ball, 24 x 12 In., Pair	1190
2-Light, Bronze, French Napoleon, 19 In., Pair	1063
2-Light, Bronze, Iron, Figural, Till Eulenspiegel, Gothic Style, c.1865, 13¾ In. ....*illus*	675
2-Light, Bronze, Porcelain, Parrot, Flowers, Twisting Branches, c.1900, 11 In., Pair	1599
2-Light, Figural, C.G. Schierholz & Son, Germany, c.1890, 7 x 9 In., Pair	343
2-Light, Gilt Bronze, Louis XV Style, Vines, c.1900, 17 x 9 In., Pair	1750
2-Light, Gilt Metal, Molded Glass Phoenix, France, c.1910, 18 x 9 In.	1125
2-Light, Patinated Bronze, Putti Holding Arms, Kneeling, Footed, 12 In., Pair	840
2-Light, Pewter, Trumpet Shape Stem, J.M. Olbrich, Germany, 14 x 7 In., Pair	2875
2-Light, Porcelain, Winged Putti, Flowers, White, Pink, Green, 12 x 11 In.	2400
2-Light, Sconce, Cupid Holding Flowers, Giltwood & Metal, c.1900, 10 In., Pair	812
2-Light, Silver Plate, Crane Shape, Tortoise Base, Chinese, 15 In., Pair	2375
2-Light, Silver, Openwork, T Shape, Archibald Knox, 1901, 11 x 9 In.	3500
2-Light, Silver, Spiraling To Round Base, Preisner, Early 1900s, 16 In., Pair	390
2-Light, Spelter, Gilt, Composition Asian Figures In Robes, 8 x 10 In., Pair	175
2-Light, Wood, Red & Green Paint, Spiral Stem, Ratchet, Domed Base, 20 In.	215
3-Light, Bronze, Figural, Seated Children, Gilt, c.1900, 27 x 16 In.	2500
3-Light, Bronze, Louis XIV Style, Scrolls, 2 Tiers, Glass Drops, 17 In., Pair	562
3-Light, Bronze, Porcelain Figures, Seated, Courting, 16 x 13 In., Pair	281
3-Light, Bronze, Shield Shape, E.T. Hurley, 1918, 15 x 10½ In.	277
3-Light, Cranberry, Glass, Bohemian, Pendants, 29 x 15 In.	125
3-Light, Gilt Bronze & Marble, France, c.1900, 37 x 9 x 6 In., Pair	2375
3-Light, Giltwood, George III, c.1770, 12½ x 26 In., Pair	2500
3-Light, Glass, Gilded, Flame Finial, Rope Twist Arms, Murano, 17 x 15 In., Pair	523
3-Light, Iron, Hammered, Stylized Flower, c.1910, 13½ x 6¾ In. ....*illus*	139
3-Light, Marble, Gilt Metal, Louis XV, Fin De Siecle, France, c.1880, 18 x 11 In.	812
3-Light, Metal, Camels, Palms, Cold Paint, c.1890, 15 x 18½ In.	750
3-Light, Parcel Gilt, Leaf & Vine Scroll, Bobeches, Infants, 14 x 9 In., Pair	350
3-Light, Parcel Gilt, Vase Shape Post, Swags, Scroll Arms, 1800s, 17 In., Pair	562
3-Light, Pewter, Openwork Shaft, Footed, Achille Gamba, 18½ In.	800
3-Light, Silver Plate, Columnar, Rocaille, Scroll Arms, c.1815, 20 x 16 In., Pair	750
3-Light, Silver Plate, Rococo, Drop Arms, 16 x 16 In., Pair	218
3-Light, Silver, English Rose, Convertible, Fisher, 1900s, 17 In.	523
3-Light, Silver, Gadrooned, Preisner, 16½ In.	425
3-Light, Silver, George V, Leaves, Joseph Heming & Co., c.1913, 17 In., Pair	3321
3-Light, Silver, Gold Wash, Ebonized, A. Salomonsen, 1950s, 13 In., Pair	2625
3-Light, Silver, Leafy Arms, Round Foot, Fisher, c.1950, 12 x 15 In., Pair	714
3-Light, Silver, Reeded Scroll Arms, Stepped Foot, Preisner, 16 In., Pair	154
3-Light, Silver, Tapered, Scroll Arms, Urn Cups, Flared Foot, 1900s, 13 In., Pair	360
3-Light, Stone, Inlay, Silver, Flowers, Emilia Castillo, 1900s, 16½ x 11 In.	531
3-Light, Vase Shape Stem, Scroll Arms, Flared Cups, Round Foot, 12 In., Pair	384
3-Light, Wrought Iron, Relief, Owl, Perched, Round Base, c.1920, 13 In.	250
4-Light, Bronze, Caryatid Stem, Swan Arms, Base, c.1815, 28 In., Pair	1750

Cambridge, Candy Jar, Lid, Rose Du Barry, Peach-Blo, Acid Etched, Silver Leaf Bands, Knob, 6 In.
$115

Ruby Lane

Cambridge, Vase, Ebony, Apple Blossom, c.1935, 12 x 5½ In.
$425

Ruby Lane

Cameo Glass, Vase, Blue Cased, Pine Trees, Lake, Mountains, Lamartine, France, 7¾ x 5 In.
$889

Ruby Lane

Cameo Glass, Vase, Pink Flowers, Leaves, Maroon Swirl, Icicle Trim, Bergun & Schverer, 5 In. $4,740

James D. Julia Auctioneers

Campbell Kids, Doll, Girl, Blond, Molded Hair, Kilt, Rubber, 10 In. $40

Ruby Lane

Campbell Kids, Spoon Rest, Red, White, c.1955, 4 In., Pair $20

Ruby Lane

4-Light, Bronze, Gilt, Eros Holds Branches, French Empire, 25 In. ....*illus*	562
4-Light, Bronze, Putti, Flower Bouquet, Black Slate Base, 24 In., Pair	561
4-Light, Bronze, Scrolling Branches, Crystal Fruit Drops, c.1935, 22 In., Pair	750
4-Light, Bronze, Scrolling Branches, Putto, Grape Clusters, 25 In., Pair	2250
4-Light, Porcelain, Applied Flowers, Woman, Child, Sitzendorf, 18 x 10 In., Pair	1062
4-Light, Silver Plate, Curved Drop Arm, Christofle, 22 x 12 In., Pair	973
4-Light, Silver, Baluster, Leaf Capped Arms, Round Base, c.1853, 20 In., Pair	3444
4-Light, Wrought Iron, C-Scroll, Waisted, Openwork, 24 x 23 In.	88
5-Light, Brass, Applied Flowers, Art Nouveau, Marked, 13 x 17 In.	245
5-Light, Broad Leaf Decor, Elkington & Co., England, 1865, 25 x 15 In.	875
5-Light, Bronze, Brass, Gothic Revival, Wild Cats, Rectangular Base, 22 In., Pair	450
5-Light, Bronze, French Restauration, Leaves, Gilt, Patina, c.1835, 34 In., Pair ....*illus*	2000
5-Light, Bronze, Patina, Kneeling Cherub, Center Arm, Marble Base, 19 In.	437
5-Light, Bronze, Renaissance Revival, Scroll, Filigree, 20 x 20 In., Pair	343
5-Light, Bronze, Wheat Sheaf, Lilies, Grape Clusters, Tripod, 30 x 14 In., Pair	188
5-Light, Classical Figure, Flower Bobeches, Electrified, 35 ½ x 15 In., Pair	9375
5-Light, Gilt Bronze, Emerald Green Porcelain, 1800s, 21 ¼ In.	246 to 531
5-Light, Gilt Bronze, Figural, Woman, 20 In.	2500
5-Light, Gilt Bronze, Figures On Base, England, 1800s, 22 ½ x 19 In.	468
5-Light, Gilt Bronze, Louis XV, Rocaille, France, c.1880, 24 x 13 In., Pair	812
5-Light, Gilt Bronze, Putti, Flowers, Red Marble Plinth, 40 x 21 In., Pair	1159
5-Light, Gilt, Bronze, Marble, French Neoclassical, 1800s, 19 ½ x 9 In.	384
5-Light, Porcelain, Flower Cartouches, Leaf Arms, Sevres Style, 15 x 12 In.	413
5-Light, Silver, Art Nouveau, W. Binder, Germany, 1800s, 10 x 11 In.	354
5-Light, Silver, Baroque, Beaded, Leaves, Domed Base, Mexico, 15 x 15 In.	2200
5-Light, Silver, Knopped Stem, Leafy Scrolls, Pierced Shades, 17 In.	3437
5-Light, Silver, Openwork Base, Holland, Miniature, c.1900, 2⅞ In. ....*illus*	225
5-Light, Silver, Rococo Style, Putti Crested Base, Italy, 1900s, 16 x 7 In.	437
5-Light, Silver, Scroll Arms, Knop Stem, Lobed Base, c.1810, 24 In.	1599
5-Light, Silver, Tree Trunk, Flowers, Leaves, Rocaille, Bracket Feet, 24 x 16 In., Pair	1320
6-Light, Brass & Marble, Black Spherical Glass, Russia, 27 x 12 In.	1750
6-Light, Bronze, Baroque Style, Beaded Swags, France, c.1980, 32 x 17 In., Pair	812
6-Light, Bronze, Cherubs Holding Tree Of Lights, 29 ½ In., Pair	1250
6-Light, Bronze, Empire, Figural, Woman, Arms Up, Square Base, 34 In., Pair	4000
6-Light, Bronze, Gilt, Leaves, Flowers, Women, Buds, Bobeches, 32 In.	2750
6-Light, Bronze, Marble, Putti, Scroll Handles, Pierced, c.1865, 48 In., Pair	937
6-Light, Bronze, Seated Putti, Gilt Leaf Arms, Napoleon III, 25 x 13 In.	1220
6-Light, Gilt Bronze, Rococo Style, France, 1800s, 21 x 11 In., Pair	3000
6-Light, Gilt Bronze, Scroll Flowers, Putti, Pierced Base, c.1885, 26 In., Pair	812
6-Light, Neoclassical, Maiden, Griffin, Stepped Base, 29 x 14 In., Pair	383
6-Light, Ormolu, Louis XV, Flower Cups, Twist, Leaves, 1900s, 23 In.	1750
6-Light, Silver Plate, Daffodils, Weedon Grossmith, c.1890, 35 x 22 In.	549
6-Light, Silver, Baluster Stem, Garland, Scroll Arms & Feet, 34 In., Pair	9225
6-Light, Stainless Steel, Ball, Long Cone, Italy, 28 x 12 ½ In. ....*illus*	650
6-Light, Standing Figure, Classical Dress, 26 ½ In., Pair	562
7-Light, Bronze, Ormolu, Acanthus, 1800s, 35 In.	3000
7-Light, Cherub, Flowers, Scroll, 38 x 18 In.	2000
7-Light, Gilt Bronze, Griffins & Garland, 1800s, 30 x 15 In., Pair	805
7-Light, Gilt Bronze, Nymph, Rocaille, Scroll Arms, c.1885, 29 x 17 In., Pair	5000
7-Light, Gilt Bronze, Winged Women, France, 1800s, 34 x 13 In.	2990
7-Light, Gilt, Green Glass, 3-Footed, 26 In., Pair	500
7-Light, Silver Gilt, Scroll, Leafy, Continental, 1800s, 36 In.	850
7-Light, Silver, Circle, Triangle Candle Lip, Rafi Landau, 11 ½ x 14 In.	1445
7-Light, Wrought Iron, Arrow Shape, ½ In., Pair	625
8-Light, Bronze, Wrought Iron, Triangles, Curves, 12 ½ x 20 In. ....*illus*	325
9-Light, Giltwood, Leaf Scroll Arms, Carved Posts, c.1915, 86 In., Pair	5850
9-Light, Wrought Iron, Early 1900s, 72 x 24 In.	748
10-Light, Gilt Bronze, Ornate, France, 1800s, 38 x 15 ½ In.	4025
18-Light, Silver, Trumpet Vase Topper, Leaves, Iran, c.1950, 37 In., Pair	7500
Bronze, Gilt, Baroque Revival, Cherub, Horn, Leaves, 20 x 9 In., Pair	297
Girandole, Bohemian Cut To Clear Ruby Glass, 10 In.	63

Girandole, Clear, Bohemian, 12 In., Pair 438
Girandole, Tulip Shape, Milk White Overlay, Gilding, Flowers, 11 In., Pair 960
Wrought Iron, Flower Openwork, Germany, c.1910, 13 x 4 In., Pair.................. 177

CANDLESTICKS were made of brass, pewter, glass, sterling silver, plated silver, and all types of pottery and porcelain. The earliest candlesticks, dating from the sixteenth century, held the candle on a pricket (sharp pointed spike). These lost favor because in times of strife the large church candlesticks with prickets became formidable weapons, so the socket was mandated. Candlesticks changed in style through the centuries, and designs range from Classical to Rococo to Art Nouveau to Art Deco.

Altar, Giltwood, Molded Crosses, France, Late 1800s, 28 x 7 In., Pair.................. 1500
Baluster & Urn, Pricket, Turned, Cream & Gold, Base, c.1900, 16 In., Pair........... 593
Blown Glass, Green, Cobalt Blue Band, Applied Flower Sprays, 11 In., Pair.......... 162
Blown Glass, Stacked Balls, Round Base, 7 In., Pair....................................... 50
Brass, Alpha, Bobeche, Robert Riddle Jarvie, 11 x 5 In., Pair............................ 1098
Brass, Barley Twist Stem, Octagonal Base, c.1700, 5 In., Pair...............*illus* 123
Brass, Bulbous Stem, Dome Base, Mid-Drip Pan, Threaded Posts, Spain, 1600s, 10 In., Pair.... 660
Brass, Chamber, Adjustable Tole Shade, Urn Nozzle, Dished Base, 15 In., Pair.......... 330
Brass, Continental, Turned Stem, Drip Pan, 17th Century, 9 In. 354
Brass, Cut Glass, Orange, Square, 14 In., Pair.. 63
Brass, Cylindrical Cup, Turned Stem, Domed Foot, Europe, c.1710, 9 In. 100
Brass, Cylindrical Stem, Bulbous Cup, Disc Foot, R. Jarvie, Signed, 13 In., Pair...... 900
Brass, Georgian, Square, Fluted Stem, Flared, Ringed, c.1750, 12 In. 275
Brass, Knopped Seamed Stem, Twist Up, Petal Base, England, 1700s, 9 In. 1300
Brass, Knopped Stem, Incised Design, Reeded Holder, Round Foot, 48 In., Pair........ 160
Brass, Pricket, Relief Portraits, Jesus, Tripartite Base, Scroll Feet, c.1835, 44 In. 1000
Brass, Pricket, Turned, Domed Base, 11 In., Pair... 120
Brass, Shaped Stem, Square Base, 1800s, 6 ¼ In., Pair...............*illus* 35
Brass, Thin Support, Bobeche, Round Base, Robert Jarvie, 11 x 5 In., Pair............ 610
Brass, Trumpet Shape, Tapering Knopped Stem, Round Base, 1700s, 8 In., Pair....... 215
Brass, Turned Stem, Drip Pan, Continental, 17th Century, 9 In., Pair.................. 355
Brass, Twist, Round Foot, 22 In., Pair... 30
Brass, Wax Guards, 6 Domes, Lobed Edge, Leaf Twist Stems, 1800s, 13 In. 650
Bronze, Crane, Open Beak, 11 x 4 ½ In., Pair.. 714
Bronze, Double Gourd, Ring Handles, Relief Design, 8 In., Pair......................... 125
Bronze, Empire, Gilt, Busts, Round Foot, c.1825, 41 In................................... 1250
Bronze, Empire, Gilt, Turned Columns, Flower Bands, France, 1800s, 10 In. 480
Bronze, Fluted, Jessie Preston, 14 x 4 In.. 375
Bronze, Frog, Lifting Weights, Balls, Shorts, 4 ½ In., Pair................................ 96
Bronze, Gilt Lions, Standing On Hands, Tails Wraped Around Stem, 12 In. 400
Bronze, Gilt, Figural Putti, Wall Sconces, France, 1800s, 14 x 5 ½ In., Pair.......... 1020
Bronze, Gilt, Louis XV, Entwined Leaves, Wood Base, Electrified, 16 x 7 In. 1200
Bronze, Gilt, William IV, Flowers & Scrolls, 1800s, 7 x 6 In., Pair..................... 687
Bronze, Glass, Classical Women, Column, 3 Socles, Paw Feet, 15 In., Pair............. 330
Bronze, Gothic, Hexagonal, Openwork, Pinnacles, 3 Scroll Feet, 30 In., Pair 330
Bronze, Iris Shape, 11 ½ x 7 In., Pair... 1342
Bronze, Napoleon III, Rococo, c.1870, 10 In., Pair 305
Bronze, Pricket, Turned, Knopped Stem, Germany, 14 x 6 In., Pair..................... 141
Bronze, Rearing Dragons, Opposing, Painted, Chinese, 1900s, 19 In., Pair 550
Bronze, Seahorse, Round Base, Lip, E.T. Hurley, 6 x 5 In. 500
Bronze, Tapered, Square, Bell Flower, Egg & C-Scroll, Bobeche, 9 x 5 In. 82
Bronze, Torch, Stone Base, Tony Stapells, 16 x 9 In....................................... 200
Chamber, Copper, Hammered, G. Stickley, Als Ik Kan Stamp, 9 x 7 In., Pair........... 938
Chamber, Silver Plate, Candlecup, Snuffer, Henry Wilkinson & Co., 6 ½ In. 31
Chamber, Silver Plate, Reeded, Barker Bros., J. Dixon & Sons, 1800s, 4 In., Pair..... 63
Copper, Hammered, Round Foot, Apollo Studios, 10 ½ x 5 ½ In. 125
Copper, Leaves, Bulbous Cup, Domed Base, Handles, Onondaga, 10 In., Pair........... 780
Copper, Silver Plate, Jewels, Scroll Handle, Bradley & Hubbard, 1885, 12 In., Pair.... 3125
Cut Glass, Cane Cutting, Honeycomb, Hobstar, 10 In., Pair.............................. 270
Ecclesiastical, Wood, 3-Footed, 1700s, 28 In., Pair...................................... 529

Candelabrum, 2-Light, Bronze, Iron, Figural, Till Eulenspiegel, Gothic Style, c.1865, 13 ¾ In.
$675

Ruby Lane

Candelabrum, 3-Light, Iron, Hammered, Stylized Flower, c.1910, 13 ½ x 6 ¾ In.
$139

Ruby Lane

Candelabrum, 4-Light, Bronze, Gilt, Eros Holds Branches, French Empire, 25 In.
$562

New Orleans Auction Galleries

Candelabrum, 5-Light, Bronze, French Restauration, Leaves, Gilt, Patina, c.1835, 34 In., Pair
$2,000

New Orleans Auction Galleries

Candelabrum, 5-Light, Silver, Openwork Base, Holland, Miniature, c.1900, 2⅞ In.
$225

Ruby Lane

Candelabrum, 6-Light, Stainless Steel, Ball, Long Cone, Italy, 28 x 12½ In.
$650

Rago Arts and Auction Center

Enamel, Gilt, Louis XVI, Figural, Busts, 9¾ In., Pair	375
Figural, Black, Basalt, Wedgwood, 11 In.	125
Figural, Gilt, Crouching Lion, Banana Leaves, Beaker Vase, c.1800, 5 In.	246
Figural, Silver, Figures Represent Season, Urn Sconce, Marble Base, 12 In.	1230
Gilt Bronze, Palmettes, Flower, Cobalt Blue, Porcelain, France, 23 x 8 In., Pair	4200
Gilt Bronze, Vase Shape, Leaves, Obelisk, Torch Mount, c.1815, 21 In., Pair	750
Giltwood, Archangel, Robed, Angels, Scroll, Bombe Base, c.1700, 34 In., Pair	3125
Giltwood, Gesso, Leaves, Footed, Belgium, c.1900, 29 x 10¼ In. ....*illus*	395
Giltwood, Pricket, Knopped Stem, Leaf & Scroll, Carved, Bobeche, 21 x 7 In.	225
Giltwood, Pricket, Relief Carved Leaf, Tripod, 26 x 7 In.	225
Glass & Metal, Stan Hawk, Hawk House, c.1950, 9 x 8 In., Pair	2000
Glass, Gilt Bronze, Leaves, 6½ x 2¾ In., Pair	100
Glass, Millefiori, Blown, Rose Gold Spiral Twist, 12 In.	512
Glass, Yellow, Column, Petal Rim, Stepped Base, New England, 9 In., Pair ....*illus*	177
Hog Scraper, Wedding Band, Push-Up, Lip Hanger, 1800s, 7 In., Pair	450
Iron, Candlestand, Adjustable Candleholder, Box Base, 1800s, 34 x 11 In.	1560
Iron, Conical Base, Rod, Scroll Cup Support, Adjustable, 1800s, 16 In.	950
Iron, Cylindrical Stem, Stepped Slot, Flat Catcher, Hook, Footed, 1700s, 8 In.	350
Iron, Extendable, 5 Iron Bars, Wall Mount Spike, 1800s, 31 In.	584
Iron, Hog Scraper, Cylindrical, Hooked Catcher, Scalloped Base, 1800s, 7 In.	250
Iron, Hog Scraper, Hollow Tube, Push-Up, 8 In. ....*illus*	125
Iron, Painted White, Trumpet Socket, Leafy Scrolls, 3 Paw Feet, 9 In., Pair	183
Iron, Ratchet, Cup, Scroll Finial, 1700s, 17 In.	900
Lucite, Nickel Plated Metal, Pretzel Shape, Dorothy Thorpe, 7 In., Pair	277
Mahogany, Brass, George III, Ring & Spiral Turned Stem, England, 15 In.	480
Mahogany, Georgian, Twisting, Round Base, 21 In., Pair	343
Malachite, Louis XVI, Leaf Capital, Gilt Mount, 12 x 6 In.	500
Marble, Black, Blue John, England, 1800s, 9 In.	854
Metal, Jack-In-The-Pulpit, Leaf Base, Pained, Art Nouveau, 10 In., Pair	177
Metal, Snake Charmer, Palm Tree, Cold Paint, Metal, 8¾ In.	438
Metal, Spider, Web, Germany, 6½ In., Pair	438
Oak, Figural, King, Chain Mail Tunic, Sword, Cornucopia, c.1815, 61 In.	2500
Oak, Twist, Round Foot, Bobeche, 10 In., Pair	75
Parcel Gilt, Pricket, Articulating, Phoenix, Dragon, 23 x 21 In., Pair	1190
Pewter, Baluster Shape Column, Push Rods, Homan, c.1850, 10 In., Pair ....*illus*	153
Porcelain, Bell Shape, Gilt, Orange, Birds, Flowers, 1900s, 9 x 4 In.	125
Porcelain, Figural, Girl, Red Hat, Brown Plaid Skirt, Grass, Staffordshire, 5½ In. ....*illus*	45
Porcelain, Green Parrot, Leaves, Candlecup On Neck, Pedestal, 17 In., Pair	938
Porcelain, Pyramid Shape, Blood Red, Chinese, 8 In.	120
Pottery, Boat Shape, Speckled, Brown, Orange, Cream, Footed, 1970s, 2 x 4¾ In. ....*illus*	14
Pressed Glass, Hexagonal, Yellow, Boston & Sandwich Glass, c.1850, 11 In.	300
Silver Plate, Baluster Standard, Sheffield, 1900s, 11 x 6 In., 8 Piece	687
Silver Plate, Columnar, Swag & Trophy, Base, England, 13 In., Pair	240
Silver Plate, Corinthian Column, Gorham, 1901, 12½ x 5 In., Pair	750
Silver Plate, Lyre Shaped Stem, Lion, Urn Cups, Sheffield, 12 In., Pair	180
Silver Plate, Skyscraper, Brass, Richard Meier, 9 In., Pair	590
Silver Plate, Zigzag Stem, Ettore Sottsass, 13 x 3½ In.	593
Silver, Armorial Lion On Base, Ribbed, Sheffield, 1796, 11 In.	120
Silver, Beaded, Round Base, 3 Applied Feet, 1900s, 13 In.	406
Silver, Column, Reeded, Round Foot, Georg Jensen, 10 In., Pair	3125
Silver, Corinthian Column, Swags, Tassels, Square Base, 10 x 4 In., 4 Piece	1663
Silver, Crystal Base, Silver Frond Finials, William Yeoward, 9¾ In.	600
Silver, Dolphin Stem, Scroll Base, Buccellati, Italy, 8 In., Pair	3120
Silver, Empire, Belgian Second Standard, H. Becker, c.1800, 11 x 6 In., Pair	1500
Silver, Flower, Sconce To Stem Tendrils, Round Foot, 1901, 8 In., Pair	7688
Silver, George II, Crested Figural, John Cafe, 1750, 10 In., Pair	8640
Silver, George II, Leafy, Knopped Stem, John Cafe, 1752, 4 Piece	4000
Silver, George II, Shells, Fluted, Knopped Stem, Lion, Base, 9 In., Pair	3840
Silver, Helmet Shape Cup, Arts & Crafts, 6 x 3 In., Pair	1750
Silver, Hurricane, Glass Shades, Redlich & Col, 1900s, 15 x 5 In., Pair	937
Silver, Knopped Baluster Stem, Shaped Foot, c.1915, 10 In., 4 Piece	2500

Silver, Knopped Monogrammed Stem, Inscribed Base, 1917, 10 In., Pair	369
Silver, Nautilus Shape, 3 ½ In., Pair	1111
Silver, Petal Shape Base, Maciel, Mexico, c.1950, 4 In., Pair	185
Silver, Scroll, Shell & Acanthus, Shaped, Gorham, 1917, 11 In., 4 Piece	2280
Silver, Serpentine Base Swirls To Stem, Rolled Cup Rim, Towle, 8 In., Pair	95
Silver, Taper, Joseph Clare, Maker's Marks, London, 1724, 4 ½ In.	688
Silver, Turned Baluster Stem, Scalloped Base, Petal Cup, 1969, 10 In., Pair	812
Silver, Woman, Holding Torch, 2nd Woman, Holding Branch, 16 x 6 In., Pair	1625
Steel, Blackened, Sculptural, Albert Paley, 1998, 21 ½ x 6 In., Pair	6250
Tin, Push-Up, Sand Weighted Base, 1800s, 10 In., Pair	390
Wood, Gilt, Torchere, George II, Scroll, Leaf Carved, c.1880, 53 x 22 In., Pair	1875
Wood, Poplar, Round Top, Turned Stem, Painted, Nails, 1800s, 27 In.	2280
Wood, Pricket, Cylinder, Red Paint, Iron Mounts, X-Base, c.1800, 26 In., Pair	1770

CANDLEWICK *items may be listed in the Imperial Glass category.*

CANDY CONTAINERS have been popular since the late Victorian era. Collectors have long favored the glass containers, but now all types, including tin and papier-mache, are collected. Probably the earliest glass container sold commercially was the Liberty Bell made in 1876 for sale at the Centennial Exposition. Thousands of designs were made until the cost became too high in the 1960s. By the late 1970s, reproductions were being made and sold without the candy. Containers listed here are glass unless otherwise described. A Belsnickle is a nineteenth-century figure of Father Christmas. Some candy containers may be listed in Toy or in other categories.

Alligator, Composition, Glass Eyes, 10 ½ In.	450
America's Defenders, Airplane, Grumman, Cardboard, 1942, 7 x 3 In.	270
Antique Car, 6 ½ x 9 In.	36
Belsnickle, Gold Robe, Tree, Papier-Mache, Mica Flecks, c.1905, 10 In.	449
Black Boy, Piglet, Bursting From Egg, Branch Feet, c.1910, 8 In.	741
Boy On Sled, Papier-Mache, Paint, Wool Hat & Clothes, c.1910, 5 In.	265
Bucket, Owls At Night, Nill & Jess Co., Chocolate Creams, 13 x 13 In.	518
Cartoon, Tin, Teenie Weenie Toffies, Murdoch & Co., 15 x 12 In.	719
Cat, Brown, Green Eyes, Collar, Composition, Germany, c.1880, 3 x 5 In.	565
Dog, Pug, Pink Bow, Bell Collar, Glass Eyes, Composition, 4 x 4 In.	281
Doll, Bisque, Glass, Cardboard, Fur Coat, Bunny Ears, Germany, 10 In.	1008
Easter Egg, Chicks, Lambs, Bells, Paper, Color Lithograph, 1940s, 4 In.	25
Gnome, Red Hat, 8 In.	61
Hen, Seated, Twig Nest, Composition, Marked, Dorothy, 1923, 5 x 5 In.	145
Horse Head, Dresden, Gilded Silver, Silk Pouch, c.1890, 2 x 3 In.	1495
Jack-O'-Lantern, Papier-Mache, Wire Handle, 1940s, 5 In.	105
Leprechaun, Pipe, 4 In. *illus*	175
Pelican, Top Hat, Papier-Mache, Composition, 1930s, 5 ½ In.	59
PEZ, Curious George	1
PEZ, Halloween, Laughing Ghost	1
Reindeer, Removable Head, Santa, Blue Coat, Composition, c.1910, 8 In.	795
Rooster, Plaster, Red, Yellow Head, Black Feathers	125
Santa Claus, Blue Robe, 13 In.	1722
Taxi Cab, Glass, Yellow, Pennsylvania, 1920s, 4 ¼ In. *illus*	61
Truck, Red, Tin Litho, Toffee De Luxe, Macintosh, 1920s, 8 In.	1200
Veggie Man, Nodder, Cardboard, Germany, 7 ½ In. *illus*	305

CANES and walking sticks were used by every well-dressed man in the nineteenth century, but by World War I the style had changed. Today canes are used by few but the infirm. Collectors prize old canes made with special features, like hidden swords, whiskey flasks, or risqué pictures seen through peepholes. Examples with solid gold heads or made from exotic materials are among the higher-priced canes. See also Scrimshaw.

Alligator, Stipple Carved Shaft, Brass Tip, c.1925, 35 In.	177
Animal Handle, Crosshatched Shaft, c.1910, 33 In.	600
Antler, Carving, Skull, Stars, Charleston Zouave Cadets, J.F. Burke, 1861, 7 In. *illus*	1200

Candelabrum, 8-Light, Bronze, Wrought Iron, Triangles, Curves, 12 ½ x 20 In.
$325

Kamelot Auction House

Candlestick, Brass, Barley Twist Stem, Octagonal Base, c.1700, 5 In., Pair
$123

Cowan's Auctions

Candlestick, Brass, Shaped Stem, Square Base, 1800s, 6 ¼ In., Pair
$35

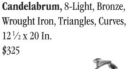

Hess Auction Group

Candleholders Glossary
A chamberstick is a candlestick that was used to light the way to the bedchamber. It was usually made with a wide saucer-like base that caught the wax drippings. It sometimes had a handle.
A candlestand is a candleholder tall enough to stand on the floor.
A torchere is a tall stand used to hold candles in the eighteenth century.

CANE

Candlestick, Giltwood, Gesso, Leaves, Footed, Belgium, c.1900, 29 x 10¼ In.
$395

Ruby Lane

Candlestick, Glass, Yellow, Column, Petal Rim, Stepped Base, New England, 9 In., Pair
$177

Hess Auction Group

Candlestick, Iron, Hog Scraper, Hollow Tube, Push-Up, 8 In.
$125

Ruby Lane

Bone, Wood, Inlay, Woman's Leg, 33½ In.	250
Carved Wood, Hand Shape Handle, Openwork, Balls, Tapered, c.1900, 36 In.	338
Carved, Snakes & Leaves, Red & Green Stain, c.1950, 36 In.	210
Ebonized, Gold Filled Tip, 36½ In.	590
Flag, 39-Star, United States, 35 In.	418
Maple, Carved Bird Grip, Schtockschnitzler Simmons, 35½ In. ....*illus*	885
Shark Spine, Vertebrae, Ivory Handle, Monogram, Wood Ferrule, c.1900, 37 In.	210
Silver Handle, Wood, Ebonized, 35½ In.	150
Silver, Wood, Automobile Shape, England, 35 In.	1625
Walking Stick, Root Carved, Intertwined Snakes, Multicolor, c.1910, 61 In.	360
Walking Stick, Silver, Woman Mask, Leaves, Cartouche, Horn, Italy, 1900s, 36½ In.	206
Walking Stick, Whalebone, Ivory, Clenched Fist Handle, Ropework, 33¼ In.	1800
Walking Stick, Wood Shaft, Silver Engraved Handle, Presentation, c.1797, 38 In.	1250
Walking Stick, Wood, 2 Resting Alligators, 48 In.	360
Walking Stick, Wood, Ball Grip, Hexagonal Cage, Entwined Snake, 1900s, 38 In.	129
Walking Stick, Wood, Bird, Fish, Horseshoe, Serpent, 1800s, 35 In.	644
Walking Stick, Wood, Carved, Tree Branch & Leaves, Folk Art, c.1910, 35 In.	270
Walking Stick, Wood, Greyhound Head Handle, Resin, Golden Eyes, c.1930, 36 In.	110
Walking Stick, Wood, Hearts, Clover, Leaves, Ribbed Grip, Inscribed, c.1890, 37 In.	936
Walking Stick, Wood, Intertwined Snake, Tack Eyes, Folk Art, c.1925, 36 In.	660
Wood, Carved, Figural Rebel Head Handle, Glass Eyes, 34½ x 2 In.	1872
Wood, Dog Head Handle, 33 In.	359
Wood, Relief Carved, Snake, Coiled Around Shaft, Copperheads, 1864	480

CANTON CHINA is blue-and-white ware made near the city of Canton, in China, from about 1795 to the early 1900s. It is hand decorated with a landscape, building, bridge, and trees. There is never a person on the bridge. The "rain and cloud" border was used. It is similar to Nanking ware, which is listed in this book in its own category.

Basket, Pierced Weave, 2 Handles, c.1850, 5 x 11 In.	270
Basket, Undertray, Reticulated, 1800s, 5 x 11 In.	277
Basket, Undertray, Reticulated, 4½ In.	330
Bowl, Vegetable, Lid, 1800s, 4½ x 11 In., Pair	185
Candlestick, Tapered, Flared Foot, 10 In.	270
Candlestick, Tapered, 1800s, 10 In.	111
Coffeepot, Lid, Foo Dog Knop, Strap Handle, 8 In.	390
Nut Dish, Mountains, 12 Piece	720
Pitcher, Water, Narrow Neck, 12 In.	330
Pitcher, Water, Waisted, 9½ In.	570
Plate, Landscape, Mountain, Lake, 10 In.	93
Platter, Hexagonal, Houses, Hills, 20 In.	720
Platter, Landscape, 11½ In., Pair	625
Platter, Well & Tree, Buildings, Landscape, 15½ x 18½ In.	180
Punch Bowl, Leaves, Lake, Landscape, 5 x 16 In.	125
Shrimp Dish, Landscape, Buildings, Mountains, Bridge, 10½ x 9½ In. ....*illus*	123
Soup, Dish, House, Boat, 9 In. ....*illus*	175
Sugar & Creamer, Landscapes, 2 Piece	61
Tea Caddy, Hexagonal, 6 x 5 In.	510
Teapot, Ships, Hills, Arched Finial, 4 x 7 In.	510
Tureen, Soup, Pavilions, Mountains, 13½ In.	480
Tureen, Stem Knop, Boar's Head Handles, 7 x 9½ In.	360
Tureen, Undertray, 9 x 13 In.	480
Vase, Stoneware, Seated Man, Crane, Raised Stylized Clouds, 10½ In.	250

CAPO-DI-MONTE porcelain was first made in Naples, Italy, from 1743 to 1759. The factory moved near Madrid, Spain, and operated there from 1771 until 1821. The Ginori factory of Doccia, Italy, acquired the molds and began using the crown and *N* mark. It eventually became the modern-day firm known as Richard Ginori, often referred to as Ginori or Capo-di-Monte. This company also used the crown and *N* mark. Richard Ginori was purchased by Gucci in 2013. The Capo-Di-Monte mark is still being used.

Box, Classical Figures, Chariot, Horse, Faces, Flowers, 4 x 8 In.	163

Centerpiece, Lemons, Pyramid, 29 In.	208
Dish, Lid, Cherub Finial, Lion Heads, Multicolor, 5¾ In. .... *illus*	345
Group, Man, 2 Seated Women, 18 In.	188
Group, Musicians, Dancers, 20 In.	125
Plaque, Bacchus, Festival, Multicolor, 17½ x 9½ In.	141
Plaque, Fruit Offered To Zeus, Shield Shape, 17 x 15 In.	504
Plaque, Prometheus, Holding Fire, Eagle, Gods, Shield Mount, Ginori, 23 In.	312
Plate, Armorial, Heraldic Crests, Cherubs, Serpentine Rim, 11 In., 14 Piece	365
Stein, Knight, Feathers, Bulbous Belly, Spread Foot, Helmet Lid, 1 Liter	480
Tray, 5 Sections, Handles, Red, Blue & Yellow Flowers, 16 x 21 In.	59

CAPTAIN MARVEL was introduced in February 1940 in Whiz comic books. An orphan named Billy Batson met the wizard, Shazam, and whenever he said the magic word he was transformed into a superhero. A movie serial was released in 1940. The comic was discontinued in 1954. A second Captain Marvel appeared in 1966, a third in 1967. Only the original was transformed by shouting "Shazam."

Bank, Mechanical, Magic Dime Saver, Flying, Tin Litho, 1940s, 2½ In.	268
Comic Book, Captain Marvel Adventures, No. 7, Fawcett, 1942	633
Comic Book, Captain Marvel Adventures, No. 29, 1943	418
Doll, Plush Body, Velveteen, Composition, Felt, Cape, Tag, 1946, 17 In.	5891
Figure, Wood, Composition, Paint, Standing, Arms Crossed, Base, 1945, 5 In.	575
Pin, Captain Marvel Club, Shazam, Portrait, Red, Blue, Celluloid, 1941, 1 In.	69
Poster, Captain Marvel Flying, Space Background, 1978, 14½ x 10 In.	80
Puzzle, Rides Engine Of Doom, Box, 25 Cent, 1941 .... *illus*	225
Racer, Tin Litho, Rubber Tires, Multicolor, Windup, 1947, 4 In., Set Of 4	411
Ring, Compass, Rocket Raider, Lighting Bolt, Brass, Enamel, Adjustable, c.1946	253
Watch, Leather Band, Metal, Glass, Full Figure Captain Marvel, 1948	85
Watch, Metal, Captain Marvel, Jet, Vinyl Over Leather Band, Box, 3 x 5 In.	190

CAPTAIN MIDNIGHT began as a network radio show in September 1940. The first comic book appeared in July 1941. Captain Midnight was really the aviator Captain Albright, who was to defeat the Nazis. A movie serial was made in 1942 and a comic strip was published for a short time. The comic book version of Captain Midnight ended his career in 1948. Radio premiums are the prized collector memorabilia today.

Badge, Decoder, Portrait, Propeller, Goldtone, Pinback, 1930s, 2 x 2 In.	83
Badge, Decoder, Premium, Pinback, 1940s	70
Blackout Kit, Magic Lite-Ups, Premium, Original Mailer, 1942	306
Decoder, Goldtone, Aluminum Knob, Cutouts, Red Cover, 1948, 2¼ In.	93
Folder, Secret Instructions, Squadron, Flight Commander, 3 x 7 In.	115
Game, Mexican Ringo Jumpo, Beans, Newspaper, 1939, 11 x 17 In.	173
Kit, Aeroplane, Spartan Bomber, Letter, Assembly Sheet, Poster, 1939	173
Membership Medal, Necklace Hole, 1940	5
Photograph, Signed, c.1940, 10 x 8 In.	10
Ring, Mining Ore, Goldtone Metal, Stones, Premium, 1947, 1 In.	153
Ring, R Initial, Brass, Logo, Raised Plastic Circle, Ink Stamp, 1948	115

CARDS listed here include advertising cards (often called trade cards), baseball cards, playing cards, and others. Color photographs were rare in the nineteenth century, so companies gave away colorful cards with pictures of children, flowers, products, or related scenes that promoted the company name. These were often collected and stored in albums. Baseball cards also date from the nineteenth century, when they were used by tobacco companies as giveaways. Gum cards were started in 1933, but it was not until after World War II that the bubble gum cards favored today were produced. Today over 1,000 cards are issued each year by the gum companies. Related items may be found in the Christmas, Halloween, Movie, Paper, and Postcard categories.

Baseball, 1963 Rookie Stars, P. Gonzalez, P. Rose, K. McMullen, A. Weis, Topps	1800

Candlestick, Pewter, Baluster Shape Column, Push Rods, Homan, c.1850, 10 In., Pair
$153

Hess Auction Group

Candlestick, Porcelain, Figural, Girl, Red Hat, Brown Plaid Skirt, Grass, Staffordshire, 5½ In.
$45

Ruby Lane

Candlestick, Pottery, Boat Shape, Speckled, Brown, Orange, Cream, Footed, 1970s, 2 x 4¾ In.
$14

Ruby Lane

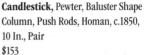

Candy Container, Leprechaun, Pipe, 4 In.

$175

Ruby Lane

Candy Container, Taxi Cab, Glass, Yellow, Pennsylvania, 1920s, 4 ¼ In.

$61

Morphy Auctions

Candy Container, Veggie Man, Nodder, Cardboard, Germany, 7 ½ In.

$305

Morphy Auctions

Baseball, 1968 Mets Rookie Stars, Jerry Koosman, Nolan Ryan, No. 177	3900
Baseball, 1968 Reds Rookie Stars, Johnny Bench, Ron Tompkins, Topps, No. 247	3300
Baseball, Babe Ruth, Bat On Shoulder, Red Ground, Goudey, No. 149, 1933	2700
Baseball, Babe Ruth, No. 6, York Caramels, Black & White, Frame, 1927, 2 ½ In.	696
Baseball, Bob Feller, Dixie Lids, 1938	540
Baseball, Bobby Mathews, Kalamazoo Bats, 1887, 4 In.	1989
Baseball, Box Of 36 Wax Packs, Unopened, O-Pee-Chee, 1974	9000
Baseball, Box Of 36 Wax Packs, Unopened, O-Pee-Chee, 1977	3300
Baseball, Buck Ewing, Walking Pose, Old Judge, N172, 1887	960
Baseball, Charles Comiskey, Arms Folded, Old Judge, N172, 1887	1320
Baseball, Christy Mathewson, Blue Ground, Sporting Life, 1910-11	2400
Baseball, Christy Mathewson, Throwing, Dockman & Sons, 1909	3900
Baseball, Clyde Milan, Gold Border, T205, 1911	360
Baseball, Connie Mack, Lincoln Publishing, 1906	1080
Baseball, Cy Young, Dockman & Sons, 1909	1200
Baseball, Cy Young, Standard Caramel, 1910	2040
Baseball, Dizzy Dean, Throwing, Rice Stix, 1935	1680
Baseball, Duke Snider, Rookie, Bowman, No. 226, 1949	960
Baseball, Ernie Banks, Topps, No. 510, 1965	600
Baseball, George Bell, Gold Border, T205, 1911	420
Baseball, George Herman Ruth, R340, Sport Kings, Green Border, 1933, 6 x 9 In. ....*illus*	7200
Baseball, George Perring, E145, Cracker Jack, 1914.........................*illus*	960
Baseball, Gil Hodges, Berk Ross, 1952	1440
Baseball, Harmon Killebrew, Rookie, Topps, No. 124, 1955	600
Baseball, Henry Aaron, Topps, No. 128, 1954	3900
Baseball, Honus Wagner, D322, Tip Top Bread, 1910........................*illus*	19200
Baseball, Honus Wagner, E145, Cracker Jack, 1914 ....*illus*	2040
Baseball, Jackie Robinson, Bowman, No. 22, 1950	1920
Baseball, Jackie Robinson, Fleetwood Slacks, 1947	600
Baseball, Jackie Robinson, Rookie, Leaf Gum, 1948-49	5400
Baseball, Jimmie Foxx, Batting, Goudey, No. 154, 1933	1080
Baseball, Joe DiMaggio, Goudey Heads Up, No. 250, 1938	4800
Baseball, Joe Tinker, Bat Off Shoulder, Sovereign 350, 1909-11	960
Baseball, Johnny Bench, Catching, Topps, No. 95, 1969	1920
Baseball, Johnny Evers, Standard Caramel, E93, 1910	480
Baseball, Lou Gehrig, Bat On Shoulder, Goudey, No. 61, 1934	3900
Baseball, Mickey Mantle, Bowman, No. 101, 1952	2160
Baseball, Mickey Mantle, Topps, No. 82, 1953	3000
Baseball, Mickey Mantle, World Series Game 2, No. 307, Topps, 1960	70
Baseball, Nap Lajoie, Sepia, 1910	840
Baseball, Nolan Ryan, Topps, No. 595, 1972	3300
Baseball, Pee Wee Reese, Bowman, No. 33, 1953	480
Baseball, Pete Rose, Rookie, Topps, No. 537, 1963	720
Baseball, Phil Rizzuto, Topps, No. 189, 1955	1560
Baseball, Reggie Jackson, Rookie, Topps, No. 260, 1969	1800
Baseball, Roberto Clemente, Rookie, Topps, No. 164, 1955	4200
Baseball, Rocky Colavito, Topps, No. 380, 1965	540
Baseball, Roger Bresnahan, Blue Ground, Sporting Life, 1910-11	840
Baseball, Roy Campanella, Topps, No. 314, 1952	960
Baseball, Sandy Koufax, Rookie, Topps, No. 123, 1955	600
Baseball, Satchel Paige, Bowman, No. 224, 1949	1920
Baseball, Stan Musial, Leaf Gum, No. 4, 1948	4500
Baseball, Ted Williams, Rookie Year, Play Ball, 1939	5400
Baseball, Tris Speaker, Batting, White Border, Piedmont, 1909-11	420
Baseball, Ty Cobb, Bat On Shoulder, White Border, Piedmont, 1909-11	3900
Baseball, Ty Cobb, Detroit Tigers, Red Ground, Sweet Caporal, T206, 1909-11	960
Baseball, Ty Cobb, Detroit Tigers, With Bat, Cracker Jack, 1914	19200
Baseball, Uncut Sheet, Includes Brett & Yount Rookie Cards, Topps, 1975	2160
Baseball, Walter Johnson, Portrait, White Border, 1909-11	2160
Baseball, Warren Spahn, Leaf Gum, 1948-49	3000
Baseball, Willie Mays, Rookie, Bowman, No. 305, 1951	2280

Baseball, Yogi Berra, Topps, No. 191, 1952	540
Basketball, Jerry West, Autograph, Rookie, Fleer, No. 43, 1961-62	600
Basketball, Michael Jordan, Rookie, Star, No. 101, 1984-85	11400
Basketball, Oscar Robertson, Rookie, Fleer, No. 36, 1961-62	2400
Basketball, Tom Heinsohn, Rookie, Topps, No. 19, 1957-58	1920
Basketball, Wilt Chamberlain, Rookie, Fleer, No. 8, 1961-62	9600
Boxing, Cassius Clay (Muhammad Ali), Rookie, Hemmets Journal, No. 23, 1960	1080
Boxing, Rocky Marciano, Rookie, Topps Ringside Boxing, 1951	1440
Football, 1958 Complete Set, Topps, 132 Cards	840
Football, Bart Starr, Rookie, Autograph, Topps, No. 119, 1957	1800
Football, Frank Gifford, Rookie, Bowman, No. 16, 1952	540
Football, Jim Brown, Autograph, Topps, No. 62, 1958	960
Football, Johnny Unitas, Rookie, 2 Images, Topps, No. 138, 1957	1320
Football, Otto Graham, Bowman, No. 2, 1952	960
Football, Paul Brown, Rookie, Bowman, No. 14, 1952	1080
Football, Tom Landry, Bowman, No. 142, 1952	1200
Greeting, New Years, 3 Cherubs, Seashell, Flower Bouquet, c.1880	12
Greeting, Valentine, Embossed Lace, Honeycomb, Tissue, Girl, Dog, c.1860, 4 x 3 In.	95
Gum, Addams Family, Photo, Cast Members, Puzzle Backs, 1964, 66 Cards	463
Gum, James Bond, Photos, Movie Scenes, Black & White, 1965, 3 x 4 In., 66 Cards	278
Gum, Spooky Stories, Photos, Monster Movie Scenes, c.1964, 3 x 4 In., 144 Cards	253
Hockey, Boom Geoffrion, Parkhurst, No. 3, 1952-53	1080
Hockey, Complete Set, Topps, 1954-55, 60 Cards	3600
Hockey, Gordie Howe, Rookie, Parkhurst, No. 66, 1951-52	4800
Hockey, Henri Richard, Parkhurst, No. 82, 1963-64	480
Hockey, Tim Horton, Rookie, Parkhurst, No. 58, 1952-53	7800
Playing, Edison Mazda, Ecstasy, Parrish, 52 Cards, Case, Box, 1930, 2 x 4 In.	154
Playing, Great Northern Railway, Winold Reiss, Boxed, 3¾ x 4¾ In., 2 Pack	53
Playing, Marlin Fire Arms Co., Annie Oakley Ace, 44 Cards	840
Playing, Marquis De Lafayette, Portrait, Cream, Yellow, Green, 1824, 3½ x 2½ In.	406
Playing, Stevens Patent, Habeas Corpus Protection, 1869	350
Playing, Tiffany, Light Blue, Light Green, Boxed, Sealed, 5 x 4 In., 2 Pack	34
Tarot, The Nile Fortune Telling, Gold Edges, Text, Box, c.1900, 4 x 3 In., 52 Cards	145
Trading, Auto, Color Photo Fronts, Model Detail Backs, 1953, 2 x 4 In., 63 Cards	229
Trading, Auto, World On Wheels, No. 177, Cadillac, 1955 Eldorado, Show Car	139
Trading, Auto, World On Wheels, Red, Back, No. 173, Buick Wildcat, Dreamcar	139
Trading, Bewitched, Practicing Witchcraft, Photo, Elizabeth Montgomery, Test, 1965	173
Trading, Display Box, Munsters, 24 Wax Packs, Wrappers, Photos, 1964, 4 x 8 In.	3536
Trading, Hood Ice Cream, Planes, Color Photo Fronts, Spec Backs, 1950s, 42 Cards	209
Trading, Pinup Art, American Beauties Gum Inc., 9 Cards, 1 Sheet, 1944, 8 x 10 In.	177
Trading, Shmoo Sealtest Ice Cream, Text Backs, c.1950, 2 x 3 In., 10 Cards	1328
Trading, Shredded Wheat, Movie Stars, Color Photos, 1951, 2½ x 3 In., 48 Cards	597
Trading, Skelly Gasoline, Space Fleet, Space Theme Art, Text Backs, 1953, 24 Cards	815
Trading, TV Western Stars, 5 Cents, Display Box, c.1959, 6 x 7 In., 30 Packs	379

CARDER, *see Aurene and Steuben categories.*

CARLTON WARE was made at the Carlton Works of Stoke-on-Trent, England, beginning about 1890. The firm traded as Wiltshaw & Robinson until 1957. It was renamed Carlton Ware Ltd. in 1958. The company went bankrupt in 1995, but the name is still in use.

Humidor, Petunia, Flow Blue, Gold Highlights, Marked Stoke On Trent, 5¼ In. ...... *illus*	94
Match Striker, Heraldic Crest, Red, Blue, Black, 2½ x 3 In.	69
Pitcher, Bouquets, Cobalt & Gold Draping Around Shoulder, c.1880, 7 In.	145
Teapot, Figural, Austin 35 Car, Gray, 9½ x 4 x 6 In.	450

CARNIVAL GLASS was an inexpensive, iridescent pressed glass made from about 1907 to about 1925. More than 1,000 different patterns are known. In September 2014 an important collection was sold and resulted in very high prices. Some of them are included here. Carnival glass is currently being reproduced.

Amethyst, Bowl, Ribbed, Ruffled Edge, Isaac Millersburg, 6½ In.	133

Cane, Antler, Carving, Skull, Stars, Charleston Zouave Cadets, J.F. Burke, 1861, 7 In.
$1,200

Cowan's Auctions

Cane, Maple, Carved Bird Grip, Schtockschnitzler Simmons, 35½ In.
$885

Hess Auction Group

Canton, Shrimp Dish, Landscape, Buildings, Mountains, Bridge, 10½ x 9½ In.
$123

John McInnis Auctioneers

Canton, Soup, Dish, House, Boat, 9 In.
$175

Ruby Lane

This is an edited listing of current prices. Visit **Kovels.com** to check thousands of prices from previous years and sign up for free information on trends, tips, reproductions, marks, and more.

Capo-Di-Monte, Dish, Lid, Cherub Finial, Lion Heads, Multicolor, 5¾ In. $345

Ruby Lane

Captain Marvel, Puzzle, Rides Engine Of Doom, Box, 25 Cent, 1941 $225

Ruby Lane

Card, Baseball, George Herman Ruth, R340, Sport Kings, Green Border, 1933, 6 x 9 In. $7,200

Robert Edward Auctions

Beaded Shell, Mug, Blue	145
Butterfly & Berry, Vase, Amber, 10 In.	77
Butterfly, Bonbon, Folded, Beaded Edge, Handles, Green, 2 x 8 In.	585
Captive Rose, Bowl, Ruffled Edge, Fenton, Blue, 9 In.	20
Captive Rose, Plate, Scalloped Edge, Electric Blue, Purple Iridescent, 9 In.	265
Cherry Chain, Plate, Blue, 6 In.	135
Comet, Bowl, Ruffled Edge, Green, Fenton, 1911, 8¾ In. ......*illus*	45
Dragon & Lotus, Bowl, Ice Cream, Scalloped Edge, Gold, Green Opal, 8 In.	450
Fanciful, Plate, Basketweave, Cobalt Blue, Piecrust Edge, Dugan, 1910-11, 9 In. ......*illus*	775
Fanciful, Plate, White, 9 In.	301
Fine Rib, Vase, Fenton, Amethyst, 15½ In.	45
Fishscale & Beads, Plate, Marigold, 7 In.	52
Fishscale & Beads, Plate, Marigold, 8 In.	83
Fishscale & Beads, Plate, Purple, 7 In.	176
Fishscale & Beads, Plate, White, 7 In.	15
Fruits & Flowers, Plate, Green, 7 In.	72
Good Luck, Bowl, Basketweave, Marigold, 3 x 9 In.	480
Grape & Cable, Bowl, Footed, Fenton, 12 x 7 In.	79
Grape & Cable, Bowl, Ruffled Edge, Octagonal, Marigold, 10 In.	20
Grape & Cable, Bowl, Ruffled Edge, Crimped Edge, Amethyst, Northwood, 11 In.	67
Grape & Cable, Dessert Bowl, Green, Northwood, 5 In.	32
Grape Arbor, Water Set, Pitcher, 6 Tumblers, Dark Marigold, 7 Piece	135
Grapevine Lattice, Bowl, Ruffled Edge, Purple, 7 In.	46
Hearts & Flowers, Compote, Ruffled Edge, Pedestal Foot, Aqua Opal, 1900s	650
Hearts & Vine, Bowl, Ruffled Edge, Fenton, Blue, 6 In.	20
Heavy Grape, Plate, Amber, 8 In.	78
Heavy Grape, Plate, Marigold, 8 In.	26
Holly & Berry, Bowl, Ruffled Edge, Amethyst, Dugan, 7½ In. ......*illus*	75
Holly, Plate, Aqua Teal, 9 In.	364
Holly, Plate, Blue, 9 In.	41
Honeycomb & Beads, Plate, Crimped Edge, Green, 7 In.	254
Imperial Grape, Decanter, Gourd Shape, Stopper, Electric Purple, 12 In.	465
Imperial Iron Cross, Plate, Stretch Panels, Smoke, 10½ In.	50
Imperial Open Rose, Plate, Pastel Marigold, 9 In.	10
Imperial Ripple, Vase, Swung, Purple, 9 x 3 In.	35
Imperial Ripple, Vase, Swung, Purple, 13½ x 3 In.	25
Leaf & Beads, Rose Bowl, Marigold, Northwood, 1905, 4 x 5½ In. ......*illus*	75
Leaf Chain, Bowl, Folded Crimped Rim, Blue, Purple, 7 In. Diam.	1100
Leaf Chain, Bowl, Ruffled Edge, Hexagonal, Fenton, Green, 9 In.	20
Leaf Chain, Plate, Blue, 7 In.	31
Little Flowers, Berry Bowl, Green, 6 In.	73
Orange Tree, Bowl, Ruffled Edge, Ball Feet, Pumpkin Iridescent	325
Orange Tree, Plate, Blue, 9½ In.	20
Orange Tree, Plate, Blue, 9 In.	83
Oriental Poppy, Pitcher, Amethyst, 13 In.	169
Oriental Poppy, Plate, Northwood, Marigold, Clear Base, 9½ In.	226
Pansy, Bowl, Ruffled Edge, Electric Purple, 9 In.	325
Peacock & Grape, Bowl, Fenton, Green, 9 In.	40
Peacock & Urn, Ice Cream Set, c.1912, 10 In., 7 Piece	1025
Peacock At The Urn, Bowl, Ruffled Edge, Fenton, Marigold, 9 In.	25
Peacocks, Bowl, Ruffled Edge, Crimped Edge, Electric Purple, 9 In.	675
Persian Medallion, Fruit Bowl, Ruffled Edge, Gold, Green, 9 In.	355
Persian Medallion, Plate, Blue, 6 In.	21
Pinecone, Plate, Crimped Edge, Blue, 6 In.	40
Pinecone, Plate, Crimped Edge, Amethyst, 6 In.	158
Pinecone, Plate, Marigold, 6 In.	18
Raspberry, Tumbler, Green	36
Ribbon Tie, Bowl, 3-In-1 Edge, Fenton, Blue, 8 In.	20
Rose Garden, Vase, Boat Shape, Scalloped Edge, Blue, Iridescent, 9 In.	275

C

Sailboat, Plate, Blue, 6 In.	169
Sailboat, Plate, Marigold, 6 In.	40
Ski Star, Bowl, Wavy Rim, Amethyst Iridescent, c.1910, 8 In.	426
Stippled Rays, Bowl, Ruffled Edge, Crimped, Northwood, Marigold, 11 In.	11
Stippled Rays, Plate, Blue, 6 In.	15
Stippled Rays, Plate, Green, 6 In.	15
Strawberry, Bowl, Northwood, Marigold, 8 ½ In.	34
Strawberry, Plate, Basketweave, Sawtooth Edge, Purple Iridescent, 9 In.	345
Thin Rib, Vase, Fenton, Blue, 12 ½ In.	11
Three Fruits, Bowl, Light Green, 8 ½ In.	56
Three Fruits, Plate, Ribbed Back, Purple, 9 In.	156
Trout & Fly, Bowl, Ice Cream, Green, Iridescent, Scalloped Edge, 2 x 8 In.	1000
Vase, Trumpet Shape, Orange, Red, Yellow, 17 In.	38
Vineyard, Pitcher, Clear Applied Handle, Marigold, Dugan, 9 ½ x 5 ¾ In. *illus*	59
Vintage, Plate, Marigold, 7 In.	11
Windsor, Juice, Blue, Federal Glass, 5 In.	11
Wishbone, Console, Beaded Crimped Edge, Green, Purple, 9 In.	299

CAROUSEL or merry-go-round figures were first carved in the United States in 1867 by Gustav Dentzel. Collectors discovered the charm of the hand-carved figures in the 1970s, and they were soon classed as folk art. Most desirable are the figures other than horses, such as pigs, camels, lions, or dogs. A stander has all four feet on the carousel platform; a prancer has both front feet in the air and both back feet on the platform; a jumper has all four feet in the air and usually moves up and down.

Camel, Stander, Carved Wood, Paint, Swirled Marble Eyes, Dare, 1885, 69 In.	9500
Camel, Walking, Carved, Painted, Platform Seat, Glass Eyes, c.1910, 45 x 63 In. *illus*	1840
Cat, Jumper, Carved Wood, Paint, Pink Saddle, Bayol, c.1900, 32 x 18 In.	3999
Chariot, Wood, Paint, Cherubs, Flowers, Velvet Seats, c.1914, 53 x 84 In.	7500
Deer, Jumper, Antlers, 48 In.	246
Donkey, Running, Painted, Bells, Tassels, Glass Eyes, Brass Holt, 1800s, 54 In.	8190
Elephant, Stander, Carved Wood, Seat, Kiddie Ride, c.1920, 32 x 36 In.	1000
Goat, Jumper, Blue Saddle, Charles Looff, c.1886, 60 x 64 In.	4920
Horse, Carved, Saddle, Asymmetrical Mane, Horsehair Tail, c.1880, 51 x 51 In.	3555
Horse, Jumper, Carved Wood, Gold, Purple Saddle, Roses, 1920s, 69 x 36 In.	1200
Horse, Jumper, Multicolor, c.1900, 23 x 62 In.	550
Horse, Jumper, Wood, Carved, Multicolor Paint, C.W. Parker, 59 x 65 In. *illus*	1180
Horse, Jumper, Wood, White, Saddle, Friedrich Heyn, Germany, 1880s, 35 x 53 In. *illus*	2500
Horse, Jumper, Yellow, Green, Purple, 57 In.	125
Horse, Prancer, Carved Wood, Paint, Brown, Pink, Bayol, 1900, 58 x 54 In.	3000
Horse, Prancer, Wood, Carved, Gray Crackle, Leather Strap, Stirrups, 45 x 42 In.	813
Horse, Stander, Coney Island Style, Cream, Inset Colored Gems, 62 x 62 In.	12500
Mule, Prancer, Paint, Raised Mane & Saddle, Glass Eyes, 1900s, 60 In.	8775
Panel, Wood, Paint, Lake Scene, Scroll, Flowers, Frame, c.1905, 21 x 105 In.	1100
Pig, Jumper, Carved Wood, Paint, Tongue Out, Plaque, Bayol, c.1900, 69 In.	7500
Rabbit, Jumper, Carved Wood, Paint, 2nd Row, Bayol, 1920s, 48 x 30 In.	3000
Rooster, Prancer, Carved Wood, Paint, Mauve, Anderson, c.1905, 36 x 31 In.	2999
Rounding Board, Carved Wood, Paint, Landscape, Scroll, PTC, 104 x 46 In.	2900
Seat, Swinging, Gilt, Carved, Shells, Leaves, Tufted Back, Hooks, 26 x 60 In.	413
Shield, Jester Head, Carved Wood, Shield Shaped, Herchell-Spillman, c.1907	850
Zebra, Jumper, Carved Wood, Paint, Herschell, 1920s, 52 x 42 In.	3800

CARRIAGE means several things, so this category lists baby carriages, buggies for adults, horse-drawn sleighs, and even strollers. Doll-sized carriages are listed in the Toy category.

Baby Buggy, Metal, Cloth Seat, Rubber Tires, Reclining, Folds, c.1905, 34 x 16 In.	595
Baby, Wicker, Black, Metal Frame & Wheels, Wood, Corduroy, 1920s, 30 x 30 In.	355
Buggy Seat, Wood, Green, 8 x 36 In.	180
Buggy, Doctor's, Columbus Carriage Manufacturing Co., Late 1800s	1800

Card, Baseball, George Perring, E145, Cracker Jack, 1914
$960

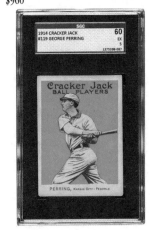

Robert Edward Auctions

Card, Baseball, Honus Wagner, D322, Tip Top Bread, 1910
$19,200

Robert Edward Auctions

Card, Baseball, Honus Wagner, E145, Cracker Jack, 1914
$2,040

Robert Edward Auctions

Carlton Ware, Humidor, Petunia, Flow Blue, Gold Highlights, Marked Stoke On Trent, 5¼ In.
$94

Woody Auction

Carnival Glass, Comet, Bowl, Ruffled Edge, Green, Fenton, 1911, 8¾ In.
$45

Ruby Lane

Carnival Glass, Fanciful, Plate, Basketweave, Cobalt Blue, Piecrust Edge, Dugan, 1910-11, 9 In.
$775

Ruby Lane

Carnival Glass, Holly & Berry, Bowl, Ruffled Edge, Amethyst, Dugan, 7½ In.
$75

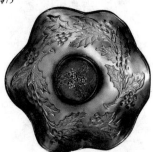

Ruby Lane

Sleigh, 1-Horse Open, Black, Cane Seat, Late 1800s, 46½ x 45½ x 80 In.	480
Sleigh, 1-Horse Open, Black, Maroon Seat, Red Rails, c.1900, 46½ x 89 In.	375
Sleigh, Horse Drawn, Wood, White Paint, Rails, Tufted Seat, c.1880, 66 x 44 In.	900

CASH REGISTERS were invented in 1884 because an eye on the cash was a necessity in stores of the nineteenth century, too. John and James Ritty invented a large model that resembled a clock and kept a record of the dollars and cents exchanged in the store. John Patterson improved the cash register with a paper roll to record the money. By the early 1900s, elaborate brass registers were made. More modern types were made after 1920.

National Cash Register, TF Marlett, 15 In.	615
National, Model 33, Embossed, Brass, c.1890, 18 x 15 In.	402
National, Model 312, Brass, 17 x 10¼ In.	354
National, Model 313, Brass, Marble Till, Drawer, Embossed Design, 17 In.	300
National, Model 313, Brass, Milk Glass, Labels, 1910, 21 x 10 x 16 In. *illus*	384
National, Model 313, Candy Store, Copper	887
National, Model 317, Brass, Marble, Drawer, Scroll, Wood Base, 16 In.	277
National, Oak Drawer, 31½ x 30½ In.	413
National, Oak, Veneer, Grain Painted, 8 Drawers, Door, 57 x 28 In.	177

CASTOR JARS for pickles are glass jars about six inches in height, held in special metal holders. They became a popular dinner table accessory about 1890. Each jar had a top that was usually silver or silver plate. The frame, also of a silver metal, had a handle that arched above the jar and a hook that held a pair of tongs. By 1900, the pickle castor was out of fashion. Many examples found today have reproduced glass jars in old holders. Additional pickle castors may be found in the various Glass categories.

Pickle, 3 Colors, Yellow, Blue, Flowers, Yellow Leaves, Silver Plate, Homon Mfg., 11½ In., *illus*	695
Pickle, Amber Glass, Swirl, Silver Frame, Leaves, Beaded, Lid, Finial, Tongs, 1800s	522
Pickle, Amber Jar, Button & Cane Pattern, Silver Plated Openwork Frame, 11 In.	71
Pickle, Blue, Cylindrical, Daisy & Button, Embossed Caddy, 11½ In.	96
Pickle, Blue, Thumbprint, Enamel, Leaves, Berries, Silver Twist Frame, Lid, 1800s	195
Pickle, Cranberry Glass, Coin Dot, Silver Plated Frame & Lid, Finial, 1920s, 11 In.	258
Pickle, Cranberry Glass, Enamel, Flowers, Silver Plated Stand, Tongs, 12 In.	69
Pickle, Cranberry Glass, Swirl, Silver Plate, Paw Feet, Handle, Bird Finial, 11 In.	160
Pickle, Cranberry, Dairy, Fern, Meriden Caddy, Northwood, 11 In.	121
Pickle, Cranberry, Daisy, Paneled, Etched, Silver Frame, Lid, Finial, c.1905, 12 In.	234
Pickle, Cranberry, Opalescent, Coin Spot, Silver Plated Caddy, Crane Finial, 12 In.	121
Pickle, Cruet, Sterling Silver, Scroll & Shell, 10 x 10 In.	800
Pickle, Lighthouse Shape, Bell Shape Lid, Pierced Design, Acorn Finial, 6 In.	36
Pickle, Pink Satin Glass, Eagle Finial, 10 x 5 In.	88
Pickle, Ruby Red, Coin Spot, Silver Plate, 4-Footed, Tongs, 12 In.	174

CASTOR SETS holding just salt and pepper castors were used in the seventeenth century. The sugar castor, mustard pot, spice dredger (shaker), bottles for vinegar and oil, and other spice holders became popular by the eighteenth century. These sets were usually made of sterling silver. The American Victorian castor set, the type most collected today, was made of silver plated Britannia metal. Colored glass bottles were introduced after the Civil War. The sets were out of fashion by World War I. Be careful when buying sets with colored bottles; many are reproductions. Other castor sets may be listed in various porcelain and glass categories in this book.

4 Bottles, Amber Glass, Metal Shakers, Glass Stoppers, Wire Stand, c.1905	98
4 Bottles, Milk Glass, Flower Sprigs, Metal Tops, Stand, Handle, c.1910, 8 In.	115
4 Bottles, Turquoise Glass, Paneled, Starburst Pattern, Scalloped Stand, c.1900	95
5 Bottles, Ruby Red Glass, Etched Roses, Metal Tops, Silver Stand, 1920s	235
7 Cut Glass Cruets, Silver Plated Frame, Lattice, Grapevine, Handle, 13 In. *illus*	187

CATALOGS are listed in the Paper category.

CAUGHLEY porcelain was made in England from 1772 to 1814. Caughley porcelains are very similar in appearance to those made at the Worcester factory. See the Salopian category for related items.

Asparagus Server, Blue, White, Fisherman, Wavy Sides, Tapered, 1780, 3 x 3 In.	461
Creamer, Alternating Stars & Dots, Gold, Cream Ground, 1780s, 3 x 4 5/8 In. ....*illus*	119
Cup & Saucer, Blue & White, Gilt, Fisherman, c.1790, 1 3/4 In.	134
Egg Drainer, Blue & White, Pleasure Boat, Round, Branch Handle, c.1770, 3 In.	659
Jug, White, Blue, Flower Spray, Molded, Scroll Handle, Mask Spout, c.1775, 8 In.	564
Mustard Pot, Blue, White, Fisherman, Scroll Handle, Lid, Finial, c.1775, 3 In.	664
Relish, Blue, Fisherman & Cormorant, Leaf Shape, Raised Foot, c.1785, 4 In.	95
Saucer, White, Cobalt Blue, Flower Sprig, Crosshatch Border, 1700s, 5 In. Diam.	174
Spoon Holder, Blue, White, Boy On Buffalo, Gilt, Crown Shape, c.1780, 5 x 3 In.	141
Tea Bowl, Blue & White, Woman, Sleeping In Woods, Paneled, c.1820, 3 x 4 In.	85
Tea Caddy, Blue, White, Gilt, Temple, Pagoda, Baluster, Ribbed, Lid, c.1790, 5 In.	186

CAULDON Limited worked in Staffordshire, Great Britain, and went through many name changes. John Ridgway made porcelain at Cauldon Place, Hanley, until 1855. The firm of John Ridgway, Bates and Co. of Cauldon Place worked from 1856 to 1859. It became Bates, Brown-Westhead, Moore and Co. from 1859 to 1862. Brown-Westhead, Moore and Co. worked from 1862 to 1904. About 1890, this firm started using the words *Cauldon* or *Cauldon Ware* as part of the mark. Cauldon Ltd. worked from 1905 to 1920, Cauldon Potteries from 1920 to 1962. Related items may be found in the Indian Tree category.

Game Plate, Mallard, Shore, Marsh, Gilt, Signed J. Birbeck Sr., 1800s, 8 3/4 In. ....*illus*	245
Plate, 6 Sections, White Leafy Center, Gilt, Roses, 9 3/4 In., Pair	144
Plate, Fox Hunting, Cream, Brown, Beaded, Scalloped Rim, 1940s, 10 In. Diam.	230
Plate, Gilt, Flower Wreath Medallion, Teal, Twist Rim, 1900, 10 In., 12 Piece	688
Plate, Luncheon, Dark Pink, Gilt Rim, c.1910, 12 Piece	960
Plate, Pink Rosebuds, Gold Scroll, Leaves, Scalloped Rim, c.1915, 10 In., 8 Piece	795
Platter, Turkey, Tall Grass, Pink Flower Border, Scalloped Rim, 1800s, 21 x 17 In.	400

CELADON is the name of a velvet-textured green-gray glaze used by Chinese, Japanese, Korean, and other factories. This section includes pieces covered with celadon glaze with or without added decoration.

Beaker, Crackle Glaze, Flared Rim, Flared Foot, 6 x 5 1/2 In.	1888
Bowl, Fish & Wave Design, Incised, Wide Rim, Footed, 2 x 7 In.	390
Bowl, Stylized Dragons & Flowers, Flared, Korea, 2 1/2 x 7 1/2 In.	540
Brush, Carved Handle, Chilong Design, Russet Markings, 15 In.	123
Brushpot, Rolled Lotus Leaf Shape, Flower Branches, Gray Spotting, 1 x 4 In.	123
Cachepot, Ormolu, Crackleware, Ribbon Bows, Pomegranate Finial, 12 x 9 In.	952
Censer, Squat, Ribbed, Lion Head Handles, Incised, Flared Rim, c.1800, 7 In.	4740
Charger, Barbed Rim, Chinese, 14 1/4 In.	2526
Charger, Incised Design, Scalloped Rim, Dark Green Glaze, 14 In. Diam.	840
Cup, Openwork, Branch Handle, Carved, Root Shape Base, Chinese, 1800s, 2 In.	1534
Dish, Divided, Petaled Lobes, Steep Sides, 6 In. Diam.	1353
Figurine, Dove, 8 In., Pair	250
Figurine, Duck, 1900s, 9 2/3 x 5 1/2 In. ....*illus*	170
Figurine, Duck, Rockery, 9 1/2 x 4 1/2 In., Pair	119
Figurine, Elephant, Pierced Cases, 9 x 10 In.	238
Figurine, Elephant, Rider, 7 x 6 1/2 In.	147
Jar, Cherry Blossom, Korea, 9 In.	250
Jar, Oval, Stick Neck, Dish Shape Mouth, Lug Handles, Incised Rings, 13 In.	185
Platter, Butterflies, Birds, Flowers, Chinese, 10 x 7 3/4 In. ....*illus*	189
Umbrella Stand, Hexagonal, Bush, Grasses, Blue Birds, Japan, 23 x 10 In.	143
Vase, Applied Dragon, Crackle, 12 In.	500
Vase, Blue Glaze, Flaming Pearl, Carnations, Cloud Scrolls, c.1870, 23 x 7 In.	178
Vase, Bottle, Teardrop Shape, 9 1/2 In.	156

Carnival Glass, Leaf & Beads, Rose Bowl, Marigold, Northwood, 1905, 4 x 5 1/2 In.
$75

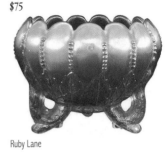

Ruby Lane

Carnival Glass, Vineyard, Pitcher, Clear Applied Handle, Marigold, Dugan, 9 1/2 x 5 3/4 In.
$59

Ruby Lane

Carousel, Camel, Walking, Carved, Painted, Platform Seat, Glass Eyes, c.1910, 45 x 63 In.
$1,840

Cottone Auctions

TIP

Permanent marker stains can be removed from most wood or textiles by wiping with a cloth soaked in rubbing alcohol.

Carousel, Horse, Jumper, Wood, Carved, Multicolor Paint, C.W. Parker, 59 x 65 In. $1,180

Hess Auction Group

Carousel, Horse, Jumper, Wood, White, Saddle, Friedrich Heyn, Germany, 1880s, 35 x 53 In. $2,500

Ruby Lane

Carousel Ladies

All horses on a carousel are mares.

Cash Register, National, Model 313, Brass, Milk Glass, Labels, 1910, 21 x 10 x 16 In. $384

Neal Auctions

Vase, Bulbous, Beast & Ring Handles, Trumpet Neck, Flared Foot, c.1910, 12 In.	95
Vase, Bulbous, Long Neck, Mask & Ring Handles, Splay Foot, c.1910, 11 In.	415
Vase, Carved Line Design, Ribbon, Ring Foot, 9 In.	123
Vase, Double Gourd, Incised Tendrils, Molded Rope Waist, Chinese, 6 x 5 In.	468
Vase, Double Gourd, Korea, 6 ½ In.	400
Vase, Fluted Mouth, Crackle Glaze, 7 In.	187
Vase, Garlic Bulb Shape, Fluted, Chinese, c.1920, 6 In. ....*illus*	850
Vase, Green, Dark Green Leaves, Purple Flowers, Black Birds, Chinese, 25 In.	62
Vase, Pear Shape, Bird, Flower, Crackle Glaze, Cup Rim, Stem Foot, c.1800, 10 In.	123
Vase, Pear Shape, Tubular Lug Handles, Brown Crackle Glaze, 5 In.	7995
Vase, Reserve, Figures, Houses, Landscape, Hawk Head Handles, 8 In., Pair	2125

CELLULOID is a trademark for a plastic developed in 1868 by John W. Hyatt. Celluloid Manufacturing Company, the Celluloid Novelty Company, Celluloid Fancy Goods Company, and American Xylonite Company all used celluloid to make jewelry, games, sewing equipment, false teeth, and piano keys. The name celluloid was often used to identify any similar plastic. Celluloid toys are listed under Toy.

Dresser Set, Mirror, Brush, Comb, Nail File, Buffer, Powder, Shoehorn, Pink, 1920s	80
Letter Opener, Page Turner, Cream Color, Girl In Bonnet Finial, 1920s, 10 In.	215
Mirror, Amber, Shaped Top, Tapered Handle, Marked, Amerith, 1900s, 15 x 6 In.	25
Nodder, Bulldog, Sitting, c.1920, 3 ¼ In.	24
Rattle, Girl, Playing Mandolin, Pink, Blue, Viscoloid, c.1910, 5 ½ In.	49

CELS *are listed in this book in the Animation Art category.*

CERAMIC ART COMPANY of Trenton, New Jersey, was established in 1889 by Jonathan Coxon and Walter Scott and was an early producer of American belleek porcelain. It became Lenox, Inc. in 1906. Do not confuse this ware with the pottery made by the Ceramic Arts Studio of Madison, Wisconsin.

Mug, 2 Monks, Cobalt Blue, Loop Handle, Sterling Silver Lid, 1896, 7 In.	443
Mug, Gooseberries, Leaves, Gilt Trim, Belleek, Olive Becht, 1897, 6 In.	61
Pitcher, Cider, Grapes, c.1900, 6 In.	95
Pitcher, Cider, Red Apples, 1901, 6 In.	95
Tankard, Hunting Dogs, Gilt Handle, Margaret B., 1906, 5 x 5 In.	245

CERAMIC ARTS STUDIO was founded about 1940 in Madison, Wisconsin, by Lawrence Rabbitt and Ruben Sand. Their most popular products were molded figurines. The pottery closed in 1955. Do not confuse these products with those of the Ceramic Art Co. of Trenton, New Jersey.

Figurine, Dancing Peasant Girl, c.1950, 6 In.	19
Plaque, Cockatoo, White, Gilt, 1950s, 8 x 4 In.	40
Shelf Sitter, Ballerina, White Tutu, Black Hair, c.1950, 5 In.	45

CHALKWARE is really plaster of Paris decorated with watercolors. One type was molded from Staffordshire and other porcelain models and painted and sold as inexpensive decorations in the nineteenth century. This type is very valuable today. Figures of plaster, made from about 1910 to 1940 for use as prizes at carnivals, are also known as chalkware. Kewpie dolls made of chalkware will be found in the Kewpie category.

Figurine, Cat, Nodder, Fur Details, Stripes, Mustard, Black, Red Collar, 4 x 7 In.	1230
Figurine, Cat, Nodder, Paint, Striped, Handwritten Birthday Underside, 1800s, 4 x 7 In.	1680
Figurine, Cat, Painted & Smoke Decorated, 15 In.	7500
Figurine, Cat, Painted, White, Red & Black Polka Dots, Pennsylvania, c.1855, 6 In.	1476
Figurine, Cat, Seated, Tan, Black Splotches, Pink Ears, 1800s, 6 In.	780
Figurine, Cat, Sitting, Spots, Red Ears, Painted Features, 10 In.	923
Figurine, Deer, Reclining, Paint & Mica Flecks, Oval Base, c.1940, 11 x 9 In.	585
Figurine, Dog, Seated, Painted Black Ears, 1800s, 5 ¾ In. ....*illus*	142

Figurine, Dove, Yellow Paint, Molded Leaf & Berry Base, 11 In., Pair		350
Figurine, Fruit Tree, Hollow Molded, Painted, Pennsylvania, 13 ½ In.	*illus*	501
Figurine, Lovebirds, Paint, Red, Green Feathers, Fluted Pedestal, c.1855, 7 In.		400
Figurine, Owl, Hollow, Painted Natural Colors, Pennsylvania, 1800s, 13 ¼ In.	*illus*	177
Figurine, Parrot, Multicolor, 12 ½ In.		96
Figurine, Pigeon, Orange Tin Feet, 1800s, 7 In.		209
Figurine, Pigeon, Painted Base, 11 In., Pair		221
Figurine, Rooster, Yellow, Green Beak, 1800s, 7 In.		123
Figurine, Rooster, Yellow, Red, Black, Banded, Base, Penn., c.1850, 7 In., Pair		1845
Figurine, Santa Claus, 1800s, 7 ½ In.		1353
Figurine, Squirrel, Mottled Brown, Yellow & Red, Pennsylvania, c.1850, 6 In.		369
Figurine, Squirrel, White, Black Tail, Eating Nut, 1800s, 7 In., Pair		540
Garniture, Fruit Compote, Lovebirds On Top, White Pressed Glass, 11 In.		492
Garniture, Fruit, Red, Lime Green, White, 1800s, 13 ¼ In.		390
Garniture, Fruit, Zigzag Leaves, Pedestal, Multicolor, 1800s, 14 x 10 In., Pair		2800
Garniture, Leaves, Brown, Yellow, 1800s, 10 ¼ In.		270
Plaque, Twisted Tree, Rocky Shoreline, Sea Gulls, Boats, c.1975, 35 x 15 In.		125
Statue, Woman With Jug, Collecting Water, Brown, Pale Blue, 1920s, 17 In.		130
Watch Hutch, Angel In Grotto, 1800s, 11 ½ In.		120

CHARLIE CHAPLIN, the famous comedian, actor, and filmmaker, lived from 1889 to 1977. He made his first movie in 1913. He did the movie *The Tramp* in 1915. The character of the Tramp has remained famous, and in the 1980s appeared in a series of television commercials for computers. Dolls, candy containers, and all sorts of memorabilia with the image of Charlie's Tramp are collected. Pieces are being made even today.

Doll, Little Tramp, Flocked Head, Cloth, Spins, Windup, 1920s, 7 In.		1100
Figurine, The Tramp, Holding Flower, Lladro, c.1980, 11 In.		329
Lamp, Electric, Black, Charlie Hugging Reeded Post, Bottle, 1920s, 15 In.		395
Movie Poster, The Vagabond, Playing Violin, Linen Mounted, 44 x 30 In.		431
Statue, Bowler Hat, Cane, Chalkware, Paint, Round Base, 1970s, 15 In.		265

CHARLIE McCARTHY was the ventriloquist's dummy used by Edgar Bergen from the 1930s. He was famous for his work in radio, movies, and television. The act was retired in the 1970s. Mortimer Snerd, another Bergen dummy, is also listed here.

Doll, Composition, Shoulder Head, Stitch Jointed, Effanbee, Box, c.1935, 19 In.	*illus*	570
Game, Radio Party, 1938		75
Puppet, Ventriloquist, Plastic, Tuxedo, Hat, Monocle, 28 In.		65
Spoon, Silver Plate, Name On Handle, Portrait, Duchess Silver Co., 6 In.		22
Toy, Mortimer Snerd, Crazy Car, Tin Lithograph, Clockwork, Marx, 7 In.		236
Toy, Ventriloquist, Celluloid, Tuxedo, Cane, Windup, Box, 1930s, 7 In.		209

CHELSEA porcelain was made in the Chelsea area of London from about 1745 to 1769. Some pieces made from 1770 to 1784 are called Chelsea Derby and may include the letter *D* for *Derby* in the mark. Ceramic designs were borrowed from the Meissen models of the day. Pieces were made of soft paste. The gold anchor was used as the mark, but it has been copied by many other factories. Recent copies of Chelsea have been made from the original molds. Do not confuse Chelsea porcelain with Chelsea Grape, a white pottery with luster grape decoration. Chelsea Keramic is listed in the Dedham category.

Dish, Double Leaf Shape, Green Rim, Flower Spray, c.1755, 9 In., Pair		2812
Figurine, Dove, Blue, White & Pink, Grass, C-Scroll, Round Base, 1800s, 9 In., Pair		297
Fob, Seal, Figural, Chicken, Chicks, French Text, Paint, Hardstone Base, c.1765		1995
Plate, Bird, Flowers, White Ground, Scrolling Border, Gold Anchor Mark, 10 In.		480
Scent Bottle, Bouquet Shape, Purple, Yellow, Stopper, 3 In.		7500
Scent Bottle, Cauliflower Shape, Stopper, 3 In.		1250
Tureen, Melon Shape, Yellow Green, c.1735, 6 ½ In.		5000

Castor, Pickle, 3 Colors, Yellow, Blue, Flowers, Yellow Leaves, Silver Plate, Homon Mfg., 11 ½ In., $695

Ruby Lane

Castor Set, 7 Cut Glass Cruets, Silver Plated Frame, Lattice, Grapevine, Handle, 13 In. $187

New Orleans Auction Galleries

Caughley, Creamer, Alternating Stars & Dots, Gold, Cream Ground, 1780s, 3 x 4 ⅝ In. $119

Ruby Lane

CHELSEA GRAPE

Cauldon, Game Plate, Mallard, Shore, Marsh, Gilt, Signed J. Birbeck Sr., 1800s, 8¾ In.
$245

Ruby Lane

Celadon, Figurine, Duck, 1900s, 9⅔ x 5½ In.
$170

Ruby Lane

Celadon, Platter, Butterflies, Birds, Flowers, Chinese, 10 x 7¾ In.
$189

Ruby Lane

TIP
Rub soap on noisy door hinges.

CHELSEA GRAPE pattern was made before 1840. A small bunch of grapes in a raised design, colored with purple or blue luster, is on the border of the white plate. Most of the pieces are unmarked. The pattern is sometimes called Aynsley or Grandmother. Chelsea Sprig is similar but has a sprig of flowers instead of the bunch of grapes. Chelsea Thistle has a raised thistle pattern. Do not confuse these Chelsea patterns with Chelsea Keramic Art Works, which can be found in the Dedham category, or with Chelsea porcelain, the preceding category.

Butter Chip, Copper Luster, c.1860	20
Cup & Saucer, Paneled, Angled Handle, Purple Luster, 1800s	25
Plate, Shaped Rim, Blue, Copper Luster, c.1925, 10 x 9 In.	20
Teapot, Bulbous, Paneled, Dome Lid, White, Purple, 1960s, 7 x 8 In.	150

CHELSEA SPRIG is similar to Chelsea Grape, a pattern made before 1840, but has a sprig of flowers instead of the bunch of grapes. Chelsea Thistle has a raised thistle pattern. Do not confuse these Chelsea patterns with Chelsea Keramic Art Works, which can be found in the Dedham category, or with Chelsea porcelain.

Cup & Saucer, Paneled, Blue Luster, c.1905, 3 x 4 In., 4 Piece	45
Cup & Saucer, Reeded Foot, Purple Luster, 2½ In.	15

CHINESE EXPORT porcelain comprises the many kinds of porcelain made in China for export to America and Europe in the eighteenth, nineteenth, and twentieth centuries. Other pieces may be listed in this book under Canton, Celadon, Nanking, Rose Canton, Rose Mandarin, and Rose Medallion.

Basin, Blue Fitzhugh, Butterflies, Flowers, Spearhead, Trellis, 16 In.	2640
Basket, Fruit, Oval, Black Enamel, Gilt Rim, Latticework, c.1770, 4 x 8 In.	225
Basket, Fruit, Stand, Blue, White, Shell Handles, Openwork, c.1810, 5 In.	500
Bowl, Blue, White, Monteith Shape, Scalloped Rim, 1800s, 4¾ In.	250
Bowl, Famille Verte, Flowers, Globular, Rolled Rim, Bell Foot, 5 In.	123
Bowl, Figures, Dragon, Fruit, Flat Rim, 4 x 12 In.	357
Bowl, Fish, Birds, Flowers, 24½ In., Pair	6875
Bowl, Gilt, Hunting Scenes, Cobalt Blue Ground, 5 x 10 In.	150
Bowl, Salad, Blue, White, Pagoda, River, Boats, Diaper Band, 1800s, 10 In.	250
Bowl, Serving, Famille Rose, Hand Painted, 1800s, 5 x 11½, Pair	1093
Bowl, Tea, Lid, Bell Shape, Flowering Peony Branch, c.1900, 4 In.	1476
Bowl, Yellow & Green, Dragons, Waves, Raised Foot, c.1885, 4 In.	584
Brushpot, Famille Rose, Bulbous, Roundels, Coiled Dragons, c.1900, 6 In.	800
Brushpot, Famille Rose, Cylindrical, Flower Ball, Roundels, Gilt, c.1900, 6 In.	246
Brushpot, Famille Rose, Figures, Playing Instruments, Tree, c.1910, 9 x 9 In.	60
Centerpiece, Stand, Gilt, Scalloped, Blue, White Landscape, 8 x 14 In.	833
Charger, Arms, Mills Impaling Webber, c.1745, 13 In.	900
Charger, Famille Rose, Ducks, Garden, Lotus Border, Octagonal, 12 In.	180
Charger, Famille Rose, Flower Spray Border, Octagonal, c.1790, 15 In.	711
Cider Jug, Blue, White, Strap Handle, Lid, Flowers, Houses, 1800s, 10 In.	475
Cider Jug, Lid, Blue & White, Fitzhugh, Foo Dog, 10 In.	1140
Cider Jug, Lid, Blue & White, Reclining Foo Dog Knop, 11 In.	660
Coffeepot, Figures, Landscape, 9¼ In.	438
Coffeepot, Lighthouse Shape, Birds, Strap Handle, Lid, c.1810, 10 In.	148
Coffeepot, Shield Crests & Anchors, Gilt Initials CK, c.1810, 9 In.	425
Creamer, Helmet Shape, Paneled, Vignettes, Figures, Roses, Handle, 4 In.	189
Cup, Bell Shape, Dragons, Iron Red Glaze, Raised Foot, c.1900, 2 In., Pair	246
Cup, Blue & White, Paneled, Flowers, Ring Foot, c.1715, 2½ In.	240
Decanter, 4 Chambers, Dragons, Openwork, Late 1800s, 12 x 5 In.	312
Dish, Famille Rose, Quatrefoil, Lobes, Warriors, Poems, 1800s, 10 In.	615
Dish, Green Fitzhugh, Armorial, c.1820, 9½ In.	472
Dish, Magpie, Prunus, Famille Rose, White, 10 In., Pair	3750
Dish, Ring, Molded Coiled Dragon, Wave Pattern, Cream Glaze, 8 In.	1230
Dish, Shrimp, Bird, Tree, Multicolor, 1800s, 10½ x 9½ In.	120
Dish, Shrimp, Birds, Butterflies, Flowers, Stream, 10 In.	168

Dish, Shrimp, Famille Rose, Celadon, Gilt, Bird, Butterfly, c.1850, 10 In.	180
Figurine, Boy, Riding 3-Legged Toad, Peach, Coin, Green, 1800s, 5 In.	923
Figurine, Cockerels, Enameled Red Comb, Porcelain, 1800s, 14 In., Pair	1020
Figurine, Dog, Seated, Sideways, Hind Legs Folded, c.1900, 4 In., Pair	338
Figurine, Phoenix, Famille Rose, 14 x 4 ½ In., Pair	238
Figurine, Phoenix, Famille Rose, Red & Blue, Porcelain, 1800s, 20 In.	610
Figurine, Pigeon, Teal Head, Multicolor Feathers, Base, c.1875, 7 In., Pair	875
Figurine, Rooster, Famille Rose, 1800s, 11 ¾ In. ....*illus*	366
Flask, Moon Shape, Dragon Handles, Mandarin, Phoenix, 9 In., Pair	1750
Garniture, Mandarin Scenes, Figural Handles, 1900s, 26 x 9 x 6 In., Pair	468
Ginger Jar, Blue & White, Plum Branches, c.1800, 16 ½ x 8 In.	1375
Ginger Jar, Bulbous, Yellow, Incised, Flowers, c.1800, 15 x 7 In., Pair	1375
Ginger Jar, Famille Noire, Cranes, Cracked Ice Border, c.1800, 6 In.	3075
Ginger Jar, Famille Noire, Phoenix, Cranes, Flowers, 1900s, 15 x 12 In.	250
Ginger Jar, Famille Verte, Pierced Wood Base, 1800s, 12 x 7 ½ In.	1062
Ginger Jar, Phoenix, Lotus, Pale Green, Swollen Top, c.1935, 23 In., Pair	875
Jar, Octagonal, Blue & White, Symbols, Waves, Clouds, 1800s, 19 In.	533
Jar, Ostrich, Deer, Blue, White, Bulbous, Flared Rim, c.1885, 6 In.	123
Jar, Roundels, Stylized Shou, Pink Bats, Lid, Bud Finial, c.1900, 8 x 9 In.	356
Kettle, On Stand, Burner, Dragon, Lid, c.1974, 12 In.	2583
Kettle, Repousse With Irises, On Stand, 1800s, 14 In.	5175
Lantern, Wedding, Flowers, Turquoise, Hexagonal, 1900s, 12 x 6 In., Pair	406
Mug, Blue & White, Elegant Women With Bat, Late 1700s, 5 ¼ In.	183
Pillow, Famille Rose, Figures, Cartouches, Birds, Flowers, Lotus Ground, c.1890, 6 x 7 In. *illus*	128
Pitcher, Water, Landscape, Mountains, Lake, Buildings, 1800s, 10 In.	135
Plaque, Famille Rose, River, Boat, Figures, Calligraphy, 1900s, 7 x 5 In.	492
Plate, Armorial, Red, Gilt Border, Flower Sprays, Fraser Arms, c.1755, 9 In.	200
Plate, Arms Of Izod, 6 Jaguar Heads, Multicolor, c.1730, 9 In. ....*illus*	4500
Plate, Famille Rose, Pink Flowers, Diaper Border, Gilt, 9 In., 12 Piece	1200
Plate, Famille Rose, Pomegranate, 1700s, 9 In.	183
Plate, Octagonal, Flowers, Crab, Cobalt Blue, Gilt, Iron Red, 1700s, 9 In.	450
Platter, Famille Rose, Figures, Trees, Gilt Border, Oval, 1800s, 17 In.	948
Platter, Famille Rose, Peacocks, Rocks, Porcelain, 1700s, 1 ½ x 16 In.	500
Platter, Figures & Landscape, Reserve, Blue Tracery, 1800s, 13 x 11 In.	300
Platter, Flowers, Puce Rim, Cut & Notched Corners, c.1800, 2 x 18 In.	300
Platter, Orange Fitzhugh, Shield, Stag Head, 1800s, 22 In. ....*illus*	3750
Platter, Oval, Salmon Red, Flower, Bird, c.1840, 16 In.	360
Punch Bowl, Blue & White, Rain, Clouds, 1800s, 11 ½ x 4 ½ In.	800
Punch Bowl, Blue, White, Landscape, Flower Border, 1800s, 14 In. Diam.	923
Punch Bowl, Famille Rose, Bacchanalian Picnic, Bamboo, Vines, 13 In.	1125
Punch Bowl, Famille Rose, Group, Courtyard, Flowers, 5 x 11 In.	812
Punch Bowl, Famille Verte, Warriors, Flowers, c.1815, 7 x 16 In.	738
Punch Bowl, Panels, Castle, Roundels, Flower Border, c.1790, 5 x 12 In.	1185
Saucer, Mandarin Palette, Acrobats, c.1790, 5 x 5 ½ In.	271
Strainer, Blue, House, Landscape, 1800s, 14 x 10 In.	152
Tankard, Famille Rose, Multicolor Flowers, Maiden, Children, 1700s, 5 In.	356
Teapot, Armorial, Blue, White, Blue Finial, 5 x 9 ½ In.	375
Teapot, Arms Of Graham, Paint, Gilt, Husk Swag, Foo Dog Knop, 10 In.	420
Teapot, Famille Verte, Dome Lid, Squat, Landscape, Figures, 8 x 11 In.	540
Teapot, Foo Dog, Dancers Under Cape, Figural Feet Base, c.1905, 8 x 10 In.	980
Teapot, Lid, Blue, Seascape, Square, Early 1900s, 4 In.	439
Teapot, Medallion, Figures, Hunt, Landscape, Bridge, Pond, Green, 6 In.	74
Tureen, Blue Willow, Boar's Head Handles, Lid, Finial, 1800s, 9 x 14 In.	330
Tureen, Shell Handles, Lid, Finial, Landscape, Cobalt Blue, Gilt, 1800s, 8 In.	750
Tureen, Tray, Blue, Boar's Head Handles, Blossom Finial, 1800s, 8 x 15 In.	120
Tureen, Undertray, Carp, Sea Grasses, Entwined Gilt Handles, 14 In.	510
Umbrella Stand, Famille Rose, Cylindrical, Flowers, Animals, 1800s, 29 In.	1185
Urn, Cover, Famille Rose, Garniture, Late 1700s, 20 x 6 x 4 In.	2500
Urn, Famille Rose, Butterflies, Birds, Flowers, Animal, Gilt, Lid, 16 In.	468

Celadon, Vase, Garlic Bulb Shape, Fluted, Chinese, c.1920, 6 In.
$850

Ruby Lane

Chalkware, Figurine, Dog, Seated, Painted Black Ears, 1800s, 5 ¾ In.
$142

Hess Auction Group

Chalkware, Figurine, Fruit Tree, Hollow Molded, Painted, Pennsylvania, 13 ½ In.
$501

Hess Auction Group

Chalkware, Figurine, Owl, Hollow, Painted Natural Colors, Pennsylvania, 1800s, 13¼ In.
$177

Hess Auction Group

Charlie McCarthy, Doll, Composition, Shoulder Head, Stitch Jointed, Effanbee, Box, c.1935, 19 In.
$570

Theriault's

Chinese Export, Figurine, Rooster, Famille Rose, 1800s, 11¾ In.
$366

Neal Auctions

Vase, Dark Blue, Pink Flower Heads, Swollen Shoulder, Tapered, 15 In.	150
Vase, Domestic Scenes, Blossoms, Birds, 12½ In.	100
Vase, Eagle, E Pluribus Unum, Starburst, 16 In.	305
Vase, Famile Rose, Squat, Stick Neck, Lotus Scroll, Bats, c.1900, 11 In.	3690
Vase, Famille Rose, 5 Boys, Turquoise, Tapered, Figures, Lotus, 12 In. ....*illus*	1476
Vase, Famille Rose, Flowers, Leafy Scroll, Trumpet Neck, 1800s, 9 In.	154
Vase, Famille Rose, Landscapes, Birds, Flowers, Stand, 1800s, 13 In.	296
Vase, Famille Verte, Figures, Building, Phoenix, Marked, 1900s, 15 In. ....*illus*	121
Vase, Famille Verte, Pear Shape, Flowers, Reserves, Pale Blue, 10 In.	400
Vase, Fan, Turquoise & Gilt Leaf, 1900s, 19 x 16 x 6 In., Pair	687
Vase, Flask Shape, Scroll Handles, Yellow, Incised Dragons, 1900s, 15 In.	90
Vase, Flowers, Court Scene, Landscape, Horse, Foo Dog, 14 x 11 In.	1190
Vase, Foo Dog Ring Handles, Leaves, Swollen Rim, 1900s, 22 In., Pair	1000
Vase, Morning Glories, Pink, Yellow, Green, Insects, 9 In., Pair	184
Vase, Woman, Sword, American Shield & Eagle, c.1930, 12 In.	425
Wall Pocket, Famille Rose, Vase Shape, Ruyi, Openwork Foot, 8 In., Pair	296
Warming Dish, Blue Band, Gold Stars, Family Crest, 1700s, 2 x 10 In.	240
Warming Dish, Blue, White, Swags, Center Medallion, 1800s, 10 In.	135

CHINTZ is the name of a group of china patterns featuring an overall design of flowers and leaves. The design became popular with English makers about 1928. A few pieces are still being made. The best known are designs by Royal Winton, James Kent Ltd., Crown Ducal, and Shelley. Crown Ducal and Shelley are listed in their own sections.

Balmoral, Bonbon, Royal Winton, 6 In.	84
Balmoral, Bowl, Vegetable, Oval, Royal Winton, 9 In.	190
Balmoral, Cup & Saucer, Royal Winton, Demitasse	98
Bedale, Creamer, Countess, Royal Winton, Gold Trim, 4 Oz., 2¼ In.	45
Bedale, Dish, Sweetmeat, Square, Royal Minton, 4¾ In.	41
Bedale, Plate, Dinner, Royal Winton, Gold Trim, Square, 9 In.	175
Bedale, Relish, 3 Sections, Royal Minton	182
Beeston, Vase, Bud, Shouldered, Royal Winton, 5 In.	145
Blue Pansy, Tray, Shelley, 14 In.	98
Cheadle, Butter, Cover, Royal Winton, ½ Lb.	219
Cheadle, Candy, Dish, Triangular, Royal Winton, 5¼ In.	56
Cheadle, Cup & Saucer, Footed, Royal Winton	44
Cheadle, Teapot, Lid, Albans, Royal Winton, 3 Cup, 4 In.	879
Clevedon, Creamer, Royal Winton, 4 Oz., 2¾ In.	86
Clevedon, Plate, Salad, Royal Winton, 8 In.	69
Crazy Paving, Cup & Saucer, Footed, James Kent	88
Cromer, Creamer, Countess, Royal Winton, 3 In.	52
Cromer, Cup & Saucer, Royal Winton	45
English Rose, Cup & Saucer, Royal Winton	84
English Rose, Teapot, Lid, Countess, Royal Winton, 1 Cup, 3 In.	489
Esther, Coffeepot, Flowers, Saucer Foot, Lid, Finial, Royal Winton, c.1948, 8 In.	495
Florita, Bowl, Fruit, James Kent, 6¼ In.	48
Florita, Sugar, James Kent	69
Hazel, Bonbon, Footed, Royal Winton, 6¼ In.	218
Hazel, Creamer, Bulbous, C-Scroll Handle, Royal Winton, 1930s, 5 In.	160
Hazel, Jug, Globe Shape, Royal Winton, 16 Oz., 3¾ In.	290
Hazel, Plate, Dinner, Royal Winton, 10 In.	179
Hazel, Relish, Royal Winton, 8 In.	47
Jardiniere, Multicolor, Shaped Mouth, Grimwades, Royal Winton, 8 In.	52
Marion, Butter, Cover, Royal Winton, ½ Lb.	254
Marion, Cake Plate, Open Handles, Scalloped, Royal Winton, 10 In.	198
Marion, Plate, Dinner, Royal Winton, 10 In.	169
Nantwich, Sugar & Creamer, Square Shape, Royal Winton, 1943, 2 In. & 2½ In.	80
Old Cottage, Jug, Roses, Blue Flowers, Yellow Flowers, Royal Winton, 5 In. ...*illus*	195
Peach Tree, Creamer, Red, Flowers, Gilt, Wavy Rim, Royal Standard, 1940s, 3 In.	36
Primula, Bowl, Vegetable, Rectangular, James Kent, 9 In.	119

Chinese Export, Pillow, Famille Rose, Figures, Cartouches, Birds, Flowers, Lotus Ground, c.1890, 6 x 7 In.
$128

Neal Auctions

Chinese Export, Plate, Arms Of Izod, 6 Jaguar Heads, Multicolor, c.1730, 9 In.
$4,500

Brunk Auctions

Chinese Export, Platter, Orange Fitzhugh, Shield, Stag Head, 1800s, 22 In.
$3,750

Neal Auctions

Chinese Export, Vase, Famille Rose, 5 Boys, Turquoise, Tapered, Figures, Lotus, 12 In.
$1,476

Skinner, Inc.

Chinese Export, Vase, Famille Verte, Figures, Building, Phoenix, Marked, 1900s, 15 In.
$121

James D. Julia Auctioneers

To Clutter or Not to Clutter
Modern design is simple, uncluttered, and neat. But some need clutter in their lives, so old trunks as tables, a row of green vases, or old toys must be included. Several modern designers are taking pieces of old machinery or buildings and transforming them into new lamps and tables.

Chintz, Old Cottage, Jug, Roses, Blue Flowers, Yellow Flowers, Royal Winton, 5 In.
$195

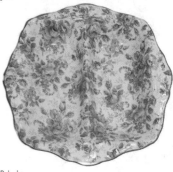

Ruby Lane

Chintz, Rosalynde, Relish, Roses, Forget-Me-Nots, 2 Sections, James Kent, 1930s, 6 1/2 In.
$22

Ruby Lane

Chintz, Rosebud, Chop Plate, Pink Vine, Spode, 1949, 13 In.
$65

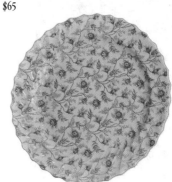

Ruby Lane

Christmas, Match Safe, Merry
Christmas, Happy New Year, E.B. Pool,
Celluloid, 3 In.
$218

Rachel Davis Fine Arts

Christmas, Pin, Your Old Friend Santa
Is At Bailey's, Portrait, c.1910,
1 ¼ In.
$411

Hake's Americana & Collectibles

Christmas, Postcard, Father Christmas,
Joyeux Noel, White Robe, Fanny Pack,
1905, 5 x 3 In.
$50

Ruby Lane

Primula, Cup & Saucer, Footed, James Kent	96
Primula, Dish, Shell Shape, James Kent, 7 ½ In.	62
Primula, Relish, 3 Sections, James Kent, 9 ½ In.	113
Primula, Salt & Pepper, James Kent, 2 ½ In.	101
Rosalynde, Relish, Roses, Forget-Me-Nots, 2 Sections, James Kent, 1930s, 6 ½ In. ....*illus*	22
Rosebud, Chop Plate, Pink Vine, Spode, 1949, 13 In. ....*illus*	65
Royalty, Cup & Saucer, Royal Winton	97
Sunshine, Bowl, Vegetable, Oval, Royal Winton, 9 In.	167
Sunshine, Nut Dish, Royal Winton, 4 In.	43
Sunshine, Plate, Dinner, Royal Winton, 10 In.	147
Sunshine, Teapot, Lid, Royal Winton, 4 Cup, 4 ¾ In.	678
Vase, Purple, Fruit, Round Foot, H & K Tunstall, 12 In.	116
Vase, Roses, Flowers, Birds, Multicolor, White Ground, 11 ½ In., Pair	162
Waste Dish, Blue, Multicolor Flowers, Copeland, 11 In.	70
Waste Dish, Blue, Red Flowers, Copeland, 11 In.	58
Welbeck, Creamer, Countess, Royal Winton, 6 Oz., 3 In.	119
Welbeck, Plate, Dinner, Square, Royal Winton, 9 ¾ In.	146
Welbeck, Salt & Pepper, Tray, Royal Winton, 3 Piece	239

 CHOCOLATE GLASS, sometimes mistakenly called caramel slag, was made by the Indiana Tumbler and Goblet Company of Greentown, Indiana, from 1900 to 1903. It was also made at other National Glass Company factories. Fenton Art Glass Co. made chocolate glass from about 1907 to 1915. More recent pieces have been made by Imperial and others.

Cactus, Butter, Scalloped Rim, Cover, Shaped Finial, c.1903, 5 x 8 In.	114
Leaf Bracket, Dish, 3-Toed, Tricornered, Greentown, 3 ¾ In.	50
Leaf Bracket, Relish, Boat Shape, Scalloped Rim, Oval Feet, 5 x 7 In.	72

CHRISTMAS *plates that are limited edition are listed in the Collector Plate category or in the correct factory listing.*

 CHRISTMAS collectibles include not only Christmas trees and ornaments listed below, but also Santa Claus figures, special dishes, and even games and wrapping paper. A Belsnickle is a nineteenth-century figure of Father Christmas. A kugel is an early, heavy ornament made of thick blown glass, lined with zinc or lead, and often covered with colored wax. Christmas cards are listed in this section under Greeting Card. Christmas collectibles may also be listed in the Candy Container category. Christmas trees are listed in the section that follows.

Andirons, Santa Claus, Cast Iron, 15 x 20 In.	438
Candy containers are listed in the Candy Container category.	
Cookie Jar, Woodland Santa, Deer, Squirrel, Fitz & Floyd, 12 In.	199
Creamer, Santa Claus, Red Robe, Fur Trim, Green Sack, Royal Bayreuth, 4 In.	885
Doll, Santa Claus, Cloth Body, Painted Face, Red Coat & Hat, c.1922, 30 In.	125
Doll, Santa Claus, Composition, Black Boots, Red Cheeks, 18 ½ In.	142
Figure, Elf, Sitting, Laughing, Green, Ceramic, c.1950, 2 ½ x 4 In.	18
Match Holder, Santa Claus Holding Sack Out, Royal Bayreuth, 5 ½ In.	3835
Match Safe, Merry Christmas, Happy New Year, E.B. Pool, Celluloid, 3 In. ....*illus*	218
Menu, Higbee Toytown, Santa, Superman, Cardstock, 1940s, 5 x 6 In.	1740
Music Box, Carolers, 4 Children, Ceramic, Silent Night, 1970s, 8 x 5 In.	22
Pin, Kresge Department Store, Newark, Santa Claus Face, c.1920, 1 ½ In.	315
Pin, Santa Claus, Sibley, Linsay & Curr, New Store, c.1900, 1 ¼ In.	345
Pin, Your Old Friend Santa Is At Bailey's, Portrait, c.1910, 1 ¼ In. ....*illus*	411
Pitcher, Santa Claus, Fur Trimmed Robe, Sack, Royal Bayreuth, 7 ¼ In.	4720
Postcard, A Fond Christmas, Santa Claus On Rooftop, 1908	10
Postcard, Father Christmas, Joyeux Noel, White Robe, Fanny Pack, 1905, 5 x 3 In. ....*illus*	50
Postcard, Santa Claus, Held Up By Children, Tree, Embossed Cardstock, 1907	33
Postcard, Santa Claus, Tree, Fairy, Child, Cardstock, c.1905, 5 ½ x 3 ½ In.	26
Postcard, Santa Claus, Working On List, Candlestick, Maroon Coat, c.1905	20
Postcard, Santa Putting Toys In Bed, Sleeping Kids, Embossed, c.1910, 3 x 5 In.	32

C

Postcard, Uncle Sam As Santa, Jolly Christmas To You, Squeaker, 4 x 6 In. ....*illus*	767
Salt & Pepper, Figural Candy Cane, Red, White, Green, Japan, 1950s, 5 In.	48
Santa Claus, Nodder, Composition, c.1955, 5 In.	83
Santa Claus, Pipe, White Hair & Beard, Composition, Feather Sprig, 14 In.	1415
Santa Claus, Plastic, Blown, Green Toy Sack, Internal Light, 47 In.	40
Sign, St. Nick Boots, Unika, Laughing Santa Claus, Die Cut, 12 x 5½ In.	1438
Sign, Welcome To Toytown, Santa, Mickey, Donald, 2-Sided, 1930s, 7 x 11 In.	408
Toy, Roly Poly, Santa Claus, Holding Presents, Weighted, Viscoloid, 1920s, 5 In.	125
Toy, Santa Claus, Sleigh, Reindeer, Red Paint, Cast Iron, 1900s, 16 x 7 In.	2800
Vase, Santa Claus, Gift, Sack, Claire Burke, 1980s, 8 x 7 In.	18
Wreath, Cellophane, Red, White Poinsettia, Candle, Electric, 12 x 7 In.	16

CHRISTMAS TREES made of feathers and Christmas tree decorations of all types are popular with collectors. The first decorated Christmas tree in America is claimed by many states, including Pennsylvania (1747), Massachusetts (1832), Illinois (1833), Ohio (1838), and Iowa (1845). The first glass ornaments were imported from Germany about 1860. Paper and tinsel ornaments were made in Dresden, Germany, from about 1880 to 1940. Manufacturers in the United States were making ornaments in the early 1870s. Electric lights were first used on a Christmas tree in 1882. Character light bulbs became popular in the 1920s, bubble lights in the 1940s, twinkle bulbs in the 1950s, plastic bulbs by 1955. In this book a Christmas light is a holder for a candle used on the tree. Other forms of lighting include light bulbs. Other Christmas collectibles are listed in the preceding section.

Bronze, Gilt, Neiman Marcus, 1980s, 23½ x 21 In.	448
Light Set, Glass, Colored Bulbs, Wire Cord, Box, Glolite, 1940s	52
Ornament, Belsnickle, White Robe, Papier-Mache, Mica, 1930s, 10 In.	268
Ornament, Book, Candy Container, Portrait, Child, Germany, 3 x 2 In.	100
Ornament, Boy As Court Jester, Spun Cotton, Multicolor, 5 In.	175
Ornament, Duck, Cap, Papier-Mache, Wood, Yellow, Orange, 1920s, 6 In.	284
Ornament, Elaine's Santa Claus, Gardening Can, Multicolor, P. Breen, 3 In.	60
Ornament, Fish, Gilt Scales, Blue Fins, Tail, Brown Gills, Dresden, 5 In.	175
Ornament, Flapper Girl, Face, Round, Glass, Paint, c.1920, 2½ In.	250
Ornament, Kugel, Acorn Shape, Mercury Glass, 8 In.	48
Ornament, Kugel, Ball, Blown Glass, Cobalt Blue, 2⅝ In. Diam. ....*illus*	224
Ornament, Kugel, Berry, Gold, Germany, 3½ In. ....*illus*	1534
Ornament, Kugel, Grape Cluster, Cobalt Blue, 1800s, 8½ In.	225
Ornament, Kugel, Grape Cluster, Green Glass, Germany, 4 In.	295
Ornament, Kugel, Grapes, Amethyst Glass, Ring, 3 In. ....*illus*	332
Ornament, Kugel, Green Grapes, Brass Cap, Hanger, Germany, 1800s, 6 In.	350
Ornament, Moose, Dresden, 2 In.	80
Ornament, Mouse, Spun Cotton, Pink Paper Ears, 2½ In.	60
Ornament, Nautilus, Paper, Embossed, Pieced, Painted, Dresden, 3 x 2 In.	1950
Ornament, Pinocchio, Mercury Glass, Red, 6 In.	45
Ornament, Pocket Watch, Glass, Gold, Red, Iridescent, Molded Star, 3 In.	70
Ornament, Rocking Chair, Tin, Red, Cream, 2¼ In.	30
Ornament, Rocking Horse, Sterling Silver, 2 x 1¾ In.	35
Ornament, Santa Claus, Glass, Multicolor, 5 In.	175
Ornament, Santa Claus, Lauscha, Germany, 5 In.	68
Ornament, Snowflake, Sterling Silver, Gorham, 1973, 3 In.	30
Stand, Cast Iron, Green Enamel, 3 Legs, Log Shape Screw Heads, c.1910.............................	195
Stand, Metal, Tree Branch Tripod Feet, Silver Patina, c.1905, 6 x 10 In.	125
Stand, Tree Stump, Cement, 11 In.	58
Topper, Church, Steeple, Glitter Tree, Blown Glass, Victorian, 8 In.	250

CHROME items in the Art Deco style became popular in the 1930s. Collectors are most interested in high-style pieces made by the Connecticut firms of Chase Brass & Copper Co., Manning-Bowman & Co., and others.

Bookends, Jacks, Chrome Finish, Jeff Curry, 6 x 7½ In.	118
Fireplace Tool Set, Horseshoe Shape, Brush, Tongs, Poker, Shovel, Art Deco, 5 Piece	40

Christmas, Postcard, Uncle Sam As Santa, Jolly Christmas To You, Squeaker, 4 x 6 In.
$767

Bertoia Auctions

Christmas Tree, Ornament, Kugel, Ball, Blown Glass, Cobalt Blue, 2⅝ In. Diam.
$224

Hess Auction Group

Christmas Tree, Ornament, Kugel, Berry, Gold, Germany, 3½ In.
$1,534

Bertoia Auctions

Christmas Tree, Ornament, Kugel, Grapes, Amethyst Glass, Ring, 3 In. $332

Norman Heckler & Company

Cigar Store Figure, Indian Maiden, Feathered Headdress, Tobacco Leaves, c.1900, 68 In. $16,800

Cowan's Auctions

Model, Signal Cannon, 12 In.	1750
Pitcher, Brass, Hatchet Shape, Peter Muller-Munk, c.1935, 12 x 10 In.	2684
Sculpture, Steel, Loop, Curved Over Like Wave, 1990, 19 ½ x 17 In.	976
Shaker, Footed, Engraved Grape Leaves, Farberware, c.1950, 12 x 8 In.	78
Tray, Art Deco, Scroll Form, Ebonized Wood, c.1930, 19 In.	106
Tree, Enameled Wood, Steel Trunk, C. Jere, 1970s, 48 x 21 In.	469
Vase, Bud, Metal Tube, Stone Base, Angelo Mangiarotti, c.1960, 12 x 8 In., Pair	500

CIGAR STORE FIGURES of carved wood or cast iron were used as advertisements in front of the Victorian cigar store. The carved figures are now collected as folk art. They range in size from counter type, about three feet, to over eight feet high.

Bust, Turk's Head, Carved Pine, Paint, Turban, c.1890, 20 x 14 In.	1481
Indian Maiden, Feathered Headdress, Tobacco Leaves, c.1900, 68 In. *illus*	16800
Indian, Chief, Bundle Of Cigars, Headdress, Drum Base, 71 In.	296
Indian, Chief, Pine, Right Hand To Brow, Plinth, 1800s, 76 In.	34000
Indian, Headdress, Holding Cigars & Pipe, 17 x 11 In.	4095
Indian, Headdress, Holding Cigars, 73 x 15 In.	480
Indian, Princess, Cigars In Hand, 65 ½ x 14 In.	510
Indian, Tobacconist, Feathered Headdress, Robe, c.1910, 58 x 16 In.	2214
Indian, Warrior, War Bonnet, Arm Up, Hand Over Eyes, 70 In.	855
Indian, Yellow Shirt, Arm Across Chest, 1800s, 40 In.	5856
Sailor, Missionary Figure, Holding Box, Give A Penny, 55 x 11 In.	1521
Woman, Seminude, Gold Feathered Skirt, Hands Aloft, 1800s, 48 In.	2100

CINNABAR is a vermilion or red lacquer. Pieces are made with tens to hundreds of thicknesses of the lacquer that is later carved. Most cinnabar was made in the Orient.

Box, Carved, Group, Table, Landscape, 6 Petal Shape, 1 ¼ x 4 In.	687
Box, Covered, Animals & Landscape, 6 ½ x 6 ½ In.	3680
Box, Diamond Shape, Peach Baskets, Sword, 8 ¼ In.	660
Box, Dome Lid, Round, Peony, Blooms, Buds, Leaves, 4 In.	11250
Box, Gander, Carved, Brass Rim, 9 x 12 ½ In.	885
Box, Landscape, 3 ¼ In.	120
Box, Lobed, Pewter Core, Scholar, Attendant, Landscape, Scroll Border, 4 In.	4062
Box, Peony, Divided Interior, 7 x 5 ¼ In.	168
Box, Round, Carved, Pagoda, Landscape, Laquer Interior, 1800s, 7 x 14 In.	6600
Box, Round, Landscape, Pavilions, Chinese, 5 ¾ In.	175
Ginger Jar, Lid, Lacquer, Lotus Flowers, 5 x 4 In. *illus*	213
Lamp, Outdoor Scenes, Flowers, Panels, Black Wood Base, 30 x 5 ½ In.	767
Panel, Carved, Scholar & Attendants, Pierced Rosewood Stand, c.1890, 13 In.	1046
Urn, Stand, Figures, Mountains, 16 In.	2000
Vase, Flared Neck, Foot, Carved Flowers, 14 ½ x 7 ½ In., Pair	324
Vase, Globular, Trumpet Neck, Carved, Flowers, Lotus Scrolls, c.1800, 21 In.	4920
Vase, Squat, Cylindrical Neck, Birds, Flowers, 6 ¾ In.	270

CIVIL WAR mementos are important collectors' items. Most of the pieces are military items used from 1861 to 1865. Be sure to avoid any explosive munitions.

Ambrotype, Triple Armed Union Soldier, Uniform, Pressed Paper Case	1152
Belt Buckle, Brass, Stamped OVM, Ohio Volunteer Militia, c.1860, 2 x 3 In.	600
Broadside, Butler's Proclamation, General, Infamous Orders, 11 x 14 In.	1778
Broadside, Recruitment, Louisiana Volunteers, Union Army, 1862, 23 x 18 In.	1920
Broadside, Recruitment, Rensselaer County, N.Y., Lansingburgh, 18 x 24 In.	461
Broadside, Recruitment, Your Country Calls, Mass., 1862, 18 x 23 In.	1680
Broadside, Spread Wing Eagle, Cavalry Headquarters, New York, 12 x 14 In.	1230
Button, Confederate, Coat, Brass, Van Wart Son & Co., c.1860s, 1 In.	222
Button, Confederate, Gettysburg Battlefield, Back Loop, ⅞ In.	33

Cap, Shako, Leather, Infantry Horn, Eagle Brass Plate, Strap, 9 x 6 In............................... *illus*	345
Cartridge Box, .59 Caliber, Metal Trays, Model 1863, Embossed Flap....................................	90
Carving, Cotton Stone, Confederate P.O.W., Gratiot Prison, c.1860s, 4 x 4 In.	2304
Church Bell, Confederate, G.W. Coffin, Buckeye Bell Foundry, 17 x 21 In.	8640
Coat, Officer's, Union, Infantry Regiment, c.1862-64...	5536
Cutlass, Leather Scabbard, Capture Tag, Cook & Brother, Union, c.1864, 21 In.	9775
Dog Tag, Abraham Lincoln Portrait, War Of 1861, Fdk. B. Rathbun, N.Y.	1100
Field Drum, Wood, Stain, Red Hoops, Label, Porter Blanchard, 1861, 11 x 18 In.	480
Fife, Rosewood, Brass Fixtures, 15 ¼ In.	115
Kepi, Chasseur Style, Blue Wool Broadcloth, Trefoil Piping, Leather Brim, Strap...............*illus*	2040
Kepi, Union Soldier's, 7th Regiment, Artillery Buttons, New York, 1865	375
Map, Hand Drawn, Camps, Fortifications, Suffolk, Virginia, 1863, 15 x 21 In.	7920
Patriotic Ribbon, New York, Silk, Flag, Verse, Scalloped Edge, c.1863, 4 x 5 In.	190
Pipe, Carved Stone, Pelican & Flag, Confederate, Folk Art, 2 x 2 ½ In....................................	1080
Pipe, Carved Wood, Fluted, Battle Of Antietam, Sept. 17, 1862, 3 ½ In.	2400
Pipe, Carved, Soldier, Kepi Attached With Hinge, Folk Art, 3 x 7 In.....................................	576
Powder Horn, Carved, John Delong, Confederate, July 1862, 11 In..	308
Spoon & Fork, Prisoner Of War, Carved, Richmond, Virginia, 1863, 11 In.	308
Sword, Confederate, Artillery, Scabbard, Double Edge Blade, Brass Hilt, 18 In.	805
Tintype, Disabled Man On Mule, Pressed Paper Case, ½ Plate...	792
Tintype, Union Infantryman Sergeant, Musket & Bayonet, Pressed Paper Case	720

CKAW, *see Dedham category.*

CLARICE CLIFF was a designer who worked in several English factories, including A.J. Wilkinson Ltd., Wilkinson's Royal Staffordshire Pottery, Newport Pottery, and Foley Pottery after the 1920s. She is best known for her brightly colored Art Deco designs, including the Bizarre line. She died in 1972. Reproductions have been made by Wedgwood.

Autumn, Tea & Coffee Set, Balloon Tree, Coffee, Teapot, Sugar, Creamer, 4 Cups & Saucers	812
Autumn, Vase, Orange, Yellow, Gold, Square Shape, Canted Side, c.1932, 5 In.	490
Bizarre, Plate, Mustard Center, Cream Border, Flowers, Grass, 7 In., 6 Piece..........................	390
Fantasque, Vase, Red, Green Melons, Lemons & Limes, 8 In.	1200
Sunburst, Demitasse Set, Teapot, 6 Cups & Saucers, Sugar & Creamer, 15 Piece .... *illus*	2340
Teepee, Teapot, Demon, Indian, Headdress, Porcelain, 7 In.	250

CLEWELL was made in limited quantities by Charles Walter Clewell of Canton, Ohio, from 1902 to 1955. Pottery was covered with a thin coating of bronze, then treated to make the bronze turn different colors. Pieces covered with copper, brass, or silver were also made. Mr. Clewell's secret formula for blue patinated bronze was burned when he died in 1965.

Jardiniere, Copper, Bronze & Green, Tapered, Swollen Rim, 10 x 14 In.	3250
Vase, Copper Clad Stick Neck, Flared Mouth, Blue, Green, 4 x 6 ½ In....................................	687
Vase, Copper Clad, 2 Handles, 2 Buttresses, Brown With Green Trim, 3 In.	489
Vase, Copper Clad, 4 Handles, Footed, 3 ½ x 3 In...	375
Vase, Copper Clad, Angel, Armor, 8 x 4 In..	250
Vase, Copper Clad, Brown Shoulders, Teal Bottom, 8 x 5 In.	250
Vase, Copper Clad, Carved, Reticulated, Ferock, F. Ferrell, c.1910, 2 ¾ x 8 In....................*illus*	944
Vase, Copper Clad, Flask Shape, Narrow Neck, 6 x 4 In.	610
Vase, Copper Clad, Flowers, Stamped, 11 In.	345
Vase, Copper Clad, Owens, Twist, Flowers, Marked, 5 ⅝ In...	431
Vase, Copper Clad, Shouldered, Green, Rust, 11 x 8 ½ In..	1098
Vase, Copper Clad, Teal Green, Signed, 12 ¾ x 7 In...*illus*	750
Vase, Copper Clad, Trumpet, Gourd, 7 ¼ x 2 ½ In.	305
Vase, Copper Clad, Turquoise, Rust, Mottled, 3 x 5 ½ In.	562
Vase, Copper Over Ceramic, Blue Green, Engraved, 8 ¼ In..	259
Vase, Sunflower, Brown, Stamped Mark, 3 x 7 ½ In...	750
Plate, Arrival Of General Marquis De Lafayette, c.1825, 6 ¾ In.	153
Plate, Historic, Views, Transfer, Staffordshire, Brown, White, Black, 10 In., 6 Piece	238

Cinnabar, Ginger Jar, Lid, Lacquer, Lotus Flowers, 5 x 4 In.
$213

Ruby Lane

Civil War, Cap, Shako, Leather, Infantry Horn, Eagle Brass Plate, Strap, 9 x 6 In.
$345

Leonard Auction

Civil War, Kepi, Chasseur Style, Blue Wool Broadcloth, Trefoil Piping, Leather Brim, Strap
$2,040

Cowan's Auctions

Clarice Cliff, Sunburst, Demitasse Set, Teapot, 6 Cups & Saucers, Sugar & Creamer, 15 Piece
$2,340

Weiss Auctions

85

Clewell, Vase, Copper Clad, Carved, Reticulated, Ferock, F. Ferrell, c.1910, 2¾ x 8 In.
$944

Humler & Nolan

Clewell, Vase, Copper Clad, Teal Green, Signed, 12¾ x 7 In.
$750

Rago Arts and Auction Center

Clock, Abbott, Samuel, Giltwood, Mirror, 8-Day, Weight, Brass Movement, 35 In.
$2,530

Cottone Auctions

CLIFTON POTTERY was founded by William Long in Newark, New Jersey, in 1905. He worked there until 1909 making lines that included Crystal Patina and Clifton Indian Ware. Clifton Pottery made art pottery until 1911 and then concentrated on wall and floor tile. By 1914, the name had been changed to Clifton Porcelain and Tile Company. Another firm, Chesapeake Pottery, sold majolica marked Clifton Ware.

Jug, Terra-Cotta, Crab Design, Squat, Loop Handle, Indian Ware, c.1908, 5 x 6 In.	135
Pitcher, Terra-Cotta, Black, Geometric Design, Squat, Indian Ware, c.1908, 4 x 7 In.	105
Vase, Green, Amber Drip, Crystal Patina, Bulbous, Tubular Neck, c.1905, 11 In.	340

CLOCKS of all types have always been popular with collectors. The eighteenth-century tall case, or grandfather's, clock was designed to house a works with a long pendulum. The name on the clock is usually the maker but sometimes it is a merchant or other craftsman. In 1816, Eli Terry patented a new, smaller works for a clock, and the case became smaller. The clock could be kept on a shelf instead of on the floor. By 1840, coiled springs were used and even smaller clocks were made. Battery-powered electric clocks were made in the 1870s. A garniture set can include a clock and other objects displayed on a mantel.

Abbott, Samuel, Giltwood, Mirror, 8-Day, Weight, Brass Movement, 35 In. ....*illus*	2530
Advertising, A&W Root Beer, Ice Cold, Red, White, Black, Double Bubble, 15 In.	492
Advertising, Alarm, Big Ben Type, Starkist, Charlie The Tuna, Box, c.1970	100
Advertising, Ben Schneider Jewelry Co., Ingraham, Early 1900s, 36 x 16 In.	390
Advertising, Chero-Cola, Make The Test, We'll Do The Rest, Regulator, Oak, 32 In.	180
Advertising, Duquesne Beer, Wood, Metal, Blue, Art Deco Style, Light-Up, 25 In.	123
Advertising, Edwards' Desiccated Soups, Composition, 8-Day, Baird, 31 In. ....*illus*	1150
Advertising, Fire Ring Spark Plugs, Yellow, Orange, Flames, Plastic, Light-Up, 16 In.	390
Advertising, Gem Damaskeene Razor, 1 Dollar, Man, Baby, Wood, 28 x 23 In.	360
Advertising, Lang's Dairy Products, Plastic, Milk Carton Image, 1950s, 17 In. ......*illus*	170
Advertising, Pontiac Auto Co., Alabaster Case, Red Indian Logo, 6 x 7 x In.	690
Alarm, Walnut, Illuminated, Incised Design, B. Bradley & Co., 15 In.	1035
Annular, Enameled, Hand Painted, Rotating Dial, Onyx Base, France, c.1890, 5 In.	2875
Ansonia, Flowers, Cobalt Blue, Gilt, Scroll Crest, Sides & Skirt, 1800s, 11 In.	1999
Ansonia, Goblin, Daisies, Scrolling Crest & Feet, Round Dial, Gilt, c.1904	150
Ansonia, La Landes, Amber, Green, Flowers, Scroll Crest & Feet, 1882, 11 In.	995
Ansonia, Navy, Brass, Spelter, Ship's Wheel, Jewel Rim, Ropework, c.1898, 11 In.	250
Ansonia, Office, Wall, Wood, Roman Numerals, Spring Motor, N.Y., c.1910, 16 In.	114
Atkins, Shelf, Rosewood, Painted Metal Dial, Mirror & Glass, London, 17 In.	1725
Atkins, Shelf, Rosewood, Signed & Painted Metal Dial, London, 1800s, 17 In.	4025
Atmos, LeCoultre, Brass, Glass, Revolving Pendulum, Swiss, 1900s, 9 In.	720
Bakelite, Glass, Arched, Timer, Hawkeye Measured Time, 1932, 6 x 5 In.	1750
Banjo, Dunning, Mahogany, Metal Dial, Reverse Painted, 8-Day, Brass, 40 In. ....*illus*	2875
Banjo, Howard & Davis, No. 2, Original Glass, 44 In. ....*illus*	4520
Banjo, Howard, E., No. 4, Cherry, Enamel Dial, Eglomise Panels, Gilt, c.1865, 32 In.	1481
Banjo, Mahogany, Kilbourn & Proctor, Painted Dial, Weight, 1900s, 39 x 11 In.	1062
Banjo, Mahogany, Lyre, Grand Ma's Cap Tablet, Patent, Boston, c.1825, 44 In.	300
Banjo, Mahogany, Metal Dial, Floral Panel, Brass Pendulum, Crank, c.1820, 42 In.	2100
Banjo, Mahogany, P. P. Quimby, Harp Pattern, Belfast, Maine, c.1820, 38 In.	1600
Banjo, Mahogany, Tapered Support, Square Base, John Currier, 1800s, 29½ In.	360
Banjo, New England Clock Co., Gilt, Metal Dial, 8-Day, Brass, c.1810, 40 In. ......*illus*	2990
Banjo, Oak, Pendulum, 39 In.	125
Banjo, Tiffany & Co., Mahogany, Reverse Painted, Ships, Eagle Finial, 32 In.	354
Banjo, Walnut, Mt. Vernon, George Washington, Reverse Painted, c.1910, 21 In.	460
Banjo, Waltham, Mahogany, Gilt Throat, 8-Day Movement, 1900s, 42 In.	1000
Banjo, Willard, A. Jr., Mahogany, Reverse Painted Tablets, c.1810, 49½ In.	5290
Banjo, Willard, A., Mahogany, Brass Eagle Finial, Brass Sidearms, 34 In.	1680
Banjo, Willard, A., Mahogany, Brass, Enamel Dial, Reverse Painted, c.1810, 35 In. ......*illus*	3993
Banjo, Willard, S., Mahogany, Wood Acorn Finial, Oak Leaves, 33¼ In.	2280
Berthoud, Enamel On Silver, Champleve Dial, Heron Base, Signed, 1800s, 7 x 3 In.	2990
Birge & Fuller, Shelf, Steeple, Fusee, c.1845, 25 x 12¾ In.	1200

Clock, Advertising, Edwards' Desiccated Soups, Composition, 8-Day, Baird, 31 In.
$1,150

Cottone Auctions

Clock, Advertising, Lang's Dairy Products, Plastic, Milk Carton Image, 1950s, 17 In.
$170

Tom Harris Auctions

Clock, Banjo, Dunning, Mahogany, Metal Dial, Reverse Painted, 8-Day, Brass, 40 In.
$2,875

Cottone Auctions

Clock, Banjo, Howard & Davis, No. 2, Original Glass, 44 In.
$4,520

Tom Harris Auctions

Clock, Banjo, New England Clock Co., Gilt, Metal Dial, 8-Day, Brass, c.1810, 40 In.
$2,990

Cottone Auctions

Clock, Banjo, Willard, A., Mahogany, Brass, Enamel Dial, Reverse Painted, c.1810, 35 In.
$3,993

James D. Julia Auctioneers

Timepiece or Clock?
Originally a clock was used to tell time and had a bell or other sound-making parts, while a timepiece kept time but was silent. Today people tend to call all sorts of timekeepers "clocks," including wall clocks, shelf clocks, and church tower clocks.

Clock, Cuckoo, Black Forest, Walnut, Birds, Leaves, 3 Weights, Germany, 1900s, 28 In.
$395

Tom Harris Auctions

CLOCK

Clock, Cuckoo, Stag, Rabbit Rifles, Birds, Carved, Painted, c.1948, 20 x 30 In.
$354

Fox Auctions

Clock, Jones, Abner, Shelf, Mahogany, Metal Dial, Mirror, 8-Day, Brass, c.1830, 45 In.
$5,980

Cottone Auctions

Clock, Marti, S., Shelf, Black Slate, Red Marble Accents, France, c.1895, 12 x 19 In.
$154

Cowan's Auctions

Clock, Nelson, George, Ball, Brass, Wood, 1949
$704

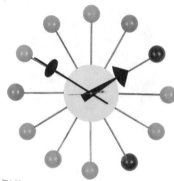

Wright

Clock, Sawin, Mahogany, Reverse Painted, Iron Dial, Brass Bezel, Bell, c.1829, 33 In.
$482

Skinner, Inc.

Clock, Shelf, Acorn, Laminated Rosewood, Painted Metal Dial, 8-Day, J.C. Brown, 24 In.
$7,475

Cottone Auctions

Clock, Shelf, Boulle, Gilt Bronze, 8-Day, Spring Driven, Brass Movement, 1800s, 22 x 11 In.
$1,093

Cottone Auctions

Birge, John, Shelf, Triple Decker, Wood, Eagle, Painted Panels, c.1830, 37 x 17 In.	615
Black Forest, Shelf, Walnut, Carved Dogs, Building, Gilt Dial, c.1885, 13 x 16 In.	937
Bracket, Black Lacquer, Bronze, Scrollwork, Louis XIV, France, c.1880, 13 x 7 In.	1500
Bracket, Boulle, Lacquer, Tortoiseshell Inlay, Louis XIV Style, 1880s, 25 x 15 In.	2375
Bracket, Bronze, Tortoiseshell, Pierced, Rocaille, Flowers, Phoenix, c.1885, 44 x 17 In.	4250
Bracket, Ebonized, Ormulu, 8 Bells, Arched, Finials, Leaf Scroll Feet, c.1800, 24 In.	4720
Bracket, Empire, Black Lacquer, Ormolu Mounts, 8-Day Gong Hour Strike, 30 In.	1500
Bracket, George III, Mahogany, Brass, Engraved Dial, Jas. Forsythe, London, 20 In.	3120
Bracket, Gilt Bronze, Ebonized Wood, Winterhalder & Hofmeier, 1900s, 27 x 17 In.	750
Bracket, Mahogany, Brass Lions, Thomas Cox Savory, England, 1800s, 15 In.	900
Bracket, Mahogany, Broken Arch Case, Maple & Co., London, 1800s, 15 x 12 In.	590
Bracket, Mahogany, Bronze, Pierced Gilt, Handle, Finials, c.1910, 20 x 13 In.	625
Bracket, Mahogany, Silvered Rings, Gilt Spandrels, Wm. Chaps, London, 23 In.	437
Bracket, Musical, Bells, Satinwood, Brass, Finials, Talon Feet, c.1790, 19 x 15 In.	3792
Bracket, Wood, Brass, Moon Phase, Date Wheel, Holland, 16 In.	550
Brown, J.C., Forestville, Shelf, 2 Steeples, Carved, Ripples, Gothic, c.1850, 20 x 12 In.	1320
Brown, J.C., Shelf, Mahogany, Beehive, Ripple Front, 19 x 10 1/2 x 4 In.	600
Brown, J.C., Shelf, Rosewood, Ripple, Onion Top, Frosted & Etched Glass, 20 In.	1955
Brown, J.C., Wall, Acorn, Mahogany, Ebonized Doors, 28 1/2 In.	3565
Carriage, Brass, Round, Column, France, 5 In.	840
Carriage, Bronze, Repeater, Beveled Glass Panels, 1900s, 7 x 4 x 4 In.	875
Cartel, Gilt, Sunburst, Eros, Leaves, Flowers, Louis XIV Style, France, c.1879, 23 In.	1500
Chandler, Abiel, Wall, Mirror, Painted Metal Dial, Reverse Painted Glass, 29 In.	2070
Charpentier, Shelf, Gilt Bronze, Porcelain Dial, Signed, 30 x 22 x 13 In.	5175
Chelsea, Metal Dial, Wind, From Biplane, Mounted In Propeller, 1917, 4 In. Diam.	655
Cuckoo, Black Forest, Grapes, 33 In.	281
Cuckoo, Black Forest, Walnut, Birds, Leaves, 3 Weights, Germany, 1900s, 28 In. illus	395
Cuckoo, Stag, Rabbit Rifles, Birds, Carved, Painted, c.1948, 20 x 30 In. illus	354
Desk, Agate, Round Face, Enamel Wreath, Silver Winged Claw Feet, 5 x 4 In.	1185
Desk, Bronze, Ormulu Mount, 30-Hour Movement, France, 6 In.	275
Empire, Gilt Bronze, Figural, Urn Form, Swans, Early 1800s, 16 x 9 1/2 In.	2432
Figural, Czarina Elizabeth, Gilt Metal, Porcelain, Germany, 1900s, 26 x 21 In.	531
Figural, Elephant, Rider, Porcelain, Bronze, Gilt, Multicolor, France, 23 x 13 1/2 In.	4760
Figural, Fan, Wood Case, Stepped, Openwork Hours On Ribs, Minute Dial, 12 In.	1073
Figural, Napoleon, Horse, Bronze Egg & Dart Molding, Sienna Marble, 16 x 7 In.	714
Figural, Parcel Gilt, Neoclassical Woman, Holding Clock In Left Arm, 20 x 11 In.	2677
Figural, Peasant, Holding Fan, Hours On Ribs, Serpents, Composition, 70 In.	1228
Figural, Woman, Seated, White Metal, Footed Base, c.1890, 22 1/2 In.	350
Forestville, Shelf, Mahogany, Ogee, c.1840, 29 x 16 x 4 In.	60
Forestville, Shelf, Steeple, Hot Air Balloon, American Flags, c.1850, 20 x 10 In.	738
French, Comtoise, Brass Frame, Flowers, Enamel Dial, LaPlagne Argentat, c.1860	682
French, Comtoise, Brass Frame, Peasant & Plow, Darmais Au Coteau, c.1870	273
Hills & Goodrich, Shelf, Ogee, Door, Mirror, c.1841, 31 x 18 x 5 In.	450
Hoadley, Silas, Shelf, Pillar & Splat, Upside Down, c.1820, 36 x 17 x 4 1/2 In.	180
Hoadley, Silas, Shelf, Upside Down, 30-Hour Time & Alarm, c.1820, 25 x 12 In.	900
Hooper, Henry, Shelf, Gilt Metal Watch Hutch, Boston, c.1860s, 6 x 5 x 3 In.	580
Howard, E., Regulator, Walnut, Burl, Ebonized Pillars & Molding, Signed, 52 In.	4888
Ithaca Clock Co., Wall, Calendar, Walnut, Brass, Nickel, 28 In.	1380
Ives, Joseph, Shelf, Mahogany, Scroll Top, Mirror, c.1820, 56 x 19 1/2 x 6 In.	1320
Ives, Joseph, Shelf, Rosewood, Reverse Painted, Chariot, Dial Refreshed, 17 1/2 In.	920
Jaeger-LeCoultre & Cie, Atmos, Shelf, Glass, Brass, Black Dial, Stamped, 9 x 6 In.	546
Japy Freres, Shelf, Figural, Bronze, Patina, Tropical Landscape, c.1880, 19 x 13 In.	325
Jerome, Chauncey, Shelf, Mahogany, Fusee, c.1840, 23 In.	180
Jones, Abner, Shelf, Mahogany, Metal Dial, Mirror, 8-Day, Brass, c.1830, 45 In. illus	5980
Junghans, Acrobat, Trapeze, Mahogany, Brass, Circus, Scalloped Roof, 15 x 9 In.	343 to 531
Junghans, Shelf, Mahogany, Steeple, Quarter Hour Strike, c.1900, 19 1/2 x 13 In.	100
Juvet & Co., Globe, Time, Brass, Gargoyles, Claw Feet, Floor Model, 48 x 12 In.	9488
Knox, A., Liberty, Shelf, Pewter, Copper, Enamel, Turquoise Dial, Leaves, c.1910, 8 In.	4053
Knox, A., Liberty, Tudric, Shelf, Brass, Blue Enamel Dial, Arts & Crafts, 8 x 6 In.	3335

Clock, Shelf, Empire, Gilt, Bronze, Greek Vase Case, Signed, Lepaute, c.1790, 16 x 6 In. $1,920

Neal Auctions

Clock, Shelf, Rolling Ball, Wood, Steel, Bronze, 8-Day, Thermometer, Barometer, 22 In. $308

Cowan's Auctions

TIP
Clocks that are wound from the back should be wound counterclockwise because that is really clockwise from the front of the clock. Never wind an old clock counterclockwise.

CLOCK

Clock, Tall Case, George III, Oak, Mahogany, Brass & Rosettes, Painted Face, 87 In. **$468**

New Orleans Auction Galleries

Clock, Tall Case, Gowland, C., Mahogany, 8-Day, Calendar Dial, England, c.1840, 94 In. **$840**

Cowan's Auctions

Leavenworth, Mark, Shelf, Mahogany, Columns, Paw Feet, Painted Dial, 22 In.	5520
Marti, S., Shelf, Black Slate, Red Marble Accents, France, c.1895, 12 x 19 In. ....*illus*	154
Munger, S.A., Shelf, Walnut, Iron Dial, 8-Day, Eagle Pendulum, c.1830, 39 In.	878
Mystery, Dog, Boxer, Composition, Brass Case & Pendulum, 25 In.	409
Nelson, George, Ball, Brass, Wood, 1949 ....*illus*	704
Nelson, George, Table, Watermelon, Wood, Howard Miller, c.1954, 5 x 8 x 4 In.	2500
Nelson, George, Wall, Sunflower, Howard Miller Clock Co., c.1958, 29 ½ In.	2200
Orton Preston, Shelf, Mahogany, Cutout Crest, Farmington, Ct., c.1830, 33 In.	211
Oswald, Shelf, Rolling Eye, Devil, Wood, Carved, Germany, 5 ½ x 4 ¼ In.	1342
Oswald, Shelf, Rolling Eye, French Bulldog, Wood, Carved, Germany, 6 x 3 ½ In.	187
Oswald, Shelf, Rolling Eye, Poodle, Wood, Carved, Germany, 5 x 3 ¼ In.	1527
Oswald, Shelf, Rolling Eye, Sitting Cat, Wood, Carved, Germany, 12 ½ x 4 ½ In.	1250
Picture, Erotic, Hotel 69, 4 x 5 In.	187
Picture, Oil On Canvas, Church, Mountains, Dial In Steeple, Musical, c.1860, 29 In.	1229
Picture, Oil On Canvas, Procession, Dial In Building, Gong, Chimes, c.1870, 38 In.	8871
Portico, Empire, Flame Mahogany, Bronze, Enameled Dial, France, 1800s, 21 In.	720
Portico, Louis-Philippe, Rosewood, Marquetry, Gilt Bronze, Glass Dome, 24 x 12 In.	531
Recorder, International, 50 Employees, Oak, Glass, Iron, Brass, c.1915, 39 x 35 In.	600
Regimental, Terra-Cotta, Soldier, Esk., Ulanen Regt. Nr. 16, Salzwedel, c.1909, 15 In.	690
Regulator, Brass, Porcelain Dial, Beveled Glass, Doors, Plinth, France, c.1885	652
Regulator, Oak, Jeweler's, Columns & Carvings, Porcelain Dial, 1800s, 75 In.	1150
Regulator, Paper Over Tin Dial, Round Hinged Door, Molded, Pendulum, 31 In.	90
Regulator, Terry, Silas B., Rosewood, Painted Metal Dial, 33 In.	1610
Regulator, Wall, Mahogany, Banded Inlay, Painted Glass Dial, 1800s, 42 In.	3163
Regulator, Walnut, Carved, Columns, Finials, Glass Door, Brass, c.1915, 57 x 20 In.	1778
Sawin, Mahogany, Reverse Painted, Iron Dial, Brass Bezel, Bell, c.1829, 33 In. ....*illus*	482
Seth Thomas, Figural, Goats, Glass Eyes, Black Forest Style, 1800s, 34 x 22 In.	4888
Seth Thomas, Shelf, Brass Case, 1900s, 13 x 8 In.	270
Seth Thomas, Shelf, Mahogany, Paint, Scroll, Columns, Tin Dial, c.1880, 32 x 19 In.	150
Seth Thomas, Shelf, Pillar & Scroll, Mahogany, Brass Finials, c.1820, 31 x 17 In.	2091
Seth Thomas, Shelf, Pillar & Scroll, Mahogany, Repainted Glass, 30 In.	1610
Seth Thomas, Shelf, Walnut, Ebonized, Calendar Dial, No. 6, c.1878, 24 x 15 In.	562
Shelf, 2 Metal Figures, 8-Day, Arabic Numerals, Pendulum, Key, 20 In.	850
Shelf, Acorn, Laminated Rosewood, Painted Metal Dial, 8-Day, J.C. Brown, 24 In. ....*illus*	7475
Shelf, Acorn, Rosewood, Reverse Painted, 8-Day, J.C. Brown, c.1830, 24 In.	46000
Shelf, Alabaster, Gilt Bronze, Figural, Woman, Animals, Base, c.1885, 15 x 14 In.	1046
Shelf, Arched Crest, Enamel Dial, Malachite, Vines, Glass Door, c.1865, 13 x 16 In.	208
Shelf, Art Deco, Metal, Arched, Beveled Glass, Stepped Base, 6 x 8 In.	200
Shelf, Belle Epoque, Gilt Bronze, Hangs From Frame, France, c.1890, 8 x 6 In.	687
Shelf, Biedermeier, Fruitwood, White Onyx, Temple Shape, c.1950, 22 x 13 In.	461
Shelf, Boulle, Gilt Bronze, 8-Day, Spring Driven, Brass Movement, 1800s, 22 x 11 In. ....*illus*	1093
Shelf, Brass, Cloisonne, Glass Doors, Enamel Dial, Flowers, Columns, 18 x 15 In.	460
Shelf, Bronze Dore, Figural, Shakespeare, Seated, Footed, Scroll, 1800s, 17 x 14 In.	189
Shelf, Bronze, Dore & Patinated, Gothic Revival, France, 1800s, 15 x 9 x 5 In.	1000
Shelf, Bronze, Fig Leaf Case, Kneeling Satyrs, Porcelain Dial, Marble Base, 10 In.	600
Shelf, Bronze, Gilt Figurine, Silvered Dial, 1800s, 18 x 12 In.	937
Shelf, Bronze, Gilt, Cavalier, Scrolls, Grange Et Betout, France, c.1880, 15 x 10 In.	812
Shelf, Bronze, Nymph, Garden, Round Dial, Gilt, Footed, Art Nouveau, 14 x 8 In.	136
Shelf, Compendium, Marble, Malachite Inlay, Barometer Dial, 21 x 21 In.	896
Shelf, Empire Style, Putto, Bow & Arrow, Black Marble Base, Animal Feet, 15 In.	180
Shelf, Empire, Gilt Bronze, Angel, Footed, 15 In.	1750
Shelf, Empire, Gilt, Bronze, Greek Vase Case, Signed, Lepaute, c.1790, 16 x 6 In. ....*illus*	1920
Shelf, Figural, Bronze, Boy, Basket Of Fish, Enamel Dial, Scroll Feet, c.1885, 28 In.	1107
Shelf, Gilt Bronze, Diana, Cherub, Animals, Leaves, France, 1800s, 25 x 38 x 11 In.	8625
Shelf, Gilt Bronze, Figure, Porcelain Plaque, Angel, France, c.1880 15 x 21 In.	1750
Shelf, Gilt Bronze, French Style, Porcelain Dial, Leaves, Urn Top, 22 In.	225
Shelf, Gilt Bronze, Pierced Scrolls, Putto, Flute, Cupid, Urn, France, 20 x 22 In.	4000
Shelf, Gilt Bronze, White Marble, Enamel Dial, Late 1800s, 13 ½ x 11 In.	384

Shelf, Gothic Revival, Cast Iron, Mother-Of-Pearl Landscapes, 1800s, 21 x 18 In.	500
Shelf, Lapis Lazuli, Gilt Bronze, Empire Style, 1900s, 4 x 3 In.	875
Shelf, Louis XV Style, Bronze, Enamel, Cupids, Lyre Case, Paw Feet, France, 24 In.	312
Shelf, Mahogany, Broken Arch Crest, Pillars, Village Scene, Finials, 31 x 16 In.	649
Shelf, Mahogany, Painted Wood Dial, Reverse Painted Glass, Early 1800s, 26 In.	5060
Shelf, Marble, Amber, Ormolu Mount, Round, Fruit, Leaves, c.1900, 18 x 21 In.	2500
Shelf, Marble, Gilt Bronze, Carved Woman, Lunar Face, France, 1800s, 17 x 14 In.	3998
Shelf, Marble, Gilt, Figural, Cupid Finial, France, 21 x 12 x 6 In.	750
Shelf, Marble, Porcelain Dial, Round, Scroll Sides, Columns, Molded Base, 17 In.	413
Shelf, Napoleon III, Gilt Metal, Onyx, Maiden With Leaves, 1800s, 11 x 10 ½ In.	305
Shelf, Nobleman & Dog, Seated, c.1890, 15 x 13 In.	125
Shelf, Pillar & Scroll, Mahogany, Jeromes & Darrow, c.1830, 19 x 5 In.	360
Shelf, Porcelain, Gold Pot Metal, Lovebirds, Satyrs, Transfer Print, 20 x 14 ½ In.	360
Shelf, Red Jasper, Female Figure, Gilt Legs, 8-Day, Pendulum, Dial, Key, 24 In.	300
Shelf, Rolling Ball, Wood, Steel, Bronze, 8-Day, Thermometer, Barometer, 22 In. _illus_	308
Shelf, S. Marti, Bronze, Scrolling Leaves, Porcelain Dial, Pendulum, France, 14 In.	600
Shelf, T.R., Timby, Globe, Walnut, Paper Dials, 1860, 27 In.	3450
Shelf, Terry & Sons, Pillar, Scroll, Mahogany, Tablet, Reverse Painted, 30-Hour, 30 In.	480
Shelf, Terry, Eli, Pillar & Scroll, Mahogany, Brass Finials, c.1810, 31 In.	920
Shelf, Walnut, Brass, Windmill, Swivel Case, France, 1800s, 26 x 17 In.	1000
Shelf, Walnut, Carved & Ebonized Trim, Strike, Spring, Brass Calendar, 20 In.	1725
Shelf, Walnut, Mirrored Panels, Glass Door, 8-Day Movement, 1800s, 25 In.	425
Shelf, White Onyx, Bronze Ornamental Mounts, c.1880, 9 ½ x 14 In.	50
Shelf, Willard, A., Mahogany, 8-Day, Painted Dial, Mirrror, c.1900, 33 ½ In.	4800
Shelf, Wood, Carved, Eagle, Wreath On Ship, German POW, 1942, 25 x 9 In.	1800
Silver, Harp Shape, Enamel Design, Key Wind, Vienna, Austria, 8 In.	3600
Skeleton, Francis Abbott, Brass Movement, Signed, Engraved, Glass Dome, 13 In.	3795
Studley, David, Shelf, Mahogany, Metal Dial, Lyre, Flower Spandrels, c.1840, 35 In.	5750
Tall Case, A. & C. Edwards, Pine, Engraved Silvered Chapter Ring, 86 In.	2530
Tall Case, Boynton, Calvin, Pine, Brass, Painted Numerals, Dwarf, c.1820, 49 In.	1955
Tall Case, Cheney, E., Cherry, Swan's Neck Crest, 8-Day, Iron Dial, c.1800, 83 In.	2457
Tall Case, Cherry, Broken Arch Crest, Finials, Shaped Door, Flowers, c.1820, 88 In.	1875
Tall Case, Chinoiserie, Molded Crown, Brass Works, 92 x 18 In.	2700
Tall Case, Chippendale, Mahogany, 8-Day, Chime, Dwarf, c.1930s, 57 ½ In.	1100
Tall Case, Ellis, Richard, Chinoiserie, Westminster Chimes, c.1800, 97 x 20 In.	1250
Tall Case, Empire, Mahogany, Moon Face, Chimes, B.J. Cookes Sons, c.1910, 92 In.	800
Tall Case, Federal, Cherry, Walnut, Arched Face, Painted Flowers, c.1824, 78 In.	1080
Tall Case, French Provincial, Limed Wood, 94 In.	200
Tall Case, George III, Oak, Mahogany, Brass & Rosettes, Painted Face, 87 In. _illus_	468
Tall Case, Georgian, Mahogany, Shaped Skirt, Painted Dial, 88 x 20 In.	750
Tall Case, Gillows, George III, Arched Dial, Naval Scene, Gothic Door, 90 In.	16800
Tall Case, Gowland, C., Mahogany, 8-Day, Calendar Dial, England, c.1840, 94 In. _illus_	840
Tall Case, Hoadley, Silas, Pine, Eagle, Early 1800s, 84 x 18 ½ In.	813
Tall Case, Krause, John J., Hepplewhite, Cherry, Broken Pediment, Date, 96 In.	1060
Tall Case, Mahogany, Arched Crest, Late 1700s, 95 x 17 x 11 In.	750
Tall Case, Mahogany, Broken Arch Crest, Glazed Panel Door, Brass, 87 x 19 In.	1600
Tall Case, Mahogany, Carved, Broken Arch Pediment, Finial, Columns, 104 In.	10620
Tall Case, Mahogany, Iron Dial, Ship, Roses, Door, Bracket Feet, c.1800, 93 x 24 In.	2400
Tall Case, Mahogany, Silvered Moon Phase Dial, c.1770, 98 x 25 In.	3738
Tall Case, Maple, Broken Pediment, Flowers, 8-Day, Flared Feet, 1800s, 98 In.	3393
Tall Case, Needham, Jesse, Chippendale, Walnut, c.1830, 90 x 19 ½ In.	12000
Tall Case, Oak, Mahogany, Inlaid, Broken Scroll Crest, Georgian, 88 x 23 In.	1098
Tall Case, Painted, Flowers, Brass Pendulum, Porcelain Flowers, c.1835, 89 In.	593
Tall Case, Pine, Federal, Arched Hood, 1800s, 82 ½ x 19 x 11 In.	420
Tall Case, Pine, Grain Paint, Broken Pediment, Tombstone Face, c.1820, 88 In.	7380
Tall Case, Pine, Molded Crown, 30-Hour Birdcage Movement, 74 x 14 In.	750
Tall Case, Shaker, Pine, Square Dial, Frame, Door, I. Youngs, 1834, 79 x 14 In.	24600
Tall Case, Taber, Stephen, Fretwork, Moon & Sun, R. Swift Case, c.1810, 90 In.	8000
Tall Case, Walnut, Arched Crest, Finials, Spires, Columns, Ship, c.1810, 95 In.	5925

Clock, Tall Case, Waltham, Mahogany, Silvered & Brass Dial, Chimes, c.1900, 99 In.
$1,200

Cowan's Auctions

Clock, Vienna Regulator, Long Drop, Mahogany, 8-Day, Time & Strike, 52 In.
$240

Cowan's Auctions

Cloisonne, Bowl, Birds, Flowers, Ormolu, Dragon Handles, Chinese, 1800s, 16 x 19 In.
$1,375

New Orleans Auction Galleries

Cloisonne, Box, Figural, Crane, Multicolor, 9 x 4½ In.
$450

Cloisonne, Figurine, Woman, Celluloid Head, Hands, Multicolor Dress, Flowers, 12½ x 3 In.
$245

Cloisonne, Ink Blotter, Flowers, Red, Blue, 4¼ x 2½ In.
$225

Tall Case, Walnut, Cutout Feet & Skirt, Va., c.1820, 87½ x 17 In.	644
Tall Case, Waltham, Mahogany, Silvered & Brass Dial, Chimes, c.1900, 99 In. ....*illus*	1200
Tall Case, Welcher, Frederic, Georgian, Japanned, Bird & Flowers, 1800s, 87 In.	492
Tall Case, Willard, A., Mahogany, Roxbury Style, Pierced, Finials, c.1775, 97 In.	9480
Tall, Mahogany, Inlaid, Bird's-Eye Maple, 8-Day, c.1810, 93 x 19 x 10 In.	7800
Terry & Sons, Shelf, Mahogany, Gilt, Paint, Eagle Crest, 1830, 31 x 18 In.	215

Tiffany clocks that are part of desk sets made by Louis Comfort Tiffany are listed in the Tiffany category. Clocks sold by the store Tiffany & Co. are listed here.

Tiffany, Shelf, Champleve, Gilt Bronze, Cherubs, Garland, Signed, 1800s, 14 In.	3680
Vienna Regulator, Long Drop, Mahogany, 8-Day, Time & Strike, 52 In. ....*illus*	240
Wag-On-Wall, Walnut, Round, Molded Frame, Chain, Germany, 11 In. Diam.	106
Wall, Keyhole, Painted Black, Original Reverse Painted Tablet, 16 In.	1610
Wall, Oak, Painted, English Tavern, Bells, Ludston Hall, Shropshire, c.1924, 58 In.	4600
Wall, Rolling Pin, Inlaid, 8-Day, Caledonian, England, c.1870, 38 x 16 In.	150
Waltham, Banjo, Wood, Carved, Reverse Paint, Flags, Old Ironside, c.1900, 40 In.	523
Water, Time Flow, Glass Pipes, Pendulum, B. Gitton, France, 1980s, 89 x 33 In.	5795
Welch Spring, Wall, Rosewood, Cary V.P., c.1880, 20 In.	863
Welch, E.N., Regulator, Wall, Mahogany, Octagonal, Point Drop, Door, 8-Day, 31 In.	472
Whiting, Riley, Shelf, Portrait, George Washington, c.1832, 32 x 18½ In.	2460

CLOISONNE enamel was developed during the tenth century. A glass enamel was applied between small ribbons of metal on a metal base. Most cloisonne is Chinese or Japanese. Pieces marked China were made after 1900.

Basket, Silver, Dark Blue & Green, Flowers, Russia, 4 x 5 In.	3565
Beaker, Silver, Round Bottom, Roll Rim, Shapes, Waves, c.1910, 3 In.	2214
Bird, Green, Black, White, Brown Stump, 8½ In., Pair	175
Bowl, Birds, Flowers, Ormolu, Dragon Handles, Chinese, 1800s, 16 x 19 In. ....*illus*	1375
Bowl, Black, Turquoise, Dragons, Flaming Pearl, Squat, c.1900, 6 x 2 In.	201
Bowl, Coiled Dragons, Shou Symbol, Stylized Peach Branches, c.1885, 6 In.	154
Box, Duck Shape, Multicolor, Cream, c.1925, 5¼ In.	345
Box, Figural, Crane, Multicolor, 9 x 4½ In. ....*illus*	450
Box, Gilt, Phoenix, Diaper Pattern, Japan, 2 x 4 In.	357
Box, Irises, Grass, Water, Round, Japan, 4¼ In.	100
Box, Oval, Dragon Finials, Handles, 4 In.	150
Box, Rickshaw Figures, Flowers & Stylized Ground, Japan, c.1910, 4 x 9 In.	1495
Box, Round, Water, Irises, Flowers, Multicolor, 1900s, 2 x 4 In.	100
Box, Silver, Woman, Art Nouveau, Stylized Flowers, Oval, Russia, 1 x 3 In.	1718
Censer, Blue, 3-Footed, Multicolor, 24½ In.	469
Censer, Blue, Peonies, Fretwork Handles, Lid, Bats, Tripod, c.1935, 16 x 12 In.	1750
Censer, Gilt & Bronze, Purple, Original Patina, Chinese, 5½ x 6½ In.	316
Censer, Mythical Animal, Phoenixes, Scrolling, Chinese, 1900s, 13 x 9 In., Pair	1125
Censer, Squat, Upright Handles, Gilt, Openwork Lid, 1900s, 10 In., Pair	1482
Charger, 3 Interlocked Circles, Birds, Branches, Blue, 12 In.	149
Charger, Blue, Cranes Amid Branches & Flowers, c.1890, 3½ x 24 In.	976
Charger, Blue, Flowers, Chinese, 23¾ In.	187
Charger, Dragon Center, Fan Shape Cartouches, Flowers, Navy, Japan, 24 In.	780
Charger, Flared Rim, Foo Dogs, Ball, Scrolling Lotus, Gilt, 1900s, 21 In. Diam.	738
Charger, Flying Crane, Blue Ground, 15½ In., Pair	313
Cigarette Case, Temple, Dragon, Multicolor, Rounded Corners, c.1900, 5 x 3 In.	369
Creamer, Silver, Dark Blue & Green, Flowers, Russia, 2 x 4½ x 2½ In.	2300
Ewer, Bombe, Spreading Foot, Flowers, Leaves, Blue Ground, 12 x 7 In.	610
Figurine, Rooster & Hen On Flowered Knoll, Chinese, 1800s, 9 In.	720
Figurine, Woman, Celluloid Head, Hands, Multicolor Dress, Flowers, 12½ x 3 In. ....*illus*	245
Incense Burner, Figural Bull, Masks, Dragons, Chinese, 1900s, 10 x 17 In., Pair	593
Ink Blotter, Flowers, Red, Blue, 4¼ x 2½ In. ....*illus*	225
Jar, Bulbous, Stylized Lotus, Leafy Tendrils, Turquoise Ground, 6 In.	246
Jardiniere, Bat, Gourd, Plum, Chinese, 17 x 21½ In.	750
Kovsh, Green & Pink & Violet, Dark Blue Ground, Russia, c.1917, 4 x 3 In.	1875

Kovsh, Silver Gilt, Textured Ground, Turquoise, Green, Gold, c.1915, 9 In.	12500
Kovsh, Silver, Cabochons, Inscription, Moscow, c.1910, 6 x 12 In. ....*illus*	24600
Kovsh, Silver, Hooked Prowl, Handle, Flowers, Leaves, Turquoise, c.1910, 8 In.	2214
Kovsh, Silver, White & Blue & Red, Flowers, Russia, 2 ½ x 5 x 3 In.	2760
Lamp, Dragon, Electric, Converted Vases, Chinese, c.1890, 16 In., Pair	600
Mahjong Box, Drawers, Bracket Feet, Handles, Dragons, c.1800, 8 x 10 In.	1599
Planter, Hundred Antiques, Carved Headstone Lilies, Chinese, 1900s, 22 x 7 In.	593
Plate, Men, Desk, Book, Stars, Grass, Chinese, 9 In.	875
Scepter, Scrolling, Brocade, Lotus Flowers, Green, Chinese, 1900s, 22 In.	312
Sculpture, Horse, Blue, Multicolor Dragons, c.1900, 51 x 67 In.	360
Sculpture, Woman On Elephant, Flower Skirt & Blanket, 21 x 18 In.	655
Smoking Set, Bay & Boats, Pine Trees, Blue, Tray, 1900s, 4 Piece, 12 x 8 In.	1875
Tea Set, Tray, Teapot, Sugar & Creamer, 2 Tea Caddies, Black, 6 Piece	483
Teapot, Brass, Green, Lotus Petals, Handle, Lid, Frog Finial, 1900s, 5 x 8 In.	1500
Teapot, Dome Lid, Turquoise, Flowers, Scroll, Loop Handle, c.1905, 6 x 9 In.	675
Teapot, Light Blue, Dragons, 5 x 6 ½ In.	374
Tray, Fan Shape, Pheasants, Flowers, Patterned Border, Scrolls, c.1900, 11 In.	111
Tumbler, Flowers, Ovchinnikov, Signed, Russia, 4 x 3 In.	575
Vase, 4 Panels, Blue, Green, 21 x 11 In.	625
Vase, Birds, Leaves, Blue, High Shoulders, 10 In., Pair	92
Vase, Black, Swirling Dragons & Scrollwork, Japan, c.1900, 12 ½ x 4 In.	3000
Vase, Blue, Flowers, Ormolu Mounts, Etienne Enot, Paris, c.1880, 14 x 7 In., Pair	885
Vase, Blue, Flowers, Trees, White, Red, Japanese Characters, 7 x 5 In., Pair	416
Vase, Blue, White, Long Tapered Neck, Flared Mouth, Lotus, 10 ¼ In.	53
Vase, Blue, White, Ring Handles, c.1925, 6 ½ In., Pair	125
Vase, Brass, Aquamarine Base, Leaves, Blossoms, Scrolls, c.1890, 13 In., Pair	250
Vase, Bronze, Leaves, Berries, Blue, Purple, 19 ¼ In.	156
Vase, Brown, Peacock, Japan, 1800s, 10 In.	2760
Vase, Brown, Phoenixes & Dragons, Small Area Of Loss, Japan, 15 In.	1610
Vase, Chrysanthemums, Lotus Flowers, Yellow, Stylized Clouds, 10 In., Pair	218
Vase, Cranes, Leaves, Black Ground, 5 x 2 ½ In., Pair	88
Vase, Dragon, Chrysanthemum, Brown, Teal, Stripes, 12 In.	525
Vase, Dragons, Waves, Swollen Shoulder, Pinched Neck, 1900s, 13 In., Pair	1422
Vase, Elephant Head Handles, Cartouches, Buddah, Lid, Figural Feet, 12 x 17 In.	189
Vase, Flared Neck, Dragon, Phoenix, Flaming Pearl, Flowers, Blue, 5 In., Pair	83
Vase, Flask Shape, Landscape, Rainbow, Trumpet Neck, c.1910, 12 In.	948
Vase, Flowering Branch, Green Ground, Japan, 7 x 4 In.	82
Vase, Flowering Roses, Bamboo, Sparrow, 8 In., Pair	135
Vase, Flowers, Birds, Hexagonal, Attributed To Hayashi Chuzo, 12 In., Pair	1000
Vase, Flowers, Butterflies, Chinese, 12 ¼ In., Pair	281
Vase, Flowers, Prunus Fruit, Wide Rim, Domed Foot, 30 ½ x 13 In., Pair	590
Vase, Fluted, Long Neck, Dragons, Phoenix, Leaves, Bands, Japan, 9 x 4 In., Pair	375
Vase, Flying Dragon, Flames, Stippled, Shouldered, Rolled Rim, c.1900, 10 In.	2192
Vase, Genie Bottle Shape, Garlic Mouth, Handles, Lotus, 1900s, 15 In., Pair	830
Vase, Gilt, Serpentine Dragon, Pine Trees, Clouds, 17 x 6 ½ In., Pair	1309
Vase, Grapevine, Cream Ground, 7 In.	120
Vase, Green Maple Leaf, Red Ground, 1920-50, 7 ¼ In., Pair	325
Vase, Hexagonal, Birds, Flowers, Panels, Flower Medallions, Bands, 12 In.	8610
Vase, Light Blue, Heron & Irises, Japan, Early 1900s, 6 In., Pair	460
Vase, Light Green, Flowers, 9 ¾ In.	45
Vase, Lotus Scrolls, Turquoise Ground, Chinese, 1900s, 25 x 12 In., Pair	750
Vase, Oval, Mottled Glaze, Butterflies In Flight, c.1900, 6 In.	593
Vase, Oval, Tapered, Rolled Rim, Banded, Birds & Flowers, c.1900, 6 In., Pair	593
Vase, Pagoda, Landscape, Scrolled Leaves, Pink Flowers, Octagonal Foot, 10 In.	595
Vase, Panels, Phoenix, Dragons, Butterflies, Amphora Shape, Japan, 10 In. ....*illus*	875
Vase, Pheasants, Flowering Trees, Banding, Silver Rim, c.1900, 12 In.	2460
Vase, Phoenix Birds & Dragons, Orange Ground, Japan, c.1890, 6 x 2 ¼ In.	875
Vase, Purple Iris, Pale Green, Rolled Gilt Rim, Ring Foot, c.1910, 4 In.	3496
Vase, Red Dragons, Flaming Pearl, Bottle Shape, Flared Rim, c.1910, 12 In.	119
Vase, Rooster, Dragon, Red, White, Green, 6 In., Pair	187

Cloisonne, Kovsh, Silver, Cabochons, Inscription, Moscow, c.1910, 6 x 12 In.
$24,600

Skinner, Inc.

Cloisonne, Vase, Panels, Phoenix, Dragons, Butterflies, Amphora Shape, Japan, 10 In.
$875

New Orleans Auction Galleries

Clothing, Caftan, Velour, Blue & Pink, Long Sleeves, Zipper, Emilio Pucci, Size 10
$236

Leslie Hindman Auctioneers

This is an edited listing of current prices. Visit **Kovels.com** to check thousands of prices from previous years and sign up for free information on trends, tips, reproductions, marks, and more.

Clothing, Coat, Cape, Wool, Fox Trim, Revillon, Paris, London, New York, 38 In.

$625

New Orleans Auction Galleries

Clothing, Coat, Fur, Coyote, White Fox, Notched Collar, Leather Button, Hook, Size 10

$468

New Orleans Auction Galleries

Clothing, Coat, Mink, Blond, ¾ Length, Notched Collar, Pompom Buttons, 30 In.

$812

New Orleans Auction Galleries

Vase, White, Irises, Green Leaves, Red Ground, 7 In.	96
Vase, White, Yellow Flowers, Red Ground, 12 In., Pair	250
Vase, Yellow, Mt. Fuji, Flying Birds, Ando, 7⅜ In.	247
Vase, Yellow, Pear Shape, Pink Mums, Leaves, Porcelain, Japan, 12 In., Pair	1071
Vase, Yellow, White, Flowers, Blue Ground, Ring Handles, c.1925, 18 x 14 In.	200

 CLOTHING of all types is listed in this category. Dresses, hats, shoes, underwear, and more are found here. Other textiles are to be found in the Coverlet, Movie, Quilt, Textile, and World War I and II categories.

Belt, Gold, Hammered, Medallions, Hook Closure, Rader, 1970s, 39 x 1 In.	168
Belt, Leather, Silver Studs, Horses, Pouch, 2 Straps, Buckles, Argentina, 2 x 45 In.	237
Caftan, Botanical Print, Lime Green, Buttons, Emilio Pucci	251
Caftan, Flowers, Butterflies, Long Sleeve, V-Neck, Floor Length, Pulitzer, Size S	236
Caftan, Flowers, Long Sleeves, Keyhole Neck, Back Zipper, L. Pulitzer	236
Caftan, Flowers, Long Sleeves, V-Neck, Back Zipper, Lily Pulitzer, Size S	220
Caftan, Pink Flowers, Sleeveless, Shear Overlay, Keyhole Neck, Lilly Pulitzer	95
Caftan, Thai Silk, ¾ Sleeves, Pleated, Zipper, Sash, J. Thompson, Size P	95
Caftan, Velour, Blue & Pink, Long Sleeves, Zipper, Emilio Pucci, Size 10 ....*illus*	236
Cape, Evening, Opera, Gold, Black Lame, Fur Collar, Silk & Velvet Trim	810
Coat, Cape, Wool, Fox Trim, Revillon, Paris, London, New York, 38 In. ....*illus*	625
Coat, Fur, Coyote, White Fox, Notched Collar, Leather Button, Hook, Size 10......*illus*	468
Coat, Fur, Muskrat, Vertical Pelts, Squared Shoulders, 44 In.	180
Coat, Mink, Blond, ¾ Length, Notched Collar, Pompom Buttons, 30 In..........*illus*	812
Coat, Mink, Brown, Stroller, Shawl Collar, Banded, c.1960s, Size 10-12, 32 In.	468
Coat, Sable, Mink Cuffs & Collar, Label, Douglas Furs, 48 In.	2280
Collar, Irish Lace, Ivory, Shawl, Flowers, Trailing Leaf Border, c.1910, 11 x 46 In.	50
Dress, Black Silk, Flower Brocade, White, Blue, Rushed Insert, Demi-Train, 1875	570
Dress, Cotton, White, Crochet Bodice, Lace Cap Sleeves, Tiered Petticoat, c.1900, Size S	1650
Dress, Front Wrap, Sleeveless, Gathered Skirt, Kick Pleat, Zipper, Balenciaga, Size 36.......*illus*	126
Dress, Halter Top, Elastic Strap, Back Tie Closure, Side Zipper, Label, Stephen Burrow's World...*illus*	315
Dress, Ivory Dotted Mulle & Satin, Gathered Bodice, Puff Sleeves, c.1820	228
Dress, Sundress, Cotton & Polyester, Rose Print, Mid Length, Lilly Pulitzer, 1970s,	150
Dress, Tea, Black Silk, Puffed Sleeves, V-Neck, Lace Ruffles, c.1875	285
Dunce Cap, Cotton, Bells, Tassels, Faux Jewels, Embroidery, c.1910, 3 Piece	320
Ear Muffs, Beige Fur, Orange Patches, Bendable Headband, 1950s, 17 In.	25
Hat, Bowler, Pitkin The Hatter, Tailor Made Hats, England, 1900s, 4½ In.	42
Hat, Official's, Qing Court, Silk, Gauze, Chin Strap, Brass Button,1800s, 8 x 12 In.	2460
Hat, Straw, Lacquered, Flowers, Green Velvet Band, Size S, c.1955	30
Hat, Toque Bonnet, Chin Ties, Maroon Velvet, Black Silk Lining, 1800s, 16 In.	75
Hat, Trilby, Man From U.N.C.L.E., Wool, Braided Trim, Feather, 1965, 9 x 9 In.	380
Jacket, Brown Fur, Mandarin Collar, Fur Buttons, Braided Loops, Petite	228
Jacket, Brown Velvet, Flowers, Pagoda Sleeves, Chenille, Beaded Tassels, 1800s	684
Jacket, Leather, Brown, 1 Button Closure, Breast Flap Pockets, Chanel, Size 46	413
Jacket, Leather, Lamb, Reversible Mink, Sakowitz, c.1990, Size 8-10, 29 In.	812
Kilt, Davidson, Wool, Leather Straps, Lined White Serge, Canada, Early 1900s	332
Mittens, White Rabbit Fur, Red Leather, Felt Lined, Women's, 1960s, 12½ In.	70
Robe, Blue Silk, Embroidered, China, 1900s, 50 x 29 In.	218
Robe, Gauze, Embroidery, Dragons, Bats, Buddhist Emblems, c.1900, 44 In.	9225
Robe, Silk, Brocade, Dragons, Flaming Pearls, Buddhist Emblems, c.1890, 54 In.............*illus*	3690
Robe, Silk, Embroidered, Birds & Butterflies, Waves, Cream, Chinese, 43 In.	415
Robe, Silk, Embroidery, Brocade, Flowers, Fruit, Birds, Chinese, Women's, 40 In.	1722
Scarf, Eperon D'Or, Red, Blue, Yellow, Henri D'Origny, Hermes, 1974, 35 x 35 In.	375
Scarf, Jumping, Pink, Philippe Ledoux, Hermes, 1980s, 35 x 35 In.	281
Scarf, Quilted Flap Bay, Red, Green, Black, Chanel, 33½ x 33½ In.	218
Scarf, Shoes, Multicolor, Ferragamo, 34 x 34 In.	312
Scarf, Silk, 2 Horses, Blue, Teal, Cream Ground, Hermes, 35 x 35 In.	123
Scarf, Silk, Bolduc, Orange, Gray Ribbons, Hermes, 35 x 35 In.	578
Scarf, Silk, Brise De Charme, Fans, Yellow, Julia Abadie, Hermes, 35 x 35 In.	129
Scarf, Silk, Courtly Pavilion, Black Border, Multicolor, Hermes, 36 x 36 In., Pair	344

Scarf, Silk, Dark Brown & Burgundy Stripe, Beige, 26 x 26 In.	182
Scarf, Silk, Fantasies Indiennes, Coral, Green, Flowers, Tree, Hermes, 1983, 35 In.	384
Scarf, Silk, Flowers, Blue, Purple, Emilio Pucci, 35 ½ x 35 ½ In.	75
Scarf, Silk, Hanging Tassels, Gold, White Ground, Hermes, 36 x 36 In., Pair	468
Scarf, Silk, Hola Flamenca, Hermes, 35 x 35 In.	660
Scarf, Silk, Inspired By Giverny, L. Bourthomieux, Hermes, 35 x 35 In.	212
Scarf, Silk, Kaleidoscope, Multicolor, Black, Hermes, 36 x 36 In.	438
Scarf, Silk, Mythical Hunting Scenes, Knights, Dragons, Lions, Gucci, 35 x 35 In.	359
Scarf, Silk, Navy Blue, Belts, Purple, Red, Brown, Gucci, 34 x 34 In.	212
Scarf, Silk, Pampa, Hermes, 35 x 35 In.	418
Scarf, Silk, Panther, Black Ball, Yellow Ground, Cartier, 34 x 34 In.	182
Scarf, Silk, Sunflowers, Fall Leaves, Chanel, 37 ½ x 38 In.	247
Scarf, Silk, Tassels, Red, Purple, Green Border, Bottega Veneta, 33 ½ x 34 In.	50
Shawl, Silk, Embroidered, Peonies, Birds, Macrame, Fringe Trim, 63 x 63 In.	800
Shawl, Silk, Lame, Silk & Metal Thread, Art Deco, France, c.1920, 44 x 45 In.	185
Shoes, Ivory Silk, Embroidered Flowers, Ribbon Ties, Leather Sole, c.1750	2800
Shoes, Wool, Red Broadcloth Uppers, Covered Heel, Braid, c.1735, 9 In.	3750
Veil, Bridal, Ivory Lace, Flowers, Cathedral, Point De Gaze, c.1890, 65 x 105 In.	5665
Vest, Sonny & Cher, Faux Fur, Loop Hook, Signatures, C. Brent, 1966, 20 x 22 In.	115
Wedding Dress, Skirt, Blouse, Flowers, Silk, Embroidery, Red, Chinese, 1920s	665

CLUTHRA glass is a two-layered glass with small bubbles and powdered glass trapped between the layers. The Steuben Glass Works of Corning, New York, first made it in 1920. Victor Durand of Kimball Glass Company in Vineland, New Jersey, made a similar glass from about 1925. Durand's pieces are listed in the Durand category. Related items are listed in the Steuben category.

Tazza, White, Cone Shape Base, Wide Bowl, Flat Rim, Pink Border, 5 x 8 In.	354
Vase, Blue, Incised, Steuben, 8 ¼ In.	800
Vase, Mottled Opal, Yellow, Red, Shouldered, Pontil, Signed, 8 ½ In. ....*illus*	201
V ase, Mottled White & Periwinkle, Clear Ground, 8 ½ In.	120
Vase, Opalescent White To Mottled Blue, Cone Shape, Trumpet Rim, 10 In.	354
Vase, Opalescent White To Mottled Bright Pink, Lobed, Flared Rim & Foot, 8 In.	472
Vase, Opalescent White To Mottled Pink, Bulbous, Shouldered, Flared Rim, 5 In.	212
Vase, Pink Mottled, Flared Rim, Tapered, Shouldered, Steuben, c.1910, 8 In.	531

COALBROOKDALE was made by the Coalport porcelain factory of England during the Victorian period. Pieces are decorated with floral encrustations.

Basket, Green, Flowers, Upright Handle, Wavy Rim, 1830, 8 x 10 In.	510
Platter, Kirkstall Abbey, Molded Flowers, Gilt, Scrolling Rim, c.1850, 13 In.	612
Sugar, Applied Flowers, Bird Finial, Signed, c.1830, 3 ¾ x 5 ⅛ In. ....*illus*	195
Umbrella Stand, Allegorical, Hercules Fighting Snake, 33 x 19 In.	531
Umbrella Stand, Figural, Child Holding Snake, Cast Iron, 1800s, 33 In.	738
Urn, Encrusted Flowers, Cherubs, Lid, Flower Cluster Finial, c.1810, 8 In.	465
Vase, Cobalt Blue, Molded Flowers, Gilt, Ruffled Rim, Handles, 1800s, 12 In.	365

COALPORT ware was made by the Coalport Porcelain Works of England beginning about 1795. Early pieces were unmarked. About 1810–25 the pieces were marked with the name *Coalport* in various forms. Later pieces also had the name *John Rose* in the mark. The crown mark was used with variations beginning in 1881. The date 1750 is printed in some marks, but it is not the date the factory started. Coalport was bought by Wedgwood in 1967. Coalport porcelain is no longer being produced. Some pieces are listed in Indian Tree.

BONE CHINA
COALPORT
MADE IN ENGLAND
EST.1750

Cooler, Fruit, Bengal Tiger, Multicolor, Gold Creatures, Liner, Lid, 10 In., Pair	6000
Jardiniere, Comet, Stripes, Celestial Collection, c.1980, 5 ½ x 4 ½ In., Pair	28
Plaque, Still Life, Flower Bouquet, Hand Painted, Frame, c.1820, 17 x 15 In.	1920
Plate, Dessert, Landscape In Reserve, Yellow, Flowers, 9 In., 4 Piece	150
Plate, Flower Sprays, Dash & Bead Border, Shaped Medallions, 11 In., 10 Piece	357

Clothing, Dress, Front Wrap, Sleeveless, Gathered Skirt, Kick Pleat, Zipper, Balenciaga, Size 36
$126

Leslie Hindman Auctioneers

Clothing, Dress, Halter Top, Elastic Strap, Back Tie Closure, Side Zipper, Label, Stephen Burrow's World
$315

Leslie Hindman Auctioneers

Clothing, Robe, Silk, Brocade, Dragons, Flaming Pearls, Buddhist Emblems, c.1890, 54 In.
$3,690

Skinner, Inc.

Cluthra, Vase, Mottled Opal, Yellow, Red, Shouldered, Pontil, Signed, 8 ½ In. $201

Early Auction Company

Coalbrookdale, Sugar, Applied Flowers, Bird Finial, Signed, c.1830, 3 ¾ x 5 ⅛ In. $195

Ruby Lane

Coalport, Sugar, Lid, Gilt, Bands Of Leaves & Red Ribbons, 2 Handles, Finial, 7 ½ x 5 ½ In. $325

Ruby Lane

Cobalt Blue, Eye Wash Cup, Blown, Pedestal, c.1910, 2 ½ x 1 ¾ In. $38

Ruby Lane

Plate, Hand Highlighted Flower Sprays, Shaped Medallions, 10 ¾ In., 10 Piece	357
Plate, Marron, Gilt Borders, 10 ½ In., 12 Piece	350
Platter, Pearlware, Oval, Green Border, Sprays, Scalloped Rim, 1800s, 8 x 11 In.	125
Sugar, Lid, Gilt, Bands Of Leaves & Red Ribbons, 2 Handles, Finial, 7 ½ x 5 ½ In. ....*illus*	325
Urn, Blue Beading, Scenic Cartouche, Gilt, Handles, Pedestal Foot, c.1895, 6 In.	1450
Urn, Green Bands, 3 Festive Women, Cherubs, Leafy Foot, 11 ¾ In., Pair	125
Vase, Gilt Handles, Jeweled Decoration, 7 ¾ In.	281

COBALT BLUE glass was made using oxide of cobalt. The characteristic bright dark blue identifies it for the collector. Most cobalt glass found today was made after the Civil War. There was renewed interest in the dark blue glass in the late 1930s and dinnerware was made.

Eye Wash Cup, Blown, Pedestal, c.1910, 2 ½ x 1 ¾ In. ....*illus*	38
Urn, Louis XVI, Ormolu, Handles, Round Foot, 8 In., Pair	750
Vase, Cut To Clear, Flowers, Notched Mouth, 18 x 5 In.	125
Vase, Overlay, 5 ¾ In., Pair	125

COCA-COLA was first served in 1886 in Atlanta, Georgia. It was advertised through signs, newspaper ads, coupons, bottles, trays, calendars, and even lamps and clocks. Collectors want anything with the word *Coca-Cola*, including a few rare products, like gum wrappers and cigar bands. The famous trademark was patented in 1893, the *Coke* mark in 1945. Many modern items and reproductions are being made.

3D Glasses, Verigraph, Drink Coca-Cola, 5 Cents, Cardboard, Plastic, 1914, 5 x 2 In.	554
Ashtray, Drink Coca-Cola, Bottle, Bakelite, Metal, Pull Match, 1930s, 7 In.	1095
Bank, Coca-Cola, Figural, Sprite Boy, Bottle Cap Hat, Cast Iron, Enamel, 1800s, 8 In.	225
Bank, Pig, Red, Plastic, Drink Coca-Cola, c.1950, 2 ¼ x 4 x 2 In.	35
Bank, Soda Dispenser, Refresh Yourself, Ice Cold, Tin, Cups, Box, 1950s, 10 In.	277
Belt Buckle, Drink Coca-Cola, Delicious & Refreshing, Brass, Red, 1960s	243
Bookmark, Heart Shape, Portrait, Girl, 5 Cent, 1898, 2 ¼ In.	660
Bottle & Can Opener, Steel, Logo, Ekco, c.1960	10
Bottle Carrier, 6 Bottle, Masonite, Rope Handle, 1940s, 5 ½ x 8 In.	67
Bottle Carrier, 12 Bottle, Aluminum, Bail Handle, c.1950, 16 x 7 In.	150
Bottle Carrier, Drink Coca-Cola, Paint, Plated Wire, Handles, 1950s, 13 x 20 In.	115
Bottle Opener, Drink Coca-Cola, Cast Iron, Paint, Wall Mount, 1920s, 3 x 3 In.	275
Bottle Opener, Stainless Steel, Bottle Shape, Flat, c.1980s, 7 ½ In.	8
Bottle Opener, Wall Mount, Plastic, Cap Catcher, Starr, Brown Mfg., 6 In.	55
Bottle, ACL Lettering, Cap, 12 ¼ In.	184
Bottle, Coke Is It!, At The Super Bowl, Tampa, Florida, 1984	10
Bottle, Tin Lithograph Cap, 1930s, 20 In., 3 Piece	480
Calendar, 1903, Hilda Clark, Holding Glass, 1903, 23 x 14 In.	2000
Calendar, 1904, Lillian Nordica, Side Table, June, 23 ¼ x 14 In.	850
Calendar, 1908, Good To The Last Drop, March-December Pad, Cardboard, 7 x 14 In.......*illus*	5800
Chalkboard, Masonite, Menu, Bottle, Blue, It's The Real Thing, 30 x 18 In.	92
Chalkboard, Masonite, Menu, Bottle, Things Go Better With Coke, 30 x 18 In.	92
Clock, Coca-Cola, The Ideal Brain Tonic, Wood, Red, Gold, Circles, 31 x 19 In.	923
Clock, Drink Coca-Cola, 5 Cents, Sold Here, Delicious & Refreshing, Oak Case, Sample, 20 x 10 In. *illus*	800
Clock, Drink Coca-Cola, Brass, Glass, c.1960, 15 x 15 In.	130
Clock, Fishtail Logo, Metal, Green Numbers, Electric, 1950s, 15 x 15 In.	250
Clock, Ice Cold Coca-Cola, Red, White, Green, Octagonal, Neon, 1941, 19 In.	3000
Clock, Walnut Case, Quartz, Drink Coca-Cola In Bottles, 1930s, 16 x 16 In.	349
Cooler, AM Radio, Drink Coca-Cola, Ice Cold, Red & White, Plastic, 10 In.	369
Cooler, Drink Coca-Cola In Bottles, Red Metal, Aluminum, Handle, 1950s	250
Cooler, Red, Handle, Acton Manufacturing, 17 x 12 In.	117
Coupon Ad, Girl With Fan, 2-Sided, c.1905, 10 x 6 ½ In.	201
Crate, Drink Coca-Cola In Bottles, Wooden Slats, Metal Mounts, 1960s	95
Display, Circus, Clown, Holding Bottle, 1932, 44 In.	915
Display, Girl, Holding Glass, White Ruffled Collar, Die Cut, 1926, 45 x 33 In.	600

Coca-Cola, Calendar, 1908, Good To The Last Drop, March-December Pad, Cardboard, 7 x 14 In.
$5,800

Coca-Cola, Clock, Drink Coca-Cola, 5 Cents, Sold Here, Delicious & Refreshing, Oak Case, Sample, 20 x 10 In.
$800

Coca-Cola, Fan, Hand, Bamboo, Paper, Drink Coca-Cola, 10 x 15 In.
$385

Coca-Cola, Glass Holder, Silver Plate, Openwork, 1800s, 2 ¼ x 2 ¼ In.
$2,200

Coca-Cola, Knife, Folding, Leaf Work, Corkscrew, Bottle Opener, Kastor & Co., c.1900, 3 ½ In.
$495

Coca-Cola, Sign, Drug Store, Drink Coca-Cola, Delicious & Refreshing, Enamel, 60 x 46 In.
$848

Coca-Cola, Thermometer, Silhouette, Drink Coca-Cola, Delicious, Refreshing, 1939, 16 x 7 In.
$395

Coca-Cola, Toy, Truck, Delivery, Flat Top, Yellow, The Pause That Refreshes, 1950s, 6 ½ x 14 ½ In.
$350

Coca-Cola, Tray, Girl In Yellow, Drink Coca-Cola, Gold Rim, 13 ¼ x 10 ½ In.
$299

Coffee Mill, Enterprise, 2 Wheel, No. 209, Red, Decals, Eagle Finial, 34 x 25 In.

$986

Showtime Auction Services

Coin Spot, Cruet, Opalescent, White Faceted Stopper, c.1940, 6⅝ x 3½ In.

$125

Ruby Lane

Coin-Operated, Grip Tester, Round Dial, Red, Metal Stand, Curved Legs, 1930s, 19 x 47 In.

$593

Morphy Auctions

Display, Refresh Yourself, Cardboard, Trifold, Arched, Desert, 1925, 39 x 39 In.	4920
Door Push, Drink Coca-Cola, Porcelain, Metal, Red & White, 1930s, 27 In.	461
Door Push, Here's The Real Thing, Metal, c.1970, 18½ x 2 In.	70
Fan, Hand, Bamboo, Paper, Drink Coca-Cola, 10 x 15 In. ....*illus*	385
Figure, Elf, Drink Coca-Cola, Apron, Holding Bottle & Bell, Plastic, 1950s, 23 In.	615
Glass Holder, Silver Plate, Openwork, 1800s, 2¼ x 2¼ In. ....*illus*	2200
Handle, Pull, Aluminum, Bottle, Red Coca-Cola Logo, 11 In., Pair	184
Hat, Soda Jerk, White Cotton, Red Trim, 1950s, 10½ In.	35
Ice Pick, Yellow, Red, Coca-Cola In Bottles, 1940s, 10 In.	14
Knife, Folding, Leaf Work, Corkscrew, Bottle Opener, Kastor & Co., c.1900, 3½ In. ....*illus*	495
Lighter, Ribbed, Gold, Japan, 4¼ In., Pair	153
Megaphone, Cardboard, Tin Mouthpiece, Red & White, 10 In.	25
Menu Board, Red Button Logo, 6-Pack Carrier, Cardboard, c.1940, 29 x 16 In.	1555
Mirror, Calendar Girl, Hat, Red Flowers, Celluloid, 1911, Pocket, 2 x 1 In.	177
Mirror, Portrait, Girl, Driving, Drink Coca-Cola In Bottles, 2¼ In.	3600
Napkin Holder, Coca-Cola Lollipop Sign, 1950s, 12¼ In.	461
Notepad, Black, 1908, 4½ In., Pair	30
Pinback, Floral Ring, Bottle In Center, 1 In.	25
Playing Cards, 2 Couples, On Beach, Be Really Refreshed, 1960s, 2 x 3½ In.	40
Poster, Drink Coca-Cola 5 Cents, Lillian Nordica, On Board, 1903, 18 x 26 In.	85
Pull Plate, Pull, Refresh Yourself, Porcelain, Green, White, Red, 1950s, 8 x 4 In.	660
Ruler, Coke Adds Life To Everything, White, Red, Plastic, 1970s, 12 In.	10
Service Pin, 1930s Uniform Award Pin For 10 Years Of Service, Round, ¾ In.	59
Sewing Kit, Victorian Girl Holding Coca-Cola Bottle, Tin, Oval, 2⅝ In.	10
Sheet Music, Ben Bolt, Girl, Purple Hydrangeas, Wolf & Co., 1905, 13 x 10 In.	62
Sheet Music, My Coca-Cola Bride, Girl, Purple Hydrangeas, 1905, 13 x 10 In.	92
Sign, Coca-Cola 5 Cents, Girl's Face, Soda, Flower, Die Cut, c.1912, 15 x 10 In.	2091
Sign, Coca-Cola, Button, Red & White, Porcelain, Enamel, 1950s, 48 In. Diam.	550
Sign, Coca-Cola, Sign Of Good Taste, Take Home A Carton, Tin, 1950s, 28 x 20 In.	485
Sign, Drink Coca-Cola, 5 Cents, Figural, Christmas Bell, Cardboard, 12 In.	2091
Sign, Drink Coca-Cola, Fountain Service, Porcelain, Metal, 1941, 27 x 14 In.	3075
Sign, Drink Coca-Cola, Red, Yellow, Fishtail, Metal, Neon, 1960s, 37 x 57 In.	1400
Sign, Drink Coca-Cola, Swimmer Girl, Festoon, Die Cut, Cardboard, 28 x 14 In.	677
Sign, Drug Store, Drink Coca-Cola, Delicious & Refreshing, Enamel, 60 x 46 In. ....*illus*	848
Sign, Fountain Service Drink Coca-Cola, Tin, Enamel, 63 x 48 In.	2925
Sign, Girl, Blue Ribbon, Bottle In Hand, Umbrella, 27 x 23 In.	2280
Sign, Good Taste Coca-Cola, 3 Glasses, 1927, 32½ In.	2400
Sign, Groceries, Drink Coca-Cola, Rectangular, Sheet Metal, 72 x 36 In.	643
Sign, Neon, Reverse Painted, Countertop, 26 In.	7500
Sign, Pause Refresh, Sign Of Good Taste, Bottles, Cardboard, 1950s, 11 x 16 In.	100
Sign, Rack, Metal, Please Place Empties Here, The Real Thing, 1970s, 12 x 7 In.	92
Sign, Refreshing, Girl, Holding Mask, Hair Up, Gown, Mat, 1946, 36 x 19 In.	800
Sign, Tin Lithograph, Red, White Letters, Green Frame, 1930s, 10½ x 32 In.	1093
Syrup Bottle, Delicious, Also Refreshing, Fired-On Enamel, 11¼ In.	4800
Thermometer, Cigar Shape, Red, White, Sign Of Good Taste, 29 x 8 In.	295
Thermometer, Drink Coca-Cola, 2 Bottles, Arched, Red, Metal, Enamel, 16 In.	325
Thermometer, Figural Bottle, Tin, Embossed Coca-Cola, 1930, 16 In.	246
Thermometer, Silhouette, Drink Coca-Cola, Delicious, Refreshing, 1939, 16 x 7 In. ....*illus*	395
Thermometer, Silhouette, Girl, Robertson Dualife Co., 1939, 15 x 6 In.	395
Thermometer, Silhouette, Girl Drinking Out Of Bottle, Green, 1939, 15 x 6 In.	395
Tip Tray, 1904, Exhibition Girl, 6¼ x 4½ In.	435
Tip Tray, 1909, Exhibition Girl, Tin Lithograph, Oval, 6 x 4 In.	435
Tip Tray, 1910, Coca-Cola Girl, Drink Delicious Coca-Cola, Tin Litho, 6 x 4 In.	345
Tip Tray, 1913, Hamilton King Girl, Oval, 6 x 4 In.	142
Tip Tray, 1916, Elaine, Holding Glass, Oval, Passaic Metal Ware Co., 6 x 4 In.	71
Toy, Car, Coca-Cola, Refresh With Zest!, Metal, Friction, Box, 1960s, 10 In.	499
Toy, Truck, Delivery, Flat Top, Yellow, The Pause That Refreshes, 1950s, 6½ x 14½ In. ....*illus*	350
Tray, 1914, Betty, Hat With Ribbon, Delicious & Refreshing, Oval, 13 x 15 In.	185

Tray, 1916, Elaine, Holding Glass, Hat, Roses On Table, 19 x 8 ½ In.		275
Tray, 1926, Golfing Couple, Man Pouring Glass For Girl, 13 x 10 ½ In.		475
Tray, 1938, Girl At Shade, Yellow Dress & Hat, Holding Bottle, 13 x 10 In.		299
Tray, 1939, Springboard Girl, White Bathing Suit, With Bottle, 13 x 10 ½ In.		150
Tray, 1941, Skater Girl, Red Skirt, Scarf, 13 x 10 ½ In.		85
Tray, 1942, 2 Girls At Car, 13 x 10 ½ In.		175
Tray, Girl In Yellow, Drink Coca-Cola, Gold Rim, 13 ¼ x 10 ½ In.	*illus*	299
Tray, Thirst Knows No Season, Have A Coke, Girl, Bottle, 1950s, 13 x 11 In.		150
Umbrella, Drink Coca-Cola In Bottles, Alternating, Orange & White, 67 In.		275
Vending Machine, Red Metal, Embossed Coca-Cola, Glass, 1950s, 65 x 24 In.		1600

COFFEE MILLS are also called coffee grinders, although there is a difference in the way each grinds the coffee. Large floor-standing or counter-model coffee mills were used in the nineteenth-century country store. Small home mills were first made about 1894. They lost favor by the 1930s. The renewed interest in fresh-ground coffee has produced many modern electric mills and hand mills and grinders. Reproductions of the old styles are being made.

Enterprise Mfg. Co., Iron, Wood Base, Red Paint, 12 x 7 x 9 In.		633
Enterprise, 2 Wheel, No. 2, Red Paint, Drawer, 11 ½ In.		1080
Enterprise, 2 Wheel, No. 209, Red, Decals, Eagle Finial, 34 x 25 In.	*illus*	986
Enterprise, 2 Wheel, No. 3, Red Paint, Drawer, 14 In.		676
Enterprise, 2 Wheel, Red Paint, Drawer, 29 In.		1080
Enterprise, 2 Wheel, Red Paint, Stencil, Drawer, c.1880, 13 In.		431
Enterprise, 2 Wheel, Red Text, Yellow Ground, 26 x 21 In.		275
Enterprise, Cast Iron, Countertop, Tin Hopper, Wood Drawer, c.1880, 22 In.		960
Enterprise, Wheel, Red, No. 18, 56 x 30 ½ In.		1416
Landers, Frank & Clark, 2 Wheel, Black Paint, Drawer, 12 In.		720
Landers, Frary & Clarke, Iron, Red, No. 11, 12 In.		221
None-Such Coffee, Bronson Walton, Tin Lithograph, Wood Base, 10 x 6 In.		633

COIN SPOT is a glass pattern that was named by collectors for the spots resembling coins, which are part of the glass. Colored, clear, and opalescent glass was made with the spots. Many companies used the design in the 1870–90 period. It is so popular that reproductions are still being made.

Cruet, Opalescent, White Faceted Stopper, c.1940, 6 ⅝ x 3 ½ In.	*illus*	125
Lamp, Oil, Pale Blue & Opal, Bulbous, Saucer Foot, Loop Handle, 1800s, 13 In.		342
Pitcher, Green Opalescent, Yellow, Baluster, Crimped Rim, 1800s, 10 In.		200
Sugar Shaker, Cranberry & White, Squat, Metal Dome, c.1895, 5 In.		190
Vase, Hat, White, 8 In.		40

COIN-OPERATED MACHINES of all types are collected. The vending machine is an ancient invention dating back to 200 B.C., when holy water was dispensed from a coin-operated vase. Smokers in seventeenth-century England could buy tobacco from a coin-operated box. It was not until after the Civil War that the technology made modern coin-operated games and vending machines plentiful. Slot machines, arcade games, and dispensers are all collected.

Arcade, Kicker & Catcher, 1 Cent, Cherry, Cast Metal, c.1935, 18 In.		1169
Arcade, Pinball, Brownie Pool, Wood Case, Glass Marbles, 1930s, 15 x 21 In.		230
Gambling, Big Six, Money Wheel, Star, Dollars, Green, Gold, Wood, 86 In.		677
Gambling, Poker Game, 1 Cent, Deuces Wild Marquee, Wood, Metal, 17 In.		492
Gambling, Roulette, Walnut, Boxing Scenes, 3 Coin Slots, France, c.1940, 27 In.		1638
Grip Tester, Round Dial, Red, Metal Stand, Curved Legs, 1930s, 19 x 47 In.	*illus*	593
Skill, Baseball, World Champion, Aluminum, Wood Base, 10 x 9 x 17 In.		600
Skill, Sweets, Wood, Penny Slot, Chocolate Payout, O. Whales, England, 31 In.		682
Skill, Take Your Pick, Wood, Metal, O. Whales, England, c.1955, 32 In.		614
Slot, 10 Cent, Pace 8 Star Bell, Metal Cabinet, Paint, 1940s, 16 x 24 In.		424

Coin-Operated Machine, Trade Stimulator, Sun Cabinet, 2-Wheel Bicycle, Oak, Crank, 19 x 13 In.
$7,380

Morphy Auctions

Coin-Operated, Vending, Gumball, Card, 5 Cent, Red, Oak Mfg. Co., 1950s, 14 x 13 In.
$265

Burchard Galleries

Coin-Operated, Vending, Gumball, Mouthy Marvin, Northwestern Co., 1960, 46 In.
$264

Milestone Auctions

99

C

Collector Plate, Royal Copenhagen, Hans Christian Andersen, Silhouette, E. Hasserlis, 9 In.

$45

Ruby Lane

Collector Plate, Villeroy & Boch, Cathedral Of Trier, 1891, 10 In.

$299

Ruby Lane

Compact, Metal, Goldtone, Filigree, Blue Enamel, Portrait, Marie Antoinette, Estee Lauder, 2 In.

$48

Ruby Lane

Cookie Jar, Irish Wolfhounds, Driving, Classic Convertible, Porcelain, 8¼ In.

$93

Wiederseim Associates

Slot, Jennings, Governor, 1 Cent, Chrome, Handle, 3 Reels, c.1965, 27 x 17 In.	1534
Slot, Mills, 1 Cent, High Top, Chrome, Red & Black, Wood Base, 26 x 16 In.	923
Slot, Mills, Castle Front, Blue, Green, 5 Cent, c.1930, 25½ x 16 In.	826
Slot, Silver Palace, 25 Cents, Castle Shape, Red, Chrome, Mills, 27 x 16 In.	738
Slot, The Operators Bell, 5 Cent, Cast Iron, Scroll Feet, c.1910, 24 x 14 In.	1353
Trade Stimulator, Fairest Wheel, Cigar Store, Carved Wood, 1895, 21 x 9 In.	738
Trade Stimulator, Sun Cabinet, 2-Wheel Bicycle, Oak, Crank, 19 x 13 In. ...*illus*	7380
Vending, Cigarettes, Pick-A-Pack, 1 Cent, Baker Novelty, 1939, 11 In.	1228
Vending, Gum, 5 Cent, Red Aluminum, Glass Globe, Key, Regal, c.1945	225
Vending, Gumball, 1 Cent, Glass Globe, Red, Cast Iron, Star, 1950s, 15 x 8 In.	740
Vending, Gumball, 1 Cent, Mint Green, Decal, Countertop, c.1950, 14 In.	150
Vending, Gumball, Card, 5-Cent, Red, Oak Mfg. Co., 1950s, 14 x 13 In. ...*illus*	265
Vending, Gumball, Mouthy Marvin, Northwestern Co., 1960, 46 In. ...*illus*	264
Vending, Hand-EE-Kerchief, Men's, 10 Cent, Mirror, Key, 1928, 34 In.	246
Vending, Postcard, 5 Cent, Wooden, Slot, Decal, Exhibit Supply Co., 13 In.	523
Vending, Seat Cover & Toilet Tissue, 1 Cent, Kitco, Porcelain, 13 x 8 In.	277

 COLLECTOR PLATES are modern plates produced in limited editions. Some may be found listed under the factory name, such as Bing & Grondahl, Royal Copenhagen, Royal Doulton, and Wedgwood.

Alfred Meakin, Mother's Day, 1974, Children, Fishing On Bridge, 8 In.	10
American Greeting, Mother's Day, 1978, Holly Hobbie	20
Berlin Design, Mother's Day, 1971, Gray Poodles, 7¾ In.	10
Bradford Exchange, Jack Russell Terrier, Portrait, Faience, 1890, 12 In.	193
Braford Exchange, Winnie The Pooh, Forever Friends, 1st Issue, 1970s, 8 In.	22
Dresden, Mother's Day, 1974, Tiger & Cub, Gilt Trim, 8¼ In.	35
Fenton, Mother's Day, 1984, Custard Satin, Panda, Scalloped Edge, 8 In.	34
Franklin Mint, Countryside Cats, Time To Play, 8 In.	18
Knowles, Annie Series, Daddy Warbucks, 1983	15
Knowles, Norman Rockwell, The Cobbler, 1978, 8 In.	65
Norman Rockwell, Christmas, 1980, Scotty Plays Santa, 8¼ In.	20
Norman Rockwell, Heritage Series, Lighthouse Keeper's Daughter, 1979, 8 In.	12
Norman Rockwell, Mother's Day, 1981, After The Party, Box	20
Norman Rockwell, Mother's Day, 1984, Grandma's Courting Dress, 8 In.	15
P. Buckley Moss, 1984, Christmas, Noel, Family, Horse & Buggy, 8 In.	500
Reco, Circus Series, Tommy The Clown, 1982	25
Royal Copenhagen, Christmas, 1953, Frederiksborg Castle, 7 In.	49
Royal Copenhagen, Christmas, 1972, Osterland, In The Desert, 7¼ In.	25
Royal Copenhagen, Hans Christian Andersen, Silhouette, E. Hasserlis, 9 In. ...*illus*	45
Svend Jensen, Mother's Day, 1974, Daisies For Mother, 7½ In.	10
Villeroy & Boch, Cathedral Of Trier, 1891, 10 In. ...*illus*	299

 COMIC ART, or cartoon art, includes original art for comic strips, magazine covers, book pages, and even printed strips. The first daily comic strip was printed in 1907. The paintings on celluloid used for movie cartoons are listed in this book under Animation Art.

Concept Art, G.I. Joe, Jeep Driver, Skid Mark, Ink & Watercolor, 14 x 19 In.	1149
Cover, Mighty Mouse, No. 5, Pen & Ink, Artboard, E. Colon, Marvel, 11 x 17 In.	380
Cover, Starfire No. 8, Pen & Ink, Artboard, Sci-Fi, DC Comics, 1977, 11 x 17 In.	381
Drawing, Grinch, Color Pencil, Animation Paper, Signed, Ross, c.1966, 11 x 13 In.	173
Drawing, Mighty Thor, Portrait, Pencil, Artboard, Frame, Joe Sinnott, 15 x 16 In.	115
Gum Card, Wrapper, Film Funnies, Movie Star Caricatures, Gum Inc., 1935, 5 x 6 In.	129
Page, Comic, Justice League Of America, No. 101, Pg. 15, Pen & Ink, 1972	604
Page, Comic, X-Men No. 30, Pg. 18, Pen & Ink, Artboard, 1967, 13 x 21 In.	1139
Page, Magazine, Tomb Of Dracula, No. 1, Pen, Ink, Board, Marvel, 1979, 11 x 17 In.	3163
Postcard, Daredevil, Lev Gleason, Squeeks, Monkey, Golden Age, 1944, 3 x 6 In.	1518
Shmoo, Seashells, Cowry Shell Body, Scallop Shell Base, 1948, 4½ In.	115
Sketch, Batman & Robin, Felt Pen, Artboard, Frame, Bob Kane, 1976, 17 x 19 In.	506

Strip, Al Capp, 3 Panels, My Tests Show That You Are Neat, 1974, 12 x 39 94
Strip, Al Capp, A Mother's Tears, 1974 94

COMMEMORATIVE items have been made to honor members of royalty and those of great national fame. World's Fairs and important historical events are also remembered with commemorative pieces. Related collectibles are listed in the Coronation and World's Fair categories.

Box, Charles James Fox, Britain's 1st Foreign Secretary, Brass, c.1801, 3 In. 285
Coin, Gold, 300 Yuan, Olympics, 1980 550
Medal, Athens Olympic Stadium, Olympics, Wreath, Brass, 1896, 1 In. 386
Medal, Normandy Transatlantic, Ship, Bronze, Woman, Case, 1935, 3 In. 450
Plaque, 1798 Irish Rebellion, Death Of Father Michael Murphy, 1890s, 9 In. 280
Plate, Bicentennial, Independence Hall, Amber, Avon, 1976, 8 In. 15

COMPACTS hold face powder. A woman did not powder her face in public until after World War I. By 1920, the beauty parlor, permanent waves, and cosmetics had become acceptable. A few companies sold cake face powder in a box with a mirror and a pad or puff. Soon the compact was designed by jewelers and made of gold, silver, and precious materials. Cosmetic companies began to sell powder in attractive compacts of less valuable metal or plastic. Collectors today search for Art Deco designs, famous brands, compacts from World's Fairs or political events, and unusual examples. Many were made with companion lipsticks and other fittings.

18K Gold, Engine-Turned Allover, Rectangular, Interior Compartments 4920
Boucheron, Pierced, Engraved, Flowers, 5 Cabochon Rubies, Square, 3 x 3 In. 1375
Chatelaine, Silver, Hand Mirror-Shape Charm, Gilded Well, c.1915, 5 x 3 In. 125
Coro, Metal, Enamel, Rhinestone Swirl Design, Clip Closure, Square, 1950s 96
Dante & Beatrice, Silver, Imitation Malachite, Cut Corners, c.1875, 3 In. 180
Gilt, Filigree, Blue Cabochons, Glass, Mirror, Powder Puff, Chain, c.1910, 3 x 2 In. 160
Mappin & Webb, Portrait, Girl, Chain, 3 1/2 x 2 1/2 In. 250
Metal, Goldtone, Filigree, Blue Enamel, Portrait, Marie Antoinette, Estee Lauder, 2 In......*illus* 48
Minaudiere, Silvertone, Enamel, Mirror, Powder Puff, Chain, 1930s, 3 x 2 In. 800
Ormolu, Goldtone, Enamel, Flowers, Pearls, Mirror, Powder Puff, c.1880, 2 x 3 In. 1025
Silver, Rectangular, Reticulated, Birds, Flowers, Urn, Gilt, 3 In. 144
Silver, Round, Green, Gilt, Red, Bamboo, Continental, 1925, 1 3/4 In. 238
Silver, Round, Green, White, Bamboo, Continental, 1925, 2 In. 313

CONSOLIDATED LAMP AND GLASS COMPANY of Coraopolis, Pennsylvania, was founded in 1894. The company made lamps, tablewares, and art glass. Collectors are particularly interested in the wares made after 1925, including black satin glass, Cosmos (listed in its own category in this book), Martele (which resembled Lalique), Ruba Rombic (1928–32 Art Deco line), and colored glasswares. Some Consolidated pieces are very similar to those made by the Phoenix Glass Company. The colors are sometimes different. Consolidated made Martele glass in blue, crystal, green, pink, white, or custard glass with added fired-on color or a satin finish. The company closed for the final time in 1967.

Bowl, Swallows, Yellow, Frost, Etched, Flared Rim, 1920s, 10 In. Diam. 158
Compote, Amethyst, Fish, Water Lilies, Pedestal, Flared Rim, c.1933, 3 x 6 In. 102
Plate, Catalonian, Galactic Clear, Swirl Pattern, Bubbles, Wavy Rim, 1927, 8 In. 75
Tray, Catalonian, Honey, 6 Sections, Swirls, Lobed Rim, 1920s, 1 x 12 In. 650
Trinket Box, Regent Violet, Milk Glass, Tufted, Gold Beads, Lid, 1950s 120
Vase, Catalonian, Amber, Conical, Wavy Rim, Bubble Ribbed, 1920s, 10 In. 125
Vase, Catalonian, Lavender, Fan Shaped, Ribbed, Curved Rim, 1920s, 7 In. 92
Vase, Nude Woman, Blue Robing, 12 In. 150
Vase, Sea Gull, Orange Birds, Blue Ground, 11 In. 25

CONTEMPORARY GLASS, *see Glass-Contemporary.*

Cookie Jar, Old Shoe House, Red Roof, California Originals, 1950s, 7 x 11 In. $49

Ruby Lane

Coors, Plate, Orange, 10 1/4 In. $46

Replacements, Ltd.

TIP
Re-key all locks when you move to a new house or apartment or if you lose a key.

Copeland, Figurine, Robinette, Nymph Seated, Bird On Arm, Tree, Parian, c.1875, 13 In. $554

Skinner, Inc.

C

Copeland, Vase, Urn, Courtship, Seascape, Gold Trim, Winged Female Handles, 16 In.
$277

Cowan's Auctions

Copeland Spode, Plate, Byron, Grape Trellis, Woman, Boy, Water Jug, Green, Octagonal, 10 In.
$20

Ruby Lane

Copeland Spode, Wine Cooler, Peacock, Flowers, Green, 8 ½ In.
$139

Strawser Auction Group

 COOKBOOKS are collected for various reasons. Some are wanted for the recipes, some for investment, and some as examples of advertising. Cookbooks and recipe pamphlets are included in this category.

Holiday Goodies & How To Make Them, Peter Pauper Press, 1952, 7 ½ In.	22
Italian Cookbook, Maria Luisa Taglienti, 310 Pages, 1955	30
Italian Family Cooking, E. Giobbi, Hardcover, Random House, 252 Pgs., 1971, 9 x 6 In.	10
Money-Saver Chicken Cookbook, Supermarket Book Co., Color, Spiral, 128 Pgs., 1976	7
Pots & Pans: A Slovenian-American Cookbook, H. Dicke, 212 Pgs., 1982	60

 COOKIE JARS with brightly painted designs or amusing figural shapes became popular in the mid-1930s. Many companies made them and collectors search for cookie jars either by design or by maker's name. Listed here are examples by the less common makers. Major factories are listed under their own names in other categories of the book, such as Abingdon, Brush, Hull, McCoy, Metlox, Red Wing, and Shawnee. See also the Disneyana category.

Bear & Beehive, Flasher, Relief, Lid, Finial, American Bisque, 1940s, 9 x 7 In.	230
Bear, Romper, Cookie, Brown, Rosy Cheeks, American Bisque, c.1958, 10 In.	145
Clown Head, Red Nose, Yellow Hat, Curly Hair, Japan, 1950s, 7 ¾ In.	40
Dog, Bone In Mouth, Cream, Fitz & Floyd, 1977, 9 In.	65
Dog, Muggsy, Toothache, White, Blue Ribbon Around Head, Bow, Shawnee, 1950s	195
Hen & Chick, Brown Glaze, FAPCO, USA, 4 ½ x 5 ½ In.	30
Hexagon, Wexford Pattern, Anchor Hocking, c.1970, 11 x 6 ½ In.	25
Irish Wolfhounds, Driving, Classic Convertible, Porcelain, 8 ¼ In. ....*illus*	93
Old Shoe House, Red Roof, California Originals, 1950s, 7 x 11 In. ....*illus*	49
Owl, Collegiate, Brown, Tan, Bisque, 11 ¼ In.	95
Owl, Collegiate, Tasseled Cap, Glasses, Book, American Bisque Co., 11 In.	135
Owl, Winking, White, Orange, Green, Ceramic, 1950s, 12 x 8 In.	300
Raggedy Ann, Sitting On Barrel, California Originals, 13 ¾ In.	146

COORS U.S.A. **COORS** ware was made by the Coors Porcelain Company of Golden, Colorado, a company founded with the help of the Coors Brewing Company. Its founder, John Herold, started the Herold China and Pottery Company in 1910. The company name was changed in 1920, when Herold left. Dishes were made from the turn of the century. Coors stopped making nonessential wares at the start of World War II. After the war, the pottery made ovenware, teapots, vases, and a general line of pottery, but no dinnerware—except for special orders. The company is still in business making industrial porcelain. For more prices, go to kovels.com.

Biscuit Jar, Pink Flowers, Green Leaves, Banded Collar, Lug Handles, 1930s, 9 In.	95
Pitcher, Batter, Teal Glaze, Rosebud, Yellow Leaves, Angular Handle, 1920s, 10 In.	85
Plate, Dessert, Rosebud Yellow, 7 In.	12
Plate, Luncheon, Rosebud Blue, 9 In.	32
Plate, Orange, 10 ¼ In. ....*illus*	46
Vase, Blue Matte Glaze, Conical, Lower Handles, Stepped Dome Foot, 1940s, 8 In.	120

 COPELAND pieces listed here are those that have a mark including the word *Copeland* used between 1847 and 1976. Marks include *Copeland Spode* and *Copeland & Garrett.* See also Copeland Spode, Royal Worcester, and Spode.

Bust, Queen Victoria, Ermine Cape, Sash, Order Of The Garter, Parian, 11 In.	76
Candelabrum, 3-Light, Figural Cherub Stem, Holding Leafy Scroll, 9 In., Pair	381
Figurine, Robinette, Nymph Seated, Bird On Arm, Tree, Parian, c.1875, 13 In. ....*illus*	554
Pitcher, Flowers, Purple, Pink, Blue, Squat, Ruffled Rim, Saucer Foot, c.1880, 12 In.	295
Pitcher, Leaves, Blossoms, Venus In Shell, Cherub, Dolphin, c.1875, 10 In.	156
Plate, Luncheon, Jacobean Flowers, Blue & Gray, Scalloped, 1887, 8 In., 4 Piece	300
Plate, Roses, Cobalt Blue Border, Gilt, Beaded, c.1880, 9 In. Diam., 12 Piece	1250
Vase, Urn, Courtship, Seascape, Gold Trim, Winged Female Handles, 16 In. ....*illus*	277

COPELAND SPODE appears on some pieces of nineteenth-century English porcelain. Josiah Spode established a pottery at Stoke-on-Trent, England, in 1770. In 1833, the firm was purchased by William Copeland and Thomas Garrett and the mark was changed. In 1847, Copeland became the sole owner and the mark changed again. W.T. Copeland & Sons continued until a 1976 merger when it became Royal Worcester Spode. The company was bought by the Portmeirion Group in 2009. Pieces are listed in this book under the name that appears in the mark. Copeland, Royal Worcester, and Spode have separate listings.

Dinner Set, Creamware, Transfer Print Hunt Scene, Service For 12	500
Jar, Lid, Pink Flowers, Green Leaves & Vines, White Ground 13 In.	30
Ladle, Delhi Pattern, Blue, Scrolling Flowers, Tapered Handle, c.1860	250
Pitcher, Blue, White Figural Reserve, 7 ¾ In.	188
Pitcher, Gilt Rim, Branches, Pink Flowers, Urn, Band At Shoulder, 8 In.	200
Plate, Byron, Grape Trellis, Woman, Boy, Water Jug, Green, Octagonal, 10 In. ....*illus*	20
Platter, Pagoda, Butterflies, Blue, White, Octagonal, 1870, 11 x 15 In.	350
Platter, Tower Pattern, Bridge, Stream, Trees, Blue & White, 14 x 18 In.	106
Teapot, Chintz, Blue & White	98
Teapot, Mayflower, Blue, White, Red, Angular Handle, Lid, 1800s, 10 In.	270
Tureen, Lid, Tray, Gilt, Flow Blue, Imari, 12 ½ x 14 In.	125
Tureen, Tower Pattern, Bridge Of Salaro, Rope Rim, Lid, 1930s, 5 x 7 In.	235
Urn, Chintz, Blue, 12 In.	139
Wine Cooler, Peacock, Flowers, Green, 8 ½ In. ....*illus*	139

COPPER has been used to make utilitarian items, such as teakettles and cooking pans, since the days of the early American colonists. Copper became a popular metal with the Arts & Crafts makers of the early 1900s, and decorative pieces, like desk sets, were made. Other pieces of copper may be found in Arts & Crafts, Bradley & Hubbard, Kitchen, Roycroft, and other categories.

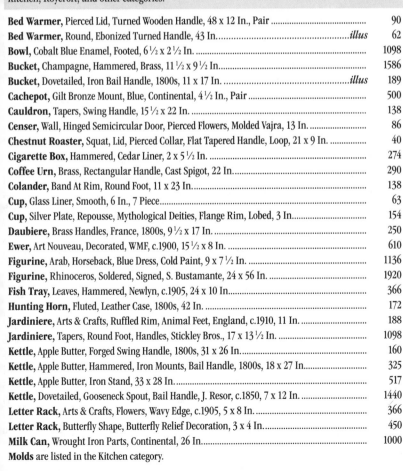

Bed Warmer, Pierced Lid, Turned Wooden Handle, 48 x 12 In., Pair	90
Bed Warmer, Round, Ebonized Turned Handle, 43 In. ....*illus*	62
Bowl, Cobalt Blue Enamel, Footed, 6 ½ x 2 ½ In.	1098
Bucket, Champagne, Hammered, Brass, 11 ½ x 9 ½ In.	1586
Bucket, Dovetailed, Iron Bail Handle, 1800s, 11 x 17 In. ....*illus*	189
Cachepot, Gilt Bronze Mount, Blue, Continental, 4 ½ In., Pair	500
Cauldron, Tapers, Swing Handle, 15 ½ x 22 In.	138
Censer, Wall, Hinged Semicircular Door, Pierced Flowers, Molded Vajra, 13 In.	86
Chestnut Roaster, Squat, Lid, Pierced Collar, Flat Tapered Handle, Loop, 21 x 9 In.	40
Cigarette Box, Hammered, Cedar Liner, 2 x 5 ½ In.	274
Coffee Urn, Brass, Rectangular Handle, Cast Spigot, 22 In.	290
Colander, Band At Rim, Round Foot, 11 x 23 In.	138
Cup, Glass Liner, Smooth, 6 In., 7 Piece	63
Cup, Silver Plate, Repousse, Mythological Deities, Flange Rim, Lobed, 3 In.	154
Daubiere, Brass Handles, France, 1800s, 9 ½ x 17 In.	250
Ewer, Art Nouveau, Decorated, WMF, c.1900, 15 ½ x 8 In.	610
Figurine, Arab, Horseback, Blue Dress, Cold Paint, 9 x 7 ½ In.	1136
Figurine, Rhinoceros, Soldered, Signed, S. Bustamante, 24 x 56 In.	1920
Fish Tray, Leaves, Hammered, Newlyn, c.1905, 24 x 10 In.	366
Hunting Horn, Fluted, Leather Case, 1800s, 42 In.	172
Jardiniere, Arts & Crafts, Ruffled Rim, Animal Feet, England, c.1910, 11 In.	188
Jardiniere, Tapers, Round Foot, Handles, Stickley Bros., 17 x 13 ½ In.	1098
Kettle, Apple Butter, Forged Swing Handle, 1800s, 31 x 26 In.	160
Kettle, Apple Butter, Hammered, Iron Mounts, Bail Handle, 1800s, 18 x 27 In.	325
Kettle, Apple Butter, Iron Stand, 33 x 28 In.	517
Kettle, Dovetailed, Gooseneck Spout, Bail Handle, J. Resor, c.1850, 7 x 12 In.	1440
Letter Rack, Arts & Crafts, Flowers, Wavy Edge, c.1905, 5 x 8 In.	366
Letter Rack, Butterfly Shape, Butterfly Relief Decoration, 3 x 4 In.	450
Milk Can, Wrought Iron Parts, Continental, 26 In.	1000

Molds are listed in the Kitchen category.

Copper, Bed Warmer, Round, Ebonized Turned Handle, 43 In.

$62

Turner Auctions + Appraisals

Copper, Bucket, Dovetailed, Iron Bail Handle, 1800s, 11 x 17 In.

$189

Hess Auction Group

Copper, Pitcher, Wide Mouth Spout, Narrow Lobed Band, 8 ¼ x 3 ½ In.

$48

Ruby Lane

COPPER

Copper, Sculpture, Lighthouse, Side Building, Openwork Stairs, Slate, 13 x 14 In.
$175

Ruby Lane

Copper, Watering Can, Brass Rain Head, 1 Pt., 4 x 13¾ In.
$65

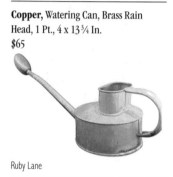

Ruby Lane

Coralene, Porringer Set, Lid, Underplate, Cranes, Leaves, Green, c.1890, 5½ In., 3 Piece
$150

Ruby Lane

Coronation, Cup, Queen Elizabeth II, Coat Of Arms, Flags, Brown, Royal Doulton, 1953, 11 In.
$62

Roland Auctioneers & Valuers

Pitcher, Wide Mouth Spout, Narrow Lobed Band, 8¼ x 3½ In. ....*illus*	48
Plaque, Ain't It Funny, Peacock, Multicolor, Colland & Co., 10 x 6 In.	250
Plaque, Crab, Leaves, Hexagon, 10 In.	427
Plaque, Lion, Bas Relief, Repousse, Frame, 34 x 28½ In.	767
Plaque, Portrait, Alfred E. Smith, 1928, 9 In.	263
Plaque, Relief, Robert Graham, L2, Nude Figure, 1992, 14 x 14 In.	8125
Plaque, Round, Surface Mottling, Benedict Art Studio, 15 In.	281
Plaque, Woman's Portrait, Profile, Flowing Hair, Embossed, Russia, 18 x 10 In.	35
Pot, Brass Handles, Gallard Paris, France, 15½ x 17 In.	500
Sculpture, Buddha, Cloisonne, Seated, Crossed Legs, Jar, Lotus Throne, 11 In.	984
Sculpture, Flying Sea Gulls, Agate Bolder Base, Curtis Jere, c.1950, 34 x 11 In.	119
Sculpture, Horse, Blue, Enamel, Gio Ponti, 8 x 16 In.	5185
Sculpture, Lighthouse, Side Building, Openwork Stairs, Slate, 13 x 14 In. ....*illus*	175
Teakettle, Dovetailed, Swing Handle, Finial, Stamped H. Reigart, c.1810, 7 In.	270
Teakettle, Gooseneck Spout, Handle, John Wolf, Cincinnati, 7 x 11 In.	369
Teakettle, Iron Mounts, Wood Agitator, Swing Bail Handle, 1800s, 18 x 26 In.	295
Teakettle, Lid, Mushroom Finial, Gooseneck Spout, Swing Handle, c.1810, 6 In.	767
Teakettle, Urn Shape, S-Spout, Thorn Handle, Scalloped, Flared Rim, Lid, c.1900, 9 In.	499
Teapot, Brown, Yellow Flowers, Japan, 6 In.	163
Tray, Bittersweet Nightshade, Vine, Acid Etched, Carence Crafters, 5 x 9 In.	183
Tray, Hammered, Handles, G. Stickley, 19 x 15 In.	732
Tray, Round, Handles, Wrought, Falick Novick, 17½ x 12 In.	305
Tray, Shaped, Rectangle, Handles, Robert Riddle Jarvie, 20 x 12 In.	1250
Umbrella Stand, Art Nouveau, Tapered, Raised Butterflies, Flowers, 21 In.	900
Umbrella Stand, Hammered, Tapered, Handles, British Arts & Crafts, 25 x 13 In.	2250
Urn, Octagonal, Faceted, Swags, Tapering Pedestal Foot, Gilt, c.1860, 23 In.	4444
Vase, 2 Handles, Fluted, Japan, 18 x 6 In.	406
Vase, Buttressed, Riveted, Frederick Fifield, 9½ x 8 In.	488
Vase, Hammered, Cylindrical, Buttressed, Paneled, K. Kipp, c.1912, 8 In.	1476
Vase, Hammered, Cylindrical, Flared, Rolled Rim, G. Stickley, c.1910, 11 In.	984
Vase, Hammered, Fluted Mouth, Tapered Round Foot, Stickley, 8 x 6 In.	250
Vase, Hammered, Pear Shape, Stick Neck, Jean Dunand, 17½ x 5 In.	3660
Water Pump, Iron Handle, Pine Backplate, 90 x 9 In.	325
Watering Can, Brass Rain Head, 1 Pt., 4 x 13¾ In. ....*illus*	65

COPPER LUSTER *items are listed in the Luster category.*

 CORALENE glass was made by firing many small colored beads on the outside of glassware. It was made in many patterns in the United States and Europe in the 1880s. Reproductions are made today. Coralene-decorated Japanese pottery is listed in the Japanese Coralene category.

Compote, Amber, Peaches, Branches, Silver Rim, Squat, 1800s, 6 x 8 In.	650
Jar, Blue Green To White, Gold Beaded Leaves, Shouldered, c.1890, 4 In.	165
Perfume Bottle, Blue To White, Gold Seaweed Design, Stopper, c.1900, 7 In.	110
Pitcher, Cranberry Glass, Gold & Blue Beaded Leaves, Baluster, Ring Foot, 5 In.	147
Pitcher, White To Fuchsia, Yellow Beaded Twig Design, Reeded Handle, 7 In.	1250
Porringer Set, Lid, Underplate, Cranes, Leaves, Green, c.1890, 5½ In., 3 Piece.........*illus*	150
Rose Bowl, Gold Mother-Of-Pearl, Wheat, In-Folding Rim, Footed, c.1890, 5 In.	400
Rose Bowl, Turquoise To Yellow, Gold Seaweed, Squat, Ruffled Rim, c.1890, 4 In.	340
Shade, Pink To Frosted, Flowering Stems, Ruffled Rim, c.1900, 6 In.	128
Vase, Amber Glass, Beads, Gold Trim, Ball Shape, Trumpet Neck, 1950s, 5 In.	105
Vase, Blue Satin, Beaded Flowers, Footed Urn, Trumpet Neck, 1800s, 7 In.	145
Vase, Cobalt Blue, Yellow & Pink Roses, Gold Band, Japanese, 7 In., Pair	360
Vase, Gilt, Roses, Green, Blue, Japanese, 5 x 4½ In.	72
Vase, Iridescent Yellow To Cream, Beaded, Seaweed Clusters, c.1900, 7 In.	310
Vase, Lavender, White, Teal, Gold Seaweed Overlay, Bulbous, c.1880s, 7 x 5 In.	315
Vase, Orange To Peach, Gold Seaweed Overlay, Jar Shape, c.1900, 6 In.	127
Vase, Satin Pink To White, Gold Beading, Star Design, Oval, c.1900, 5 In.	375
Vase, Yellow, Beaded Dragonflies, Leafy Branches, Lobed Collar, 1800s, 6 In.	550
Vase, Yellow, Gold, Flowers, Round, Double Handles, 3-Footed, 4 x 3½ In.	540

CORDEY CHINA COMPANY was founded by Boleslaw Cybis in 1942 in Trenton, New Jersey. The firm produced gift shop items. In 1969 it was acquired by the Lightron Corp. and operated as the Schiller Cordey Co., manufacturers of lamps. About 1950 Boleslaw Cybis began making Cybis porcelains, which are listed in their own category in this book.

Figurine, Victorian, Woman, Blue Dress, Flowers In Hair, 14 In.	195
Figurine, Woman, Pastel Dress, Lace Trim, Ringlet Hair, Hat, Scrolled Base, 11 In.	117

CORKSCREWS have been needed since the first bottle was sealed with a cork, probably in the seventeenth century. Today collectors search for the early, unusual patented examples or the figural corkscrews of recent years.

Bone, Coaching Scene, 7 In.	157
Gilt Metal, 17 In.	51
Indian Head, Carved Wood, Stained, 1950s, 7 ½ In.	199
Little Brown Jug, Silver Plate, 1930s, 4 In.	94
Penis, Ebony, 5 x 5 In.	468
Skeleton Key, Brass, 1970s, 7 In.	52
Tangent Lever, Steel & Brass, Scroll, Marked, c.1875, 8 x 5 In.	185

CORONATION souvenirs have been made since the 1800s. Pottery, glass, tin, silver, and paper objects with a picture of the monarchs and date have been sold at many coronations. The pieces that mention King Edward VIII, the king who was never crowned, are not rare; collectors should be sure to check values before buying. Related pieces are found in the Commemorative category.

Container, Tin, King George VI, Queen Elizabeth, Oval Portraits, 1937, 5 x 6 In.	25
Cup, Queen Elizabeth II, Coat Of Arms, Flags, Brown, Royal Doulton, 1953, 11 In. ....*illus*	62
Medal, Queen Anne, Silver, Engraved, Bust, 1702, 1 ¼ In. Diam.	225
Mug, Queen Elizabeth, Commemorative, 1953, 4 In.	323
Plate, King Edward VIII, Portrait, Flags, Fluted Border, Scalloped Rim, 1937	80

COSMOS is a pressed milk glass pattern with colored flowers made from 1894 to 1915 by the Consolidated Lamp and Glass Company. Tablewares and lamps were made in this pattern. A few pieces were also made of clear glass with painted decorations. Other glass patterns are listed under Consolidated Lamp and also in various glass categories. In later years, Cosmos was also made by the Westmoreland Glass Company.

Butter, Dome Cover, White Opalescent, Flowers, Pink, Blue, Finial, c.1905, 8 x 7 In.	285
Condiment Set, Salt, Pepper, Mustard, Stand, 7 ¼ x 6 In., 4 Piece	402
Lamp, Oil, Milk Glass, Pink, Blue, Yellow Flowers, Dot Pattern, c.1910, 4 In.	88
Pitcher, Milk Glass, Pink Band, Crisscross Pattern, Flowers, c.1905, 9 In.	106
Sugar & Creamer, Lobed, Pastel Multicolor, 2 Piece	345
Sugar & Creamer, Milk Glass, Crisscross Pattern, Pink Band, Flowers, 1800s, 6 In.	152

COVERLETS were made of linen or wool during the nineteenth century. Most of the coverlets date from 1800 to the 1880s. There was a revival of hand weaving in the 1920s and new coverlets, especially geometric patterns, were made. The earliest coverlets were made on narrow looms, so two woven strips were joined together and a seam can be found. The weave structures of coverlets can include summer and winter, double weave, overshot, and others. Jacquard coverlets have elaborate pictorial patterns that are made on a special loom or with the use of a special attachment. Quilts are listed in this book in their own category.

Blue & White, Flowers, Birds, Jos. Klar, 1839, 74 x 88 In.	292
Double Weave, Flowers, Stars, Red, White, Blue, Border Buildings, 87 x 73 In.	523
Jacquard, American Eagles, Deer, Capitol Building, Red, White, 1850, 90 x 96 In.	219
Jacquard, Blue, White, Liberty, Great Seal, 88 x 81 In.	780
Jacquard, Blue Wool & Cotton, c.1825, 72 x 102 In.	240
Jacquard, Blue, White, Signed Naomi Bradley & J. Impson, 1841, 80 x 88 In.	292
Jacquard, Corner Block, Michael Franz, Miami, Ohio, 1830, 2 Panel, 72 x 80 In.	210
Jacquard, Flowers, Blue, White, Inscription, Sally Newell, 1848, 84 x 91 In.	388

Coverlet, Jacquard, Flowers, J. Witmer, Red, Dark Blue, Pa., 1847, 2 Panel, 78 x 97 In.
$413

Hess Auction Group

Coverlet, Jacquard, Flowers, Signed, Lancaster, New Holland, 1842, 2 Panel, 76 x 81 In.
$266

Hess Auction Group

Coverlet, Jacquard, Flowers, Turkey, Rooster, Blocks, H. Oberly, 2 Panel, 74 x 92 In.
$295

Hess Auction Group

Coverlet, Jacquard, Wool, Cotton, Tulips, Willow Tree, Wm. Craig, 1849, 76 x 88 In.
$132

Garth's Auctioneers & Appraisers

Cowan, Vase, Pillow, October Glaze, U Shape, Scroll Base, 1928, 6½ x 4¼ In.
$89

Ruby Lane

Cracker Jack, Toy, Fortune-Teller, Wheel Spinner, Sailor Jack, Bingo, 1930s, 1¾ In.
$46

Ruby Lane

Cranberry Glass, Bowl, Cut Glass, Oval Bull's-Eye, Strawberry Diamonds, Bohemia, 1820s, 5 x 9 In.
$1,150

Ruby Lane

Jacquard, Flowers, Grapevine Border, Anna Kumler, 1868, 72 x 96 In.	125
Jacquard, Flowers, J. Witmer, Red, Dark Blue, Pa., 1847, 2 Panel, 78 x 97 In. ....*illus*	413
Jacquard, Flowers, Signed, Lancaster, New Holland, 1842, 2 Panel, 76 x 81 In. ....*illus*	266
Jacquard, Flowers, Turkey, Rooster, Blocks, H. Oberly, 2 Panel, 74 x 92 In. ....*illus*	295
Jacquard, M. Hoke In Dover 1837, C. Henry, 97 x 85 In.	197
Jacquard, Navy Stripes, Pink, White, 90 x 74½ In.	63
Jacquard, Navy, Green, Circular Patterns, Henry Womelsdorf, 1841, 96 x 80 In.	150
Jacquard, Red, Blue, Flowers, Roosters, Turkeys, Wreaths, Fringe, 1800s, 82 x 93 In.	413
Jacquard, Red, Cream, Green, Blue, Flowers, Birds, Trees, Fringe, c.1843, 90 x 78 In.	215
Jacquard, Red, Floral, Fringe, 1900s, 90 x 95 In.	199
Jacquard, Red, Green, Black, Grapevines, Bird Border, Fringe, 1844, 66 x 92 In.	540
Jacquard, Red, Green, Yellow, c.1850, 83 x 80 In.	160
Jacquard, Red, White, Mermaids, Fish, 1800s, 67 x 84 In.	380
Jacquard, Rose Pattern, Snowflake Border, Name Blocks, 1838, 78 x 94 In.	236
Jacquard, Star Medallions, Floral Vine Border, 1850, 2 Panel, 68 x 86 In.	600
Jacquard, Stars, Flowers, Red, White, Double Cloth, 1846, 95 x 87 In.	785
Jacquard, Washington, Steamboat Corners, Philip Schum, c.1869, 76 x 80 In.	210
Jacquard, Wool & Cotton, Flowers, Indiana, 2 Panel, c.1858, 78 x 84 In.	300
Jacquard, Wool, Black, Cream, Snowflake & Window Pattern, 1800s, 88 x 78 In.	800
Jacquard, Wool, Cotton, Tulips, Willow Tree, Wm. Craig, 1849, 76 x 88 In. ....*illus*	132
Jacquard, Wreath, Flower Vine Border, Corner Block, S. Kuder, 1847, 80 x 92 In.	355
Overshot, Blue, White, Cotton, Scrolling Flowers, 1845, 91 x 88 In.	240
Overshot, Blue, White, Grid Pattern, 86 x 106 In.	192
Overshot, Navy, Natural, Geometrics, Fringe, Va., 1800s, 76 x 96 In.	199
Overshot, Orange & White, Grid Pattern, c.1850, 93 x 72 In.	135
Overshot, Red, Blue, Green, Geometric, Plaid, Fringe, 2 Panel, c.1850, 76 x 82 In.	384
Overshot, Red, Green, Blue, Central Quatrefoil Flowers & Leaves, 73 x 81 In.	180
Overshot, Red, White Cotton, Flowers, Marked J & D, 1841, 94 x 72 In.	300
Overshot, Red, White, Blue, Grid, 71 x 90 In.	271

COWAN POTTERY made art pottery and wares for florists. Guy Cowan made pottery in Rocky River, Ohio, a suburb of Cleveland, from 1913 to 1931. A stylized mark with the word *Cowan* was used on most pieces. A commercial, mass-produced line was marked *Lakeware*. Collectors today search for the Art Deco pieces by Guy Cowan, Viktor Schreckengost, Waylande Gregory, or Thelma Frazier Winter.

Bowl, Blue, Ring Foot, Curved Walls, 6 x 2 In.	45
Bowl, Center, Delft Blue, Ribbed, Footed, 1920s, 4 x 12 In.	65
Bowl, Square, Footed, Scalloped, Pink, 1920s, 11 x 11 In.	65
Candelabrum, 2-Light, Dancer, Ivory Glaze, Flower Cups, 1927, 10 x 8 In., Pair	1850
Candleholder, Byzantine, Guava Yellow, c.1927, 9 x 6 In.	99
Candlestick, Groundhog, Holding Candleholder, Book, Green, 1912-31, 9 In.	1121
Flower Frog, Dancing Nude, Scarf, Opaque White, Anna Pavlova, 1925, 6 In.	160
Planter, Peacock Blue, Matte Glaze, Oval, Marked, c.1930, 10 x 7 In.	367
Plate, Glazed, Tennis Players, Viktor Schreckengost, c.1929, 11 In.	438
Vase, Fan, Seahorse, Footed, Channeled, Ivory, c.1926, 7 In.	79
Vase, Pillow, October Glaze, U Shape, Scroll Base, 1928, 6½ x 4¼ In. ....*illus*	89
Vase, Pillow, Yellow Glaze, Scroll Base, c.1928, 6 In.	89
Vase, Stepped Base, Flared, Green Glaze, c.1929, 6 In.	69
Vase, Teal, Azure Matrix Glaze, Bulbous, Trumpet Neck, Marked, c.1930, 7 In.	199

CRACKER JACK, the molasses-flavored popcorn mixture, was first made in 1896 in Chicago, Illinois. A prize was added to each box in 1912. Collectors search for the old boxes, toys, and advertising materials. Many of the toys are unmarked.

Card, Endangered Species, Cougar	4
Card, Tail Slide, Alligator	8
Card, Tilt, Bucking Bronco	12
Card, Tilt, Eye, Opens & Closes	12
Card, Tilt, Girl With Umbrella, Dog, Doghouse	10

Charm, French Horn, Dark Metal, 1 ¼ In.	9
Charm, Orphan Annie, Plastic, Embossed	25
Charm, Pistol, Metal, 1 ⅛ In.	7
Charm, Stylized Bee, Plastic, Dark Blue	10
Charm, Tennis Racket, Silver Metal, 2 ½ In.	8
Game, Board, Milton Bradley, 1976	25
Pitch Fork, Metal, Silvertone, 2 ¼ In.	7
Toy, 2 Owls On Crescent Moon, Metal, ⅝ In.	8
Toy, Bugle, Metal, 1 In.	6
Toy, Clicker, Frog, Green Metal, 2 In. Diam.	35
Toy, Clip-On, Pocket Clips Peeper, Indian, Green, Plastic	9
Toy, Dexterity Game, Circus	11
Toy, Dial A Face, Pink, Plastic, Top Hat	15
Toy, Eye Ticklers, Optical Illusions	12
Toy, Fortune-Teller, Wheel Spinner, Sailor Jack, Bingo, 1930s, 1 ¾ In. *illus*	46
Toy, Hen, Metal	13
Toy, How To Make Your Own Finger Prints	10
Toy, I.D. Tag, Plastic, Yellow, Mascot	6
Toy, Majorette, Plastic, Blue, Raised Leg	6
Toy, Motor Boat, Driver, Dark Metal, 1 ¼ In.	10
Toy, Pocket Clip, Owl, Blue, Plastic	5
Toy, Popper, Beard, Red	12
Toy, Shovel, Sheet Metal, Navy Front, Silver Back, 3 In.	25
Toy, Wrench, Plastic, Blue	7

CRACKLE GLASS was originally made by the Venetians, but most of the wares found today were made since the 1800s. The glass was heated, cooled, and refired so that many small lines appeared inside the glass. Most was made from about 1930 to 1980, although some is made today. The glass is found in many colors, but collectors today pay the highest prices for amberina, cranberry, or ruby red. Cobalt blue is also popular. More crackle glass may be listed in those categories in this book.

Creamer, Olive Green To Silvery Blue, Squat, Loop Handle, c.1960, 4 In.	25
Decanter, Topaz, Double Lobed, Flared Rim, Ball Finial, 1950s, 12 In.	80
Pitcher, Tangerine, Yellow Loop Handle, Baluster, Ruffled Rim, c.1955, 5 In.	75
Vase, Green, Applied Filigree Swirl, Ruffled Rim, 7 x 4 In.	48

CRANBERRY GLASS is an almost transparent yellow-red glass. It resembles the color of cranberry juice. The glass has been made in Europe and America since the Civil War. It is still being made, and reproductions can fool the unwary. Related glass items may be listed in other categories, such as Rubina Verde.

Basket, Enamel, Girl, Flower, Twist Bail Handle, Loop Feet, 1800s, 6 x 4 In.	235
Bowl, Cut Glass, Oval Bull's-Eye, Strawberry Diamonds, Bohemia, 1820s, 5 x 9 In. *illus*	1150
Bride's Basket, Pillar, Brass Frame, Handle, Scroll Feet, c.1950, 8 x 8 In.	80
Dresser Jar, Luster, Clear Finial, Flowers, Leaves, 6 x 6 In.	49
Epergne, 4 Trumpet Shapes, Shell Shape Base, c.1880, 17 In.	200
Epergne, Dolphins, Italy, 23 x 11 ½ In.	501
Epergne, Fluted Mouth, Square Base, 23 In.	344
Epergne, Lily Pad Shape Plates, Bowl, Gilt, Continental, 10 x 18 In.	1062
Ewer, Flowers, Bronzed Metal Mounts, 14 In.	61
Marriage Cup, Gilt, Flowers, Handles, Honesdale, 7 In.	100
Pitcher, Opalescent Swirl, Baluster, Ruffled Rim, Handle, c.1885, 9 In.	465
Pitcher, Opalescent, Hobnail, Bulbous, Ruffled Rim, Handle, c.1890, 8 In.	218
Pitcher, Woman Feeding Scottish Terrier, c.1955, 10 In.	23
Rose Bowl, Cut To Clear, Overlay, Cut Swag, 5 In.	108
Salt, Master, Applied Glass Decoration, 1 ½ x 4 In.	96
Vase, Cut To Clear, Strawberry Diamond Pattern, Ruffled Rim, 12 In.	216
Vase, Horn Shape, Faceted, Foldover Rim, Bronze Ram's Head, c.1850, 10 In., Pair	1187
Vase, Stick, Opaque Bands, 7 x 4 In.	98

Creamware, Jug, Black Transfer Banding, Leaves, Rosettes, c.1950, 12 In. **$135**

Leland Little Auctions

Creil, Charger, Woman, Putti, Vine, Star, Cobalt Blue, Multicolor Border, 1840-80, 11 In. **$425**

Ruby Lane

Crown Milano, Biscuit Jar, Enamel, Blossom, Embossed Silver Plated Lid, Marked, 7 In. **$259**

Early Auction Company

TIP

Antique glass should be handled as if it has been repaired and might fall apart. Hold a pitcher by the body, not the handle. Pick up stemware by holding both the stem and the bowl. Hold plates in two hands, not by the rim.

Cruet, Amber, Hobnail, Blue Reeded Handle & Stopper, c.1890, 8 In.
$150

Ruby Lane

Cruet, Green Glass, Pear Shape, Pewter Overlay, Swirl, Flowers, Art Nouveau, 8¾ x 4½ In.
$175

Ruby Lane

Currier & Ives, Ice Boat On The Hudson, 8½ x 13 In.
$660

Cowan's Auctions

Vase, Swirl, Chimney, 10 In.	205
Vase, Trumpet, Wide Flared Mouth, Pair, 11 x 7 In.	171
Vase, White To Cranberry, Gilt, Reserve, Cherub, Landscapes, 10 In., Pair	1080
Water Set, Pitcher, Inverted Thumbprint, 8 Tumblers, 9 Piece	258
Wine, Cut Clear To Leaf, St. Louis Crystal, 8 x 3½ In., 11 Piece	300

CREAMWARE, or queensware, was developed by Josiah Wedgwood about 1765. It is a cream-colored earthenware that has been copied by many factories. Similar wares may be listed under Pearlware and Wedgwood.

Basket, Oval, Scalloped Rim, Pierced, Festoons, Twisted Handles, c.1785, 6 In.	738
Candlestick, Vase Shape Stem, Scroll Handles, Masks, Base, c.1785, 11 In.	461
Charger, Molded Feather Edge, Rothwell, England, c.1800, 17 In.	492
Coffeepot, Birds, Multicolor, Ridged Neck & Base, Molded Masks, 1800s, 6 In.	60
Creamer, Oval, Wavy Rim, Roundels, Pierced, Honeycombs, c.1780, 4 In.	2214
Fruit Plate, Anemone Flowers, Sprigs, Molded Shells, c.1780, 9 In. Diam.	185
Jug, Black Transfer Banding, Leaves, Rosettes, c.1950, 12 In. ....*illus*	135
Jug, Ship, Eagle, Shield, Peace, Commerce, Honest Friendship, 1804, 10 In.	2706
Mug, Cylindrical, Pagoda, Verse, Blue, Ear Shape Handle, 1777, 4 In.	1230
Pitcher, 3-Masted Ship, Ribbon, God Speed The Plow, J. Barr, 5 In.	1968
Plaque, Nude Nymph, Hammock, Putti In Trees, Frame, c.1860, 14 x 16 In.	1046
Plate, Brown Mottled Glaze, Green, Tan, Molded Rim, c.1790, 10 In. Diam.	210
Plate, Molded Ribbons, Interlaced, Wavy Rim, Tortoiseshell Glaze, c.1760, 9 In.	1968
Platter, Charleston, Green, Black Transfer Printed, c.1800, 15 In.	240
Teapot, Chinoiserie, Pavilion, Rocks, Birds, Landscape, c.1780, 7 In.	480
Teapot, Cylindrical, Ribbed, Entwined Handles, Cutout Rim, Lid, c.1780, 4 In.	523
Teapot, Lid, Cybele, Chariot, Cylindrical, Flower Knop, Beaded, c.1775, 6 In.	1046
Teapot, Lid, Oval, Leaf Molded Handle & Spout, Flowers, c.1775, 5 In.	2829
Teapot, Octagonal, Diagonal Spout, Rose Sprays, 1805, 6 x 9½ In.	831
Teapot, Prodigal Son In Excess, Staffordshire, 5 In.	660
Tureen, Tray, Cabbage, 7½ In.	1188
Tureen, Wheat Sheaves, Yellow Band, Artichoke Finial, c.1800, 11 x 15 In.	425

CREIL, France, had a faience factory as early as 1794. The company merged with a factory in Montereau in 1819. It made stoneware, mocha ware, and soft paste porcelain. The name *Creil* appears as part of the mark on many pieces. The Creil factory closed in 1895.

Bowl, View Of Aqueduct, Oval, Creamware, 1808-18, 10½ x 7½ In.	480
Cake Stand, Wildflowers, Red Transfer, Wave Border, Domed Foot, c.1910, 5 x 10 In.	99
Charger, Middle Eastern Woman, Hand Painted, Frame, 13 In.	400
Charger, Woman, Putti, Vine, Star, Cobalt Blue, Multicolor Border, 1840-80, 11 In...........*illus*	425
Coffeepot, Cupid Vignettes, Transfer Design, Shaped, Footed, c.1815, 10 In.	813
Coffeepot, Origin Of Dalliance, Cupid Offering Rose, Creamware, c.1810, 10 In.	780
Creamer, Flowers, Blue & White, Squat, Wide Spout, Saucer Foot, 1800s, 4½ In.	105
Dish, Majolica, Molded Asparagus, Hand Painted, 3½ x 15 x 10 In.	216
Jug, Frogs, Leaping & Playing Music, Reeds, Lily Pad, Cream, Brown, 1800s, 11 In.	163
Plate Set, Roman Vignettes, Et Montereau, Creamware, c.1900, 8½ In., 8 Piece	705
Plate, Cavalier King Charles Spaniel, Portrait, Gilt Rim, Montereau, c.1880, 12 In.	192
Plate, Commemorative, Earthenware, Russian Emperor, Troops, 1880, 8 In.	245
Plate, Commemorative, Yellow, Charles X Allant A La Chasse, Scratches, 9 In.	25
Plate, Dueling, Champagne Bottles, Transfer, French Text, Portraits, c.1850, 8 In.	125
Plate, Scroll Medallion, White, Blue, Transfer, Swag Border, Saucer Foot, c.1900, 9 In.	95
Plate, Voyages En Balloon, Man, Top Hat, Hot Air Balloon, Montereau, 8 In.	59
Plate, Yellow, Landscape, Horse, Rider, Charles X, 9¼ In.	24
Teapot, Caesar, Mark Antony, Transfer, Paneled, Creamware, c.1815, 7 In.	375
Tile, Winter Scene, 2 Boys Sledding, Tumbling, Paint, Montereau, 1800s, 8 x 8 In.	248
Tureen, Lid, King Louis XVI, Napoleon, Josephine, Creamware, c.1818, 15 In.	1152
Tureen, Undertray, King Louis XVI, Creamware, 10½ x 15 In.	1080
Undertray, Caesar Pardoning Marcellus, Reticulated, 14 x 9½ In.	360

CROWN DERBY is the name given to porcelain made in Derby, England, from the 1770s to 1935. Andrew Planche and William Duesbury established Crown Derby as the first china-making factory in Derby. Pieces are marked with a crown and the letter *D* or the word *Derby*. The earliest pieces were made by the original Derby factory, while later pieces were made by the King Street Partnerships (1848–1935) or the Derby Crown Porcelain Co. (1876–90). Derby Crown Porcelain Co. became Royal Crown Derby Co. Ltd. in 1890. It is now part of Royal Doulton Tableware Ltd.

Ewer, Pink, 22K Gilding, Leaves, Blossoms, c.1890, 7 In.	232
Teapot, White, Blue, Gilt, Scroll Handle, Lid, Finial, Marked, c.1782, 5 x 9 In.	435
Vase, Bud, Butterflies, White, Bulbous, Stick Neck, Marked, 1800s, 4 In.	325
Vase, Cobalt Blue, Gilt Leaves, Butterflies, c.1890, 5 In.	290

CROWN DUCAL is the name used on some pieces of porcelain made by A.G. Richardson and Co., Ltd., of Tunstall and Cobridge, England. The name has been used since 1916. Crown Ducal is a well-known maker of chintz pattern dishes. The company was bought by Wedgwood in 1974.

Plate, Octagonal, Blue, Birds, Flowers, 8 ½ In.	88
Platter, Tulip Pattern, Oval Center, Shaped Border, 1920s, 14 x 10 In.	86
Teapot, Lid, Pink Flowers, Bulbous, Scalloped Rim, Finial, 1930s, 6 x 9 In.	395
Wash Pitcher, Bowl, Marigold, Orange, Purple, 2 Piece	110

CROWN MILANO glass was made by the Mt. Washington Glass Works about 1890. It was a plain biscuit color with a satin finish decorated with flowers and often had large gold scrolls. Not all pieces are marked.

Biscuit Jar, Enamel, Blossom, Embossed Silver Plated Lid, Marked, 7 In. ....*illus*	259
Humidor, Flowers, Red, Yellow, Silver Plate, 6 ½ x 5 ¾ In.	153
Jar, Lid, Cream, Pink, Yellow, Turtle Finial, 4 ¾ In.	240
Lamp, Victorian Hall, Melon Ribbed Insert, Enamel Flower, Globe, 14 In.	144
Vase, Bird, Branch, Flowers, White, 13 x 5 In.	98
Vase, Flowers, Oval, Pinched Neck, Ruffled Rim, c.1900, 13 ½ In.	531

CRUETS of glass or porcelain were made to hold vinegar, oil, and other condiments. They were especially popular during Victorian times and have been made in a variety of styles since the eighteenth century. Additional cruets may be found in the Castor Set category and also in various glass categories.

Amber, Hobnail, Blue Reeded Handle & Stopper, c.1890, 8 In. ....*illus*	150
Amberina, Amber Cased, Ribbing, Arched Handle, Faceted Stopper, 6 ½ In.	3000
Cranberry Glass, 10 Cups, Applied Handle, Gilt Stylized Flowers, 11 Piece	98
Cranberry Glass, Opalescent, Herringbone, Applied Handle, Faceted Stopper, 6 In.	450
Cranberry Glass, Opalescent, Seaweed, Faceted Finial, Hobbs, Brockunier, 6 In.	216
Cut Glass, Wide Base, Long Stopper, 4 x 7 In.	22
Earthenware, Delft, Tin Glaze, Blue, White, Stand, 6 ½ In., Pair	1020
Glass, Coin Dot, Light Blue, Stopped, 7 In.	24
Glass, Dew Drop, Hobnail, Yellow Neck, Hobbs, Brockunier & Co., 7 In.	96
Glass, Opalescent, Lattice, Ribbed, Blue, Faceted Stopper, c.1886, 6 ½ In.	108
Glass, Pink, Melon Shape, Multicolor Enamel Beading, Scrolling, 7 In.	570
Glass, Ruby Cabochons, Gilt, Scroll, Squat, Lobed, Metal Spout & Handle, 1800s, 5 In.	215
Glass, Silver Overlay, Applied Flower Garlands, Stopper, 7 ¼ In.	72
Green Glass, Pear Shape, Pewter Overlay, Swirl, Flowers, Art Nouveau, 8 ¾ x 4 ½ In. ....*illus*	175
Porcelain, Faces, Bjorn Winbland For Rosenthal, 6 ½ x 3 In., Pair	48
Red Crackle Glass, Ruffled Rim, Swirl Handle, Triple Ball Stopper, c.1960, 7 In.	20
Slag Glass, Green, White, Pineapple Stopper, 7 x 3 In.	18

CT GERMANY was first part of a mark used by a company in Altwasser, Germany (now part of Walbrzych, Poland), in 1845. The initials stand for C. Tielsch, a partner in the firm. The Hutschenreuther firm took over the company in 1918 and continued to use the *CT*.

Custard Glass, Persian Medallion, Basket, Fruit, Berries, Ruffled Rim, Fenton, 7 ½ In.
$35

Ruby Lane

Cut Glass, Compote, Hobstar, Sawtooth, Teardrop, Averbeck, 8 x 5 In.
$275

Ruby Lane

Cut Glass, Vase, Stars, Waffle & Burst, Pinched Waist, 19 ½ In.
$726

James D. Julia Auctioneers

TIP
The best time to buy an antique is when you see it.

Cybis, Figurine, Sharmaine, Sea Nymph, 1978, 13 In.
$775

Ruby Lane

Czechoslovakia Glass, Sculpture, Space Garden In Green, V. Prochazka, 2005, 48 In.
$5,625

Rago Arts and Auction Center

Bowl, Lily Of The Valley, Violets, Pink Embossed Border, 14 x 9 In.	75
Bowl, Magenta Roses, Leaves, Oval, Gold Rim, Pierced Handles, 14 x 9 In.	50
Centerpiece, Gold, Leafy Border, Flowers, Reticulated, Pedestal, 12 x 5 In.	150
Tray, Ruffled Rim, Yellow Flowers, Fern Fronds, Shaped Border, 5 x 4 In.	95
Trivet, Pink Flowers, Green Leaves On Border, Ivory Ground, 1890s, 6 In.	45

 CUP PLATES are small glass or china plates that held the cup while a diner of the mid-nineteenth century drank coffee or tea from the saucer. The most famous cup plates were made of glass at the Boston and Sandwich factory located in Sandwich, Massachusetts. There have been many new glass cup plates made in recent years for sale to gift shops or collectors of limited editions. These are similar to the old plates but can be recognized as new.

Flower & Dots, Bubbled, Rope Twist Band, Scalloped Rim, Sandwich Glass, 4 In.	48
Inverted Lacy Hearts, Clear, Scalloped Rim, Flint Glass, 4 In. Diam.	38
Milk Glass, Green, Striations, Flower, Beaded, Ring Foot, 1800s, 4 In. Diam.	35
Porcelain, Acorn & Oak Leaf, Scudder's American Museum, c.1825, 4 In.	540
Porcelain, White House, Washington, Shell Border, Dark Blue, c.1830, 5 In.	7800
Porcelain, White House, Washington, Shell Border, Dark Blue, c.1830, 6 In.	1620
Porcelain, Woodlands Near Philadelphia, c.1825, 4 In.	600
Roman Rosette, Amethyst Iridescent, Crimped Rim, Flint Glass, 1800s, 5 In.	325

 CURRIER & IVES made the famous American lithographs marked with their name from 1857 to 1907. The mark used on the print included the street address in New York City, and it is possible to date the year of the original issue from this information. Earlier prints were made by N. Currier and use that name from 1835 to 1847. Many reprints of the Currier or Currier & Ives prints have been made. Some collectors buy the insurance calendars that were based on the old prints. The words *large, small,* or *medium folio* refer to size. The original print sizes were very small (up to about 7 x 9 in.), small (8.8 x 12.8 in.), medium (9 x 14 in. to 14 x 20 in.), large (larger than 14 x 20 in.). Other sizes are probably later copies. Other prints by Currier & Ives may be listed in the Card category under Advertising and in the Sheet Music category. Currier & Ives dinnerware patterns may be found in the Adams or Dinnerware categories.

Across The Continent, Empire Takes Its Way, Palmer, 1809, 20 x 28 In.	3500
American Express Train, F.F. Palmer, 1864, Large Folio	985
Cares Of A Family, Quail & Chicks, A.F. Tait, Frame, 1856, Large Folio	3800
Frozen Up, Winter Scene, Oxen, Frame, 1872, Small Folio	2885
Hudson Highlands, c.1900, Large Folio	725
Ice Boat On The Hudson, 8½ x 13 In. *illus*	660
Lincoln Family, Black & White, Frame, 1867, Medium Folio	499
Rocky Mountains, Emigrants Crossing Plains, 1800s, 22 x 29 In.	1000
The Levee, New Orleans, Signed, 1883, 22 x 31 In.	8540

 CUSTARD GLASS is a slightly yellow opaque glass. It was made in England in the 1880s and was first made in the United States in the 1890s. It has been reproduced. Additional pieces may be found in the Cambridge, Fenton, and Heisey categories. Custard glass is called Ivorina Verde by Heisey and other companies.

Bowl, Flowers, Gilt Trim, Bulbous, Wide Rim, c.1910, 4 x 8 In.	160
Chrysanthemum Sprig, Compote Jelly, Gold Trim, Northwood, 4 x 5 In.	32
Creamer, Cylindrical, Wavy Spout, Loop Handle, Gilt, 1920s, 5 In.	58
Ewer, Enameled, Leaves, Orange, Green, Blue, Lime, 8 x 3½ In.	24
Ivory Crest, Basket, Gilt Rim, Fenton, c.1940, 8½ x 7 In.	39
Log Cabin, Basket, Fenton, 8 In.	73
Maize is its own category in this book.	
Persian Medallion, Basket, Fruit, Berries, Ruffled Rim, Fenton, 7½ In. *illus*	35
Pink Blossom, Fairy Light, 4¾ In.	20
Poppy, Basket, Fenton, 7 In.	45
Satin Drapery, Vase, Ruffled Rim, Fenton, c.1975, 8 In.	37
Satin Hobnail, Fairy Light, Fenton, 5 In.	34

Starburst, Compote, Fenton, c.1960, 5½ x 4 In.		30
Washington, Toothpick Holder, Beaded Base, 2½ In.		45

CUT GLASS has been made since ancient times, but the large majority of the pieces now for sale date from the American Brilliant period of glass design, 1875 to 1915. These pieces have elaborate geometric designs with a deep miter cut. Modern cut glass with a similar appearance is being made in England, Ireland, Poland, and the Czech and Slovak republics. Chips and scratches are often difficult to notice but lower the value dramatically. A signature on the glass adds significantly to the value. Other cut glass pieces are listed under factory names, like Hawkes, Libbey, and Sinclaire.

Berry Bowl, Waldorf Pattern, Clark Waldorf, 4 x 9 In.	236
Bowl, Gilt, Swan Head Handles, Diamond Point, France, c.1880, 10 x 23 In.	937
Bowl, Hobstar, 3 x 8 In.	60
Bowl, Hobstar, Flower Bottom, 4 x 9 In.	84
Bowl, Hobstar, Grape & Vine Intaglio, Footed, Tuthill, 4 x 8 In.	120
Bowl, Hobstar, Quill, 3½ x 8 In.	132
Bowl, Hobstar, Wavy, Hoare, 9 In.	300
Bowl, Starburst, Gorham Mounts, Flowers, 14 In.	168
Bowl, Strawberry Diamond & Fan Pattern, Scalloped, 6 In.	250
Brandy Set, Cartier, Decanter & 4 Snifters, France, 1900s, 7 x 3 In.	375
Bread Tray, Princeton Pattern, Empire, 13 x 8 In.	200
Butter, Cover, Domed, Starburst, Ball Finial, 7¾ In.	60
Centerpiece, Ruby, Gilt Bronze, Wyvern Shape Handles, 1900s, 24 x 19 In.	1000
Cheese Dish, Hobstar, Flattened Diamond Point, Fan Cut, Lid, 6 x 8 In.	72
Cheese Dish, Octagonal, Hobstar, Strawberry Diamond Pattern, Lid, 7 x 9 In.	400
Compote, Hobstar Variant, Zipper Cut Stem, c.1900, 12 x 8 In.	366
Compote, Hobstar, Sawtooth, Teardrop, Averbeck, 8 x 5 In. ....*illus*	275
Cruet, Hobstar, Vesica & Fan Motif, Signed, Hawkes, Footed, 8 In.	90
Cruet, Intaglio Grape, Dual Neck, Silver End Caps, c.1885, 10 In.	185
Decanter & Sherry Glass Set, Stopper, 8 Sherries, Decanter, 7½ In.	510
Decanter, Bergen, Glenwood Pattern, 9¼ In.	92
Decanter, Florence Star Type Pattern, Facet Cut Ring Neck, 12 In.	100
Decanter, Hobstar, Vesica, Diamond & Fan, Mushroom Stopper, 10 In.	100
Decanter, Hobstar, Vesica, Engraved Flowers, Steeple Stopper, 11 In.	100
Decanter, Liqueur, Thistle, Wheat, Silver Mounted Corks, 1900s, 13 In., Pair	100
Decanter, Swags, Rosette, Mushroom Stopper, 1800s, 13 In.	180
Ewer, Stick Neck, Flowers, Silver Handle & Spout, Stopper, c.1906, 13 In.	1046
Fruit Basket, Laurel Leaf, Starburst, Silver Handle, c.1900, 12 x 8 In.	390
Humidor, Carolyn Pattern, Shouldered, Square Jar Shape, J. Hoare, 9 In.	650
Ice Cream Tray, Camilla Single Petal Pattern, W.C. Anderson, 14 x 7 In.	125
Pitcher, Hobstar, Strawberry Diamond, Cane & Fan, Handle, 11 In.	225
Pitcher, Hobstar, Zipper Cuts, Silver Collar With Flowers & Scrolls, 13 In.	492
Pitcher, Swirl, Silver Rim, Applied Handle, 11 In.	300
Punch Bowl, Conjoined Hobstar Circles, Fan, 13 x 14 In.	420
Punch Bowl, Lotus Blossoms, Silver Rim & Undertray, Inlay, c.1900, 14 In.	5625
Serving Dish, Cart Shape, Hobstar, Cane, Fan, 4 x 11½ In.	600
Sugar & Creamer, Duchess, Pitkin & Brooks	350
Tankard, Hobstar, Strawberry Diamond, Harvard, Prism & Star, 11 In.	500
Tray, Field Of Flashed Daisy Blossoms, Round, 14 In.	150
Tray, Ice Cream, Central Hobstar, Strawberry, Diamond, Fan Cut, 11 x 8 In.	72
Tray, Ice Cream, Zephyr, Blackmer, 18 x 10 In.	1380
Tray, Round, Gravic, Strawberry, Hawkes, Round, 11 In.	550
Tray, Round, Starburst, Silver Border & Handles, Bun Feet, c.1900, 15 x 12 In.	484
Vase, Bowling Pin, Hobstar, Strawberry Diamond, Zipper & Star, 10 In.	150
Vase, Cylinder, Cut Glass, J. Hoare, Sawtooth Rim, 14 In.	150
Vase, Fan Shape, Hobstar, Fan, 9 x 10½ In.	192
Vase, Flared, Kohinoor & Honeycomb, Hawkes, 10 In.	125
Vase, Hobstar, Cane, Prism & Bull's-Eye, Footed, Scalloped Base, 8 In.	125
Vase, Irises, Engraved, Gilt Metal, France, Edmond Enot, c.1890, 7 x 4 In.	1125
Vase, Pinched Waist, Hobstar, Vesica, Cane, Strawberry Diamond & Fan, 17 In.	225

D'Argental, Vase, Field, Trees, Pond, Amber, Ocher, Frosted, Oval, Acid Cut, Cameo, c.1920, 6 In.
$1,885

Ruby Lane

Daum, Bowl, Blackberries, Vines, Mottled Ground, Footed, Cross Of Lorraine, 5 x 8 In.
$1,363

James D. Julia Auctioneers

Daum, Figurine, Love Owl, Pate-De-Verre, Red, Orange, Blue, Xavier Carnoy, 4½ x 3 In.
$650

Ruby Lane

This is an edited listing of current prices. Visit **Kovels.com** to check thousands of prices from previous years and sign up for free information on trends, tips, reproductions, marks, and more.

Daum, Vase, Banjo Shape, Lake, Tree, Leaves, Blue, Green, 6½ In. $3,700

Ruby Lane

Daum, Vase, Catkins, Leafy Branches, Orange & Brown Over Pale Blue, Footed, 12¾ In. $2,950

Humler & Nolan

Daum, Vase, Rain Scene, Trees, Barrel Shape, Cut & Enameled, Signed, 1½ In. $1,955

Early Auction Company

Vase, Star & Chair Bottom, American, 10¼ In.	214
Vase, Stars, Waffle & Burst, Pinched Waist, 19½ In. ....*illus*	726
Vase, Trumpet, Alhambra, Meriden, 15 In.	650
Vase, Trumpet, Tricorner Top, Hobstar Base, Elmira, 12 In.	200

CYBIS porcelain is a twentieth-century product. Boleslaw Cybis came to the United States from Poland in 1939. He started making porcelains in Long Island, New York, in 1940. He moved to Trenton, New Jersey, in 1942 as one of the founders of Cordey China Co. and started his own company, Cybis Porcelains, about 1950. The firm is still working. See also Cordey.

Bust, Indian Girl, Running Deer, Headband, Feather, 10 In.	399
Figurine, Baby Birds, Nest, 5 x 4 In.	110
Figurine, Bear, Brown, 4 x 8 x 3 In.	195
Figurine, Dog, Boxer, Flowered Base, 5 x 6 In.	295
Figurine, Duckling, Baby Brother, 4 x 4 In.	65
Figurine, Girl, Seated, Book On Lap, Alice, 1978, 8 x 4 x 4 In.	329
Figurine, Great Thunder Crow Dancer, 18½ In.	1875
Figurine, Horse Head & Forelegs With Mermaid Tail, White, Teal Wave, 13 In.	200
Figurine, Horseback Acrobat, Ribbons, White Horse, 16 In.	281
Figurine, Little Red Riding Hood, 1973, 7 In.	59
Figurine, Rabbit, Mr. Snowball, 1970s, 4½ In.	40
Figurine, Red Tailed Hawk, Praying Mantis, Branch, 1977, 18 In.	1100
Figurine, Sharmaine, Sea Nymph, 1978, 13 In. ....*illus*	775
Figurine, Woman, Blue Dress, Applied Flowers, Ruffles, 1940s, 14 In.	195
Group, Indian Men, Peace Pipes, 16 x 13 In.	750
Ornament, Angel, Bust, Blond, Wings, 1985, 4 In.	43
Vase, Blue Birds, Leaves, 1960s, 9¾ In.	200

CZECHOSLOVAKIA is a popular term with collectors. The name, first used as a mark after the country was formed in 1918, appears on glass and porcelain and other decorative items. Although Czechoslovakia split into Slovakia and the Czech Republic on January 1, 1993, the name continues to be used in some trademarks.

CZECHOSLOVAKIA GLASS

Bowl, Clear & Cranberry, Incised, Ring Foot, c.1960, 4 x 7 In.	349
Bowl, Yellow, Large Red Splotches, 11½ In.	25
Compote, Double Handles, Opalescent, 5½ x 8½ In.	36
Dresser Box, Blue, Gold Enamel, Flowers, Paw Feet, Hinged Lid, 4 In.	87
Powder Box, Iridescent, Leaves, Diamond Quilted, 1930s, 4 x 6 In.	299
Sculpture, Basket, Spattered Flowers & Leaves, c.1920, 18 In.	1025
Sculpture, Space Garden In Green, V. Prochazka, 2005, 48 In. ....*illus*	5625
Shade, Red, Yellow, Diamond Cut, Spherical, 6 In.	38
Vase, Green, Oil Spot, Ruffled Rim, Tapered Neck, 7 x 3½ In.	150
Vase, Iris, Purple, Frosted, Josef Inwald Weil, c.1920, 9½ In.	74
Vase, Orange, Wrapped, Brown, 4½ In.	19
Vase, Purple, Blue, Mottled, Applied Glass, 10 In.	25
Vase, Purple, Nude Women Dancing, Square, Tapered, 1930s, 8 In.	499
Vase, Satin Glass, Ormolu, Medallion Mount, Sea Gulls, 14 x 11 In.	120

CZECHOSLOVAKIA POTTERY

Basket, Black, Orange, Squat, Upright Handle, Wavy Rim, 1930s, 5 In.	64
Bell, Figural, Woman, Wide Skirt, Hands On Hips, c.1930, 5 In.	65
Pitcher, Cobalt Blue, Geometric Design, Bulbous, 1920s, 6 In.	150
Vase, 3 Open Tulips, Stem Base, Crimped Rim, Orange, Green, 5 In.	95
Vase, Bud, Bird, Stump, 3 Openings, Green, Peach, 1930s, 6 x 3 In.	65
Vase, Medallion, Flowers, Cobalt Blue, Mottled, 1920s, 10 In.	155

DANIEL BOONE, a pre–Revolutionary War folk hero, was a surveyor, trapper, and frontiersman. A television series, which ran from 1964 to 1970, was based on his life and starred Fess Parker. All types of Daniel Boone memorabilia are collected.

Postcard, Linen, Reading, Pennsylvania, Birthplace, Stichler & Co., c.1935	4
Postcard, Wagon Train, Boone, N.C., Pioneers	4

Ring, Red Plastic, Daniel Boone Head, 1960s..	15
Toy, Figure, Daniel Boone, Rifle, Name On Base, Plastic, Marx, 3 In................................	15

D'ARGENTAL is a mark used in France by the Compagnie des Cristalleries de St. Louis. The firm made multilayered, acid-cut cameo glass in the late nineteenth and twentieth centuries. D'Argental is the French name for the city of Munzthal, home of the glassworks. Later the company made enameled etched glass.

Perfume Bottle, Flowers & Leaves, Brown, Red & Yellow, Atomizer, 6 In..................................	460
Shade, Hanging, Nasturtiums, Round, 4 Patinated Metal Chains, 17 In.	1063
Vase, Field, Trees, Pond, Amber, Ocher, Frosted, Oval, Acid Cut, Cameo, c.1920, 6 In. ....*illus*	1885
Vase, Landscape, Rose Cased, Amethyst Overlay, France, 1900, 8¼ In................................	625
Vase, Narrow Mouth, Smoky Violet, Clematis, Cameo, 6¾ In..	185
Vase, Purple Wisteria On White, Signed, Early 1900s, 13⅛ x 3½ In..............................	500
Vase, Red Flower Vines, Yellow Ground, Early 1900s, 12 x 4 In....................................	937
Vase, Red Raspberries Against Yellow, Signed, 7¾ In...	518
Vase, Red Trumpet Flowers & Vine, Bird, Frosted Yellow Ground, Oval, 17¾ In...............	2903
Vase, Squat, Fringe Indigo Flower Heads Over Yellow, 2¼ x 4 In.................................	633

DAUM, a glassworks in Nancy, France, was started by Jean Daum in 1875. The company, now called *Cristalleries de Nancy*, is still working. The *Daum Nancy* mark has been used in many variations. The name of the city and the artist are usually both included. The term *martele* is used to describe applied decorations that are carved or etched in the cameo process.

Bowl, Blackberries, Vines, Mottled Ground, Footed, Cross Of Lorraine, 5 x 8 In.................*illus*	1363
Bowl, Enamel, Leaves & Flowers, Amber, Signed, c.1920, 2¾ x 5¾ x 4 In.	812
Bowl, Enamel, Red Flowers, Yellow Ground, Flared, 3 x 4½ In......................................	406
Bowl, Gold Foil Inclusions, Iron, Blue, Majorelle, 3½ x 10¼ In....................................	875
Bowl, Gold Foil Inclusions, Iron, Yellow, Majorelle, 5 x 10 In.	1000
Bowl, Green & Gold, Etched, Iron Scroll Overlay, Bubble Bottom, Flared Rim, 5 x 10 In...........	1000
Bowl, Morning Glory, French Silver Mounts, Green, Yellow, c.1900, 4 x 9 In........................	1500
Bowl, Pale Blue & Amber, Gold Inclusions, Etched Iron Glass Scroll, Ball Feet, 4 x 10 In...........	875
Bowl, Palm Magnum, Pate-De-Verre, c.1980, 10¼ x 22 In..	8125
Bowl, Poppies, Purple, Mauve, Red, Squat, Square Handles, Saucer Foot, 4 x 10 In.	2500
Bowl, Thistle, Green Shaded To Pink Shaded To Frosted, Gilt, Folded Rim, Cameo, 6 In.	1778
Bowl, Trees, Grasses, Lake Shore, Mottled Blue Sky, Round, Folded-In Sides, 3 x 4½ In...........	2963
Box, Lid, Orange Berries On Branches, Mottled Purple Shaded To Cream, Flared, 3 x 6 In........	1778
Box, Lid, Spring Scene, Trees, Mottled & Shaded Yellow Ground, Dome Lid, 3½ In.	2844
Centerpiece, Two Amber Dragons Encircling Blue Bowl, Pate-De-Verre, 4 x 8½ In.	1725
Figurine, Cheetah, Seated, Head Turned, Curled Tail, Amber Pate-De-Verre, 11 x 10 In.	2360
Figurine, Eron In Rushes, Amber & Pale Aqua, Engraved, Pate-De-Verre, 9¾ In.	748
Figurine, Love Owl, Pate-De-Verre, Red, Orange, Blue, Xavier Carnoy, 4½ x 3 In..............*illus*	650
Figurine, Venus De Milo, Pink, Blue, Abstract Female, Pate-De-Verre, 17½ x 8¾ In.	531
Lamp, Base, Dark Amethyst Foot, Orange Body, Cameo Cut Blossoms, Signed, 7½ In.	115
Lamp, Base, Green Trees On Lake At Night, Cameo Glass, 11 In.......................................	3824
Lamp, Electric, Water Carrier, Marble, Glass, Pierre Le Faguays, 1920s, 22 x 4½ In.	6250
Lamp, Landscape, Ruffled Shade, Baluster Stem, Ruffled Foot, Cameo Glass, 20 x 11 In..........	6875
Lamp, Winter Scene, Enameled, Double Domed Shade, Cameo Glass, 1900s, 14 x 7 In.	13750
Liquor Set, Decanter, Teardrop Stopper, 5 Cordials, Black Enamel, Trees, Hills, 6 Piece.........	2500
Salt Cellar, Winter Landscape, Enamel, Cameo, 1¼ x 1¾ In..	975
Sculpture, Ballerine Ambre, Yellow To Green, Pate-De-Verre, c.1980, 12½ In.	2250
Sculpture, Horse, Blue, Silvered Metal, Hilton McConnico, Pate-De-Verre, 12¼ x 12½ In.	2125
Sculpture, Persphata, Amber Glass, Marble Stand, c.1980, 13½ In....................................	9375
Toothpick Holder, Etched & Gilt Trimmed, Pink, Raised Flowers, 1900s, 2 x 1¼ In.	125
Tray, Shell Shape, Thistle Design, Cameo, 10¾ In..	259
Tumbler, Bleeding Heart Flowers, Shaded, Mottled Ground, Barrel Shape, 3½ In.....................	1150
Tumbler, Winter Scene, Barren Trees, Snow, Mottled Yellow Shaded To Orange, 5 In................	2370
Vase, 2 Trees In Farm Field, House, Mottled Blue Sky, Squat Pillow Form, 4½ x 7 In.	8295
Vase, Amaryllis, Green, Blue, Pate-De-Verre, 15⅛ In...	1000
Vase, Aquatic, Enameled, Gilt, Etched, Green & Brown, Signed, c.1900, 9 x 5 In.	11250

Davenport, Plate, Church, Shore, Flowers, Ironstone, 1820-60, 10¼ In. $170

Ruby Lane

Davy Crockett, Chest, Toy, Teepee, Lake, Mountains, Gray, 16 x 28 In. $108

Milestone Auctions

De Morgan, Vase, Stylized Animals, Birds & Vines, 2 Red Handles, 13 In. $2,963

James D. Julia Auctioneers

TIP

A damaged porcelain clockface is difficult to repair. It will lower the price of a clock by 20 to 30 percent.

De Vez, Vase, Woman Of High Fashion, Double Handles, Art Nouveau, 10 x 5 In. $292

Rago Arts and Auction Center

Decoy, Brant, Hollow Body, Glass Eyes, Lead Weight, Bill Brown, Repaint, 17 In. $275

Ruby Lane

Decoy, Killdeer Plover, Carved, Painted, Stamped, A.E. Crowell, 1940, 7 x 9 In. $6,050

James D. Julia Auctioneers

Decoy, Merganser, Carved, Painted, Signed W.C., 15 In. $142

Hess Auction Group

Vase, Banjo Shape, Lake, Tree, Leaves, Blue, Green, 6 ½ In. ....*illus*	3700
Vase, Barrel, Cameo Scene With Tree & Boat, Dark Brown & Red, Signed, 4 ¾ In.	575
Vase, Bees, Stems, Yellow, Green, Gilt, Pedestal Foot, Flared, Cameo Glass, c.1885, 9 In.	9375
Vase, Black Shore Scene, Yellow & Orange Ground, Signed, 1900s, 7 ¾ x 5 In.	937
Vase, Bluebells, Mottled Blue Shaded To Green Ground, Flared, Bulbous Foot, 21 In.	13035
Vase, Brown Trees Against Orange Lake, Cameo, Signed, 6 In.	460
Vase, Catkins, Leafy Branches, Orange & Brown Over Pale Blue, Footed, 12 ¾ In. ....*illus*	2950
Vase, Crocuses, Blue, Black, White, Etched, Swollen Stick, c.1910, 12 x 2 In.	5938
Vase, Cyclamen, Green, Cream, Tapered, Handles, Metal Overlay, Martele, 10 In.	4063
Vase, Enamel, Windmill & Houses & Boats, Black Over White, Signed, 3 ¼ x 1 ⅜ In.	288
Vase, Etched, Enamel, Mottled, Foliage With Cobwebs, c.1915, 8 ½ In.	687
Vase, Forest, Lake, Green, Turquoise, Gilt, Poem, Etched, Cylinder, Cameo, c.1910, 5 In.	1250
Vase, Foxglove, Orange, Yellow, Golden Brown, Swollen Base, Stick Stem, Cameo, 31 In.	2596
Vase, Frosted, Plate Yellow, Blue Flowers, Leaves, Cameo, 5 ⅞ In.	2952
Vase, Glass With Iron Cage, Mottled Orange, Signed, 10 ¼ x 8 ¾ In.	1187
Vase, Gold Enamel, Etched Peacock Feather Design, Cream & Tan, 1920s, 13 x 8 In.	4688
Vase, Green Leaves, Lavender Ground, Applied Glass Dragonflies, Cylinder, 1900s, 9 In.	1230
Vase, Lily Of The Valley, Opalescent Ivory, Pink, Cone Shape, Cameo, 11 In.	2596
Vase, Line Of Orange & Red Orchids Above Green Against Frost, 4 ½ x 5 ½ In.	1840
Vase, Mottled Aqua, Yellow Spots, Matte, Squat, Wide Rim, Ring Foot, Signed, 4 x 6 In.	283
Vase, Off-White With Bees, Cameo, Signed, Late 1800s, 9 x 3 ½ In.	9375
Vase, Overlay, Mottled, Purple, Amber, c.1900, 23 ¾ In.	3750
Vase, Pillow, Mottled Green, Blue & Orange, Signed, c.1918, 4 ¾ x 6 ¾ x 2 ¼ In.	937
Vase, Pinecones, Distant Shore, Gray, Mottled Pink, Yellow & Cream Sky, Cylinder, 5 In.	1600
Vase, Pink Rose, Green, Pate-De-Verre, 6 ¾ In.	325
Vase, Purple Flowers, Mottled, Enameled, 1900, 4 ⅜ In.	3250
Vase, Rain Scene, Trees, Barrel Shape, Cut & Enameled, Signed, 1 ½ In. ....*illus*	1955
Vase, Red Flowers, Leaves, Mottled Yellow Shaded To Citron Ground, Swollen Top, 7 In.	2963
Vase, Red, Amber, Burgundy, Caramel, Mottled, Foil Inclusions, Oval, Stick Neck, 28 In.	2360
Vase, Rounded Square, Winter Scene, Trees, Crows, Roll Rim, Cameo, c.1910, 5 In.	8125
Vase, Stick, Bleeding Hearts & Leaves, Orange Over White, Cameo, Signed, 4 ½ In.	1093
Vase, Sweet Peas, Green & Red, Cameo, Signed, 1800s, 15 ¼ x 5 In.	2500
Vase, Sweet Peas, Stems, White, Green, Pink, Oval, Swollen Ring Neck, c.1885, 15 In.	2500
Vase, Tapered, Thistle Stems, Pale Blue, Spotted, Cameo, 20 x 5 ⅞ In.	7000
Vase, Tobacco Flowers, Deep Yellow Shaded To Brown, Tapered, Footed, Cameo, 14 ½ In.	1500
Vase, Trees In Spring, Frosted & Mottled Yellow & Green, 14 In.	4500
Vase, Wheat Stalks, Mottled & Textured Blue To Cream, Cylindrical, Bulbous Foot, 11 In.	5036
Vase, Winter Scene With Black Crows, France, Early 1900s, Signed, 5 ⅜ x 5 ¼ In.	8125
Vase, Winter Scene, Trees, Snow, Mottled Yellow Shaded To Orange, Square, 7 ½ In.	4740
Vase, Wisteria, Opaque White, Plum, Stick, Swollen Dome Foot, Cameo, c.1910, 13 In.	938
Vase, Wisteria, Purple, Green, Orange Shaded To Purple, 2 Jewels, Rolled Rim, 6 In.	4740
Vase, Zigzag Bands, Clear Green, Textured Green Ground, Flared, Art Deco, 9 In.	1185
Wine, Pate-De-Verre, Amethyst Bowl, Green Foot, Human Face, 4 ¼ In.	300

DAVENPORT pottery and porcelain were made at the Davenport factory in Longport, Staffordshire, England, from 1793 to 1887. Earthenwares, creamwares, porcelains, ironstone, and other ceramics were made. Most of the pieces are marked with a form of the word *Davenport.*

DAVENPORT LONGPORT STAFFORDSHIRE

Biscuit Jar, Old Imari, White, Red Flowers, Blue Ground, Barrel Shape, 6 x 5 In.	129
Cup & Saucer, Gilt Scrolls & Shells, c.1820.	145
Dessert Plate, Old Imari, Molded Handles, 10 x 9 In.	82
Gravy Boat, Pagoda, Trees, Paneled, Octagonal Base, Underplate, c.1840, 8 x 3 x 5 In.	75
Ice Bucket, Silver Plate Mounts, Old Imari, Handle, 5 x 5 In.	141
Plate, Church, Shore, Flowers, Ironstone, 1820-60, 10 ¼ In. ....*illus*	170
Plate, Imari Colors, Gold Edge, Church, Flowers, 10 ¼ In.	170
Platter, Pagodas, Fences, River, Butterfly & Geometric Border, c.1800, 9 x 6 In.	110
Platter, Pagodas, Fences, River, Butterfly Border, Pearlware, Blue & White, c.1800, 9 x 6 In.	110
Soup, Dish, Fisherman, Flower Border, Gothic Ruins, c.1812, 9 ¾ In.	90
Soup, Dish, Flower & Leaf Border, Men Fishing, House In Trees, c.1810, 9 ¾ In.	90

Teapot, Woman Milking Cow, Cobalt Blue & White, Child's, c.1800, 5¾ In.		85
Tray, Vase Of Flowers, Flower & Fruit Border, c.1820, 12½ In.		385

DAVY CROCKETT, the American frontiersman, was born in 1786 and died in 1836. The historical character gained new fame in 1954 when the Walt Disney television show ran a series of episodes featuring Fess Parker as Davy Crockett. Coonskin caps and buckskins became popular and hundreds of different Davy Crockett items were made.

Box, Display, Gum, Tattoo, 1 Cent, Wood Grain, Gun Images, 1955, 5 x 7 In.		173
Box, Gum Card, Display, Picture Card Bubble Gum, 1 Cent, Photo, 6 x 8 In.		384
Card Set, Gum, 2nd Series, Green Back, 1956, 80 Cards		388
Chest, Toy, Teepee, Lake, Mountains, Gray, 16 x 28 In.	*illus*	108
Clock, Figural, Log Cabin, Lighted Window, Animated Davy, c.1955, 7 x 12 In.		181
Cookie Jar, Davy Holding Rifle, Brush, 1956, 10 In.		300
Coonskin Cap, Faux Fur, Real Racoon Tail, 4 x 7 In.		21
Costume, Frontier King, Rifle, Powder Horn, Pistol, Sling, Canteen, Box, 1955, 35 In.		803
Fork, Stainless Steel, Walt Disney, c.1955, 6 In.		10
Game, Target, Rifle, Bullets, Indian & Bear Targets, Box, c.1955, 19 x 23 In.		139
Handkerchief, Embroidered, Crossed Swords, Bird, Basket, Cotton, 10 x 10 In.		15
Hat, Indian Fighter, Coonskin, Fur, Label, Box, Weathermac, c.1955, 9 x 13 In.		115
Lunch Box, Thermos, The Alamo, Kit Carson, Metal, Handle, c.1955, 9 In.		411
Mug, Davy On Horse, Rifle, Signature, Fire King, 3½ In.		12
Planter, Young Davy, Bear, Tree Trunk, Gold Trim, McCoy, 5¼ In.		39
Record, 3 Adventures Of Davy Crocket, Disneyland Records, 33 RPM, 1950s		9
Record, Ballad Of Davy Crockett, Little Golden, 1950s, 78 RPM		10
Standee, Davy Holding Rifle, Cardboard, Easel Back, c.1955, 12 x 27 In.		139
Toy, Plastic, Embossed, Star Shape, Davy, Coonskin Hat		20
Tumbler, Davy Fought For Texas, Orange, c.1960, 4¼ In.		6

DE MORGAN art pottery was made in England by William De Morgan from the 1860s to 1907. He is best known for his luster-glazed Moorish-inspired pieces. The pottery used a variety of marks.

Tile, Boar, Seated, Blue, Cream, Sands End, c.1880, 6 x 6 In.		1168
Vase, Cobalt, Flowers, Leaves, For Cantagali Iznik, Italy, 1800s, 16½ x 8 In.		1845
Vase, Stylized Animals, Birds & Vines, 2 Red Handles, 13 In.	*illus*	2963

DE VEZ was a signature used on cameo glass after 1910. E. S. Monot founded the glass company near Paris in 1851. The company changed names many times. Mt. Joye, another glass by this factory, is listed in its own category.

deVez

Vase, Amber, Trees & Lake, Cristallerie De Pantin, France, Early 1900s, 8 x 3¾ In.		937
Vase, Brown, Amber, Ivory, Dusk Reflecting On Lake, Cottage On Shore, Cameo, 8¼ In.		900
Vase, Conical, Pink, Green, Cascading Branch, Castle, Mountains, Cameo, 7 In.		390
Vase, Distant Village, Vertical Bands, Apple Trees, Clouds, Yellow, Green, Red, 8¼ In.		600
Vase, Exotic Birds, Yellow, Cameo, 7½ In.		312
Vase, Frosted, Olive Green, Lemon Yellow, Water, Boat, Village, 1900s, 13¾ x 4 In.		375
Vase, Olive Green, Yellow, Frosted, Trees, Water, Boat, Distant Village, 1900s, 13¾ x 4 In.		360
Vase, Red, Yellow, Lake, Boatman, Mountains, Trees, 5¼ In.		360
Vase, Woman Of High Fashion, Double Handles, Art Nouveau, 10 x 5 In.	*illus*	292

DECORATED TUMBLERS *may be listed in Advertising, Coca-Cola, Pepsi-Cola, Sports, and other categories.*

DECOYS are carved or turned wooden copies of birds, fish, or animals. The decoy was placed in the water or propped on the shore to lure flying birds to the pond for hunters. Some decoys are handmade; some are commercial products. Today there is a group of artists making modern decoys for display, not for use in a pond. Many sell for high prices.

Black Duck, Attributed To Benjamin Holmes, 16 In.		321
Black Duck, Carved, Painted, Relief Wings, c.1950, 15 In.		73

Dedham, Rabbit, Plate, Blue & White, 8½ In.
$73

Hess Auction Group

Dedham, Vase, Oxblood & Mahogany Drip Glaze, Stoneware, Experimental, Robertson, 8¾ In.
$3,750

Rago Arts and Auction Center

Dedham, Vase, Pillow, Blue Flowers, Leaves, Impressed CKAW, Black R Inside G, 2⅜ In.
$443

Humler & Nolan

Valuable Old Glass
If you have valuable old glass you should keep it in a safe environment. It should be stored or displayed where there is some air movement to dry off the surface; store glass bottles and containers with the stoppers and lids open.

D

Dedham, Vase, Stylized Flowers, Raised
Panels, Blue Glaze, Chelsea Keramic,
c.1885, 8 In.
$185

Skinner, Inc.

Degenhart, Figurine, Owl, Delft Blue,
3 ½ In.
$38

Ruby Lane

Degue, Basket, Amber Glass, Mottled,
Wrought Iron, Flowers, Leaves,
10 ½ x 20 In.
$910

Treadway Toomey Auctions

Blue-Winged Teal, Hen, 1900s, 5 ¾ x 11 ¼ In.	410
Brant, Black & White, New Jersey, 9 ¼ x 18 ¾ In.	840
Brant, Hollow Body, Glass Eyes, Lead Weight, Bill Brown, Repaint, 17 In. ....*illus*	275
Canada Goose, Carved & Painted, A. Elmer Crowell, Early 1900s, 4 ¾ In.	700
Canada Goose, Carved, Wing Detail, Weathered, Early 1900s, 10 ½ x 18 In.	150
Canada Goose, Hollow Carved, Glass Eyes, 28 ½ In.	228
Canada Goose, Life Size, Paint, Glass Eyes, Metal Tripod Legs, Canada, c.1950, 23 x 28 In.	840
Canada Goose, Spread Wings, Painted, Wood, Corrugated Tin Wings, 40 x 58 In.	649
Canada Goose, Wood, Painted, A.E. Crowell, Mass., 4 ½ In.	1300
Canada Goose, Working, Black & White, Tack Eyes, 9 x 26 ¾ In.	1800
Canvasback Drake, Hollow, Delineated Wings, Mid 1900s, 8 x 17 In.	120
Canvasback Drake, Painted, Brown, Green, Beige, R. Madison Mitchell, 16 In.	106
Canvasback Duck, Wood, Glass Eyes, Painted, c.1910, 12 ¾ In.	375
Common Scoter Hen, Working, Applied Head, American, 1900s, 5 x 12 In.	420
Cormorant, Marv Bernet, 23 ½ In.	160
Duck, Multicolor, F.M. Barteau, 1900s, 5 ¾ In.	162
Eider Drake, 4-Part Construction, Applied Head, 1900s, 7 x 15 In.	1020
Eider, Carved Pine, Black & White Paint, Green Beak, c.1965, 8 x 16 In.	1837
Fish, Carved, Black Spine, Silver Gray, Bob Foster, Signed, 1900s, 9 In.	98
Fish, Catfish, Yellow, Black, 9 ¼ In.	123
Fish, Orange, Red, Spotted, Oscar Peterson Style, 1900s, 8 In.	443
Fish, Yellow, Factory Carved, c.1950, 6 ¾ In.	74
Frog, Ice Fishing, Carved, Black Spotted Frog, White, c.1950, 12 ¼ In.	111
Golden Plover, Frank Adams, 1910.	540
Grouse, On Log, Wood, Painted, George R. Huey, Maine, 7 ½ In.	800
Heron, Blue, Carved, Mounted On Wood Base, Late 1800s, 30 x 32 ¾ In.	8400
Herring Gull, Solid, Glass Eyes, Original Paint, Incised Wing, 1900s, 7 ½ x 17 In.	281
Killdeer Plover, Carved, Painted, Stamped, A.E. Crowell, 1940, 7 x 9 In. ....*illus*	6050
Merganser Hen, Leather Crest, 1910	2750
Merganser, Carved, Painted, Signed W.C., 15 In. ....*illus*	142
Redhead Duck, Madison Mitchell, 13 ½ In.	172
Sea Gull, Turned Head, Ron Andrus, Original Paint, Mid 1900s, 12 In.	188
Swan, Solid Wood, Painted Tack Eyes, Mid 1900s, 20 x 20 In.	375

DEDHAM POTTERY was started in 1895. Chelsea Keramic Art Works was established in 1872 in Chelsea, Massachusetts, by members of the Robertson family. The factory closed in 1889 and was reorganized as the Chelsea Pottery U.S. in 1891. The firm used the marks *CKAW* and *CPUS*. It became the Dedham Pottery of Dedham, Massachusetts. The factory closed in 1943. It was famous for its crackleware dishes, which picture blue outlines of animals, flowers, and other natural motifs. Pottery by Chelsea Keramic Art Works and Dedham Pottery is listed here.

Golden Gate, Plate, San Francisco, Poppy Border, Blue & White, Inscribed, 10 In.	738
Grape, Bread Plate, 10 In.	180
Grapevine, Plate, Blue, White, 8 ⅝ In.	150
Pond Lily, Plate, Blue & White, Rabbit Mark, 8 ½ In., Pair	123
Rabbit, Coffeepot, White, Blue, Oval, Lid, c.1910, 8 In.	30
Rabbit, Plate, Blue & White, 8 ¼ In., 4 Piece	180
Rabbit, Plate, Blue & White, 8 ½ In. ....*illus*	73
Rabbit, Plate, Blue & White, 10 In.	120
Vase, Mottled Brown & Celadon Glaze, Stoneware, Hugh Robertson, 10 x 4 ½ In.	5000
Vase, Oxblood & Mahogany Drip Glaze, Stoneware, Experimental, H. Robertson, 8 ¾ In. ..*illus*	3750
Vase, Pillow, Blue Flowers, Leaves, Impressed CKAW, Black R Inside G, 2 ⅜ In. ....*illus*	443
Vase, Stylized Flowers, Raised Panels, Blue Glaze, Chelsea Keramic, c.1885, 8 In.............*illus*	185

DEGENHART is the name used by collectors for the products of the Crystal Art Glass Company of Cambridge, Ohio. John and Elizabeth Degenhart started the glassworks in 1947. Quality paperweights and other glass objects were made. John died in 1964 and his wife took over management and production ideas. Over 145 colors of glass were made. In 1978, after the death of Mrs. Degenhart, the molds were sold. The *D* in a heart trademark was removed, so collectors can easily recognize the true Degenhart pieces.

Figurine, Dog, Blue Marble Slag, c.1978, 3 In.	41
Figurine, Dog, Peach, Marbled, 3 x 2⅜ In.	35
Figurine, Dog, Periwinkle, c.1978, 3 In.	27
Figurine, Owl, Cobalt Blue, 3½ In.	8
Figurine, Owl, Dark Green, 3½ In.	10
Figurine, Owl, Delft Blue, 3½ In. ....*illus*	38
Figurine, Owl, Slag Glass, 3½ In.	16
Slipper, Vaseline, Green, 1⅞ x 3⅞ In.	40
Toothpick Holder, Amberina, Bird At Base, 3 In.	19
Toothpick Holder, Opalescent, Dark Yellow, 2¼ x 2¼ In.	23
Toothpick Holder, Toffee Slag, 2½ In.	35

DEGUE is a signature acid etched on pieces of French glass made by the Cristalleries de Compiegne in the early 1900s. Cameo, mold blown, and smooth glass with contrasting colored rims are the types most often found.

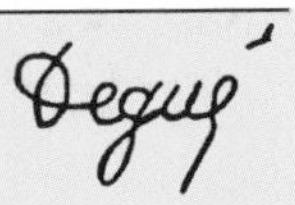

Degué

Basket, Amber Glass, Mottled, Wrought Iron, Flowers, Leaves, 10½ x 20 In. ....*illus*	910
Bowl, Mauve & Green Glass, Iron Frame, Early 1900s, 11¼ x 18½ x 10¼ In.	562
Vase, Lamp, Electrified, 2 Handles, Red, Black, Mottled, 15¾ In.	90
Vase, Mottled Burgundy, Mauve, Lilac, Applied Black Handles, c.1926, 17 x 7½ In.	510
Vase, Pale Pink, Swirls, Frost, Cameo, 17½ x 7½ In.	660

DELATTE glass is a French cameo glass made by Andre Delatte. It was first made in Nancy, France, in 1921. Lighting fixtures and opaque glassware in imitation of Bohemian opaline were made. There were many French cameo glassmakers, so be sure to look in other appropriate categories.

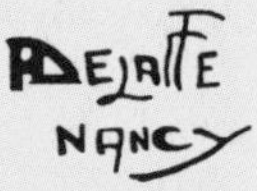

DELATTE NANCY

Bowl, Red, Mottled, 12 In.	60
Lamp, Base, Cameo, Orange Flowers Against Lighter Orange Back, Signed, 14 In.	633
Vase, Gourd, Grapes, Grass, Amethyst, Yellow, Cameo, 7¾ In.	300
Vase, Roses, Orange, Red, Flecks, Frosted, Short Neck, 1920s, 5 x 5 In. ....*illus*	1205
Vase, Round, Etched Geometric Pattern, Red Patina, c.1925, 10 In.	563
Vase, Yellow, Blue, Metal Mount, Handles, 1925, 14 In.	3003
Vase, Yellow, Purple, Green, Lobed, France, 11 In.	3219

DELDARE, *see Buffalo Pottery Deldare.*

DELFT is a special type of tin-glazed pottery. Early delft was made in Holland and England during the seventeenth century. It was usually decorated with blue on a white surface, but some was polychrome, decorated with green, yellow, and other colors. Most delftware pieces were dishes needed for everyday living. Figures were made from about 1750 to 1800, and are rare. Although the soft tin-glazed pottery was well-known, it was not named delft until after 1840, when it was named for the city in Holland where much of it was made. Porcelain became more popular because it was more durable, and Holland gradually stopped making the old delft. In 1876 De Porceleyne Fles factory in Delft introduced a porcelain ware that was decorated with blue and white scenes of Holland that reminded many of old delft. It became popular with the Dutch and tourists. By 1990 all of the blue and white porcelain with Dutch scenes was made in Asia, although it was marked *Delft.* Only one Dutch company remains that makes the traditional old-style delft with blue on white or with colored decorations. Most of the pieces sold today were made after 1891, and the name *Holland* usually appears with the Delft factory marks. The word *Delft* appears alone on some inexpensive twentieth- and twenty-first-century pottery from Asia and Germany that is also listed here.

Birdcage, White, Blue, Green, Flowers, Leaves, Scrolls, Footed, Dome Top, Bell Finial, 26 In.	124
Bowl, Blue, White, Flowers, Pierced Handles, Lid, c.1760, 3¼ In.	351
Bowl, Blue, White, Scalloped Rim, Fluted Sides, Boats, Flowers, Landscape, 1700s, 4 In.	293
Bowl, Flowers, Round Foot, 1700s, 5 x 10¼ In.	840

Delatte, Vase, Roses, Orange, Red, Flecks, Frosted, Short Neck, 1920s, 5 x 5 In.
$1,205

Ruby Lane

Delft, Bowl, Marriage, Stylized Bouquets, Friendship & Love, Inscribed, Dated, 4 x 10⅞ In.
$2,214

Leland Little Auctions

Delft, Bowl, Tulip, 7 Openings, Flowers, Fronds, Blue, White, 8 x 9½ In.
$338

William H. Bunch Auctions

TIP
Never unplug an electrical cord by pulling the cord. Always hold the plastic part of the plug. Weak cords cause fires.

Delft, Charger, Blue & White, Flowers, Cornucopia, 1700s, 13⅜ In.
$222

Jeffrey S. Evans

Delft, Honey Pot, Flip Lid, Red Outlined Flowers, Yellow, Green, Leaves, 3½ In.
$146

Copake Auction

Denver, Pitcher, Molded, Men, Animals, Trees, Plants, Brown, Green Glaze, c.1905, 7 x 6 In.
$125

Ruby Lane

Depression Glass, Adam, Cake Plate, Footed, Pink, Jeannette Glass, 10 In.
$20

Ruby Lane

Bowl, Marriage, Stylized Bouquets, Friendship & Love, Inscribed, Dated, 4 x 10⅞ In........*illus*	2214
Bowl, Multicolor, Flowers, Dutch, Early 1700s, 6 x 12½ In.	960
Bowl, Tulip, 7 Openings, Flowers, Fronds, Blue, White, 8 x 9½ In. ....*illus*	338
Candlestick, Rouen Style, Faience, Winged Griffins, 9¼ x 3½ In., Pair,	472
Castor, Sugar, Blue & White Flowers, Cylindrical, Pierced Dome Top, 1700s, 5 In.	738
Charger, 2 Parrots, Initialed LV, England, Early 1700s, 13½ In.	720
Charger, Bird & Landscape, Hand Painted, 12 In.	978
Charger, Blue & White, Basket Of Flowers, Crosshatched Border, 13 In., Pair	738
Charger, Blue & Yellow Flowers, 13⅜ In.	1046
Charger, Blue & White, Flowers, Cornucopia, 1700s, 13⅜ In. ....*illus*	222
Charger, Flower Basket, Flower Swirl Band & Border, White, Blue, Orange, 1700s, 13 In.	406
Charger, Grapes & Lemon, Blue & Yellow, Brown & Green, England, 1700s, 13½ In.	200
Charger, Man, Landscape, Multicolor, London, 1765-75, 11⅞ In.	720
Charger, Multicolor, Bird In Branch, Dutch, Early 1700s, 13¾ In.	600
Charger, Satyrs & Woman, Putti Border, Blue & White, Tin Glazed, c.1800, 24 In.	360
Charger, Yellow Border, Songbird, Dutch, Early 1700s, 14 In.	480
Charger, Yellow Tulip Border, Man Carrying Doors, Dutch, Early 1700s, 13½ In.	570
Figurine, Dog, Pink, Standing, Collar, 14½ In.	1063
Flower Brick, Blue, White, Vines, Flowers, Raised Rim, 1700s, 4½ x 2½ In.	497
Honey Pot, Flip Lid, Red Outlined Flowers, Yellow, Green, Leaves, 3½ In. ....*illus*	146
Horn, Hunting, Decorative, Blue, White, Flowers, Early 1800s, 24 In.	1900
Inkstand, Blue, White, Birds, Flowers, 1700s, 3 x 7 In.	468
Plaque, Oval, Shaped, Landscape, 23¾ In.	188
Plate, Blue, Flowers, Feathers, Butterfly Rim, 1600s, 13¾ In.	425
Plate, Octagonal, Blue, White, Woman Fishing, Pier, Flowers, 1700s, 6½ In.	222
Plate, Painted, White Ground, Peafowl, Trees, Yellow, Brown, Blue, 1700s, 9 In.	2300
Plate, Sporting, Fish, Multicolor, White Ground, 1700s, 8¾ In., Pair	1560
Punch Bowl, Freehand Flower & Vine Design, Text, Footed, c.1800, 5 x 10 In.	1169
Shoes, Heel, Flowers, Blue & Yellow Flowers, Green Leaves, White, 7 In.	1187
Shoes, Heel, Flowers, Blue, White, 5¾ In.	312
Shoes, Heel, Flowers, Heart, Cherub, Blue, White, 5⅞ In.	1250
Shoes, Heel, Flowers, Stripes, Yellow, Blue, White, 1700s, 5⅛ In.	312
Tazza, Blue, White, Flowers, Pedestal Foot, Late 1600s-Early 1700s, 3¼ In.	2808
Teapot, Blue, White, C-Shape Handle, High Short Spout, Flowers, 1700s, 4¾ In.	1112
Tile, Blue & White, Round Vignettes, Metal Frame, Metal Frame, 23 x 26 In., 9 Tiles	263
Tobacco Jar, Maryland Taback, Oval, Tin Glaze, Blue, Netherlands, Early 1600s, 8½ In.	1680
Toby Jug, Aristocrat, Broadcoat, Ruffled Shirt, Seated, Keg Of Beer, Tin Glaze, c.1905, 11 In.	389
Tray, Chips & Dip, Turntable, Blue & White, Windmill, Swags, Bowl, Lid, c.1950, 4 x 14 In.	290
Vase, Blue, White, Cartouche, Flowers, Bird, 1700s, 10½ In.	263
Vase, Earthenware, Blue, White, Flowers, 19¼ In.	125

DENTAL cabinets, chairs, equipment, and other related items are listed here. Other objects may be found in the Medical category.

Cabinet, Burl Walnut, Roll Opening, Black Marble Desk, Drawers, 1800s, 64 x 33 x 16 In.	1375
Cabinet, Lift Top, Black, Ivory, Art Deco, 1930s, 42 x 15 In.	1275
Cabinet, Light Green, 4 Cabinets, Multiple Drawers, 1910, 47 x 58 In.	527
Cabinet, Oak, Black Leather, 13 Drawers, H. Gerstner & Sons, 15½ x 16¼ In.	186
Mannequin, Facial, Metal Head, Teeth, Stand, 20 In.	992
Model, Full Mouth Of Teeth, Gold Filled Molars, Plastic Hinge, Life Size, England, c.1955	110
Model, Tooth, 2 Parts, 1950s, 7¼ In.	225
Teaching Model, Aluminum, Chromed Steel, Teeth, Gums, Head, 22½ x 6 In.	732
Tin, Floss, Curity, Nylon, 10 Yards, Bauer & Black, Blue Border, ⅜ x 1⅛ In.	18
Tray, Milk Glass, Beige, American Cabinet Co., 8 x 4 In., Pair	18

DENVER
CT&
PTCo

DENVER is part of the mark on an American art pottery. William Long of Steubenville, Ohio, founded the Lonhuda Pottery Company in 1892. In 1900 he moved to Denver, Colorado, and organized the Denver China and Pottery Company. This pottery, which used the mark *Denver*, worked until 1905, when Long moved to New Jersey and founded the Clifton Pottery. Long also worked for Weller Pottery, Roseville Pottery, and

American Encaustic Tiling Company. Do not confuse this pottery with the Denver White Pottery, which worked from 1894 to 1955 in Denver.

Pitcher, Molded, Men, Animals, Trees, Plants, Brown, Green Glaze, c.1905, 7 x 6 In..........*illus*   125
Vase, Tulips, Embossed, Crystalline Matte Glaze, 1903, 8½ In...   1920

DEPRESSION GLASS is an inexpensive glass that was manufactured in large quantities during the 1920s and early 1930s. It was made in many colors and patterns by dozens of factories in the United States. Most patterns were also made in clear glass, which the factories called *crystal*. If no color is listed here, it is clear. The name *Depression glass* is a modern one and also refers to machine-made glass of the 1940s through 1970s. Sets missing a few pieces can be completed through the help of a matching service.

Adam, Cake Plate, Footed, Pink, Jeannette Glass, 10 In. ....*illus*   20
Baltimore Pear, Sugar, Handles, Pedestal, Jeannette Glass, 4½ In.   10
Block Optic, Bowl, Cereal, Green, Anchor Hocking, 5¼ In..   15
Block Optic, Plate, Bread & Butter, Anchor Hocking, 6 In.   4
Block Optic, Plate, Dinner, Green, Anchor Hocking, 10 In..   30
Block Optic, Saucer, Green, Anchor Hocking, 6¼ In..   8
Burple, Bowl, Dessert, Anchor Hocking, 4⅝ In.   5
Burple, Goblet, Forest Green, Anchor Hocking, 5¾ In...   13
Burple, Tumbler, Footed, Forest Green, Anchor Hocking, 5 In..   8
Burple, Tumbler, Iced Tea, Forest Green, Anchor Hocking, 6¾ In....................................   16
Cherry Blossom, Cake Plate, Green, Scalloped Rim, Jeannette Glass, 10¼ In..................*illus*   35
Cherry Blossom, Sugar, Pink, Angular Handles, Scalloped Rim, c.1935, 3 x 6 In.....................   20
Colony, Bowl, Salad, Hazel Atlas, 6 In..   6
Colony, Dish, Hazel Atlas, 9½ In..   12
Colony, Serving Bowl, Hazel Atlas, 10¾ In..   24
Columbia, Bowl, Ruffled, Federal Glass, 11 In..   35
Columbia, Butter, Federal Glass, ½ Lb.   5
Columbia, Candy Jar, Oval Body, Pointed Lid, Round Foot, 30 In....................................   1045
Columbia, Chop Plate, Federal Glass, 11 In...   21
Columbia, Plate, Bread & Butter, Federal Glass, 6 In...   6
Criss Cross, Bowl, Mixing, Cobalt Blue, Raised Circular Foot, Hazel Atlas, 8 x 4 In...........*illus*   42
Criss Cross, Butter, Cover, Hazel Atlas, ¼ Lb.   8
Criss Cross, Dish, Square, Hazel Atlas, 8½ In...   25
Cubist, Plate, Bread & Butter, Green, Jeannette Glass, 5⅝ In.   9
Cubist, Sugar & Creamer, Amber, Jeannette Glass..   10
Cubist, Sugar & Creamer, Pink, Jeannette Glass...   20
Dewdrop, Snack Set, Cup & Plate, Jeannette Glass...   8
Doric, Berry Bowl, Pink, Jeannette Glass, 8¼ In..*illus*   35
Floragold, Bowl, Dessert, Jeannette Glass, 5½ In..   16
Floragold, Bowl, Ruffled Edge, Jeannette Glass, 9½ In..   21
Floragold, Torte Plate, Jeannette Glass, 13⅝ In..   32
Harvest, Goblet, Amber, Indiana Glass, 5¼ In..   6
Hellenic Blue, Tumbler, Jeannette Glass   8
Hellenic Green, Bowl, Fruit, Jeannette Glass, 2⅜ In.   12
Hellenic Green, Bowl, Gold Trim, Jeannette Glass, 3¾ In..   12
Hellenic Green, Ice Bucket, Jeannette Glass, 5 In..   20
Hellenic Green, Juice, Jeannette Glass...   10
Hellenic Green, Pitcher, Jeannette Glass, 9¼ In..   35
Hellenic Green, Tumbler, Jeannette Glass, 6½ In..   12
Iris, Butter, Cover, Round, Jeannette Glass, ½ Lb..   45
Iris, Creamer, Jeannette Glass..   10
Iris, Fruit Bowl, Ruffled Edge, Jeannette Glass   2
Iris, Plate, Dinner, Jeannette Glass, 9 In..   40
Iris, Sherbet, Jeannette Glass   12
Iris, Vase, Footed, Flared, Jeannette Glass, 9 In...*illus*   20
Laurel, Goblet, 5½ In.   7
Laurel, Iced Tea, 7 In.   10

Depression Glass, Cherry Blossom, Cake Plate, Green, Scalloped Rim, Jeannette Glass, 10¼ In.
$35

Ruby Lane

Depression Glass, Criss Cross, Bowl, Mixing, Cobalt Blue, Raised Circular Foot, Hazel Atlas, 8 x 4 In.
$42

Ruby Lane

Depression Glass, Doric, Berry Bowl, Pink, Jeannette Glass, 8¼ In.
$35

Ruby Lane

Depression Glass, Iris, Vase, Footed, Flared, Jeannette Glass, 9 In.
$20

Depression Glass, Old Colony, Bowl, Pink, Anchor Hocking, 7 In.
$24

Ruby Lane

Depression Glass, Ovide, Creamer
$20

Ruby Lane

Depression Glass, Patrician, Sugar & Creamer, Amber, Federal Glass
$17

Ruby Lane

Depression Glass, Pressed Jewel, Relish, 3 Sections, Hazel Atlas, 11 x 5¾ In.
$12

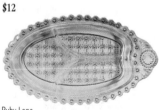

Ruby Lane

Mayfair Open Rose

Mayfair Open Rose was made by Hocking Glass Company from 1931 to 1937. It was made primarily in Light Blue and Pink, with a few Green and Yellow pieces. Crystal examples are rare. The cookie jar and the whiskey glass have been reproduced since 1982.

Laurel, Sherbet, 3½ In.	5
Loganberry, Bonbon, Indiana Glass, 7 In.	8
Loganberry, Grill Plate, Indiana Glass, 8⅞ In.	15
Madrid, Bowl, Fruit, Amber, Federal Glass, 5 In.	8
Madrid, Bowl, Vegetable, Oval, Federal Glass, 10 In.	15
Madrid, Cup, Amber, Federal Glass	4
Madrid, Sugar, Handles, Amber, Federal Glass	12
Manhattan, Bowl, Dessert, Anchor Hocking, 5⅜ In.	21
Manhattan, Cup, Anchor Hocking	10
Manhattan, Sherbet, Anchor Hocking	8
Manhattan, Tumbler, Anchor Hocking, 5⅜ In.	15
Monarch, Goblet, Royal Ruby, Anchor Hocking, 5⅜ In.	12
Moroccan Amethyst, Bowl, Handle, Oval, Hazel Atlas, 7¾ In.	14
Moroccan Amethyst, Bowl, Hazel Atlas, 6 In.	11
Mt. Vernon, Goblet, Water, Indiana Glass, 6 In.	4
No. 620, Cake Plate, Amber, Indiana Glass, 11¼ In.	21
No. 6045, Candy Dish, 3-Sided, Turquoise, Hazel Atlas, 6¾ In.	8
Old Cafe, Ashtray, Round, Hocking Glass, 4¼ In.	6
Old Cafe, Plate, Bread & Butter, Hocking Glass, 6 In.	5
Old Cafe, Relish, 3 Sections, Hocking Glass, 12 In.	15
Old Colony, Bowl, Hocking Gass, 9½ In.	12
Old Colony, Bowl, Pink, Anchor Hocking, 7 In. ....*illus*	24
Old Colony, Compote, Hocking Glass	14
Ovide, Creamer ....*illus*	20
Patrician, Sugar & Creamer, Amber, Federal Glass ....*illus*	17
Pebble Leaf, Goblet, Indiana Glass, 5¾ In.	8
Pebble Leaf, Relish, 6 Sections, Amber, Indiana Glass, 15 In.	28
Pebble Leaf, Relish, 6 Sections, Blue, Indiana Glass, 15 In.	62
Petalware, Plate, Cherries, 8 In.	28
Pheasants, Juice, Hazel Atlas, 3¾ In.	3
Pioneer, Plate, Smoke, Federal Glass, 11⅜ In.	10
Pressed Jewel, Relish, 3 Sections, Hazel Atlas, 11 x 5¾ In. ....*illus*	12
Princess, Candy Dish, Lid, Amber, Indiana Glass	18
Princess, Candy Dish, Lid, Blue, Indiana Glass	21
Royal Lace, Bowl, Green, Wavy Rim, Footed, Hazel Atlas, c.1940	35
Soreno, Bowl, Fruit, Hocking Glass, 4¾ In.	4
Stars & Bars, Sugar & Creamer, Hocking Glass	20
Stars & Stripes, Plate, Dessert, Hocking Glass, 8½ In.	25
Swedish Modern, Bowl, Anchor Hocking, 3½ x 7¼ In.	12
Wexford, Butter, Cover, Anchor Hocking, ¼ Lb.	12
Wexford, Goblet, Anchor Hocking, 6⅝ In.	5
Wexford, Plate, Dinner, Anchor Hocking, 9½ In.	20
Wild Rose, Bowl, Fruit, Indiana Glass, 6 In.	4
Wild Rose, Cake Plate, Handles, Indiana Glass, 12¼ In.	21
Wild Rose, Nappy, Indiana Glass, 6½ In.	5
Windsor, Bowl, Blue, Indiana Glass, 10½ In.	35
Windsor, Bowl, Federal Glass, 7½ In.	15
Windsor, Bowl, Mayonnaise, Federal Glass, 5⅝ In.	10
Windsor, Bowl, Pink, Indiana Glass, 5½ In.	10
Windsor, Butter, Cover, Federal Glass, ¼ Lb.	15
Windsor, Cake Stand, Federal Glass, 4¼ x 11 In.	32
Windsor, Candy Dish, Blue, Indiana Glass, 7½ In.	12
Windsor, Pitcher, Federal Glass, Pt., 5⅝ In.	20
Windsor, Plate, Dinner, Blue, Indiana Glass, 11 In.	23
Windsor, Plate, Dinner, Federal Glass, 11 In.	12
Windsor, Sugar & Creamer, Federal Glass	21
Windsor, Tumbler, Federal Glass, 5 In.	8
Windsor, Tumbler, Forest Green, Anchor Hocking, 4 In.	8
Windsor, Tumbler, Royal Ruby, Anchor Hocking, 4 In.	9

D

DERBY has been marked on porcelain made in the city of Derby, England, since about 1748. The original Derby factory closed in 1848, but others opened there and continued to produce quality porcelain. The Crown Derby mark began appearing on Derby wares in the 1770s.

Bowl, Birds, Red, Purple, Ruffled Edge, 10¾ In., Pair		313
Plate, Octagonal, Diamond Chain Border, Strawberry Plant, Pansies, c.1775, 9 In.		246
Sugar, Lid, Gilt, Bands, Leaves, c.1815, 6 x 7 In.	*illus*	75
Teapot, Roses, Oval, Lid, Flower Knop, Diamond Pattern Spout, Red, Enamel, c.1765, 4 In.		308

DICK TRACY, the comic strip, started in 1931. Tracy was also the hero of movies from 1937 to 1947 and again in 1990, and starred in a radio series in the 1940s and a television series in the 1950s. Memorabilia from all these activities are collected.

Badge, Pouch, Brass Shield, Relief Embossed, Eagle, Spread Wings, c.1937, 3 In.		115
Button, Cartoon Portrait, Dick Tracy & Junior, Brown Hat, c.1933, 1 In.		153
Card Set, Tip-Top Bread, Character Art Fronts, Ad Backs, 1952, 2 x 3 In., 10 Cards		278
Outfit, Crime Stoppers, Holster, Box.	*illus*	120
Poster, Dick Tracy Vs. Crime Inc., Chapter 15, Retribution, 1941, 27 x 41 In.		168
Wrist Radio, Plastic Crystal Dial, Leather Strap, Antenna, Instructions, Box, c.1947		258 to 425

DICKENS WARE *pieces are listed in the Royal Doulton and Weller categories.*

DINNERWARE used in the United States from the 1930s through the 1950s is listed here. Most was made in potteries in southern Ohio, West Virginia, and California. A few patterns were made in Japan, England, and other countries. Dishes were sold in gift shops and department stores, or were given away as premiums. Many of these patterns are listed in this book in their own categories, such as Autumn Leaf, Azalea, Coors, Fiesta, Franciscan, Hall, Harker, Harlequin, Red Wing, Riviera, Russel Wright, Vernon Kilns, Watt, and Willow. For more prices, go to kovels.com. Sets missing a few pieces can be completed through the help of a matching service.

Apple Blossom, Platter, Johnson Brothers, 12¼ In.		21
Athena, Butter, Cover, Round, Johnson Brothers		50
Autumn Monarch, Platter, Johnson Brothers, 13 In.	*illus*	43
Ballerina, Bowl, Dessert, Forest Green, Universal Potteries, 5⅜ In.		7
Ballerina, Cup & Saucer, Forest Green, Universal Potteries		10
Ballerina, Plate, Bread & Butter, Forest Green, Universal Potteries, 6¼ In.		3
Biscayne, Sugar, Turquoise Lid, Flower, Green, Blue Leaf, Paden City, 1950s, 3½ In.	*illus*	20
Blue Nordic, Plate, Dinner, Johnson Brothers, 9¾ In.		24
Blue Willow, Teapot, Johnson Brothers, 1913	*illus*	220
Boutonniere, Creamer, Taylor, Smith & Taylor		10
Boutonniere, Cup & Saucer, Taylor, Smith & Taylor		5
Boutonniere, Gravy Boat, Taylor, Smith & Taylor		7
Boutonniere, Plate, Bread & Butter, Taylor, Smith & Taylor, 6¾ In.		4
Chintz, Butter, Vernonware, ¼ Lb.		25
Chintz, Chop Plate, Vernonware, 13¾ In.		42
Chintz, Cup, Vernonware		10
Country Sage, Bowl, Cereal, Homer Laughlin, 6¼ In.		5
Country Sage, Bowl, Vegetable, Lid, Homer Laughlin		25
Country Sage, Butter, Cover, Homer Laughlin		18
Country Sage, Cup & Saucer, Homer Laughlin		6
Country Sage, Plate, Dinner, Homer Laughlin, 10 In.		8
Country Strawberry, Plate, Dinner, Homer Laughlin, 10 In.		12
Dairy Maid, Bowl, Fruit, Crooksville, 5⅜ In.		11
Dairy Maid, Cup & Saucer, Crooksville		12
Dairy Maid, Plate, Bread & Butter, Crooksville, 6 In.		10
Dairy Maid, Plate, Dinner, Crooksville, 10¼ In.		15
Desert Sand, Plate, Bread & Butter, Johnson Brothers, 6½ In.		5
Desert Sand, Plate, Dinner, Johnson Brothers, 10½ In.		13

D

Derby, Sugar, Lid, Gilt, Bands, Leaves, c.1815, 6 x 7 In.
$75

Alex Cooper Auctioneers

Dick Tracy, Outfit, Crime Stoppers, Holster, Box
$120

Milestone Auctions

Dinnerware, Autumn Monarch, Platter, Johnson Brothers, 13 In.
$43

Replacements, Ltd.

Dinnerware, Biscayne, Sugar, Turquoise Lid, Flower, Green, Blue Leaf, Paden City, 1950s, 3½ In.
$20

Ruby Lane

DINNERWARE

Dinnerware, Blue Willow, Teapot,
Johnson Brothers, 1913
$220

Ruby Lane

A Broken Mark

In 1910 Dirk Van Erp
stamped his copper ware
with a mark that pictured a
windmill above a rectangular
box enclosing his printed
name. In 1913 the stamp was
damaged and one side of the
box was gone. The resulting
mark is the "broken box"
mark used from 1913 until
about 1930.

Dinnerware, French Peasant, Dish,
Relish, Blue Ridge, 9 In.
$143

Ruby Lane

Dinnerware, Golden Wheat, Sugar, Lid,
Homer Laughlin, 2 ½ In.
$28

Replacements, Ltd.

Eggshell Georgian, Platter, Homer Laughlin, 13 ½ In.	25
Family Affair, Bowl, Fruit, Steubenville, 5 ⅜ In.	7
Family Affair, Plate, Bread & Butter, Steubenville, 6 ¼ In.	6
French Peasant, Dish, Relish, Blue Ridge, 9 In. ....*illus*	143
Friendly Village, Cup & Saucer, Johnson Village	8
Friendly Village, Plate, Dinner, Covered Bridge, Johnson Brothers, 10 ½ In.	25
Golden Apple, Plate, Dinner, Johnson Brothers, 10 In.	16
Golden Bell, Cup & Saucer, Paragon	25
Golden Wheat, Sugar, Lid, Homer Laughlin, 2 ½ In. ....*illus*	28
Golden Willow, Cup & Saucer, Crooksville	9
Golden Willow, Plate, Bread & Butter, Crooksville	7
Goldendawn, Platter, Scalloped, Johnson Brothers, 11 ½ In. ....*illus*	14
Granite, Bowl, Vegetable, Taylor, Smith & Taylor	10
Greenbriar, Chop Plate, Paden City, 12 ¾ In.	62
Greenbriar, Plate, Dinner, Paden City, 9 ¼ In.	13
Greenbriar, Soup, Dish, Paden City, 6 ⅛ In.	10
Greenbrier, Casserole, Cover, Paden City	55
Greendawn, Cup & Saucer, Johnson Brothers	14
Greendawn, Gravy Boat, Johnson Brothers	25
Greendawn, Plate, Bread & Butter, Johnson Brothers, 6 ⅜ In.	6
Greendawn, Plate, Dinner, Johnson Brothers, 10 In.	14
Greendawn, Platter, Johnson Brothers, 13 ¾ In.	25
Greydawn, Bowl, Vegetable, Lid, Blue, Johnson Brothers, 8 In.	55
Greydawn, Plate, Dinner, Blue, Johnson Brothers, 9 ⅝ In.	14
Greydawn, Platter, Blue, Johnson Brothers, 12 ¼ In.	20
Heritage Hall, Bowl, Vegetable, Johnson Brothers, 8 ¼ In.	28
Heritage Hall, Plate, Bread & Butter, Johnson Brothers, 6 ¾ In.	8
Heritage Hall, Plate, Salad, Johnson Brothers, 8 In. ....*illus*	16
Hibiscus, Cup & Saucer, Salem	17
Hibiscus, Plate, Bread & Butter, Salem	6
Hostess, Cup & Saucer, Edwin Knowles	30
Jamaica Bay, Plate, Bread & Butter, Taylor, Smith & Taylor, 6 ⅝ In.	5
Jamaica Bay, Saucer, Taylor, Smith & Taylor	2
Lazy Daisy, Bowl, Cereal, Taylor, Smith & Taylor, 7 ⅜ In.	7
Lazy Daisy, Casserole, Cover, Taylor, Smith & Taylor, 2 Qt.	45
Lazy Daisy, Plate, Bread & Butter, Taylor, Smith & Taylor, 7 In.	6
Lu-Ray, Creamer, Green, Taylor, Smith & Taylor	18
Lu-Ray, Creamer, Yellow, Taylor, Smith & Taylor, 2 ½ In.	12
Lu-Ray, Gravy Boat, Yellow, Taylor, Smith & Taylor	25
Lu-Ray, Platter, Green, Taylor, Smith & Taylor, 11 ¾ In.	16
Madras, Gravy Boat, Underplate, Alfred Meakin	56
Malvern, Soup, Dish, Johnson Brothers, 8 In.	21
Marble, Plate, Dinner, Taylor, Smith & Taylor, 10 In.	15
Marble, Platter, Oval, Taylor, Smith & Taylor, 13 ½ In.	21
Margaret Rose, Chop Plate, Johnson Brothers, 12 In. ....*illus*	60
Margaret Rose, Platter, Johnson Brothers, 12 ¼ In.	35
Margaret Rose, Soup, Dish, Rimmed, Johnson Brothers, 8 In.	28
Melody, Bowl, Vegetable, Round, Johnson Brothers, 8 ⅛ In.	18
Melody, Plate, Bread & Butter, Johnson Brothers, 6 ⅛ In.	6
Monion, Bowl, Dessert, Paden City, 5 ½ In.	8
Old Mill, Charger, Johnson Brothers, 11 ⅜ In.	24
Old Mill, Mug, Johnson Brothers, 3 ⅜ In.	20
Oriental Garden, Plate, Bread & Butter, Johnson Brothers, 6 ¼ In.	7
Oriental Garden, Plate, Dinner, Johnson Brothers, 10 In.	21
Peach Bloom, Plate, Bread & Butter, Johnson Brothers, 6 ⅛ In.	11
Pebbleford, Plate, Bread & Butter, Sunburst Yellow, Taylor, Smith & Taylor, 6 ¼ In.	3
Pebbleford, Plate, Dinner, Sand, Taylor, Smith & Taylor, 10 ¼ In.	10
Pebbleford, Plate, Dinner, Sunburst Yellow, Taylor, Smith & Taylor, 10 ⅛ In.	9
Pebbleford, Plate, Dinner, Turquoise, Taylor, Smith & Taylor, 10 ¼ In.	9
Regency, Plate, Salad, Johnson Brothers, 8 In.	8

Rosalee, Plate, Dinner, Paden City, 9⅞ In.	15
Rose & Leaf, Coffeepot, Edwin Knowles, 1950s, 8¾ In. ....*illus*	38
Sheraton, Plate, Salad, Square, Johnson Brothers, 7¾ In.	15
Skytone, Cup & Saucer, Homer Laughlin	12
South Wood, Cup & Saucer, Homer Laughlin	17
Splatter Blue, Bowl, Cereal, Homer Laughlin, 7¼ In.	12
Splatter Blue, Bowl, Vegetable, Homer Laughlin, 9¼ In.	35
Splatter Blue, Plate, Dinner, Homer Laughlin, 10⅝ In.	21
Spring Song, Cup & Saucer, Homer Laughlin	49
Sugar & Spice Brown, Bowl, Vegetable, Johnson Brothers, 8½ In. ....*illus*	20
Swing Moss Rose, Bowl, Oval, Pink Rim, Homer Laughlin, 1940s, 9¼ x 7 In. ....*illus*	22
Trend, Gravy Boat, Steubenville	15
Victory Needlepoint, Berry Bowl, Basket Of Flowers, Salem, 5⅝ In. ....*illus*	5
Village, Bowl, Cereal, Pfaltzgraff, 6⅛ In.	4
Village, Butter, Cover, Pfaltzgraff	15
Village, Gravy Boat, Pfaltzgraff	14
Village, Plate, Dinner, Pfaltzgraff, 10⅜ In.	6
Village, Relish, 3 Sections, Pfaltzgraff, 12 In.	15
Wheat, Bowl, Cereal, Taylor, Smith & Taylor, 6⅝ In.	5
Wheat, Bowl, Vegetable, Oval, Taylor, Smith & Taylor, 13½ In.	15
Wheat, Cup & Saucer, Taylor, Smith & Taylor	6
Wheat, Plate, Bread & Butter, Taylor, Smith & Taylor, 6¼ In.	3
Wheat, Sugar & Creamer, Taylor, Smith & Taylor	21
Yorktowne, Butter, Cover, Pfaltzgraff	17
Yorktowne, Creamer, Pfaltzgraff	5
Yorktowne, Cup & Saucer, Pfaltzgraff	5
Yorktowne, Gravy Boat, Pfaltzgraff	14
Yorktowne, Plate, Dinner, Pfaltzgraff, 10¼ In.	8
Yorktowne, Platter, Pfaltzgraff, 14¼ In.	21
Yorktowne, Salt & Pepper, Pfaltzgraff	15

DIONNE QUINTUPLETS were born in Canada on May 28, 1934. The publicity about their birth and their special status as wards of the Canadian government made them famous throughout the world. Visitors could watch the girls play; reporters interviewed the girls and the staff. Thousands of special dolls and souvenirs were made picturing the quints at different ages. Emilie died in 1954, Marie in 1970, Yvonne in 2001. Annette and Cecile still live in Canada.

Doll, Composition, Jackets, Blankets, Hot Water Bottle, Case, 6¾ In., 5 Babies	615
Doll, Composition, Sleep Eyes, Molded Hair, Jointed, Madame Alexander, 11 In., 5 Babies	492
Doll, Composition, Toddlers, Sleep Eyes, Jointed, 12 In., 5 Toddlers	523
Doll, Composition, Wood Low Chairs, Gowns, Bonnets, 7 In., 5 Babies ....*illus*	995
Doll, Crib, Original Clothing, Badge, Madame Alexander, 7 In., 5 Babies	580
Doll, Trunk, Original Clothing, 6½ In., 5 Babies	150

DIRK VAN ERP was born in 1860 and died in 1933. He opened his own studio in 1908 in Oakland, California. He moved his studio to San Francisco in 1909 and the studio remained under the direction of his son until 1977. Van Erp made hammered copper accessories, including vases, desk sets, bookends, candlesticks, jardinieres, and trays, but he is best known for his lamps. The hammered copper lamps often had shades with mica panels.

Bookends, Copper, Hammered, Cutout Overlay, Scalloped Crest, 1906, 5 x 5 In.	400
Box, Copper, Hammered, Steamer Trunk Shape, Riveted Straps, Handles, 3 x 7 In.	1003
Charger, Copper, Hammered, Turned Back Edge, Impressed, 12 In.	561
Jardiniere, Hammered Copper, c.1915, 11½ x 5½ In.	3660
Lamp, Copper, Bean Pot, Hammered, Conical Mica Shade, Riveted Straps, 13 In.	8260
Lamp, Copper, Hammered, Bulbous, Orange, Paneled Mica Shade, c.1920, 19 In.	6875
Lamp, Hammered Copper, 20 x 22 In.	9760
Matchbox Holder, Undertray, Copper, Hammered, Marked, 3½ x 5 In. ....*illus*	472
Vase, Copper, Flared Bottom, 22½ x 10½ In.	5490

Dinnerware, Goldendawn, Platter, Scalloped, Johnson Brothers, 11½ In. $14

Ruby Lane

Dinnerware, Heritage Hall, Plate, Salad, Johnson Brothers, 8 In. $16

Replacements, Ltd.

Dinnerware, Margaret Rose, Chop Plate, Johnson Brothers, 12 In. $60

Replacements, Ltd.

Dinnerware, Rose & Leaf, Coffeepot, Edwin Knowles, 1950s, 8¾ In. $38

Ruby Lane

Dinnerware, Sugar & Spice Brown, Bowl, Vegetable, Johnson Brothers, 8½ In.
$20

Ruby Lane

Dinnerware, Swing Moss Rose, Bowl, Oval, Pink Rim, Homer Laughlin, 1940s, 9¼ x 7 In.
$22

Ruby Lane

Dinnerware, Victory Needlepoint, Berry Bowl, Basket Of Flowers, Salem, 5⅝ In.
$5

Ruby Lane

TIP

Don't use a repaired plate for food. It could be a health hazard.

Dionne Quintuplets, Doll, Composition, Wood Low Chairs, Gowns, Bonnets, 7 In., 5 Babies
$995

Ruby Lane

DISNEYANA is a collectors' term. Walt Disney and his company introduced many comic characters to the world. Collectors search for examples of the work of the Disney Studios and the many commercial products modeled after his characters, including Mickey Mouse and Donald Duck, and recent films, like *Beauty and the Beast* and *The Little Mermaid*.

Bank, Donald Duck, Mechanical, Tin Litho, House, Tongue Push Button, 3½ x 6½ x 3 In......	142
Bank, Donald Duck, Registering, Tin, Louis Marx, 4¼ In............................*illus*	250
Bank, Mickey Mouse, Hands On Hips, Brown Shirt, Aluminum, Paint, c.1935, 9 In.	493
Bank, Mickey Mouse, Leaning, Treasure Chest, Composition, Paint, 1938, 6 In.	115
Book, Big Little, Mickey Mouse, 1st Issue, 2nd Version, Mickey Waving, 1933	489
Book, Mickey Mouse, Paper Doll, Cutout, Cardstock, 1933, 10 x 19 In...........................	460
Box, Mickey Mouse Cookies, Animal Crackers, Nabisco, 2¾ x 5⅛ x 1⅞ In.....................	130
Bracelet, Mickey & Minnie, Silver Plate, Cuff, c.1932, ⁷⁄₁₆ x 2¼ In..............................	115
Cel, see Animation Art category.	
Chamber Pot, Mickey Mouse, Piano, Enameled, R.G. Kreuger, Germany, 1930s, Child's, 6 In..	165
Container, Mickey Mouse, Toothy Smile, Red Eyes, Blue Shorts, Bisque, 1930, 6 In..................	1020
Cover, Comic Book, Mickey Mouse, No. 226, Pen & Ink, Board, 1987, 11 x 16 In...............	708
Cup, Mickey Mouse, The Cactus Kid, Paragon Fine China, England, 1930s, 3 In.................	3232
Display Figure, Donald Duck, Composition, Old King Cole Inc., 1940, 26 x 32 In.............*illus*	3289
Display, Pluto, Ears Up, Composition, Paint, Old King Cole Inc., 1940, 30 x 40 In.	3486
Doll, Mickey & Minnie, Cloth, Head Moves, Knickerbocker, 1930s, 12 In., Pair	443
Doll, Mickey Mouse, Cloth, 2 Guns, Cowboy, Hat, Chaps, Rope, c.1935, 12 In. ....*illus*	4250
Drawing, Mickey Mouse, Mallets, Pencil, Animation Paper, 1928, 10 x 12 In.	1083
Eggcup, Mickey Mouse Series, 2 Baby Birds, Royal Paragon, 1930, 2¼ In...........................	1645
Figurine, Donald Duck, Golfing, Checkered Hat, Swinging Club, c.1947, 8 In.......................	950
Figurine, Ferdinand The Bull, Painted & Glazed, Zaccagnini, 1947, 5 x 8 x 9 In....................	672
Figurine, Geppetto, Pinocchio, Chair, R. John Wright, 18 In................................*illus*	462
Figurine, Mickey Mouse, Bisque, Movable Arms, c.1928, 4¾ In.	127
Figurine, Mickey Mouse, Playing Instruments, Tin, Tab Base, 1930s, 2 In., 5 Piece.................	1546
Figurine, Mickey Mouse, Pluto The Pup, Bisque, Movable Arm, Leash, 1930s, 6 In..................	215
Figurine, Mickey Mouse, Wood, Oil Cloth Ears, Lollipop Hands, Jointed, c.1931, 7 In.	443
Fire Truck, Donald Duck As Fire Chief, Tin Lithograph, Windup, Box, 1950s, 5 x 6 In.	1392
Flashlight, Mickey Mouse, Minnie & Pluto, Tin Lithograph, Cardboard Box, 6¼ In.	945
Game, Mickey Mouse, Le Cameleon, Wood, Painted, 2 Figures, Arcade, c.1935, 34 In.........*illus*	736
Game, Mickey Mouse, Table Quoits, Board, Figure, Hoops, Box, 1930s, 7 x 10 In.	748
Game, Mickey Mouse, Tidleywinks, Cardboard, Wood Cup, Box, 1930s, 6 x 10 In.	822
Hand Puppet, Minnie Mouse, Cloth, Composition, 1950s, 10 x 8 In.	35
Knife, Pocket, Mickey Mouse, Full Body, White Grip, 2 Blades, 5 In..............................	127
Lunch Box, Mickey Mouse, School Days, 8¼ x 7 In..	579
Movie Projector, Mickey Mouse, 3 Films, Keystone Mfg., Box, c.1930, 11 In.	710
Nodder, Mickey Mouse, String Instrument, Celluloid, Windup, 1930s, 6 In.	267
Painting, Donald Duck, Picnic Day, Nephews, Frame, c.1960, 20 x 26 In.	1150
Pencil Box, Mickey Mouse, Figural, Cardboard, Dixon, 1930s, 6 x 9 In.	177
Pencil Holder, Donald Duck, Lamp Shape, Celluloid, 1930s, 3¼ In................................	430
Pencil Sharpener, Mickey Mouse, 5 In..	24
Pencil Sharpener, Mickey Mouse, Donald Duck, Celluloid, 1930s, 3 In., Pair......................	196
Pencil Sharpener, Mickey Mouse, Full Figure Decal, Orange Ground, c.1935, 1 In..................	222
Picture Card, Mickey & Minnie, Brave Little Tailor, Cardstock, c.1939, 5 x 7 In.......................	2215
Picture Card, Snow White, Features Scene, Let Go My Pants, 1939, 5 x 7 In.......................	1072
Pin, Mickey Mouse, 30 Comics, Sunday Herald & Examiner, Lithograph, 1930s, 1 In.	411
Pin, Mickey Mouse, Waving, Walt Disney, Red & White, Dome, 1 In...........................	115
Pinocchio, Geppetto, R. John Wright, 19 In..	625
Pitcher, Lucifer The Cat, Figural, Ceramic, Painted, Cinderella Ware, 1950s, 5 In.	188
Plate, Mickey & Minnie, Playing Piano & Singing, Octagonal, Paragon, 1930s, 6 In.	230
Playing Cards, Mickey & Minnie, Cardboard Slipcase, Deck Of 52, 1930s, 3 x 4 In.	695
Pocket Watch, Mickey Mouse, Metal Case, Celluloid Dial, Ingersoll, Box, 3 x 4 In.	765
Pocket Watch, Mickey Mouse, Steel Case, Mickey Dial, Wind, Ingersoll, 1935, 2 In.	650
Record Cover, Mickey & The Beanstalk, Artboard, 1968, 19 x 20 In.	468
Sign, Donald Duck, Ducky Double, Popsicle, Cardboard, Easel Back, 1950s, 13 In.	209

Dirk Van Erp, Matchbox Holder, Undertray, Copper, Hammered, Marked, Tray 3 ½ x 5 In.
$472

Humler & Nolan

Disneyana, Bank, Donald Duck, Registering, Tin, Louis Marx, 4 ¼ In.
$250

Morphy Auctions

Disneyana, Display Figure, Donald Duck, Composition, Old King Cole Inc., 1940, 26 x 32 In.
$3,289

Hake's Americana & Collectibles

Disneyana, Doll, Mickey Mouse, Cloth, 2 Guns, Cowboy, Hat, Chaps, Rope, c.1935, 12 In.
$4,250

Pook & Pook

Disneyana, Figurine, Geppetto, Pinocchio, Chair, R. John Wright, 18 In.
$462

Susanin's Auctioneers & Appraisers

Disneyana, Game, Mickey Mouse, Le Cameleon, Wood, Painted, 2 Figures, Arcade, c.1935, 34 In.
$736

Auction Team Breker

Disneyana, Sign, Mickey Mouse, RPM Motor Oil, Blue, Tin, 1939, 24 In.
$1,905

Morphy Auctions

Disneyana, Toy, Donald Duck Whirligig, Celluloid, Spins, Moves, Borgfeldt, Japan, Prewar, 10 In.
$420

Bertoia Auctions

Disneyana, Toy, Pluto, Sniffing Dog, Lever Tail
$60

American Antique Auctions

Mickey Mouse Watches
The Mickey Mouse watch by Ingersoll was made in 1933 with Mickey wearing yellow gloves. The word *Ingersoll* was on the watch face. In 1934 *Made in U.S.A.* was added, and in 1938 ©*W.D. Ent.* was added.

Doll, A.M., 390, Automaton, Sleeping Mother, Baby, Music, Bisque, Celluloid, c.1910, 16 In.
$602

Auction Team Breker

Doll, Advertising, RCA Radiotrons, Composition, Wood, Cameo Doll Co., c.1930, 16 In.
$633

Hake's Americana & Collectibles

Sign, Mickey Mouse, RPM Motor Oil, Blue, Tin, 1939, 24 In. ....*illus*	1905
Tape Measure, Pluto, Figural, Back Tape Pull, Yellow, Black, Celluloid, 1930s, 3 In.	209
Tea Set, Mickey & Minnie, Donald, Pluto, Yellow, Chien, 15 In., 20 Piece	210
Tea Set, Mickey Mouse & Friends, Tin Lithograph, Ohio Art, 1930s, 14 Piece	260
Tea Set, Snow White, Seven Dwarfs, Tin Litho, Box, 1937, 10 x 15 In., 12 Piece	886
Thermometer, Mickey Mouse, Pluto, Doghouse, Steel Frame, Tin Lithograph, 1930s, 3 In.	316
Tin, Coffee, Donald Duck, Free Sample, Goyer Coffee Co., 2¼ x 3 In.	201
Toothbrush Holder, Doc, Brush Your Teeth, Porcelain, 1950s, 4½ In.	67
Toothbrush Holder, Donald Duck, Long Bill, Bisque, Hanging, 1934, 5 In.	239
Toothbrush Holder, Mickey Mouse, Hands On Hips, Bisque, 1930s, 4 In.	115
Toy, Cart, Delivery, Pinocchio, Tin Lithograph, Masonite, Multicolor, Windup, Marx, 1940, 8 x 9 In. ..	1082
Toy, Donald Duck Duet, Goofy Dances, Donald Drums, Windup, 1946, 7 x 11 In.	291
Toy, Donald Duck Whirligig, Celluloid, Spins, Moves, Borgfeldt, Japan, Prewar, 10 In. ....*illus*	420
Toy, Donald Duck, Waddling, Moves Arms, Long Bill, Celluloid, Windup, 1930s, 5 In.	201
Toy, Dopey, Dwarf, Waddles, Eyes Move, Tin Litho, Painted, Windup, Marx, Box, 1938, 8 In.	1904
Toy, Figaro, Tin Lithograph, Rubber Ears, Black, Orange, Yellow, Windup, Box, 1939, 5 In.	348
Toy, Mickey & Donald, Drum, Wooden, Green Metal Rims, c.1937, 4 x 6½ In.	285
Toy, Mickey & Donald, Hand Car, Track, Tin Lithograph, Wells, England, 12 x 14 In.	960
Toy, Mickey & Minnie, Sand Play Set, Tin Lithograph, Cardboard Box, 8 x 8 In., 5 Piece	612
Toy, Mickey Mouse, Fun-E-Flex Racer, Wood Car, Pull Toy, 1930s, 4 In.	538
Toy, Mickey Mouse, Hand Car, Mickey, Minnie, Windup, Box, Lionel, 1930s, 11 In.	886
Toy, Mickey Mouse, Jazz Drummer, Tin Lithograph, Spring Plunger, 1931, 6⅕ In.	610
Toy, Mickey Mouse, Minnie Mouse, Hand Car, Track, Box, 13¾ x 11½ In.	960
Toy, Mickey Mouse, Rollerskater, Pulling Wheels, Bell, Pull, 1935, 7 x 14 In.	658
Toy, Mickey Mouse, Rollerskater, Rubber Ears, Tin Lithograph, Windup, Box, 1950s, 6 In.	506
Toy, Mickey Mouse, Sparkler, Head, Cutout Mouth & Eyes, Tin Lithograph, 1931, 6 In.	165
Toy, Pinocchio, Multicolor, Tin Lithograph, Windup, Marx, 9 x 3 In.	242
Toy, Pluto, Sniffing Dog, Lever Tail, 9 In. ....*illus*	60
Toy, Sand Pail, Three Little Pigs, Big Bad Wolf, Pigs Dancing, Tin Lithograph, c.1934, 4 In.	173
Toy, Sand Shovel, Mickey & Minnie, Tin Lithograph, Wood Handle, 1930s, 7 x 21 In.	595
Toy, Saxophone, Mickey Mouse, Tin Litho, Jointed, Cymbals On Feet, Germany, c.1930, 6 In. ...	950
Umbrella, Mickey & Minnie Mouse, Light Rust Fabric, Walt Disney Enterprises, Ltd., 1930s	195
Underwear, Mickey & Minnie Mouse, Store Box, 12 Pair, Sylcraft, 1930s, 8 x 11 In.	557
Wristwatch, Mickey Mouse, Leather Band, Full Figure Mickey Dial, Box, Ingersoll, 1938	332

DOCTOR, *see Dental and Medical categories.*

 DOLL entries are listed by marks printed or incised on the doll, if possible. If there are no marks, the doll is listed by the name of the subject or country or maker. Notice that Barbie is listed under Mattel. G.I. Joe figures are listed in the Toy section. Eskimo dolls are listed in the Eskimo section and Indian dolls are listed in the Indian section. Doll clothes and accessories are listed at the end of this section. The twentieth-century clothes listed here are in mint condition.

A.M., 390, Automaton, Sleeping Mother, Baby, Music, Bisque, Celluloid, c.1910, 16 In. ....*illus*	602
A.M., Bisque Head, Sleep Eyes, Teeth, Molded Dimple, Wig, Late 1800s, 24 In.	70
A.M., Porcelain & Composition, Open Mouth, Shaker Dress, Signed, 14 In.	960
Advertising, Olde Tyme Comfort Shoes, Felt, Hollow Skirt, Egg Cover, Lenci, c.1927, 5 In.	689
Advertising, RCA Radiotrons, Composition, Wood, Cameo Doll Co., c.1930, 16 In. ....*illus*	633
Alexander dolls are listed in this category under Madame Alexander.	
Alt, Beck & Gottschalk, 639, Bisque Head, Red Mohair Wig, Curls, Blue Eyes, c.1910, 24 In. ...	626
Alt, Beck & Gottschalk, 1362, Nell, Bisque Head, Jointed, Human Hair, Glass Eyes, 30 In.	550
Armand Marseille dolls are listed in this category under A.M.	
Automaton, Bisque, Sleep Eyes, Wooden Limbs, Velvet Music Box, Late 1800s, 18 In.	94
Automaton, Black Man, Smoking, Composition, Velvet Coat, France, c.1910, 24 In.	5294
Automaton, Box, Harlequin Drummers, Dances, 14 x 29 In.	3835
Automaton, Charcuterie, Surreal Butcher Eats, Papier-Mache, Metal, c.1940, 18 x 51 In.	1092
Automaton, Girl With Guitar, Bisque Swivel Head, Carton Torso, Mohair Wig, 1882, 13 In.	7410
Automaton, Gustav Vichy, The Happy Drunkard, France, c.1890, 22½ x 13 In.	8750
Automaton, Leopold Lambert, Polichinelle, Cymbals, Bisque Head, Carton Torso, c.1890, 18 In.*illus*	9120

Doll, Automaton, Leopold Lambert,
Polichinelle, Cymbals, Bisque Head, Carton
Torso, c.1890, 18 In.
$9,120

Theriault's

Doll, Chad Valley, Princess Elizabeth, Felt,
Glass Eyes, Mohair Curls, Jointed, c.1935,
18 In.
$1,232

Theriault's

Doll, French, Mignonette, Bisque, Peg-Jointed,
Painted Boots, Costume, c.1882, 6 In.
$1,904

Theriault's

Doll, Automaton, Whistler, Bisque Head,
Paperweight Eyes, Carton Body & Legs, c.1893,
27 In.
$47,880

Theriault's

Doll, Emma Adams, Cloth Head, Oil Paint,
Stitch-Jointed, World's Fair Jacket, 1892, 15 In.
$3,192

Theriault's

Doll, French, Mignonette, Bisque, Swivel
Head, Glass Eyes, Jointed Elbows, c.1882, 5 In.
$2,352

Theriault's

Doll, Carved Wood, Wig, Dowel-Jointed,
Lord & Lady Clapham Series, c.1680, 16 In.
$21,660

Theriault's

Doll, French, Mignonette, Bisque, Eiffel Tower
Headdress, Exposition Paris 1889, 5 In.
$2,016

Theriault's

Doll, French, Mignonette, Jeanne D'Arc,
Bisque, Glass Eyes, Mohair, Jointed, c.1900,
4 1/2 In.
$1,008

Theriault's

Doll, Gaultier, Gentleman, Porcelain Shoulder Head, Painted, Kid Body, c.1860, 17 In.
$7,840

Theriault's

Doll, German, Bisque Head, Glass Eyes, Human Hair, Metal Torso, Edison Phonograph, c.1890, 22 In.
$5,244

Theriault's

Doll, German, Composition Head, Flanged Neck, Painted, Cloth Body, Stitch-Jointed, 1930s, 17 In.
$399

Theriault's

Doll, German, Mabel Lee, Porcelain Shoulder Head, Sculpted Hair, Muslin Body, c.1855, 22 In.
$4,104

Theriault's

Doll, Heubach, Pouty Boy, Bisque Head, Glass Sleep Eyes, Ball-Jointed, c.1912, 16 In.
$1,680

Theriault's

Doll, Kestner, 221, Toddler, Bisque, Googly Eyes, Mohair Wig, Composition, Ball-Jointed, c.1912, 13 In.
$3,762

Theriault's

Doll, Kestner, Baby Jean, Bisque Socket Head, Composition, Bent Limb Body, c.1912, 11 In.
$336

Theriault's

Doll, Kuhnlenz, Brown Bisque, Swivel Head, Glass Eyes, Mohair, Peg-Jointed, c.1890, 6 In.
$672

Theriault's

Automaton, Leopold Lambert, Smoker, Pink Coat, Jumeau Bisque Head, c.1885, 24 x 7¾ In. .	2000
Automaton, Leopold Lambert, Smoker, Red Coat, Jumeau Bisque Head, 23½ x 5¾ In.	2074
Automaton, Man, Playing Violin, Papier-Mache, Blinks Eyes, Taps Foot, 1860, 14 In.	4560
Automaton, Moorish Harpist, Papier-Mache, Brown Skin, Glass Eyes, c.1867, 30 In.	17670
Automaton, Rabbit, Glass Eyes, Rises & Falls From Cabbage, 6½ x 6 In.	900
Automaton, Roullet & Decamps, St. Anthony Of Padua, Blesses Child, c.1905, 20 In.	2528
Automaton, Symphonion, Dice Magician, Musical Disc, Bells, 31¼ x 15 In.	3172
Automaton, Vichy, Clown, Plays Sieve As Banjo, Composition, Laughing Eyes, c.1900, 21 In.	5459
Automaton, Vichy, Elegant Woman, Flutters, Fans Herself, Composition, c.1895, 24 In.	2862
Automaton, Vichy, Nurse Pushes Baby In Stroller, Bisque, Metal, Fabric, Box, c.1880, 12 In.	4006
Automaton, Whistler, Bisque Head, Paperweight Eyes, Carton Body & Legs, c.1893, 27 In.*illus*	47880
Averill, Bonnie Babe, Boy, Girl, Bisque, Sleep Eyes, Loop-Jointed, c.1925, 6 In., Pair	840
Babe Ruth, Celluloid Head, Stuffed Body, Felt Arms, Baseball Uniform, Bat, 1930s, 13 In.	210
Bahr & Proschild, 220, Asian Child, Bisque, Amber Tint, Glass Eyes, Jointed Wood, 12 In.	1344
Bahr & Proschild, Scowling Indian, Bisque, Brown Glass Eyes, Mohair Wig, 12 In.	900
Barbie dolls are listed in this category under Mattel, Barbie.	
Bing, Dutch Boy & Girl, Cloth, Stitched & Painted Face & Hair, Jointed, c.1915, 10 In., Pair	280
Bisque, Girl, Blond, Mohair Wig, Fixed Eyes, Composition Body, Germany, c.1898, 8 In.	225
Bisque, Sculpted Hair & Bodice, Painted Features, Muslin Body, Blue Dress, Germany, 8 In.	336
Bisque, Sculpted Hair & Bodice, Painted Features, Muslin Body, Blue Gown, Germany, 9 In.	224
Blampoix, Porcelain Shoulder Head, Glass Eyes, Gusset-Jointed Body, c.1860, 21 In.	2508
Bone, Carved Head, Brown Enameled Glass Eyes, Wood Body, Dowel Joints, c.1760, 13 In.	1254
Bru Jne, Bisque Swivel Head, Blue Glass Eyes, Brunette Mohair, Kid, Wood, Dress, 20 In.	15390
Bru Jne, Bisque Swivel Head, Glass Eyes, Human Hand-Tied Hair, Satin Dress, c.1886, 19 In.	5700
Bru Jne, Fashion, Ebony Bisque, Swivel Head, Brown Glass Eyes, Black Mohair, Gown, 16 In.	5985
Bruckner, Cloth, Topsy Turvy, Mammy & White Baby, Molded Faces, c.1900	850
Bruno Schmidt, Wendy, Bisque Head, Sleep Eyes, Composition Body, c.1912, 8 In.	6840
Bye-Lo, Baby, Bisque Swivel Head, Glass Sleep Eyes, Painted Hair, Dress & Bonnet, 6 In.	228
Bye-Lo, Baby, Bisque, 1-Piece Head & Torso, Painted, Loop-Jointed, Wicker Basket, 5 In.	399
Carved Wood, Wig, Dowel-Jointed, Lord & Lady Clapham Series, c.1680, 16 In.*illus*	21660
Chad Valley, Prince Edward, Felt Head, Glass Eyes, Mohair Wig, Muslin Torso, 1936, 15 In.	448
Chad Valley, Princess Elizabeth, Felt, Glass Eyes, Mohair Curls, Jointed, c.1935, 18 In. *illus*	1232
Chatty Cathy, Vinyl Head, Hard Plastic Body, Blond Hair, Blue Eyes, c.1962, 20 In.	200
Czech, Morning Glory Lady, Porcelain Shoulder Head, Flowers In Hair, Gown, 24 In.	2850
Door Of Hope, Asian Men & Women, Wood, Painted, Costumes, c.1925, 11 In., 7 Piece	2912
Effanbee, Child, Boy, Wood, Composition, Painted, Human Hair Wig, Suit, 1930s, 17 In.	850
Effanbee, Dy-Dee Wee, Baby, Plastic Head, Rubber Body, Flannel Pajamas, 9 In.	855
Effanbee, Lovums, Toddler, Composition Head, Cloth Body, Chubby Cheeks, 1930s, 29 In.	579
Emma Adams, Cloth Head, Oil Paint, Stitch-Jointed, World's Fair Jacket, 1892, 15 In. *illus*	3192
English, Wood, Dark Glass Eyes, Pink Cheeks, Brunette Human Hair, Kid Arms, c.1790, 5 In.	13680
Fashion, Bisque, Painted, Mohair, Kid Body, Marked, Au Magasin Des Enfants, 17 In.	3990
Fashion, Bisque Socket Head, Glass Eyes, Mohair Wig, Gown & Hat, France, c.1865, 9 In.	2280
Fashion, Bisque Swivel Head, Blue Glass Eyes, Articulated Wood Body, 17½ In.	6840
Fashion, Bisque Swivel Head, Glass Eyes, Blond Wig, Kid Body, Silk Gown, c.1860, 14 In.	2964
Fashion, Bisque Swivel Head, Pale Complexion, Blue Eyes, Folklore Gown, c.1860, 15 In.	3876
Fashion, Radiquet & Cordonnier, Bisque, Statuette, Swivel Head, France, 1880, 17 In.	9120
Fashion, Wax Head, Slender Face, Tilted, Sculpted Wax Body, Harem Dress, c.1915, 18 In.	2508
Franz Schmidt, Bisque Head, Brown Sleep Eyes, Mohair, Composition Body, c.1917, 8 In.	513
French, Bisque Swivel Head, Glass Eyes, Jointed Arms, Long Mohair Wig, 1880, 6 In.	2736
French, Bisque Swivel Head, Glass Eyes, Jointed, Braids, Folklore Costume, 1885, 6 In.	1140
French, Bisque Swivel Head, Glass Eyes, Mohair, Wood Articulated Body, c.1867, 13 In.	4218
French, Bisque Swivel Head, Human Hair, Articulated Wood Body, c.1870, 21 In.	10830
French, Carton Moule Head & Body, Painted, Brown Mohair, Kid, Trousseau, c.1810, 22 In.	4560
French, Mignonette, Bisque, Eiffel Tower Headdress, Exposition Paris 1889, 5 In.*illus*	2016
French, Mignonette, Bisque, Peg-Jointed, Painted Boots, Costume, c.1882, 6 In.*illus*	1904
French, Mignonette, Bisque, Swivel Head, Glass Eyes, Jointed Elbows, c.1882, 5 In.*illus*	2352
French, Mignonette, Jeanne D'Arc, Bisque, Glass Eyes, Mohair, Jointed, c.1900, 4½ In. *illus*	1008
French, Papier-Mache Shoulder Head, Glass Eyes, Cloth Body, Empire Gown, 1840, 33 In.	3876
French, Papier-Mache, Grenadier Garde Imperiale, 1804, Wood, Painted, Label, 15 In.	513
French, Papier-Mache, Soldier, Wood, Painted, Uniform, Pull String Arms, c.1840, 16 In.	1083

Doll, Lenci, Child, Felt, Swivel Head, Blond Mohair Wig, Jointed, Label, 1930s, 15 In.
$456

Theriault's

Doll, Lenci, Dutch Girl, Felt, Muslin, Painted, Side-Glancing Googly Eyes, c.1935, 9 In.
$112

Theriault's

Doll, Lenci, Girl, Felt, Swivel Head, Side-Glancing Eyes, Blond Mohair, Box, 1925, 23 In.
$1,254

Theriault's

Doll, Liberty Boy, Porcelain Shoulder Head, Painted, Cloth, Composition, A.D.P. Mfg., 16 In.
$672

Theriault's

Doll, Mannequin, Wood, Ball-Jointed, Ink Lettered Body Parts, Continental, c.1860, 20 In.
$1,232

Theriault's

Doll, Marseille, Just Me, Bisque Socket Head, Glass Eyes, Mohair Wig, Jointed, c.1926, 9 In.
$741

Theriault's

French, Papier-Mache, Wood, Painted, Jointed, Nurse Costume, Red Cross, c.1840, 7 In.	570
French, Petit Et Dumoutier, Bisque Head, Glass Eyes, Pewter Hands, Hat, c.1882, 20 In.	9690
French, Porcelain, Fortune-Teller, Folded Paper Skirt, Black Painted Hair, 1800s, 10 In.	969
Frozen Charlotte, Porcelain, Painted Details, Bathing, Germany, 8 ½ In.	336
Gaultier, Bisque Socket Head, Glass Eyes, Composition Body, Jointed, c.1882, 24 In.	5700
Gaultier, Bisque Socket Head, Wood & Composition, Jointed, Mohair, c.1882, 42 In.	18240
Gaultier, Bisque Swivel Head, Blue Glass Eyes, Mohair, Fashion, c.1865, 13 In.	2850
Gaultier, Bisque Swivel Head, Fashion, Glass Eyes, Kid, Jointed, 2 Piece Dress, c.1875, 11 In.	840
Gaultier, Gentleman, Porcelain Shoulder Head, Painted, Kid Body, c.1860, 17 In. ....*illus*	7840
Gebruder Heubach dolls may also be listed in this category under Heubach.	
Gebruder Heubach, Dolly Dimples, Bisque Socket Head, Sleep Eyes, c.1910, 19 In.	2015
Gebruder Heubach, Whistler Boy, Bisque Swivel Head, Cloth Body, Side-Glancing Eyes, 14 In.	670
German, Bisque Head, Blue Glass Inset Eyes, Human Hair, Carton Body, c.1890, 8 In.	684
German, Bisque Head, Glass Eyes, Human Hair, Metal Torso, Edison Phonograph, c.1890, 22 In... *illus*	5244
German, Bisque Head, Glass Googly Eyes, Papier-Mache Body, Folklore Dress, c.1920, 9 In.	741
German, Bisque Shoulder Head, Sculpted Hair, Dresden Ornaments, Muslin Body, 22 In.	1938
German, Bisque Socket Head, Sleep Eyes, Dimple, Jointed, Bent Limb, Baby, 1900s	59
German, Bisque, Socket Head, Blue Sleep Eyes, Wig, Composition Body, c.1910, 22 In.	80
German, Bride, Porcelain, Dome Shoulder Head, Painted, Muslin, Stitch Jointed, 16 In.	684
German, China Head, Shoulders, Black Flat Top Hair, Cloth Body, c.1870, 25 In.	94
German, Composition Head, Flanged Neck, Painted, Cloth Body, Stitch-Jointed, 1930s, 17 In.*illus*	399
German, Grape Lady, Porcelain, Sculpted Hair In Snood, Muslin Body, Silk Gown, 18 In.	1824
German, Lady, Bisque, Sculpted Hair & Bonnet, Dresden Flowers, Kid Body, c.1870, 18 In.	5016
German, Lady, Papier-Mache, Kid, Wood, Brown Sculpted Updo, Comb, Dress, c.1830, 14 In.	4104
German, Lady, Porcelain Shoulder Head, Sculpted Snood, Cloth Body, Gown, c.1870, 18 In.	2280
German, Mabel Lee, Porcelain Shoulder Head, Sculpted Hair, Muslin Body, c.1855, 22 In.*illus*	4104
German, Papier-Mache Shoulder Head, Black Sculpted Curls, Muslin Body, Gown, 31 In.	3876
German, Peddler Lady, Bisque, Sculpted Hair, Kid Body, Dress, Basket Of Wares, 14 In.	1368
German, Porcelain Shoulder Head, Plump Face, Sculpted Hair, Kid, Folklore Costume, 21 In.	855
German, Porcelain, Painted, Sculpted Chignon, Muslin, Stitch-Jointed, Dress, c.1860, 25 In.	1008
German, Tauflinge, Baby, Porcelain Head, Painted, Muslin Arms, Curled Fingers, c.1860, 7 In.	855
German, Tauflinge, Baby, Swaddled, Papier-Mache, Painted, Silk Bunting, c.1860, 5 In.	513
German, Tauflinge, Baby, Wax Over Papier-Mache Head, Lever Sleep Eyes, 1860, 9 In.	798
German, Tauflinge, Child, Crier, Porcelain, Wax Over Papier-Mache Body, Bellows, 12 In.	4332
German, Wax Over Papier-Mache Head, Glass Eyes, Muslin Body, Mohair, c.1875, 15 In.	285
German, Wood, Heart Shape Face, Painted, Dowel-Jointed, Gown, Hat, Grodner Tal, c.1830, 15 In.	20520
Goebel, Bisque, Baby, Woven Basket, Scowl, Painted Eyes, c.1912, 6 In.	399
Half Dolls are listed in the Pincushion Doll category.	
Handwerck, Bisque Head, Blond Wig, Glass Sleep Eyes, Composition, Jointed Body, 18 In.	95
Hertel Schwab, Toddler, Bisque Socket Head, Glass Googly Sleep Eyes, c.1917, 11 In.	4332
Hertwig, Laurel & Hardy, Papier-Mache, Dancing, Bisque, Clockwork, Key, c.1930, 8 In.	2289
Heubach, see also Gebruder Heubach.	
Heubach, Googly Girl, Bisque Head, Blue Glass Eyes, Jointed Composition, Dress, 8 In.	2688
Heubach, Native American Woman, Bisque Shoulder Head, Intaglio Eyes, Costume, 13 In.	2128
Heubach, Pouty Boy, Bisque Head, Glass Sleep Eyes, Ball-Jointed, c.1912, 16 In. ....*illus*	1680
Horsman, Baby Dimples, Composition, Stuffed, Blue Sleep Eyes, Teeth, c.1928, 22 In.	23
Huret, Bisque Swivel Head, Plump Face & Body, Painted, Mohair, Wood, Costume, 18 In.	18240
Ideal, Grumpy, Oilcloth Head, Arms, Fabric Body, Felt Outfit, Illustrated Box, 1938, 11 In.	240
Ideal, Pinocchio, Composition Head, Wood, Jointed Body, Felt Bow Tie, Box, 7 ½ In.	145
Ideal, Samantha, Bewitched TV Show, Posable, Red Felt Dress, Witch's Hat, Box, 12 In.	1115
Ideal, Snow White, Oilcloth Head & Arms, Black Hair, Red & Pink Dress, 1938, 15 ½ In.	127
Indian dolls are listed in the Indian category.	
J.D.K. dolls are listed in this category under Kestner.	
Japanese, Ichimatsu, Papier-Mache, Gofun Finish, Painted Hair, Costume, 1930s, 21 In.	1368
Japanese, Ichimatsu, Papier-Mache, Muslin, Painted, Silk Costume, Label, 1920s, 21 In.	1254
Japanese, Lady, Wood, Gofun, Painted, Silk Floss Hair, Silk Costume, Maruhei, c.1885, 12 In.	513
Japanese, Mitsuore, Papier-Mache, Gofun, Glass Eyes, Silk Locks, Jointed, c.1850, 17 In.	4275
Japanese, Mitsuore, Wood, Carved, Enamel Eyes, Black Silk Floss Hair, Jointed, 11 In.	1026
Japanese, Ningyo, Unmarried Lady, Wood, Gofun Finish, 3 Costumes, 7 Wigs, c.1910, 13 In.	627
Japanese, Samurai, Seated, Wood, Gofun Finish, Silk Hair, Kimono, Chrysanthemum, 16 In.	399

Doll, Martha Chase, Cloth Body, Pressed Face, Oil Paint, Cotton Sateen Body, c.1910, 17 In.
$513

Theriault's

Doll, Mattel, Barbie, No. 1, Blond Ponytail, Swimsuit, Stand, Box, c.1958, 11 In.
$3,990

Theriault's

Doll, Mattel, Barbie, Color Magic, Golden Hair, Diamond Print Swimsuit & Headband, 1966
$270

McMasters Harris Auction Co.

F & B
Dolls marked Effanbee were made by Fleischaker & Baum, a company founded in 1912 by Bernard Fleischaker and Hugo Baum. The mark can help you date your doll. If the word "Effanbee" has a capital letter at the beginning, followed by lowercase letters, it is an early mark. All capital letters were used beginning in 1923. After 1923, the middle letters, "an," were written in smaller capital letters. The company changed hands several times and is now owned by Tonner Doll Co. of Kingston, N.Y.

Doll, Nancy Ann Storybook, Style Show, Hard Plastic, Socket Head, Sleep Eyes, c.1950, 18 In.
$171

Theriault's

Doll, S.F.B.J., 227, Bisque Socket Head, Glass Eyes, Painted Face, Composition, Jointed, c.1912, 14 In.
$1,482

Theriault's

Doll, Schoenhut, Girl, Wood, Intaglio Eyes, Mohair Bob, Spring-Jointed, c.1912, 15 In.
$1,008

Theriault's

Doll, Simon & Halbig, 905, Bisque, Glass Eyes, Mohair, Peg-Jointed, c.1890, Miniature
$1,568

Theriault's

Doll, Simon & Halbig, 949, Bisque Socket Head, Ball-Jointed, Composition & Wood, 11 In.
$1,232

Theriault's

Doll, Simon & Halbig, Bisque Head, Sleep Eyes, Mohair Wig, Gusset-Jointed, c.1890, 17 In.
$570

Theriault's

Doll, Steiner, Nun, Bisque Socket Head, Jointed Composition & Wood, Cloth Habit, 10 In.
$3,248

Theriault's

Doll, Unis, 301, Bebe, Bisque, Composition, Wood, Schoolgirl Costume, c.1925, 14 In.
$616

Theriault's

Doll, Wax Shoulder Head, Glass Eyes, Muslin Stitch-Jointed Body, England, c.1880, 27 In.
$1,232

Theriault's

Japanese, Takeda, Wood, Gofun Finish, Expressive Hands, Silk Hair, Kabuki Costume, 16 In..		798
Japanese, Warrior On Horse, Papier-Mache, Painted Features, Horsehair Tail, c.1920, 15 In...		228
Jumeau, Bebe, Bisque Head, Blue Glass Eyes, Blond Mohair, Composition, Silk Dress, 28 In. ...		4275
Jumeau, Bebe, Bisque Head, Brown Glass Eyes, Brunette Wig, Jointed, Silk Dress, 20 In.		3135
Jumeau, Bebe, Bisque Head, Brown Glass Eyes, Composition, Wood, Jointed, Size 10, 22 In......		3135
Jumeau, Bebe, Bisque Head, Brown Paperweight Eyes, Mohair, Sailor Dress, Size 1, 9 In.........		7125
Jumeau, Bebe, Bisque, Cafe-Au-Lait, Black Hair, Original Gown, Coins, Size 11, 24 In.............		3990
Jumeau, Bisque Head, Laughing, Crinkled Eyes, Composition, Mohair, c.1900, 20 In.		74100
Jumeau, Bisque Head, Paperweight Eyes, Closed Mouth, Pierced Ears, 1800s, 12 In.................		211
Jumeau, Bisque Socket Head, Amber Glass Eyes, Composition, Jointed, c.1878, 14 In.		4800
Jumeau, Bisque Socket Head, Composition & Wood Body, Depose Mark, c.1882, 25 In.		5700
Jumeau, Bisque Swivel Head, Blue Paperweight Eyes, Leather Gloved Hands, 1800s.................		878
Jumeau, Bisque Swivel Head, Pale Blue Inset Eyes, Mohair, Fashion Body, c.1875, 17 In.		7410
Jumeau, Dapper Gentleman, Bisque Swivel Head, Wood Body, Wool Coat, Top Hat, 20 In. *illus*		12540
Juro, Dick Clark, Bandstand, Vinyl Head, Fabric Body, Signed Jacket, Box, 1950s, 28 In.		173
K * R, 101, Marie, Bisque Socket Head, Blue Eyes, Pouty, Folk Costume, c.1909, 12 In.		896
K * R, 114, Gretchen, Bisque Socket Head, Blue Eyes, Coiled Braids, Folk Costume, 9 In.		672
K * R, 115A, Phillip, Bisque Socket Head, Sleep Eyes, Pouting, Hat, Toddler, 1912, 12 In.		1596
K * R, 192, Bisque Head, Fixed Eyes, Open Mouth, Teeth, Jointed, c.1890, 30 In........................		222
K * R, 717, Girl, Celluloid Head & Body, Open Mouth, Teeth, Mohair, Eyelet Dress, c.1900		300
K * R, Hans, Bisque Socket Head, Plump Pouty Face, Blond Mohair Bob, Ball-Jointed, 17 In.....		2128
K * R, Mein Liebling, Bisque Head, Brown Sleep Eyes, Brunette Mohair, Antique Dress, 26 In...		2520
K * R, Peter, Bisque Socket Head, Painted, Blue Eyes, Wood, Composition, Overalls, 18 In.		896
Kathe Kruse, 1613, Peasant Girl, Cloth, Pressed & Oil Painted Features, Pouty Lips, 17 In.......		4256
Kathe Kruse, Dutch Girl, Molded Oilcloth Head, Jointed, Human Hair, 1936, 17 In.................		1020
Kathe Kruse, Girl, Cloth Swivel Head, Painted, Human Hair Wig, Jointed, Pink Dress, 20 In...		1780
Kathe Kruse, Girl, Cloth, Oil Painted Face, Pouting, Blue Dress, Polka Dots, c.1945, 18 In.		1260
Kenner, Six Million Dollar Man, Red Jogging Suit, Elastic Cuff Sleeves, Box, 1975, 13 In.........		320
Kestner, 10, Bisque Head, Blue Glass Eyes, Blond Mohair Curls, Red Dress & Cape, 17 In.........		5700
Kestner, 221, Googly Toddler Girl, Bisque Head, Sleep Eyes, Composition, Pinafore, 14 In........		3640
Kestner, 221, Toddler, Bisque, Googly Eyes, Mohair Wig, Composition, Ball-Jointed, c.1912, 13 In.*illus*		3762
Kestner, Baby Jean, Bisque Socket Head, Composition, Bent Limb Body, c.1912, 11 In.......*illus*		336
Kestner, Bisque Head, Blue Glass Sleep Eyes, Mohair, Bisque Body, Child, c.1880, 6 In..........		3192
Kestner, Bisque Swivel Head, French Wrestler, Glass Eyes, Mohair Wig, 1880, 9 In.............		2280
Kestner, Bisque Swivel Head, Jointed, Mohair, Blue Boots, Pup On Pillow, 1885, 8 In.............		2052
Kestner, Hilda, 14, Bisque Head, Sculpted Forelock, 2 Upper Teeth, Bent Limb Baby, 18 In.......		1140
Kewpie dolls are listed in the Kewpie category.		
Kley & Hahn, 526, Bisque Head, Painted, Brunette Bob, Jointed, Velvet Suit, 14 In..............		1008
Kling, Woman, Bisque, Sculpted Wavy Hair, Dresden Flowers, Glass Eyes, Muslin, 13 In..........		448
KPM, Scottish Gentleman, Porcelain, Painted, Sculpted Hair, Muslin, Leather, 17 In.		21660
Kuhnlenz, Brown Bisque, Swivel Head, Glass Eyes, Mohair, Peg-Jointed, c.1890, 6 In. ....*illus*		672
Lenci, Aviatrix, Felt, Painted, Mohair Bob, Gray Jacket, Jodhpurs, Cap, c.1928, 16 In.		1008
Lenci, Boudoir, Felt, Swivel Head, Blond Mohair Curls, Roses, Slender Body, 1933, 20 In..........		2166
Lenci, Child, Felt, Swivel Head, Blond Mohair Wig, Jointed, Label, 1930s, 15 In. ....*illus*		456
Lenci, Clown, Felt, Black Swivel Head, Oil Paint, Googly Eyes, Ruffled Collar, c.1920, 13 In.		1368
Lenci, Cowboy, Felt, Big Nose, Side-Glancing Eyes, Costume, Fur Chaps, 1923, 18 In.		4480
Lenci, Dutch Girl, Felt, Muslin, Painted, Side-Glancing Googly Eyes, c.1935, 9 In..............*illus*		112
Lenci, Fashionable Girl, Felt, Painted, Blue Eyes, Pink Dress, Applied Flowers, c.1923, 13 In.		504
Lenci, Fashionable Girl, Felt, Painted, Long Blond Braids, Red Coat & Shoes, c.1935, 16 In.		784
Lenci, Felt, Swivel Head, Plump Cheeks, Forelock Curl, Pajamas, Candlestick, 1930, 17 In........		2964
Lenci, Flapper, Felt, Gish Face, Blond Bob, Long Limbs, Organdy Dress, c.1927, 24 In.		1792
Lenci, Flora, Felt, Swivel Head, Seated, Tiered Organdy Dress, Flower Wreath, c.1930, 35 In.		4200
Lenci, Girl, Felt, Swivel Head, Side-Glancing Eyes, Blond Mohair, Box, 1925, 23 In............*illus*		1254
Lenci, Little Annie Rooney, Felt, Swivel Head, Googly Eyes, Braided Pigtails, Broom, 9 In.........		741
Lenci, Mexican Boy, Felt, Painted, Pouty, Mohair, Braided Trousers, Jacket, Hat, 17 In.........		1456
Lenci, Pan, Felt, Wide Grin, Looped Wool Hair, Horns, Fantasy Costume, c.1929, 8 ½ In.		728
Lenci, Scottish Boy, Pouty, Felt, Swivel Head, Side-Glancing Eyes, c.1930, 17 In.		1254
Lenci, Skier, Felt, Swivel Head, Googly Eyes, Mohair Curls, Skis & Poles, 1933, 10 In.		456
Lenci, Toddler Girl, Felt, Pouty Cheeks, Ringlets, Organdy Dress & Bonnet, c.1935, 17 In.		784
Lenci, Torino Girl, Pressed Felt, Swivel Head, Lace Bonnet, Bird In Cage, 1930s, 20 In.		800

Doll, Wood, Carved, Bobbed Hair, Jointed, Painted, Huggler, Swiss, c.1930, 9 ½ In.

$392

Theriault's

Bread Head

Early Ravca dolls had heads made of French bread that was molded, then treated. Later the dolls were made with silk-stocking faces. Bernard Ravca (1904–1998) made the dolls in Paris from 1924 to 1939, when he moved to the United States. His wife, Frances, worked with him.

Doll Clothes, Dress, Hat, Green Silk, Box Pleats, Juliette Sleeves, Rose Silk Bow, c.1890, 16 In.

$672

Theriault's

This is an edited listing of current prices. Visit **Kovels.com** to check thousands of prices from previous years and sign up for free information on trends, tips, reproductions, marks, and more.

Doll Clothes, Sac Du Voyage, Carpetbag, Canvas, Leather Straps, Wood Handles, c.1875, 6 In.
$1,083

Theriault's

Doll Clothes, Shoes, Black Kidskin, Silk Rosettes, Bead Closure, Jumeau, c.1884, 2 ¼ In.
$1,120

Theriault's

Doorstop, Flowers, Dahlias, Multicolor, Basket, Handle, Hubley 204, 9 ⅜ In.
$118

Bertoia Auctions

Lenci, Wabi-Sabi, Japanese Girl, Felt, Swivel Head, Side-Glancing, Kimono, 1930s, 14 In.	685
Lenci, Woman, Series 250, Felt, Painted, Googly Eyes, O Mouth, Upswept Hair, Gown, 19 In.	1120
Leotine Rohmer, Wax Shoulder Head, Blue Enamel Eyes, Wooden Body, c.1858, 20 In.	3420
Liberty Boy, Porcelain Shoulder Head, Painted, Cloth, Composition, A.D.P. Mfg., 16 In.....*illus*	672
Madame Alexander, Binnie, Plastic, Blue Sleep Eyes, Honey Blond, Tag, 1954, 15 In.	140
Madame Alexander, Cissy, Brunette, 18 In.	450
Madame Alexander, Cissy, Plastic, 1950s, 21 In.	250
Madame Alexander, Godey, Wendy Face, Composition, Tags, 1946, 21 In.	700
Madame Alexander, Margaret O'Brien, Composition, Socket Head, Sleep Eyes, 21 In.	900
Madame Alexander, Marlo Thomas, That Girl, Black Hair, Sleep Eyes, Box, c.1965, 9 In.	65
Madame Alexander, Snow White, Composition, Black Human Hair Wig, 1940s, 18 In.	485
Madame Alexander, St. Patty's Day, Wendy, Plastic, Jointed, Red Hair, Freckles, Box, 8 In.	70
Madame Alexander, Susie Q, Mask Pressed Face, Side-Glancing Eyes, Yarn Hair, 13 In.	250
Man & Woman, Black Sateen, Stuffed, Fleece Hair, Costumes, c.1790, 23 In., Pair	399
Mannequin, Wood, Ball-Jointed, Ink Lettered Body Parts, Continental, c.1860, 20 In.......*illus*	1232
Marseille, Baby, Asian, Bisque, Painted Hair, Brown Eyes, Composition Body, Costume, 12 In.	672
Marseille, Baby, Googly, Bisque, Sculpted Topknot, Blue Side-Glancing Eyes, Gown, 9 In.	224
Marseille, Boy, Bisque Dome Head, Painted Hair & Face, Folklore Clothes, c.1912, 11 In.	228
Marseille, Just Me, Bisque Socket Head, Glass Eyes, Mohair Wig, Jointed, c.1926, 9 In.......*illus*	741
Marseille, Just Me, Girl, Bisque, Sleep Eyes, Mohair, Composition Toddler Body, Dress, 8 In.	672
Martha Chase, Cloth, Pressed & Oil Painted Face, Sculpted Hair, c.1910, 15 In.	1254
Martha Chase, Cloth Body, Pressed Face, Oil Paint, Cotton Sateen Body, c.1910, 17 In. ....*illus*	513
Mattel, Barbie, Bubble Cut, Blond, White Lips, Jacket & Shorts, Resort Set, No. 963, 1964-67	70
Mattel, Barbie, Bubble Cut, Brunette, American Airlines Stewardess, No. 984	120
Mattel, Barbie, Color Magic, Golden Hair, Diamond Print Swimsuit & Headband, 1966....*illus*	270
Mattel, Barbie, No. 1, Blond Ponytail, Swimsuit, Stand, Box, c.1958, 11 In..........................*illus*	3990
Mattel, Barbie, No. 3, Blond Ponytail, Black & White, Striped Swimsuit, Shoes, Sunglasses	225
Mattel, Barbie, No. 4, Brunette Ponytail, Solo In The Spotlight Dress, No. 982	375
Mattel, Barbie, No. 5, Blond Ponytail, Striped Swimsuit	70
Mattel, Barbie, No. 5, Blond Ponytail, Wedding Day Dress, No. 972	80
Mattel, Barbie, No. 6, Brunette Ponytail, Red Swimsuit	45
Morimura, Bisque Socket Head, Sleep Eyes, Open Mouth, Dimple, Japan, 20th Century, 18 In.	94
Nancy Ann Storybook, Style Show, Hard Plastic, Socket Head, Sleep Eyes, c.1950, 18 In..*illus*	171
Paper dolls are listed in their own category.	
Papier-Mache, Cobalt Blue Eyes, Mohair Wig, Fabric, Leather Arms & Legs, 14 ¾ In.	156
Papier-Mache, Shoulder Head, Glass Eyes, Painted Features, Stuffed, 1800s, 22 ½ In.	187
Papier-Mache, Shoulder Head, Molded Hair, Silk Bows, Painted Shoes, c.1840, 9 ½ In.	825
Parian, Bisque, Cloth, Molded Face & Hair, Long Gown, 1900s, 10 In.	50
Pincushion Dolls are listed in their own category.	
Porcelain, Lady, Painted, Sculpted Finger Curls, Muslin, Stitch-Jointed, Silk, 25 In.	6270
Porcelain, Plump Cheeks, Arms & Legs, Bare Feet, Painted Features, Mohair, c.1860, 27 In.	2166
Puppet, Hand, Morticia, Addams Family, Fabric Body, Vinyl Head, Bag, c.1965, 10 In.	338
Puppet, Marotte, Bisque Head, Round Body, Bone Handle, Jester Costume, c.1885, 13 In.	570
Rag, Lucille Ball, I Love Lucy, Stuffed Cloth, Plastic Face, Thread Hair, Apron, 1953, 28 In.	253
Rag, Oswald The Lucky Rabbit, Velveteen, Felt Ears, Glass Eyes, Cotton Tail, c.1931, 11 In.	4111
Rohmer, Porcelain Shoulder Head, Plump, Painted, Blond Mohair, Stuffed Kid, 17 In.	5895
Rohmer, Porcelain Shoulder Head, Plump Face, Painted, Fashion Body, c.1865, 16 In.	11400
Rohmer, Porcelain Swivel Head, Painted, Lamb's Wool Wig, Kid Body, Silk Gown, 18 In.	11400
Roxana Cole, Cloth, Muslin, Stitched & Painted Details, Stitch-Jointed, 1880s, 21 In., Pair	10830
S & H dolls are listed here as Simon & Halbig.	
S.F.B.J., 226, Sailor, Bisque Dome Head, Painted Hair, Glass Eyes, c.1912, 19 In.	969
S.F.B.J., 227, Boy, Bisque Socket Head, Glass Eyes, Painted Face, Composition, Jointed, c.1912, 14 In.*illus*	1482
S.F.B.J., Bluette, Bebe, Bisque, Mohair Wig, Jointed Composition & Wood, c.1907, 11 In.	1120
S.F.B.J., Woman, Bisque Head, Blue Glass Googly Side-Glancing Eyes, Costume, 8 In.	2016
Sailor, Whalebone, Inset Glass Eyes, Jointed, Hair, 1800s, 8 In.	1780
Schlaggenwald, Lady, Porcelain Head & Limbs, Painted, Human Hair, Muslin Body, 18 In.	2736
Schlaggenwald, Lady, Porcelain Shoulder Head & Limbs, Human Hair Curls, Gown, 26 In.	3135
Schmitt Et Fils, Bisque, Glass Eyes, Mohair, Jointed Wood, Composition, Eyelet Dress, 17 In.	6160
Schoenhut, Barney Google & Sparkplug, Googly Eyes, c.1923, 7 In.	448

Schoenhut, Boy, Wood, Carved, Pouty Lower Lip, Blond Wig, Spring-Jointed, 1911, 16 In.	5040
Schoenhut, Boy, Wood, Paint, Mohair, Jointed, Blue & White School Uniform, 17 In.	250
Schoenhut, Boy, Wood, Sculpted Hair, Blue Intaglio Eyes, Spring-Jointed, 1912, 16 In.	616
Schoenhut, Girl, Wood, Intaglio Eyes, Carved Braids & Bow, Spring-Jointed, c.1912, 16 In.	896
Schoenhut, Girl, Wood, Intaglio Eyes, Mohair Bob, Spring-Jointed, c.1912, 15 In.....illus	1008
Schoenhut, Girl, Wood, Intaglio Eyes, Spring-Jointed, Dotted Dress, c.1912, 16 In.	1120
Schoenhut, Japanese Man, Wood, Sculpted Hair, Spring-Jointed, Costume, 1920s, 15 ½ In.	4200
Schoenhut, Wood, Socket Head, Sculpted Braids, Painted Face, c.1912, 16 In.	1368
Schoneau & Hoffmeister, Nun, Bisque Head, Composition, Jointed, Habit, c.1900, 15 In.	684
Shirley Temple dolls are included in the Shirley Temple category.	
Simon & Halbig dolls are also listed here under S & H.	
Simon & Halbig, 9, Bisque Shoulder Head, Brown Glass Eyes, Freckles, Straw Hat, 24 In.	546
Simon & Halbig, 151, Bisque Head, Painted Eyes, Open Smile, Wood & Composition, 21 In.	5600
Simon & Halbig, 886, Bisque Swivel Head, Sleep Eyes, Blue Stockings, c.1890, 7 In.	798
Simon & Halbig, 886, Bisque, Swivel Head, Glass Sleep Eyes, Mohair Wig, c.1885, 9 In.	1938
Simon & Halbig, 905, Bisque, Glass Eyes, Mohair, Peg-Jointed, c.1890, Miniature.....illus	1568
Simon & Halbig, 949, Bisque Socket Head, Ball-Jointed, Composition & Wood, 11 In. .....illus	1232
Simon & Halbig, 1009, Black Boy, Bisque Head, Glass Eyes, Mohair Wig, Suit, 11 In.	672
Simon & Halbig, 1249, Bisque Head, Composition, Jointed, Human Hair, Sleep Eyes, 19 In.	1010
Simon & Halbig, 1329, Oriental, Bisque Head, Open Mouth, Teeth, Pierced Ears, 1900s,	761
Simon & Halbig, Asian Child, Bisque Head, Glass Sleep Eyes, Wood Body, c.1890, 21 In.	1938
Simon & Halbig, Bisque Head, Sleep Eyes, Mohair Wig, Gusset-Jointed, c.1890, 17 In.....illus	570
Simon & Halbig, Bisque Socket Head, Sleep Eyes, Open Mouth, Teeth, Wig, 1900s, 30 In.	129
Simon & Halbig, Bisque Swivel Head, Jointed, Sleep Eyes, Mohair Wig, 1885, 7 In.	2166
Simon & Halbig, Bisque Swivel Head, Sculpted Hair, Muslin Body, Gown, c.1874, 9 In.	1710
Simon & Halbig, Bisque Swivel Head, Sculpted Waves, Peg-Jointed, c.1875, 6 In.	2508
Simon & Halbig, Bisque Swivel Head, Twill Body, Glass Eyes, Mohair, c.1880, 10 In.	3534
Simon & Halbig, Bisque Swivel Head, Twill Over Wood Body, Jointed, c.1875, 11 In.	3420
Simon & Halbig, Blue Glass Eyes, Blond Human Hair Wig, Jointed Body, c.1905, 26 In.	1200
Simon & Halbig, Girl, Bisque, Sculpted, Painted, Pink Dress, Bare Feet, c.1870, 4 ½ In.	280
Sleeping Beauty, Bisque Head & Arms, Pale, Red Lips, Green Eyes, Black Mohair, c.1905	240
Sonneberg, 136, Bisque Head, Composition, Jointed, Glass Eyes, Human Hair, c.1885, 18 In.	2776
Steiner, Bebe Gigoteur, Bisque, Glass Eyes, Open Mouth, Clockwork, Cries Mama, 18 In.	2052
Steiner, Bebe Mascotte, Bisque Head, Paperweight Eyes, Dimple, Pierced Ears, c.1890, 26 In.	2691
Steiner, Bisque Head, Glass Eyes, Human Hair, Composition, Jointed, c.1890, 11 In.	1824
Steiner, Nun, Bisque Socket Head, Jointed Composition & Wood, Cloth Habit, 10 In.....illus	3248
Sweet Dolly, Sleep Eyes, Plastic Hair, 16 In.	34
Thuillier, Bisque Head, Glass Eyes, Blond Mohair, Composition, Wood, Velvet, 16 In.	13110
Unis, 301, Bebe, Bisque, Composition, Wood, Schoolgirl Costume, c.1925, 14 In. .....illus	616
Unis, Bluette, Bisque Head, Sleep Eyes, Teeth, Blond Curls, Jointed, 1930s, 11 In.	840
Walking, Baby, Bisque Dome Head, Painted, Carton Body, Hinged Legs, Germany, 11 In.	560
Walking, Carton Moule Head, Glass Eyes, Black Wig, Muslin Arms, Wooden Mechanism, 28 In.	3990
Wax Over Papier-Mache, Black Glass Eyes, Stuffed Muslin Body, Original Costume, 16 In.	912
Wax Shoulder Head, Glass Eyes, Muslin Stitch-Jointed Body, England, c.1880, 27 In. ....illus	1232
Wood, 1 Piece, Paint Over Gesso, Inset Eyes, Original Silk Gown, Continental, c.1790, 13 In.	1596
Wood, Carved, Bobbed Hair, Jointed, Painted, Huggler, Swiss, c.1930, 9 ½ In.....illus	392
Wood, Egg Shape Head, Painted Features, Human Hair Wig, Jointed Hips, 1772, 18 In.	11970
Zinner & Sohne, Acrobat, Bisque Shoulder Head, Spiral Wire Legs, Hoop, Tumbles, 10 In.	392

DOLL CLOTHES

Bonnet, Woven, Brown, Wide Brim, Blue Silk Ribbon, Bows, Flowers, c.1870, 5 In.	252
Coat, Boy's, Navy Velvet, 2 Rows Of Gold Buttons, Gold Stars On Cap, For 14-In. Doll	728
Coat, Cream Mohair, Round Collar, 3 Pearl Buttons, c.1890, For 24-In. Doll	336
Coin Purse, Doll's, Metal, Bronze Finish, Silk Ribbon, Medallion, France, 1878, 3 In.	570
Dress, Cream Pique Print, Red Embroidery, Pagoda Sleeves, c.1860, For 6-In. Doll	1680
Dress, Hat, Green Silk, Box Pleats, Juliette Sleeves, Rose Silk Bow, c.1890, 16 In.....illus	672
Evening Coat, Black Satin, Beads, Gold Silk Embroidery, Tassels, House Of Worth, 1910	627
Gown, Mauve Taffeta, Pleated Lace & Muslin Garlands, 2 Piece, For 13-In. Doll	784
Gown, Pale Green Silk, Ribbon Candy Ruching, Lace Collar, c.1859, For 21-In. Doll	504
Gown, Rose Silk, Sheer Crepe De Chine Overlay, Pouffed Sleeves, Rose Bands, c.1870	1026
Pinafore, Blue Chambray, Flared, White Blouse Underneath, For 15-In. Doll	280

Doorstop, Frog, Sitting On Mushroom, Green, Yellow, 4 ½ In.
$600

Bertoia Auctions

Doorstop, Nude Child, Reaching, Signed, Ella Rood Studios, Whitman, Mass., 17 In.
$1,652

Bertoia Auctions

Doorstop, Ship, 3-Masted, Cannon Portals, Cross Cutout, Footed, Iron, 9 ½ x 9 In.
$65

Ruby Lane

Doulton, Pitcher, Bitter Must Be The Cup, Profile, Leaves, Tan, 9 In.
$30

Norman Heckler & Company

Doulton, Vase, Storks & Bats, Salt Glaze, Lambeth, c.1895, c20 In., Pair
$3,750

Heritage Auctions

Dresden, Plate, Portrait, Auguste Strobl, Raised Gilt, Enamel Border, Klemm, 1900s, 6 In.
$360

Cowan's Auctions

Sac Du Voyage, Carpetbag, Canvas, Leather Straps, Wood Handles, c.1875, 6 In..............*illus*	1083
Shoes, Black Kidskin, Silk Rosettes, Bead Closure, Jumeau, c.1884, 2 1/4 In. ....*illus*	1120
Shoes, Boots, Tan Leather, Grommets, Twisted Laces, Pompom, c.1885, 2 3/4 In.	392
Shoes, Cream Kidskin, Silk Rosettes, Leather Soles, Marked, Bru Jne Paris 5, 2 1/2 In.	741
Shoes, Cream Kidskin, Twill Edges, Silk Rosettes, Silver Butterflies, c.1880, 2 1/2 In...............	280
Suit, Young Man's, Tan Linen, Velvet Collar, Patterned Vest, c.1820, 24-In. Jacket	560

DONALD DUCK *items are included in the Disneyana category.*

DOORSTOPS have been made in all types of designs. The vast majority of the doorstops sold today are cast iron and were made from about 1890 to 1930. Most of them are shaped like people, animals, flowers, or ships. Reproductions and newly designed examples are sold in gift shops.

2 Footmen Joined, Red & Gold Jackets, Painted, Cast Iron, Hubley, c.1920, 12 In.....................	1422
Angel, Wings, Trumpet, Running, 17 In.	63
Aunt Jemima, Cast Iron, 11 3/4 In.	120
Baseball, Pitcher, Batter, Catcher, Painted, Cast Iron, 7 x 6 1/4 In.	480
Biplane, Green, Red, White & Blue Tail, Cast Iron, c.1920, 8 1/2 x 18 In.	584
Black Man, Seated On Cotton Bale, Top Hat, White Shirt, Cast Iron, c.1920, 9 x 7 In.	1541
Boy With Pail & Pole, Painted, Cast Iron, 12 1/2 In.	18
Butler, Formal Attire, Standing, Parquet Floor, Cast Iron, Paint, c.1920, 12 In.	1422
Cat, Siamese, Sitting, Blue Eyes, Black, White, 10 1/2 In.	375
Cat, Sitting, Black Paint, Cast Iron, Hubley, 9 1/2 In.	144
Cat, Sitting, Flat, Greenblatt, Boston, Ma., 1927-49, 9 In.	468
Cats, Sitting, Composition, 5 1/2 In.	111
Clown, Bent Over Laughing, Red Costume, White Fluted Collar, Cast Iron, 10 In.	677
Clown, Flat Back, Pleated Collar, Hat, Full Body, Square Base, Cast Iron, c.1920, 10 In.	1422
Dog, Basset Hound, Brass, c.1920, 7 x 11 In.	95
Dog, Boston Terrier, Painted, Leather Collar, Iron, 10 1/2 In.	207
Dog, German Shephard, Cast Iron, 12 In..	94
Dog, Whippet, Lying Down, Iron, 27 1/4 x 12 In.	2040
Duck, Walking, Top Hat, Yellow, Cast Iron, c.1920, 8 x 4 1/4 In.	535
Flamingo, Green Leaves, Cast Iron, 10 1/4 In.	570
Flower, Urn, Purple, Yellow, Green, Iron, 7 In., Pair	250
Flowers, Dahlias, Multicolor, Basket, Handle, Hubley 204, 9 3/8 In. ....*illus*	118
Flowers, Poppies & Daisies, Yellow, White & Pink, Blue Vase, Iron, Hubley, 7 In...........	118 to 120
Fox, Brass Over Iron, England, 10 In..	155
Frog, Sitting On Mushroom, Green, Yellow, 4 1/2 In. ....*illus*	600
Gnome, Full Figure, Cast Iron, 10 5/8 In.	164
Heron, Perched, Red, Yellow, Green, Cast Iron, 1900s, 8 x 5 In.	267
Horse, Standing, Reins, Black & White Paint, Cast Iron, Hubley, 10 In.	266
Huck Finn, Multicolor, Cast Iron, Littco, 1920s, 13 In.	175
Lighthouse, Cape Hatteras, Painted Metal, Molded Base, c.1925, 21 x 9 In.	1541
Little Red Riding Hood, Wolf, 1920s, 7 1/2 In..	585
Lobster, Red, Cast Iron, 9 In..	840
Mammy, Hubley, 9 In..	321
Mouse, Sitting Up, Painted, Shaped Base, Felt-Lined Bottom, Cast Iron, c.1905, 4 In.	60
Nude Child, Reaching, Signed, Ella Rood Studios, Whitman, Mass., 17 In......................*illus*	1652
Old Salt, Yellow Rainsuit, 15 In...	480
Owl, Painted, Cast Iron, Bradley & Hubbard, 15 3/4 In..	1169
Owl, On Branch, Cast Iron, 8 3/4 In.	527
Peter Rabbit, Carrot, Blue Overalls, Cast Iron, 8 1/2 x 5 In..	178
Rabbit, Seated On Log, Cast Iron, Bradley & Hubbard, c.1920, 15 x 8 In.............................	2370
Rabbit, Top Hat & Tails, Painted, Green Grassy Dome Base, Cast Iron, 1920, 10 In....................	1422
Rooster, Ball, Stepped Square Base, Composite, 13 In.	13
Rooster, Crowing, Cast Iron, 10 In.	222
Santa Maria, Multicolor, Cast Iron, 11 3/4 In.	72
Ship, 3-Masted, Cannon Portals, Cross Cutout, Footed, Iron, 9 1/2 x 9 In..........................*illus*	65

Shoe, Iron, Black Paint, J.R. Palmenberg's Sons, 1900s, 6 ½ x 10 In., Pair	450
Snooper Man, Painted, Early 1900s, 13 ¼ In.	600
Southern Belle, Salmon Colored Dress, Iron, 11 ½ In.	60
Street Singers, Trio, Multicolor, 8 In.	335
Swan, White, Green, 15 ¼ In.	780
Victorian Woman, Flower Basket, Square Base, Paint, Cast Iron, B&H, c.1900, 11 In.	240
Winnie The Pooh, Seated, Arms Above Head, Resin, Paint, c.1975, 21 x 12 In.	145

DOULTON pottery and porcelain were made by Doulton and Co. of Burslem, England, after 1882. The name *Royal Doulton* appeared on the company's wares after 1902. Other pottery by Doulton is listed under Royal Doulton.

Biscuit Jar, Tan Cranes, Lake, Brown Ground, Silver Plated Lid, Burslem, 6 ⅜ In.	48
Ewer, Dragon Handle, Burslem, 15 ½ In.	187
Ewer, Flowers, Green Leaves, 8 In.	62
Pitcher, Bitter Must Be The Cup, Profile, Leaves, Tan, 9 In. *illus*	30
Punch Bowl, Blue, White, Transfer, Flowers, Stripes, Burslem, 14 In.	60
Vase, Cattle, Incised, H. Barlowe, 18 ¼ In.	885
Vase, Center Band, Grazing Horses, Tan, Blue, Hannah Barlow, Lambeth, 11 ¼ In., Pair	3000
Vase, Center Band, Grazing Horses, Tan, Olive Green, Hannah Barlow, Lambeth, 9 ½ In.	600
Vase, Gold, Dark Blue, Swirls, 3 Handles, 3-Footed, 6 ¾ In.	150
Vase, Storks & Bats, Salt Glaze, Lambeth, c.1895, 20 In., Pair *illus*	3750

DRESDEN and Meissen porcelain are often confused. Porcelains were made in the town of Meissen, Germany, beginning about 1706. The town of Dresden, Germany, has been home to many decorating studios since the early 1700s. Blanks were obtained from Meissen and other porcelain factories. Some say porcelain was also made in Dresden in the early years. Decorations on Dresden are often similar to Meissen, and marks were copied. Some of the earliest books on marks confused Dresden and Meissen, and that has remained a problem ever since. The Meissen "AR" mark and crossed swords mark are among the most forged marks on porcelain. Meissen pieces are listed in this book under Meissen. German porcelain marked "Dresden" is listed here. Irish Dresden and Dresden made in East Liverpool, Ohio, are not included in this section.

Bowl, European Town Scene, Bouquets, Putti Raising Goblet Finial, 1890, 18 x 16 In.	3000
Compote, Pierced Basket, Dancing Putti, Flowers, Gilt Feet, Round Base, c.1900, 28 In.	2040
Figurine, Cat, White, Brown & Gray Spots, 12 ¼ x 6 ¼ In.	357
Figurine, Monkey, Holding Apple, Flowers, 16 x 10 ½ In.	826
Figurine, Monkey, White, Stump, Eating Apple, Flowering Vines, 16 x 11 In.	1708
Gravy Boat, Tray, Flower Sprays, 12 x 12 ½ In.	98
Group, 4 Winged Angels, Birds Escaping Cage, 10 x 9 ½ In.	281
Group, Courting Couple, Red Coat, Side Table, 6 In.	38
Pin Tray, Dog, Terrier, Seated, Figural, Black & White, Gold Trim, c.1950, 3 x 2 In.	150
Plate, Portrait, Auguste Strobl, Raised Gilt, Enamel Border, Klemm, 1900s, 6 In. *illus*	360
Plate, Portrait, Woman, Hat, Gilt Rim, Multicolor, 9 ⅝ In.	163
Vase, Gilt, Blue, Tapers, 11 ¼ In.	313
Vase, Mossware, Applied Flowers & Putti, 8 ½ In., Pair *illus*	120
Vase, Portrait, Gilt, Blue, Handles, 11 In.	593
Vase, Portrait, Woman, Gilt, Teal, Handles, Round Foot, 9 In.	1500
Vase, Reticulated Lattice, Applied Pink & White Flowers, 20 x 10 ¼ In.	595

DUNCAN & MILLER is a term used by collectors when referring to glass made by the George A. Duncan and Sons Company or the Duncan and Miller Glass Company. These companies worked from 1893 to 1955, when the use of the name *Duncan* was discontinued and the firm became part of the United States Glass Company. Early patterns may be listed under Pressed Glass.

Box, Clematis, 4 ¾ x 3 ¾ In. *illus*	17
Cane & Arch, Punch Bowl, Scalloped Rim, Sawtooth Edge, 1930s, 7 x 14 In.	225

Dresden, Vase, Mossware, Applied Flowers & Putti, 8 ½ In., Pair
$120

Cowan's Auctions

Duncan & Miller, Box, Clematis, 4 ¾ x 3 ¾ In.
$17

Martin Auction Co.

Durand, Vase, Gold Luster, Applied Webbing, Iridescent Red, Flared Neck, 7 In.
$259

Early Auction Company

Durant Kilns, Bowl, Blue Volcanic Glaze, Funnel Shape, Signed, 1915, 5 ¾ x 15 In.
$110

Rago Arts and Auction Center

D

Enamel, Bowl, Copper, Standing Figure, Fish, Sailing, Karl Drerup, Signed, 2 x 7¼ In.
$438

Rago Arts and Auction Center

Enamel, Charger, Giraffes, Elephants, Zebras, Copper, Signed, Edward Winter, 1939, 17 In.
$1,125

Rago Arts and Auction Center

Enamel, Plaque, Multicolor, Geometrics, Arthur Ames, Frame, c.1965, 12 x 14 In.
$1,125

Los Angeles Modern Auctions

TIP

If there are raised applied decorations on your art glass, be careful when cleaning it. Gold or silver accents, painted enamel decoration, and beads must be kept in fine condition to maintain the value.

Canterbury, Vase, Blue Opalescent, Fluted, Ruffled Rim, 4 x 4 In.	25
Caribbean, Pitcher, Wavy Swirl, Sapphire Blue, Shaped Rim, 1930s, 6 In.	250
Compote, White Stem, Clear Glass, c.1885, 8 In.	28
Daisy & Button, Bowl, Fruit, Amberette, Paneled, Petal Rim, 1800s, 9 In.	95
Daisy & Button, Pitcher, Amberette, Paneled, Scalloped Rim, 1800s, 8 In.	200
Festive, Punch Bowl Set, Cobalt Blue Handles, Underplate, Ladle, 12 Cups	60
First Love, Cocktail Shaker, Clear, Etched, Cylindrical, 1930s, 7 In.	190
Hobnail, Bowl, Salad, Blue Opalescent, Beaded Edge, 1940s, 12 In.	89
Mardi Gras, Nut Dish, Sawtooth Edge, c.1900, 3 x 7 In.	99
Sandwich, Plate, Deviled Egg, Round, 12 Eggs, c.1940, 12 In. Diam.	85
Sanibel, Bowl, Shell Shape, Opalescent Canary Yellow, 10 x 13 In.	135
Shell & Tassel, Compote, Lid, Shell Finial, Square Shape, 1800s, 9 x 5 In.	160
Sylvan, Centerpiece, Pink Opalescent, Blue Swirl, Lobed, 1930s, 4 x 12 In.	95
Teardrop, Pitcher, Clear, Bulbous, Ice Guard Lip, C-Scroll Handle, 1930s, 9 In.	110
Three Feathers, Vase, Cornucopia, Blue Opalescent, 1930s, 8½ In.	95

DURAND art glass was made from 1924 to 1931. The Vineland Flint Glass Works was established by Victor Durand and Victor Durand Jr. in 1897. In 1924 Martin Bach Jr. and other artisans from the Quezal glassworks joined them at the Vineland, New Jersey, plant to make Durand art glass. They called their gold iridescent glass Gold Luster.

Bowl, Gold Luster, Turned-Out Rim, Stretch Border, Green Iridescent, Signed, 14 In.	200
Candlestick, Cobalt Blue & Green, Opal Feathering, 3 x 5 In.	575
Jar, Iridescent Blue, Matching Lid, Amber Finial, Signed, 7 In.	259
Jar, Lid, Shouldered, Gold Iridescent, Signed, 10 In.	460
Lamp Base, Gold Luster Shouldered Body, Iridescent Spider Webbing, 19 In.	144
Lamp, Gold Torchiere Shade, Iridescent Spider Webbing, Metal & Black Marble Base, 66 In.	690
Lamp, Pulled Feathers, Luster Glass, Metal Mount, 1910, 29 In.	1375
Vase, Beehive, Blue Iridescent, 6 Horizontal Rims, Signed, c.1930, 6½ In.	351
Vase, Blue Pulled Feather, Orange Flecks, Golden Threading, Gold Aurene Foot, 13 In.	944
Vase, Cut Glass, Geometric, Amethyst, 8½ In.	201
Vase, Genie Bottle, Gold Luster, Signed, 15½ In.	604
Vase, Gold Iridescent, Random Opaque White Pulled Decoration, Signed, 4¾ In.	142
Vase, Gold Luster, Applied Webbing, Iridescent Red, Flared Neck, 7 In. *illus*	259
Vase, Gold Luster, Inverted Rim, Applied Iridescent Spider Webbing, Signed, 10 In.	230
Vase, Gold Luster, Round Foot, 5 In.	143
Vase, Iridescent Blue, Narrow Neck, Footed, 9½ In.	201
Vase, King Tut, Green & Gold Iridescent, Inverted Saucer Foot, 11¼ In.	1185
Vase, King Tut, Lady Gay Rose, Gold Decoration, c.1930, 18¼ In.	1053
Vase, King Tut, Opal Coiled Pattern In Iridescent Gold, Signed, 15 x 9 In.	1955
Vase, Opal Ground, Gold & Blue Hearts, Spider Webbing, Signed, c.1930, 5 In.	117
Vase, Translucent, Green Peacock Design, Shouldered, Footed, 6¾ In.	288

Durant

DURANT KILNS was founded by Jean Durant Rice in 1910 in Bedford Village, New York. He hired Leon Volkmar to oversee production. The pottery made both tableware and artware. Rice died in 1919, leaving Leon Volkmar to run the business. After 1930 the name Durant Kilns was changed and only the Volkmar mark was used.

Bowl, Blue Volcanic Glaze, Funnel Shape, Signed, 1915, 5¾ x 15 In. *illus*	110
Plate, Gold, Volkmar, 9½ In.	118
Plate, Leon Volkmar, Gold Luster Over Mustard Glaze, Chain Link Border, c.1919, 9½ In.	115

ELVIS PRESLEY, the well-known singer, lived from 1935 to 1977. He became famous by 1956. Elvis appeared on television, starred in 27 movies, and performed in Las Vegas. Memorabilia from any of the Presley shows, his records, and even memorials made after his death are collected.

Folio Page, Photo, Black & White, Signed, Mat, Frame, 1957, 19 x 22 In.	1531
Guitar, 4-String, Styron, Purple Marble, Silver Luster, Strap, Signature, 1957, 32 In.	173

D

Record, All Shook Up, RCA, 45 RPM, 1957		10
Trading Card, Gum, Color Photos, Text, 1956, 3 x 4 In., Set Of 65		230

ENAMELS listed here are made of glass particles and other materials heated and fused to metal. In the eighteenth and nineteenth centuries, workmen from Russia, France, England, and other countries made small boxes and table pieces of enamel on metal. One form of English enamel is called *Battersea* and is listed under that name. There was a revival of interest in enameling in the 1930s and a new style evolved. There is now renewed interest in the artistic enameled plaques, vases, ashtrays, and jewelry. Enamels made since the 1930s are usually on copper or steel, although silver was often used for jewelry. Graniteware is a separate category, and enameled metal kitchen pieces may be included in the Kitchen category. Cloisonne is a special type of enamel and is listed in its own category.

Bonbonniere, Hand Painted, People On Coast, England, Late 1700s, 3 ¼ x 1 ¾ In.		875
Bowl, Copper, Standing Figure, Fish, Sailing, Karl Drerup, Signed, 2 x 7 ¼ In.	*illus*	438
Bowl, Elongated Oval, Red Swirl, Gold Mottle, Black, Copper, c.1962, 9 x 5 In.		175
Bowl, Gilt Bronze, Hand Painted, Fin De Siecle, France, Late 1800s, 16 ¼ x 12 ¾ In.		3250
Box, Sewing, Round Body, Hinged Lid, Portrait Of Edwardian Lady, Velvet Interior, 2 x 4 In.		86
Casket, Silver, Red & Blue, Gold Washed Interior, Rudolf Vyurst, Russia, c.1891, 2 ⅝ In.		7995
Charger, Giraffes, Elephants, Zebras, Copper, Signed, Edward Winter, 1939, 17 In.	*illus*	1125
Cigarette Case, Oval Panel, Couple, Blue, White, Beading, Gilt Trim, c.1925, 4 x 2 In.		330
Font, Holy Water, Green Onyx, Champleve, France, Early 1900s, 13 x 8 ½ In.		1250
Picture Frame, Champleve, Brass & Glass, Early 1900s, 9 x 9 ¾ x 3 ¼ In.		406
Plaque, Abstract, Circles, Vertical Stripes, Blue, Red, Yellow, Virgil Cantini, 1971, 30 x 9 In.		2499
Plaque, Multicolor, Geometrics, Arthur Ames, Frame, c.1965, 12 x 14 In.	*illus*	1125
Plaque, Orchids & Hummingbirds, Copper, Wood Frame, France, Early 1900s, 15 In., Pair		3750
Salt, Open, Flowers, Leaves, Panels, Round Foot, c.1910, 1 ½ x 2 ½ In.		1230
Salt, Red, White, Spoon, 1 ¼ In., 2 Pair		50
Tazza, People, Animals, Forest, Round Foot, Portrait Medallions, 5 In.		1375
Teapot, Dragon, Teal Ground, Korea, 1900s, 6 ½ In.		37
Tray, Pansy, Multicolor, White Ground, Piero Fornasetti, Italy, 1950s, 23 ½ In.		244
Vase, Copper, Lid, Woman & Unicorn, Camille Faure, France, 16 x 8 In.	*illus*	6250

ERPHILA is a mark found on Czechoslovakian and other pottery and porcelain made after 1920. This mark was used on items imported by Ebeling & Reuss, Philadelphia, a giftware firm that was founded in 1866 and out of business sometime after 2002. The mark is a combination of the letters *E* and *R* (Ebeling & Reuss) and the first letters of the city, Phila(delphia). Many whimsical figural pitchers and creamers, figurines, platters, and other giftwares carry this mark.

Dresser Box, Doll, Green, Madame Pompadour, 6 ½ In.		125
Figurine, Horse, Leaping, Blanc De Chine, Gray Spots		18
Pitcher, Toucan, Red Beak, Black, Cream, 1930s, 6 x 5 In.	*illus*	55
Teapot, Cat, Tan, Black, Red Ribbon, 8 In.		125
Teapot, Dog, Brown, Black, 8 In.		125
Teapot, Dog, White, Black Spots, Red Bow, 1920-40, 7 ½ In.		168
Vase, Nudes, Women, 4 Panels, Cream, 10 x 4 ¾ In.		18

ES GERMANY porcelain was made at the factory of Erdmann Schlegelmilch from 1861 to 1937 in Suhl, Germany. The porcelain, marked *ES Germany* or *ES Suhl*, was sold decorated or undecorated. Other pieces were made at a factory in Saxony, Prussia, and are marked *ES Prussia*. Reinhold Schlegelmilch made the famous wares marked *RS Germany*.

Cake Plate, White Iridescent Border, Woman With Flower, 11 In.		47
Game Plate, Grouse, Meadow, Shaped, Multicolor, 1900s, 11 ½ In.	*illus*	100
Plate, Gold, English Ivy Rim, Women In Garden, Cupid, 9 ½ In.		425

Enamel, Vase, Copper, Lid, Woman & Unicorn, Camille Faure, France, 16 x 8 In.
$6,250

Rago Arts and Auction Center

Erphila, Pitcher, Toucan, Red Beak, Black, Cream, 1930s, 6 x 5 In.
$55

Hudson Valley Auctions

ES Germany, Game Plate, Grouse, Meadow, Shaped, Multicolor, 1900s, 11 ½ In.
$100

Ruby Lane

Eskimo, Sculpture, Carved Wood, Inuit Man, Holding Fish, Square Base, 1961, 10½ in.
$246

Cowan's Auctions

Eskimo, Sculpture, Man, Standing, Hooded Coat, Inuit, 11 In.
$700

Ruby Lane

Eskimo, Snow Goggles, Carved Wood, Slits, Child's, c.1925, 5 x 1¼ In.
$127

Allard Auctions

ESKIMO artifacts of all types are collected. Carvings of whale or walrus teeth are listed under Scrimshaw. Baskets are in the Basket category. All other types of Eskimo art are listed here. In Canada and some other areas, the term Inuit is used instead of Eskimo.

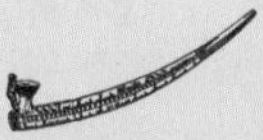

Basket, Lid, Flowers, Red, Pink, Green, c.1925, 8½ x 11½ In.	100
Blanket, Mountain Goat Wool, Tan, Black, Cedar Bark Fringe, c.1900, 45 x 63 In.	12000
Book Holder, Walrus Heads, Inked Eyes, 16⅛ x 11¼ In.	546
Book Holder, Walrus Heads, Inked Eyes, Male, Female, Sturgeon, Polar Bear, 13 x 11½ In.	1840
Box, Walrus Tusk, Blue Stone, 4 In.	720
Cane Handle, Carved Antler, 2 Stylized Eskimos, Holding On To Shaft, 1800s, 4 x 3 In.	948
Cribbage Board, Ivory, Beluga Whales, Polar Bears, 1900s, 1 x 12 In.	316
Cribbage Board, Ivory, Hunter, Polar Bears, Dog, Ellie Kulrh, c.1950, 4¾ x 30 In.	920
Cribbage Board, Ivory, Walrus, People, Boat, 1900s, 2 x 11½ In.	402
Cribbage Board, Walrus Tusk, Seal Shape, Decoration, 2 Pegs, 9½ x 1½ In.	460
Doll, Bone, Wood, Ink Painted Features, Hide & Fur Costume, Kid Mittens, c.1910, 6 In., Pair..	114
Doll, Carved Wood, Painted, Hide Clothes, Boots, 8¾ In.	95
Doll, Cedarwood, Sealskin Moccasins, Red Tunic, c.1900, 14 In.	172
Doll, Sealskin, Boots, Mitts, Carved Wooden Face, Cloth Clothing, 1900-25, 10½ In.	258
Drum, Round, Hide, Carved Wood Handle, Frame, Paint, Animal, c.1890, 26 x 15 In.	2400
Figure, Eskimo In Kayak, Wood, Carved, Kidskin Jacket, Bone Accents, c.1910, 26 In.	285
Figurine, Eskimo, Bird, Stone, 4¾ In.	100
Figurine, Man Fishing, Jade, 3½ x 3 In.	123
Knife, Snow, Bone, Curved Blade, Notched Handle, Circles & Lines, 2 x 11 In.	1304
Sculpture, 3 Walruses, 5½ In.	62
Sculpture, Carved Wood, Inuit Man, Holding Fish, Square Base, 1961, 10½ in. ....*illus*	246
Sculpture, Man, Standing, Hooded Coat, Inuit, 11 In. ....*illus*	700
Sculpture, Standing Man, 1 Hand Behind Back, Kaka Ashoona, Stone, 17 In.	600
Snow Goggles, Bone, Humans, Walruses, 1900-20s, 5¼ x 2¼ In.	1725
Snow Goggles, Carved Wood, Slits, Child's, c.1925, 5 x 1¼ In. ....*illus*	127
Totem Pole, Wood, Green, Red & Black Paint, 4 Figures, Tlingit, c.1900, 27 In.	1968
Totem Pole, Wood, Paint, Mosquito, Frog, Human Face, Blue, Tlingit, c.1915, 16 In.	1440
Totem Pole, Wood, Spread Wing Thunderbird, Creature, Multicolor Paint, c.1910, 15 In.	780
Tusk, Ivory, Etched, Inked, Northern Scenes, Multicolor, 1980s, 1 x 15 In.	546

 FABERGE was a firm of jewelers and goldsmiths founded in St. Petersburg, Russia, in 1842, by Gustav Faberge. Peter Carl Faberge, his son, was jeweler to the Russian Imperial Court from about 1870 to 1917. The rare Imperial Easter eggs, jewelry, and decorative items are very expensive today.

Creamer, Silver, Tapered Cylinder, Matte Finish, c.1890, 3½ In.	998
Goblet, Xenia, Cut To Clear, Multicolor, 8⅜ In., 6 Piece	400
Vase, Globular, Meandering Swags, Flat Rim, Narrow Mouth, Signed, Box, 8 x 9 In.	83

FAIENCE refers to tin-glazed earthenware, especially the wares made in France, Germany, and Scandinavia. It is also correct to say that faience is the same as majolica or Delft, although usually the term refers only to the tin-glazed pottery of the three regions mentioned.

Bowl, Flowers, Green, Blue, Orange, c.1800, 12 In.	61
Cachepot, Flowers, Pink, Purple, Bugs, Scalloped Rim, Handles, France, 4¾ x 12 In.......*illus*	59
Centerpiece, Oval Basin, Molded Mask, Serpent, Mythological, Double Dolphin, 16 x 19 In.	250
Jar, Lid, Cobalt Blue Lobed Cartouches, Yellow, Brown, Green, 1900, 5½ In.	132
Plate, Shaped, Armorial, Blue, Green, Red, Flowers, Leaves, 11½ In.	38
Platter, Shepherds, Landscape, Blue, White, Italy, 23 x 15½ In.	100
Portrait Plate, Vendeenne, Initialed On Back, M.C., Tiny Chip, 10⅜ In.	12
Sculpture, Horse Head, White Crackle Glaze, Faux Marble Plinth, 28 x 12 In.	185
Sculpture, Rooster, White, Italy, 29 x 17 In.	225
Sculpture, Turquoise Glaze, Putti Standing On Dolphin, Holding Shell, 24¼ In., Pair	5000
Tile, Circular, Blue Peacock, Yellow Background, 5⅜ In.	345
Tile, Circular, Mission, Rich Matte Glazes, Yellow & Blue & Red, 5⅜ In.	345
Vase, Moon Flask, Bird, Branch, Flowers, Multicolor, c.1880, 12 In.	2000

FAIRINGS are small souvenir boxes and figurines that were sold at country fairs during the nineteenth century. Most were made in Germany. Reproductions of fairings are being made, especially of the famous *Twelve Months after Marriage* series.

Box, Boy, Sitting In Boat, Shell Border, 2¾ In.	25
Box, Cradle, Baby Dresser, Flower Lid, Staffordshire, c.1875, 2 x 2 x 3 In.	52
Box, Dog, Lying On Grass, Basket Weave, 19th Century, 3½ x 1¾ In.	75
Box, Girl Holding Basket, Dog, Porcelain, 1800s, 4½ x 3 In.	145
Box, Woman's Hand, Holding Box, Blue & Orange Trim, Conte & Boheme, c.1890, 3 In.	75
Box, Monkey Playing Drum, Tassels, Porcelain, Staffordshire, c.1876, 4 x 3 In.	65
Box, Tea Set, Shell Border, 2¾ In.	20
Box, Twelve Months After Marriage, Woman In Bed, Man Holding Baby, 3⅜ In.	90
Box, Vanity, Framed Cameos, Woman With Fan, Victorian, 4 In.	60
Dresser Box, Clock, 2 Urns, Numbered, 2¼ In.	45
Figurine, Old Woman With Children, In Shoe, Bisque, 2⅛ In.	22
Figurine, Pigs, In Green Car, Germany, c.1910, 3½ x 2 In.	85
Ring Box, Kissing Pigeons, Nest, On Dresser, c.1895, 2⅛ x 1½ x 2 In.	90
Trinket Box, Shells, Burgundy, Light Blue, Dogs, Rabbit, Staffordshire, 3 x 1½ In.......*illus*	50

FAIRYLAND LUSTER *pieces are included in the Wedgwood category.*

FAMILLE ROSE, *see Chinese Export category.*

FANS have been used for cooling since the days of the ancients. By the eighteenth century, the fan was an accessory for the lady of fashion and very elaborate and expensive fans were made. Sticks were made of ivory or wood, set with jewels or carved. The fans were made of painted silk or paper. Inexpensive paper fans printed with advertising were giveaways in the late nineteenth and early twentieth centuries. Electric fans were introduced in 1882.

Advertising, French Theater, People, Landscape, 16¼ In.	192
Bone, Engraved Paper, Empress Matilda, Frame, France, c.1850, 17 x 24 In. ....*illus*	562
Electric, Robbins & Myers, Brass Tone, 19 x 16¾ In.	184
Folding, 18th Century Figures, Reticulated Mother-Of-Pearl, Paint, Gilt, Shadowbox, 28 In.	244
Folding, Grecian Scenes, Reticulated Mother-Of-Pearl, Gilt, Ormolu, Shadowbox, 18 In.	488
Folding, Paper, Pink Border, Reserves, Figures, Frame, 19 In.	213
Mother-Of-Pearl, Gauze, Birds, Flowers, 25½ In.	120
Sandalwood, Figural Landscape, Carved, 18 In.	390
Silk, Bone, 4 Cartouches, Pink, Blue, Beige, Yellow, 20 In.	270
Silk, Bone, Exotic Bird, 15½ In.	390
Silk, Bone, Young Woman, Cherubs, Blue, Brown, 17¼ In.	132
Silk, Silver, Multicolor, Frame, 23 In.	138
Wood, Painted, Portrait, Dancers, Linen, Flowers, 9 x 16½ In.	35

FAST FOOD COLLECTIBLES *may be included in several categories, such as Advertising, Coca-Cola, Toy, etc.*

FEDERZEICHNUNG, *see Loetz category.*

FENTON ART GLASS COMPANY was founded in 1905 in Martins Ferry, Ohio, by Frank L. Fenton and his brother, John W. Fenton. They painted decorations on glass blanks made by other manufacturers. In 1907 they opened a factory in Williamstown, West Virginia, and began making glass. The company stopped making art glass in 2011 and assets were sold. A new division of the company makes handcrafted glass beads and other jewelry. Copies are being made from leased original Fenton molds by an unrelated company, Fenton's Collectibles. The copies are marked with the Fenton mark and Fenton's Collectibles mark. Fenton is noted for early carnival glass produced between 1907 and 1920. Some of these pieces are listed in the Carnival Glass category. Many other types of glass were also made. Spanish Lace in this section refers to the pattern made by Fenton.

Acorn, Bowl, Flared Ruffled Edge, Blue Iridescent, 7½ x 2 In.	80

Faience, Cachepot, Flowers, Pink, Purple, Bugs, Scalloped Rim, Handles, France, 4¾ x 12 In.
$59

Ruby Lane

Fairing, Trinket Box, Shells, Burgundy, Light Blue, Dogs, Rabbit, Staffordshire, 3 x 1½ In.
$50

Ruby Lane

Fan, Bone, Engraved Paper, Empress Matilda, Frame, France, c.1850, 17 x 24 In.
$562

New Orleans Auction Galleries

Top Ten Fenton Patterns
Hundreds of thousands of users visit our website, Kovels.com, each month. The Fenton patterns that are the most popular among our visitors are:

1. Coin Dot
2. Hobnail
3. Daisy Fern
4. Silver Crest
5. Burmese
6. Spanish Lace
7. Moonstone
8. Rose Crest
9. Water Lily
10. Aqua Crest

F

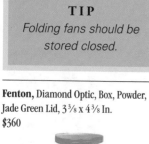

Fenton, Diamond Optic, Box, Powder, Jade Green Lid, 3 3/8 x 4 3/8 In.
$360

Fenton Art Glass Collectors of America

Fenton, Hobnail, Vase, Burmese, Sample, 18 3/4 In.
$373

Fenton Art Glass Collectors of America

Fenton, Ruby Slag, Figurine, Deer, Seated, 1980s
$135

Fenton Art Glass Collectors of America

Celeste Blue, Bowl, Footed, Stretched, Flared Rim, 3 In.	20
Christmas Poinsettia, Compote, Plum Opal, Carnival Glass, 5 x 10 In.	475
Coin Spot, Bowl, Cranberry Opalescent, c.1945-54, 3 1/2 x 6 1/2 In.	45
Daisy & Button, Bell, Green, Ribbed Handle, 5 3/4 In.	25
Daisy & Fern, Cruet, Satin, Topaz Opalescent, Handle, Stopper, c.1940-60, 5 In.	175
Daisy & Fern, Lemonade Set, Cranberry, Clear Handle, Tumblers, 9 1/2-In. Pitcher, 7 Piece	240
Dancing Ladies, Bowl, Footed, Scroll Handles, Jade Green, 11 x 6 x 5 In.	461
Dancing Ladies, Dish, Yellow, Urn Shape, Handles, Footed, 1920s, 7 In.	595
Diamond Lace, Compote, White Opalescent, Lid, 10 1/2 In.	50
Diamond Optic, Box, Powder, Jade Green Lid, 3 3/8 x 4 3/8 In. ....*illus*	360
Diamond Optic, Compote, Tangerine, Dolphin Handles, c.1920, 4 In.	180
Dogwood, Fairy Lamp, Domed, Glass Center, Folded Rim Base, Burmese, 6 In.	70
Dot Optic, Water Set, Clear, White Opalescent Dots, Pitcher, 6 Glasses, 1940s, 7 Piece	180
Epergne, Silver Plate & Glass, William IV., Early 1900s, 11 3/4 x 22 3/4 In.	406
Georgian, Sugar & Creamer, Amber	32
Hanging Vine, Vase, Karnak Red, 2 Blue Handles, Shouldered, 7 1/4 In.	1750
Hanging Vine, Vase, Karnak Red, Blue Foot, Flared Rim, 12 In.	5605
Hanging Vine, Vase, Karnak Red, Blue Foot, Stick Neck, 7 In.	3680
Hobnail, Bowl, Double Ruffle, Blue Opalescent, 1940-55, 11 In.	58
Hobnail, Slipper, Amber, 6 1/2 In.	23
Hobnail, Vase, Burmese, Sample, 18 3/4 In. ....*illus*	373
Mandarin Red, Candlestick, Opaque, Footed, c.1933, 3 In.	75
Milk Glass, Goblet, 5 1/2 In.	15
Rose, Compote, Sapphire, 7 5/8 In.	40
Ruby Slag, Figurine, Deer, Seated, 1980s ....*illus*	135
Ruby Slag, Figurine, Mouse, Seated, Big Ears ....*illus*	165
Silver Crest, Candy Dish, Footed, Lid, 6 1/2 In.	175
Spiral Optic, Vase, Pink Cranberry, Crimped Rim, 4 1/2 In.	70
Strawberry & Currant, Compote, Vaseline, Ruffled Lip, 5 1/2 In.	47
Vase, Blue, 3 Ruffles, 4 1/2 In.	20
Vase, Fan, Rose, Green, Vasa Murrhina, 1970, 7 1/2 x 7 In. ....*illus*	92
Vase, Hat, Opalescent, Hobnail, Vaseline, 8 In.	150
Vase, Mosaic, Iridescent Amethyst, Threading, Footed, Fake Tiffany Mark, 6 1/2 In. ....*illus*	1093

FIESTA, the colorful dinnerware, was introduced in 1936 by the Homer Laughlin China Co., redesigned in 1969, and withdrawn in 1973. It was reissued again in 1986 in different colors and is still being made. New colors, including some that are similar to old colors, have been introduced. One new color is introduced in March every year. The simple design was characterized by a band of concentric circles beginning at the rim. Cups had full-circle handles until 1969, when partial-circle handles were made. Harlequin and Riviera were related wares. For more prices, go to kovels.com.

Apricot, Cup & Saucer	12 to 20
Apricot, Gravy Boat	42
Apricot, Sugar, Handles, 5 1/2 In.	10
Black, Plate, 8 In.	27
Chartreuse, Eggcup	87
Chartreuse, Platter, 11 In.	90
Cobalt Blue, Bowl, 2 3/4 x 8 1/2 In.	5
Cobalt Blue, Cup	19
Cobalt Blue, Cup & Saucer	18
Cobalt Blue, Marmalade, 3 1/2 In. ....*illus*	360
Cobalt Blue, Syrup	232
Cobalt Blue, Tumbler, Water, 8 Oz.	63
Dark Green, Cup & Saucer	14
Gray, Plate, 9 In.	11 to 17
Gray, Plate, Salad, 7 3/8 In.	9
Ivory, Plate, 6 1/2 In.	5 to 10
Ivory, Plate, 10 In.	18
Ivory, Tumbler, Juice, 3 1/2 In.	13 to 15

F

Light Green, Creamer	20
Light Green, Cup	7
Light Green, Plate, 6 In.	4
Light Green, Salt & Pepper, Ball Shape, 2¾ In.	20
Medium Green, Bowl, No. 4, 5½ x 7½ In. ....*illus*	149
Medium Green, Plate, Dinner, 10 In.	175
Periwinkle, Teapot, Lid	55
Red, Compote, 3½ x 5 In.	85
Red, Mixing Bowl, No. 3, 6½ In.	22
Red, Tumbler, Water	56
Rose, Plate, Dinner, 10½ In.	9
Rose, Soup, Dish, 7 In.	8
Rose, Sugar & Creamer	28
Turquois, Plate, 7 In.	8
Turquoise, Casserole, Lid, 7¾ x 5½ In.	80
Turquoise, Cup	9
Turquoise, Cup & Saucer	13 to 36
Turquoise, Mug	50
Turquoise, Pitcher, Disc, 6⅞ In.	40
Turquoise, Plate, Dinner, 9⅜ In.	15
Turquoise, Saucer, 6 In.	5
White, Cup & Saucer	11
Yellow, Bowl, 1936-43, 5¾ x 8½ In.	70
Yellow, Cup & Saucer	13
Yellow, Pitcher, Ice Lip, 4¼ In.	90
Yellow, Pitcher, Disc ....*illus*	125
Yellow, Plate, 6 In.	4
Yellow, Plate, 9 In.	12
Yellow, Plate, 10 In.	15
Yellow, Platter, Oval, 13 x 10 In.	26
Yellow, Saucer	6
Yellow, Soup, Dish, 8½ In.	17
Yellow, Sugar & Creamer	30
Yellow, Sugar, Lid	13 to 21

FINCH, *see Kay Finch category.*

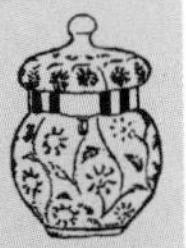

FINDLAY ONYX AND FLORADINE are two similar types of glass made by Dalzell, Gilmore and Leighton Co. of Findlay, Ohio, about 1889. Onyx is a patented yellowish white opaque glass with raised silver daisy decorations. A few rare pieces were made of rose, amber, orange, or purple glass. Floradine is made of cranberry-colored glass with an opalescent white raised floral pattern and a satin finish. The same molds were used for both types of glass.

Celery Vase, Silver Inclusions, 6½ In.	181
Spooner, Floradine, Red, Opal White Flowers, Opaque, 4½ In.	302
Spooner, Floradine, Red, Opal White Flowers, Translucent, 4½ In.	423
Toothpick Holder, Onyx, Green, Leaves, Flowers, Opalescent Glass, 2½ x 2 In.	210

FIREFIGHTING equipment of all types is collected, from fire marks to uniforms to toy fire trucks. It is said that every little boy wanted to be a fireman or a train engineer 75 years ago, and the collectors today reflect this interest.

Bucket, A. Kidson No. 6, Black, 1800s, 12 x 9 In.	204
Bucket, Coat Of Arms, 1900s, 16½ In.	156
Bucket, Leather, B.M.C. No. 19, Handle, Painted, 1825, 12 In.	524
Bucket, Leather, Black, Strap Handle, 21 In.	330
Bucket, Leather, Canvas Bags, Federal Fire Society, c.1914, 18½ In., Pair	1920
Bucket, Leather, J. French, 1830, 18 In.	720
Bucket, Leather, Paint, Banner, Reuben Dow, Eagle, Handle, 1806, 13 In., Pair	2370

F

Fenton, Ruby Slag, Figurine, Mouse, Seated, Big Ears
$165

Fenton Art Glass Collectors of America

Valuable Glass Vases
If you use valuable glass vases like Fenton or pottery vases like Roseville for flowers, use dried plants unless you protect the vase. Put a slightly smaller glass vase inside to hold the water and the flowers. "Hard" water will leave a stain on pottery or glass.

Fenton, Vase, Fan, Rose, Green, Vasa Murrhina, 1970, 7½ x 7 In.
$92

Ruby Lane

Fenton, Vase, Mosaic, Iridescent Amethyst, Threading, Footed, Fake Tiffany Mark, 6½ In.
$1,093

Early Auction Company

Fiesta, Cobalt Blue, Marmalade, 3 ½ In. $360

Replacements, Ltd.

Fiesta, Medium Green, Bowl, No. 4, 5 ½ x 7 ½ In. $149

Ruby Lane

Fiesta, Yellow, Pitcher, Disc $125

Ruby Lane

TIP

Smoke stains can be removed from a stone fireplace with an art gum eraser. Soot on the carpet in front of the fireplace can be removed with salt. Sprinkle dry salt on the soot, wait 30 minutes, then vacuum.

Bucket, Leather, Paint, E.A. Smith, Banner, Cylindrical, Handle, c.1810, 18 In.	2844
Bucket, Leather, Painted, Firefighters Spraying Burning Building, 1826, 14 ½ In.	1900
Bucket, Leather, Reddish Brown, Handle, 12 ½ In.	270
Bucket, Leather, Stencil, J Wilson WFC, Washington, Penn. Fire Co., c.1840, 10 In.	960
Bucket, Leather, Warren, Yellow Ground, Red Drapes, 1829, 12 ½ In.	738
Bucket, Red Paint, Banner, Medallion, Agile, J. Chickering, No. 1, 1809, 12 In.	1230
Bucket, Tole, Pump Room No. 2, Coat Of Arms, c.1890, 25 x 17 In.	300
Bucket, Tole, Yellow, Bird, Handles, 12 ¼ In.	213
Engine Bell, Cast Iron Bracket, Red, 16 x 23 In.	344
Extinguisher, Hand Grenade Shape, Star Harden, Blue, 1884	165
Extinguisher, Hero Can, Red & White, Canada, 1940s, 5 In.	30
Fire Extinguisher, Copper, Pyrene, 5 Gallon, 1900s, 22 x 10 ½ In. *illus*	250
Fire Horn, Tole, Red, Green, 1900s, 26 In.	369
Grenade, Babcock Hand, Fire Extinguisher Co., Cobalt Blue, 1880-1900, 7 ½ In. *illus*	3450
Grenade, Hayward's Hand, Light To Medium Lime Green, Tooled Lip, 1871-95, 6 ⅜ In. *illus*	288
Grenade, Perfection, Horseshoe Banner, Fish Scale Pattern, Amber, 1885, 8 In.	13800
Grenade, Rockford Kalamazoo Automatic, Extinguisher, Cobalt Blue, 1880-1900, 10 In. *illus*	316
Helmet, Brass, Village Plate, Leather Liner, Baileval France, 7 ½ x 10 ¾ In.	147
Lantern, Silvered Brass, Cage, Tapered Glass Globe, Loop Handle, Inscribed, 17 In.	1024
Relay Panel, Walnut, 12 ¾ In.	102
Trumpet, Brass, Silver Plate, 1865, 19 In.	2522
Trumpet, Silver Plate, c.1810, 20 In.	296

FIREPLACES were used to cook food and to heat the American home in past centuries. Many types of tools and equipment were used. Andirons held the logs in place, firebacks reflected the heat into the room, and tongs were used to move either fuel or food. Many types of spits and roasting jacks were made and may be listed in the Kitchen category.

Accessory Box, Tortoiseshell, 2-Part Tower With Lid & Silver Mounts, Early 1800s, 8 In.	360
Andirons, Baroque Style, Bronze, Scrolled Base, Putti, Satyr, Bacchante, 36 x 16 In.	1750
Andirons, Brass & Iron, Nathaniel Johnson, Boston, c.1816, 24 ½ x 13 ½ x 26 ½ In.	650
Andirons, Brass & Iron, Neoclassical Urn, Early 1800s, 16 x 23 In.	488
Andirons, Brass & Iron, Steeple Top, James Davis, Boston, 18 ½ x 11 x 15 ½ In.	500
Andirons, Brass With Ball Finials, American, Early 1800s, 13 ½ x 26 In.	183
Andirons, Brass, Arts & Crafts, Stylized Openwork Flower, Splayed Feet, c.1910, 27 In.	500
Andirons, Brass, Federal, Urn Top, Cabriole Legs, Late 1700s, 26 ¼ In.	322
Andirons, Brass, Regency, Torches, c.1900, 16 ⅜ x 12 In.	750
Andirons, Brass, Ribbed Urn, Spur Legs, Eagle, Spread Wings, Plinth, c.1800, 21 x 23 In.	770
Andirons, Brass, Stylized Cats, Sitting, Chrome Plating Co., Tenn., 20 In.	250
Andirons, Brass, Stylized Dogs, Curled Tail, 12 ¾ x 7 ¼ In.	295
Andirons, Bronze & Wrought Iron, Renaissance, Seated Lion Finials, 1800s, 49 In.	2640
Andirons, Bronze, Dore Et Patine, Continental, c.1900, 29 ¾ x 15 ½ x 22 ½ In.	1000
Andirons, Bronze, Figural, Kneeling Indian, Arm On Head, c.1900, 22 x 14 In.	8750
Andirons, Bronze, Polished, Rectangular, Overlapping Circles, Iron Fire Dogs, 14 ¾ x 6 In.	2375
Andirons, Cast Iron, Armorial, Figures, Fleur-De-Lis, Arched Base, 1640, 25 x 15 In.	330
Andirons, Cast Iron, Arts & Crafts, Electric, Owl, Lit Eyes, 11 x 21 In.	457
Andirons, Cast Iron, Boston Terrier, Black, White, Howes, 17 In.	300
Andirons, Cast Iron, Cat, Seated, c.1880, 17 ¾ In.	2040
Andirons, Cast Iron, Dog, Dachshund, Whimsical, Sitting, Elongated, Art Deco, 18 In.	600
Andirons, Cast Iron, Dog, Elongated Figure, Seated, Looking Down, 1900s, 18 In.	492
Andirons, Cast Iron, Duck, Black Paint, Memphis, Tenn., 14 x 29 In.	1169
Andirons, Cast Iron, Figural, Butler, In Uniform, 1830, 17 x 10 In.	749
Andirons, Cast Iron, G. Washington Figure, Holding Hat, Plinth, c.1875, 20 x 16 In.	415
Andirons, Federal, Brass, 1800s, 16 In.	37
Andirons, Fender, Brass, Pierced Scrollwork, Dolphins, c.1900, 26 ½ x 59 x 6 In.	562
Andirons, Figural, Bronze, Eros & Psyche, 1900s, 32 ½ x 17 x 11 ½ In.	1000
Andirons, Indian Chief, Multicolor, 21 ½ In.	9000
Andirons, Iron, Dragons, Human Legs, Red Enamel, Art Deco, 1930s, 21 x 15 ½ In. *illus*	130
Andirons, Iron, Turned Post, Ducks In Flight Finials, Circle Frame, 37 In.	142

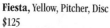

F

Firefighting, Fire Extinguisher, Copper, Pyrene, 5 Gallon, 1900s, 22 x 10½ In.
$250

Ruby Lane

Firefighting, Grenade, Babcock Hand, Fire Extinguisher Co., Cobalt Blue, 1880-1900, 7½ In.
$3,450

Glass Works Auctions

Firefighting, Grenade, Hayward's Hand, Light To Medium Lime Green, Tooled Lip, 1871-95, 6⅜ In.
$288

Glass Works Auctions

Firefighting, Grenade, Rockford Kalamazoo Automatic, Extinguisher, Cobalt Blue, 1880-1900, 10 In.
$316

Glass Works Auctions

Fireplace, Andirons, Iron, Dragons, Human Legs, Red Enamel, Art Deco, 1930s, 21 x 15½ In.
$130

Rago Arts and Auction Center

Fireplace, Bellows, French Provincial, Walnut, Leather, Carved, Lyre Shape, c.1875, 23 x 9 In.
$976

Neal Auctions

Fireplace, Bellows, Peat, Wood, Leather, Brass, Mechanical, Wheel Handle, 1800s, 9 x 28½ In.
$78

Thomaston Place Auction Galleries

Fireplace, Matchbox Holder, Brass, Monogram, Dirk Van Erp, 12¾ x 4 In.
$325

F

Rago Arts and Auction Center

Fireplace, Screen, Art Nouveau, Walnut, Carved, Brass Insert, A. Ruetsch, 1903, 40 x 25 In.
$3,259

James D. Julia Auctioneers

Fireplace, Screen, Victorian, Mahogany, Needlepoint, Carved, Turnings, c.1850, 45 x 12 In.
$366

Neal Auctions

Fireplace, Screen, Walnut, Pole, Needlework, King Charles Spaniel, Victorian, 59 In.
$468

New Orleans Auction Galleries

Fireplace, Tinder Lighter, Flintlock, 5½ In.
$610

Norman Heckler & Company

Andirons, Phoenix, H-Shape, Flying, J. Miller, 17½ x 17¾ In.	615
Andirons, Sheet Iron, Pine Trees, c.1980, 18 x 17½ In.	338
Andirons, Steel, 3 Curled Panels, 1900s, 21 x 21 In.	800
Andirons, Wrought Iron, Faceted Finials, Arch Base, Pad Feet, 1700s, 19 x 20 In.	120
Andirons, Wrought Iron, Heart, Faceted Shaft, Mushroom Top, Arched Legs, 21 In.	1353
Andirons, Wrought Iron, Paint, Dragon, Shield Fronts, Paw Feet, c.1910, 28 x 23 In.	240
Andirons, Wrought Iron, Rotating Pot Hanger, 1800s, 52 In.	960
Andirons, Wrought Iron, Swan's Head Finial, Double Arched Feet, Roasting Hooks, 23 In.	369
Basket, Regency, Urn With Ram's Head, Hotbox Drawer, 1800s, 22 In.	240
Bellows, French Provincial, Walnut, Leather, Carved, Lyre Shape, c.1875, 23 x 9 In. ....*illus*	976
Bellows, Ivory Ground With Fruit, Shaped Handles, Henry Porter, 1800s, 20 In.	150
Bellows, Leather, Wrought Iron, Green Paint, Stenciled Hearts, Snake Form Spout, 44 In.	120
Bellows, Peat, Wood, Leather, Brass, Mechanical, Wheel Handle, 1800s, 9 x 28½ In. ....*illus*	78
Bellows, Smoked On Yellow With Cornucopia, Releathered, Early 1800s, 17½ In.	420
Chenets, Andirons, Bronze, Iron, Louis XV, 1800s, 23½ x 19 x 22 In., Pair	687
Chenets, Andirons, Bronze, Louis XV, Gilt, Leafy Scrolls, 18 x 23 In.	500
Chenets, Andirons, Bronze, Louise XV, Leaf & Scroll Bases, Putti, 9½ x 11¾ In., Pair	1500
Chenets, Andirons, Fender, Gilt Bronze, Lyre Shape, Flame Finials, 1900s, 17 x 46 In.	180
Chenets, Andirons, Gilt Bronze, Figural, Cherub, Rocaille Work Base, Late 1800s, 11 x 11 In.	875
Chenets, Andirons, Brass, Louis XV, Scroll Leaves, Branches, 18½ In.	125
Chenets, Andirons, Gilt Bronze, Louis XVI, Cherubs, 11 x 10 In., Pair	375
Chenets, Andirons, Gilt, Louis XVI, Gadrooned Urn, Flaming Finial, 15 x 16 In.	714
Coal Scuttle, Brass, Scoop, Helmet Shape, 16¾ x 12¾ In.	238
Coal Scuttle, Helmet, Brass, Wood Handles, Matching Iron Tongs & Shovel, 13 x 25 In.	122
Coal Scuttle, Tole, Flower Spray, 4-Footed, 25 In.	42
Fender & Chenet Set, Brass, Rococo Style, France, 1900s, 15 x 37½ x 8 In.	343
Fender, Brass, Art Nouveau, Naturalistic Scrolled Ends, Late 1800s, 53 In.	180
Fender, Brass, Colonial Williamsburg Virginia Metalcrafters, c.1975, 6½ x 50 In.	95
Fender, Brass, Serpentine, Pierced, Etched Design, 1800s, 5½ x 50 In., Pair	215
Fender, Brass, Upholstered, Molded Bases, Urn, 14½ x 53 In.	475
Fender, Bronze, Dore Et Patine, England, Early 1800s, 12½ x 56½ x 5 In.	2125
Fender, Iron, Wirework, Brass Belted Ball Finials, Early 1800s, 12 x 45¾ In.	750
Fender, Spherical Finials, Rectangular, c.1900, 54 x 16 In.	119
Fireback, Cast Iron, Arched Top, Relief Thistle, 2 Crowns, Lion Rampant, 31⅞ x 30½ In.	425
Fireback, Iron, Rococo Scroll Work, Flowers, Winged Medallion, 22⅜ In.	780
Firescreen, Tole, Shaped Panel, Birds On Branches, Brass Scroll Feet, 39½ x 29 In.	531
Fork, Wrought Iron, 3 Tines, Arrow Ends, Twisted Handle, 48 In.	720
Guard, Art Deco, Stylized Swan, Serpentine, Wave Scrolls, H. Boutet, c.1925, 59½ In.	7500
Hearth Broom, Hard Wood, Pennsylvania, 51 In.	664
Hearth Broom, Hard Wood, Pennsylvania, 56½ In.	603
Log Holder, Spirals, Handles, 18 x 20 In.	149
Mantel is listed in the Architectural category.	
Matchbox Holder, Brass, Monogram, Dirk Van Erp, 12¾ x 4 In. ....*illus*	325
Plaque, Eagle Hose No. 2, Oval, 8¾ x 11 In.	234
Screen, Art Nouveau, Walnut, Carved, Brass Insert, A. Ruetsch, 1903, 40 x 25 In. ....*illus*	3259
Screen, Art Nouveau, Walnut, Fabric, Nancy School, 40½ x 23¼ In.	475
Screen, Arts & Crafts, Iron, Arched Crest, Fiddlehead & Flowers, 1900s, 20½ x 35 In.	461
Screen, Biedermeier, Bird's-Eye, Needlework Floral Spray, 1800s, 38½ x 25¼ In.	500
Screen, Brass, Wreath Crest, Branches, Birds, Swags, Scroll Feet, c.1950, 27 x 29 In.	1062
Screen, Bronze, Patina, Blackened Steel, Glass, Abstract, 36 x 44½ In.	2500
Screen, Ebonized, 2 Porcelain Panels, Borders, Turned Posts, c.1890, 39 x 24 In.	1169
Screen, Federal, Brass & Iron Wirework, 1800s, 25¼ x 50¼ x 12 In.	540
Screen, Grapes, Fruit, Pot, Painted, Multicolor	25
Screen, Marble Veneer, Gilt, Scroll, Rectangular Foot, 41 In.	125
Screen, Needlepoint & Fruitwood, France, c.1900, 47½ x 29 x 21 In.	375
Screen, Neoclassical, 3-Panel, Gilt Metal, Molded Glass Discs, 32 In.	42
Screen, Openwork Hearts Pattern, Black, Iron, U.S.A., 30½ x 18 In.	338
Screen, Rococo, Giltwood, Drapery, 51½ x 40¾ In.	1250
Screen, Victorian, Mahogany, Needlepoint, Carved, Turnings, c.1850, 45 x 12 In. ....*illus*	366
Screen, Walnut, Pole, Needlework, King Charles Spaniel, Victorian, 59 In. ....*illus*	468
Screen, Wirework, Vertical Wires, Scroll & Swag, Brass Molding, Early 1800s, 24 x 41 In.	1800

Screens are also listed in the Architectural and Furniture categories.

Set, Louis Philippe, Bronze, Finial, Fire Screen, Fender, Andirons, 29 x 61 In.	1250
Shovel, Ember, Wrought Iron, Flared, Flower Basket Stem, Acorn Finial, 13 In.	800
Tinder Box, Hammered Copper, Removable Liner, Iron, 15 x 18 In.	396
Tinder Box, Iron, Tinned, Candleholder, Round, Circle Handle, Snuffer, Flint, c.1810, 4 In.	275
Tinder Lighter, Flintlock, 5 ½ In. ....*illus*	610
Tongs, Iron, Heart Shape Handle, 2 Heart Hooks With Faceted Ends, c.1780, 31 In.	500
Tongs, Iron, Long Arms, Loop Handle, Pierced Disk, Hanging Loop Pick, 1700s, 18 In.	2700
Tool Rest, Brass, Dual Spherical Finials, Horizontal C-Scroll, England, 1800s, Pair	30
Tool Set, Gilt Brass & Steel, Stand, Urn & Flower Handles, Late 1900s, 28 In.	1440
Tool Set, Iron, Shovel, Tongs, Poker, Brush, Handles, Stand, Scroll Feet, c.1915, 33 In.	1185
Trammel, Iron, Brass, Incised Sawtooth Blade, Pierced Crest, Leaves, 1657, 36 In.	1778
Trammel, Iron, Sawtooth, Heart Finial, Loop End, Scroll Handle, 1700s, 44 In.	325
Trammel, Iron, Scrollwork, Engraved Design, c.1810, 36 In. ....*illus*	600

FISCHER porcelain was made in Herend, Hungary. The wares are sometimes referred to as Herend porcelain. The pottery was originally founded in Herend in 1826 and was bought by Moritz Fischer in 1839. Fischer made replacement pieces for German and Far Eastern dinnerware and later began making its own dinnerware patterns. Figurines were made beginning in the 1870s. The company was nationalized in 1948. Martin's Herend Imports, Inc., began importing Herend china into the United States in 1957. The company was privatized in 1993 and is now in business as Herend.

MF

Bowl, Rothschild Bird, Flared Border, 10 ¾ x 2 In.	59
Bowl, Salad, Rothschild Bird Pattern, Insects, Birds, 10 x 10 In.	345
Cachepot, Birds, Leaves, Branches, Green Handles, 10 In.	500
Candy Dish, Gilt, Shell Shape, Birds, Branches, Butterflies, Insects, Blue, White, 9 x 8 ¾ In.	188
Decanter, Blue Flower, Green Leaves, Impressed Mark, 15 ⅛ In.	390
Dish, Sweetmeat, Tri-Lobed, Scalloped Rim, Scroll Handle, Flowers, Gilt, Herend, 12 In.	124
Figurine, Conch Shell, Pink, Cream, 6 ¼ In.	375
Figurine, Duck With Golden Egg, Red, Blue, Teal, Pink, c.1980, 7 ½ In.	237
Figurine, Elephant, Trunk Up, Green Fishnet, 10 x 14 In.	813
Figurine, Frog Prince, Blue, White, Gilt, 1 ½ In.	126
Figurine, Hussar Military Man, Sword, Signed K. Strobl, 16 In.	218
Figurine, Owl, Perched On Books, Blue, Pink, Green, 11 ½ In.	625
Figurine, Panther, Prowling, Black Fishnet, 17 ½ In.	688
Figurine, Parrot, Red Head, Stump, 4 ⅞ x 3 ¼ In.	118
Figurine, Rabbit, Gold Nose & Paws, Pink Fishnet, 11 ⅞ In.	688
Figurine, Rabbit, Paw Up, Green Fishnet, 24K Gold, Herend, c.1950, 4 In.	300
Group, Man & Bull, 9 ½ x 16 ½ In.	312
Group, Man On Donkey, 15 ¼ In.	250
Plate, Flowers, 10 In., 12 Piece	531
Teapot, Green Bouquet, Rose Stem Handle, Rose Stem Finial, 8 ½ x 15 ½ In.	125
Tureen, Soup, Queen Victoria, Bulbous, Handles, Dome Lid, Finial, 1960s, 9 x 12 In.	500
Vase, Reticulated, Shaped Rim, Flowers, Multicolor, 6 ½ x 11 ½ In. ....*illus*	400

FISHING reels of brass or nickel were made in the United States by 1810. Bamboo fly rods were sold by 1860, often marked with the maker's name. Lures made of metal, or metal and wood, were made in the nineteenth century. Plastic lures were made by the 1930s. All fishing material is collected today and even equipment of the past 30 years is of interest if in good condition with original box.

Bait Bucket, Tin, Bail Handle, B & B Keep's Em Alive	198
Creel, Woven Splint, Leather Strap, String Hinges, Early 1900s, 8 ½ x 14 In.	54
Float, Glass, Sphere, Blue, Japan, 11 ½ In.	290
Lure, 2 Hooks, Wood, Blue, White, Red Tip, 6 ⅛ In. ....*illus*	10
Lure, Box, Shmoo Plug Bait, Wood, Metal Hook, c.1948, 5 In., Pair	348
Reel, Fin-Nor, Tycoon, 2 Speed, Case, 9 ½ x 9 ½ In.	1062
Reel, Fly, Cortland, Graphite GRF-1000, Fitted Carrying Bag, Late 1900s, 29 In.	63
Skewer, Curved Handle, Asian, 40 In.	86

Fireplace, Trammel, Iron, Scrollwork, Engraved Design, c.1810, 36 In. $600

Garth's Auctioneers & Appraisers

Fischer, Vase, Reticulated, Shaped Rim, Flowers, Multicolor, 6 ½ x 11 ½ In. $400

Ruby Lane

Fishing, Lure, 2 Hooks, Wood, Blue, White, Red Tip, 6 ⅛ In. $10

Ruby Lane

Flash Gordon, Toy, Rocket Fighter, Tin, Shoots Sparks, Windup, 4 ½ x 12 In. $413

Woody Auction

Florence Ceramics, Figurine, Abigail, Blue, White, 8 ½ x 5 ½ In. $55

Ruby Lane

Flow Blue, Plate, Morning Glory, Fluted Border, Leaves, Green, Brown, 9 ½ In. $60

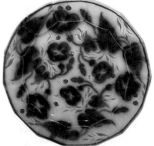

Ruby Lane

FLAGS *are included in the Textile category.*

FLASH GORDON appeared in the Sunday comics in 1934. The daily strip started in 1940. The hero was also in comic books from 1930 to 1970, in books from 1936, in movies from 1938, on the radio in the 1930s and 1940s, and on television from 1953 to 1954. All sorts of memorabilia are collected, but the ray guns and rocket ships are the most popular.

Comic Book, Flash, Trickster Appears, No. 152, 1965	285
Comic Book, Showcase, 4th Silver Age Flash, 1958	1879
Comic Book, The Flash, 1st Mirror Master, No. 105, 1959	1411
Movie Poster, Conquers The Universe, Destroying Ray, 1940, 27 x 41 In.	1006
Toy, Air Ray Gun, Shoots Air, Aluminum, Paint, Red & White, Box, 1948, 10 In.	425
Toy, Ray Pistol, Clicker, Tin Litho, Raised Spiral Rings, Box, Marx, 1950s, 10 In.	506
Toy, Rocket Fighter, Tin, Shoots Sparks, Windup, 4 ½ x 12 In. ....*illus*	413

FLORENCE CERAMICS were made in Pasadena, California, from World War II to 1977. Florence Ward created many colorful figurines, boxes, candleholders, and other items for the gift shop trade. Each piece was marked with an ink stamp that included the name *Florence Ceramics Co.* The company was sold in 1964 and although the name remained the same, the products were very different. Mugs, cups, and trays were made.

Bust, Gilt Embellishment, c.1945, 8 ⅛ x 5 ¾ In.	199
Figurine, Abigail, Blue, White, 8 ½ x 5 ½ In. ....*illus*	55
Figurine, Adeline, Pink With Blue, 9 In.	190
Figurine, Clarissa, Blue, 7 ½ In.	170
Figurine, Clarissa, Green, 8 ¼ In.	375
Figurine, Clarissa, Pink, 7 ½ In.	81
Figurine, Georgette, Green Dress, Bonnet, 10 In.	750
Figurine, Jeanette, Blue, 7 ¾ In.	280
Figurine, Jennifer, Pink, 8 In.	68
Figurine, Jim, Man Holding His Top Hat, 7 x 4 ½ In.	53
Figurine, Josephine, Aqua Dress, Hat, Red Gloves, 1960s, 9 In.	375
Figurine, Lavon, Pink Dress, 1960s, 9 In.	555
Figurine, Louise, White Gown, Pink Scarf & Parasol, 1950s, 7 In.	109
Figurine, Martha, Blue, 8 ¼ In.	375
Figurine, May, Flower Holder, 6 ½ In.	24
Figurine, Musette, Ruby Dress, Lace Collar, Hat, 1960s, 9 In.	500
Figurine, Princess, Green, 10 ½ In.	1050
Figurine, Rosalie, Maroon Dress, Lace Ruffle, Ringlets, 1960s, 10 In.	1100
Figurine, Storybook Hour, Mother Reading To Child	41
Figurine, Victoria, Woman On Loveseat, 7 x 8 ¼ In.	655
Plaque, Raised Bust, Woman In Bonnet, Brown Edge, c.1950, 2 x 7 x 6 In.	32

FLOW BLUE was made in England and other countries about 1830 to 1900. The dishes were printed with designs using a cobalt blue coloring. The color flowed from the design to the white body so that the finished piece has a smeared blue design. The dishes were usually made of ironstone china. More Flow Blue may be found under the name of the manufacturer.

Basin, Flower Garlands, Squat, Fluted Rim, Out-Rolled Rim, c.1885, 15 In. Diam.	265
Butter Chip, Flowers, Shaped Rim, 3 ¼ In.	15
Chamber Pot, Ironstone, Victoria Pattern, Gilt, Loop Handle, Squat, 1800s, 6 x 11 In.	200
Jug, Marine Pattern, Flattened, Round, Tubular Neck, Handle, Burslem, 1880, 8 x 6 In.	110
Pitcher, Ironstone, Roses, Cylinder, Shaped Foot & Rim, Handle, 1800s, 7 x 7 In.	55
Plate, Dinner, Italianate Garden, Wavy Gilt Edge, 1800s, 10 In. Diam.	81
Plate, Ironstone, Skeleton Flower, Zigzag Pattern Border, 9 ½ In. Diam., 3 Piece	142
Plate, Morning Glory, Fluted Border, Leaves, Green, Brown, 9 ½ In. ....*illus*	60
Platter, Flowers, Scalloped, Oval, Ford & Sons, c.1900, 16 x 12 In.	292
Platter, Kin Shan Pattern, 16 x 20 In.	59

F

Platter, Kyber, 12 x 15 ⅝ In., Pair		188
Platter, Oval, Shaped Rim, Embossed Leaves, Flower Border, c.1905, 16 x 12 In.		210
Platter, Scinde, Blue, Ironstone, J. & G. Alcock, 12 ¾ x 16 ¼ In.		153
Platter, Scinde, Landscape, 12 x 9 In.		110
Platter, Temple, Landscape, 14 x 10 ¾ In., Pair		242
Tureen, Togo Pattern, Castle, Lake, Roses, Oval, Scallop, Handles, Lid, c.1900, 6 x 12 In.		275

FLYING PHOENIX, *see Phoenix Bird category.*

FOLK ART is also listed in many categories of this book under the actual name of the object. See categories such as Box, Cigar Store Figure, Paper, Weather Vane, Wooden, etc.

Angel, Sandstone, Standing & Holding A Baby, Ernest Reed, Signed, 23 x 17 In.		3900
Birdhouse, Gables, Trim, Shutters & Weathervane, 1800s, 24 x 21 x 16 In.		600
Birdhouse, Wood, Steep Pitched Roof, 2 Windows & Door, 21 x 21 In.		60
Boat, Great Lakes, Wooden, White, Red & Black, Rigging & Anchor, Early 1900s, 35 x 37 In.		1200
Bottle, With American Flags & Shields Inside, Late 1800s, 9 ½ In.		2640
Bust, Emmylou Harris, Wooden Carved & Painted, Signed, c.1986, 12 In.		240
Carnival Toss Target, Black Americana, Swivel Eyes, Attached Canvas Bag, c.1930, 33 In.		2574
Cartouche, Painted, Drapes, Tassels, 19th Century, 41 In.		702
Chair, Red Cedar, Carved Alligator Crest, 3 Slats, Woven Rush Seat, c.1900, 35 ½ In.		840
Dancing Chinese Man, Carved Wood, Paint, Jointed Body, Iron Base, 14 ½ In.		325
Diorama, Shack, 2 Figures, Wood, Paint, Tray Base, Jail House Carvers, 9 x 24 In.		620
Dog, Crosshatch, Brown, Putty, Paint, Gesso, 2 x 3 In.	*illus*	158
Dresser, Child's, Chip Carved, Mirror, 42 x 19 In.		300
Duck, Mosaic, Chinese Blue & White Porcelain Fragments, 9 x 15 In.		360
Eagle, Perched On Square Base, Spread Wings, Hand Carved, Pine, c.1875, 20 In.		530
Eagle, Perched, Carved Wood, Yellow & Red Paint, Green Dome Base, Strawser, 5 In.		201
Eagle, Pine, Spread Wings, Perched, 1800s, 40 In.		995
Ear Of Corn, Carved Hardwood, Eye Screw For Hanging, 32 In.		399
Figure, Blacksmith Or Iron Worker With Anvil, Carved From Log, 1900s, 24 x 13 In.		2125
Figure, Carved Eagle, Standing Upright, Curved Beak, Plinth, Turned Finials, 52 x 19 In.		237
Figure, Horse & Rider, Carol Anthony, Papier-Mache, Mixed, c.1970, 47 x 50 x 17 ¾ In.		183
Figure, Santo, Outstretched Arms, Hand Carved Wood, Paint, Mexico, 1800s, 13 In.		125
Frog, Jointed, Wood, Weathered, 27 ½ x 6 In.	*illus*	86
Frog, Sandstone, Added Green Paint, Ernest Reed, Signed, 6 ½ x 10 In.		300
Fruit Basket, Slats, Rings, Yellow, Pink & Blue Paint, Wire Handles, 10 x 14 In.		118
Hat Rack, Eagle, Spread Wings, Perched On Branch, Wood, Carved, 3 Hooks, 18 x 29 In.		1353
Iron Carnival Target, Heavy Ram, Yellow, Mid 1900s, 13 ½ In.		211
Jalopy, Wooden & Tin, Cloth Top & Rubber Tires, Moving Front Axle, 1900s, 13 x 20 In.		63
Mirror, Oval, Pierced Wood Frame, Leaves, Birds, Flowers, Deer, c.1900, 54 x 35 In.		3321
Parrot, Carved Wood, Original Paint, Mounted On Wall Plaque, Late 1800s, 8 ½ In.		270
Picture, Watercolor On Paper, Portrait, John Christian, By Jacob Maentel, 1808, 10 ¾ x 7 ¾ In.		3600
Picture, Watercolor, Potted Tulip, Orange, Yellow, Frame, Signed, Yoder, c.1825, 15 x 13 In.		300
Pipe Stand, Limestone, 2 Women & Cat, Log Rack On Top, Early 1900s, 6 x 9 In.		1250
Plaque, Sperm Whale, Carved, Ridged Back, Conical Teeth, Bead Eye, c.1990, 45 In.		1126
Plaque, Wood, Paint, White & Gray, Pigeon Coop, Pigeons, Corner Fit, c.1900, 19 In.		450
Portrait, Indian Chief, Oil On Bark, Headdress, Woven Birch Frame, 32 In. Diam.		593
Retablo, Virgin Mary, Circle Of Jose Rafael Aragon, 8 ½ x 6 In.	*illus*	512
Rocking Horse, Carved, Painted Wood, Yellow & Green, Signed, W. Gotshall, 11 In.		354
Rooster, Red, Brown, Wood, 25 ½ x 20 In.		1420
Rooster, Standing, Blue Glaze, Edwin Meaders, Signed, c.1921, 16 In.		480
Rooster, Wood, John Reber, c.1900, 7 In.		2400
Sculpture, Band, Guitar, Drum, Bell, Arms Move With String, 18 ½ x 9 In.	*illus*	24
Sculpture, Farm, Farmers, Well, Dog, White Fence, 7 ½ x 11 In.		63
Sculpture, Painted Iron, Laughing Clown, 1900s, 32 x 18 In.		625
Sculpture, Red Crown Feathers, Upswept Wings, 18 x 5 ¼ In.		118
Snake, Slithering, Carved Root, Painted, 38 ½ In.		83

Folk Art, Dog, Crosshatch, Brown, Putty, Paint, Gesso, 2 x 3 In.
$158

Norman Heckler & Company

Folk Art, Frog, Jointed, Wood, Weathered, 27 ½ x 6 In.
$86

Hudson Valley Auctions

Folk Art, Retablo, Virgin Mary, Circle Of Jose Rafael Aragon, 8 ½ x 6 In.
$512

Jackson's International Auctioneers & Appraisers

F

Folk Art, Sculpture, Band, Guitar, Drum, Bell, Arms Move With String, 18½ x 9 In.
$24

Cowan's Auctions

Folk Art, Washboard, Chicken, Oil Paint, Clementine Hunter, 1900s, 23⅝ x 12½ In.
$1,375

New Orleans Auction Galleries

Folk Art, Whirligig, Washer Woman, Tub, Bonnet, Stand, Tin, Wood, 21½ x 28½ In.
$660

Thomaston Place Auction Galleries

Snake, Wood, Carnival Ride, Original 3-Color Paint & Surface, c.1930, 54 In.	510
Songbird, Perched, Muted Plumage, Wall Mount, Early 1900s, 8½ In.	105
State Seal, Virginia, Blue Ground, Reverse C-Scroll Frame, Late 1800s, 29 x 20 In.	1638
Statue, Uncle Sam, Flag, Standing On Box, Red, White, Blue, 54 In.	497
Suitcase, Wood, Paint, Skaters, Flowers, Green, Red, Brass Hardware, c.1910, 13 x 21 In.	338
Toy, Wagon, Wood Box, Wood Wheels, Painted, Express, Handle, 11-In. Box	71
Wall Hanging, Wool, Applied Crocheted Figures, Tree, Animals, K. Donaldson, 31 x 22 In.	840
Washboard, Chicken, Oil Paint, Clementine Hunter, 1900s, 23⅝ x 12½ In. ......*illus*	1375
Whirlygig, 2 Men Sawing, Propeller, Red, White, Black, Yellow, 19 In.	72
Whirligig, Airplane, Tin, J. Hinkley c.1923, 30 x 22 In.	1386
Whirligig, Figural, Man In Top Hat, Black Paint, Cube On Square Base, 1900s, 18 In.	210
Whirligig, Man, Wearing Red Jacket, Black Trousers, Cap, Weathered Surface, 22 In.	677
Whirligig, Washer Woman, Tub, Bonnet, Stand, Tin, Wood, 21½ x 28½ In. ......*illus*	660

 FOOT WARMERS solved the problem of cold feet in past generations. Some warmers held charcoal, others held hot water. Pottery, tin, and soapstone were the favored materials to conduct the heat. The warmer was kept under the feet, then the legs and feet were tucked into a blanket, providing welcome warmth in a cold carriage or church.

Brass, Peafowl, Engraved, Hinged Lid Pan, Turned Walnut Handle, 1800s, 43½ In.	35
Cherry, Old Red Paint, Heart Vent Holes, Iron Wire Bail Handle, Penn., 1800s	236
Tin & Wood, Box, Paint Design, Metal Top Handle, Signed, Smith, 10 x 8 In.	295
Tin, Pierced, Circle, Heart, Red Wash Finish, 6 x 9 In.	96

FOOTBALL *collectibles may be found in the Card and the Sports categories.*

 FOSTORIA glass was made in Fostoria, Ohio, from 1887 to 1891. The factory was moved to Moundsville, West Virginia, and most of the glass seen in shops today is a twentieth-century product. The company was sold in 1983; new items will be easily identifiable, according to the new owner, Lancaster Colony Corporation. Additional Fostoria items may be listed in the Milk Glass category.

American, Bonbon, 3-Toed, 6¾ In.	14
American, Bowl, Inverted Rim, 7½ In.	63
American, Bowl, Lid, Milk Glass, 7½ x 6 In. ......*illus*	135
American, Butter, Cover, ¼ Lb.	69
American, Butter, Cover, 1915-82, 2 x 7¾ In.	50
American, Celery Dish, 10 In.	20
American, Jug, Ice Lip, 70 Oz.	78
American, Nappy, Handle, Cornered, 5¾ In.	12
American, Pitcher, 8 In.	48
American, Relish, 3 Sections, 10½ In.	24
American, Relish, Gondola Shape, Divided, Handles, 12 x 5½ In. ......*illus*	10
American, Vase, Bud, Flared, Octagonal Base, 8¼ In.	24
American, Vase, Flared, Square Foot, 10 In.	48
Argus, Juice, Green, 2⅞ In.	8
Arlington, Banana Stand, Milk Glass, 7¾ In.	53 to 55
Baroque, Candleholder, Triple Light, 1937-58, 5⅝ In.	30
Biscayne, Goblet, Water, Blue, 6⅜ In.	14
Biscayne, Sherbet, Blue, 4½ In.	9
Biscayne, Tumbler, Iced Tea, Blue, 6¼ In.	16
Century, Creamer, 4 In.	15
Century, Sugar, 1950-82, 4 In.	8 to 18
Cherish, Sherbet, Platinum Rim, 5⅛ In.	14
Coin Glass, Dish, Oval, Light Blue, Scalloped, 3¼ x 6 In.	45
Coin Glass, Vase, Blue, Footed, 1958-62, 8 In.	45
Coin Glass, Wedding Bowl, Ruby Red, Lid, 8 In.	65
Colony, Bonbon, Swirl, Curved, 1940-73, 6¼ In.	15
Corsage, Tumbler, Juice, Footed, 1935-59, 4⅞ In.	15

Georgian, Sherbet, 5¼ In.	20
Glamour, Goblet, Green, 7⅛ In.	19
Glamour, Sherbet, Green, 5 In.	9
Glamour, Tumbler, Iced Tea, Green, 6½ In.	17
Glamour, Tumbler, Iced Tea, Onyx, 6½ In.	17
Jamestown, Butter, Cover, Amber, ¼ Lb.	38
Jamestown, Goblet, 5⅞ In.	15
Jamestown, Goblet, Pink, 5⅞ In.	22
Jamestown, Juice, Amber, 4¾ In.	12
Jamestown, Tumbler, Iced Tea, 6⅛ In.	21
Jamestown, Tumbler, Iced Tea, Green, 6⅛ In.	19
Jenny Lind, Pitcher, Cameo, Amethyst, Satin, 8½ In.	68
June, Candy Container, Lid, Fleur-De-Lis, Blue......................	174
June, Candy Container, Lid, Topaz, Lid	90
June, Cup & Saucer, Topaz	52
June, Vase, Pink, Straight-Sided, 8 In.	185 to 220
June, Vase, Topaz, 8 In.	127
Luxemburg Crown, Candle Bowl, Ruby Red, c.1963, 7¼ x 4⅝ In. ...	95
Mayfair, Relish, 5 Sections, 13¼ In.	46
Moonstone, Goblet, Blue, 6½ In. ....*illus*	5
Navarre, Ice Bucket, Etched, 1940-50, 5½ x 6 In.	65
New Garland, Bowl, Topaz, Crystal, Leaves, Flowers, 5½ x 12 In. ...	47
Oak Leaves & Acorns, Sugar Pail, Handle, 1927-31, 3½ In. ...	75
Paradise Brocade, Ice Bucket, Green, Bail Handle, c.1930, 6 x 5 In. ...*illus*	115
Paradise, Vase, Green, Footed, c.1927-31, 7¼ In.	125
Pebble Beach, Tumbler, Flaming Orange, Footed, c.1968-73, 6 In. ...	20
Reflection, Goblet, Platinum Band, 6¼ In.	17
Reflection, Tumbler, Iced Tea, Platinum Band, 5⅞ In.	21
Rosalie, Tumbler, Iced Tea, 6⅝ In.	44
Sentimental, Sherbet, 5¼ In.	15
Sheraton, Sherbet, 5¼ In.	10
Sheraton, Tumbler, Iced Tea, 6½ In.	21
Silhoutte, Goblet, Water, 7 In.	22
Silhoutte, Sherbet, 5⅛ In.	9
Sorrento, Goblet, Water, Green, 6 In.	10
Sorrento, Tumbler, Iced Tea, Blue, 6¾ In.	16
Sorrento, Tumbler, Iced Tea, Green, 6¾ In.	10
Sprite, Cup & Saucer	18
Venise, Goblet, 7 In.	27
Virginia, Goblet, Light Blue, 7¼ In.	13
Woodland, Champagne, Brown, 5¼ In.	13

FOVAL, *see Fry category.*

FRAMES *are included in the Furniture category under Frame.*

FRANCISCAN is a trademark that appears on pottery. Gladding, McBean and Company started in 1875. The company grew and acquired other potteries. It made sewer pipes, floor tiles, dinnerware, and art pottery with a variety of trademarks. It began using the trade name *Franciscan* in 1934. In 1936, dinnerware and art pottery were sold under the name *Franciscan Ware.* The company made china and cream-colored, decorated earthenware. Desert Rose, Apple, El Patio, and Coronado were best sellers. The company became Interpace Corporation and in 1979 was purchased by Josiah Wedgwood & Sons. The plant was closed in 1984, but a few of the patterns are still being made. For more prices, go to kovels.com.

Amapola, Platter, 14⅜ In. ....*illus*	20
Apple, Bowl, Vegetable, Lid, 9 x 4 In.	53
Apple, Butter, Cover, Finial, ¼ Lb.	50

Fostoria, American, Bowl, Lid, Milk Glass, 7½ x 6 In.
$135

Ruby Lane

Fostoria, American, Relish, Gondola Shape, Divided, Handles, 12 x 5½ In.
$10

Ruby Lane

Fostoria, Moonstone, Goblet, Blue, 6½ In.
$5

Ruby Lane

This is an edited listing of current prices. Visit **Kovels.com** to check thousands of prices from previous years and sign up for free information on trends, tips, reproductions, marks, and more.

Fostoria, Paradise Brocade, Ice Bucket, Green, Bail Handle, c.1930, 6 x 5 In. $115

Ruby Lane

Butter Pats

Butter pats are round dishes 3 ½ inches in diameter that held a square pat of butter at a dinner table. It can be confused with an ashtray, salt dish, doll dish, and even a saucer. There is an indentation in a saucer to hold a cup. A butter pat often has a rim.

Franciscan, Amapola, Platter, 14 ⅜ In. $20

Ruby Lane

Franciscan, Chelan, Bowl, Vegetable, 9 ¾ x 7 In. $38

Ruby Lane

Apple, Creamer, 3 In.		16 to 22
Apple, Cup & Saucer		21
Apple, Gravy		35
Apple, Mug, 9 Oz., 2 ⅞ In.		30
Apple, Plate, Bread & Butter		10
Apple, Plate, Dinner		11
Apple, Platter, 14 In.		35
Apple, Relish, 3 Sections, Oval, 12 In.		45
Apple, Utensil Holder, 6 In.		42
Arcadia Green, Cup & Saucer		50
Autumn, Coffeepot, 10 ¼ In., 6 Cup		99
Autumn, Cup & Saucer		12
Autumn, Platter, 13 ¾ In.		22
Autumn, Serving Bowl, 9 ¼ In.		22
Autumn, Teapot, Lid, 5 ¼ In., 5 Cup		89
Bird 'N Hand, Plate, Dinner		13
Camel, Bowl, Fruit, 4 ¾ In.		25
Camel, Platter, 12 ½ In.		75
Chelan, Bowl, Vegetable, 9 ¾ x 7 In.	*illus*	38
Chestnut Weave, Plate, Dinner, 10 ⅝ In.		25
Cloud Nine, Berry Bowl, 5 In.		8 to 10
Cloud Nine, Gravy Boat, Attached Underplate		35
Cloud Nine, Plate, Bread & Butter, 6 ⅛ In.		6
Cloud Nine, Plate, Dinner, 10 ¼ In.		12
Desert Rose, Creamer, 4 ½ In.	*illus*	15
Desert Rose, Cup & Saucer		15
Desert Rose, Cup & Saucer, Rounded Sides		15
Desert Rose, Lasagna Dish, 13 x 10 ¼ In.		70
Desert Rose, Plate, Dinner, 10 ½ In.		20
Desert Rose, Platter, 12 In.		50
Desert Rose, Platter, 14 ¼ In.		42
Desert Rose, Sugar, 4 ½ In.		89
Desert Rose, Teapot, Lid		80
Elsinore, Cup & Saucer		28
Floral, Plate, Dinner, 10 ½ In.		15
Floral, Plate, Salad, 8 ½ In.		8
Floral, Salt & Pepper		22
Forget-Me-Knot, Cup & Saucer		16
Forget-Me-Knot, Plate, Salad, 8 In.		18
Huntington Rose, Plate, Dinner, 10 ⅝ In.		50
Jamocha, Cup & Saucer, Footed		9
Madeira, Bowl, Fruit, 5 ⅜ In.		18
Madeira, Bowl, Vegetable, Round, 7 ¾ In.		25
Madeira, Plate, Bread & Butter		4
Madeira, Plate, Dinner, 10 ½ In.		12
Merry Go Round, Gravy Boat		22
Merry Go Round, Plate, Dinner		12
Merry Go Round, Platter, 13 ¼ In.		30
October, Baker, 9 ⅝ x 8 ¾ In.	*illus*	35
October, Bowl, Cereal, 7 ⅛ In.		25
October, Plate, Dinner, 10 ¾ In.		30
Padua, Chop Plate, 11 ¾ In.	*illus*	42
Pink-A-Dilly, Ashtray, 3 ¾ In.		8
Pink-A-Dilly, Gravy Boat		26
Pink-A-Dilly, Plate, Dinner, 10 ⅜ In.		13
Pink-A-Dilly, Sugar & Creamer		41
Radiance, Casserole, Round, Lid, Qt., 7 In.		86
Sierra Sand, Plate, Dinner, 10 ¾ In.		10
Silver Pine, Cup & Saucer		24

F

Starburst, Creamer, 4 In.	23
Starburst, Cup & Saucer, 1950s	10 to 20
Starburst, Mug, 2¾ In.	75
Starburst, Mustard Jar, 1950s, 3 In. .....illus	45
Starburst, Plate, Dinner, 10¼ In.	40
Starburst, Soup, Dish	45
Tahiti, Cup & Saucer	8
Tulip Time, Platter, Oval, 14 In.	35
Westwood, Plate, Dinner, 10⅝ In.	25
Wheat, Chop Plate, 13 In.	25
Wheat, Plate, Bread & Butter, 6⅜ In.	5
Wheat, Salt & Pepper	20
Wilshire, Plate, Bread & Butter	8
Wilshire, Plate, Dinner	15
Wilshire, Plate, Salad	12
Woodside, Teapot, Lid, 5½ In.	102

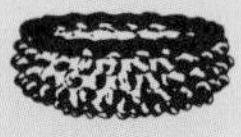

FRANCISWARE is the name of a glassware made by Hobbs, Brockunier and Company of Wheeling, West Virginia, in the late 1800s. It is a clear or frosted hobnail or swirl pattern glass with an amber-stained rim. Some pieces were made by a pressed glass method, others were mold blown.

Butter, Cover, Frost, Amber Band, Ribbed Swirl, Squat, Knob Finial, 1800s, 5 x 5 In.	95
Candy Dish, Frosted Satin Dew Drop, Amber Ribbon, Hobnail, c.1880, 3 x 5 In.	65
Celery Vase, Frosted Dew Drop, Canary Edge, Hobnail, Ruffled Rim, c.1886, 6 In.	75
Drink Set, Pitcher, Tumbler, Yellow, Hobbs Bruckner, 2 Piece	50
Pitcher, Dew Drop, Amber To Frost, Hobnail, Baluster, Wavy Rim, 8 In.	206
Server, Dew Drop, Frost, Amber Rim, Hobnail, Oval, Sawtooth Edge, 1880s, 7 x 10 In.	76
Sugar & Creamer, Amber To Frost, Hobnail, Crimped Rim, 1880s, 4 x 5 In.	235

FRANKART INC., New York, New York, mass-produced nude "dancing lady" lamps, ashtrays, and other decorative Art Deco items in the 1920s and 1930s. They were made of white lead composition and spray-painted. *Frankart Inc.* and the patent number and year were stamped on the base.

Ashtray, Figural, Nude Woman, Holds Bowl, Green, c.1927, 11¼ In.	750
Bookends, Nude, On Book, Painted, Spelter, 10½ In.	567
Lamp, Figural, Angel, Arched Back, Frosted Glass Wings, c.1920, 10 In.	1750

FRANKOMA POTTERY was originally known as The Frank Potteries when John F. Frank opened shop in 1933. The factory is now working in Sapulpa, Oklahoma. Early wares were made from a light cream-colored clay from Ada, Oklahoma, but in 1956 the company switched to a red clay from Sapulpa. The firm made dinnerware, utilitarian and decorative kitchenwares, figurines, flowerpots, and limited edition and commemorative pieces. John Frank died in 1973 and his daughter, Joniece, inherited the business. Frankoma went bankrupt in 1990. The pottery operated under various owners for a few years and was bought by Joe Ragosta in 2008. It closed in 2010. The buildings, assets, name, and molds were sold at an auction in 2011.

Brown, Vase, Art Deco, Ringed, 3 In.	145
Lazy Bones, Cup & Saucer, Blue	22
Lazy Bones, Plate, Bread & Butter, Blue, 7¼ In.	8
Mayan Aztec, Ashtray, Prairie Green, 4½ x 3½ In.	15
Mayan Aztec, Flowerpot, Prairie Green, 4 x 4½ In.	26
Mayan Aztec, Platter, Prairie Green, Round, 13¾ In.	38
Plainsman, Honey Pot, Lid, Green	32
Plainsman, Votive, Brown, 7¼ In.	45
Prairie Green, Pitcher, 1940s, 2½ In.	35
Wagon Wheel, Creamer, Onyx Black, 2½ In.	35

Franciscan, Desert Rose, Creamer, 4½ In.
$15

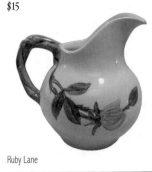

Ruby Lane

Franciscan, October, Baker, 9⅝ x 8¾ In.
$35

Ruby Lane

Franciscan, Padua, Chop Plate, 11¾ In.
$42

Ruby Lane

TIP

Dust mites are the subject of many articles today. The more humid the environment, the more quickly they multiply. Dust mites eat dust particles, then will turn to paints and glazing materials on wooden pieces. The only way to avoid damage is to clean regularly.

F

Franciscan, Starburst, Mustard Jar, 1950s, 3 In.
$45

Ruby Lane

Frankoma, Wall Pocket, Cowboy Boot, Tan, 7 In.
$35

Ruby Lane

Fraternal, Odd Fellows, Helmet, Brass Spike, Visor, 10¾ x 10 In.
$145

Ruby Lane

Wall Pocket, Cowboy Boot, Tan, 7 In. ....*illus*	35
Westwind, Mug, Prairie Green, 2½ In.	8

FRATERNAL objects that are related to the many different fraternal organizations in the United States are listed in this category. The Elks, Masons, Odd Fellows, and others are included. Also included are service organizations, like the American Legion, Kiwanis, and Lions Club. Furniture is listed in the Furniture category. Shaving mugs decorated with fraternal crests are included in the Shaving Mug category.

Ancient Order Of Foresters Of America, Shaving Mug, T.G. Murray	55
Eastern Star, Ashtray, Triangular, Logo, Lefton, 4 x 4 In.	19
Eastern Star, Bracelet, Hinged, 14K Gold, Diamonds, Gemstones, 2½ In.	660
Eastern Star, Cup & Saucer, 5-Pointed Star, Lefton	20
Eastern Star, Pin, 10K Gold, Laurel Wreath, F.A.T.A.L., ½ In.	24
Eastern Star, Pin, Masonic Star, Laurel Wreath, 14K Gold, 1½ In.	240
Eastern Star, Ring, Black Onyx, Filigree, 14K, Size 7	60
Elks, Ashtray, Raised Elk, B.P.O.E., Brown, Monmouth Western Co., 1 x 4 In.	18
Elks, Belt Buckle, Brass, Raised Elk, Clock Face, B.P.O.E., 1970s, 3 x 2 In.	49
Elks, Watch Fob, Elk Tooth, Red Stone Eyes, Antlers, 1⅛ In.	165
Lions Club, Pin, Bow, Lion Pendant, 1900s, 1⁹⁄₁₆ In.	45
Lions Club, Sign, Round, Porcelain, Multicolor, 30¾ In.	96
Masonic, Apron, Kidskin Front With Ink Symbols, Silk Backing, c.1808, 13 In.	420
Masonic, Artillery Shell, Emblems, Embossed, 13½ x 4 In.	174
Masonic, Banner, Elizabeth No. 309, Black, Brown Fringe, 36 x 19 In.	877
Masonic, Box, Inlaid Mother-Of-Pearl, Symbols, Early 1800s, 3 x 12½ x 6½ In.	123
Masonic, Cabinet, Carved Crest, Walnut, French Country, 1900s, 76¾ x 65¼ In.	295
Masonic, Medal, Queen Victoria 60th Jubilee, Gilt, Silver, Silk Ribbon, Box, 4 x 1⅜ In.	365
Masonic, Mirror, Carved Symbols In Frame, Late 1800s, 30½ x 21½ In.	2500
Masonic, Poster, Fraternal Order Of Eagles, Eagle, Spread Wings, Cloth, c.1925, 36 In.	23
Masonic, Walking Stick, Carved, Duck Head Handle, Sun, Cross, Heart, Fish, c.1940, 35 In.	119
Odd Fellows, Bank, Still, Architectural, Brass, 1900, 4½ In.	36
Odd Fellows, Doorstop, Iron, Crescent, Down, FLT, R, 7¾ In.	90
Odd Fellows, Helmet, Brass Spike, Visor, 10¾ x 10 In. ....*illus*	145
Odd Fellows, Hourglass, Turned Wood, Glass, Paint, c.1890, 9 x 6½ In.	300
Odd Fellows, Medal, Blue Ribbon, 25 Years, Date Of Joining 1891 ....*illus*	85
Odd Fellows, Poster, Symbolic, Copy Of 1883 Print, Mat, Frame, 21 x 16 In.	30
Odd Fellows, Sign, Broad Ax, Wood, c.1930, 33 In.	510
Shriner, Button, Convention, Isis Temple, Shriner On Locust, Celluloid, 1901, 2 In.	696
Sons & Daughters Of Liberty, Pin, Silvertone, Clear & Sapphire Crystals, 1920s, 1½ In.	35

FRY GLASS was made by the H.C. Fry Glass Company of Rochester, Pennsylvania. The company, founded in 1901, first made cut glass and other types of fine glasswares. In 1922 it patented a heat-resistant glass called Pearl Ovenglass. For two years, 1926–1927, the company made Fry Foval, an opal ware decorated with colored trim. Reproductions of this glass have been made. Depression glass patterns made by Fry may be listed in the Depression Glass category. Some pieces of cut glass may also be included in the Cut Glass category.

FRY

Basket, Etched Glass, 14 In.	100
Bowl, Bluish Purple, Applied Fuchsia Threading, Controlled Bubbles, 13¾ x 10½ In. ......*illus*	175
Bowl, Cut Glass, Elsie, Stars, Feathers, Diamonds, Ribs & Cross Hatching, 8 x 4 In.	208
Bowl, Pinwheel, Hobstar, Star Center, Sawtooth Rim, Signed, 5½ x 5 x 1¼ In.	78
Casserole, Etched Lid With Finial, 1932, 9 x 7 x 3⅝ In.	18
Cookie Jar, Sunnybrook, Green, 7 In.	239
Creamer, Radio Wave, 3½ In.	325
Pitcher, Cut Glass, Signed	51
Platter, Cut Glass, Star Pattern, 9 In.	139
Sugar, Radio Wave, 3 In.	325
Vase, Radio Wave, Cobalt Blue, 8 In.	195

FRY FOVAL

Basket, Opalescent White, Cobalt Blue, Fan Shape, Petal Rim, 8 x 7 In.	185
Bowl, Blue Footed Base, Opalescent, 2 1/2 x 4 1/2 In.	35
Bowl, Pale Yellow To Opalescent White, Dome Foot, Tapered, 8 x 11 In.	320
Bowl, Silver Trim, Fuchsia Rim, Jade Foot, 1920s, 10 x 3 1/4 In. ....*illus*	225
Candlestick, Opaque White, Turquoise Blue Treading, Stick, Disc Foot, 10 In., Pair	375
Cordial, Diamond Optic, Pink & Green	79
Creamer, Blue Opalescent, 2 1/2 x 5 1/2 x 1 1/2 In.	37
Creamer, Radio Wave, Milky White, Green Handle, 3 1/2 In.	325
Cup & Saucer, Child's, Opalescent, Green Handle, 1 3/4 x 4 1/2 In.	27
Martini, Diamond Optic, Pink & Green, 6 3/8 x 4 1/2 In.	29
Sugar, Radio Wave, Milky White, 2 Green Handles, 3 In.	324
Teapot, Jade Green, Frosted, Bulbous, Lid, Ball Finial, 1920s, 7 In.	324
Teapot, Lid, Opalescent, Green Spout Handle & Finial, c.1920, 7 x 8 In.	324
Vase, Trumpet, Opalescent, Blue Round Base, 11 1/4 In.	90

FULPER POTTERY COMPANY was incorporated in 1899 in Flemington, New Jersey. It made art pottery from 1909 to 1929. The firm had been making bottles, jugs, and housewares from 1805. Doll heads were made about 1928. The firm became Stangl Pottery in 1929. Stangl Pottery is listed in its own category in this book.

Bookends, Book Shape, Green, Beige, 3 x 5 In., Pair	274
Bowl, Brown Flambe Over Green Glaze, 5 Fish Encircling Interior, 2 7/8 x 11 3/8 In.	489
Bowl, Pedestal, Mottled Flambe Glaze, 3 In.	110
Centerpiece, Tan, Squat, 3 Feet Extending Into Candleholders, c.1910, 6 x 10 In.	120
Flower Frog, Green Brown, Cream, Mushroom Shape, 7 7/8 x 3 1/2 In.	90
Flower Frog, Green, Frog Shape, 7 In.	61
Jar, Temple, Cobalt Blue Over Mirror Black Glaze, Bulbous Shoulder, Marked, 12 In.	384
Lamp, Leaded Glass, Mottled, Mushroom Shape, 17 x 17 In.	9760
Perfume Light, Ballerina, Lamp Center, Bisque, Diffuses Perfume, 1920s, 6 In. ....*illus*	228
Vase, 7-Sided, Chinese Blue Over Mahogany Over Ivory Flambe Glazes, Marked, 9 3/4 In.	345
Vase, Blue Flambe Glaze, Molded Bird, Impressed, 12 7/8 In.	431
Vase, Blue Flambe Over Purple Matte Glaze, Shouldered, Tapered, c.1920, 15 In.	1188
Vase, Blue Snowflake Crystals, Bulbous, Upright Handles, Saucer Foot, 12 In.	236
Vase, Bronze Green, Mottled, Cylindrical, Marked, 17 In.	431
Vase, Cobalt Blue, Mahogany Over Yellow, Flambe Glaze, 7-Sided, Stamped, 10 In.	177
Vase, Cream, Blue, Handles, Impressed Signature, 11 1/2 x 8 In.	400
Vase, Crystalline Blue, Multicolor Near Base, Handles, Round Foot, 12 x 9 In.	793
Vase, Crystalline Glaze, Blue, White, Ocher Ground, 5 1/2 x 9 In.	244
Vase, Crystalline Green, 3 Handles, Round Foot, 6 x 8 In.	457
Vase, Cucumber Crystalline Glaze, Maidens, Relief, Oval, 1920s, 12 x 6 In.	750
Vase, Cucumber Green Matte Glaze, Gourd Shape, Fluted Neck, 2 Handles, 9 x 11 In.	875
Vase, Dripping, Green Crystalline Glaze, Marked, 16 3/4 In.	805
Vase, Flambe Glaze, Green, Brown, Artichoke, Impressed, 5 1/2 x 8 1/2 In.	2318
Vase, Frothy Brown & Black Flambe Over Mustard Matte, 3 Handles, Vasekraft, 9 x 10 In.	750
Vase, Gold Matte, Cream, Brown & Black Flambe, Dripped, Squat, c.1915, 7 x 11 In.	1125
Vase, Green Crystalline Glaze, Shouldered, Square Handles At Neck, Stamped, 9 In.	177
Vase, Green Flambe Drip Glaze, Round, Squat, 9 x 10 1/2 In.	2625
Vase, Green To Rose, Frothy, Slotted Handles, 1922-28, 11 x 5 In. ....*illus*	495
Vase, Green, 2 Ring Handles, Tapers To Mouth, 12 1/2 x 8 In.	1586
Vase, Green, 6-Sided, 11 In.	260
Vase, Green, Tan, Leopard Skin Crystalline, Flambe Glaze, Barrel Shape, c.1915, 11 In.	1750
Vase, Ivory Flambe Over Mustard Matte Glazes, Rotund, Marked, 7 1/2 x 10 1/2 In.	1840
Vase, Mirror Black Glaze, Bulbous, Tapered, Lobed, Footed, 11 1/2 x 8 1/2 In.	1625
Vase, Mirror Black, Chinese Blue & Rose Flambe Glaze, Pear Shape, Handles, 11 x 8 In.	313
Vase, Olive Green Matte, Gourd Shape, 4 Handles, Round Foot, 8 x 6 1/2 In.	396
Vase, Rose Matte Glaze, Squat, Bulbous Shoulder, Rolled Rim, Marked, 7 In.	120
Vase, Triple, Cat's-Eye Flambe Glaze, 3 Cylindrical Holders, Round Base, 11 x 8 In.	3375
Vase, Turquoise, Crystallized, Oblong Loop Handles, 12 3/8 x 5 3/4 In.	200

Fraternal, Odd Fellows, Medal, Blue Ribbon, 25 Years, Date Of Joining 1891
$85

Ruby Lane

Fry, Bowl, Bluish Purple, Applied Fuchsia Threading, Controlled Bubbles, 13 3/4 x 10 1/2 In.
$175

Ruby Lane

Fry Foval, Bowl, Silver Trim, Fuchsia Rim, Jade Foot, 1920s, 10 x 3 1/4 In.
$225

Ruby Lane

TIP

Install large windows in your house—burglars avoid shattering them because of noise.

Fulper, Perfume Light, Ballerina, Lamp Center, Bisque, Diffuses Perfume, 1920s, 6 In.

$228

Theriault's

Fulper, Vase, Green To Rose, Frothy, Slotted Handles, 1922-28, 11 x 5 In.
$495

Ruby Lane

Furniture, Armoire, Contemporary, Walnut, Parcel Gilt Wings, Shelves, Doors, 82 x 50 In.
$3,125

Neal Auctions

Vase, Wisteria Glaze, 2 Angled Handles, Round Finger Holes, Stamped, 6½ x 8 In.	312
Wall Pocket, Blue, Greek Key, 8 In.	225

FURNITURE of all types is listed in this category. Examples dating from the seventeenth century to the 2000s are included. Prices for furniture vary in different parts of the country. Oak furniture is most expensive in the West; large pieces over eight feet high are sold for the most money in the South, where high ceilings are found in the old homes. Condition is very important when determining prices. These are NOT average prices but rather reports of unique sales. If the description includes the word *style* , the piece resembles the old furniture style but was made at a later time. It is not a period piece. Small chests that sat on a table or dresser are also included here. Garden furniture is listed in the Garden Furnishings category. Related items may be found in the Architectural, Brass, and Store categories.

Armchairs are listed under Chair in this category.

Armoire, Art Deco, Mahogany, Ebony, Dessin Furniture, 78 x 59 In.	301
Armoire, Cherry, Flared Cornice, Recessed Panel Doors, c.1810, 90 x 62 In.	4270
Armoire, Cherry, Removable Cornice, Shaped Door Panels, c.1800, 81 x 46 In.	800
Armoire, Contemporary, Walnut, Parcel Gilt Wings, Shelves, Doors, 82 x 50 In. ....*illus*	3125
Armoire, French Provincial, Fruitwood, Carved Flowers, c.1825, 87 x 57 In. ....*illus*	1178
Armoire, French Provincial, Walnut, 90½ x 58 In.	1750
Armoire, Fruitwood, Marquetry, Scroll Crest, Corbel, Doors, 1700s, 97 x 75 In.	9225
Armoire, Louis Philippe, Fruitwood, 2 Paneled Doors, Hidden Drawer, 93 x 55 In.	625
Armoire, Louisiana Creole, Cypress, Doors, Drawers, Pegged, c.1875, 76 In. ....*illus*	5000
Armoire, Mahogany, Inlaid Compass Star, Fluted Column, Louisiana, 80 x 57 In.	6710
Armoire, Rococo, Rosewood, Arch Crest, Flowers, Mirrored Door, c.1850, 92 x 50 In.	711
Armoire, Rococo, Walnut, Arched Pediment, 2 Doors, Italy, 97 x 64 In.	187
Armoire, Walnut, Flared Cornice, Plain Frieze, 1800s, 78 x 64 x 21 In.	1220
Bar Cart, Nicked Brass, Mahogany, Casters, c.1950, 36 x 37 In.	594
Bar, Walnut, Carved Panels, Rose Marble Top, Continental, 1800s, 42 x 124 In.	4500
Barstool, Chrome, Leather, Red, c.1980, 39¼ x 19½ In., 5 Piece	625
Barstool, Swivel, Midcentury, Teak, Brass, 51 x 15 In., 4 Piece	100
Bed Steps, Chinoiserie, Leather Treads, Open Shelves, c.1910, 28 x 26 x 18 In.	244
Bed Steps, Commode, Mahogany, 3 Steps, Lift Top, Pullout Seat, c.1835, 25 x 19 In., Pair	2000
Bed Steps, English Regency, Inset Leather Treads, Drawer, Scroll, 1800s, 30 In.	325
Bed Steps, Regency, Mahogany, 3 Steps, Leather, Hinged, Eng., 1800s, 26 x 19 In.	480
Bed Steps, William IV, Mahogany, Gold Trim, Leather Treads, Bun Feet, 24 x 20 In.	468
Bed, Aesthetic Revival, Faux Bamboo, Spindles, Ball Finials, c.1875, 54 x 37 In. ....*illus*	488
Bed, Canopy Frame, Federal, Maple, Scroll Headboard, 89 x 84 In.	1140
Bed, Canopy, Black Walnut, Victorian Revival, England, 1800s, 98 x 69 x 92 In.	1560
Bed, Cast Iron, Victorian Style, Headboard, Footboard, Rails, 64¾ In.	125
Bed, Cream Paint, Parcel Gilt, Putti In Wreath, Italy, 1800s, 63 x 74 In., Pair ....*illus*	4000
Bed, Empire, Maple, Turned Posts & Acorn Finial, Side Rails, 46 x 49 x 82 In.	156
Bed, Four-Poster, Federal, Mahogany, 77 x 55 In.	500
Bed, Four-Poster, Frame, Chrome, King, Pace Collection, Mid 1900s	720
Bed, Four-Poster, George III, Red, 82 In., Pair	188
Bed, Four-Poster, Mahogany, Carved Leaf Posts, Pineapple Finials, 79 x 54 x 80 In.	812
Bed, Four-Poster, Mahogany, Ribbed, Scalloped Rails, c.1875, 114 x 78 x 87 In.	8750
Bed, Four-Poster, Molded Cornice, Turned Post, c.1875, 105 x 80 x 90 In.	2375
Bed, Four-Poster, Walnut, Chamfered Posts, Mississippi, 98 x 78 In.	3355
Bed, L. & J.G. Stickley, Twin, 3 Wide End Slats, c.1905, 42 x 79 In.	1250
Bed, Limbert, Double, 7 End Slats, c.1910, 50 x 80 In.	1625
Bed, Mixed Wood, Blue Paint, Rope Style, Acorn Finial, c.1840, 52 x 72 In.	360
Bed, Pine, Blue Paint, Rope Design, Flowers, Scroll Headboard, c.1875, 54 x 78 In.	510
Bed, Red Paint, Rope Tension, Shaped Headboard, Ball Finials, 1700s, 74 x 50 In.	2000
Bed, Rococo Revival, Half-Tester, Arched Canopy, Ohio, c.1875, 97 x 79 In.	2250
Bed, Rococo, Rosewood, Carved, Fruit & Flower Crest, Bowed Footboard, c.1855, 67 x 58 In. ....*illus*	14640
Bed, Sleigh, P. Deux, Galvanized Metal, Tube Legs, Ball Feet, 40 x 77 In., Pair	200
Bed, Trundle, Rope, Walnut, Ball Finials, Pegged Rails, c.1810, 59 x 39 In.	1100
Bed, Walnut, Peaked Back, Urn Crest, Finials, Paneled, Disk Feet, 103 x 71 In.	1888

F

Furniture, Armoire, French Provincial, Fruitwood, Carved Flowers, c.1825, 87 x 57 In.
$1,178

New Orleans Auction Galleries

Furniture, Armoire, Louisiana Creole, Cypress, Doors, Drawers, Pegged, c.1875, 76 In.
$5,000

New Orleans Auction Galleries

Furniture, Bed, Aesthetic Revival, Faux Bamboo, Spindles, Ball Finials, c.1875, 54 x 37 In.
$488

Neal Auctions

Furniture, Bed, Cream Paint, Parcel Gilt, Putti In Wreath, Italy, 1800s, 63 x 74 In., Pair
$4,000

New Orleans Auction Galleries

Furniture, Bed, Rococo, Rosewood, Carved, Fruit & Flower Crest, Bowed Footboard, c.1855, 67 x 58 In.
$14,640

Neal Auctions

Furniture, Bookcase, Barrister, Mahogany, 3 Stack, Globe-Wernicke, 53 x 34 In.
$213

Hess Auction Group

Furniture, Bookcase, Console, Regency, Rosewood, Drawers, Doors, Mirror, 1800s, 55 x 42 In.
$780

Selkirk Auctioneers & Appraisers

Furniture, Bookcase, On Chest, Burl Decoration, Adirondack, N.Y., c.1915, 86 x 46 In.
$6,150

Skinner, Inc.

Coat Racks

Coat racks are an ignored furniture form. The oak coat rack once favored by offices can still be found in antiques shops. Less common but more unusual are the coat racks designed by Eames, Sottsass, and other twentieth-century designers. These often look more like sculpture than furniture.

FURNITURE

Furniture, Bookcase, Revolving, Mahogany, 4 Tiers, Trubner & Co., London, c.1910, 66 x 22 In.
$750

Neal Auctions

Furniture, Bookstand, Wood, Scroll Sawn Backplate, Portable, c.1850, 10 x 18 x 12 In.
$812

New Orleans Auction Galleries

Furniture, Bureau, George III, Mahogany, Drop Front, Fitted Interior, c.1780, 40 x 39 In.
$1,500

New Orleans Auction Galleries

Furniture, Bureau, Louis XV Style, Kingwood, Kneehole, Drawers, Inlay, Bronze, c.1910, 31 x 37 In.
$1,830

Neal Auctions

Furniture, Bureau, Mahogany, Block Front, Cock-Beaded, Brass, c.1770, 30 x 36 In.
$7,380

Skinner, Inc.

Furniture, Cabinet, Display, Edwardian, Mahogany, Glazed Doors, Drawers, c.1900, 92 In.
$1,098

New Orleans Auction Galleries

Furniture, Cabinet, Drawers, Flexible Home Arrangements, Johnson Furniture Co., c.1945, 48 x 30 In.
$1,750

Wright

Furniture, Cabinet, French Provincial, Pine, Scroll, Shaped Glazed Doors, 96 x 56 In.
$750

New Orleans Auction Galleries

Furniture, Cabinet, G. Nelson, CSS, Walnut, Heated Surface, Flip Top, Herman Miller, c.1960, 36 x 25 In.
$1,803

Wright

Bench, Biedermeier, Mahogany, H Shape, 28 In.	750
Bench, Bucket, Blue Paint, 1800s, 40½ x 41 x 15 In.	1140
Bench, Bucket, Dovetailed Shelf, Hinged Doors, Shaped Feet, c.1850, 44 In.	527
Bench, Corner, Softwood, Painted, Plank Seat, Cutout Legs, 1800s, 19 x 52 In.	266
Bench, Dragon, Openwork, Crest, Clouds, Fighting Cocks, Arms, 51 x 54 In.	826
Bench, Elm, Lacquer, Woven Rattan Top, Open Apron, Square Legs, 19 x 46 In.	120
Bench, Foot, Shaker, Pine, Painted, Cutout Ends, Square Feet, 1800s, 13 x 38 In.	185
Bench, Fruitwood, Tapestry Seat, Carved Flowers, Scroll Toes, 1800s, 18 x 45 In.	625
Bench, Giltwood, Turned Stretcher, Curule Legs, Velvet Pillow Top, 71 In., Pair	3198
Bench, Jacobean, Walnut, Canted Corners, 27¾ In.	238
Bench, Lacquer, 3 Scenic Panels, Openwork Legs, c.1880, 39 x 76 In.	625
Bench, Oak, Molded Top, Splayed, Turned End Supports, Stretcher, 19 x 92 In.	1476
Bench, Phillip Lloyd Powell, Walnut, Sculpted, Round Legs, 1960s, 146 In.	15000
Bench, Pine, Shaped Arms & Square Nails, Child's, 26 x 27 In.	1320
Bench, Prayer, Pine, Molded Lip, Scroll Shoe Feet, 1800s, 4½ x 30 x 11 In.	41
Bench, Regency Style, Silk, Beech, Gilt Metal Mounts, c.1900, 34 x 36 In., Pair	885
Bench, Shaker Meetinghouse, Spindle Back, 10 Legs, 1800s, 32 x 107 In.	732
Bench, Shaker, Pine, Red Stain, Plank Seat, Stretchers, 1800s, 18 x 35 In.	4613
Bench, Shaker, Pine, Yellow Stain, Arch Cutout Legs, Scribe, 1800s, 14 x 27 In.	697
Bench, Softwood, Plank Back, Scroll Cutout Arms, Arch Feet, 1800s, 38 x 83 In.	165
Bench, Softwood, Red Paint, Beaded Crest, Open Backrest, 1800s, 33 x 72 In.	3775
Bench, Steel Frame, Leather Tufted Seat, Square Legs, 1900s, 18 x 145 In.	2750
Bench, Walnut, Carved, 19th Century, 19½ x 88 In., Pair	450
Bench, Wegner, Oak, Upholstered, Curved Seat, 1960s, 17 x 28 In., Pair	4275
Bench, Window, Mahogany, Upholstered, Rolled Arms, Stretcher, 1700s, 25 x 50 In.	600
Bench, Window, Wood, Carved, Scalloped Apron, Scroll Arms, 1800s, 25 x 41 In.	1020
Bench, Wood-Box, Pine, Birdcage Back, Hinged Lift Seat, 1800s, 36 In.	1521
Bench, Wright, Folding, Plywood, Upholstered, Steel Chain, 27 x 42 x 24 In.	1000
Book Mill, Burl Walnut, Revolving, Round Top, Turned Post, c.1880, 30 x 18 In.	812
Bookcase, Barrister, 4-Stack, Globe-Wernicke, 112 x 81½ In.	442
Bookcase, Barrister, Mahogany, 3 Stack, Globe-Wernicke, 53 x 34 In. ....illus	213
Bookcase, Barrister, Pivoted Glass Doors, Mahogany, Lundstrum, 49 x 34 In.	236
Bookcase, Beacon Hill, Dome Top, 2 Doors, 85 x 30 In., Pair	562
Bookcase, Chippendale, Mahogany, Swan's Neck Crest, Doors, 1780, 108 x 46 In.	6814
Bookcase, Chippendale, Molded Crest, 4 Sections, Glass Doors, c.1810, 99 x 43 In.	1659
Bookcase, Console, Regency, Rosewood, Drawers, Doors, Mirror, 1800s, 55 x 42 In. ....illus	780
Bookcase, Danner Co., Walnut, 3 Shelves, Revolving, c.1890, 47 x 24 x 24 In.	895
Bookcase, Evans Clark, Walnut, Masonite Panels, Hinged, 1950s, 64 x 60 In.	2500
Bookcase, Fruitwood, Arched Crest, Glazed Door, Claw Feet, 1800s, 76 x 41 In.	2214
Bookcase, G. Stickley, 2 V-Shaped Troughs, Cutout Ends, c.1907, 31 x 32 In.	1125
Bookcase, G. Stickley, Double Door, Eastwood, N.Y., c.1905, 56 x 57 x 13 In.	4375
Bookcase, G. Stickley, Oak, 2 Glazed Panel Doors, c.1904, 56 x 42 In.	5625
Bookcase, Louis XVI Style, Marble Top, Banded Doors, Chevron, c.1910, 62 x 74 In.	400
Bookcase, Mahogany, 2 Sections, Glazed Doors, Cutout Circles, c.1810, 85 x 38 In.	1080
Bookcase, Mahogany, 3 Sections, Reeded Columns, Glazed Door, 78 In.	1125
Bookcase, Mahogany, 4 Shelves, Shaped Sides, Drawer, Casters, c.1885, 41 x 19 In.	948
Bookcase, Mahogany, Directoire Style, 2 Glass Doors, Bun Feet, 102 x 54 In.	2400
Bookcase, On Chest, Burl Decoration, Adirondack, N.Y., c.1915, 86 x 46 In. ....illus	6150
Bookcase, Pine, 2 Sections, Glass Panel Doors, Base Molding, c.1865, 90 x 48 In.	356
Bookcase, Revolving, Mahogany, 4 Tiers, Trubner & Co., London, c.1910, 66 x 22 In.........illus	750
Bookcase, Revolving, Victorian, Oak, Wicker, 4 Tiers, Openwork, 39 x 19 In.	1541
Bookcase, T. Evan Hughes, Cherry, 3 Stack, U-Shape, c.1987, 79 x 100 In.	3437
Bookcase, Van Keppel & Green, Folding Screen Supports, 72 x 96 In.	4375
Bookcase, Walnut, 3 Glazed Panel Doors, Projecting Center, c.1865, 60 x 66 In.	1375
Bookcase, Walnut, 3 Sections, 3 Glass & 2 Wood Doors, Drawers, 70 x 67 In.	406
Bookcase, Wood, Shelves, Cupboard, Brass Butterfly Mounts, c.1975, 61 x 22 In.	123
Bookstand, Georgian, Mahogany, Upholstered, Demilune, 3 Tiers, Faux Books, 46 In.	12000
Bookstand, Wood, Scroll Sawn Backplate, Portable, c.1850, 10 x 18 x 12 In....................illus	812
Breakfront, Mahogany, 4 Astragal Glazed Doors, Urn Finials, c.1815, 96 x 104 In.	4750
Breakfront, Oak, 2 Sections, 3 Glazed Doors, Shaped Apron, c.1965, 74 x 71 In.	593

Furniture, Cabinet, Hardwood, Carved, Doors, Brass, Chinese, c.1890, 97 x 49 In. $2,400

Brunk Auctions

Furniture, Cabinet, James Mont, Wood, Silvered, Mirror, Doors, 1960s, 34 x 76 In. $1,750

Rago Arts and Auction Center

Furniture, Cabinet, Louis XVI Style, Inlay, Marble Top, Drawer, Door, Bronze Mounts, 45 x 52 In. $1,708

Neal Auctions

Furniture, Cabinet, Macassar Ebony, Mahogany, Inlaid, Bone Pulls, Art Deco, 59 In.
$1,625

New Orleans Auction Galleries

Furniture, Cabinet, Mahogany, Gilt Bronze, Glass, Marble, Mirror, 1800s, 44 x 58 In.
$8,050

Cottone Auctions

Furniture, Cabinet, Oak, Hanging, Japanned, Butterfly Hinges, 3 Shelves, England, 1700s, 35 In.
$480

Cowan's Auctions

Breakfront, Walnut, Carved, Hunt Cabinet, Mirror, U.S.A., 1800s, 110 x 84 x 27 In.		3360
Buffet, Breakfront, Mahogany, Marble, Brass Trim, Canted Corners, 39 x 102 In.		4687
Buffet, Cherry, Bowfront, Drawers, Brass Handles, Tapered Legs, c.1930, 38 x 60 In.		1400
Buffet, Fruitwood, Shaped Panel Cupboard Doors, Scroll Apron, c.1850, 34 x 54 In.		625
Buffet, Oak, Chamfered, Drawers, Cabinet Doors, Cabriole Legs, 1900s, 37 x 67 In.		400
Bureau, George III, Mahogany, Drop Front, Fitted Interior, c.1780, 40 x 39 In.	*illus*	1500
Bureau, Louis XV Style, Kingwood, Kneehole, Drawers, Inlay, Bronze, c.1910, 31 x 37 In.	*illus*	1830
Bureau, Mahogany, Block Front, Cock-Beaded, Brass, c.1770, 30 x 36 In.	*illus*	7380
Bureau, Mahogany, Roll Top, Slide, Drawers, Pilasters, 1800s, 49 x 47 In.		660
Bureau, Painted, Scroll Back, Projecting Drawer, Columns, 51 x 42 In.		1476
Bureau, Walnut, Slant Front, Banded Drawers, Square Legs, 1800s, 37 x 36 In.		937
Cabinet, Altar, Rosewood, Shaped Corbels, Tapered, Drawer, Asia, 31 x 29 In.		206
Cabinet, Baker's, Wood, Hutch, Work Top, Drawers, Block Legs, c.1890, 56 x 46 In.		165
Cabinet, Biedermeier, Fruitwood, Recessed Door, Drawer, Ebonized Columns, 31 In.		625
Cabinet, Biedermeier, Granite Top, 3 Drawers, 1900s, 31 ½ x 32 ½ In.		50
Cabinet, Boule Bowfront, Serpentine Sides, Inlaid Brass, Gilt, 45 x 65 x 21 In.		4600
Cabinet, Boule, Burl, Ebonized, Gilt, Serpentine, 1800s, 44 x 79 x 19 In.		4888
Cabinet, Byrdcliffe, Hanging, Carved Lily, Woodstock, N.Y., 1909, 20 x 40 In.		6250
Cabinet, China, Chippendale, Mahogany, Drawer, 4 Doors, 74 x 37 In.		50
Cabinet, Display, Bowfront, Flowers, Glass, Gilded Gallery, c.1910, 55 x 28 In.		1185
Cabinet, Display, Edwardian, Mahogany, Glazed Doors, Drawers, c.1900, 92 In.	*illus*	1098
Cabinet, Display, Gilt, Glass, Shaped, Carved Apron, Cabriole Legs, 57 x 27 In.		443
Cabinet, Display, Walnut, Zebrawood, 2 Sliding Glass Doors, Cupboard, 58 In.		200
Cabinet, Display, Wood, Glass Shelves, Hinged Door, Dentil Cornice, 61 x 20 In.		201
Cabinet, Drawers, Flexible Home Arrangements, Johnson Furniture Co., c.1945, 48 x 30 In.	*illus*	1750
Cabinet, Ebonized, Brass Gallery, Portrait Plaques, Ormolu, c.1865, 60 x 54 In.		1375
Cabinet, Edwardian, Bowfront, 2 Doors, Drawer, 40 x 41 In.		875
Cabinet, Filing, Oak, Drawers, Brass Handles, Derby Desk, 51 ½ x 16 In.		110
Cabinet, Florence Knoll, Marble Top, Rosewood, Chrome Base, 1960s, 26 x 75 In.		3375
Cabinet, French Provincial, Pine, Scroll, Shaped Glazed Doors, 96 x 56 In.	*illus*	750
Cabinet, G. Nakashima, Walnut, Brass, Overhang Top, Drawers, 1959, 32 x 106 In.		8750
Cabinet, G. Nakashima, Walnut, Oak, Overhang Top, Sliding Doors, 1987, 32 x 88 In.		13750
Cabinet, G. Nakashima, Walnut, Overhang Top, Sliding Doors, 1956, 32 x 83 In.		12500
Cabinet, G. Nelson, CSS, Walnut, Heated Surface, Flip Top, Herman Miller, c.1960, 36 x 25 In.	*illus*	1803
Cabinet, Hardwood, Carved, Doors, Brass, Chinese, c.1890, 97 x 49 In.	*illus*	2400
Cabinet, Hardwood, Dome Top, Notched Molding, Panel Door, 16 x 27 In.		308
Cabinet, James Mont, Wood, Silvered, Mirror, Doors, 1960s, 34 x 76 In.	*illus*	1750
Cabinet, Library, Oak, Card Filing, 120 Drawers, Cupboard, c.1910, 74 x 40 In.		3995
Cabinet, Louis XVI Style, Inlay, Marble Top, Drawer, Door, Bronze Mounts, 45 x 52 In.	*illus*	1708
Cabinet, Macassar Ebony, Mahogany, Inlaid, Bone Pulls, Art Deco, 59 In.	*illus*	1625
Cabinet, Mahogany, Gilt Bronze, Glass, Marble, Mirror, 1800s, 44 x 58 In.	*illus*	8050
Cabinet, Mahogany, Glass Door, Painted Flowers, Scroll Crest, c.1900, 59 x 24 In.		237
Cabinet, Mahogany, Inlay, 2 Astragal Glazed Doors, 1800s, 88 x 43 In.		2375
Cabinet, Mahogany, Marble Top, 2 Doors, Flowered Frieze, 1900s, 38 x 62 In.		4500
Cabinet, Mahogany, Marquetry, Serpentine Crest, Glass Doors, c.1910, 83 x 51 In.		1375
Cabinet, Maple, Iron Frame, Memphis, c.1960, 63 ½ x 38 ½ In.		400
Cabinet, Moroccan Design, Paint, Raised Panel Doors, 1940s, 41 x 55 In.		1670
Cabinet, Music, Mahogany, Mirror, Scroll Supports, Cupboard, c.1900, 58 x 33 In.		800
Cabinet, Oak, Demilune, Barrel Shape, Dentil Cornice, Spiral Carved, 14 x 18 In.		1845
Cabinet, Oak, Ebonized Trim, Walnut, 4 Doors, Lion's Head, Cupid, 77 x 71 In., Pair		2125
Cabinet, Oak, Hanging, Japanned, Butterfly Hinges, 3 Shelves, England, 1700s, 35 In.	*illus*	480
Cabinet, P. Evans, Cityscape, Chrome Metal, Wood, 24 ½ x 72 In.		5625
Cabinet, P. Evans, Wood, Steel, Multicolor, Shelves, Revolves, 1960s, 74 x 20 In.		8125
Cabinet, Painter's, Blue, 20 Drawers, Contents Name Scroll, 24 x 48 In.		12300
Cabinet, Paolo Buffa, Rosewood, Cupboards, Cross Legs, 1940s, 60 x 69 In.		6250
Cabinet, Poplar, Yellow Paint, Dovetailed, Doors, Pa., c.1835, 52 x 43 In.	*illus*	9000
Cabinet, Raymond Loewy, Wood, Steel, Enamel, Plastic, Drawers, c.1969, 36 x 79 In.	*illus*	6875
Cabinet, Record, C. Webb, Cherry, Spindled, Compartments, 64 x 20 In.		984
Cabinet, Record, Wood, Crossband, Guilloche, Speaker, Fluted, c.1930, 43 x 43 In.		120
Cabinet, Red Lacquer, Butterflies, Flowers, Doors, Chinese, c.1880, 24 x 16 In.		120

Furniture, Cabinet, Poplar, Yellow Paint, Dovetailed, Doors, Pa., c.1835, 52 x 43 In. $9,000

Brunk Auctions

Furniture, Cabinet, Raymond Loewy, Wood, Steel, Enamel, Plastic, Drawers, c.1969, 36 x 79 In. $6,875

Los Angeles Modern Auctions

Furniture, Cabinet, Sewing, Walnut, Veneer, 3 Tiers, Pulls, Spool Holders, 15 x 10 In. $875

New Orleans Auction Galleries

TIP
Have an extra key made to fit doors and drawers in old furniture. Stick it to the bottom of the piece with a wad of gum or tape.

Furniture, Cabinet, Specimen, Walnut, 2 Doors, 4 Glass Panes, 4 Fitted Drawers, 96 x 60 In. $2,280

Cowan's Auctions

Furniture, Cabinet, Spoon, Hanging, Door, Paint, AHL, 1829, 11 Spoons, 19 In. $1,320

Brunk Auctions

Furniture, Cabinet, Storage, Eames, ESU 270-C, Birch Plywood, Herman Miller, 1950, 24 x 32 In. $5,625

Wright

Furniture, Candlestand, Mahogany, Serpentine Tilt Top, Tripod Base, c.1790, 29 x 20 In. $1,353

Skinner, Inc.

Furniture, Candlestand, Windsor, Walnut, Adjustable, 2 Arms, Shelf, 1800s, 25 x 23 In. $450

Cowan's Auctions

Furniture, Canterbury, Edwards & Roberts, Rosewood, Carved, Eng., c.1875, 23 x 26 In. $768

Neal Auctions

Furniture, Canterbury, Walnut, Inlaid Urn Panel, 2 Dividers, Drawer, Victorian, 24 x 25 In.
$1,000

New Orleans Auction Galleries

Furniture, Carving Trolley, Louis XVI Style, Oak, Silver Plated Revolving Dome, 44 x 26 In.
$1,220

Neal Auctions

Furniture, Chair, Art Deco, Venturi, Plywood, Laminated, Applied Decoration, Knoll, 1986, 23 x 31 In.
$3,328

Wright

Cabinet, Red Lacquer, Hinged Mirror, Drawers, Chinese, 1900s, 7 x 8 x 10 In.	313
Cabinet, Rococo, Oak, Bombe, Carved, Leaves, Tassels, Doors, 1700s, 91 x 67 In.	296
Cabinet, Rosewood, Carved, Panel Doors, Flowers, Pierced, c.1915, 35 x 35 In.	625
Cabinet, Sewing, Walnut, Veneer, 3 Tiers, Pulls, Spool Holders, 15 x 10 In. *illus*	875
Cabinet, Smoking, G. Stickley, Door, Drawer, Blackened Mounts, 28 x 20 In.	2875
Cabinet, Specimen, Walnut, 2 Doors, 4 Glass Panes, 4 Fitted Drawers, 96 x 60 In. *illus*	2280
Cabinet, Spice, Hanging, Wood, Lift Top Cubby, Labeled Drawers, 19 x 11 In.	120
Cabinet, Spice, Walnut, Pine, 11 Drawers, Signed, T. Fisher 1887, 11 x 16 x 5 In.	1107
Cabinet, Spoon, Hanging, Door, Paint, AHL, 1829, 11 Spoons, 19 In. *illus*	1320
Cabinet, Stand, Lacquer, 2 Doors, Oval Panels, Flowers, c.1835, 42 x 11 In.	1875
Cabinet, Stickley Bros., Shaped Gallery, Glazed Doors, Copper Pulls, 74 x 48 In.	8750
Cabinet, Storage, Eames, ESU 270-C, Birch Plywood, Herman Miller, 1950, 24 x 32 In. *illus*	5625
Cabinet, Strapwork Hinges, Chinoiserie, Mid 1700s, 17½ x 22 x 9 In.	1250
Cabinet, Streamlined Design, Open Shelves, Doors, Drawers, 62 x 72 In.	1230
Cabinet, Vitrine, Napoleon III, Mahogany, Hinged Top, Glass, Mirrors, 46 In.	750
Cabinet, Wood, Carved, 2 Glazed Doors, Cupboards, Dragons, 1900s, 74 x 37 In.	984
Cabinet, Wood, Paint, Serpentine Crest, 6 Rows Of 4 Drawers, 22 x 19 In.	266
Cabinet, Wood, Trapezoid, 2 Tiers, Bamboo Openwork, 1900s, 74 x 36 In.	246
Cabinet, Wormley, Mahogany, Woven Design, Brass Legs, 1950s, 36 x 61 In.	2250
Cabinet, Wormley, Walnut & Brass, Natzler Tiles, 42 x 60 x 19 In.	3250
Candlestand, Cherry, Butternut, Round Top, Cleat, Drawer, 1800, 29 x 16 In.	1020
Candlestand, Cherry, Square, Vase Turned Post, Tripod Base, c.1780, 24 x 13 In.	1800
Candlestand, Cherry, Tilt Top, Inlay, Turned Post, Snake Feet, 1700s, 27 x 18 In.	400
Candlestand, Cherry, Tilt Top, Tripod Base, Downswept Spider Legs, c.1820, 29 In.	152
Candlestand, Chippendale, Maple, Octagonal Top, Tripod Base, American, 24½ In.	187
Candlestand, Hepplewhite, Tilt Top, Curly Maple, c.1810, 28½ In.	489
Candlestand, Mahogany, Queen Anne, Tilt Top, Late 1700s, 38 x 22 In.	180
Candlestand, Mahogany, Serpentine Tilt Top, Tripod Base, c.1790, 29 x 20 In. *illus*	1353
Candlestand, Mahogany, Shaped Tilt Top, Bulbous Post, Reeded, 1800s, 26 x 25 In.	154
Candlestand, Mahogany, Tilt Top, Inlaid Eagle, Swollen Post, 1810, 31 x 22 In.	3851
Candlestand, Painted, Octagonal, Swollen Stem, Pendant, Tripod, c.1785, 25 In.	1500
Candlestand, Queen Anne, Cherry, Dish Top, Turned Post, Snake Feet, 1700s, 28 x 14 In.	330
Candlestand, Queen Anne, Cherry, Octagonal, Flowerhead, Tripod, c.1760, 28 x 19 In.	296
Candlestand, Queen Anne, Cherry, Tray Top, Drawer, Urn, Tripod, c.1770, 26 x 16 In.	3259
Candlestand, Shaker, Maple, Rotating Round Top, Threaded Post, 1800s, 34 x 16 In.	615
Candlestand, Walnut, Red Paint, Round Top, Carved Stem, Tripod, c.1710, 26 In.	3000
Candlestand, Walnut, Scalloped Top, Spiral Post, Cabriole Legs, Pad Feet, 26 In.	240
Candlestand, Windsor, Walnut, Adjustable, 2 Arms, Shelf, 1800s, 25 x 23 In. *illus*	450
Canterbury, American Classical Mahogany, Lyre Ends, 24 x 19 x 16 In.	1586
Canterbury, Bamboo, Demi-Lune, 20 In.	150
Canterbury, Edwards & Roberts, Rosewood, Carved, Eng., c.1875, 23 x 26 In. *illus*	768
Canterbury, Mahogany, Drawer, 20½ x 18⅛ In.	350
Canterbury, Mahogany, Scroll Dividers, Shell Crest, Bulbous Feet, c.1855, 20 x 20 In.	711
Canterbury, Regency, 1800s, 19 x 19 In.	197
Canterbury, Walnut, Dividers, Scroll Panels, England, c.1850, 20 x 25 x 17 In.	549
Canterbury, Walnut, Inlaid Urn Panel, 2 Dividers, Drawer, Victorian, 24 x 25 In. *illus*	1000
Cart, Book, Mahogany, 3 Shelves, Spoke Wheels, Casters, 30 x 8 In.	161
Cart, Dessert, Brass, Glass, Mirror Top, Towel Rods, Wine Rack, 26 x 30 In.	175
Carving Trolley, Louis XVI Style, Oak, Silver Plated Revolving Dome, 44 x 26 In. *illus*	1220
Cassone, Walnut, Carved, Lift Top, Figural Frieze, Paw Feet, Italy, 1700s, 26 x 70 In.	600
Cassone, Walnut, Carved, Sarcophagus Shape, Flowers, Guilloche, c.1900, 27 x 68 In.	3500
Cellarette, G. Stickley, Single Door, Copper Inset, Flip Top, 1905, 43 x 24 In.	1875
Cellarette, George III, Mahogany, Brass Bound, 3 Bands, 28 x 19 In.	2812
Cellarette, Hepplewhite, Mahogany, Tapered, c.1820, 29½ x 21 In.	700
Cellarette, Hollywood Regency, Beverly Hills Hotel, 1950s, 26 In.	240
Cellarette, Mahogany, Carved, Sarcophagus, Gadrooned Lid, c.1850, 20 x 28 In.	1098
Cellarette, Mahogany, Coffin Shape, Turned Post, Curved Legs, c.1810, 32 x 17 In.	1187
Cellarette, Mahogany, Shaped, Lift Top, Beaded, Brass Handles, 1800s, 22 x 27 In.	2000
Cellarette, On Stand, Federal Style, Walnut, Dividers, 33 x 22 x 16 In.	649
Cellarette, Regency, Mahogany, Brass Mount, Molded Rim, Tapered, 20 x 28 In.	1900

F

Furniture, Chair, Baroque, Leaf & Scroll Carving, Needlepoint Upholstered, 47 In. $500

New Orleans Auction Galleries

Furniture, Chair, Bugatti, Walnut, Pewter, Copper, Vellum, Italy, 1910s, 32 x 16 In. $2,125

Rago Arts and Auction Center

Furniture, Chair, C. Pollock, Sling, Chrome Plate, Lambskin, Arms, Knoll, 1970s, 28 In., Pair $1,625

New Orleans Auction Galleries

Furniture, Chair, C. Wynn, Alice In Wonderland, Enamel, Reclaimed Parts, 2016, 43 In. $3,000

Rago Arts and Auction Center

Furniture, Chair, Carved Crest, 4 Turned Spindles, Upholstered Seat, Spain, 1700s, 33 In. $180

Cowan's Auctions

Furniture, Chair, Carved, Flowers, Vines, A.J. Sutton Feb. 4-1950, Child's $30

Cowan's Auctions

Furniture, Chair, Chippendale, Mahogany, Carved, Needlepoint, Slip Seat, Arms, 1700s $512

Neal Auctions

Furniture, Chair, Chippendale, Mahogany, Carved, Urn Shape Splat, Slip Seat, Arms, 38 In. $224

Hess Auction Group

Furniture, Chair, Chippendale, Venturi, Plywood, Knoll, 1985, 37 ½ In., Pair $4,375

Wright

Furniture, Chair, Clamshell, Walnut, Upholstered, S.J. Wiener, Kodawood, 1960s, 32 In.
$154

Skinner, Inc.

Furniture, Chair, Clare Graham, Tin Can Lids, Metal Studs, 2000s, 28 x 23 In.
$2,875

Rago Arts and Auction Center

Furniture, Chair, Club, Walnut, Cane Barrel Back, Upholstered Seat, c.1950, 28 In., Set Of 3
$800

Cowan's Auctions

Cellarette, Walnut, Hinged Lid, Stand, Slide, Square Legs, c.1810, 43 x 20 In.	6000
Chair Set, A. Umanoff, Mayan Sun, Metal, Pierced Sunburst, Saddle Seat, 36 In., 4	600
Chair Set, G. Nelson, Pretzel, Plywood, Vinyl Seat, H. Miller, 1950s, 29 In., 4	3000
Chair Set, G. Stickley, Dining, Slat Back, Leather Seat, 1 Armchair, 36 In., 8	4688
Chair Set, Georgian Style, Mahogany, Ribbonback, Marlboro Legs, 37 In., 10	2250
Chair Set, Hollywood Regency, Mahogany, Urn Back, Grosfeld House, 36 In., 4	1800
Chair Set, Leather, Ribbed Back & Cushion, Straight Sides & Arms, 32 In., 6	875
Chair Set, Louis XVI Style, Carved, Leather Back & Seat, c.1940, 38 In., 6	900
Chair Set, Louis XVI Style, Multicolor, Cane, c.1910, 34 ½ In., 6	475
Chair Set, Lucite, Continuous Back & Legs, Panel, Velvet Seat, 1970s, 29 In., 4	500
Chair Set, Midcentury, Teak, Fiberglass, Arm, White, 33 x 24 In., 4	100
Chair Set, Peter Danko, Eco-Eden, Bentwood, Ash, Plywood, 32 x 21 In., 6	375
Chair Set, Ron Arad, Empty Chair, Curves, Chrome Legs, 36 ½ x 17 In., 6	5625
Chair Set, V. Magistretti, Resin, Black, Arm, Italy, 29 x 23 In., 4	343
Chair, Andre Arbus, Mahogany, Bronze, Upholstered, Arms, c.1948, 33 x 27 In.	10000
Chair, Art Deco, Venturi, Plywood, Laminated, Applied Decoration, Knoll, 1986, 23 x 31 In....*illus*	3328
Chair, Banister Back, Bow Heart, Paint, Spindles, Splint Seat, Arms, c.1750, 47 In.	3250
Chair, Banister Back, William & Mary, Black Paint, Carved Crest, 1700s, 52 In.	510
Chair, Banister Back, William & Mary, Scroll Crest, Downswept Arms, c.1765, 43 In.	1422
Chair, Banister Back, Wood, Black Paint, Heart Cutout, c.1750, 45 In.	9000
Chair, Banister, Black, Carved, Pierced, Scroll Crest, Woven Seat, c.1750, 45 In.	1600
Chair, Banister, Brown Paint, Cutout Heart Crest, Turned Legs, c.1750, 47 In.	4750
Chair, Barcelona, Tufted, Black, Leather, 29 x 30 In., Pair	1500
Chair, Baroque, Leaf & Scroll Carving, Needlepoint Upholstered, 47 In. ...*illus*	500
Chair, Bergere, Louis XVI Style, Giltwood, Cane Back, Arms, c.1930, 41 In.	400
Chair, Bergere, Louis XVI Style, Giltwood, Scroll, Oval Back, Arms, 36 In.	1062
Chair, Bergere, Mahogany, Stepped Crest, Pineapple Finials, Arms, c.1865, 43 In.	937
Chair, Bergere, Upholstered, Gilt, Fluted Legs, Padded Arms, c.1910, 43 In.	3250
Chair, Birch, Square Back, Tapered Legs, Tubular Stretcher, c.1938, 33 In.	4688
Chair, Black Forest, Parquetry, Stencil, 35in.	375
Chair, Black Forest, Walnut, Carved, Bear, Twig Shape Legs, c.1875, Child's, 39 In.	885
Chair, Bugatti, Walnut, Pewter, Copper, Vellum, Italy, 1910s, 32 x 16 In....*illus*	2125
Chair, Bugatti, Walnut, Round Suede Seat, Square Back, Tassels, 1900s, 53 In.	11875
Chair, C. Pollock, Sling, Chrome Plate, Lambskin, Arms, Knoll, 1970s, 28 In., Pair....*illus*	1625
Chair, C. Wynn, Alice In Wonderland, Enamel, Reclaimed Parts, 2016, 43 In. ...*illus*	3000
Chair, Carved Crest, 4 Turned Spindles, Upholstered Seat, Spain, 1700s, 33 In....*illus*	180
Chair, Carved, Flowers, Vines, A.J. Sutton Feb. 4-1950, Child's....*illus*	30
Chair, Carved, Horseshoe Back, Folding, Openwork Splat, Arms, 1900s, 42 In.	1067
Chair, Chippendale, Cherry, Woven Slip Seat, Frame, Square Legs, c.1775, 39 In.	117
Chair, Chippendale, Mahogany, Carved, Needlepoint, Slip Seat, Arms, 1700s ...*illus*	512
Chair, Chippendale, Mahogany, Carved, Urn Shape Splat, Slip Seat, Arms, 38 In. ...*illus*	224
Chair, Chippendale, Mahogany, Shaped, Pierced Splat, Claw Feet, c.1780, 38 In.	415
Chair, Chippendale, Venturi, Plywood, Knoll, 1985, 37 ½ In., Pair....*illus*	4375
Chair, Clamshell, Walnut, Upholstered, S.J. Wiener, Kodawood, 1960s, 32 In....*illus*	154
Chair, Clare Graham, Tin Can Lids, Metal Studs, 2000s, 28 x 23 In. ...*illus*	2875
Chair, Club, Walnut, Cane Barrel Back, Upholstered Seat, c.1950, 28 In., Set Of 3....*illus*	800
Chair, Corner, Aesthetic Revival, Ebonized, Spindle Back, Uprights, c.1875, 30 In., Pair	549
Chair, Corner, Chippendale, Maple, Birch, Pierced Splats, Plank Seat, 31 In.	720
Chair, Corner, George II, Walnut, Shell & Flower Crest, Rosettes, 1700s, 31 In.	1416
Chair, Corner, Louis XV, Cane Back, Seat, 36 x 21 In.	156
Chair, Corner, Maple, Splint Seat, Bird Heads, Turned Spindles, c.1710, 31 In.	1300
Chair, Corner, Queen Anne, Maple, Shaped Splats, Pegged, U.S.A., 32 In....*illus*	625
Chair, Corner, Smoking, Chippendale, Mahogany, Scalloped Rails, c.1770, 33 In.	497
Chair, Corner, Walnut, Flowerhead & Shell Crest, George II, 31 ½ In.	1415
Chair, De Sede, Aluminum, Steel, Leather, Post, 5 Legs, Swivel, 1970s, 34 In., Pair	1125
Chair, Eames, Lounge, Ottoman, Rosewood, Leather & Aluminum, 33 x 32 In.	4025
Chair, Eames, Lounge, Ottoman, Wood, Leather, H. Miller, c.1995, 2 Piece ...*illus*	4375
Chair, Eames, Wire Chair, DKR Model, 2 Piece Bikini Cushion, Blue, 32 x 18 In.	125
Chair, Edwardian, Shieldback, Carved, Flowers, Downswept Arms, c.1910, 37 In.	562
Chair, Egg, Arne Jacobsen, Cotton Upholstery, Swivel, Denmark, c.1960, 41 In.	780

F

Furniture, Chair, Corner, Queen Anne, Maple, Shaped Splats, Pegged, U.S.A., 32 In.
$625

New Orleans Auction Galleries

Furniture, Chair, Eames, Lounge, Ottoman, Wood, Leather, H. Miller, c.1995, 2 Piece
$4,375

Los Angeles Modern Auctions

Furniture, Chair, Esherick, Captain's, Walnut, Saddle Leather Strap Seat, 31 x 23 In.
$9,375

Rago Arts and Auction Center

Names for Mission-Style Furniture
Craftsman was the name used by Gustav Stickley. Furniture by other makers was called Arts & Crafts, Crafts-Style, Hand-Craft, Mission, Quaint, or Roycroft. To add to the confusion, the family name was used by Gustav's relatives.

Furniture, Chair, Fauteuil, Charles X, Rosewood, Upholstered, Open Arms, c.1835, 33 In., Pair
$2,375

New Orleans Auction Galleries

Furniture, Chair, Fruitwood, Carved, Child, Fruit, Branches, Padded Back & Seat, 1800s, 54 In.
$4,500

New Orleans Auction Galleries

Furniture, Chair, G. Nelson, Lounge, Metal, Upholstered, Wood Arms, H. Miller, 1950, 29 In.
$1,250

Los Angeles Modern Auctions

Furniture, Chair, G. Stickley, Morris, Spindles, Drop Arm, Leather Cushions, c.1905, 41 x 37 In.
$2,875

Rago Arts and Auction Center

Furniture, Chair, G. Stickley, Willow, Leather Seat Cushion, Arms, 1912-15, 35 x 32 In.
$2,000

Rago Arts and Auction Center

Furniture, Chair, G. Stickley, Willow, Woven, Cushion, Arms, Eastwood, 1912, 36 x 24 In.
$1,625

Rago Arts and Auction Center

FURNITURE

Furniture, Chair, Gerrit Rietveld, Zigzag, Cherry, Laminated, Cassina, 1990s, 29 x 17 In., Pair
$1,500

Rago Arts and Auction Center

Furniture, Chair, Gothic Revival, Venturi, Plywood, Grandmother Pattern, Knoll, 1984, 41 In.
$6,250

Wright

Furniture, Chair, Hollowed Maple Log, Hornbeam, Carved, Nails, c.1710, 28 x 18 In., Child's
$3,630

James D. Julia Auctioneers

Furniture, Chair, House Of Representatives, Oak, Carved, Shield, Arms, c.1857, 42 In.
$12,500

Neal Auctions

Furniture, Chair, Hunzinger, Walnut, Upholstered, Turned Stiles, Legs, c.1868, 33 In.
$492

Skinner, Inc.

Furniture, Chair, Joe, Leather, Grommets, Baseball Mitt, Poltronova, 1970s, 36 x 67 In.
$6,875

Rago Arts and Auction Center

Furniture, Chair, Kagan-Dreyfuss, Lounge, Contour, Walnut, Leather, 1954, 30 x 34 In., Pair
$30,000

Wright

Furniture, Chair, Louis XV Style, Gilt, Upholstered, Carved, Arms, c.1900, 43 In., Pair
$9,000

Brunk Auctions

Furniture, Chair, Mahogany, Inlay, Flower Baskets, Shaped Crest, Arms, Dutch, 1800s, 46 In.
$180

Cowan's Auctions

Chair, Esherick, Captain's, Walnut, Saddle Leather Strap Seat, 31 x 23 In.........................*illus*	9375
Chair, Fauteuil, Charles X, Rosewood, Upholstered, Open Arms, c.1835, 33 In., Pair...........*illus*	2375
Chair, Fauteuil, Gilt, Guilloche, Upholstered, Carved, Open Arms, c.1900, 39 In., Pair	2500
Chair, Fauteuil, Louis XVI Style, Painted, Upholstered, Open Arms, 40 In., Pair......................	593
Chair, Fauteuil, Mahogany, Dome Crest, Upholstered, Open Arms, c.1835, 36 In., Pair..............	937
Chair, Fauteuil, Upholstered, Leaf Crest, Urn Splat, Saber Legs, Arms, c.1890, 36 In., Pair........	2125
Chair, Finn Juhl, Teak, Upholstered, Brass, Curved, Arms, 1950s, 30 In.	6250
Chair, Frank Lloyd Wright, Usonian, Sturges Residence, 1939, 29 x 20 In.	10000
Chair, French Restoration Style, Leaves, Scroll, Saber Legs, 1800s, 38 In.	275
Chair, Fruitwood, Carved, Child, Fruit, Branches, Padded Back & Seat, 1800s, 54 In. ....*illus*	4500
Chair, G. Nakashima, Walnut, Canted Stiles, Spindle Back, Dish Seat, 35 In.	3250
Chair, G. Nelson, Coconut, Cream, 34 x 41 In.	937
Chair, G. Nelson, Lounge, Metal, Upholstered, Wood Arms, H. Miller, 1950, 29 In..............*illus*	1250
Chair, G. Stickley, Morris, Spindles, Drop Arm, Leather Cushions, c.1905, 41 x 37 In.........*illus*	2875
Chair, G. Stickley, Morris, Wood, Cushions, Flared Legs, Bow Arms, 38 In.	11250
Chair, G. Stickley, Willow, Leather Seat Cushion, Arms, 1912-15, 35 x 32 In.....................*illus*	2000
Chair, G. Stickley, Willow, Woven, Cushion, Arms, Eastwood, 1912, 36 x 24 In...................*illus*	1625
Chair, Gazing, Wood, Tilt Back, Rotating Headrest, Arms, 1800s, 34 x 60 In.	1481
Chair, Gehry, Vitra Wiggle, Laminated Cardboard, Masonite, 1990s, 31 In.	1188
Chair, Georgian, Mahogany, Upholstered, Cabriole Legs, Shaped Arms, c.1760..........................	1404
Chair, Gerrit Rietveld, Zigzag, Cherry, Laminated, Cassina, 1990s, 29 x 17 In., Pair.........*illus*	1500
Chair, Gothic Revival, Mahogany, Upholstered, Intertwining Splat, c.1770, 39 In.	468
Chair, Gothic Revival, Venturi, Plywood, Grandmother Pattern, Knoll, 1984, 41 In..........*illus*	6250
Chair, H. Bertoia, Steel, Paint, Open Diamond, Red, Black, 31 x 33 In., Pair	554
Chair, H. Probber, Lounge, High Back, Angular, Piping, c.1960, 36 x 32 In., Pair	1500
Chair, H. Thor-Larsen, Ovalia, Fiberglass, Aluminum, Knit Upholstery, 1968, 50 In.................	3750
Chair, Hollowed Maple Log, Hornbeam, Carved, Nails, c.1710, 28 x 18 In., Child's.............*illus*	3630
Chair, Hollywood Regency, Gilt, Black Paint, Tapestry, Suede Back, 35 In., Pair	480
Chair, Hollywood Regency, Paint, Upholstered, Carved, Spiral Arms, 1950s, 43 In.	375
Chair, Horn, Leather, Serpentine, Steer Horn Crest, Bone Inlay, c.1885, 57 In.	9375
Chair, House Of Representatives, Oak, Carved, Shield, Arms, c.1857, 42 In.......................*illus*	12500
Chair, Hunzinger, Walnut, Upholstered, Turned Stiles, Legs, c.1868, 33 In.......................*illus*	492
Chair, I. Kenmochi, Kashiwado Chair, Cedar, 1961, 32 x 27 In.	4062
Chair, James Mont, Club, Wood, Enamel, Upholstered, Rolled Trim, 30 x 33 In.........................	1000
Chair, Jean Prouve, Vitra, White, Black Metal...	406
Chair, Jeanneret, Lounge, Birch, Metal, Scissor Style, 1950s, 30 In., Pair	4688
Chair, Joe, Leather, Grommets, Baseball Mitt, Poltronova, 1970s, 36 x 67 In. ....*illus*	6875
Chair, John Jeliff, Walnut, Needlepoint, Flowers, 1870	319
Chair, Kagan-Dreyfuss, Lounge, Contour, Walnut, Leather, 1954, 30 x 34 In., Pair...........*illus*	30000
Chair, Ladder Back, Curved Slats, Woven Seat, Stretcher, c.1840, 30 In., Pair	356
Chair, Laminated Rosewood, Pierced, Carved, Old Finish, 1800s, 34 In.	259
Chair, Louis XV Style, Carved Back, Loose Cushion, Cabriole Legs, 56 In.	375
Chair, Louis XV Style, Gilt, Upholstered, Carved, Arms, c.1900, 43 In., Pair......................*illus*	9000
Chair, Louis XVI, Aubusson Tapestry Back, c.1910, 37 x 23 In., Pair.....................................	1063
Chair, Louis XVI, Fruitwood, Upholstered, 36 x 16 In., Pair	375
Chair, Lounge, Rocking, Walnut, Upholstered, Curved, Pearsall, 1960s, 36 x 60 In....................	4063
Chair, Lounge, Teak, Sheepskin, Serpentine, Curved Seat & Arms, 1960, 40 In.	840
Chair, Mahogany, Carved Crest, Pierced, Vase Shape Splat, Scroll Arms, 40 In.........................	1750
Chair, Mahogany, Carved, Shells, Flowers, Pierced Splat, Scroll Arms, c.1900, 54 In................	948
Chair, Mahogany, Dome Back, Eagle Head, Scroll Arms, 1900s, 44 In., Pair............................	500
Chair, Mahogany, Inlay, Flower Baskets, Shaped Crest, Arms, Dutch, 1800s, 46 In...........*illus*	180
Chair, Mahogany, Serpentine, Shield Shape Splat, Cabriole Legs, 1800s, 45 In.	492
Chair, Mahogany, Tufted, Reeded, Top Shape Feet, Padded Arms, c.1835, 46 In.	1250
Chair, Mahogany, Upholstered, Carved, Vines, Shieldback, Slats, 1790, 38 In., Pair	4444
Chair, Maple, Ash, Vase & Ring-Turned Stiles, Spindles, Arms, c.1700, 46 In...................*illus*	1845
Chair, Marcel Breuer, Birch, Plywood, For Bryn Mawr College, 1938, 33 In......................*illus*	4375
Chair, Marcel Breuer, Chrome & Leather, 1900s, 30 In..	120
Chair, Masonic, Wood, High Back, Carved, Symbols, Finials, 49 In., Pair................................	1067
Chair, Metamorphic, Oak, Carved, Masks, Cabriole Legs, Step Stool, Arms, c.1850, 38 In. ..*illus*	1708
Chair, Milo Baughman, Steel, Bronzed, Upholstered, T. Coggin, 1970s, 27 In., Pair.................	4375

Furniture, Chair, Maple, Ash, Vase & Ring-Turned Stiles, Spindles, Arms, c.1700, 46 In.
$1,845

Skinner, Inc.

Furniture, Chair, Marcel Breuer, Birch, Plywood, For Bryn Mawr College, 1938, 33 In.
$4,375

Rago Arts and Auction Center

Furniture, Chair, Metamorphic, Oak, Carved, Masks, Cabriole Legs, Step Stool, Arms, c.1850, 38 In.
$1,708

Neal Auctions

FURNITURE

Furniture, Chair, Raked Arrow Back, Bamboo Turned Legs, Painted, Pa., 1800s, 25 In., Child's
$472

Hess Auction Group

Furniture, Chair, Ray Lewis, Cast Aluminum, Fauna Impala, 35 In., Pair
$2,530

Cottone Auctions

Furniture, Chair, Rococo Revival, Walnut, Carved, Charles White, Arms, c.1850, 35 In., Pair
$11,285

Neal Auctions

Furniture, Chair, Rohlfs, Hall, High Back, Carved, R. Cipher, c.1904, 57 In.
$20,000

Rago Arts and Auction Center

Furniture, Chair, Rosewood, Upholstered, Brass Casters, Swan Arms, c.1810, 36 In.
$575

Cottone Auctions

Furniture, Chair, V. Kagan, Lounge, Tri-Symmetric, Aluminum, Leather, 1970s, 42 x 21 In.
$3,000

Rago Arts and Auction Center

Furniture, Chair, Viennese Secessionist, Bentwood, Mahogany, c.1905, 39 In., Pair
$4,305

Skinner, Inc.

Furniture, Chair, W. McArthur, Lounge, Upholstered, Aluminum, Tubular Frame, Arms, 1933, 32 In.
$1,067

James D. Julia Auctioneers

Furniture, Chair, Wegner, Woven Seat, Arms, Carl Hansen & Son, 1951, 28 In.
$6,563

Los Angeles Modern Auctions

Chair, Necessary, Potty, Scroll Crest, Cutout, Canted Sides, Arms, c.1710, 27 In.	1481
Chair, Oak, Carved, Lollipop, George Hunzinger, 38 x 25 x 18 In.	1610
Chair, Oak, Leather Seat, Mark On Rail, GPI, Grove Park Inn, Furniture, 40¾ In.	1680
Chair, Office, Heywood-Wakefield, Walnut, Curved Back, Casters, 30 x 30 In.	584
Chair, Ottoman, Eames, Tan Leather, Herman Miller, c.1980	5625
Chair, Ottoman, Wegner, Teak, Upholstered, Curved Back, Arms, 1960s, 39 In.	7500
Chair, Ottoman, Wormley, Leather, Swivel, Casters, Dunbar, 1950s, 30 In.	1250
Chair, P. Paulin, Artifort Ribbon, Upholstered, Beech Base, 28 In., Pair	3750
Chair, Queen Anne Style, Mahogany, Upholstered, Barrel Back, Cabriole Legs, 44 In., Pair	1187
Chair, Queen Anne, Leather, Arched Crest, Wings, Scroll Arms, c.1950, 43 In.	1185
Chair, Queen Anne, Mahogany, Vase Splat, Stretcher, Spanish Feet, c.1750, 41 In.	240
Chair, Queen Anne, Maple, Upholstered Over Rail, Turned Stretchers, 1700s, 40 In.	708
Chair, Raked Arrow Back, Bamboo Turned Legs, Painted, Pa., 1800s, 25 In., Child's *illus*	472
Chair, Ray Lewis, Cast Aluminum, Fauna Impala, 35 In., Pair *illus*	2530
Chair, Rocker, is listed under Rocker in this category.	
Chair, Rococo Revival, Walnut, Carved, Charles White, Arms, c.1850, 35 In., Pair *illus*	11285
Chair, Rohlfs, Hall, High Back, Carved, R. Cipher, c.1904, 57 In. *illus*	20000
Chair, Rosewood, Grained, Fruit Basket, Flowers, Stencil Design, c.1850	90
Chair, Rosewood, Upholstered, Brass Casters, Swan Arms, c.1810, 36 In. *illus*	575
Chair, Rosewood, Vase Shape Splat, Swirl Feather Crest, Carved, c.1710, 49 In.	7000
Chair, Salterini, John, Iron, Caned, Arm, 1960s, 32 x 27 In.	175
Chair, Shaker, Pine, Stain, Spindle Back, Block Crest, Splayed Legs, 1800s, 24 In.	523
Chair, Shaker, Tilter, Maple, Slat Back, Stencil Marked, c.1840, 40 In.	1169
Chair, Slipper, Serpentine Crest, Fruit, Pierced Scroll Leaf Splat, c.1865, 38 In.	687
Chair, V. Kagan, Lounge, Tri-Symmetric, Aluminum, Leather, 1970s, 42 x 21 In. *illus*	3000
Chair, V. Kagan, Nautilus, Swivel, 1900s, 29 x 36 In., Pair	1035
Chair, Viennese Secessionist, Bentwood, Mahogany, c.1905, 39 In., Pair *illus*	4305
Chair, W. Friedrich, Steer Horn, Acorn Tips, Claw Feet, 37 x 32 In.	3900
Chair, W. McArthur, Lounge, Upholstered, Aluminum, Tubular Frame, Arms, 1933, 32 In.*illus*	1067
Chair, W. Platner, Steel Wire, Nickeled, Upholstered, Arms, c.1970, 30 In., Pair	2952
Chair, Walnut, Arched Back, Caryatids, Pendant Finial, Arms, c.1885, 49 In.	1599
Chair, Walnut, Webbed Back, Damask Upholstery, Claw Feet, George II, 40 In.	720
Chair, Wassily, Steel, Chrome Plate & Leather, 29 x 31 In., Pair	1046
Chair, Wegner, Teak, Spindled Splat, Padded, Continuous Arm, 1986, 32 In.	1625
Chair, Wegner, Woven Seat, Arms, Carl Hansen & Son, 1951, 28 In. *illus*	6563
Chair, Wendell Castle, Molar, Fiberglass, Gel Coated, c.1971, 27 x 37 x 32 In.	1955
Chair, William IV, Mahogany, Cane Back, Saber Legs, Arms, c.1835, 38 In.	1250
Chair, Windsor, Elm, Plank Seat, Cabriole Legs, Pad Feet, Arms, 1700s, 39 In.	177
Chair, Windsor, Elm, Plank Seat, Shaped Splat, Spindles, Arms, 1700s, 39 In. *illus*	780
Chair, Windsor, Fanback, Curved Crest, Paint, Initials, c.1790, 37 In., Pair *illus*	861
Chair, Windsor, Fanback, Mixed Wood, Plank Seat, c.1775, 36 In.	140
Chair, Windsor, Fanback, Shaped Crest, Scroll Ears, Plank Seat, 1700s, 37 In. *illus*	300
Chair, Windsor, Fanback, Spindles, Dark Green, Knuckle Arms, 42 In.	330
Chair, Windsor, Paint, Bow Back, Vase & Ring Turned, Saddle, c.1775, 36 In.	6500
Chair, Windsor, Paint, Scroll Crest, Drawer Under Seat, Paddle Arm, c.1785, 45 In.	1541
Chair, Windsor, Sack Back, Bowed, Spindles, Incised, Swollen Legs, c.1815, 35 In.	119
Chair, Windsor, Sack Back, Mixed Wood, Oval Seat, Arms, c.1790, 35 In. *illus*	360
Chair, Windsor, Sack Back, Spindles, Black, Turned Supports & Legs, Arms, 42 In.	130
Chair, Windsor, Sack Back, Spindles, Mahogany Armrests, 1700s, 39 In. *illus*	308
Chair, Windsor, Sack Back, Spindles, Paint, Scroll Arms, Turned Legs, 1800s, 36 In.	492
Chair, Windsor, Splayed Legs, Shaped Handrests, Continuous Arm, 37 In.	1476
Chair, Windsor, Wood, Bow Back, Spindles, Saddle Seat, Shaped Arms, 37 In.	47
Chair, Windsor, Yellow Paint, Bow Back, Spindles, Writing Arm, 48 In.	240
Chair, Windsor, Yew, Oak, Pierced Splat, Saddle Seat, Arms, c.1785, 39 ½ In. *illus*	121
Chair, Wing, Federal, Mahogany, Upholstered, Scroll Arms, Reeded Legs, 1800s, 45 In.	510
Chair, Wing, George III, Mahogany, Dome Back, Outscrolled Arms, c.1810, 46 In.	875
Chair, Wood, Bar Crest Rail, Armrest, Graining, Chinese, c.1900, 27 In.	246
Chair, Wood, Hemp, Horseshoe, Pierced Splat, Footrest, Folds, 1900s, 43 In., Pair	615
Chair, Yacht, Leather, Brass Finials, Ship's Wheel Supports, Arms, c.1935, 36 In.	356
Chair-Table, Pine, Lift Top Seat, 3-Board Scrub Top, 30 x 53 In.	600

Furniture, Chair, Windsor, Elm, Plank Seat, Shaped Splat, Spindles, Arms, 1700s, 39 In.
$780

Brunk Auctions

Furniture, Chair, Windsor, Fanback, Curved Crest, Paint, Initials, c.1790, 37 In., Pair
$861

Cowan's Auctions

Furniture, Chair, Windsor, Fanback, Shaped Crest, Scroll Ears, Plank Seat, 1700s, 37 In.
$300

Cowan's Auctions

Furniture, Chair, Windsor, Sack Back, Mixed Wood, Oval Seat, Arms, c.1790, 35 In.
$360

Cowan's Auctions

Furniture, Chair, Windsor, Sack Back, Spindles, Mahogany Armrests, 1700s, 39 In.
$308

Cowan's Auctions

Furniture, Chair, Windsor, Yew, Oak, Pierced Splat, Saddle Seat, Arms, c.1785, 39½ In.
$121

James D. Julia Auctioneers

Chair-Table, Pine, Red Wash, Early 1800s, 28 x 49 In.	780
Chair-Table, Writing, Bamboo, Spindles, Drawers, Round Legs, c.1815, 34 In.	266
Chaise Longue, After Le Corbusier, 62 In.	468
Chaise Longue, Louis XV Style, Carved, Downswept Arms, Extended Seat, 36 In.	900
Chaise Longue, O.M. Bouloum, Fiberglass, Man Shaped, c.1972, 24 x 60 In.	750
Chaise Longue, Upholstered, Paint, Arch Crest, Cane Back, Arms, c.1965, 34 x 65 In.	237
Chaise Longue, Walter Lamb, Bronze, Brown-Jordan, c.1950, 68½ In. *illus*	4688
Chest, American Empire, Mahogany, Poplar, Veneer, 4 Drawers Over 1, 15 x 15 In.	840
Chest, Arts & Crafts, Oak, Hinged Top, Paneled, Reeded Legs, c.1910, 18 x 21 In.	150
Chest, Bachelor's, Georgian, Mahogany, Drawers, Brass Pulls, c.1800, 36 x 27 In.	1230
Chest, Bachelor's, Mahogany, Cock-Beaded, Scroll Bracket Feet, c.1790, 36 x 37 In.	687
Chest, Bedding, Futon Storage, 2 Parts, Flame Grained, Japan, 67 x 71 In.	2400
Chest, Biedermeier, Birch, 36 x 48 In.	437
Chest, Blanket, Arts & Crafts, Oak, Bench Top, Copper Hardware, 20 x 36 In.	1625
Chest, Blanket, Baroque, Oak, Carved, Flowers, Leaves, Bun Feet, c.1800, 38 x 20 In. *illus*	360
Chest, Blanket, Blue, Dovetailed, New England, 21½ x 53 In.	1320
Chest, Blanket, Butternut, Drawers, Tombstone Panel, Beaded, 1881, 26 x 45 In.	3720
Chest, Blanket, Cedar, Green & Red Sponge Paint, Till, 1800s, 26 x 54 In. *illus*	1200
Chest, Blanket, Cherry, Maple, Hinged Lid, Dovetailed Bracket Base, 1800s, 9 In.	1872
Chest, Blanket, Chippendale, Pine, Drawers, Hinged Lid, Bracket Feet, c.1785, 48 x 38 In.	356
Chest, Blanket, Gray To Black Paint, Breadboard Ends, N.C., 1800s, 20 x 34 In.	360
Chest, Blanket, Mahogany Grain, Hinged, Drawers, French Feet, c.1835, 44 x 43 In.	237
Chest, Blanket, Molded Lift Top, Drawers, Turnip Feet, c.1700, 44 x 41 In.	17000
Chest, Blanket, Paint, 6-Board, Lift Top, Cutouts, Heart Pendant, 1710, 27 x 48 In.	6500
Chest, Blanket, Pine, 6-Board, Shaped Ends, c.1880, 27 x 42 x 18 In.	300
Chest, Blanket, Pine, Blue Paint, Sprays, Iron Handles, Block Feet, 1825, 26 x 55 In.	450
Chest, Blanket, Pine, Burnt Sienna Grain, Drawers, Interior Till, 1800s, 25 x 44 In.	300
Chest, Blanket, Pine, Dark Blue Green, John Bellinger, 1814, 19 x 44 x 19 In.	960
Chest, Blanket, Pine, Double Tilled, Drawers, Molded Base, New England, 17 x 42 In.	120
Chest, Blanket, Pine, Hinged Lid, Dovetailed, Painted, Fitted, Till, Pa., c.1810, 22 x 45 In. *illus*	242
Chest, Blanket, Pine, Hinged Top, Molded, 3 Drawers, Pilasters, c.1750, 52 x 41 In.	830
Chest, Blanket, Pine, Paint, Brass Lock, Leather Straps, Arch Legs, c.1830, 18 x 30 In.	2583
Chest, Blanket, Pine, Paint, Molded Lift Top, Drawer, Cutout Ends, c.1745, 27 x 40 In.	2500
Chest, Blanket, Pine, Paint, Nailed Construction, Shaped Skirt, c.1850, 24 x 43 In. *illus*	360
Chest, Blanket, Pine, Paint, Yellow, Green, Turned Ball Feet, c.1870, 30 x 51 In.	840
Chest, Blanket, Pine, Red, Drawer, Arched, Shaped, 35 x 40½ In.	480
Chest, Blanket, Pine, Umber, Breadboard Top, Columns, Drawers, c.1835, 28 x 44 In.	240
Chest, Blanket, Poplar, Grain Paint, Red, Yellow, Molded Lid, c.1840, 24 x 44 In.	240
Chest, Blanket, Poplar, Grain Painted, Stencil, Till, Original Feet, c.1880, 25 x 44 In. *illus*	3360
Chest, Blanket, Poplar, Hinged Lid, c.1830, 27¼ x 48 In.	702
Chest, Blanket, Poplar, Mustard Vinegar Graining, c.1810, 10 x 15 x 9 In.	1560
Chest, Blanket, Pumpkin Pine, Drawer, Clothespin Pulls, 51 x 17 In.	216
Chest, Blanket, Red Brown, Stencils, Urn, Flowers, Birds, Compass Stars, 48 In.	1800
Chest, Blanket, Red Paint, Lift Top, 3 False Drawers, Shaped Apron, 1700s, 41 x 18 In.	2900
Chest, Blanket, Shaker, Paint, Hinged, Lift Top, Iron Handles, 1800s, 17 x 36 In.	738
Chest, Blanket, Shaker, Pine, Painted, Flip Top, Bracket Feet, c.1810, 24 x 46 In.	2460
Chest, Blanket, Shaker, Poplar, Paint, Lift Top, Angled Feet, c.1815, 36 x 41 In.	738
Chest, Blanket, Slate Blue, Pine, Dovetailed, New England, 16 x 40 In.	150
Chest, Blanket, Softwood, Paint, Green, Flowers, G. Heilig, Ephrata, Pa., 24 x 38 In.	148
Chest, Blanket, Softwood, Paint, Red, Scalloped Base, Turned Feet, 10 x 17 In.	1534
Chest, Blanket, Sponge Paint, Rust Red, Black, Turned Feet, 49½ In.	562
Chest, Blanket, Sponge Paint, Yellow, Red, 1800s, 23 x 49½ In.	500
Chest, Blanket, Walnut, Inlaid Fans, Iron Strap Hinges, Miniature, 12 x 23 In.	1800
Chest, Bonnet, Federal, Walnut, Figured Panels, 4 Drawers, 1825, 45 x 42 In.	1560
Chest, Bowfront, Drawers, Diamond Escutcheon, French Feet, 1800s, 35 x 29 In.	885
Chest, Bowfront, Mahogany, Gallery, Turned Legs, Twist Post, c.1800, 44 x 42 In.	300
Chest, Burl, Serpentine Top, Molded, Drawers, Bracket Feet, 1900s, 30 x 32 In.	1784
Chest, Campaign, Camphor, Carved Shell Gallery, Inlay, c.1835, 48 x 44 In.	1007
Chest, Campaign, Mahogany, Brass, 2 Sections, Drop Front, England, 1800s, 43 In. *illus*	1680
Chest, Cherry, 3 Drawers, Paneled, Diminutive Turned Feet, c.1835, 15 x 17 In.	4388

Furniture, Chaise Longue, Walter Lamb, Bronze, Brown-Jordan, c.1950, 68½ In.
$4,688

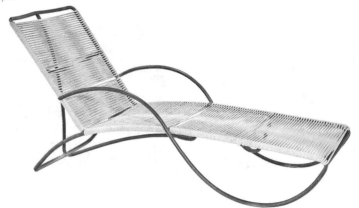

Los Angeles Modern Auctions

Furniture, Chest, Blanket, Baroque, Oak, Carved, Flowers, Leaves, Bun Feet, c.1800, 38 x 20 In.
$360

Cowan's Auctions

Furniture, Chest, Blanket, Cedar, Green & Red Sponge Paint, Till, 1800s, 26 x 54 In.
$1,200

Cowan's Auctions

Furniture, Chest, Blanket, Pine, Hinged Lid, Dovetailed, Painted, Fitted, Till, Pa., c.1810, 22 x 45 In.
$242

James D. Julia Auctioneers

Furniture, Chest, Blanket, Pine, Paint, Nailed Construction, Shaped Skirt, c.1850, 24 x 43 In.
$360

Cowan's Auctions

Furniture, Chest, Blanket, Poplar, Grain Painted, Stencil, Till, Original Feet, c.1880, 25 x 44 In.
$3,360

Garth's Auctioneers & Appraisers

Bigger Is Better
Extra-tall cupboards and high-boys, large dining room tables, and other huge pieces of furniture are no longer sold at bargain prices. New homes with cathedral ceilings and large rooms have space for these large antique pieces, so prices are high.

Furniture, Chest, Campaign, Mahogany, Brass, 2 Sections, Drop Front, England, 1800s, 43 In.
$1,680

Cowan's Auctions

Furniture, Chest, Dower, Paint, Flower Panels, Tulips, Leaves, Hinged Lid, c.1780, 20 x 44 In.
$2,460

Skinner, Inc.

Furniture, Chest, Dower, Softwood, Architectural, Till, Panels, Lancaster Co., 1783, 51 x 25 In.
$3,540

Hess Auction Group

FURNITURE

Furniture, Chest, Empire Style, Mahogany, Marble Top, Bronze Mounts, 1800s, 52 x 32 In.
$854

Neal Auctions

Furniture, Chest, Georgian, Walnut, Double Banded, Long & Short Drawers, 1700s, 37 x 36 In.
$4,500

New Orleans Auction Galleries

Furniture, Chest, Mule, Pine, Grain Paint, Lift Lid, Dovetailed Drawers, New Eng., c.1850, 34 In.
$600

Garth's Auctioneers & Appraisers

Furniture, Chest, Sheraton, Bowfront, Drawers, Reeded Pilasters, New England, c.1835, 41 x 43 In.
$3,328

James D. Julia Auctioneers

Furniture, Chest, Softwood, 10 Graduated Drawers, Grain Painted, Miniature, 25 x 15 In.
$295

Hess Auction Group

Furniture, Chest, Sugar, Cherry, Pine, Lift Top, Hinged, 2 Doors, c.1810, 29 x 24 In.
$1,200

Brunk Auctions

Furniture, Chest, Tansu, Elm, Metal Mounts, 2 Doors, Drawer, Korea, 31 x 36 In.
$500

New Orleans Auction Galleries

Furniture, Chest, Traveling, Teak, Lift Lid, Doors, 11 Drawers, Brass, 1900s, 36 x 31 In.
$27,012

Garth's Auctioneers & Appraisers

Furniture, Chest, Walnut, 5 Drawers, Brass Handles, Block Feet, Johnson Furniture Co., c.1950, 47 x 38 In.
$420

Cowan's Auctions

Chest, Cherry, Drawers, Porcelain Pulls, Flowers, Gallery, c.1875, 56 x 39 In.	3360
Chest, Cherry, Inlaid Arrows, Diamonds, Eagle, Pilasters, c.1835, 47 x 45 In.	1185
Chest, Cherry, Poplar, 4 Drawers, Inlaid Initials, 49 x 42 x 22 In.	1000
Chest, Chippendale, Birch, Drawers, Bracket Base, Pendant, c.1790, 55 x 40 In.	267
Chest, Chippendale, Birch, Molded Top, Drawers, Bracket Feet, 1800s, 33 x 39 In.	600
Chest, Coin, Mahogany, Maple, Inlaid Door, 16 Drawers, c.1800, 18 x 13 In.	6600
Chest, Dower, Chippendale, Walnut, Drawers, Iron Strap Hinges, Lock, Till, 28 x 50 In.	189
Chest, Dower, Chippendale, Walnut, Inlaid Eagle, Drawers, Iron Strap Hinges, 28 x 50 In.	295
Chest, Dower, Paint, Flower Panels, Tulips, Leaves, Hinged Lid, c.1780, 20 x 44 In. ....*illus*	2460
Chest, Dower, Pine, Paint, Iron Strap Hinges, Eagle, Tulip, S.R./S.R. 1829, 52 In.	2640
Chest, Dower, Softwood, Architectural, Till, Panels, Lancaster Co., 1783, 51 x 25 In. ....*illus*	3540
Chest, Dower, Walnut, Diamond Panels, Iron Hinges, Bracket Feet, c.1800, 9 x 15 In.	5925
Chest, Ed Roos Co., Mahogany, Cedar, 21 x 45 In.	40
Chest, Empire Style, Mahogany, Marble Top, Bronze Mounts, 1800s, 52 x 32 In. ....*illus*	854
Chest, Empire Style, Mahogany, Ormolu, 6 Drawers, Saber Feet, 62 In.	562
Chest, Empire, Curly Maple, Cherry, 1 Over 3 Graduated Drawers, 56 x 42 In.	480
Chest, Faux Paint, 5 Drawers, c.1900, 43 x 36 In.	450
Chest, Federal, Cherry, 4 Drawers, Late 1700s, 33 x 38 x 23 In.	549
Chest, Federal, Cherry, Bowfront, Inlay, Drawers, French Feet, c.1815, 35 x 43 In.	1067
Chest, Federal, Cherry, Brass, Drawers, Shaped Apron, Flare Feet, c.1815, 38 x 38 In.	625
Chest, George III, Mahogany, Fret Carved Frieze, Pilasters, c.1785, 40 x 43 In.	1000
Chest, George III, Mahogany, Serpentine, Beaded, Bracket Feet, c.1815, 37 x 44 In.	1625
Chest, Georgian, Mahogany, Beaded, Shaped Apron, French Feet, 1800s, 42 x 37 In.	270
Chest, Georgian, Mahogany, Inlay, 5 Drawers, Brass Handles, 1800s, 44 x 49 In.	369
Chest, Georgian, Mahogany, Scroll Top & Apron, Paw Feet, 1800s, 29 x 34 In.	420
Chest, Georgian, Walnut, Double Banded, Long & Short Drawers, 1700s, 37 x 36 In. ....*illus*	4500
Chest, Gilt, Paint, Glass Panel Top, Drawers & Sides, Fluted Legs, 35 x 43 In., Pair	5000
Chest, H. Probber, Walnut, Ebonized, 48 x 36 In.	562
Chest, Hepplewhite, Mahogany, Beaded Drawers, Brass Pulls, c.1800, 36 x 40 In.	1062
Chest, Hepplewhite, Mahogany, Bowfront, String Inlay, Drawers, 1800s, 41 x 46 In.	585
Chest, High, Queen Anne, Maple, 5 Over 4 Drawers, c.1760, 75 x 42 In.	1920
Chest, Jacobean, Oak, 3 Geometric Panel Drawers, Bun Feet, c.1700, 37 x 40 In.	523
Chest, Lingerie, Restoration Style, Mahogany, Marble Top, Drawers, c.1920, 55 x 23 In.	250
Chest, Louis XVI Style, Mahogany, Marble Top, 3 Drawers, c.1940, 32 In.	400
Chest, Mahogany, 5 Drawers, Brass Handles, Ogee Bracket Feet, c.1800, 30 x 31 In.	1125
Chest, Mahogany, Bowfront, Reeded Stiles, Gallery, Oval Ends, c.1835, 40 x 36 In.	593
Chest, Mahogany, Brass, 2 Sections, Drawers, Turned Feet, c.1810, 46 x 39 In.	2429
Chest, Mahogany, Maple, Bowfront, Inlay, Paneled Drawers, c.1800, 39 x 43 In.	4148
Chest, Mahogany, Maple, Bowfront, Inlay, Paneled Drawers, c.1815, 38 x 42 In.	2370
Chest, Mahogany, Maple, Bowfront, Paneled Drawers, Scallop Apron, c.1815, 36 x 41 In.	498
Chest, Mahogany, Oxbow, Serpentine, Graduated Drawers, Ogee Feet, 39 x 34 In.	2460
Chest, Mahogany, Paneled, Inlaid, Beaded, Bracket Feet, c.1815, 46 x 47 In.	875
Chest, Mahogany, Serpentine Front, String Inlay, French Feet, 1800s, 34 x 41 In.	738
Chest, Mahogany, Serpentine, Beaded Drawers, Bracket Feet, c.1800, 37 x 44 In.	1250
Chest, Marquetry, Walnut & Seaweed, 2 Over 3 Drawers, c.1780, 35 x 40 In.	4000
Chest, Mule, Pine, Grain Paint, Lift Lid, Dovetailed Drawers, New Eng., c.1850, 34 In. ....*illus*	600
Chest, Mule, Pine, Red & Black Grain, Dovetailed, Bootjack Ends, c.1810, 51 x 38 In.	420
Chest, Paint, Red, White, Blue, Eagles, Dot Heart, Hinged Lid, 1803, 24 x 49 In.	21600
Chest, Pine, Birch, Overhanging Drawer, 3 Graduated Drawers, c.1830, 41 In.	263
Chest, Pine, Blue Paint, Lift Lid, Hinged, Drawer, Till, 1800s, 10 x 15 In.	2006
Chest, Pine, Dome Top, Wrought Iron Straps, c.1840, 23 In.	105
Chest, Pine, Grain Paint, Dovetailed Drawers, Turned Feet, c.1850, 46 x 41 In.	360
Chest, Pine, Paint, Molded Edge, Fruit, Urn, Squat Ball Feet, c.1835, 16 x 32 In.	1778
Chest, Queen Anne, Maple, Drawers, Fan Carved, Scroll Apron, c.1750, 73 x 40 In.	3120
Chest, Queen Anne, Tiger Maple, Cornice Cap & Fan Drawers, 1700s, 70 x 41 In.	3776
Chest, Red Paint, 6-Board, Molded Lid, Hinges, Sawtooth Cutouts, 16 x 20 In.	2829
Chest, Red Paint, Beaded Drawers, Mushroom Pulls, Cutouts, c.1835, 46 x 48 In.	390
Chest, Shaker, Black Walnut, Stain, Hinged Lift Lid, 23 x 91 In.	2583
Chest, Shaker, Maple, Red Paint, 6 Cubby Drawers, Turned Pulls, 1800s, 13 x 26 In.	2091
Chest, Shaker, Pine, Paint, Lift Top, Iron Hinges, Bracket Feet, c.1830, 27 x 30 In.	11070

Furniture, Chest, Walnut, Cane Front Doors, Drawers, Peg Feet, American Of Martinsville, c.1950, 45 x 36 In.

$180

Cowan's Auctions

Furniture, Chest-On-Frame, Federal, Walnut, Bandy Legs, North Carolina, 44 x 41 In.

$2,280

Brunk Auctions

Furniture, Commode, American Restauration, Walnut, Marble Top, Drawers, c.1850, 35 x 50 In.

$1,125

New Orleans Auction Galleries

F

Furniture, Commode, Louis XV, Kingwood, Marble Top, Bombe, Paint, Drawers, 33 x 46 In.
$1,187

New Orleans Auction Galleries

Furniture, Commode, Provincial, Fruitwood, Drawers, Bracket Base, 1800s, 38 x 50 In., Pair
$2,250

New Orleans Auction Galleries

Furniture, Cupboard, Corner, Federal, Cherry, 2 Sections, Glazed Door Over 2 Doors, 84 In.
$840

Brunk Auctions

Chest, Shaker, Pine, Red Stain, 4 Drawers, Knob Center Pulls, c.1840, 27 x 25 In.	1845
Chest, Shaker, Pine, Red Stain, 7 Drawers, Wood Knobs, Molded, 1800s, 73 x 41 In.	18450
Chest, Shaker, Pine, Red Stain, 11 Molded Drawers, Ball Knobs, c.1830, 73 x 52 In.	22140
Chest, Shaker, Pine, Yellow, Flip Top, Brass Hook, Iron Handles, c.1900, 12 x 28 In.	2583
Chest, Shaker, Walnut, Fruitwood Knobs, Beaded Drawers, c.1850, 56 x 45 In.	11685
Chest, Sheraton, Bowfront, Drawers, Reeded Pilasters, New England, c.1835, 41 x 43 In. *illus*	3328
Chest, Sheraton, Cherry, Barber Pole Inlay, Brass, French Feet, c.1810, 43 x 38 In.	984
Chest, Sheraton, Maple, Cock-Beaded Drawers, Turned Feet, c.1855, 44 x 41 In.	570
Chest, Softwood, 10 Graduated Drawers, Grain Painted, Miniature, 25 x 15 In. *illus*	295
Chest, Storage, Mixed Wood, Paint, Diamond Paneled, 1800s, 35 x 44 In.	210
Chest, Sugar, Cherry, Pine, Lift Top, Hinged, 2 Doors, c.1810, 29 x 24 In. *illus*	1200
Chest, Sugar, Federal, Cherry, Inlaid, Dovetailed Drawer, Southern, 36 x 29 In.	3360
Chest, Tansu, Elm, Metal Mounts, 2 Doors, Drawer, Korea, 31 x 36 In. *illus*	500
Chest, Tansu, Japan, c.1920, 64 x 35 In.	246
Chest, Tiger Maple, Scrolled Crest, Pinwheels, 11 Drawers, 80 x 39 In.	4305
Chest, Traveling, Teak, Lift Lid, Doors, 11 Drawers, Brass, 1900s, 36 x 31 In. *illus*	27012
Chest, Walnut, 5 Drawers, Brass Handles, Block Feet, Johnson Furniture Co., c.1950, 47 x 38 In. *illus*	420
Chest, Walnut, Brass, Pilasters, Trophy Mounts, Leaves, Square Legs, c.1950, 55 x 38 In.	1185
Chest, Walnut, Cane Front Doors, Drawers, Peg Feet, American Of Martinsville, c.1950, 45 x 36 In. *illus*	180
Chest, Walnut, Collector's, Inlaid Panel Doors, 3 Drawers, 1800s, 13 x 12 x 8 In.	390
Chest, Walnut, Cove Molded Cornice, 9 Drawers, Ogee Bracket Feet, 69 x 42 In.	3658
Chest, Watchmaker's, Wellington Style, Mahogany, Brass, 24 x 11 In.	1500
Chest, Wormley, Walnut Veneer, Leather, Metal, Drawers, Tapered Feet, 36 x 74 In.	1845
Chest-On-Chest, Cherry, 9 Drawers, Shaped Bracket, 70 ½ x 37 In.	625
Chest-On-Chest, Mahogany, Molded, 8 Drawers, Bracket Feet, c.1785, 69 x 43 In.	1750
Chest-On-Chest, Oak, Dovetailed, Carved Facades, Bracket Feet, c.1875, 71 x 43 In.	1920
Chest-On-Chest, Queen Anne, Maple, Graduated Drawers, Pad Feet, c.1775, 81 x 39 In.	2400
Chest-On-Frame, Federal, Walnut, Bandy Legs, North Carolina, 44 x 41 In. *illus*	2280
Chest-On-Frame, Walnut, Satinwood, Serpentine Apron, Angels, Doors, 37 x 15 In.	154
Coat Rack, Costumer, G. Stickley, 2 Supports, 5 Hooks, Trestle Base, 72 In.	2750
Coffer, Oak, Hinged, Carved, Cross, Sunburst, Block Feet, c.1715, 31 x 65 In.	1500
Commode, American Restauration, Walnut, Marble Top, Drawers, c.1850, 35 x 50 In. *illus*	1125
Commode, French Empire, Walnut, Marble Top, 4 Drawers, 1800s, 34 x 45 In.	900
Commode, French Provincial, Marble Top, Fruitwood, c.1910, 33 x 45 In.	1342
Commode, Fruitwood, Banded Design, Paneled, c.1750, 38 x 50 In.	4750
Commode, Fruitwood, Bombe, Hinged, Drawers, Hoof Feet, c.1810, 28 x 21 In.	750
Commode, Fruitwood, Bowfront, Shaped Top, Scroll Apron, 1700s, 34 x 44 In.	1250
Commode, George III, Mahogany, Dovetailed, Flared Feet, c.1800, 40 x 44 In.	2596
Commode, Kingwood, Marble Top, Diamond Parquetry, c.1890, 35 x 31 In.	875
Commode, Kingwood, Marble Top, Inlay, Saber Legs, Scroll, c.1910, 34 x 46 In.	531
Commode, Kingwood, Marble Top, Parquetry, Pendant Apron, c.1810, 37 x 46 In.	1000
Commode, Louis XV, Continental, Bombe Shape, Veneered, 1900s, 25 x 12 In.	240
Commode, Louis XV, Gilt Bronze, 2 Drawers, Rocaille Mounts, 35 x 59 In.	5185
Commode, Louis XV, Kingwood, Marble Top, Bombe, Paint, Drawers, 33 x 46 In. *illus*	1187
Commode, Louis XV, Ormolu, Flower Inlay, 3 Drawers, 37 x 46 In., Pair	750
Commode, Louis XV, Walnut, Inlay, Drawers, Dovetailed, Iron, 1700s, 32 x 30 In.	885
Commode, Louis XVI Style, Marble Top, 2 Drawers, Fluted Columns, 35 In.	550
Commode, Mahogany, Demilune, Swing Doors, False Drawers, 1800s, 34 x 28 In.	1353
Commode, Mahogany, Marble Top, Fabric Panel Doors, Pilasters, 1800s, 37 x 51 In.	1187
Commode, Mahogany, Marble Top, Frieze Drawer, Bracket Feet, c.1835, 36 x 52 In.	1375
Commode, Mahogany, Marble Top, Gilt Leaf Bands, Red Figures, 1800s, 34 x 47 In.	1750
Commode, Mahogany, Marble Top, Inlay, Crossband, Spade Feet, 1900s, 33 x 43 In.	300
Commode, Mahogany, Marble Top, Ormolu, Flower Basket, c.1910, 35 x 51 In.	4250
Commode, Mahogany, Marble Top, Ormolu, Pilasters, Turret Feet, 39 x 44 In.	812
Commode, Mahogany, Marble Top, Ormolu, Pillars, Turret Feet, c.1850, 35 x 45 In.	2750
Commode, Mahogany, Marble Top, Ormolu, Pillars, Turret Feet, c.1850, 36 x 50 In.	1125
Commode, Marble Top, Gilt, Doors, Leaf Garland, Wreath, Tapered Legs, 36 x 41 In.	250
Commode, Multicolor, Scrolls, Portraits, 3 Drawers, Cabriole Legs, Italy, 38 x 47 In.	812
Commode, Neoclassical, Walnut, Drawers, Tapered Legs, c.1800, 36 x 51 In.	5250
Commode, Neoclassical, Walnut, Marquetry, Diana The Huntress, 31 x 35 In.	480

Furniture, Cupboard, Corner, Maple, 2 Sections, Doors, Cutout Foot, Pa., c.1820, 77 x 47 In.
$3,000

Garth's Auctioneers & Appraisers

Furniture, Cupboard, Corner, Pine, Paneled Doors, Mustard Paint Over Red, c.1825, 84 x 44 In.
$1,200

Garth's Auctioneers & Appraisers

Furniture, Cupboard, Corner, Pine, Raised Panel Door, Drawer, Tabletop, c.1825, 51 x 32 In.
$720

Garth's Auctioneers & Appraisers

Furniture, Cupboard, Dutch, Federal, Softwood, 2 Sections, Pennsylvania, 84 x 54 In.
$708

Hess Auction Group

Furniture, Cupboard, Dutch, Federal, Walnut, Doors, Drawers, Pie Shelf, Pa., 85 x 64 In.
$3,186

Hess Auction Group

Furniture, Cupboard, Dutch, Softwood, Glazed Doors, Shelf, Drawers, Pa., 85 x 61 In.
$826

Hess Auction Group

Furniture, Cupboard, Federal, Cherry, 2 Sections, 12-Pane Door, Panel Doors, Pa., 88 x 44 In.
$1,180

Hess Auction Group

Furniture, Cupboard, Hanging, Pine, Mirrors, Doors, Drawers, Towel Bar, c.1910, 27 x 32 In.
$1,440

Cowan's Auctions

Furniture, Cupboard, Jelly, Pine, Poplar, Grain Painted, Dovetailed, Mirror, c.1845, 55 x 42 In.
$360

Garth's Auctioneers & Appraisers

Furniture, Cupboard, Pine, 2 Sections, Glass Doors, Drawers, Doors, 1800s, 112 x 46 In.
$2,400

Garth's Auctioneers & Appraisers

Furniture, Cupboard, Pine, Grain Painted, Open Top, Scalloped, Door, c.1875, 78 x 45 In.
$720

Garth's Auctioneers & Appraisers

Furniture, Cupboard, Pine, Paint, Shelves, Plank Doors, New England, c.1810, 76 In.
$480

Cowan's Auctions

Commode, Neoclassical, Walnut, Veneer, Drawers, Block Legs, c.1800, 36 x 51 x 25 In.	5250
Commode, Provincial, Fruitwood, Drawers, Bracket Base, 1800s, 38 x 50 In., Pair.........*illus*	2250
Commode, Regency Style, Kingwood, Marble Top, Ormolu, Bowfront, 35 x 60 In.	1187
Commode, Regency Style, Kingwood, Marble, Ormolu, Bombe, Drawers, 34 x 47 In.	625
Commode, Rosewood, Marble Top, Gilt, Bowfront, Pendant Apron, 30 x 38 In.	1187
Commode, Tulipwood, Rose Marble Top, Gilt, Bombe, c.1910, 36 x 42 In.	492
Commode, Venetian Style, Serpentine, Mirror, Shaped, Doors, Flared Legs, 38 In.	150
Commode, Walnut, Fruitwood, Bombe, Banded Drawers, 33 x 39 In., Pair.	2125
Commode, Walnut, Inlay, Flowers, Demilune, Drawers, Door, c.1930, 33 x 36 In.	406
Commode, Walnut, Marble Top, Carved, Scroll Skirt & Feet, 1900s, 34 x 43 In.	570
Commode, Walnut, Marble Top, Curved, Inlay, Peg Feet, c.1790, 36 x 48 In.	1500
Cradle, Oak, Paneled, Molded, France, 29 x 38 In.	250
Cradle, Rocking, Cherry, Knuckle Arms, Pennsylvania, 1800s, 25 x 43 In.	35
Credenza, Baroque, Walnut, Carved, Italy, c.1690, 42 x 71 In.	7930
Credenza, Paint, Canted Sides, Drawers, Paneled Doors, Italy, 40 x 60 In.	2074
Credenza, Scandinavian, Teak, 3 Doors, Drawers, Tabergsmobler, 1950s, 31 x 35 In.	780
Credenza, Widdicomb, Walnut, Parquetry, 4 Hinged Doors, c.1950, 31 x 83 In.	354
Crib, Bird's-Eye Maple, Ring Turned, Hinged, 42 x 25 In.	236
Cupboard, Bench, Poplar, Bucket Shelf, 2 Hinged Doors, c.1850, 37 In.	644
Cupboard, Cherry, 2 Sections, Panel Doors, 12 Panes, c.1850, 85 x 44 In.	1440
Cupboard, Chinese, Elm, Opera Scenes, Doors, Drawers, Dovetailed, c.1890, 66 x 52 In.	270
Cupboard, Corner, Cherry & Pine, Hanging, 1700s, 36 x 29 x 17 In.	720
Cupboard, Corner, Cherry, 2 Doors, 12-Panes, Stepped Cornice, c.1835, 86 x 51 In.	2000
Cupboard, Corner, Cherry, 2 Panel Doors, 2 Lower Doors, c.1815, 88 In.	4680
Cupboard, Corner, Cherry, Glazed Mullion & Panel Doors, c.1810, 107 x 51 In.	2400
Cupboard, Corner, Federal, Cherry, 2 Sections, 12 Pane Door, 2 Doors, 87 x 44 In.	1770
Cupboard, Corner, Federal, Cherry, 2 Sections, Glazed Door Over 2 Doors, 84 In.........*illus*	840
Cupboard, Corner, Maple, 2 Sections, Doors, Cutout Foot, Pa., c.1820, 77 x 47 In. ....*illus*	3000
Cupboard, Corner, Maple, 12-Pane Door, Cove & Bead, c.1825, 90 x 44 In.	4800
Cupboard, Corner, Pine, Green, 3 Shelves, Hinged Plank Door, 1800s, 76 In.	1287
Cupboard, Corner, Pine, Paint, Glazed Door, 4 Tombstone Arches, 95 In.	3998
Cupboard, Corner, Pine, Paneled Doors, Mustard Paint Over Red, c.1825, 84 x 44 In.......*illus*	1200
Cupboard, Corner, Pine, Raised Panel Door, Drawer, Tabletop, c.1825, 51 x 32 In.........*illus*	720
Cupboard, Corner, Pine, Yellow, Molded Cornice, Lower Door, c.1800, 83 In.	7605
Cupboard, Corner, Poplar, 2 Section Cornice, 2 Doors, Rosette Pattern, c.1850	702
Cupboard, Corner, Poplar, American, Early 1800s, 86 x 52 ½ In.	6600
Cupboard, Corner, Poplar, Glass Pane Doors, Cutout Feet, c.1840, 83 x 58 In.	840
Cupboard, Corner, Walnut, 2 Hinged Doors, Bracket Base, c.1790, 86 x 45 In.	5265
Cupboard, Corner, Walnut, 2 Sections, Glazed Doors, Scroll Corners, 1800s, 90 x 55 In.	470
Cupboard, Corner, William & Mary, Burl, Scrolled Crest, Seaweed Inlay, 41 In.	1140
Cupboard, Corner, Yellow Pine, Poplar, Grain Painted, c.1780, 81 x 51 In.	9000
Cupboard, Crock, Pine, Stain, 3 Upper Shelves, Lower Shelf, 1800s, 82 x 71 In.	600
Cupboard, Dutch, Federal, Softwood, 2 Sections, Pennsylvania, 84 x 54 In.........*illus*	708
Cupboard, Dutch, Federal, Walnut, Doors, Drawers, Pie Shelf, Pa., 85 x 64 In.........*illus*	3186
Cupboard, Dutch, Softwood, Glazed Doors, Shelf, Drawers, Pa., 85 x 61 In.........*illus*	826
Cupboard, Federal, Cherry, 2 Sections, 12-Pane Door, Panel Doors, Pa., 88 x 44 In.........*illus*	1180
Cupboard, George III, Oak, Shelves, Scalloped, Turned Legs, 1800s, 90 x 66 In.	1845
Cupboard, Hanging, Pine, Mirrors, Doors, Drawers, Towel Bar, c.1910, 27 x 32 In. ....*illus*	1440
Cupboard, Hanging, Pine, Salmon, 2 Shelves, Early 1800s, 36 x 24 x 7 ½ In.	344
Cupboard, Hanging, Wood, Door, Leaping Stag, Drawer, Shelf, 2005, 35 In.	1053
Cupboard, Hanging, Yellow Faded Design, Shelf, 19 x 15 ½ x 10 In.	360
Cupboard, Hepplewhite, Walnut, 2 Sections, Glazed Doors, 85 x 70 In.	2714
Cupboard, Jelly, Cherry, 2 Hinged Doors, Drawers, Turned Feet, 1800s, 30 x 44 In.	439
Cupboard, Jelly, Pine, Paint, Shaped Crest, Panel Doors, 1840, 59 x 49 In.	660
Cupboard, Jelly, Pine, Pickled, 2 Drawers Over 2 Doors, 51 x 41 In.	420
Cupboard, Jelly, Pine, Poplar, Grain Painted, Dovetailed, Mirror, c.1845, 55 x 42 In. ....*illus*	360
Cupboard, Jelly, Pine, Red Paint, Panel Doors, Cutout Base, 1800s, 57 x 46 In.	420
Cupboard, Jelly, Poplar, Pine, 2 Hinged Doors, Drawers, Cutout Bracket Base, 48 In.	234
Cupboard, Jelly, Softwood, 2 Drawers Over 2 Paneled Doors, 63 x 47 In.	413
Cupboard, Jelly, Softwood, Green Paint, Paneled Doors, Arch Feet, Pa., 49 x 50 In.	1062

Cupboard, Maple, 2 Sections, Glazed Panel Doors, Pilasters, c.1835, 79 x 47 In.	830
Cupboard, Painted, Blue, Green, 2 Doors, Scroll Top, Cutouts, c.1865, 83 x 48 In.	1200
Cupboard, Pastry, Wood, Metal, 2 Sections, Pie Cooler, Casters, c.1910, 68 x 40 In.	1300
Cupboard, Pine, 2 Sections, Glass Doors, Drawers, Doors, 1800s, 112 x 46 In. ....*illus*	2400
Cupboard, Pine, 2 Sections, Panel Doors, Drawer, Bracket Base, c.1850, 93 x 47 In.	3240
Cupboard, Pine, Brown Paint, 2 Panel Doors, Shelves, c.1800, 43 x 43 In.	1422
Cupboard, Pine, Grain Painted, Open Top, Scalloped, Door, c.1875, 78 x 45 In. ....*illus*	720
Cupboard, Pine, Paint, Shelves, Plank Doors, New England, c.1810, 76 In. ....*illus*	480
Cupboard, Pine, Red Paint, Shelves, Hinged Panel Door, c.1790, 82 x 31 In.	6000
Cupboard, Pine, Red Wash, 2 Paneled Blind Doors, Brass, Tabletop, 1800s, 26 x 44 In.	510
Cupboard, Pine, Red Wash, Doors, Shelves, Brass Pulls, Tabletop, c.1850, 34 x 34 In.	330
Cupboard, Pine, Slant Back, 3 Shelves Over Single Door, Pa., 77 x 42 In.	1968
Cupboard, Pine, Worn Blue Paint, Iron Butt Hinges, c.1885, 72 x 35 x 22 In.	660
Cupboard, Red Paint, Rosettes, Pilasters, 2 Panel Doors, c.1750, 87 x 53 In.	1700
Cupboard, Red Paint, Shelf Back, 2 Doors, 1800s, 54 x 42 In.	1840
Cupboard, Shaker, Pine, Pantry, 2 Doors, Paneled, Knobs, c.1830, 74 x 42 In.	7380
Cupboard, Shaker, Pine, Printing Press, Hinged Door, Racks, c.1875, 45 x 28 In.	400
Cupboard, Shaker, Pine, Raised Panel Door, Shelf, Iron Hinges, c.1860, 18 x 23 In.	492
Cupboard, Shaker, Pine, Red Paint, Molded, Paneled Door, 1800s, 32 x 25 In.	861
Cupboard, Shaker, Pine, Step Back, Raised Panel Door, c.1820, 84 x 33 In.	1845
Cupboard, Sheraton, Walnut, 2 Sections, 2 Glazed & 2 Paneled Doors, Pa., 87 In.	2006
Cupboard, Sheraton, Wood, 2 Parts, Glazed Door, 9 Panes, Footed, 83 x 38 In.	1534
Cupboard, Step Back, Pine, 4 Paneled Doors, 3 Drawers, Bracket Feet, 1800s, 85 In. ....*illus*	540
Cupboard, Step Back, Softwood, 2 Sections, Spice Drawers, Shelves, 87 x 67 In.	710
Cupboard, Wall, Pine, Open Top, Plank Door, Shelf, New England, c.1810, 68 x 35 In.......*illus*	1560
Cupboard, Wall, Walnut, 2 Hinged Doors, 8 Panes, 2 Panel Doors, Va., c.1840, 81 In.	2691
Cupboard, Walnut, 2 Sections, Beaded Doors, 12 Panes, Drawers, c.1835, 88 x 53 In.	2750
Cupboard, Wood, Paint, Overhang Top, Doors, Recessed Panels, 1900s, 72 x 66 In.	711
Daybed, Brass Hinged, Carved, Flowers, 36 x 39 ½ In.	187
Daybed, G. Stickley, Oak, Bars, 29 x 79 In.	2684
Daybed, Jean Prouve, Steel, Enamel, Upholstered, Roll Pillow, 1940s, 23 x 74 In.	11250
Daybed, L. & J.G. Stickley, Slatted Ends, Cushion, c.1904, 28 x 80 In.	813
Daybed, Limbert, Oak, 27 x 74 In.	732
Daybed, Louis XV Style, Shaped Apron, 6 Cabriole Legs, 1800s, 24 x 76 In.	350
Daybed, Louis XVI, Painted, Cushion, 30 x 59 ½ In.	813
Daybed, Mies Van Der Rohe, Walnut, Leather, Tufted, Steel Legs, 1970s, 25 x 80 In.	5938
Daybed, Padded Ends, Carved Urn Peak, Top Shape Feet, 1800s, 36 x 75 In.	2000
Daybed, Paint, Peak Paneled Head & Footboard, Columns, c.1850, 43 x 72 In.	2125
Daybed, Poplar, Paint, Red, Blue, Turned Posts, Beaded Rails, 1800s, 24 x 67 In.	469
Daybed, Sleigh, Walnut, Scrolled Ends, Slat Seat, Paneled Back, c.1850, 39 x 78 In.........*illus*	300
Daybed, William & Mary, Oak, Spiral Stiles & Legs, Cane Seat, 1900s, 39 x 66 In.	800
Daybed, Wood, Spool-Turned Arms & Feet, Plank Base, Cushions, 30 x 72 In.	107
Desk, A.W. Iversen, Student, Teak, Gallery, 4 Drawers, Denmark, 1960s, 33 x 39 In.	3250
Desk, American, Queen Anne On Base, Fitted Interior, Cabriole Legs, 51 x 37 In.	570
Desk, Arne Vodder, Teak, 2 Sections, L-Shape, Cabinet, Denmark, 1960s, 80 x 66 In.	3125
Desk, Art Nouveau, Walnut, Brass, 6 Drawers, Spain, c.1900, 31 ½ x 59 In.	5625
Desk, Biedermeier, Drop Front, Maple Inlay, Ebonized, Drawers, 59 x 36 In.......*illus*	615
Desk, Birch, Plank Top, Side Drawers, Open Frame Support, c.1938, 29 x 50 In.	2750
Desk, Butler's, American Empire, Drop Front, Cherry, Maple, Drawers, 45 x 42 In.	236
Desk, Butler's, Neoclassical, Mahogany, Tiered Marble, c.1810, 54 x 37 x 22 In.	3450
Desk, Campaign, Baker Furniture, Milling's Road, 30 ½ x 54 In.	1062
Desk, Campaign, Mahogany, Brass, Gallery, Slope, Pigeonholes, c.1850, 39 x 53 In.	1185
Desk, Chippendale, Slant Front, Mahogany, Fitted Interior, Drawers, Pa., 41 x 45 In. ....*illus*	649
Desk, Chippendale, Slant Front, Maple, Pine, Drawers, Ogee Feet, c.1765, 45 x 40 In. ....*illus*	3000
Desk, Chippendale, Slant Front, Tiger Maple, c.1890, Child's, 22 x 22 x 12 In.	660
Desk, Chippendale, Slant Front, Walnut, 7 Cubbies & Drawers, c.1790, 46 In.	4388
Desk, Davenport, Mahogany, Dovetailed Drawers, Casters, 1800s, 32 x 21 In.	390
Desk, Davenport, Pierced Arch Crest, Sloped, Lion Feet, c.1865, 52 x 25 In.	1250
Desk, Drop Front, Cherry, Diamond Band At Base, c.1810, 42 x 43 In.	995
Desk, Drop Front, Walnut, 2 Parts, Arched Door, Paw Feet, 1800s, 74 x 46 In.	2214

Furniture, Cupboard, Step Back, Pine, 4 Paneled Doors, 3 Drawers, Bracket Feet, 1800s, 85 In.

$540

Cowan's Auctions

Furniture, Cupboard, Wall, Pine, Open Top, Plank Door, Shelf, New England, c.1810, 68 x 35 In.

$1,560

Cowan's Auctions

Furniture, Daybed, Sleigh, Walnut, Scrolled Ends, Slat Seat, Paneled Back, c.1850, 39 x 78 In.

$300

Garth's Auctioneers & Appraisers

Furniture, Desk, Biedermeier, Drop Front, Maple Inlay, Ebonized, Drawers, 59 x 36 In.
$615

Skinner, Inc.

Furniture, Desk, Chippendale, Slant Front, Mahogany, Fitted Interior, Drawers, Pa., 41 x 45 In.
$649

Hess Auction Group

Furniture, Desk, Chippendale, Slant Front, Maple, Pine, Drawers, Ogee Feet, c.1765, 45 x 40 In.
$3,000

Garth's Auctioneers & Appraisers

Furniture, Desk, Edwardian, Satinwood, Painted, Side Cabinets, c.1910, 49 x 42 In.
$738

Skinner, Inc.

> **TIP**
> The more elaborate the interior fittings for a desk, the more valuable the piece.

Furniture, Desk, House Of Representatives, Oak, Lift Top, Carved, Shield, c.1857, 36 x 29 In.
$17,920

Neal Auctions

Furniture, Desk, Mahogany, Cabinet In Kneehole, Bracket Feet, England, c.1785, 30 x 30 In.
$420

Cowan's Auctions

Furniture, Desk, Mahogany, Carved Scrolls, 2 Drawers, Shell Pulls, Victorian, 29 x 46 In.
$1,000

New Orleans Auction Galleries

Furniture, Desk, Plantation, Mahogany, Raised Cabinets, Sloping Lid, Leather, Drawers, c.1850, 50 x 54 In.
$212

James D. Julia Auctioneers

Furniture, Desk, Plantation, Walnut, Drop Front, Bookcase, Kneehole, Victorian, 92 x 48 In.
$295

Hess Auction Group

F

Desk, Drop Front, Walnut, 5 Drawers, c.1875, 44 In.	498
Desk, Edwardian, Satinwood, Painted, Side Cabinets, c.1910, 49 x 42 In. ....*illus*	738
Desk, House Of Representatives, Oak, Lift Top, Carved, Shield, c.1857, 36 x 29 In. ....*illus*	17920
Desk, J. Quistgaard, Hinged Foldover Top, Lovig, 1972, 34¾ x 64 In.	1062
Desk, Jean Royere, Mahogany, Cane, Lamp, Open Frame, 1950s, 46 x 48 In.	12500
Desk, Jeanneret, Rosewood, Teak, Leather Top, Shelf, Plank, c.1957, 28 x 48 In.	6250
Desk, Kingwood, Ormolu, Leather Top, Busts, Scroll Apron, 1900s, 31 x 67 In.	3750
Desk, Kneehole, George III, Satinwood, Banded, c.1770, 31 x 43 In.	6250
Desk, Library, Warren McArthur, Laminate, Aluminum, Tubular, 34 x 50 In.	2125
Desk, Limbert, Drop Front, 2 Slatted Shelves, Branded Mark, 40 x 34 In.	938
Desk, Louis XV Style, Slant Front, Walnut, Parquetry, Cabriole Legs, c.1900, 36 x 24 In.	1000
Desk, Louis XV, Gilt Bronze, Parquetry, Cartonnier, c.1890, 52 x 39 x 12 In.	6000
Desk, Louis XVI Style, Mahogany, Leather Top, Drawers, Fluted Legs, 30 In.	1400
Desk, Mahogany, Banded, Frieze Drawers, Peg Feet, c.1890, 31 x 60 In.	2750
Desk, Mahogany, Cabinet In Kneehole, Bracket Feet, England, c.1785, 30 x 30 In. ....*illus*	420
Desk, Mahogany, Carved Scrolls, 2 Drawers, Shell Pulls, Victorian, 29 x 46 In. ....*illus*	1000
Desk, Milo Baughman, Chrome Steel, Burl, 28½ x 54 In.	1500
Desk, Oak, Gallery, Shaped, Drawer, Cutouts, Block Legs, c.1905, 33 x 40 In.	4500
Desk, Ormolu, Leather Top, Inlay, Fluted Trumpet Legs, 1900s, 30 x 45 In.	1062
Desk, Partners, Esherick, Pine, Plank Top, 2-Sided, Folding, c.1950, 29 x 68 In.	9375
Desk, Partners, Mahogany, Leather Top, Gilt, Fluted Legs, 1900s, 30 x 72 In.	937
Desk, Partners, Mahogany, Leather Top, Molded, Drawers, Shelf, c.1915, 30 x 50 In.	800
Desk, Partners, Oak, Drawers On 2 Sides, Casters, Glass Top, 30 x 72 In.	110
Desk, Partners, Oak, Leather, Arched, 4 Drawers, Turned Legs, 1880s, 32 x 60 In.	1187
Desk, Partners, Pine, Stain, Drop Leaf, 2 Leaves, Side Drawers, c.1950, 29 x 68 In.	6250
Desk, Plantation, Mahogany, Raised Cabinets, Sloping Lid, Leather, Drawers, c.1850, 50 x 54 In. *illus*	212
Desk, Plantation, Walnut, Drop Front, Bookcase, Kneehole, Victorian, 92 x 48 In. ....*illus*	295
Desk, Postmaster's, Pine, Poplar, Blue Paint, Paneled Doors, c.1825, 85 x 52 In.	3360
Desk, Reception, Slant Front, Green Leather, Side Tables, Drawers, 33 x 66 In.	125
Desk, Renaissance Revival, Oak, Carved, Lion's Mask Drawers, 1800s, 31 x 56 In.	433
Desk, Roll Top, Carved Medallions, Side Doors, Etched, 50¾ x 51 In.	187
Desk, School, Hepplewhite, Slant Front, Walnut, Hinged, Tapered Legs, 31 x 24 In.	60
Desk, School, Shaker, Maple, Lift Top, Swollen Post, Tripod, c.1840, 28 x 21 In.	7380
Desk, Sewing, Shaker, Butternut, Overhang Top, Hutch, c.1815, 45 x 33 In.	7380
Desk, Sewing, Shaker, Maple, Paint, Slide, Step Back Gallery, c.1830, 40 x 31 In.	67650
Desk, Shaker, Sister's, Birch, Pine, Slide, Beadboard Ends, c.1845, 41 x 30 In. ....*illus*	10800
Desk, Shaker, Slant Front, Pine, Poplar, Butternut, Drawers, Hinged, 44 x 30 In.	1560
Desk, Slant Front, Mahogany, Candle Slides, Bracket Feet, c.1810, 37 x 31 In.	431
Desk, Slant Front, Mahogany, Serpentine, Bracket Feet, c.1765, 42 x 38 In.	3851
Desk, Slant Front, Maple & Poplar, 4 Drawers, Refinished, 43 x 38 x 20 In.	600
Desk, Slant Front, Maple, Lift Top, Hinged, Bracket Feet, c.1760, 43 x 37 In.	415
Desk, Tambour, Mahogany, Enamel, Roll Top, Chrome, T-Legs, 34 x 54 In.	1187
Desk, Teak, American, Modern, L Configuration, c.1950, 29 x 72 x 30 In.	375
Desk, Travel, Mahogany, Brass Bound, Hinged Lid, c.1835, 6½ In.	70
Desk, Walnut, Overhang Marble Top, Carved, Cabriole Legs, 1900s, 30 x 59 In.	300
Desk, William & Mary Style, Slant Front, Maple, Turned, Nutting, 1930s, 38 In.	1353
Desk, Wood, Lift Top, Drawer, Serpentine Apron, Baluster Legs, 1800s, 32 x 32 In.	380
Desk, Wood, Shaped, Brass Edge, Cabriole Legs, Hoof Feet, c.1910, 29 x 43 In.	360
Dining Set, Round Glass Top, Tubular Steel, Memphis Style, 5 Piece	984
Dresser, American Federal, Cherry, c.1800, 40½ x 43 In.	610
Dresser, Eastlake, Pine, 5 Drawers, Locks, Maple & Co., London, 40 x 42 In.	50
Dresser, Georgian, 5 Drawers, Crossbanded, Brass Pulls, Bracket Feet, 39 x 38 In.	500
Dresser, H. Probber, Walnut, Ebonized, 9 Drawers, 31 x 83 In.	531
Dresser, Kittinger, Mandarin, Lacquered Wood, White, 1950s, 32 x 30 In., Pair	4688
Dresser, Marble Top, Bowfront, Turret Ends, Leaves, Bun Feet, c.1790, 35 x 57 In.	1375
Dresser, Oak, Plank Top, Frieze Drawers, Serpentine Apron, c.1810, 36 x 78 In.	1230
Dresser, Parzinger, Wood, Grass, Linen, 4 Drawers, 34 x 36 In., Pair	750
Dresser, Roycroft, Panel Gallery, 2 Short Over 4 Long Drawers, 58 x 41 In.	6875
Dresser, Saginaw Furniture, Federal Style, Mahogany, Serpentine, 35 x 46 In.	90

Furniture, Desk, Shaker, Sister's, Birch, Pine, Slide, Beadboard Ends, c.1845, 41 x 30 In.
$10,800

Willis Henry Auctions

Furniture, Dresser, Serpentine Front, Painted Flowers & Scrolls, 1800s, 41 x 51 In.
$2,500

New Orleans Auction Galleries

Furniture, Dry Sink, Cupboard, Blue Paint, Raised Panel Doors, Drawers, c.1890, 89 x 65 In.
$5,400

Garth's Auctioneers & Appraisers

Roll-Top Desks
The first American patent for a horizontal tambour roll-top desk was issued to Abner Cutler in 1850. He worked in Buffalo, New York.

Furniture, Dry Sink, Hood, Poplar, Blue Paint, Drawers, Doors, Cutout Feet, c.1825, 42 x 49 In.
$4,200

Garth's Auctioneers & Appraisers

Furniture, Easel, Aesthetic Revival, Cherry, Carved, Spindles, Adjustable, 1880s, 74 In.
$1,680

Brunk Auctions

Furniture, Etagere, Galle, Shaped, Art Nouveau, Flowers, Shelves, Inlay, c.1900, 63 x 36 In.
$7,703

James D. Julia Auctioneers

Dresser, Serpentine Front, Painted Flowers & Scrolls, 1800s, 41 x 51 In. ....*illus*	2500
Dresser, Shaker, Pine, Overhang Top, Drawers, Tapered Legs, c.1810, 31 x 44 In.	1476
Dresser, Victorian, Walnut, Curved, Drawers, Cabriole Legs, 31 x 38 In.	375
Dry Sink, Blue Paint, 2 Cabinets, 3 Drawers, Shelf, 76 x 42 In.	2000
Dry Sink, Cherry & Pine, Gallery Top, 2 Doors, c.1850, 31 x 49 In.	420
Dry Sink, Cupboard, Blue Paint, Raised Panel Doors, Drawers, c.1890, 89 x 65 In............*illus*	5400
Dry Sink, Hood, Poplar, Blue Paint, Drawers, Doors, Cutout Feet, c.1825, 42 x 49 In.........*illus*	4200
Dry Sink, Pine, Overhanging Well, 2 Hinged Doors, Shelf, 1800s, 41 In.	761
Dry Sink, Pine, Paint, High Back, Shelf, Black, Green, c.1890, 52 x 60 In.	1200
Dry Sink, Pine, Square Gallery Top, Drain Hole, Stretcher Base, 30 x 73 In.	1320
Dry Sink, Softwood, Backsplash, Drawer, Paneled Doors, 1800s, 34 x 51 In.	236
Dry Sink, Softwood, Red Paint, Open, Drawer, Shelf, Serpentine Sides, 33 x 48 In.	472
Dry Sink, Softwood, Zinc Well, Drawer, Paneled Doors, Cutout Feet, 34 x 40 In.	561
Dry Sink, Walnut, Zinc, Dovetailed Trough, Brass Tacking, c.1875, 34 x 41 In.	531
Dry Sink, Wood, Paint, Flowers, Fruit, Cupboard Doors, Shaped Skirt, 16 x 19 In.....................	189
Dumbwaiter, George III, Mahogany, England, c.1800, 36 x 22 In.	316
Dumbwaiter, Mahogany, Brass, Cloverleaf Top, Revolving, c.1880, 33 ½ In.	976
Easel, Aesthetic Revival, Cherry, Carved, Spindles, Adjustable, 1880s, 74 In.......................*illus*	1680
Easel, Eastlake, Mahogany, Swan Supports, 77 In..	840
Etagere, Art Deco, Burl, 70 x 47 In.	687
Etagere, Federal, Mahogany, 4 Shelves, Drawer, c.1820, 54 x 26 In.	2640
Etagere, Galle, Shaped, Art Nouveau, Flowers, Shelves, Inlay, c.1900, 63 x 36 In..............*illus*	7703
Etagere, Mahogany, French Empire, Gilt Mounts, c.1810, 74 x 36 x 18 In.	2588
Etagere, Mahogany, Shelves, Frieze Drawer, Turned Supports, 1800s, 54 x 20 In.	584
Etagere, Milo Baughman, Chrome Steel, Glass Shelves, 1970s, 79 x 42 In.	531
Etagere, Neoclassical, Mahogany, Shelves, Turned Columns, Drawers, 63 In.	625
Etagere, Pine, Rattan, Cane, 5 Shelves, Adirondack, c.1920, 63 x 25 In............................*illus*	154
Etagere, Victorian, Wicker, 5 Tiers, Gallery, Open Scroll, Curved Legs, 63 x 29 In......................	593
Etagere, Walnut, Fruitwood, 3 Scalloped Tiers, Pierced, Gallery, 39 x 21 In., Pair	1062
Etagere, William IV, Walnut, Demilune, Graduated Shelves, Drawer, c.1835, 81 x 54 In....*illus*	5250
Etagere, Wood, Mirror Back, Gargoyle, Twist Columns, Shelves, 83 x 51 In.	649
Footstool, Arts & Crafts, Oak, Leather Upholstery, Brass, Partial Label, 5 x 13 In.............*illus*	767
Footstool, Cabriole Legs, Pad Feet, England, 18 x 17 x 21 In.	420
Footstool, Center Handle, Blue, Trefoil, Splayed Base, 10 x 17 In.	180
Footstool, G. Stickley, Leather Top, Square Legs, c.1912, 15 x 20 In...	469
Footstool, Giltwood, Beaded Cushion, Round, Carved, Reeded Frame, Disc Feet, 6 x 11 In., Pair *illus*	305
Footstool, Green Paint, Rectangular, Chamfered, Arched Sides, c.1810, 7 x 15 In.	950
Footstool, P. Evans, Steel, Bronze, Cube Base, Cushion, Casters, 1969, 18 x 18 In.	2500
Footstool, Red Brown Paint, Skirt Drawer, Pa., 1800s, 6 x 12 In.....................................*illus*	165
Footstool, Shaker, Basswood, Upholstered, Swollen Legs, c.1880, 7 x 12 In.	369
Footstool, Sheraton, Cherry, Shaped Skirt, Turned Legs, Ball Feet, c.1815, 8 x 15 In.	236
Footstool, Splint Top, Vase & Ring-Turned Legs, Stretchers, c.1790, 11 x 13 In.	450
Footstool, Walnut, Cabriole Legs, 1800s...	183
Footstool, Walnut, Cushion, Pierced Apron, Pendant, c.1865, 17 x 21 In., Pair......................	296
Hall Stand, Edwardian, Mirrors, Paint, Flower Urns, Umbrella Rack, 89 x 56 In..............*illus*	1062
Hall Stand, Iron, Twig Pattern, Mirror, Candle Cups, Corneau Freres, France, 84 In........*illus*	1000
Hall Stand, Mahogany, Brass Hooks, Barleytwist Post, c.1880, 70 x 34 In.	3100
Hall Stand, Mahogany, Carved Crest, Mirror, Turned Columns, 85 x 31 In.	413
Hall Stand, Walnut, Cartouche, Mirror, Brass Hooks, Marble Bench, c.1850, 127 x 60 In........... *illus*	976
Hall Stand, Wood, Nautical Design, Beaded, Mirror, Seat, c.1910, 82 x 45 In.	420
Hammock, Hand Woven, Wood Spreaders, Yellow, Red, 1975, 122 x 45 In.	5000
Hat Rack, Redware, Dog's Head, Stick In Mouth, Glass Eyes, c.1875, 10 x 20 In.	1005
Hat Rack, Wood, Red Paint, Tapered Shaft, Spindles, Knobs, Tripod, 69 In...............................	11993
Headboard, Art Deco Style, Mahogany, Inlaid Satinwood, Wall Mount, 55 x 77 In...........*illus*	2000
Headboard, Flowers, Birds, Castle, Sailing Ship, c.1950, 50 ½ x 75 In.	125
Headboard, Louis XVI, Gilt, Leaves & Flowers, Molded Pediment, 89 x 80 In.	472
Headboard, Max Kuehne, Wood, Gilt, Silver Leaf, Plants, Carved, 1940s, 48 x 58 In.	4375
Highboy, Mahogany, Bonnet Top, Cabriole Legs, Pad Feet, 31 x 16 In.	240
Highboy, Queen Anne, Cherry, 10 Drawers, Cabriole Legs, 73 x 39 In.	1062
Highboy, Queen Anne, Maple, American, 1700s, 69 x 38 In.	1610

Furniture, Etagere, Pine, Rattan, Cane, 5 Shelves, Adirondack, c.1920, 63 x 25 In.
$154

Cowan's Auctions

Furniture, Etagere, William IV, Walnut, Demilune, Graduated Shelves, Drawer, c.1835, 81 x 54 In.
$5,250

New Orleans Auction Galleries

Furniture, Footstool, Arts & Crafts, Oak, Leather Upholstery, Brass, Partial Label, 5 x 13 In.
$767

Hess Auction Group

Furniture, Footstool, Giltwood, Beaded Cushion, Round, Carved, Reeded Frame, Disc Feet, 6 x 11 In., Pair
$305

Neal Auctions

Furniture, Footstool, Red Brown Paint, Skirt Drawer, Pa., 1800s, 6 x 12 In.
$165

Hess Auction Group

TIP
Ordinary beer is great for cleaning a gilded mirror frame. Just pour it on a soft rag, rub gently, and dry.

Furniture, Hall Stand, Edwardian, Mirrors, Paint, Flower Urns, Umbrella Rack, 89 x 56 In.
$1,062

New Orleans Auction Galleries

Furniture, Hall Stand, Iron, Twig Pattern, Mirror, Candle Cups, Corneau Freres, France, 84 In.
$1,000

New Orleans Auction Galleries

Furniture, Hall Stand, Walnut, Cartouche, Mirror, Brass Hooks, Marble Bench, c.1850, 127 x 60 In.
$976

Neal Auctions

181

FURNITURE

Furniture, Headboard, Art Deco Style, Mahogany, Inlaid Satinwood, Wall Mount, 55 x 77 In.
$2,000

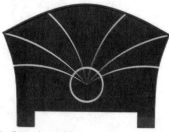

New Orleans Auction Galleries

Furniture, Huntboard, Cherry, Walnut, Inlaid, South Carolina, c.1825, 39 x 54 In.
$12,000

Brunk Auctions

Furniture, Jardiniere, Aesthetic Revival, Tiles, Tole Liner, Mintons China, c.1880, 39 x 44 In.
$1,125

New Orleans Auction Galleries

Furniture, Kneeler, Prie-Dieu, Mahogany, Pierced, Medallion, Needlepoint, Victorian, 37 In.
$312

New Orleans Auction Galleries

Furniture, Knife Box, Wood, Gilt Flowers, Acorns, Brass Handle, Rose Baize Inside, 11 In.
$812

New Orleans Auction Galleries

Furniture, Lap Desk, Burl Walnut, Brass Plaque, Presentation, 1872, Stand, 22 x 19 In.
$812

New Orleans Auction Galleries

Furniture, Library Steps, Chair, Mahogany, Caned, Carved, Treads, Eng., 1800s, 36 In.
$2,440

Neal Auctions

Furniture, Library Steps, V. Kagan, Walnut, Sculpted, 3 Steps, Triangular Frame, 1970s, 31 x 23 In.
$11,250

Rago Arts and Auction Center

Furniture, Lowboy, Chippendale, Mahogany, Drawers, Carved, Cabriole Legs, c.1770, 31 x 30 In.
$3,025

James D. Julia Auctioneers

Highboy, Queen Anne, Maple, Swan's Neck Crest, 2 Sections, c.1790, 36 x 20 In.	948
Huntboard, Cherry, Walnut, Inlaid, South Carolina, c.1825, 39 x 54 In. ....*illus*	12000
Huntboard, Pine, Blue Paint, Nail & Pin Construction, 38 x 51 x 22 In.	1200
Jardiniere, Aesthetic Revival, Tiles, Tole Liner, Mintons China, c.1880, 39 x 44 In. ....*illus*	1125
Jardiniere, Napoleon III, Mahogany, Gilt Bronze, 1900s, 12 x 11 x 11 In.	625
Kneeler, Prie-Dieu, Mahogany, Pierced, Medallion, Needlepoint, Victorian, 37 In. ....*illus*	312
Knife Box, Wood, Gilt Flowers, Acorns, Brass Handle, Rose Baize Inside, 11 In. ....*illus*	812
Lap Desk, Burl Walnut, Brass Plaque, Presentation, 1872, Stand, 22 x 19 In. ....*illus*	812
Lap Desk, Mahogany, Fruitwood Veneers, 4 ½ x 12 ½ In.	84
Lap Desk, Rosewood, Mother-Of-Pearl Plaque, 3 ½ x 12 In.	62
Lap Desk, Stand, Burl Walnut, Mahogany, Brass Inlay, 1800s, 20 x 13 ½ In.	132
Lap Desk, Stand, Rosewood, Mother-Of-Pearl Inlay, 20 x 14 In.	192
Lectern, Mahogany, Slant Front, Inset Leather, Drop Leaf Sides, Victorian, 51 In.	1187
Library Steps, Chair, Mahogany, Caned, Carved, Treads, Eng., 1800s, 36 In. ....*illus*	2440
Library Steps, George III, Mahogany, Gilt Treads, Hinged, Handles, 31 x 19 In.	2100
Library Steps, Gothic Revival, Metamorphic, 4 Steps, Folds To Chair, Oak, 36 In.	437
Library Steps, Regency, Mahogany, Railing, Casters, c.1810, 83 x 21 In.	11875
Library Steps, V. Kagan, Walnut, Sculpted, 3 Steps, Triangular Frame, 1970s, 31 x 23 In. *illus*	11250
Linen Press, Cherry, Doors, 6 Panes, Drawers, Columns, c.1830, 85 x 47 In.	938
Linen Press, Cherry, Molded Crest, Arched Doors, Fluted Stiles, 74 x 52 In.	1298
Linen Press, Chippendale, Cherry, 2 Panel Doors Over 3 Drawers, 75 x 47 In.	590
Linen Press, Georgian, Figured Mahogany, Paneled Doors, Drawer, 73 x 47 In.	360
Linen Press, Georgian, Oak, Carved, Mid 1800s, 104 x 74 In.	2562
Linen Press, Harbor Scene, Dusk, 2 Doors, 3 Drawers, 86 x 51 In.	2125
Linen Press, Hepplewhite Style, Inlaid, 2 Doors, Drawers, Bone Pulls, Miniature, 13 In.	420
Linen Press, Mahogany, Federal, 2 Drawers, Paneled Doors, 1800s, 55 x 49 In.	2745
Linen Press, William IV, Mahogany, 2 Paneled Doors, Fitted, Turned Feet, 82 In.	687
Love Seat, Wood, Wool, Leather, Ball Feet, Arms, Mobelvaerk, 1950s, 61 In.	3750
Lowboy, Cherry, Walnut, Drawers, Scroll Apron, Beaded, Block Legs, 28 x 36 In.	590
Lowboy, Chippendale, Mahogany, Drawers, Carved, Cabriole Legs, c.1770, 31 x 30 In. ....*illus*	3025
Lowboy, Queen Anne, Maple, Drawers, Shaped Apron, Pad Feet, c.1785, 32 x 38 In.	593
Lowboy, Queen Anne, Oak, Cusped Corners, Skirt, Cabriole Legs, 1700s, 29 x 30 In.	413
Mirror, Arched Frame, Beveled Glass, 2 Sections, Scrollwork, 42 x 19 In.	1230
Mirror, Art Deco, Cobalt Blue Glass, Convex Inset Mirrors, 45 x 30 In.	1968
Mirror, Art Deco, Steel Frame, Fountain, 48 x 39 In.	813
Mirror, Arts & Crafts, Hammered Copper, Enamel, Flowers, 23 x 17 ½ In.	3294
Mirror, Baroque, Brass Scrollwork, Faux Tortoiseshell, 48 x 31 In.	1625
Mirror, Baroque, Enamel Frame, Branches, Ribbons, Inset Crystals, 23 x 14 In.	708
Mirror, Baroque, Giltwood, Cartouche Shape, Palmette Crest, Flowers, 24 x 18 In., Pair	1250
Mirror, Biedermeier, Mahogany, Veneer Panel, Ebonized Beading, Inset, 80 In.	750
Mirror, Brass Beaded, Inset Costume Jewelry, Round Corners, 1900s, 32 x 24 In.	437
Mirror, Cast Iron, Giltwood, Paint, Eagle, Portrait, Admiral Dewey, c.1875, 20 In.	360
Mirror, Cheval, Mahogany, Carved, Grapes, Paw Feet, Tilting, c.1885, 77 x 48 In.	2000
Mirror, Cheval, Mahogany, Faceted Finials, Mid 1800s, 81 x 45 In.	976
Mirror, Cheval, Mahogany, Reeded Columns, Garland, Trestle, c.1890, 73 x 34 In.	770
Mirror, Chippendale Style, Giltwood, Pierced, Rocaille & Vine, 42 x 26 In.	562
Mirror, Chippendale, Mahogany, Carved, Scrollwork, Shell Inlay, c.1790, 42 x 21 In. ....*illus*	242
Mirror, Chippendale, Mahogany, Eagle Crest, Gilt Liner, c.1875, 39 x 18 In.	219
Mirror, Chippendale, Mahogany, Gilt, Scrollwork, Eagle, Carved, c.1810, 40 x 19 In.	600
Mirror, Chippendale, Mahogany, Scrolled Ornamentation, Bird Crest, 30 x 17 In.	140
Mirror, Chippendale, Rococo, 2-Part Mirror, Carved, Giltwood, c.1785, 68 x 45 In. ....*illus*	968
Mirror, Convex, William IV, Giltwood, Ebonized Liner, Gilt Spheres, 24 In.	500
Mirror, Dessus De La Porte, Giltwood, Ribbon, Leaf Swag, c.1900, 15 x 42 In.	1750
Mirror, Dressing, Cast Iron, Ivy, Swivel Frame, C-Scroll, Shell Base, c.1890, 19 In.	82
Mirror, Dressing, Mahogany, Columns, Scroll Brackets, Drawers, c.1810, 24 x 23 In. ....*illus*	5535
Mirror, Dressing, Tilts, Oval, 30 x 20 In.	157
Mirror, Driftwood, Octagonal, 36 In.	250
Mirror, Federal, Giltwood, American, Early 1800s, 36 x 22 In.	60
Mirror, Federal, Giltwood, Reverse Paint, Delmarone & Cermananti, c.1800, 43 x 26 In.	649
Mirror, Federal, Giltwood, Reverse Paint, Glass Panel, Woman, Rock, 24 x 14 In.	533

F

Furniture, Mirror, Chippendale, Mahogany, Carved, Scrollwork, Shell Inlay, c.1790, 42 x 21 In.
$242

James D. Julia Auctioneers

Furniture, Mirror, Chippendale, Rococo, 2-Part Mirror, Carved, Giltwood, c.1785, 68 x 45 In.
$968

James D. Julia Auctioneers

Furniture, Mirror, Dressing, Mahogany, Columns, Scroll Brackets, Drawers, c.1810, 24 x 23 In.
$5,535

Skinner, Inc.

Furniture, Mirror, Girandole, Carved, Giltwood, c.1810, 50 x 35 In. $4,888

Cottone Auctions

Furniture, Mirror, Hollywood Regency, 3 Ovals, Giltwood, Scrolling, c.1935, 46 x 84 $1,125

New Orleans Auction Galleries

Furniture, Mirror, Lodge, Wood, Paint, Composition, Carved, Eagle, c.1910, 83 x 38 In. $2,280

Garth's Auctioneers & Appraisers

Mirror, Federal, Giltwood, Scrolled Flower Crest, Pendant, Urn, 1800s, 52 x 18 In.	300
Mirror, G. Nakashima, Black Walnut, Free Edge, 46 x 28 In.	4305
Mirror, George II, Giltwood, Eagle's Head Crest, Reeded, 1700s, 52 x 29 In.	860
Mirror, George II, Leaves & Birds, 3 Sections, Giltwood, 31 ½ x 75 In.	343
Mirror, George III, Parcel Gilt, Mahogany, Eagle Pediment, 58 x 28 In.	900
Mirror, Giltwood, Beaded, Gadrooned, Scroll, Cartouches, c.1885, 69 x 41 In.	1750
Mirror, Giltwood, Bull's-Eye, Spherules, Eagle Crest, c.1915, 32 x 22 In.	750
Mirror, Giltwood, Carved Leaves, Scrollwork, Blue Panels, c.1850, 34 x 25 In.	1000
Mirror, Giltwood, Convex, Entwined Dolphins, Reeded Ebony, c.1980, 42 x 24 In.	1185
Mirror, Giltwood, Cove Molded, Paneled, Relief Scrollwork, c.1800, 52 x 36 In.	937
Mirror, Giltwood, Egyptian Revival, Convex, Alligators, Candleholders, 52 In.	550
Mirror, Giltwood, Figural, Masks, Wings, Leaves, 34 x 29 In.	500
Mirror, Giltwood, Leaf Crest, Plaque, Scroll Branch Apron, c.1800, 56 x 34 In.	2250
Mirror, Giltwood, Leaf Spray Crest, Swags, Beading, Flowers, c.1885, 75 x 49 In.	5250
Mirror, Giltwood, Leaves, Dolphins, Eagle Crest, Candle Arms, c.1815, 55 x 48 In.	8750
Mirror, Giltwood, Medallion Shape, Scroll, Rocaille, Leaves, c.1765, 17 x 45 In.	2125
Mirror, Giltwood, Molded, Egg & Dart Frame, Branches, c.1935, 41 x 28 In.	875
Mirror, Giltwood, Oval, Continental Rococo, Carved, 1800s, 77 x 30 In.	1342
Mirror, Giltwood, Oval, Pierced Frame, Rocaille, Leaf Crest, 1900s, 53 x 29 In.	531
Mirror, Giltwood, Panel Of Alpine Village Above, Late 1800s, 64 x 34 In.	4575
Mirror, Giltwood, Part Ebonized, Scrollwork, 64 x 42 In.	188
Mirror, Giltwood, Pierced Ribbon Crest, Music Symbols, Tassels, 49 x 27 In.	468
Mirror, Giltwood, Rococo, Wire Flowers, Ho Ho Birds, Italy, 1800s, 68 x 33 In.	687
Mirror, Giltwood, Shaped, Nationalist, Eagles, Crossed Flags, Rosette, 25 x 43 In.	535
Mirror, Giltwood, Shell Carved Crest, 1700s, 53 x 28 In.	3500
Mirror, Giltwood, Shells, Mask Crest, Dragons, Dolphins, Pierced, c.1885, 69 x 29 In.	2375
Mirror, Giltwood, Sunburst, Continental, 26 ½ In.	700
Mirror, Giltwood, Swan's Neck Crest, Cartouche, Vine Scrolls, c.1735, 47 x 24 In.	875
Mirror, Girandole, Carved, Giltwood, c.1810, 50 x 35 In. ....*illus*	4888
Mirror, Girandole, Federal, Giltwood, Eagle, Spread Wings, c.1810, 47 x 27 In.	677
Mirror, Hollywood Regency, 3 Ovals, Giltwood, Scrolling, c.1935, 46 x 84 ....*illus*	1125
Mirror, Japanned, Red, Gilt Figures, Shaped Surround, Slant Front Base, 39 In.	312
Mirror, Jin-Di-Sugi, Cypress, Brass Roundel, Minneapolis Crafthouse, 32 x 24 In.	625
Mirror, Lodge, Wood, Paint, Composition, Carved, Eagle, c.1910, 83 x 38 In. ....*illus*	2280
Mirror, Louis XV Style, Giltwood, Pierced Crest, C-Scrolls, Leaves, 48 x 29 In.	437
Mirror, Louis XVI, Giltwood, Lotus Leaves, Flower Swag Crest, c.1715, 51 x 37 In.	3500
Mirror, Mahogany Veneer, Reverse Painted, Continental, c.1850, 50 x 32 In.	185
Mirror, Mahogany, Gilt, Scalloped Crest, Eagle, Pendant Apron, c.1890, 37 x 23 In.	119
Mirror, Mirrored Tiered Surrounds, Octagonal, Italy, 42 x 30 In., Pair	812
Mirror, Neoclassical, Giltwood, Pierced Ribbon, Scroll, Italy, 1900s, 59 x 33 In. ....*illus*	937
Mirror, P. Evans, Copper, Bronze, Pewter, Patchwork Design, 1970s, 30 x 30 In.	1375
Mirror, Paint, Heart & Crown Crest, Cutouts, Molded, Black c.1710, 20 x 12 In.	950
Mirror, Parcel Gilt, Scroll Framed Tablet, Pilasters, Urns, c.1950, 60 x 40 In.	1187
Mirror, Pier, Giltwood, Louis XV, Maidens Bathing, c.1900, 60 x 28 In.	2250
Mirror, Pier, Giltwood, Oval Inset Painting, Rocaille, Scroll, c.1885, 76 x 42 In.	3500
Mirror, Pier, Mahogany, Triangle Crest, Ormolu Griffins, Urn, c.1835, 91 x 37 In.	593
Mirror, Pier, Neoclassical Style, Giltwood, Egg & Dart, Panels, Urn, Roses, 69 In.	1375
Mirror, Pier, Oil Painting, Tombstone Shape, Cartouche Crest, c.1735, 65 x 31 In.	531
Mirror, Queen Anne Style, Japanned, Nature Designs, Scroll Crest, 48 x 23 In.	780
Mirror, Queen Anne, Giltwood, Tombstone Shape, Leaves, c.1965, 53 x 27 In.	3500
Mirror, Queen Anne, Walnut, Giltwood, Arched Crest, Scroll, c.1765, 32 x 16 In.	415
Mirror, Raindrops, Mixed Metals, C. Jere, 1972, 30 x 7 In. ....*illus*	2625
Mirror, Red Paint, High Shaped Crest, Swirls, Molded Frame, 1787, 20 x 10 In.	8000
Mirror, Regency Style, Giltwood, 3 Sections, Columns, Swags, c.1900, 41 x 70 In.	625
Mirror, Rococo, Giltwood, Leaves, Continental, 1900s, 42 x 30 ½ In., Pair	500
Mirror, Rococo, Giltwood, Phoenix Crest, Rocaille, England, 1700s, 48 x 22 In.	1920
Mirror, Shaving, Mahogany, Walnut, Brass Inlay, 1-Drawer Base, 22 ½ In.	120
Mirror, Shaving, Pink, Green, Peter Hunt, 22 x 18 In.	357
Mirror, Tabernacle, Giltwood, Acorn Drops, Pilasters, c.1835, 42 x 24 In.	1062
Mirror, Table, Beveled, Metal Stepped Frame, Red, Black, Art Deco, 1935, 20 x 14 In.	431

Furniture, Mirror, Neoclassical, Giltwood, Pierced Ribbon, Scroll, Italy, 1900s, 59 x 33 In.
$937

New Orleans Auction Galleries

Furniture, Mirror, Raindrops, Mixed Metals, C. Jere, 1972, 30 x 7 In.
$2,625

Rago Arts and Auction Center

Furniture, Mirror, Wendell Castle, Biomorphic, Wood, Stack Laminated, Carved, 1970s, 16 In.
$8,913

Cottone Auctions

Furniture, Pedestal, Bugatti, Walnut, Inlaid Pewter, Copper, Studio, c.1902, 46 x 18 In.
$12,500

Los Angeles Modern Auctions

Furniture, Pedestal, Onyx, Classical Column, Gilt Metal Bands, 30 In.
$660

Cowan's Auctions

Furniture, Pedestal, Renaissance Revival, Ebonized, Gilt, Velvet Panel, c.1870, 37 x 17 In.
$1,024

Neal Auctions

Furniture, Pie Safe, Chestnut, Pinwheels, Cut Corner Tins, Doors, Indiana, c.1850, 73 x 52 In.
$1,800

Garth's Auctioneers & Appraisers

Furniture, Recamier, Neoclassical, Faux Rosewood, Scrolled, Stencil, c.1815, 33 x 78 In.
$3,750

New Orleans Auction Galleries

Antimacassar

An antimacassar is a doily or cover put on the top of the upholstered back of a chair. It was used to keep hair oil used by men from staining the upholstery. Hair oil used in the nineteenth century was said to have been imported from Macassar in the East Indies.

F

FURNITURE

Furniture, Rocker, Adirondack, Twig, Bentwood, Slat Back, Stain, c.1975, Child's, 27 In.
$240

Garth's Auctioneers & Appraisers

Furniture, Rocker, V. Kagan, Walnut, Sculpted, Wool, Leather, 1970s, 39 x 32 In.
$11,875

Rago Arts and Auction Center

Furniture, Rocker, Windsor, Bench, Faux Figured Maple Crest, Plank Seat, c.1810, 30 x 67 In.
$976

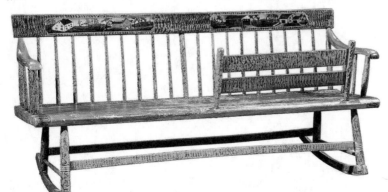

Neal Auctions

Furniture, Screen, 6-Panel, Eames, Rosewood, Canvas, H. Miller, 1990s, 68 x 57 In.
$2,625

Rago Arts and Auction Center

Furniture, Secretary, Biedermeier, Mahogany, Drop Front, Stepped Crest, c.1835, 79 x 43 In.
$2,500

New Orleans Auction Galleries

Furniture, Secretary, George II, Slant Front, Burl, Mirror Doors, Fitted, 1700s, 80 In.
$3,240

Cowan's Auctions

Furniture, Secretary, Queen Anne, Drop Front, Chinoiserie, Fitted, 1700s, 87 x 41 In.
$4,500

New Orleans Auction Galleries

Mirror, Tessellated, Decorated Frame, Greek, 48 ½ In.	375
Mirror, Venetian Glass, Lattice Border, Aventurine Rosettes, c.1935, 40 x 30 In.	3998
Mirror, Venetian, Queen Anne, Smoked, Giltwood, 1900s, 60 x 23 In.	1200
Mirror, Walnut, Pickled, Swan's Neck Crest, Raised Panels, 1800s, 50 x 49 In.	812
Mirror, Wendell Castle, Biomorphic, Wood, Stack Laminated, Carved, 1970s, 16 In. ....*illus*	8913
Mirror, William & Mary, Walnut, Fruitwood, Cushion Frame, Inlay, c.1690, 29 In.	1680
Mirror, Woman, Driving, Embossed, Mermaids, Lilies, Celluloid, Brass, 9 x 5 In.	374
Mirror, Wood, Black Paint, Molded Frame, Stepped, c.1710, 17 x 14 In.	4250
Mirror, Wood, Gesso, Carved, Openwork Scroll, Leaves, Chevron, 25 x 28 In.	502
Mirror, Wood, Resin, Glass, Sunburst, Line Vautrin, 37 In.	1900
Mirror, Wood, Sunburst, Raised Rays, 36 In.	1250
Ottoman, Leather, Pig Shape, Floppy Ears & Tail, Button Eyes, c.1900, 24 In.	710
Ottoman, Tapestry, Velvet, Fringe, 18 ½ x 51 In.	500
Ottoman, Tortoise, Stitched Leather, 1900s, 14 x 29 In.	480
Ottoman, William IV Style, Mahogany, Leather, Brass Tacks, Casters, 16 x 37 In.	1250
Overmantel Mirror, see Architectural category.	
Parlor Set, Shanghai Deco, Rosewood, Leather, Round Arms, c.1970, 3 Piece	6560
Pedestal, Bugatti, Walnut, Inlaid Pewter, Copper, Studio, c.1902, 46 x 18 In. ....*illus*	12500
Pedestal, French Empire, Bronze Mounted, Paneled, Trim, 44 In.	200
Pedestal, French Neoclassical Style, Composition, Paint, Garlands, 30 In., Pair	180
Pedestal, Marble, White, Orange, Square Top & Base, Gilt Banding, 40 x 13 In.	780
Pedestal, Neoclassical, Mahogany, Granite Top, Tapered, Swags, Torches, 48 In.	343
Pedestal, Onyx, Classical Column, Gilt Metal Bands, 30 In. ....*illus*	660
Pedestal, Renaissance Revival, Ebonized, Gilt, Velvet Panel, c.1870, 37 x 17 In. ....*illus*	1024
Pie Safe, Blue Paint, Glass Paneled Door, Ring-Turned Legs, c.1850, 45 x 31 In.	1007
Pie Safe, Cherry & Pine, Punched Tin Panels, Tulips, Mid 1800s, 57 x 39 In.	1560
Pie Safe, Chestnut, Pinwheels, Cut Corner Tins, Doors, Indiana, c.1850, 73 x 52 In. ....*illus*	1800
Pie Safe, Mahogany, Punched Tin Panels, Scrolled Apron, c.1880, 64 x 42 In.	2100
Pie Safe, Paint, Scroll Backsplash, Doors, Punched Tin Panels, 1800s, 60 x 42 In.	295
Pie Safe, Pine, 2 Doors, Punched Tin Panels, Drawer, 59 x 33 In.	295
Pie Safe, Pine, Green, Square, Tall Square Legs, Door, c.1850, 66 In.	2340
Pie Safe, Pine, Poplar, 8 Tin Panels, c.1900, 58 x 31 In.	230
Pie Safe, Pine, Red Paint, Punched Tin Panels, Pinwheels, Shapes, 1868, 70 x 47 In.	480
Pie Safe, Punched Tin Panels, Eagles, Ohio, Mid 1800s, 73 x 41 x 17 In.	660
Pie Safe, Sheraton, Wood, Plank Top, Punched Tin Panels, Turned Feet, 56 x 41 In.	590
Pie Safe, Softwood, Cream Over Blue, 12 Tin Panels, Stars In Circles, 58 In.	885
Pie Safe, Softwood, Plank Top, Punched Tin Panels, Arch Feet, 1800s, 59 x 41 In.	826
Pie Safe, Wall, Mixed Wood, Paint, Punched Tin Door, Stars, c.1885, 37 x 41 In.	354
Pie Safe, Walnut, Punched Tin Panels, 2 Hinged Doors, 1800s, 50 x 53 In.	1989
Pie Safe, Walnut, Punched Tin Panels, 2 Hinged Doors, Drawer, c.1850, 54 In.	4680
Pie Safe, Wood, Punched Tin Panels, Doors, Stars, Spandrels, c.1850, 61 x 42 In.	948
Rack, Baking, Steel, Brass, 2 Shelves, 83 x 48 In.	125
Rack, Bread, Fruitwood, Scroll Crest, Urn Finials, Spindles, c.1850, 37 x 34 In.	1000
Rack, Drying, Pine, Square Shaft, Staggered Dowels, 96 x 8 In.	62
Rack, Game, Wrought Iron, Silver Paint, Scrolled Ends, 1800s, 72 In.	600
Rack, Hanging, Mixed Wood, Green Paint, Star Shape, Wire Hooks, c.1915, 45 In.	250
Rack, Hanging, Softwood, 11 Hand-Carved Mushroom Pegs, 1800s, 66 In.	107
Rack, Luggage, Roycroft, Wood, Slatted Top, Open Sides, Trundle, 26 x 30 In.	938
Rack, Magazine, Inlaid Mother-Of-Pearl, Black, c.1950, 23 x 16 In.	187
Rack, Magazine, Teak, Denmark, 20 ½ x 22 In.	87
Rack, Quilt, Walnut, Shaped, Cutout Feet, Chamfered Edge, c.1850, 38 x 31 In.	240
Rack, Towel, Pine, Red Paint, 3 Bars, Uprights, Arch Feet, 1800s, 36 x 32 In.	367
Recamier, Biedermeier, Maple, Upholstered, 1900s, 32 x 69 In.	1125
Recamier, Neoclassical, Faux Rosewood, Scrolled, Stencil, c.1815, 33 x 78 In. ....*illus*	3750
Recamier, Rosewood, Serpentine, Carved, Arms, Block Feet, c.1835, 36 x 75 In.	4250
Rocker, Adirondack, Bent Willow, Yellow, 1900s, 43 ½ x 22 In.	156
Rocker, Adirondack, Twig, Bentwood, Slat Back, Stain, c.1975, Child's, 27 In. ....*illus*	240
Rocker, David Barr, Walnut, 1980s, 39 x 23 In.	1220
Rocker, Eames, Fiberglass, Birch, For Herman Miller, 1950s, 27 x 25 In.	812
Rocker, G. Stickley, Flattened Arms, 2 Cushions, c.1907, 40 x 29 In.	594

Furniture, Server, Federal, Mahogany, Drawers, Butterfly Doors, Cock-Beaded, c.1815, 43 x 42 In.
$2,541

James D. Julia Auctioneers

Furniture, Settee, Carved, 4-Panel Back, Arms, Continental, 1700s, 47 x 77 In.
$1,416

Hess Auction Group

Furniture, Settee, Louis XV, Fruitwood, Shaped Seat & Back, Tapestry, c.1790, 76 In.
$1,250

New Orleans Auction Galleries

Furniture, Settle, G. Stickley, Willow, Cushions, Arms, 1912-15, 33 x 88 In.
$2,375

Rago Arts and Auction Center

Furniture, Settle, L. & J.G. Stickley, Even Arms, Slats, Leather Cushion, c.1910, 39 x 75 In.
$3,250

Rago Arts and Auction Center

Fake Carving
A faker will often carve an extra design on the lid of a desk or the leg of a table to add to the value.

Furniture, Shelf, Paint, D-Shape Tiers, Leaf Carved Edges, Continental, 80 x 53 In.
$1,187

New Orleans Auction Galleries

Furniture, Sideboard, Art Nouveau, Mahogany, Mirror, Carved, England, c.1900, 78 In.
$1,320

Garth's Auctioneers & Appraisers

Rocker, L. & J.G. Stickley, 4 Splats, Upholstered Seat, 37 x 31 In.	244
Rocker, L. & J.G. Stickley, Brown Leather, Fayetteville, N.Y., c.1910, 38 x 29 In.	1375
Rocker, L. & J.G. Stickley, Brown Leather, Fayetteville, N.Y., c.1912, 36 x 31 In.	3125
Rocker, Mahogany, Cutouts, Shaped Sides, Scroll Arms, c.1815, Child's, 27 In.	443
Rocker, Milo Baughman, Iron, Birch, Upholstered, 1950s, 30 ½ x 27 In.	793
Rocker, Neoclassical, Rosewood, Tablet, Cane Back, Scroll Arms, American, 41 In.	793
Rocker, Oak, Bent-Spindle Back, Plank Seat, Shaped Arms, c.1850, 42 ½ In.	380
Rocker, Oak, Ladder Back, 4 Slats, Tiger Maple, Acorn Finials, 1800s, 44 In.	176
Rocker, Rococo, Mahogany, Lincoln, American, Mid 1800s, 40 x 33 In.	732
Rocker, Shaker, Birch, 3 Slats, Harvard, Mass., c.1830s, 38 ½ x 14 ½ In.	600
Rocker, Shaker, Cylinder Crest Rail, Slat Back, Shaped Arms, Stretcher, c.1885	615
Rocker, Shaker, Maple, Woven Tape Seat & Back, Acorn Finials, c.1885, 35 In.	150
Rocker, Shaker, Mixed Wood, Black Paint, Upholstered, c.1885, Child's, 23 In.	720
Rocker, Shaker, Tiger Maple, Ladder Back, Curved Arms, c.1820, 45 In.	2640
Rocker, Stickley, Inlaid Sewing, Maple, Pewter, Cane Seat, 35 x 17 In.	1952
Rocker, V. Kagan, Walnut, Sculpted, Wool, Leather, 1970s, 39 x 32 In. ....*illus*	11875
Rocker, Windsor, Bench, Faux Figured Maple Crest, Plank Seat, c.1810, 30 x 67 In. ......*illus*	976
Screens are also listed in the Architectural and Fireplace categories.	
Screen, 2-Panel, Hardwood, Bone Embellished, Early 1900s, Japan, 71 ¾ In.	610
Screen, 2-Panel, Mirrored, Panes, Painted, 86 x 58 In.	563
Screen, 3-Panel, Arched Panels, Animals In Room, Paint, c.1975, 96 x 24 In.	354
Screen, 3-Panel, Arts & Crafts, Mahogany, Leather, Poppy, Serpent, 53 x 49 In.	4880
Screen, 3-Panel, Birds, Flowers, Red, Green, Scandinavia, 1800s, 74 x 81 In.	1119
Screen, 3-Panel, Dressing, Gilt, Columns, Carved, Ruins, c.1890, 86 x 76 In.	2370
Screen, 3-Panel, Gilt, Alternating Mirrored Panels, Crossbars, 97 x 78 In.	563
Screen, 3-Panel, Lake, Buildings, Boat, 60 In.	250
Screen, 3-Panel, Landscape, Monkeys, Classical Ruins, Blue, 35 x 72 In.	1625
Screen, 3-Panel, Mahogany, Arched, Columns, Nymph, Pierced, c.1935, 73 x 57 In.	937
Screen, 3-Panel, Mahogany, Paint, Flowers, Recessed Center Panel, 78 x 74 In.	250
Screen, 3-Panel, Watercolor On Silk, Figures, Landscape, c.1910, 70 x 60 In.	1185
Screen, 3-Panel, Wood, Pyrographic, Early To Bed, Now I Lay, 66 x 45 In.	313
Screen, 4-Panel, Bamboo, Circles, 16 Square Grid, 73 In.	250
Screen, 4-Panel, Chinoiserie Scenes, Leather, Brass Tacks, c.1875, 81 x 79 In.	590
Screen, 4-Panel, Countryside, Pond, Swan, Leather, 75 x 93 In.	1000
Screen, 4-Panel, Grecian Key, Lacquer, Wood, Black, White, 86 x 64 In.	343
Screen, 4-Panel, Hardwood, Inset Porcelain, Blue, White, Landscapes, 69 x 73 In.	950
Screen, 4-Panel, Landscape, Tan, Silk, Black Framing, Asia, 40 x 49 In.	281
Screen, 4-Panel, Leather, Scroll Cartouches, Eagles, Embossed, c.1910, 63 x 92 In.	1000
Screen, 4-Panel, Mahogany, France, 18th Century, 76 x 88 In.	550
Screen, 4-Panel, Oak, 12 European Scenes, 65 x 80 In.	156
Screen, 4-Panel, Oil On Canvas, Scenes, Genji Tale, Japan, 1800s, 66 x 96 In., Pair	2280
Screen, 4-Panel, Table, Wood, Porcelain Reserves, Landscape, Chinese, 23 x 32 In.	2375
Screen, 4-Panel, Tooled Leather, Multicolor, 74 ½ x 72 In.	188
Screen, 4-Panel, Village Scenes, Lion Cartouches, Paint, Leather, c.1900, 72 x 88 In.	118
Screen, 6-Panel, Eames, Rosewood, Canvas, H. Miller, 1990s, 68 x 57 In. ....*illus*	2625
Screen, 8-Panel, Asian, Birds, 85 x 128 In.	950
Screen, 8-Panel, Eames, Molded Ash Plywood, 68 x 60 In.	1375
Screen, Mahogany, Copper, Slag Glass, Thistle, Scottish Arts & Crafts, 39 x 30 In.	2000
Screen, Table, 3-Panel, Gilt Bronze, Porcelain Inset, Courting Couples, 17 x 23 In.	688
Screen, Table, Carved Jade, Embroidered Silk, Wood Frame, 13 x 10 In.	1250
Screen, Tapestry, Basket, Flowers, Parrot, Serpentine Gilt Frame, 39 x 28 In.	1125
Secretary, Applewood, Slant Front, Scroll Crest, Finials, Doors, c.1790, 79 x 36 In.	4250
Secretary, Biedermeier, Mahogany, Drop Front, Stepped Crest, c.1835, 79 x 43 In. ....*illus*	2500
Secretary, Broken Scroll Pediment, 2 Cabinet Doors, Swags, c.1810, 85 x 49 In.	1230
Secretary, Drop Front, 4 Serpentine Drawers, Maddox Colonial, 41 x 36 In.	275
Secretary, Drop Front, Burl Veneer, Carved Trim, Fluted Columns, 59 x 37 In.	1118
Secretary, Federal, Cherry, Marquetry, Tulips, 2 Tambour Doors, Drawers, 48 In.	1375
Secretary, Fruitwood, Dome Crest, Mirror Door, Bowed Drawers, 96 x 43 In.	3000
Secretary, George II, Slant Front, Burl, Mirror Doors, Fitted, 1700s, 80 In. ....*illus*	3240
Secretary, George III, Oak, Cabinet, 3 Drawers, 92 x 46 In.	687

Secretary, Mahogany, Bowfront, Columns, Hinged Lid, Bracket Feet, 1922, 64 x 41 In.	830
Secretary, Mahogany, Cylinder, Cupboards, Turk Heads, Columns, 56 x 44 In.	3250
Secretary, Mahogany, Drop Front, Drawer Faced, Granite Top, 58 x 33 In.	1187
Secretary, Maple, Rosewood, Drawers, Green Marble, 58 ½ x 38 In.	375
Secretary, Oak, Slant Front, Mirror Doors, Gesso Trim, Bracket Feet, 83 x 37 In.	1625
Secretary, Queen Anne, Drop Front, Chinoiserie, Fitted, 1700s, 87 x 41 In. ....*illus*	4500
Secretary, Slant Front, Stone Veneer, Brass Inlay, Maitland Smith, 84 In.	3750
Secretary, Walnut, 2 Sections, 3 Glazed Doors, Fretwork, 1800s, 100 x 66 In.	738
Semainier, Mahogany, Marble Top, Cove Molded, Fluted Stiles, c.1900, 52 x 27 In.	1750
Server, Federal, Mahogany, Cherry, Drawer, Baltimore, Md., c.1825, 51 x 41 In.	556
Server, Federal, Mahogany, Drawers, Butterfly Doors, Cock-Beaded, c.1815, 43 x 42 In. .....*illus*	2541
Server, G. Stickley, Eastwood, N.Y., c.1907, 39 x 48 x 20 In.	1750
Server, G. Stickley, Maple, Backsplash, Drawers, Block Legs, c.1907, 39 x 48 In.	1750
Server, G. Stickley, Rectangular Gallery, 4 Drawers, 39 x 48 In.	3125
Server, Hepplewhite, Mahogany, Bowfront, Flower Inlay, Baltimore, 34 x 44 In.	1298
Server, Hepplewhite, Maple, Bowfront, Dovetailed Drawers, 1800s, 30 x 48 In.	944
Server, Mahogany, Dovetailed, Reeded, Leaves, Colby's, c.1950, 27 x 83 x 20 In.	360
Server, Mahogany, Drawer, 2 Open Shelves, Marquetry, c.1920, 43 x 44 In.	350
Server, Marble Top, Black, Grilled Door, 31 x 40 In.	100
Server, Marble Top, Directoire Style, 3 Drawers, 3 Doors, c.1910, 44 x 63 In.	650
Server, Oak, Paneled Doors, Carved, Hinges, 3-Board Top, American, 30 x 66 In.	330
Server, Pine, 4 Paneled Doors, Flowers, Turned Feet, 1800s, 40 x 58 In.	480
Server, Provincial Louis XV, Oak, Burl, Drawers, 3 Paneled Doors, 38 x 78 In.	1800
Server, Provincial, Walnut, Carved, Cupboards, Bracket Feet, c.1800, 34 x 44 In.	270
Server, Walnut, 4 Paneled Doors, Refinished, 59 x 46 x 15 In.	840
Server, Walnut, Marble Top, Carved, Flowers, Cabriole Legs, 1900s, 34 x 39 In.	677
Server, Welsh Pickled Pine, 2 Drawer, Tenon, c.1850, 32 x 54 x 17 In.	826
Settee, Anglo-Colonial, Rosewood, Pierced, X-Splat, Cane Seat, 33 x 64 In.	1500
Settee, B. Rouzie, Cherry, Walnut, 2 Seats, 31 x 66 In.	776
Settee, Carved, 4-Panel Back, Arms, Continental, 1700s, 47 x 77 In. ....*illus*	1416
Settee, Charles X, Mahogany, Reeded Crest Rail, Paw Feet, c.1810, 38 x 71 In.	854
Settee, French Empire, Gilt Carved, Bronze Mounts, Swan Arms, 1800s, 37 x 78 In.	300
Settee, French Napoleon III, Upholstered, Turned Legs, Arms, c.1870, 36 x 53 In.	450
Settee, Fruitwood, Triple-Back, Vase Shape Splats, Serpentine, c.1880, 46 x 61 In.	431
Settee, Georgian, Molded Panel, 4 Seats, Cabriole Legs, 42 x 72 In.	1000
Settee, Giltwood, Masks, Swan's Heads, Griffins, Shoefoot Base, c.1885, 41 x 46 In.	308
Settee, Grain Paint, Spindle Back, Scroll Arms, Turned Legs, 1800s, 34 x 73 In.	413
Settee, Leather, Padded, Sloped Arms, Iron Scroll Apron, c.1910, 37 x 69 In., Pair	2000
Settee, Louis XV, Fruitwood, Shaped Seat & Back, Tapestry, c.1790, 76 In. ....*illus*	1250
Settee, Louis XVI Style, Cane Back, Twist Cane Legs, c.1940, 16 In.	550
Settee, Louis XVI, Giltwood, Ribbon Carved, 37 x 53 In.	1464
Settee, Louis XVI, Parcel Gilt, Upholstered, 40 x 72 In.	2000
Settee, Mahogany, Leaf Carved Crest Rail, 1800s, 30 x 44 ½ x 20 In.	384
Settee, Maple, Triple Chairback, Turned Crest, Pierced, Arms, c.1825, 36 x 65 In.	2370
Settee, Napoleon III Style, Leather Button Back, Arms, Turned Feet, 32 x 46 In.	500
Settee, Neoclassical, Paint, Shieldback, Lyre Splats, Block Legs, c.1810, 37 x 64 In.	1000
Settee, Regency, Cane, Medallions, Classical Figure, Putti, 8 Legs, 35 x 66 In.	708
Settee, Shaker, Pine, Stain, Spindle Back, Shaped Seat, 5 Legs, c.1850, 32 x 82 In.	2829
Settee, Sheraton, Upholstered, Curved Reeded Crest, Arms, c.1800, 37 x 81 In.	948
Settee, Wood, Shaped Crest, Spindles, Flowers, Scroll Arms, 1800s, 34 x 72 In.	189
Settle, Arts & Crafts, Oak, Back Slats, c.1912, 36 x 76 In.	1046
Settle, Dark Gray Brown, 3 Drawers, c.1810, 63 x 61 ½ In.	5160
Settle, English Oak, Paneled Back, Hinged Seat, Early 1700s, 45 x 55 In.	677
Settle, G. Stickley, Eastwood, N.Y., c.1902, 39 x 69 ½ x 33 ½ In.	3250
Settle, G. Stickley, Willow, Cushions, Arms, 1912-15, 33 x 88 In. ....*illus*	2375
Settle, High Back, Cutouts, Pointed Handrests, Arch Base, 1700s, 53 x 60 In.	11000
Settle, L. & J.G. Stickley, Even Arms, Slats, Leather Cushion, c.1910, 39 x 75 In. ....*illus*	3250
Settle, Limbert, Grand Rapids, Mich., c.1910, 31 x 86 x 33 ½ In.	2125
Settle, Oak, Arts & Crafts, Shaped Posts, c.1912, 77 x 31 ½ In.	1353
Settle, Stickley, Arts & Crafts, Quartersawn Oak, 5 Splats, 28 x 72 In.	570 to 720
Shelf, Blackamoor, Green Cape, Bracket, 14 x 11 In., Pair	365

Furniture, Sideboard, Sheraton, Mahogany, Drawer 2 Doors, Turned Legs, American, 36 x 60 In.
$354

Hess Auction Group

Furniture, Sideboard, Walnut, String Inlay, Doors, Beaded Drawers, 6 Legs, c.1810, 43 x 58 In.
$8,610

Skinner, Inc.

Furniture, Sideboard, Widdicomb, Bowfront, Mahogany, Inlay, Gilt Banding, 37 x 78 In.
$687

New Orleans Auction Galleries

Hollywood Deco

Hollywood Deco is a modern term describing the extreme Art Deco designs used for the decorating in movies like *The Thin Man* (1934). The furnishings look glamorous and theatrical. The Hollywood-inspired furniture, with round mirrors, chrome, blue glass, plastic, and blond wood, ranged from poor quality to expensive custom-made.

F

FURNITURE

Furniture, Sofa, Empire, Mahogany, Carved, Pierced Crest, Scroll Arms, H.B. Mudge, 1800s, 84 In.
$492

Cowan's Auctions

Furniture, Sofa, Neoclassical, Mahogany, Carved, Outscrolled Arms, c.1810, 34 x 91 In.
$3,050

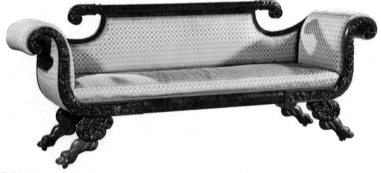

Neal Auctions

Furniture, Sofa, Neoclassical, Mahogany, Upholstered, Scroll Arms, Paw Feet, c.1825, 89 In.
$1,750

New Orleans Auction Galleries

Furniture, Sofa, V. Kagan, Tiger Maple, Floating Seat & Back, 1970s, 84 x 36 In.
$20,000

Rago Arts and Auction Center

Furniture, Stand, 8-Sided Marble Top, Openwork, Dragon Head Feet, Chinese, c.1900, 38 In.
$369

Skinner, Inc.

Furniture, Stand, Hardwood, Carved, Openwork, Porcelain Tile Top, Chinese, c.1890, 18 In.
$363

James D. Julia Auctioneers

Furniture, Stand, Hepplewhite, Cherry, Drawer, Square, Tapered Legs, Pa., 28 x 16 In.
$94

Hess Auction Group

Shelf, Bucket Bench, Pine, Dovetailed, Crescent Cutouts, c.1850, 44 x 34 In.	660
Shelf, Clock, Walnut, Dovetailed Drawer, Shaker, c.1850, 42 x 16 In.	810
Shelf, G. Nelson, Omni, Walnut, Aluminum Supports, 1960s, 92 x 129 In.	3375
Shelf, George III, Pickled Pine, Hanging, 4 Tiers, Shaped Supports, 48 x 48 In.	120
Shelf, Gilt, Figural, Seated Blackamoor, Bracket, 15 In., Pair	2375
Shelf, Hanging, Cast Iron, Projecting Back, Convex Ends, c.1850, 10 x 6 In.	431
Shelf, Hanging, Chippendale, Oak, Carved, Stepped Cornice, c.1850, 34 x 54 In.	767
Shelf, Hanging, Mahogany, 4 Scroll Shelves, Carved Crest, 1800s, 33 x 33 In.	154
Shelf, Hanging, Oak, Molded Cornice, 4 Tiers, 3 Sections, c.1800, 46 x 52 In.	150
Shelf, Hanging, Shaker, Pine, Paint, 2 Tiers, Planks, Arched Ends, 1800s, 29 x 50 In.	369
Shelf, Hanging, Tiger Maple, 1800s, 14 x 40 x 5 In.	374
Shelf, Hanging, Walnut, 4 Tiers, Shaped Side Panels, c.1850, 36 x 36 In.	533
Shelf, Louis XV, Giltwood, Scroll, Leaves, Bracket, 20 x 17 In.	469
Shelf, Mahogany, Dentil Molded, Acorn Bracket Base, c.1850, Eng., 17 x 18 In.	325
Shelf, Mahogany, Open Shelves, Shaped Whaleside Panels, c.1890, 33 x 27 In.	474
Shelf, P. Evans, Bronze, Sculpted, Smoky Glass Shelves, 1970, 79 x 96 In.	16250
Shelf, Paint, D-Shape Tiers, Leaf Carved Edges, Continental, 80 x 53 In. ....illus	1187
Shelf, Walnut, Carved, Bracket, 18 In.	44
Shelf, Walnut, Iron, 4 Tiers, Serpentine, Pierced, Lattice Crest, c.1865, 41 x 31 In.	474
Sideboard, Art Nouveau, Mahogany, Mirror, Carved, England, c.1900, 78 In. ....illus	1320
Sideboard, Banded, Oval Convex Glass Doors, 7 Drawers, 36 x 66 In.	250
Sideboard, Burl Walnut, Gadrooned, Leaves, Cabriole Legs, Paw Feet, 49 x 92 In.	177
Sideboard, Chrome, Lacquer, 1950s, 33 x 89 ½ In.	437
Sideboard, Ebony Inlay, Bowfront, Curved Door, Reeded Legs, c.1870, 36 x 65 In.	356
Sideboard, Edwardian, Mahogany & Satinwood, c.1880, 46 x 88 x 21 In.	4880
Sideboard, Federal, Mahogany, Inlaid, 2 Cellarette Drawers, c.1800, 42 x 85 In.	2160
Sideboard, French Provincial, Cherry, Carved, 3 Drawers, 2 Doors, 39 x 61 In.	450
Sideboard, G. Stickley, Eastwood, N.Y., c.1905, 49 x 60 x 21 In.	2500
Sideboard, G. Stickley, Slatted Gallery, 2 Doors, 4 Drawers, 49 x 56 In.	2625
Sideboard, George III Style, Mahogany, Banded, Drawers, Spade Feet, 35 x 60 In.	687
Sideboard, George III Style, Serpentine, Towel Rack, Drawers, 1900s, 47 x 68 In.	649
Sideboard, Georgian, Mahogany Inlay, Banded, England, 1800s, 44 x 73 In.	1560
Sideboard, Gothic Revival, Leafy Scroll, Paw Feet, Drawers, 4 Doors, 39 x 84 In.	472
Sideboard, Hepplewhite, Mahogany, Inlay, Serpentine, 2 Doors, 1800s, 39 x 70 In.	492
Sideboard, Hepplewhite, Mahogany, Inlay, Serpentine, Doors, 1800s, 40 x 72 In.	1560
Sideboard, Hepplewhite, Mahogany, Serpentine, Cupboards, Round Legs, 36 x 71 In.	384
Sideboard, Hepplewhite, Mahogany, String Inlay, Bellflowers, c.1950, 39 x 54 In.	1200
Sideboard, Italian Renaissance, Walnut, Carved, 3 Doors, Paw Feet, c.1930, 40 In.	600
Sideboard, L. & J.G. Stickley, Fayetteville, N.Y., c.1910, 44 x 48 x 20 In.	1500
Sideboard, Limbert, Oak, Brass, 6 Drawers, 2 Doors, 58 x 60 In.	2500
Sideboard, Louis Philippe, Cherry, 2 Frieze Drawers, Doors, 40 x 53 In.	450
Sideboard, Mahogany, Bowfront, Inlay, Tapered Legs, Spade Feet, c.1815, 35 x 64 In.	461
Sideboard, Mahogany, Brass Rail, D-Shape Top, Concave, c.1815, 53 x 85 In.	1750
Sideboard, Mahogany, Brass Rail, Serpentine, Bellflower Inlay, c.1915, 56 x 78 In.	1750
Sideboard, Mahogany, Broken-Arch Gallery, Spiral Legs, c.1815, 42 x 48 In.	1250
Sideboard, Mahogany, Demilune, Inlay, Drawers, Spade Feet, c.1815, 37 x 66 In.	738
Sideboard, Mahogany, Inlay, Serpentine Banded Top, c.1780, 35 x 57 In.	732
Sideboard, Neoclassical Style, Bronze, 4 Doors, France, c.1950, 36 x 83 In.	550
Sideboard, Neoclassical, Mahogany, Serpentine, 2 Paneled Doors, 44 In.	312
Sideboard, Pine, Salmon Paint, 3 Drawers, Scalloped Skirt, Nails, 38 x 40 In.	1680
Sideboard, Renaissance Revival, Walnut, Carved, Drawers, Scroll Legs, 50 x 84 In.	384
Sideboard, Roycroft, Wood, East Aurora, N.Y., c.1905, 59 x 57 x 20 In.	8125
Sideboard, Sheraton, Mahogany, Drawer 2 Doors, Turned Legs, American, 36 x 60 In. .....illus	354
Sideboard, Stickley Bros., Stepped, Shaped Gallery, Copper Pulls, 70 In.	7500
Sideboard, Walnut, Linenfold Panel Doors, Carved Monkeys, 1800s, 47 x 62 In.	2100
Sideboard, Walnut, Marble Top, 4 Paneled Doors, Cabriole Legs, c.1880, 40 In.	1000
Sideboard, Walnut, String Inlay, Doors, Beaded Drawers, 6 Legs, c.1810, 43 x 58 In. ....illus	8610
Sideboard, Widdicomb, Bowfront, Mahogany, Inlay, Gilt Banding, 37 x 78 In. ....illus	687
Sideboard, Wormley, Oak, Mahogany, c.1958, 38 x 69 In.	2583
Sofa, Brass, Upholstered, Wormley, Dunbar, 1960s, 28 x 93 ½ x 34 In.	2625
Sofa, De Sede, Terrazza, Leather, Stepped Rolls, 2 Sections, 1970s, 26 x 126 In.	10625

Furniture, Stand, Music, Mahogany, Adjustable, England, 1800s, 29 In. $123

Cowan's Auctions

Furniture, Stand, Overhang Top, Cock-Beaded Drawer, Square Legs, Paint, c.1815, 29 x 24 In. $4,018

Skinner, Inc.

Furniture, Stand, Shaving,
Quartersawn Oak, Mirror, Drawer, Door,
Shelf, 65 x 10 In.
$1,276

Showtime Auction Services

Furniture, Stand, Shaving,
Renaissance Revival, Mirror, Marble
Top, Drawers, c.1850, 64 In.
$576

Neal Auctions

Sofa, Eileen Gray, Monte Carlo, Red, Leather, Chrome, Asymmetrical, 111 x 34 In.	1476
Sofa, Empire, Mahogany, Carved, Pierced Crest, Scroll Arms, H.B. Mudge, 1800s, 84 In. *illus*	492
Sofa, Federal, Bird's-Eye Maple, Rosewood, Bands, Reeded Legs, 36 x 79 In.	7800
Sofa, Federal, Mahogany, Roll Ends, Cornucopia Arms, Paw Feet, 35 x 94 In.	325
Sofa, G. Nakashima, Cherry, Upholstered, Plank Seat, c.1950, 32 x 72 In.	6250
Sofa, G. Nelson, Marshmallow, Green, Blue, Purple, 30 ½ x 52 In.	4575
Sofa, Leather, Rosewood, Fiberglass, Yellow, Brazil, P. Lafer, 1970s, 28 x 89 In.	3125
Sofa, Mahogany, Upholstered, Curved Crest, Reeded Arms, c.1810, 37 x 78 In.	1750
Sofa, Neoclassical, Carved & Gilded, Mahogany, Grecian, c.1825, 78 x 32 In.	10065
Sofa, Neoclassical, Mahogany, Carved, Outscrolled Arms, c.1810, 34 x 91 In. *illus*	3050
Sofa, Neoclassical, Mahogany, Upholstered, Scroll Arms, Paw Feet, c.1825, 89 In. *illus*	1750
Sofa, Oak, Leather, Cantilevered Arms, Curved Block Feet, 1900s, 25 x 95 In.	1560
Sofa, Regency, Tufted, Rhinestone Buttons, Ball & Claw Feet, 68 x 69 In.	708
Sofa, Sample, Mahogany Veneer, Horsehair, 7 x 11 In.	900
Sofa, V. Kagan, Tiger Maple, Floating Seat & Back, 1970s, 84 x 36 In. *illus*	20000
Sofa, V. Kagan, Walnut, Mohair Upholstery, Bean Shape, 1960s, 29 x 113 In.	12500
Sofa, V. Kagan, Walnut, Upholstered, Sculpted Feet, 1950s, 30 x 79 In.	5313
Sofa, Victorian, Mahogany, Upholstered, Scroll Crest, Casters, 48 x 72 In.	170
Sofa, Walnut, Scroll Arms, Upholstered, Early 1800s, 35 x 70 In.	360
Stand, 2-Board Top, Splay Leg, Drawer, Early 1800s, 30 x 20 In.	344
Stand, 3 Tiers, Rosewood, Marble, Gilt Metal Gallery, 34 x 15 ½ In.	406
Stand, 8-Sided Marble Top, Openwork, Dragon Head Feet, Chinese, c.1900, 38 In. *illus*	369
Stand, Butler, Bald Man In Tails, Holding Tray, Wood, Painted, 2-Sided, 39 In.	71
Stand, Carved Hardwood, Soapstone Top, Chinese, Late 1800s, 32 In.	1035
Stand, Contemporary, Birds, Wrought Iron, Glass Top, 27 x 9 In.	112
Stand, Corner, Federal Style, Maple, Cherry, Drawer, 29 ½ In.	531
Stand, Dictionary, Regency, Mahogany, Rotating, Telescoping Tripod, 1800s, 36 In.	885
Stand, Drop Leaf, Sheraton, Drawers, Bird's-Eye Maple, Tapered Legs, 18 x 19 In.	270
Stand, Elm, Lacquer, Carved Apron, Open Geometric Stretcher, 31 x 15 In.	118
Stand, G. Nelson, Rosewood, Metal, Cube, Shelves, Drawer, 1950s, 24 x 18 In., Pair	5000
Stand, G. Stickley, Copper Top, Block Legs, X-Stretcher, c.1912, 29 x 18 In.	1375
Stand, Game, Checkers, Red, Black, Wrought Iron, 3-Footed, 29 x 15 In.	163
Stand, Hardwood, Carved, Openwork, Porcelain Tile Top, Chinese, c.1890, 18 In. *illus*	363
Stand, Hardwood, Marble Top, Fretwork Apron, Paw Feet, c.1900, 19 In., Pair	1046
Stand, Hardwood, Square Top, Braced Block Legs, Stretcher, Chinese, 1900s, 13 In.	60
Stand, Henry II, Walnut, Carved, Drawer, Ring Turned, Stretcher, c.1900, 33 x 16 In.	150
Stand, Hepplewhite Style, Cherry, Overhang Top, Splayed Legs, 28 x 21 In.	118
Stand, Hepplewhite, Cherry, Drawer, Square, Tapered Legs, Pa., 28 x 16 In. *illus*	94
Stand, Italian Renaissance, Black Walnut, Putti Backsplash, c.1835, 60 x 19 In., Pair	3480
Stand, Kettle, Chippendale, Mahogany, Dish Top, Ring-Turned Support, 20 In.	3304
Stand, Louis Philippe, Drawer, Cupboard, Painted Medallion, Yellow, 30 x 15 In.	100
Stand, Louis XV Style, Fruitwood, Marble Top, Cabriole Legs, France, 35 x 21 In.	675
Stand, Luggage, Slate Work, Brass Highlights, England, 1800s, 18 x 24 In.	480
Stand, Magazine, L. & J.G. Stickley, Fayetteville, N.Y., c.1910, 42 x 21 In.	1250
Stand, Magazine, L. & J.G. Stickley, Slat Sides, 4 Shelves, c.1912, 42 x 21 In.	1500
Stand, Magazine, Limbert, Oak, Half-Circle Cutouts, 20 x 14 In.	976
Stand, Mahogany, Brass, Drawers, Bulbous Post, Scroll Legs, c.1835, 42 x 24 In.	207
Stand, Marble Top, Lobed Flower, Openwork, Animal Feet, c.1900, 18 In.	123
Stand, Marble Top, Pierced Apron, Shelf, Scroll, Paw Feet, c.1900, 32 In., Pair	800
Stand, Music, Iron, Fleur-De-Lis, Twist Post, Tripod Scroll Base, 1900s, 61 x 37 In.	1020
Stand, Music, Mahogany, Adjustable, England, 1800s, 29 In. *illus*	123
Stand, Overhang Top, Cock-Beaded Drawer, Square Legs, Paint, c.1815, 29 x 24 In. *illus*	4018
Stand, Painted, Salmon, Red & Green Flower, Vines, Tapered Legs, 28 x 20 In.	923
Stand, Parlor, Walnut, Marble Top, Turned Posts, Carved Stretcher, 32 x 27 In.	213
Stand, Parlor, Walnut, Marble, Turtle Top, X-Stretcher, Curved Legs, 30 x 39 In.	213
Stand, Pastry, Wood, Arched, 3 Octagonal Tiers, Tilting, Flowers, 1890, 32 x 11 In.	450
Stand, Plant, Empire, Giltwood, Marble, Green, Flowers, Hoof Feet, 35 x 17 In.	4880
Stand, Plant, Hardwood, Octagonal, Inset Marble, Beaded Trim, Vines, 23 In.	123
Stand, Plant, Mahogany, Inlaid, Mother-Of-Pearl, Morocco, c.1880, 41 x 15 In.	850
Stand, Plant, Marble Insert, Octagonal, Carved Skirt, Paw Skirt, 24 x 17 In.	236
Stand, Plant, Marble Top, Flower Trim, Openwork, Carved, Chinese, 33 x 15 In.	236

F

Furniture, Stand, Sheraton, Walnut, Dovetailed Drawer, Turned Legs, 1800s, 27 x 28 In.
$390

Cowan's Auctions

Furniture, Stand, Victorian, Oak, Wicker, 2 Tiers, Round, Heywood Bros., 29 x 26 ½ In.
$2,429

James D. Julia Auctioneers

Furniture, Stool, 3 Legs, Paint, Star On Top, Star Of Good Luck, Pa., 10 x 8 In.
$60

Cowan's Auctions

Furniture, Stool, Neoclassical, Curly Maple, Cane Seat, Saber Legs, c.1810, 9 x 15 In.
$305

Neal Auctions

Furniture, Stool, Oak, Carved Apron, Turned Legs, England, 18th Century, 1700s, 21 x 16 In.
$600

Cowan's Auctions

Furniture, Table, Center, Cypress, Extending Shelves, John S. Bradstreet, c.1905, 33 x 28 In.
$24,000

Cowan's Auctions

FURNITURE

Furniture, Table, Center, Renaissance Revival, Walnut, Framed Marble Top, 1800s, 29 x 38 In.
$2,300

Cottone Auctions

Furniture, Table, Chrome Steel, Stacked Tubular Rings, Round Glass Top, 28 x 48 In.
$812

New Orleans Auction Galleries

Furniture, Table, Cigarette, McCobb, Milk Glass Top, Brass Tripod Base, c.1956, 22 x 20 In.
$2,813

Los Angeles Modern Auctions

Furniture, Table, Coffee, Contemporary, Smoked Glass, Chrome Plate, Steel, 21 x 46 In.
$531

New Orleans Auction Galleries

Furniture, Table, Coffee, I. Noguchi, Wood Base, Glass Top, Herman Miller, c.1944, 15 x 30 In.
$1,008

Leslie Hindman Auctioneers

Furniture, Table, Coffee, Kagan-Dreyfuss, Walnut, Glass, Tri-Symmetric, c.1955, 72 x 32 In.
$5,625

Wright

Furniture, Table, Coffee, Karl Springer, Brass, Curled Under Ends, 1960s, 42 x 42 In.
$1,890

Leslie Hindman Auctioneers

Stand, Plant, Marble Top, Octagonal, Openwork, Flowers, Cabriole Legs, c.1900, 24 In.		125
Stand, Plant, Marble Top, Shaped, Flowers, Square Stretcher, Chinese, 32 x 22 In.		295
Stand, Portfolio, Renaissance Revival, Carved Walnut, Late 1800s, 42 x 25 In.		610
Stand, Renaissance Revival, Walnut, Inlay, Panels, Buttons, c.1870, 30 x 18 In.		895
Stand, Shaving, Quartersawn Oak, Mirror, Drawer, Door, Shelf, 65 x 10 In.	*illus*	1276
Stand, Shaving, Renaissance Revival, Mirror, Marble Top, Drawers, c.1850, 64 In.	*illus*	576
Stand, Shaving, Victorian, Mahogany, Bowfront, Tilt Mirror, c.1890, 71 x 20 In.		356
Stand, Sheraton, Maple, Alligatored, Reeded Edge, Drawer, Turned Legs, 30 x 20 In.		720
Stand, Sheraton, Maple, Red Paint, 2-Board Top, Gallery, c.1835, 30 x 22 In.		450
Stand, Sheraton, Walnut, Dovetailed Drawer, Turned Legs, 1800s, 27 x 28 In.	*illus*	390
Stand, Sheraton, Wood, Red Paint, 2-Board Top, Dovetailed, c.1835, 27 x 27 In.		450
Stand, Square, Carved Supports, Stretchers, Bamboo Design, c.1900, 8 x 8 In.		338
Stand, Telephone, O. Bach, Art Nouveau, Bronze, Onyx, Nude Figures, 47 x 24 In.		425
Stand, Victorian, Oak, Wicker Beaded Skirt, Scroll Supports, 30 x 25 In.		1778
Stand, Victorian, Oak, Wicker, 2 Tiers, Round, Heywood Bros., 29 x 26½ In.	*illus*	2429
Stand, Victorian, Oak, Wicker, 3 Tiers, Curved Legs, C-Shape Shelf, 35 x 30 In.		415
Stand, Walnut, Door Over Drawer, England, Mid 1800s, 31 x 18 x 15 In.		240
Stand, Yellow Paint, Vines, Red Buds, Overhang Top, Drawer, Maine, 25 x 20 In.		8610
Stool, 2 Steps, Pine, Maple, Rectangular, Cutout Ends, 1800s, 15 In.		431
Stool, 3 Legs, Paint, Star On Top, Star Of Good Luck, Pa., 10 x 8 In.	*illus*	60
Stool, Backless, Curved Wood Seat, Slats, c.1950, 29 x 16 In., 4 Piece		5000
Stool, Chippendale, Mahogany, Carved, Animal Print Upholstery, Eng., 1800s, 19 x 19 In.		600
Stool, Cricket, Limbert, Oak, Leather, 21 x 16 In.		671
Stool, Doctor, Metal, Leather Seat, Adjustable, Scroll Legs, Casters, 1920s, 28 x 13 In.		1700
Stool, Dressing, French Empire, Scroll Arms, Gilt Mask, Putti Mounts, 28 x 27 In.		812
Stool, Ebonized, Round Top, Griffin Apron, Elephant Head Legs, 28 In., Pair		2250
Stool, Egyptian Revival, Ostrich, Gilt, Wings Down, Ball & Claw Feet, 32 x 28 In.		812
Stool, Esherick, Walnut, Hickory, Triangular Seat, Cylindrical Legs, 1956, 19 In.		4375
Stool, George III, Mahogany, Upholstered, 1770		1250
Stool, Lift Top, Chippendale, Mahogany, Needlepoint Upholstery, c.1900, 20 x 23 In.		530
Stool, Mahogany, Thebes, Liberty & Company, England, c.1890, 15 x 17 In.		732
Stool, Maple & Pine, Round Seat, Tapered Splay Legs, Stretchers, 1800s, 23 x 11 In.		185
Stool, Neoclassical, Curly Maple, Cane Seat, Saber Legs, c.1810, 9 x 15 In.	*illus*	305
Stool, Oak, Carved Apron, Turned Legs, England, 18th Century, 1700s, 21 x 16 In.	*illus*	600
Stool, Oak, Splayed Vase & Ring-Turned Legs, Box Stretchers, 20 x 17 In.		1845
Stool, Piano, Mahogany, Carved, Velvet Upholstery, American, c.1825, 23 In.		540
Stool, Piano, Swivel, Mahogany, Carved, Dolphin Side Rails, c.1820, 18 In.		222
Stool, Walnut, Hand Caned, Round Seat, 4 Turned Legs, Mid 1800s, 7 In.		120
Stool, Windsor, Brown Paint, Concave Seat, Splayed Bamboo Legs, 31 In.		523
Stool, Wood, Boot Finial, Carved, Cats, Figures, Folding, H. Hayden, c.1850, 34 In.		600
Stool, Wood, Rush Seat, Drawer, Brass Ring, Turned Legs, Ball Feet, c.1915, 14 x 13 In.		225
Table & Chair Set, Walter Lamb, Glass, Brown Jordan Co., 1950, 3 Piece		3750
Table, Afra & Tobia Scarpa, Smoky Glass, Chrome, 45 x 45 In.		281
Table, Altar, Carved, Hardwood, Chinese, 38½ x 76½ In.		250
Table, Altar, Elm, Heaven Soaring Ends & Aprons, Chinese, c.1890, 39 x 116 In.		593
Table, Altar, Elm, Red Lacquer, Stepped Edge, Block Legs, 1800s, 33 x 38 In.		295
Table, Altar, Elm, Saber Legs, Double Stretchers, Shaped Feet, 1800s, 31 x 55 In.		443
Table, Altar, Hardwood, Rounded Corners, Tapered Legs, Dragons, 31 x 27 In.		4444
Table, Altar, Zitan, Flared Ends, Carved Apron, Columnar Trestle, 34 x 61 In.		10665
Table, Arts & Crafts, Oak, Pierced Stretchers, Cutouts, Limbert, c.1908, 29 x 30 In.		944
Table, Baker's, Mahogany, Inlay, Crossbanded, Leaves, Hinged, 46 x 96 In.		500
Table, Biedermeier, Birch, Round, Lyre, Griffin, 4 Drawers, Pedestal, 31 x 41 In.		1169
Table, Biedermeier, Pedestal, 31 x 44 In.		360
Table, Birch, Hepplewhite, Maple, Red Paint, Drop Leaf, Figured Top, c.1940, 29 x 36 In.		390
Table, Birch, Sycamore, Round, Star Medallion, Splay Feet, c.1815, 28 x 25 In.		1353
Table, Bronze, Marble, Round, Claw Feet, Casters, 29 x 28 In.		500
Table, Butcher's, Cast Iron, Marble Top, Scroll, Bull's Heads, 1900s, 30 x 48 In.		540
Table, Candle, Pewter, Iron, Gold Paint, Offering Slot, Flowers, 1920s, 19 x 57 In.		795
Table, Card, Aldo Tura, Lacquer, Kings & Queen Cards, 4 Chairs, 32 x 32 In., 5 Piece		3750
Table, Card, Chippendale, Mahogany, Hinge Top, c.1765, 31 x 35 In.		4444
Table, Card, Flip Top, Mahogany, Birch Veneer, Oval Corners, c.1815, 29 x 37 In.		1476

Furniture, Table, Coffee, McCobb, Travertine, Brass, Primavera, Calvin, c.1952, 16 x 66 In.
$1,750

Los Angeles Modern Auctions

Furniture, Table, Coffee, Mesa Baum, Sumauma Wood, Glass, J. Krantz, R & Co., 2005, 36 In.
$1,000

Rago Arts and Auction Center

Furniture, Table, Coffee, Milo Baughman, Glenn Of California, c.1950, 16 x 48 In.
$625

Los Angeles Modern Auctions

TIP
Serious collecting of antique furniture began in the 1920s. Prices went up and fakers began to make great pieces from average pieces. Butterfly tables were made from tavern tables, block-front bureaus from plain bureaus; inlaid eagles and other designs were added to furniture and clocks. Plain highboys were "improved" with scroll tops. Plain legs of tea tables were carved. Birdcage supports and piecrust edges were added to plain tables.

F

Furniture, Table, Coffee, P. Evans, Glass Top, Chrome & Brass Blocks, Cityscape, 15 x 42 In.
$840

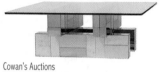

Cowan's Auctions

Furniture, Table, Coffee, Vignelli, Oak, Glass Top, Geometric Wood Shapes, 13 x 48 In.
$3,250

Rago Arts and Auction Center

Furniture, Table, Coffee, W. Platner, Bronze Plated Steel Rods, Glass Top, Knoll, 1965, 15 x 40 In.
$630

Leslie Hindman Auctioneers

Furniture, Table, Console, Brass, Chrome, Black Lucite, Tubular Frame, 27 x 62 In.
$468

New Orleans Auction Galleries

Table, Card, Grain Painted, Salmon, Overhang Top, Oval Corners, Tapered Legs, 28 In.	923
Table, Card, Mahogany, Fluted Legs, New England, c.1815, 30 x 35 In.	1112
Table, Card, Mahogany, Grain Painted, Swivel Top, Turned Legs, c.1850, 30 x 33 In.	120
Table, Card, Mahogany, Serpentine, Hinged Top, Oval Corners, c.1810, 31 x 36 In.	652
Table, Center, Boulle, Tortoiseshell, Brass, Shaped Top, 1800s, 30 x 51 In.	780
Table, Center, Bronze, Scroll Design Top, Scalloped Apron, France, 31 In.	150
Table, Center, Cypress, Extending Shelves, John S. Bradstreet, c.1905, 33 x 28 In. *illus*	24000
Table, Center, Directoire Style, Bronze Plateau, 4 Legs, Platform Base, 30 In.	500
Table, Center, Ebony, Scroll Supports, Triangle Stretcher, 1900s, 31 x 44 In.	2250
Table, Center, Gilt, Marble Top, Pierced Apron, Stretcher, c.1890, 32 x 63 In.	2375
Table, Center, Granite Top, Leaf Carved Post, Flared Base, c.1890, 29 x 40 In.	625
Table, Center, Mahogany, Inlay, Sunburst, Sphere Support, Gilt Paw Feet, 31 x 52 In.	2500
Table, Center, Mahogany, Ormolu, Marble Top, Round Legs, 1900s, 30 x 28 In.	625
Table, Center, Mahogany, Parcel Gilt, Neoclassical, 1800s, 31 x 47 In.	976
Table, Center, Marble Top, X-Carved Banding, Fluted Legs, c.1910, 29 x 28 In.	3750
Table, Center, Metal, Glass Top, Base, Tree With Limbs, Root Legs, 31 x 38 In.	875
Table, Center, Mission Oak, Mortise & Tenon Stretcher Joints, 29 x 40 In.	170
Table, Center, Neoclassical, Mahogany, Marble Top, Scroll Feet, c.1850, 30 x 41 In.	2562
Table, Center, Parcel Gilt, Ebonized, Carved Flowers, Leaves, Vines, 28 x 39 In.	6000
Table, Center, Regency, Mahogany, Beaded Band, Pedestal, c.1815, 28 x 54 In.	5535
Table, Center, Regency, Rosewood, Marble, Round, 34 In.	5250
Table, Center, Renaissance Revival, Walnut, Framed Marble Top, 1800s, 29 x 38 In. *illus*	2300
Table, Center, Rosewood, Marble Top, Carved Flowers, Pierced, c.1890, 32 x 22 In.	450
Table, Center, Rosewood, Marble Top, Pierced, Basket, c.1850, 31 x 40 In.	4500
Table, Center, Rosewood, Scroll Carved, Quatrefoil Post, c.1850, 31 x 46 In.	3250
Table, Center, Rosewood, Serpentine, Openwork, Stretcher, c.1900, 30 x 38 In.	625
Table, Center, Walnut, Inlay, Shaped Ends, Segmented Legs, c.1865, 30 x 42 In.	1500
Table, Cherry, Pine, Breadboard Top, Vase & Ring-Turned Legs, New Eng., 24 x 20 In.	2091
Table, Chrome Steel, Stacked Tubular Rings, Round Glass Top, 28 x 48 In. *illus*	812
Table, Cigarette, McCobb, Milk Glass Top, Brass Tripod Base, c.1956, 22 x 20 In. *illus*	2813
Table, Coffee, Burl Top, Metal Base, Gilt Design, c.1970, 14 x 47 ½ In.	450
Table, Coffee, Burl, 20 x 46 In.	112
Table, Coffee, Cast Iron, Paint, Ebonized Frame, Rosettes, 1900s, 17 x 45 In.	295
Table, Coffee, Cloud, Wendell Castle, Gel Coated Fiberglass, c.1969, 22 x 37 In.	3335
Table, Coffee, Contemporary, Smoked Glass, Chrome Plate, Steel, 21 x 46 In. *illus*	531
Table, Coffee, Eames, Round, Wide Rim Lip, Tube Legs, 15 x 34 In.	1250
Table, Coffee, G. Nakashima, Walnut, Slab, Corner Plank Base, 1973, 14 x 53 In.	9375
Table, Coffee, Giltwood, Gesso, Silver Leaf, Paint, Block Legs, 1940s, 17 x 46 In.	5625
Table, Coffee, Glass Top, Brass Frame, Antler Legs & Apron, 20 x 50 In.	1500
Table, Coffee, Glass Top, Nickeled Steel, Wire, Pedestal Base, 15 In.	431
Table, Coffee, Hardwood, Parquetry, Geometric Patterns, Curule Base, 21 x 38 In.	593
Table, Coffee, Herbier, Tile Top, Stained Wood Legs, 1960s, 12 x 47 x 18 In.	504
Table, Coffee, I. Noguchi, Glass Top, Ebonized Wood, Interlocking Base, 15 x 50 In.	984
Table, Coffee, I. Noguchi, Walnut & Glass, Herman Miller, c.1969, 15 x 50 In.	1000
Table, Coffee, I. Noguchi, Wood Base, Glass Top, Herman Miller, c.1944, 15 x 30 In. *illus*	1008
Table, Coffee, Kagan-Dreyfuss, Walnut, Glass, Tri-Symmetric, c.1955, 72 x 32 In. *illus*	5625
Table, Coffee, Karl Springer, Brass, Curled Under Ends, 1960s, 42 x 42 In. *illus*	1890
Table, Coffee, Karl Springer, Silvered Wood, 48 x 36 In.	1875
Table, Coffee, Lacquer Top, Brass Chrome Banding, Belgium, c.1970, 14 x 47 In.	500
Table, Coffee, Louis XV Style, Marble, Carved, Cabriole Legs, Stretchers, 17 In.	300
Table, Coffee, Lucite & Brass, Vitrine Sliding Top, c.1970, 15 x 33 In.	550
Table, Coffee, M. Pergay, Stainless Steel, Squared, 1970s, 12 x 46 x 21 In.	1250
Table, Coffee, Mahogany, Brass, Glass Top, Ship's Wheel, 3 Legs, 17 In.	400
Table, Coffee, McCobb, Travertine, Brass, Primavera, Calvin, c.1952, 16 x 66 In. *illus*	1750
Table, Coffee, Mesa Baum, Sumauma Wood, Glass, J. Krantz, R & Co., 2005, 36 In. *illus*	1000
Table, Coffee, Milo Baughman, B. Saltman, Walnut, Laminate, 1950s, 16 x 40 In.	2500
Table, Coffee, Milo Baughman, Glenn Of California, c.1950, 16 x 48 In. *illus*	625
Table, Coffee, Neoclassical Style, Glass, Reverse Painted, Leaves, 3 Gilt Feet, 43 In.	2500
Table, Coffee, Oak, Drum, Ceremonial, Glass Top, Ball Feet, 1800s, 17 x 29 In.	1067
Table, Coffee, P. Evans, Glass Top, Chrome & Brass Blocks, Cityscape, 15 x 42 In. *illus*	840
Table, Coffee, P. Evans, Marble Top, Cut Steel, Open Loops Base, 1960s, 38 In.	12500

Table, Coffee, Philip LaVerne, Bronze, Asian Scene, Panel Base, 1960s, 18 x 56 In.		5625
Table, Coffee, Philip LaVerne, Bronze, Reclining Figure, 1960s, 19 x 63 In.		10625
Table, Coffee, Puzzle, Amoeba Shape Top, Interlocking Furniture Co., 16 x 34 In.		250
Table, Coffee, Reverse Painted, Molded Frame, Jansen, c.1960, 16 x 39 In.		500
Table, Coffee, S. Inui, Rosewood, Round Corners, Plank Legs, 1960s, 13 x 71 In.		3750
Table, Coffee, Seandel, Steel, Copper, Bronze, Circles, Sunspots, 1970s, 20 x 46 In.		2125
Table, Coffee, Studio Furniture, Walnut, 2-Board Top, Stretcher, 15 x 50 In.		923
Table, Coffee, Teardrop, Steel, Glass, 19 x 39 x 53 In.		567
Table, Coffee, Triangular, Ebonized Top, Turned Legs, c.1960, 22 In.		150
Table, Coffee, Turtle Top, Brass Trim, Faux Bamboo Base, c.1975, 17 x 33 In.		240
Table, Coffee, V. Kagan, Snail, Walnut, Glass Top, 15 x 42 In.		1062
Table, Coffee, V. Kagan, Walnut, Mosaic Crescent Top, 1950s, 32 x 56 In.		13750
Table, Coffee, Vignelli, Oak, Glass Top, Geometric Wood Shapes, 13 x 48 In.	*illus*	3250
Table, Coffee, W. Platner, Bronze Plated Steel Rods, Glass Top, Knoll, 1965, 15 x 40 In.	*illus*	630
Table, Coffee, Walnut, Surfboard Shape, Tapered Square Legs, c.1950, 16 x 67 In.		431
Table, Coffee, Wood, Glass, Top, Italy, 1950s, 19 x 34 x 64 In.		378
Table, Console, A. Magnoni, Walnut, Urn Shaped Supports, 1920s, 32 x 73 In.		1353
Table, Console, Arabesque, Sphinx, Trestle Supports, Bearded Mask, 36 x 63 In.		3540
Table, Console, Art Deco, Burl, 2 Drawers, U-Shape, 40 x 46 In.		187
Table, Console, Art Deco, Burl, Rosewood, U-Shape, 33 x 49 In.		406
Table, Console, Beech, Marble Top, Serpentine, Pierced, 1900s, 35 x 38 In.		492
Table, Console, Brass, Chrome, Black Lucite, Tubular Frame, 27 x 62 In.	*illus*	468
Table, Console, Dunbar, Red Lacquer, Beveled Glass Panels, Wire, 27 x 56 In.		1599
Table, Console, Empire Style, Mahogany, Brass Inlay, Scroll Base, American, c.1910, 52 In.	*illus*	2400
Table, Console, Faux Marble Top, Pierced Frieze, Scroll Legs, c.1815, 32 x 40 In.		1750
Table, Console, Giltwood, Marble Top, Pierced, Stretcher, c.1890, 30 x 45 In.		8750
Table, Console, Giltwood, Red Marble Top, Stepped Foot, c.1800, 35 x 71 In.		5228
Table, Console, Gio Ponti, Walnut, Brass, Flip Top, Block Legs, 1960s, 30 x 65 In.		6875
Table, Console, Iron, Marble Top, Mask, Pierced Leaf Scroll, Curled Feet, 36 x 73 In.		625
Table, Console, J. Bearden, Steel, Torch Cut, Welded, Textured, Enamel, 29 x 48 In.	*illus*	1625
Table, Console, Louis XV, Marble Top, Gilt, Carved, Pierced Frieze, 36 x 37 In.		492
Table, Console, Louis XV, Provincial, Walnut, Carved, Faux Marble, 1700s, 42 x 25 In.	*illus*	1664
Table, Console, Louis XVI, Giltwood, Marble Top, Pierced, Stretcher, 49 x 20 In.		3900
Table, Console, Mahogany, Copper Color, Carved Legs, c.1915, 30 x 43 In.		219
Table, Console, Mahogany, Marble Top, Brass Busts, Leaves, c.1965, 31 x 51 In.		1185
Table, Console, Mahogany, Marble Top, Shell Carved, Reeded Legs, 35 x 41 In.		468
Table, Console, Mahogany, Serpentine Marble Top, Lyre, 1800s, 29 x 33 In.		240
Table, Console, Oak, Marble Top, Curved Legs, Leaf Toes, c.1850, 35 x 59 In.		500
Table, Console, Oak, Wrought Iron, 2 Tiers, Arch Back, Scroll, 1940s, 49 x 59 In.		11875
Table, Console, Rococo Style, Marble Top, Serpentine, Cabriole Legs, 34 x 48 In., Pair		3750
Table, Console, Silver Gilt, Paint, Drawer, Mirrored Skirt, c.1930, 35 x 58 In.		1200
Table, Console, Somerset Bay, Mahogany, Koi Fish, Blue, Yellow, 33 x 64 In.		230
Table, Coromandel Style, Lacquer, 19 x 46 In.		2000
Table, Curly Maple, 3-Board Top, Breadboard Ends, Trestle, 1960s, 30 x 84 In.		1680
Table, Danish, Teak, Pullout Leaves, 29 x 55 In.		45
Table, Dining, A. Paley, Steel, Stone, Molded, Swirled Base, 1982, 31 x 51 In.		9375
Table, Dining, Elm, Square Frieze, Shaped Supports, Block Legs, 33 x 58 In.		413
Table, Dining, Farm, Cherry, Pine Top, Stretcher Base, Turned Legs, 30 x 65 In.		354
Table, Dining, Fermin Verdeguer, Veneers, Stainless Steel, 29 x 83 In.	*illus*	3075
Table, Dining, Florentine Style, Pine, Paint, Harp Legs, 1950s, 30 x 150 In.		4880
Table, Dining, French, Mahogany, Bronze Mounts, Fluted Legs, 2 Leaves, 30 In.		450
Table, Dining, French, Parquetry, Tapered Legs, Bronze Mounts, c.1940, 29 In.		400
Table, Dining, G. Nakashima, Walnut, Plank Top, Trestle Legs, 1956, 29 x 60 In.		7500
Table, Dining, G. Stickley, Eastwood, N.Y., c.1908, 30 x 54 In.		1875
Table, Dining, G. Stickley, Round, 5 Squared Legs, 8 11-In. Leaves, 28 x 54 In.		4063
Table, Dining, Georgian, Drop Leaf, Walnut, Leaf Knees, Hoof Feet, 30 x 60 In.		6000
Table, Dining, H. Probber, Teak, Mahogany, Curved, Slab Legs, 1960s, 29 x 78 In.		5625
Table, Dining, Italian Rococo, Walnut, Carved, Rope Twist Skirt, 30 x 77 In.		4160
Table, Dining, Italian, Ico Parisi, Downswept Supports, Tapered Legs, c.1960, 45 In.		500
Table, Dining, John Stuart, Danish Modern, Teak, Drop Leaf, X-Shape, c.1950, 64 x 18 In.		730
Table, Dining, Karl Springer, Goatskin, Lacquer, Parchment, c.1978, 29 x 54 In.		4688

Furniture, Table, Console, Empire Style, Mahogany, Brass Inlay, Scroll Base, American, c.1910, 52 In.
$2,400

Cowan's Auctions

Furniture, Table, Console, J. Bearden, Steel, Torch Cut, Welded, Textured, Enamel, 29 x 48 In.
$1,625

Rago Arts and Auction Center

TIP

If the screw holding a hinge is loose, try this old-fashioned remedy. Break off the heads of several large wooden kitchen matches or toothpicks. Put the wooden strips in the hole with some glue, then screw the old screw back into place.

Furniture, Table, Console, Louis XV, Provincial, Walnut, Carved, Faux Marble, 1700s, 42 x 25 In.
$1,664

Neal Auctions

Furniture, Table, Dining, Fermin Verdeguer, Veneers, Stainless Steel, 29 x 83 In.
$3,075

Skinner, Inc.

Furniture, Table, Dining, Mahogany, Reeded Pedestal, Concave Base, Casters, 30 x 119 In.
$7,380

Skinner, Inc.

Furniture, Table, Dining, P. Evans, Burl Walnut, Glass, Chrome Steel, Faceted, 30 x 84 In.
$20,000

Rago Arts and Auction Center

Furniture, Table, Dining, Parzinger, Mahogany, Satinwood, Brass, Charak, 1950s, 30 x 68 In.
$3,129

Rago Arts and Auction Center

Furniture, Table, Dining, Venturi, Urn, Plywood, Laminated, Knoll, 1984, 59 x 29 In.
$2,500

Wright

Furniture, Table, Dining, P. Shire, Memphis, Enameled Metal, Glass, 1980s, 33 x 64 In.
$4,688

Rago Arts and Auction Center

Furniture, Table, Dressing, Beau Brummel, Georgian, Mahogany, Carved, Fitted, c.1800, 34 x 25 In.
$875

Neal Auctions

Furniture, Table, Dressing, Pine, High Gallery, False Drawers, Paint, c.1850, 39 x 33 In.
$510

Cowan's Auctions

Furniture, Table, Drop Leaf, Curly Maple, Frieze Drawer, Turned Tapered Legs, c.1910, 54 x 48 In.
$640

Neal Auctions

F

Table, Dining, Knoll Noguchi, White Top, Pedestal, Weighted Base, 29 In.	475
Table, Dining, L. & J.G. Stickley, Drop-Down Legs, c.1907, 29 x 54 In., 6 Leaves	2500
Table, Dining, Mahogany, 2 Pedestals, Columnar Posts, Splayed Legs, 30 x 132 In.	1500
Table, Dining, Mahogany, 2 Pedestals, Turned Posts, Splayed Legs, 29 x 120 In.	1375
Table, Dining, Mahogany, Banded, Columnar Pedestal, Splayed Legs, 30 x 72 In.	2750
Table, Dining, Mahogany, D-Shape Ends, Inlay, Square Legs, c.1800, 30 x 161 In.	2250
Table, Dining, Mahogany, Folding Hinged Top, c.1825, 30 x 44 In.	105
Table, Dining, Mahogany, Pedestal, Reeded Splay Legs, c.1935, 30 x 83 In.	2375
Table, Dining, Mahogany, Reeded Pedestal, Concave Base, Casters, 30 x 119 In. ....*illus*	7380
Table, Dining, Mahogany, Tilt Top, Carved Circles, Splay Legs, c.1850, 28 x 36 In.	1500
Table, Dining, Oak, Pickled, Shaped, Carved, Flowers, Cabriole Legs, 31 x 81 In.	937
Table, Dining, Oval Glass Top, Acrylic C-Form Supports, 29 x 42 In.	750
Table, Dining, P. Evans, Burl Walnut, Glass, Chrome Steel, Faceted, 30 x 84 In..........*illus*	20000
Table, Dining, P. Shire, Memphis, Enameled Metal, Glass, 1980s, 33 x 64 In..........*illus*	4688
Table, Dining, Parzinger, Mahogany, Satinwood, Brass, Charak, 1950s, 30 x 68 In. ....*illus*	3129
Table, Dining, Pine & Oak Top, Parquetry, Spiral Iron Legs, 1900s, 38 x 96 In.	1875
Table, Dining, Rococo, Oak, Oval, Carved, Leaves, Fruits, Pedestal, c.1865, 28 x 58 In.	652
Table, Dining, Rosewood, Round Onyx Top, Sloped Legs, 1940s, 30 x 48 In.	5313
Table, Dining, Shaker, Drop Leaf, Birch, Paint, Overhang Top, c.1840, 27 x 36 In.	4305
Table, Dining, Sheraton, Walnut, 3-Board Top, Beaded, Turned Legs, 29 x 54 In.	384
Table, Dining, Softwood, Painted, 3-Board Scrub Top, Tapered Legs, 29 x 49 In.	708
Table, Dining, Stickley Bros., Round, Block Post, Curved Supports, 1910, 30 x 54 In.	2250
Table, Dining, Travertine, Cube, 29 x 36 In.	687
Table, Dining, Venturi, Urn, Plywood, Laminated, Knoll, 1984, 59 x 29 In.........*illus*	2500
Table, Dining, Victorian, Round, Carved, Winged Dragon Legs, 1800s, 30 x 63 In.	3450
Table, Dining, Walnut, Carved, Scallop Apron, Flowers, Cabriole Legs, 30 x 61 In.	474
Table, Dining, Walnut, Carved, Scallop Apron, Fruit, Scroll Legs, 1800s, 31 x 114 In.	295
Table, Dining, Walnut, Lazy Susan Top, Beaded Tapered Legs, 32 x 46 In.	708
Table, Dining, Walnut, Louis XV Style, Molded Apron, 4 Leaves, 1800s, 30 In.	550
Table, Dining, Willy Beck, Extension, Rosewood, 28 ½ x 40 In.	1968
Table, Dressing, Beau Brummel, Georgian, Mahogany, Carved, Fitted, c.1800, 34 x 25 In. *illus*	875
Table, Dressing, Bird's-Eye Maple, Poplar, 3 Drawers, c.1820, 40 x 30 In.	322
Table, Dressing, Chippendale, Mahogany, Dovetailed, Batwing Pulls, 1700s, 30 x 30 In.	649
Table, Dressing, Chippendale, Walnut, Pilasters, Claw Feet, c.1760, 28 x 34 In.	4800
Table, Dressing, Elm, 3 Section Lift Top, Mirror, Cabriole Legs, 1700s, 34 x 20 In.	875
Table, Dressing, Fruitwood, Chinoiserie, Drawers, Scrollwork, 1900s, 30 x 40 In.	1375
Table, Dressing, Georgian, Walnut, Shaped, 1700s, 27 x 30 x 18 In.	1664
Table, Dressing, Mahogany & Burl, Shaped, Stool, c.1810, 77 x 43 In.	1725
Table, Dressing, Marble Lift Top, Tilt Mirror, Columns, Paw Feet, c.1835, 70 x 38 In.	1875
Table, Dressing, Neoclassical, Mahogany, Mirror, Swans, Columns, 1800s, 55 x 33 In.	510
Table, Dressing, Pine, High Gallery, False Drawers, Paint, c.1850, 39 x 33 In.........*illus*	510
Table, Dressing, Queen Anne, Cherry, Fan Carved, Cabriole Legs, 1700s, 31 x 34 In.	2950
Table, Dressing, Queen Anne, Pine, Cabriole Legs, c.1880, 30 x 44 In.	780
Table, Dressing, Rococo Revival, Mahogany, Mirror, Serpentine, c.1850, 61 x 39 In.	515
Table, Dressing, Satinwood, Mirror, Kidney Shape, Gilt Bronze, 60 x 46 In.	437
Table, Dressing, Tiger Maple, Grain Paint, Scroll Back, Shaped Top, 31 In.	1046
Table, Dressing, Walnut, Queen Anne, 1700s, 29 x 35 x 20 ½ In.	1440
Table, Dressing, William & Mary, Walnut Veneer, Pierced Escutcheon, 30 x 29 In.	826
Table, Drop Leaf, Curly Maple, Frieze Drawer, Turned Tapered Legs, c.1910, 54 x 48 In. ....*illus*	640
Table, Drop Leaf, Danish, Curved Side, Tapered Legs, c.1960, 29 x 54 In.	150
Table, Drop Leaf, George II, Mahogany, c.1750, 28 x 26 In.	2125
Table, Drop Leaf, Handkerchief, Mahogany, Faceted Legs, 1775, 28 x 44 In.	5036
Table, Drop Leaf, Mahogany, Molded Block Legs, 1700s, 27 x 48 In.	70
Table, Drop Leaf, Oak, Gateleg, Oval Top, Drawer, Turned Legs, 29 x 44 In.	338
Table, Drop Leaf, Oak, Gateleg, Pierced Baluster Supports, c.1910, 25 x 26 In.	246
Table, Drop Leaf, Plusquellec, Whirling Dervish, Cherry, Marble, 1992, 54 x 54 In.	861
Table, Drop Leaf, Queen Anne, America, Late 1700s	125
Table, Drop Leaf, Queen Anne, Mahogany, Round, Pad Feet, 1700s, 29 x 48 In.	354
Table, Drop Leaf, Queen Anne, Maple & Oak, America, 1700s, 27 x 48 In.	360
Table, Drop Leaf, Tiger Maple, Swing Leg Supports, 1800s, 30 x 48 In.........*illus*	369
Table, Drop Leaf, Walnut, 2 Swing Leg Supports, 1800s, 29 x 43 In.........*illus*	210

Furniture, Table, Drop Leaf, Tiger Maple, Swing Leg Supports, 1800s, 30 x 48 In.

$369

Cowan's Auctions

Furniture, Table, Drop Leaf, Walnut, 2 Swing Leg Supports, 1800s, 29 x 43 In.

$210

Cowan's Auctions

Furniture, Table, Federal, Mahogany, Carved, 4 Foldover Sections, c.1810, 132 x 48 In.

$1,920

Neal Auctions

Furniture, Table, G. Stickley, Leather Top, Eastwood, c.1908, 31 x 41 In.

$3,750

Rago Arts and Auction Center

FURNITURE

Furniture, Table, G. Stickley, Oak, Grueby Tiles, Through Tenon, Shelf, Red Decal, c.1902, 26 In.
$19,200

Brunk Auctions

Furniture, Table, Game, Backgammon, George III, Mahogany, Cherry, Brass Inlay, c.1800, 27 x 45 In.
$3,738

Cottone Auctions

Furniture, Table, Game, Sheraton, Mahogany, Foldover Top, Inlays, Portsmouth, c.1810, 31 x 36 In.
$3,509

James D. Julia Auctioneers

TIP
Dark-colored candle wax can bleed into the finish on a wooden table. If the hot wax drips, the color may remain.

Table, Eastlake, Tiger Oak, Stick & Ball, Carved Apron, 30 x 30 In.	20
Table, Elm, Soapstone, Shelf, Fretwork Apron, Shaped Feet, Chinese, c.1900, 32 x 16 In.	420
Table, Extension, Oak, Pullout Leaves, Twist Base, Stretchers, c.1875, 29 x 30 In.	118
Table, Extension, Pine, Tapered Legs, 2-Board Top, 30 x 42 x 30 In.	420
Table, Farm, Batten Top, Well, Storage Drawer, Peg Legs, c.1810, 32 x 42 In.	1536
Table, Farm, Oak, 3-Board, Cutlery Drawer, Square Legs, c.1950, 30 x 107 In.	1304
Table, Federal, Mahogany, Carved, 4 Foldover Sections, c.1810, 132 x 48 In. .....*illus*	1920
Table, Federal, Pine, Overhang Top, Drawer, Cut Nails, Southern, 28 x 31 In.	300
Table, Federal, Pine, Walnut, Lazy Susan Center, 1800s, 31 x 55 In.	3120
Table, Florence Knoll, Rosewood, Chrome Plated Steel, 1950s, 17 x 45 In.	690
Table, Fruitwood, Scroll Lyre-Shape Supports, Spain, 1700s, 30 x 32 x 72 In.	2125
Table, G. Nakashima, Walnut, Shaped Slab Top, Plank Post, 1975, 17 x 35 In.	11875
Table, G. Stickley, Eastwood, N.Y., c.1905, 29 x 24 In.	1375
Table, G. Stickley, Leather Top, Eastwood, c.1908, 31 x 41 In. .....*illus*	3750
Table, G. Stickley, Oak, Grueby Tiles, Through Tenon, Shelf, Red Decal, c.1902, 26 In. .....*illus*	19200
Table, G. Stickley, Plank Top, Mouse Hole Supports, c.1912, 30 x 54 In.	1250
Table, Game, Backgammon, George III, Mahogany, Cherry, Brass Inlay, c.1800, 27 x 45 In.*illus*	3738
Table, Game, Billy Haines, Capiz Shells, Inlay, 29 ½ x 36 In.	2560
Table, Game, Chess, Regency, Penwork, Ebonized, 28 x 21 In.	343
Table, Game, Chippendale, Mahogany, Foldover Top, Carved, c.1770, 29 x 31 In.	1560
Table, Game, Drop Leaf, 2 Drawers, Yellow & Black, 28 x 15 x 17 x 31 In.	1680
Table, Game, Empire, Mahogany, Lyre Base, Casters, 29 ½ x 35 In.	236
Table, Game, Federal, Mahogany, Tilt & Twist Top, Leaf Pedestal, 36 x 36 In.	425
Table, Game, Fruitwood, Removable Top, Starburst, Splay Legs, c.1915, 29 x 34 In.	1062
Table, Game, Hepplewhite, Flame Birch, Inlaid, Tapered Legs, c.1810, 29 x 36 In.	595
Table, Game, Mahogany, D-Shape, Hinged Top, Brass Banding, c.1850, 31 x 43 In.	625
Table, Game, Mahogany, Foldover, Serpentine, Inlaid Urn, c.1915, 30 x 36 In.	625
Table, Game, Neoclassical, Fruitwood, Parquetry, Wreaths, Hinged, Italy, 30 x 32 In.	500
Table, Game, Neoclassical, Mahogany, Foldover, Crossbanded, Pedestal, Paw Feet, 30 In.	343
Table, Game, Paint, Board Top, Block Pedestal, Stepped Base, Tapered Feet, 25 In.	826
Table, Game, Pine, Paint, Breadboard Lift Top, Turned Legs, c.1880, 30 x 48 In.	390
Table, Game, Queen Anne, Mahogany, Leather, Foldover, Scalloped, 28 x 37 In., Pair	1625
Table, Game, Queen Anne, Mahogany, Foldover, Frieze Drawer, 1700s, 29 x 33 In.	450
Table, Game, Sheraton, Mahogany, Foldover Top, Inlays, Portsmouth, c.1810, 31 x 36 In. ..*illus*	3509
Table, Game, Tilt Top, Cherry, Checkerboard Inlay, Tripod, Spider Legs, 29 In.	1112
Table, Game, Walnut, Serpentine Flip Top, Carved, Tapered Legs, c.1870, 29 x 34 In.	1195
Table, Gilt, Marble Top, Louis XVI, c.1880, 29 ½ x 20 In.	1000
Table, Glass, Brass, Frieze Knobs, End Handles, Shaped Legs, 16 x 39 In. .....*illus*	375
Table, Hall, Marble Top, Carved, Scalloped, Fluted Legs, Black, 1900s, 34 x 49 In.	614
Table, Handkerchief, Chippendale Style, Mahogany, Cabriole Legs, Eng., 28 x 38 In.	840
Table, Harvest, Plank Top, Blue, Tapered Legs & Base, 1800s, 29 x 102 In.	700
Table, Hepplewhite, Drop Leaf, Walnut, Skirt Drawer, Pa., 29 x 18 x 38 In. .....*illus*	83
Table, Hepplewhite, Mahogany, Line Inlay, Drop Leaf Center Sections, 3 Piece .....*illus*	443
Table, Invalid, Telescopic Column Support, American, c.1880, 40 In.	1063
Table, Iron Base, White Marble Top, Scroll Frame, France, c.1880, 36 x 64 In.	2880
Table, Jacobean, Oak, Carved, Foldover, Barley Twist Legs, 1800s, 30 x 35 In.	122
Table, Jacobean, Stretcher, 6 Arches, 30 x 20 ½ In.	125
Table, L. & J.G. Stickley, Media Shelf, Shoe Feet, 29 x 48 In.	615
Table, L. & J.G. Stickley, Trestle, Mousehole Cutout Sides, 29 x 54 In.	1625
Table, Lab, Swing Stools, Writing Board, Doors, Iron Handles, 1920s, 31 x 60 In.	2800
Table, Library, G. Stickley, 2 Frieze Drawers, Stretcher Shelf, 30 x 48 In.	1250
Table, Library, G. Stickley, Clip Corners, Stretcher, Block Legs, c.1901, 29 x 54 In.	1625
Table, Library, L. & J.G. Stickley, Onondaga, Fayetteville, N.Y., c.1904, 30 x 48 In.	1125
Table, Library, Limbert, Oak, Copper, 29 x 48 In.	976
Table, Library, Neoclassical Style, Carved Pedestal, Urn, Dolphin, c.1920, 29 x 72 In.	250
Table, Louis Sognot, Mahogany, Bentwood, 2 Tiers, 22 x 36 In.	687
Table, Louis XV, Mahogany, Canted Corners, Inlay, Drawer, c.1825, 30 x 34 In.	875
Table, Louis XVI, Parquetry, Marble, France, c.1880, 31 x 24 ½ In.	960
Table, Low, Marcel Breuer, Laccio, Black Laminate Top, Steel, 1960s, 14 x 53 x 19 In.	347
Table, Low, Rosewood, Carved, Ruyi Heads, Pentagram Stretcher, 33 x 14 In.	1050

Furniture, Table, P. Evans, Patchwork, Copper, Bronze, Pewter, Granite, 1970s, 22 x 29 In.
$2,250

Rago Arts and Auction Center

Furniture, Table, Philip LaVerne, Spring Festival, Bronze, Pewter, 1960s, 15 x 28 In.
$5,313

Rago Arts and Auction Center

Furniture, Table, Porcelain, Sevres Style, Dish Top, Painted, Flowers, Tripod, 19 x 24 In.
$1,107

Cowan's Auctions

Furniture, Table, Glass, Brass, Frieze Knobs, End Handles, Shaped Legs, 16 x 39 In.
$375

New Orleans Auction Galleries

Furniture, Table, Hepplewhite, Drop Leaf, Walnut, Skirt Drawer, Pa., 29 x 18 x 38 In.
$83

Hess Auction Group

Furniture, Table, Hepplewhite, Mahogany, Line Inlay, Drop Leaf Center Sections, 3 Piece
$443

Hess Auction Group

Furniture, Table, Majorelle, Art Nouveau, 2 Tier, Oval, Inlaid Flowers, Signed, 1918, 32 x 33 In.
$2,370

James D. Julia Auctioneers

Furniture, Table, Nakashima, Wohl, Black Walnut, 3 Splayed Legs, 1975, 21 x 27 In.
$4,063

Rago Arts and Auction Center

Furniture, Table, Nesting, Walnut, Crossbanded Inlay, England, c.1920, Largest 23 In., 3 Piece
$240

Cowan's Auctions

F

Furniture, Table, Serving, Stickley Bros., Oak, Hammered Copper Pulls, Quaint, Tag, 37 x 34 In.
$1,080

Brunk Auctions

Furniture, Table, Sewing, Edwardian, Lift Top, Drawer, Painted Designs, c.1900, 28 x 24 In.
$185

Cowan's Auctions

Furniture, Table, Side, French Provincial, Walnut, Drawer, Turned Legs, 1700s, 35 x 21 In.
$1,024

Neal Auctions

Table, Low, Tilt Top, Rosewood, Carved Post, Cabochon, Tripod, c.1885, 28 x 47 In.	1875
Table, Mahogany, Decagon Top, Turned Pedestal, Tripod Legs, 27 x 22 In.	240
Table, Mahogany, Round Marble Top, Columns, 3-Part Base, 27 x 20 In.	615
Table, Mahogany, Round, Sunburst, 4 Turned Posts, Splayed Legs, 29 x 60 In.	1625
Table, Mahogany, Ship's Wheel, Brass Hub, Glass Top, Pedestal, 1896, 28 x 60 In.	3852
Table, Majorelle, Art Nouveau, 2 Tier, Oval, Inlaid Flowers, Signed, 1918, 32 x 33 In. *illus*	2370
Table, Malachite, Gilt, Round, Pierced Frieze, Urn, Stretcher, 1800s, 32 x 26 In.	22500
Table, Maple, Pine, Overhang Top, Drawer, Turned Legs, 1700s, 26 x 51 In.	3690
Table, Maple, Pine, Red Paint, Breadboard Top, Beaded, New Eng., 26 x 48 In.	5228
Table, Maple, Shaped Leaves, Drawer, Gateleg, c.1880, 29 x 49 In.	500
Table, Maple, Sponge Paint, Flower Spray, Overhang Top, c.1765, 29 x 33 In.	3259
Table, Marble Top, Brushed Steel, Pierced Tapered Legs, 1950s, 38 x 47 In.	937
Table, Marble Top, Round, Pierced Gallery, Candle Slide, c.1880, 30 x 26 In.	738
Table, Marble Top, Round, Rays, Brass Gallery, Swirls, Square Legs, 32 x 28 In.	356
Table, Marquetry, Bronze Mounts, Drawer, France, 1800s, 30 x 45 x 29 In.	1150
Table, Nakashima, Wohl, Black Walnut, 3 Splayed Legs, 1975, 21 x 27 In. *illus*	4063
Table, Neoclassical, Gilt Bronze, Black Granite Top, Round, 25 x 16 In., Pair	1830
Table, Neoclassical, Marble Top, Iron Tripod Base, Italy, 1800s, 28 x 28 In.	2440
Table, Nesting, Galle, Marquetry, Plants, Butterflies, 27 x 19 In., 3 Piece	1625
Table, Nesting, H. Mobler, Denmark, c.1950, 19 x 17 To 20 x 22 In., 3 Piece	406
Table, Nesting, Hardwood, Incised Floral, Asia, c.1910, 28 x 22 x 15 In., 3 Piece	812
Table, Nesting, Lacquer, Gilt, Village, Dragon Feet, 1800s, 26 x 27 In., 3 Piece	1375
Table, Nesting, Walnut, Crossbanded Inlay, England, c.1920, Largest 23 In., 3 Piece *illus*	240
Table, Nesting, Wormley, Bleached Walnut, Dunbar, 1940s, 20 x 26 In., 5 Piece	1250
Table, Oak, Oval Top, Turned Swing Legs, Center Finial, c.1900, 28 x 53 In.	246
Table, Oak, Plank Top, Molded, Drawer, Turned Legs, Stretchers, 29 x 40 In.	984
Table, Oak, Projecting Top, Frieze Drawer, Stretcher, Turned Legs, 28 x 36 In.	2337
Table, Oak, Twist Legs, Stretcher, Hinged Leaves, Gateleg, c.1900, 27 x 12 In.	356
Table, P. Evans, Copper, Enamel, Granite Top, Patchwork, 1970s, 22 x 30 In.	3750
Table, P. Evans, Patchwork, Copper, Bronze, Pewter, Granite, 1970s, 22 x 29 In. *illus*	2250
Table, Paint, Tilt Top, Flowerhead, Baluster Post, Tripod, c.1865, 27 x 36 In.	1375
Table, Pembroke, Cherry, 21 x 17 ½ In.	281
Table, Pembroke, Federal, Mahogany, Bellflower, Urn, Inlay, 28 x 30 x 41 In.	19200
Table, Pembroke, Federal, Mahogany, Inlay, Tapered Legs, c.1810, 28 x 21 In.	338
Table, Pembroke, Federal, Tiger Maple, c.1800, 28 In.	413
Table, Pembroke, George III, Satinwood, Inlaid, Drawer, 1700s, 29 x 33 x 44 In.	488
Table, Pembroke, Mahogany, Beaded Drawer, Apron Ends, 28 In.	129
Table, Pembroke, Mahogany, Demilune, Flower Inlay, Hinged Leaves, c.1815, 30 In.	4740
Table, Pembroke, Satinwood, Paint, Demilune, Inlay, c.1800, 28 x 32 In.	1220
Table, Philip LaVerne, Bronze, Pewter, Etched, Textured Top, 1960s, 17 x 48 In.	5313
Table, Philip LaVerne, Spring Festival, Bronze, Pewter, 1960s, 15 x 28 In. *illus*	5313
Table, Phillip Powel, Wood, Triangular Marble Top, 1960s, 19 x 29 In.	2000
Table, Pier, Louis Philippe, Mahogany, Marble Top, Dolphin Support, 36 x 52 In.	1750
Table, Pine, 3 Drawers, Turned Legs, England, 1900s, 30 x 72 In.	375
Table, Pine, 3-Board Top, Stretcher, Base, Scalloped Apron, 1800s, 30 x 86 In.	1440
Table, Pine, Demilune, Bootjack Cutout Ends, Box Stretcher, 30 x 70 In.	1107
Table, Pine, Hutch, Lift Top, Hinged, Demilune Ends, Base, 1700s, 28 x 72 In.	4750
Table, Porcelain, Sevres Style, Dish Top, Painted, Flowers, Tripod, 19 x 24 In. *illus*	1107
Table, Queen Anne, Drop Leaf, Mahogany, England, 1700s, 28 x 42 In.	180
Table, Queen Anne, Maple, Pine, Turned Legs, Pad Feet, Oval, 1700s, 26 x 43 In.	413
Table, Reading, Literary Machine, John Carter, Mahogany, Iron Base, 1800s, 51 In.	2457
Table, Red Paint, Round, Ring-Turned Post, Tripod Base, Pa., 1700s, 27 x 24 In.	3690
Table, Regency, Chinoiserie, Raised Mandarin Figures, Brass Feet, 30 x 28 In.	500
Table, Regency, Mahogany, Inlay, Star, Pedestal, Claw Feet, 60 In. Diam.	687
Table, Regency, Mahogany, Round, Rope Twist Supports, c.1810, 29 x 19 In.	2074
Table, Regency, Pullout Board, Drawers, Carved Lyre Base, c.1810, 27 x 26 In.	518
Table, Rosewood, Porcelain Plaques, Round, Bulb Pedestal, c.1880, 29 x 29 In.	4018
Table, Rosewood, Turned Pedestal, 4 Spindles, Curved Base, c.1840, 29 x 38 In.	270
Table, Rosewood, William IV, Oval Top, Pedestal, c.1835, 30 x 48 x 71 x 47 In.	2091
Table, Salon, Louis XIV Style, Marquetry, Urn & Garland Inlay, 29 x 46 In.	2176

Table, Serving, Oak, Pine, Red, Sawbuck, 2-Board Top, c.1785, 34 In.	498
Table, Serving, Stickley Bros., Oak, Hammered Copper Pulls, Quaint, Tag, 37 x 34 In......*illus*	1080
Table, Sewing, Amboyna Wood, Lift Top, Columnar Legs, c.1810, 29 x 23 In.	1722
Table, Sewing, Butternut, Overhang Top, Drawer, Round Legs, c.1850, 31 x 36 In.	14760
Table, Sewing, Edwardian, Lift Top, Drawer, Painted Designs, c.1900, 28 x 24 In. ......*illus*	185
Table, Sewing, Federal, Mahogany, Oval, Lift Top, Philadelphia, 1810, 29 x 24 In.	600
Table, Sewing, Lift Top, Bag, Rails, Trestle Supports, Stretcher, 27 x 24 In.	100
Table, Sewing, Mahogany, Carved, Leaves, Fluted Legs, Mass., 1810, 29 x 21 In.	3120
Table, Sewing, Mahogany, Drawers, Columns, Swollen Post, 1840, 31 x 21 In.	593
Table, Sewing, Pine, Paint, Scrub Top, Arched Apron, Cutouts, 1850, 29 x 44 In.	330
Table, Sewing, Rosewood, Brass, Lift Top, Drawer, Turned Legs, c.1810, 19 x 30 In.	708
Table, Sewing, Satinwood, Drawers, Bag Slide, Reeded Legs, c.1810, 29 x 18 In.	1560
Table, Sewing, Sheraton, Mahogany, Octagonal, Hinged, 1810, 28 x 22 In.	1067
Table, Sewing, Softwood, Drawer, Plank Top, Beaded, Turned Legs, 29 x 27 In.	266
Table, Shaker, Maple, Stain, 2-Board Overhang Top, Drawer, c.1830, 26 x 33 In.	14760
Table, Shaker, Ministry, Birch, Plank Top, Trestle Base, c.1840, 28 x 66 In.	4920
Table, Shaker, Paint, 5-Board Top, X-Legs, Breadboard Ends, Folds, 1800s, 26 x 36 In.	431
Table, Side, Birch, Mahogany, 30 x 15 In.	281
Table, Side, Blackamoor, Round, Figural Black Woman, c.1910, 31 x 24 In., Pair	3750
Table, Side, Brass, Oval Glass Top, 3 Tiers, Pierced, Fluted Legs, 23 x 17 In.	130
Table, Side, Burl, Brass, Octagonal, Painted Flowers, Inlay, Drawer, 18 x 14 In.	41
Table, Side, Elm, 2 Frieze Drawers, Block Legs, Scroll Brackets, 33 x 29 In.	236
Table, Side, Elm, Mortised, Carved, Red, Green Lacquer, Brackets, c.1900, 34 x 55 In.	120
Table, Side, Esherick, Mahogany, Triangular, Block Legs, 1932, 20 x 17 In.	17500
Table, Side, F. Harer, Walnut, Ebony, Overhang Top, Drawer, 1930s, 28 x 34 In.	2875
Table, Side, French Provincial, Walnut, Drawer, Turned Legs, 1700s, 35 x 21 In. ......*illus*	1024
Table, Side, Fruitwood, Dovetailed Drawer, Trestle, Pegged, 1800s, 26 x 18 In.	472
Table, Side, Fruitwood, Marble Top, Brass, Flower Inlay, c.1850, 28 x 22 In.	625
Table, Side, Fruitwood, Starburst, Curved Legs, Triangular Base, 29 x 22 In.	1625
Table, Side, G. Nakashima, Black Walnut, Free Edge Top, Plank Sides, 18 x 21 In.	9225
Table, Side, G. Nakashima, Walnut, Slab Top, Tripod, Round Legs, 17 x 29 In.	1750
Table, Side, G. Stickley, Leather Top, X-Stretcher, Block Legs, c.1904, 30 x 41 In.	6250
Table, Side, G. Stickley, Mahogany, Cutouts, Block Legs, c.1905, 29 x 36 In.	2000
Table, Side, Gilt, Marble Top, Guilloche Frieze, Column Legs, Urn, 27 x 20 In.	3000
Table, Side, Gilt, Marble Top, Reeded, Ribbed Legs, Stretcher, c.1910, 27 x 24 In.	875
Table, Side, Giltwood, Octagonal, Figural Chinese Man Post, c.1910, 20 x 22 In., Pair	625
Table, Side, Italian Bombe, Inlay, Serpentine, 2 Drawers, 28 x 22 In.	1320
Table, Side, Kem Weber, Designed For Disney, c.1938, 28 x 15 In.	3125
Table, Side, Kingwood, Gilt Mounts, Oval, Inlaid Landscape, c.1900, 30 x 20 In.	875
Table, Side, Mahogany, Inlay, Hinged Glass Top, Tapered Legs, Splay Feet, 31 x 24 In.	83
Table, Side, Mahogany, Marble Top, Ormolu, 3-Part Base, c.1810, 30 x 16 In.	750
Table, Side, Maple, Overhang Top, Drawers, Crosshatched Legs, c.1840, 27 x 22 In.	1067
Table, Side, Maple, Serpentine, Carved, Shelf Stretcher, Cabriole Legs, 1920s	200
Table, Side, Marble Top, Gallery, Leather Faced Door, Books, c.1890, 16 x 12 In., Pair	937
Table, Side, Marble Top, Parquetry Inlay, Ormolu, Bowfront, 29 x 24 In., Pair	812
Table, Side, Metal, Porcelain Flower Top, Pierced Gallery, c.1910, 31 x 39 In.	3750
Table, Side, Milo Baughman, Wood, L Shape, c.1950, 21 x 32 In., Pair	1000
Table, Side, Mixed Wood, Red Stain, Overhang Top, Block Legs, 28 x 18 In.	212
Table, Side, Olive Wood, Round, Columns, Ebonized, Tripod, c.1810, 25 x 20 In.	492
Table, Side, P. Shire, Aluminum, Glass, Triangle, Orange, Burgundy, 16 x 29 In.	1250
Table, Side, Pine, Sponge Paint, Demilune, Overhang Top, c.1810, 32 x 36 In.	1067
Table, Side, Rosewood, Chrome, Danish, 24 x 27 In.	75
Table, Side, Seated Dog Pedestal, Marble Top, 31 ½ In., Pair	1000
Table, Side, Shaker, Stain, Gallery, Overhang Top, Block Legs, 1800s, 33 x 27 In.	923
Table, Side, Tiger Oak, Clover Shape Top, Spindle Legs, Shelf, c.1890, 29 x 24 In.	275
Table, Side, Tile Top, Iron, Arched Legs, Rope Twist Stretcher, 1920s, 22 x 31 In.	9375
Table, Side, Tilt Top, Column Post, Concave Base, Bun Feet, c.1835, 30 x 26 In.	437
Table, Side, Tray Top, Mahogany, Fluted Legs, Top Shape Feet, c.1790, 28 x 33 In.	1250
Table, Side, Walnut, Marquetry Patera, 3 Carved Griffin Legs, c.1950, 28 x 18 In.	148
Table, Side, William IV, Mahogany, Banding, Drawers, Ribbed Legs, c.1850, 32 x 83 In.	200
Table, Side, William IV, Mahogany, Bands, Peg Feet, c.1850, 32 x 83 x 17 In.	200

Furniture, Table, Specimen Stone & Mosaic Checkerboard, Custom Base, 1800s, 36 In. Diam.

$690

Cottone Auctions

Furniture, Table, Tavern, Oak, Drawer, Brass Drop Pull, Turned Legs, England, c.1820, 30 x 24 In.

$450

Cowan's Auctions

Furniture, Table, Tea, Queen Anne, Maple, Oval, Valance Apron, Turned Legs, 1700s, 27 x 37 In.

$1,353

Skinner, Inc.

Shaker Chairs
Some Shaker chairs have a number impressed on the top of the front leg or back post. This indicated where the chair belonged. Each room had a number.

F

Furniture, Table, Tortoise & Hare, Bronze, Glass Top, Frank Fleming, c.1990, 29 x 72 In.
$6,250

New Orleans Auction Galleries

Furniture, Table, Trestle, Walnut, Plank Top, Iron Stretchers, Spain, 1800s, 30 x 43 In.
$2,214

Cowan's Auctions

Furniture, Table, Tulip, E. Saarinen, Bronze, Enameled Aluminum, Pedestal, Round, 16 x 20 In.
$45,000

Wright

TIP

Look at the dovetails on dresser drawers. They should all match if the drawer is original. Replaced drawers or drawer fronts lower value.

Table, Side, Wood, Geometric Top, Twigs, Trunk, Roots Base, c.1920, 28 x 32 In.	1845
Table, Side, Wormley, Mahogany, Metal Labels, Dunbar, 22 x 22 x 14 In., Pair	1000
Table, Specimen Stone & Mosaic Checkerboard, Custom Base, 1800s, 36 In. Diam. ...*illus*	690
Table, Sunburst Top, Angular Base, c.1950, 24 In.	650
Table, Tavern, Maple, Drop Leaf, Turned Legs, Beaded Stretcher, 1700s, 28 x 38 In.	6000
Table, Tavern, Maple, Overhang Top, Breadboard Ends, Drawer, 1800s, 27 x 41 In.	450
Table, Tavern, Maple, Paint, Ring-Turned Legs, Stretchers, c.1790, 23 x 24 In.	1422
Table, Tavern, Oak, Drawer, Brass Drop Pull, Turned Legs, England, c.1820, 30 x 24 In....*illus*	450
Table, Tavern, Paint, Oval Top, Beaded, Turned Legs, c.1710, 27 x 32 In.	17000
Table, Tavern, William & Mary, Pine, Scrub Top, Box Base, c.1735, 27 x 32 In.	1481
Table, Tavern, Wood, Pine Top, Drawer, Turned Legs, Stretcher, 1700s, 27 x 37 In.	236
Table, Tea, Chippendale, Mahogany, Dish Top, 1700s, 28 x 27 In.	660
Table, Tea, Chippendale, Tilt Top, Mahogany, Octagonal, Pierced, 1700s, 31 x 35 In.	650
Table, Tea, Ebonized, Gilt, Gallery, Cluster Column Legs, X-Stretcher, 29 x 34 In.	1250
Table, Tea, George III, Mahogany, Tilt Top, Carved Base, England, c.1780, 28 x 23 In.	518
Table, Tea, Mahogany, Gallery Top, Marquetry, Inlaid Vase, Drawer, Dutch, 30 x 37 In.	1250
Table, Tea, Mahogany, Piecrust Tilt Top, Spiral Post, Claw Feet, c.1800, 28 x 31 In.	308
Table, Tea, Mahogany, Tilt Top, Carved Post, 3-Part Base, 1770, 29 x 34 In.	2963
Table, Tea, Maple, Red Paint, Oval Top, Turned Legs, Pad Feet, 1700s, 27 x 33 In.	950
Table, Tea, Queen Anne, Chinoiserie, Dish Top, Fluted Post, Tripod, c.1760, 28 x 30 In.	237
Table, Tea, Queen Anne, Mahogany, Tilt Top, Snake Feet, 1700s, 29 x 33 In.	277
Table, Tea, Queen Anne, Mahogany, Turret Corners, Birdcage Support, 27 x 28 In.	360
Table, Tea, Queen Anne, Maple, Oval, Valance Apron, Turned Legs, 1700s, 27 x 37 In. .....*illus*	1353
Table, Tea, Queen Anne, Maple, Tilt Top, Birdcage, Urn Post, c.1750, 28 x 36 In.	1422
Table, Tea, Queen Anne, Walnut, Tilt Top, Ring-Turned Post, 1800s, 45 x 21 In.	185
Table, Tea, Tray Top, Mahogany, Cabriole Legs, Salem, Mass., 25 x 25 x 18 In.	7380
Table, Telephone, Mahogany, Drop Front, Scroll, Turned Legs, 1950s, 49 x 31 In.	700
Table, Tilt Top, Regency, Penwork, People, Black, 29 x 18 In.	750
Table, Tilt Top, Walnut, Tripodal Base, Downswept Legs, c.1835, 25 In.	702
Table, Tilt Top, Walnut, Turned, Leaf Carved Pedestal, Tripod, 1800s, 29 x 34 In.	90
Table, Tortoise & Hare, Bronze, Glass Top, Frank Fleming, c.1990, 29 x 72 In. ...*illus*	6250
Table, Travertine, Square, Toe Base, c.1975, 21 ½ x 20 In.	492
Table, Tray, Brass, Glass Top, Bamboo X-Legs, Handles, Folding, 30 x 31 In.	425
Table, Trestle, Walnut, Plank Top, Iron Stretchers, Spain, 1800s, 30 x 43 In. ...*illus*	2214
Table, Tulip, E. Saarinen, Bronze, Enameled Aluminum, Pedestal, Round, 16 x 20 In....*illus*	45000
Table, W. Platner, Glass Top, Patinated Steel Wire Base, Knoll, 15 x 48 In.	875
Table, W. Platner, Glass, Nickeled Steel, Wire Base, Knoll, 1960s, 28 x 54 In.	3125
Table, Walnut, Carved, Flowers, Multicolor, Cherubs, Italy, 1700s, 31 x 72 x 32 In.	3750
Table, Walnut, Stretcher Base, Turned Legs, American, 1800s, 30 x 51 x 29 In.	2070
Table, William IV, Carved Mahogany, Tilt Top, 1800s, 29 x 52 ½ In.	1750
Table, Work, Gothic Revival, Mahogany, Slide Top, Drawers, Cast Iron, 1800s, 31 x 23 In..*illus*	562
Table, Work, Mahogany & Rosewood, Carved, Classical, c.1810, 29 x 22 In.	1464
Table, Work, Painted, Yellow Pine & Poplar, Drawer, 28 x 60 In.	644
Table, Work, Pine Top, Drawer, Dovetailed Battens, Tapered Legs, c.1780, 27 In.	152
Table, Work, Regency, Mahogany, Brass Gallery, Drawers, Trestle Base, 29 In.	468
Table, Work, Regency, Rosewood, Veneer, Drawer, Mahogany Lined, 29 x 19 In.	531
Table, Work, Shaker, Pine, Maple, Paint, 2-Board Top, Drawer, c.1860, 28 x 42 In.	600
Table, Work, Tortoiseshell, Octagonal Lift Top, Pedestal, Fabric Well, 29 In.	3250
Table, Work, Walnut, 2-Board Pine Top, Scalloped Apron, Drawer, 1700s, 28 In.	439
Table, Work, Walnut, Single Drawer, 2-Board Top, Octagonal Legs, 1800s, 29 In.	152
Table, Work, Wood, Marble, Fluted Legs, Cutouts, Brass Label, c.1900, 33 x 58	2040
Table, Wormley, Mosaic Top, Glass, Brass, Walnut Base, Dunbar, 1960s, 16 x 60 In.	3000
Table, Wormley, Open Shelf, Drawer, 24 ¾ x 17 In.	1046
Table, Writing, Bonheur Du Jour, Louis XV Style, Rosewood, c.1885, 50 x 37 In....*illus*	605
Table, Writing, Chippendale Style, Maple, Dovetailed, Heart Cutout, 29 x 48 In.	590
Table, Writing, Fruitwood, Plank Top, Frieze Drawer, c.1880, 27 x 35 In.	523
Table, Writing, Mahogany, Banded, String Inlay, Drawer, Stretcher, 29 x 41 In.	348
Table, Writing, Mahogany, Leather Top, Frieze Drawer, Turned Legs, c.1850, 30 x 43 In.	861
Table, Writing, Ring-Turned Tapered Legs, Stretcher, 29 x 35 In.	225
Table, Writing, Walnut, Leather Top, Drawers, Pullout Slide, 1900s, 30 x 69 In.	490
Table, Writing, Walnut, Round, Piecrust Veneers, c.1850, 29 x 42 In.	1000

F

Furniture, Table, Work, Gothic Revival, Mahogany, Slide Top, Drawers, Cast Iron, 1800s, 31 x 23 In.
$562

New Orleans Auction Galleries

Furniture, Table, Writing, Bonheur Du Jour, Louis XV Style, Rosewood, c.1885, 50 x 37 In.
$605

James D. Julia Auctioneers

Furniture, Tea Cart, Edwardian, Mahogany, Shelves, Drawer, W. Walker, c.1890, 48 x 54 In.
$1,098

Neal Auctions

Furniture, Tea Cart, Nakashima, Walnut, Rolls, Adjustable Shelf, Casters, 1965, 30 x 47 In.
$9,375

Rago Arts and Auction Center

Furniture, Teapoy, William IV, Mahogany, Hinged Top, Fitted, Tin-Lined Section, c.1835, 32 x 20 In.
$968

James D. Julia Auctioneers

Furniture, Umbrella Stand, Fornasetti, Sheet Metal, Decorated, Casa Con Calonne, Italy, 23 In.
$2,375

New Orleans Auction Galleries

Furniture, Umbrella Stand, Mission, Oak, 36 Compartments, Tin Drip Pans, 28 x 45 In.
$130

Hess Auction Group

Furniture, Umbrella Stand, Rococo Style, Grotesque Mask, Scrolled Feet, Cast Iron, 36 x 19 In.
$366

Neal Auctions

Furniture, Vanity, J. Adnet, Illuminated, Macassar Ebony, Nickeled Brass, Mirror, 1930s, 72 x 60 In.
$2,625

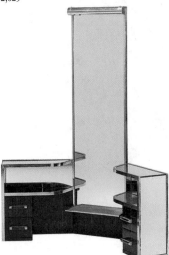

Rago Arts and Auction Center

Furniture, Wall Shelf, Blackamore, Giltwood, Painted, Seated Boy, Shelf, c.1900, 13 x 11 In., Pair
$854

Neal Auctions

Furniture, Wall Unit, McCobb, Walnut, Brass, Open Tiers, 6 Narrow Drawers, Label, c.1950, 76 x 60 In.
$960

Cowan's Auctions

Furniture, Wardrobe, Poplar, Sponge Painting, Stencil, Mennonite, Ohio, 1851, 80 x 51 In.
$3,360

Cowan's Auctions

Table, Writing, William IV, Mahogany, Turned Stretcher, c.1830, 30 x 59 In.	7500
Table, Wrought Iron, Repeating X-Shape Base, Glass Top, 1970s, 20 x 30 In.	35
Tabouret, G. Stickley, Hexagonal Top, Flat Legs, Stretcher Shelf, 18 x 20 In.	2125
Tabouret, L. & J.G. Stickley, Oak, Cut-Corner, 17 x 17 In.	1000
Tabouret, L. & J.G. Stickley, Oak, Octagonal, 18 x 18 In.	687
Tabouret, Limbert, Oak, 18 ½ x 20 In.	305
Tabouret, Limbert, Oak, Octagonal, A-Frame Legs, 17 x 17 In.	2000
Tabouret, Oak, Square, Plank Legs, Shelf, Curved Block Feet, c.1900, 15 x 14 In.	390
Tea Cart, Edwardian, Mahogany, Shelves, Drawer, W. Walker, c.1890, 48 x 54 In. ....*illus*	1098
Tea Cart, Nakashima, Walnut, Rolls, Adjustable Shelf, Casters, 1965, 30 x 47 In. ....*illus*	9375
Tea Cart, Teak, Lift-Off Tray Top, Casters, Danish, 1950s, 26 x 28 In.	120
Teapoy, Mahogany, Hinged Top, Pedestal, Animal Feet, England, 1800s, 31 In.	600
Teapoy, William IV, Mahogany, Hinged Top, Fitted, Tin-Lined Section, c.1835, 32 x 20 In..*illus*	968
Umbrella Stand, Fornasetti, Sheet Metal, Decorated, Casa Con Calonne, Italy, 23 In. ....*illus*	2375
Umbrella Stand, Garouste & Bonetti, Ceramic, Blue, Green, Black, 23 x 10 In.	1187
Umbrella Stand, Mission, Oak, 36 Compartments, Tin Drip Pans, 28 x 45 In. ....*illus*	130
Umbrella Stand, Oak, Barley Twist Legs, Backsplash, Tin Plate, c.1890, 32 x 36 In.	735
Umbrella Stand, Plaster, Figural, Boy, Apprentice, Apron, Tree Stump, c.1910, 36 In.	780
Umbrella Stand, Rococo Style, Grotesque Mask, Scrolled Feet, Cast Iron, 36 x 19 In........*illus*	366
Umbrella Stand, Sheraton Style, Mahogany, Stick-And-Ball, Tole Pan, 28 x 24 In.	500
Vanity, J. Adnet, Illuminated, Macassar Ebony, Nickeled Brass, Mirror, 1930s, 72 x 60 In..*illus*	2625
Vanity, Mahogany, Ormolu, Shaped Top, Scroll Apron, 1800s, 30 x 36 In.	795
Vanity, Maple, Relief Carved, Mirror, Doors, Turned Feet, c.1925, 72 x 46 In.	1200
Vanity, Wood, Chalk Paint, Caned Bench, Trifold Mirror, 1920s, 65 x 47 In.	595
Vitrine, Art Deco, Iron, Chrome, 2 Glass Doors, Peaked Top, Paw Feet, 64 In.	1100
Vitrine, Art Nouveau, Walnut, France, 81 ½ x 44 In.	625
Vitrine, Giltwood, Carved, Baroque, Italy, 1800s, 87 ½ x 37 In.	4880
Vitrine, Louis XV, Bronze Mount, Frolicking Putti, Cabriole Legs, 62 x 45 In.	8540
Vitrine, Louis XVI, Walnut, 3 Shelves, Gilt Mount, Inlay, 49 x 23 In.	281
Vitrine, Mahogany, Ormolu, Marble Top, Bowed, Glass Doors, c.1935, 29 In. Diam.	593
Vitrine, Oak, Glass Front, Sliding Doors, Tapered Feet, c.1900, 66 ½ In.	800
Vitrine, Painted, Dome Crest, Glazed Panel Door, Scroll Toes, c.1865, 66 x 35 In.	1250
Vitrine, Parcel Gilt, Vernis Martin, Continental, c.1910, 66 x 26 In.	512
Vitrine, Philip Reinisch, Corner, Brass, 1970s, 72 x 27 In., Pair	187
Vitrine, Rosettes, Leaves, Ribbon, Beading, 2 Doors, 5 Shelves, 81 x 21 In.	2196
Wall Shelf, Blackamore, Giltwood, Painted, Seated Boy, Shelf, c.1900, 13 x 11 In., Pair....*illus*	854
Wall Unit, McCobb, Walnut, Brass, Open Tiers, 6 Drawers, Label, c.1950, 76 x 60 In. ....*illus*	960
Wardrobe, Art Nouveau, Rosewood, Oak, Carved, Etched Glass, 106 x 105 In.	10625
Wardrobe, Bird's-Eye Maple, Mirrored Doors, England, c.1850, 81 x 92 In.	540
Wardrobe, Louis XV, Burl Veneer, 2 Paneled Doors, Drawer, 82 x 49 In.	2400
Wardrobe, Poplar, Sponge Painting, Stencil, Mennonite, Ohio, 1851, 80 x 51 In..............*illus*	3360
Wardrobe, Shrank, Walnut, Doors, Ogee Molding, Iron Hinges, Lancaster County, Pa......*illus*	16520
Wardrobe, Shrank, Walnut, Ogee Cornice, Raised Panel Doors, Inlaid 1779, 79 x 54 In.	3835
Wardrobe, Walnut, Carving, Health & Peace, Italy, c.1850, 98 x 91 In.	2375
Washstand, Burl, Walnut, Marble, Bronze, Leon Jallot, c.1900, 39 x 24 x 18 In.	938
Washstand, Federal, Mahogany, Fluted Panels, Reeded Legs, Drawer, c.1835, 31 x 18 In.	120
Washstand, Federal, Maple, Cutout Backsplash, Drawer, Shelf, Turned Legs, 38 x 22 In.	826
Washstand, George III, Mahogany, 2 Tiers, Backsplash, Copper Basin, Shelf, 1800s, 45 In.	177
Washstand, Louis Philippe, Pine, Marble, 38 ½ x 31 ½ In.	175
Washstand, Mahogany, American Classical, c.1850, 38 x 35 x 20 In.	610
Washstand, Mahogany, Carved, Classical, Well, c.1810, 32 x 16 x 17 In.	732
Washstand, Mahogany, England, c.1875, 48 x 23 In.	250
Washstand, Poplar, Backsplash, Drawer, Lower Shelf, Ring-Turned Legs, 35 In.	82
Washstand, Sheraton, Black, Grain, Stencil Painted, Drawer, 33 x 35 In.	250
Washstand, Walnut, Marble Top, Tile Backsplash, Doors, c.1850, 64 x 54 In.	360
Wastebasket, G. Stickley, Vertical Wood Strips, Studs, 1907, 14 x 12 In.	1875
Window Seat, Mahogany, Turned Legs, Top Shape Feet, 19 x 48 In.	500
Wine Cooler, George III, Mahogany, Inlay, Hinged Lid, Handles, c.1810, 28 x 22 In. ....*illus*	360
Wine Cooler, Georgian, Marquetry, Brass Bands, Hexagonal, c.1800, 24 In.	1180
Wine Cooler, Regency, Rosewood, Gadrooned Carving, 4 Bun Feet, 18 x 18 ½ In.	1428
Wine Cooler, Table, Mahogany, Marble Top, 2 Tin Wells, 1800s, 28 x 26 In.	1250

FURSTENBERG PORCELAIN WORKS was started in Furstenberg, Germany, in 1747. It is still working and is still using the *F* with crown mark. Many of the modern products are made in the old molds.

Compote, Lid, Peacock, Red & Turquoise, Caryatid Handles, Seedpod Finial, 9 x 8 In.	349
Vase, Trumpet, Courting Couples Dressed In Green, 5¾ In.	40

G. ARGY-ROUSSEAU is the impressed mark used on a variety of glass objects in the Art Deco style. Gabriel Argy-Rousseau, born in 1885, was a French glass artist. In 1921, he formed a partnership that made pate-de-verre and other glass. The partnership ended in 1931 and he opened his own studio. He worked until 1952 and died in 1953.

Bowl, Blackberries, Purple, Frosted, Flared, Footed, Pate-De-Verre, Signed, 4 In.	1185
Box, Lid, Cornflowers, Blue, Black, Red, Frosted Ground, Pate-De-Verre, Round, 3 In.	2370
Lamp, 2 Kneeling Women, Amethyst, Pate-De-Verre, 2 Socket, 19 x 6 In.	3304
Lamp, Amber, Red, Pate-De-Verre, Wrought Iron, 8 x 5 In.	1708
Nightlight, Masques, 3 Red Faces, Ribs, Pate-De-Verre, Iron Base, 6 In. ....*illus*	5333
Paperweight, Moth, Brown, Tan, On Square Mottled Amber Block, 2¾ In.	2074
Vase, Frosted, Blue Trees, Green, Blue, Red Flowers, Marked, 5⅞ In.	5535
Vase, Spiders & Brambles, Brown & Red Pate-De-Verre Leaves, Frosted, 5 In.	7110

GALLE was a designer who made glass, pottery, furniture, and other Art Nouveau items. Emile Galle founded his factory in France in 1874. After Galle's death in 1904, the firm continued to make glass and furniture until 1931. The *Galle* signature was used as a mark, but it was often hidden in the design of the object. Galle cameo and other types of glass are listed here. Pottery is in the next section. His furniture is listed in the Furniture category.

Bowl, Dragonfly, Purple, Cream Ground, Navette Shape, 2¾ x 7 x 3 In.	2625
Decanter & Cordial Set, Amber Cut, Medieval, 6 Cordials, Signed, 9½ In., 7 Piece	10350
Dish, Lid, Orchid, White, Enamel, Forget-Me-Nots, Bowknots, Insects, Flared Foot, 6 In.	720
Lamp, Art Nouveau, Amber Flowers, Frosted Ground, Bronze Base, Early 1900s, 19 x 11 In.	4500
Lamp, Wild Roses, Red, Pale Yellow, Tapered Stem, Domed Shade, Cameo, c.1900, 23 In.	27638
Perfume Bottle, Enameled Glass, Signed, 1880s, 4 x 2½ In.	1500
Sconce, Corner, Red Iris, Butterfly, Frosted Yellow Ground, Brass Mount, Flowers, 11 In.	3022
Tray, Wood Medieval Castle, Inlaid, Octagonal, Owl Handles, 19 x 23¼ In.	805
Tumbler, Ribbed, Woman Dancing, Inscription, 4½ In.	185
Vase, Amber & Red, Grapes, Grapevine, Cameo, Early 1900s, 10¼ x 4¾ In.	937
Vase, Amber Flowers & Leaves, Swollen Top, Tapered, Ring Foot, Cameo, c.1900, 8 In.	1060
Vase, Amber Over Green, Flowering Vine, Cameo, Signed, 7¾ x 5 In.	812
Vase, Amethyst Foot, Citron, Cut Flower & Lily Pads, Cameo, 7¼ In.	604
Vase, Banjo Shape, Dragonfly, Lily Pad, Purple, Yellow, 6¾ In.	1020
Vase, Bats, Flying, Moon, Village, Purple, 5¼ x 4 In. ....*illus*	9600
Vase, Berry, Branch, Leaf, Mottled Seaweed, Green, Translucent, 13¾ In. ....*illus*	9000
Vase, Blue Flowers, Purple Leaves, Cream Ground, Footed, Signed, 6¾ In. ....*illus*	2666
Vase, Blue Windowpane Flowers, Frosted Yellow Ground, Cameo, 5¾ In.	1422
Vase, Bonheur Bon An Bon Sicle, Flowers, Pink, Purple, 5½ In. ....*illus*	7800
Vase, Bottle Shape, Green & Pink, Trailing Vines, Cameo, Signed, c.1825, 6 x 3 In.	562
Vase, Brown Violets, Yellow Ground, Cameo, Signed, 3¼ x 2⅛ In.	575
Vase, Bud, Angelica, Lime Green, Pink Frost, Amber, Acid Etched, c.1900, 7 In. ....*illus*	576
Vase, Bulbous, Red Crocuses Against Yellow, Cameo, Signed, 8⅜ x 5 In.	3680
Vase, Bulbous, Ribbed Tube Neck, Enamel, Gilt, Trailing Vines & Flowers, c.1885, 18 In.	5750
Vase, Bulbous, Stick Neck, Sunflower, Amber, Silver Flower Foot & Collar, c.1910, 7 In.	1750
Vase, Cicada, Yellow Ground, Bottle Form, Cameo, 6¾ x 3 In.	2125
Vase, Cornflowers, Red, Yellow, Cameo, c.1925, 5 x 4 In. ....*illus*	461
Vase, Cranberry Flowers, Cream Ground, Round Foot, Cameo, 22½ In.	383
Vase, Crocus, White, Purple, Frosted Citrine Ground, Oval, Blown, Flared Rim, 8 In.	948
Vase, Cut Pond Scene, Green On Peach, Cameo, Signed, 4¾ In.	748
Vase, Dark Blue, Dark Red Trees, Lake, Mountains, Cameo, 1900s, 14 x 6 In.	3500
Vase, Dark Brown Set Over Olive Green, Cameo, 11⅝ In.	460
Vase, Dark Red Grapes Over Pink & White & Orange Frost, Cameo, Signed, 12⅜ In.	805
Vase, Desert Rose, Overlay, Cameo, c.1900, 4 In.	425

Furniture, Wardrobe, Shrank, Walnut, Doors, Ogee Molding, Iron Hinges, Lancaster County, Pa.
$16,520

Hess Auction Group

Furniture, Wine Cooler, George III, Mahogany, Inlay, Hinged Lid, Handles, c.1810, 28 x 22 In.
$360

Brunk Auctions

G.Argy-Rousseau, Nightlight, Masques, 3 Red Faces, Ribs, Pate-De-Verre, Iron Base, 6 In.
$5,333

James D. Julia Auctioneers

Galle, Vase, Bats, Flying, Moon, Village, Purple, 5 ¼ x 4 In.
$9,600

Galle, Vase, Berry, Branch, Leaf, Mottled Seaweed, Green, Translucent, 13 ¾ In.
$9,000

Galle, Vase, Blue Flowers, Purple Leaves, Cream Ground, Footed, Signed, 6 ¾ In.
$2,666

Galle, Vase, Bonheur Bon An Bon Sicle, Flowers, Pink, Purple, 5 ½ In.
$7,800

Galle, Vase, Bud, Angelica, Lime Green, Pink Frost, Amber, Acid Etched, c.1900, 7 In.
$576

Galle, Vase, Cornflowers, Red, Yellow, Cameo, c.1925, 5 x 4 In.
$461

Galle, Vase, Moths, Glazed, Gilt Faience, Signed, 1880s, 14 x 5 In.
$6,250

Galle, Vase, Nasturtium, Orange, Frost, France, c.1900, 10 ¾ x 6 In.
$422

Galle Pottery, Figurine, Cat, Seated, White, Yellow Flowers, Green Eyes, Signed, c.1910, 13 ½ In.
$2,400

Vase, Dragonfly, Lily Pads, Purple, White Ground, Bottle Form, 7 x 3 In.	2375
Vase, Flowers, Blue, Purple, Cream Ground, Squat, Cameo, 4 x 5 In.	1625
Vase, Flowers, Pink, Cameo, Signed, c.1900, 5 1/2 x 4 3/4 In.	2500
Vase, Flowers, Yellow, Brown, Cameo, 7 x 2 1/2 In.	793
Vase, Frosted Amber, Red Leafy Flowers, 6 In.	937
Vase, Frosted, Amber Glass, Purple Vine, Cameo, 1900, 9 4/5 In.	812
Vase, Frosted, Orange Flowering Vines, Cameo, 1900, 8 1/2 In.	812
Vase, Fuchsia Blossoms, Purple, Pink, Cameo, Signed, 4 1/2 x 4 In.	489
Vase, Green Thistle, Cream Shaded To Pink Frosted Ground, Tapered, Cameo, 14 5/8 In.	593
Vase, Hibiscus, Blue & Purple Over Orange, Cameo, Signed, Early 1900s, 10 3/4 x 8 In.	7500
Vase, Hibiscus, Blue Blossoms, Brown Leaves, Amber, Gourd Shape, c.1910, 11 In.	7500
Vase, Hyacinth, Brown & Lavender Over Yellow, Cameo, Signed, c.1910, 12 x 5 x 4 In.	8750
Vase, Iris, Brown, Tapered, Flared, Lavender, Frost Ground, Cameo, 16 1/2 x 7 In.	1300
Vase, Landscape, Mountains, Trees, Tan Ground, Bottle Shape, Cameo, 6 3/4 x 3 1/4 In.	1125
Vase, Lily Pads On Pond, Arrowroot, Blue, Frosted Cream Ground, Oval, Footed, 14 In.	4266
Vase, Moths, Glazed, Gilt Faience, Signed, 1880s, 14 x 5 In. ...illus	6250
Vase, Nasturtium, Orange, Frost, France, c.1900, 10 3/4 x 6 In. ...illus	422
Vase, Overlay, Flowers, Mottled, Foil, Orange, Cream, c.1900, 9 In., Pair.	10000
Vase, Overlay, Flowers, Purple, Lavender, Cameo, c.1900, 5 3/4 In.	375
Vase, Plum, Pendant Flowers, Branches, Vines, Cameo, 9 1/2 In.	750
Vase, Plum, Seaweed, Lime Green Ground, Cameo, 10 3/4 In.	1000
Vase, Purple Clematis Vine Against Yellow, Cameo, Signed, 15 x 6 1/2 In.	1725
Vase, Red & Gold, Footed, Tapered Body, Pond Scene, Cameo, Signed, 9 1/2 In.	920
Vase, Red Flowers On Yellow, Cameo, Early 1900s, 13 1/2 x 8 In.	6875
Vase, Red Flowers, Frosted Cream Ground, Bulbous, Boat Shape Rim, Cameo, 8 1/2 In.	3259
Vase, Red Glass, Berry & Leaf Cameo, Bulbous Inverted Funnel, Ring Collar, c.1910, 3 In.	492
Vase, Stick, Gourds, Vines, Blossoms, Purple Ground, Gold Trim, 18 In.	4148
Vase, Stick, Leaves, Purple, Orange Ground, Cameo, 6 1/4 In.	625
Vase, Stick, Lilies, Opalescent, Enamel, c.1890, 13 In.	3750
Vase, Sunflower, Orange, Silver Accents, Cameo, 7 x 5 x 3 3/4 In.	1750
Vase, Sunflowers, Mushrooms & Spider Web, Signed, Early 1900s, 12 1/2 x 4 1/2 In.	10000
Vase, Tall Neck, Green, Pale Blue, Flowers, Leaves, Cameo, 6 1/2 In.	492
Vase, Trees, Lake, Amber & Pink, Cameo, Signed, c.1900, 8 1/2 x 2 3/4 In.	1000
Vase, Trumpet Flowers, Yellow, Orange, Round Top, Tapered, Cameo, c.1910, 14 x 8 In.	6875
Vase, Vine & Berries, Purple, Blue, Shaded Blue & Yellow Ground, Oval, Footed, 9 5/8 In.	8295
Vases, Purple Overlay, Blue, Cameo, 8 5/8 In.	3125

GALLE POTTERY was made by Emile Galle, the famous French designer, after 1874. The pieces were marked with the initials *E. G.* impressed, *Em. Galle Faiencerie de Nancy,* or a version of his signature. Galle is best known for his glass, listed above.

Figurine, Cat, Seated, White, Yellow Flowers, Green Eyes, Signed, c.1910, 13 1/2 In. ...illus	2400
Vase, Cicada, Maroon & Green Vertical Bands, Faience, Bulbous, 3 3/4 In. ...illus	711

GAME collectors like all types of games. Of special interest are any board games or card games. Transogram and other company names are included in the description when known. Other games may be found listed under Card, Toy, or the name of the character or celebrity featured in the game. Gameboards without the game pieces are listed in the Gameboard category.

Addams Family, Spinner, Cards, Player Pieces, Box, Ideal, 1964, 10 x 20 In.	811
Bingo, Cage, Wire, Spinning Ball Dispenser, Slide Shoot, 73 Wood Balls, 1960s, 12 x 14 In.	75
Board, All Aboard For Chicago, Railroad Tracks On Board, Train Station, Box, 8 x 11 In.	978
Board, Life Savers, Sinking Ship, Lifeboat, Spinner, Playing Pieces, Box, 9 x 12 In.	604
Bocce Ball Set, 8 Balls, A.G. Spalding & Bros., England, Early 1900s, 6 x 16 x 16 In.	420
Box, Lacquer, Gilt, Shaped, Rectangular, Chinoiserie, 7 Card Trays, 2 Card Boxes, 3 x 12 In.	450
Cards, Women Are Trumps, Historical Figures, 31 Of 54 Cards, Bailey, Banks & Biddle	375
Carnival Target, Pig, Orange, Iron, c.1925, 4 3/4 x 7 3/4 In.	300
Checkers, Chess, Dominoes, England, Box, 7 1/2 x 15 1/4 In.	450
Chess Set, Amber & Aqua Glass Tiles, Metal Board, Elongated Figures, 1970s, 21 x 21 In.	803
Chess Set, Carved Walrus Tusk, Eskimo & Animal Figures, Case, c.1935, 30 Piece	1722

Galle Pottery, Vase, Cicada, Maroon & Green Vertical Bands, Faience, Bulbous, 3 3/4 In.
$711

James D. Julia Auctioneers

TIP
Bright sunlight may fade colors of gameboard boxes.

Game, Chess Set, Military Civil War, Charles Stadden, Mahogany Box, c. 1975, In.
$3,410

Ahlers & Ogletree Auction Gallery

Game, Dominoes, Monogram, Presentation, Sterling Silver Case, 1 3/4 x 5 1/2 In.
$720

Thomaston Place Auction Galleries

Game, Fish Pond, Fish, Poles, McLoughlin Bros., 1890s, 18 x 9 In.
$216

Milestone Auctions

209

Game, Shut The Door, Dice, Leather Cup, Wood Board, 19 x 11 In.
$122

Showtime Auction Services

Gameboard, Checkerboard, Black & White Paint, Red Border, Corner Flowers, 1800s, 18 x 17 In.
$1,722

Skinner, Inc.

Gameboard, Checkered, Diamond Shaped Play Area, 2-Board Construction, c.1900, 21 x 21 In.
$2,420

James D. Julia Auctioneers

Gameboard, Checkers, Pine, Painted, 15 x 9³⁄₈ In.
$295

Hess Auction Group

Chess Set, Military Civil War, Charles Stadden, Mahogany Box, c. 1975............*illus*	3410
Chess Set, White, Portland Blue, Wood Case, Chessboard Top, c.1973, 20 x 20 In......	1230
Clock Golf, Wood Box, F. Hayres Ltd., England, Late 1800s, 7³⁄₄ x 15¹⁄₂ In.	150
Domino Set, Sterling Silver, Monogrammed, Engraved, Lid, 1917, 1³⁄₄ x 5¹⁄₂ In.	600
Dominoes, Monogram, Presentation, Sterling Silver Case, 1³⁄₄ x 5¹⁄₂ In...........*illus*	720
Fish Pond, Fish, Poles, McLoughlin Bros., 1890s, 18 x 9 In............*illus*	216
Fortune Teller, Parlor Base Ball, Bostons Vs. Chicagos, Wood Case, Ball, Paint, 13 x 10 In.	1560
Jeu De Construction, Wood Blocks, Lithographed Architectural Details, France, c.1865, 14 In.	798
Mahjong, 144 Bone On Wood Tiles, Chips, Fitted Box, O & M Hauser, c.1925, 12 x 10 In...........	819
Mahjong, Copper & Wood Case, Bone, Bamboo Pieces, Racks, Pung Chow, 6 x 9 In.	189
Mahjong, Rosewood, Brass Trim, 5 Drawers, 7¹⁄₄ x 9¹⁄₂ In.	177
Ouija, Board, Wood, Black Letters & Symbols, Instructions, W. Fuld, 1915, 12 x 18 In.	300
Penny Toss, Tabletop, Carnival, Wood, 4 Raised Boards, 5 Red Pockets, c.1930-40, 48 In.	250
Poker Set, Clay Chips, Numbered Disks, Chip Rack, Wooden Lift Top Box, Latch, 1800s...........	875
Puzzle, Lithograph, Papier-Mache, Farm Animal Sounds, Box, c.1900, 13 x 8 In.....................	600
Puzzle, Wooden Sphere, Carved Pyramid Shapes, Leather Straps, Victorian, 8 In.	895
Roulette Wheel, Wood Base, Late 1800s, 23¹⁄₂ In...	480
Scrabble, Crossword, 100 Wood Letters, Board, 4 Wood Stands, 1950s, 14 x 8 In......................	20
Shut The Door, Dice, Leather Cup, Wood Board, 19 x 11 In..*illus*	122
Target, Bird, Tin Base, Tin Litho, Hinged, Rubber Darts, Cardboard Box, 1930s, 12 x 12 In......	127
Target, Eagle Form, Cast Iron, Painted, Red, White & Blue Bull's-Eye Center, 26 x 13 In.	6765
Target, Ramar Of The Jungle, Blow Gun, Cardboard Stand, Balls, c.1953, 15 x 20 In..............	177
Target, Shooting, Paper, Ground Hog, Sold By Sears, Roebuck & Co., 1950s, 6 x 9 In..............	10
Uncle Wiggily, Pin The Hat, Milton Bradley, Frame, Original Packaging, Hats, 24 x 30⁷⁄₈ In...	71
Wheel, Chance, Casino Style, Carnival, Bicycle Wheel Hub, Oak Rim, c.1910, 34¹⁄₂ In.	200
Wheel, Gambling, Carnival, Bike Tire, Wood Frame, Playing Cards, 1930s, 31 In.	1300
Wheel, Wood, 1-Sided, Original Paint, Metal Trim, Early 1900s, 30 In.	300
Wheel, Wood, 2-Sided, Numbers & Dominos, Early 1900s, 25 In.	480
Wheel, Wood, Wall Mounted, Made From Bicycle, Late 1800s, 33¹⁄₂ x 30¹⁄₂ In............	813

 GAME PLATES are plates of any make decorated with pictures of birds, animals, or fish. The game plates usually came in sets consisting of 12 dishes and a serving platter. These sets were most popular during the 1880s.

Birds, Flowers, Gilt Rim, Cobalt, Porcelain, Limoges, 9¹⁄₂ In., 8 Piece.	125
Deer, Stags, Rabbits, Squirrels, Ducks, Pheasants, Fox, Limoges, 9¹⁄₂ In., 9 Piece	324
Fish, Gilded Grillwork, Spode, c.1875, 8³⁄₄ In., 8 Piece..	1445
Fish, Water Plants, Multicolor, MZ Austria, 8¹⁄₂ In..	168

 GAMEBOARD collectors look for just the board without the game pieces. The boards are collected as folk art or decorations. Gameboards that are part of a complete game are listed in the Game category.

Checkerboard, Black & White Paint, Red Border, Corner Flowers, 1800s, 18 x 17 In.........*illus*	1722
Checkered, Diamond Shaped Play Area, 2-Board Construction, c.1900, 21 x 21 In. ....*illus*	2420
Checkers & Parcheesi, Applied Edge, Early 1900s, 19¹⁄₂ x 22¹⁄₂ In..........................	360
Checkers & Parcheesi, Painted, Black, Puce, Red, Square Nails, 18 x 20 In.	3321
Checkers & Parcheesi, Pine, Walnut, Cherry, 30 x 18¹⁄₂ In.	225
Checkers & Parcheesi, Reversible, Mid 1800s, 27¹⁄₂ In.....................	700
Checkers & Parcheesi, Round With Red Stain, 26 In.......................	300
Checkers, 2-Sided, Salmon, Black Squares, 1800s, 18⁵⁄₈ x 18⁵⁄₈ In........................	351
Checkers, Black, Yellow, Pine, 29 x 18¹⁄₂ In........................	275
Checkers, Lacquer, Gilt, Chinese, c.1900, 16¹⁄₂ x 16¹⁄₂ In.......................	148
Checkers, Pine, Painted, 15 x 9³⁄₈ In...*illus*	295
Checkers, Pine, Wear & Hinge Marks, Early 1900s, 16 x 16 In.....................................	406
Checkers, Pine, Yellow, Black, 1800s, 19¹⁄₂ x 29 In.	381
Folk Art, Red, Black, Yellow, White, Geometric, 9 Patch, 1960-70, 27 x 27 In................	1625
Good Luck, Central Horse & Jockey, Applied Horseshoe, 25¹⁄₄ x 20¹⁄₄ In.	1680
Parcheesi & Backgammon, Folding, Wear & Yellow Varnish, Early 1900s, 20 x 24 In.	360
Parcheesi, Oak, Painted, Green, Yellow, Red, Blue, 19 In..	2460
Parcheesi, Wood, American Flag Center, 18¹⁄₄ x 20¹⁄₂ In.	321

GARDEN FURNISHINGS have been popular for centuries. The stone or metal statues, urns and fountains, sundials, small figurines, and wire, iron, or rustic furniture are included in this category. Many of the metal pieces have been made continuously for years.

Arbor, Arch, Columns, Pine, 72 ½ In.	469
Arbor, Arch, Curlicues, 96 x 72 In.	427
Arbor, Latticework, Pitched Top, White, 103 x 60 In.	406
Armillary, Green, Strong Man Support, Cast Iron, 30 In.	234
Bench, Baroque Style, Composite, 50 x 18 In., Pair	313
Bench, Blue, Flowers, Cast Iron, 30 In.	117 to 234
Bench, Cathedral Window, Central Motif, Iron, England, 1800s, 39 x 60 x 24 In.	2250
Bench, Curved Back, Joined Tubes, Scroll Arms, Shaped Legs, Iron, c.1900, 38 x 48 In.	2500
Bench, Fern Pattern, Serpentine Crest, Cast Iron, 1800s, 35 x 55 In. ....*illus*	854
Bench, Grape, Leaf, White Paint, Metal, 27 x 57 In., Pair	1000
Bench, Grotto, Figural, Shell, Fish, 22 In.	1250
Bench, Minerva Head Back, Acanthus Scroll Legs, Iron, c.1880s, 37 ½ x 45 In.	660
Bench, Neoclassical, Scroll Arms, Flared Feet, Stone, 37 x 55 ¾ In.	1071
Bench, Paint, Scalloped, Scroll & Flower Back, Open Weave Seat, Iron, 1930s, 39 x 33 In.	795
Bench, Pierced Back, Spires, Scrollwork, Wood Slat Seat, Cast Iron, 39 x 64 In., Pair	1500
Bench, Ram's Mask, Arms, White Paint, 34 ½ x 44 In., Pair	1250
Bench, Scroll Back, Cog & Wheel Seat, Cast Iron, 1800s, 15 In.	900
Bench, Scroll Design, Rosette Medal Lions On Seat, Cabriole Legs, Cast Iron, 34 x 45 In.	330
Bench, Shaped Back, Open Honeycomb Pattern, Painted, Cast Iron, Victorian, 45 In., Pair	1680
Bench, Twig Form, Cast Iron, 32 x 50 In.	944
Birdbath, 2-Piece, Tapered Column, Flared Foot, Granite, 32 x 24 In.	1200
Birdbath, Bowl, Lily Pad, Cement, 23 ½ In.	23
Birdbath, Flowers & Leaves, Black, Tripod Feet, Cast Iron, Marked, England, 29 x 13 In.	254
Birdbath, Gradated Circles, Copper, Iron, 21 ½ x 17 In.	180
Birdbath, Tree Trunk, Figural, 3-Part, Limestone, 1900s, 25 x 25 In.	870
Boot Scraper, 2 Stakes, Scrolled Ends, Iron, c.1810, 11 ¼ In. ....*illus*	266
Boot Scraper, Back To Back Griffins, Green, Round Tray, 10 x 13 In.	263 to 343
Boot Scraper, Cat, Tail Up, Mud Tray, c.1888, 6 ¾ In.	120
Boot Scraper, H Shape, Brass, Iron, 7 ½ In., Pair	50
Boot Scraper, Horse, c.1900, 17 In.	566
Chair Set, Slat Back & Seats, Kingsley Bate, 55 x 23 In., 6	900
Chair, Bent Tubes, Continuous Seat & Back, Curlicue Arms, Pad Feet, Iron, 31 In., Pair	3250
Chair, Cast Iron, Profile Of C. Vanderbilt, Vanderbilt Univ., 31 In.	1187
Chair, Fern Pattern, Iron, c.1900, 32 ½ x 22 x 22 In., Pair	2750
Chair, Folding, Wood Back & Slat Seat, Wrought Iron, 18 In.	300
Chair, Lyre Back, Swan's Head Finial, Padded, Iron, Brass, 36 In., Pair	240
Chair, Neoclassical, Arched Back, Fleur-De-Lis Splat, Wrought Iron, 38 ¾ x 18 In., 6 Piece	476
Chair, Octagonal Table, Pierced Geometrics, White Paint, Aluminum, 5 Piece	480
Chair, Regency Style, Faux Verdigris, X & O Back, Wrought Iron, 36-In. Settee, 3 Piece	1920
Chair, Treebark Decoration, White, Composition, 4 Piece	625
Chair, White, Removable Ottoman, Salterini, 58 In.	526
Chair, Wire, Victorian, Rolled Iron, c.1900, 36 x 39 ½ In.	119
Dining Set, Table, 4 Chairs, Sunbursts, Francois Carre, 5 Piece	354
Dining Set, Table, 4 Chairs, Wrought Iron, White, 5 Piece	204
Figure, Bust, Demon, Molded Plateau, Sandstone, Concrete Base, 1900s, 28 In.	3000
Figure, Dolphins, Leaping, Bronze, 56 ½ In.	7250
Figure, Egret, Standing, Bronze, Patina, 1900s, 30 In., Pair ....*illus*	313
Figure, Flamingo, Standing, Cast Iron, Pink Paint, Round Base, 24 x 19 In., Pair ....*illus*	875
Figure, Fountain, Mermaid, Fish, Bronze, Mid 1900s, 42 In.	6500
Figure, Frog, 5 Frogs On Back, Bronze, 39 In.	1320
Figure, Frog, Leaping, Bronze, 28 x 17 In.	952
Figure, Gnome, Standing, Electrified Lantern, Pat Nydea Pend 347, 27 In. ....*illus*	4425
Figure, Gnome, Reading, Stone, 23 x 12 In.	416
Figure, Horned Ewe, Lamb, Limestone, Royston Clapp, 1950, 15 ½ x 16 In.	480
Figure, Lion, Seated, Cast Stone, 26 In., Pair	500
Figure, Mermaid, Seated, Arms Behind Head, 36 In.	125

Garden, Bench, Fern Pattern, Serpentine Crest, Cast Iron, 1800s, 35 x 55 In.
$854

Garden, Boot Scraper, 2 Stakes, Scrolled Ends, Iron, c.1810, 11 ¼ In.
$266

G

TIP

Set heavy garden urns or statues on a foundation, usually a cement block set in the ground.

Garden, Figure, Egret, Standing, Bronze, Patina, 1900s, 30 In., Pair
$313

This is an edited listing of current prices. Visit Kovels.com to check thousands of prices from previous years and sign up for free information on trends, tips, reproductions, marks, and more.

Garden, Figure, Flamingo, Standing, Cast Iron, Pink Paint, Round Base, 24 x 19 In., Pair

$875

Neal Auctions

Garden, Figure, Gnome, Standing, Electrified Lantern, Pat Nydea Pend 347, 27 In.

$4,425

Bertoia Auctions

Garden, Fountain, Figural, Boy Holding Carp, Bronze, France, 1800s, 25 ½ x 15 In.

$1,408

Neal Auctions

Figure, Peacock, Flaring Feathers, Scalloped Edge, Shaped Base, Lead, c.1900, 24 In.	540
Figure, Putti Carrying Wheat, Continental, Stone, 1900s, 32 x 10 x 12 In., Pair	437
Figure, Putto, Posed With Outstretched Arms, Lead, 1800s, 31 ½ x 24 x 24 In.	640
Figure, Shepherd, Shepherdess, Lead, 55 ¾ In., 2 Piece	2750
Figure, Squirrel, Tail Up, Lead, 11 In.	313
Fountain, Bubbler, Ceramic, Art Deco, 38 ½ x 17 ¼ In.	1000
Fountain, Cherub & Shells, Lily, Frog & Turtle Border On Basin, White Cast Metal, 90 In.	3438
Fountain, Child, Fish, Blossom Shape Base, Lead, 31 ½ In.	1680
Fountain, Figural, Boy Holding Carp, Bronze, France, 1800s, 25 ½ x 15 In. ....*illus*	1408
Fountain, Fishbowl, Black, Pedestal, Scalloped Rim, Cast Iron, Victorian, 52 x 28 In.	1416
Fountain, Fiske Style, Painted, Egrets, Metal, 1900s, 58 x 33 In. ....*illus*	640
Fountain, Frog, Lily Pad, Egrets, Boy Holding Fish, Cast Iron, Zinc, c.1880, 96 x 72 In.	4444
Fountain, Head, Neptune, Shell Crown, Cast Iron, 24 x 12 ½ In.	400
Fountain, Nude Boy & Swan, Wings Up, Upraised Beak, Spout, c.1865, 47 x 40 In.	7703
Fountain, Pyramid, Sundial, Verdigris, 38 x 17 In.	906
Fountain, Seated Nude Woman, Seashell, Fish, Scudder Style, Bronze, 46 x 30 In.	3895
Fountain, Sphere, Layered Strips, Beige, Concrete, 34 x 30 In.	2500
Fountain, Tortoise, Bronze, Patina, 63 ¼ x 34 In.	5900
Fountain, White Storks, 3 Sections, J.W. Fiske & Co., N.Y. ....*illus*	4720
Fountain, Woman, Dolphins, Shell Shape Basin, Bronze, Patina, 95 x 49 In., 2 Piece ....*illus*	7015
Gate, 2-Panel, Flower Basket, 82 x 66 ½ In., Pair	437
Gate, Heart Scrolls, Wrought Iron, 66 x 56 In., 2 Piece	750
Gate, Tree, Painted Green Leaves, Filigree, c.1890, 41 ¾ x 28 In.	1230
Gazebo, Classical, Scrolling Cast Iron Dome, Travertine Columns, 174 x 118 In.	4550
Guideposts, Pagoda Shape, Granite, 41 x 24 ½ In., Pair	2360
Hitching Post, Back Boy, Green Pants, White Shirt, Iron, 46 x 15 In.	731
Hitching Post, Black Boy, Open Shirt, Blue Pants, Cast Iron, 45 In.	738
Hitching Post, Black Boy, Seated, Barefoot, 18 ½ In.	92
Hitching Post, Black Man, Hand In Pocket, Holding Loop, Cast Iron, 26 In.	246
Hitching Post, Painted, Block & Turned Column, Ball Cap, Iron, c.1885, 48 In., Pair	300
Hitching Post, Suten, Iron, Old Green Paint, 54 In.	900
Jardiniere, Neoclassical Style, Bronze, Relief, Angels, Putti, Pedestal, 56 In., Pair ....*illus*	6563
Jardiniere, Putti, Tree Stump, Flowers, Iron, 32 ¾ x 15 ½ In., Pair	297
Jardiniere, Shaped Rim, Round Foot, Lead, Italy, 15 In.	138
Lantern, Japanese Style, Hexagonal, Stone, 28 In.	780
Lantern, Yellow Glass, Hexagonal, Wrought Iron, 24 In.	63
Lawn Stag, Full Antler Rack, Opposite Directions, Iron, 56 x 26 x 38 In., Pair	5750
Patio Set, Iron, Mesh, White, Fiberglass Tabletop, American, c.1960, 7 Piece	576
Patio Set, Table, Chairs, Chairs, Glass Top, Ribbon, M. Tempestini, 7 Piece, 33 x 20 In.	2812
Pedestal, Stepped Top, Wasted Stem, Acanthus Base, Stepped Plinth, 30 ½ x 19 ½ In.	1200
Plant Stand, see also Furniture, Stand, Plant	
Planter, Barrel Shape, Slanted Sides, Rope Banding, Orange Glaze, c.1900, 15 In.	2583
Planter, Black Paint, Pierced Scroll, Gilt Pinecone Finials, 1900s, 25 x 71 In., Pair	1375
Planter, Boat, Anchor, Rope, Gilt Wave Marking, Bronze, 12 In.	156
Planter, Campana Shape, Masks, Socle, Round Foot, Bronze, Iron, 11 ⅜ x 11 ⅜ In.	175
Planter, Circle Handles, Zinc, 23 ½ x 23 ½ In., Pair	1250
Planter, Famille Rose, Flared Rim, Willow, Peony, Lotus Branches, Ruyi, c.1900, 13 In.	738
Planter, Famille Verte, Bulbous, Butterflies, Insects, White Ground, 10 x 12 ½ In.	1353
Planter, Famille Verte, Octagonal, Flared Flat Rim, Boys, Garden, 1800s, 6 x 12 In.	1599
Planter, Medallions, Earthenware, Continental Glazed, 21 In.	100
Planter, Neoclassical, Lions, Swags, Fruit, Grapes, Apples, Stone, Cast, 28 x 33 In.	295
Planter, Pedestal, Container, Walter Lamb, Brown Jordan Co., 1950, 25 x 16 In., Pair ....*illus*	1500
Planter, Round, Quatrefoil Lobed, Ruyi Legs, Gray, Black Crackle Glaze, 1700s, 3 x 6 In.	2214
Planter, Saddle Shape, Molded Fleurs-De-Lis, Lion's Head, Stone, c.1950, 23 x 24 In., Pair	812
Planter, Stoneware, Red, Unglazed, David Cressey, 6 x 12 In.	562
Pot, Flared, Gadrooned Neck, Round Foot, 41-In. Square Plinth Base, 68 x 41 In.	1071
Sculpture, Bacchus Riding A Goat, 2 Putti, Laurel Grapevine, Stone, 40 x 17 x 31 In.	492
Sculpture, Cherub, Seated, Looking Down, Quiver, Oxidation, Iron, 24 ¾ x 11 In.	595
Sculpture, Dog, Seated, White, Cast Iron, 23 In.	6150
Sculpture, Eagle, Spread Wings, Attacking, Cast Iron, Granite Base, 18 In.	1100

G

Garden, Fountain, Fiske Style, Painted, Egrets, Metal, 1900s, 58 x 33 In.
$640

Neal Auctions

TIP
Outdoor bronze garden figures should be waxed twice a year for protection.

Garden, Fountain, White Storks, 3 Sections, J.W. Fiske & Co., N.Y.
$4,720

Hess Auction Group

Garden, Fountain, Woman, Dolphins, Shell Shape Basin, Bronze, Patina, 95 x 49 In., 2 Piece
$7,015

Neal Auctions

Garden, Jardiniere, Neoclassical Style, Bronze, Relief, Angels, Putti, Pedestal, 56 In., Pair
$6,563

Neal Auctions

Garden, Planter, Pedestal, Container, Walter Lamb, Brown Jordan Co., 1950, 25 x 16 In., Pair
$1,500

Los Angeles Modern Auctions

Garden, Seat, Water Lilies, Cattails, Birds, George Jones, Majolica, England, 1800s, 19 x 14 In.
$3,220

Cottone Auctions

Garden, Settee, Fern Pattern, Cast Iron, c.1850, 33 x 54 x 20 In.
$3,072

Neal Auctions

G

213

Garden, Settee, Wire Frame, Black Paint, Victorian, 37 x 76 x 22 In.
$354

Hess Auction Group

Garden, Sprinkler, Duck, Red Breast, Yellow Beak, Iron, 12 In.
$570

Milestone Auctions

Gaudy Dutch, Creamer, Butterfly, Flowers, Blue, Yellow, Helmet Shape
$518

Hess Auction Group

Gaudy Dutch, Creamer, Multicolor, Pink Luster, Petrus Regout, 1830, 4½ In.
$375

Ruby Lane

Sculpture, Pig, Rust, White Paint, Tin, 33 In.	117
Sculpture, Pineapple, Cast Iron, 24 In., Pair	593
Sculpture, Praying Monk, Monastic Robes, Plinth Base, Stone, 46 x 7 In.	952
Sculpture, Torch Shape, Flame Finial, Tin, 64 x 21 In.	2380
Seat, Birds, Flowers, Blue & White, Openwork, Hexagonal, Porcelain, c.1900, 19 In., Pair	984
Seat, Blue & White, Bamboo Forest, Warriors, Barrel Seat, Slat Back, Arms, 26 x 22 In.	1250
Seat, Dragon, Flaming Pearl, Barrel Shape, Relief Carved, Marble, 1900s, 19 In.	296
Seat, Hexagonal, Blue & White, Lotus Blossoms, Openwork, Porcelain, 1800s, 19 In.	948
Seat, Hexagonal, Foo Dog Handle, Concrete, Chinese, 20 x 19 In., Pair	438
Seat, Openwork Design, Blue, White, Barrel Shape, Flat Top, Porcelain, 1800s, 18 In.	800
Seat, Water Lilies, Cattails, Birds, George Jones, Majolica, England, 1800s, 19 x 14 In. *illus*	3220
Settee & Chair, Laurel Pattern, White, Winged Griffin Legs, Cast Iron, 42-In. Settee	1586
Settee, Fern Pattern, Cast Iron, c.1850, 33 x 54 x 20 In. *illus*	3072
Settee, Wire Frame, Black Paint, Victorian, 37 x 76 x 22 In. *illus*	354
Settee, Wirework, Mesh Back, Scrolls, Bracket Legs, Stretcher, England, 1800s, 34 x 61 In.	425
Shrine Lantern, Iron, Helmet Top, Japan, 62 x 26 In.	4800
Sprinkler, Duck, Red Breast, Yellow Beak, Iron, 12 In. *illus*	570
Sundial, Armillary, Bronze, Ringed Sphere, Arrow, Roman Numerals, Pedestal, c.1910, 10 x 7 In.	140
Sundial, Iron, Red, Disc, Arched Support, 10 In.	840
Sundial, Pewter, Roman Numeral Scale, Dotted Border, Triangular Gnomon, 2 In.	431
Table, Cast Iron, Red, c.1910, 27 x 47½ In.	225
Table, Floral Top, Griffin-Form Legs, Cast Iron, 23 In.	200
Table, Iron, Round Top, Curvy Legs, Ring At Base, Stretcher, Scrollwork, 29 x 24 In.	937
Table, Iron, Round Top, Shaped Legs, Cast Spider Stretcher, Scrolls, c.1900, 29 x 40 In.	1067
Table, Ram's Head, Drapery, Green, White, Marble, Carved, 35 x 45¼ In.	1875
Table, Wrought Iron, Round Terrazzo Top, Scroll Base, Painted, Italy, 33½ x 33 In.	895
Tool, Dibber, Ribbed, Redware, 1800s, 9½ In.	62
Trellis, Obelisk, Openwork, Cast Iron, Square Base, 72 x 18 In., Pair	535
Urn, 2 Seated Winged Cherubs On Rim, Flower Garlands, 31½ x 31 In.	1180
Urn, 2 Sections, Flower Blossom, Plinth Form Base, Cast Iron, 32 In.	234
Urn, Animal Heads, Scroll Handles, Zinc, 1880-90, 21 x 30 In., Pair	1200
Urn, Applied Handles, England, Cast Iron, Early 1900s, 17 x 12½ In., Pair	313
Urn, Black, Egg & Dart, Gadrooned, Tapering, Round Foot, Plinth Base, Iron, 30 x 22 In., Pair	535
Urn, Bluegreen, Molded Rim, Leafy Mounts, Square Base, 20¼ x 17 In., Pair	840
Urn, Bouquet Of Flowers, Classical Urn, White Paint, Cast Iron, 1800s, 51½ x 29 x 14 In.	854
Urn, Campana, Egg & Dart, Grapevines, Ram's-Head Handles, Stone, 50 x 33 In., Pair	1190
Urn, Campana, Rolled Rim, Gadrooned, Cast Iron, 37½ x 23¾ In., Pair	590
Urn, Campana, Round Rolled Rim, Egg & Dart, Plinth, Iron, 37½ x 37 In., Pair	1190
Urn, Classical Figures, Grape Arbor, Mask Handles, Fluted Base, 32 x 25½ In.	1920
Urn, Double Handle, Square Plinth, Cast Iron, 41½ x 18½ In.	375
Urn, Egg & Dart, Flared Rim, Ridge Fan, Iron, 24 x 18½ In., 4 Piece	1071
Urn, Georgian, Lid, Tapered Stone Bases, Cast Iron, 29 x 13 In., Pair	1900
Urn, Lid, Campana Shape, Swag, Pineapple Finial, Iron, 48¾ x 14½ In.	714
Urn, Lion, Dolphin, Verdigris, Kramer Bros., Cast Iron, 42 x 35 In., Pair	4105
Urn, Neoclassical, Scroll Handles, Iron, 14¼ In., Pair	1250
Urn, Scroll Handles, Square Base, Cast Iron, 17 In., Pair	138

GAUDY DUTCH pottery was made in England for the American market from about 1810 to 1820. It is a white earthenware with Imari-style decorations of red, blue, green, yellow, and black. Only sixteen patterns of Gaudy Dutch were made: Butterfly, Carnation, Dahlia, Double Rose, Dove, Grape, Leaf, Oyster, Primrose, Single Rose, Strawflower, Sunflower, Urn, War Bonnet, Zinnia, and No Name. Other similar wares are called Gaudy Ironstone and Gaudy Welsh.

Coffeepot, War Bonnet, Dome Lid, 10½ In.	2950
Creamer, Butterfly, Flowers, Blue, Yellow, Helmet Shape	518
Creamer, Carnation, 4½ In.	649
Creamer, Multicolor, Pink Luster, Petrus Regout, 1830, 4½ In. *illus*	375
Creamer, Oyster, Bulbous, Loop Handle, Saucer Foot, c.1840, 5 In.	80
Creamer, Single Rose, 4½ In.	561

G

Creamer, Single Rose, Helmet Shape, c.1850, 4½ In.	1180 to 2242
Cup & Saucer, Double Rose, 5½ In.	295 to 354
Cup & Saucer, Oyster, 5½ In.	177 to 266
Cup & Saucer, Single Rose, 5½ In.	177
Cup & Saucer, Sunflower, 5½ In.	384 to 412
Cup & Saucer, Urn, 5½ In.	413
Plate, Butterfly, 7⅜ In.	531
Plate, Butterfly, 8½ In.	561 to 826
Plate, Carnation, Dot Design Rim, 1800s, 8½ In.	649
Plate, Carnation, Yellow & Green Leaves, Blue Border, 7½ In. ....*illus*	335
Plate, Dove, 8¼ In.	325
Plate, Grape, Minor Wear, 9¾ In.	295
Plate, Oyster, 6½ In.	325
Plate, Single Rose, 5½ In.	153 to 236
Plate, Single Rose, 10 In.	130
Plate, Single Rose, Minor Wear, 6¾ In.	354
Plate, Sunflower, 7½ In. ....*illus*	335
Plate, Sunflower, 7⅜ In.	89
Plate, Sunflower, 8¼ In.	295
Plate, Sunflower, 9⅝ In.	59
Plate, Urn, 7½ In.	106 to 295
Plate, Urn, 8 In.	303
Plate, Urn, Yellow & Green Leaves, 8¼ In.	266
Platter, Leaf, Rectangular, Canted Corners, 10 x 12½ In.	75
Plate, Zinnia, 8⅜ In.	472
Soup, Dish, War Bonnet, 9¾ In.	169
Sugar Lid, War Bonnet, Squat, Boat Shape Lid, Wreath Finial, 1800s, 5¼ In.	3186
Sugar, Lid, Carnation, Knob Finial, Square Handles, Pink Luster Highlights, 5 In.	708
Sugar, Lid, Grape, 5½ In.	1003
Teapot, Lid, War Bonnet, Squat, Curved Handle, 1800s, 6¼ In.	2006
Toddy Plate, Single Rose, 5¾ In.	384
Waste Bowl, Carnation, 3 x 6½ In.	1003
Waste Bowl, Carnation, 5⅝ In.	266
Waste Bowl, Dove, 2⅞ x 5½ In. ....*illus*	590
Waste Bowl, Oyster, 5½ In.	472
Waste Bowl, Single Rose, 3 x 6½ In.	236
Waste Bowl, Single Rose, 5½ In.	590
Waste Bowl, Urn, 6½ In.	236
Waste Bowl, Urn, Flowers & Leaves, 5½ In.	561

GAUDY IRONSTONE is the collector's name for the ironstone wares with the bright patterns similar to Gaudy Dutch. It was made in England for the American market after 1850. There may be other examples found in the listing for Ironstone or under the name of the ceramic factory.

Bowl, Seeing Eye, Rolled Rim, c.1850, 4 x 5¼ In.	57
Pitcher, Octagonal, Red Flowers, Blue Leaves, 1840-50, 8¼ In. ....*illus*	248
Plate, Dinner, Flowers & Fern, Shaped Rim, c.1860, 10 In.	89
Plate, Strawberry, Red, Cobalt Blue Leaves, Green Stems, c.1855, 9 In.	251
Platter, Pinwheel, Blue, Red, Luster, Gilt, Oval, Scalloped, c.1855, 12 x 16 In.	149
Punch Bowl, Pink Luster, Scroll Rim, Dome Foot, c.1855, 5 x 10 In.	186
Sugar, Dome Lid, Pinwheel, Paneled, Squat, Handles, Flared, Finial, c.1850, 8 In.	95

GAUDY WELSH is an Imari-decorated earthenware with red, blue, green, and gold decorations. Most Gaudy Welsh was made in England for the American market. It was made from 1820 to about 1860.

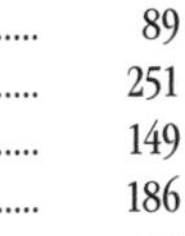

Cup & Saucer, Green & Red Flower, c.1840, 6 In.	88
Mug, Oyster Pattern, Blue, Red, Green, White Ground, c.1890, 4 x 4 In. ....*illus*	48
Pitcher, Flower, Blue, Orange, Pink, Copper Luster, Diamond Pattern, c.1840, 6 In.	92
Plate, Grape Cluster, Leaves, Canted Rim, c.1840, 7 In.	87
Plate, Green & Red Flowers, Shaped Rim, c.1840, 8 In.	95

Gaudy Dutch, Plate, Carnation, Yellow & Green Leaves, Blue Border, 7½ In.
$335

Hess Auction Group

G

> **TIP**
> *If you wash vintage dishes in a dishwasher, use a no- or low-phosphate (under 1.7 percent) dishwashing product. Read the label. Also remember that lemon-oil products are not good for silverware.*

Gaudy Dutch, Plate, Sunflower, 7½ In.
$335

Hess Auction Group

Gaudy Dutch, Waste Bowl, Dove, 2⅞ x 5½ In.
$590

Hess Auction Group

Gaudy Ironstone, Pitcher, Octagonal, Red Flowers, Blue Leaves, 1840-50, 8¼ In.
$248

Ruby Lane

Gaudy Welsh, Mug, Oyster Pattern, Blue, Red, Green, White Ground, c.1890, 4 x 4 In.
$48

Ruby Lane

Gene Autry, Collector Plate, Horses, Guitar, Fences, Nostalgia Collectibles, 1984, 9⅜ In.
$50

Ruby Lane

GEISHA GIRL porcelain was made for export in the late nineteenth century in Japan. It was an inexpensive porcelain often sold in dime stores or used as free premiums. Pieces are sometimes marked with the name of a store. Japanese ladies in kimonos are pictured on the dishes. There are over 125 recorded patterns. Borders of red, blue, green, gold, brown, or several of these colors were used. Modern reproductions are being made.

Chocolate Pot, Geisha, Garden Scene, Flower Border, c.1900, 9¾ In.	70
Cup & Saucer, Geisha, Umbrellas, Trees	20
Sake Set, Geisha, Red Kimono, Paper Label, Carafe, Cups, 4 Piece	75
Tray, Geisha, Bridge, Trees, Reticulated Corners, Cobalt Blue, 11 x 8 In.	55

GENE AUTRY was born in 1907. He began his career as the "Singing Cowboy" in 1928. His first movie appearance was in 1934, his last in 1958. His likeness and that of the Wonder Horse, Champion, were used on toys, books, lunch boxes, and advertisements.

Collector Plate, Horses, Guitar, Fences, Nostalgia Collectibles, 1984, 9⅜ In. ....*illus*	50
Comic Book, Gene Autry Comics, No. 5, 1943	230
Holster Outfit, Leather Belt, Pockets, Cuffs, Spurs, Cap Gun, Box, 1950s, 14 x 21 In.	436
Lunch Box, Thermos, Melody Ranch, Autry On Rearing Champion, Lasso, 1954, 8 In.	683
Standee, World's Greatest Cowboy, & Champion, Cardboard, 1940s, 31 x 59 In.	253
Watch, Tooled Leather Straps, Glow-In-The-Dark Hands, Box, 1948, 4 x 7 In.	253

GIBSON GIRL black-and-blue decorated plates were made in the early 1900s. Twenty-four different 10½-inch plates were made by the Royal Doulton pottery at Lambeth, England. These pictured scenes from the book *A Widow and Her Friends* by Charles Dana Gibson. Another set of 12 9-inch plates featuring pictures of the heads of Gibson Girls had all-blue decoration. Many other items also pictured the famous Gibson Girl.

Plate, A Quiet Dinner With Dr. Bottles, 10½ In.	54
Plate, Failing To Find Rest, 10½ In.	86
Plate, Head, Portrait, 9 In.	152
Plate, Miss Babbles, The Authoress Calls & Reads Aloud, 10½ In.	61
Plate, She Contemplates The Cloister, 10½ In.	86
Plate, She Is Disturbed By A Vision, 10½ In.	111
Plate, Some Think That She Has Remained In Retirement, 1900, 10½ In.	265
Plate, They Take A Morning Ride, 10½ In.	112

GIRL SCOUT collectors search for anything pertaining to the Girl Scouts, including uniforms, publications, and old cookie boxes. The Girl Scout movement started in 1912, two years after the Boy Scouts. It began under Juliette Gordon Low of Savannah, Georgia. The first Girl Scout cookies were sold in 1928.

Compass, Fob, Silver Plate, Nickel, Round Glass Top, US Gauge Co., c.1935, 1½ In.	95
Cup, Travel, Telescoping, Emblem, Aluminum, c.1930	20
Doll, Uniform, Box, Terri Lee Doll Co., 1950s, 8 In.	90
Pin, Gold Tone, Green, Girl Scouts, Girls Profile, c.1980, ⅞ In.	10
Pin, Member, Mariners, 1950s, 1⅛ In. ....*illus*	35
Uniform, Jumper, Pants, Green, Blouse, Girl Scout Label, Pleated Pockets, Polyester, Size 10	15

GLASS factories that are well known are listed in this book under the factory name. This category lists pieces made by less well-known factories. Additional pieces of glass are listed in this book under the type of glass, in the categories Glass-Art, Glass-Blown, Glass-Bohemian, Glass-Contemporary, Glass-Midcentury, Glass-Venetian, and under the factory name.

Bowl, Rocaille Molded, Pierced Gilt Base, France, c.1900, 11¾ x 12½ In.	1500
Cake Stand, Clear Baluster Stem, Round Foot, Ruby Thumbprint Rim, c.1850, 7 x 9 In.	360

Canister, Blown, Clear With Applied Cobalt Bands, Mid 1800s, 10 ½ In.	390
Cocktail Set, Ice Bowl, 6 Blue Wine Glasses, Tray, Art Moderne, 8 Piece	112
Compote, Incised, Gilt, Pair, 12 ½ x 9 ¾ In.	250
Compote, Iridescent Blue, Purple & Gold, Flower & Leaves, Ruffled Rim, 1910s, 9 In.	375
Compote, Thumbprint Pattern, Round Foot, Wide Rim, Shaped Stem, c.1850, 11 x 12 In.	420
Pitcher, Cut & Enameled, Flower & Gold Scrolling, Trefoil Rim, Gold Accents, 10 ½ In.	374
Sculpture, 2 Fish, Loop Shape, 11 In.	875
Sugar, Pillar, Clear, Wafter Stem, Folded, Flat Rim, Etched Garland Design, 1846, 4 x 5 In.	480
Vase, Hyacinth, Pattern Molded, Teal Green, 12 Ribs, Pontil, 1840-70, 5 ¾ In. ....*illus*	173
Wine, Blanka, Josair Crystal, Petal Shape Bowl, Tapered Square Stem, 7 In., 12 Piece	129

GLASS-ART. Art glass means any of the many forms of glassware made during the late nineteenth or early twentieth century. These wares were expensive when they were first made and production was limited. Art glass is not the typical commercial glass that was made in large quantities, and most of the art glass was produced by hand methods. Later twentieth-century glass is listed under Glass-Contemporary, Glass-Midcentury, or Glass-Venetian. Even more art glass may be found in categories such as Burmese, Cameo Glass, Tiffany, and other factory names.

Blue, Green, Ruffled Rim, Pulled Feathers, 12 ¾ In.	63
Bowl, Frosted, Red, Yellow, Sand Cast, 9 x 16 In.	248
Bowl, Iron Stand, Mottled Mauve, Verrerie D'Art, France, Early 1900s, 8 ¾ x 10 In.	687
Bowl, Pink, Blue, Gold Flecks, 16 In.	81
Bowl, Thumbprint, Iridescent Gold, Blue, Green, WMF, German, 3 x 5 In.	212
Charger, 2 Golden Fish, Signed Cole, Vermont, 19 ¼ In.	144
Dresser Jar, Carved Red Flowers, Frosted White, Silver Rim, St. Louis, France, c.1900, 3 x 5 In.	1625
Flower Frog, Clear, France, 4 ½ x 3 In.	30
Goblet, Iridescent, Trumpet, Flowers, Amedee Duc De Caranza, c.1902, 6 x 3 In.	875
Panel, Bird & Basket, Secessionist Style, Cream Slag Ground, Donaldson, c.1912, 11 x 13 In.	2500
Sherbet, Iridescent Gold, Twisted Stem, Round Foot, 4 ½ In., 12 Piece	134
Tumbler, Aqua Blue, Opalescent Poinsettias, Leaves, Frosted Scrolls, c.1890, 4 In.	80
Tumbler, Poinsettias & Leaves, Aqua Blue, Opalescent, Frosted Scrolls, c.1890, 4 In.	80
Vase, Applied Green Tadpoles, Stuart & Sons, 1920s, 8 In. ....*illus*	300
Vase, Blue, Gilt Band, France, 1900, 12 ½ In.	225
Vase, Bulbous, Iridescent Green, Blue, Dripping Handles, 7 ¼ x 5 In.	206
Vase, Clear, Turquoise Threading, Flared Rim, Ball Stem, Dome Foot, c.1900, 8 In.	42
Vase, Controlled Bubble, Green, Maurice Marinot, 1920s, 5 ¾ x 4 ¾ In. ....*illus*	3300
Vase, Gilt Trim, Clear Cased In Cobalt, Chrysanthemum, Iris, 6 x 3 ¾ In.	212
Vase, Gilt, Bronze, Rooster, France, 22 In.	4000
Vase, Gold Iridescent, Swirl, 7 In.	84
Vase, Green & Pink Iridescent, Twist Stripes, Low, Ruffled, c.1900, 3 ½ x 7 In.	475
Vase, Green Iridescent, Ripples, Pinched, c.1900, 3 ¼ In.	137
Vase, Green, Gold Iridescent, Tapered, 9 x 4 ¼ In.	312
Vase, Internally Decorated Crackled Glass, Signed, Eugene Leveille, 1880s, 7 ½ x 3 ½ In.	1000
Vase, Iridescent Blue, Applied Flowers, Silver Lip, Signed Albert Baker, 1898, 6 x 3 In.	112
Vase, Iridescent Gold, Small Mouth, 6 In.	246
Vase, Iridized Myra, Blue, Green, Fluted Mouth, 3 x 2 ½ In.	76
Vase, Luster Glaze, Snails, France, 1900s, 20 ¾ x 6 In.	1125
Vase, Multicolor, Angelfish, Seagrasses, 10 ½ In.	120
Vase, Opaque Lavender, Swirl, Bust Beadwork, Torches, J. Riedel, 1870s, 5 x 2 In.	112
Vase, Pompeian, Pinched, Red, Iridescent, c.1900, 6 In.	437
Vase, Red, Dangling Berries, 1920, 23 In.	468
Vase, Streaks, White, Green Red, Wavy Cylinder, Scroll Rim, Crackled, 1880s, 8 In.	1000

GLASS-BLOWN. Blown glass was formed by forcing air through a rod into molten glass. Early glass and some forms of art glass were hand blown. Other types of glass were molded or pressed.

Basket, Clear, Cobalt Blue, Black Lines, Round, Wavy Rim, 8 x 10 In., 5 Piece	8750

G

Girl Scout, Pin, Member, Mariners, 1950s, 1 ⅛ In.
$35

Ruby Lane

Glass, Vase, Hyacinth, Pattern Molded, Teal Green, 12 Ribs, Pontil, 1840-70, 5 ¾ In.
$173

Glass Works Auctions

Glass-Art, Vase, Applied Green Tadpoles, Stuart & Sons, 1920s, 8 In.

$300

Woody Auction

Glass-Art, Vase, Controlled Bubble, Green, Maurice Marinot, 1920s, 5¾ x 4¾ In.

$3,300

Woody Auction

Glass-Blown, Creamer, Aquamarine, Flared To Rim, Hollow Handle, Zanesville, Ohio, c.1840, 4⅝ In.

$2,925

Norman Heckler & Company

Bowl, Orange, Round Bottom, Wide Rim, Gold Leaf Inclusions, 1930s, 4 x 9 In.	1875
Cake Plate, Clear, Folded Rim, Footed, 4 Stems, Panel Cut, Flint Glass, c.1840, 7 In.	300
Carafe, Pillar Mold, Clear, Deep Ribbing, Squat, Flared Rim, c.1850, 4½ In.	313
Carboy, Green, 1800s, 25½ x 19 In.	100
Carboy, Wine, Pale Green, 18 x 12½ In.	125
Champagne, Cranberry, Twisted Stems, Italy, 1900s, 7½ In., 10 Piece	750
Champagne, Etched, Flowers, Leaves, Aspinwall Crest, c.1900, 4⅜ In., 6 Piece	141
Compote, Clear, Baluster Stem, Folded Rim, Flint Glass, c.1840, 10 x 11 In.	270
Creamer, Aquamarine, Flared To Rim, Hollow Handle, Zanesville, Ohio, c.1840, 4⅝ In...*illus*	2925
Creamer, Cobalt Blue, Vertical Ribs, Horizontal Bands, Curled Handle, 4⅜ In.	2185
Decanter, 8-Pillar Mold, Clear, Cobalt Blue Ribs, Bell Form, Neck Ring, Stopper, 14 In.	403
Decanter, Bell Shape, Ribbed, Original Shaped Stopper, 13 In., Pair	448
Fishbowl, Leech Jar, Clear, Folded Rim & Feet, Flint Glass, c.1840, 15½ In.	450
Fly Catcher, Etched Bamboo Design, Shouldered, Spherical Stopper, Scroll Feet, c.1890, 13 In. .*illus*	732
Jar, Apothecary, Pillar Mold, Folded Rim, Pedestal Foot, Lid, Finial, c.1850, 18 In.	375
Jug, Cobalt Blue, Bulbous, Wavy Rim, White Loop Handle At Neck, 1930s, 7 x 5 In.	2500
Pitcher, Folded Lip, Threaded Neck, Loop Handle, Aqua Glass, c.1840, 7 In.	1200
Pitcher, Marbrie Loop Pattern, Clear, Opaque White Looping, Footed, 7 In.	300
Plate, Salad, Flowers, Leaves, Gilt Rim, Aspinwall Crest, c.1900, 8 In., 9 Piece	413
Porringer, Saratoga Green, Bulbous Bowl, Applied Ear Handle, 3⅞ In.	2691
Salt, Diamond Pattern, Cobalt Blue, Cup, Pedestal Foot, Flint Glass, c.1840, 3 In.	5880
Salt, Hat Shape, Yellow Green, Annular Rings, Flared Brim, Pontil, 2 x 3¾ In. *illus*	6435
Sculpture, Bird, Frosty White, Bubble Pattern, Black Feet, Gold Leaf, 1930s, 12 In.	2125
Sculpture, Horse, Clear To Orange, Standing, Shaped Mane & Tail, 15 x 14 In.	1750
Sculpture, Mallard Duck, Multicolor Swirls, 1960s, 4 x 8 In.	1188
Syrup, Clear, Teardrop Shape, Ribs, Handle, Pewter Lid, Bird Finial, c.1850, 11 In.	480
Urn, Emerald Green, Applied Side Handles, 9¼ In.	108
Vase, Cobalt Blue Leaf Shapes, Bulbous, Tapered Neck, Flat Rim, 1930s, 8 In.	938
Vase, Filigree, Bubbles, Clear, Pear Shape, Flared Rim, Ring Foot, 1950s, 15 In.	1000
Vase, Frosted White, Lines, Swollen Shoulder, Pinched Neck, Flat Rim, 1940, 10 In.	5313
Vase, Silver Metallic, Black Crackle, Dots, Dimpled, Cutout Rim, c.1950, 7 x 6 In.	4013
Vase, White Frost, Swirly Stripe Texture, Square, Arched Rim, c.1935, 8 x 5 In.	1063

GLASS-BOHEMIAN. Bohemian glass is an ornate overlay or flashed glass made during the Victorian era. It has been reproduced in Bohemia, which is now a part of the Czech Republic. Glass made from 1875 to 1900 is preferred by collectors.

Basket, Cobalt Blue, Clear, Rose, Leaves, 8 x 7½ x 5 In.	249
Basket, Flared Rim, Amber Glass, Diamonds, Yellow To Blue, 4¾ x 10¾ In.	265
Beaker, Huntsman, Dog, Opal Glass, Pink, 1850, 4¼ In.	932
Box, Molded, Blown, Brass Trim, Applied Flowers, 5¾ x 6¼ In.	318
Box, Red Cut To Clear, Oval, Lid, c.1900, 5 x 3 x 4 In.	1036
Compote, Bronze, Red Cut To White, 14 x 13 In.	250
Compote, Nude Women, Fountain, White Horses, 6⅜ x 5¾ In.	123
Decanter Set, Cut, Hobstars, Decorated Gilt Bands, 10 In. Decanter, 6 Piece	312
Decanter, Amber, Threaded, Spot, Tadpoles, 11 x 6 In., Pair	354
Decanter, Cobalt Blue Cased, Decorated, Scrollwork, Spire Stoppers, Gilt, 19 In., Pair ..... *illus*	5000
Decanter, Gilt, Long Neck, Squat Body, Lace Pattern, 12¼ x 5½ In.	212
Pokal, Cased Glass, White, Gilt, Rococo Gilt Reserve, Flowers, 18½ x 4½ In.	76
Pokal, Intaglio Hunt, Landscape, Stags, Squirrels, Birds, Dogs, Castles, 1800s, 14¼ In.	96
Pokal, Intaglio, Hunt, Landscape, c.1880, 14 In.	625
Pokal, Lid, Ruby Flashed, Engraved Hunter, Dog & Stag, 13 In., Pair. *illus*	500
Punch Bowl, Lid, Green & White, Leaves, Cattails, c.1890, 17 In.	895
Urn, Lid, Ruby Flashed, Engraved Deer In Forest, Square Base, 13 In., Pair	360
Vase, Art Nouveau, Ruffled Rim, Iridescent Yellow, Spatter, Kralik, 9 x 13 In.	1003
Vase, Cranberry, Opaque White, Waisted, 11 In., Pair	625
Vase, Cut Glass Bands, Amber & Blue Stain Cut To Clear, Footed, 11 In., Pair	480
Vase, Flared Rim, Iridescent Gold, Pulled Feather, Blue, Lavender, 9¼ In.	738
Vase, Flower Reserves, Crosshatch, Red, White, Flared Neck, 10 x 3⅝ In., Pair	177

Glass-Blown, Fly Catcher, Etched Bamboo Design, Shouldered, Spherical Stopper, Scroll Feet, c.1890, 13 In.
$732

Neal Auctions

Dale Chihuly
Dale Chihuly (1941–) is the best-known of the late-twentieth-century studio glassmakers. Chihuly blew early pieces himself. After several injuries, he had others do the glassblowing. He still designs the pieces.

Glass-Bohemian, Decanter, Cobalt Blue Cased, Decorated, Scrollwork, Spire Stoppers, Gilt, 19 In., Pair
$5,000

New Orleans Auction Galleries

Glass-Bohemian, Pokal, Lid, Ruby Flashed, Engraved Hunter, Dog & Stag, 13 In., Pair
$500

New Orleans Auction Galleries

Glass-Bohemian, Wedding Cup, Woman, Skirt, Gilt, Daisies, Cherub, F. Heckert, 11 In.
$1,440

The Stein Auction Company

Glass-Contemporary, Bowl, Macchia, Spots, Dale Chihuly, 2002, 14½ x 21 In.
$10,625

Rago Arts and Auction Center

Glass-Contemporary, Bowl, Pilchuck Basket, Blown, Dale Chihuly, 1977, 5½ In.
$3,750

Rago Arts and Auction Center

TIP
Forged glass signatures, including Steuben, Quezal, and Tiffany, are appearing on newer glass. This has been true for years. Do not trust a signature. Be sure the glass is the proper shape and type to have been produced by the original factory or artist. Fake marks are written with a diamond-tipped drill or are acid-stamped. All look real.

Glass-Blown, Salt, Hat Shape, Yellow Green, Annular Rings, Flared Brim, Pontil, 2 x 3¾ In.
$6,435

Norman Heckler & Company

Glass-Contemporary, Sculpture, Emergence, Dominick Labino, 1980, 7 x 4 In.
$4,688

Rago Arts and Auction Center

Glass-Contemporary, Sculpture, Esmeralda, Sandblasted, Carved, Wood, Steel, Keke Cribbs, 1994, 19 In.
$8,125

Rago Arts and Auction Center

Glass-Contemporary, Sculpture, Geometry Of Meaning-80 Degrees, Laminated, M. Taylor, 31 In.
$5,313

Rago Arts and Auction Center

Glass-Contemporary, Sculpture, Muse In Mist, Cast, Cut, Polished, Mark Peiser, 14 x 9½ In.
$9,375

Rago Arts and Auction Center

Glass-Contemporary, Teapot, Checkerboard, Murrine, Aventurine, R. Marquis, 1978, 6 In.
$4,375

Rago Arts and Auction Center

Glass-Contemporary, Vase, Applied Turquoise Glass Knobs, Geometric Designs, Dan Dailey, 1992, 21 In.
$10,800

Brunk Auctions

Vase, Fritz Heckert Changeant, Curlicue Rim, Dimpled Body, 8 In.	115
Vase, Gold, Cranberry, Swirls, Pinched, Rolled Rim, Kralik, 12 ¾ x 6 In.	276
Vase, Green Rim, 3 Green Tadpoles, Kralik, 5 ¼ In.	204
Vase, Iridescent Green, Flat Threaded, Gourd Base, Long, Narrow Neck, 8 ½ x 4 ½ In.	76
Vase, Iridescent, Blue Green, Pewter Overlay, Kralik, 10 ½ x 8 ½ In., Pair.	3294
Vase, Lid, Cobalt Blue, Cut To Clear, Urn Shape, Deer, Landscape, 54 x 13 In., Pair.	708
Vase, Mold Blown, Blue, Gilt, Flowers, Leaves, 1900, 19 ¾ In.	531
Vase, Oil Spot, Iridescent Gold, Magenta Highlights, Pallme-Koenig, 14 x 7 In.	200
Vase, Opal Over Brown With Dark Threading, Ruffled Rim, Kralik, 3 ¾ x 5 In.	207
Vase, Red, Applied Glass Band, Kralik, 8 ½ x 6 In.	61
Vase, Ruby, Gilt Decoration, Flattened Rim, Narrow Neck, Red, Pedestal Foot, 15 x 7 In., Pair..	8271
Vase, Ruby, Gilt, Checkerboard Decoration Band, Scalloped Base, 15 ¾ In.	188
Vase, Ruffled Lip, Kralik, 17 In.	50
Vase, Trumpet, Diamonds, 18 In.	313
Vase, White Cut To Green, Spots, Flowers, 9 In.	75
Wedding Cup, Woman, Skirt, Gilt, Daisies, Cherub, F. Heckert, 11 In. ....*illus*	1440

GLASS-CONTEMPORARY includes pieces by glass artists working after 1970. Many of these pieces are free-form, one-of-a-kind sculptures. Paperweights by contemporary artists are listed in the Paperweight category. Earlier studio glass may be found listed under Glass-Midcentury or Glass-Venetian.

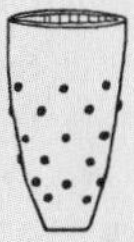

Basket, Clear To Green, Applied Handle, Blown, R. Levin, 1993, 16 In.	126
Bowl, Clear, White Ribbon Swirl Pattern, Tapered, Wide Rim, c.1978, 5 x 9 In.	1188
Bowl, Cornflower Blue, Pulled Feathers, Blue Outline, Opal Ground, Charles Lotton, 5 x 7 In..	690
Bowl, Fan Shape, Multicolor, Fused Threads, Folded Rim, 8 x 15 In.	7500
Bowl, Fish Shape, Green Enameled With Red Dots, Maurice Heaton, 2 ⅝ x 14 ¾ In.	460
Bowl, Macchia, Moroccan, Ruffled Edge, D. Chihuly, Signed, 2003, 5 ½ x 10 x 9 In., Pair.........	5000
Bowl, Macchia, Poppy Red, Black Rim, D. Chihuly, 8 In.	2750
Bowl, Macchia, Spots, Dale Chihuly, 2002, 14 ½ x 21 In. ....*illus*	10625
Bowl, Macchia, Wavy Free-Form, Swirls, Blue, D. Chihuly, 1982, 15 In.	8125
Bowl, Pilchuck Basket, Blown, Dale Chihuly, 1977, 5 ½ In. ....*illus*	3750
Bowl, Ruby, Gold, Wavy Lines, Spotting, Tapered, Ruffle Rim, 1983, 3 Piece.............	5313
Bowl, Seaform, D. Chihuly, c.1984, 9 x 22 ½ x 18 In.	6325
Bowl, Shell Shape, Folding Rim, Pink, Feathery Edge, 1986, 6 x 14 In.	8750
Bowl, Undulating Rim, Brown, Green, Blue, Brian Heritage, 6 ½ x 15 In.	188
Box, Liuli, Gold & Silver Leaf Inclusions, Hexagonal, K. Fujita, 3 x 3 ½ In.	3625
Bust, Relax Series, Pastel Swirls, Black Base, Dino Rosin, 21 ½ x 10 ½ In.	1298
Bust, Woman, Swirls, Frosted, Black Base, Dino Rosin, Italy, 13 x 5 ¼ In.	1416
Group, Lovers, Gold Leaf, Black Glass Base, Dino Rosin, Italy, 29 In.	325
Platter, Translucent Yellow, Spiral Splatter With Stand, Kent Ibsen, 15 ¼ In.	115
Sculpture, Amber & Gold Luster Rings, Swirling, Black, 1980s, 9 x 17 In.	430
Sculpture, Amethyst Glass Medallion, Applied Buttons, T.P. Sand, 18 In.	236
Sculpture, Brick-Like Grid, Brown, Blue, c.1980, 42 x 36 In.	1968
Sculpture, Cobra, Calcedonia, Loredano Rosin, c.1975, 19 ¾ x 9 ¾ x 10 ¾ In.	5250
Sculpture, Emergence, Dominick Labino, 1980, 7 x 4 In. ....*illus*	4688
Sculpture, Esmeralda, Sandblasted, Carved, Wood, Steel, Keke Cribbs, 1994, 19 In. ....*illus*	8125
Sculpture, Frosty White, Blue, Free-Form, Waves, Shards, 1987, 9 x 12 In.	6250
Sculpture, Geometry Of Meaning-80 Degrees, Laminated, M. Taylor, 31 In...............*illus*	5313
Sculpture, Muse In Mist, Cast, Cut, Polished, Mark Peiser, 14 x 9 ½ In..............*illus*	9375
Sculpture, Seaform, Parrot Green Persian, D. Chihuly, 2 Piece	7200
Sculpture, Stacked Wavy Shapes, Clear, Amber & Aqua, 1975, 3 x 4 In.	2750
Sculpture, Teapot Goblet, White, Yellow Threading, Marquis, 1989, 10 In.	5000
Sculpture, Tripod, Purple, White, Scroll Legs, Flower Shape Top, 1981, 7 x 11 In.	688
Sculpture, Tropical Fish, Richard Jolley, 11 ¼ x 8 ¾ In.	4216
Teapot, Checkerboard, Murrine, Aventurine, R. Marquis, 1978, 6 In...................*illus*	4375
Teapot, Dome Lid, Orange & White Squares, Lid, Swollen Spout, 1980, 7 x 10 In.	4063
Teapot, Inverted Funnel, Wavy Squares, Loop Handle, Lid, 1980, 6 x 7 In.	3625
Teapot, Multicolor, Cased, Spotted Lid, Rick Eckerd, 10 ½ x 5 In.	241

Glass-Contemporary, Vase, Catena, Canes, Murrine & Powder Inserts, Etched Yoichio Ohira, 1998, 6 x 5 In. $7,500

Rago Arts and Auction Center

G

Glass-Contemporary, Vase, Hopi, Blown, Lino Tagliapietra, Italy, 1994, 8 x 11 In. $13,750

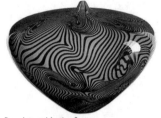

Rago Arts and Auction Center

Glass-Contemporary, Vase, Oggigiorno, Fused Threads, Signed Z. M. Zynsky, 2002, 12 In. $11,250

Rago Arts and Auction Center

GLASS-CONTEMPORARY

Glass-Contemporary, Vase, Orange Bird Of Paradise, Orient & Flume, S. Beyers, 5¾ x 3½ In. $395

Ruby Lane

Glass-Contemporary, Vase, Pink, White Blossoms, Vines, Iridescent Blue, Charles Lotton, 1979, 7¾ In. $518

Early Auction Company

Glass-Contemporary, Vase, Teasers Series, Murrine, S.R. Powell, 1989, 31½ In. $11,250

Rago Arts and Auction Center

Tray, Raised Edge, Gold Flecked Panels, Red Diamonds, Lynn Latimer, 12 x 9 In.	23
Vase, Amber, Wavy Bands, Blue Splashes, Red Rim, Folded, Dale Chihuly, 8 In.	3259
Vase, Applied Turquoise Glass Knobs, Geometric Designs, Dan Dailey, 1992, 21 In. ...*illus*	10800
Vase, Aurene Blue, Opal, Gold, Pulled Swirls, Tapered, Flared Rim, 1974, 8 In.	826
Vase, Black, Multicolor Shapes, Shouldered, Tapered, Narrow Lip, 1980, 8 In.	5625
Vase, Blue & Green, King Tut Swirls, Globe Bottle Shape, 1974, 7 x 7 In.	354
Vase, Blue Iridescent, Pink Neck, Tapered, Lundberg Studios, c.1994, 14⅛ In.	450
Vase, Bright Yellow, White Feather, Folded Rim, Charles Lotton, 8¼ In.	288
Vase, Cabinet, Opal Body, Iridescent Blue Heavy, Mark Cantor, Lundberg, c.1975, 3½ In.	604
Vase, Cased Layers, Purple, Gold, Correia, 1980s, 12 In.	74
Vase, Catena, Canes, Murrine & Powder Inserts, Etched Yoichio Ohira, 1998, 6 x 5 In.......*illus*	7500
Vase, Cinnamon, Stripes, 7 In.	4250
Vase, Circle Slash, Sandblasted, Copper, Spherical, Dome Rim, 1981, 4 In.	5625
Vase, Clear Base, Wide Blue Bowl, Mark Sudduth, 10 x 8 In.	165
Vase, Cobalt Blue, Abstract Face, Black, Red, Carlos Pebaque, 6½ In.	246
Vase, Cobalt Blue, Orange Flower Petals, Swollen Oval, 1978, 5 In.	531
Vase, Cone, Frosted, Green, Leaves, Flowers, Tommie Rush, c.1990, 12½ In.	154
Vase, Contemporary, Green Body, Shoulder, Iridescent Pulled Silver Swirl, 6½ In.	1150
Vase, Cylinder, Navajo Blanket, Yellow, Streaks, D. Chihuly, 1975, 11 In.	22500
Vase, Dark To Pale Amber, Bottle Shape, Stick Neck, c.1975, 32½ In.	495
Vase, Faces, Multicolor, Acid Etched, Tapered, Poland, 1986, 5 x 7 In.	1625
Vase, Flume, Bruce Sillars & Greg Held, Aurene Blue & Red Flowers, c.1983, 14¾ In.	460
Vase, Frosted, Green, Cutwork, Joseph Becker, 1999, 12¼ In.	277
Vase, Glass & Brass Box, Silver & Lime Green & Burgundy, Jack Ink, 8 x 10 In.	920
Vase, Green Iridescent, Flaring Rim, Dan Shuara, Orient & Flume, Dan Shura, 1982, 5¼ x 3½ In.	383
Vase, Green, Flowers, Orient & Flume, 6½ In.	63
Vase, Hopi, Blown, Lino Tagliapietra, Italy, 1994, 8 x 11 In. ...*illus*	13750
Vase, Internal Bands, Mottled Green, Red, White Rim, Free-Form, W. Morris, 19 In.	1778
Vase, Jack-In-The-Pulpit, Deep Red Form, Iridescent Silver Face, Signed, Lundberg, 13 In.	518
Vase, Kent Ibsen, Aqua Bulbous Base, Gold Swirl, Cased In Crystal, Signed, c.1975, 15 In.	345
Vase, Lime Green, Dark Green Dots, Cranberry Ground, Pinched, Dale Chihuly, 8 In.	2370
Vase, Lincoln Drape Light Blue & Gold Aurene, Signed, Charles Lotton, c.1973, 7⅞ x 6 In.	345
Vase, Macchia, Cinnamon, D. Chihuly, Signed, 2001, 6¼ x 7½ x 6½ In.	3438
Vase, Multi Flora With Pink Flowers Against Dark Blue, Signed, c.1981, 8 In.	633
Vase, Multi Flora, Pink Lilies, Leaves, Charles Lotton, 1990, 12¼ x 4¾ In.	944
Vase, Murine, Multicolor, Bottle Shape, Stick Neck, Marked, 34 x 18 In.	8750
Vase, Oggigiorno, Fused Threads, Signed Z. M. Zynsky, 2002, 12 In. ...*illus*	11250
Vase, Orange Bird Of Paradise, Orient & Flume, S. Beyers, 5¾ x 3½ In....*illus*	395
Vase, Paperweight, Berry Color, Flower Reeds, Green Leaves, Oval, 1978, 6 x 4 In.	3750
Vase, Pink Cameo, Footed, Amethyst, Dancing Nudes, Signed, K. Murphy, c.1996, 7½ In.	288
Vase, Pink Coral & Jellyfish, Signed, Chris Hellman & Joyce Roessler, c.1987, 6 x 6½ In.	374
Vase, Pink, Red Wavy Lines, Squat, Bulbous, Bumps, 1985, 2 x 5 In.	1875
Vase, Pink, Threaded, Silhouettes, Free-Form, Dale Chihuly, 1980, 13 In.	8125
Vase, Pink, White Blossoms, Vines, Iridescent Blue, Charles Lotton, 1979, 7¾ In. ...*illus*	518
Vase, Purple Fish & Green Plants Against Cobalt, Lee Hudin, Orient & Flume, Signed, 5 In.	316
Vase, Purple Haze, Silvery White, Applied Purple Shapes, Oval, 1978, 7 In.	1875
Vase, Running Man, Blue, Iridescent Sand, 9¼ x 8¾ In.	1091
Vase, Seafoam, Teal, Blue, Amber Wave, D. Chihuly, 8 x 7½ In.	4484
Vase, Silvery Blue Feather Patterns Over Cobalt, Signed, David Lotton, c.1988, 5¾ In.	115
Vase, Squat, Gold, Green Iridescent, Orient & Flume, 6 In.	108
Vase, Teasers Series, Murrine, S.R. Powell, 1989, 31½ In. ...*illus*	11250
Vase, Tulip Shape, Iridescent Blue, Steven Maslach, 1983, 10 In.	108
Vase, White, Orange, Cobalt Blue Slashes, Etched, Tubular, Rounded, 1985, 10 In.	4375
Vase, Yellow, Green Interior, Flowers, Orient & Flume, 12 In.	218
Wine, Champagne, Iridescent, David Fogi, c.1980, 7 In., 6 Piece	53

GLASS-CUT, *see Cut Glass category.*

GLASS-DEPRESSION, *see Depression Glass category.*

G

GLASS-MIDCENTURY refers to art glass made from the 1940s to the early 1970s. Some glass factories, such as Baccarat or Orrefors, are listed under their own categories. Earlier glass may be listed in the Glass-Art and Glass-Contemporary categories. Italian glass may be found in Glass-Venetian.

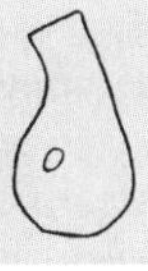

Bowl, Blue, Transparent, Mottled, 20 x 21 In.		279
Pitcher, Swirls, Red, Yellow, Blue, Dark Red Handle, 13½ In. ....*illus*		97
Sculpture, Amber, Arch Shape, Signed, H. Littleton, 1972, 5 x 4½ In.		1750
Sculpture, Blue Irises, Clear Leaves, Ronnie Hughes, 12½ In.		113
Sculpture, Curved Horn, Bird's-Eye, Turquoise, Copper Stem & Base, 1960s, 12 In.		4063
Sculpture, Figural, Blue, Round Base, c.1970, 23 x 11 In.		590
Sculpture, Flared Triangle, Orange Stripes, Copper Stem & Base, 1960s, 7 x 9 In.		4375
Sculpture, Red Flower, Clear Leaves, Ronnie Hughes, 16½ In.		156
Sculpture, Running Horse, Pino Signoretto, 1970s, 15½ x 25 In.		590
Sculpture, Yellow Sunflower, Clear Leaves, Ronnie Hughes, 12½ In.		113
Vase, Amber, Applied Shapes, Bowl, Wavy Rim, Tubular Foot, 1960s, 8 x 10 In.		875
Vase, Applied Balls & Spears, Cobalt Blue, Yellow, Pear Shape, 1965, 14 In.		3625
Vase, Aqua Marine, Bulbous, Molded Tendrils, Turn Down Rim, 1970, 6 In.		295
Vase, Ariel, Blue Black, Angelfish, Bubbles, Reflection Glaze, 1973, 5 In.		384
Vase, Black Amethyst, Iridescent Silver, Lavender, King Tut, 1972, 8 In.		472
Vase, Blue, Blown, Sandblasted, Copper Plated, Marvin Lipofsky, 1962, 12 x 6½ In...........*illus*		4375
Vase, Blue, Green, Lines & Streaks, Beaker, Asymmetrical Angled Rim, 1950s, 14 In.		2625
Vase, Blue, Marvin Lipofsky, Signed, 1966, 9 x 7 x 6¼ In.		2250
Vase, Citron Yellow, Brown, King Tut Pattern, Tubular, Peiser, 1971, 14 In.		266
Vase, Dark Green, Copper Threading, Oval, Tubular Neck, 1960s, 8 x 5 In.		594
Vase, Elongated Gourd, Sculpted Collar, Rolled Rim, Dark Amber, 1965, 9 In.		1375
Vase, Frosted, Pleated, Wavy Cylinder, Crimped Rim, Wirkkala, c.1950, 8 In.		469
Vase, Gooseneck, Slender Form, Engraved, Dominick Labino, 1963, 15⅛ In.		288
Vase, Gourd, Blue Flowers & Green Leaves Against White, Signed, c.1973, 6 In.		288
Vase, Green Swirl, D. Labino, H. Littleton, 1965, 12 x 4 In. ....*illus*		938
Vase, Green, Blue, Amber, Streaked, Bulbous, Dimpled, Pinched Neck, 1970, 7 In.		450
Vase, Mini-Me, Stacked Multicolor Discs, Baluster, Flared, S. Hutter, 9 In.		1422
Vase, Ruby Red, Paneled, Rounded Top, 3 Arched Swirl Feet, D. Labino, 1965, 10 In..........*illus*		584
Vase, Smoky To White Frost, Drips, Triangular, Swollen Stick Neck, 1960s, 13 In.		2375
Vase, White & Topaz, Oval Bubble Design, Wavy Square Shape, 1962, 12 In.		3750

GLASS-PRESSED, *see Pressed Glass category.*

GLASS-VENETIAN. Venetian glass has been made near Venice, Italy, since the thirteenth century. Thin, colored glass with applied decoration is favored, although many other types have been made. Collectors have recently become interested in the Art Deco and 1950s designs. Glass was made on the Venetian island of Murano from 1291. The output dwindled in the late seventeenth century but began to flourish again in the 1850s. Some of the old techniques of glassmaking were revived, and firms today make traditional designs and original modern glass. Since 1981, the name *Murano* may be used only on glass made on Murano Island. Other pieces of Italian glass may be found in the Glass-Contemporary and Glass-Midcentury categories of this book.

Aquarium, Stefano Toso, 9¾ x 14¼ In.		3050
Bottle, Banded, Blown, Etched, Bands, Ball Stopper, Fulvio Bianconi, 1960s, 18 In...........*illus*		1063
Bowl, Black, White, Amber, Green, Swirls, Speckled, Flared, Wavy Rim, 3 x 9 In.		549
Bowl, Clamshell, Iridescent, Ercole Barovier, 1930s, 8½ x 8½ In., Pair		1000
Bowl, Dancing Mouse, Enamel, V. Zecchin, 12¼ In.		2375
Bowl, Label, Archimede Seguso Murano, c.1970, 4 x 10½ In. ....*illus*		1063
Bowl, Multicolor Streaks, Copper Inclusions, Ring Foot, c.1955, 4 x 8 In.		3000
Compote, Latticinio, Pink, Copper, Swirl, Gold, Flared, Murano, c.1875, 4 x 8 In.		250
Console Set, Yellow, 2 Candlesticks, Centerpiece, 3 Piece		2812
Decanter, Dark Purple, Spun Thread, Matching Stopper, Paolo Venini, 7 x 4⅝ x 3¼ In.		748
Decanter, Round Bottom, Swollen Neck, Smoky Topaz, Murano, 1987, 11 In.		1375
Dish, Sea Shell, Opalescent, 3⅛ x 8⅝ In.		100

Glass-Midcentury, Pitcher, Swirls, Red, Yellow, Blue, Dark Red Handle, 13½ In. $97

Cowan's Auctions

Glass-Midcentury, Vase, Blue, Blown, Sandblasted, Copper Plated, Marvin Lipofsky, 1962, 12 x 6½ In. $4,375

Rago Arts and Auction Center

Glass-Midcentury, Vase, Green Swirl, D. Labino, H. Littleton, 1965, 12 x 4 In. $938

Rago Arts and Auction Center

Glass-Midcentury, Vase, Ruby Red, Paneled, Rounded Top, 3 Arched Swirl Feet, D. Labino, 1965, 10 In.

$584

Cowan's Auctions

Glass-Venetian, Bottle, Banded, Blown, Etched, Bands, Ball Stopper, Fulvio Bianconi, 1960s, 18 In.

$1,063

Rago Arts and Auction Center

Glass-Venetian, Bowl, Label, Archimede Seguso Murano, c.1970, 4 x 10½ In.

$1,063

Rago Arts and Auction Center

Ewer, Multicolor & Layered, Somerso Technique, 1960s	395
Figurine, Bird, Cased Purple, White, Applied Eyes & Feet, 7 x 9 In.	69
Figurine, Cat, Blue, Green, Luigi Onesto, 1900s, 5¾ x 5½ In.	118
Figurine, Hat, Lattimo, Orange, White, 12¾ x 4½ In.	406
Figurine, J-Shape Bird, Teal, Round Murine Eyes, 13¼ In.	1947
Figurine, Mother & Children, Blue, Green, 19 In.	218
Figurine, Pulcini Bird, Blue, Green Stripes, Metal Legs, Alessandro Pianon, 7¾ x 3¾ In.	7500
Perfume Bottle, Round, Sommerso, Blue, Red, Green, Stopper, Murano, 16 x 9 In.	449
Sculpture, 2 Parts, Blue & White Swirls, Ball, Folded Rim, c.1977, 13 x 16 In.	5313
Sculpture, Aquarium, Clear Square, Multicolor Fish & Lines, 1950s, 9 x 9 In.	1125
Sculpture, Bird, Orange, Blown, Copper Feet, Alessandro Pianon, 1960s, 9 x 5 In. ....*illus*	5000
Sculpture, Bird, Yellow, Fuchsia, Green, Curved Shape, 1960s, 11 x 4 In., Pair	1250
Sculpture, Devil, Blown, Applied Glass, Attributed To Pino Signoretto, 15 x 7½ In..........*illus*	1875
Sculpture, Pulcini Bird, Perched, Frosty & Cobalt Blue, Green, 1960s, 10 In.	2625
Sculpture, Sailfish, Blue, Purple, Murano, 16 In.	40
Sculpture, Stylized Phoenix, Flame Wings, 27 x 10 In.	590
Sculpture, Teapot, Multicolor Swirls, Loop Handle, Bell Base, 1986, 15 x 13 In.	1625
Sculpture, Violin, Black, Cobalt Blue, Purple & Pink Striations, Base, 26 In.	2537
Sculpture, Wavy Angular Edge, Bell Base, Splotches, 1953, 12 x 12 In.	1500
Urn, Red, Melon Ribbed, Black Scroll Handles, Shouldered, 1930s, 9 x 8 In.	2000
Vase, 2 Necks, Blown, Murano, A. Fuga, Italy, Mid 1900s, 18¼ x 6 x 4 In.	3125
Vase, Amber, Yellow Rim, Round Foot, 7 In.	108
Vase, Basilissa, E. Sottsass, Vistosi, Memphis, 1977, 8¾ x 8¾ In.................*illus*	2625
Vase, Black & Red, Blue Cane Swirls, Swollen Rim, Murano, 1986, 12 x 12 In.	1500
Vase, Blown, Murrine, Murano, L. Ferro, Italy, 1952, 9 x 7 x 7 In.	3250
Vase, Blue Bubbles, Crinkled Metal, Squat, Ring Foot & Neck, 1980s, 5 x 8 In.	2500
Vase, Blue Sommerso, Multicolor Circles, Bubbles, Oval, Murano, 11 x 9 In.	366
Vase, Blue, Green, Stripe, Frosted, 15½ x 6½ In.	125
Vase, Blue, Multicolor Inclusions, 14¾ In., Pair	75
Vase, Blue, Red, Green, Patchwork Design, Conical, Murano, c.1950, 9 In.	2214
Vase, Blue, Splotches & Streaks, Applied Ribbon, Ruffle Rim, Murano, c.1890, 6 In.	117
Vase, Clear & Red, Spherical, Swollen Stick Neck, Zigzag Handles, 1930s, 9 In.	1875
Vase, Clear, Cobalt Blue & Fuchsia Squares, Tapered Square, c.1948, 12 In.	3125
Vase, Cobalt Blue To Clear, Applied Ribs, Scalloped & Ruffled Rim, 14 x 10¼ In.	129
Vase, Cobalt Blue, Red Cane Bands, Tapered Neck, Fulvio Bianconi, 1951, 9¾ In.	500
Vase, Cobalt Blue, White, Peleus & Thetis, Greek Key Banding, 1800s, 17 In.	3444
Vase, Coral Branches, Lattimo, E. Nason, Murano, Italy, Mid 1900s, 8¾ x 8¾ x 5¼ In.	1875
Vase, Cranberry, Cracked, 10 x 4 In.	2250
Vase, Cylindrical, Round Base, Yellow, Red, Green, Brush Strokes, c.1950, 12 In.	3500
Vase, Diagonal Grid, Bubbles, Gold Inclusion, Clear, Seguso, 9¼ x 6 In.	488
Vase, Donna, Cased Red, Female Shape, Arms Akimbo, Bellybutton, 9½ x 6½ In.	12200
Vase, Filigrana, Clear Swirls, Pale Green Lines, Bottle Shape, Murano, 20 In.	3500
Vase, Fine Canes, Black, Yellow, Carlo Scarpa, 5¼ x 3¾ In.	1187
Vase, Frosty White, Black Shapes, Tapered, Teardrop Top, Murano, 19 In.	12500
Vase, Green, Blue, Transparent, Opaque, Stick Neck, Gio Ponti, c.1948, 13¾ x 4¼ In.	1375
Vase, Incalmo, Black, Orange Threaded Band, Spherical, Murano, 1982, 10 In.	1063
Vase, Iridescent Blue, Patches, Dino Martens, c.1950, 14 x 8 In.	2000
Vase, Merletto, Blown, Archimede Seguso, Murano, 1950s, 8¼ x 4½ In. ....*illus*	6250
Vase, Metallic Gold Crackle, Turquoise Dots, Pinched Neck, c.1950, 6 In.	2250
Vase, Millefiori, Ruffled, Gold Aventurine, 12¼ x 7½ In.	118
Vase, Multicolor Curvy Squares, Tapered, Wavy Rim, 1950s, 9 x 6 In.	6875
Vase, Multicolor Iridescent, Ribbon Swirls, Cylindrical, Flat Rim, 1940, 9 In.	5000
Vase, Multicolor Squares, Elongated Oval, Short Stick Neck, 1950s, 14 In.	6875
Vase, Multicolor, Pink & Purple Circles, Metallic, Tube Neck, c.1950, 10 In.	4375
Vase, Opalescent, Gold Leaf Inclusions, Pinwheels, 11¾ x 6 In.	1220
Vase, Orange, Red Spiral Design, Black Base, Tubular, 1960s, 15 x 4 In.	6250
Vase, Orange, Red, Interlocking Diamond Shapes, Stripes, Tapered, 1981, 10 In.	1875
Vase, Ormolu Mount, Diaper, Fan, 8 In., Pair	240
Vase, Osellaria Trombone, Copper Inclusions, Pinwheel, c.1952, 9¼ x 7 In.	7930
Vase, Pale Blue, Flared Rim, Silver Foot & Beaded Handles, 1924, 9 In.	1625

G

Glass-Venetian, Sculpture, Bird, Orange, Blown, Copper Feet, Alessandro Pianon, 1960s, 9 x 5 In.
$5,000

Rago Arts and Auction Center

Glass-Venetian, Sculpture, Devil, Blown, Applied Glass, Attributed To Pino Signoretto, 15 x 7 ½ In.
$1,875

Rago Arts and Auction Center

Glass-Venetian, Vase, Basilissa, E. Sottsass, Vistosi, Memphis, 1977, 8¾ x 8¾ In.
$2,625

Rago Arts and Auction Center

> **TIP**
> To remove stains from a glass vase, fill it with warm water and drop in a denture-cleaning tablet.

Glass-Venetian, Vase, Merletto, Blown, Archimede Seguso, Murano, 1950s, 8¼ x 4½ In.
$6,250

Rago Arts and Auction Center

Glass-Venetian, Vase, Pezzato, Green, Yellow, Black, Bianconi, Murano, Acid Stamp, 1950s, 11 In.
$4,375

Rago Arts and Auction Center

Glass-Venetian, Vase, White, Applied Glass, Face, Arm Handles, Feet, E. Nason, 1950s, 14 x 10 In.
$3,625

Rago Arts and Auction Center

G

Goebel, Doll, Bisque, Composition, Googly, 1920s, 7 In.
$29

Ruby Lane

Goldscheider, Bust, Girl, Red Hair, Glazed Ceramic, 1930s, 6 x 6½ In.
$750

Treadway Toomey Auctions

Gonder, Vase, Greenish Brown Exterior, Lavender Interior, 1941-57, 7 x 5¼ In.
$40

Ruby Lane

Vase, Patchwork, Fulvio Bianconi, 7 x 7 In.	4880
Vase, Pear Shape, Fine Canes, Black, Yellow, Carlo Scarpa, 5¼ x 3¾ In.	1187
Vase, Pezzato, Green, Yellow, Black, Bianconi, Murano, Acid Stamp, 1950s, 11 In. ......*illus*	4375
Vase, Pink, Orange, Purple, Control Bubble, Multicolor, 10¾ x 8¼ In.	324
Vase, Plum, Mauve, Turquoise, Striped, Pear Shape, Stick Neck, c.1949, 14 In.	2750
Vase, Red & Turquoise Triangular Shapes, Cup Shape, Ring Foot, 1960s, 8 In.	4375
Vase, Red Band, Blue Ground, Fulvio Bianconi, 7½ x 4 In.	1000
Vase, Red, Blue, Streaks, Free-Form, Pinched Waist, Wavy Rim, 1959, 12 In.	5938
Vase, Red, Green, Sommerso, Laura De Santillana, 16¾ x 17½ In.	12500
Vase, Red, Spherical, Swollen Stick Neck, Arched Handles, 1930s, 8 In.	813
Vase, Round, 2 Tube Necks, Dimples, Orange, Green Stripes, 1950s, 11 x 6 In.	6250
Vase, Scavo With Leaves, Dark Blue, Cenedese, E. Nason, Murano, Italy, 1950s, 11 x 6 x 4 In. ...	2000
Vase, Square, Fine Canes, Black, Yellow, Carlo Scarpa, 5¼ x 3¾ In.	1187
Vase, Square, Tapering, Tutti-Frutti, Fused Glass, Foil Inclusions, Red, 6⅜ x 4 In.	600
Vase, Trumpet, 4-Sided, Bright Orange, Heart Shape Gilded Base, Carlo Moretti, 11 In.	94
Vase, Turquoise & Cobalt Blue, Circles, Swollen, Tapered, 1960s, 10 x 6 In.	813
Vase, Turquoise Glass, Gold Leaf, Applied Foot, Handles, N. Martinuzzi, 9½ x 6½ In.	1125
Vase, Vertical Striations, Red, Yellow, Blue, Green, Cream, 19 x 7½ In.	389
Vase, White Checkerboard, Gold & Yellow, Metallic, Egg Shape, 1940s, 10 In.	2250
Vase, White Ground, Green, Red, Blue Shapes, Bottle, Stick Neck, c.1948, 11 In.	3125
Vase, White, Applied Glass, Face, Arm Handles, Feet, E. Nason, 1950s, 14 x 10 In. ......*illus*	3625
Vase, White, Cobalt Blue, Teardrop, Handles At Rim, Spread Foot, 1930s, 13 In.	1500
Vase, Yellow Stripes, Red, Murines, 14½ x 6½ In.	62
Vase, Yokohama Series, Murrine, Murano, A. Nason, Italy, Mid 1900s, 11 x 6 In.	3750
Vase, Zipper Panels, Red, White, Blue & Orange, Flared, Schiavon, Murano, 19 In.	1778
Wine, Red, Gold Gilt, Menorah, Star Of David, Twist Stem, Murano, 1950s, 5 In.	150

 GLASSES for the eyes, or spectacles, were mentioned in a manuscript in 1289 and have been used ever since. The first eyeglasses with rigid side pieces were made in London in 1727. Bifocals were invented by Benjamin Franklin in 1785. Lorgnettes were popular in late Victorian times. Opera Glasses are listed in the Opera Glass category.

Ski Goggles, Bakelite Side Shields, Steel Frame, Case, 1920s	345
Steel Frame, Clam Top Case, John Anderson	126

 GLIDDEN POTTERY worked in Alfred, New York, from 1940 to 1957. The pottery made stoneware, dinnerware, and art objects.

Bowl, Blue Gray Speckles, Scalloped, 1947, 13 x 8 In.	32
Planter, Gray, Black & Brown Speckles, Turquoise Interior, 4 x 4 x 4 In.	28

Goebel **GOEBEL** is the mark used by W. Goebel Porzellanfabrik of Oeslau, Germany, now Rodental, Germany. The company was founded by Franz Detleff Goebel and his son, William Goebel, in 1871. It was known as F&W Goebel. Slates, slate pencils, and marbles were made. Soon the company began making porcelain tableware and figurines. Hummel figurines were first made by Goebel in 1935 and are now being made by another company. Goebel is still in business. Old pieces marked *Goebel Hummel* are listed under Hummel in this book.

Candleholder, Angel, Yellow Accordion, 2½ In.	18
Doll, Bisque, Composition, Googly, 1920s, 7 In. ......*illus*	29
Figurine, Baby Leaning On Basket, Starfish Hands, 3 x 1¾ In.	95
Figurine, Barn Owl, Brown, Tan, Black, White, 1972-79, 2¼ x 1¾ In.	35
Figurine, Parrot, Macaw, Red, Green, Yellow, White, 7½ x 7 In.	65
Vase, Baby Hatching Out Of Egg, 4 x 3 In.	125

Goldscheider Wien **GOLDSCHEIDER** was founded by Friedrich Goldscheider in Vienna in 1885. The family left Vienna in 1938 and the factory was taken over by the Germans. Goldscheider started factories in England and in Trenton, New Jersey. The New Jersey factory started in 1940 as Goldscheider–U.S.A. In 1941 it became Goldscheider–Everlast

G

Corporation. From 1947 to 1953 it was Goldcrest Ceramics Corporation. In 1950 the Vienna plant was returned to Mr. Goldscheider, but it closed in 1953. The Trenton, New Jersey, business, called Goldscheider of Vienna, is a wholesale importer.

Bust, Girl, Red Hair, Glazed Ceramic, 1930s, 6 x 6 ½ In. ....*illus*	750
Figurine, Dancer, Butterfly, c.1937, 18 x 16 In.	2142
Figurine, Woman, Blue Dress, Dog, 17 In.	2125

GOLF, *see Sports category.*

GONDER CERAMIC ARTS, INC., was opened by Lawton Gonder in 1941 in Zanesville, Ohio. Gonder made high-grade pottery decorated with flambe, drip, gold crackle, and Chinese crackle glazes. The factory closed in 1957. From 1946 to 1954, Gonder also operated the Elgee Pottery, which made ceramic lamp bases.

Pitcher, Chartreuse, Green Volcanic Glaze, Square, Wavy Handle, c.1950, 8 In.	43
Pitcher, Gold, Turquoise Crackle, Pink Interior, Pear Shape, Wavy Spout, Handle, 10 In.........	75
Vase, Greenish Brown Exterior, Lavender Interior, 1941-57, 7 x 5 ¼ In..............................*illus*	40
Vase, Turquoise & Gold, Crackle Design, Square Trumpet Neck, Handles, 1940s, 8 In..............	60

GOOFUS GLASS was made from about 1900 to 1930 by many American factories. It was originally painted gold, red, green, bronze, pink, purple, or other bright colors. Colors were cold painted or sprayed on, not fired on, and were not permanent. Many pieces are found today with flaking paint, and this lowers the value. Both goofus glass and carnival glass were sold at carnivals, but carnival glass colors are fired on and don't flake off.

Bowl, Red Roses, Gold Leaves, Flared, Crimped Ruffle Rim, 3 x 9 In..............................	35
Candy Dish, Red & Gold, Diamond Cut, Round, Reeded Lid, Swan Finial, 6 x 5 In...................	52
Plate, Carnations, Red, Gold, Octagonal, c.1900, 11 In...*illus*	30
Serving Bowl, Gold & Red, Narcissus Spray, Star Center, Leaves, c.1905, 3 x 9 In.	38
Vase, Purple, Molded Blooming Roses, Tapered, Rolled Rim, c.1905, 7 x 5 In.	59

GOSS china has been made since 1858. English potter William Henry Goss first made it at the Falcon Pottery in Stoke-on-Trent. The factory name was changed to Goss China Company in 1934 when it was taken over by Cauldon Potteries. Production ceased in 1940. Goss China resembles Irish Belleek in both body and glaze. The company also made popular souvenir china, usually marked with local crests and names.

Bust, Parian, W. Irving, 13 ½ In...	582
Jug, Souvenir, Newhaven Crest, Anchor, Harbor, Red, Blue, Brown, c.1890, 4 In. ....*illus*	105
Mug, Naughty Bear, 1922, 2 ⅞ x 2 ½ In.	70
Vase, Lincoln Cathedral, 2 ¾ In...	42
Vase, Nautilus Shell, Coral Stand, 6 ½ x 6 x 2 ½ In...	66
Wall Pocket, Shield, Lion Crest, Red & White & Gold, 7 ⅛ x 4 ¼ x 2 ¼ In.	57

GOUDA, Holland, has been a pottery center since the seventeenth century. Two firms, the Zenith pottery, established in the eighteenth century, and the Zuid-Hollandsche pottery, made the brightly colored art pottery marked *Gouda* from 1898 to about 1964. Other factories followed. Many pieces featured Art Nouveau or Art Deco designs. Pattern names in Dutch, listed here, seem strange to English-speaking collectors.

Chamberstick, Black Trim, Flowers, Multicolor, 3 In., Pair	30
Jardiniere, Damascus, Flower Band, Blue, Pink, Green, Black Ground, 13 x 9 In. ....*illus*	159
Pitcher, Milk, Tulips, Orange, Yellow, Green Trim, 8 In.	22
Pitcher, Zuid, Sredbo, Stylized Flower, Multicolor, 6 In.	47
Plate, Daisy, Gold Outline, Tan, Black, 11 ½ In.	48
Tray, Black Shaped Rim, Red, Blue, Green Repeating Leaf Shape Pattern, 14 x 10 In.	33
Vase, Flowers, Cream, Teal, Brown, Blue, 4 x 4 In..	12
Vase, Flowers, Orange Band At Neck, 10 ¼ In.	130
Vase, Yellow Bursts, Blue Ground, Brown Swirls, 8 ⅛ In.	70

Goofus Glass, Plate, Carnations, Red, Gold, Octagonal, c.1900, 11 In
$30

Ruby Lane

G

Goss, Jug, Souvenir, Newhaven Crest, Anchor, Harbor, Red, Blue, Brown, c.1890, 4 In.
$105

Ruby Lane

Gouda, Jardiniere, Damascus, Flower Band, Blue, Pink, Green, Black Ground, 13 x 9 In.
$159

William H. Bunch Auctions

GRANITEWARE

Graniteware, Coffeepot, Green, Swing,
Bail Handle, Turned Knob,
8½ x 11½ In.
$61

Forsythe's Auctions

Graniteware, Kettle, Lid, Green &
White Swirl, Berlin Style, Bail Handle,
7¼ In.
$200

Hess Auction Group

TIP

*Want to be "green"?
Recyclable bags, boxes,
sealing tape, plastic
peanuts, and bubble
wrap are available.*

Greentown, Cactus, Butter, Chocolate
Glass, c.1903, 5¼ x 7¼ In.
$145

Ruby Lane

GRANITEWARE is enameled tin or iron used to make kitchenware since the 1870s. Earlier graniteware was green or turquoise blue, with white spatters. The later ware was gray with white spatters. Reproductions are being made in all colors. There is a second definition of the word *graniteware* meaning a blue speckled pottery. Only the metal graniteware is listed here.

Canister, Red, Flowers, c.1900, 7 x 5 In.	50
Coffee Kettle, Green, Swing Bail Handle, Turned Wood Grip, 8½ x 11½ In.	61
Coffeepot, Brown, Fluted Top, Wood Finial, Handle, Manning-Bowman, 1889, 7 In.	45
Coffeepot, Daisy & Rose Bouquet, Blue Ground, c.1900, 8¾ In.	130
Coffeepot, Green, Swing, Bail Handle, Turned Knob, 8½ x 11½ In. ....*illus*	61
Cup, Blue & White Spatterware, 3½ x 3½ In.	19
Ember Pot, Blue Veined, Handles, c.1900, 9 x 8 x 5 In.	167
Funnel, Gray Enamel, Mottled, Handle, Haberman Mfg. Co., c.1900, 4¼ In.	18
Funnel, White, Loop Handle, Germany, 5 In.	29
Jardiniere, White, Green Band, Oval, 17 x 15 x 7 In.	130
Kettle, Lid, Green & White Swirl, Berlin Style, Bail Handle, 7¼ In. ....*illus*	200
Muffin Pan, Hoosier Blue, White Specks, 12 Sections, 12 x 15 In.	39
Pitcher, Squat, Trees, Flowers, c.1875, 6 x 4 In.	88
Roasting Pan, Cobalt Blue & White Speckles, Domed Lid, 14 x 10 x 6 In.	45
Tray, Gray, c.1870, 16¾ x 13½ In.	60
Utensil Hanger, White, Blue, Roses, 1930s, 20 x 14 In.	95

GREENTOWN glass was made by the Indiana Tumbler and Goblet Company of Greentown, Indiana, from 1894 to 1903. In 1899, the factory became part of National Glass Company. A variety of pressed glass was made. Additional pieces may be found in other categories, such as Chocolate Glass, Holly Amber, Milk Glass, and Pressed Glass.

Austrian, Cordial, Vaseline, 3 In.	72
Austrian, Spooner, Vaseline, 4¾ In.	48
Cactus, Butter, Chocolate Glass, c.1903, 5¼ x 7¼ In. ....*illus*	145
Fighting Cocks, Dish, Lid, Cock Finial, White, c.1902, 3¾ x 4⅛ In.	3932
Squirrel, Pitcher, Tail Out, Scalloped Rim, c.1898, 8¾ In.	84
Teardrop & Tassel, Pitcher, Blue, 8⅞ In.	145

GRUEBY FAIENCE COMPANY of Boston, Massachusetts, was founded in 1894 by William H. Grueby. Grueby Pottery Company was incorporated in 1907. In 1909, Grueby Faience went bankrupt. Then William Grueby founded the Grueby Faience and Tile Company. Grueby Pottery closed about 1911. The tile company worked until 1920. Garden statuary, art pottery, and architectural tiles were made until 1920. The company developed a green matte glaze that was so popular it was copied by many other factories making a less expensive type of pottery. This eventually led to the financial problems of the pottery. Cuerda seca and cuenca are techniques explained in the Tile category. The company name was often used as the mark, and slight changes in the form help date a piece.

Bowl, Bulb, Green Matte Glaze, Mottled, Marked, 2 x 7¾ In.	369
Bowl, Leaves, Green Glaze, Squat, Pinched Stand-Up Rim, 2 x 6 In.	750
Frieze, The Pines, Trees In Landscape, 8 Tiles, Half Tile Border, Oak Frame, 12 x 55 In.	16250
Paperweight, Scarab, Green, Mottled, c.1900, 4 In.	625
Tile, Bird In Five Different Pastel Glazes, Nicks At Corners, Impressed, 6 x 6 In.	1840
Tile, Green Matte Glaze, Griffin, Oak Frame, 8 In.	1220
Tile, Landscape, Ocean, Clouds, Hilltop Huts, Trees, Sky, 4 x 4 In., Pair	1188
Tile, Leaf, Brown, Beige, Frame, 6 x 6 In.	125
Tile, Oak Tree, Cloud, Green, Blue, Addison LeBoutillier, Wood Frame, 6 x 6 In.	6710
Tile, Pines, Green, Brown, Frame, 6 x 6 In.	3965
Tile, Yellow Tulip, Green Leaf Outlines & Ground, Square, Wood Frame, c.1910, 6 In.	1625
Tray, Dresser, Inlaid, Tile, Undulating Silver Rim, Bigelow Kennard Co., 1¼ x 11 x 5 In.	540
Vase, Blue Drip Glaze, Arches, Stamped, c.1905, 11 x 7¾ In. ....*illus*	10000
Vase, Bottle Shape, Green, Sword Blade Leaf Tips, 6⅛ In.	650
Vase, Daffodils, 2-Color, Ruth Erickson, Stamped, 14 In. ....*illus*	12500

Vase, Flowers, Overlapping Stylized Leaves Below, Green, Swollen, Straight Neck, 13 In.	4375
Vase, Green Glaze, Elongated Flutes, Bulbous, Squat, 9 x 10 In.	2250
Vase, Green Matte Glaze, 7 Handles, Stamped, c.1900, 10 x 8 ½ In. ....*illus*	31250
Vase, Green Matte Glaze, High Shoulders, Round Foot, Signed ER, 6 x 9 ½ In.	3050
Vase, Green Matte Glaze, Leaf Blades, Tapered, Round Bottom, Flare Rim, c.1905, 8 In.	1599
Vase, Green Matte Glaze, Leaves & Buds, Squat, Trumpet Neck, c.1905, 7 In.	1625
Vase, Green Streaked Glaze, Leaves & Buds, Pear Shaped, c.1905, 7 In.	1875
Vase, Green, Petals, Ruth Erickson, 4 ½ x 7 In.	1464
Vase, Incised Leaf Design, Green Matte Glaze, Swollen Rim, 1902, 9 x 7 In.	3500
Vase, Leaves, Carved, Green Glaze, Elongated, Tapered, 14 x 4 ½ In.	2500
Vase, Leaves, Green Glaze, Cylindrical Neck, Squat Base, 8 x 4 ¾ In.	1250
Vase, Leaves, Green Glaze, Yellow Buds, Bulbous, Squat, Flared Rim, 6 x 8 In.	5313
Vase, Leaves, Green Leathery Glaze, Bulbous, Squat, Ruth Erickson, 6 ¾ x 9 ½ In.	6250
Vase, Leaves, Green, Yellow Buds, Swollen Cylinder, 9 x 4 In.	2875
Vase, Leaves, Green, Yellow Buds, Swollen Cylinder, 11 ½ x 5 ½ In.	3750
Vase, Leaves, Wide, Vertical, Oval, Flared Rim, 5 x 4 In.	2000
Vase, Lilies, Carved, Green & Cream Matte Glaze, Swollen Base, Leaves, 14 x 7 In.	12500
Vase, Melon Shape, 2-Color Matte, Cream, Brown, 11 ½ x 8 In.	6100
Vase, Overlapping Leaves, Green Matte Glaze, Bulbous, Cylindrical Neck, 1905, 19 In.	8125
Vase, Squat, Broad Foliage, Thick Green Leathery Matte Glaze, 2 ¾ x 4 ¼ In.	1265
Vase, Stylized Flowers, Yellow Bud, Green, Partial Paper Label, c.1905, 12 x 5 ½ In. ....*illus*	4063
Vase, Tapering, Thick Green Matte Glaze, Impressed Logo, 7 ¾ In.	575
Vase, Vertical Leaves, Green Matte Glaze, Bulbous, Pinched Neck, c.1905, 6 In.	1125

GUN, *see Toy*

GUSTAVSBERG ceramics factory was founded in 1827 near Stockholm, Sweden. It is best known to collectors for its twentieth-century artwares, especially Argenta, a green stoneware with silver inlay. The company broke up and was sold in the 1990s.

Gustafsberg

Bowl, Rust & Brown Glaze, Incised, Tire Shape, Flat Rim, Cylindrical Foot, 2 x 4 In.	325
Dish, Green, Silver Grid With Dots On Intersections, 8 ¼ x 8 ¼ In.	182
Vase, Aquatic Rider, Horse, Fish, Teal, Mottled, Inscribed Svenska Simforbundet, 7 x 6 In.	98
Vase, Necklace Of Leaf Blades, White Over Aqua, Laurel Wreath, 4 In. ....*illus*	118
Vase, Sculpted Figures, Fish, Paper Label, Berndt Friberg, 1959, 19 x 5 In. ....*illus*	2750
Vase, Tall Cylinder, Brick Design, Turquoise, Electroplated Silver, 1950s, 13 In.	1000

HAEGER POTTERIES, INC., Dundee, Illinois, started making commercial artwares in 1914. Early pieces were marked with the name *Haeger* written over an *H.* About 1938, the mark *Royal Haeger* was used in honor of Royal Hickman, a designer at the factory. The firm closed in 2016. See also the Royal Hickman category.

Haeger

Figurine, Rooster, Oxblood, 20 In., Pair	69
Pitcher, Bright Orange, White Interior, Handle, 8 In. ....*illus*	25
Planter, Green, 11 x 6 In.	26
Vase, Blue Lava Glaze, Peach Agate, Squat, Trumpet Neck, Handles, c.1937, 7 In.	60
Vase, Footed, Embossed, Yellow, 8 x 3 ½ In.	23
Vase, Mauve Agate Glaze, Blue, Leaf Shape, c.1935, 7 In.	50

HALF-DOLL, *see Pincushion Doll category.*

HALL CHINA COMPANY started in East Liverpool, Ohio, in 1903. The firm made many types of wares. Collectors search for the Hall teapots made from the 1920s to the 1950s. The dinnerware of the same period, especially Autumn Leaf pattern, is also popular. The Hall China Company merged with Homer Laughlin China Company in 2010. Autumn Leaf pattern dishes are listed in their own category in this book.

HALL'S SUPERIOR QUALITY KITCHENWARE

Cameo Rose, Platter, Oval, 11 ⅝ In.	35
Flower Decorated Handle, Pitcher, Light Blue, 7 ¼ In.	11
Hallcraft, Peach Blossom, Pitcher, 6 In.	55
Moderne Ivory, Teapot, Gold Trim, 6 Cup	65

Grueby, Vase, Blue Drip Glaze, Arches, Stamped, c.1905, 11 x 7 ¾ In.
$10,000

Rago Arts and Auction Center

H

Grueby, Vase, Daffodils, 2-Color, Ruth Erickson, Stamped, 14 In.
$12,500

Rago Arts and Auction Center

Grueby, Vase, Green Matte Glaze, 7 Handles, Stamped, c.1900, 10 x 8 ½ In.
$31,250

Rago Arts and Auction Center

Grueby, Vase, Stylized Flowers, Yellow Bud, Green, Partial Paper Label, c.1905, 12 x 5 ½ In.
$4,063

Rago Arts and Auction Center

Gustavsberg, Vase, Necklace Of Leaf Blades, White Over Aqua, Laurel Wreath, 4 In.
$118

Humler & Nolan

Gustavsberg, Vase, Sculpted Figures, Fish, Paper Label, Berndt Friberg, 1959, 19 x 5 In.
$2,750

Rago Arts and Auction Center

Mt. Vernon, Bowl, Vegetable, Lid, Oval, 9 ¼ In.	65
Mt. Vernon, Cup & Saucer, Footed	12
Mt. Vernon, Plate, Dinner, 10 ⅛ In.	15
Mt. Vernon, Platter, Oval, 13 ½ In.	28
Peach, Pitcher, 9 ¼ In. _illus_	12
Red Poppy, Coffeepot, Lid, 8 In.	50
Refrigerator Ware, Leftover, Lid, Yellow, 1940, 6 ½ x 4 ¼ In. _illus_	36
Royal Rose, Mixing Bowl, 7 ½ In.	29
Silhouette, Teapot, 5 Bands, 8 Cup	128
Star, Teapot, Gold Paint, 1940s, 6 Cup, 6 x 5 ½ In. _illus_	49

 HALLOWEEN is an ancient holiday that has changed in the last 200 years. The jack-o'-lantern, witches on broomsticks, and orange decorations seem to be twentieth-century creations. Collectors started to become serious about collecting Halloween-related items in the late 1970s. The papier-mache decorations, now replaced by plastic, and old costumes are in demand.

Button, Hallowe'en Findlay, Witch, Celluloid, St. Louis Button Co., c.1920, 1 ½ In. _illus_	139
Doorstop, Halloween Girl, Cast Iron, Littco Products, c.1936, 14 ¼ x 8 ½ In. _illus_	29500
Figure, Pumpkin Man, Felt, 20 ½ In. _illus_	3250
Jack-O'-Lantern, Papier-Mache, Gap Toothed Grimace, 1930s, 6 In.	48
Lantern, Cat On Fence, Papier-Mache, Molded, Black & Orange, 1940s, 8 In., Pair	226
Lantern, Devil Head, Papier-Mache, Molded, Bail Handle, 1940s, 6 In.	115
Mold, Pumpkin, Brass, 13 x 9 In.	146
Pumpkin, Papier-Mache, 8 x 8 In.	46
Pumpkin Man, Felt, Black Vest, Black Pants, Pumpkin Head, Teeth, 20 ½ In.	3900
Skeleton Dancer, Paper, Stretch Arms & Legs, Black, White, Beistle Co., c.1950, 7 In.	29

 HAMPSHIRE pottery was made in Keene, New Hampshire, between 1871 and 1923. Hampshire developed a line of colored glazed wares as early as 1883, including a Royal Worcester–type pink, olive green, blue, and mahogany. Pieces are marked with the printed mark or the impressed name *Hampshire Pottery* or *J.S.T. & Co., Keene, N.H.* Many pieces were marked with city names and sold as souvenirs.

Lamp, Pillow, Green Matte Glaze, Marked, 20 In.	154
Vase, Bulbous, Green Matte Glaze, Four Embossed Leaves, 3 ½ In.	184
Vase, Greek Key, Green Matte Glaze, 5 ¼ x 6 In.	366
Vase, Green Matte Glaze, Geometric, 6 ½ x 8 In.	343
Vase, Leaf, Green Matte Glaze, Flared Rim, Early 1900s, 10 In.	250
Vase, Mottled Blue Matte, Green, Marked, 8 ½ In.	276
Vase, Mottled Green, Squat, Incised Panels, 3 ½ In.	246

HANDEL glass was made by Philip Handel working in Meriden, Connecticut, from 1885 and in New York City from 1893 to 1933. The firm made art glass and other types of lamps. Handel shades were made not only of leaded glass in a style reminiscent of Tiffany but also of reverse painted glass. Handel also made vases and other glass objects.

Chandelier, 1-Light, Globe Pendant, Forest & Birds, 1910s, 27 ½ x 9 ½ In.	2750
Chandelier, 4-Light, Ginko Leaves, Etched Obverse Painted Glass, 20 x 18 In.	7500
Chandelier, Hammered Metal Ring, Chains, 4 Prairie School Style Shades, 38 x 22 In.	10000
Lamp Base, Bronze, Ribbed Leaf Stem, Openwork Leaf Base, Acorn Pulls, 23 In. _illus_	1046
Lamp, 2-Light, Reverse Painted Shades, Green, 24 ½ x 22 ½ In.	976
Lamp, Arts & Crafts, Copper, Stylized Leaves, Landscape, Bell Shape Shade, c.1915, 12 In.	750
Lamp, Cast Bronze, Brown Ice Mosserine Shade, Bell Shape Post, 57 In.	4956
Lamp, Chipped Ice Shade, Blue Pheasant, Flowers, Bronze 3-Legged Platform Base, 24 In.	8710
Lamp, Chipped Ice Shade, Moon, Trees, Orange, Bronze Baluster Stem, Ringed Foot, 14 In.	2242
Lamp, Chipped Ice Shade, Palm Trees, Shore, Orange Sky, 6-Sided, Bronze Vine Base, 15 In.	4740
Lamp, Chipped Ice Shade, Treasure Island, Ship, Moon, Bronze Urn Base, Greek Key Bands, 23 In.	7703
Lamp, Daffodil, Obverse Painted Glass, Original Patina, 23 x 18 In.	4375
Lamp, Desk, Forest Green Shade, Original Patina, Shade Signed, 14 x 10 ½ In.	2000
Lamp, Desk, Green Slag Glass Shade, Red, Rooftop, Metal Baluster Stem, c.1915, 16 In.	1188

H

Lamp, Domed Shade, Egyptian Ruins, Patinated Base, 26 x 18 In. ....*illus*	5175
Lamp, Domed Shade, Nautical Scene, Peach, Gold, Bronze Stem, Lobed Foot, 24 In.	5310
Lamp, Floor, Glass Shade, Coral, Iridescent Green Droplets, Ruffled, Bronze Base, 57 In.	826
Lamp, Flowers, Butterflies, Chinese Base, Scrolled Foot, 23 In.	7500
Lamp, Flowers, Long Stems, Shaded, Cylindrical, Bronze Cap & Foot, 15 In.	1185
Lamp, Glass Scarlet Macaw, Domed Shade, Bronze Base, Branch & Roots, c.1921	4920
Lamp, Glass Shade, Paneled, Palm Trees, Bronze Base, Fretwork, c.1915, 26 x 21 In.	2875
Lamp, Green, Mosserine Shade, c.1910s-20s, Original Patina, Signed, 57 x 13 ½ In.	1625
Lamp, Leaded Glass, Black-Eyed Susan Metal Base, Early 1900s, 25 x 20 In.	3738
Lamp, Leaded Glass, Geometric Panels, Striated Green, Stylized Leaf Base, 26 In.	2074
Lamp, Leaded Shade, Dragonfly, Tapered Column, 20 ¼ x 17 In.	960
Lamp, Mermaid, Bronzed Spelter Base Only, Early 1900s, 21 ¾ In.	2640
Lamp, Metal Overlay Shade, Trees, Caramel Slag, Ribbed Base, Acorn Pulls, 21 In. ....*illus*	1353
Lamp, Mushroom Shade, Frosted Glass, Berries, Squared Patinated Metal Base, 19 x 11 In.	938
Lamp, Night Seascape, Patina, c.1910, 23 ⅝ x 17 ¾ In.	8750
Lamp, Original Patina Base, Early 1900s, 23 ¾ x 16 In.	2375
Lamp, Parrot, Flowers, Bronzed, Joseph Palme, c.1920, 23 ⅛ x 17 ⅞ In.	6562
Lamp, Parrot, Signed, Early 1900s, 22 ½ x 18 In.	10350
Lamp, Parrots, Henry Bedigie, c.1921, 23 ½ x 17 ¾ In.	9375
Lamp, Parrots, Leaves, Cylindrical, Metal Base, 6 Feet, 59 In., Pair...............................	4375
Lamp, Pendant, Globe, Parrots, Flowers, Iridescent Amber, Metal, c.1910, 21 x 9 In.	1375
Lamp, Pine Woods Sunset Shade, Slag Glass, 4-Footed, 64 ¾ In.	3690
Lamp, Scenic Lake Shade, Trees, Bronze Tree Trunk Stem, Spreading Roots Base, 24 In.	4130
Lamp, Ships, Rocky Shore, Round Bronze Base, Curled Handles, 19 In.	4148
Lamp, Stylized Leaves, Obverse Painted, Original Patina, 1920s, 15 ¼ x 7 In.	2500
Lamp, Table, Arborvitae Sunset Panel Shade, Bronze Tree Trunk Base, c.1910, 31 In.	2250
Lamp, Treasure Island, Ship, Full Moon Over Water, Palm Trees, Bronze Harp Base, 57 In.	4148
Lamp, Trees, Winter Landscape, Yellow Sky, Bronze, Copper, Brass, 22 x 17 In. ....*illus*	390
Lamp, Trees In Meadow, Stream, Bronze Base, Stylized Leaves, 25 In.	2963
Lamp, Wooded Stream Scene, Bronze Tree Trunk Base, 24 In.	17775
Lamp, Umbrella Shade, Tan Slag Glass Panels, 3-Socket Tree Trunk Base, 23 x 19 In.	4148
Vase, Teroma, Treescape At Sunset, Mauve, Cream, Green, Beaker, Swollen Collar, 9 In.	923

HARDWARE, *see Architectural category.*

HARKER POTTERY COMPANY was incorporated in 1890 in East Liverpool, Ohio. The Harker family had been making pottery in the area since 1840. The company made many types of pottery but by the Civil War was making quantities of yellowware from native clays. It also made Rockingham-type brown-glazed pottery and whiteware. The plant was moved to Chester, West Virginia, in 1931. Dinnerware was made and sold nationally. In 1971 the company was sold to Jeannette Glass Company, and all operations ceased in 1972. For more prices, go to kovels.com.

Alpine, Chop Plate, 11 In.	11
Bamboo, Platter, Oval, Brown, Cameo, 11 ⅜ x 9 ¾ In. ....*illus*	15
Blue Cameoware, Teapot, Lid, 6 ¼ In.	25
Corinthian, Platter, Oval, Teal, 11 In.	15
Magnolia, Platter, Serving, Oval, 13 ½ In.	46
Modern Tulip, Casserole, Round, Lid, Qt., 7 In.	78
Petit Point Rose, Soup, Dish, 7 ½ In.	5
Tulip, Pitcher, Hotoven, 5 ½ In.	20
White Cap, Cup & Saucer	6

HARLEQUIN dinnerware was produced by the Homer Laughlin Company from 1938 to 1964, and sold without trademark by the F. W. Woolworth Co. It has a concentric ring design like Fiesta, but the rings are separated from the rim by a plain margin. Cup handles are triangular in shape. Seven different novelty animal figurines were introduced in 1939. For more prices, go to kovels.com.

Chartreuse, Dish, Salad, 7 In.	74
Gray, Cup	5

Haeger, Pitcher, Bright Orange, White Interior, Handle, 8 In.
$25

Ruby Lane

Hall, Pitcher, Peach, 9 ¼ In.
$12

Wilton Gallery

Hall, Refrigerator Ware, Leftover, Lid, Yellow, 1940, 6 ½ x 4 ¼ In.
$36

Ruby Lane

H

Hall, Star, Teapot, Gold Paint, 1940s, 6 Cup, 6 x 5 ½ In.
$49

Ruby Lane

Halloween, Button, Hallowe'en Findlay, Witch, Celluloid, St. Louis Button Co., c.1920, 1 ½ In.
$139

Hake's Americana & Collectibles

Halloween, Doorstop, Halloween Girl, Cast Iron, Littco Products, c.1936, 14 ¼ x 8 ½ In.
$29,500

Bertoia Auctions

Gray, Cup & Saucer		21
Mauve Blue, Creamer, 2 ½ In.		32
Mauve Blue, Eggcup, Double, 3 ¾ x 2 In.	*illus*	29
Mauve Blue, Figurine, Duck		196
Rose, Cup & Saucer		8
Rose, Teapot, Lid, 5 In.		143
Spruce Green, Cup & Saucer		98
Turquoise, Cup		4
Yellow, Creamer		23
Yellow, Gravy Boat		28
Yellow, Tumbler, 4 In.		35

HATPIN collectors search for pins popular from 1860 to 1920. The long pin, often over four inches, was used to hold the hat in place on the hair. The tops of the pins were made of all materials, from solid gold and real gemstones to ceramics and glass. Be careful to buy original hatpins and not recent pieces made by altering old buttons.

Brass, Teddy Bear, Rhinestone Eyes, c.1905, 8 In.		125
Cabochon Amethyst, Rhinestones, Beaded Ring, Flower Shape, Brass, 10 In.		145
Carnival Glass, Bat, Triangular, Purple, Gold, Iridescent		325
Carnival Glass, Flying Bat, Rounded Triangle, Dark Amethyst		120
Carnival Glass, Round, Good Luck, Amethyst		15
Carnival Glass, Round, Rooster, Amber		40
Carnival Glass, Round, Rooster, Black, Cobalt Blue		15
Carnival Glass, Round, Rooster, Celeste Blue		50
Celluloid, Calla Lily Shape, 3 ¾ In.	*illus*	80
Gold, Lion Of St. Mark, Rope Twist Surround, 1 ¼ In.		421
Papillon, Glass, Green, Mother-Of-Pearl Luster, c.1900, 1 ¾ In.		445

HATPIN HOLDERS were needed when hatpins were fashionable from 1860 to 1920. The large, heavy hat required special long-shanked pins to hold it in place. The hatpin holder resembles a large saltshaker, but it often has no opening at the bottom as a shaker does. Hatpin holders were made of all types of ceramics and metal. Look for other pieces under the names of specific manufacturers.

Carnival Glass, Amethyst, Grape & Cable, Northwood, 6 ¾ x 2 ½ In.		54
Elfinware, Flowers, 3 Sections, c.1900, 4 x 3 In.		125
Figural, Monkey, Squatting, Ring Tree, 1909, 4 ⅛ x 2 ⅛ In.		796
Imperial Glass, Open Edge Lace, Diamond Point, Blue, 1930, 4 ½ x 4 ½ In.		21
Porcelain, Blue Flowers, Scallop Edges, Gold Leaf, 4 ½ In.		89
Porcelain, Cylindrical, Pink Flowers, Gilt Trim, Belleek, 5 In.		165
Porcelain, Flowers, Pink, Green, Cream, Royal Dux, 7 ¼ In.		84
Porcelain, Pink Roses, RS Prussia, 4 ½ In.	*illus*	42
Pottery, Green, Pierced Lid, 3 Roundels, Moorcroft, c.1914, 5 In.		124
Pressed Glass, Scalloped Edge, Broad Base, 6 ¼ In.		195

HAVILAND & CO. **HAVILAND** china has been made in Limoges, France, since 1842. David Haviland had a shop in New York City and opened a porcelain company in Limoges, France. Haviland was the first company to both manufacture and decorate porcelain. Pieces are marked *H & Co., Haviland & Co.,* or *Theodore Haviland.* It is possible to match existing sets of dishes through dealers who specialize in Haviland china. Other factories worked in the town of Limoges making a similar chinaware. These porcelains are listed in this book under Limoges.

Decanter, Cat Shape, Seated, White, Edouard Marcel Sandoz, 11 ½ In.		250
Fish Plate, Mollusk Decoration, Gold Rim, 7 ½ In., 6 Piece		60
Oyster Plate, 5 Wells, Used in White House, President Rutherford B. Hayes, 1879	*illus*	1320
Plate, Blue Rim, Woman, Parasol, Signed S. Athrand, 9 ¼ In.		144
Plate, Portrait, Woman, Long Hair, Pink Dress, Yellow Flowers, 9 ½ In.		875

H

Plate, Red & Purple Grapes, Leaves, Stems, Gilt Rim, c.1910, 9 In.	95
Table Set, Platter, Plates, Cobalt Border, Gilt Flowers, 13 In., 11 Piece	125
Vase, Applied Vines, Fruit, Blue, c.1880, 13 In.	312
Vase, Mottled High Glaze, Flowers, Signed, c.1880, 14 In.	960
Vase, Textured, Impressionistic, Flowers, Footed, Brown, Limoges, c.1890, 10 In., Pair	600

HAWKES cut glass was made by T. G. Hawkes & Company of Corning, New York, founded in 1880. The firm cut glass blanks made at other glassworks until 1962. Many pieces are marked with the trademark, a trefoil ring enclosing a fleur-de-lis and two hawks. Cut glass by other manufacturers is listed under either the factory name or in the general Cut Glass category.

Bowl, Klondike, 9 In.	2000
Bowl, Victor, Low, Marked, 8 1/2 In.	201
Bowl, Zipper, 7 In.	60
Compote, Sheraton Pattern, Intaglio Flower Baskets, Cornucopia, 6 3/4 x 7 1/2 In. ....*illus*	550
Dish, Hobstar, 7 In.	42
Dresser Box, Iris, Hinged, Cut Base, Round, Marked, 3 x 6 In.	345
Dresser Jar, Domed Lid, Amber Flashed, Bell Shape, Paneled, c.1930, 3 x 4 In.	360
Match Holder, Hobstar & Diamonds, Cloverleaf Logo, 2 1/4 In.	80
Plate, Festoon, 7 In.	2250
Vase, Flower Center Resting On Rayed Disc Base, Gladys, 6 1/2 x 12 1/2 In.	805
Vase, Funnel Neck, Chrysanthemum & Vine, Sterling Silver Base, 1900s, 12 1/2 In.	310

HEAD VASES, generally showing a woman from the shoulders up, were used by florists primarily in the 1950s and 1960s. Made in a variety of sizes and often decorated with imitation jewelry and other lifelike accessories, the vases were manufactured in Japan and the U.S.A. Less elaborate examples were made as early as the 1930s. Religious themes, babies, and animals are also common subjects. Other head vases are listed under manufacturers' names and can be located through the index in the back of this book.

Girl, Blond, Hands Out To Hold Card, Enesco Foil Label, Japan, c.1960, 3 In.	18
Girl, Teenage, Pigtails, Hat, Long Eyelashes, White, 4 In.	25
Woman, Auburn Hair, Headband, Black Bow, Topline, 8 1/2 In.	195
Woman, Blond, Black Hat & Gloves, Eyes Closed, Foil Label, 4 In.	35
Woman, Blond, Dimple, Curly Pigtails, Flowers, Hat, Lefton, 8 In.	45
Woman, Blond, Pink Iridescent Dress & Hat, Closed Eyes, 1940s, 6 In.	35
Woman, Gray Hat & Dress, Red Lips & Nails, Pearls, Relpo, 7 In.	98
Woman, Hat, Flowers On Shoulder, White Eyelashes, 5 In.	60
Woman, Pink Glass Hat, Blond Hair, Long Eyelashes, 6 x 6 In. ....*illus*	750

HEDI SCHOOP emigrated from Germany in 1933 and started Hedi Schoop Art Creations, North Hollywood, California, in 1940. Schoop made ceramic figurines, lamps, planters, and tablewares. The business burned down in 1958. Some of the molds were sold and Schoop began designing for other companies. She died in 1995.

Hedi Schoop S

Cookie Jar, Figural, Woman, Darner Doll, Blue & Green Striped Skirt, 12 In.	126
Dish, Lettuce Edge, Red Interior, Mottled Blue Green Exterior, 1940s, 12 x 7 In.	32
Figurine, Spanish Senorita, Baskets, Blue Dress, 12 3/4 x 4 1/2 In.	125
Planter, Green, Yellow, Red, 14 In.	35

HEINTZ ART METAL SHOP used the letters HAMS in a diamond as a mark. In 1902, Otto Heintz designed and manufactured copper items with colored enamel decorations under the name Art Crafts Shop. He took over the Arts & Crafts Company in Buffalo, New York, in 1903. By 1906 it had become the Heintz Art Metal Shop. It remained in business until 1930. The company made ashtrays, bookends, boxes, bowls, desk sets, vases, trophies, and smoking sets. The best-known pieces are made of copper, brass, and bronze with silver overlay. Similar pieces were made by Smith Metal Arts and were marked *Silver Crest*. Some pieces by both companies are unmarked.

Halloween, Figure, Pumpkin Man, Felt, 20 1/2 In.
$3,250

Morphy Auctions

H

Handel, Lamp Base, Bronze, Ribbed Leaf Stem, Openwork Leaf Base, Acorn Pulls, 23 In.
$1,046

Skinner, Inc.

Handel, Lamp, Domed Shade, Egyptian Ruins, Patinated Base, 26 x 18 In.
$5,175

Cottone Auctions

Handel, Lamp, Metal Overlay Shade, Trees, Caramel Slag, Ribbed Base, Acorn Pulls, 21 In.
$1,353

Skinner, Inc.

Handel, Lamp, Trees, Winter Landscape, Yellow Sky, Bronze, Copper, Brass, 22 x 17 In.
$390

Rago Arts and Auction Center

Harker, Bamboo, Platter, Oval, Brown, Cameo, 11 ³⁄₈ x 9 ³⁄₄ In.
$15

Ruby Lane

> **TIP**
> Don't use gold- or silver-decorated glasses if the trim has turned chalky gray. This is a source of lead poisoning.

Box, Art Deco Pattern, Sterling On Bronze, Wood Lined, 2 x 4 x 3 In.	165
Candlestick, Landscape, Triangular Base, Handle, Sterling On Bronze, 4 x 4³⁄₄ In.	156
Lamp, Berry Sprig, Bell Swivel Shade, Harp Frame, Sterling On Bronze, 11 In.	767
Lamp, Domed Tambourine Shape Shade, Sterling On Bronze, 11 x 10 In.	1952
Lamp, Electric, Gilt, Overall Decoration, Sterling On Bronze, 9 x 7¹⁄₄ In.	750
Lamp, Metal Overlay Shade, Repeating Balusters, Mica, Sterling On Bronze, 11 In., Pair	2000
Lamp, Stylized Clover, Sterling On Bronze, Wicker Shade, 1910s, 26 x 22 In.	1125
Lamp, Woodbine Mushroom, Sterling On Bronze, 15 x 15 In.	5625
Planter, Fern, Sterling On Bronze, 4¹⁄₂ x 7 In.	732
Trophy, Embossed Center Medallion, Corinthian Yacht Club, 9¹⁄₂ x 5¹⁄₂ In.	342
Vase, Bamboo, Sterling On Bronze, 8¹⁄₂ x 5 In.	468
Vase, Berries & Leaves, Beaker, Trumpet Rim, Sterling On Bronze, 8 In.	236
Vase, Bronze, Flowers, 1875, 8³⁄₄ In. *illus*	825
Vase, Bronze, Stylized Silver Flowers, Patina, 12 x 4¹⁄₂ In. *illus*	430
Vase, Cup Shape Mouth, Sterling On Bronze, 9¹⁄₂ x 3¹⁄₂ In.	468
Vase, Daffodil, Sterling On Bronze, 6 In.	259
Vase, Flowers, Leaves, Sterling On Bronze, 12 x 4¹⁄₂ In.	457
Vase, Silver Crest, Brown, Windmill, Sterling On Bronze, 1900-20, 12 In.	125
Vase, Silver Crest, Green, Waisted, Flowers, Sterling On Bronze, 1900-20, 6 In.	125
Vase, Silver Crest, Leafy Trailing Branches, Sterling On Bronze, 1900-20, 12 In.	188
Vase, Silver Crest, Tan, Waisted, Flower Overlays, Sterling On Bronze, 1900-20, 8 In.	125
Vase, Stick, Berry & Sprig, Impressed, Sterling On Bronze, 11³⁄₄ In.	196
Vase, Thistle Stem, Impressed, Sterling On Bronze, 7¹⁄₄ In.	403
Vase, Vines, Linked By Flower Garland, Sterling On Bronze, Marked, 8 In.	224

HEISEY glass was made from 1896 to 1957 in Newark, Ohio, by A. H. Heisey and Co., Inc. The Imperial Glass Company of Bellaire, Ohio, bought some of the molds and the rights to the trademark. Some Heisey patterns have been made by Imperial since 1960. After 1968, they stopped using the *H* trademark. Heisey used romantic names for colors, such as Sahara. Do not confuse color and pattern names. The Custard Glass and Ruby Glass categories may also include some Heisey pieces.

Animal, Dog, Scottie	128
Bookends, Fish	45
Colonial, Pitcher, Scalloped Edge, Footed, c.1930-40, 5¹⁄₂ x 7 In.	32
Continental, Toothpick Holder	10
Course Rib, Plate, Ground Bottom, 8 In.	27
Crystolite, Celery Tray, 1938-57, 12 In.	32
Crystolite, Relish, 3 Sections, Flat Bottom, 12¹⁄₂ x 8 In.	35
Crystolite, Sugar & Creamer, Round	25
Double Rib & Panel, Mustard, Lid	14
Fandango, Nappy, Tricorner, 7 In.	40
Flat Panel, Sugar, Floral Cutting, Open, 3 In.	24
Greek Key, Jelly, Handle	22
Lariat, Relish, 4 Sections, 8¹⁄₂ In.	15
Lariat, Vase, Crimped, Footed, 1942-57, 7¹⁄₂ In.	38
Locket On Chain, Spooner, Vaseline, 1896-1904, 4 In. *illus*	871
Moongleam, Sugar & Creamer, Wide Flat Panel	32
No. 393, Sugar, Lid, Hotel, Double Handles, Panels, Diamond H, c.1900, 5 x 3¹⁄₄ In. *illus*	30
Octagon, Bowl, Footed, 6 In.	32
Old Gold, Ashtray	20
Old Queen Anne, Plate, 5¹⁄₂ In.	14
Plantation, Relish, 3 Sections, 10 In.	10
Plantation, Vase, 5¹⁄₂ In.	25
Pleat & Panel, Compote, Lid	45
Prince Of Wales, Toothpick Holder, Plumes	76
Provincial, Creamer, Clear, c.1950, 3³⁄₄ In.	12
Puritan, Butter, Cover, ¹⁄₄ Lb.	20
Puritan, Cruet, 4 Oz.	8

H

Harlequin, Mauve Blue, Eggcup, Double, Homer Laughlin, 3¾ x 2 In.
$29

Ruby Lane

Hatpin, Celluloid, Calla Lily Shape, 3¾ In.
$80

Ruby Lane

Hatpin Holder, Porcelain, Pink Roses, RS Prussia, 4½ In.
$42

Ruby Lane

Haviland, Oyster Plate, 5 Wells, Used in White House, President Rutherford B. Hayes, 1879
$1,320

Strawser Auction Group

Hawkes, Compote, Sheraton Pattern, Intaglio Flower Baskets, Cornucopia, 6¾ x 7½ In.
$550

Ruby Lane

TIP
To remove coffee or tea stains from cups put some salt on a piece of orange or lemon rind and rub the marks. Then wash the usual way.

Head Vase, Woman, Pink Glass Hat, Blond Hair, Long Eyelashes, 6 x 6 In.
$750

Ruby Lane

Heintz Art, Vase, Bronze, Flowers, 1875, 8¾ In.
$825

Ruby Lane

Heintz Art, Vase, Bronze, Stylized Silver Flowers, Patina, 12 x 4½ In.
$430

Forsythe's Auctions

Heisey, Locket On Chain, Spooner, Vaseline, 1896-1904, 4 In.
$871

Jeffrey S. Evans

Heisey, No. 393, Sugar, Lid, Hotel, Double Handles, Panels, Diamond H, c.1900, 5 x 3¼ In.
$30

Ruby Lane

Heubach, Candy Container, Baby, Egg, 6 x 4¼ In.
$315

Ruby Lane

Hochst, Figurine, Fish Seller, Apron, Buckle Shoes, Gold Wheelmark, 8½ In.
$128

Susanin's Auctioneers & Appraisers

Puritan, Jug, Squat, 3 Qt.		35
Puritan, Relish, Oval, 5 Sections, 13½ In.		25
Revere, Lemon Dish, 1913-57, 5 In.		16
Rib & Star, Plate, 8 In.		24
Ridgeleigh, Centerpiece, 11 In.		25
Ridgeleigh, Nappy, 4½ x 4½ In.		22
Ridgeleigh, Tumbler		121
Sunburst, Candlestick, Square Base		75
Sunburst, Nappy, Cupped, 7½ In.		22
Sunburst, Toothpick Holder		85
Sunflower, Torte Plate, 13 In.		23
Tudor, Celery Dish, 11 In.		5
Tudor, Cruet, 6 Oz.		10
Tudor, Plate, Cheese, Handles, 1923-39, 6¼ In.		14
Twist, Celery Dish, Pink, 13 In.		35
Twist, Cruet, Vinegar, 1928-37, 5½ In.		30
Twist, Jelly, 2 Handles		20
Twist, Nappy, 8 In.		35
Victorian, Bowl, Sherbet, Pressed Block Pattern, 1933-52, 4 In.		10
Warwick, Vase, Cobalt Blue, 9 In.		110
Whirlpool, Butter, ¼ Lb.		17
Yeoman, Puff Box, Lid, Base, Round, Hawthorne, 1913-57, 4 In.		195

HEREND, *see Fischer category.*

 HEUBACH is the collector's name for Gebruder Heubach, a firm working in Lichten, Germany, from 1840 to 1925. It is best known for bisque dolls and doll heads, the principal products. The company also manufactured bisque figurines, including piano babies, beginning in the 1880s, and glazed figurines in the 1900s. Piano Babies are listed in their own category. Dolls are included in the Doll category under Gebruder Heubach and Heubach. Another factory, Ernst Heubach, working in Koppelsdorf, Germany, also made porcelain and dolls. These will also be found in the Doll category under Heubach Koppelsdorf.

Candy Container, Baby, Egg, 6 x 4¼ In.	*illus*	315
Figurine, 2 Boys, In 1 Oversized Nightshirt, White, Blue, c.1910, 4 In.		215
Figurine, Baseball Player, Pitching, Multicolor, 10 In.		104
Figurine, Boy & Girl, Playing Dress-Up, Adult Clothes, Green, c.1905, 7½ In., Pair		225
Figurine, Dancing Girl, Pink Dress, White Lace, Blue Bow, Blond, c.1900, 8 In., Pair		489
Figurine, Dog, King Charles Spaniel, Seated, White, Gray, Hand Painted, c.1895, 4 In.		298
Figurine, Dutch Boy & Girl, Kissing, c.1905, 7½ In.		270
Figurine, Dutch Girl, Feeding Doves, Jar, Kneeling, Base, c.1910, 7 In.		257
Figurine, Farmer's Wife, Seated, Smiling, Bonnet, White, Gray, Black, c.1910, 6 In.		250
Figurine, Puppy, St. Bernard, Wearing Baby Bonnet, White, Brown, Blue, c.1900, 4 In.		160
Jewelry Box, Sage Green, White, Indian, Beaded Swag, Hexagonal, c.1905, 3 x 5 In.		220
Planter, Boy With Blanket, Laundry Basket, Floppy Hat, Ivory, 1930s, 6 x 4 In.		65
Vase, Amsterdam Woman, Holding Book, Pink, Tan, Black, Tapered, c.1900, 8 In.		85

HISTORIC BLUE, *see factory names, such as Adams, Ridgway, and Staffordshire.*

 HOBNAIL glass is a style of glass with bumps all over. Dozens of hobnail patterns and variants have been made. Clear, colored, and opalescent hobnail have been made and are being reproduced. Other pieces of hobnail may also be listed in the Duncan & Miller and Fenton categories.

Ashtray, Opaque White, Center Ring, Squat, Scalloped Rim, Ring Foot, 1970s, 8 In.		28
Banana Boat, Milk Glass, Footed, 9 x 12 In.		56
Basket, Fuchsia To Pink, Thorny Twisted Clear Handle, Scalloped Rim, 1800s, 7 x 5 In.		159
Bowl, Rose Color To Pale Pink, Opalescent, Crimped Ruffled Rim, c.1920, 5 x 10 In.		195
Cruet, Clear & Frosted Glass, Round, Neck Rings, Wavy Rim, Ball Stopper, c.1885, 8 In.		305

H

Pitcher, Cranberry To Vaseline, Applied Handle, Hobbs, 7 ½ x 8 In.	184
Plate, Opalescent, 8 ½ In.	18
Vase, Fan Shape, Vaseline Glass, Opalescent, 8 ½ In.	17
Vase, Opalescent White, Round, Scalloped Rim, 1960s, 5 In.	52

HOCHST, or Hoechst, porcelain was made in Germany from 1746 to 1796. It was marked with a six-spoke wheel. Be careful when buying Hochst; many other firms have used a very similar wheel-shaped mark. Copies have been made from the original molds.

Figurine, Dog, Pug, Seated, Faience, 1750-60, 3 ¾ In.	2798
Figurine, Drummer, Turkish Chapel, Turban, Red Jacket, 7 In.	254
Figurine, Fish Seller, Apron, Buckle Shoes, Gold Wheelmark, 8 ½ In. ....*illus*	128
Plate, Flower Sprays, Insects, Rococo Scenes, Gilt, Strap Handles, c.1750, 7 In.	515

HOLLY AMBER, or golden agate, glass was made by the Indiana Tumbler and Goblet Company of Greentown, Indiana, from January 1, 1903, to June 13, 1903. It is a pressed glass pattern featuring holly leaves in the amber-shaded glass. The glass was made with shadings that range from creamy opalescent to brown-amber.

Butter, Scalloped, Beaded, Dome Lid, Greentown, c.1895, 6 x 7 In.	1300
Butter, Scalloped, Dome Lid, Greentown, c.1905, 6 x 7 In.	1300
Master Berry, Golden Agate, Greentown, 1902, 2 ⅞ x 7 ½ In.	108 to 205
Plate, Golden Agate, Greentown, 7 ½ In.	302
Sugar, Dome Lid, Knob Finial, Lobed, Greentown, c.1903, 6 ½ x 4 In.	3500
Sugar, Golden Agate, Beading, Dome Lid, Finial, Greentown, 1903, 7 In.	3500

HOLT-HOWARD was an importer that started working in New York City in 1949 and moved to Stamford, Connecticut, in 1955. The company sold many types of table accessories, such as condiment jars, decanters, spoon holders, and saltshakers. Its figural pieces have a cartoon-like quality. The company was bought out by General Housewares Corporation in 1968. Holt-Howard pieces are often marked with the name and the year or *HH* and the year stamped in black. The *HH* mark was used until 1974. The company also used a black and silver paper label. Holt-Howard production ceased in 1990 and the remainder of the company was sold to Kay Dee Designs. In 2002, Grant Holt and John Howard started Grant-Howard Associates and made a new piece, a retro pixie cookie jar marked *GHA* that sold from a mail order catalog. Other retro pixie pieces were made until 2006.

Ashtray, Figural, Smoking Man, Checkered Shirt, Hat, 1950s, 5 ¼ In.	21
Bank, Kitten, Nodder, Coin Kitty, Black Letters, Blue Bow, Sticker, 5 ¾ x 4 ¾ In.	45
Bell, Christmas Girl, Holding Tree, Red, Pointed Hat, 3 In.	11
Bottle Brush, Christmas Tree, Glitter, Glass Ornaments, 9 In.	30
Butter, Cover, Cozy Cat, Pixieware, 1958, 7 ½ x 2 ¼ In.	125
Candleholder, Angel, Muff, Spaghetti Trim, c.1960, 4 In.	6
Coffeepot, Coq Rouge, Red Rooster, Electric, 1960s, 7 ¼ x 4 ½ In. ....*illus*	74
Cookie Jar, Coq Rouge, Rooster, 1961, 8 x 6 In.	35
Cruet, Pixie Ware, Russian Salad Dressing, Beard, Vertical Stripes, c.1959, 7 In. .....*illus*	50
Eggcup, Cog Rouge, Rooster, 2 ⅞ In.	10
Figurine, Cat, Sitting, Green, Marked, 1960s	297
Head Vase, Daisies, Heart Shape Lips, Closed Eyes, c.1960, 5 ½ In.	80
Jar, Cottage Cheese, Green Border, Kissing Kittens, 1958, 4 In. ....*illus*	39
Jar, Ketchup, Winking, Foil Label, 6 In.	45
Jar, Mustard, Rooster, 4 ½ x 3 In.	16
Jar, Pixie Ware, Olives, Winking, 5 In.	115
Jar, Pixie Ware, Onions, X-Eyes ....*illus*	150
Planter, Christmas Angel, White, Red Bow, 1958, 4 x 2 x 3 In.	25
Salt & Pepper, Christmas Birds, Holly & Bow On Head, Green, 1950s, 3 ½ In.	65
Salt & Pepper, Cozy Cats, Side-Glancing Eyes, Scarves, c.1961, 4 ¼ In.	12
Stringholder, Cat Head, Plaid Scarf, Blue Eyes, c.1958	40

Holt-Howard, Coffeepot, Coq Rouge, Red Rooster, Electric, 1960s, 7 ¼ x 4 ½ In.
$74

Ruby Lane

Holt-Howard, Cruet, Pixie Ware, Russian Salad Dressing, Beard, Vertical Stripes, c.1959, 7 In.
$50

Holt-Howard, Jar, Cottage Cheese, Green Border, Kissing Kittens, 1958, 4 In.
$39

Holt-Howard, Jar, Pixie Ware, Onions, X-Eyes
$150

Holt-Howard

The bowl of a Holt-Howard Pixie is sometimes crazed even though the lid is perfect. The color of the stripes on the bowl always matches something on the lid like a hairbow. The stripes are always vertical on Holt-Howard pieces. Horizontal stripes are used on similar pieces that are "knock-offs" made in the 1950s–1970s.

Hopalong Cassidy, Camera, Original Box, 5 x 4 x 5 ½ In.
$345

Wm Morford Auctions

Hopalong Cassidy, Velocipede, 3 Wheels, Steerhorn Handlebars, Rollfast, D.P. Harris, 24 x 28 In.
$468

Hake's Americana & Collectibles

HOPALONG CASSIDY was a character in a series of 28 books written by Clarence E. Milford, first published in 1907. Movies and television shows were made based on the character. The best-known actor playing Hopalong Cassidy was William Lawrence Boyd. His first movie appearance was in 1919, but the first Hopalong Cassidy film was not made until 1934. Sixty-six films were made. In 1948, William Boyd purchased the television rights to the movies, then later made 52 new programs. In the 1950s, Hopalong Cassidy and his horse, named Topper, were seen in comics, records, toys, and other products. Boyd died in 1972.

Bank, Figural Bust, Mint Green, Plastic, Box, 1950s, 5 In.	115
Button, For Democracy 100 Per Cent, Bill Boyd Portrait, Cowboy Hat, 1942, 1 In.	173 to 190
Camera, Original Box, 5 x 4 x 5 ½ In. ....*illus*	345
Cookie Jar, Hopalong Cassidy & Topper, Barrel, Saddle Lid, Glazed Ceramic, 1950, 11 In.	115
Holster Set, Leather, Gold Plated Cap Gun, Incised, Box, 1955, 7 x 12 In.	209
Lamp, Milk Glass Base, Paper Shade, Hoppy Images, 1950s, 4 x 17 In.	437
Lunch Box, Desert, Decal, Red Metal, Thermos, Aladdin, 1952, 4 x 4 In.	285
Lunch Box, Thermos, Riding Horse, 8 x 7 In.	549
Pinback, Celluloid, Hopalong, Topper, 1 9/16 In.	14
Punch-Out Card, Tell-A-Tale, Hoppy Scenes, Text, 1951, 2 x 3 In., Pair	1265
Radio, Black Metal, Embossed Foil, Hoppy On Topper, c.1950, 8 x 5 In.	209
Ring, Removable Hat & Compass, Brass, HC Initials, Post Cereal, 1952	127
Toy, Hoppy & Topper, Lasso, Rocking, Tin Lithograph, Windup, 1950s, 11 x 10 In.	285
Velocipede, 3 Wheels, Steerhorn Handlebars, Rollfast, D.P. Harris, 24 x 28 In. ....*illus*	468

HORN was used to make many types of boxes, furniture inlays, jewelry, and whimsies. The Endangered Species Act makes it illegal to sell many of these pieces.

Box, Incised Tulips, Compass Star, Red Ink, Hinged Lift Lid, c.1850, 4 ½ In. ....*illus*	450
Carving, Guanyin, Standing, Holding Child, 13 In.	246
Rhinoceros, Trophy, To Frederick T. Martin, Hunt With Teddy Roosevelt, 1907, 14 ½ In.*...illus*	22990
Tobacco Cutting Board, Moose Antler, 5-Point, Filed, c.1910, 16 In. ....*illus*	360
Tumbler, Incised Design Of Husband & Wife, J. Dorrell, 1800s, 4 In.	150

Howard Pierce

HOWARD PIERCE began working in Southern California in 1936. In 1945, he opened a pottery in Claremont. He moved to Joshua Tree in 1968 and continued making pottery until 1991. His contemporary-looking figurines are popular with collectors. Though most pieces are marked with his name, smaller items from his sets often were not marked.

Bust, Woman, Brown Glaze, Speckled Hair, Elongated Neck, Marked, 7 ¾ x 4 In. ....*illus*	90
Figurine, Parent & Child, Modernist, Cobalt Blue Glaze, 10 In.	31
Figurine, Pelican, 8 ½ In.	50
Figurine, Raccoon, 5 In.	27
Vase, Branch With 2 Sitting Birds, 9 In.	22
Vase, Green, White Giraffe Figurine Attached To Base, 7 ¼ x 5 In.	56

HOWDY DOODY and Buffalo Bob were the main characters in a children's series televised from 1947 to 1960. Howdy was a redheaded puppet. The series became popular with college students in the late 1970s when Buffalo Bob began to lecture on campuses.

Cookie Jar, Bumper Car, Yellow, c.1980, 8 x 9 x 5 In.	325
Costume, Buffalo Bob, Blue Suit, Leather Fringe, Belt, Buckle, 30 x 18 In. Shirt	3163
Cue Card, Gallery, Applause Please, O-O-O, Ahhh, 1950s, 11 x 14 In., 3 Piece	934
Display, Hey Kids!, Colgate Dental Cream, Riser, Cardboard, 1954, 30 x 31 In.	127
Lamp, Scout, Seated, Plastic, Blue, White, Round Base, Electric, 1950s, 7 In.	85
Lunch Box, Howdy Holding Frying Pan, Chuck Wagon, Tin Lithograph, 1954	675
Toy, Band, Bob Smith At Piano, Howdy Dancing, Tin Litho, Windup, Unique Art, 8 In. ......*illus*	561
Trading Card, Sheet, Characters, 1951, 6 Cards Per Sheet, 3 Sheets, 7 x 7 In.	115
Watch, Chrome Case, Portrait, Vinyl Band, Movable Eyes, Box, 1950s, 4 x 7 In.	115

HULL pottery was made in Crooksville, Ohio, from 1905. Addis E. Hull bought the Acme Pottery Company and started making ceramic wares. In 1917, A. E. Hull Pottery began making art pottery as well as the commercial wares. For a short time, 1921 to 1929, the firm also sold pottery imported from Europe. The dinnerware of the 1940s (including the Little Red Riding Hood line), the matte wares of the 1940s, and the high gloss artwares of the 1950s are all popular with collectors. The firm officially closed in March 1986.

Bank, Brown Drip, 1957, 5 x 7 In.	39
Bank, Pink & Blue, 1957, 5½ x 7 x 4½ In.	20
Brown Drip, Bowl, Fruit, 5⅜ In.	7
Brown Drip, Cookie Jar	50
Brown Drip, Cup & Saucer	18
Brown Drip, Mug, 4⅛ In.	8
Brown Drip, Pitcher, 8 x 8 In.	20
Brown Drip, Plate, Bread & Butter, 6⅝ In.	7
Brown Drip, Salt & Pepper	20
Cornucopia, Vase, Pink, Black Rim, White Speckles, 6¼ x 11½ In. ....*illus*	24
Figurine, Accordion Player, Swing Band, White, 1940s, 5¾ In.	70
Gray Drip, Cookie Jar, Gingerbread Man, 12 x 9½ In.	215
Green Drip, Mug, Pair	27
Heartland, Creamer	29
Heartland, Sugar & Creamer	64
Little Red Riding Hood, Bank, Standing, 1940s, 6¾ In.	124
Little Red Riding Hood, Cookie Jar, Blond, Yellow Basket ....*illus*	65
Little Red Riding Hood, Sugar & Creamer, Side Pour, 5 In.	25
Little Red Riding Hood, Teapot, Marked, 1940s, 8¼ x 8 x 7 In.	39
Open Rose, Planter, Ram's Head Handles, 6 x 9 In.	25
Pine Cone, Pitcher, White, 11¾ In.	19
Rosella, Cornucopia, White Flowers, Leaves, 1946, 7 x 8½ In.	70
Serenade, Pitcher, Pink, Birds, Flared, 6½ In.	18
Sunglow, Bowl, Pink, Green, Ribbed Rim, 7½ In.	9
Sunglow, Wall Pocket, Iron Shape, Pink, Twisted Handle, c.1952	80
Tawny Ridge, Butter, Cover, ¼ Lb.	27
Tokay, Pitcher, Grapes & Vines, Pink, Twig Handle, Spout, 12 In.	25
Tulip, Basket, Blue Matte Glaze, Red, Yellow, Green Leaves, Scalloped Handle, 8 x 6 In.	58
Tulip, Vase, Footed, Offset Handles, c.1938, 6 In.	40
Vase, Flower, Leaves, Pink, Light Blue, Double Handles, 15½ In. ....*illus*	48
Wildflower, Creamer	69
Wildflower, Pitcher, 7½ In.	40
Wildflower, Vase, Footed, 2 Handles, Scalloped, Yellow, Blue, Mauve, 9 x 8 x 4 In.	36
Woodland, Basket, Pink, Green Handle, Footed, 1940s, 12 x 11 In.	190
Woodland, Jardiniere, Pink, Blue Scalloped Rim & Handles, 7 In.	28
Woodland, Vase, Double, 1950, 8 In.	67

HUMMEL figurines, based on the drawings of the nun M.I. Hummel (Berta Hummel), were made by the W. Goebel Porzellanfabrik of Oeslau, Germany, now Rodental, Germany. They were first made in 1935. The *Crown* mark was used from 1935 to 1949. The company added the *bee* marks in 1950. The *full bee*, with variations, was used from 1950 to 1959; *stylized bee*, 1957 to 1972; *three line mark,* 1964 to 1972; *last bee*, sometimes called *vee over gee,* 1972 to 1979. In 1979 the V bee symbol was removed from the mark. *U.S. Zone* was part of the mark from 1946 to 1948; *W. Germany* was part of the mark from 1960 to 1990. The Goebel *W. Germany* mark, called the *missing bee* mark, was used from 1979 to 1990; *Goebel, Germany*, with the crown and *WG*, originally called the new mark, was used from 1991 through part of 1999. A new version of the bee mark with the word *Goebel* was used from 1999 to 2008. A special *Year 2000* backstamp was also introduced. Porcelain figures inspired by Berta Hummel's drawings were introduced in 1997. These are marked *BH* followed by a number. They were made in the Far East, not Germany. Goebel discontinued making Hummel figurines in 2008 and Manufaktur

Horn, Box, Incised Tulips, Compass Star, Red Ink, Hinged Lift Lid, c.1850, 4½ In.
$450

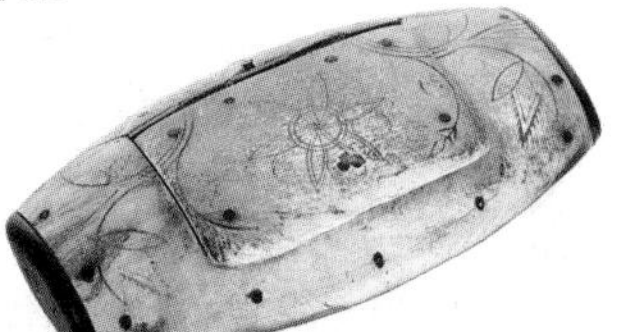

Garth's Auctioneers & Appraisers

Horn, Rhinoceros, Trophy, To Frederick T. Martin, Hunt With Teddy Roosevelt, 1907, 14½ In.
$22,990

James D. Julia Auctioneers

Horn, Tobacco Cutting Board, Moose Antler, 5-Point, Filed, c.1910, 16 In.
$360

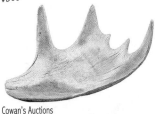

Cowan's Auctions

TIP
Hand-wash dishes and glasses with gold or platinum trim.

Howard Pierce, Bust, Woman, Brown Glaze, Speckled Hair, Elongated Neck, Marked, 7¾ x 4 In.
$90

Ruby Lane

Howdy Doody, Toy, Band, Bob Smith At Piano, Howdy Dancing, Tin Litho, Windup, Unique Art, 8 In.
$561

Bertoia Auctions

Hull, Cornucopia, Vase, Pink, Black Rim, White Speckles, 6¼ x 11½ In.
$24

Ruby Lane

TIP

To remove coffee stains, try wiping the cup with a damp cloth and baking soda.

Rodental took over the factory in Germany and began making new Hummel figurines. Hummel figurines made by Rodental are marked with a yellow and black bee on the edge of an oval line surrounding the words Original M.I. Hummel Germany. The words *Manufaktur Rodental* are printed beneath the oval. Manufaktur Rodental was sold in 2013 and new owners have taken over. Hummel Manufaktur GmbH is the new company. Other decorative items and plates that feature Hummel drawings have been made by Schmid Brothers, Inc., since 1971.

Bell, No. 775, Ornament, Ride Into Christmas, 1989, 3¼ In.	12
Box, Singing Lessons, Little Boy, Yellow Bird, Stylized Bee, 5¼ x 4¾ In.	125
Figurine, No. 43, March Winds, 5 In.	94
Figurine, No. 45, Madonna, Full Bee, 13 In. ....*illus*	37
Figurine, No. 58, Play Mates, Full Bee.	150
Figurine, No. 65, Farewell, Stylized Bee, 4¾ In.	145
Figurine, No. 70, Holy Child, Full Bee, 1950s, 7½ In.	795
Figurine, No. 71, Stormy Weather, Full Bee, c.1945, 6¾ In.	400
Figurine, No. 81, School Girl, Stylized Bee, 5¼ In.	71
Figurine, No. 84, Worship, Stylized Bee, 5¼ In.	116
Figurine, No. 94, Surprise, Full Bee, 4 In.	46
Figurine, No. 127, Doctor, Full Crown Mark, 5 In.	70
Figurine, No. 129, Band Leader, Full Bee, 5 In.	80
Figurine, No. 133, Mother's Helper, Stylized Bee, 5 In.	58
Figurine, No. 142/X, Apple Tree Boy, 1991-2000, 32 x 14 In. ....*illus*	3360
Figurine, No. 152, Umbrella Boy, Missing Bee, 4¾ In.	415
Figurine, No. 169, Bird Duet, Stylized Bee, 4¼ In.	85
Figurine, No. 203, Signs Of Spring, Full Bee, 4 In. ....*illus*	30
Figurine, No. 217, Boy With Toothache, Full Bee, 1950s, 5½ In.	110
Figurine, No. 258, Which Hand, Missing Bee, 5½ In.	125
Figurine, No. 321, Wash Day, 3 Line Mark, 5¾ In.	125
Figurine, No. 336, Close Harmony, 3 Line Mark, 1955, 5½ In.	45
Figurine, No. 340, Letter To Santa Claus, Last Bee, 1957, 7¼ In.	175
Figurine, No. 353/1, Spring Dance, 3 Line Mark, 5⅝ In.	145
Figurine, No. 396, Ride Into Christmas, Missing Bee, c.1971, 6 In.	180
Figurine, No. 429, Hello World, Hummel Mark, 5½ In.	78
Figurine, No. 758, Nimble Fingers, Wood Bench, Hummel Mark, 4½ In.	129
Lamp, No. 223, To Market, Full Bee, c.1965, 19½ x 5 In.	148
Lamp, No. 223, To Market, Stylized Bee, 11½ x 5 In.	148
Pitcher, No. 130/3/0, Man With Sword, Full Bee, Goebel, 3¾ In.	24
Plate, Annual Christmas, Angel Walking With Child, 1974, 7½ In.	6
Plate, Annual Christmas, Angel's Light, 1990, 7¾ In.	15
Plate, Annual Christmas, Feeding Time, 1987, 7½ In.	150
Plate, Annual Christmas, Postman, 1983, 7½ In.	75
Plate, Annual Mother's Day, Der Kleine Fischer, 1973	22
Plate, Annual, Apple Tree Boy, Bas Relief, 1977, 7½ In.	39
Plate, Little Explorers, Danbury Mint, 1980s, 8¼ In.	35
Wall Plaque, No. 30/0, Ba-Bee, Girl, Crown Mark, 5 In.	185
Wall Plaque, No. 48, Madonna & Jesus, Stylized Bee, 4 x 3¼ In.	210
Wall Pocket, No. 360/A, Boy In Tree, Playing Flute, Girl, Flowers, Goebel, 5¾ x 4½ In.	135
Water Font, No. 7, Angelic Prayer, 4¼ x 3¼ In.	126

LORENZ HUTSCHEN REUTER
GERMANY

HUTSCHENREUTHER PORCELAIN FACTORY was founded by Carolus Magnus in Hohenburg, Bavaria, in 1814. A second factory was established in Selb, Germany, in 1857. The company made fine quality porcelain dinnerware and figurines. The mark changed through the years, but the name and the lion insignia appear in most versions. Hutschenreuther became part of the Rosenthal division of the Waterford Wedgwood Group in 2000. Rosenthal became part of the Arcturus Group in 2009.

Bird Of Prey, Wings Up, 17 In.	175
Cake Plate, Flower Bouquets, Gray, Pink, Gilt Rim & Handles, 1920s, 10 In.	150
Figurine, Mother's Darling, Woman Holding Baby In Air, 1950s, 8 In.	1200

H

Figurine, Nude, Ball, Arms Up, 8¾ In.	112
Figurine, Woman, Nude, Arms Up, Stepping Forward, 9 In.	156
Figurine, Woman, Nude, Balancing Gold Spheres, c.1940, 9 In.	400
Figurine, Woman, Nude, Hands In Hair, 13½ In.	343
Figurine, Woman, Nude, Seated, Holding Flowers, Deer, 1940s, 9 In.	295
Figurine, Woman, Nude, Seated, Underwear, Red Polka Dots, 4 x 7 In.	218
Group, May Dance, 3 Girls Dancing In Circle, 1940s, 9 x 9 In.	1500
Group, Nude Woman, Deer, 1995-69, 8½ x 8½ In. ....illus	410
Group, White Horse, Black Colt, 14 In.	150
Jewelry Box, Bronze, 5 Plaques, Women, Landscapes, 4¾ x 7 In.	885
Pitcher, Orange Poppies, Green Leaves, Trim, c.1930, 7 In.	230
Plaque, Maiden With Veiled Bodice, Gilded Wood Frame, Maroon Mat, 5¾ x 7⅝ In.	460
Plaque, Portrait Of Gypsy Woman With Tambourine & Harp, Signed, 5¾ x 8½ In.	89
Plate, Roundels, Art Nouveau, Gold Encrusted Border, 1925-32, Frame, 15 In.	49
Plate, Selb, Navy Blue, Handles, 12¼ In.	13
Platter, Bellevue, 1977-79, 15 In. ....illus	190
Tea Set, Flowers, Purple, Yellow, Pink, Gilt, Teapot, Sugar, Creamer, 1910s	255
Tea Set, Teapot, Creamer, Cup & Saucer, Scenes Of Munich, Blue, Gold, c.1860, 8 Piece	719
Teapot, Dandelion, Blue Gray, Cylindrical, Dome Lid, Finial, c.1950s, 8 In.	169
Vegetable Bowl, Underplate, Revere, 1958-88, 10¼ In. ....illus	95

ICONS, special, revered pictures of Jesus, Mary, or a saint, are usually Russian or Byzantine. The small icons collected today are made of wood and tin or precious metals. Many modern copies have been made in the old style and are being sold to tourists in Russia and Europe and at shops in the United States. Rare, old icons have sold for over $50,000. The riza is the metal cover protecting the icon. It is often made of silver or gold.

Bibical Figures, One Holding Scroll, One With Man's Head In Alms Bowl, 8½ x 6¾ In.	132
Biblical Figures, Silver, Wood Frame, Blue Enameling, Russia, 13¾ x 12 In.	2125
Christ The Pantocrator, Gilt Brass, Painted Wood & Glass, 1800s, 12 x 8¾ x 2¾ In.	562
Christ, Halo, Plaque, Oil On Canvas, Silk, Wood, Pierced Brass Frame, 1800s, 23 In. Diam.	330
Christ, Halo, Tempera On Wood, Gilt & Enamel, Russia, 1800s, 12 x 10 In.	450
Holy Trinity, Silver, Repousse Leafy Scrolling Border, Russia, Marked, 1842, 13 x 11 In.	1250
Kazan Mother Of God, Silver, Mark Of Semyon Galkin, Russia, 1908-17, 9 x 8¾ In.	1063
Kovcheg Panel, 4 Pictures, Mother Of God, 2 Patron Saints, Russia, 1800s, 12⅜ x 12⅝ In.	246
Madonna & Child, Stamped Silver, Russia, 7½ x 5⅛ In.	125
Madonna, Child, Silver, Russia, 5 x 7¾ In.	594
Mary, Christ Child, Arched Panel, Rope Twist Border, Plique-A-Jour, Russia, 2¾ In.	276
Mary, Jesus, Angels, Brass, Ukraine, 22 x 18 In.	156
Mother & Child, Oklad, Silvered, 9 x 7 In.	125
Mother Of God, Silver Plate, 12 Saints, Oklad, Russia, 12½ x 10¾ In. ....illus	1750
Our Lady Of Pomata, Child, Crown, Roses, Oil On Canvas, Frame, Peru, c.1790, 19 x 15 In.	1230
Serafine, Rove, 1700s, 12½ x 11 In.	500
St. Dimitry, Wood, c.1869, 17½ x 14½ In.	406
St. George, Plaque, Slaying Dragon, Giltwood Frame, Spiral Columns, c.1780, 12 x 9 In.	875
Virgin Mary, Holding Christ, Oil On Copper, Shadowbox, 1600s, 18 x 16 In.	180

IMARI porcelain was made in Japan and China beginning in the seventeenth century. In the eighteenth century and later, it was copied by porcelain factories in Germany, France, England, and the United States. It was especially popular in the nineteenth century and is still being made. Imari is characteristically decorated with stylized bamboo, floral, and geometric designs in orange, red, green, and blue. The name comes from the Japanese port of Imari, which exported the ware made nearby in a factory at Arita. Imari is now a general term for any pattern of this type.

Bowl, Central Medallion, Boat, Waves, Crane, Pine Trees, Bamboo, Plum Blossoms, 9¾ In.	68
Bowl, Hexagonal, Red, Blue, 1900s, 2¼ x 6½ In.	43
Bowl, Lobed, Chrysanthemum, Serpentine Rim, Gilt, 4⅝ x 9 In.	123
Bowl, Panels, Trees, Flowers, Gilt, Multicolor, Fukagawa, c.1890, 7½ x 15 In. ....illus	805

Hull, Little Red Riding Hood, Cookie Jar, Blond, Yellow Basket
$65

Strawser Auction Group

Hull, Vase, Flower, Leaves, Pink, Light Blue, Double Handles, 15½ In.
$48

Milestone Auctions

Hummel, No. 45, Madonna, Full Bee, 13 In.
$37

Leighton Galleries

Hummel, Figurine, No. 142/X, Apple Tree Boy, 1991-2000, 32 x 14 In. $3,360

Weiss Auctions

Hummel, Figurine, No. 203, Signs Of Spring, Full Bee, 4 In. $30

Ruby Lane

Hutschenreuther, Group, Nude Woman, Deer, 1995-69, 8½ x 8½ In. $410

Ruby Lane

Charger, Blue, Flower Designs, Red, Yellow, Green, Gold Lines, Leaf Scrolls, 1700s, 14 In.	246
Charger, Blue, Orange, Gold, Green, c.1870, 19 In.	197
Charger, Central Peony, Alternating Landscape, Tree Branch Cartouches, 18½ In.	132
Charger, Flowers, Peonies, Birds, Fan Shape Cartouches, 17½ In.	240
Charger, Folding Screen, Red, Blue, 18 In.	112
Charger, People, Courtyard, 24 In.	480
Charger, Reserve, Text, Covered Dining, Blue Rim, 24 In.	1000
Charger, Scalloped Border, Leaves, Birds, Flower Urn Reserve, Red, Blue, 17¾ In.	375
Charger, Scalloped, Ribbed, Gilt, Flowers, Animals, Birds, 15 In.	228
Compote, Gilt Metal, Flowers, Pedestal Foot, Geometric Fret Handles, 1800s, 13 x 18 In.	461
Condiment Stand, Davenport, Silver Plate, c.1880, 3 Piece, Tallest 4¾ In.	250
Ginger Jar, Lid, Ribbed, Flowers, Birds, Butterflies, Tapered, 10⅞ x 4⅞ In.	275
Jar, Flowers, Garden, Hexagonal, 7 In.	132
Jar, Foo Dog Finial, Dragons, Trees, Flowers, 1850-99, 32 In. ....*illus*	1250
Jardiniere, Gilt Mask Handles, Flowers, Blue, Red, 8 x 11½ In.	135
Jardiniere, Landscape & Flower Panels, Red, Blue, Green, Japan, c.1900, 11½ x 14¾ In.	354
Plate, Dinner, Lotus Flowers, Orange, Blue, Gilt Trim, c.1910, 11 In., 12 Piece	1062
Plate, Leafy Border, Red, Blue & Gold, Paint, 1800s, 1½ x 5 In.	31
Platter, Deer, Landscape, Scroll & Leaf Border, 15½ In.	156
Platter, Reserves, Flowers, Lobed Rim, 24 In.	343
Punch Bowl, Flowers, Landscape, Hand Painted, c.1880, 6 x 15 In.	288
Punch Bowl, Orange & Blue, Late 1800s, 6 x 14½ In.	1062
Tazza, 2 Tiers, Bronze Mount, Figural, Mermen, Fish, Acanthus, c.1890, 10¾ x 12 In.	1000
Teapot, Brocade & Flower Panels, Vines, Red, White, Gilt, Inset Lid, 1800s, 10 x 5 In.	1135
Teapot, Cobalt Blue, Burnt Orange, Figural Finial, Lobed Body, 4¾ In.	94
Vase, Bottle Shape, Blue, Flowers, Multicolor, Ormolu Base, 17¼ In., Pair	500
Vase, Elephant Head Handles, Square, Ironstone, 15 x 4¾ In., Pair	300
Vase, Flowers, Red, Blue, 25 x 14½ In.	472
Vase, Garden, Urn, Stairs, Flowers, 29 In.	531
Vase, Shaped Reserves, Flowers, Scrolling Vines, Blue, Red, Flared Rim, 1800s	830

IMPERIAL GLASS CORPORATION was founded in Bellaire, Ohio, in 1901. It became a subsidiary of Lenox, Inc., in 1973 and was sold to Arthur R. Lorch in 1981. It was sold again in 1982, and went bankrupt in 1984. In 1985, the molds and some assets were sold. The Imperial glass preferred by the collector is freehand art glass, carnival glass, slag glass, stretch glass, and other top-quality tablewares. Tablewares and animals are listed here. The others may be found in the appropriate sections.

Candlewick, Bowl, 10 In.	45
Candlewick, Bowl, 4⅞ In.	15
Candlewick, Bowl, Ebony, 9 In.	81
Candlewick, Candlestick, 2-Light, Pair	45
Candlewick, Celery Dish, Crimped, 8 In.	90
Candlewick, Creamer	10
Candlewick, Plate, Salad, 8 In.	10
Candlewick, Platter, Round, 13 In.	25
Candlewick, Relish, 2 Sections	11
Candlewick, Salt & Pepper	15
Candlewick, Soup, Cream, 5 In.	40
Cape Cod, Cordial, 3¾ In.	6
Cape Cod, Wine, 5 In.	10
Cape Cod, Tumbler, Iced Tea, Footed, 6 In.	12
Crocheted, Bowl, Fluted, Footed, 8 x 4 In.	25 to 41
Crocheted, Compote, Etched, 4¾ In.	30
Crocheted, Dish, Mayonnaise, Underplate	22
Fashion, Pitcher, Water, Marigold, 8 In.	75
Free Hand, Vase, Blue Iridescent, c.1925, 11½ In. ....*illus*	140
Free Hand, Vase, Orange, Blue Decoration, c.1925, 8½ In.	105
Luster Rose, Butter, Cover, Green, ½ Lb.	201

Hutschenreuther, Platter, Bellevue, 1977-79, 15 In.
$190

Replacements, Ltd.

Hutschenreuther, Vegetable Bowl, Underplate, Revere, 1958-88, 10¼ In.
$95

Replacements, Ltd.

Icon, Mother Of God, Silver Plate, 12 Saints, Oklad, Russia, 12½ x 10¾ In.
$1,750

Ruby Lane

Imari, Jar, Foo Dog Finial, Dragons, Trees, Flowers, 1850-99, 32 In.
$1,250

AntiqueAdvertising.com

TIP
Never use hot or cold water on glass. Use dishwashing liquid, a soft toothbrush, and warm water. Rinse, then dry with a terrycloth towel.

Imari, Bowl, Panels, Trees, Flowers, Gilt, Multicolor, Fukagawa, c.1890, 7½ x 15 In.
$805

Cottone Auctions

Imperial Glass, Free Hand, Vase, Blue Iridescent, c.1925, 11½ In.
$140

Jeffrey S. Evans

Imperial, Vase, Gold Luster, Cylindrical, Gray Interior, Flared Rim, Footed, 11½ In.
$58

Early Auction Company

Indian, Bag, Central Plains, Hide, Beaded, Geometric Designs, Tin Danglers, Horsehair, 1870s, 6 x 3 In. $1,353

Skinner, Inc.

Skookum

Skookum Indian dolls can be dated by the material used for the parts. The earliest dolls from the mid–to–late 1910s had apple heads, no feet, and a block of wood for a body. In the early 1920s, some apple-head dolls had composition shoes. In the 1930s, the feet were leather-over-wood moccasins. From the 1910s to the 1940s, dolls had composition masks, some marked "Germany." In the 1940s, plastic masks were used.

Indian, Bag, Doctor's, Lakota, Buffalo, Beaded, Cross Designs, 1880, 6½ x 11 In. $9,225

Skinner, Inc.

TIP
Leather that crumbles to red powder has "red rot." It is caused by absorption of sulfur dioxide and cannot be stopped.

Old Williamsburg, Goblet, Amber, 6½ In.	12
Old Williamsburg, Sherbet, Amber, 4¾ In.	7
Provincial, Goblet, Amethyst, 5 In.	18
Provincial, Goblet, Olive Green, 5 In.	13
Provincial, Sherbet, Olive Green, 4 In.	7
Star Medallion, Pitcher, 5½ In.	23
Star Medallion, Sugar	18
Starlight, Perfume, Bottle Stopper, 6½ In.	35
Vase, Gold Luster, Cylindrical, Gray Interior, Flared Rim, Footed, 11½ In. ....*illus*	58
Vintage Grape, Cordial, 4 In.	25

 INDIAN art from North and South America has attracted the collector for many years. Each tribe has its own distinctive designs and techniques. Baskets, jewelry, pottery, and leatherwork are of greatest collector interest. Eskimo art is listed under Eskimo in this book.

Apron, Great Lakes, Beaded, Tassels, Yarn Pompons, Flowers, c.1890, 48 x 15 In.	593
Awl Case, Apache, Beaded Hide, Dangling Tin Cone Tiers, Handle, c.1885, 13 In.	2583
Backrest, Blackfoot, Peeled Willow, Beaded Panels, Poles, Tapered, c.1910, 66 In., Pair	2280
Bag, Beaded, Zipper, Indian Chief Profile, Flowers, White Ground, 1930s, 11½ x 14 In.	375
Bag, Central Plains, Hide, Beaded, Geometric Designs, Tin Danglers, Horsehair, 1870s, 6 x 3 In.*illus*	1353
Bag, Cheyenne, Hide, Beading, Line Design, Dangles, Fabric Fringe, c.1885, 13 x 18 In.	4800
Bag, Chippewa, Bandolier, Tassels, 1800s	2185
Bag, Cree, Beaded, Round, Drawstring, Seed Beads, Concentric Circles Of Petals, 5 x 5 In.	287
Bag, Doctor's, Lakota, Buffalo, Beaded, Cross Designs, 1880, 6½ x 11 In. ....*illus*	9225
Bag, Doctor's, Sioux, Beaded, Sinew Sewn, Lazy Stitch Beaded, Hinged Satchel, 12 x 17 In.	2380
Bag, Iroquois, Beaded, Flowers, Double Flap, Niagara Style, 1900-25, 7 x 7 In.	195
Bag, Iroquois, Snap Closure, Velvet Ground, Beaded Flowers, 12½ x 7½ In.	258
Bag, Iroquois, Velvet, Beaded, Niagara Style, 2-Sided, Double Flap, c.1910, 7 x 7 In.	81
Bag, Octopus, Tlingit, Indigo Trade Cloth, Brown Ribbon Trim, Flowers, 1900s, 18 x 12 In.	1265
Bag, Tipi, Cheyenne, Geometric Design, Beads, Red Yarn Fringe, 1800s, 18 x 12 In.	593
Bag, Tipi, Sioux, Beaded, Hide, Horsehair, Crosses, Shapes, Tin Cones, c.1890, 14 x 23 In.	2963
Bag, Tobacco, Cheyenne, Hide, Beads, Horsehair, Cone Dangles, Fringe, c.1885, 37 In.	7800
Bag, Tobacco, Ho-Chunk, Beaded Hide, Flowering Vines, Fringe, c.1885, 35 In.	1440
Bag, Yakima, Beaded, Seated Indian, Pipe, Birds, Water, Rose, Mountains, 1940s, 12 x 13 In.	575
Bandolier, Anishinaabe, Beaded, Vine, Leaves, Flowers, Multicolor, c.1890, 14 In.	1045
Bandolier, Anishinaabe, Beaded, Vining Leaves, Flower, Fringe, c.1885, 42 x 16 In.	960
Basket, Apache, 2-Tone, Dogs, Human Figures, Alternating Pattern, c.1900, 3 x 13 In.	3000
Basket, Apache, Meandering Lines, Tan & Dark Brown, Wide Rim, c.1900, 4 x 15 In.	1680
Basket, Apache, Quadrants, Man, Dogs, 1940s, 2 x 9½ In.	207
Basket, Apache, Willow, Coiled, Devil's Claw Zigzag, c.1915, 3¼ x 11½ In. ....*illus*	420
Basket, Bowl, Apache, Woven, Geometric Designs, c.1910, 2½ x 11¾ In. ....*illus*	546
Basket, Chechalis, Flared, Geometric Patterns, Pink, Orange, 1990s, 5 x 7½ In.	287
Basket, Choctaw, Storage, Lid, Natural Cane, Diamond Design, 25 x 21 x 17 In. ....*illus*	500
Basket, Hopi, Braided Rim, Diamonds, 1950s, 3 x 14 In.	161
Basket, Hopi, Coiled, Katsina, Brown, Tan, 9¾ x 12 In.	632
Basket, Hopi, Mesa Coiled, Pictorial Plaque, Katsina, Hair, Retta Lou Adams, 1½ x 17 In.	373
Basket, Lid, Attu, Knob Handle, 3 Color Bars, Wool Threads, 1900, 6 x 7½ In.	862
Basket, Lid, Mono Lake, Beaded, Geometric Designs, Minnie Mike, 7 x 9 In. ....*illus*	4305
Basket, Lid, Nuu Chah Nulth, Horizontal Flowers, Starburst, Knob Handle, c.1900, 6 x 9 In.	546
Basket, Lid, Tlingit, Beaded, Openwork, Multicolor Vertical Zigzag, 1900s, 6 x 4 In.	431
Basket, Mission, Flared, 2-Color Flowers, 2 x 7¼ In.	258
Basket, Peach, Hopi, 6 Katsina Heads, Crosses, Multicolor, Talaheftewa, 10 x 12 In.	488
Basket, Pima, Flared Sides, Maze-Like Design, 5½ x 9½ In.	57
Basket, Pima, Flared, Rattlesnake Design, Diamond Symbols, 1920s, 4 x 8½ In. ....*illus*	259
Basket, Pomo, Coiled, Stepped Symbols, c.1900, 1¼ x 3⅛ In.	230
Belt Buckle, Silver, Oval, Turquoise Stone, James Williams, Arizona, c.1967, 3 x 4 In. ....*illus*	259
Belt Pouch, Plateau, Beads, Orange & Fuchsia, Turquoise Cross, Tassel, c.1910, 6 x 6 In.	1080
Belt, Crow, Leather, Beaded Squares & Border, Brass Tack Designs, Buckle, c.1885, 4 In.	480
Belt, Navajo, 8 Conchas, Radiating Stamp Work, Arland Ben, 1980-90s, 3 x 3¼ In.	2587

Belt, Navajo, 8 Conchas, Silver, Repousse, Large Buckle, Leather Belt, 1970s, 44 In...........*illus*	431
Belt, Navajo, 12 Silver & Turquoise Medallions, Lura Moses Begay, 55 In.	540
Belt, Navajo, Conchas, Silver, Stamped, Turquoise Cabochon, Starburst, 42 x 1 ¾ In.	402
Belt, Plateau, Harness, Leather, Thread, American Flag, Blue, Brass Tacks, 31 ½ x 2 ¾ In...........	747
Belt, Zuni, Concha, Turquoise, Sterling Silver, Weekoty Touchmark, 47 In......................*illus*	4305
Belt, Zuni, Silver & Turquoise, Black Leather, 8 Conchas, 9 Butterflies, c.1965, 47 In..............	1722
Blanket, 3rd Phase Variant, 9 Red Squares, Blue Bars, 1900s, 34 x 40 In................................	431
Blanket, Navajo, Chief's, Banded With Purple Stripes In Four Corners, 1890s, 52 x 56 In.	1500
Blanket, Navajo, Chief's, Third Phase, Red, Gray, Brown, c.1880, 55 x 82 In.	1000
Blanket, Navajo, Chief's, White, Red, Black, Zigzag, Diamond, Stripes, c.1915, 98 x 62 In.	1080
Blanket, Saddle, Navajo, Diamond Design, Minor Imperfections, c.1890, 26 ½ x 29 ½ In.........	406
Blanket, Saddle, Sioux, Beaded Hide, Diamond Shapes, Fringe, c.1885, 75 x 14 In.	3600
Bolo, Hopi, Overlay, Disc, Key Design, Katsina Head, Fernando Puhuhefvaya, 1980, 3 In.	207
Bolo, Navajo, Concentric Turquoise, Coral Bands, 1960-70s, 3 ½ In...	195
Bolo, Navajo, Katsina Slide, Silver, Turquoise, Marked G, 1975-2000, 6 ½ In.	369
Bolo, Navajo, Silver, Leaf Work, Turquoise, Coral, Bear Claws, 4 ½ x 3 ½ In.	460
Bolo, Silver, Leaf Work, Matrix Turquoise Nuggets, 12K Gold Platform, 1980s, 3 x 2 ½ In.	184
Bolo, Zuni, Katsina Head, Wrought Silver, Myron Panteah, 2 x 2 ½ In.	316
Bolo, Zuni, Katsina, Mosaic, Mudhead Oval Tips, Ronnie Calabaza, 1980s, 3 ½ x 2 ¼ In.	1265
Bolo, Zuni, Mosaic Inlay, Silver, Dancer, Carved, c.1972, 45 In., Bolo 7 x 3 In......................*illus*	863
Bolo, Zuni, Rainbow Yei Figure, Mosaic Inlay, Silver, c.1970s, 4 ¼ x 2 ¼ In. ....*illus*	345
Bonnet, Sioux, Beaded, Sinew, Beads, Bars, Four Winds Flag, Velvet Lining, 6 x 5 In.	805
Bottle, Pit River, Basketry Covered Glass, Geometrics, Black, White, c.1910, 12 x 3 In.........*illus*	403
Bow, Great Lakes, Wood, Curved, Painted Designs, Sinew String, Arrows, 1800s, 20 In..............	840
Bowl, Hopi, Cupped, Deep Burgundy, Abstract, Geometric, 4 In..	439
Bowl, Pipe, Great Lakes, Human Hand Effigy, 1 ½ x 3 In...*illus*	738
Bowl, Santa Clara, Blackware, Carved, Waves, Madeline Naranjo, 2 ¾ x 7 In.	360
Bowl, Tlingit, Otter Shape, Carved Alderwood, Abalone Eyes, c.1915, 12 x 5 In.	2370
Box, Navajo, Silver, Stampwork, Spider Web Turquoise, Suzie James, 1980s, 2 ¼ x 5 In.	460
Bracelet, Hopi, Gold, Silver, Etched, Kokopellis, Pueblo, Cloud, 5 ½ x 1 ½ In.	460
Bracelet, Hopi, Silver On Silver, Arch, 3 Panels, Pueblos, Eagle Head, 1980s, 6 ¾ x 1 ½ In.	316
Bracelet, Navajo, Cuff, Buffalo Head, Silver, Turquoise Border, 1975-2000, 6 x 3 ½ In.	308
Bracelet, Navajo, Silver Cuff, Turquoise, Rope Bezel, Stampwork, c.1955, 5 x ⅞ In..........*illus*	173
Bracelet, Navajo, Silver, Turquoise, Rectangles, Circles, Triangles, 1950s, 5 ⅞ x 1 ½ In........	460
Bracelet, Navajo, Turquoise Cluster, Silver Openwork Cuff, 1975-2000, 6 x 2 ¼ In.	554
Bracelet, Navajo, Turquoise, Oval, Silver Mount, Marked, Lois Mike, 6 x 3 ¼ In.	923
Bracelet, Zuni, Cuff, 84 Petit Point Turquoise, Paul Livingston, 1980-90s, 5 ½ x 1 In.	373
Bracelet, Zuni, Cuff, Mosaic, Inlay, Geometric Panels, 5 ⅛ x 1 ⅛ In.	690
Bracelet, Zuni, Inlay, Katsina Dancer, Mosaic, Blue, Red, Cream, 1970s, 5 ½ x 2 ¼ In.	316
Bracelet, Zuni, Needlepoint Style, Silver, Coral Stones, Ray & Eva Wyaco, 5 x 1 ¼ In.	230
Bracelet, Zuni, Shell, Mudhead Dancer, Mosaic Inlay, Red, Black, White, 5 ½ x 2 ½ In.	345
Breastplate, Plains, Bone, 4 Row Mystic Warrior, Shell Rosette, Quilled, Tin, 24 x 18 In.	2300
Breastplate, Plains, Bone, Hair Pipe, Dangling Pennies, 1910, 41 In.	1440
Breastplate, Sioux, Quilled, Bandolier Style, Cloth Beads, Pony Bead Fringe, Red, 36 x 24 In. ...	402
Bridle Cover, Nez Perce, Beaded, Red & Blue Stars, White Ground, 1940s, 17 x 18 In.............	258
Buckle, Hopi, Silver Overlay, Geometric Pattern, Coral Stone, Signed Lomawywisa, 2 x 3 In....	1725
Buckle, Navajo, Copper, Silver Overlay, Stamped, Randy Secatero, 2 x 3 In.............................	230
Buckle, Navajo, Silver Overlay, Shadowbox Style, Radiating Feathers, J.M. Begay, 4 In.	431
Buckle, Navajo, Silver, Oval, Royston Turquoise Nuggets, 3 ⅛ x 3 ⅞ In.	195
Buckle, Navajo, Silver, Overlay, Stamped, 2 x 3 In..	258
Buckle, Zuni, Covered Wagon, Silver, Turquoise, Mother-Of-Pearl, Coral, 3 x 4 In. ....*illus*	360
Buckle, Zuni, Inlaid Stones, Channel Style, Katsina Head, Radiating Feathers, 2 x 2 ⅞ In.	258
Canteen, Cap, Navajo, Tobacco, Chain, Stamped, Coral, 1980s, 3 ½ x 3 In.	345
Canteen, Hopi, Red, Black Zigzag, Round, Ear Handles, Cylinder Spout, c.1885, 9 x 8 In.	5700
Canteen, Tobacco, Zuni, Shell, Silver Detail, Link Chain Strap, c.1935, 4 In......................*illus*	4305
Cherokee, Basket, Lidded, Woven Cane, 2-Tone, Rectangular, 1900s, 17 x 12 x 12 In.	150
Clothing, Navajo, Velvet Blouse, Silver, Cotton Skirt, Ribbon Trim, c.1985, 27 x 36 In. ....*illus*	92
Clothing, Seminole, Jacket & Skirt, Patchwork, Ribbon, 1970s, 28 In., Length 41 In.........*illus*	230
Club, Arapaho, Stone, Double-Headed, Thin Cylindrical Handle, 1800s, 37 In.	1800
Cradle, Apache, Beaded Hide, Wood Frame, Sinew, Navajo Doll, c.1885, 14 x 5 ¾ In........*illus*	1800
Cradle, Cheyenne, Hide, Beaded, Cotton Lined, Wood Slats, Brass Tacks, c.1885, 40 In.	1599

Indian, Basket, Apache, Willow, Coiled, Devil's Claw Zigzag, c.1915, 3 ¼ x 11 ½ In.
$420

Cowan's Auctions

Indian, Basket, Bowl, Apache, Woven, Geometric Designs, c.1910, 2 ½ x 11 ¾ In.
$546

Allard Auctions

Indian, Basket, Choctaw, Storage, Lid, Natural Cane, Diamond Design, 25 x 21 x 17 In.
$500

Neal Auctions

Indian, Basket, Lid, Mono Lake, Beaded, Geometric Designs, Minnie Mike, 7 x 9 In.
$4,305

Skinner, Inc.

> **TIP**
> Beads that are still strung on the original thread have more value than restrung pieces. If you plan to wear the jewelry, be sure the string has not weakened.

Indian, Basket, Pima, Flared, Rattlesnake Design, Diamond Symbols, 1920s, 4 x 8 ½ In.
$259

Allard Auctions

Indian, Belt Buckle, Silver, Oval, Turquoise Stone, James Williams, Arizona, c.1967, 3 x 4 In.
$259

Allard Auctions

Indian, Belt, Navajo, 8 Conchas, Silver, Repousse, Large Buckle, Leather Belt, 1970s, 44 In.
$431

Allard Auctions

Indian, Belt, Zuni, Concha, Turquoise, Sterling Silver, Weekoty Touchmark, 47 In.
$4,305

Cowan's Auctions

Indian, Bolo, Zuni, Mosaic Inlay, Silver, Dancer, Carved, c.1972, 45 In., Bolo 7 x 3 In.
$863

Allard Auctions

Indian, Bolo, Zuni, Rainbow Yei Figure, Mosaic Inlay, Silver, c.1970s, 4 ¼ x 2 ¼ In.
$345

Allard Auctions

Indian, Bottle, Pit River, Basketry Covered Glass, Geometrics, Black, White, c.1910, 12 x 3 In.
$403

Allard Auctions

Indian, Bowl, Pipe, Great Lakes, Human Hand Effigy, 1 ½ x 3 In.
$738

Skinner, Inc.

Cradleboard, Doll, Kiowa, Beaded, Atah, 1900s, 27 x 8 In..............................	10925
Cup, Woodlands, Stylized Bear Handle, Wood, Relief Carved, Figures, 1800s, 5 x 2 In......*illus*	2460
Dispatch Case, Central Plains, Leather, Beaded, Multicolor, c.1900, 11 ½ x 7 In.............*illus*	1968
Doll Cradle, Woven Ash & Split Oak, Basket Weave, Maine, c.1900, 12 x 18 In...........	575
Doll, Central Plains, Hide, Canvas, Horsehair Braids, Beaded Dress, c.1885, 13¾ In. ....*illus*	900
Dress, Paiute, Buckskin, Beaded Figures, Symbols, Cut-In & Tied Fringe, c.1950	546
Dress, Shoshone, Buckskin, Lazy Stitch Beaded Top, Orange, Red, Fringe, Size Large, 1930s.....	1150
Dress, Sioux, Beaded, Buckskin, Yellow, Red, Tin Cone Danglers, Fringe, c.1950, 54 In............	2074
Drum Head, Plains, Painted Hide, Thunderbird, War Eyes, c.1880, 17 x 19 In.	9500
Drum, Log, Taos, Hollowed, Peeled, Stretched Rawhide, 31 x 14 In............................	230
Earrings, Zuni, Flower Head, Turquoise Beads, Silver Dangles, c.1950, 2½ In.....................	240
Envelope, Hide, Parfleche, Paint, Multicolor Shapes, Laced Closure, c.1900, 24 x 14 In.	1200
Figure, Kwakiutl, Shaman, Carved Cedar, Red & Black Paint, c.1890, 16 In.	20145
Gloves, Plains, Hide, Flowers, Side Fringe, Fur Opening, Velvet Lining, c.1875	199
Gloves, Plateau, Beaded, Buckskin, Flowers, Fringe, 1920, 11 In.	316
Gloves, Yakima, Beaded, Buckskin, 5-Point Star, Horses, Horseshoe, 1930s, Size Large..........	489
Hair Ornament, Northern Plains, Quilled Hide Drop, Red & Tan, c.1885, 34 In.	600
Headdress, Northern Plains, Buffalo Hide & Horn, Brass Bells, Abalone, c.1900, 48 In.	3900
Headdress, Plains, Buffalo, Horns, Sinew Sewn, Lazy Stitch, 7 x 19 In...............................	747
Holster, Plains, Beaded, Lazy Stitch, Stripes, Crosses, Fringe, Pink, Green, 1900s, 10½ In.......	460
Horse Rosette, Crow, Keyhole, Beaded, Horsehair Tufts, 15 x 9 In....................................	690
Jar, Acoma, Lattice, Stylized Flowers, Squat, 8¼ In..*illus*	720
Jar, Acoma, Parrots, Pottery, Red, White Ground, Emma Lewis, 5 x 7½ In.	747
Jar, San Ildefonso, Lid, Black Glaze, Gray, Cylindrical, Squared Finial, c.1920, 7 In.	1968
Jar, San Ildefonso, Tan, Orange, Shapes, Bulbous, Tapered Bottom, c.1900, 10 x 12 In............	5100
Jar, Water, Hopi, Pottery, Avian Designs, Red, Black, Flared Rim, 1970-90, 12 x 16 In...............	575
Katsina, Hopi, Eagle, Outstretched Wings, Red & Black Tips, Blue Face, 1980s, 29 x 36 In.......	80
Knife Sheath, Northern Plains, Beaded Hide, Leather Strap, Brass Rivets, c.1885, 9 In.	2400
Knife, Northern Plains, Brass Tacks, Buffalo Hide Beaded Sheath, c.1870, 12¼ In...........*illus*	2640
Ladle, Great Lakes, Carved Maple, Figural Otter, Curved Handle, 1800s, 9 x 5 In.	3998
Ladle, Iroquois, Carved Walnut, Shaped Notched Handle, Wide Bowl, c.1850, 7 x 5 In.	770
Leggings, Cheyenne, Deer Hide, Beading, Tan, Orange, White, Laced, c.1885, 17½ In.	1046
Leggings, Great Lakes, Beading, Black, Flower Vines, Frame, c.1890, 24 x 26 In.	1140
Martingale, Crow, Beaded, Blue, Red Stars, Diamonds, Arrows, Fringe, 46½ x 19½ In.	1150
Martingale, Plateau, Beaded Panels, Buffalo Hide, Shell Discs, c.1885, 36 x 16 In.	3600
Mask, Iroquois, Carved Wood, Painted, Horsehair, Tin Clad Eyes, c.1980, 12 x 7 In...........*illus*	288
Mask, Iroquois, False Face, Horsehair, Tin Eyes, Drooping Red Mouth, 1970-90, 10½ In..........	230
Mask, Mohawk, False Face, Brown, Copper Clad Eyes, Black Hair, 10 x 7 In..............................	230
Mask, Northwest Coast, Carved, Painted, Face, Radiating Extensions, 20 x 24 x 5 In.........*illus*	259
Mask, Northwest Coast, Raven, Feathers, Felt, Pull String Opens Jaw, 1920s, 13 x 5 In.	2370
Mask, Seneca, False Face, Red, Copper Clad Eyes, Spoon Mouth Blower, 10 x 7 In......................	172
Moccasins, Arapaho, Sinew Sewn, Lazy Stitch, Moose Hide, Diamonds, Green, White, 11 In....	287
Moccasins, Boot, Southern Plains, Beaded Hide, Sinew, c.1885, 18 x 9½ In. ....*illus*	3075
Moccasins, Cheyenne, Beaded Hide, Blue, White, Green, Red, 9½ In.	250
Moccasins, Cheyenne, Green Rectangle, 3 White Triangles, Hard Sole, Elkhide, 10½ In.	575
Moccasins, Cheyenne, Hide, Beaded, Fringe, Multicolor Designs, 1880s, 11 In..................*illus*	2337
Moccasins, Cree, White Buckskin, Flowers, Rawhide Soles, 1900s, 9½ In.	184
Moccasins, Crow, Classic Band Design, Leather Soles, c.1950, Child's, 6 x 5½ In.............*illus*	316
Moccasins, Iroquois, Doeskin, Scalloped Borders, Rolled Seam, Child's, c.1900	90
Moccasins, Plains, Hide, White, Red, Green, Laces, 1880s, 10¾ In.	187
Moccasins, Shoshone, White Buckskin, Pink Diamonds, 1980s, 9¾ In.	184
Moccasins, Sinew Sewn, Lazy Stitch, Hard Soled, Green, Red, White, c.1900, 9 In.	161
Moccasins, Sioux, Beaded, Center Seam, Vamp Tabs, Multicolor, 10 In.	1092
Moccasins, Sioux, Hide, Beaded, Quill Wrapped, Multicolor, c.1910, 9½ In.......................*illus*	984
Moccasins, Ute, Buffalo Soles, Lazy Stitch, Antelope Hide, Blue Triangles, 10 x 18 In.	4025
Moccasins, Ute, Sinew Sewn, Lazy Stitch Beaded, Red, Triangles, 1930s, 10 In.	460
Necklace, Hopi, Concha, 9 Disc Plaques, Kokopelli In Maze, Silver, c.1980, 26 In.	1599
Necklace, Navajo, 12 Liberty Dimes, Turquoise Stone Pendant, 1950s, 25 In. ....*illus*	230
Necklace, Navajo, Butterfly Pendant, Turquoise, Sleeping Beauty Stones, 31 In........................	632
Necklace, Navajo, Silver Overlay Box & Triangle Beads, Tommy Singer, 1980-90s, 28½ In..........	977
Necklace, Navajo, Silver, Sand Case, Fleur-De-Lis, Spider Web Turquoise, Signed DTB, 27 In. .	1035

Indian, Bracelet, Navajo, Silver Cuff, Turquoise, Rope Bezel, Stampwork, c.1955, 5 x ⅞ In.

$173

Allard Auctions

Indian, Buckle, Zuni, Covered Wagon, Silver, Turquoise, Mother-Of-Pearl, Coral, 3 x 4 In.

$360

Brunk Auctions

Indian, Canteen, Tobacco, Zuni, Shell, Silver Detail, Link Chain Strap, c.1935, 4 In.

$4,305

Skinner, Inc.

TIP

If you are having antique jewelry repaired, be sure the jeweler uses old stones. New ones are cut differently and will seem brighter. Pearls and turquoise change color with age.

Indian, Clothing, Navajo, Velvet Blouse, Silver, Cotton Skirt, Ribbon Trim, c.1985, 27 x 36 In.
$92

Allard Auctions

Indian, Clothing, Seminole, Jacket & Skirt, Patchwork, Ribbon, 1970s, 28 In., Length 41 In.
$230

Allard Auctions

Indian, Cradle, Apache, Beaded Hide, Wood Frame, Sinew, Navajo Doll, c.1885, 14 x 5¾ In.
$1,800

Cowan's Auctions

Necklace, Navajo, Silver, Turquoise Cabochons, Squash Blossom, Figures, c.1930, 23 In.	584
Necklace, Navajo, Squash Blossom, 15 Coral Stones, 3⅝ In. Naja, 1970s, 32 In.	632
Necklace, Navajo, Squash Blossom, Pueblo Style, Small Beads, 1970s, 24 In.	862
Necklace, Navajo, Squash Blossom, Silver, Turquoise, Marked, 1975-2000, 22 In............*illus*	677
Necklace, Navajo, Turquoise, Silver, 4 Stone Cross, Spaced Stone Choker, 17½ In.	184
Necklace, Plains, Amulet, Bear Claw, Twisted Hide, Beads, Brass Rings, c.1875, 18 In.......*illus*	1363
Necklace, Pueblo, 10 Strands, Turquoise Nuggets, Brown Shells, 1980s, 28 In.	218
Necklace, Pueblo, Mosaic Turquoise, Strung Graduated Coral Beads, 2 In. Pendant, 22 In.	517
Necklace, Santo Domingo, Polar Bear Fetish, Faux Ivory Bears & Heishi, 30 In.	74
Necklace, Zuni, Choker, Inlay, Carico Lake Turquoise, Geometric, Silver, c.2000	977
Necklace, Zuni, Rainbow Figures, Silver, Inlaid Turquoise, Jet, Shell, Coral, 27 In.	523
Necklace, Zuni, Rainbow, 11 Inlaid Figures, Turquoise, Jet, Shell, Coral, Silver Chain, 27 In...	523
Olla, Apache, 2-Tone Basket, Geometric Designs, Dogs, Flared Rim, c.1900, 8 In.	1230
Olla, Basket, Apache, Black Diamonds, 1800s, 24 x 21 In.	3450
Olla, Hopi, Winged Figure & Other Figures, Symbols, Nettie Ami, 1950s, 7 x 9 In............*illus*	489
Olla, Zuni, White, Black & Red Abstract Design, Round, Tapered, c.1885, 12 x 13 In.	4500
Panel, Northwest Coast, Potlatch, Wood Carved, Mythical 2-Headed Serpent, 34 x 7 In.	316
Pipe Bag, Plains, Lazy Stitch, 2-Sided, Blue, Brown, White, 33 x 6 In.	431
Pipe Bag, Plains, Sinew, Lazy Stitch, Front Beaded Box, Blue Bar Design, 1900s, 17 x 6½ In...	485
Pipe Bag, Sioux, 2-Sided, Lazy Stitch, Horse, Rider, Triangles, Fringe, 1990s, 18½ x 6 In.	862
Pipe, Bag, Arapaho, Hide, Beaded, Painted, Geometric & Cross Designs, 1870s, 30 In.......*illus*	6150
Pipe, Plains, Red, Catlinite, File Burned Stem, 4 x 8½ In.	184
Pipe, Sioux, Stone Bowl, Catlinite Inlay, Puzzle Design Carved Handle, c.1885, 28 In.	3075
Pot, Acoma, Water, Handle, Orange & Black & White With Birds, c.1900, 10 x 8 In.	920
Pot, Acoma, Water, Orange & Black & White, c.1900, 13 x 12 In.	460
Pot, Santa Domingo, Orange & Black & Cream, 1800s, 9½ x 10 In.	1610
Pouch, Apache, 2-Sided, Deer Hide, Glass Bead, Fringe, Flap, Late 1880s, 6 x 5 In.	275
Pouch, Northern Plains, Tab, Beaded Hide, Light Blue, Tapered, Tassels, c.1885, 11 In.	1680
Pouch, Plains, Ration Ticket, Beads, Tin Cone Fringe, Label, Albuquerque, c.1885, 6 x 4 In.	360
Pouch, Plains, Strike-A-Light, Beaded Hide, Flap Closure, Tin Cone Fringe, c.1885, 5 In.	1080
Purse, Heart Shape, Beaded, Horse Heads, Flowers, Hide Handle, c.1910, 12 x 11 In.	3500
Purse, Iroquois, Handmade Souvenir, Beaded, Fringe, Box Style, 1906, 4 x 5 In.	65
Purse, Sioux, Sinew, Lazy Stitch, Snap Closure, Lavender, c.1910, 6 x 7½ In.	575
Quirt, Wooden, Carved, Painted, Grass Dance, Wrist Straps, 15½ In.	450
Rattle, Northwest Coast, Bird Human Spirit Transformation, 1980s, 6 x 18 In.	862
Rattle, Northwest Coast, Coyote, Carved, Black, Red, White, Coyote Fur, 1950-80, 12 x 4 In.	184
Rattle, Shaman's, Northwest Coast, Long-Necked Bird, Carved, Multicolor, 7½ x 16 In.	632
Robe, Northern Plains, Bear Skin, Painted Geometric Designs, c.1890, 84 x 68 In.	711
Rug, Navajo, 2 Gray Hills, Earth Tones, 35 x 22½ In.	373
Rug, Navajo, 4 Yei Figures, Black Border, Homespun, 1960s, 39 x 77 In.	632
Rug, Navajo, Chief's, Woven Wool, Stepped Diamonds, Cross, c.1900, 84 x 62 In............*illus*	4800
Rug, Navajo, Feathers, Mirror Image Women, Crosses, Tan, Red, White, Black, 32 x 20 In.	488
Rug, Navajo, Fylfot Crosses, Spools, Diamonds, Serrated Triangles, Red, Black, 17 x 18 In.	431
Rug, Navajo, Ganado, Crosses, Diamond Medallions, Black, Gray, Red, Brown, 43 x 72 In.	180
Rug, Navajo, Ganado, Geometric Pattern, Diamonds Border, 1940s, 42 x 60 In..............*illus*	805
Rug, Navajo, Ganado, Ivory, Linked Medallions, Gray, Brown, Red Border, 33 x 55 In.	228
Rug, Navajo, Opposing Red & White Fylfot Cross, Red, Brown, Swastikas, 73 x 44 In.	920
Rug, Navajo, Wool, Hourglasses, Diamonds, Feathers, 2 Figures, c.1910, 64 x 48 In..........*illus*	2091
Rug, Navajo, Yei Figures, Red, Brown, Green, White Ground, Black Border, 40 x 60 In.	488
Rug, Navajo, Zigzag, Red, Green, Yellow, White, c.1910, 44 x 31 In.	293
Saddlebag, Sioux, Parfleche, U-Shape, Rawhide, Painted Designs, c.1910, 11 x 12 In........*illus*	690
Sand Painting, Navajo, Sandstone, Ceremonial Yei Dancer, Whirling Log, 31½ x 31½ In.	266
Sash, Seminole, Finger Woven, Wool, Dyed, Beads, Long Fringe, Tassels, c.1815, 117 In.	9600
Scabbard, Rifle, Athabaskan, Beaded, Quilled Hide, Flower Vines, Fringe, c.1885, 47 In.	780
Scoop, Northeast Woodlands, Maple, Bear Effigy Handle, Chip Carved, 1800s, 9 x 6 In.	948
Seed Jar, Hopi, Cream, Black & Rust, Panels, Squat, Roll Rim, c.1900, 7 x 14 In.	3900
Sheath & Knife, Sioux, Beads & Hide, Beaded Hanging Tab, Fringe, c.1885, 11 In.	1920
Shirt, Sioux, Tanned Hide, Beaded, Poncho Cut, Paint, Fringe Trim, c.1915, 38 x 62 In.	2370
Spoon, Haida, Hardwood, Black, Totemic Handle, c.1950, 6½ x 2 In.	488
Spoon, Northwest Coast, Goat Horn, Carved, Eagle Tip, Animal Heads, 1950s, 12 In. ....*illus*	431
Spoon, Northwest Coast, Silver, Coastal Figures, Russel Smith Kwakiutl, 1980s	258

Indian, Cup, Woodlands, Stylized Bear Handle, Wood, Relief Carved, Figures, 1800s, 5 x 2 In.
$2,460

Skinner, Inc.

Indian, Dispatch Case, Central Plains, Leather, Beaded, Multicolor, c.1900, 11 ½ x 7 In.
$1,968

Cowan's Auctions

Indian, Doll, Central Plains, Hide, Canvas, Horsehair Braids, Beaded Dress, c.1885, 13 ¾ In.
$900

Cowan's Auctions

Indian, Jar, Acoma, Lattice, Stylized Flowers, Squat, 8 ¼ In.
$720

Brunk Auctions

Indian, Knife, Northern Plains, Brass Tacks, Buffalo Hide Beaded Sheath, c.1870, 12 ¼ In.
$2,640

Cowan's Auctions

Indian, Mask, Iroquois, Carved Wood, Painted, Horsehair, Tin Clad Eyes, c.1980, 12 x 7 In.
$288

Allard Auctions

Indian, Mask, Northwest Coast, Carved, Painted, Face, Radiating Extensions, 20 x 24 x 5 In.
$259

Allard Auctions

> **TIP**
> Many collectors think using leather dressing lowers the value of leather collectibles.

Indian, Moccasins, Boot, Southern Plains, Beaded Hide, Sinew, c.1885, 18 x 9 ½ In.
$3,075

Cowan's Auctions

Indian, Moccasins, Cheyenne, Hide, Beaded, Fringe, Multicolor Designs, 1880s, 11 In.
$2,337

Skinner, Inc.

Indian, Moccasins, Crow, Classic Band Design, Leather Soles, c.1950, Child's, 6 x 5 ½ In.
$316

Allard Auctions

Indian, Moccasins, Sioux, Hide, Beaded, Quill Wrapped, Multicolor, c.1910, 9 ½ In.
$984

Cowan's Auctions

Indian, Necklace, Navajo, 12 Liberty Dimes, Turquoise Stone Pendant, 1950s, 25 In.
$230

Allard Auctions

Spoon, Tlingit, Carved Bowl, Flowering Vines, Incised Tapered Handle, 10 In.		415
Store Display, Doll, Skookum Woman, Dress, Wood Beads, Moccasins, c.1910, 34 In.	*illus*	1380
Ticket, Col. Cummins' Wild West Indian Congress, Portrait Of Geronimo, 1906, 4 x 2 ¼ In.		246
Tomahawk, Plains, Cast Brass Pipe, Burnt Ash Handle, Hide & Tack, c.1890, 22 In.		1659
Tomahawk, Plains, Rocker Blade, Engraved, Scallop Handle, Brass Tacks, 1800s, 20 In.		7200
Totem Pole, Haida, Argillite, Frog, Raven, Salmon, Cat, Black, 11 ½ x 3 In.		805
Totem Pole, Tlingit, Carved Cedar, Paint, Figures, Bird, Fish, Man, c.1900s, 17 x 10 In.		5333
Tray, Apache, Radiating Stepped Pattern, 1 ½ x 15 In.		546
Vase, Cochiti, Figural, Painted Eyes, 2 Strap Handles, Pottery, c.1910, 10 x 9 In.	*illus*	1045
Vase, Navajo, Silver Double Holder, Pillow Base, Copper Inlay, Turquoise Trim, 4 In.		295
Vase, San Ildefonso, Blackware, Matte, Signed, Linda Dunlap, 6 ¼ x 6 In.		437
Vest, Blackfoot, Hide, Beaded, Cloth Lined, Geometric Designs, 1890, 23 In.	*illus*	861
Vest, Northern Plains, Beaded, Elkhide Back, Flowers, White Ground, 20 x 19 In., 1920s		862
Vest, Plateau, Beaded Front, Red & Green Flowers, White Ground, c.1910, 23 x 19 In.		1610
Vest, Sioux, Hide, Beading, Horses, Ponies, Stars, Silver Domed Buttons, c.1885, 22 In.		4613
War Club, Root, Birchwood, Carved Face, Spiked, Tubular Handle, c.1910, 34 x 10 In.		74
Weaving, Navajo, Brown, White, Geometric Border, 1930s, 47 x 70 In.		200
Weaving, Navajo, Diamonds, Crimson Field, c.1910, 92 x 58 ½ In.		2200
Weaving, Navajo, Pictorial, Coal Field, Trucks, Farm, Animals, Border, 1900s, 35 x 43 In.		900
Weaving, Navajo, Red Ground, Black & White Diamond Pattern, c.1900, 95 x 59 In.		1353
Weaving, Navajo, Yei, Dancers, Stepped Border, Germantown, c.1910, 53 x 37 In.	*illus*	2460
Yoke, Plateau, Beaded Front, Stripes, Blue, Green, Red, White, c.1900, 16 ½ x 27 ½ In.		517

INDIAN TREE is a china pattern that was popular during the last half of the nineteenth century. It was copied from earlier Indian textile patterns that were very similar. The pattern includes the crooked branch of a tree and a partial landscape with exotic flowers and leaves. Green, blue, pink, and orange were the favored colors used in the design. Coalport, Spode, Johnson Brothers, and other firms made this pottery.

Creamer, Spode		66
Cup & Saucer, Johnson Brothers		10
Plate, Bread & Butter, Johnson Brothers, 6 ¼ In.		6
Plate, Dinner, Johnson Brothers, 10 In.		17
Plate, Dinner, Spode, 10 In.		72
Plate, Rust, Scalloped Edges, 10 ½ In.	*illus*	30
Platter, Indian Tree, Tree & Well, Ironstone, W & H London, 18 x 23 In.		275
Platter, Johnson Brothers, 12 ¼ In.		24
Tureen, Spode, Lid, 3 Qt.		878

INKSTANDS were made to be placed on a desk. They held some type of container for ink, and possibly a sander, a pen tray, a pen, a holder for pounce, and even a candle to melt the sealing wax. Inkstands date to the eighteenth century and have been made of silver, copper, ceramics, and glass. Additional inkstands may be found in these and other related categories.

Brass, Georgian, 6 x 7 In.		330
Bronze, Beehives, Ormolu, Harpy Mask Shoulders, Footed, 5 x 8 ¾ In.		476
Bronze, Gilt Pageboy, Mottled Black Marble Base, 2 Bronze Inkwells, 10 ½ x 14 In.		240
Bronze, Marble, Musical Putto, Glass Ink Pots, Pen Tray, 6 x 8 ¾ In.		300
Bronze, Porcelain, Mounted Japanese Lacquer, Early 1900s, 3 ½ x 19 x 13 In.		1024
Bronze, Portagent Marble, Napoleon Bust, Eagle Wells, 1800s, 13 x 15 x 12 In.		1024
Cameo Inset, Black, Twist, Italy, 4 ¼ x 5 In.		1250
Cast Metal, Brass Patination, Indian Chief, Glass Inset Well, c.1920, 4 ½ In.		164
Cinnabar, Carved, Figures In Landscape, Pyramid Form, Flower Cover, Chinese, 4 In.		360
Ebony, 4 Elephants, 2 Candleholders, Glass Inkwell, Inlay, Ball Feet, 5 ⅞ x 5 ¾ In.		125
Gilt, Winter, Treestump Inkwells, Leaves, Berries, Vines, 5 ½ x 14 ⅞ In.		570
Horn, Brass, 2 Green Glass Inkwells, 4 ½ x 12 In.		125
Old Paris, Courting Couple, Purple, Gilt Decoration, 8 ½ In.		125
Pagoda Sides, Mandarin Feet, Octagonal, Silver, England, c.1845, 7 x 10 ½ x 7 ½ In.		687
Papier-Mache, 2 Wells, Stamp Box, 14 x 8 In.		62

Indian, Necklace, Navajo, Squash Blossom, Silver, Turquoise, Marked, 1975-2000, 22 In.
$677

Cowan's Auctions

Indian, Necklace, Plains, Amulet, Bear Claw, Twisted Hide, Beads, Brass Rings, c.1875, 18 In.
$1,363

Skinner, Inc.

Indian, Olla, Hopi, Winged Figure & Other Figures, Symbols, Nettie Ami, 1950s, 7 x 9 In.
$489

Allard Auctions

Indian, Pipe, Bag, Arapaho, Hide, Beaded, Painted, Geometric & Cross Designs, 1870s, 30 In.
$6,150

Skinner, Inc.

Indian, Rug, Navajo, Chief's, Woven Wool, Stepped Diamonds, Cross, c.1900, 84 x 62 In.
$4,800

Cowan's Auctions

Indian, Rug, Navajo, Ganado, Geometric Pattern, Diamonds Border, 1940s, 42 x 60 In.
$805

Allard Auctions

Indian, Rug, Navajo, Wool, Hourglasses, Diamonds, Feathers, 2 Figures, c.1910, 64 x 48 In.
$2,091

Cowan's Auctions

Indian, Saddlebag, Sioux, Parfleche, U-Shape, Rawhide, Painted Designs, c.1910, 11 x 12 In.
$690

Allard Auctions

Indian, Spoon, Northwest Coast, Goat Horn, Carved, Eagle Tip, Animal Heads, 1950s, 12 In.
$431

Allard Auctions

I

Indian, Store Display, Doll, Skookum Woman, Dress, Wood Beads, Moccasins, c.1910, 34 In.
$1,380

Allard Auctions

Indian, Vase, Cochiti, Figural, Painted Eyes, 2 Strap Handles, Pottery, c.1910, 10 x 9 In.
$1,045

Cowan's Auctions

Indian, Vest, Blackfoot, Hide, Beaded, Cloth Lined, Geometric Designs, 1890, 23 In.
$861

Skinner, Inc.

Porcelain, Ruyi Shape, Dragon & Phoenix, Banding, Blue & White Glaze, 5 In.	615
Porcelain, Stand, Pot, 2 Inkwells, Bleu Celeste, Bouquets, Garlands, Sevres, 6⅝ x 11⅝ In.	1220
Silver Plate, Glass Inkwells, Removable Candlestick, 9½ In.	175
Silver Plate, Glass, Pierced Gallery, 8½ x 5 In.	63
Silver, 2 Glass Inkwells, 9¼ In.	213
Silver, Acanthus Scrolling, Cut Glass Wells, E. Barnard & Sons, London, 10 In. ....*illus*	343
Wood, Black Forest, Antlered, 2 Glass Inkwells, 7 x 9 In.	813

INKWELLS, of course, held ink. Ready-made ink was first made about 1836 and was sold in bottles. The desk inkwell had a narrow hole so the pen would not slip inside. Inkwells were made of many materials, such as pottery, glass, pewter, and silver. Look in these categories for more listings of inkwells.

Bisque, Figurine, 3 Women & A Secret, Dreamy Eyes, Curtain, 2 Wells, Germany, 10 In.	285
Bronze, Dog, Cold Painted, Multicolor, Marble Base, Early 1800s, 4½ In.	240
Bronze, Gilt, Bouquet, North Wind Face, 9 x 9 In.	87
Bronze, Gilt, Champleve, Pierced Shell Border, 4 x 10¾ In.	1500
Bronze, Grand Tour, 3 Bull Heads, 3 Bacchus Heads, Grapes, Cupid, Dolphin, 7½ x 4 In.	265
Bronze, Napoleon III, Putti, Urn, Square Base, 4½ In.	406
Bronze, Owl On Book, c.1900, 3 In.	320
Bronze, Urn Shape, Hinged Lid, Baroque Style, Heroes, Acanthus, Underplate, 1800s, 7 x 7 In.	188
Brown, Green Glaze, Drum Shape, 4 Quill Holes, Yellowware, c.1875, 4½ In. Diam.	65
Copper, Arrowheads, Gourd Shape, Shreve & Co., c.1900, 3 x 5½ In.	1500
Cut Glass, Scenic Repousse, Kirk & Son Co., 4⅝ x 4 In.	150
Gilt Bronze, Glass, Renaissance Style, Lions, Early 1900s, 4 x 10 x 10 In.	750
Gilt Bronze, Pierced Base, 2 Pots, 2 Candle Cups, Pink Silk Screen, c.1880, 18 In. ......*illus*	1187
Gilt Metal, Walrus Head, Porcelain Interior, Hinged, Round Marble Base, 6 x 8 In.	254
Glass, Beaded Silver Lid, Carved Carnelian, Pink Gem, D. Donaldson, 3 x 2½ In.	1000
Glass, Multi-Cane, Rod, Cobalt Blue, Multicolor, Clear Coin Spot, Stopper, 7½ In.	120
Glass, Oak Leaves, Purple, Daum, c.1920, 4½ x 3⅞ In.	2750
Jade, Rosewood, Silver, Flared, Reticulated Handles, Flowers, c.1900, 4 x 4 In.	1180
Metal, Glass, Elephant Head, Monkey Atop, Decorated For Parade, 1920s, 6 x 4 In.	265
Metal, Rebecca At The Well, Cold Painted, Metal, Franz Bergmann, 28 x 9½ In.	62
Onyx, Dome Lid, Flowers, Alabaster Base, Fluted, Green, 5 x 9¾ In.	156
Ormolu, Malachite, Dragon Handles, Phoenix, Scroll, Flowers, 4 x 9 In.	687
Ormolu, Sailboat, Mother-Of-Pearl Sails, 2 Glass Wells, 9 In. ....*illus*	396
Pearlware, Figural, Seated Women, Pink Clothing, Multicolor, 4¼ x 5¾ In.	600
Porcelain, Clown, Ruffled Collar, Red, White, Becquerel, Pierrot, 4 x 3¼ In.	687
Porcelain, Figurine, Best Friends, 2 Women, Embracing, Top Half Removes, 2 Wells, 10 In.	114
Porcelain, Figurine, Young Ladies At Dressing Table, 1 Sits, 1 Combs Hair, 2 Wells, 9 In.	285
Porcelain, Glazed, Cherry Amethyst Finial, Jade, E. Farmer, Early 1900s, 5½ x 3½ In.	2125
Porcelain, Glazed, Repurposed Chinese Jade, Edward Farmer, Early 1900s, 4 x 2½ In.	1250
Porcelain, Mother, Seated In Chair, Girl On Lap, Boy Leaning, Germany, 9 x 9 In.	399
Porcelain, Trio Of Children At Play, Hidden Wells, Germany, Mid 1800s, 6 In.	171
Redware, Manganese Stripes, 1800s, 2¾ x 3½ In.	540
Silver Plate, Round Base, Beaded Border, Glass Liner, Elkington, Eng., 3 x 9 In.	120
Silver, Candle Sconce, Snuffer, Scroll Arms Form Pen Rest, Shell, Base, c.1832, 5 In.	492
Silver, Round, Openwork Rim, Faux Tortoiseshell Lid, Mappin & Webb, 2 x 4 In.	60
Sterling Silver, Gilt Wood, Agate, Lotus Flower, E. Farmer, Early 1900s, 5¼ x 3¼ In.	1125
Wood, Black Forest, Carved, Figural Dog Head, Pen Tray, 1800s, 11 x 7 In. ....*illus*	1350
Wood, Bulldog Head, Black Forest, Glass Eyes, Hinged Lid, c.1875, 2⅞ x 3 x 2¼ In.	425
Wood, Diver's Helmet Shape, Ebonized, Siebe Gorman & Co., 1910, 5 In.	2125
Yellowware, Figural, Deer, Variegated Glaze, East Liverpool, Ohio, c.1875, 7 In.	240
Yellowware, Man Reclining On Rocky Base, Rockingham Glaze, c.1875, 3¼ x 5 In.	120

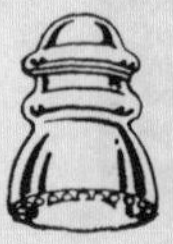

INSULATORS of glass or pottery have been made for use on telegraph or telephone poles since 1844. Thousands of styles of insulators have been made. Most common are those of clear or aqua glass; most desirable are the threadless types made from 1850 to 1870. CD numbers are Consolidated Design numbers used by collectors to indicate shape.

CD 100, Surge Glass, Embossed, Reg. U.S. Pat. Off., 2¾ In.	20
CD 102, Diamond, Mustard Yellow	1540
CD 106, Hemingray, No. 9, Clear Glass	25
CD 110.6, National, Corkscrew, Blue Aqua	880
CD 123, EC & M Co. S.F., Green	330
CD 134, No. 16, Pat Dec 19 1871, Yellow Olive Green	2750
CD 134, Standard, Straw, Threadless	3135
CD 152, Hemingray, No. 40, Green Glass	69
CD 154, Whitall Tatum, Deep Red Amber	2145
CD 155, Kerr, Clear With Cobalt Blue Splotch	743
CD 155.6, Hemingray, Aqua	10670
CD 164, Hemingray, No. 20, Blue Glass, Embossed	40
CD 228, Brookfield, Deep Green Aqua	688
CD 242, Hemingray, No. 66, Blue	468
CD 247, Ribbed Power, Blue Aqua	495
CD 265, Fisher, Light Green	7700
CD 268, The Crown, Pat Allowed, Deep Aqua	7810
CD 317, Chambers, Candlestick, Light Green	825
CD 735, Tillotson, Teal Green	413
CD 737, Lefferts, Aqua	2915
CD 790, Teapot, Dark Teal	5720
CD 1003, Block, Non-Tapering Wire Groove, Light Blue	1430
CD 1038, Cutter, Pat Apr 26, 04, Green	468

IRISH BELLEEK, *see Belleek category.*

IRON is a metal that has been used by man since prehistoric times. It is a popular metal for tools and decorative items like doorstops that need as much weight as possible. Items are listed here or under other appropriate headings, such as Bookends, Doorstop, Kitchen, Match Holder, or Tool. The tool that is used for ironing clothes, an iron, is listed in the Kitchen category under Iron and Sadiron.

Ashtray, Giraffe, Wrought, Thomas Molesworth, 30 x 8 In.	2875
Ashtray, Skillet Shape, Handle, 2 Cigarette Rests, Wagner Ware, 4¾ In.	15
Bed Warmer, Long Handle, Perforated, 33 In.	58
Brush Holder, Tinned, Can & Handle, Cylindrical Tubes, Dome Lid, Brush, c.1900, 11 x 8 In.	246
Burglar Alarm, Trip Mechanism, Domed, Marked Patd	173
Bust, Apollo, Eyes Cast Over Shoulder, 26 In. *illus*	2318
Censer, Squat, Bulbous, Loop Handles, Tripod Feet, Rust Glazed, c.1800, 5 x 6 In.	1476
Coal Heater, Louis XV, Blue, Porcelain Enamel, Pierced Flowers, Deville & Cie., 24 x 16 In.	375
Cow, Head, 21 x 20 In.	380
Cross, Leaves, Black Paint, 41½ x 21 In.	265
Cuspidor, Derby Hat Shape, White Enamel Interior, 3 In.	875
Cuspidor, Top Hat Shape, Black, 7¼ In.	593
Eagle, Pilot, House, Cast, 12 In.	610
Eagle, Spread Wings, Banner, Gold Paint, Late 1800s, 24¼ x 29 In.	2160
Figure, Butler, Holding Tray, Elongated Flat Figure, Patent Applied For, 1920s, 25 In. *illus*	228
Figure, Gargoyle, Seated, Spread Wings, Open Mouth, Black Paint, c.1890, 34 x 43 In. *illus*	1024
Group, Farmer, Horse Drawn Plow, c.1901, 5 x 14 In.	2768
Harness Holder, Horse, Red Paint, c.1900, 35½ In.	300
Hook, Beam, Cutout Heart, Single Loop Hook, c.1800, 5 x 2 x 6¼ In.	375
Ice Shaver, Wheel, Square Base, Red, Green, White, 24¼ x 12¾ In.	206
Mask, Face, 17 x 23 In.	134
Pipe Kiln, 4-Footed, 1700s, 14¼ In.	351
Porringer, Lid, Openwork Arched Tab Handle, Eagle, 13 Stars, 1800s, 2½ x 7 In.	800
Porringer, Wide Rim, Tab Handle With Double Heart Cutout 1800s, 2 x 8 In.	150
Rush Holder, Turned Wood Base, 10½ In.	480
Shooting Gallery Target, Clown With Bell & Clapper, Early 1900s, 19 In.	510
Shooting Gallery Target, Man In Top Hat, Early 1900s, 14 In.	660
Spatula, Thistle, Twisted Handle, Canada, 10¾ In.	80

TIP

Turn a telephone insulator upside down and you can plant a small cactus in the top hole. Use quake wax or the wax used by orthodontists to prevent braces from rubbing to hold the insulator on a saucer or jelly jar cover.

Indian, Weaving, Navajo, Yei, Dancers, Stepped Border, Germantown, c.1910, 53 x 37 In.
$2,460

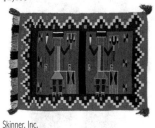

Skinner, Inc.

Indian Tree, Plate, Rust, Scalloped Edges, 10½ In.
$30

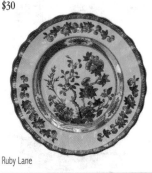

Ruby Lane

Inkstand, Silver, Acanthus Scrolling, Cut Glass Wells, E. Barnard & Sons, London, 10 In.
$343

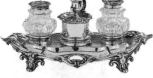

New Orleans Auction Galleries

Inkwell, Gilt Bronze, Pierced Base, 2 Pots, 2 Candle Cups, Pink Silk Screen, c.1880, 18 In.
$1,187

New Orleans Auction Galleries

Inkwell, Sailboat, Mother-Of-Pearl Sails, Ormolu, 2 Glass Wells, 9 In.
$396

Ruby Lane

Inkwell, Wood, Black Forest, Carved, Figural Dog Head, Pen Tray, 1800s, 11 x 7 In.
$1,350

Cottone Auctions

Stag, Gray Painted Surface, Rust Showing Through, Late 1800s, 58 x 40¼ x 16½ In.	2400
Statue, Man, Wearing Armor, Beard, Standing, Footed Base, Chinese, c.1880, 13 In.	237
Stick, Hasty Pudding, Shaped Handle, Openwork Double Scroll Finial, 1700s, 15 x 2 In.	350
Stick, Hot Toddy, Shaped Flat Handle, Loop Finial, Round Rod, Ball Tip, 1800s, 11¼ In.	550
Strong Box, Baroque, Painted, Handles, Leaves & Flowers, Double Eagle, 1800s, 19 x 42 x 22 In.	944
Umbrella Stand, Circles, 30½ x 21 In.	112
Umbrella Stand, Jack Tar, Sailor, Drip Pan, Anchor, Spade, 26 x 18 In. ....*illus*	415
Umbrella Stand, Stylized Coral, Figural Dolphin Feet, 31½ x 21½ In.	560
Windmill Weight, Bell, Embossed, Early 1900s, 9 In.	270
Windmill Weight, Buffalo, Mounted On Stand, Early 1900s, 15½ In.	600
Windmill Weight, Bull, White Head, Red Body, Fairbury Windmill Company, c.1910-20	672
Windmill Weight, Eagle, Feather Detailing, Mounted On Metal Base, Early 1900s, 15¼ In.	900
Windmill Weight, Eagle, Head Turned, 15 In.	936
Windmill Weight, Eagle, Spread Wings, 24 In.	555
Windmill Weight, Elgin Wind Power & Pump Co., Old Black Paint, Early 1900s, 10 In.	250
Windmill Weight, Football Shape, Baker Manufacturing Co., c.1916-18	175
Windmill Weight, Horse, Dempster, Mounted On Stand, Early 1900s, 10 In.	360
Windmill Weight, Horse, Long Tail, Brown, Black Paint, Dempster, c.1905, 15 x 16 In.	975
Windmill Weight, Letter W, Althouse Wheeler Company, c.1910-20	409
Windmill Weight, Oval, Plattner Yale Embossed, Lincoln, Neb., Stand, Early 1900s, 11 In.	330
Windmill Weight, Rooster, 20 x 18 In.	175 to 292
Windmill Weight, Round, Embossed, Myers Imperial, Ashland, Ohio, 6½ x 2¾ In.	2700
Windmill Weight, Spearhead, Challenge, Batavia, Ill., Stand, Early 1900s, 12 x 23¾ In.	120
Windmill Weight, Squirrel, Silver Paint, Elgin Wind Power & Pump Co., 17½ In.	1046
Windmill Weight, Star, 5 Points, Old Gray Paint, On Stand, Early 1900s, 14 In.	600
Windmill Weight, Waupun W, Althouse-Wheeler Co., Waupun, Wis., Early 1900s, 16½ In.	461

IRONSTONE china was first made in 1813. It gained its greatest popularity during the mid-nineteenth century. The heavy, durable, off-white pottery was made in white or was decorated with any of hundreds of patterns. Much flow blue pottery was made of ironstone. Some of the decorations were raised. Many pieces of ironstone are unmarked, but some English and American factories included the word *Ironstone* in their marks. Additional pieces may be listed in other categories, such as Chelsea Grape, Chelsea Sprig, Flow Blue, Gaudy Ironstone, Mason's Ironstone, Moss Rose, Staffordshire, and Tea Leaf Ironstone.

Bowl, Vegetable, Wheat Pattern, China Blue, Oval, Lid, Side & Top Handles, 12 In., Pair	295
Feeder, Blue, White, Pagoda, Bridge, Blue Willow, 7 In.	187
Feeder, Blue, White, River, Landscape, Copeland Spode, 7 In.	475
Feeder, Blue, White, Transfer Printed, Flowers, Branches, 6½ In.	275
Feeder, Blue, White, Transfer Printed, Leaves, Flowers, 7 In.	237
Pitcher, Relief Molded, Death Of Ellsworth & Killing Of Jackson By Brownell, 9 In.	2500
Plate, Rabbit & Frog Transfer Scenes, Stick Spatter Border, 9⅜ In. ....*illus*	106
Platter, Abbey Pattern, Green Transfer, Flower Border, Shaped Rim, 17 x 21 In.	142
Punch Bowl, Furnival, Rustic Pattern, Impressed, c.1870, 9⅞ x 19½ In.	488
Toddy Plate, Recallers, Alphabet Border, 5½ In. Diam.	95

ISPANKY figurines were designed by Laszlo Ispanky, who began his American career as a designer for Cybis Porcelains. He was born in Hungary and came to the United States in 1956. In 1966 he went into business with George Utley in Trenton, New Jersey. Islpanky made limited edition figurines marked with his name and Utley Porcelain Ltd. The company became Ispanky Porcelains Ltd. in 1968 and moved to Pennington, New Jersey. Ispanky worked for Goebel of North America beginning in 1976. He worked in stone, wood, or metal, as well as porcelain. He died in 2010.

Bust, Brown Hair, Pulled Back, Blue Bow In Hair And On Shoulder, 9 x 5 In.	125
Bust, Susie, Blond, Ponytail, Pink Band, Goebel, 8 In.	45
Figurine, Autumn, On Stump, Holding Bowl Of Fruit, Limited Edition, 7 In. ....*illus*	60
Figurine, Ballerina, Stretching, Green Flowered Tights, 15 In.	70
Figurine, Indian On Horseback, Buffalo, 16 x 17 In.	175

Figurine, Indian Woman, Horse, Papoose, 12 ¾ In.	180
Figurine, Pegasus, Leaping, White, 12 In.	50 to 156
Figurine, Sitting, Flowered Chair, Blond Hair, Yellow Dress, Goebel, 8 x 7 ½ In.	40
Figurine, Waist Up, Elizabeth, Blond, Pink Gown, Holding Flowers, 8 In.	275

IVORY from the tusk of an elephant is thought by many to be the only true ivory. To most collectors, the term *ivory* also includes such natural materials as walrus, hippopotamus, or whale teeth or tusks, and some of the vegetable materials that are of similar texture and density. Other ivory items may be found in the Scrimshaw and Netsuke categories. Collectors should be aware of the recent laws limiting the buying and selling of elephant ivory and scrimshaw.

Basket, Village Scene, Insects, Flowers, 8 ¼ In.	750
Box, Dragon Shape Handles, Bamboo Legs, Foo Dog Finial, 6 In.	250
Box, Hinged Lid, Carved, Knights, Rose Garlands, Beadwork, Cylindrical, Ball Feet, 4 In.	224
Figurine, Ada May, Holding Glass Sphere, Bronze Dress, Onyx Base, c.1925, 14 In.	20268
Figurine, Butterfly Dancers, 2 Girls, Legs Extended, Flowing Tunic, c.1925, 17 In.	46063
Figurine, Diana, With Bow, Bronze Borzoi Dog At Her Side, Onyx Base, c.1925, 13 In.	18425
Figurine, Emperor, Empress, 15 ½ x 3 ¾ In., Pair.	2100
Figurine, Foo Dog, Seated, Carved Base, 8 In.	312
Figurine, Japanese Woman, Robe, Holding Fan, Headpiece, Butterflies, Wood Stand, 13 In.	502
Figurine, Man, Goods Hanging From Shoulders, 6 ¾ In.	187
Figurine, Phoenix, Carved Post, 11 In., Pair.	125
Figurine, Woman, Dog, Seated, Knee Up, 6 ⅝ x 3 In.	600
Flask, Dragon, Bat, Leaves, Rings, 12 In.	187
Group, Woman, Child, Basket, Fish, Pole, Holds Skirts, 7 ½ In.	189
Plaque, Joan Of Arc, Gothic Frame, 1800s, 9 x 4 ¼ In.	2070
Tusk, Figures, Trees, Landscape, 17 ½ In. ....*illus*	545
Tusk, Leaves, Dragons, Birds, 42 In.	1875
Urn, Figures, Temple, Dragon Handles, Foo Dog, Frame, 9 In.	437
Vase, People, Everyday Life, Frame, 4 In., Pair.	437

JACK-IN-THE-PULPIT vases, shaped like trumpets, resemble the wildflower named jack-in-the-pulpit. The design originated in the late Victorian years. Vases in the jack-in-the-pulpit shape were made of ceramic or glass.

Vase, Glass, Blue Opalescent, 11 ¾ x 6 ¾ In.	24
Vase, Glass, Gold Iridescent, Applied Leaves, 8 In.	816
Vase, Glass, Green Opalescent, Lundberg Studios, 17 In.	453
Vase, Glass, Matte Green, Matte Red, 18 x 7 ½ In.	60
Vase, Glass, Opalescent, Cranberry Peppermint, 10 ½ In.	96
Vase, Iridescent Gold, Magenta, Green, Pulled Leaves, Ribbed, 11 In.	236

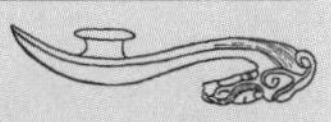

JADE is the name for two different minerals, nephrite and jadeite. Nephrite is the mineral used for most early Oriental carvings. Jade is a very tough stone that is found in many colors from dark green to pale lavender. Jade carvings are still being made in the old styles, so collectors must be careful not to be fooled by recent pieces. Jade jewelry is found in this book under Jewelry.

Archer's Ring, Tubular, Angled Top, Flat Rim, Pale Green, Translucent White, 1 x 1 In.	246
Belt Buckle, Dragon Head Hook, Openwork Chilong, Flowers, Oval, 4 In.	1230
Belt Hook, Spinach Green, Carved, Figural Dragon, Chilong, 1900s, 5 ¼ In.	237
Bowl, Carved, Green, Rounded Corners, Rosewood Stand, Chinese, Early 1900s, 5 x 9 In.	4500
Bowl, Carved, Shallow, 8 Buddhist Symbols, Chinese, c.1973, 6 ½ In.	15600
Bowl, Green, Flared Rim, Stand, Boxed, 2 ¾ x 4 In., 14 Piece.	357
Brushwasher, Celadon, Unfurling Lotus Leaf, 8 ½ In.	11875
Citron, Buddha's Hand, Leafy Branch, Carved, Incised, Pale Green, White, 1700s, 3 In.	1107
Cup, White, Carved, 1700s, 1 ⅛ In.	1562
Figurine, Black, White, Woman, Cliff, Flowers, Rabbit, Stand, 10 ¾ In.	406
Figurine, Buddha, Bottle Of Elixir, 1 ¾ x 1 In.	64

Iron, Bust, Apollo, Eyes Cast Over Shoulder, 26 In.
$2,318

Copake Auction

Iron, Figure, Butler, Holding Tray, Elongated Flat Figure, Patent Applied For, 1920s, 25 In.
$228

Theriault's

Iron, Figure, Gargoyle, Seated, Spread Wings, Open Mouth, Black Paint, c.1890, 34 x 43 In.
$1,024

Neal Auctions

Iron, Umbrella Stand, Jack Tar, Sailor, Drip Pan, Anchor, Spade, 26 x 18 In.
$415

James D. Julia Auctioneers

Ironstone, Plate, Rabbit & Frog Transfer Scenes, Stick Spatter Border, 9 3/8 In.
$106

Hess Auction Group

Figurine, Buddha, White, Spinach Green, 2 3/8 x 1 3/8 In. ....*illus*	450
Figurine, Goat, Horned, Reclining, White, 1 1/2 x 2 In.	159
Figurine, Goat, Reclining, Branch In Mouth, Rosewood Footed Base, Chinese, c.1900, 4 x 4 In.....	3750
Figurine, Horse, Reclining, Head Turned, Carved, Incised, Pale Green, Russet Marks, 2 x 3 In.	4920
Figurine, Horse, White, Carved, Based Fitted Into Wood Stand, Chinese, Early 1900s, 6 In.......	960
Figurine, Horse, White, Seated, Stand, Chinese, 2 1/2 x 3 1/2 In.	562
Figurine, Mirror, Hand, White, Silver, Dragon, Eel, Elephant, 9 In.	3596
Figurine, Monkey, Sitting, White, 2 1/4 In..	4760
Figurine, Panther, Crouched, Stalking Prey Pose, Spinach Green, Stand, Carved, 1900s, 6 In.	356
Figurine, Phoenix, Cabbages, Leaves, Wood Base, 14 In., Pair	1500
Figurine, Phoenix, Celadon, 9 3/8 In.	687
Figurine, Rooster, Carnelian, Gilt Metal, Edward Farmer, Early 1900s, 6 x 5 x 3 In....	2000
Figurine, Seal, Russet, Chinese Characters, 1 1/2 x 1 3/4 In.	187
Figurine, White, Lavender, Gown, Fruit, Vine, 7 x 3 In.	613
Figurine, White, Standing Goddess In Robe, Wooden Stand, Chinese, Early 1900s, 8 1/2 In.......	720
Figurine, Woman, Flowing Robe, Holding Bottle, Pale Green, Wood Stand, 1900s, 10 In.	415
Figurine, Woman, Holding Peach & Branch, Rockery Base, Wood Stand, c.1910, 8 In., Pair.....	3851
Group, 3 Immortals, Lavender & Bits Of Green, Carved, Chinese, c.1950, 6 1/2 x 2 In.........	937
Group, Duck, Ducklings, Cattails, White, Stand, 1900s, 3 In.	1187
Group, Monkeys, Climbing, Playing, Drinking, 2 1/2 x 3 3/4 In.	750
Group, Qilin, Reclining With Cub, Pale Green, Russet, White Striations, Carved, 1 x 3 In........	1599
Group, Soldier, Horse, Gilt, Silver, Bone, Turquoise, Box, 7 1/2 In.	1500
Jar, Carved Dragons, Pearls & Clouds, Hardwood Stand, Chinese, c.1950, 6 x 7 1/2 In.	343
Page Turner, Brass, Chased, Relief Decorated, Peach & Bat, Dragon, 13 1/4 x 1 In..........	4200
Plaque, Lock, Peony, 1800s, 3 3/8 In.	1770
Sculpture, Disc, Carved, Spinach Green, Wood Base, 1368-1644, 12 1/2 x 5 1/2 In.	3738
Tea Set, Teapot, 4 Cups, Tray, Cherry Blossom, Serpentine, 6 Piece	125
Teapot, Foo Dog Handle, 5 1/4 x 8 1/2 In..	3570
Toggle, Stylized Chilong, Phoenix, Bat, Relief Carved, Openwork, Olive Green, Russet, 3 In.....	984
Tree, 2 Hardstone Eagles On Top, Pine Base, Carved, Chinese, c.1900s, 26 x 13 x 9 3/4 In.........	875
Urn, Spinach Green, Loose Ring Handles, 9 In.	1375
Vase, Carved Layered Leaves, Birds, Lingzhi, Pale Green, Flared Petal Rim, 1900s, 6 In.	1067
Vase, Carved, Scrollwork, Dragon Head Handles, China, 1900s, 13 x 5 1/2 x 1 1/2 In., Pair..........	5937
Vase, Lotus Leaf Shape, Carved, Chinese, Early 1900s, 7 3/8 x 4 In........................	180
Vase, Nephrite, Fungi Finial Lid, Dragons, Green & White, Chinese, Early 1900s, 6 1/2 In.	960
Vase, Stepped, Greek Key, 6 1/2 x 3 1/2 In.	5937

JAPANESE WOODBLOCK PRINTS *are listed in this book in the Print category under Japanese.*

JASPERWARE can be made in different ways. Some pieces are made from a solid-colored clay with applied raised designs of a contrasting colored clay. Other pieces are made entirely of one color clay with raised decorations that are glazed with a contrasting color. Additional pieces of jasperware may also be listed in the Wedgwood category or under various art potteries.

Cheese Dome, Brown, Molded Rope Handle, Fern Fronds, Grass, Cattails, 11 x 12 1/2 In.	826
Plaque, Frolicking Putti, 10 1/4 x 9 In.	49

JEWELRY, whether made from gold and precious gems or plastic and colored glass, is popular with collectors. Values are determined by the intrinsic value of the stones and metal and by the skill of the craftsmen and designers. Victorian and older jewelry has been collected since the 1950s. More recent interests are Art Deco and Edwardian styles, Mexican and Danish silver jewelry, and beads of all kinds. Copies of almost all styles are being made. American Indian jewelry is listed in the Indian category. Tiffany jewelry is listed here.

Belt Buckle, Bronze, Dragon, Chilong Head Hook, Curved, Silver & Gold Inlay, 6 In.	984
Belt Hook, Inlay, Turquoise, Gold, Bronze, S-Shape, Dragon Head, Chinese, 5 In.	5312
Bibelot, Cased Comb, Lipstick Brush, Frame, 18K Gold, Van Cleef & Arpels, 1900s....................	1062
Bracelet & Earrings, Concave Discs, 22K Textured Gold, Diamond Centers, S. Shaw..............	1968
Bracelet & Pendant, Silver, Moonstone Cabochons, Marked, Danecraft, 1950s	250

J

Bracelet, 5 Plaques, Fish, Tackle, Reverse Painted Glass, 14K Links, Sloan & Co., 7 In..............	2214
Bracelet, 14 Victorian Slides, Gemstones, 10K Gold, 7⅜ In.....................................*illus*	593
Bracelet, Amethysts, Turquoise Beads, Gilt Silver, Arts & Crafts, D. Nossiter, 7 In.	3690
Bracelet, Bakelite, Cuff, Black, Hinged, Sterling Swirl Design, Diamonds, 1½ x 7 In...............	1375
Bracelet, Bakelite, Cuff, White, Hinged, Diamond Starburst, Silver, Pearls, 5 x 7 In.	1250
Bracelet, Bangle, Brazil Pattern, Gold, Enamel, Hermes, Box, 8 In.	406
Bracelet, Bangle, Hinged, Athena Wearing Helmet, Enamel, 18K Gold, Tiffany & Co., 6 In........	584
Bracelet, Bangle, Hinged, Coiled Snake, Black & Colorless Diamonds, 14K Gold, Effy, 7 In.	1169
Bracelet, Bangle, Hinged, Diamonds, Old European Cut, Gold, 1940s, 6½ In.	2706
Bracelet, Bangle, Hinged, Scarab, Faience, 18K Gold, Cloisonne Lotus, T.B. Starr, 7 In.............	4182
Bracelet, Bangle, Hinged, Scarab, Hardstone, Plique-A-Jour Wings, Lotus, Art Deco, 7 In.	2460
Bracelet, Bangle, Hinged, Scottish Agate Tablets, Engraved 15K Gold, Victorian, 7 In.	1046
Bracelet, Bangle, Hinged, Snake, 18K Gold, Kieselstein-Cord, 6⅜ In..	6765
Bracelet, Bangle, Inset Tambours, Gold, Beading & Wirework, c.1865, 6½ In.	2583
Bracelet, Bangle, Love, Screw, Box, Screwdriver, 18K Gold, Marked, Cartier, 7 In.	4920
Bracelet, Bangle, Nineveh Relief, Assyrian Revival, Gold, c.1870, 1 x 6¾ In.	3321
Bracelet, Bangle, Pink Stones, Faux Pearls & Turquoise, Goldtone, ModeArt, 1960s	191
Bracelet, Bead, Nephrite, Rock Crystal Discs, Chain, Gold, Enameled Key, Art Deco, 8 In.	615
Bracelet, Cameo, Citrine, Maiden, Upswept Hair, 18K Gold Floral Mount, c.1920, 7¼ In.	1968
Bracelet, Cerisier, Blue Glass Plaques, Etched, Lalique, c.1928, 2¾ In.	2750
Bracelet, Charm, Double Chain, 14K Gold, 5 Charms, Gemstone Accents, 8 In.	1534
Bracelet, Charm, Double Link, 5 Charms, Gemstones, Ballerina, Birthday, 14K Gold, 8 In.	1534
Bracelet, Charm, Double Round Link, 14 Charms, Heart, Clover, Buddha, 14K Gold, 7 In........	2124
Bracelet, Charm, Fish, Pearl In Mouth, Shells, Starfish, Goldtone, Marked, HAR, 7¼ In.	65
Bracelet, Charm, Round Link, 10 Charms, Carousel, Nantucket Basket, Shell, 14K Gold, 8 In.	2006
Bracelet, Charm, Square Link Chain, 4 Charms, 2 Lockets, 14K Yellow Gold, 7 In............*illus*	1652
Bracelet, Charm, Square Link Chain, 8 Charms, 14K Yellow Gold, 7½ In........................*illus*	1652
Bracelet, Charm, Woven, 5 Disc Charms, Piano, Pearl Heart, Poodle, Key, 14K Gold, 7½ In....	2950
Bracelet, Charm, Woven, Piano, Pearl Heart, Birthday Wish, Poodle, Key, 14K, 7½ In	2950
Bracelet, Clamper, Cobra Heads, Enamel, Brushed Goldtone, Hattie Carnegie, 7 In.	525
Bracelet, Clamper, Glass Cabochons, Rhinestones, Rhodium, Judy-Lee, 1950s, 7 In.	42
Bracelet, Cuff, 14K Gold, Hammered, Scalloped Edges, Keith, 6¼ In.	1107
Bracelet, Cuff, Circles, CC, 18K Gold Plate, Marked, Chanel, 1980s, 8 x 2 In............................	1450
Bracelet, Cuff, Engraved Scrolls, Gold, Bead & Ropework Accents, Etruscan Revival, 7 In........	2952
Bracelet, Cuff, Flexible, Cross & Barbell Links, 18K Gold, Boucheron, 6 In.	4920
Bracelet, Cuff, Flexible, Silver, Homeric Coin Fringe, G.W. Shiebler, 7 In...............................	1599
Bracelet, Cuff, Hinged, Textured Gold, Applied Flowers, Pearls, Rubies, Victorian, 6½ In.	375
Bracelet, Cuff, Silver, Embossed, Red Coral Cabochon, Hopi, Marked, c.1980, 2 x 6 In..............	246
Bracelet, Cuff, Tapered, Overlapping End, Gold, Ed Wiener, 2⅜ In.	800
Bracelet, Cuff, Wave Form, Textured & Polished 14K Gold, Marked, Wiener, 5 In.............*illus*	660
Bracelet, Cuff, Wood, 7 Turquoise Cabochons, 18K Gold Bezels, F. Visconti, 5¾ In.	584
Bracelet, Cuff, Wood, Silver, Shaped Turquoise, Coral & Onyx, E. Cummings, 5¼ In.	840
Bracelet, Diamond Strips, Alternating With Rope Twists, 18K Gold, Platinum, D. Webb, 8 In...	6000
Bracelet, Line, Alternating Emeralds & Diamonds, Platinum, Beaded, Art Deco, 7¼ In.............	4613
Bracelet, Link, Angular & Heavy, 18K Rose Gold, Marked, SD, Retro, 7¾ x 1⅝ In...................	4800
Bracelet, Link, Box, 5 Sapphires, 4 Diamonds, Platinum, Bailey, Banks & Biddle, 6 In.............	1481
Bracelet, Link, Brickwork, Arched, Retro, 7 In..	523
Bracelet, Link, Crescent Shape, 18K Rose Gold, Retro, 7⅝ In.	1722
Bracelet, Link, Leaves & Beaded Buds, Silver, Marked, Georg Jensen, 7⅜ In.	523
Bracelet, Link, Moonstones, Rubies, Diamonds, 14K Bicolor Gold, Retro, 7 In.................*illus*	2952
Bracelet, Link, Pendant, Wax Seal, Monogram, Silver, Hester Bateman, 1-In. Seal, 7 In.	840
Bracelet, Link, Scalloped, Gold, Hairwork, Oval Clasp, Painted Landscape, c.1845, 7 In...........	677
Bracelet, Link, Summer Flowers, Multicolor Enamel, 18K Gold, Adrian, 7½ In.	1722
Bracelet, Mesh, Woven, 18K Gold, Diamond Melee Swish, Gubelin, 6¾ In.	2460
Bracelet, Micro Mosaic, Cherub In Chariot, Lions, Gold Beading & Wirework, c.1860, 7 In......	13530
Bracelet, Opal, 17 Round Cut Diamonds, Silver, 7 In. ....*illus*	343
Bracelet, Pin & Earrings, Micro Mosaic, Roman Ruins, Gold, 8¼, 2 & 1 In., Set.............*illus*	2583
Bracelet, Plaques, 6 Garnet Cabochons, Gold Openwork Spacers, France, c.1900, 8 In.	2460
Bracelet, Plaques, Buds, Links, Silver, Moonstone Cabochons, Georg Jensen, 7¼ In.................	1353
Bracelet, Plaques, Scottish Agates, Faceted, Gold Terminals & Links, 8 In........................*illus*	523

Ispanky, Figurine, Autumn, On Stump, Holding Bowl Of Fruit, Limited Edition, 7 In.
$60

Ruby Lane

Ivory, Tusk, Figures, Trees, Landscape, 17½ In.
$545

Time & Again Auction Galleries

Jade, Figurine, Buddha, White, Spinach, 2⅜ x 1⅜ In.
$450

Ruby Lane

TIP
You can tell a piece of jade by the feel. It will be cold, even in warm weather.

Jewelry, Bracelet, 14 Victorian Slides, Gemstones, 10K Gold, 7 ⅜ In.
$593

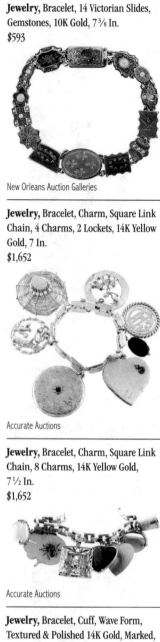

New Orleans Auction Galleries

Jewelry, Bracelet, Charm, Square Link Chain, 4 Charms, 2 Lockets, 14K Yellow Gold, 7 In.
$1,652

Accurate Auctions

Jewelry, Bracelet, Charm, Square Link Chain, 8 Charms, 14K Yellow Gold, 7 ½ In.
$1,652

Accurate Auctions

Jewelry, Bracelet, Cuff, Wave Form, Textured & Polished 14K Gold, Marked, Wiener, 5 In.
$660

Brunk Auctions

Bracelet, Roman Soldier, Gold, Wirework, Archaeological Revival, c.1865, 6 ½ In...........*illus*	2706
Bracelet, Snowflake, 10 Tanzanites, Oval, Alternating Diamond Flakes, Tiffany & Co., 7 In.....	5843
Bracelet, Stars, Wide Strap, Silver, Victorian, 7 ⅜ In.	277
Bracelet, Strap, Link, Wide Arched Ovals, Bead Accents, Gold, Victorian, 8 In............	4920
Bracelet, Strap, Woven, Engraved Disk Slide, Split Pearl, Black Tracery, Victorian, 8 In.	1599
Charm, Zodiac, Cancer, Crab, 18K Gold, Van Cleef & Arpels, 1 ¼ In.......................................	2214
Clip, Dress, Shield, Diamonds, Platinum, Pierced, Udall & Ballou, Art Deco, 1 In., Pair	3936
Clip, Dress, Stylized Scroll, Curled End, Diamonds, Platinum, Art Deco, 1 ¼ In.	2460
Clip, Dress, Turtle, 18K Gold, Turquoise Beads On Shell, Ruby Eyes, 1 In., Pair.....................	984
Clip, Fur, Unicorn, Enamel, Diamonds, Rubies, Sapphires, 18K Gold, Depose, 3 ½ In........*illus*	5625
Cuff Links, Amethyst, Oval, Faceted, 18K Gold..	800
Cuff Links, Bat, Figural, Onyx, 18K White Gold, ⅞ In.	492
Cuff Links, Citrine, Oval, Faceted, 18K Gold Bezel Frame, Cartier	1845
Cuff Links, Coins, Gold, Indian Head, 5 Dollar, 1908 & 1911, 1 ⅛ In.....................................	1625
Cuff Links, Disc, Inlaid Stripes, Blackened Steel, 18K Gold, Faraone..	738
Cuff Links, Garnet, Faceted, 14K Gold, Lucien Piccard	308
Cuff Links, Mesh Loop, Open, Ruby Terminals, 18K Gold, France	1230
Cuff Links, Moonstones, Bezel Set, 2-Sided, 18K Gold, Edwardian, Tiffany	738
Cuff Links, Reverse Painted Glass, Skye Terrier, Mother-Of-Pearl Ground	615
Cuff Links, Ruby, Oval Cabochon, 18K White Gold Mount, Link, Diamonds, S. Schepps	1353
Cuff Links, Silver, 4 Irregular Sides, Cutout Center, Marked, Paul Lobel	308
Cuff Links, Square, Pyramidal, 18K Gold, Blackened Steel Top, Faraone................................	523
Cuff Links, Stylized Steer Head, Gemstone Eyes, 18K Gold, 1960s, 1 x ¾ In. ....*illus*	288
Dress Set, Man's, Abalone, Pearl Center, Octagonal Mount, Platinum Over Gold, Larter	492
Dress Set, Man's, Chevron, Rectangular, Ruby Stripe, 18K Gold, Van Cleef & Arpels, 5 Piece....	2829
Dress Set, Man's, Gold Bead, Star Set Sapphires, Van Cleef & Arpels, 5 Piece	2829
Dress Set, Man's, Lion's Heads, Emerald Eyes, Enamel, 18K Gold, David Webb, 5 Piece.............	3383
Dress Set, Man's, Penguins, 18K Gold, Enamel	1599
Dress Set, Man's, Ribbed Baton, Rubies, Van Cleef & Arpels, Marked, Box	4613
Dress Set, Man's, White Guilloche Discs, 18K Gold Rope Twist Frame, Cartier, 8 Piece	2829
Earrings, 2 Leaves, Curving, Sapphires, Diamonds, 18K Gold, Van Cleef & Arpels, 1 In.	4920
Earrings, Amethyst, Oval, Pear Drops, Turquoise Border, D. Nossiter, 1 ¾ In.	1353
Earrings, Amphora Drop, Suspended From Scarabs, Gold, c.1865, 1 ⅜ In.	1845
Earrings, Aurora Borealis Rhinestones, Dangles, Rhodium, Clip-On, Marked, Coro, 2 In........	30
Earrings, Ball, Radiating Rods Around Half, 14K Gold, Retro, 1 ⅜ In.	861
Earrings, Chandelier, Amethysts, Foil Back, Gold Scrollwork Mount, c.1835, 2 ⅜ In.	6150
Earrings, Chandelier, Rhinestones, Goldtone, Clip-On, Mimi Di Niscemi, 1960s, 3 In.	395
Earrings, Cirolit Stones, Green Faceted Oval & Clear, Clip-On, Box, Ciro, 1960s, 1 ¼ In.	80
Earrings, Coin, Veiled Figure, Bronze, 18K Gold Beaded Frame, E. Locke, ¾ In.	2214
Earrings, Coral, Fluted Strips, Diamond Strips, 18K Gold, Clip-On, Charles Turi, 1 In..............	2337
Earrings, Coral, Oval, Melon Carved, 18K Gold Mount, Diamond Edge, S. Kelly, 1 In.	923
Earrings, Dangle, 3 Interlocking Squares, Ropetwist, 18K Gold, Tiffany & Co., 2 In.................	1845
Earrings, Dangle, Hoop, Ropework, 18K Gold, Diamond, Georg Jensen, 1 In.	861
Earrings, Dangle, Snake, 18K Gold, Reticulated Body, Elsa Peretti, Tiffany & Co., 4 In.............	7995
Earrings, Dangle, Urn, Bead & Ropework Accents, Etruscan Revival, 1 ⅜ In.	615
Earrings, Dome, Basket Weave Inlay, Coral, Black Jade, 18K Gold, Tiffany & Co., 1 In.	3998
Earrings, Dome, Oval, Blue Enamel, Raised Gold Bars, Schlumberger, Tiffany, ½ In.	1599
Earrings, Drop, Amethysts, Pear Shape, Open Gold Flower & Leaf Frame, c.1835, 3 In.............	1230
Earrings, Drop, Hand Holding Flowers, Textured Gold, Georgian, c.1825, 3 In........................	1230
Earrings, Drop, Opal, Diamonds, Gold Vermeil, Oxidized Finish, 1 ½ In............................*illus*	531
Earrings, Flower, Rock Crystal Petals, Sapphire & Diamond Center, Aletto Bros., 1 In.	4305
Earrings, Fly By Night, Bat, Diamonds, Blackened 18K Gold, Open Center, S. Webster, 1 In......	584
Earrings, Green Tourmaline, Rectangular, White Gold Frame, Pearl Drop, S. Webster, 2 In.	1722
Earrings, Hoop, Alternating Gold Beads & Pearls, 18K Gold, LeGi, 1 ½ In.	296
Earrings, Huggie, Pave Diamonds, 18K Gold, Rounded Rectangular Mount, L. Pizzo, ⅝ In.	2706
Earrings, Leaf, Rhinestones, Faux Pearls, Rhodium, Clip-On, Marked, Charel, 1940s, 1 In.....	55
Earrings, Monete, Roman Coin, Constantine, 18K Gold, Clip-On, Bulgari, 1 In.	3075
Earrings, Pearls Over Diamond, Platinum Mount, Tiffany & Co., Box	3075
Earrings, Pink, Rhinestones, Oval Cabochons, Goldtone, Warner, 1950s, 1 In........................	30
Earrings, Red, Blue & Green Rhinestones, Goldtone, Clip-On, Marked, Boucher, 1 In.	85

J

Jewelry, Bracelet, Plaques, Scottish Agates, Faceted, Gold Terminals & Links, 8 In.
$523

Skinner, Inc.

Jewelry, Bracelet, Roman Soldier, Gold, Wirework, Archaeological Revival, c.1865, 6 ½ In.
$2,706

J

Skinner, Inc.

Jewelry, Clip, Fur, Unicorn, Enamel, Diamonds, Rubies, Sapphires, 18K Gold, Depose, 3 ½ In.
$5,625

Jewelry, Bracelet, Link, Moonstones, Rubies, Diamonds, 14K Bicolor Gold, Retro, 7 In.
$2,952

Skinner, Inc.

Jewelry, Bracelet, Opal, 17 Round Cut Diamonds, Silver, 7 In.
$343

New Orleans Auction Galleries

Jewelry, Bracelet, Pin & Earrings, Micro Mosaic, Roman Ruins, Gold, 8 ¼, 2 & 1 In., Set
$2,583

 Skinner, Inc.

JEWELRY

Jewelry, Cuff Links, Stylized Steer Head, Gemstone Eyes, 18K Gold, 1960s, 1 x ¾ In.
$288

Allard Auctions

Jewelry, Earrings, Drop, Opal, Diamonds, Gold Vermeil, Oxidized Finish, 1 ½ In.
$531

New Orleans Auction Galleries

Jewelry, Necklace & Earrings, Flowers, Turquoise, Gold, Converts To 2 Bracelets, 14 & 1 In., Set
$1,599

Skinner, Inc.

Jewelry, Necklace & Earrings, Fringe, Lotus & Palmette Drops, Etruscan Revival, 16 & 2 In., Set
$3,998

Skinner, Inc.

Chokers

Choker necklaces are back in style, especially for expensive jewelry. They were popular in the 18th century. The wide chokers cover an old wrinkled neck. New thin chokers can look sexy.

Jewelry, Necklace, Cameo, Coral, Bearded Figures, Gold Frames, c.1825, 16 In.
$2,583

Skinner, Inc.

Jewelry, Necklace, Emerald Roundels, Carved, Rose Cut Diamonds, Silver, Diamond Clasp, 19 In.
$468

New Orleans Auction Galleries

Eisenberg Jewelry Marks

Eisenberg Ice was a mark used on rhinestone jewelry from 1945 to 1958. The words were written in block letters. From 1970 to 1985, the block letter mark was used with a copyright symbol.

Jewelry, Medallion, Tete Du Masque, Abstract Face, 23K Gold, P. Picasso, P. Hugo, Box, 2 In.
$31,980

Skinner, Inc.

TIP

Broken silver jewelry may have melt-down value. Check to see if the metal is really silver.

Earrings, Sunflower, Diamond Melee, 18K Textured Gold, Clip-On, Asprey, 1¼ In.	4920
Earrings, Thorn Noir, Overlapping Thorns, Diamonds, 18K Gold, S. Webster, 2 In.	1230
Earrings, Thunderbolt, Diamond Melee, Blackened 18K Gold, I. Makri, 1¾ In.	923
Fob, Seal, Carnelian, Intaglio UK, 18K Stirrup Frame, Swivels, Hinged Bail, c.1800, 2 In.	1000
Hatpins are listed in this book in the Hatpin category.	
Lavaliere, Oval Citrine, Leafy Frame, Diamonds, 14K Gold, Festoon Chain, Art Nouveau, 16 In.	800
Locket, Bird, Bamboo, Pierced Silver, Japonesque Style, Victorian, England, 2 In.	338
Locket, Black Enamel, Split Pearl & Diamond Star, Oval, Gold, Victorian, 2⅜ In.	800
Locket, Heart Shape, Blue Enamel, Guilloche, Diamonds, 18K Gold, 1800s, 3 x 3 In.	4575
Locket, Mourning, Gold, Oval, Quartz, Diamonds, Leaves, c.1878, 2¾ In.	615
Locket, Pearl Star, On Blue Enamel Dome, Oval Bead & Wirework Frame, c.1875, 2 In.	984
Locket, Scarab, Coral, Pearls, Gold Wirework, Etruscan Revival, c.1870, 2 In.	1353
Lorgnette, Flowers, Diamonds, Blue Enamel, 18K Gold, Hidden Watch, Swiss, 3¼ In.	4500
Lorgnette, Iris, Woman With Flowing Hair, 14K Gold, Art Nouveau, 5 In.	861
Lorgnette, Overlapping Acanthus Leaves, 14K Gold, Beaded Woven Case, Art Nouveau, 5 In.	1353
Lorgnette, Platinum, Engraved, Diamond Melee, Chain, Art Deco, 34 In.	861
Medallion, Tete Du Masque, Abstract Face, 23K Gold, P. Picasso, P. Hugo, Box, 2 In. ....*illus*	31980
Necklace & Bracelet, Pink Panther, Pink Crystal Navettes, Weiss, 1960s, 17 & 7 In.	180
Necklace & Earrings, Coral, Bacchante, Grapes, Baton Links, Head Drops, c.1870, 17 In.	4613
Necklace & Earrings, Enamel Leaves, Rainbow Stones, Silver, Chico's, 1980s, 21 In.	98
Necklace & Earrings, Flowers, Red & Peacock Crystals, Leaves, B.S.K., 1950s, 19 In.	156
Necklace & Earrings, Flowers, Turquoise, Gold, Converts To 2 Bracelets, 14 & 1 In., Set....*illus*	1599
Necklace & Earrings, Fringe, Lotus & Palmette Drops, Etruscan Revival, 16 & 2 In., Set ...*illus*	3998
Necklace, 3 Filigree Plaques, Cannetille Work, Drops, Swag Chains, c.1825	1968
Necklace, 4 Charms, House & Tree, Phone, Dancer, Basket, Platinum, Gold, Art Deco, 22 In.	984
Necklace, 5 Jade Beads, Navette Links, 14K Gold Filigree, 22 In.	1353
Necklace, 5 Pendants, Turquoise Cabochons, Pearl, Knife Edge Bars, Gold, 17 In.	1169
Necklace, 7 Cameo Plaques, Gods, Goddesses, Chain Swags, Seed Pearls, Drops, c.1860, 18 In.	3444
Necklace, 10 Flowers, Turquoise Beads & Seed Pearls, Gold Chain, Victorian, 16 In.	1845
Necklace, Amber Beads, 6 Silver Mounted Tiger Claws, Coins, Mongolia, Late 1800s	3600
Necklace, Beads, 5 Strands, Banded & Fluted, 18K Gold, Lalaounis, 15½ In.	11685
Necklace, Beads, Lapis, 20 Graduated, Faceted 18K Gold Spacers, Carvin French, 22 In.	2214
Necklace, Beads, Mixed Metal, Ebony, 22K Gold & Silver, Rena Koopman, 20 In.	2952
Necklace, Bracelet & Earrings, Alligator Heads, Silver, Links, Clip-On, Kieselstein-Cord	1230
Necklace, Cameo, Coral, Bearded Figures, Gold Frames, c.1825, 16 In. ....*illus*	2583
Necklace, Chain, 14K Gold, Grotesque, Maiden, Dragon & Lotus Plaques, C. Howe, 62 In.	8610
Necklace, Chain, Fancy 18K Links, Sodalite Batons, N. Cola, 1970s, 36 In.	3690
Necklace, Charm, Curb Link, 14K Gold, 33 Charms, 28 In.	3245
Necklace, Charm, Curb Link, 33 Charms, Airplane, Umbrella, Golf Clubs, 14K Gold, 28 In.	3245
Necklace, Choker, Butterfly, Plastic Amber Cabochons, Goldtone, Rader, 1980s, 12 In.	250
Necklace, Choker, Trumpet Flowers, Pink, Rhinestones, Silver, Bond-Boyd, 15 In.	25
Necklace, Citrine Drop, Platinum, Diamonds, Link Chain, Art Deco, 2-In. Drop, 29 In.	2706
Necklace, Coin, Bezel Set, Thick Curb Link Chain, Bulgari, 14 In.	5925
Necklace, Collar, 14K Gold, Forged, Shaped, Hinged, Ed Wiener, 14 In.	840
Necklace, Collar, 18K Gold, Articulated, Geometric End, Lalaounis, 15 In.	1107
Necklace, Collar, Chrome, Carnelian, Onyx, Lapis & Turquoise Shapes, Munari, 1984, 7 In.	7370
Necklace, Coral, 10 Strands Clustered Into 1, Italy, Mid-1900s, 15 In.	120
Necklace, Dragonfly, Garnet, Diamonds, 18K Rose Gold, Marked, Chaumet, 18 In.	3750
Necklace, Emerald Roundels, Carved, Rose Cut Diamonds, Silver, Diamond Clasp, 19 In.*...illus*	468
Necklace, Fringe, Scalloped, Baluster, Gold, Egyptian Revival, c.1865, 17 In.	1845
Necklace, Fringe, Scalloped, Beaded Baluster Drops, Etruscan Revival, c.1865, 16 In.	2460
Necklace, Fringe, Tubular Links, Graduated, 18K Gold, France, Retro, 15 In.	2214
Necklace, Hiroko, Pendant, Elongated Rings, Teardrop Link Chain, Mattioli, 42 In.	3690
Necklace, Kissing Swans, Clear & Red Stones, Goldtone, Atwood & Sawyer, 17 In.	130
Necklace, Lariat, Bird Of Prey, 18K Gold, Mabe Pearls, Diamond Melee, SeidenGang	1599
Necklace, Link, Emeralds, Diamond Edges, Clover Drop, White Gold, M. Cristoff, 18 In.	5925
Necklace, Link, Rolo, 3 Charms, Elephant, Clown, Bear, Sapphire Eyes, 18K, Chopard, 17 In.	2963
Necklace, Link, Thick, Oval, Clasp With 2 Rubies, Lily Fitzgerald, Box, 20 In.	4613
Necklace, Lucite Teardrop Cabochon, Crystals, Black Multi-Chain, Chico's, 20 In.	49
Necklace, Nike, Nude Form With Wings, Silver, Paul Wunderlich, 5 x 3½ In.	3000

Jewelry, Necklace, Opal, Diamond Surround, Bicolor Gold Chain, 1½-In. Pendant
$3,500

New Orleans Auction Galleries

J

Jewelry, Necklace, Pendant, 48 Black Stone Beads, 8 Coral Openwork Beads, Chinese, 16 In.
$338

Skinner, Inc.

Jewelry, Necklace, Pendant, Silver, Freshwater Pearl, Kalo, c.1910, 13 In.
$2,500

Rago Arts and Auction Center

Jewelry, Necklace, Portrait, Elliptical Frame, White Gold, Diamonds, Plojoux, Geneva, 22 In.
$1,250

New Orleans Auction Galleries

Jewelry, Necklace, Silver, Flowers, Amber & Green Onyx Accents, Georg Jensen, 18 In.
$6,765

Skinner, Inc.

Jewelry, Necklace, Snake, Flexible Link, Pearls, Garnets, Emeralds, Locket, Victorian, 14 In.
$1,845

Skinner, Inc.

Jewelry, Pendant, Baroque Pearls, 18K Gold, Hammered, Beaded, E. Locke, 1 ½ In.
$4,000

New Orleans Auction Galleries

Jewelry, Pendant, Coin, 1975 Krugerrand, 14K Yellow Gold, Rope Twist Frame, 1 ½ In.
$1,375

New Orleans Auction Galleries

Jewelry, Pendant, Nose & Lips, Abstract, Gold Plate, Cord, Salvador Dali, 1 ½-In. Pendant
$492

Skinner, Inc.

Jewelry, Pin & Earrings, Fly, Amethyst Body, 14K Gold, Retro, 1 ½ & 1 In., Set
$1,169

Skinner, Inc.

Jewelry, Pin, 12 Old Mine Cut Diamonds, 18K & 10K Gold, 1 ¾ In.
$2,040

Brunk Auctions

Jewelry, Pin, Abstract, Silver, 14K Gold, Enamel, Mother-Of-Pearl, Earl Pardon, 1950, 2 x 2 In.
$1,375

Rago Arts and Auction Center

Necklace, Opal, Diamond Surround, Bicolor Gold Chain, 1 ½-In. Pendant ....*illus*	3500
Necklace, Pearls, 109 Graduated, Platinum & Diamond Clasp, Art Deco, 20 In.	984
Necklace, Pearls, 2 Strands, 18K Gold Lion & Ring Clasp, Van Cleef & Arpels.	3444
Necklace, Pendant, 48 Black Stone Beads, 8 Coral Openwork Beads, Chinese, 16 In. ....*illus*	338
Necklace, Pendant, Bud & Leaves, Silver, Labradorite, Paper Clip Chain, Georg Jensen, 24 In.	3444
Necklace, Pendant, Heart, Pearls, 16 Round Diamonds, 18K Gold, 20th Century, 16 In.	410
Necklace, Pendant, Platinum, Diamond & Pearls Pendant, Y Chain, Edwardian, 18 In.	4888
Necklace, Pendant, Silver, Freshwater Pearl, Pendant, Kalo, c.1910, 13 In. ....*illus*	2500
Necklace, Pin & Earrings, Rock Crystals, Cross Drop, Gold Cannetille Frames, 1820s, 16 In., Set ..	7995
Necklace, Portrait, Elliptical Frame, White Gold, Diamonds, Plojoux, Geneva, 22 In. ......*illus*	1250
Necklace, Riviere, 28 Amethysts, Cushion Cut, Foil Backed, Silver Over Gold, c.1800, 16 In.	3444
Necklace, Scarab, Pearl Drop, Enamel, Gold & Turquoise Chain, Art Deco, 21 In.	3075
Necklace, Silver, Flowers, Amber & Green Onyx Accents, Georg Jensen, 18 In. ....*illus*	6765
Necklace, Snake, Flexible Link, Pearls, Garnets, Emeralds, Locket, Victorian, 14 In.........*illus*	1845
Necklace, Snake, Gold, Turquoise, Rubies, Ring Slide, Heart Drop, Victorian, 15 ½ In.	2583
Necklace, Star Designs, Silver, Victorian, 16 In.	523
Necklace, Thief Of Bagdad, Multicolor Stones, Pearls, Goldtone, Korda, 1940s, 15 In.	425
Pendant, 10 Concentric Rings, Silver, Amethyst Center, Georg Jensen, 4 ¼ In.	2583
Pendant, Aquamarine Drop, Platinum Flower Mount, Diamonds, Black, Starr & Frost, 1 In.	1107
Pendant, Baroque Pearls, 18K Gold, Hammered, Beaded, E. Locke, 1 ½ In.................*illus*	4000
Pendant, Circle, 18K Gold, Rutilated Quartz & Blue Hardstone Detail, Bulgari, 1 ½ In.	1722
Pendant, Circle, Twisted Rope, Diamonds, Gemstones, 18K Gold, D. Yurman, 2 x 1 In.	82
Pendant, Coin, 1975 Krugerrand, 14K Yellow Gold, Rope Twist Frame, 1 ½ In.................*illus*	1375
Pendant, Corncob, 18K White Gold Cob, Yellow Gold Husk, Cord, Cartier, 2 In.	948
Pendant, Garnet, Oval, Gold Cannetille Work Frame, Seed Pearl Accents, c.1825, 2 ⅜ In.	984
Pendant, Hands, Fish, Scorpions, Owl, Anchor, Horn, Frame, 14K Gold, E. DeKolb, 3 In.	1722
Pendant, Heart, Pink Tourmaline, Diamond Bail, Platinum Over Gold, Edwardian, 1 In.	2583
Pendant, Jackknife, Pave Diamonds, 18K White Gold, Retractable Blade, Salavetti, 1 ¼ In.	652
Pendant, Jade, Carved Peapod, Emerald Green, Luster, 14K Gold Bail, 1900s, 1 In.	2133
Pendant, Jasper Plaque, Muses, Purple Guilloche, Diamonds, Belle Epoque, Cartier, 2 In.	9840
Pendant, Maltese Cross, Garnet, Gold Wirework, Flared Chalcedony Ends, c.1820, 2 In.	615
Pendant, Micro Mosaic, Flower Basket, Dog, Bird & Garland On Reverse, Gold, 1 ¼ In.	861
Pendant, Mourning, Reverse Painted Glass, Willow, Woman, Gold Case, Woven Hair, 3 In.	2706
Pendant, Nose & Lips, Abstract, Gold Plate, Cord, Salvador Dali, 1 ½-In. Pendant.........*illus*	492
Pendant, Shell, Mottled, Bezel Set Lapis & Ruby, 14K White Gold, M. Stix, 2 In.	677
Pendant, Spirit Of Driftwood, Arrow Shape Dangles, Silver, Signed, 1987, 3 In.	660
Pendant, Woman, Blowing Diamond Dandelion Seeds, Gold, Enamel, Art Nouveau, 17 In.	1968
Pendant, Woman's Profile, Long Hair, Gilt Silver, Diamonds, Pearl Drop, Art Nouveau, 2 In.	2952
Pendant, Zodiac, Lion, 18K Gold, Marked, Cartier, 1 ½ x 1 ¼ In.	3776
Pin & Earrings, Coral Cabochon, Textured 18K Gold, Knot Pin, H. Dunay, 3 ⅜ & 1 In., Set.	5843
Pin & Earrings, Fly, Amethyst Body, 14K Gold, Retro, 1 ½ & 1 In., Set.................*illus*	1169
Pin & Earrings, Orchids, Aqua & Clear Rhinestones, Goldtone, Avon, 1940s, 2 & 1 In., Set	165
Pin & Earrings, Pinecones On Branch, 14K Gold, Retro, 2-In. Pin, Set	590
Pin & Earrings, Red Rhinestones, Goldtone, Crescents, Emmons, 1950s, 2 & 1 In., Set	145
Pin & Earrings, Willow Tree, Pink Moonstones, Gold Wash, Reja, 1947, 2 & ¾ In., Set	1250
Pin, 2 Crowned Hearts, Thistles, M Monogram, Silver, Luckenbooth, c.1860, 2 ½ In.	123
Pin, 2 Griffins, 18K Gold, Ruby Eyes, Holding Oval Cabochon Emerald, Art Nouveau, 2 In.	1476
Pin, 2 Horsemen, Spears, Gold Beading & Wirework, Glass Compartment, 1870, 2 ⅜ In.	1353
Pin, 2 Swallows, Branch, Diamonds, Ruby Eyes, 2 ½ In.	2214
Pin, 2-Masted Ship, 18K Rose Gold, Sapphire & Ruby Accents, Patek Philippe, Retro, 2 In.	2337
Pin, 3 Flowers, Lapis Blossoms, Diamonds, 18K Gold, La Triomphe, 1 ⅝ In.	923
Pin, 5 Pearls, Diamonds, Flared Platinum Openwork Mount, Edwardian, 1 ¼ In.	1230
Pin, 12 Old Mine Cut Diamonds, 18K & 10K Gold, 1 ¾ In.................*illus*	2040
Pin, Abstract, Silver, 14K Gold, Enamel, Mother-Of-Pearl, Earl Pardon, 1950, 2 x 2 In......*illus*	1375
Pin, Acorns, Pearlized, Clear Stones, Goldtone Leaves, C-Clasp, Marked, Coro, 1 ¾ In.	22
Pin, Amethysts, Gold Scrolling Frame, Removable Pendant, Compartment, c.1835, 3 ¾ In.	6150
Pin, Aquamarine, Rectangular, Step Cut, Diamond Melee Edge, Onyx Plaques, c.1940, 1 In.	3321
Pin, Bar, 2 Owls, Flanking ROMA & Columns, Gold Bead & Wirework, c.1875, 2 In.	523
Pin, Bar, Green Tourmaline, Diamond Edge, Platinum On Gold, Black, Starr & Frost, 2 In.	1476
Pin, Bar, Onyx, 23 Seed Pearls, Fish Hook Catch, 14K Gold, 1800s, 2 ¼ x ½ In.	562

Jewelry, Pin, Butterfly, Lacquer, Diamonds, 18K Gold, J. Hakose, Van Cleef & Arpels, 1 ⅝ In.
$13,530

Skinner, Inc.

Jewelry, Pin, Butterfly, Pink Sapphires, Diamonds, 18K White Gold, 1 In.
$4,750

New Orleans Auction Galleries

Jewelry, Pin, Circle With Bow, Diamonds, Synthetic Emerald, Platinum, 1 ¼ In.
$660

Brunk Auctions

Gold Jewelry

We've heard a theory that yellow gold jewelry was popular in the days of gaslights. When electric lights came into general use about 1900, white gold became popular. Whatever the reason, white gold and platinum were not often used on fine jewelry before 1900.

Jewelry, Pin, Dog, Golden Retriever, Reverse Painted Glass, Oval, 14K Gold, R. Yard, 1 ¾ In.
$1,722

Skinner, Inc.

Jewelry, Pin, Flowers, Amethyst & Diamond Petals, 2 Nephrite Leaves, 14K Gold, 1 ¾ In.
$1,125

New Orleans Auction Galleries

Jewelry, Pin, Flutist, Turtle, Sterling Silver, William Hunt Diederich, c.1900, 1 ¾ x 2 ¼ In.
$4,063

Rago Arts and Auction Center

Pin, Bar, Owl, Chased Wings, Gold, Beaded, Wirework, Ball Ends, Etruscan, c.1865, 3 In.	615
Pin, Bar, Portrait, Bacchante, Grapes, Enamel On Porcelain, 18K Gold, Art Nouveau, 3 In.	523
Pin, Bee, Pink Enamel Cherry Blossoms, Crystals, Gold Plated, J. Rivers, 1 x 2 In.	125
Pin, Bird In Wreath, Silver, Marked, No. 70, Georg Jensen, 2 ½ In.	461
Pin, Bird, Swallow, Diamonds, Old Mine, Rose Cut, Ruby Eye, Silver On Gold, c.1870, 3 In.	15990
Pin, Bird, Swallow, Silver, Marcasite, Green Stone Eyes, Germany, c.1940, 1 x 2 In.	60
Pin, Bow, Diamonds, Platinum, Art Deco, 2 In.	2214
Pin, Bow, Diamonds, Sapphires Inside, Platinum, J.E. Caldwell & Co., 1 In.	1968
Pin, Buddha, Seated, Tasseled Pillow, Peking Glass, Goldtone, Hattie Carnegie, 1960s, 1 ½ In.	228
Pin, Butterfly, Diamond Body, 18K Gold Cutout Wings, Van Cleef & Arpels, 2 In.	3444
Pin, Butterfly, Enamel & Marcasite, 14k Gold, 1 ⅛ In.	288
Pin, Butterfly, Lacquer, Diamonds, 18K Gold, J. Hakose, Van Cleef & Arpels, 1 ⅝ In. ....*illus*	13530
Pin, Butterfly, Old Mine Cut Diamonds, 14K Gold, Jewels, Russia, c.1915, 2 ½ In.	5000
Pin, Butterfly, Pink Sapphires, Diamonds, 18K White Gold, 1 In. ....*illus*	4750
Pin, Cameo, Carnelian, Bearded Man, Classical Drape, Oval Gold Frame, 1800s, 2 In.	1353
Pin, Cameo, Hardstone, 2 Cherubs, Leaning On Plinth, 14K Gold Frame, Arts & Crafts, 1 In.	584
Pin, Cameo, Hardstone, Moses, 18K Gold Openwork, Diamonds & Pearls, L. Rosi, 2 In.	1230
Pin, Cameo, Sardonyx, Woman's Profile, Curls, Black Enamel, Gold Frame, Pearls, 2 In.	923
Pin, Cameo, Shell, Medusa Profile, 14K Gold Mount, Zaccagnini, 3 In.	1599
Pin, Cameo, Shell, Venus & Cupid, Platinum, Beaded, Diamonds, Pearls, Edwardian, 1 ⅝ In.	923
Pin, Carnelian, Intaglio, Greek Warrior, Round Frame, 14K Gold Bands, 1 ½ In.	492
Pin, Carnelian, Oval, Spiral Scroll Frame, 18K Gold, 1930s, 1 ½ In.	738
Pin, Circle With Bow, Diamonds, Synthetic Emerald, Platinum, 1 ¼ In. ....*illus*	660
Pin, Citrine, Oval, Gold Repousse Frame, c.1835, 1 ¼ In.	308
Pin, Clock, Oval Dial, Silver, Blue Guilloche, Edwardian, Golay Fils & Stahl, 1 ½ In.	461
Pin, Confederate Soldier, Gray Uniform, Sword, Chain, 18K Gold, Enamel, Tiffany & Co., 2 In.	1200
Pin, Coral Beads, Star Set, Diamond, Gold Wirework, c.1875, 1 ¾ In.	388
Pin, Cross, 19 Diamonds, Mine Cut, Gold, Lobed Sides, c.1865, 1 ¼ In.	4305
Pin, Diamonds, Platinum, Elliptical, Openwork, Art Deco, 2 ¾ In.	3690
Pin, Dog, Bulldog, 18K Gold, Enamel, Wood, Emerald & Diamond Collar, J. Roca, 1 ⅝ In.	1107
Pin, Dog, Golden Retriever, Reverse Painted Glass, Oval, 14K Gold, R. Yard, 1 ¾ In. ....*illus*	1722
Pin, Dog, Poodle, 18K Gold, Beaded, Ruby Eye, Garnet Collar, Van Cleef & Arpels, 1 In.	5166
Pin, Dog, Scottish Deerhound, In Pursuit, Silver, Gold Collar, c.1900, 2 ½ In.	861
Pin, Dog, Terrier, 18K Gold, Sapphire Eyes, Tag Says Lottie, Cartier, c.1950, 1 ¼ In.	3690
Pin, Dog's Head, Setter, Enamel, Round, Platinum & Gold Mount, Diamonds, Art Deco, 1 In.	1353
Pin, Doodle, Bird, Openwork, 14K Gold, Tiffany & Co., 1 In.	308
Pin, Dragonfly, Gold, Pearl, Ruby Eyes, Pink Topaz & Aquamarine Wings, c.1900, 1 ⅜ In.	1599
Pin, Elegant Woman, Diamond Necklace, Plique-A-Jour Enamel, Gold, Art Nouveau, 1 In.	1722
Pin, Elephant, 14K Gold, Diamond Tusks, Ruby Eyes, Uwe Koetter, 1 ¼ In.	1169
Pin, Endless Knot, Pearls, Diamonds, 14K Gold, Pearl Locket Drop, Russia, 3 In.	2706
Pin, Flower, 4 Petals, Coral Enamel, 18K Gold, Diamond Stamens, Boucheron, 1 ¾ In.	3690
Pin, Flower, Green Chalcedony Bead, Diamond, 14K Gold, Cartier, Retro, 1 In.	738
Pin, Flower, Pink Rhinestones, Goldtone Leaves, Marked, D. Lisner, 2 ½ x 1 ½ In.	41
Pin, Flower, Rock Crystal Petals, Ruby & Diamond Melee Accents, Tiffany & Co., 1 In.	923
Pin, Flowers, Amethyst & Diamond Petals, 2 Nephrite Leaves, 14K Gold, 1 ¾ In. ....*illus*	1125
Pin, Flutist, Turtle, Sterling Silver, William Hunt Diederich, c.1900, 1 ¾ x 2 ¼ In. ....*illus*	4063
Pin, Frog, 14K Gold, Emerald Eyes, On Coral Branch, 2 ¼ x 3 ¾ In. ....*illus*	2750
Pin, Frog, Leaping, 14K Gold, Diamond & Emerald Body, Ruby Eyes, 2 ¼ In. ....*illus*	584
Pin, Goldfish, 18K Gold, Enamel, Orange Body, Green Fins, Diamonds, Serafini, 3 In.	3851
Pin, Golf Club, Platinum, Diamond Melee, Pearl Ball, Art Deco, 2 ⅜ In.	400
Pin, Grape Cluster, Amethysts, Pearls, Diamonds, 14K Gold, Seaman Schepps, 1 ¾ In.	923
Pin, Hebe, Fish, Diamonds, 18K Gold, Green Enamel Seaweed, G. Braque, c.1962, 3 In.	4920
Pin, Jabot, Oval Moonstone Ends, Circular Diamond Frames, Platinum, Edwardian, 3 In.	948
Pin, Jade Plaque, Vines, Carved, Pierced, Platinum On Gold, Diamonds, Art Deco, 1 ¼ In.	1107
Pin, Jade, Ducks, Flowers, Carved, Pierced, Platinum Frame, Diamond Ends, Cartier, 2 In.	3444
Pin, Leaf, Abstract, 18K Gold, Openwork, 7 Bezel Set Moonstones, c.1960, 2 ⅜ In.	923
Pin, Leaf, Hardstone, Brown, Diamond Accents, Enamel Stem, 18K Gold, 1 ⅜ In.	1046
Pin, Leaves, Silver, Green Agate Cabochons, Amber Drops, Hentze, Georg Jensen, 3 In.	5228
Pin, Leaves, Silver, Protruding Amber Buds, Drops, Green Agate Accents, Georg Jensen, 4 In.	18450

Jewelry, Pin, Frog, 14K Gold, Emerald Eyes, On Coral Branch, 2¼ x 3¾ In. $2,750

New Orleans Auction Galleries

Jewelry, Pin, Frog, Leaping, 14K Gold, Diamond & Emerald Body, Ruby Eyes, 2¼ In. $584

Skinner, Inc.

Jewelry, Pin, Lion, Diamonds, Emerald Eye, Ruby Tongue, 18K Gold, Marked, HB, 2¾ In. $2,460

Skinner, Inc.

Jewelry, Pin, Lizard, Diamonds, Tsavorite Garnets, Ruby, Eyes, 14K White Gold, 2¾ In. $3,250

New Orleans Auction Galleries

Jewelry, Pin, Micro Mosaic, Cat, 18K Gold, Sapphire Cabochons, E. Locke, 2½ In. $7,812

New Orleans Auction Galleries

Jewelry, Pin, Micro Mosaic, Moonstones, Pearls, Diamonds, 18K Gold, E. Locke, 2 In. $4,500

New Orleans Auction Galleries

Jewelry, Pin, Pave Turquoise, Locket Back, Woven Hair, 15K Gold, Engraved, 1870 $274

Neal Auctions

Jewelry, Pin, Peacock, Demantoid Garnet, Diamonds, Platinum Over 18K Gold, 1 In. $3,321

Skinner, Inc.

Jewelry, Pin, Portrait, Cleopatra, Enamel, 18K Gold Asp, Emerald, Leresche & Fils, 1¼ In.
$2,583

Skinner, Inc.

Jewelry, Pin, Portrait, Dog, Porcelain, 18K Gold, Removable Bail, E. Locke, 1½ In.
$3,000

New Orleans Auction Galleries

Jewelry, Pin, Rabbit Waiter, Diamonds, Sapphires, Rubies, Platinum, R. Yard, 1930s, 2 In.
$45,000

New Orleans Auction Galleries

Jewelry, Pin, Songbird, Round Multicolor Gemstones, 18K Gold, Jean Vitau, 1 In., Pair
$2,091

Skinner, Inc.

Jewelry, Pin, Stylized Ribbon, Gold, Sapphire Spray, Diamonds, Retro, Tiffany, 1940s, 2¾ In.
$2,074

James D. Julia Auctioneers

Jewelry, Pin, Sunburst, 24 Diamonds, Seed Pearls, 1¼ In.
$900

Brunk Auctions

Jewelry, Pin, Tiger's Head, Enamel, Diamonds, Ruby Eye, 18K Gold, Missiaglia, 1¼ In.
$3,998

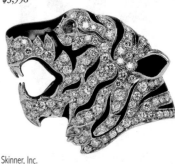

Skinner, Inc.

Jewelry, Pin, Woman, Dragonfly Wings, 18K Gold, Enamel, Diamonds, Pearls, Carreras, 2 In.
$6,150

Skinner, Inc.

Jewelry, Ring, Aquamarine, Emerald Cut, Diamonds On Sides, Size 4¾
$960

Brunk Auctions

TIP

Changing the size of a necklace or bracelet? Save the links, pearls, or stones removed from the piece. Someday you might want to make it bigger again.

Pin, Lion, Diamonds, Emerald Eye, Ruby Tongue, 18K Gold, Marked, HB, 2¾ In.............*illus* 2460

Pin, Lizard, Diamonds, Tsavorite Garnets, Ruby, Eyes, 14K White Gold, 2¾ In.................*illus* 3250

Pin, Locket, Raised Scrolls, Engraved, Oval, Rose Gold, Silver, England, c.1880, 1½ In. 185

Pin, Malachite, Oval Turquoise, Square Silver Frame, J. Hoffmann, Wiener Werkstatte, 2 In.... 27500

Pin, Man In Moon, Crescent, 18K Gold, Mother-Of-Pearl, Jade Eye, Tiffany, Hong Kong, 2 In. .. 984

Pin, Maple Leaf, 14K Textured Gold, Single Diamond, Cartier, Italy, 1⅝ In. 861

Pin, Micro Mosaic, Cat, 18K Gold, Sapphire Cabochons, E. Locke, 2½ In..........................*illus* 7812

Pin, Micro Mosaic, Moonstones, Pearls, Diamonds, 18K Gold, E. Locke, 2 In....................*illus* 4500

Pin, Moth, Silver, Garnet Eyes, Turquoise Wings, Art Nouveau, 2⅝ x 3½ In. 633

Pin, Mourning, Maiden, Holding Plaque, Memento, Spaniel, Navette, 18th Century, 1½ In. 677

Pin, Old Car, 18K Gold, Diamond Fender, Enamel Grill & Tires, Rubies, Milano Piero, 2 In. 2666

Pin, Opal Doublet, Oval, 14K Granulated Gold Mount, Ed Wiener, 1½ In........................... 840

Pin, Pave Turquoise, Locket Back, Woven Hair, 15K Gold, Engraved, 1870.........................*illus* 274

Pin, Peacock, Demantoid Garnet, Diamonds, Platinum Over 18K Gold, 1 In....................*illus* 3321

Pin, Peacock, Enamel, Filigree, David Andersen, Norway, c.1950, 1 x 1 In......................... 60

Pin, Peacock, Pearl, Turquoise, Amethysts, Diamonds, 18K Gold, Meister Zurich, 3 In. 1845

Pin, Pearls, 15 Round Cultured 14K Gold, 20th Century, 2 In....................................... 187

Pin, Pharaoh's Head, Gold, Agate Face, Cloisonne Nemes, Diamond Collar, Art Deco, 2 In........ 4920

Pin, Portrait, Cleopatra, Enamel, 18K Gold Asp, Emerald, Leresche & Fils, 1¼ In.............*illus* 2583

Pin, Portrait, Dog, Porcelain, 18K Gold, Removable Bail, E. Locke, 1½ In. ....*illus* 3000

Pin, Rabbit Waiter, Diamonds, Sapphires, Rubies, Platinum, R. Yard, 1930s, 2 In. ....*illus* 45000

Pin, Roses, Pink Marquise Rhinestones, Goldtone, Marked, Weiss, 1960s, 3 In. 125

Pin, Sailboat, 14K Gold, Split Pearl Sails, Marked, Sloan & Co., 1½ In.............................. 431

Pin, Sapphire, Diamonds, 14K White Gold, Elliptical, Openwork, Art Deco, 1½ In. 142

Pin, Scallop Shell, 14K Gold, Marked, McTeigue, 1½ In... 481

Pin, Scarab, Amethyst, Gold, Enamel Wings, Ruby Accents, Egyptian Revival, 1½ In. 1722

Pin, Scarf, Winged Dragon, Gold, Plique-A-Jour Enamel, Art Nouveau, ¾ In. 1046

Pin, Seahorse, Silver, Marked, Paul Lobel, 2½ In. 677

Pin, Ship, Schooner, Enamel, 22K Gold Wire Rigging, Pearl Fringe, 2½ In. 1476

Pin, Silver, 14K Gold, Enamel, Rectangular, Geometric, Earl Pardon, 1950, 1 x 2 In................. 2250

Pin, Snowflake, Diamonds & Pearls, 14K Gold, Open, c.1910, 1 In................................. 1550

Pin, Songbird, Round Multicolor Gemstones, 18K Gold, Jean Vitau, 1 In., Pair..................*illus* 2091

Pin, Squirrel, Nut, Green Hardstone Belly, Ruby Eye, Van Cleef & Arpels, 2 In. 5166

Pin, Stylized Leaf, 18K Gold Rope Twist, Sapphire Vein, Van Cleef & Arpels, 2½ In. 1230

Pin, Stylized Ribbon, Gold, Sapphire Spray, Diamonds, Retro, Tiffany, 1940s, 2¾ In. ....*illus* 2074

Pin, Sunburst, 24 Diamonds, Seed Pearls, 1¼ In..*illus* 900

Pin, Tiger's Head, Enamel, Diamonds, Ruby Eye, 18K Gold, Missiaglia, 1¼ In.................*illus* 3998

Pin, Tropical Fish, 18K Gold, Mother-Of-Pearl, Black Jade, Hematite, Tiffany & Co., 2½ In. 2829

Pin, Turquoise, Pave Set, Greek Key Border, Gold, Compartment, Victorian, 1½ In................. 492

Pin, Umbrella, 18K Gold, Open Canopy, Diamond Drops, Twisted Handle, K. Wayne, 2 In........ 615

Pin, Woman, Dragonfly Wings, 18K Gold, Enamel, Diamonds, Pearls, Carreras, 2 In. ....*illus* 6150

Ring, 2 Peacock Feathers, Crossed, 18K Gold, 2 Heart Shape Opals, Art Nouveau, 4 In. 2583

Ring, 3 Pearls, 14K Gold, Leaf & Scroll Shoulders, 1920s, Size 6½.................................. 1599

Ring, 6 Diamonds, 14K Gold Nugget Setting, Ed Wiener, Size 5.................................... 1440

Ring, Abstract, Red Hardstone Triangular Bead, Silver, M. De Patta, Mexico, Size 6½............. 1845

Ring, Amethyst, Oval Cut, Blue Topaz & Diamond Chip Accent, 14K Gold, Size 6.................... 160

Ring, Amethyst, Oval, Diamond Border, Textured 18K Gold, Buccellati, Size 5¾ 1968

Ring, Aquamarine, Emerald Cut, Diamonds On Sides, Size 4¾........................*illus* 960

Ring, Band, 18K White Gold, Mother-Of-Pearl Inlay, Line Of Diamonds, L. Pizzo, Size 6¼....... 523

Ring, Band, 3 Flowers, 18 Rubies, Diamonds, 18K White Gold Openwork, Le Vian, Size 6¾...... 500

Ring, Band, B. Zero1, Concave, Steel, 18K Rose Gold Edges, A. Kapoor, Bulgari, Size 7¾........... 369

Ring, Band, Thick, 18K Gold, Diamond Heart, Center Row Of Diamonds, Mauboussin, Size 6.. 593

Ring, Basket, Ruby, 5 Diamonds, 14K Gold, 20th Century, Size 6.................................... 187

Ring, Black Opal, 14K Textured Gold, Cast & Forged, Adjustable Hoop, Size 5 ....*illus* 1625

Ring, Citrine, Emerald Cut, 4 Round Diamonds, 4 Square Rubies, 14K Gold, Retro, Size 7........ 2963

Ring, Coin, Silver, 14K Gold Bezel, Beaded Accents, Susan Sarantos, Size 6¾ 984

Ring, Coral Cabochon, 18K Gold, Geometric Frame, Diamonds, Di Modolo, Size 8.................... 968

Ring, Diamonds, Old European Cut, Oval Cluster, Platinum Over Gold, c.1920, Size 9.............. 1845

Jewelry, Ring, Black Opal, 14K Textured Gold, Cast & Forged, Adjustable Hoop, Size 5
$1,625

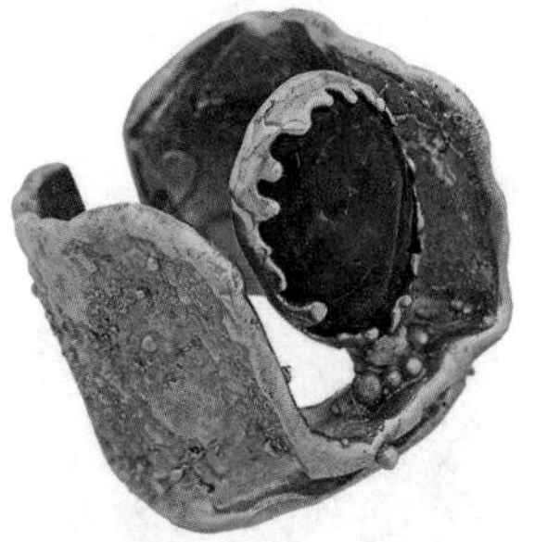

Rago Arts and Auction Center

Jewelry, Ring, Snake, Coiled, 18K Gold, Ruby Cabochons, Lalaounis, Box, Size 5, 2 In.
$3,198

Skinner, Inc.

Jewelry, Ring, Synthetic Tourmaline, Diamonds, 14K Gold Scrolling Mount, Size 6
$360

Brunk Auctions

Josef Originals, Figurine, Isolde, From Tristan & Isolde Opera, Yellow, 8½ In. $195

Ruby Lane

Judaica, Seder Plate, Black, White, Hebrew, Transferware, Ridgway, 1924, 10 In. $250

Ruby Lane

Jugtown, Vase, Blue, Mottled, Incised Bands, Flared Neck, Marked, 9¾ x 7 In. $1,000

Rago Arts and Auction Center

Ring, Diamonds, Pearls, Alternating Rings, Beaded Platinum Mount, c.1920, Size 2		3567
Ring, Dome, Citrine Beads, 18K Gold, Pomellato, Size 6½		2214
Ring, Dome, Rock Crystal, Diamond Inside, 18K Gold Mount, Mauboussin, Size 5		1476
Ring, Elongated Ruby, Hammered 22K Gold Mount, H. Alvin Sharpe		1800
Ring, Flower, Pave Ruby Petals, Green Plique-A-Jour Leaves, Diamonds, Moira, Size 5¾		1968
Ring, Frog, On Riverbank, Sun, Plique-A-Jour, 18K Gold, Masriera Y Carreras, Size 5½		1968
Ring, Garnet, Oval, 18K Gold Mount, Beaded Shoulders, Temple St. Clair, Size 6¾		677
Ring, Green Chalcedony, Oval, 14K Gold Abstract Mount, 1960s, Size 7½		615
Ring, Intaglio, Lion Attacking Gazelle, Oval Textured Frame, Size 7¼		738
Ring, Lover's Eye, Left, Brown, Yellow Gold, 1800s, ½ x ⅜ In.		2625
Ring, Mabe Pearl, 19K Textured Gold Wing Frame, David Webb, Size 5½		1046
Ring, Mourning, Maiden, Sepia, Hairwork Willow Tree, Gold, Navette, 1781, Size 6¾		523
Ring, Mourning, Urn, Willow Tree, Hairwork, Blue Enamel Border, Gold, Navette, Size 5¾		677
Ring, Pave Diamond Rectangle, 18K Stepped & Hammered Mount, D. Webb, Size 8		3998
Ring, Pink Sapphires, Diamonds, Platinum, 14K Gold, Faceted Center, c.1925, Size 8		4800
Ring, Poison, 2 Entwined Snakes, Diamond Melee, 18K Gold, I. Makri, Size 6		1845
Ring, Sapphire, Elongated, Diamond Baguette Sides, Platinum, France, 1950, Size 6½		9225
Ring, Scarab, Amethyst, Oval, 14K Gold, Purple & White Enamel Rays, Art Deco, Size 7		431
Ring, Seal, Carnelian, Roman Soldier, Ribbed 18K Gold Mount, Size 9		840
Ring, Silver, Green Stone, Carved Clover Setting, Mid 1900s, Size 8, Man's		60
Ring, Skeleton Key, Sterling Silver, Wrapped, Box, Avon, 1976, Size 8		85
Ring, Skull, Wood, Carved, Diamond Eyes, 14K Gold & Onyx Mount, Amedeo, Size 7		523
Ring, Snake, Coiled, 18K Gold, Brown Diamond Head, Marked, Susan Sarantos, Size 8		492
Ring, Snake, Coiled, 18K Gold, Ruby Cabochons, Lalaounis, Box, Size 5, 2 In. *illus*		3198
Ring, Snake, Coiled, 18K Gold, Ruby Eyes, Victorian, Size 8		923
Ring, South Sea Pearl, Ridged 18K Gold Shank, Diamonds, C. Walling, Size 5¼		1107
Ring, Sputnik, Aquamarine, Amethyst, Topaz, Citrine, Garnet, 18K Gold, H. Stern, Size 5		600
Ring, Star Sapphire, Oval, Platinum, Diamond Shoulders, Art Deco, Size 7¼		3998
Ring, Synthetic Tourmaline, Diamonds, 14K Gold Scrolling Mount, Size 6 *illus*		360
Ring, Tete De Mort, Skull & Crossbones, Diamond Melee, 18K White Gold, Dior, Size 6		1107
Ring, Tiger's Eye, Blue, 14k White Gold, America, 1900s, Size 8, Man's		240
Ring, Trinity, 3 Interlocking Bands, Ribbed, 14K Gold, Cartier, Size 3¼		431
Stickpin, Amethyst Glass Stone, Shield Shape, Goldtone Metal, 3½ In.		52
Stickpin, Art Glass Cabochon, Green, Caramel Edges, Brass, Fretwork, c.1890, 2½ In.		24
Stickpin, Man In The Moon, Moonstone, Diamonds, Gold, ⅜ In.		554
Tie Bar, Man's, Diamond, Flanked By Sapphires, 14K Bicolor Gold, Retro, 2¼ In.		201
Tie Set, 18K Gold, Crystal, Diamond, Longmire, England, 1900s		1875

Watches are listed in their own category.

Wristwatches are listed in their own category.

 JOHN ROGERS statues were made from 1859 to 1892. The originals were bronze, but the thousands of copies made by the Rogers factory were of painted plaster. Eighty different figures were created. Similar painted plaster figures were produced by some other factories. Rights to the figures were sold in 1893, and the figures were manufactured until about 1895 by the Rogers Statuette Co. Never repaint a Rogers figure because this lowers the value to collectors.

Group, Charity Patient, 1866, 22 In.		380
Group, Checker Players, 1860, 15 In.		4500
Group, Mail Day, 1864, 16 In.		875
Group, Village Schoolmaster, 1862, 9¾ In.		1776

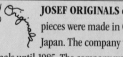 **JOSEF ORIGINALS** ceramics were designed by Muriel Joseph George. The first pieces were made in California from 1945 to 1962. They were then manufactured in Japan. The company was sold to George Good in 1982 and he continued to make Josef Originals until 1985. The company was sold two more times. The last owner went bankrupt in 2011.

Figurine, Dog, Cocker Spaniel, Seated, Tan, Sticker, 4 In.		30
Figurine, Isolde, From Tristan & Isolde Opera, Yellow, 8½ In. *illus*		195

Figurine, Mary, Holding Jesus, Sticker, c.1955, 8 ½ In. 35
Figurine, November Harvest, Foil Sticker, 3 ¾ In. 48

JUDAICA is any memorabilia that refers to the Jews or the Jewish religion. Interests range from newspaper clippings that mention eighteenth- and nineteenth-century Jewish Americans to religious objects, such as menorahs or spice boxes. Age, condition, and the intrinsic value of the material, as well as the historic and artistic importance, determine the value.

Chalice, Moses, 10 Commandments, King Solomon, Green, 8 ¼ In. 250
Charity Box, Cupped Hand, Half-Moon Cylinder, Brass, c.1875, 21 In. 2000
Etrog Container, Roses, Lobed, Footed, 1950-99, 5 ½ x 5 ¾ In. 625
Kiddush Cup, Hand Painted, Goblet Form, Biblical Scene, Italy, Early 1900s, 5 ¾ In. 492
Kiddush Cup, Square Foot, Poland, 4 ¾ In. 156
Kiddush Cup, Sterling Silver, Flowers, Leaves, Relief, Russia, 5 ¼ In. 135
Menorah, 8 Oil Fonts, Detachable Light, Silver, Marked, Bezalel, c.1910, 5 x 6 In. 980
Menorah, Art Deco, Silver, Poland, c.1920, 17 In. 3000
Menorah, Candle Cups, Openwork Scales, Silver, Continental, 8 ¼ In. 150
Menorah, Hanukkah, Openwork, Leaves, Scroll, Footed, Silver, 8 ¼ x 10 In. 4062
Menorah, Hexagon Red Marble Base, Salvador Dali, 1981, 19 ⅝ In. 3750
Seder Plate, Birds, Mandalas, Moses, Mt. Sinai, 10 Commandments, Persia, 13 In. 590
Seder Plate, Black, White, Hebrew, Transferware, Ridgway, 1924, 10 In. ....*illus* 250
Seder Tray, Engraving, Portrait, Floral Border, 8 ¾ In. 94
Seder Tray, Engraving, Star Of David, Shield Crest, Eagle, Pewter, 13 ½ In. 184
Torah Finials, Star Of David, Faceted Stems, Bells, Silver, 1913, 15 ¾ In. 3000

JUGTOWN POTTERY refers to pottery made in North Carolina as far back as the 1750s. In 1915, Juliana and Jacques Busbee set up a training and sales organization for what they named Jugtown Pottery. In 1921, they built a shop at Jugtown, North Carolina, and hired Ben Owen as a potter in 1923. The Busbees moved the village store where the pottery was sold to New York City. Juliana Busbee sold the New York store in 1926 and moved into a log cabin near the Jugtown Pottery. The pottery closed in 1959. It reopened in 1960 and is still working near Seagrove, North Carolina.

Bowl, Tan, Blue Inside, Incised Decoration, Flared, 5 x 9 ½ In. 1000
Vase, Angled, Ring Decoration, Blue, Red, Flared Rim, 10 ¼ In. 640
Vase, Blue, Mottled, Incised Bands, Flared Neck, Marked, 9 ¾ x 7 In. ....*illus* 1000
Vase, Round, Shouldered, Pale Blue Mottled, Red Speckles, Marked, 6 In. 224
Vase, Turquoise, High Glaze, 7 ½ In. 215

JUKEBOXES play records. The first coin-operated phonograph was demonstrated in 1889. In 1906 the Automatic Entertainer appeared, the first coin-operated phonograph to offer several different selections of music. The first electrically powered jukebox was introduced in 1927. Collectors search for jukeboxes of all ages, especially those with flashing lights and unusual design and graphics.

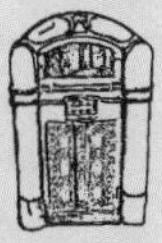

AMI, Model A, Plastic, Art Deco, Faux Wood Frame, 1946, 40 x 30 In. 1888
AMI, Model JCH-100, Curved Glass, Manual Selector, 60 45-RPM Records, 1957, 60 In. 5459
Seeburg, Model ESE 100, 4 Speakers, 100 45-RPM Discs, 1970 1717
Wurlitzer, Arched Case, Lighted, 24 Discs, c.1941, 57 x 32 In. ....*illus* 2400
Wurlitzer, One More Time, Arched Glass, Bubbles, 100 45-RPM Records, c.1988, 60 In. 6868
Wurlitzer, Teledisc, The Egg, Domed Bubble Top, 5-Legged, Chrome Stand, 1982 5294

KATE GREENAWAY, who was a famous illustrator of children's books, drew pictures of children in high-waisted Empire dresses. She lived from 1846 to 1901. Her designs appear on china, glass, napkin rings, and other pieces.

Book, Marigold Garden, 1st Edition, Illustrated, Color, Hardcover, 1885 195
Button, Children, Ring Around The Rosie, Iridescent, Dark Pearl, 1 ³/₁₆ In. ....*illus* 225
Doll, Big Sister, Porcelain Head & Hands, White Dress & Hat, Blue Sash, 11 In. 85

Jukebox, Wurlitzer, Arched Case, Lighted, 24 Discs, c.1941, 57 x 32 In.
$2,400

Brunk Auctions

Kate Greenaway, Button, Children, Ring Around The Rosie, Iridescent, Dark Pearl, 1 ³/₁₆ In.
$225

K

Ruby Lane

Kelva, Dresser Box, Blue, Pink Flowers, Hinge, 5 x 8 In.
$476

Morphy Auctions

What's A Can Without An Opener
The can opener was invented 48 years after the can.

Kenton Hills, Vase, Cherries, Red, Blue, William Hentschel, 9¾ In. $145

Humler & Nolan

Kew Blas, Vase, Pulled Feather, Gold Iridescent, Green, c.1910, 8¾ In. $1,206

K

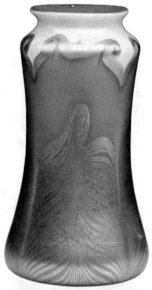

Morphy Auctions

Figurine, Ellen, Girl, Seated, Yellow Pillow, Doll, Porcelain, c.1980, 4 In.	147
Figurine, Nell, Bonnet, Seated In Wagon, Square Base, c.1980, 4 In.	100
Plate, Children Playing, Fence, River, c.1890, 10 In. Diam.	87
Vase, Figural, Woman With Basket, Pink Dress, Bonnet, Stump, 10 In.	283

Kay Finch
CALIFORNIA

KAY FINCH CERAMICS were made in Corona del Mar, California, from 1935 to 1963. The hand-decorated pieces often depicted whimsical animals and people. Pastel colors were used.

Figurine, Cat, Pink, White Whiskers, 6½ In.	50
Figurine, Cat, Seated, Matte Cream, Pink, Mauve, Swirled Fur, 1940s, 11 In.	390
Figurine, Chick, Standing, Looking Down, Open Beak, White, Green, Black, 1940s, 4 In.	99
Figurine, Dog, Cocker Spaniel, Seated, White, Gray Nose, Signed, 1950s, 13 x 13 In.	996
Figurine, Lamb, Prancing, Pink, White, Blue Eyes, Flower Wreath, 1940s, 10½ In.	250
Figurine, Peanut The Elephant, Raised Foot & Trunk, Pink, Flowers, Signed, 1950s	289
Figurine, Pig, Winking, Pale Pink, Yellow, Green, Mauve Cheeks, 1940s, 4 x 4 In.	125
Figurine, Rabbit, Teal Scarf, 22½ In.	300

KAYSERZINN, *see Pewter category.*

KELVA

KELVA glassware was made by the C. F. Monroe Company of Meriden, Connecticut, about 1904. It is a pale, pastel-painted glass decorated with flowers, designs, or scenes. Kelva resembles Nakara and Wave Crest, two other glasswares made by the same company.

Dresser Box, Blue, Pink Flowers, Hinge, 5 x 8 In. ......*illus*	476
Dresser Box, White Lilies, Pink Streaks, Shaped, Paneled, Hinged Lid, c.1910, 7 In.	614
Jewelry Box, Green, Pink Flower, Beading, Scalloped Oval, Hinged Lid, 1900s, 3 x 5 In.	760
Powder Box, Flowers, Green, Pink, Beaded, Hexagonal, Hinged Puff Lid, c.1900, 4 In.	335
Powder Box, Red Poppy, Opaline, Mottled Green, Squat, Metal, Hinged Lid, c.1900, 3 x 5 In.	600
Trinket Box, Moss Green, Orange & White Flowers, Shaped, Hinged Lid, c.1910, 4 In.	31
Trinket Box, Mottled Gray, Pink, Flowers, Beaded, Hexagonal, Ormolu Feet, Hinged Lid, 4 In.	574

KENTON HILLS POTTERY in Erlanger, Kentucky, made artwares, including vases and figurines that resembled Rookwood, probably because so many of the original artists and workmen had worked at the Rookwood plant. Kenton Hills opened in 1939 and closed during World War II.

Lamp, Yellow Glaze, Mottled Leaves, Double Gourd, Brass Base, c.1939, 18 In.	663
Vase, Cherries, Red, Blue, William Hentschel, 9¾ In. ......*illus*	145
Vase, Turquoise, Crackle Glaze, Gourd Shape, Marked, 1940s, 10 In.	495

KFW·BLAS **KEW BLAS** is the name used by the Union Glass Company of Somerville, Massachusetts. The name refers to an iridescent golden glass made from the 1890s to 1924. The iridescent glass was reminiscent of the Tiffany glass of the period.

Candlestick, Gold Iridescent, Mauve, Ribbed Swirl, Swollen Stick, Disc Foot, 8 In.	176
Compote, Gold Iridescent, Twisted Stem, Flared Ruffled Rim, Signed, 1900s, 7 In.	1015
Creamer, Gold Iridescent, Amber Aurene, Cylindrical, Scroll Handle, c.1905, 3 x 4 In.	595
Finger Bowl, Gold Iridescent, Purple Highlights, Flowerhead Shape, c.1905, 7 In.	249
Vase, Calcite Blue, Orange & Gold Iridescent, Coil Design, Flared Rim, 7 In.	295
Vase, Pulled Feather, Gold Iridescent, Green, c.1910, 8¾ In. ......*illus*	1206
Vase, White, Gold Iridescent, Pulled Feather, Squat Disc, Pedestal, c.1910, 3 x 4 In.	613
Vase, White, Green Pulled Ribbon, Iridescent Gold, Trumpet Shape, Ruffled Rim, 9 In.	590

KEWPIES, designed by Rose O'Neill, were first pictured in the *Ladies' Home Journal.* The figures, which are similar to pixies, were a success, and Kewpie dolls and figurines started appearing in 1911. Kewpie pictures and other items soon followed. Collectors search for all items that picture the little winged people.

Bisque, 1 Piece, Holds Broom, Dust Bin, Rose O'Neill, c.1912, 5 In. ......*illus*	392

Bisque, Composition, Glass Eyes, Marked, O'Neill, JDK 12, c.1912, 14 In............................*illus*	4200
Bisque, Fireman, Helmet, Jointed, Starfish Hands, Side-Glancing Eyes, c.1915, 5 In.	3078
Bisque, Side-Glancing Eyes, Blue Wings, Helmet, Belt, Sword, Gilt Trumpet, 5 In.............*illus*	728
Bisque, The Hugger, Twin Babies, Starfish Hands, c.1915, 3 ½ In..	105
Bisque, Topknot, Blue Wings, Flocked Teddy Bear, Rose O'Neill, c.1912, 5 ½ In.................*illus*	336
Huggers, Bride & Groom, Bisque, Blue Wings, Germany, c.1915, 3 ½ In.	224

KING'S ROSE, *see Soft Paste category.*

KITCHEN utensils of all types, from eggbeaters to bowls, are collected today. Handmade wooden and metal items, like ladles and apple peelers, were made in the early nineteenth century. Mass-produced pieces, like iron apple peelers and graniteware, were made in the nineteenth century. Also included in this category are utensils used for other household chores, such as laundry and cleaning. Other kitchen wares are listed under manufacturers' names or under Advertising, Iron, Tool, or Wooden.

Bird Spit, 3-Footed, Flat Feet, Iron, 14 In...	555
Bird Spit, Rectangular, Pins, Iron, 14 x 14 In...	234
Blender, Hollywood Liquefier Co., Cream, Art Deco, 14 ½ x 6 ¼ In.	305
Bowl, Dough, Black, Loop Handle, 33 x 14 ½ In..	270
Bowl, Dough, Wood, Roughhewn, 1800s, 5 ¾ x 26 ⅝ In.	80
Box, Candle, French Provincial, Walnut, Slant Top, Scrolls, Drawer, Arched Backplate..............	366
Box, Pantry, Pine, Dark Blue Green, 1800s, 9 ¼ In.	600
Box, Utensil, Walnut, Shaped Edges & Divider, Cutout Center Handle, 6 x 15 x 8 In...............	118
Box, Utensil, Wooden, Blue Paint, Rectangular, Center Divider, 1800s, 3 x 11 In.	189
Bread Box, Yellowware, Molded, Urn, Grapes, Variegated Brown & Green, 13 x 16 In.	360
Bread Slicer, Cast Iron, Wood Handle, Slice Tray, Alexanderwerk, 1930s, 11 x 15 In.	165
Broiler, Electric, Chrome, Quik Chef, 1952, 9 x 13 ½ In. ....*illus*	129
Broiler, Rotating, Iron, 12 x 22 In.	82
Broiler, Rotating, Iron, Rectangular, 4 Half Circle Stands For Toast, 18 In.	70
Broiler, Rotating, Iron, Round, 29 In.	117
Bucket, Sugar, Green Paint, Bentwood Swing Handle, Late 1800s, 12 ½ x 11 ¾ In....................	570
Butter Mold, look under Mold, Butter in this category.	
Butter Paddle, Tiger Maple, Wide Scoop, Straight Handle, 1800s, 11 In.	95
Butter Paddle, Wood, Carved, Wide Spoon, Curved Hook Handle, Thumb Rest, 1800s, 10 In. .	225
Butter Stamp, 2 Parts, 2 Pineapples, Carved, Rectangular, Turned Handle, 1800s, 5 In.	236
Butter Stamp, 2-Sided, 6-Point Star & Pinwheel, Lollipop Handle, 1800s, 7 In.	443
Butter Stamp, 2-Sided, 6-Point Star & Pinwheel, Lollipop Handle, 1880s, 8 ½ In.	325
Butter Stamp, 6-Point Star, Leafy Design, Round, Lollipop Handle, 1800s, 7 In.	189
Butter Stamp, Cherry, Radial Center, 2 ¼ x 3 ¾ In.................................*illus*	150
Butter Stamp, Circular, Eagle & Swan, 1800s, 4 ⅜ In., Pair	129
Butter Stamp, Eagle, Spread Wings, Maple, Turned, Single Piece, 4 ¼ In. ....*illus*	118
Butter Stamp, Flower, Carved, Round, Tapered, Lollipop, Handle, Hole, 1800s, 8 In...............	236
Butter Stamp, Heart, Crosshatched, Turned & Carved Wood, Round, 2 ¾ In. Diam.	201
Butter Stamp, Letter M, Carved, Mahogany, Single Piece, 1800s, 3 x 5 In. ....*illus*	106
Butter Stamp, Lollipop, Carved American Eagle, Turned Handle, Mid 1800s, 8 ¼ In.	1375
Butter Stamp, Pinwheel, Concentric Circles, Canada, 1800s	200
Butter Stamp, Sheaf Of Wheat, Leaves, Crescent Shape, Turned Handle, 1800s, 7 In., Pair	325
Butter Stamp, Stylized Eagle, Spread Wings, Carved, Pa., 1800s, 3 ¼ In.....................*illus*	1180
Butter Stamp, Turned, Carved Flower, Pennsylvania, 1800s, 4 ½ In.........................*illus*	30
Butter, Lid, Flashed, Glass, 12 Panels, Scalloped Edge, Red, Gold, Flowers, c.1840....................	253
Cabbage Cutter, Pine, Heart Cutouts, Dovetailed Box, Patina, c.1850, 50 In.	120
Cabbage Cutter, Walnut, Handwrought Screws On Box, Mid 1800s, 44 In.	60
Cake Board, Flower Medallion With Man On Horseback, Late 1800s, 11 x 11 In.	1625
Cake Board, Mahogany, Carved, Dove, Flower & Wreath Surround, Scalloped, 8 ½ In.	523
Cake Board, Mahogany, Carved, Elliptical, Decoration, 13 ½ x 23 ½ In.	3437
Cake Board, Mahogany, Carved, New York Coat Of Arms, Wreath, 11 In.	3690
Cake Pan, Oscar The Grouch, Garbage Can Shape, Tin, Wilton, 1977, 16 In.	15
Cheese Mold, Punched Tin, Swivel Wire, 2 x 7 In. ....*illus*	146
Chopper, Cutout Heart, Iron Blade, Maple Handle, 12 ½ In.	585

Kewpie, Bisque, 1 Piece, Holds Broom, Dust Bin, Rose O'Neill, c.1912, 5 In.
$392

Theriault's

Kewpie, Bisque, Composition, Glass Eyes, Marked, O'Neill, JDK 12, c.1912, 14 In.
$4,200

Theriault's

Kewpie, Bisque, Side-Glancing Eyes, Blue Wings, Helmet, Belt, Sword, Gilt Trumpet, 5 In.
$728

Theriault's

This is an edited listing of current prices. Visit Kovels.com to check thousands of prices from previous years and sign up for free information on trends, tips, reproductions, marks, and more.

Kewpie, Bisque, Topknot, Blue Wings, Flocked Teddy Bear, Rose O'Neill, c.1912, 5½ In.
$336

Theriault's

A Lot of Bread
A Griswold No. 28 bread pan can be worth $25,000.

Kitchen, Broiler, Electric, Chrome, Quik Chef, 1952, 9 x 13½ In.
$129

Ruby Lane

Kitchen, Butter Stamp, Cherry, Radial Center, 2¼ x 3¾ In.
$150

Ruby Lane

Chopper, Garnish, Stainless Steel, Kenberry, U.S.A., 1950s, 4½ In.	12
Chopping Block, Birch, Wrought Iron Chopper, 1800s, 14¼ x 9 In.	74
Chopping Block, Pine, Clover Shape, Green Sides, c.1920, 16¼ x 14 In.	357
Churn, Blue, 1800s, 47 x 10 In.	393
Churn, Blue, Iron Bands & Lid, Dasher Repaired Or Replaced, 23½ x 11 In.	300
Churn, Softwood, Round, Hand Crank, 17 In. ....*illus*	59
Churn, Tabletop, Pine Walnut Interior, Mid 1800s, 14 x 14 x 11 In.	219
Churn, Walnut, Turned Posts, Urn Finials, Hand Crank, Glass Jar, Ball Feet, 17 x 9 In.	1968
Churn, Yellow, Crank, 4 Legs, 1800s, 29 x 19 In.	175
Clothes Wringer, Wooden Hand Crank, c.1880, 9 In.	49
Coffee Grinders are listed in the Coffee Mill category.	
Coffee Mills are listed in their own category.	
Cooker, Oats, Enamel, Speckled, 3 Parts, Squat Pot, Interior Container, Lid, 1930s, 23 In.	75
Cookie Cutter, Church, Tin, 6¾ In.	472
Cookie Cutter, Horse & Rider, Handle, Tin, 9½ In.	1298
Cookie Cutter, Horse, Square, Applied Handle, Tin, 6 In.	177
Cookie Cutter, Horse, Tin, Thos. Miller & Bro., 1880-90, 7½ x 12¼ In.	461
Cookie Cutter, Horse, Trotting, Sheet Iron, 1800s, 10 x 9 In.	263
Cookie Cutter, Rooster, Tin, 19th Century, 10¾ x 8½ In. ....*illus*	134
Cookie Cutter, Rooster, Tin, Pennsylvania, 19th Century, 8½ In.	59
Cookie Mold, Cast Iron, 8 Squares, Goose, Dog, Man, Woman, Fruit, Flower, Cat, Rooster, 7 In.	53
Cookie Mold, Maple, 2-Sided, Elizabethan Woman & Man, Springerle, 4½ x 12½ In.	89
Cookie Mold, Maple, Mounted Man, Wheeled Vehicle, Springerle, 5¾ x 16¾ In.	78
Cranberry Scoop, A.D. Makepeace Co., Painted, Red, c.1890, 20½ x 21½ In.	246
Cranberry Scoop, Wood, 18½ x 19 In.	360
Cutlery Box, Walnut, Two Sections, 10¼ x 12¾ In.	140
Cutting Board, Pig, Figural, Softwood, Tail Forms Circle Crest, Eyelet, 16 In.	153
Cutting Board, Pine, Round, Lollipop Handle, Pennsylvania, 22 In.	354
Cutting Board, Wood, Carved Circle Hex Signs, Arched Side Handle, Hole, 1800s, 5 x 14 In.	530
Dish, Wood, Leaf Shape, Acorns, 1941, 14¾ In.	148
Dough Box, Freehand Decoration, Dovetailed, Legs, c.1850, 28 x 39 x 17 In.	600
Dough Box, Hepplewhite, Red Paint, Early 1800s, 29 x 36 x 22½.	1200
Dough Box, Softwood, Recessed Ends, Single Board Lid, Mid 1800s, 11 x 28 In.	293
Dough Box, Wood, Paint, Saint, Holding Skull, Robe, Turquoise Scroll, c.1910, 6 x 35 In.	1200
Dough Box, Yellow Pine, Red Paint, Mid 1800s, 28½ x 35½ x 20 In.	780
Dough Scraper, Iron & Brass, Peter Derr, c.1860, 3¾ In.	875
Dough Scraper, Iron Blade, Tapered Brass Handle, Marked, Peter Derr, 1854, 4 In.	1062
Dough Scraper, Steel & Brass, Split At Handle & Blade, Peter Derr, c.1853, 4 In.	219
Dough Scraper, Wrought Iron, 1800s, 4 In.	49
Dutch Oven, Lid, Wide Rim, Bail Handle, Loop Finial, Peg Feet, Cast Iron, 1800s, 7 x 14 In.	375
Eggcup, Turned Wood, Paint, Pussy Willow & Decal, Dome Foot, Lehnware, 3 In.	266
Flour Bin, Green, Iron Bands, 30 x 21½ In.	450
Flour Bin, Poplar, Plank Top, 1800s, 37½ x 30 x 15⅜ In.	576
Flour Sifter, Metal, Wooden Crank Handle, Scroll Base, Lid, Fries, 1930s, 12 x 9 In.	200
Food Chopper, Steel, Crescent Blade, Sculpted Scroll Edge, Handsaw Handle, 10 In.	584
Food Chopper, Steel, Leafy Heart Scrolls, 6⅞ In.	1260
Food Chopper, Wheels, L.S. Starrett, c.1880, 13 In.	86
Fork, 2 Prongs, Iron, Flattened Handle, Center Heart & Cutout Heart Finial, 1700s, 17 x 3 In.	1800
Fork, 2 Prongs, Iron, Shaped Handle, Openwork Heart Finial, c.1800, 14 x 2 In.	500
Fork, Flesh, 2 Prongs, Iron, Long Rod Handle, Diamond Shape Handle, Loop Finial, 1800s, 23 In.	200
Fork, Flesh, 2 Prongs, Wrought Iron, Twisted, Punched Decoration, Dated 1785, 17 In.	325
Grater, Nutmeg, Figural, Acorn, 3 In., Pair	375
Grater, Nutmeg, Turned Maple, Pierced Handle, Compartment Base, 1700, 6 In.	900
Hatchel, Wood, Box Cover, Heart Cutout, Plank Slide, c.1815, 24¼ In.	54
Herb Grinder, Iron, Grinding Wheel, Wooden Handle, Iron Trough, 1800s	212
Ice Bucket, Teak, Aluminum, Dansk Style, c.1965, 11 x 9 In.	71
Ice Cream Maker, Shepard's Lightning Freezer, Bucket, Crank Handle, 7 In.	153
Iron, Rose Brass, Wedge, Oak Handle, Incised Crown, Scrollwork, Flowers, 1782, 7 In.	3555
Juice Press, Fruitwood, Wrought Iron, 1800s, 15 x 10¾ In.	62

K

Juice Press, Fruitwood, Wrought Iron, Round Base, Turned Handles, 1800s, 12 In.	62
Juice Press, Tiger Maple, Turned Legs, Plank Base, Tapered Handle, c.1810, 10 x 18 In.	295
Kettle Pusher, Iron, Wide Loops, Wish Scroll Design, Straight Leg, Hooked Foot, 1700s, 5 x 8 In.	300
Kettle Tilter, Iron, Scrollwork, Wavy Handle, Brass Finial, Twisted Hook, 1700s, 14 x 16 In.	950
Kettle, Lid, Loop Lift, Bulbous, Bail Handle, Marked 28, Cast Iron, 1800s, 9 x 12 In.	150
Kettle, Squat, Peg Feet, Bail Handle, Curved Spout, Lid, Finial, Cast Iron, 1800s, 4 x 6 In.	600
Ladle, Butter, Maple, Openwork Handle, Canada, 1850s, 8 ¼ In.	325
Ladle, Gourd Bowl, Tin Rim, Turned Wood Handle, Heart Shape Lug, 14 In. ....*illus*	48
Lemon Press, Iron, Landers, Frary & Clark Co., 1880s, 7 ½ x 3 ¾ In. ....*illus*	60
Mangle Board, Beech, Carved, Horse Shape Handle, Rondels, c.1800, 5 x 22 In., Pair	2370
Mangle Board, Chestnut, Carved, Horse Handle, Incised Pinwheel Design, 1827, 24 In. ....*illus*	325
Match Holders can be found in their own category.	
Match Safes can be found in their own category.	
Measures, Copper, Graduated, 1800s, Largest 8 In., 4 Piece	360
Mixer, Milk Shake, Hamilton Beach, 3 Heads, Green, c.1950, 20 x 13 In.	387
Mixer, Milk Shake, Model 40DM, Green, Hamilton Beach, 18 ½ In.	60 to 272
Mixer, Milk Shake, Western Electric, Marble Base, Wood Crank Handle, Cup, 19 In.	210
Mixer, Myers Bullet, Mint Green, Cups, 1900s, 18 ½ In.	123
Mold, Bundt Cake, Redware, Impressed John Bell Waynesboro, 4 x 9 In.	330
Mold, Butter, Eagle, Spread Wings, Flower & Leaves, Late 1800s, 4 x 4 In., Pair	439
Mold, Cake, Wood, Sow, Piglets, Tree, Garland Circle, 6 ½ In. ....*illus*	175
Mold, Candle, see Tinware category.	
Mold, Cheese, Heart Shape, Punched Tin, Loop Handle, 3 Tin Feet, 3 ¾ In.	59
Mold, Cheese, Heart Shape, Punched Tin, Top Handle, 3 ¾ In.	130
Mold, Chocolate, Lamb Shape, 2 Sections, Glazed Interior, Redware, Marked 7, Pa., 3 ¾ In.	106
Mold, Chocolate, Shmoo Shape, Plated Metal, 20 Wells, Loop Top, c.1948, 6 x 13 In.	115
Mold, Fish Shape, Shaded Glaze, Redware, Pa., 1800s, 10 In.	189
Mold, Fish, Figural, Open Mouth, Scales, Curved, Redware, Interior Glaze, 1800s, 12 ¼ In.	118
Mold, Glove Form, Metal, Tapered, McBride Glove Finisher Co., Toledo, 30 ½ In.	47
Mold, Ice Cream, see also Pewter category.	
Mold, Turk's Head, Handles, Redware, 1800s, 4 x 13 In. ....*illus*	495
Mold, Turk's Head, Glazed, Redware, 5 ½ x 9 In.	41
Mold, Turk's Head, Mottled Glaze, Redware, 1800s, 4 x 9 In.	42
Mold, Turk's Head, Mottled Glaze, Redware, John Bell, Waynesboro, Pa., 7 x 10 In.	212
Mold, Yellow Glaze Rim, Redware, 1800s, 3 ¼ x 9 ½ In.	123
Molds may also be found in the Pewter and Tinware categories.	
Mortar & Pestle, Ash, Turned Foot, 19th Century, 7 x 6 ⅝ In.	523
Mortar & Pestle, Brass, Fluted, Double Handle, 1700s, 7 ½ In.	111
Mortar & Pestle, Burl, Turned, 1800s, 6 ¼ x 5 ¼ In.	250
Mortar & Pestle, Tiger Maple, Stepped Base, 19th Century, 6 ¾ x 6 In.	984
Mortar & Pestle, Wood, Lignum Vitae, 1800s, 14 ¾ In., 2 Piece	111
Mortar & Pestle, Wood, Turned, Green Paint, 1800s, 8 In.	150
Pan, Round Pierced & Hinged Lid, Iron, Long Chamfered Edge Handle, c.1800, 12 x 45 In.	200
Pasta Cutter, Cast Iron, Paint, Table Mount, Crank, Baccellieri Bros., c.1910	95
Pie Board, Softwood, Round, Short Tapered Handle, Circle Crest, Eyelet, 1800s, 23 In.	189
Pitcher, Oak, Staves, 1800s, 15 In.	86
Pitcher, Underplate, Aluminum, Steel, Teal, Henry Dreyfuss, Thermos, 6 In., 2 Piece	210
Posset Pot, Cast Iron, 3-Footed, 1700s, 8 ½ x 7 ½ In.	98
Pot, 3-Footed, Long Handle, 1700s, 28 In.	292
Pot, Copper, Straight Sides, Dovetailed, Straight Handle, 4 ½ x 9 In.	18
Pot, Indigo, Cast Iron, Deep, Rounded, Flared Rim, 2 Rod Handles, 1800s, 21 x 40 In.	1098
Pot, Iron, 3-Footed, Swing Handle, 1700s, 14 x 14 In.	526
Press, Sandwich, Square Side Handles, Front Top Handle, Cord, Footed, 1930s	12
Rack, Herb Drying, Pine, Mustard Paint, 1800s, 43 x 42 In.	420
Rack, Plate, Oak, Hanging, c.1825, 44 ⅜ x 54 ¾ In.	450
Rack, Utensil, Wrought Iron, Wavy Bracket, Center Hook, Scroll Finial, 1700s, 3 x 12 In.	475
Reamers are listed in their own category.	
Rolling Pin, Wood, Turned Spool Top Handle, Shaped Side Supports, 1800s, 13 In.	118
Sadiron, Flatiron, Combination, Revolving, Wood Handle, Family Laundry Iron, 1894, 5 x 7 In.	71
Sadiron, Slug, Brass, Engraved Flowers & Leaves, Initials, 5 x 6 ½ In.	47

Kitchen, Butter Stamp, Eagle, Spread Wings, Maple, Turned, Single Piece, 4 ¼ In.

$118

Hess Auction Group

Kitchen, Butter Stamp, Letter M, Carved, Mahogany, Single Piece, 1800s, 3 x 5 In.

$106

Hess Auction Group

Kitchen, Butter Stamp, Stylized Eagle, Spread Wings, Carved, Pa., 1800s, 3 ¼ In.

$1,180

K

TIP

Never clean an iron cooking utensil with soap. Wipe it with paper towels, wash it in hot water with a plastic bristle brush, and dry it well.

Kitchen, Butter Stamp, Turned, Carved Flower, Pennsylvania, 1800s, 4½ In. $30

Hess Auction Group

Kitchen, Cheese Mold, Punched Tin, Swivel Wire, 2 x 7 In. $146

Norman Heckler & Company

Kitchen, Churn, Softwood, Round, Hand Crank, 17 In. $59

Hess Auction Group

Old Stoves

Enameled gas stoves for the kitchen made in the 1920s and 1930s are selling quickly at flea markets. Be sure they have been inspected by an expert gas stove company before you use them. They can be used with a gas line or a butane gas tank.

Sadiron, Slug, Round Open Back, Shaped Wood Hand Grip, 5¾ x 7 In.	12
Salt & Pepper Shakers are listed in their own category.	
Salt Box, Hanging, Oak, Crescent Top, Drawer, Canted Lift Lid, Wooden Pull, England, 18 In.	360
Scale, Cast Iron, Brass, Fan, Paint, Early 1900s, 25½ x 27 In.	180
Scoop, Ice Cream, Heart Shape, Trigger Pull, 11 In. *illus*	7200
Scoop, Ice Cream, Round, Flat, Thumb Press, Shaped Wooden Handle, 10 In.	277
Scouring Box, Arched Sides, 2 Compartments, Tray, Slide Lid, 1800s, 3 x 9 x 13 In.	354
Slough Board, Chestnut, Cutout Handle & Initials H.B., 17¼ In.	47
Slough Board, Walnut, Arched Top, Heart, Diamond Cutout, 1800s, 26¼ In.	95
Slough Board, Walnut, Cutout Heart Handle, 16½ In.	106
Slough Board, Wooden, Rectangular, Circle Crest, 1 Blade, Hanging Eyelet, 1800s, 24 In.	42
Smoothing Board, Machete Shape, Carved Wood, Continental, 1800s, 21 In. *illus*	83
Spatula, Rod Handle, Flat Top, Heart Shape Finial, Punchwork Initials, Iron, c.1800, 16 x 3 In.	750
Spatula, Thistle, Twisted Handle, Iron, Canada, 10¾ In.	80
Spatula, Wrought Iron, Pierced Blade, Shaped Beveled Handle, E.P. Sebastian, 20 In.	5900
Spice Box, Bird's-Eye Maple, Fitted Interior, Slide Lid, 7½ In.	295
Spice Jar, Lid, Wood, Turned, Painted Red, Green & Yellow Bands, Footed, c.1860, 9 In.	1722
Spice, Chest, Pine, 9 Drawers, Paneled Sides, 15½ x 21 In.	240
Spit Jack, Iron, Heart Motif, Clockwork, Walnut Base, 12½ In.	177
Spoon Rack, Pine, Carved Candle Box Base, Early 1900s, 28½ x 12 In.	480
Strainer, Tin, Heart Shape, 6½ x 5¼ In.	111
Tap, Champagne, Soda, 2 Parts, Treaded Shaft, Ribbed Wooden Handle, c.1900, 7 In.	160
Teakettle, Copper, Gooseneck Spout, Handle Marked H. Dehuff, 1800s, 11¾ In.	556
Teapot, Iron, Gooseneck, 1700s, 15 x 16 In.	81
Teapot, Iron, Heart Shape Leaf, Red, Japan, 5½ x 6 In.	250
Teapot, Iron, Molded Rockery On Lid, Molded Landscape On Sides, 11¼ In.	120
Teapot, Iron, Raised Dots, Fish, Swing Handle, Japan, 14½ In.	139
Toaster, Iron, Double Concentric Half Circles, 1800s, 17 In.	98
Toaster, Iron, Rectangular, 4-Footed, 1800s, 12½ x 18 In.	123
Toaster, Porcelain, Pop-Up, 2 Bread Slots, White, Gilt, Scrolls, Porcelier, 1930s	500
Toaster, Wrought Iron, Loops, Hearts Merging Into Fish, Handle, c.1800, 6 x 12 In.	250
Tongs, Sugar, Walnut, Carved, Cutout Heart & Circles, Sawtooth Edge, Germany, c.1889	82
Tray Set, Nested, Oak, Gallery Rim, 2 Handles, Largest 3 x 23½ In., 4 Piece	360
Tray, Cutlery, Pine, Heart, Diamond, Arthur Rogers, 2½ x 10½ In.	144
Tray, Flatware, Pine, Red, Yellow, Blue, Stencils, Cutout Center Handle, c.1850, 5 x 13 In.	420
Tray, Utensil, Pine, Black, Leaves, 1825, 5¼ x 12 In.	480
Trencher, Burl, Layers Of Paint On Exterior, 1800s, 6 x 17 x 20 In.	1000
Trencher, Wood, Elongated Oval, Raised & Flared Sides, Wide Rim, Flat Base, 5 x 26 In.	180
Trencher, Wood, Roughhewn, Green & Red Paint, 1800s, 4½ x 20 In.	180
Trencher, Wood, Roughhewn, Red Paint, Mid 1800s, 4½ x 13½ x 20½ In.	390
Trivet, see Trivet category.	
Vacuum Cleaner, Pneumatic, Steel, Tin, Wood, Cylindrical, Reeves Co., 1915, 49 x 8 In.	210
Waffle Iron, Brass, Fish Shape Body, Scales, Wrought Iron Handle, 1700s, 31 In.	1400
Waffle Iron, Cast Iron, Folk Art Flower, Oval, Handles, c.1910, 21 x 5 In.	220
Waffle Iron, Cast Iron, Round, 5 Hearts, Star Center, Tiny Hearts Within, Griswold, c.1905	450
Washboard, Carved Heart, 20½ x 7½ In.	180
Washing Machine, Woman's Friend, Wood Basin, Iron Base, Wringer, 1920s, 41 x 44 In.	210

KNIFE collectors usually specialize in a single type. In the 1960s, the United States government passed a law that required knife manufacturers to mark their knives with the country of origin. This seemed to encourage the collectors, and knife collecting became an interest of a large group of people. All types of knives are collected, from top quality twentieth-century examples to old bone- or pearl-handled knives in excellent condition.

Bayonet & Shoulder Belt, Cartridge Box, Leather, England, Early 1800s	2066
Bowie, Black Walnut Handle, Leather Scabbard, Schmid, Providence, R.I., 11 In. *illus*	10200
Bowie, Confederate D-Guard, Hand Forged Spear, Pointed Blade, c.1863, 17 In.	1320
Bowie, Enoch Drabble, Single Edge Point Blade, Etched Panels, 12½ In.	3105
Bowie, S.C. Wragg, Texas Ranger, 25 Furnace Hill, Sheffield, Eagles, Shields, Stars, 13 In.	8250
Bowie, Silver Handle, Chased Leaves, Stamped Blade, Leather Sheath, c.1850, 12 In.	510

K

Iron Pans Smooth

Vintage cast-iron pans were hand-cast in sand, while modern pieces are made by a different method that leaves a rough surface. The old ones bring the highest cost.

Kitchen, Cookie Cutter, Rooster, Tin, 19th Century, 10¾ x 8½ In.
$134

Norman Heckler & Company

Kitchen, Ladle, Gourd Bowl, Tin Rim, Turned Wood Handle, Heart Shape Lug, 14 In.
$48

Hess Auction Group

Kitchen, Lemon Press, Iron, Landers, Frary & Clark Co., 1880s, 7½ x 3¾ In.
$60

Ruby Lane

> **TIP**
> Old cast-iron cookware is smoother inside than pans cast recently. Griswold pans over 90 years old have a line on the bottom of the pan that was made during the casting. It is called a "gatemark."

Kitchen, Mangle Board, Chestnut, Carved, Horse Handle, Incised Pinwheel Design, 1827, 24 In.
$325

Hess Auction Group

Kitchen, Mold, Cake, Wood, Sow, Piglets, Tree, Garland Circle, 6½ In.
$175

Ruby Lane

Kitchen, Mold, Turk's Head, Handles, Redware, 1800s, 4 x 13 In.
$495

Ruby Lane

Kitchen, Scoop, Ice Cream, Heart Shape, Trigger Pull, 11 In.
$7,200

Morphy Auctions

Kitchen, Smoothing Board, Machete Shape, Carved Wood, Continental, 1800s, 21 In.
$83

Hess Auction Group

Knife, Bowie, Black Walnut Handle, Leather Scabbard, Schmid, Providence, R.I., 11 In.
$10,200

Cowan's Auctions

K

Kosta, Vase, Autumn, Internal Decoration, Vicke Lindstrand, 7 x 4 In. $750

Rago Arts and Auction Center

Kutani, Chocolate Pot, Geisha, Fans, Swirls, Flowers, Gilt, 9½ x 6¼ In. $113

Ruby Lane

Butcher, Buffalo Hunter's, Wood Scale Grip, Pin Point Pitting, c.1880s, 11 In.	85
Dagger, Bone Handle, Gold Damascene, Steel Tapered Blade, Velvet Scabbard, 12 In.	875
Dagger, Carved Ivory Handle & Sheath, Pointed Etched Blade, c.1850, 17 In.	3259
Dagger, Carved Jade Hilt, Pineapple, Lotus, Wootz Steel Curved Blade, Wood Scabbard, 9 In.	2500
Dagger, Chained, SS, Portepee, Capture Papers, Ebony Grip, Nazi Symbols, c.1936	4600
Dagger, Curved Blade, Brass Sheathed Base, Bone Scale Grip, Turkey, c.1750-1800, 6¾ In.	375
Dagger, Jade Hilt, Inset Cabochon Rubies, Steel Curved Blade, Wood Scabbard, 12 In.	2750
Dagger, Left Hand, Deep Grooved & Decoratively Pierced Blade, Italy, c.1600, 11 In.	3400
Dagger, Left Hand, Main Gauche, Spain, c.1660, 17⅞ In.	8500
Dagger, Ram's Head Handle, Gold Inset Seal On Blade, Sheath, Persia, 1900s	593
Fighting, Reinforced Forte Blade, Octagonal Brass & Copper Grip, Spain, c.1800, 9⅝ In.	2850
Katana, Ivory Scabbard, Carved, c.1880, 15½ In.	381
Kindjal, Silver & Niello, Russia, c.1900, 14 In.	2550
Ovambo, Slaver's, Wood Carved Grip, Wood Scabbard, Late 1800s, 5 In.	315
Pike, Excavated, Fort Ticonderoga, Tapered Ridge Point, c.1775-77, 23¾ In.	445
Pike, Leaf Shape Blade, Long Langets, Hardwood Pole, Europe, 1600s, 101¼ In.	517
Plug Bayonet, Jacobite Mottos, Silver Decoration, Bog Oak Grip, Scotland, c.1690, 9 In.	4500
Pocket, Franklin Mint, John Deere, Tractor On Handle, Late 1900s	63

KNOWLES, *Taylor & Knowles items may be found in the KTK and Lotus Ware categories.*

KOSTA

KOSTA, the oldest Swedish glass factory, was founded in 1742. During the 1920s through the 1950s, many pieces of original design were made at the factory. Kosta and Boda merged with Afors in 1964 and created the Afors Group in 1971. In 1976, the name Kosta Boda was adopted. The company merged with Orrefors in 1990 and is still working.

Decanter, Bird, Clear, Etched Neck, Bulbous, Head Stopper, c.1950, 8 In., Pair	123
Vase, 2 Leaping Men, Nude, Purple, Citron & Black, Rounded Bottom, Flared Rim, 6 In.	472
Vase, Autumn, Internal Decoration, Vicke Lindstrand, 7 x 4 In. ....*illus*	750
Vase, Black Swirls, 6 x 10½ In.	172
Vase, Cobalt Blue, Yellow & White Zipper, Round, Wide Rolled Rim, 5 x 8 In.	177
Vase, Multicolor, Cylindrical, Inscribed, 7½ x 6 In.	110

K.P.M **KPM** refers to Berlin porcelain, but the same initials were used alone and in combination with other symbols by several German porcelain makers. They include the Konigliche Porzellan Manufaktur of Berlin, initials used in mark, 1823–47; Meissen, 1723–24 only; Krister Porzellan Manufaktur in Waldenburg, after 1831; Kranichfelder Porzellan Manufaktur in Kranichfeld, after 1903; and the Krister Porzellan Manufaktur in Scheibe, after 1838.

Box, White, Square, Berlin, 4¼ In.	37
Bust, Bisque, Pensive Woman, Flower Wreath, Cricket On Shoulder, 10¼ x 4¼ In.	129
Candle Screen, Courting Couple, Rifle, Pup, Town, Lithophane, 13-In. Stand, 4 x 6 In.	495
Chocolate Pot, Flowers, Gilt Trim, Swirl Texture, Loop Handle, Lid, Marked, 1800s, 7 In.	1200
Coffeepot, White, Waves, 7½ In.	63
Figurine, Goddess Calliope, Holding Tablet & Pen, Gilt, Red & Blue Mark, 7¾ In.	409
Lithophane, see also Lithophane category.	
Plaque, Arab Man, Horseback, Holding Rifle, Giltwood Frame, 10 x 7½ In.	2745
Plaque, Children, Girl, Boy, Arm Over Shoulder, 13 x 8 In., Pair	10883
Plaque, Cupid & Venus, Garden, Winged Putti, Frame, 7¼ x 5 In.	4500
Plaque, Girl, Gazing Upward, 11 x 8 In.	562
Plaque, Mythological Scene, Goddesses, Celebration, Pastoral Landscape, 1855, 6 x 9 In.	861
Plaque, Woman, Red, Blue Robe, Flowers, Gilt Frame, 6 x 4¾ In.	219
Plate, Green Leaves, Red Insect, Handles, Gilt Rim, 10½ In.	25
Plate, Pink Flowers, Gilt Trim, Reticulated Border, 9½ In.	875
Plate, Soup, Flowers, Pink, 9¾ In., 12 Piece	750
Vase, Leaves, People, Gilt Bronze Mount, Flared Neck, Split Handles, 15 x 9 In.	1830
Vase, Marbleized, Griffin Handles, c.1875, 16½ In., Pair	11250
Vase, Moths, Glazed, 2 Handles, T. Schmuz-Baudiss, Germany, c.1900, 12½ x 5 In.	625
Vase, Oval Scene, Military Biplane, Garland Border & Band, White Ground, c.1915, 14 In.	885
Vase, White, Parcel Gilt, Fiddlehead Handles, c.1900, 28 In.	750

KTK are the initials of the Knowles, Taylor & Knowles Company of East Liverpool, Ohio, founded by Isaac W. Knowles in 1853. The company made many types of utilitarian wares, hotel china, and dinnerware. It made the fine bone china known as Lotus Ware from 1891 to 1896. The company merged with American Ceramic Corporation in 1928. It closed in 1934. Lotus Ware is listed in its own category in this book.

K.T.&K.
CHINA

Chamber Pot, Pink Roses, Leaves, Bulbous, Handle, Dome Lid, Loop Finial, 1920s, 5 x 9 In. ..	109
Creamer, Violets, Mottled Cream Ground, Shouldered, Wavy Spout, 1930s, 5 x 7 In.	66
Pitcher, Leaf & Wheat, Opaque White, Bulbous, Scrolled Rim, Handle, c.1905, 11 In.	150
Planter, Mottled, Pink & Gray, Incised Feathers, Swirling Stems, Cube, Fan Rim, 1920s, 5 In..	102
Platter, Flower Sprays, Cream Ground, Oval, Reeded Band, Gilt Rim, 1920s, 11 In.	80
Relish, White, Pink Roses, Elongated Oval, Serpentine, Swirled Rim, c.1905, 6 In.	72

KU KLUX KLAN items are now collected because of their historic importance. Literature, robes, and memorabilia are seen at shows and auctions. Laws passed in 1870 and 1871 caused the decline of the Klan. A second group calling itself the Ku Klux Klan emerged in 1915. There are still local groups using the name.

Statue, Klansman, Standing, Arms Folded, Base, Plaster, 1920s, 8 In.	633

KUTANI porcelain was made in Japan after the mid-seventeenth century. Most of the pieces found today are nineteenth century. Collectors often use the term *Kutani* to refer to just the later, colorful pieces decorated with red, gold, and black pictures of warriors, animals, and birds.

Bowl, Lid, Gilt, Rectangular Cartouches, Portraits, Marked, 4 x 7 In.	937
Bowl, Warrior, Snow Scene, 13 In.	187
Censer, Lid, Red, White Reserves, Peasants, Landscape, Footed, Foo Dog Finial, c.1875	476
Charger, Cranes, Patterned Banding, Emblems, Raised Foot, 1800s, 2 ½ x 18 In.	584
Charger, Festival, Snow, 14 In.	250
Charger, Figures, Animal, Flowers, Reserves, Orange, c.1880, 14 ¼ In.	96
Charger, Samurai, Winter, 14 In.	312
Chocolate Pot, Geisha, Fans, Swirls, Flowers, Gilt, 9 ½ x 6 ¼ In. ......*illus*	113
Cup, Lid, Shells, 3 In	120
Figurine, Frog, Brown, Cream, 9 In.	450
Figurine, Goddess Kwannon, Rockery Throne, Vase, Scepter, 11 In.	300
Incense Burner, Lion Lid, Dragons, Pierced, Upright Handles, Footed, Blue, White, 5 x 5 In...	165
Jar, Dome Lid, Relief Fan Shape Cartouches, Flowers, Green Flower Ground, 11 In.	180
Plate, Central Bird, Tree, Orange Rim, Gilt, Cartouche, 9 In.	60
Punch Bowl, Flower Panels On Red & Gilt Ground, Marked, Late 1800s, 5 x 14 ⅝ In.	732
Vase, People, Flowers, Cartouches, Gilt, Salmon, 9 ¾ In.	168

L.G. WRIGHT Glass Company of New Martinsville, West Virginia, started selling glassware in 1937. Founder "Si" Wright contracted with Ohio and West Virginia glass factories to reproduce popular pressed glass patterns like Rose & Snow, Baltimore Pear, and Three Face, and opalescent patterns like Daisy & Fern and Swirl. Collectors can tell the difference between the original glasswares and L.G. Wright reproductions because of colors and differences in production techniques. Some L.G. Wright items are marked with an underlined *W* in a circle. Items that were made from old Northwood molds have an altered Northwood mark—an angled line was added to the *N* to make it look like a *W*. Collectors refer to this mark as "the wobbly W." The L.G. Wright factory was closed and the existing molds sold in 1999.

Daisy & Button, Toothpick Holder, Blue	10
Daisy & Cube, Goblet, Green Forest, 5 ¾ In.	35
Eyewinker, Bowl, Fruit, Amber, 4 In.	10
Moon & Stars, Ashtray, Ruby, 8 ½ In.	22
Paneled Grape, Goblet, Ruby, 6 In.	35
Paneled Thistle, Candy Dish, Lid, Handles, 7 ½ In.	55
Priscilla, Compote, Flared, Amber, 7 ¾ x 6 ⅜ In.	25
Strawberry & Currant, Wine, Ruby, 4 ¾ In.	40

Lacquer, Box, Cosmetic, Flowers, E-Scroll, 4 Hooks, 2 Drawers, Japan, 1800s, 25 ½ x 10 ¾ In.
$687

Heritage Auctions8

Lalique, Figurine, Tete De Cheval, Horse's Head, Clear, Etched Mark, 15 ¾ In.
$3,900

Cowan's Auctions

Lalique, Lamp, Gros Fruits, Fruit, Frosted, Sepia, Footed Metal Base, Etched, 11 x 9 In.
$5,625

Rago Arts and Auction Center

Lalique, Vase, Archers, Frosted, Clear, Gray Patina, Etched R. Lalique France, 1921, 10 x 8 In.

$4,063

Rago Arts and Auction Center

Lalique, Vase, Monnaie Du Pape, Money Plant, Mauve, Molded R. Lalique, 1914, 9 In.

$8,750

Rago Arts and Auction Center

Lamp, Argand, Bronze, Gilt Bands, Frosted Shade, Henry Hooper, Boston, Electrified, c.1810, 15 In., Pair

$1,830

Neal Auctions

Three Faces, Sugar, Lid, 4 7/8 In.	35
Wild Rose, Goblet, Blue, 6 3/8 In.	18

LACQUER is a type of varnish. Collectors are most interested in the Chinese and Japanese lacquer wares made from the Japanese varnish tree. Lacquer wares are made from wood with many coats of lacquer. Sometimes the piece is carved or decorated with ivory or metal inlay.

Bottle, Sake, Black, Gold, Crane, Flowers, 8 1/4 In.	216
Bowl, Red, Brown, Gold, Butterfly, 4 1/2 In.	120
Box, Circles, Cube, 10 1/4 x 7 In.	125
Box, Cosmetic, Black, Gold Inlay, Silver Rim, Japan, 10 x 7 3/4 x 5 In.	2880
Box, Cosmetic, Flowers, E-Scroll, 4 Hooks, 2 Drawers, Japan, 1800s, 25 1/2 x 10 3/4 In. .... *illus*	687
Box, Cosmetic, Scrolling Flowers, 2 Doors, Drawers, Metal Lock, c.1920, 19 x 15 In.	12
Box, Cranes, 2 Friends, Zohiko, 11 3/4 In.	156
Box, Fan, Cranes, Pine Tree, 3 Drawers, Hinged Lid, 7 1/2 In.	180
Box, Gold, Peacock's Eye Design, 7 3/4 x 6 1/4 In.	96
Box, Lid, 4 Koi, Teal, Koho, c.1940, 13 x 13 In.	3125
Box, Lid, Bears, Morning, Pine Forest, Hinged, 5 1/2 In.	96
Box, Lid, Plum Branches, Mountains, Stippled Ground, Japan, c.1900, 5 x 8 x 5 In.	562
Box, Medallion, Dragons, Cranes, Phoenix, Fishnet, 2 1/4 x 10 1/2 In.	240
Box, Peony, 5 1/4 x 7 1/2 In.	960
Box, Red, Spiral Shape, Burma, 23 In.	218
Box, Writing, Gold Suzuribako, Writing Utensils, 8 3/4 x 7 3/4 x 3 In.	3900
Jewelry Box, Sprinkled, Red, Gold, Mother-Of-Pearl, Dragonflies, c.1800, 7 x 8 In.	7994
Plate, Red, Geisha Scenes, Mother-Of-Pearl, Bone, 21 x 16 In.	75
Tray, Black, Rabbit, Field, 10 x 10 In.	330

LADY HEAD VASE, *see Head Vase.*

R.LALIQUE **LALIQUE** glass and jewelry were made by Rene Lalique (1860-1945) in Paris, France, between the 1890s and his death in 1945. Beginning in 1921 he had a manufactuing plant in Alsace. The glass was molded, pressed, and engraved in Art Nouveau and Art Deco styles. Most pieces were marked with the signature *R. Lalique.* Lalique glass is still being made. Most pieces made after 1945 bear the mark *Lalique.* After 1980 the registry mark was added and the mark became *Lalique ® France.* In the prices listed here, this is indicated by Lalique (R) France. Some pieces that are advertised as ring dishes or pin dishes were listed as ashtrays in the Lalique factory catalog and are listed as ashtrays here. Names of pieces are given here in French and in English. Jewelry made by Rene Lalique is listed in the Jewelry category.

Ashtray, Archers, Amber, Round, 1922, 5 In. Diam.	500
Ashtray, Athletes, Clear, Blue Tint, Domed Cylinder, Dish Base, c.1910, 4 x 4 In.	1188
Ashtray, Serpentine Border, Beveled Edge, Engraved, 4 x 4 In.	120
Atomizer, Drapees Dansant, Nudes, Green Tint, Marked R. Lalique, 5 In.	403
Bowl, Opalescent, Molded Flower Bands, Rolled Rim, Marked, c.1920, 4 x 10 In.	369
Chandelier, Noisetier, Hazel, Frosted, Star Form, 7 Lights, 1924, 30 In.	11250
Figurine, 2 Doves, Frosted, Connected At Chest, Round Base, Signed, 9 x 7 In.	330
Figurine, Cat, Frosted, Engraved Signature, Late 1900s, France, 3 3/4 x 8 1/2 In., Pair	750
Figurine, Cochon, Pig, Frosted Pink, Clear Sticker, Signed, 6 In.	150
Figurine, Dancer, Woman, 9 1/2 In.	160
Figurine, Dove, Marked, 8 1/4 x 7 x 4 In.	156
Figurine, Elephant, Frosted, Signed, 6 In.	288
Figurine, Falcon, Frosted, Naturalistic Base, Inscribed, 1900s, 9 x 5 x 7 In.	431
Figurine, Leopard, Black, Prowling, Signed, 14 1/2 In.	920
Figurine, Leopard, Crouching, Arm Outstretched, Inscribed, 1900s, 4 x 14 1/2 x 3 In.	431
Figurine, Leopard, Prowling, Frosted, Signed, 14 1/2 In.	518
Figurine, Lion, Amber, Clear Lalique Sticker, Signed, 8 In.	748
Figurine, Lion, Frosted, Signed, 8 In.	546
Figurine, Polar Bear, Abstract, Frosted & Clear, 6 x 8 In.	196
Figurine, Rhinoceros, Black Hardstone, Mounted, Marked, 1900s, 4 7/8 x 12 x 4 In.	523

Figurine, Rooster, Clear, Hexagonal Base, 1953, 18 ½ x 14 In.	2250
Figurine, Tete De Cheval, Horse's Head, Clear, Etched Mark, 15 ¾ In. ....*illus*	3900
Lamp, Gros Fruits, Fruit, Frosted, Sepia, Footed Metal Base, Etched, 11 x 9 In. ....*illus*	5625
Perfume Bottle, Ambre De Siam, Nude, Amber Patina, Clear, Frosted, Pierced, 1920, 4 In.	10000
Perfume Bottle, Coty, Styx, Clear, Amber Dabber, c.1911, 4 ½ In.	1125
Perfume Bottle, Houbigant, La Belle Saison, Woman's Head, Leaves, Clear, Sepia, 1925, 4 In.	1187
Perfume Bottle, Lucien LeLong, Skyscraper, Inner Container, Contents, 4 ½ In.	546
Perfume Bottle, Nina Ricci, Coeur Joie, Cutout Heart, Butterfly Stopper, Box, 5 In.	30
Perfume Bottle, Piver, Scarabee, Beetle Shoulders, France, 1910, 3 ¼ x 2 ½ In.	2125
Perfume Bottle, Roger & Gallet, Narkiss, Starfish, France, 1912, 4 x 3 In.	1625
Perfume Bottle, Worth, Vers Le Jour, Chevrons, Amber, Flask Form, c.1926, 6 ¼ x 4 ½ In.	594
Perfume Tester, D'Orsay, La Renommee, Clear & Frosted, c.1922, 1 ¾ x 8 ¾ In.	938
Pitcher, Langeais, Vertical Ribs, Frosted, Cylindrical Neck, Scroll Handle, 9 In.	496
Plate Set, Annual, Clear & Frosted, 1966 Through 1970, 8 ¼ In., 5 Piece	94
Plate, Algues Noir, Tree Of Life, Black, Frosted, 1900s, 11 ¼ In., 8 Piece	812
Powder Box, Dancing Women, Clear & Frosted, Teal Patina, c.1929, 2 ¾ In.	176
Vase, Aigrettes, Egrets, Fern Leaves, Frosted, Bulbous, Engraved R. Lalique, 10 In.	6221
Vase, Ara, 3 Pairs Of Molded Parrots, Frosted Signed, 10 ⅝ In.	575
Vase, Archers, Frosted, Clear, Gray Patina, Etched R. Lalique France, 1921, 10 x 8 In. ....*illus*	4063
Vase, Bagatelle, Sparrows, Foliage, Frosted, 6 ½ In.	190
Vase, Bamako, Frosted, Clear Protrusions, Flared, Etched R. Lalique France, 1934, 7 In.	625
Vase, Dahlias, Molded, Frosted Black Enamel, Squat, Bulbous, 1932, 5 x 7 In.	1003
Vase, Domremy, Thistle, Opalescent, Rolled Rim, 1927, 8 In.	984
Vase, Epis, Leaves & Flared Ribs, Clear & Frosted, Green Patina, Marked, c.1931, 6 ½ In.	406
Vase, Gobelet, 6 Figurines, Smoky Topaz, Etched R. Lalique, 1912, 7 ½ x 5 ½ In.	2125
Vase, Graines, Rows Of Bubbles, Alexandrite, Flared Neck, 1930, 8 x 8 In.	3000
Vase, Graines, Seeds, Alexandrite, Flared, France, 7 ¾ x 7 ¾ In.	3000
Vase, Leaves, Molded, Dark Amber, Spherical, Pinched Neck, Flared Rim, 1926, 10 In.	8125
Vase, Malesherbes, Loquat Leaves, Jade Green, White Patina, Pear Shape, 1927, 9 x 7 In.	3625
Vase, Marisa, Vertical Fish, Opalescent, c.1927, 9 x 9 In.	4375
Vase, Martinet, Flying Birds, Frosted, Tapered, Handles, Marked, c.1980, 10 In.	277
Vase, Monnaie Du Pape, Money Plant, Mauve, Molded R. Lalique, 1914, 9 In. ....*illus*	8750
Vase, Ondines, Nude Water Nymphs, Frosted, Flared, Lalique France, c.1965, 9 In.	660
Vase, Opalescent, Molded, Spherical, Pinched Neck, Flat Flared Rim, 1927, 9 x 9 In.	4375
Vase, Poissons, Fish, Cased Opalescent, Round, Molded R. Lalique, 1921, 9 ¼ x 10 In.	3125
Vase, Royat, Notched, Ribs, Semicircular Protrusions On Rim, c.1936, 6 ¼ In.	400
Vase, Versailles, Grapevine Band, Clear & Frosted, Urn, Etched Lalique France, 13 ¾ In.	1230
Vase, Xian, Dragon, Fish Scales, Frosted, 7 ½ x 9 In.	403

LAMPS of every type, from the early oil-burning Betty and Phoebe lamps to the recent electric lamps with glass or beaded shades, interest collectors. Fuels used in lamps changed through the years; whale oil (1800–40), camphene (1828), Argand (1830), lard (1833–63), turpentine and alcohol (1840s), gas (1850–79), kerosene (1860), and electricity (1879) are the most common. Other lamps are listed by manufacturer or type of material.

Aladdin, Perfume, Woman, Urn, 6 In.	1187
Argand, Brass, Frosted Glass Shades, Etched Flowers, Grapes, 2-Light, c.1850, 15 In., Pair	369
Argand, Bronze & Gilt, Single Light, Etched Glass Shade, c.1835, 12 x 10 x 5 In.	183
Argand, Bronze, Gilt Bands, Frosted Shade, Henry Hooper, Boston, Electrified, c.1810, 15 In., Pair.. *illus*	1830
Arredoluce, Wall, Chrome, Glass, Enamel Shapes, 6-Light, 1960s, 21 x 8 In.	4063
Betty, Grease, Copper, Iron, Stamped, 1800s, 6 In.	295
Betty, Grease, Peter Derr, Brass, Iron, Copper, Hook, Wick Pick, Signed, P.D. 1850, 6 ⅜ In.... *illus*	1180
Betty, Grease, Tin, Stick Stems, Round Top, Saucer Base, Scroll Handle, 1800s, 13 In.	165
Bradley & Hubbard lamps are included in the Bradley & Hubbard category.	
Chandelier, 1-Light, Glass Dome, Greek Key, Continental, Early 1900s, 45 x 24 In.	240
Chandelier, 1-Light, Leaded Glass, Yellow, Cast Metal, 23 x 34 In.	500
Chandelier, 2-Light, Bronze, Basket Form, Strands Of Crystal Drops, 31 x 29 In.........*illus*	2500
Chandelier, 2-Light, Gilt Bronze, Putti, Flame Shape Frosted Shades, 26 In.	1500
Chandelier, 3-Light, Antler Horn, Mica, American Rustic, 33 x 51 In.	1500
Chandelier, 3-Light, Brass, Frosted Shades, Etched Flowers, 19th Century, 29 ½ In.	82

Lamp, Betty, Grease, Peter Derr, Brass, Iron, Copper, Hook, Wick Pick, Signed, P.D. 1850, 6 ⅜ In.
$1,180

Hess Auction Group

Lamp, Chandelier, 2-Light, Bronze, Basket Form, Strands Of Crystal Drops, 31 x 29 In.
$2,500

New Orleans Auction Galleries

Lamp, Chandelier, 4-Light, Iron, Crown, Twisted, Fleur-De-Lis, Electrified, 42 In.
$960

Cowan's Auctions

Lamp, Electric, Art Nouveau, Bronze, Trees, Prisms, Spurious Tiffany Mark, c.1900, 24 In.
$1,500

New Orleans Auction Galleries

Lamp, Electric, Bergman, Bronze, Harem Girl, Middle East Setting, Cold Painted, Austria, 1800s, 15 In.
$7,320

Neal Auctions

Lamp, Electric, Brass, Red Enameled Aluminum, Adjustable, Italy, c.1950, 14 x 15¼ In.
$2,250

Wright

Chandelier, 3-Light, Bronze Frame, Tiers, Crystal Pendants, Glass Finial, 1900s, 36 x 15 In.....	625
Chandelier, 3-Light, Mixed Metal, Frosted Teardrop Shade, 19th Century, 48½ In................	380
Chandelier, 3-Light, Tin, Crimped Drip Pans, c.1850, 14 x 12½ In., Pair.............................	5100
Chandelier, 4-Light, Bronze, Glass Shades, Art Deco, Marked, c.1925, 37 In......................	1800
Chandelier, 4-Light, Bronze, Molded Glass, Louis XIV, 1900s, 19 x 18 In., Pair	1125
Chandelier, 4-Light, Copper, Hammered, Amber Glass, Arts & Crafts, 42 x 24 In.	2196
Chandelier, 4-Light, Gilt Bronze, Basket, Swirling Leaves, Flower Shades, c.1910, 28 x 18 In. ..	875
Chandelier, 4-Light, Gilt Bronze, Frosted Glass, Rococo, Bell Epoque, France, 23 x 19½ In.....	687
Chandelier, 4-Light, Iron, Crown, Twisted, Fleur-De-Lis, Electrified, 42 In. ....*illus*	960
Chandelier, 5-Light, Amber Glass, Downswept Arms, Serpentine Stem, 27½ x 14½ In.........	297
Chandelier, 5-Light, Bronze, Sunbursts, Pink Acid Etched, Shades, Art Deco, 34 x 32 In.........	708
Chandelier, 5-Light, Tole, Birds, Flowering Branches, Multicolor, 34 x 32 In......................	313
Chandelier, 5-Light, Wedgwood, Porcelain Blue Jasper Dip, Ceiling Plate, c.1890, 19 x 10 In...	431
Chandelier, 6-Light, Bow Top Ribbon, Reeded, Leaves, Porcelain Flowers, 33½ x 23 In...........	1220
Chandelier, 6-Light, Brass, Conical Arms, Linen Shades, Glass Beading, 1950s, 44 In.............	3750
Chandelier, 6-Light, Brass, Gas, Dragon Motif, 19th Century, 34¾ In................................	556
Chandelier, 6-Light, Bronze, Cut Glass, Ring, Flower Pendants Shapes, France, 38 x 21 In......	500
Chandelier, 6-Light, Center Stem, Hunt Scene Etched Globes, Prisms, 40 x 39 In................	2900
Chandelier, 6-Light, Chrome, Acrylic, Amber, 15 In.	63
Chandelier, 6-Light, Cranberry Glass, Hobnail, Scroll Arms, Brass, c.1900, 41 x 29 In.	625
Chandelier, 6-Light, Enamel, Bronze, Porcelain, Flower Basket, 34 x 21½ In.......................	1125
Chandelier, 6-Light, Gilt Bronze, Scroll Arms, Putti, Pierced Canopy, c.1965, 36 x 20 In.	1625
Chandelier, 6-Light, Gilt Bronze, Tole, Ribbon Form Supports, Eagle Mounts, 37 x 27 In.	563
Chandelier, 6-Light, Gilt Metal, Flower Stems, Folding Leaves, Faux Candles, 34 x 38 In..........	95
Chandelier, 6-Light, Gilt Metal, Glass Beads, Pendants, Flowers, France, 1900s, 33 x 29 In......	1375
Chandelier, 6-Light, Gilt Metal, Leaves, Hanging Crystals, Faux Candles, 21 x 17 In.	271
Chandelier, 6-Light, Glass, Blue, Putti, Garland, Prisms, 27½ x 17 In.	354
Chandelier, 6-Light, Iron, Twisted, Scrolled, Wax Cup, 13½ x 25½ In.	354
Chandelier, 6-Light, Medallion, Open, Scrolled, Fleur-De-Lis, 3 Rod Standard, 33 x 25 In.......	295
Chandelier, 6-Light, Metal Frame, Rock Crystal Drops, Glass Spray, 1900s, 39 x 37 In............	4500
Chandelier, 6-Light, Palmettes, Swags, Bells, Prisms, Scroll Arms, 40 x 26 In......................	1000
Chandelier, 6-Light, Pinecone Finial, French Empire, 1900s, 24½ x 18½ In........................	406
Chandelier, 6-Light, Porcelain, Bronze, Sevres Style, France, Late 1800s, 58 x 19 In.	1375
Chandelier, 6-Light, Scroll Arms, Candle Cups, Drip Pans, 19½ x 28½ In.........................	1800
Chandelier, 6-Light, Silvered Metal, Prisms, Louis XV Style	2759
Chandelier, 6-Light, Tole, Tapered Hexagon, Gilt Leaves, Reeded Ball, c.1865, 48 x 29 In........	1185
Chandelier, 7-Light, Gilt Bronze, Tole, Artichoke Finial, 25½ x 26½ In.	1125
Chandelier, 7-Light, Gilt Metal, Leaded Slag Glass, Arts & Crafts, Early 1900s, 25 x 21 In.	1750
Chandelier, 8-Light, Bronze Shades, Zebra, Leaves, 52 x 48 In.	3094
Chandelier, 8-Light, Bronze, Leaf Arms, Teardrop Prisms, Neoclassical Style, 29 x 25 In.........	593
Chandelier, 8-Light, Bronze, Pierced Frame, Hanging Spears, Leaves, c.1865, 18 x 25 In.	1500
Chandelier, 8-Light, Emerald & Clear Glass, Hanging Prisms, Teardrops, 1900s, 29 In............	270
Chandelier, 8-Light, Empire, Oil Lamp Shape, Flame Center, Crown Ceiling Plate, 37½ x 26 In...	1100
Chandelier, 8-Light, Gilt Metal, Cut Glass, Scroll Arms, Flowers, 1900s, 34 x 35½ In.	875
Chandelier, 8-Light, Glass Fringe, Tiers, Blue, Ormolu, Russia, c.1900, 46½ x 29 In.	5000
Chandelier, 8-Light, Ormolu, Cut & Pressed Glass, Louis XVI Style, 1900s, 40 x 23½ In..........	1250
Chandelier, 8-Light, Ormolu, Porcelain, Pink, Blue, Sevres, 38 x 27 In..............................	472
Chandelier, 8-Light, Quiver, Arrows, Ball, Urn, Acorn Drop Finial, Louis XVI Style, 34 x 36 In.	354
Chandelier, 8-Light, Scroll Arms, Hanging Prisms, Pendants, c.1970, 42 x 28 In.	711
Chandelier, 8-Light, Tole, Crystal, Balloon Frame, France, 1900s, 34 x 21 In.	625
Chandelier, 8-Light, Tole, Flowers, Pink, Green, 26 x 30 In...	250
Chandelier, 8-Light, Venetian Glass, Rope Twist Arms, Floral Pendants, 37 x 33 In.	1500
Chandelier, 8-Light, Iron, Glass Shades, c.1950, 35 x 32 In...	150
Chandelier, 9-Light, Fawn, Satyr & Putto, Gas & Electric, c.1900, 66 x 38½ In.	9687
Chandelier, 10-Light, Brass, Scroll & Pierced Arms, Baldwin, 1900s, 27½ x 39 In.................	875
Chandelier, 10-Light, Brass, Sputnik, Italy, 20 x 17 In.	457
Chandelier, 10-Light, Bronze, Patinated, Scroll Arms, Sprays Of Prisms, France, 30 In.	1500
Chandelier, 10-Light, Gilt Metal, Murano, Glass, Scroll Arms, Bell Shades, 48 x 27 In., Pair...	2500
Chandelier, 10-Light, Glass, Silver Metal, Italian Argent, 1900s, 37 x 35 In..........................	2074
Chandelier, 12-Light, Brass, 2 Tiers, Scroll Arms, Center Ball, 1800s, 25 x 24 In.	948

Chandelier, 12-Light, Bronze, Glass, Louis XVI, 1900s, 33 x 35 In.	500
Chandelier, 12-Light, Chromed Metal, Molded Glass Discs, Spherical, Italy, 45 x 24 In............	594
Chandelier, 12-Light, Chromed Steel, Brushed Aluminum, Boxy Shades, 13 x 18 In.................	593
Chandelier, 12-Light, Gilt Bronze, Rock Crystal, Louis XV, France, Late 1800s, 37 x 21 In........	3500
Chandelier, 12-Light, Gilt Metal, Cut Glass Pendants, Napoleon III, 29 x 27 In.....................	406
Chandelier, 12-Light, Gio Ponti, Nickel Plated, Italy, Mid 1800s, 36 x 42 In.	1250
Chandelier, 12-Light, Glass, Tiered, Twist Arms, Pendant Drops, Swags, 1900s, 26 x 24 In.	875
Chandelier, 12-Light, Lions, Brackets, Renaissance Revival, 31 x 31 In.	708
Chandelier, 15-Light, 2 Tiers, Scrolls, Glass Bead Festoons, Maria Theresa Style, 37 x 33 In...	2125
Chandelier, 15-Light, Brass, Ball Finial, 2 Tiers, Scroll Arms, Holland, 1900s, 23 x 32 In.	343
Chandelier, 16-Light, Bronze, Cut Glass, Louis XIV Style, France, Early 1900s, 37 x 33 In.	4500
Chandelier, 16-Light, Bronze, Pear Shape, Flowers, Urn, Spiral Twist, Louis XV, 41 x 42 In.....	10000
Chandelier, 16-Light, Chrome, Glass, Bubble Shade, 29 x 22 In.	125
Chandelier, 16-Light, Chromed Steel, Brushed Aluminum, Boxy Shades, 26½ x 26½ In.........	875
Chandelier, 17-Light, E. Stejnar, Brass, Glass, Acrylic, 1960s, 24 x 15 In.	2000
Chandelier, 22-Light, Cut Pressed Glass, Ormolu, Louis XIV Style, 1900, 51½ In......................	3750
Chandelier, 28-Light, Bronze, Glass, Fin De Siecle, France, Late 1800s, 47 x 44 In...................	10000
Chandelier, Copper, France, 6 Shades, Frosted Glass, Art Deco, c.1930, 30 In...........................	500
Chandelier, Gilt Brass, Frosted Etched Glass, Art Nouveau, Spain, 1906, 70 x 36 In..................	6250
Chandelier, Gilt Metal, Basket, Frosted Glass Leafy Shades, 23 x 20 In.	219
Chandelier, Murano Glass, Twisted Central Shaft, Beaded Scroll Arms, c.1950, 38 In...............	950
Chandelier, S. Seandel, Copper, Enameled Steel, Domed Pierced Texture, 1970s, 36 x 15 In. ...	4375
Chandelier, Waterfall, Capiz Shell, 72 In..	90
Electric, 2-Light, Student, Tin, Yellow Paint, Conical Base, Umbrella Shade, 24 In.	944
Electric, 3-Light, Chromed, Enamel, Adjustable, Italy, 69 x 12 In.	300
Electric, 3-Light, Magistretti, Mezza Chimera, Acrylic, Enameled Metal, 1970s, 31 x 9 In., Pair.	813
Electric, 12-Light, Bronze, Gold Iridescent Lily Shades, Lily Pad Base, c.1910, 20 In.................	4920
Electric, Adrian Pearsall, Wood, 3-Footed, Midcentury, 38 x 15 In., Pair	436
Electric, Alabaster, Alabaster Shade, Crystal Finial, 4-Footed, 59¼ In.................................	206
Electric, Alabaster, Pillar, Figural Mime, Domed Shade, Square Base, Art Deco, 17 In.............	185
Electric, Aluminum, Bakelite, Tiered Cylindrical Post, Tiered Disc Shade, 1930s, 20 In..........	4063
Electric, Art Deco, Dancing Girl Kicking Ball, Millefiori Shade, 8½ x 7¾ In.............................	708
Electric, Art Deco, Gold Kneeling Woman, Holding Up Frosted Lamp Ball, 16¾ In....................	188
Electric, Art Deco, Pairs Of Parakeets, Pierced Metal Base, 12 In.....................................	108
Electric, Art Deco, Pink Glass, Ribbed, Square Stepped Base, 11½ In., Pair.............................	188
Electric, Art Glass Shade, Green Oil Spot, Gold, Bronze Arm, Marble Base, 31 In......................	1778
Electric, Art Nouveau, 6 Caramel Slag Panels, 6 Blue Slag Panels, Lake Shore, 24 x 9 In.........	354
Electric, Art Nouveau, Bronze, Original Patina, Glass Cabochons, c.1900, 24½ x 16 In.............	4375
Electric, Art Nouveau, Bronze, Trees, Prisms, Spurious Tiffany Mark, c.1900, 24 In..........*illus*	1500
Electric, Baroque Revival, Giltwood, Putti, Acanthus Leaves, Scrolls, 78½ In.............................	535
Electric, Baroque Revival, Parcel Gilt, Barley Twist, Paneled Square Base, 76½ x 14 In...........	833
Electric, Benedict Studio, Copper, Hammered, Triangular Shade, Mica Panels, 1910, 14 In.	1500
Electric, Bergman, Bronze, Harem Girl, Middle East Setting, Cold Painted, Austria, 1800s, 15 In...*illus*	7320
Electric, Bigelow & Kennard, Leaded Glass, Autumn Leaf Band, Green, Amber, Ribbed Base, 18 In.	5036
Electric, Blackamoor, Red Pants, 33 x 8½ In.	236
Electric, Brass, Champleve Enamel, Tao Tich Masks, Brocade Ground, Japan, 1900s, 62 In.....	437
Electric, Brass, Embossed, Arabic Text, Camel, Pierced Shade, Bead, Moon & Star Finial, 21 x 9 In.	206
Electric, Brass, Marble, Rubber, Arredoluce, c.1950, 7 x 9 x 23 In.	5000
Electric, Brass, Red Enameled Aluminum, Adjustable, Italy, c.1950, 14 x 15¼ In.............*illus*	2250
Electric, Brass, Tole, Black, Pierced Rotating Shade, Chapman, c.1980, 45 In.......................	660
Electric, Bronze, Arab Carpet Merchant, Bergman, Marked Geschulzt, Austria, 21 In.......*illus*	1815
Electric, Bronze, Arabic Nomad, Camel, Palm Trees, Cold Painted, Vienna, c.1915, 13 In..*illus*	2000
Electric, Bronze, Atlas, Figural, Durand Lava Art Glass Bowl Shade, 20½ x 7 In.	3068
Electric, Bronze, Blacksmith, Furnace, Anvil, Hammer, c.1880, 18¾ In...................................	344
Electric, Bronze, Figural, Dancer, Millefiori Shade, c.1930, 8½ x 8½ x 5 In.	1125
Electric, Bronze, Gilt, 3 Graces, Paw Feet, White Shade, France, 1800s, 29 x 15 In.....................	1062
Electric, Bronze, Lighthouse Form, Rocky Base, c.1925, 15½ In..	360
Electric, Bronze, Male & Female Classical Forms, 1800s, 15 x 14 x 6½ In., Pair.......................	5490
Electric, Bronze, Nymph, Draped, Figural, Rose Shape Bulb, France, c.1900, 23 x 8 In.	1250
Electric, Bronze, Parrot, Birdcage In Beak, Candlestick Base, Stone Sphere, 1920s, 15 In.........	711

Lamp, Electric, Bronze, Arab Carpet Merchant, Bergman, Marked Geschulzt, Austria, 21 In.
$1,815

James D. Julia Auctioneers

Lamp, Electric, Bronze, Arabic Nomad, Camel, Palm Trees, Cold Painted, Vienna, c.1915, 13 In.
$2,000

New Orleans Auction Galleries

Lamp, Electric, Kurt Versen, Enameled Steel, Adjustable, c.1955, 17 x 19 In.
$1,375

Wright

How Bright the Light?

The light from one regular 60-watt lightbulb is equal to the light from twenty-five double-wick whale-oil lamps used in the nineteenth century.

Lamp, Electric, Newel Post, Bronze, Draped Woman, 3-Light, Art Nouveau, France, c.1890, 36 In.
$420

Cowan's Auctions

Lamp, Electric, Poul Henningsen, Copper, Brass, PH 3/2, 1927, 17 x 11 In.
$6,875

Wright

Lamp, Electric, Riviere, Leaded Glass, Grapes, Leaves, Bronze Organic Base, 21 In.
$3,555

James D. Julia Auctioneers

TIP
Reverse-painted lampshades should never be washed. Just dust them.

Lamp, Electric, Robj, Bellhop, Figural, Ceramic, Umbrella Shade, France, 1920s, 13 x 8 In.
$2,875

Rago Arts and Auction Center

Lamp, Electric, Rock Crystal, Art Moderne Style, Graduated Spheres, Plinth Base, 19 In., Pair
$1,464

Neal Auctions

Lamp, Electric, T. Wirkkala, Brass, Enameled Aluminum, Leather, 1958, 16 ½ x 15 In.
$4,688

Wright

Lamp, Electric, Wilkinson, Water Lily & Cattail, Leaded Glass, Bronze Base, c.1910, 30 In.
$5,463

Cottone Auctions

Electric, Bronze, Umbrella Shade, Mosaic Slag Glass, Pink, Green, c.1910, 21 In.		2091
Electric, Carl Thieme, 2-Light, Porcelain, Yellow, Putti, Germany, 1900s, 22 x 7 In.		531
Electric, Chrome Plated Brass, Enameled Aluminum, Blackened Silver, Italy, 1964, 24 In.		1524
Electric, Chrome Plated Steel, Red Enameled Aluminum, Robert Sonneman, c.1965, 20 In.		406
Electric, Chrome, Cased Glass, Square Banded Column, Vinyl Shades, 1950-90, 81 x 21 In., Pair		2500
Electric, Cobra, Birch Veneer, Frosted Glass Sphere, Brass, 1977, 58 x 9 ½ In.		625
Electric, Copper, Hammered, Tapered Shade, Mica Panels, S-Handles, Arts & Crafts, 24 In.		2500
Electric, Cupid Holding Torch, Pink, Blue Drapery, Tin, 14 x 14 In., Pair		238
Electric, Duffner & Kimberly, Leaded Glass, Pink Water Lilies, Tapered, Bronze Base, 24 In.		7110
Electric, Elephant, Trunk Holds Up Socket, 24 In., Pair		438
Electric, Feu Follet, Woman, Holding Stained Glass Lanterns, Plaster, c.1910, 43 In.		370
Electric, G. Stickley, Copper, Hammered, Tapered, Wicker & Silk Shade, 1910s, 24 x 18 In.		3125
Electric, Gilt Metal, Wood, Sheaf Of Wheat, Italy, 1900s, 27 ¼ x 10 ¼ In., Pair		562
Electric, Gilt, Bronze, Lily Pad Base, Frog, Stem, Leaves, Bird, Art Nouveau, 18 In., Pair		1845
Electric, Glass, Controlled Bubbles, Gold Leaf Inclusions, 21 In., Pair		1125
Electric, Glass, Diamond & Fan, Baluster, Gilt Nozzle, Hurricane Shade, c.1885, 17 In., Pair		812
Electric, Green Marble, Urn Form, Bronze Mount, Putti, Silk Shade, France, 34 In.		468
Electric, Hand Shape, Wood, Carved, Dark Gray, 12 In., Pair		125
Electric, Hands Holding Shade, Cast Plaster, White, 16 x 9 ½ In.		375
Electric, Hanging, Birdcage, Ceramic, White, Red Flowers, 18 x 10 ½ In.		238
Electric, Hanging, Duffner & Kimberly, Bell Shape, Green, Blue, Red, Twist, 11 x 19 ¾ In.		6490
Electric, Heifetz, Baseball Pitcher, Wood, Trapezoid Shade, Art Deco, 1930s, 24 In.		360
Electric, Iridescent Glass, Tulip Shape, c.1910, 18 ⅞ In.		187
Electric, Iron, Lemon Tree, Black, Gilt, 24 x 10 In.		425
Electric, James Harvey Crate, Aluminum, Cork, Heifetz Manufacturing Co., 1950, 24 x 13 In.		7500
Electric, Jefferson, Reverse Painted, Flowers, Red, Green, c.1915, 21 x 18 In.		2750
Electric, Jielde, Enameled Steel & Aluminum, Adjustable, France, 1950s, 63 x 18 In.		1250
Electric, Kurt Versen, Enameled Steel, Adjustable, c.1955, 17 x 19 In.	*illus*	1375
Electric, L. Poulsen, Artichoke, Copper, Enameled Aluminum, Stainless Steel, 24 x 24 x 25 In.		8125
Electric, Lapis Lazuli, Gold Veined, Gilt Bronze, Urn Form, Louis XV Style, c.1920, 30 x 8 In., Pair.		3000
Electric, Leaded Glass Shade, Poinsettia, Bronze Base, 78 In.		1750
Electric, Leaded Glass, Green, Mushroom Shade, 1900s, 26 x 10 ½ In.		593
Electric, Leaded Glass, Pink & Green Teardrops, Brass, Classique Lamp Co., 18 x 23 In.		500
Electric, Leaded Glass, Pink Flowers, Bark, 18 x 23 In.		500
Electric, Lucite, Brown, Infused Palm Leaves, 16 ½ x 11 ½ In., Pair		535
Electric, Lucite, Cut Corner Rectangles, 34 In., Pair		500
Electric, Lucite, Stacked Discs, Alternating Frosted & Clear, 1900s, 30 x 10 ¼ In., Pair		812
Electric, Lunel, Brass, Enamel, Cylindrical Paper Shades, 3-Light, 1950s, 72 In., Pair		5625
Electric, Mangiarotti, Chrome, Acrylic, Mushroom Shade, Cased White Glass, 1970s, 12 In.		813
Electric, Moe Bridges, Metal, Butterflies, Flowers, Painted Glass Shade, c.1910, 13 In.		575
Electric, Murano Glass, Blue, Neoclassical Design, 1900s, 37 x 15 x 15 In.		562
Electric, Neoclassical, Beige Marble, Gilt Bronze Mount, Swags, 21 ½ x 5 In., Pair		952
Electric, Newel Post, Bronze, Draped Woman, 3-Light, Art Nouveau, France, c.1890, 36 In.	*illus*	420
Electric, Nicola L., Eye, Orange, Green, Steel, Plastic, 79 x 19 In.		6875
Electric, Nicola R., Red Lips, Steel, Plastic, Signed, Nicola 1969, 52 ½ x 28 In.		4880
Electric, O. Torlasco, Aluminum, Enameled Brass, Cinched Stem, Lumi, 1950s, 15 In., Pair		1250
Electric, Onyx, Brass, Embossed Shaft, Green Onyx Urn, 4 Sockets, 57 ¾ In.		413
Electric, P. Evans, Copper, Pewter, Linen Shade, Conical Base, c.1960, 66 In.		8750
Electric, P. Powell, Walnut Turned, Conical Standard, Linen Shade, 2-Light, 1960s, 43 In.		6875
Electric, Palm Tree, Chrome, Glass, 30 In.		100
Electric, Peter Shire, Olympic Torch, Multicolor, Wavy Support, 1984, 102 In.		1750
Electric, Pittsburgh, Reverse Painted, Lake House, Stormy Sky, Ribbed Metal Base, 21 In.		474
Electric, Poul Henningsen, Copper, Brass, PH 3/2, 1927, 17 x 11 In.	*illus*	6875
Electric, Praying Mantis, Red & Green Leaded Glass, Cast Metal, 18 x 6 ½ In.		1586
Electric, R. Larche, Gilt Bronze, Dancer, Flowing Draper, Art Nouveau, 16 ½ In.		1812
Electric, Reverse Painted, Tudor House, Country, Winter, 1900-20, 9 ⅜ In.		112
Electric, Riviere, Leaded Glass, Grapes, Leaves, Bronze Organic Base, 21 In.	*illus*	3555
Electric, Robj, Bellhop, Figural, Ceramic, Umbrella Shade, France, 1920s, 13 x 8 In.	*illus*	2875
Electric, Rock Crystal, Art Moderne Style, Graduated Spheres, Plinth Base, 19 In., Pair	*illus*	1464
Electric, Roy Hamilton, Ceramic, Linen Design, Double Gourd, c.1950, 30 x 10 In., Pair		1875

Lamp, Hanging, Modernist, Steel, Orb, Rods, Glass Flowers, c.1950, 22 x 15 In. $369

Skinner, Inc.

Lamp, Kettle, Brass, Copper, Iron, Peter Derr, Stamped P.D. 1850, 10 ¼ In. $3,540

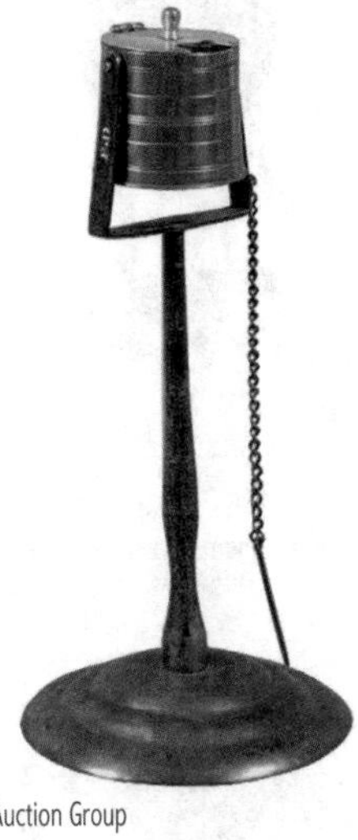

Hess Auction Group

Lamp, Sinumbra, Bronze, Flora-Cut Shade, H.N. Hooper, c.1850, Electrified, 24 In. $3,000

Neal Auctions

LAMP

Lamp, Solar, Bronze, Acanthus, Bacchantes, Eagles, Fluted Glass, c.1810, 34 In.
$4,880

Lamp, Solar, Gilt Bronze, Glass, Blue, Cut To Clear, Prisms, Marble Base, 1800s, 24 In.
$4,270

Electric, Rudi Stern, Halogen, Black Steel, Neon, Stripe, Torchere, 1970s, 72 x 14 In.	500
Electric, Satsuma, Rising Sun, Gilt, Squared Tapered Body, Japan, 14 ½ In.	238
Electric, Scandinavian, Leather, Copper, Linen, c.1950, 62 x 18 x 18 In., Pair	6250
Electric, Sconce, Kurt Versen, Metal, c.1948, 5 ½ x 14 x 28 In., Pair	1375
Electric, Slag Glass Shade, Caramel, 8 Panels, Bronzed Vase, 17 ½ In.	228
Electric, Slag Glass Shade, Domed, Copper Overlay Tulip, Daisy, 22 In.	144
Electric, Spelter, Cavalier, Armor, 52 In.	2142
Electric, Still Life, Fruit, White Glaze, Silk Shade, 34 In., Pair	150
Electric, Student, Jerry Martin, Tin, 2-Light, Green Flared Shade, Conical Base, 24 In.	590
Electric, T. Wirkkala, Brass, Enameled Aluminum, Leather, 1958, 16 ½ x 15 In. ....*illus*	4688
Electric, Tommi Parzinger, Pyramid, Walnut, Brass, Stiffel, 1960s, 20 ½ In., Pair	687
Electric, Topless Woman, Tree, Figural, Octagonal Base, 22 In.	344
Electric, Tubular Stem, Tiered Aluminum Discs Shade, Stepped Base, c.1940, 22 x 16 In.	4500
Electric, Turtle Shell, Brass Support, Lucite Base, c.1975, 16 ½ In.	150
Electric, Warrior, Figural, Green Columns, Parcel Gilt, Flame Finial, 40 In., Pair	750
Electric, Wilkinson, Water Lily & Cattail, Leaded Glass, Bronze Base, c.1910, 30 In. ....*illus*	5463
Electric, Wood Shade, Bottle Shape, Lava Glaze, Plinth, Scheurich, 29 In.	277
Electric, Wood, Dragon Post, Carved Claw Feet, Silk Lantern Shade, 1920s, 72 x 16 In.	2995
Fairy, Cranberry Opalescent Glass, Swirled Feather, Fenton, 1950s	381
Fairy, Green Opalescent Glass, Swirled Feather, Fenton, c.1953	510
Fat, Brass, Iron, Adjustable, Drip Pan, c.1825, 20 In.	277
Fat, Iron, Oval, Twisted Handle	420
Fat, Tin, Stand, 1800s, 12 In.	246
Fluid, Art Glass, Aventurine, Pink & White Spatter, 11 In.	70
Fluid, Glass Cranberry Cut To Clear, Swirl, Gilt Collar, Threaded Cap, 6 In.	86
Fluid, Glass, Cobalt Blue Font, Shield & Stars, Clear Chimney, c.1880, 6 ⅜ In.	489
Fluid, Milk Glass, Blue, Flowers, Etched, Brass Fitting, 12 In.	106
Fluid, Opaline Glass, Blue, Ribbon, White Font, 10 ¾ In.	94
Fluid, Pewter, 2 Wick Burners, Round Foot, Pedestal, Banding, Scroll Handle, 1800s, 7 In.	118
Fluid, Silver, Frosted Glass Globe, Glass Chimney, Sheffield, c.1900, 22 ¾ In.	84
Gas, Billiard Table, Brass, 2-Light, Electrified, 13 x 52 In.	240
Gasolier, 5-Light, Frosted Glass, Cut Strawberry Finial, France, Late 1800s, 40 x 32 In.	1500
Gasolier, 12-Light, Bronze, Cut Glass Hanging Prisms, Globe Shades, c.1850, 57 x 38 In.	7812
Gasolier, Chandelier, Gilt Bronze, Ring & Urn Form, Scroll Arms, 1800s, 53 x 29 In.	1000
Gasolier, Glass, Standing Figure, Arm Holding Up Globe Shade, 11 ⅝ In.	200
Gasolier, Metal, Figural, Goddess Diana, Holding Up Slag Glass Shade, Plinth, c.1865, 66 In.	4000
Gasolier, Winged Putti, Holding Torch, Renaissance Revival, 16 ¾ x 6 In., Pair	1071
Grease, Tin, Stick Stem, Cylindrical Top, Wick Pick, Saucer Base, 1800s, 7 In.	118
Handel lamps are included in the Handel category.	
Hanging, Brass, Urn, Glass, Shade & Smoke Bell, Cut Dove & Garland, 1800s, 27 In.	1708
Hanging, Cut Glass, Clear, Frosted, Flowers, 14 ½ In.	410
Hanging, Dome, Glass Panels, Brass Frame, Leafy Vines, Chain, c.1900, 35 x 32 In.	3555
Hanging, Emil Stejnar, Sputnik, 22 x 16 In.	1521
Hanging, Faux Marble, Resin, Inverted Dome, 40 x 30 In.	267
Hanging, Faux Tortoiseshell, Resin, Bronze, Inverted Dome, 38 x 30 In.	476
Hanging, Gilt Metal, Beaded Glass, Louis XVI Type, 24 In.	344
Hanging, Modernist, Steel, Orb, Rods, Glass Flowers, c.1950, 22 x 15 In. ....*illus*	369
Hanging, Panton, Mother-Of-Pearl Discs, Clusters, Chain, 1960s, 79 x 40 In.	6250
Hanging, Sputnik, 23 x 16 In.	1287
Hurricane, Glass, Cranberry Flashed, Painted White Flowers, Cut Prisms, 21 x 6 In., Pair	365
Kerosene, Aladdin, Short Lincoln Drape, Amber Glass Base, Clear Shade, 12 In.	30
Kerosene, Glass, Sulphide, 2 Male Portraits, Wide Circular Foot, Electrified, 1800s, 32 In.	450
Kettle, Brass, Copper, Iron, Peter Derr, Stamped P.D. 1850, 10 ¼ In. ....*illus*	3540
Oil, Black, Round Foot, 1800s, 11 In., Pair	35
Oil, Brass, Green Glass, Reeded Column, Stepped Square Base, England, 19 ½ x 5 In.	200
Oil, Bronze & Marble, Barbedienne, 2-Light, France, 1800s, 24 x 6 ½ In., Pair	1000
Oil, Cut Glass, Cranberry, Gilt Metal Mount, Marble Base, 14 In.	366
Oil, Cut Glass, Shell Shape Shade, Button & Spear Prisms, 25 x 9 ½ In.	175
Oil, Etched Glass, Sailing Ship, Fluted Top, Zigzag Band On Foot, 10 In., Pair	120

L

Oil, Hanging, Oval Pan, Curved Arm & Hook, Iron Wire Pick, c.1800, 10 In.	1700
Oil, Milk Glass, Green Cut To Clear Font, Mid 1800s, 13 ¾ In.	120
Oil, Portrait Bust, Enamel, Strapwork, Bouquets, Rose Ground, 17 x 9 In., Pair	225
Oil, Pressed Glass Font, Green Dimpled Canopy, Juno Country Store, 29 In.	218
Oil, Pull Down, Parlor, Smoke Bell, Roses, Victorian, 13 In.	177
Oil, Silver Plate, Magic Lamp Form, Hugo Leven, Kayserzinn, c.1900, 10 In.	187
Oil, Spelter, Urn, Winged Griffin Handles, Etched Glass Globe, 30 x 7 In., Pair	150
Pairpoint lamps are in the Pairpoint category.	
Peg, Oil, Brass Beehive Stem, Green Glass Font, Enamel Flowers, Ruffled Rim, 6 x 3 In.	265
Peg, Oil, Pressed Glass, Star & Bulls-Eye, Gilded Girandole Base, Mother & Child, 24 In., Pair .	640
Perfume, Buddha, Red, Yellow, 8 x 5 In.	187
Perfume, Genie, Holding Bowl, Green, White, 6 ½ x 5 In.	312
Perfume, Hunter, 2 Deer, Toga, 10 x 9 In.	625
Perfume, Pierrot, Draping Shawl On A Woman, Art Deco, 9 x 6 In.	312
Perfume, Porcelain, Polar Bear, Night-Light, Bohne & Soehne, c.1925, 10 x 7 In.	410
Sconce, 1-Light, Bronze, Urn, Eagle Finials, Late 1800s, 45 x 11 ½ x 5 In., Pair	812
Sconce, 1-Light, Chrome, Tubular Glass, Art Deco, France, 1900s, 16 x 6 ½ x 4 In., Pair	468
Sconce, 1-Light, Cornucopia, Robed Arm, Parcel Gilt, Continental, 25 In., Pair	1875
Sconce, 1-Light, Figural, Mermaid, Gilt Wings, Glass Shade, 18 x 4 ½ x 9 In., Pair	1062
Sconce, 1-Light, Giltwood, Alabaster, Baroque, Italy, Early 1900s, 15 ¾ x 8 ¾ x 11 In.	687
Sconce, 1-Light, Giltwood, Pierced, Rocaille, Tassels, Mirror Back, c.1865, 26 x 14 In., Pair	906
Sconce, 1-Light, H. Hoffmann-Lederer, Acrylic, Brass, Blue, Crumpled, 15 x 9 In., Pair	250
Sconce, 1-Light, Iron, Crimped Arch Top, Punched Heart & Diamonds, 1800s, 13 x 5 In.	800
Sconce, 1-Light, Starburst, Leaves, Gilt Metal, 17 ½ x 15 In., Pair	250
Sconce, 1-Light, Tin, Balloon Shape Back, Crimped Edges, 1800s, 13 x 7 In., Pair	1000
Sconce, 1-Light, Tin, Pewter, 5 Blossoms, Pair, 9 ⅜ In.	4320
Sconce, 1-Light, Tinned Iron, Crimped Arch Top, Reeded Sides, 13 x 3 In., Pair	1100
Sconce, 1-Light, Tinned Iron, Round Plate, Star & Ray, Ruffled Cup, 10 In. Diam.	1900
Sconce, 1-Light, Wood, Paint, Wheat Sheaves, Green, Gilt, Bulb Or Candle, 19 x 18 In., Pair	950
Sconce, 2-Light, 3 Ships, Relief, White Sails, Blue Sky, 9 x 12 In., Pair	125
Sconce, 2-Light, Brass, Enameled Aluminum, Articulated, Italy, 1950s	1062
Sconce, 2-Light, Brass, Griffin, Torch Arms, Pierced Shades, Scroll, c.1900, 17 In., 4 Piece	615
Sconce, 2-Light, Brass, Scroll Arms, Faceted Prisms, c.1910, 27 x 13 In., 4 Piece	677
Sconce, 2-Light, Brass, Shell Shape Backplate, Scroll Arms, 1900s, Spain, 7 x 7 In., Pair	437
Sconce, 2-Light, Bronze, Flower, Leaf, Jansen, c.1940, 19 In., Pair	450
Sconce, 2-Light, Bronze, Ribbon Backplate, France, 1900s, 20 ½ x 10 ¾ x 6 In., Pair	687
Sconce, 2-Light, Cherub, Standing, Ormolu, Empire, c.1810, 11 ½ In., Pair	1750
Sconce, 2-Light, Flame Mahogany, Square Panel, Mirrored Arch, Empire, 38 x 21 In., Pair	250
Sconce, 2-Light, Flower Spray, Blue Ovals, Sevres Style, 14 ½ In., Pair	250
Sconce, 2-Light, Flowers, Fruit, Feathers, Shades, Composition, Louis XV, 27 x 11 ¼ In.	500
Sconce, 2-Light, Gilt Bronze, Art Nouveau, c.1910, 39 ½ x 24 In., Pair	1000
Sconce, 2-Light, Gilt Bronze, Bowknot Finials, France, 1900s, 21 x 10 x 5 ½ In., Pair	406
Sconce, 2-Light, Gilt Bronze, Ram's Heads, France, 1900s, 25 ¾ x 12 ½ x 6 ¾ In., Pair	468
Sconce, 2-Light, Gilt Bronze, Swag, Torch Backplate, Flaming Urn, 17 x 11 In., Pair	750
Sconce, 2-Light, Gilt Leafy Branches, Scrolling, Parrot, Crystal Drops, 1900s, 28 In., Pair	4920
Sconce, 2-Light, Giltwood, Carved, Louis XVI Style, Early 1900s, 37 x 12 In., Pair	488
Sconce, 2-Light, Giltwood, Flowers, Bronze Arms, Glass Drops, c.1915, 15 x 12 In., Pair	1375
Sconce, 2-Light, Giltwood, Tasseled Ribbons, Italy, 1900s, 35 x 13 x 10 In., Pair	875
Sconce, 2-Light, Glass, Cut, Molded, Red Discs, Starbursts, 16 ½ x 16 In., Pair	125
Sconce, 2-Light, Iron, Oval Cartouche, Acanthus Leaf Finial, Drop & Candle Cups, 10 x 9 In.	206
Sconce, 2-Light, Limewood, Metal, Tan, Turquoise, Scroll Openwork, Flowers, 18 In., Pair	124
Sconce, 2-Light, Metal, Baronial Style, Continental, 1900s, 17 ½ x 12 x 7 ¼ In., Pair	437
Sconce, 2-Light, Mirrored Backplate, Chinoiserie, Italy, 1900s, 29 x 8 x 5 ½ In., Pair	562
Sconce, 2-Light, Plaques, Ceramic, Leaf & Ribbon, 18 x 12 In.	312
Sconce, 2-Light, Wood, Brass, Chinoiserie, Mirror, Pastoral Scene, c.1940, 20 In., Pair	275
Sconce, 3-Light, Bronze Dore, Mirror, Openwork Leaf, Wreath, Trumpet, 38 x 17 In., Pair	3570
Sconce, 3-Light, Cut Glass, Gilt Metal, Teardrop Shape, Eagles, Beaded Swags, 18 In., Pair	2400
Sconce, 3-Light, Gilt Bronze, Leaves, Spiral Twist Arms, 29 ¼ x 20 ¾ In.	800
Sconce, 3-Light, Gilt, Scroll Back, Leaf & Rocaille Scroll Arms, c.1935, 21 In., Pair	531

Lamp, Solar, Gilt Bronze, Shell, Scroll & Flowers, Cut Glass Shade, c.1850, 30 x 9 In.
$1,792

Neal Auctions

Lampshade, Hurricane, Milk Glass, Melon Shape, Fluted, Panels, Violets, 8 ¼ In.
$295

Ruby Lane

Lantern, Candle, Punched Tin, Lines & Dots, Hinged Door, Human Face, c.1800, 15 In.
$584

Cowan's Auctions

Lantern, Tin, Frosted Panels, Glass Font, Burner, J. Sangster Patent March 25th 1862, 17 In.
$200

Hess Auction Group

Lantern, Wrought Iron, Linked Rings, 3-Light, Mica, Samuel Yellin, Philadelphia, 38 x 11 In.
$5,938

Rago Arts and Auction Center

Le Verre Francais, Vase, Berries, Branches, Cobblestone Neck, Cameo, Engraved Mark, 7⅝ In.
$502

Humler & Nolan

Sconce, 3-Light, Giltwood, Eagles, Masks, French Neoclassical, 1800s, 31 x 14 In.	1500
Sconce, 3-Light, Giltwood, Scrolling Leaves, Phoenix, Mirror Back, c.1935, 47 In., Pair	1500
Sconce, 3-Light, Rocaille, Laurel, Berry, Nymph, Acanthus, 19¾ x 20 In.	531
Sconce, 4-Light, Bacchus, Head & Torso, Cornucopias, 36½ x 17¾ In.	4800
Sconce, 4-Light, Brass, Abstract Antler, Dagobet Peche Style, 1920s, 13 x 17 In., Pair	732
Sconce, 4-Light, Gaetano Sciolari, Chromed Steel, Enamel, Lightolier, 11 x 11 In., Pair	531
Sconce, 4-Light, Gilt Metal, Rock Crystal, Glass, Urn Backplate, Louis XV, 36 x 19 In., Pair	5000
Sconce, 4-Light, Wood, Silver, Tree, Leaf Arms, Tassels, Tulip Cups, c.1965, 21 In., Pair	562
Sconce, 5-Light, Brass, Shaped Fretwork Back, Scroll Arms, 23 In., Pair	480
Sconce, 5-Light, Gilt Bronze, Female Bust Backplate, Pendants, Beads, 16 x 15 In., Pair	1000
Sconce, 5-Light, Gilt Leaves, Glass Flowers, 16 x 16 In., Pair	48
Sconce, 5-Light, Gilt, Metal Frame, Rosettes, Swags, Glass Drops, c.1915, 21 In., Pair	937
Sconce, Arts & Crafts, Slag Glass, Iron, Cone Shape, 5½ x 8 In., Pair	1464
Sconce, Cornucopia, Overflowing With Flowers, Branches, c.1850, 14¾ x 16 In., Pair	436
Sconce, Eagle, Tassels, Ribbon, Bow, Federal, 35¾ x 16 In., Pair	450
Sconce, Giltwood, Carved, Tulips & Leaves, Bowknot, Mid 1900s, 15 x 8 x 4 In., Pair	531
Sconce, Giltwood, Shaped Back, Needlework Panel, Brass Arm, 29 x 14 In., Pair	6000
Sconce, Glass, Mottled Purple & White, Iron, Art Deco, 21½ In.	250
Sconce, Murano, Glass, Fluted, Ribbed, Light Amber, 18 In., Pair	375
Sconce, Tin, Ruffled Candleholder, Oval Mosaic Mirror Back, 10 In., Pair	660
Sconce, Tin, Sunflower, Candle, 1800s, 11 x 10 In., Pair	240
Sconce, Tobacco Leaf, Gold Flecks, Italy, c.1940, 18 x 9½ In., Pair	1875
Sinumbra, Brass, Square Base, Floral Shade, 15 Prisms, c.1850, 18 In.	819
Sinumbra, Bronze, Candlestick Form, Cut Flower Shade, H. Hooper, Boston, c.1840, 25 In.	1024
Sinumbra, Bronze, Cut Glass, Marble, Frosted & Cut Glass Shade, 1800s, 31 x 10¼ In.	593
Sinumbra, Cut Glass, Brass Mount, Bulbous Shade, Ferns, E. Glass Co., Boston, 17 In.	4270
Sinumbra, Bronze, Flora-Cut Shade, H.N. Hooper, c.1850, Electrified, 24 In. *illus*	3000
Sinumbra, Silver Plate, Engraved Glass Shade, American, Mid 1800s, 31 x 9 In., Pair	1952
Sinumbra, Silvered Bronze, Atlas On Pedestal, Bulbous Shade, Messenger & Son, 10 In.	3500
Solar, Brass, Lip Burner, Chimney, Frosted Shade, Square Marble Base, c.1850, 29½ In.	380
Solar, Bronze, Acanthus, Bacchantes, Eagles, Fluted Glass, c.1810, 34 In. *illus*	4880
Solar, Camphene, Gilt Bronze, Baluster, Leaves, Eagle, Marble Base, Globe, Hooper, 25 In.	640
Solar, Gilt Bronze, Fluted Ionic Column, Cut Glass Shade, c.1850, 30 x 8½ In.	1664
Solar, Gilt Bronze, Glass, Blue, Cut To Clear, Prisms, Marble Base, 1800s, 24 In. *illus*	4270
Solar, Gilt Bronze, Leafy Stem, Star Form Base, Double Gourd Glass Shade, c.1850, 24 In.	1586
Solar, Gilt Bronze, Marble, Etched Glass Globe, Cornelius & Co., c.1850, 22 x 8½ In.	2440
Solar, Gilt Bronze, Shell, Scroll & Flowers, Cut Glass Shade, c.1850, 30 x 9 In. *illus*	1792
Solar, Gilt Bronze, Vase Form, Frosted Globe, Prisms, Marble Base, c.1850, 30 In.	500
Solar, Hanging, Gilt Brass, Squat Glass Shade, Cut Leaves, Smoke Bell, Chains, 17 x 10 In.	1342
Solar, White & Cranberry Cased Glass, Cornelius & Baker, 1848, 33½ x 7½ In.	562
Tiffany Lamps are listed in the Tiffany category.	
Torchere, 3-Light, Alabaster, Rope Twist, Urn Shape, Flowers, Putti, 71¼ In.	1187
Torchere, 6-Light, Blackamoor Figure, Multicolor, Pedestal, 76 In., Pair	1625
Torchere, 16-Light, Ormolu, Acanthus, 91 In., Pair	11875
Torchere, Art Deco, Stylized Tree, Pierced Leaves, Openwork, Black, 80¼ In., Pair	1250
Torchere, Art Deco, Tole, Fruitwood, Caryatid, Human Feet, Faux Marble, 67 In., Pair	625
Torchere, Bronze, Acanthus, Swags, Leaves, Marble Base, 72 In., Pair	8750
Torchere, Composite, Paint, Molded Palm Tree, Rock Base, Art Deco, 72 In., Pair	4613
Torchere, Giltwood, Acanthus, Laurel, Louis XVI, 62½ x 18 In., Pair	2074
Torchere, Iron, Pricket Stick, 3-Footed, 46 x 15 In.	300
Trammel, 4-Light, Iron, Twist Hanger, Candle Cups, 19 In.	93
Whale Oil, Blown Glass, Tin Mount, Stars, Diamonds, Ring Handles, 17¼ In.	540
Whale Oil, Brass, Tapered Stem, Square Base, Peg Font, Swags, 19th Century, 14 In., Pair	660
Whale Oil, Ceiling, Gilt Bronze, Gadrooned Ring, Scroll Mount, Glass Shade, 19 x 14 In.	1586
Whale Oil, Flared, Cone Shape Foot, Brass Burner, Bent Wire Hanger, 2½ x 9¾ In.	184
Whale Oil, Gilt Bronze, Scroll Feet, Opaque Shade, Putti, Plume & Atwood, 64 x 18 In.	1190
Whale Oil, Glass, Clear, Turned Baluster Stem, Stepped Square Foot, 12½ In.	95

LAMPSHADE

Bohemian Glass, Green Veins, Pallme-Koenig, 4¾ x 15½ In.	177

L

Bristol Glass, Gold Flake, Umbrella Shape, Opaque White, Ribs, 6 x 10 In.	360
Cranberry Glass, Hurricane, Eagle, Stars, 11 In.	188
Glass, Bell Shape, Etched, 15 In.	177
Glass, Globe, White & Blue Swirls, 8 In.	323
Hurricane, Cut Class, 15 In., Pair	250
Hurricane, Milk Glass, Melon Shape, Fluted, Panels, Violets, 8¼ In. *illus*	295
Leaded, Slag Glass, Tulips, Red, 12 Panels, Arts & Crafts, 15 x 25 In.	345
Satin Glass, Landscape, Blue, 12 x 17 In.	36
Slag Glass Panels, Blue, Caramel, Cream Openwork Frame, c.1920, 10 x 18 In.	5200
Slag Glass, Green, Tan, Flowers, Octagonal, 18½ x 18½ In.	789
Slag Glass, Yellow, Flowers, Hammered Metal, Arts & Craft, 43 x 14½ In.	708

LANTERNS are a special type of lighting device. They have a light source, usually a candle, totally hidden inside the walls of the lantern. Light is seen through holes or glass sections.

Brass, 6 Panels, Square Handle, 16 In., Pair	35
Brass, Frosted Glass Shade, Cut Tendrils On Lower Portion, 1800s, 25 x 8 In.	687
Brass, Handles, Dietz, 11 In., Pair	153
Bronze, Patinated, 4-Light, Bowknots & Anthemion, Neoclassical, France, 1900s, 33 x 15 In.	562
Candle, Punched Tin, Lines & Dots, Hinged Door, Human Face, c.1800, 15 In. *illus*	584
Cased Glass, Melon Shape, Gold Foil Inclusions, Barovier Style, Italy, c.1970, 42 x 12 In.	750
Gas, Tole, Pagoda Form, Directoire Style, Electrified, 25 x 18 x 9 In.	512
Hall, 3-Light, Glass, Etched, 9⅝ In., Pair	813
Hall, 3-Light, Glass, Etched, 12 In., Pair	688
Hall, Brass, C-Scroll Supports, 4 Curved Glass Panels, 4 Lights, Electrified, 20 x 12 In.	225
Hall, Gilt Bronze, Rococo Style, France, Early 1900s, 58½ x 32 In.	5500
Hanging, 3-Light, George III, Chains, Engraved Bands, Stars, Bell Shape, 17 In.	375
Hanging, 4-Light, Iron, Brass, Gilbert Poillerat Style, 1900s, 23¼ In., Pair	1230
Hanging, Brass, Etched Glass, Acorn Shape, 35 In.	188
Hanging, Brass, Leaded Slag Glass, Arts & Crafts, 10½ x 10½ In.	549
Hanging, Bronze, Banded Swag, Regency Style, 22 In.	1200
Hanging, Classical, Brass Support, Frosted Globe, Etched Flowers, 1800s, Electrified, 32 In.	425
Hanging, George III, Chains, Engraved, Bell Shape, 23 x 12½ In., Pair	2250
Iron, H. Balmer, Onion Form, Candle Prick, Brutalist, Flemington Iron Works, 1960, 25 x 25 In.	250
Iron, Pierced, Cylindrical, Crescent, Dot & Linked Piercings, Late 1700s, 15½ x 6 In.	100
Miner's, Brass, Mesh, Hook, 14½ In.	37
Oil, Barn, Glass, Tin, Pierced, Bail Handle, Domed Disc Base, Burner, Fluid Jar, 13 In.	236
Peacock Silhouette, Blue, White Ground, Orange Iron, Art Deco Style 1950-90, 26 x 12 In.	100
Tin, Frosted Panels, Glass Font, Burner, J. Sangster Patent March 25th 1862, 17 In. *illus*	200
Tin, Glass Panes, Wire Guards, E.F. Parker's Patents, c.1854, 16 In.	156
Tin, Glass, 4 Bays, 4 Crowns On Top, Octagonal Ogee Base, 19 In., Pair	420
Tin, Pierced, Cylindrical, Strap Handle, Cone Shape Top, Candleholder, 1800s, 16 In.	234
Tin, Pierced, Cylindrical, Tapered Top, Molded Glass Globe, 17 In.	416
Tin, Rectangular, Crossbars, Ring Handle, 1800s, 15 In.	308
Tole, Yellow, 16 x 11½ In.	250
Wood, Chamfered Top, Lift Door, Arched Handle, 3 Glass Panes, 16 x 8 In.	3198
Wrought Iron, 3-Light, Linked Rings, Mica, Samuel Yellin, Philadelphia, 38 x 11 In. *illus*	5938

LE VERRE FRANCAIS is one of the many types of cameo glass made by the Schneider Glassworks in France. The glass was made by the C. Schneider factory in Epinay-sur-Seine from 1918 to 1933. It is a mottled glass, usually decorated with floral designs, and bears the incised signature Le Verre Francais.

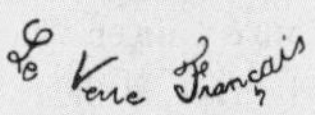

Ewer, Pink, Brown, Round Foot, Cameo, 1920, 10¼ In.	1750
Lamp, Hanging, Pendant, Garance Pattern, Gilt Metal, Cameo, 28 x 5½ In.	813
Vase, Algues Pattern, Red & Orange White Ground, 7 x 8¼ In.	625
Vase, Berries, Branches, Cobblestone Neck, Cameo, Engraved Mark, 7⅝ In. *illus*	502
Vase, Conical, Burnt Sienna, Flowers, Cameo, 13¾ In.	677
Vase, Flowers, Red, Blue, Yellow Ground, Narrow Mouth, Cameo, 9½ In.	677

Leather, Saddle, Parade, Martingale, Black, White, Silver, Conchas, Mexico, 1700s, 28 x 18 In.
$600

Cowan's Auctions

Leeds, Basket, Chestnut, Scalloped, Handles, Lid, Underplate, Creamware, 8¾ x 10½ In.
$656

Heritage Auctions

Lefton, Figurine, Siamese Cat, Seated, 5¼ x 4¾ In.
$14

Ruby Lane

L

Legras, Vase, Pate-De-Verre, Acid Cut, Purple Flowers, Marked, 8 x 4 In.
$675

Ruby Lane

Lenox, Jar, Lid, Flowers, Gold Trim, Arts & Crafts, A. Booker, Belleek, c.1906-24, 5 x 3 In.
$265

Ruby Lane

Lenox, Plate, Salad, Blue Tree, Yellow Flowers, 8¼ In.
$30

Ruby Lane

Vase, Holly & Pebble Border Yellow, Pink Ground, Cameo, Signed, 4 x 8 In.	489
Vase, Plum Pendant Flowers, Mottled Yellow, Tapered, 1920s, 19 x 9 In.	1250
Vase, Red Foxglove, Mottled Pink Ground, Cameo, 19⅞ In.	1093
Vase, Red Poppies, Yellow Ground, Swollen Mouth, Cameo, 15 In.	1625
Vase, Rubaniers, Brown, Orange, Mottled White, Ebony Handles, Bottle, 17 In.	1003
Vase, Stylized Blossom & Stem, Plum, Mottled Pink, Waisted Cylinder, Cameo, 24 In.	2250
Vase, Stylized Leaves, Red, Pale Yellow Ground, 8¾ In.	677

LEATHER is tanned animal hide and has been used to make decorative and useful objects for centuries. Leather objects must be carefully preserved with proper humidity and oiling or the leather will deteriorate and crack. This damage cannot be repaired.

Bridle, Bit & Breast Strap, Dragoon, Yellow & Blue Strap Heads, Mexican War	1495
Saddle Bags, Model 1904, Double, Brown, 3 Buckles, 1917	180
Saddle Bags, Model 1904, Double, Brown, Brass, Canvas Liner Bags, 1918	180
Saddle Bags, Throw Over, Hand Laced, 2 Buckle Straps, 13 x 12 In.	115
Saddle, Antelope, Ernst Bauman, Custer Scout, Western, Tooled Seat, Rogers, c.1876	7475
Saddle, Civil War, McClelland, Rawhide Seat, Black Leather Harness, Straps, Skirts, Stirrups..	1495
Saddle, Eagle Pommel, Officer's, Half Spanish, Black Patent Leather Seat, c.1830	2300
Saddle, McClelland, Brass Fittings, Wood Stirrups, c.1903, 11¼ In.	156
Saddle, Military Issue, Black, c.1900	402
Saddle, Parade, Martingale, Black, White, Silver, Conchas, Mexico, 1700s, 28 x 18 In.......*illus*	600
Saddle, Sinaloa, Jineta Pattern Tree, Owned By General Santa Ana, Mexico, c.1840	4025
Saddle, Western Seat, Mound Pommel, Stirrups, Flower Embossed	173
Valise, Dragoon, Mexican War, Dark Blue Wool, Black Leather Trim, 18 x 6¼ In.	690

LEEDS POTTERY

LEEDS pottery was made at Leeds, Yorkshire, England, from 1774 to 1878. Most Leeds ware was not marked. Early Leeds pieces had distinctive twisted handles with a greenish glaze on part of the creamy ware. Later ware often had blue borders on the creamy pottery. A Chicago company named Leeds made many Disney-inspired figurines. They are listed in the Disneyana category.

Basket, Chestnut, Scalloped, Handles, Lid, Underplate, Creamware, 8¾ x 10½ In. ....*illus*	656
Charger, Blue Feather Edge, Yellow Urn, Flowers, c.1840, 13¼ In.	443
Plate, Blue Feather Edge, Transfer Image, Woman Feeding Chickens, 7¼ In.	59
Plate, Green Feather Edge, Peafowl, 7⅜ In.	177
Plate, White, Eagle, Spread Wings, Shield, Blue Feather Edge, Wavy Rim, c.1815, 8 In. Diam. ..	480
Platter, Pearlware, Blue Feather Edge, Eagle & Shield Center, 1800s, 15¼ x 12¼ In.	923

LEFTON is a mark found on pottery, porcelain, glass, and other wares imported by the Geo. Zoltan Lefton Company. The company began in 1941. George Lefton died in 1996 and the company was sold in 2001. The company mark has changed through the years, but because marks have been used for long periods of time, they are of little help in dating an object.

Bank, Pig, Red Ears & Bow, 1940s, 6 In.	45
Bonbon, Reticulated, Pink Flowers, Pedestal, Gold Trim, 3¾ x 7 In.	18
Bookends, Horse's Head, c.1960, 3 x 5 x 5 In.	59
Candle Climber, Angel, Hands Folded, Sticker, 3¾ In., Pair	35
Cup & Saucer, Wheat, Gilt	30
Figurine, Birthday Angel, May, Bouquet, 4 In.	19
Figurine, Bunny, Albino, On Hind Legs, 4 In.	20
Figurine, Siamese Cat, Seated, 5¼ x 4¾ In. ....*illus*	14
Figurine, Woman, Washing Child, Red & Gold Foil Label, 7 x 4 In.	85
Group, Dog, Collie & Pup, Foil Label, 5 x 5¾ In.	75
Pitcher, Heritage Green, Pink Roses, Gilt, Crimped Rim, Scalloped Foot, c.1950, 7 In.	210
Plaque, Madonna & Child, Hand On Face, Gold Trim, 7 x 4 x 2 In.	52
Plaque, Mermaid, Turquoise, Marked, 1950s, 6½ In.	98
Salt & Pepper, Cat, He & She, Bow, Tie, Lashes, Whiskers, Foil Label	12

LEGRAS was founded in 1864 by Auguste Legras at St. Denis, France. It is best known for cameo glass and enamel-decorated glass with Art Nouveau designs. Legras merged with Pantin in 1920 and became the Verreries et Cristalleries de St. Denis et de Pantin Reunies.

Ice Tub, Emerald Green, Gilt Oak Leaves, Silver Acorns, Signed, c.1900, 3¾ x 6 x 5 In.	687
Lamp, Acid Cut, Landscape, Autumn, Bronze Shade Mount, 12 In.	369
Vase, Art Deco, Green, Locust Wing & Scallop Design, Waterfall, Triangular, Signed, 8 In.	205
Vase, Berry, Acid Etched, Leaves, France, c.1910, 8 In.	187
Vase, Chrysanthemums, Multicolor Enamel Flowers, Bulbous, Tube Neck, c.1905, 12 In.	549
Vase, Cranberry, White, Leaf Decoration, Cameo, 1950, 14 In.	375
Vase, Enameled, Orange Flowers, Green Mottled Ground, 5½ x 4 In.	150
Vase, Landscape, Trees, Brown, Tan, 24 x 6½ In.	2091
Vase, Mountain Lake With Trees, Amber Ground, Early 1900s, 10¾ x 4¾ In.	593
Vase, Orange Poppies, Green Ground, Signed, 12¼ In.	369
Vase, Pate-De-Verre, Acid Cut, Purple Flowers, Marked, 8 x 4 In. *illus*	675
Vase, Stone Bridge, Stream, Bushes, Trees, Greens, Browns, Cameo, Bulbous, 4 x 4¼ In.	711
Vase, White, Green & Blue, Etched & Enameled, Elongated, Geometric Design, 21 In.	812

LENOX porcelain is well-known in the United States. Walter Scott Lenox and Jonathan Coxon founded the Ceramic Art Company in Trenton, New Jersey, in 1889. In 1896 Lenox bought out Coxon's interest, and in 1906 the company was renamed Lenox, Inc. The company makes porcelain that is similar to Irish Belleek. In 2009, after a series of mergers, Lenox became part of Clarion Capital Partners. The marks used by the firm have changed through the years, so collectors can date the ceramics. Related pieces may also be listed in the Ceramic Art Co. category.

Candleholder, Nantucket, Dutch Colonial Style, C-Shape Handle, 7 x 3 In.	30
Cup & Saucer, Holiday, Footed.	40
Figurine, Princess & Firebird, c.1990, 8½ In.	40
Frame, Wedding Promises, Embossed Flowers, Gadroon Edge, 7 x 10 In.	63
Jar, Lid, Flowers, Gold Trim, Arts & Crafts, A. Booker, Belleek, c.1906-24, 5 x 3 In. *illus*	265
Plate, Commemorative, Balsam Fir Tree, Gold Ivy Border, 1979	29
Plate, Dinner, Brookdale, 10½ In.	35
Plate, Salad, Blue Tree, Yellow Flowers, 8¼ In. *illus*	30
Platter, Poppies On Blue, Oval, c.1980, 14 In.	45
Punch Bowl, Grape Leaf, Stand, Cups, Tendrils, Belleek, 1910, 12 x 16 In., 13 Piece	250
Salt & Pepper, Santa Claus & Mrs. Claus.	14
Stein, Monk, Drinking, Cellar, Transfer, Copper Lid, Silver Overlay, Stamped, c.1905, 10 In.	431
Trinket Box, Fuchsia Carnations, Gilt Trim, Hinged, 1¾ x 2¼ In.	69
Trinket Box, Heart Shape, Rose, Gilt Trim, Embossed Rose Border, 5 x 5 In.	34
Vase, Bud, Eternal Pattern, c.1960, 8 In.	35
Vase, Embossed Roses & Leaves, Oval, Pillow Shape, 7¾ In.	59
Vase, Gourd Shape, Ribbed, Gilt Trim, c.1960, 4¾ In.	21
Vase, Silver Footed, Stick Neck, c.1970, 8 In.	195
Vase, Urn Shape, Footed, Raised Poppies, Gold Trim, 9 In.	34

LETTER OPENERS have been used since the eighteenth century. Ivory and silver were favored by the well-to-do. In the late nineteenth century, the letter opener was popular as an advertising giveaway and many were made of metal or celluloid. Brass openers with figural handles were also popular.

Art Nouveau, Patina, Jade Finial, 10¼ In.	80
Brass, Swashbuckler Sword, Hilt, 8½ In. *illus*	14
Bronze, Renaissance Revival, Sword Shape, 1800s, 11 In.	80
Horse Head, Gilded Silver, Jade, Nephrite, Faberge, Box, c.1880, 9¾ In.	3995
Napoleonic, Figural, 4 Scenes, Mother-Of-Pearl Blade, 5⅝ In.	70
Owl, Sterling Silver, Gorham, 6¾ In.	195
Silver, Carnelian, Beaded Border, Curled Handle, D. Donaldson, 8 In.	1500
Silver, Magnifying Glass, Cartier, 8¾ x 2½ In.	400
Silver, Turquoise Cabochon, 4¾ In.	25

Letter Opener, Brass, Swashbuckler Sword, Hilt, 8½ In.
$14

Ruby Lane

Zippo First
Recent research by Zippo Manufacturing Company confirms that the first Zippo windproof lighter was not actually made until 1933, although it was designed and planned for in 1932. The lighter was an improved version of an Austrian design. Today the company makes 80,000 lighters a day and says one-third sell to collectors.

Lighter, Cigar, Dog, Hunting, Wand Stores In Tree Trunk, Silver Plate, c.1900, 4 x 8 In.
$234

Treasureseeker Auctions

Lighter, Cigar, Jerome & Co., Wood Barrel, Clock, Flame Adjust, Match Holders, 1900, 9 In.
$468

Treasureseeker Auctions

L

Lighter, Cigar, Ronson, Black Bartender, Art Deco, Chrome, Black, Red, Marked, c.1930, 7½ In.
$1,170

Treasureseeker Auctions

Novelty Lighters
Novelty cigarette lighters made before 1980 are exempt from a law in Louisiana that forbids the sale of newer lighters.

Lighter, Dragon, Ferdinand, Fuchs & Bros., Silver, Raised Head, Boar Tusk Tail, c.1890, 6 In.
$1,845

Skinner, Inc.

Lighter, Flintlock, Tinder, Walnut, Steel Hardware, Pistol Grip, Compartment, c.1810, 6 In.
$531

Garth's Auctioneers & Appraisers

TIP
Take off your rings and bracelets before you start to wash figurines or dishes.

Lighter, Tinder, Flintlock, 5½ In.
$590

Hess Auction Group

Limoges, Jardiniere, Stand, Children, Umbrella, Sheep, Gilt, Marcadet, Tressemann & Vogt, c.1900, 13 In.
$812

New Orleans Auction Galleries

Limoges, Vase, Portrait, Neoclassical Style, Funnel Shape Neck, Gilt, Swags, c.1890, 14 In., Pair
$492

Skinner, Inc.

Lindbergh, Button, Slim Did It, Red, White, Blue, Back Paper, 1927, 1½ In.
$345

Hake's Americana & Collectibles

Lithophane, Panel, Woman, Infant, Wagon, Door, Tree, 6½ In.
$36

Hudson Valley Auctions

Liverpool, Jug, Eagle, Shield, Banner, E Pluribus Unum, Black Transfer, Pearlware, 8 In.
$480

Brunk Auctions

L

Silver, Victorian Handle, Leafy, Aaron Hadfield, 1818, 9 In.		100
Silver, Yellow Amber Cabochon, Silver Leaves, c.1986, 6 In.		65
Sterling Silver, Acorn Pattern, Georg Jensen, 8 In.		246
Sterling Silver, Allan Scharff For Georg Jensen, 2 x 7 ½ In.		305

LIBBEY Glass Company has made many types of glass since 1888, including the cut glass and tablewares that are collected today. The stemwares of the 1930s and 1940s are once again in style. The Toledo, Ohio, firm was purchased by Owens-Illinois in 1935 and is still working under the name Libbey Inc. Maize is listed in its own category.

Libbey

Bowl, Hobstar, Grasses, 8 In.		180
Creamer, Peachblow, Ribbed, 2 ½ x 4 In.		61
Decanter, Embossed Leaf, Green, Cork Stopper, 7 ¾ In.		20
Dish, Grand Prize, 6 In.		4250
Glass Tray, Fleur-De-Lis Pattern, Round, Flower Head Shape, Crimped Edge, 10 In.		125
Tray, Somerset Pattern, Slanted Sides, Scalloped Sawtooth Rim, 12 In.		400
Vase, Cut Glass, Squat, Hobstar, Strawberry, Diamond, 5 ¾ x 8 In.		120
Vase, On Pedestal, Cut Glass, Sawtooth Rim, 9 ⅜ In.		431
Vase, Trumpet, Ruffled, Amberina, 10 x 3 ¾ In.		98

LIGHTERS for cigarettes and cigars are collectible. Cigarettes became popular in the late nineteenth century, and with the cigarette came matches and cigarette lighters. All types of lighters are collected, from solid gold to the first of the recent disposable lighters. Most examples found were made after 1940. Some lighters may be found in the Jewelry category in this book.

Camel, Turkish & Domestic Blend Cigarettes, Enamel, Japan		75
Car Shape, Buick, Silver, Occupied Japan, 3 In.		96
Cigar, Dog, Hunting, Wand Stores In Tree Trunk, Silver Plate, c.1900, 4 x 8 In.	*illus*	234
Cigar, Jerome & Co., Wood Barrel, Clock, Flame Adjust, Match Holders, 1900, 9 In.	*illus*	468
Cigar, Ronson, Black Bartender, Art Deco, Chrome, Black, Red, Marked, c.1930, 7 ½ In.	*illus*	1170
Dragon, Ferdinand, Fuchs & Bros., Silver, Raised Head, Boar Tusk Tail, c.1890, 6 In.	*illus*	1845
Flintlock, Tinder, Walnut, Steel Hardware, Pistol Grip, Compartment, c.1810, 6 In.	*illus*	531
Flintlock Tinder, Walnut Pistol Grip With Brass & Candleholders, Late 1700s, 6 ½ In.		570
Silver, Nude Woman, Waves, Dolphin Handle, Cigarette, Art Nouveau, c.1900, 4 ½ In.		1045
Tinder, Flintlock, 5 ½ In.	*illus*	590
Winged Devil & Dragon, Bronze, c.1881, 7 ½ In.		4972

LIGHTNING RODS AND LIGHTNING ROD BALLS are collected. The glass balls were at the center of the rod that was attached to the roof of a house or barn to avoid lightning damage. The balls were made in many colors and many patterns.

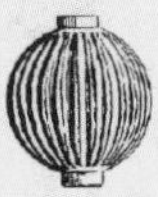

LIGHTNING ROD

Copper, Glass, Ruby Ball, Arrow Vane, Tripod Stand, c.1900, 37 In.		175
Copper, Stand, 70 In.		40
Tin, Cranberry Ball, Arrow Vane, Gray, 34 x 39 In.		150

LIGHTNING ROD BALL

Purple, 5 ½ In.		35

LIMOGES porcelain has been made in Limoges, France, since the mid-nineteenth century. Fine porcelains were made by many factories, including Haviland, Ahrenfeldt, Guerin, Pouyat, Elite, and others. Modern porcelains are being made at Limoges. The word *Limoges* as part of the mark is not an indication of age. Haviland, one of the Limoges factories, is listed as a separate category in this book.

Box, Cobalt Blue, Gilt Cartouche, Rural Scene, Cows, Goat, Man, Oval, Hinged Lid, 4 ⅜ In.		240
Box, Hinged Lid, Couple In Classical Drapery, 1800s, 1 ¾ x 3 ⅜ In.		615
Box, Teeth, Tooth Fairy, Kitten, Premiere Dents, Teddy Bear Hinge, 1930s, 2 In.		60
Coffee Set, Coffeepot, Sugar, Creamer, 2 Saucers, Cup, 16 ½ In.		468
Jardiniere, Stand, Children, Umbrella, Sheep, Gilt, Marcadet, Tressemann & Vogt, c.1900, 13 In.	*illus*	812
Oyster Plate, Hand Painted, Flowers With Gilt Highlights, France, 1900s, 10 Piece, 7 ¾ In.		120

Lladro, Figurine, Pensive Clown, No. 5130, 1982, 10 x 8 ¼ In.
$295

Ruby Lane

Loetz, Vase, Blue Iridescent, Bronze Mount, Girls Play Ring Around The Rosie, 10 ¼ x 5 In.
$1,200

Ruby Lane

Loetz, Vase, Rusticana, Green, Pinched, c.1899, 6 ¾ x 3 In.
$150

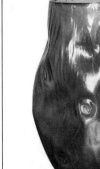

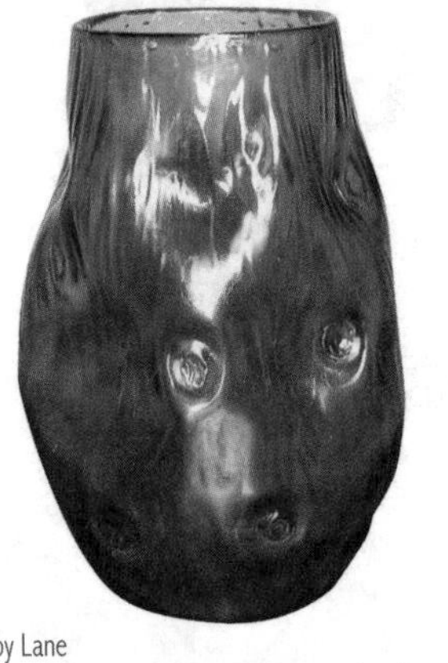

Ruby Lane

L

Lone Ranger, Game, Lone Ranger & Tonto, Red, Yellow, Warren Paper, 1978, 17 x 9 ½ In.
$28

Ruby Lane

Lone Ranger, Gun Belt, Buscadero, Double, Nickel Bullets, Sterling Silver Conchas, Buckles, 47 In.
$480

Alderfer Auction Company

Lone Ranger, Mannequin, Lone Ranger, Hat, Scarf, Double Holster, 2 Pistols, 77 In.
$300

Alderfer Auction Company

Plate, Fish Scenes, Shaped, Scalloped, Gold Trim, 11 In., 6 Piece	120
Tray, Bronze, Porcelain, Oval, Flowers, Leaves, Pierced Gallery, Paw Feet, 26 x 12 In.	472
Vase, Enamel, Flowers, Camille Faure, 4 ¼ In.	780
Vase, Portrait, Neoclassical Style, Funnel Shape Neck, Gilt, Swags, c.1890, 14 In., Pair......*illus*	492

LINDBERGH was a national hero. In 1927, Charles Lindbergh, the aviator, became the first man to make a nonstop solo flight across the Atlantic Ocean. In 1932, his son was kidnapped and murdered, and Lindbergh was again the center of public interest. He died in 1974. All types of Lindbergh memorabilia are collected.

Bracelet, Silver, New York Skyline, Eiffel Tower, Spirit Of St. Louis, 1 In.	258
Button, Slim Did It, Red, White, Blue, Back Paper, 1927, 1 ½ In. ....*illus*	345
Candy Container, Airplane, Spirit Of Goodwill, Glass, Silver, 1920s	225
Medal, Bronze, U.S. Chamber Of Commerce, 1927, 2 ½ x 3 ½ In.	50
Photograph, Press, 1930, 8 x 10 In.	20
Plaque, New York To Paris Flight, 1927, 11 ½ x 8 ½ In.	225
Tapestry, Spirit Of St. Louis Journey, Color, 36 x 54 In.	125
Toy, Airplane, Spirit Of St. Louis, Monoplane, Pressed Steel, 22 In.	275
Toy, Airplane, Spirit Of St. Louis, Pilot, Tin Lithograph, Friction, Schuco, 1927, 4 x 5 In.	664
Transfer Order, Signed, Frame, 9 ½ x 12 In.	550

LITHOPHANES are porcelain pictures made by casting clay in layers of various thicknesses. When a piece is held to the light, a picture of light and shadow is seen through it. Most lithophanes date from the 1825–75 period. A few are still being made. Many lithophanes sold today were originally panels for lampshades.

Panel, 2 Women, Reading, Sitting, Marked, 4 ½ x 5 ¼ In.	30
Panel, Angel Scene, Brass Frame, Pedestal Base, France, c.1869, Miniature, 7 In.	399
Panel, Castle, Landscape, Marked, 6 x 7 ½ In.	35
Panel, Child With Rooster & Hen, 5 x 6 In.	160
Panel, Couple At Well, Marked, 4 ¼ x 5 In.	20
Panel, Dog Saves Drowning Child, Marked, 4 ½ x 6 ½ In.	100
Panel, Woman, Infant, Wagon, Door, Tree, 6 ½ In. ....*illus*	36
Panel, Woman Writing On Trunk, Marked, 5 x 6 In.	35

LIVERPOOL, England, has been the site of many pottery and porcelain factories since the eighteenth century. Color-decorated porcelains, transfer-printed earthenware, stoneware, basalt, figurines, and other wares were made. Sadler and Green made print-decorated wares starting in 1756. Many of the pieces were made for the American market and feature patriotic emblems, such as eagles and flags. Liverpool pitchers are called Liverpool jugs by collectors.

Jug, Black & White Transfer, Sailing Ship, Flags, Anchor, Figure, Loop Handle, 8 In.	296
Jug, Cream, Black Transfer, 3-Masted Ship, Flag, Poem, Bulbous, 8 In.	830
Jug, Creamware, Transfer, Crest, Masted Ships, Washington & Colonies, c.1820, 9 In.	340
Jug, Eagle, Shield, Banner, E Pluribus Unum, Black Transfer, Pearlware, 8 In. ....*illus*	480
Jug, Herculaneum, Washington, 15 States, The True Blooded Yankee, c.1800, 8 ½ In.	861
Jug, Hope, East India Man Taking A Pilot On Board, Transfer, 8 In.	900
Jug, Marriage, George Washington's Apotheosis, 1795-1810, 11 In.	1320
Jug, Masonic Transfer, Symbols, Sailing Ship, U.S. Flag, Wreath, Baluster, 12 x 10 In.	593

LLADRO is a Spanish porcelain. Brothers Juan, Jose, and Vicente Lladro opened a ceramics workshop in Almacera in 1951. They soon began making figurines in a distinctive, elongated style. In 1958, the factory moved to Tabernes Blanques, Spain. The company makes stoneware and porcelain figurines and vases in limited and unlimited editions. Dates given are first and last years of production. Marks since 1977 have the added word "Daisa," the acronym for the company that holds the intellectual property rights to Lladro figurines.

Figurine, Centaur Girl, No. 1012, 1969-89, 9 ¼ In.	510
Figurine, Dog, Afghan, Seated, No. 1069, 1969-85, 11 ¾ In.	225

L

Figurine, Dreamer, No. 5008, 1978-99, 9 3/4 In.	85
Figurine, Feeding The Ducks, No. 4849, c.1973-95, 6 1/2 In.	145
Figurine, Girl With Piglets, No. 4572, 1968-85, 10 3/4 In.	325
Figurine, Graceful Swan, No. 5230, 1984-2000, 8 1/2 In.	45
Figurine, Iris, No. 6276, 1996-2007, 4 3/4 In.	95
Figurine, Lady Empire, No. 4719, 1970-79, 19 In.	375
Figurine, Listen To Don Quixote, Signed Salvador Furio, No. 1520, 1987-95, 20 1/2 x 20 In.	714
Figurine, Love & Marriage, No. 1802, 1995-2001, 13 3/4 In.	2600
Figurine, Madame Butterfly, No. 4991, 1978-98, 11 3/4 In.	125
Figurine, Mermaid On Wave, Vincente Martinez, No. 1347, 1978-83, 16 1/4 x 9 In.	826
Figurine, Napoleon Bonaparte, No. 5338, 1985-94, 14 In.	150
Figurine, Pensive Clown, No. 5130, 1982, 10 x 8 1/4 In. ....*illus*	295
Figurine, Pretty Pickings, Matte Glaze, No. 5222, 1984, 7 In.	110
Figurine, Rose, No. 6275, 1996-2007, 6 3/4 In.	95
Figurine, Shepherdess, Girl With Basket, No. 1034, 1969-89, 10 1/2 In.	95
Figurine, Sounds Of Love, No. 6474, 1998-2005, 9 In.	75
Figurine, The Thinker, Little Boy, No. 4876, 1974-93, 8 1/4 In.	68
Group, Satyr, Playing Pipes, No. 1108, 1969-86, 11 1/2 x 8 3/4 In.	300

LOETZ glass was made in many varieties. Johann Loetz bought a glassworks in Klostermuhle, Bohemia (now Klastersky Mlyn, Czech Republic), in 1840. He died in 1848 and his widow ran the company; then in 1879, his grandson took over. Most collectors recognize the iridescent gold glass similar to Tiffany, but many other types were made. The firm closed during World War II.

Loetz Austria

Bowl, Green, Silver Iridescent Spots & Lines, Dimpled, Squat, Folded Rim, 1900s, 4 x 6 In.	180
Bowl, Yellow Interior, Marble Exterior, Brown Swirls, Black Rim, 3 Black Feet, 4 3/4 x 9 In.	400
Compote, Orange Tango, Black Stripe, 4 1/2 x 10 In.	118
Dresser Box, Fuchsia & White Swirl, Brass Dome Lid, Cabochons, Finial, 5 x 4 In.	118
Jar, Purple, Blue, Iridescent, Pulled Trails, Silver Overlay, Squat, Stopper, c.1900, 5 In.	1125
Lampshade, Domed, green, Iridescent, 4 1/4 x 11 1/4 In.	413
Vase, 4 Handles, Iridescent, Lavender & Orange, Austria, c.1900, 4 3/4 x 5 In.	8125
Vase, Argus, Platinum Iridescent Pulled Lines & Knots, Oil Spot Ground, Folded Rim, 10 In.	5036
Vase, Blue Iridescent, Bronze Mount, Girls Play Ring Around The Rosie, 10 1/4 x 5 In. ....*illus*	1200
Vase, Chalice On Cupped Base, Iridescent Cobalt Blue With Pattern, 6 In.	288
Vase, Cobalt Blue Papillon Mounted, Brass Plated, Austria, c.1900, 14 1/2 x 6 1/2 In.	13750
Vase, Cytisus, Amber, Blue Iridescent Waves, Gold Iridescent Oil Spot, 9 In.	8295
Vase, Cytisus, Dimpled, Iridescent, Orange & Yellow, Austria, c.1902, 7 1/2 x 3 1/2 In.	3625
Vase, Cytisus, Leafy Dots, Orange, Gold, Swollen, Dimpled, Ruffled Rim, c.1902, 8 In.	3626
Vase, Cytisus, Purple & Orange, Austria, c.1902, 5 x 3 In.	2000
Vase, Cytisus, Swirls, Purple, Green, Amber, Pear Shape, Flared, c.1902, 5 x 3 In.	2000
Vase, Flowers, Leaf Blades, Orange, Blue Black, Gourd Shape, Flared Rim, Cameo, 12 In.	472
Vase, Gold Iridescent, Elongated Spots, Tapered, 3 Curvy Handles, c.1900, 5 x 4 3/4 In.	4063
Vase, Gold Iridescent, Lobed, Gilt Metal, 7 1/4 In.	1062
Vase, Gold Iridescent, Tapered, Wavy Sides, 3 Tendril Feet, 6 7/8 In.	4740
Vase, Green Iridescent, Oil Spot, Dimpled, Flared Rim, 5 1/4 In.	236
Vase, Green, Mint, White, Streaked Glaze, Swirl Ribbed, Swollen Collar, 8 x 6 In.	944
Vase, Iridescent Blue & Orange, Wavy Design, Silver Overlay, Ribbed, Shouldered, 4 In.	708
Vase, Iridescent Blue, La Pierre Silver Overlay, 1900, 12 1/8 In.	937
Vase, Iridescent Olive, Tulpen Tulip, 8 x 8 In.	383
Vase, Lid, Hunting Scene, Enameled, Gilt Glass, Adolf Beckert, Austria, 1910, 14 x 4 1/4 In.	6875
Vase, Light Blue, Stacked Donuts, White Rim, 6 1/2 x 6 3/8 In.	413
Vase, Lobed Cytisus, Blue, Green, Lemon Yellow, Swollen Collar, Folded Rim, c.1902, In.	2625
Vase, Lobed Cytisus, Green & Citrine, Austria, c.1902, 7 1/4 x 4 1/4 In.	2625
Vase, Mauve, Iridescent Metal Art Nouveau Leaves & Vine, 5 In.	1179
Vase, Metal Mounts, Blown Glass, Original Patina, Bakalowits, Austria, c.1900, 10 x 4 In.	3000
Vase, Millefiori, Ribbed, Blue, White, Twist, 8 1/2 x 6 In.	472
Vase, Mottled, Gold Iridescent, Pinched, Ruffled Rim, 9 1/4 In.	375
Vase, Octopus, Latte Brown, Mother-Of-Pearl Trails, Rolled Rim & Foot, 6 1/2 In.	649
Vase, Opaque White, Red, Bleeding Hearts, Stripes, Cylindrical, Domed Foot, 1915, 8 In.	750

Lone Ranger, Spurs, Silver, Tooled, Leather, Marked, Mexico
$720

Alderfer Auction Company

Longwy, Vase, Cruise Ship, France, Blue, Sphere, Danillo Curetti, 14 1/2 In.
$3,125

Roland Auctioneers & Valuers

Lonhuda, Vase, Flowers, Long Neck, Flared, Brown Underglaze, c.1890, 8 1/2 x 4 1/2 In.
$150

Ruby Lane

L

Losanti, Vase, Cranes, Leaves, Green, Oxblood, M.L. McLaughlin, 6 In. $2,178

Humler & Nolan

Low, Tile, Woodland Scene, Children, Blue Glossy Glaze, Frame, 14 3/8 x 10 3/4 In. $1,599

Skinner, Inc.

Vase, Orange, Green Iridescent Feather, Bulbous, Metal Mount & Collar, c.1910, 7 x 6 In.	923
Vase, Platinum Iridescent Pulled Feathers, Clambroth Ground, Squat, 3 In.	1778
Vase, Pulled Feather, Burnt Orange, Silver, Squat, Swollen Stick Neck, c.1900, 13 In.	5625
Vase, Pulled Feather, Lavender & Orange, Austria, c.1900, 13 1/4 x 7 In.	5625
Vase, Rusticana, Green, Pinched, c.1899, 6 3/4 x 3 In. .....*illus*	150
Vase, Rusticana, Light Blue Iridescent, Tree Bark Finish, Knots, Dimpled, Ruffled Rim, 7 In.	1185
Vase, Silver Flower Overlay, Twist Waves Of Iridescent Blues, 12 1/8 x 7 1/4 In.	10063
Vase, Swirl Glass, Iridescent, Green, Blue, Tendrils, Handles, Silver Plate, 18 x 10 1/4 In.	750
Vase, Swirling Design, Orange, Iridescent Green, Blue, Pink, c.1901, 8 In.	4688
Vase, Titania, Art Nouveau Silver Overlay, Iridescent Green With Red, Impressed, 8 In.	1840
Vase, Vertical Ridges, Blue Green, Gold Iridescent, 9 1/4 x 5 1/2 In.	460

LONE RANGER, a fictional character, was introduced on the radio in 1932. Over three thousand shows were produced before the series ended in 1954. In 1938, the first Lone Ranger movie was made. The latest movie was made in 2013. Television shows were started in 1949 and are still seen on some stations. The Lone Ranger appears on many products and was even the name of a restaurant chain for several years.

Box, Gum Card, Big Piece Of Chewing Gum, Picture Story, 1940, 8 x 10 In.	2468
Button, Lone Ranger Club, Republic Western, Red & White, 1938, 1 1/4 In.	158
Figure, Hat, Pistols, Rearing Silver, Reins, Saddle, Cinch Strap, Box, c.1958, 9 x 10 In.	190
Game, Lone Ranger & Tonto, Red, Yellow, Warren Paper, 1978, 17 x 9 1/2 In. .....*illus*	28
Game, Target, Hi-Yo Silver, Tin Lithograph, Original Artboard Target, 1938, 16 x 27 In.	173
Gum Card, 2-Sided Sheet, 5 Overlapping Pictures, Back Text, 1938, 8 x 10 In.	253
Gun Belt, Buscadero, Double, Nickel Bullets, Sterling Silver Conchas, Buckles, 47 In. .....*illus*	480
Horse, Silver, Fiberglass, White, 6 x 2 x 8 Ft.	660
Mannequin, Lone Ranger, Hat, Scarf, Double Holster, 2 Pistols, 77 In. .....*illus*	300
Photo, Check, Signed, Brace Beemer, Voice, Black & White, Glossy, c.1964	232
Photograph, Lone Ranger, Tonto, Horseback, Sepia, Frame, 16 x 20 In.	72
Poster, 25th Silver Anniversary, Riding Silver, Signed, 1958, 21 x 34 In.	403
Rifle Scabbard, Carved, Black, Silver Concha	120
Spurs, Silver, Tooled, Leather, Marked, Mexico .....*illus*	720
Statue, Pewter, Lone Ranger On Rearing Silver, Marble Base, Signed, 10 In.	230
Stirrups, Leather, Silver LR	360
Toy, Figures, Tonto & Scout, Stallion, Reins & Saddle, Pistol, Box, 1950s, 9 x 10 In.	463

LONGWY WORKSHOP of Longwy, France, first made ceramic wares in 1798. The workshop is still in business. Most of the ceramic pieces found today are glazed with many colors to resemble cloisonne or other enameled metal. Many pieces were made with stylized figures and Art Deco designs. The factory used a variety of marks.

Bowl, Bronze Mount, Pink Flowers, Blue Ground, 13 x 20 In.	3250
Bowl, Flower Spray, Vines, Turquoise Blue, Crackle, Ring Foot, 1920s, 10 In. Diam.	365
Cake Plate, Bird, Flower Branches, Magenta, Gilt, Scalloped, Handles, 1930s, 7 x 14 In.	520
Lamp, Perfume, Majolica, Multicolor Flowers, Blue Ground, France, 6 1/2 x 4 In.	271
Pin Tray, Flowering Branches, Multicolor, Turquoise, Wavy Oval, 1920s, 3 x 5 In.	105
Saucer, Flower Shape, Lobed Rim, Turquoise, Multicolor Flowers, Stems, 1900s, 5 In.	82
Trinket Box, Cherry Blossom Branches, Turquoise, Pink, Cobalt Blue, Lid, 1930s, 4 In.	120
Vase, Circle Clusters, Turquoise, Black, Squat, Bulbous, Flared Neck, Crackle, 1930s, 6 In.	475
Vase, Cruise Ship, France, Blue, Sphere, Danillo Curetti, 14 1/2 In. .....*illus*	3125
Vase, Trailing Flower Branches, Blue Ground, Multicolor, Trumpet Shape, 1930s, 10 In.	478

LONHUDA POTTERY COMPANY of Steubenville, Ohio, was organized in 1892 by William Long, W. H. Hunter, and Alfred Day. Brown underglaze slip-decorated pottery was made. The firm closed in 1896. The company used many marks; the earliest included the letters *LPCO*.

Vase, Blackberry, Molded, Green Matte Glaze, Oval, c.1903, 7 In.	1220
Vase, Flowers, Long Neck, Flared, Brown Underglaze, c.1890, 8 1/2 x 4 1/2 In. .....*illus*	150

L

Vase, Leaf & Berries, Brown Underglaze, Green, Smokestack, Flared Stick, 1800s, 6 In.	465
Vase, Pansy, Brown & Green Glaze, Lobed Cylinder, 1800s, 12 In.	455
Vase, Tulip Blossoms, Molded, Green Matte Glaze, Swollen Collar, c.1903, 9 In.	3010

LOSANTI was made by Mary Louise McLaughlin in Cincinnati, Ohio, about 1899. It was a hard paste decorative porcelain. She stopped making it in 1906.

Vase, Cranes, Leaves, Green, Oxblood, M.L. McLaughlin, 6 In. ....*illus*	2178

LOTUS WARE was made by the Knowles, Taylor & Knowles Company of East Liverpool, Ohio, from 1890 to 1900. Lotus Ware, a thin porcelain that resembles Belleek, was sometimes decorated outside the factory. Other types of ceramics that were made by the Knowles, Taylor & Knowles Company are listed under KTK.

Biscuit Jar, Flowers, Pink, Trickling Bronze, Lobed Swirl, Notch Rim, Gilt, c.1910, 6 In.	82
Bowl, Twig Handles, Birch Leaves, Applied Crumbled Porcelain, c.1880, 6 x 11 In.	660
Creamer, Ivory, Gilt Leafy Vines, Bulbous, Stem Handle, Flared Spout, c.1890, 4 In.	310
Cup & Saucer, Blue Flowers, Gilt Swirls & Drip Rim, c.1890, 3 x 6 In.	250
Ewer, Pink Flowers, Gilt Leaves, Pear, Angular Handle, Upright Spout, c.1890, 6 In.	250
Teapot, Cherry Blossoms, Relief, Scalloped Rim, Double Handle, c.1900, 5 x 7 In.	115
Vase, Blue Morning Glory, Cylinder Shape, Raised Lattice, 3 Gilt Ball Feet, 8 x 5 In.	295
Vase, Celadon Flowers, Umbrian, Applied Hand Molded Petals, c.1890, 9 In.	570
Vase, Tuscan, Beaded Cabochon Filigree, Cylindrical, Gilt Ball Feet, c.1900, 6 In.	1950

LOW art tiles were made by the J. and J. G. Low Art Tile Works of Chelsea, Massachusetts, from 1877 to 1902. A variety of art and other tiles were made. Some of the tiles were made by a process called "natural," some were hand-modeled, and some were made mechanically.

J. & J. G. LOW

Tile, Flower Cluster, Cobalt & Pale Blue Glaze, Allover Pattern, c.1904, 4 x 4 In.	70
Tile, Flowing Geometric Pattern, Embossed, Brick Red Glaze, Iridescence, c.1900, 6 In.	85
Tile, Mottled, Green & Gray, Crackle Design, 4 x 4 In.	21
Tile, Stylized Thistle, Relief Star, Flower Bloom, Caramel Glaze, c.1881, 4 x 4 In.	85
Tile, Woodland Scene, Children, Blue Glossy Glaze, Frame, 14 3/8 x 10 3/4 In. ....*illus*	1599

LOY-NEL-ART, *see McCoy category.*

LUNCH BOXES and lunch pails have been used to carry lunches to school or work since the nineteenth century. Today, most collectors want either early tin tobacco advertising boxes or children's lunch boxes made since the 1930s. These boxes are made of metal or plastic. Vinyl lunch boxes were made from 1959 to 1982. Injection molded plastic lunch boxes were made beginning in 1972. Legend says metal lunch boxes were banned in Florida in 1972 after a group of mothers claimed children were hitting each other with them and getting injured. This is not true. Metal lunch boxes stopped being made in the 1980s because they were more expensive to make than plastic lunch boxes. Boxes listed here include the original Thermos bottle inside the box unless otherwise indicated. Movie, television, and cartoon characters may be found in their own categories. Tobacco tin pails and lunch boxes are listed in the Advertising category.

Annie Oakley & Tagg, Yellow, Aladdin, 8 x 7 In.	327
Battle Of The Planets, G-Force Character Images, Yellow Frame, Metal, 1979	115
Children, Playing, Dog, Blue, Tin Lithograph, c.1910, 6 1/2 x 4 In. ....*illus*	95
Dukes Of Hazzard, Metal, Embossed, Bo, Luke & Daisy, Aladdin, 1980, 7 In.	127 to 195
Evel Knievel, Metal, Portrait, On Motorcycle, Jumping Cars, 1974, 7 In.	165
G.I. Joe, U.S. Army, Green Canvas, Metal Latch, Handle, Envelope, 1968, 9 x 5 In.	705
Gunsmoke, Metal, Wild West Scene, 8 x 7 In.	335
Home Town Airport, Dome Top, Metal, American Thermos Products, 1960, 8 3/4 x 6 1/4 In.	366
Incredible Hulk, Metal, Embossed, Multicolor, Aladdin, 1978	224
Land Of The Lost, Metal, Embossed, Characters, Dinosaurs, 1975	171
Movie Monsters, Embossed Metal, Plastic Thermos, Aladdin, 1979, 7 In.	611

Lunch Box, Children, Playing, Dog, Blue, Tin Lithograph, c.1910, 6 1/2 x 4 In. $95

Ruby Lane

Lustres, Amber, Cabochon, Gilt, Faceted Drop Prisms, c.1950, 12 In. $332

Leland Little Auctions

L

Maize, Sugar Shaker, Custard, Yellow Stain, Gilt, W.L. Libbey & Sons, c.1875, 5 1/2 In. $105

Jeffrey S. Evans

TIP

For removing ink prices on matte-finished pottery, try paste silver polish. It is a little abrasive and contains some cleaning chemicals that may help.

Majolica, Bowl, Butterflies, Lizards, Spider, Worm, Portuguese Palissy, Jose Cunha, 9 ½ In.
$308

Cowan's Auctions

Majolica, Cookie Jar, Sack, Ribbon, Mouse, Peek Freans Biscuits On Lid, Wm. Brownfield, c.1875, 8 In.
$570

Strawser Auction Group

TIP

The value of lustres with hanging prisms is not changed if a few of the prisms have been replaced.

Majolica, Fish Plate, 6 Fish Shape Wells, Seaweed Design, Minton, 11 ¾ In.
$1,440

Strawser Auction Group

Penguins, Parade, Upright Handle, Tin Lithograph, Red, Black, White, c.1925, 4 x 6 In.	90
Polly's Picture Party, Vinyl, Pink, Flasher Screen, Top Handle, 1960s, 7 x 9 In.	604
Scooby Doo, Metal, Headless Horseman, King-Seeley Thermos Co., 1973	115
USA, Wake Up America, Metal, Red, White, Blue, 1973, 8 ½ x 6 In.	244

LUNEVILLE, a French faience factory, was established about 1730 by Jacques Chambrette. It is best known for its fine biscuit figures and groups and for large faience dogs and lions. The early pieces were unmarked. The firm was acquired by Keller and Guerin and is still working.

Compote, Violets, Leaf Border, Marked, 9 x 4 ½ In.	150
Cup & Saucer, Pink Rose, Pink Trim, Keller & Guerin, c.1880	25
Gravy Boat, Mimosa Pattern, 1800s	45
Jardiniere, Red Flowers, Yellow Ground, Green Leaves, Handles, Keller & Guerin, 13 x 18 In...	86
Plate, Asparagus, Stalks, Swirled Leaves, 9 ¼ In.	150
Platter, Old Strausburg, Well & Tree Indentation, 18 x 12 In.	200
Vase, Cobalt Blue, Flowers, Brown, Keller & Guerin, 9 ¼ In., Pair	198
Vase, Massier, Ruby Daisies, Iridescent Green & Blue Glazes, Marked, 5 ¾ In.	805
Vase, Shepherd, Brown, Red, Blue, Green, Muller Fres., 1900s, 12 ¼ In.	744
Vase, Turtles, Handles, Keller & Guerin, 1895, 12 ¼ x 12 In.	1612

LUSTER glaze was meant to resemble copper, silver, or gold. The term luster includes any piece with some luster trim. It has been used since the sixteenth century. Some of the luster found today was made during the nineteenth century. The metallic glazes are applied on pottery. The finished color depends on the combination of the clay color and the glaze. Blue, orange, gold, and pearlized luster decorations were used by Japanese and German firms in the early 1900s. Fairyland Luster was made by Wedgwood in the 1900s. Tea Leaf pieces have their own category.

Copper, Chocolate Pot, Octagonal, Oriental Designs, 1880s, 5 In.	145
Copper, Pitcher, Band Of Stylized Leaves, Footed, 4 ½ x 5 ½ In.	89
Fairyland Luster is included in the Wedgwood category.	
Pink, Mug, Bird On Branch, Child's, c.1825, 2 x 2 In.	132
Pink, Teapot, Dome Lid, Finial, Sprig, Paneled, Angular Handle, c.1810, 7 x 11 In.	85
Pink, Teapot, Lid, Bands Of Leaves, Flowers, c.1800, 9 ½ x 6 In.	220
Pitcher, Ship, Compass, Poem, Transfer Printed, 1800s, 9 ¼ In.	281
Sunderland Luster pieces are in the Sunderland category.	

LUSTRES are mantel decorations or pedestal vases with many hanging glass prisms. The name really refers to the prisms, and it is proper to refer to a single glass prism as a lustre. Either spelling, luster or lustre, is correct.

Amber, Cabochon, Gilt, Faceted Drop Prisms, c.1950, 12 In. ....*illus*	332
Blue, Cobalt, Gilt, Flowers, Prisms, Round Foot, 14 ¼ x 7 In., Pair	1035
Blue, Leaf, Flowers, Birds, Arrow Prisms, c.1880, 13 ¼ x 6 ⅛ In., Pair	200
Bohemian Glass, Amber, Clear Prisms, Wreaths, Swirls, Scalloped Rim, 1800s, 12 In.	425
Bohemian Glass, Cut White To Cranberry, Gilt Trim, Multicolor Prisms, 13 x 7 In., Pair	413
Bohemian Glass, Green, Ball Pendants, 11 ½ In., Pair	531
Bohemian Glass, Red, Cabochons, 13 ½ In., Pair	1500
Bohemian Glass, Red, Opaque White, Swags, Prisms, 10 ½ In., Pair	938
Bohemian Glass, White, Green, 15 In., Pair	197
Cut Glass, Prisms, Clear, Round Foot, c.1930s, 13 ¾ In., Pair	4000
Green Glass, Gilt, Flowers, Spear & Button Prisms, 14 ⅛ x 7 In., Pair	750
Ruby Glass, Raised Gilt Leaves, Pink Enamel Centers, Ferns, Cut Spear Prisms, 14 In., Pair....	375

MACINTYRE, *see Moorcroft category.*

MAIZE glass was made by W.L. Libbey & Son Company of Toledo, Ohio, after 1889. The glass resembled an ear of corn. The leaves were usually green, but some pieces were made with blue or red leaves. The kernels of corn were light yellow, white, or light green.

Sugar Shaker, Custard, Yellow Stain, Gilt, W.L. Libbey & Sons, c.1875, 5 ½ In. ......*illus*	105

L

REFLECTIONS ON
50 YEARS OF COLLECTING:
PRICES, TRENDS, EVENTS, AND SURPRISES

It all began as an idea more than 50 years ago. When Ralph and I got married, we moved into an apartment and, of course, needed furniture. Our budget allowed for the "Colonial Williamsburg look," the stylish choice in the 1950s. No one who could afford the reproductions bought "used" antique or vintage things but I was told we might find some interesting lamps or ashtrays (yes ashtrays—all our friends smoked). So we went to house sales and found lamps, 18th-century dishes that could be ashtrays, a few Japanese prints, and some old figurines to put in our breakfront.

We asked about the marks on the dishes but no one knew much, just "crossed lines are Meissen" and a "beehive" is German. Library books on old porcelains were almost all written by museum curators as part of the study of art in a single country. Ralph started listing the marks by shape in a notebook with a short description.

Ralph didn't tell me that he sent his ten-page list to a publisher as an idea for a book. Six months later, he got a letter saying they wanted to publish it and offered an advance that equaled six weeks of Ralph's salary. We spent the next year writing the first general mark book for collectors. It was just like doing my high school "source theme." We listed just the basics on a card. That book, *Dictionary of Marks Pottery and Porcelain*, was a best seller, reprinted 42 times. It was followed by a second marks book in 1986 with more modern marks, and all the marks are now available on Kovels.com through a digital subscription.

We had become serious collectors, going to house sales and the few antiques shops and one antiques show in our city each year. Next came a newspaper column, soon nationally syndicated, and more books. It was all a weekend job. We had two children. Ralph was a salesman, and I taught math part-time. Looking back I realize our lack of art training may have been the reason we could write about the antiques and collectibles ignored by museums and art history classes. We were doing the research for amateurs.

In 1967, we realized that new thing called a computer could sort our price information. If we learned how to type it on "punch cards," we could write a price book in six to eight months and it would be the first up-to-date listing of prices gathered from sales in all parts of the country. There were problems, including how to code it so it would be sorted alphabetically. We selected categories—first word, furniture, doll, silver, etc.—to organize items. Entries would be one line long. Fifty thousand cards were punched and hand-sorted by our staff. For the first computer run, each line was printed with a number that was needed in case there was an error. What we didn't expect was a second proofreading of the 50,000 entries and that each error required three new cards—one with the number on the print out, one with the corrected price listing, and one with the number sending the entry where it should go. Computer runs were usually printed on lined paper used for statistics and accounting but we used the back of the paper, which was plain white. Those sheets were photographed for the pages so the price book looked like it was typewritten in a simple all-caps font. It was an instant bestseller and there was a huge mail order demand.

We have improved the book with the help of technology and readers' suggestions. Changes have included adding black and white and then color pictures, several type styles, paragraphs for each new category, a computer-generated index, special center section reports, lists of record prices, a report on the ups and downs and influences on prices, an e-book, and even a printed ruler to use to check size at a sale. We also now have more than one million of the books' entries listed online, and dated so you can tell if your antique has gone up or down in value.

Fifty years of analyzing the market and talking to experts gives me a unique view of the good and bad of collecting. So, in our usual brief style, we have created a timeline of important or just interesting events.

EVENTS THAT INFLUENCED
THE ANTIQUES AND COLLECTIBLES MARKET,
1950–2017

1922: The magazine *Antiques* started. (Its name was changed to *The Magazine Antiques* in 1928.) It was written for knowledgeable art collectors as well as museum curators. It was the first source for information we went to in 1953 when we started going to house sales, and the articles were part of the research for our first book. *The Magazine Antiques* is 95 years old this year.

1953: *Kovels' Dictionary of Marks Pottery & Porcelain 1650 to 1850.* In 1952, Ralph began to make a list of marks he saw on porcelains we admired at house sales. There was no single book on marks, just a few scholarly books about ceramics, usually from a single country. He wrote about 10 pages, sorting the marks by shape. A local antiquarian book dealer we knew looked at his work and sent it to Crown Publishing, a young company that published Seymour Wyler's book of silver marks. Six months later, Crown asked us to write our own book. It was published the next year and we had become "experts." That book, *Dictionary of Marks—Pottery and Porcelain*, had 42 printings. We wrote a similar book with more recent marks in 1986. The information and marks from both books and more are available online exclusively at Kovels.com.

1954: Our weekly newspaper column, "Know Your Antiques," begins. We were experts—that's what the book reviewers said—so we did some research and wrote a sample question-and-answer column and showed it to the *Cleveland Press*, Cleveland's evening newspaper. Ralph sold it to the newspaper for a six-week trial and we wrote for the *Press* until it closed in 1982. The column, "Know Your Antiques," ran in Cleveland's morning paper, *The Plain Dealer*, from 1982 until 2015. It was nationally syndicated in 1955 and appears in many newspapers and online sites today.

1955: Tiffany lamps were not in style and were not yet collected. We saw

1922
The magazine *Antiques* is published; its name was changed to *The Magazine Antiques* in 1928

1953
Dictionary of Marks-Pottery & Porcelain 1650 to 1850 is published

1954
"Know Your Antiques," a weekly syndicated newspaper column, begins

Antiques magazine cover from 1922. In 1928, the name became *The Magazine Antiques*

Kovels' first book, *Dictionary of Marks–Pottery and Porcelain*, 1953

a group of the glass mosaic shades displayed upside down at a Salvation Army store. Each was $25 and we wondered what we could do with one. We never thought of adding a base and restoring it as a Tiffany lamp. Record prices for a Tiffany Wisteria lamp since then are: 1974, $33,000; 1978, $48,000; 1979, $120,000; 1998, $420,500; 2001, $324,800; 2014, $1,560,000.

1959: Collectors dig bottles. Bottles, stamps, and coins were the first organized collecting interests in the United States. After the war, there was a housing boom. Some of the returned service men who had seen antiques in Europe and Japan became interested in the furniture, glass, and ceramics used in the United States. A group of California men started digging for bottles, and, in 1959, they started a club that eventually became the Federation of Historical Bottle Collectors (FOHBC), now an organization with more than 70 member clubs and thousands of individual members. Bottle collecting had become such a popular hobby we wrote a separate price book, *Kovels' Bottle Price List*, every other year from 1971 to 2006.

1960s: Outsider art, art produced by self-taught artists who are not part of the art establishment, is a new collectible getting noticed, but not yet in antiques shows or publications.

1960s: Lithographed tin sand pails made from 1930 to 1950 with color decorations of kewpies, Disney characters, and children were a new and inexpensive collectible. They became more popular and in 2017, a rare pail could cost $800.

1961: *The Mike Douglas Show*. Ralph and Terry were on the television show with Zsa Zsa Gábor who told us, "Daahlings, I only collect jewelry."

Unpopular in 1955, Tiffany Wisteria lamp, c.1906, sold for over $1 million in 2014

1955
Tiffany lamps were not in style and were not yet collected

1959
Bottle collecting becomes popular

Kovels' living room in the 1950s. Just a few antiques, all from house sales

1961: The White House restoration. Formal American antiques of the 18th and early 19th centuries went up in price because of the White House restoration. Articles in newspapers and a televised White House tour introduced collectors to antiques that had been well-known only by families that had inherited pieces. Jackie Kennedy, the president's wife, organized groups of experts to select furnishings, colors, rugs, and textiles. The White House was redecorated with historic furniture, copies of historic wallpaper, carpets, paintings, and period dishes and bronzes mostly from the Federal period. Much of it was donated. But the restoration was "too French" according to later experts, and there were gradual corrections, so much of the 1961 decorating has since been changed. The historic look was soon being copied with furnishings that were antiques or good copies and the prices went up.

Lithographed tin sand pail with Disney characters popular in the 1960s

1962: Avon bottles suddenly became a hot part of the bottle world. New bottles full of cosmetics were sold by the "Avon Lady." Empty bottles at flea markets and garage sales were in demand. Avon was the name used after 1939 by the California Perfume Company (CPC), started in 1892 in New York. It grew into a large company with more than 10,000 "depot managers" (sales ladies) by 1902. CPC started using the name "Avon" in 1928 and officially changed the name in 1939. Modern Avon bottle collecting began by 1948. One of the first figural Avon bottles, a bay rum jug, was made in 1962. In 1969 a group of collectors formed the first Avon bottle club in California. The first ceramic figurines were introduced in 1973, and collectors were buying empty bottles and creating a price explosion. In the 1970s to 1980s, glass figural bottles that held men's products went up in price. The bottles became so profitable there was a theft of empty Avon bottles at the bottle factory and the new bottles were sold at flea markets before any filled examples were advertised. Prices began to drop. The Avon

1960s

Outsider art, a new collectible, gets noticed

•

Lithographed tin sand pails made from 1930 to 1950 became new and inexpensive collectible

> # "Never walk away from something you love. Don't worry about where you'll put it or how you'll get it home."
> Terry Kovel

A vintage figural Avon bottle. Collecting began seriously around 1965

bottles went from craze in 1965 to crash in 1980. Today empty Avon bottles are sold for less than $25 and are no longer listed in their own category in our price book.

1965: THE BIGGEST SCAM of the century: FAKE BELT BUCKLES. Men's belts with large brass belt buckles were in style, and in about 1965, barrels of buckles were found in England. They had raised graphics showing Wells Fargo Company and scenes of the American West. Marked on the backs was "Tiffany Co. New York." Thousands of the buckles in over 75 different designs were offered for sale. They became a fad, and prices gradually went up. Experts followed clues: the maker's mark, source of the images, shapes of the wires on the back that held the belt, and more. In 1970, a book called *Tiffany & Gaylord Express & Exhibition Belt Plates*, seemed to prove that they were, in fact, antiques. The book was a fake, too. This was the biggest swindle of the past 50 years and many reporters claimed that millions of dollars were made by still-unknown people. Even though many cried fake, the buckles continued to sell. A 1984 ad offered a variety of designs for $25 each plus tax and 40 cents postage. A charitable auction got $700 for one buckle. Our files go back to 1971, and we even visited the book publisher who printed the fake book. (They normally printed school yearbooks.) We still get questions regarding the buckles about once a month. Some are from the 1960s to 1980s that are part of an estate. Others are brand new fakes of the fakes that are still found at flea markets, now priced at about $10 each.

Fake Wells Fargo belt buckle, c. 1965

1961
Ralph and Terry appear on *The Mike Douglas* television show

•

The White House restoration: Formal American antiques of the 18th and early 19th centuries went up in price

1962
Avon bottles become hot

1965
The biggest scam of the century: FAKE BELT BUCKLES

•

Terry and Ralph visited Picasso pottery in Vallauris, France

1965: While on a family summer trip in Cannes, France, we went to the Madoura ceramics workshop in Vallauris to see the pottery designed by Picasso. We could only afford a $25 plate with a picture of a vase of flowers and years later gave it to our daughter, Kim, as an anniversary gift. The auction price in 2017 was $2,000. We also visited the Léger Museum but couldn't afford a black and white print that we wanted that would be worth thousands today.

1967: *Know Your Antiques* was published. This was a best-selling guide to evaluating, buying, and caring for almost any antique. It included pottery, porcelain, silver, pewter, country and formal furniture, pressed and cut glass, prints, bottles, autographs, books, and much more. Revised versions were published as *Kovels' Know Your Antiques* in 1973, 1981, and 1993.

1967: Fruit jars begin to interest bottle collectors. Alice Creswick wrote the three definitive books on fruit jars, marks, shapes, and history. They are the first easy-to-understand books that priced and identified machine-made fruit jars (canning jars). The jars could be found in most basements, often filled with the peaches, pickles, or jellies made at home. Since they were easy to find and sold for very low prices, this became a new category for beginning collectors. Prices of fruit jars and many kinds of bottles rose slowly for the next 20 years but didn't reach the prices of the early blown flasks.

Pottery plate designed by Pablo Picasso, purchased by Terry and Ralph in Vallauris, France, 1965

1967: The Cleveland public television station, WVIZ, had its first fundraising auction one year after the first public television auction in Boston. The station raised $62,000. Ralph and I started appraising and selling the donated antiques in 1968, and I have worked as an auctioneer for almost every auction, including the 50th in 2017 that raised $418,000. Some of the modern items we sold are much higher priced today. We auctioned paintings by Viktor Schreckengost, Caroline Williams, Joseph O'Sickey, and Edward Henry Potthast (paintings of his beach scenes and his nephew's still life paintings); pottery by Pablo Picasso, George Ohr, Claude Conover, and Lisa McVey; and many pieces from the Cowan

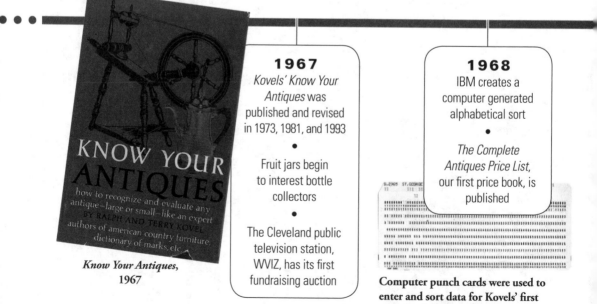

Know Your Antiques, 1967

1967
Kovels' Know Your Antiques was published and revised in 1973, 1981, and 1993

•

Fruit jars begin to interest bottle collectors

•

The Cleveland public television station, WVIZ, has its first fundraising auction

1968
IBM creates a computer generated alphabetical sort

•

The Complete Antiques Price List, our first price book, is published

Computer punch cards were used to enter and sort data for Kovels' first price book in 1968

Fruit jars became popular collectibles in 1967

and Rookwood potteries. We also sold Martele silver by Gorham, metal bookends and more by Chase Brass & Copper Company, and furniture by John Henry Belter, George and Christian Herter, Philip and Kelvin LaVerne, Charles and Ray Eames, and Gustav Stickley, long before they were high-priced. We have auctioned the antiques for the station for 49 years.

1968: IBM alphabetical sort available. We used the new program and Kovels' price book was sorted on a computer using punch cards. The machine filled a room the size of a basketball court. The space was cold to keep the computer happy, but we wore heavy sweaters.

1968: *The Complete Antiques Price List.* This was our first price book. It was hard cover, 436 pages of prices, and had no pictures. It was a bestseller and the first of our 50 antiques price guides.

1969: The Federation of Historical Bottle Collectors is formed.

1969-1972: The first national television show about antiques airs in America. Our PBS series, *Know Your Antiques*, was on television in 1970. It was broadcast in about 100 cities during the next few years and then was put in the public television library. It was recorded on film with no editing. The show won an Emmy for Outstanding Program Achievement. We took more than 800 items to the studio to use as part of the set or to show in the twenty-six 30-minute episodes. It was all ad lib, but there were cards with dates and names hidden in the props so we could sneak looks to check facts. On one show, we almost set the studio on fire with a political torch. In another segment, we got one information card behind and had to explain why we did not agree with the name showing in the corner of the coverlet on the screen. And the funniest moment was at the end of one show which ended, like all the others,

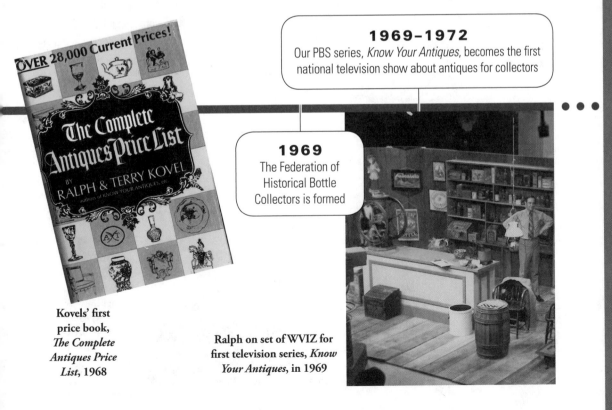

1969–1972
Our PBS series, *Know Your Antiques*, becomes the first national television show about antiques for collectors

1969
The Federation of Historical Bottle Collectors is formed

Kovels' first price book, *The Complete Antiques Price List*, 1968

Ralph on set of WVIZ for first television series, *Know Your Antiques*, in 1969

with us drinking tea and discussing what we would write about the show to our son in college. Except when I poured the tea, the camera close-up showed a floating dead fly. There were no retakes on film, so we said something silly about my bad cooking.

1970s: Asian countries started to mass produce inexpensive watches, disrupting the Swiss watch auction sales. Swiss watchmakers created clever, inexpensive watches with unusual designs that attracted young buyers who wanted a new look, not necessarily great quality. In 1983, the first collection of Swatch watches started a craze. Collectors bought new models, formed a club, and enjoyed worldwide publicity and events. Several large books were written with pictures and history. A complete collection of books and watches auctioned for $1.33 million in 2015. Out-of-production watches sold for higher and higher prices until the craze slowed by the late 1990s and most Swatch watches went back to selling for low prices. They are still made and still collected.

1970: Shaker furniture was featured in the U.S. exhibit at Expo 70, the 1970 World's Fair in Japan. The undecorated furniture with light woods and uncluttered shapes blended with the 1950s look in America that was still popular. Authentic Shaker pieces are rare and some museums and wealthy clients had bidding wars for the best Shaker pieces made and used by the Shaker communities. The chairs made to sell to the public ranged in price to $700 to $900. Pieces used by or built into Shaker community buildings still sell for thousands of dollars.

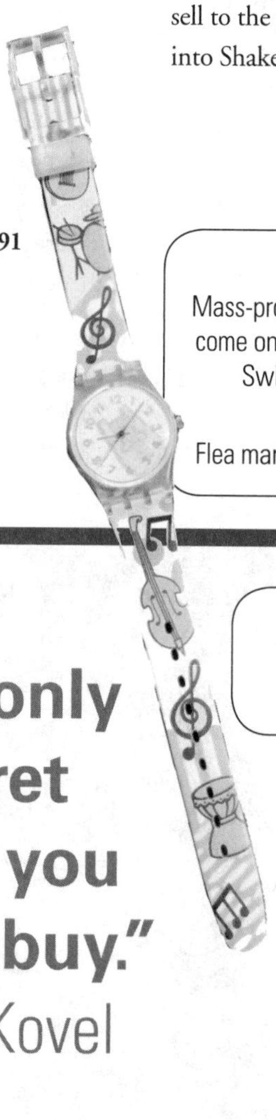

Swatch watch, 1991

1970s
Mass-produced inexpensive watches come onto the market disrupting the Swiss watch auction sales

•

Flea market shopping is mainstream

1971–2006
Bottle collecting is popular. Every other year from 1971 to 2006, a new *Kovels' Bottle Price List* was published

1970
Shaker furniture in demand

1971
Depression glass gets more popular

"You only regret what you don't buy."
Ralph Kovel

Ralph and Terry Kovel's Emmy award for "Outstanding program achievement, *Know Your Antiques* series WVIZ," 1970–71

1970s: Flea market shopping becomes mainstream. There were many new large markets, some with more than 100 dealers. Newspapers were listing sales and special events. All types of antiques were selling quickly and the dealers were making money. Salts and peppers, Depression dinnerware, and oddities priced below $50 could be found at garage sales and sold in malls. They did not, however, sell quickly at shops.

1971: Depression glass was popular enough to be listed in the 4th edition of the Kovels' price book.

1971: Interest and prices in bottle collecting rises. Every other year from 1971 to 2006, we published a new *Kovels' Bottle Price List*, which included more than 10,000 prices. There were fewer than a hundred bottle prices in our main price book and many bottle collectors wanted more.

1974 to present: We started a print newsletter, *Kovels on Antiques & Collectibles*, in 1974, then added a digital edition in 1996. Both subscription publications are still available to paid subscribers.

Example of a Shaker chair, the kind seen at 1970s World's Fair in Japan

1974: *Kovels' Collector's Guide to American Art Pottery.* Kovels' art pottery book was published at Christmastime, along with another major book about American art pottery. We wrote for the collector with pictures, marks, lists of names and short histories of the potters. The other book, *Art Pottery of the United States* by Paul Evans, was written for experts with information about potting techniques, types of glazes, and historic design influences. Now everyone could learn about the pottery made after 1876 that had been relatively unknown. Collectors started with Rookwood

The first issue of Kovels' print newsletter, *Ralph & Terry Kovel On Antiques*, September 1974

1974–present
Kovels on Antiques & Collectibles printed newsletter began. In 1996 a digital edition was added

1974
Kovels' Collectors' Guide to American Art Pottery is published

•

Kovels' Collectors Guide to Limited Editions is written during the height of the limited-edition craze

The Kovels' Collector's Guide to American Art Pottery, 1974. Many pieces are from Kovels' collection. A 1901 Rookwood vase picturing Pablino Diaz, a Kiowa, is on the cover.

and Roseville and other Ohio and East Coast art potteries. Prices went up. By the 1980s, art pottery reproductions were being made and collectors were becoming cautious buyers. The books made art pottery an important collectible and prices still continue to rise.

1974: New name: *The Kovels' Complete Antiques Price List.* We became important enough to have our name included in the title of the book.

1974: A new book, *Kovels' Collectors Guide to Limited Editions,* was written during the height of the limited-edition craze. We discovered that bookstores thought it was about limited-edition books, so the next edition in 1978 was called *Kovels' Price Guide for Collector Plates, Figurines, Paperweights, and Other Limited-Edition Items.* The limited-edition craze was over by the 1980s.

1975: The modern buyer's premium was introduced at 10 percent by Christie's and Sotheby's in London in September 1975. It started in the United States by 1982 when a few auction houses added a three-percent premium. Skinner Auctioneers and Appraisers in Boston had a 10 percent premium. It kept rising and now, in 2017, the buyer's premium is sometimes as high as 25 percent with other added charges for credit cards, checks, phone or online bidding, and, of course, sales tax.

1975: Gardner bottle sale—the bottle sale that set the prices. We were there—at the bottle auction of the century. Charles Gardner collected bottles for 46 years and had the best of the best. His first bottle was a cornucopia flask made in Coventry, Connecticut. The collection had American-made whiskeys, bitters, inks, perfumes, medicines, flasks, food, and a few English bottles. Gardner owned many rarities, some estimated at more than $10,000. We heard he was offered about $750,000 for the collection by Owens Illinois Inc., the glass company, but he chose to sell at auction. The complete auction brought $1,180,000. The highest priced bottle set the world record for an American bottle, $21,000. It was for a cobalt blue Columbia pint flask, GI-119. Bottle prices had been going up since 1970. We were already bottle collectors when in 1971 we wrote the first Kovels' bottle price guide. We wanted to record the prices from the Gardner auction in our 1976 edition.

Kovels looking over a collection of beer steins, 1974

1975
A 10% buyer's premium was introduced by Christie's and Sotheby's

•

The Gardner bottle sale changes the market

1976
Metropolitan Museum shows furniture and objects in the exhibit "American Masterpieces"

There were only 500 seats at the Gardner bottle auction and a $100 entrance fee, refundable against purchases. The parking lot was full of expensive cars with license plates like "inks," "flsks," and "bttle" at a time when you needed political connections and money for those kind of special vanity plates. Wealthy bottle collectors were there, bidding for themselves. (Art and furniture auctions usually saw collectors with an expert from the museum world to advise them on quality and price.) We had a catalog, recorded prices, and talked to many collectors and dealers. Almost everything in the 4,000-bottle auction was beyond our budget, but we had the $200 entrance fee money to spend, and we used it to by a bottle. Each bottle was sold with a "from the Gardner collection" sticker and when the bottle is sold again, the sticker will add to the price. The $20 catalog is a treasure and our bottle is now worth about four times what we paid. We wrote about the sale in a Kovels' 1975 newsletter. The sale was reported in national news media because of the celebrity bidders and high prices. Bottles had become a respected collectible, now noticed by museum and art experts and others who had ignored our world of "collectibles"—historically important, but not made to hang on a wall like a painting. Bottle prices went down a few years after the publicized auction, but went up again in 1983 when the important Blaske collection of flasks was auctioned for record prices.

A honey bottle and auction label from the Gardner bottle sale, 1975

1979–2006
The Kovels write a question-and-answer column for *House Beautiful* magazine

1977
Ralph and Terry featured in *Cleveland Magazine,* a part of "The 77 most Interesting People in Town"

1979
The British television series *Antiques Roadshow* begins

Ralph and Terry in
***Cleveland Magazine,* 1978**

1976: The Metropolitan Museum of Art in New York City had a major exhibition, "A Bicentennial Treasury: American Masterpieces from the Metropolitan." The show featured outstanding antiques created in America between 1795 and the early 20th century and was the first exhibition that displayed only American work. Included were paintings, sculpture, prints, and photographs, as well as furniture, silver, glass, and textiles. Once again, publicity and catalogs for the show created a demand for the "look" of the Philadelphia Centennial of 1876. Victorian furniture by John Jeliff, George Hunzinger, Pottier & Stymus, and John Henry Belter became fashionable again, particularly in the South in areas with large homes and high ceilings. Collectors looked for elaborate silver services, Tiffany iridescent glass vases, lamps with leaded glass shades, and stained-glass windows. American art pottery from Rookwood, Newcomb, Grueby and others went up in price. Antique silver tea sets were put in dining rooms. Other collectors saved small figurines, and fancy dinnerware. Still popular were "smalls," 18th century English porcelains, Victorian jewelry, Japanese netsukes, and 19th century dolls, toys, and mechanical banks. Advertising signs and packaging were still found at house sales and flea markets but were rising in price. Publicity and the catalogs for the show presented newly discovered information. Prices for all types of American antiques went up, especially furniture. Replicas of textiles, silver pieces, furniture, and ceramics were used to decorate the average house if authentic antiques were too expensive. Years later, many of these replicas were marketed by uninformed heirs as valuable 18th-century pieces. Experts today can spot marks from new tools, nails that are machine and not handmade, faked patina, and design flaws that tell a piece is an inexpensive 1930s replica, not a very valuable 1750s original even though it "looks just like the one on the *Antiques Roadshow*."

1978: *Kovels' Price Guide for Collector Plates, Figurines, Paperweights, and Other Limited Edition Items*, is the new name for the revised 1974 book. Limited editions are still going up in price.

1978: A major bottle book, *American Bottles & Flasks* by Helen McKearin and Kenneth M. Wilson, is published. In 1941 and 1950, Helen published two books on bottles with her father, George S. McKearin. Few books were available for serious collectors and these reference books identified American glass and bottles. Their identification system (McKearin numbers) is still used today.

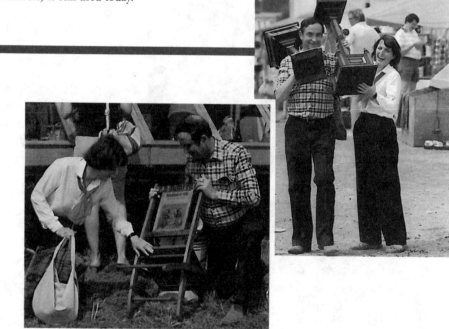

1979: *Antiques Roadshow,* the British television series, started Series 1 with eight shows or "editions" in February 1979. It is still a top-rated production in its 39th year.

1979–2000: The Kovels write a question-and-answer column for *House Beautiful* magazine. Many questions are mailed in but only about 20 percent of the items discussed were more than 100 years old.

1980+: Our book name is changed again, *The Kovels' Antiques Price List.*

1980: This was the year of the Covill ink bottle sale. William Covill wrote the first major book about antique glass inkwells in 1971, so the sale of his collection in 1980 brought high prices that lingered for a few years. But ballpoint pens made fountain pens and ink bottles less interesting, and ink bottle prices have leveled off.

Examples of flasks described in *American Bottles & Flasks and Their Ancestry,* by Helen McKearin and Kenneth Wilson, 1978

1980: The book *American Country Style* by Mary Emmerling made peeling paint and rag rugs stylish again. She created a new "country" style that changed what people were buying to furnish their houses. She featured new items that suggested colonial houses and furnishings. Antiques, and old primitive furniture, started going up in price. Many pieces were painted—good for decorating, bad for future value as an antique. Some of the items in her book were new designs that looked old, like the toy rabbit on the cover.

1980, 1983, 1988, 1991, 1995 1998, 2001, 2004: We wrote another series of price books titled *Kovels' Depression Glass & American Dinnerware Price List* from 1980 to 2004. We had written about Depression glass in the *Kovels' Antiques & Collectibles Price List.* But as collectors bought more glass, prices went up and copies of the glass were made. We noticed a parallel interest in American dinnerware.

These pictures were featured in a *Smithsonian* magazine article on the Kovels, "Life of Americana's Collectors-in-Chief is a Bowl of Treasures," November, 1980. The cameraman filming a Kovel television show caught these views of the couple.

You got "good" dishes like Wedgwood and another set of "everyday" dishes free as a premium or in the dime store. The dishes were used in the Depression but never called "Depression dishes." So, we wrote another series of price books titled *Kovels Depression Glass & American Dinnerware Price List from 1980 to 2004.* We continued the series without the word "American" in the title because foreign dishes were being used for some premiums. Autumn Leaf dinner plates cost $4.25 to $10 in the 1980 price list and $25 in 2004. Prices went up a little each year until about 2005 when they began to decrease as styles changed. Today the mix-and-match style of table setting makes prices even lower and formal dinner sets from important makers like Spode, Haviland, and Franciscan are difficult to sell at any price. A dinner set with five-piece place settings for 12 and matching serving platters, bowls, sugar and creamer, and gravy boat sells for about $150 to $250 online. But the added cost of shipping is part of the reason for the low price.

1980, 1984: *Kovels' Illustrated Price Guide to Royal Doulton* listed figurines, character jugs and some series dishes. Prices were rising each year but in the 1990s, prices started to drop. There were fewer collectors, and Royal Doulton is hard to sell today.

1980: Ralph and Terry Kovel won the Louis S. Peirce Award for Outstanding Community Service from Cleveland's WVIZ-TV public television station.

1981: *Know Your Antiques* begets *Kovels' Know Your Collectibles.* "Collectibles" was a term that was not even used in 1967, when *Know Your Antiques* was first written. It means anything that was collected that wasn't 100 years old. The book included marks with identification and histories, factory dates and pictures.

Royal Doulton Jester figurine, popular collectible in the 1980s

---

1980, 1984
Kovels' Illustrated Price Guide to Royal Doulton is published, the first of two editions

1980–2004
Kovels' Depression Glass & American Dinnerware Price List is published, the first of eight editions

1980
Our book name is changed again, to *The Kovels' Antiques Price List*

•

The Covill ink bottle sale takes place

•

The book *American Country Style* by Mary Emmerling made peeling paint and rag rugs stylish again

•

Carlyn Ring's book, *For Bitters Only*, pictures and identifies hundreds of bitters bottles

1981
Kovels' Know Your Collectibles is published

Kovels' Know Your Collectibles, 1981

1982: *Kovels' Complete Antiques Price List* is changed again to *The Kovels' Antiques & Collectibles Price List* since it includes so many items that are less than 100 years old are now known as collectibles.

1982: Martha Stewart's first book, *Entertaining*, is published. It led to her career in books and television that influenced public views of decorating, collecting, and do-it-yourself projects. She was a serious, knowledgeable collector and often discussed antiques on her television show. We appeared on a number of her shows that were produced at her studio in Connecticut starting in 1984. There was a food segment on each show,

In 1982 Martha Stewart's favorite Jadeite (plates pictured) became a "must have." Her decorating and collecting suggestions made her favorite antiques more popular and expensive.

cooked in her kitchens, and extra dishes were served in the cafeteria. It was the best food we had at any television appearance. Martha Stewart's decorating and collecting suggestions made her favorite antiques popular and more expensive. Her collection of Jadeite, a milky green glassware given away in oatmeal boxes or sold in hardware stores, was inexpensive, a few dollars for a dinner plate. By 2010, a $5 ball jug could sell for a few thousand dollars. Reproductions were made of the molded glass that were very difficult to recognize. By 2017, Jadeite is again low-priced, under $10 for common pieces.

1982: *The Kovels' Book of Antique Labels,* a very, very big picture book with full-size pictures of antique labels from the 1850s to the 1980s, is published. Each label is printed on one side of the page so it can be cut out, framed or used for decoupage.

1983: eBay starts selling many inexpensive collectibles—and a lie spreads. An interesting story about why a new online company was created is important. It gets free publicity. So a smart woman who worked for eBay got attention with a made-up story about the founder, Pierre Omidyar, that was quoted for years. Pierre's fiancé, Pam, collected Pez candy dispensers—cute, inexpensive, and there

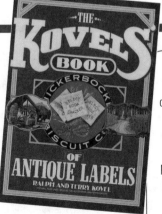

The Kovels' Book of Antique Labels, 1982. This large book (15 by 11 ¼ inches) had labels printed on one side of the page so they can be cut out, framed or used for decoupage.

1982
The book's name is changed again, to *The Kovels' Antiques & Collectibles Price List*

•

Martha Stewart's first book, *Entertaining,* is published

•

The Kovels' Book of Antique Labels with full-size labels is published

1983
eBay is launched, selling many inexpensive collectibles

•

The Blaske flasks sale pushed bottle prices way up

were new ones to buy at stores each month as well as old ones to look for that were going up in price. So the story was, eBay was created to buy and sell Pez dispensers. It wasn't until 2003 that the real story got out. It actually began as a side hobby for Omidayr and the first item sold was a broken laser pointer. eBay changed the way collectibles were bought and sold. Today, it makes more money on electronics than antiques.

1983: The Blaske collection. The Blaske flasks sale pushed bottle prices way up. Edmund and Jayne Blaske started collecting bottles in 1959. When they downsized, they decided not to give them to a museum, but to sell them so others could have the chance to own these special bottles. In 1983, Skinner Inc. had their sale in two well-thought-out auctions. In the first sale, the flasks were offered one at a time in the order of the numbers used in the McKearin book, the final word in naming and describing flasks and other bottles. All 1,114 flasks are pictured in black and white in the hardcover catalog. The second sale had a small paper-covered catalog with only 95 lots of flasks. Almost all the items sold for less than $300. Other bottles were listed in groups so a collector of inks or barber bottles didn't have to sit through the entire sale. The first sale brought $1,083,604 (including a 10 percent premium). Three record prices were set. The first was $35,200 (with premium) for a "GI-118 (McKearin number) Columbia eagle portrait flask, cobalt blue half-pint bottle from Pennsylvania c.1820–1830." It takes that entire description to be sure it isn't a similar, more common Columbia flask. Once again, the general public heard that bottles were good investments and that they were the "glue" for a group of collectors who met at sales and club meetings, had fun and interesting discussions, and became life-long friends. So there were more new collectors, more buyers, and prices for great bottles went up.

1985: Look carefully, because we dropped the word "The" in the title of the price book to make it easier to find in a library. It was changed to *Kovels' Antiques & Collectibles Price Guide.*

eBay starts in 1983, supposedly to buy and sell PEZ dispensers. Wonder Woman Pez candy dispenser, c. 1985.

Promotional pictures of Ralph and Terry for our nationally syndicated newspaper column, 1980s

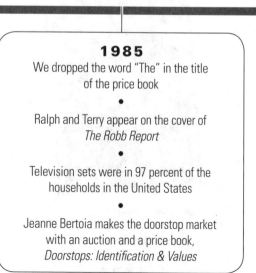

1985

We dropped the word "The" in the title of the price book

•

Ralph and Terry appear on the cover of *The Robb Report*

•

Television sets were in 97 percent of the households in the United States

•

Jeanne Bertoia makes the doorstop market with an auction and a price book, *Doorstops: Identification & Values*

1985: Television sets were in 97 percent of the households in the United States. Cable television had more than 170 cable networks offering programs. Many channels and networks failed between 1950 and the 1980s but gradually, new television shows were created about antiques and collectibles and it encouraged more people to search flea markets, shows, and shops, many planning to "invest" in antiques.

1985: Jeanne Bertoia creates the doorstop market with an auction and a price book, *Doorstops: Identification & Values.* Hundreds of reproductions were made and fakes were selling at flea markets for about $20 each. She sold her collection in three sales in 2013, 2015, and 2016 for record prices. The top price was $29,500 for a Halloween Girl doorstop made by Littco.

A cast iron rabbit doorstop. Collecting became popular in the late 1980s.

1986: Collectibles news is in a popular financial investment column. Sylvia Porter writes in her syndicated financial newspaper column that art pottery is a good investment. The only other collectible we have seen on financial "best" lists has been antique French paperweights.

1986: *The Oprah Winfrey Show* started. We did a segment with her before she had the national show. She was a reporter and she brought a floor lamp and some other antiques she owned so we could tell her more about them. Oprah went on to be a serious collector who bought Shaker furniture and other antiques. We noticed our price book on a table in one of her press pictures.

1986, 2005: *Kovels' Advertising Collectibles Price List* is another new book. Advertising is hot and pieces in good condition sell for thousands. A sign like our Grapenuts sign, for which we paid $25 in the 1950s, if in excellent condition can sell today for $7,000 to $8,000.

1986–2005
Kovels' Advertising Collectibles Price List is published, two editions.

1986
Financial writer Sylvia Porter includes art pottery as good investment

•

The Oprah Winfrey Show begins airing

•

Ralph and Terry appear on the cover feature for *The Denver Post*

1987
Kovels on Collecting, our short filler series airs

Above, the Kovels at home with their Handel lamp, November, 1987, and below, Ralph and Terry, May, 1987

1987: Our show, *Kovels On Collecting*, begins being aired as a short filler segment for other commercial television shows.

1988: The Strangest Sale. The Perelman Antique Toy Museum opened in Philadelphia in 1969. Perelman bought a building, restored it, and opened the private museum to those willing to pay $2 to see his collection of 3,000 banks and toys. In 1988, two men with guns entered the museum, tied up the curator, and stole about 100 antique marbles. They tried to take more but the bulletproof glass cases stopped them. The museum closed and the robbery was kept out of the papers. Four days later, Perelman shook hands with antiques dealer Alexander Acevedo who had offered to buy the collection before, and the building and collection were sold. The collection was inventoried and appraised and on September 16, there was a private sale for 40 invited collectors and dealers. Each had to buy $50,000 worth of toys or banks or get nothing. The preview of the three floors was at 8 o'clock. At 9:30, each buyer or pair was given a price list and one colored pen to use to sign the price tag and buy the item. At 10 o'clock, Acevedo shot a cap gun and everyone ran to sign tags. The sale is still called "The Great Grab." Leftovers were sold at two later sales. The highest prices for banks were $125,000 for the Darkie Football Freedom bank, and $150,000

for the Freedman bank. Lowest price bank was "Elephant Swinging Trunk," small, $50. The banks' sale brought $3.6 million. Other toys in the Perelman collection were sold later. Total price for Perelman's collection: $9 million.

1988: Advertising is finally selling at shows and auctions and *Kovels' Antiques and Collectibles Price List* added a section for prices. But car-related ads still are listed in "auto" and ads are also listed in other categories.

Cast iron mechanical bank, Jonah and the Whale, the type sold at the famous Perelman Antique Toy Museum sale, 1988

1988, 1989
The Occupied Japan Club is formed

1989–1992
The Discovery Channel's series, *Collector's Journal with Ralph and Terry Kovel* airs

1988
The Perelman Antique Toy Museum sale

•

Advertising is finally selling at shows and auctions

•

The International Perfume Bottle Association is created

The antiques auctioneers at WVIZ/ PBS TV Auction, 1989

1988–1989: The Occupied Japan Club was formed. Members collected and studied pottery and other decorative arts that used the mark "Made in Occupied Japan." After World War II, from 1947 to 1952, American troops occupied Japan to keep peace. The "OJ" mark was used on things exported to the United States.

Salt and pepper shakers marked Occupied Japan. The Occupied Japan Club was founded in 1988.

1988: The International Perfume Bottle Association was created and perfume bottles became expensive—and some still are. The record price is probably $178,222 for a diamond-encrusted bottle by diamond cutters Asprey and Gabi Tolkowsky sold at Christie's in 2003. The cap is a 10.36-carat diamond. A record price for a commercial bottle was the $67,650 paid for "J'Appartiens a Miss Dior" ("I belong to Miss Dior"), created to celebrate Miss Dior perfume's 10-year anniversary in 2015.

The International Perfume Bottle Association was created in 1988. This is the Miss Dior perfume 10th anniversary bottle, 1957.

1989: Barbie sale in Washington, D.C. I have strange memories of the first important Barbie doll sale. Since she was introduced in 1959, the doll and her accessories, houses, clothing, boats, a camper, airplane, swimming pool, and offices have been popular collectibles. Old, rare, and condition dictates the prices even today. We were at the sale, with our television crew, as reporters. Two larger-than-life Barbies were at the entrance. They were display models used at toy shows and special events. I didn't bid because I couldn't imagine how a giant Barbie would be comfortable in a room with our 18th-century furniture. Most of the registered bidders were men who were examining the dolls with magnifying glasses to be sure they were in perfect condition with all of the original hair. (Cut hair was a major flaw that lowered price. I still check the haircuts on dolls.) Bidding was fast, mostly by bidders in the room. The only price I remember is $60

1990, 1991
Kovel's Page-A-Day Collectibles Calendar is sold in bookstores and gift shops

1989
The first important Barbie sale.

1990
Fantasy banks made from old-style cans with photocopies of vintage labels are flooding flea markets

Kovels' Antiques & Collectibles desktop calendar, 1991

for Barbie No. 1's girdle. Her shoes were almost as expensive. I heard Barbie's price went down for a few years after the sale, then steadily rose again. Barbie No. 1 was $8,800 in 1997, $13,500 in 1999, and probably the most expensive Barbie No. 1 ever auctioned, a blonde in the black striped bathing suit, sold for $27,450 in 2003. In the last 15 years, the common dolls have been moderately priced because of the supply, but accessories, especially those still in original packaging, are going up.

1989 + 1992: The Discovery Channel's *Collectors Journal with Ralph and Terry Kovel*, twenty-six 30-minute shows, ran from 1989 to 1992. The Kovels' show on national television created interest in unusual collectibles and low-priced things like Halloween decorations or costume jewelry. The opening of the series was hosted by Malcolm Forbes, the multimillionaire publisher of *Forbes* magazine, at his gallery. It was filled with his collections of Russian Fabergé eggs, toy boats and soldiers, inscribed trophies, manuscripts, paintings, and photographs. We mentioned the Fabergé eggs, but spent most of the show on his collection of trophies. As he said, the reward for winning a race or a contest becomes one of the owner's most prized possessions, but it is often discarded after the owner dies. We later bought a "bang and go back" race trophy as a joke and later learned it was for a boat race. It was part of the new type of collecting that made unusual and everyday things popular with collectors.

A 1989 Barbie sale took place in Washington D.C.; an original blond Barbie No. 1

Our book listed a Tiffany & Co. sterling silver Larchmont Yacht Club trophy sold for $4,305 (2014), and a Dominick & Haff silver Seawanhaka Corinthian Yacht Club trophy bowl for $1,460 (2014).

1990: Fantasy banks made from old-style cans with photocopies of vintage labels and a slot in the top are flooding flea markets.

1994–2009
Kovels wrote the annual entry on collectibles for the *Encyclopedia Britannica Book of the Year*

1993
Mission-style furniture prices rise

1994
Kovels predict paperweights, movie posters, action figures, Pez candy containers, and fishing tackle will go up in price

•

The New York Times featured Kovels

1996
A blown blue Harrison's Columbian Ink master ink bottle sells at auction for $25,300

•

Google is founded

Vintage advertising tins of all types are selling in auctions, shops, and flea markets. Restaurants are decorating with vintage and reproduction metal signs, and many food companies are making specially decorated tins. I still store food in my reproduction Sun Maid Raisins and Uncle Ben's Rice tins. The value of reproduction tin is under $15 today. Old tins or cans with paper labels can cost over $100 if in good condition.

1990, 1991: *Kovels' Page-A-Day Collectibles Calendar* sold in bookstores and gift shops. A color picture was on each page with history and comments for each collectible.

1993: *Kovels' American Art Pottery: The Collector's Guide to Makers, Marks, and Factory Histories* is published. We had been collecting the pottery for years and, in 1972, we bought a group of pieces of George Ohr pottery that had been discovered in 1969. The pieces ranged from $20 to $50 and many are pictured in our book. Ohr was finally recognized as a genius by experts who could not explain how he made the twisted pieces of pottery. His work had become important and expensive. Prices continued to go up until about 2010, when some large collections were sold at auctions. Auction prices in *Kovels' Antiques & Collectibles Price Guide* for Ohr vases today range from $1,000 to $87,500.

Terry's reproduction tins from the 1990s: Uncle Ben's Converted Rice and Sun-Maid Raisins

1998, 2001, 2004
Kovels' Depression Glass & Dinnerware Price List is published

1997
The Antiques Roadshow airs on television in the United States on January 9, 1997

•

Kovels are featured in *Family Circle Magazine*

1998
www.Kovels.com. The company website is created. It's still going strong.

•

The newsletter changes to color pictures and receives the Newsletters on Newsletters Gold award

•

Ralph and Terry are on *Martha Stewart Living* television show

Kovels online homepage

1993: Prices were also moving up for late 1800s and early 1900s wooden furniture in Mission style. It was sturdy, solid wood, had simple lines, and looked new to younger collectors. Best of all, it cost less than new furniture, at least for a few years. When it got more expensive, copies were made. Mission was pictured in all the decorating magazines, and, once again, serious antiques collectors lost interest and prices for old original Mission (almost always refinished) went down.

Gustav Stickley Mission chair, a style which gained popularity in 1993

1994: Kovels predicted paperweights, movie posters, action figures, Pez candy dispensers, and fishing tackle would go up in price. They did by 2000.

1994 to 2009: Kovels wrote the annual entry on collectibles for the Encyclopedia Britannica Book of the Year. We included major events, prices, and trends.

1995: *Kovels' Quick Tips: 799 Helpful Hints on How to Care for Your Collectibles* is published. This handy, fun book had 25 years of Kovels' tips on how to care for and maintain the treasures in your home, from jewelry, heirloom silver, and childhood toys to a Coca-Cola bottle collection, kitchen utensils, books, and family photographs.

1995: The Internet was evolving and new information was appearing every day. Online forums and bulletin boards about antiques and collectibles start to appear with discussion areas and listings of items for sale.

1996: Google was founded. Search engines made research easier. Price lists, including ours, were put online.

1996: A blown blue Harrison's Columbian master ink bottle sold at auction for $25,300.

2000–2004
Ninety-one 30-minute shows of *Flea Market Finds with the Kovels,* are shown on HGTV. The series is awarded a Telly.

The Newsletter On Newsletters Gold Award, 1998

2000
The Kovels write a column, "The Kovels on Collecting," for *Forbes* magazine

DVD set of *Flea Market Finds with the Kovels*

1996: Seven bargains found at a show were listed in Kovels' newsletter: 1930s bookends, $45; tramp art popsicle stick flowerpot holder, $25; plate by fifties' artist Waylande Gregory, $35; cigarette lighters, 2 for $20; printed handkerchiefs, boxed set, "To my dearest wife, 1917," $5; Hobe costume jewelry sterling silver pin, $20; and souvenir metal Eiffel tower, 25 cents at a yard sale. Prices have gone up by more than 300 percent by 2017 for bookends, enamels, handkerchiefs, and the Eiffel tower. The Wayland Gregory plate is worth $200.

A painted tramp art bird house

1996: Kovels appear on the Home Shopping Network with the price book.

1996: The Kovels go online at www.kovels.com.

1997: *The Antiques Roadshow* starts on television in the United States on January 9, 1997. It had been on the air in England since 1979. Thousands of viewers who never thought about antiques and collectibles tuned in and antiquing became mainstream. A high appraisal of a toy or baseball card or vase immediately created a new market and higher prices at sales. But viewers didn't always understand that condition, ownership, or a special color could be the reason one piece was worth a lot and another that was similar, was not.

1998: Our book, *The Label Made Me Buy It*, was published. We have a huge collection of old labels including food cans, whiskey bottles, orange crates, ink bottles, soap, cosmetics, tobacco products, and even bananas. Discovering the history of the product and the company, the source of the pictures, and symbols was the most complicated research project we have done. The large book has 213 pages filled with color pictures of 320 labels, lists of lithographers and dating clues.

1998: Kovels add price guide prices to its website, www.Kovels.com.

Kovels' Bottles Price List, 13th (and last) edition, 2006

2001
The Kovels advised readers to buy Depression glass

2004
Kovels' American Antiques 1750–1900 is published

2006
We started writing our free weekly online eNewsletter, Kovels Komments

•

Kovels' Antiques & Collectibles Price List uses color pictures

1998: The newsletter, *Kovels on Antiques and Collectibles*, begins publishing color pictures.

2000–2001: The Kovels write a column, "The Kovels on Collecting," for *Forbes* magazine for two years.

2000–2004: Home & Garden Television Network (HGTV) airs *Flea Market Finds* with the Kovels. Ninety-one 30-minute shows were shown on HGTV. We were awarded a National Telly in 2002.

2001: The Kovels advise readers to buy Depression glass, cream and green kitchen utensils, twig furniture, Hull pottery, and 19th-century printed American textiles. Five years later Depression glass was down, the others were up in price.

2004: *Kovels' American Antiques 1750–1900* was published. Not just a revision of *Kovels' Know Your Antiques*, it was a whole new book with a whole new look, focusing on antiques made or used in America before 1900. It included 400 color pictures and tables with 340 drawings of marks and maker information.

2006: We started writing our free weekly eNewsletter called Kovels Komments. Short comments on interesting news about antiques, questions and answers or mark information, and our popular tips on care, repair, and dangers. Terry's favorite tip: "Always vacuum your taxidermied moose head from the snout up. Vacuum with the furniture attachment but go with, not against, the grain. Rinse the head every five years. Careful—too much water makes a mildewed moose head."

2006: *Kovels' Antiques & Collectibles Price List* begins using color pictures and features rainbow-colored borders on the cover.

2007: *Kovels' American Collectibles 1900 – 2000* was published. Not just a revision of *Kovels' Know Your Collectibles*, it featured 20th century furnishings, decorative and useful everyday objects, jewelry, and even toys that could be found in a home or office in the United States with histories, descriptions, marks and pictures.

Kovels' Antiques & Collectibles Price Guide 2009, **41st edition**

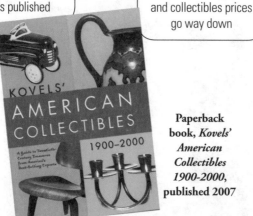

2007
Kovels' American Collectibles 1900–2000 is published

2008
The stock market crashes and antiques and collectibles prices go way down

2009
Another title change: *The Kovels' Antiques & Collectibles Price Guide*

Paperback book, *Kovels' American Collectibles 1900-2000*, published 2007

2008: The stock market crashes and antiques and collectibles prices also go way down. Only the rarest and highest quality kept selling. It was the start of the "death of brown furniture." Very low prices meant shows, auctions, and online pieces that required expensive shipping were out. A Chippendale drop-front desk that was worth $3,000 in 1960 would sell for $300. It couldn't hold a big computer and was out of style—50s and 60s collectibles and furniture was "in."

2009: Another title change: *The Kovels' Antiques & Collectibles Price Guide.* We did an online test to see if you looked for a price "guide" or a "list" and guide won.

2010: Ralph and Terry Kovel were inducted into the Cleveland Journalism Hall of Fame by The Press Club of Cleveland.

2010: Designer purses. Previously owned purses by popular designers are a new item sold at antiques auctions. A few were sold by Christie's London in 1978 in the Coco Chanel collection. The first bag sold, a navy blue flap bag, was bought by the Smithsonian Institution for $800. In 2010 Heritage Auctions decided to treat couture handbags as a special type of collectible and researched the market. They hired a special staff to learn about what might sell, pricing and presentation. Then they had a handbag auction. A few years later Christies hired these experts and started their own auctions. Heritage filed a lawsuit against Christies in 2016. Vintage name-brand bags soon sold at auction for thousands of dollars and a new market had been created. Several online stores began to specialize in couture handbags and bought and sold them online. The record price for a Hermes bag was set in 2017: $380,000 for a white crocodile skin Birkin bag with diamond-encrusted 18-karat gold hardware.

2015: Sneakers became the newest category found at auctions that now sell antiques (anything made before 1917), folk art, mid-century modern, contemporary art, and couture clothing, not just traditional art and antiques. Michael Jordan wore Air Jordans at a basketball game in 1984 and was fined $5,000 for being out of uniform. Nike and Adidas started making limited-edition sneakers by 1985.

Terry on cover of the *WVIZ Program Guide* promoting WVIZ/PBS televised auction and antiques for sale, 2013

2010
Ralph and Terry are inducted into the Journalism Hall of Fame

Previously-owned designer purses by popular designers are a new item sold at antiques auctions

2015
Sneakers appear for sale at antique auctions

PRICELESS!

WVIZ/PBS and 90.3 WCPN ideastream® congratulates the "duke and duchess of the antiques world" and all the 2010 Journalism Hall of Fame inductees.

WVIZ ad congratulating Ralph & Terry as 2010 Journalism Hall of Fame Inductees

"Sneakerheads" (shoe collectors) soon were buying, selling, and raising the price of "old" sneakers at private sales. It is now an organized group with books, apps, blogs, a website and auctions. Some shoes can sell for thousands of dollars. A pair of Michael Jordan's shoes worn in the game against Spain in the 1984 Olympics sold on June 11, 2017, for the record price of $190,373.

Michael Jordan's record-setting Converse sneaker. Sneakerheads are the newest collectors.

2016: Vintage floor lamps are wanted and selling quickly.

2017: Our 50th *Kovels Antiques & Collectibles Price Guide,* 2018 is published. It includes 20,000 prices and 2,500 color pictures, and this 50-year timeline.

2017: Items that are going up in price are big, colorful, and in excellent condition. Many contemporary Italian glass pieces were auctioned for over $25,000 in a May sale. Auctions and sales are online as well as on land, and there are fewer shows each year. Malls and shops are disappearing, but many new types of online sales are doing well. LiveAuctioneers, Bidsquare, and AuctionZip run online sales for hundreds of big and little auction houses. Many online sites sell selected items from many expensive shops, so buyers have a huge selection of merchandise from many countries, far more than 50 years ago.

Modern glass vase by Lino Tagliapietra made in 2008. Sold in 2017 for $25,000.

Technology has changed, tastes have changed, but collecting is a necessity for many of us. It seems to "be in the genes" and creates joy and even profit for many. Remember Ralph Kovels' best advice is, "If you like it, buy it," and Terry's best advice is, "Never walk away from something you love. Don't worry about where you'll put it or how you'll get it home." And we agree. "You only regret what you don't buy."

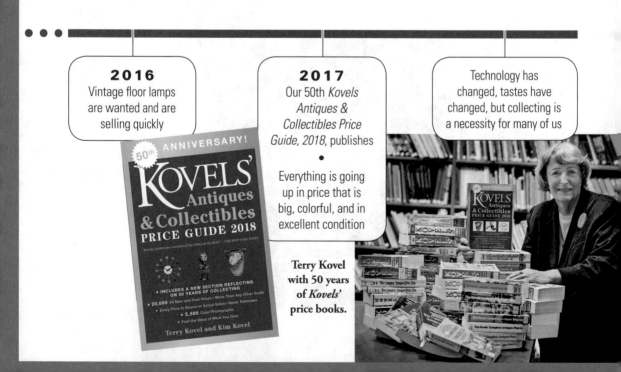

2016
Vintage floor lamps are wanted and are selling quickly

2017
Our 50th *Kovels Antiques & Collectibles Price Guide, 2018,* publishes

•

Everything is going up in price that is big, colorful, and in excellent condition

Technology has changed, tastes have changed, but collecting is a necessity for many of us

Terry Kovel with 50 years of *Kovels'* price books.

Tumbler, Creamy White, Blue Leaves, Cob Shape, c.1880, 4 In.	90
Tumbler, Custard Glass, Yellow Iridescent Leaves, Gilt Trim, 1880s, 4 In.	115
Vase, White Glaze, Blue Leaves, Creamy Ivory Interior, Oval, Tapered, 1889, 7 x 5 In.	190
Water Bottle, Opaque, Blue Leaves, Gilt Trim, Bulbous, Flared Rim, c.1880, 8 In.	185

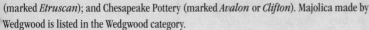

MAJOLICA is a general term for any pottery glazed with an opaque tin enamel that conceals the color of the clay body. It has been made since the fourteenth century. Today's collector is most likely to find Victorian majolica. The heavy, colorful ware is rarely marked. Some famous makers include Minton; Griffen, Smith and Hill (marked *Etruscan*); and Chesapeake Pottery (marked *Avalon* or *Clifton*). Majolica made by Wedgwood is listed in the Wedgwood category.

Apothecary Jar, Landscape, Boat, Dog, Blue, White, 12 In.	325
Asparagus Server, 6 Plates, Relief Asparagus, 7 In., 7 Piece	325
Bowl, Butterflies, Lizards, Spider, Worm, Portuguese Palissy, Jose Cunha, 9 ½ In. ....*illus*	308
Bowl, Galleon Shape, Half Nude Figurehead, Spear, c.1890, 23 x 20 ½ In.	687
Bowl, Satyr Head Masks, Putti, Scrolling Dolphins, Late 1800s, 11 ¾ x 21 x 9 In.	1046
Box, Pineapple, Monkeys, Multicolor, 9 In.	1125
Bread Basket, Blue, Brown, 12 In.	375
Bread, Tray, Ribbon & Wheat, Oval, George Jones, c.1875, 13 In.	399
Bust, Woman, Blond Hair, c.1880, 20 ½ In.	281
Bust, Woman, Hat, Lace, Blond Hair, Stand, 30 In.	281
Casserole, Lobster, George Jones, 8 ¼ x 4 ¼ In.	1000
Charger, Crab, Sea Life, Relief, Palissy Style, 13 In.	150
Charger, Female Bust, Griffin & Sun Border, Multicolor, Schutz-Cilli, 23 ¼ In.	682
Charger, Portraits, Profiles, Blue, Paulo Rubio, 12 In., Pair	177
Cheese Dish, Lid, Chestnut, Brown, Coopered Barrel Form, c.1875, 12 x 10 In.	492
Cistern, Bridge, Warriors, Blue, Yellow, Footed, Shaped Tray Base, 27 In.	2500
Cookie Jar, Sack, Ribbon, Mouse, Peek Freans Biscuits On Lid, Wm. Brownfield, c.1875, 8 In.. *illus*	570
Dish, Purple Bloom, 3 Green Leaf Trays, 7 In.	125
Ewer, Winged Angels, Fish Spout, 19 x 13 ½ In.	236
Figurine, Man With Cup, Seated, 15 ½ In.	62
Figurine, Man, Mandolin, Seated, Steps, 18 x 16 In.	218
Figurine, Rooster, Corn Husk, Multicolor, c.1915, 13 In.	861
Fish Plate, 6 Fish Shape Wells, Seaweed Design, Minton, 11 ¾ In. ....*illus*	1440
Garden Seat, Blackamoor, Villery & Boch, 1800s, 20 x 12 x 18 ½ In.	2500
Garden Seat, Passionflowers, Round, Tapered Spool, Block Feet, 1870, 18 In., Pair	4305
Humidor, Watermelon, Black Boy Seated On Lid, 1800s, 5 x 5 x 10 In.	260
Jar, Dragon, Chrysanthemum, Brown, Yellow, 15 ¼ In.	187
Jardiniere, Cattails, Cobalt Blue, 8 ¼ In.	138
Jardiniere, Grotesque, Beige, 14 ½ x 15 In.	250
Jardiniere, Pedestal, Gold & Blue, 1800s, 52 x 19 In.	748
Jardiniere, Pedestal, Raised Scrolling, Leaves, Julius Dressler, c.1900, 63 x 17 In. ....*illus*	960
Jardiniere, Red Flowers, Green Leaves, Cobalt Ground, Footed, c.1900, 9 In.	375
Jardiniere, Ribbon, Bow, Blue Ground, c.1875, 15 x 15 ½ In.	300
Jardiniere, Shells, Lattice, Openwork Scroll Handles, Blue, Tan, Scroll Feet, 23 In.	177
Jardiniere, Swags Of Fruit, Lion Masks, Dark Blue, Minton, c.1868, 21 In.	2337
Jug, Winged Cherubs, Eye Of God, Banded, Paneled Sides, 10 ¾ x 5 ½ In.	100
Pedestal, Acanthus, Bas Relief, 45 ⅝ x 14 In.	501
Pedestal, Turquoise, Lion's Head Masks, Ivy, Red Medallion, Paw Feet, 1800s, 36 x 13 In.	920
Pitcher, Bird Handle, Turquoise, George Jones, c.1875	720
Pitcher, Blue, Branch Handle, Signed, J. Holdcroft, 9 In.	105
Pitcher, Dog, Spaniel, Begging, 10 ½ In.	112
Pitcher, Frog Shape, Open Mouth, Lily Pad Base, Loop Handle, c.1900, 5 In.	413
Pitcher, Goose & Monkey, William Brownfield & Sons, c.1880, 13 ½ In.	246
Pitcher, Stork & Cattails, Punched Star Ground, Duck Head Handle, 12 In......................*illus*	266
Pitcher, Swan, 11 ¼ In.	177
Plant Stand, Blue, Pierced, 30 ½ x 14 In.	187
Plaque, Medieval Figures, High Relief, Enamel, Gilt Frame, c.1880, 14 x 22 In.	277
Plaque, Young Couple, Window, High Relief, 23 ½ x 19 In.	125

Potichomania

Potichomania, a type of decoupage, has been popular since the nineteenth century. Victorian women glued small pictures, cigar bands, and paper lace to the back or inside of a piece of glass, then sealed it with shellac or felt. The finished piece had a colorful all-over design that looked like painted porcelain. Today potichomania is easier. Pictures are glued to the back of a clear glass plate, then sealed with a special spray found at craft shops.

Majolica, Jardiniere, Pedestal, Raised Scrolling, Leaves, Julius Dressler, c.1900, 63 x 17 In. $960

Cowan's Auctions

M

Majolica, Pitcher, Stork & Cattails, Punched Star Ground, Duck Head Handle, 12 In.
$266

Hess Auction Group

Majolica, Spoon Warmer, Egg, Broken Shell, Turquoise, T.C. Brown-Westhead, Moore & Co., c.1875
$660

Strawser Auction Group

Majolica, Tobacco Jar, Sailor, Drinking, Sitting On Coiled Rope, Minton, c.1870, 9 In.
$660

Strawser Auction Group

Plate, Bird, Brown, White, Branches, Water, Flowers, Yellow Rim, Christian Dior, 4 1/2 x 10 In.	25
Plate, Hunt Scene, Horseman & Hounds, Stag, Scroll Leaf Border, c.1670, 9 In.	3305
Plate, Lobster, Shellfish, Relief, 10 In.	168
Plate, Snake, Insects, Green, Molded, Naturalistic Ground, J. Cunha, Palissy Ware, 12 In.	2160
Plate, Snake, Salamander, Lizards, Grass, Palissy Ware, c.1875, 8 1/2 In.	238
Platter, Coiled Snake, Frog, Grass, Palissy Ware, c.1900, 12 In.	238
Sardine Box, Lid, Sea Creatures, George Jones, c.1875	1020
Spoon Warmer, Egg, Broken Shell, Turquoise, T.C. Brown-Westhead, Moore & Co., c.1875 *illus*	660
Strawberry Dish, Lavender Napkin, Minton, c.1875, 11 1/2 In.	276
Strawberry Dish, Light Blue Scallop Shell, Ocher Edge, Minton, c.1875, 8 In.	221
Strawberry Dish, Pink Scallop Shell, Ocher Edge, Minton, c.1875, 8 In.	369
Strawberry Server, Leaves, Blossoms, Raised Nests, Bird On Branch, 1870	1020
Tazza, Trefoil Dish, 3-Mermaid Pedestal, Multicolor, Italy, c.1900, 10 x 12 In.	344
Tea Set, White Daisy, Brown Ground, Teapot, Sugar & Creamer, c.1875, 3 Piece	196
Teapot, Fish, Gray, Turquoise Sea, Wave Handle, c.1875, 7 1/2 x 5 In.	900
Tobacco Jar, Sailor, Drinking, Sitting On Coiled Rope, Minton, c.1870, 9 In. *illus*	660
Umbrella Stand, Water Bird, Standing, Multicolor, 40 In.	1250
Urn, Farm Landscape, Courting Scene, Bellflower, Harpy Handles, Footed, 27 3/4 x 16 1/2 In.	206
Urn, Green, Handles, 24 x 19 In.	660
Urn, Venus & Adonis, Ginori, c.1907, 12 3/4 In.	354
Vase, Adoration Of Magi, Putti, Flower Swags, Gilt Pedestal Foot, c.1740, 11 In.	2203
Vase, Blackamoor, Boy Holding Sweetmeat Basket, 1800s, 31 1/4 In.	501
Vase, Dragons, Blue, Green, White Ground, 25 1/2 In.	125
Vase, Flowers, Fruit, Snake Handles, Deruta, Italy, 27 1/4 x 13 1/2 In.	177
Vase, Goat Heads, Festoons, Blue, Urn Shape, Square Upright Handles, c.1863, 32 In.	615
Vase, Red & Yellow Glaze, Swans At Base, 3 Handles, Minton, c.1865, 40 In. *illus*	1476
Vase, Shoe, Brown, Green, 10 1/4 In.	50
Vase, Triple Stem, Branch Shape, Relief Leaves, c.1925, 8 5/8 x 7 1/4 In.	80
Vase, Tulips, Irises, Lilies, 1900-25, 17 1/4 In.	687

MALACHITE is a green stone with unusual layers or rings of darker green shades. It is often polished and used for decorative objects. Most malachite comes from Siberia or Australia.

Card Box, Caribbean Decoration, Ship, 6 3/4 x 5 3/4 In.	75
Decanter Set, Women's Heads, Decanter, 6 Cups, 7 Piece	250
Obelisk, Raised Panels, France, Mid 1900s, 18 3/4 x 4 1/4 x 4 1/4 In.	2000
Obelisk, Stepped Base, Continental, 1900s, 19 3/4 x 5 In., Pair *illus*	2500
Vase, Seminude Women, Art Deco, 10 In.	218

MAPS of all types have been collected for centuries. The earliest known printed maps were made in 1478. The first printed street map showed London in 1559. The first road maps for use by drivers of automobiles were made in 1901. Collectors buy maps that were pages of old books, as well as the multifolded road maps popular in this century.

Amsterdam, Eastern Mediterranean, Decorative Cartouche, c.1703, 19 1/2 x 23 1/4 In.	212
Carte De La Louisiane Et De La Floride, Rigobert Bonne, France, 1700s, 13 3/8 x 9 In.	1187
Charleston Harbor & Its Fortifications, A. Willimans & Co., Boston, 1861, 15 1/2 x 20 1/2 In.	792
Chatham County, Georgia, Charles G. Platen, 1875	9600
Colton's New Map Of The State Of Texas, Lithograph, Hand Colored, 1859, 16 x 25 In.	688
Delaware, Engraving, Hand Colored, William Barker, Pa., 1795, 16 1/2 x 13 3/4 In.	410
Double Hemisphere, Hand Drawn, Colored, England, Late 1700s, 19 1/4 x 29 1/4 In.	510
Florida, Engraved, Hand Colored, Herman Moll, 1736, 8 3/8 x 11 1/8 In.	1003
Florida, George F. Cram, 1900-25, Frame, 13 x 10 1/2 In.	125
Globe, Armillary, Brown, Red, Wood, Round Foot, Italy, 17 In.	136
Globe, Celestial, Parchment Paper, Revolving, Mahogany Stand, 1800s, 13 x 10 1/2 In.	595
Globe, Celestial, Wilson, 4-Footed Turned Wood Stand, 1827, 13 In.	1755
Globe, Pocket, Leather Case, Johann Georg Klinger, Germany, c.1840, Miniature, 2 1/4 In. *illus*	1536

M

Majolica, Vase, Red & Yellow Glaze, Swans At Base, 3 Handles, Minton, c.1865, 40 In.
$1,476

Map, Globe, Pocket, Leather Case, Johann Georg Klinger, Germany, c.1840, Miniature, 2¼ In.
$1,536

Map, Globe, Terrestrial, Rand McNally, Renaissance Revival, Walnut Stand, c.1910, 59 In.
$1,875

Neal Auctions

Map, Globe, Terrestrial, Maple Stand, Brass Meridian, Josiah Loring, W.H. Annin, c.1866, 14 In.
$2,562

Skinner, Inc.

Malachite, Obelisk, Stepped Base, Continental, 1900s, 19¾ x 5 In., Pair
$2,500

Neal Auctions

New Orleans Auction Galleries

Map, Planetarium, Globe, Pulley & String, Venus, Earth, Moon, Sun, Plaque, Laing's, c.1890, 13 x 22 In.
$2,806

Map, Globe, Terrestrial, Rand McNally & Co., Mahogany Base, c.1890, 31 x 18 In.
$633

Neal Auctions

New Orleans Auction Galleries

Cottone Auctions

How Old Is Your Globe?
The production date of a globe can usually be pinpointed to within 10 to 20 years based on names of countries or other geographical information. Examples: Gold Coast was changed to Ghana in 1957. If Bangladesh is officially listed as a country in South Asia, then the globe was made after 1970.

M

Marble, Lutz, Swirl, Green, Yellow, Brown, Gold Flecks 1 29/64 In.
$1,140

Morphy Auctions

Marble Carving, Bust, Fedelta, Woman, Head Turned, Ferdinando Vichi, 15 1/2 x 17 1/2 In.
$390

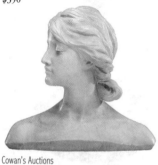

Cowan's Auctions

TIP
Never try to dry a piece of marble with a hair dryer.

Marble Carving, Obelisk, Mottled Mauve & Gray, Plinth Base, Italy, 1900s, 19 In., Pair
$468

New Orleans Auction Galleries

Globe, Stand, Steel, Aluminum, Adjustable, Writeable Surface, 1940-50s, 63 x 20 In.	549
Globe, Table, Brass Vertical Ring, Measuring Degrees, Turned Maple Base, Loring, 18 In.	2520
Globe, Terrestrial, 12 Paper Gores, Multicolor, Gilman Joslin, Cast Base, 1870, 12 In.	1080
Globe, Terrestrial, Brown, Ocher, Blue, Wood, Round Foot, 23 In.	86
Globe, Terrestrial, Cast Steel, Colored Lithograph, Tripod, Paw Feet, c.1925, 31 x 18 In.	523
Globe, Terrestrial, Mahogany, Brass, Kittinger, 16 In.	238
Globe, Terrestrial, Maple Stand, Brass Meridian, Josiah Loring, W.H. Annin, c.1866, 14 In.… *illus*	2562
Globe, Terrestrial, Mineral, Inlay, Blue, Tilting Axis, 15 1/2 x 13 1/2 In.	107
Globe, Terrestrial, Multicolor, Johnston, Edinburgh, London, Iron Base, 44 In.	1800
Globe, Terrestrial, Patinated Brass Stand, Attributed To Paul McCobb, 1960s, 38 x 22 In.	250
Globe, Terrestrial, Rand McNally & Co., Mahogany Base, c.1890, 31 x 18 In. *illus*	633
Globe, Terrestrial, Rand McNally, Renaissance Revival, Walnut Stand, c.1910, 59 In. *illus*	1875
Globe, Terrestrial, Stand, Replogle World Classic, 16 In.	116
Globe, Terrestrial, Wood, Paper, Molded Plywood Stand, C.B. Odell, c.1950, 26 x 24 In.	308
Kentucky & Tennessee, Amos Doolittle, 1796, 7 5/8 x 11 1/2 In.	2360
Mississippi River From Balise To Fort Chartres, Robert Sayer, Frame, 1765, 44 x 14 In.	3750
Mississippi, Hardee's Official Map, High Lewis, New Orleans, 1872, 36 x 23 In.	732
Nantucket, Massachusetts, Island, Geographical, Color, Frame, 1874, 11 x 18 In.	711
Negroland, Colonies & European Settlements Of Slave Trade, E. Bowen, Late 1700s, 16 x 20 In.	950
New Map Of The English Empire, John Harris, 20 x 23 In.	7380
New Orleans & City Of Lafayette, Outline Color, Mat, Frame, c.1842, 11 x 14 In.	2440
New Orleans & Suburbs, Bird's-Eye View, Color Lithograph, Gustave Koeckert, 27 x 34 In.	2684
New Orleans, Multicolor, Rand McNally Indexed Atlas, Frame, 1911, 19 5/8 x 27 1/2 In.	125
North America, Bowles New Pocket Map Of North America, Frame, 1784, 29 x 33 In.	533
Nuremberg, Eastern Mediterranean & North Africa, 20 3/4 x 24 In.	188
Planetarium, Globe, Pulley & String, Venus, Earth, Moon, Sun, Plaque, Laing's, c.1890, 13 x 22 In. *illus*	2806
Punxsutawney, Pennsylvania, Topographic, Map Guide, Frame, 1906, 17 x 20 In.	85
Tennessee, Towns, Roads, Title Cartouche, Leis & Alexander Lawson, 1804, 13 x 15 In.	2728
United States, Jacob Monk, Indian Nations Named, Original Rollers, 1854	517
World, Watercolor, Split Globe, Joining Hemispheres, Schoolgirl, Frame, 1829, 20 x 34 In.	948
York County, Pennsylvania, Shearer's, 1860, 63 x 62 In.	1416

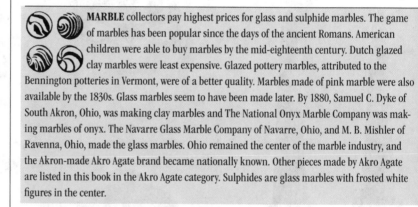

MARBLE collectors pay highest prices for glass and sulphide marbles. The game of marbles has been popular since the days of the ancient Romans. American children were able to buy marbles by the mid-eighteenth century. Dutch glazed clay marbles were least expensive. Glazed pottery marbles, attributed to the Bennington potteries in Vermont, were of a better quality. Marbles made of pink marble were also available by the 1830s. Glass marbles seem to have been made later. By 1880, Samuel C. Dyke of South Akron, Ohio, was making clay marbles and The National Onyx Marble Company was making marbles of onyx. The Navarre Glass Marble Company of Navarre, Ohio, and M. B. Mishler of Ravenna, Ohio, made the glass marbles. Ohio remained the center of the marble industry, and the Akron-made Akro Agate brand became nationally known. Other pieces made by Akro Agate are listed in this book in the Akro Agate category. Sulphides are glass marbles with frosted white figures in the center.

Akro Agate, Ace, Milky White, Opaque Yellow Ribbon, 1940s, 1 In.	145
Akro Agate, Corkscrew, White, Blue, Green, Red, Yellow, 1940s, 5/8 In.	55
Divided Core Swirl, Outer Grouping White & Yellow Latticinio Bands, 1 63/64 In.	91
Divided Core Swirl, Red, White, Blue, Birdcage White Outer Bands, 2 3/32 In.	240
Divided Core Swirl, Red, White, Blue, Birdcage Yellow Outer Bands, 2 1/8 In.	120
Double Ribbon Swirl, Yellow Latticinio, Blue, Yellow, Red, 55/64 In.	183
End Of Cane, Left Twist Swirl, Orange, Lavender, Blue, White, Yellow, 59/64 In.	61
Joseph's Coat, Blue Bands, Orange, Green, Red, White Striping, 13/16 In.	122
Joseph's Coat, Bright Yellow Bands, Blue, Red, Olive Green, 13/16 In.	120
Joseph's Coat, Oxblood Red Bands, Black, Green, White, 13/16 In.	90
Latticinio Swirl, Aqua Glass, White Latticinio Core, 7/8 In.	427
Lutz, Green Base, 1 33/64 In.	6000
Lutz, Swirl, Green, Yellow, Brown, Gold Flecks, 1 29/64 In. *illus*	1140
Onionskin Swirl, Alternating Yellow, Orange, Blue, Red, 1 1/8 In.	9150

Onionskin, Lutz, Red, Yellow, Green, White, Twist, 1 5/16 In.	1342
Single Ribbon Swirl, Multicolor, Razor Ribbon, 55/64 In.	540
Solid Yellow Core, Applied Orange & Green Bands, 4 Outer White Latticinio Bands, 1 In.	91
Sulphide, Eagle, Spread Wings, 1 1/3 In.	122
Sulphide, Woman, Dress, 1 1/2 In.	335
Tornado Twist, White Latticinio Core, Blue, Red, Green Bands, Birdcage Latticinio, 55/64 In.	390
Tornado Twist, Yellow Latticinio Core, Alternating Red & Blue, 7/8 In.	60

MARBLE CARVINGS, such as large or small figurines, groups of people or animals, and architectural decorations, have been a special art form since the time of the ancient Greeks. Reproductions, especially of large Victorian groups, are being made of a mixture using marble dust. These are very difficult to detect and collectors should be careful. Other carvings are listed under Alabaster.

Bench, Crest, Scrolls, Flowers, Birds, Dolphins, Vines, Acanthus, 47 1/2 x 61 In.	10000
Bowl, 3 x 12 In.	62
Bust, Bronze Dore, Jeune Femme, A.H. Nelson, France, c.1900, 24 x 15 x 9 In.	8750
Bust, Buddha Head, Painted Face, Black Stand, 1900s, 11 1/2 x 4 1/2 x 4 1/2 In.	625
Bust, Capuan Venus, Carrara, Italy, Late 1800s, 25 x 22 1/2 x 10 In.	3750
Bust, Courtier, Bared Shoulders, c.1875, 31 In.	3750
Bust, Diana Of Versailles, Italy, 1800s, 18 x 9 1/2 In.	1375
Bust, Fedelta, Woman, Head Turned, Ferdinando Vichi, 15 1/2 x 17 1/2 In. ....*illus*	390
Bust, Girl, Hat, Bow On Bodice, 17 1/4 In.	406
Bust, Joan Of Arc, Yellow & Gray Veining, c.1910, 21 In.	738
Bust, Johann Goethe & Friederich Schiller, Late 1800s, 22 x 11 In., Pair	875
Bust, Julius Ceasar, Cream, Yellow, Socle, Continental, 31 1/2 In.	6000
Bust, Man, Sir John Robert Steel, 22 In.	4500
Bust, Muse, Circlet, Pendant, Bouquet, Tunic, 24 3/4 x 14 3/4 In.	501
Bust, Robert Physick, 21 In.	813
Bust, Roman Emperor, Neoclassical Drapery, 1800s, 8 1/2 x 26 In.	1845
Bust, Woman, Bare Chest, Wavy Pulled Back Hair, Socle, c.1850, 17 x 11 In.	687
Bust, Woman, Clutching Bodice, 25 x 12 1/2 In.	2745
Bust, Woman, Coiled Hair, Looks Over Shoulder, 13 In.	238
Bust, Woman, Eyes Downcast, Shoulder Out, 13 1/4 In.	250
Bust, Woman, Looking Over Shoulder, 27 In.	234
Bust, Woman, Off The Shoulder Shawl, Curls, Downcast, 26 In.	3600
Bust, Young Boy, Hat, 7 1/2 In.	135
Bust, Young Girl Walking In Wind, White, Signed, c.1880, 22 In.	425
Bust, Young Gypsy Girl, Headdress, Jewelry, Signed, c.1880, 21 1/2 In.	150
Bust, Young Man, Curly Hair, Cape, 27 In.	1375
Cassoulet, Dore Bronze Mount, Dome Lid, Bacchus Masks, Swags, 15 3/4 In., Pair	1309
Column, Abstract, William Moore, 47 1/2 In.	1750
Column, Pedestal, White, 1900s, 41 1/2 x 11 1/2 In.	193
Garniture, Urn, Bronze, Louis XVI, Mottled Pink, France, 1900s, 16 1/2 x 4 1/4 In., Pair	531
Obelisk, Black, Cream, Socle, 13 1/4 In., Pair	1115
Obelisk, Circles, Black Borders, 1900s, 21 3/4 In.	2250
Obelisk, Mottled Mauve & Gray, Plinth Base, Italy, 1900s, 19 In., Pair ....*illus*	468
Obelisk, Pietra Dura, White & Green, Inlaid Stones, 1900s, 19 x 4 In.	593
Obelisk, Pyramidal, Pink, 1900s, 28 In., Pair	187
Pedestal, Gilt, Tapered, Red, Garlands, 47 x 10 1/2 In.	1062
Pedestal, Mirrored Lion's Paw, Flared Leaf, Italy, 16 1/2 x 14 1/4 x 4 1/2 In., Pair	238
Pedestal, Red, Ionic, Stepped Squared Base, 51 1/2 x 10 3/4 In.	1830
Pedestal, Rouge, Column, Square Base, 1900s, 34 x 30 x 21 In.	875
Pedestal, Rouge, Gilt Metal Mount, 43 In., Pair	1125
Pedestal, Spiral Fluted Stem, Octagonal Base, 35 3/4 In.	450
Pedestal, Tapered, Fluted, Acanthus, Octangonal Base, 36 x 11 3/4 In., Pair	413
Plaque, Relief, Birth Of Venus, 12 x 17 In.	3451
Plaque, Relief, Perseus, Head Of Medusa, 11 1/4 x 15 3/4 In.	2618
Plaque, Roman Emperors, Scagolia, Frame, 1810-15, 5 x 4 In., 4 Piece	3437
Stand, Bronze, Specimen, Marble Base, 4 Bronze Supports, France, 1800s, 9 x 6 In.	531

MARBLE CARVING

Marble Carving, Statue, Feet, Wearing Sandals, Roman Style, 1900s, 8 x 15 1/2 In., Pair
$780

Brunk Auctions

Marblehead, Vase, Stylized Plants, A. Hennessey, S. Tutt, Stamped, Ship Mark, 5 x 4 In.
$3,250

Rago Arts and Auction Center

Mardi Gras, Invitation, Ball, Two Well Known Gentlemen, Woman, Feb. 26, 1895, 13 x 10 In.
$1,159

Neal Auctions

M

TIP

Cranberry juice will stain stone, so be careful if you have marble-top tables. Other liquids will stain, but cranberry juice stains are especially bad.

Martin Brothers, Jug, Face, 2-Sided, Smiling, Handle, Glazed, Incised, 1903, 7 x 6 In.
$2,250

Rago Arts and Auction Center

Mary Gregory, Vase, Courting Couple, Bouquet, Glass, Blue, 10 1/4 In.
$240

Woody Auction

Mason's Ironstone, Cake Plate, 8 Sections, Figures, Potted Flowering Tree, Yellow, 1800s, 12 In.
$395

Ruby Lane

Statue, 3 Nude Women, Hugging, 23 3/4 In.	1625
Statue, Apollo, Looking Over Shoulder, 25 1/2 x 25 1/2 In.	3500
Statue, Crouching Venus, Italy, c.1900, 20 x 10 1/4 In.	1416
Statue, Feet, Wearing Sandals, Roman Style, 1900s, 8 x 15 1/2 In., Pair ....*illus*	780
Statue, Ginevra, Seated Child, Myriam De Kepper, 1994, 25 x 18 In.	3427
Statue, Girl Feeding Chicks, c.1900, 27 1/2 In.	750
Statue, Girl, Seated In Chair, Cesare Lapini, 28 1/2 In.	8400
Statue, Maiden, Cherub, Seminude, Roses, Rocky Base, 1800s, 40 x 31 In.	1778
Statue, Modified Fish, Red, Dean Leary, 1945, 22 x 26 In.	720
Statue, Nike, Verdigris Pedestal, Italy, 1800s, 79 x 29 In.	5750
Statue, Nude, Woman, Arms Up, Walking, White, c.1900, 35 1/2 In.	1750
Statue, Nude, Woman, Hoisting Grapevine, Sheep, 30 In.	5000
Statue, Paolo & Francesca, 34 x 19 1/2 In.	3867
Statue, Psyche, Cupid, Quiver, Arrows, 31 x 17 1/2 In.	952
Statue, Putti, Pouring Water, Jar, Bench, France, 25 In.	2750
Statue, Reclining Beauty & Admirer, Hammock, Palm Trees, 16 1/2 x 20 1/2 In.	1375
Statue, Reclining Figure, Untitled, Jose De Creeft, 9 1/2 x 14 1/4 In.	875
Statue, Rhinoceros, Green, 13 In.	450
Statue, Romeo & Juliet, Kiss, 48 x 20 In.	1309
Statue, Seminude Woman, Italy, c.1910, 72 x 20 1/2 In.	3660
Statue, Venus At Her Bath, 34 1/2 In.	3437
Statue, Venus Italica, Standing, Draped, After Canova, Marked Del Torrione, 49 In.	1062
Statue, Woman, Kneeling, Nude, Arms Crossed, 23 3/4 x 10 3/4 In.	1830
Statue, Woman, Outstretched Arms, Laurel Wreath, Putto, 40 In.	4500
Statue, Woman, Walking, Green Marble Pedestal, 42 In.	11250
Tazza, Grand Tour, Handles, Octagonal Base, 25 1/2 In.	1500
Tazza, Red, Gilt Bronze Mount, 7 x 5 1/2 In.	357
Urn, Black, Bronze Mount, Scroll Handles, Swags, Finial, 25 In., Pair	1250
Urn, Black, Gilt Bronze, Enamel, France, 1800s, 19 1/2 x 16 1/2 x 16 1/2 In., Pair	1375
Urn, Gilt, Flame Finial, Leaves, Rope, Square Base, 24 In., Pair	1500
Urn, Louis XVI, Black, Ormolu Mount, Square Base, 23 In., Pair	1000
Urn, Neoclassical Style, Hexagon Shape, 13 1/4 x 5 1/2 In., Pair	125
Vase, Cylindrical, Puck Shape Foot, Black, Gray, Angelo Mangiorotti, 6 x 8 In.	1586

MARBLEHEAD POTTERY was founded in 1904 by Dr. J. Hall as a rehabilitative program for the patients of a Marblehead, Massachusetts, sanitarium. Two years later it was separated from the sanitarium and it continued operations until 1936. Many of the pieces were decorated with marine motifs.

Tile, 2 Parrots, Fruit Basket, Hand Painted, Multicolor Glaze, Square, c.1910, 6 In.	400
Tile, Blue & Black Vase With Pink & Purple Flowers, Frame, 9 7/8 x 9 7/8 In.	460
Tile, Lone Oak Tree Landscape, Blue, Wood Frame, 4 1/4 x 4 1/4 In.	2806
Tile, Potted Tress, Signed, Wood Frame, 6 x 6 In.	3050
Trivet, Tile, Stylized Oak Tree, Green Crackle, c.1915, 6 In.	1500
Vase, Cream, Repeating Leaves & Berries, Impressed, 3 1/4 In.	1150
Vase, Cylindrical, Squat Round Base, Landscape, Sarah Tutt, 6 x 4 In.	7320
Vase, Flower Band, Green Glaze, Squat, A. Hennessey, S. Tutt, 4 x 4 In.	1375
Vase, Fruit Trees, Tan Ground, Cylindrical, Arthur Baggs, 5 x 2 3/4 In.	3125
Vase, Geese, Yellow, Blue, 3 1/2 x 3 1/2 In.	10980
Vase, Gray Matte Glaze, Blue Trees, Impressed Mark, 4 x 3 1/2 In.	1342
Vase, Green & Gray Glaze, Geometric Shapes, Bell Shape, Rolled Rim, 1910s, 4 In.	7500
Vase, Green Matte Glaze, 4 x 4 1/2 In.	3172
Vase, Green, Stems, Round Balls, Hannah Tutt, 4 1/2 x 4 1/4 In.	4575
Vase, Lavender Matte Glaze, Bulbous, Saucer Foot, Marked, 3 In.	118
Vase, Light Blue Matte Glaze, Cylindrical, 3 1/2 In.	259
Vase, Moss Green & Gray Matte Glaze, Stylized Flowers, Tapered, c.1915, 5 In.	1625
Vase, Orange Trees, Gray Ground, Arthur Hennessey, Sarah Tutt, 1910s, 7 x 4 In.	1750
Vase, Stylized Flowers, Blue, Gray Ground, Ship Mark, 1910s, 5 x 3 In.	1375
Vase, Stylized Plants, A. Hennessey, S. Tutt, Stamped, Ship Mark, 5 x 4 In. ....*illus*	3250
Vase, Stylized Rose Band, Blue Ground, Gray Outlines & Rim, Tapered, 1910s, 4 In.	938

Vase, Tall Trees, Tan Ground, Arthur Hennessey, Sarah Tutt, Ship Mark, 7 x 4 In.	2250
Vase, Tapered Middle, Dark Blue Speckled Matte, Impressed, 9 5/8 In.	403

MARDI GRAS

MARDI GRAS, French for "Fat Tuesday," was first celebrated in seventeenth-century Europe. The first celebration in America was held in Mobile, Alabama, in 1703. The first krewe, a parading or social club, was founded in 1856. Dozens have been formed since. The Mardi Gras Act, which made Fat Tuesday a legal holiday, was passed in Louisiana in 1875. Mardi Gras balls, carnivals, parties, and parades are held from January 6 until the Tuesday before the beginning of Lent. The most famous carnival and parades take place in New Orleans. Parades feature floats, elaborate costumes, masks, and "throws" of strings of beads, cups, doubloons, or small toys. Purple, green, and gold are traditional Mardi Gras colors. Mardi Gras memorabilia ranges from cheap plastic beads to expensive souvenirs from early celebrations.

Brooch, Osiris, Bride Of The Dragon King, Krewe, 1917, 1 1/4 x 1 In.	150
Dresser Box, Spelter, Gilt, Rex, 1907, 3 x 4 In.	100
Inkwell, Rex, Ball Favor, 1911, Kings Head, Scrolled Edges, 2 x 7 3/8 In.	295
Invitation, Ball, Fancy Dress & Masquerade, Feb. 3, 1894, Asian Woman, 14 In.	793
Invitation, Ball, Two Well Known Gentlemen, Woman, Feb. 26, 1895, 13 x 10 In. .... illus	1159
Mask, Bird, Long Beak, Pink, Brocade, Molded Papier-Mache, Silk Velvet, c.1930	180
Vase, 4-Sided, Green, Rex, 1916, 5 3/8 x 3 1/2 In.	150

MARTIN BROTHERS

MARTIN BROTHERS of Middlesex, England, made Martinware, a salt-glazed stoneware, between 1873 and 1915. Many figural jugs and vases were made by the four brothers. Of special interest are the fanciful birds, usually made with removable heads. Most pieces have the incised name of the artists plus other information on the bottom.

Martin Bros London

Bird, Stoneware, Signed, c.1913, 3 1/2 In.	6000
Creamer, Creature, Open Mouth, Teeth, Handle, Ivory Glaze, c.1900, 4 In.	2000
Jar, Bird, Brown, Tilted Head, Signed, c.1901, 7 5/8 In.	8000
Jar, Bird, Quizzical, Stoneware, c.1904, 6 1/2 In.	10000
Jardiniere, Brown, Cream, c.1889, 8 1/2 x 11 In.	2000
Jug, Face, 2-Sided, Smiling, Handle, Glazed, Incised, 1903, 7 x 6 In. .... illus	2250
Jug, Face, Stoneware, 1911, 6 In.	4250
Loving Cup, 1891 Harvard-Yale Boat Race, Emblems, Scrolls, 6 x 9 In.	4375
Pitcher, Birds, Brown & Peach Glaze, Paneled, Loop Handle, c.1900, 7 In.	4688
Pitcher, Blue, Gold, Shell Design, Flowers, Green Dragon Handle, 1878, 8 In.	938
Pitcher, Grotesques, Scrolls, Blue, Tan, Cream, R.W. Martin, 9 1/4 x 5 1/2 In.	1000
Spoon Warmer, Open Beak, Multicolor, 1900-10, 4 x 5 1/4 In.	1125
Vase, Dragons, Brown & Tan Streaked, Green, Jug, Pinched Neck, 1898, 8 In.	7500
Vase, Dragons, Stoneware, Glazed, Oval, Flared Rim, 1891, 13 x 10 In.	3250
Vase, Etched Lozenges, Bumps, Blue, c.1880, 2 3/4 In.	237
Vase, Jellyfish, Stoneware, Tan, 4 Panels, Tapered, 4-Sided Flared Rim, 9 x 6 In.	5938
Vase, Stems & Berries, Stoneware, Glazed, Tapered, Gargoyle Handles, 9 x 7 In.	2625
Wall Shelf, Dragon, Stoneware, Glazed, 1878, 6 x 8 x 5 In.	1000

MARY GREGORY

MARY GREGORY is the name used for a type of glass that is easily identified. White figures were painted on clear or colored glass as the decoration. The figures chosen were usually children at play. The first glass known as Mary Gregory was made in about 1870. Similar glass is made even today. The traditional story has been that the glass was made at the Boston & Sandwich Glass Company in Sandwich, Massachusetts, by a woman named Mary Gregory. Recent research has shown that none was made at Sandwich. In fact, all early Mary Gregory glass was made in Bohemia. Beginning in 1957, the Westmoreland Glass Co. made the first Mary Gregory–type decorations on American glassware. These pieces had simpler designs, less enamel paint, and more modern shapes. France, Italy, Germany, Switzerland, and England, as well as Bohemia, made this glassware. Children standing, not playing, were pictured after the 1950s.

Biscuit Jar, Blue, Metal Mount, Swing Handle, 13 In.	111
Ewer, Reverse Trumpet, Girls, Woods, Prussian Blue, 14 In.	48
Fairy Lamp, Girl, Skating, Puppy, Cobalt Blue Glass, White Enamel, Domed, c.1900, 6 In.	89

Massier, Jardiniere, Reticulated Handles, Low Relief, Turquoise, France, c.1900, 13 x 18 In.
$455

Rago Arts and Auction Center

Match Holder, Acorn, Painted Flowers, Leaves, Turned Wood, 5 1/2 In.
$189

Hess Auction Group

Match Holder, Billiards Table, Brass, Felt Type Material, Balls, Hinged Lid, Compartments, 2 x 3 1/2 In.
$834

Wm Morford Auctions

M

TIP

If you have glue from a label or piece of tape still stuck on your collectible, it may be possible to remove it by dabbing it with the sticky side of the same kind of label.

Match Holder, Wm. Miller Range & Furnace Co., Tin Lithograph, 1888 Monitor Stove, 4 x 5 In. $116

Showtime Auction Services

Match Safe, Alligator, Sterling Silver, Inscribed, Jacksonville Convention O.R.C. Of Am. 1911, 2 3/8 In. $475

Pook & Pook

Perfume Bottle, Girl, Flowers, Blue Glass, White Enamel, Bulb Stopper, 5 In.	125
Pickle Castor, Boy, Flowers, Cobalt Blue, Silver Plate, 8 In.	72
Pitcher, Cupid, Green Glass, White Enamel, Oval, Lobed, Loop Handle, 6 In.	160
Pitcher, Girl Painting, Landscape, Cranberry Glass, 10 x 6 In.	37
Pitcher, Woman In Tree, Coin Spot, Red, 9 In.	42
Trinket Box, Woman, Bicycle, Cranberry Glass, White Enamel, Squat, 1800s, 3 x 5 In.	355
Tumbler, Girl With Hoop, Cranberry, White Enamel, Victorian, 4 x 3 In.	115
Vase, Boy, Cane, Applied Clear Shells, Green Glass, White Enamel, c.1890, 7 In.	167
Vase, Child Painting, Crimped Rim, Cranberry Glass, 10 x 8 In.	70
Vase, Courting Couple, Bouquet, Glass, Blue, 10 1/4 In. ....*illus*	240
Vase, Green, Girl Painting, Ruffled Rim, Fenton, 10 1/2 x 4 In.	24
Vase, Hyacinth, Sandwich Glass, Teal, 1880s, 7 3/4 In.	65
Vase, Landscape, Opposing Women, Enamel, Blue, 6 x 2 1/2 In., Pair	73

MASONIC, *see Fraternal category.*

MASON'S IRONSTONE was made by the English pottery of Charles J. Mason after 1813. Mason, of Lane Delph, was given a patent for this improved earthenware. He usually called it *Mason's Patent Ironstone China.* It resisted chipping and breaking, so it became popular for dinnerware and other table service dishes. Vases and other decorative pieces were also made. The ironstone was decorated with orange, blue, gold, and other colors, often in Japanese-inspired designs. The firm had financial difficulties but the molds and the name *Mason* were used by many owners through the years, including Francis Morley, Taylor Ashworth, George L. Ashworth, and John Shaw. Mason's joined the Wedgwood group in 1973 and the name was used for a few years and then dropped.

Cake Plate, 8 Sections, Figures, Potted Flowering Tree, Yellow, 1800s, 12 In. ....*illus*	395
Creamer, Chinoiserie Landscape, Pavilion, Figures, Multicolor, Transferware, c.1830, 5 1/4 In.	170
Dish, Japan Pattern, Mums, Peonies, Blue, Red, Gilt, 11 x 7 1/2 In.	70
Pitcher, Cobalt Blue, Octagonal, Flowers, Gold Trim, 7 x 7 In.	50
Pitcher, Gilt, Red, Dragon, Ironstone, 13 x 9 In.	238
Pitcher, Ironstone, Transferware, Figures, Tree, Multicolor, 1830, 5 1/4 In.	212
Pitcher, Ironstone, Transferware, Flowers, White Ground, Green Handle, c.1850, 11 In., Pair	162
Platter, Asiatic Pheasant, Multicolor, 13 3/4 x 18 3/4 In.	312
Platter, Flowers, Diaper, Blue, White, Oval, 21 In.	50
Platter, Manchu, Flowering Bush, Red, White, Oval, Shaped, Handles, 12 x 15 In.	25
Tray, Manchu, Flowering Bush, Red, White, Handles, 11 In.	15
Tureen, Underplate, Lid, Flowers, Cobalt Blue Bands, Handles, 13 x 13 In.	550
Urn, Noble Urn, Old School House Pattern, Ironstone, c.1815-30, 28 1/2 In.	472
Vase, Gilt, Cobalt Blue, Chinoiserie, Circles, 8 In.	100

J.Massier fils **MASSIER,** a French art pottery, was made by brothers Jerome, Delphin, and Clement Massier in Vallauris and Golfe-Juan, France, in the late nineteenth and early twentieth centuries. It has an iridescent metallic luster glaze that resembles the Weller Sicardo pottery glaze. Most pieces are marked J. Massier. Massier may also be listed in the Majolica category.

Candlestick, Seedpod Design, Bowl Cup, Shaped Handle, Tray Base, c.1900, 19 In.	1875
Charger, Scenic, Gold Poplar Trees, Iridescent Red Sky, Marked, 13 In.	472
Jardiniere, Faun Handles, Paw Feet, Olive Green, Majolica, France, c.1880, 6 x 13 In.	312
Jardiniere, Pedestal, Art Nouveau, Figure, Inclined Head, Purple, White, c.1900, 55 In., Pair	3625
Jardiniere, Reticulated Handles, Low Relief, Turquoise, France, c.1900, 13 x 18 In. ....*illus*	455
Jardiniere, Willow Leaves, Greens, Browns, Tapered, Raised Handles, 16 x 13 In.	16250
Plaque, Landscape, Blues & Red, Signed, Clement Massier, Golfe-Juan, 1900s, 7 1/4 x 8 In.	1000
Plaque, Landscape, Multicolor, 7 x 5 1/2 In.	335
Vase, Dragonflies, Daisies, Blue, Green, Tan, Swollen Cylinder, Flattened Rim, 13 x 6 In.	1875
Vase, Fruit Branches, Green, Amber, Iridescent, Shouldered, Wavy Rim, c.1900, 10 In.	1875
Vase, Metallic Glaze, Tan Shaded To Turquoise, Tapered, 4 Asymmetric Handles, D.M., 8 In.	625
Vase, Shells & Seaweed, Gold Iridescent, Blue, Pink, Bell Shape, c.1900, 10 In.	1000

M

MATCH HOLDERS were made to hold the large wooden matches that were used in the nineteenth and twentieth centuries for a variety of purposes. The kitchen stove and the fireplace or furnace had to be lit regularly. One type of match holder was made to hang on the wall, another was designed to be kept on a tabletop. Of special interest today are match holders that have advertisements as part of the design.

Acorn, Painted Flowers, Leaves, Turned Wood, 5 ½ In. ....*illus*	189
Billiards Table, Brass, Felt Type Material, Balls, Hinged Lid, Compartments, 2 x 3 ½ In...*illus*	834
Black Boy, Pink Hat, Seated, Watermelon, Open Top, Bisque, c.1905, 6 x 6 In.	199
Black Cat, On Fence, Tin Lithograph, The Outlet, Providence, R.I., 4⅞ x 3⅜ x 1¼ In.	1610
Figural Devil, Playing Cards, Wall, Royal Bayreuth, c.1900, 4 x 5 In.	139
Figural, DeLaval Cream Separator, Original Box, Blue, 6¼ x 4 In.	288
Flowers, Painted Red & Yellow, Crimped & Shaped Hanger, Tin, 7 x 5 In.	900
Greensburg Brewing Co., Porcelain, c.1904	478
Iron, Figural, Fly, Simpson Iron Co., 2 x 4 ½ x 2⅝ In.	94
Merry War Lye, Asian Woman Washing Clothes, Tin Lithograph, 6 x 4 In...............	719
Rex Flintkote Roofing, Horse Barn, Tin Lithograph, 5 x 4 x 1 In.	546
Topsy Hosiery, Woman At Beach, Black Boy Logo, Tin Lithograph, 5 x 3 ½ In...........	518
Wm. Miller Range & Furnace Co., Tin Lithograph, 1888 Monitor Stove, 4 x 5 In..........*illus*	116

MATCH SAFES were designed to be carried in the pocket. Early matches were made with phosphorus and could ignite unexpectedly. The matches were safely stored in the tightly closed container. Match safes were made in sterling silver, plated silver, or other metals. The English call these "vesta boxes."

Alligator, Sterling Silver, Inscribed, Jacksonville Convention O.R.C. Of Am. 1911, 2⅜ In. .*illus*	475
Alligator Skin Wrap, Sterling Cartouche, c.1898, 1⅞ x 1¼ In.	69
Anheuser-Busch Brewing Assoc., 24th Knights Templar Conclave, c.1889...........................	398
Belly Dancer, Brass, Multicolor, ½ x 1 In.	94
Book, Man On Elephant, Warrior, 2⅝ In.	246
Brass, Peeing Woman, Multicolor, 1 ½ x 2 x ½ In.	218
Buggy, Parcel Gilt, Aiken Lambert, c.1890, 2¼ In.......................	150
Cardinal On Branch, Red, Yellow, Green, 5 ½ In.	90
Demon, Figural, Silver Plate, Gorham, c.1900, 2⅛ In.	197 to 246
Dog, Lying Down, Figural, Silver Plate, Gorham, c.1900, 2⅛ In.	320
Dog, Seated, Silver, Hat, Feather Plume, Ruffled Collar, Match Strike, 2¼ In.....................*illus*	319
Flag, Blue, Leaves, Silver, Reed & Barton, c.1890, 2 ½ In.	54
General Grant, Figural Bust, Nickel, c.1900, 2 ½ In........	480
Grover Cleveland, Figural Bust, Nickel, c.1900, 2 ½ In.........	480
Iris, Silver, Parcel Gilt, c.1890, 2¾ In.	106
Naked Woman In Waves With Birds, Unger, c.1905, 2⅜ In.	187
Pansies, Blue & Yellow, Variegated Green Leaves, 5 ½ In.	390
Robert E. Lee, Portrait, Flags On Reverse, 2 ½ In........................*illus*	188
Rumely Co., Threshing Machinery & Engines, Celluloid, c.1910, 3 In.	345
Snowy Owl On Branch, Green Leaf, 5 ½ In.	335
Standard Oil, 1 ½ x 2¾ x⅜ In.	153
U.S., Rifleman, Bullet, Silver, Reed & Barton, 2¾ In.	74
United Cigar Stores, Tin Lithograph, 2¼ x 1⅝ x ¼ In.........	106
Vesta, Mixed Metal, 1900, 2 ½ In.	185

MATT MORGAN, an English artist, was making pottery in Cincinnati, Ohio, by 1883. His pieces were decorated to resemble Moorish wares. Incised designs and colors were applied to raised panels on the pottery. Shiny or matte glazes were used. The company lasted less than two years.

MATT MORGAN
—CIN. O—
ART POTTERY Cº

Charger, Owls, Clouds, Landscape, Hirschfeld, 11 In.	1680
Charger, Woman, Profile, Headscarf, Yellow Olive, 1880s, 14¼ In.........	2280
Pitcher, Brown Incised Leaves, Mottled Green, 7 In.	540
Pitcher, Caramel Glaze, Gold Trim, Raised Corn Band, c. 1883, 6 ½ x 6 In......................*illus*	1650
Vase, Birds, Branches, Gold, 2 Handles, 15 ½ In.	4440

Match Safe, Dog, Seated, Silver, Hat, Feather Plume, Ruffled Collar, Match Strike, 2¼ In.
$319

Ruby Lane

Match Safe, Robert E. Lee, Portrait, Flags On Reverse, 2 ½ In.
$188

Pook & Pook

Matt Morgan, Pitcher, Caramel Glaze, Gold Trim, Raised Corn Band, c. 1883, 6 ½ x 6 In.
$1,650

Ruby Lane

M

McCoy, Cookie Jar, Flared Bowl, Cowboy Hat Lid, Western Impressions, 1950s, 12 x 12 In.
$316

Allard Auctions

McKee, Canister, Cereal, Jade, 1930s, 6¼ x 2¾ In.
$240

Ruby Lane

Medical, Cabinet, Apothecary, Mixed Wood, 36 Drawers, Slide Lip Top, 1800s, 34 x 32 In.
$2,478

Hess Auction Group

MCCOY pottery was made in Roseville, Ohio. Nelson McCoy and J.W. McCoy established the Nelson McCoy Sanitary and Stoneware Company in Roseville, Ohio, in 1910. The firm made art pottery after 1926. In 1933 it became the Nelson McCoy Pottery Company. Pieces marked McCoy were made by the Nelson McCoy Pottery Company. Cookie jars were made from about 1940 until December 1990, when the McCoy factory closed. Since 1991 pottery with the McCoy mark has been made by firms unrelated to the original company. Because there was a company named Brush-McCoy, there is great confusion between Brush and Nelson McCoy pieces. See Brush category for more information.

Bookends, Lilies, Burgundy, Green, Yellow, Gloss, 1948, 5½ x 5 In.	95
Bowl, Green Matte Glaze, Art Deco, Raised Lines, Rectangular Feet, c.1962, 8 x 4 In.	28
Cookie Jar, Barrel Shape, Nabisco, 9¼ x 7 In.	55
Cookie Jar, Flared Bowl, Cowboy Hat Lid, Western Impressions, 1950s, 12 x 12 In...........*illus*	316
Cookie Jar, Wishing Well, Brown, 9 x 7 In.	89
Dish, Open Shell, Coral, 6 x 4 In.	25
Pitcher, Buccaneer, Green Glaze, 1926, 8 In.	38
Planter, Baseball Glove, Ball, Brown, White, c.1957	145
Planter, Turtle, Green, Yellow Highlights, 5 x 8 In.	39
Planter, Wild Rose, Pink, Yellow, c.1940, 5½ In.	45
Vase, Handles, Shouldered, Collar Rim, Blue, Marked, c.1950, 18 In.	135
Vase, Poppy, Pink, Green, 8⅜ In.	65
Vase, Stoneware, Leaves, Handles, Brown, 7 In.	34
Wall Pocket, Greek Key, White, 7 x 4 In.	85

McKEE is a name associated with various glass enterprises in the United States since 1836, including J. & F. McKee (1850), Bryce, McKee & Co. (1850 to 1854), McKee and Brothers (1865), and National Glass Co. (1899). In 1903, the McKee Glass Company was formed in Jeannette, Pennsylvania. It became McKee Division of the Thatcher Glass Co. in 1951 and was bought out by the Jeannette Corporation in 1961. Pressed glass, kitchenwares, and tablewares were produced. Jeannette Corporation closed in the early 1980s. Additional pieces may be included in the Custard Glass and Depression Glass categories.

Bowl, Cereal, Jade, Lid, 5 In.	75
Bowl, Snappy, Footed, 10 In.	64
Butter, Aztec Sunburst, 1910, 7 x 5 In.	45
Cake Stand, Ball & Swirl, 5¼ x 10¾ In.	160
Canister, Cereal, Jade, 1930s, 6¼ x 2¾ In. ....*illus*	240
Compote, Majestic, c.1893, 8 In.	75
Dish, Pickle, Teutonic c.1894, 8⅜ In.	12
Pitcher, Fentec, c.1894-1914, 9¼ In.	49
Sherbet, Rock Crystal, Red, 3½ In.	75
Water Dispenser, Bright Lime Green	290

MECHANICAL BANKS *are listed in the Bank category.*

MEDICAL office furniture, operating tools, microscopes, thermometers, and other paraphernalia used by doctors are included in this category. Veterinary collectibles are also included here. Medicine bottles are listed in the Bottle category. There are related collectibles listed under Dental.

Anatomical Outline Map, Smith's American Mankin Co., Late 1800s, 44 x 20 In.	600
Bedpan, Blue, White, Transfer Print, Leaves, Staffordshire, c.1840, 13¾ In.	148
Bedpan, Brown, Glossy, Poe Pottery, 13½ In.	63
Bedpan, Tin, Removable Lid, Weiss, 19½ In.	29
Cabinet, Apothecary, Cherry, Poplar, 21 Drawers, 4 Doors, 1900s, 43 x 72 In.	1875
Cabinet, Apothecary, Hutch, Wood, Paint, Glass Knobs, Cupboards, c.1910, 58 x 36 In.	1250
Cabinet, Apothecary, Mixed Wood, 36 Drawers, Slide Lip Top, 1800s, 34 x 32 In. ....*illus*	2478
Cabinet, Apothecary, Paint, Mirrored Back, 2 Sections, Brass Pulls, 92 x 72 In.	1680
Cabinet, Apothecary, Pine, 12 Dovetailed Drawers, Painted, c.1825, 32 x 30 In. ....*illus*	605
Cabinet, Apothecary, Pine, Oak, 4 Rows Of 4 Drawers, Cast Handles, Labels, 34 x 49 In.	474

Cabinet, Apothecary, Poplar, Painted, Blue, c.1900, 41 x 39 ¾ In.	1440
Cabinet, Apothecary, Red, Chinese Export, 37 ½ x 29 ½ In.	213
Cabinet, Apothecary, Slant Front, Mixed Wood, 18 Drawers, c.1850, 30 x 16 In.	900
Cabinet, Specimen, Bird's-Eye Maple, Carved, Mirror, Drawers, Doors, c.1890, 63 x 31 In. . *illus*	1936
Chest, Apothecary, Blue Paint, Molded Edge & Base, 16 Drawers, 1900s, 14 x 25 In.	474
Chest, Apothecary, Drawer, Mahogany, 2 Glass Bottles, 6 x 5 ½ In.	178
Chest, Apothecary, Tiger Maple, 36 Drawers, 6 Rows, Mushroom Knobs, 30 x 34 In.	2785
Chest, Apothecary, William IV, Stained Oak, Maple Inlaid Edges, 3 Compartments, 6 x 12 In. .	208
Dissection Kit, 6 Scalpels, Ivory Handles, Scissors, Mahogany Case, 7 ¾ In.	437
Invalid Feeder, Blue, White, Transfer Print, Flowers, Soft Paste, 3 In.	718
Invalid Feeder, Blue, White, Transfer Print, Half Cover, Copeland, 3 x 7 ¼ In.	230
Invalid Feeder, Faience, White, Flowers, Half Lid, 3 ⅞ In.	69
Medicine Spoon, Gibson Type, Silver, Hinged Lid, England, 5 In.	225
Model, Hand, Bones, Muscles, Nerves, Multicolor, 7 ½ In.	148
Model, Maxillofacial, Nerves, Neck, Muscles, Eye, Wax, 9 x 7 In.	744
Model, Skeleton, Papier-Mache, 77 In.	687
Phrenology Bust, Glazed Ceramic, Lorenzo Fowler, 11 ¾ In.	1667
Phrenology Bust, Paper Labels, Fowler & Wells, 1872, 8 ½ In.	437
Phrenology Head, Porcelain, Molded Lines, L.N. Fowler, England, 1800s, 11 ½ In.	700
Phrenology Head, White, Black, L.N. Fowler, 12 In.	41
Pill Tile, Blue, White, Porcelain, Octagonal, England, c.1700, 10 x 12 ⅜ In.	6250
Prosthetic Stump, Boot, Shoe, Leather, 1800s, 12 In.	403
Scale, Pharmaceutical, Brass, F. Leunig & Co., London, Tripod Base, 1800s, 23 ½ In.	125
Sign, Caution Measles, White, 1800s, 9 ½ x 13 ½ In.	57
Skull, Human, 6 x 8 ¼ In.	295
Trade Sign, Chiropractic, Art Deco, Spread Wing Angel, Cast Aluminum, c.1930, 25 In.	375
Trunk, Transporting Human Blood, Lined, Metal Brackets, Hollinger Corp., 23 x 22 In. *illus*	393
Wheelchair, Wood, Padding, Nail Heads, Arms, 46 ¼ In.	138

MEISSEN is a town in Germany where porcelain has been made since 1710. Any china made in the town can be called Meissen, although the famous Meissen factory made the finest porcelains of the area. The crossed swords mark of the great Meissen factory has been copied by many other firms in Germany and other parts of the world. Pieces of Meissen dinnerware in the Onion pattern are listed in their own category in this book.

Bowl, Lid, Animals, Insects, Flower Finial, Marcolini, c.1800, 3 ¾ x 3 In.	607
Bowl, Reticulated Rim, Basket Weave, Flower Bouquets, 8 x 2 In.	118
Butter, Cover, Oval, Cartouches, Figures, Scroll, 2 Handles, Paw Feet, c.1726, 7 In.	11937
Candlestick, 2 Children, 4 Seasons Allegory, Crossed Swords Mark, 12 ¾ In., Pair	550
Candlestick, Rococo, White, Green, Flowers, 9 ½ In., 3 Piece	125
Centerpiece, 3 Women, Robes, Urn Of Flowers, Tripartite Base, Roses, c.1900, 36 In.	948
Centerpiece, Figural, Multicolor, Germany, 1900s, 14 ¾ In.	812
Centerpiece, Triton, Figural, Coiled Tail, Pierced Powel, c.1900, 17 ¼ In.	5750
Chocolate Pot, Iron Red, Panels, Figures, Flowers, Gilt Spout & Handle, c.1745, 6 In.	2387
Coffee Set, Indische Malerei Pattern, White, Pink Flowers, 9-In. Pot, 16 Piece	593
Coffeepot, Flower Sprays, Figural Spout, Gilt Trim, Blue Crossed Swords, 9 ¾ In. *illus*	192
Cup, Trembleuse, Hand Painted, 1800s, 4 ½ In., Pair	676
Cup, White, Molded Birds & Vines, Scrolled Ear Shape Handles, c.1715, 3 In., Pair	2203
Dish, 5 Lobes, Prunus Branches, Chrysanthemums, Marked, c.1730, 4 In.	2203
Dish, Lid, Figural, Gilded, 3 Putti, Flowers, Scrolling Base, Late 1800s, 8 ⅝ x 6 x 4 ⅞ In.	677
Drink Set, Teapot, Chocolate Pot, Waste Bowl, Cups, Children Playing, 10 Piece	200
Figurine, Bird & Squirrel, Crossed Swords Mark, 1800s, 16 In.	1955
Figurine, Bird Seller, Basket, 6 In.	438
Figurine, Bird, Multicolor, Naturalistic Tree Stump, 1900s, 7 ¾ In.	400
Figurine, Boy, Seated, 1800s, 5 ½ In.	489
Figurine, Child, Seated, Drinking Tea, 4 In.	500
Figurine, Chinese Woman, Carrying Sack On Back, Hat, Flower Robe, c.1745, 5 In.	6611
Figurine, Chocolate Girl, Holding Tray, Crossed Swords Mark, 1800s, 15 In. *illus*	3220
Figurine, Count Bruhl, Tailor, Riding Goat, Crossed Swords Mark, 1800s, 17 In. *illus*	14950

Medical, Cabinet, Apothecary, Pine, 12 Dovetailed Drawers, Painted, c.1825, 32 x 30 In.
$605

James D. Julia Auctioneers

Medical, Cabinet, Specimen, Bird's-Eye Maple, Carved, Mirror, Drawers, Doors, c.1890, 63 x 31 In.
$1,936

James D. Julia Auctioneers

Medical, Trunk, Transporting Human Blood, Lined, Metal Brackets, Hollinger Corp., 23 x 22 In.
$393

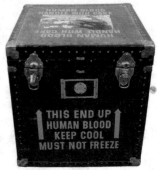

Rachel Davis Fine Arts

Meissen, Coffeepot, Flower Sprays, Figural Spout, Gilt Trim, Blue Crossed Swords, 9¾ In.
$192

Neal Auctions

Meissen, Figurine, Chocolate Girl, Holding Tray, Crossed Swords Mark, 1800s, 15 In.
$3,220

Cottone Auctions

Meissen, Figurine, Count Bruhl, Tailor, Riding Goat, Crossed Swords Mark, 1800s, 17 In.
$14,950

Cottone Auctions

Meissen, Figurine, Triton Netting Nude Nymph, 15 x 8½ In.
$8,800

Ruby Lane

Meissen, Group, 3 Cherubs, Book, Crossed Swords Mark, 1800s, 8 In.
$1,495

Cottone Auctions

Mercury Glass, Jug, Stopper, Narrow Neck, Cylindrical, 22 x 11½ In.
$295

Ruby Lane

M

Figurine, Dog, Bolognese Terrier, Brown, White, Seated, 9 In., Pair	2000
Figurine, Dog, On Stump, Licking Child's Face, White Nightgown, Gilt, c.1885, 16 In.	7434
Figurine, Girl, Holding Flower Bouquet, Lamb By Side, Marked, c.1908, 6 ½ In.	1295
Figurine, Leopard & Snake, Crossed Swords Mark, 1800s, 5 ½ x 9 In.	1265
Figurine, Malabar, Multicolor Costume, Gilded Base, Late 1800s, 7 ½ In., Pair	4613
Figurine, Man, Woman, 18th Century Clothing, Tree Trunks, Gilt Scrolls, 19 In., Pair	2880
Figurine, Muff, Book, Michael Victor Acier, 8 x 3 ¼ In.	610
Figurine, Musicians, Multicolor, 5 ½ In., Pair	615
Figurine, Servant With Swaddling Baby, Mask Face, Plaid Shawl, Ruffled Bonnet, 7 In.	1254
Figurine, St. George Slaying Dragon, Crossed Swords Mark, 1800s, 9 ½ In.	978
Figurine, Triton Netting Nude Nymph, 15 x 8 ½ In. ....*illus*	8800
Figurine, Venus With Cupid, Crossed Swords Mark, 1800s, 17 x 6 ½ In.	2760
Figurine, Woman, Birdcage, 1700s Dress, 6 x 3 ¾ In.	472
Figurine, Woman, Seated, Crossed Swords Mark, 1800s, 8 In.	920
Figurine, Young Girl With Bell Rattle & Doll, Lace Edging Detail, Bows, 5 ½ In.	570
Group, 3 Cherubs, Book, Crossed Swords Mark, 1800s, 8 In. ....*illus*	1495
Group, 4 Dancing Children, Multicolor, 6 ¼ x 6 ¼ In.	1140
Group, 4-Piece Monkey Band, Keyboard, Harp, Violin, Horn, Late 1800s, 4 ⅞ To 5 ⅞ In.	1599
Group, Bacchus, Satyr, Putto, Drinking Wine, c.1900, 16 ½ x 5 ½ In.	1920
Group, Battling Elk, Multicolor, c.1900, 4 ⅛ x 9 ½ In.	450
Group, Disciplinary Scene, Woman Holding Switch, Boy & Girl, Dog, Gilt Base, 8 In.	900
Group, Musicians, 1800s, 6 In.	1323
Group, Standing Woman, Seated Man, Wine Jug, 8 x 5 ¼ In.	793
Group, Swan, Cygnets, 1800s, 4 ¾ In.	156
Group, Venus & Attendants, Nude Women, Boy, River, Shells, Fish, 8 ¾ In.	2375
Group, Women & Children With Fishing Net, 1800s, 12 x 10 In.	2070
Jar, Lid, Green & White, Green Landscape, White Ground, Early 1900s, 9 ½ In., Pair	1046
Plate, Architectural Scene, Cobalt Blue & Gilt, Marked, 10 In., Pair	1230
Plate, Cabinet, Cobalt Blue & Gilt, Reticulated Rim, Bands, Painted Scene, c.1885	5500
Plate, Gilt, Cobalt, Center Reserve, Flower Bouquet, Scalloped Edges, 11 ½ In., 3 Piece	318
Plate, Girl, Ewer, Candlelight, Reticulated, 9 ½ In.	4000
Plate, Portrait, Woman, Reticulated, 9 ⅜ In.	4000
Platter, Blue, Flowers, Crossed Swords Mark, Early 1900s, 20 ¾ x 15 In.	70
Plinth, Multicolor, Flowers, Gilt Accents, Late 1800s, 3 ¼ x 12 x 12 In.	400
Snuffbox, Lid, Oval Panel, Figures, Gilt & Red Scrollwork, Shaped, c.1735, 3 x 2 In.	14692
Tea & Coffee Set, Teapot, Coffeepot, Sugar & Creamer, New Bradenstein Variation, 4 Piece	476
Tea Canister, Saucer Lid, Finial, Peasant Scenes, Gilt Scrollwork Border, c.1750	2203
Tray, Cobalt, Parcel Gilt, Cherubs, Undulating Rim, Quatrefoil Medallion, 11 x 8 In.	178
Tray, Gilt, Cobalt Blue Border, Shells, Purple Flowers, 16 ¼ In.	375
Tray, Shaped, Partial Gilt, Flowers, Winged Cherubs, Scrolled Leaves, Black, 11 x 8 In.	178
Tureen, Gilt Bronze Stand, Putto, Flower Basket, Leaf Handles, 13 ¾ x 8 ¼ In.	854
Tureen, Lid, Underplate, Oblong, Exotic Flowers, 10 ½ x 14 ¾ In.	357
Urn, Lid, Pate-Sur-Pate, Robed Woman, Gold Enamel, Late 1800s, 12 x 7 In.	8625
Urn, White, Gilt Relief Trim, Curled Serpent Handles, Footed, Crossed Swords, 15 In., Pair	1920
Vase, Cobalt, Gilt, Fluted, Double Serpent Handles, Crossed Swords, 18 ½ x 13 In., Pair	600
Vase, Indistinctly Painted, Blue White, High Shoulders, Narrow Neck, 1992, 27 ½ In.	12500
Vase, Pate-Sur-Pate, Multicolor, Collared Neck, Silvered Palmettes, Late 1800s, 9 ⅞ In.	10455
Vase, White, Multicolor Flowers, Gilt, Flared, Low Upturned Handles, Footed, 10 In., Pair	360

MERCURY GLASS, or silvered glass, was first made in the 1850s. It lost favor for a while but became popular again about 1910. It looks like a piece of silver.

Ball, Pedestal, c.1840, 12 x 7 In.	120
Bowl, Leaves, Sprays, Gold Interior, Lid, c.1880, 8 In.	200
Ice Bucket, Figural Apple, Lid, Red, Brass Stem Finial, Clear Glass Interior, 1920s	700
Jug, Stopper, Narrow Neck, Cylindrical, 22 x 11 ½ In. ....*illus*	295
Urn, Fluted, Double Lobe Lid, Bulbous, Waisted, Saucer Foot, 1960s, 22 In.	235
Vase, Conical, Ringed, Knob Stem, Stepped Pedestal, Frost, Gold, 1800s, 12 In.	200
Vase, Flowers, Bird, Flared Outside Rim, Frosted, c.1880, 10 ½ In.	275

Merrimac, Vase, Ribbed, Green, c.1905, 14 ¼ In.
$845

Rago Arts and Auction Center

Metlox, California Ivy, Gravy Boat, 10 ½ x 3 ½ In.
$18

Tias

Metlox, Florence, Bowl, Vegetable, Divided, Oval, Vernonware, 1970s, 12 x 9 In.
$12

M

Tias

TIP

Don't use any type of tape on porcelain or pottery that has overglazed decorations. Gilding and enamels may pull off when the tape is removed. Antiques shops often tape a lid to a bowl; when you buy, ask the dealer to remove the tape to be sure no damage has been done.

Metlox, Homestead Provincial, Pitcher, Blue, Poppytrail, 6⅞ x 6 In. $23

Ruby Lane

Metlox, Poppytrail, Mug, California Pottery, 8 Oz., 3⅜ In. $34

Tias

> **TIP**
> Most old majolica pieces have a colored bottom. The newer pieces have white bottoms.

Mettlach, Beaker, No. 2842-1171, Pilsner, Dwarf, Vines, Print Over Glaze, ¼ Liter $36

Fox Auctions

MERRIMAC POTTERY Company was founded by Thomas Nickerson in Newburyport, Massachusetts, in 1902. The company made art pottery, garden pottery, and reproductions of Roman pottery. The pottery burned to the ground in 1908.

Vase, Green Glaze, Bottle Form, Stepped Neck, 2 Loop Handles, c.1905, 6½ x 6 In.	1125
Vase, Green Glaze, Mottled, Squat, Reeded Strap Handles, c.1905, 4 x 8 In.	1750
Vase, Green Glaze, Tapered Flared Rim, c.1905, 11½ x 4½ In.	938
Vase, Green Glaze, Traces Of Black, Swollen Shape, Sturgeon Mark, 9½ x 9 In.	1375
Vase, Leaves, Textured & Shaded Green Glaze, Bulbous, c.1905, 6½ x 5 In.	875
Vase, Orange & Green Glazes, Bulbous, Cylindrical Neck, 7¾ x 6 In.	2375
Vase, Overlapping Leaves, Elongated, Green Glaze, Bulbous, c.1905, 6 x 4¾ In.	4063
Vase, Ribbed, Green, c.1905, 14¼ In. ....*illus*	845
Vase, Uranium Yellow Glaze, Swollen Shape, 2 Ear Handles, 12 x 7½ In.	1125
Wall Pocket, Applied Frog, Green Frothy Glaze, Cup Form, 5 x 6 x 3 In.	625

METLOX POTTERIES was founded in 1927 in Manhattan Beach, California. Dinnerware was made beginning in 1931. Evan K. Shaw purchased the company in 1946 and expanded the number of patterns. Poppytrail (1946–89) and Vernonware (1958–80) were divisions of Metlox under E.K. Shaw's direction. The factory closed in 1989.

Antique Grape, Bowl, Vegetable, Divided, Round, 9½ In.	42
Antique Grape, Dish, Cereal, 7 In.	19
Antique Grape, Platter, Round, 12½ In.	38
Bandero, Bowl, Vegetable, Divided, Round, 9½ In.	22
Bandero, Coffeepot, Lid	69
Bandero, Gravy Boat	21
Blueberry Hill, Platter, Square, 13½ In.	22
Blueberry Provincial, Cup & Saucer	11
California Apple, Creamer	22
California Freeform, Gravy Boat	38
California Ivy, Gravy Boat, 10½ x 3½ In. ....*illus*	18
California Ivy, Plate, Dinner, 10⅜ In.	19
California Provincial, Creamer	28
California Rose, Cup & Saucer	12
California Rose, Gravy Boat	48
California Strawberry, Butter, Cover, ½ Lb.	29
California Strawberry, Sugar, Lid	26
Camellia, Plate, Luncheon, 9 In.	18
Cape Cod, Creamer	22
Della Robia, Plate, Dinner, 10⅝ In.	18
Della Robia, Platter, 14 In.	33
Florence, Bowl, Vegetable, Divided, Oval, Vernonware, 1970s, 12 x 9 In. ....*illus*	12
Golden Fruit, Plate, Dinner, 10½ In.	14
Grape Arbor, Cup & Saucer	12
Grape Arbor, Sugar & Creamer	32
Homestead Provincial, Cup & Saucer	10 to 22
Homestead Provincial, Pitcher, Blue, Poppytrail, 6⅞ x 6 In. ....*illus*	23
Homestead Provincial, Plate, Dinner, 10 In.	12 to 25
LaMancha Gold, Cup	8
Mayflower, Chop Plate, 12 In.	32
Navajo, Cup & Saucer	15
Palm Springs, Bowl, Vegetable, Lid, Round	65
Peach Blossom, Cup & Saucer	18
Peach Blossom, Plate, Dinner, 10 In.	15
Pomegranate, Teakettle, 4½ Cup	73
Poppytrail, Mug, California Pottery, 8 Oz., 3⅜ In. ....*illus*	34
Provincial Blue, Cup & Saucer	12 to 14
Provincial Fruit, Creamer	19
Provincial Rose, Cup & Saucer	19
Provincial Rose, Plate, Dinner, 10⅝ In.	18

Provincial Rose, Plate, Salad, 7 5/8 In.	10
Provincial Rose, Salt & Pepper	30
Red Rooster, Cup & Saucer	12
Red Rooster, Plate, Dinner, 10 In.	18
Red Rooster, Platter, Oval, 13 1/2 In.	45
Rose A Day, Bowl, Vegetable, Lid, 9 1/2 In.	69
Rose A Day, Pitcher, 44 Oz., 8 1/4 In.	55
Rose A Day, Pitcher, 64 Oz., 9 3/4 In.	65
San Clemente, Cup & Saucer, Spanish Yellow	15
San Fernando, Bowl, Vegetable, Divided, 11 1/2 In.	26
San Fernando, Chop Plate, 14 1/4 In.	40
Sculptured Berry, Plate, Salad, 7 3/4 In.	20
Sculptured Daisy, Salt & Pepper	28
Sculptured Zinnia, Gravy Boat, Underplate	35
Sculptured Zinnia, Platter, 14 1/4 In.	40
Tropicana, Flowerpot, 5 In.	238
Vintage Pink, Gravy Boat, Underplate	35
Vintage Pink, Plate, Dinner, 10 1/2 In.	20
Woodland Gold, Teapot, Lid, 5 Cup, 5 In.	58

METTLACH, Germany, is a city where the Villeroy and Boch factories worked. Steins from the firm are marked with the word *Mettlach* or the castle mark. They date from about 1842. *PUG* means painted under glaze. The steins can be dated from the marks on the bottom, which include a date-number code. Other pieces may be listed in the Villeroy & Boch category.

Beaker, No. 2842-1171, Pilsner, Dwarf, Vines, Print Over Glaze, 1/4 Liter .....*illus*	36
Charger, Art Nouveau, Woman, Profile, Purple Flowers, 1900, 12 In.	950
Charger, Etched, Black Ground, Buff & Ivory, Pan Playing Flute To Maiden, c.1895, 15 1/4 In.	308
Charger, Phanolith, Green Blue Ground, White Relief, Bacchanalian, Early 1900s, 21 In.	154
Jardiniere, No. 7027, Classical Figures, Phanolith, Pedestal Base, 8 In.....*illus*	480
Pitcher, Relief, Multicolor, Green & Tan, Hunting Scene, J. Stahl, Signed, Early 1900s, 17 In.	246
Plaque, No. 1044/83, PUG, Lakeside Scene, 13 3/5 In.	72
Plaque, No. 1044/5186, Snowy Scene At Hunting Castle, Blue & White, 17 In.	144
Plaque, No. 1044/5187, Snowy Scene At Church, Blue & White, Glow In Windows, 17 In.	144
Plaque, No. 1384 & 1385, Etched, W.S., Medieval Warriors, 14 1/2 In., Pair	360
Plaque, No. 2011 & 2012, Etched, Black Eagle Shield, Red Lion Shield, 12 3/5 x 10 1/2 In., Pair	720
Plaque, No. 2022 & 2023, Etched & Glazed, 1 Blue Center, 1 Red Center, 20 1/5 In., Pair	750
Plaque, No. 2042, Etched, Stocke, 2 Riders On Horses On Road, 15 1/5 In.	450
Plaque, No. 2361A, Castle On Hill, Wartburg, 17 In.	288
Plaque, No. 2739, Etched, Munchen, Buildings Of The Town, 19 3/10 In.	2760
Plaque, No. 5178 & 5179/1044, Delft, Windmill Lake Scenes, Blue & White, 17 1/2 In., Pair	216
Plaque, No. 7049, Porcelain, Oval, Green, White, Flowers, 14 x 11 In. .....*illus*	540
Plaque, Phanolith, Pate-Sur-Pate, Maidens & Warriors, Early 1900s, 11 3/4 x 15 1/4 In., Pair	615
Plaque, Portrait, Woman, Poppies, Leafy Band, Art Nouveau Style, R. Fournier, c.1910, 19 In.	310
Plaque, White, Pate-Sur-Pate, Trojan War Figures, Johann Baptist Stahl, c.1900, 11 x 24 In.	1230
Punch Bowl, Lid, Cameo, Green & Blue & Plum, Early 1900s, 13 1/4 x 12 3/8 In.	215
Punch Bowl, Lid, Stand, Art Nouveau, Female Portrait, Grapevines, Handles, c.1910, 12 In....*illus*	615
Punch Bowl, No. 2234, Relief, Birds, Grape Leaves, Grapevine Handles, Footed, 3 Liter	144
Punch Bowl, No. 989, PUG, H. Schlitt, Gnome Figural Lid, 1 3/4 Liter .....*illus*	240
Stein, No. 1526, Mines & Mining Building, World's Fair, Chicago, Ill., Pewter Lid, 1893, 1/2 Liter	1110
Stein, No. 1851, Friedrich Jahn Bust, 4F Symbol, Gymnastic's Club, c.1900, 18 In.....*illus*	1440
Stein, No. 1909, Devil Playing Cards With Man, Print Over Glaze, Spiel, 1/2 Liter.....*illus*	204
Stein, No. 1925/639, Woman, Fancy Dress, Plumed Hat, PUG, 1 Liter .....*illus*	192
Stein, No. 2001K, Banking Book, Decorated Relief, Inlaid Lid, 1/2 Liter	192
Stein, No. 2049, Chessboard, Etched, Inlaid Lid, 1/2 Liter	1500
Stein, No. 2093, Cards, Etched, Inlaid Lid, 4 Panels With Face Cards, 1/2 Liter	570
Stein, No. 2106, Monkeys In Cage, Decorated Relief, Inlaid Lid, 2/5 Liter	2820
Stein, No. 2223, Man On Horse, Townspeople, Etched, Tapered, Pewter Lid, 22 In.	2311
Stein, No. 2282, Boy In Wine Cellar, Pewter Lid, Thumblift, 1/2 Liter	123
Stein, No. 2384/1075, Firefighting Scenes, Print Over Glaze, 2 Liter.....*illus*	600

Mettlach, Jardiniere, No. 7027, Classical Figures, Phanolith, Pedestal Base, 8 In. $480

The Stein Auction Company

Mettlach, Plaque, No. 7049, Porcelain, Oval, Green, White, Flowers, 14 x 11 In. $540

The Stein Auction Company

M

Missing Lids
Many beer steins seem to be missing their metal lids. In 1916, Germany needed metal for the war effort and citizens had to sell items made of gold, silver, brass, bronze, copper, and pewter to the government. The pewter steins and lids were melted for the war effort.

This is an edited listing of current prices. Visit **Kovels.com** to check thousands of prices from previous years and sign up for free information on trends, tips, reproductions, marks, and more.

Mettlach, Punch Bowl, Lid, Stand, Art Nouveau, Female Portrait, Grapevines, Handles, c.1910, 12 In. $615

Skinner, Inc.

Mettlach, Punch Bowl, No. 989, PUG, H. Schlitt, Gnome Figural Lid, 1 ¾ Liter $240

The Stein Auction Company

Mettlach, Stein, No. 1851, Friedrich Jahn Bust, 4F Symbol, Gymnastic's Club, c.1900, 18 In. $1,440

Cowan's Auctions

Mettlach, Stein, No. 1909, Devil Playing Cards With Man, Print Over Glaze, Spiel, ½ Liter $204

Fox Auctions

Mettlach, Stein, No. 1925/639, Woman, Fancy Dress, Plumed Hat, PUG, 1 Liter $192

Fox Auctions

TIP

Old milk glass is slightly opalescent at the edge when held up to a strong light. New glass is not.

Mettlach, Stein, No. 2384/1075, Firefighting Scenes, Print Over Glaze, 2 Liter $600

Fox Auctions

M

Stein, No. 2585, Munich Child, On Globe, Etched & Decorated Relief, Inlaid Lid, 1 Liter	216
Stein, No. 2640, Cavalier & Barmaid, Etched, Inlaid Lid, Small Glaze Flake, $\frac{1}{2}$ Liter	156
Stein, No. 2688, Bowling Scenes, Cameo, Bowling Ball Inlaid Lid, 2 $\frac{1}{2}$ Liter	960
Stein, No. 2718, David & Goliath, Etched, Inlaid Lid, 1 Liter	1320
Stein, No. 2761, Couples, 3 Panels, Blue Ground, Cameo, Inlaid Lid, Stahl, 2 Liter	1020
Stein, No. 2764, Knight On White Horse, Etched, Inlaid Lid, H. Schlitt, 5 $\frac{4}{5}$ Liter, 24 $\frac{1}{10}$ In.	5160
Stein, No. 2765, Knight On White Horse, Etched, Turret Lid, Schlitt, $\frac{1}{2}$ Liter	1560
Stein, No. 2777, People Drinking, Knights, Etched, H. Schlitt, Inlaid Lid, 3 $\frac{1}{10}$ Liter, 16 $\frac{4}{5}$ In.	1920
Stein, No. 2802, Etched, Wheat & Heart, Art Nouveau, Dark Blue & Orange, $\frac{1}{2}$ Liter	282 to 510
Stein, No. 2935, Art Nouveau Leaves, Lattice Band, Inlaid Lid, $\frac{1}{2}$ Liter	390
Stein, No. 2967, Farmer Holding Pigs, Etched, Marked P, Prototype, Pewter Lid, 1 Liter	785
Stein, No. 3143, Tirol & Eagle Shield, Couples In Ethnic Clothing, Etched, $\frac{1}{2}$ Liter	480
Stein, No. 3335, Men With Barmaids At Table, Etched, Munich Child Inlaid Lid, $\frac{1}{2}$ Liter	348
Stein, No. 3350, Playing Finger Game, Etched, Inlaid Lid, $\frac{1}{4}$ Liter	390
Stein, No. 5016, Flower Sprigs, Cartouche, Purple, Blue, Pewter Lid & Foot, 1 $\frac{1}{2}$ Liter	180
Stein, Parian Ware, Schutzen Scene, Inlaid Lid, July 1862, $\frac{1}{2}$ Liter	540
Stein, Thirsty Knight, Der Durstige Ritter, Stoneware, Marked, 1900s, $\frac{1}{2}$ Liter	300
Tureen, Working Gnomes, Handles, Multicolor, 10 $\frac{1}{4}$ x 16 In.	88
Vase, Etched, Lekythos Shape, Loop Handles, Brown, Rust & Buff, Maidens, c.1898, 13 In.	215
Vase, No. 2537, Hand Engraved, Art Nouveau, 12 In.	510
Vase, Pate-Sur-Pate, Dark Blue, Raised Flowers, 1900, 13 $\frac{4}{5}$ In.	437

MILK GLASS was named for its milky white color. It was first made in England during the 1700s. The height of its popularity in the United States was from 1870 to 1880. It is now correct to refer to some colored glass as blue milk glass, black milk glass, etc. Reproductions of milk glass are being made and sold in many stores. Related pieces may be listed in the Cosmos, Vallerysthal, and Westmoreland categories.

Pepper Shaker, Ribbed, Black Letters, Hazel Atlas Glass Co., 5 In.	15
Plate, Botanical Drawings, Multicolor, Reticulated Rim, 10 $\frac{1}{4}$ In., 7 Piece	15
Trinket Box, Figural Chicken Lid, White, Orange Speckle, Round, Wavy Rim, 1950s	10

MILLEFIORI means, literally, a thousand flowers. Many small pieces of glass resembling flowers are grouped together to form a design. It is a type of glasswork popular in paperweights and some are listed in that category.

Basket, Orange, Red, Blue, Wavy Rim, Infolded Sides, Clear Twist Handle, 5 x 5 In.	167
Bell, Black, Red, Blue, Green, Yellow, Flowers, Shapes, 4 x 2 In.	99
Centerpiece, Rainbow Color Flowers, 4 Trumpets, Crimped, Ruffled Bowl, 16 In.	1295
Cruet, Multicolor Flowers, Ball, Stick Neck, Ruffled Rim, Handle, Ball Stopper, 7 In.	165
Ewer, Red, White Flowers, Turquoise, Bottle Shape, Upright Spout, Loop Handle, 10 In.	275
Figurine, Swan, Multicolored Striations & Flowers, S-Scroll Neck, Frosted, 7 In.	310
Lamp, Dancer Kicks Multicolor Ball, Bronze, Marble, c.1940, 8 $\frac{1}{2}$ x 8 $\frac{1}{2}$ In.	600 to 1080
Paperweight, Star Pattern, Blue, Red, Green, White, 1885, 3 In.	276
Pitcher, Black, Red, Blue, Green, Flowers, Canes, Baluster, Ruffled Rim, c.1910, 5 In.	110
Pitcher, Green, White, Cobalt Blue, 3 $\frac{1}{2}$ In.	30
Vase, 2 Handles, Multicolor, c.1880, 3 $\frac{1}{2}$ x 2 In. ....*illus*	345
Vase, 2 Handles, Ruffled Mouth, Waisted Neck, 11 $\frac{1}{2}$ In.	108
Vase, Green, Blue, 2 Handles, 3 $\frac{1}{8}$ x 1 $\frac{3}{4}$ In.	24
Vase, Green, Red, Blue, Cristalleria D'Art, 12 $\frac{1}{2}$ x 7 In.	48
Vase, Handkerchief Shape, Multicolor, Italy, 8 In.	480
Vase, Multicolor Canes, Flowers, Shapes, Gold Speckled, Spherical, Flared Rim, 3 In.	85

MINTON china was made in the Staffordshire region of England beginning in 1796. The firm became part of the Royal Doulton Tableware Group in 1968, but the wares continued to be marked *Minton*. In 2009 the brand was bought by KPS Capital Partners of New York and became part of WWRD Holdings. The company no longer makes Minton china. Many marks have been used. The word *England* was added in 1891. Minton majolica is listed in this book in the Majolica category.

Chamber Pot, Pink Flowers, Leaves, Knob Handles, 10 In.	13

Millefiori, Vase, Double Handle, Multicolor, c.1880, 3 $\frac{1}{2}$ x 2 In.
$345

Ruby Lane

Minton, Jardiniere, Underplate, Lily Pad, Molded In Relief, Impressed Mark, c.1890, 11 $\frac{3}{4}$ In.
$720

Brunk Auctions

M

Minton, Plate, Gilt, Enamel, Cloisonne Style, Landscape, J. Evans, c.1880, 9 $\frac{1}{2}$ In., Pair
$660

Cowan's Auctions

TIP
Invert your old glass cake stand and use it for chips and dip. The pedestal must be hollow to hold the dip; the top plate is fine for the chips.

Minton, Vase, Pilgrim, Pate-Sur-Pate, Teal, White Slip, Maiden, Cupid, Solon, c.1879, 10 In.

$8,610

Skinner, Inc.

Mocha, Mug, Looping Earthworm, 4¾ In.

$885

Hess Auction Group

Mocha, Pitcher, Cat's-Eye, Bands, Brown, Blue, Orange, 7½ In.

$200

Hess Auction Group

TIP

Don't soak old ceramic pieces in water for a long time. Old repairs may be loosened.

Jardiniere, Underplate, Lily Pad, Molded In Relief, Impressed Mark, c.1890, 11¾ In........*illus*	720
Plaque, Landscape With Maiden, Florenze Judd, Signed, c.1870, 9⅜ x 13½ In., Pair	3321
Plaque, Pate-Sur-Pate, Nymph Tormenting Putto, 7½ x 6½ In..	9375
Plate, Cobalt Blue, Reticulated, 8⅞ In.	113
Plate, Dinner, Burgundy Border, Gilt Rim, For Tiffany & Co., 10¼ In., 12 Piece	1800
Plate, Game Birds, Pale Blue & Gilt Border, c.1918, 9 In., 12 Piece	2000
Plate, Gilt, Enamel, Cloisonne Style, Landscape, J. Evans, c.1880, 9½ In., Pair..........*illus*	660
Plate, Green Rim, Gilt, 9 In.	188
Tile, Figural, Woman, Garden, Carrying Basket, Cherub, Moss Glaze, c.1900, 18 In., Pair........	615
Urn, Ram's Head Handles, Naked Children, 1800s, 35 x 36 In.	3625
Vase, Celadon, Flared Mouth, 3 Dog Masks, Tripod Base, 36¼ In.	3272
Vase, Lid, Bright Blue, Reserve, Seated Child, Handles, 9 In.	63
Vase, Pilgrim, Pate-Sur-Pate, Teal, White Slip, Maiden, Cupid, Solon, c.1879, 10 In. ....*illus*	8610
Vase, Porcelain, Gilt, Blue, Footed, Christopher Dresser, 3¾ x 6 In.	3050
Vase, Porcelain, Lid, Gilt Trim, Swirled Blue, Rose & Flower Vines, c.1860, 15¾ In.	246

MIRRORS *are listed in the Furniture category under Mirror.*

MOCHA pottery is an English-made product that was sold in America during the early 1800s. It is a heavy pottery with pale coffee-and-cream coloring. Designs of blue, brown, green, orange, black, or white were added to the pottery and given fanciful names, such as Tree, Snail Trail, or Moss. Mocha designs are sometimes found on pearlware. A few pieces of mocha ware were made in France, the United States, and other countries.

Mug, Alternating Cable & Dot Decoration, Blue, Black, Gray, c.1825, 6 In.........................	1169
Mug, Black Seaweed Lines, Green Band, Loop Handle, 6 In.	325
Mug, Looping Earthworm, 4¾ In. ....*illus*	885
Mug, Swags, Marbled, Straight-Sided, Strap Handle, 4¾ In.	677
Pepper Pot, Yellowware, 1800s, 4¼ In.	976
Pitcher, Cat's-Eye, Bands, Brown, Blue, Orange, 7½ In. ....*illus*	200
Pitcher, Cat's-Eye, Drip Design, Barrel Shape, Loop Handle, Curved Spout, 7½ In....................	325
Pitcher, Earthworm, 2 Blue & Brown Bands, Green Border, Swollen, Loop Handle, 7 In.	1180
Pitcher, Marbleized, Swollen, Loop Handle, 1800s, 5½ In...	2360
Pitcher, Multicolor Cable, Brown Slip & Herringbone Bands, England, c.1830, 9 In.	677
Salt, Brown Bands, Cable Decoration, Footed, England, c.1820, 2 x 3 In.................................	492

MONMOUTH POTTERY COMPANY started working in Monmouth, Illinois, in 1892. The pottery made a variety of utilitarian wares. It became part of Western Stoneware Company in 1906. The maple leaf mark was used until about 1930.

Pig, Dark Brown Glaze, Embossed, Stoneware, 3½ x 7½ In...	1080
Vase, Blue, White Draping At Shoulders, Signed, 18 In.	132
Vase, Footed, Shouldered, Black, 17½ In.	794
Vase, Light Blue Slip Bands, Marked, 22 In...	30

MONT JOYE, *see Mt. Joye category.*

MOORCROFT pottery was first made in Burslem, England, in 1913. William Moorcroft had managed the art pottery department for James Macintyre & Company of England from 1898 to 1913. The Moorcroft pottery continues today, although William Moorcroft died in 1945. The earlier wares are similar to the modern ones, but color and marking will help indicate the age.

Bowl, Claremont Toadstool, Handles, 3 x 11 In..	343
Bowl, Claremont, Green Blue With Red & White Mushrooms, Signed, 8¼ In............................	259
Bowl, Clematis, Blue, Purple, Red, Pale Green Ground, 4½ x 5 In....................................*illus*	165
Bowl, Spanish, Blue With Red Flowers, 2⅞ x 7 In.	173
Bowl, Spanish, Flowerheads, Swirling Leaves, Green, Red, Yellow Glaze, 5 x 11 In.	1298
Candlestick, Cobalt Blue, Flowers, Yellow, Purple, 6½ In., Pair..	188
Candlestick, Pomegranate Bonbonniere, 7¼ In., Pair..	375

M

Ewer, Alhambra, Florian, Tapering, Red Tulips, Macintyre, 1904-13, 8¾ In.	*illus*	965
Ginger Jar, Claremont, Lid, Mushrooms, Blue & Green Ground, 8½ x 6 In.		3500
Ginger Jar, Eventide, Lid, Trees, 1918, 11¼ x 8 In.		7500
Ginger Jar, Lid, Pink Iridescent, Light Green, 10 x 8 In.		188
Ginger Jar, Lid, Poppies, Cobalt Blue Ground, Red, 1930, 16 x 12 In.		9375
Jar, Lid, Moonlit Blue Landscape, Stamped, 1918-26, 9¾ x 7 In.	*illus*	6875
Jardiniere, Landscape, Blue, Green, Impressed, c.1925, 7 x 15 In.		1187
Jug, Claremont Toadstool, c.1913, 7½ x 7 In.		625
Lamp Base, 2-Light, Rouge Flambe, Flowers, 1900-50, 22½ In.		375
Lamp Base, Cobalt Blue, Orchid, Convex Cylinder, England, 1900-50, 23 In.		250
Lamp Base, Wisteria, Plum, Oval, England, 1900-50, 21 In.		250
Planter, Poppy, c.1930, 3½ x 6½ In.		90
Plate, Leaf & Berry, Rust Red, Orange, Green, Flambe Glaze, Marked, 8½ In.		266
Urn, Pomegranate, Cobalt Blue Ground, Handles, Marked, c.1925, 8¾ In.		575
Vase, Alhambra, Florian, Red & Blue Flowers, Gilt, Macintyre, c.1903, 8 In.	*illus*	615
Vase, Anemone, Burslem, Pink, Purple, Blue, 1900s, 8¼ In.		181
Vase, Anemone, Mottled Green, Stamped Potter To H. M. The Queen, c.1945, 8¼ In.		360
Vase, Anemone, Pink, Purple, 1900s, 8¼ In.		181
Vase, Blue Flowers, Florian Ware, Burslem, For Macintyre & Co., c.1903, 10 x 5½ In.		937
Vase, Blue Flowers, Leaves, Florian Ware, Burslem, Harebell, For Macintyre & Co., 10 x 8 In.		593
Vase, Blue, Gold, Green, Florian Ware, James Macintyre, 11½ In.		325
Vase, Claremont, Mushrooms, Green, Blue Glaze, Smokestack, Handles, 8 x 8 In.		2124
Vase, Eventide, Trees, Swollen Shoulder, Spread Base, 9 x 4¼ In.		3500
Vase, Fish, Jellyfish, Blue, Green, Red, Flambe Glaze, Smokestack, c.1940, 6 In.		3000
Vase, Florian, Cornflower, Bottle Shape, Scalloped Rim, Elongated Neck, c.1900, 7¾ In.		738
Vase, Freesia, Squat, Multicolor, Red Flowers, Against Blue, c.1935, 5¾ In.		615
Vase, Grape, Flambe, Reds, Blues, Bulbous, Squat, 1928-48, 5¼ x 6 In.		750
Vase, Hazeldene, Treescape, Blue & Green Glaze, Rounded, Ring Foot, c.1900, 6 In.		2460
Vase, Landscape, Stylized Trees, Fiery Sky, Flame Glaze, Oval, 12 x 8 In.		1000
Vase, Leaf & Berry, Red, Yellow, Green, Flambe, Shouldered, Trumpet Neck, 4 In.		266
Vase, Matte Glazed, Fish & Vegetation, Mottled Blue & Green Ground, c.1930, 8¾ In.		1169
Vase, Pansies, Cobalt Blue, Pink, Green, Smokestack, Handles, Marked, 1918, 8 In.		502
Vase, Pear Shape, Flared Rim, Fruit, Blue Ground, 9 In.		360
Vase, Pomegranate, Bonbonniere, 7¼ x 4 In.		312
Vase, Pomegranate, Cobalt Blue, Peach, Bulbous, Tubular Neck, c.1910, 7 In.		400
Vase, Pomegranate, Red Fruit, Blue Ground, Bulbous, Pinched Neck, c.1915, 7 x 6 In.		2125
Vase, Pomegranate, Red, Cobalt Blue, Bulbous, Stick Neck, Flared Rim, c.1923, 11 In.		295
Vase, Pomegranate, Signed, c.1935, 9½ In.		300
Vase, Spanish, Flowers, Red, Blue, Flared, 6¾ x 7 In.		625
Vase, Trees, Hills, Fiery Sky, Blue Ground, Oval, Footed, 12¾ x 7½ In.		7500

MORGANTOWN GLASS WORKS operated in Morgantown, West Virginia, from 1900 to 1974. Some of their wares are marked with an adhesive label that says *Old Morgantown Glass.*

Bonbon, Spanish Red, Applied Golf Ball Knob, 4½ x 4½ In.	*illus*	495
Sherbet, Crinkle, Amber		19
Vase, Bud, Serenade, Jade Green, 10½ In.		43
Vase, Snowball, c.1935, 7½ In.		201

MORIAGE is a special type of raised decoration used on some Japanese pottery. Sometimes pieces of clay were shaped by hand and applied to the item; sometimes the clay was squeezed from a tube in the way we apply cake frosting. One type of moriage is called Dragonware by collectors.

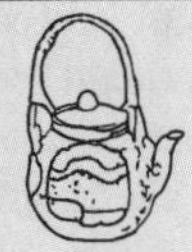

Cup & Saucer, White, Cobalt Blue, Swirls, Pink Flowers, Gilt, Footed Cup, 1930s, 3 In.	37
Dresser Box, White, Fuchsia Roses, Raised Scroll, Squat, Hinged Lid, c.1905, 4 x 5 In.	425
Ewer, Beaded, Green, White Reserve, Flower Spray, Nippon, 10 x 4½ In.	36
Platter, Pale Green, Pink Roses, Gilt Beading, Round, Cutout Handles, 1800s, 11 In.	225
Teapot, Brown Glaze, Raised Beaded Flowers, Gilt Scrolling, Flat Lid, Knob, 1920s	70

Moorcroft, Bowl, Clematis, Blue, Purple, Red, Pale Green Ground, 4½ x 5 In.

$165

Ruby Lane

Moorcroft, Ewer, Alhambra, Florian, Tapering, Red Tulips, Macintyre, 1904-13, 8¾ In.

$965

Ruby Lane

Moorcroft, Jar, Lid, Moonlit Blue Landscape, Stamped, 1918-26, 9¾ x 7 In.

$6,875

Rago Arts and Auction Center

315

Moorcroft, Vase, Alhambra, Florian, Red & Blue Flowers, Gilt, Macintyre, c.1903, 8 In.
$615

Skinner, Inc.

Morgantown, Bonbon, Spanish Red, Applied Golf Ball Knob, 4½ x 4½ In.
$495

Ruby Lane

Moriage, Vase, Couple, Seated, Terrace, Openwork, Double Handles, 12 In.
$62

Kimballs Auction & Estate Services

Vase, Beaded, Geometric Decoration, Green, Blue, Taupe, Nippon, 9 x 6 In.	150
Vase, Beaded, Green, White Tipped Flowers, 6½ x 5 In.	73
Vase, Couple, Seated, Terrace, Openwork, Double Handles, 12 In. ....*illus*	62
Vase, Opaque White, Gilt, Star, Red, Scroll, Beaded Swags, Crown Cut Rim, 1800s, 14 In.	979
Vase, Stylized Flowers, Leaves, Fronds, White, Green Ground, Double Handles, 19½ x 8 In.	184

MOSAIC TILE COMPANY of Zanesville, Ohio, was started by Karl Langerbeck and Herman Mueller in 1894. Many types of plain and ornamental tiles were made until 1959. The company closed in 1967. The company also made some ashtrays, bookends, and related giftwares. Most pieces are marked with the entwined MTC monogram.

Ashtray, Hexagonal, Blue, Art Deco, 1930, 2⅝ x 3½ x 2⅜ In.	75
Figurine, Terrier, Black & White, 2 Trinket Wells, c.1935	142
Pin Tray, Figural Hunting Dog, Black, Shaped Base, 1940s	115
Plaque, White Bust Of Lincoln, Blue Ground, 3 x 3½ In.	28
Plaque, White Trademark On Blue, N Y Rotary International, 3 x 3½ In.	25
Tile, Hand Painted, Dutch Tulips, c.1920, 4¼ x ¼, 9 Piece	195
Tile, Mother Goose, Riding Flying Goose, Brown, White, 1930s, 4 x 4 In.	225
Tile, Turtle, Crab, Fish, Green, Pink, 3 Tiles, Frame, c.1910, 12 x 24 In.	1495

MOSER glass is made by a Bohemian (Czech) glasshouse founded by Ludwig Moser in 1857. Art Nouveau-type glassware and iridescent glassware were made. The most famous Moser glass is decorated with heavy enameling in gold and bright colors. The firm, Moser Glassworks, is still working in Karlovy Vary, Czech Republic. Few pieces of Moser glass are marked.

Bowl, Cranberry Glass, Wheel Cut Concentric Circles, Gilt Decorations, 7¼ In., 4 Piece	489
Bowl, Fruit, Red, Ivory, Gold, Flowers, Scroll, Couples, Flared, c.1900, 4 x 14 In.	4500
Bowl, Stagecoach, Amber, 13 In.	187
Bowl, Underplate, Figures, Landscape, Enamel, Gilt, Cartouches, 2 Piece	247
Centerpiece, Red, White, Diamond Cut, Ruby Glass, 7 x 9 In.	3000
Compote, Teal Treetop, Brown Truck, Gilt & Enamel Leaves, Grapes, Bugs, 8 x 11¾ In.	2242
Dresser Jar, Amber Panels, Octagonal, Gilt, 4 x 3 In.	49
Ewer, Yellow & White, Swirled & Striated, Stylized Flower Band, Gilt, Jewels, 11¾ In.	356
Goblet, Art Nouveau, Flowers, Green Stem, 8 In., 6 Piece	625
Loving Cup, Cobalt Blue Glass, 3 Handles, Gilt, Heavily Decorated, 6¾ x 7 In. ....*illus*	65
Perfume Bottle, Ruby Red, Gold Overlay, Cabochons, Bulbous, Ball Stopper, 1800s, 3 In.	1000
Pill Box, Gilt, Blue Opaline, Stylized Flowers, 1½ x 2 In.	88
Pitcher, Cranberry Glass, Fan Shape Design, c.1890, 7¼ In.	62
Plaque, Opaline, Enamel, Cupids, 11 In.	937
Punch Bowl, 6 Cups, Amethyst To Clear, Raised Gilt, Rococo, 12 x 10, 7 Piece	247
Spooner, Vaseline Glass, Cherries, Opalescent, 5¾ In. ....*illus*	75
Sugar & Creamer, Prism Cut, Enamel, Medallions, Scroll, Scallop Rim, 3 & 4 In.	236
Trinket Box, Electric Blue, Flowers, Butterfly, Raised Enamel, Squat, Lid, c.1905, 3 x 4 In.	388
Trinket Box, Stylized Paw Feet, Brass, Gold, White, Flowers, 4½ x 5½ In.	126
Vase, Amber To Clear, Gold Beading & Leafy Scrolls, Beaker Shape, c.1900, 7 In.	695
Vase, Amber, Elk In The Forest, Signed, 11¾ In.	437
Vase, Animor, Amber, Baby Elephant, Trees, Green Enamel, Trumpet, Wide Ring Foot, 8 In.	413
Vase, Applied Lizard, Enamel, Flowers, Leaves, Smoke, 6 x 3¼ In.	369
Vase, Art Deco, Black Amethyst Glass, Greek Mythological Band, 8 x 5 In.	390
Vase, Clear, Flowers, Cylinder Neck, Bulbous, Turquoise Ruffle, Pedestal, c.1900, 9 In.	460
Vase, Cobalt Blue Cut Glass, Gilt Rim, 14¼ x 5½ In.	238
Vase, Cranberry Glass, Applied Clear Glass Handles, Ribbon, Bows, 7½ x 5½ In.	215
Vase, Cranberry Glass, Octagonal Panels, Gilt, 8 x 5¼ In.	61
Vase, Cranberry Red, Arched Gold Overlay Rim, Flowers, Paneled, Gilt Scroll Feet, 7 In.	1250
Vase, Cranberry, Gold, Scrolls, Flowers, Conical, Round Foot, Ruffled Band, c.1900, 12 In.	1150
Vase, Emerald Green, Gold Overlay, Enameled Flowers, Paneled, Conical, 1920s, 9 In.	850
Vase, Frost & Green Panels, Gilt, Conical, Pinched Neck, Scalloped Foot, 1930s, 19 In.	1250

M

Vase, Frosted, Forget-Me-Nots, Blue, Gold Bands & Stems, Tubular, Pedestal Foot, 7 In.	395
Vase, Gilt, Green, Enamel, Round Foot, Waisted, Zigzag Mouth, Diamond Cut, 16½ x 6 In.	360
Vase, Intaglio Carved, Lily Pads, Lilies, Green, Pink, Yellow, Flared, Shaped Rim, 11 In.	3259
Vase, Pillow, Flat Sides, Applied Pleats, Bird, Reeded Feet, 7 In.	620
Vase, Yellow Rim & Base, Intaglio Tulips, c.1890, 10 In.	275
Vase, Yellow To Clear, Intaglio Tulips, c.1890, 10 In.	300

MOSS ROSE china was made by many firms from 1808 to 1900. It has a typical moss rose pictured as the design. The plant is not as popular now as it was in Victorian gardens, so the fuzz-covered bud is unfamiliar to most collectors. The dishes were usually decorated with pink and green flowers.

Coffeepot, Maroon Lines, Bulbous, Flared Rim, Loop Handle, Lid, 1800s, 10 In.	130
Plate, Sterling Silver Rim, Rosenthal, 12 In.	62
Soup, Dish, Scalloped Rim, Gilt Trim, Rosenthal, 1950s, 8½ In.	90
Sugar, Dome Lid, Loop Finial, Bulbous, Ear Handles, Round Footed Base, 1960s, 7 In.	85

MOTHER-OF-PEARL GLASS, or pearl satin glass, was first made in the 1850s in England and in Massachusetts. It was a special type of mold-blown satin glass with air bubbles in the glass, giving it a pearlized color. It has been reproduced. Mother-of-pearl shell objects are listed under Pearl.

Ewer, Rainbow, Diamond Quilted, Ruffled Rim, Applied Handle, 7½ In. ....*illus*	144
Fan, Reticulated, Gilt, Grecian Scenes, Ormolu Mount, 17¾ In.	512
Pitcher, Turquoise Blue, Diamond Quilted, Squat, Ruffled Rim, c.1889, 9 x 6 In.	169
Rattle, Sterling Silver, Embossed Clock, Birth Record, 1900s, 3½ In.	75
Rose Bowl, Rainbow, Diamond Quilted, Frosted Feet, Bulbous, c.1890, 6 x 6 In.	385
Shade, Ocean Blue, Pink, Diamond Quilted, Squat, Ruffled Rim, 1880s, 3¼ x 5 In.	253
Tray, Wood Panels, Gilt, Fighting, Father & Child, Carved Frame, Japan, 15 x 21 In., Pair	224
Vase, Apricot To Iridescent Gold, Green, Diamond Pattern, Ruffled Rim, 9 In.	285
Vase, Diamond Quilted, Crimped Rim, Silver Plated Frame, Handles, 6 x 10 In. .....*illus*	288
Vase, Rainbow, Ribbon, Stripes, Bottle Shaped, Ruffled Rim, c.1890, 12 In.	253
Vase, Red To White, Diamond Quilted, Shouldered, Stick Neck, 12 In.	65
Vase, White Iridescent, Gold, Lobed, Squat, Metal Openwork Rim, c.1890, 5 In.	83

MOTORCYCLES and motorcycle accessories of all types are being collected today. Examples can be found that date back to the early twentieth century. Toy motorcycles are listed in the Toy category.

Badge, Cycling Falcon Club, Silver, Enamel, Falcon, 1899, 2 In.	285
Badge, Harley-Davidson, Stamped, Hinged Pin, 1 x 3 In.	106
Banner, Safety Award, American Motorcycle Ass'n, Felt, Blue, 1966, 31 x 20 In. .....*illus*	240
Belt, Kidney, 1950s, 32 In.	85
Boots, Leather, Brown, Quilted, Chanel, 10 x 9½ In.	950
Can, BSA Motorcycle Oil, It Pays To Use Only, Green, Tin, 1952, 1 Qt. .....*illus*	240
Can, Indian Motorcycle Oil, Indian Chief, Green, Tin Lithograph, 1 Gal., 11 x 8 In.	4485
Emergency Light, Harley-Davidson, Portable, Jeweled, Red Metal, 1920s	286
Helmet, Leather, White & Red, Padded, Chin Strap, France, 1940s, 8 x 10 In.	125
Horn, Cover, Chrome, 7 In.	110
Horn, King Of The Road, 14 In.	60
Jacket, Euro, Red, Black, White, AGV Sport	100
Kicker Block, Harley-Davidson, Blue, Hard Plastic	312
License Plate Topper, Aluminum, Geneva On The Lake, Female Body, 4 x 6¾ In.	130
License Plate, Calif., AAA 7 90, Porcelain, 1919	575
License Plate, Pa., 1361627	200
License Plate, W. Va., Black, Yellow, 89-727, 1950s, 12 x 5 In.	150
Motor, Indian, 1947	1200
Motorcycle, Simplex Servi-Cycle, Blue, 1950s	1550
Pin, Gold Plate, Wings & Shield, Embossed, C-Clasp, 1930s, 2 In.	184
Pin, Harley-Davidson, Dealers Conference, Orange, 1952, 2 In.	335
Poster, 20 Mile, Motorcycle Races, JC Agajanian, 25 x 22 In.	75

Moser, Loving Cup, Cobalt Blue Glass, 3 Handles, Gilt, Heavily Decorated, 6¾ x 7 In.
$65

Ruby Lane

Moser, Spooner, Vaseline Glass, Cherries, Opalescent, 5¾ In.
$75

Ruby Lane

M

Mother-Of-Pearl, Ewer, Rainbow, Diamond Quilted, Ruffled Rim, Applied Handle, 7 ½ In.
$144

Early Auction Company

Mother-Of-Pearl, Vase, Diamond Quilted, Crimped Rim, Silver Plated Frame, Handles, 6 x 10 In.
$288

Early Auction Company

Motorcycle, Banner, Safety Award, American Motorcycle Ass'n, Felt, Blue, 1966, 31 x 20 In.
$240

Milestone Auctions

Saddle Bag, Leather, Rivets, Buckles, Chains, Swiss Army, c.1905, 35 x 24 In.	420
Seat, Leather, Black	300
Seat, Saddle, Leather, Iron Spring, Lepper, 1920s, 12 x 8 In.	193
Sign, Handsom Goods At Terrible Homely Prices, Larrabee's, Wilton, Me., 11 ½ x 46 ¾ In.	978
Sign, Harley-Davidson Oil, Is It Time For A Refill?, Red, Black Border, 9 x 15 In.	600
Sign, Magnificent Sunbeam, Green Motorcycle, Multicolor, 1947, 24 x 19 In.	260
Sign, Motorcycle Shed, Wood, 16 x 37 In.	350
Tank Badge, NSU, Porcelain, Metal, 1950s, 4 x 3 In.	88

MOUNT WASHINGTON, *see Mt. Washington category.*

MOVIE memorabilia of all types are collected. Animation Art, Games, Sheet Music, Toys, and some celebrity items are listed in their own section. A lobby card is usually 11 by 14 inches, but other sizes were also made. A set of lobby cards includes seven scene cards and one title card. An American one sheet, the standard movie poster, is 27 by 41 inches. A three sheet is 40 by 81 inches. A half sheet is 22 by 28 inches. A window card, made of cardboard, is 14 by 22 inches. An insert is 14 by 36 inches. A herald is a promotional item handed out to patrons. Press books, sent to exhibitors to promote a movie, contain ads and lists of what is available for advertising, i.e., posters, lobby cards. Press kits, sent to the media, contain photos and details about the movie, i.e., stars' biographies and interviews.

Button, Gone With The Wind, Portrait, Couple, Ribbon, Atlanta Premiere, 1939, 2 In.	230
Figure, King Of The Rocket Men, Painted, Helmet, Aiming Gun, Shield Base, c.1949	652
Lobby Card, Alice In Wonderland, Original Release, 1951, 11 x 14 In., 8 Piece	863
Lobby Card, Snow White & The Seven Dwarfs, Original Film Release, 1937, 11 x 14 In.	506
Lobby Card, Three Stooges, Mutts To You, Photograph, Columbia, 1938, 11 x 14 In.	2505
Lobby Sign, My Six Loves, Cliff Robertson, Debbie Reynolds, c.1963, 28 x 44 In. ....*illus*	450
Photograph, Joan Crawford, Finger In Mouth, Mat, Signed, 1953, 5 x 7 In.	115
Photograph, Laurel & Hardy, Black & White, Autographs, Frame, 14 x 17 In.	633
Photograph, Silver Print, Greta Garbo, Arnold Genthe, 18 x 14 In. ....*illus*	480
Poster, Alfred Hitchcock, Foreign Correspondent, McCrea, 1940, 27 x 40 In.	1139
Poster, Barbarella, Jane Fonda, Moonscape, Bikini, Linen Back, Italy, 1968, 60 x 44 In.	435
Poster, Casey At The Bat, Wallace Beery, Stone Lithograph, Linen Back, 1927, 41 x 27 In.	2700
Poster, Charlie Chan, The Trap, Sidney Toler, Monogram Pictures, 1946, 27 x 41 In.	253
Poster, Jailhouse Rock, Elvis Presley, Red, Yellow, 26 x 39 ½ In.	250
Poster, Key Largo, Humphrey Bogart, Lauren Bacall, Red, White, 1948, 14 x 36 In.	633
Poster, Life Of Buffalo Bill In 3 Reels, Pawnee Bill Film Col, c.1912, 42 x 28 In.	1440
Poster, New Adventures Of Batman & Robin, The Fatal Blast, 1949, 27 x 41 In.	1271
Poster, Robinson Crusoe Of Clipper Island, Inset Film Scenes, 1936, 27 x 41 In.	127
Poster, Spy Smasher, Chapter 5, Descending Doom, 1942, 27 x 41 In.	310
Poster, The Caddy, Dean Martin, Jerry Lewis, 24 x 16 In.	200
Poster, The Green Hornet Strikes Again, Human Targets, 1941, 27 x 40 In.	696
Poster, The Phantom, Chapter 1, The Sign Of The Skull, Ace, Devil, 1943, 27 x 40 In.	1588
Poster, The Time Machine, Taylor, Morlocks, Linen Back, MGM, 1960, 78 x 80 In.	384
Poster, Warhol, The Star, Greta Garbo As Mata Hari, Pink, 33 x 23 ¼ In.	1200

MT. JOYE is an enameled cameo glass made in the late nineteenth and twentieth centuries by Saint-Hilaire Touvier de Varraux and Co. of Pantin, France. This same company made De Vez glass. Pieces were usually decorated with enameling. Most pieces are not marked.

Ewer, Purple Orchids, Gold Enamel, Cameo, Mounted, 1910-30, 12 In. ....*illus*	750
Rose Bowl, Green Satin Glass, Enamel Pink Iris, Pinched Mouth, 5 x 6 In.	100
Vase, Acid Etched, Gilt, Violets, 1900, 17 ¼ In.	937
Vase, Gilt, Amethyst Glass, Iris, 10 ¾ x 5 In.	184
Vase, Gilt, Red Poppy, Green Glass, 10 ½ x 4 ½ In.	123
Vase, Glass, Purple Mums, Gold Leaves, Gilt Rim, 1900-25, 7 ¾ In.	375
Vase, Iris, Green, Textured Finish, 14 ¾ In.	84
Vase, Trumpet Shape, Textured Green Glass, Purple, Yellow Iris, Leaves, 10 ½ In.	312

Motorcycle, Can, BSA Motorcycle Oil, It Pays To Use Only, Green, Tin, 1952, 1 Qt.
$240

Milestone Auctions

Movie, Lobby Sign, My Six Loves, Cliff Robertson, Debbie Reynolds, c.1963, 28 x 44 In.
$450

Ruby Lane

Movie, Photograph, Silver Print, Greta Garbo, Arnold Genthe, 18 x 14 In.
$480

Garth's Auctioneers & Appraisers

Mt. Joye, Ewer, Purple Orchids, Gold Enamel, Cameo, Mounted, 1910-30, 12 In.
$750

Ruby Lane

Mt. Washington, Rose Bowl, Crimped, Raised Leaves, Flowers, Yellow Ground, 4 1/2 x 5 1/2 In.
$78

Ruby Lane

Mt. Washington, Vase, Rainbow, White, Flowers, Leaves, 21 In.
$189

Case Antiques

Mulberry, Platter, Pagoda, Lake, Staffordshire, 16 In.
$73

Saco River Auction Co.

Muller Freres, Lamp, Sunset, Lake, Deer, Red, 23 x 11 In.
$4,920

Cottone Auctions

Muncie, Vase, Cream, Lavender, Signed, 5 3/4 In.
$59

Wickliff Auctioneers

M

Music, Accordion, Wurlitzer, Leather Straps, 10 1/4 x 19 3/4 In.
$449

Ruby Lane

Music, Box, Man Wearing Robes, Arm Around Seminude Woman, 4 1/2 x 5 1/2 In.
$438

Antique Reader

Music, Box, Paillard Vaucher Fils, Rosewood Veneer, Inlay, Cylinder, c.1877, 12 x 25 In.
$3,496

James D. Julia Auctioneers

Stradivarius

The label of Antonius Stradivarius has been forged and appears in many nineteenth- and twentieth-century violins of low value. One type of labeled violin was originally offered in the Sears catalog for $7.

MT. WASHINGTON Glass Works started in 1837 in South Boston, Massachusetts. In 1870 the company moved to New Bedford, Massachusetts. Many types of art glass were made there until 1894, when the company merged with Pairpoint Manufacturing Co. Amberina, Burmese, Crown Milano, Cut Glass, Peachblow, and Royal Flemish are each listed in their own category.

Biscuit Jar, Berries & Leaves, Lobed, Silver Plated Lid, 5 1/2 In.	71
Biscuit Jar, Paneled Opal Body, Pictures Sailboats, Pairpoint Lid, 6 1/2 In.	173
Biscuit Jar, Pink & White, Gold Enamel Flowers, Silver Plated Collar, Lid & Handle, 8 1/2 In. ...	144
Compote, Orange Bowl, White Leaf Design, Pairpoint Base, 5 1/4 x 7 1/2 In.	776
Condiment Set, Ribbed Melon, Silver Plated Holder, 3 Piece	307
Ewer, Mythological Face On Spout, Animal Heads, Deer, Rabbits, 12 In., Pair	230
Ewer, Royal Flemish, Paneled With Flower, Shoulder With Budded Crosses, 11 1/2 In.	2588
Pitcher, Satin Glass, Diamond Quilted, Ruffled Mouth, 9 In.	92
Rose Bowl, Crimped, Raised Leaves, Flowers, Yellow Ground, 4 1/2 x 5 1/2 In. ......*illus*	78
Rose Bowl, Flowers, Leaves, Multicolor, White Ground, 4 1/4 x 4 In.	61
Salt & Pepper, Tomato Shape, Cream, Flowers, Silver Plated Frame, 5 1/2 x 5 In.	210
Vase, Bulbous, Stick Neck, Fish, Net Design, c.1900, 10 In.	2360
Vase, Rainbow, White, Flowers, Leaves, 21 In. .....*illus*	189

MULBERRY ware was made in the Staffordshire district of England from about 1850 to 1860. The dishes were decorated with a reddish brown transfer design, now called mulberry. Many of the patterns are similar to those used for flow blue and other Staffordshire transfer wares.

Pitcher, Chrysanthemum, Branches, Cylindrical, Angled Handle, c.1850, 8 In.	84
Plate, Houses On River, Flowers & Scroll Border, c.1855, 10 In.	100
Platter, Pagoda, Lake, Staffordshire, 16 In. .....*illus*	73

MULLER FRERES, French for Muller Brothers, made cameo and other glass from about 1895 to 1933. Their factory was first located in Luneville, then in nearby Croismare, France. Pieces were usually marked with the company name.

Group, Courting Couple, Seated, Roses, Mandolin, c.1880, 7 1/2 x 7 1/2 In.	118
Lamp, Sunset, Lake, Deer, Red, 23 x 11 In. .....*illus*	4920
Vase, Cameo, Shouldered, Green & Orange, Sunset Lakeside Landscape, 5 3/4 In.	201
Vase, Dark Amber, Lake, Trees, Shore, Signed, 9 1/2 In.	500
Vase, Dark Tree Against Purple, Cameo, Muller Freres Luneville, 1900s, 5 1/2 x 2 1/4 In.	625
Vase, Mountain Landscape, Trees, Cream Ground, Green & Brown, 1900s, 8 In.	523
Vase, Overlay, Landscape, Purple, Yellow, 7 1/4 In.	875
Vase, Winter Scene, Black Trees, White Snow, Blue Night Sky, Swollen, Footed, 13 In.	6518
Vase, Woodland Landscape, Trees, Matte Green, Teal, Black, Cameo, 8 In.	826
Vase, Yellow & Blue Crystalline Glaze, Orange Swirls, Oval, Flared Rim, 13 In.	384

MUNCIE Clay Products Company was established by Charles Benham in Muncie, Indiana, in 1922. The company made pottery for the florist and giftshop trade. The company closed by 1939. Pieces are marked with the name *Muncie* or just with a system of numbers and letters, like *1A*.

Ashtray, Green Drip Over Lilac, Folded Design, c.1930, 4 x 4 In.	295
Bowl, Blue Drip Over Green Glaze, Flared, c.1930, 4 x 8 In.	125
Bowl, Blue Drip Over Pink, Squat, 2 x 7 In.	65
Pitcher, Green Over Lilac, Drip, Speckled, Cutout Handle, 6 In.	79
Vase, Blue Matte Glaze, 2-Tone, Speckled, 3 In.	32
Vase, Cream, Lavender, Signed, 5 3/4 In. .....*illus*	59
Vase, Green Drip Over Pink, Squat, Stick Neck, 9 In.	65
Vase, Ruba Rombic, Gray To Pink, Blue To Green, 4 1/8 In., Pair	188
Vase, Ruba Rombic, Green Over Purple Matte Glazes, Impressed, 4 1/8 In.	207
Wall Pocket, Salamander, Blue Over White Matte Glaze, 10 In.	1955

MURANO, *see Glass-Venetian category.*

MUSIC boxes and musical instruments are listed here. Phonograph records, jukeboxes, phonographs, and sheet music are listed in other categories in this book.

Accordion, Wurlitzer, Leather Straps, 10¼ x 19¾ In. ....*illus*	449
Amplifier, Silvertone, Model 1300, Tweed, Guitar, 1949	150
Amplifier, Vega Commander, Brown, Handle, 1950s...	525
Banjo Ukulele, Monarch Style, Green, Resonator, Star Pierced, 21¾ x 9 In.	177
Barrel Organ, Mahogany, Georgian, Astor & Co., Eng., c.1810, 52 x 25 x 19 In.	2280
Box, Black Forest, Clock, Hunter, Tree Stump, c.1880, 38 x 26½ In.	5100
Box, Bremond, Drum & Bells, Rosewood, Inlaid Pelican Crest, 14-In. Cylinder, c.1880, 24 In....	2575
Box, Cylinder, Bells, Dancing Bisque Doll, Rosewood Case, Block Feet, c.1900, 8 x 16 In...........	492
Box, Cylinder, Cherry, Hinged, Marquetry, R.C. Bornand, New York, Late 1800s, 4½ In...........	406
Box, Cylinder, Heller, Burled Fruitwood Case, 6 Tunes, Stamped, 24 x 14 In.	944
Box, Cylinder, Hinged Lid, Walnut Case, 12 Tunes, 9 Bells, Swiss, c.1865, 11 x 29 In.	948
Box, Cylinder, Organ, Rosewood Case, 12 Tunes, Piallard Vaucher, c.1877, 12 x 25 In.	3496
Box, Cylinder, Rosewood Veneer, Henry Gautschi & Sons, 1800s, 8 x 15 x 10 In.	885
Box, Cylinder, Swiss Sublimette Piccolo Zither, Painted Flowers, 8 Tunes, c.1900, 7 x 26 In.	1416
Box, Ebonized, Inlay, Flowers, Swiss, c.1880, 14½ In...	375
Box, Empress Concert Grand, Tabletop, 29 Discs, Lyon & Healy, Chicago, 14 x 28 In.	1200
Box, Grand Piano, Enameled, Men, Women, Forest, Cherubs, 5½ In..........................	2000
Box, Hinged Lid, Flower Spray, 26½ In...	500
Box, Mahogany, Carved Leaves, Crank, 17-Inch Disc, Comb, Stella, c.1910, 14 x 28 In.	1920
Box, Man Wearing Robes, Arm Around Seminude Woman, 4½ x 5½ In. ....*illus*	438
Box, Mandolin, Rosewood, Inlaid, 15-In. Cylinder, 6 Tunes, Langdorff, c.1875, 25 In.	1229
Box, Music, Stella, Mahogany, 41 15½-In. Discs, Swiss, 12 x 26 x 21 In..................	531
Box, Olympia, Mahogany, Disc Storage, America, Late 1800s, 78 x 30½ x 18 In......................	5750
Box, Paillard Vaucher Fils, Rosewood Veneer, Inlay, Cylinder, c.1877, 12 x 25 In.................*illus*	3496
Box, Paillard, Burled Walnut, Ebonized, Inlaid, 6 Interchangeable Cylinders, 11 x 43 In.	2048
Box, Polyphon, Model 41C, Wood Case, Cherub Scene, 16 8¼-In. Discs, c.1900	562
Box, Polyphon, Single Comb, Flowers, Oak, Mahogany, 8¼ x 16 In............................*illus*	615
Box, Regina, Mahogany, 8 Discs, c.1902, 11 In..	550
Box, Regina, Mahogany, Duplex Comb, 156 Teeth, 27 15½-In. Discs, c.1900...................*illus*	3854
Box, Regina, Oak, Dutch Landscape, 14 Discs, c.1897, 8 In.....................................	375
Box, Signing Bird, Gilt, Flowers Leaves, Key Wind, 11 x 6 In.................................	330
Box, Singing Bird, 2 Birds, c.1960, 21 x 12 In..	773
Box, Singing Bird, Birdcage, Moves & Chirps, Gold Leaf, c.1875, 11 In.	1710
Box, Singing Bird, Brass, Feathers, France, c.1900, 11½ In....................................	240
Box, Singing Bird, Gilt Metal, Enamel, German Landscape, Blue, Gilt Borders, 3¼ In.	4375
Box, Singing Bird, Gilt, Bronze, Blue Enamel, Landscape, 4½ In...............................	3750
Box, Singing Bird, On Piano, Vernis Martin Lacquer, Courting Scenes, c.1915, 6 In.	10918
Box, Singing Bird, Oval Hinged Lid, Filigree Design, Bronze, 2 x 4 In.	1067
Box, Singing Bird, Purple Cardinal, Scrolls, 4¼ In...	2125
Box, Singing Bird, Red Cardinal, Geometric Bands, 4½ In.......................................	2125
Box, Singing Bird, Stand, 5 Cent, Coin-Operated, 55¾ x 11½ In..............................	3125
Box, Singing Birds, 3 Feathered, Metal Dome Cage, Loop Handle, Swiss, c.1940	1140
Box, Singing Birds, Brass Birdcage, Red & Yellow Feathers, c.1900, 11 In.	738
Box, Sublime Harmony, Piccolo Comb, Rosewood Case, Inlaid Musical Symbols, c.1890, 26 In.	1365
Box, Swiss Drum & Bells, Walnut, Floral Inlay, 13-In. Cylinder, 8 Tunes, c.1885, 24 In.	3821
Box, Symphonion, c.1880, 4½ x 7½ In..	320
Box, Troll & Baker, 10 Tunes, 18-In. Inlaid Cylinder, Geneva, Wanamaker's, 9 x 33 In......	2006
Box, Wood, Organ Shape, Dancing Dolls, Window, Block Feet, Crank, c.1915, 12 In.	1824
Drum, Desi's Conga Drum, I Love Lucy, Cardboard, Conical, Metal, Box, 1950s, 19 In.....	6958
Drum, Wood, Alligatored Brown Paint, Eagle, Folk Art, Stencil, Brass Tacks, 1822, 15 x 17 In..	2040
Gong, Dragon Puzzle, Red Lacquer, Crest, Dragons, 74½ x 40 In.	767
Guitar, Acoustic, Gibson, Flat-Top, J-45, Spruce, Mahogany Sides & Back, 1955, 40 In.............	3900
Guitar, Electric, National Silver, Lap, Steel, Cast Aluminum, 1936..........................	562
Harp, Regency, Parcel Gilt, Ebonized Maple, Spruce, Fluted Column, c.1800, 67 In.	1875
Harp, Regency, Parcel Gilt, Sebastian Erard, 67¼ In...	1125
Harpsichord, Dual Keyboards, Gilt Chinoiserie, People, Flowers, Leaves, 41 x 39 In.	18300

Music, Box, Polyphon, Single Comb, Flowers, Oak, Mahogany, 8¼ x 16 In.
$615

Leland Little Auctions

TIP
Be very careful if you try to oil the mechanism of a music box. Too much oil will cause damage.

Music, Box, Regina, Mahogany, Duplex Comb, 156 Teeth, 27 15½-In. Discs, c.1900
$3,854

Auction Team Breker

M

Music, Piano, Baby Grand, Mahogany, Bench, Lester Piano, Philadelphia, c.1937, 38 x 55 In.
$590

Hess Auction Group

Mustache Cup, Pink Flowers, Green, White Enamel Beads, Lattice Vine, Gold Edging, 3 x 3 ½ In.
$30

Ruby Lane

Nailsea, Rose Bowl, Venetian Thread, Opalescent, Ruby Glass, Crimped, Ruffled, 3 ½ In.
$248

Ahlers & Ogletree Auction Gallery

Nakara, Dresser Box, Cherubs, Clouds, Amber, Enamel Beading, Marked, 2 ½ x 3 In.
$250

Ruby Lane

Harpsicord, T. Darby, Mahogany, Inlaid, York, England, 1779, 32 x 58 In.	600
Mandolin, Brown, Gibson A-2, 1921	1500
Mandolin, Gibson A3, Mother-Of-Pearl Inlay, Case, c.1919	1140
Organette, Roller, Walnut Cabinet, Hand Crank, Tournaphone Music Co., 1885, 43 x 19 In.	1102
Piano, Baby Grand, Louis XV Style, Companion Bench, H.W. Perlman, 1900s, 39 In.	1000
Piano, Baby Grand, Mahogany, Bench, Lester Piano, Philadelphia, c.1937, 38 x 55 In. *illus*	590
Piano, Chickering & Sons, White Pine, Walnut, Rosewood, Rococo Revival, 81 x 55 In.	2460
Piano, Concert Grand, Mason & Hamlin, Ebonized, Bench, c.1915, 40 x 108 In.	8125
Piano, Giltwood, Louis XV Style, Carved, Erard Paris, Late 1800s, 39 In.	8250
Piano, Grand, Rosewood, 2 Pedals, Octagonal Legs, Chickering, 1863, 37 x 77 In.	8900
Piano, Grand, Square, Rosewood, Union Co., Philadelphia, 39 x 82 In.	201
Piano, Grand, Tapered Legs, C. Bechstein, Berlin, 1900s, 39 In.	1700
Piano, Joachim Ehlers Empire, Spruce, Walnut, Alder & Limewood, Vienna, c.1815, 86 x 45 In.	11070
Piano, Steinway & Sons, Mahogany, Baby Grand, c.1931, 39 x 58 x 66 In.	5900
Saxophone, Case, Rudolph Wurlitzer, Mother-Of-Pearl Buttons, 1920s	333
Street Organ, 27-Note, Keyless, Painted Putti, 27 ½ x 23 In.	1250
Tambourine, Boxwood, Ebony, Mother-Of-Pearl, 8 In.	48
Ukulele, Roy Smeck, Case, 21 In.	50
Violin, Carved Pine, Ebony, Smiling Face Head Stock, Red Tongue, Folk Art, c.1890, 22 x 7 In.	1422
Violin, Georg Carl Kretschmann, Bow, 14 x 23 ¼ In., 2 Piece	1180
Violin, Mathias Heinicke, Wood, Scrolled Top, Case, Marked, Czechoslovakia, 1922	900

MUSTACHE CUPS were popular from 1850 to 1900 when the large, flowing mustache was in style. A ledge of china or silver held the hair out of the liquid in the cup. This kept the mustache tidy and also kept the mustache wax from melting. Left-handed mustache cups are rare but are being reproduced.

3-D Bouquet, Gold, Saucer, 3 ¼ In.	65
Bamboo Style, Yellow Violets, Gilt, Gold Trim, Footed, Saucer	95
Dogwood & Pines, Gilt Trim, RS Prussia, 1900s, 3 ¼ In.	279
Flowers, Brown, Ivory Ground, 3 In.	43
Flowers, Multicolor, 3 Loop Handle, Nippon	65
Forget-Me-Nots, Blue & White, Gilt Stems, Handle, c.1910, 2 x 4 In.	20
Fruit, Cherries, Peaches, Left Handed	434
Majolica, Butterflies, Red, Yellow, Green, Fielding	76
Pink & Yellow Roses, Netting Pattern, 3 x 3 ½ In.	40
Pink Flowers, Green, White Enamel Beads, Lattice Vine, Gold Edging, 3 x 3 ½ In. *illus*	30
Pink Roses, Leaves, c.1950	30
Purple Violets, Gold Trim, Hammersley	187
Viking, Beaded, Milk Glass, Hobbs, Brockunier, c.1867	295
Your Father's Mustache, Man, Top Hat, Japan, 1950s	28

MZ Austria   **MZ AUSTRIA** is the wording on a mark used by Moritz Zdekauer on porcelains made at his works in Altrolau, Austria, from 1884 to 1909. The mark was changed to MZ *Altrolau* in 1909, when the firm was purchased by C.M. Hutschenreuther. The firm operated under the name Altrolau Porcelain Factories from 1909 to 1945. It was nationalized after World War II. The pieces were decorated with lavish floral patterns and overglaze gold decoration. Full sets of dishes were made as well as vases, toilet sets, and other wares.

Bowl, Portrait, Constance, Pink Rose Chain Border, 9 ¾ In.	30
Bowl, Portrait, Profile, Constance, Red Half Circles, Scalloped Rim, 10 ½ In.	36
Cider Set, Pitcher, 6 Tumblers, Cherries, Heavy Gilt, 7 ½ In., 7 Piece	144
Pitcher, Flowers, White To Gold Luster, Swirl Pattern, Beaded, Crimped Rim, 6 In.	81
Plate, Portrait, 2 Women, Pink Border, Gold Laurel Chain, 9 ¾ In.	30
Plate, Portrait, Josephine, Cranberry Border, 4 Floral Reserves, 11 In.	30

NAILSEA glass was made in the Bristol district in England from 1788 to 1873. The name also applies to glass made by many different factories, not just the Nailsea Glass House. Many pieces were made with loopings of either white or colored glass as decoration.

Bowl, Blue Translucent, Opal Loopings, Squat, Ruffled Rim, Ring Foot, c.1880, 2 x 6 In.	175

M

Bowl, Ruby Glass, White, Loopings, Wavy Frilled Rim, c.1890, 5 ½ In.	188
Compote, Green & White, Drapes, Lobed, Cameo Stem, Murano, 12 x 6 ½ In.	59
Fairy Lamp, Cranberry, White, Clear Base, 5 In.	225
Fairy Lamp, Opaque Green, White, Loopings, Domed, Ruffled Feet, 1800s, 5 ½ In.	460
Pickle Castor, Blue, White Swags, Flower Embossed Holder, 2 ¾ In.	48
Rose Bowl, Blue, White, Loopings, Bulbous, Folded Rim, Frosted Feet, c.1880, 4 x 5 In.	650
Rose Bowl, Venetian Thread, Opalescent, Ruby Glass, Crimped, Ruffled, 3 ½ In. .....*illus*	248
Shade, Pale Satin Pink, Rose Colored, Loopings, Domed, c.1890, 6 In.	208
Vase, Amber Glass, White, Loopings, Squat, Ribbed, Scalloped Rim, Ring Foot, 1800s, 8 In.	210
Vase, Opaline, Yellow Orange, Oil Spot, Calla Lily Shape, 6 ¾ x 3 ½ In., Pair	123

NAKARA is a trade name for a white glassware made about 1900 by the C. F. **NAKARA**
Monroe Company of Meriden, Connecticut. It was decorated in pastel colors.
The glass was very similar to another glass, called Wave Crest, made by the company. The company closed in 1916. Boxes for use on a dressing table are the most commonly found Nakara pieces. The mark is not found on every piece.

Ashtray, Opalescent, Amber, Blossoms, Squat, Curves, Metal Band, c.1900, 2 x 4 In.	200
Box, Ivory, Hyacinth, Roses, Ribbons, Raised Design, Squat, Hinged Lid, 1800s, 7 In.	390
Dresser Box, Cherubs, Clouds, Amber, Enamel Beading, Marked, 2 ½ x 3 In. .....*illus*	250
Dresser Box, Green, Flowers, Enamel, Brass Band, Hinged Lid, Gold Satin Lined, c.1900	1210
Dresser Box, Sage Green, Blossoms, Bishop's Hat Shape, Hinged Lid, c.1900, 5 In.	715
Humidor, Green, Shaded, Cherry Blossoms, Cigars, Metal Scroll Band, Hinged Lid, 6 In.	450
Jewelry Box, Opaque Pink, Shaded, White Enamel Beading, Hinged Lid, c.1900, 4 In.	275
Match Holder, Pink, Enameled Bead Design, Brass Band, Handles, c.1900, 1 x 3 In.	461
Vase, Flowers, Shaded, Pink To Green, Beaded, Tubular, Flared Foot, Ormolu Base, 14 In.	1450

NANKING is a type of blue-and-white porcelain made in China from the late 1700s
to the early 1900s. It was shipped from the port of Nanking. It is similar to Canton
wares listed in that category, but it is of better quality. The blue design was almost
the same, a landscape, building, trees, and a bridge. But a person was sometimes on the bridge on a Nanking piece. The "spear and post" border was used, sometimes with gold added. Nanking sells for more than Canton.

Hot Water Dish, Octagonal, Blue, White, Landscape, Bridge, Flower Border, 17 In.	360
Pitcher, Cider, Diapered Border Near Rim, 8 ½ In.	480
Platter, Armorial, Gilt, Buildings, Landscape, 1700s, 12 x 14 ½ In. .....*illus*	297
Platter, Blue & White, Cracked Ice Border, Pagodas, Island, c.1800, 20 x 17 In.	1125
Platter, Oval, Blue & White, Landscape, Figures, Buildings, 1800s, 18 In.	178
Punch Bowl, Houses, Hills, 5 ½ x 13 In.	960
Punch Bowl, Scenic Medallions, Footed, 1800s, 5 ¾ x 14 ¼ In.	461
Tazza, Blue, White, Flowers, Clobbered Design, Buildings, Trees, 4 ½ x 10 In.	240

NAPKIN RINGS were in fashion from 1869 to about 1900. They were made of silver,
porcelain, wood, and other materials. They are still being made today. The most
popular rings with collectors are the silver plated figural examples. Small, realistic
figures were made to hold the ring. Good and poor reproductions of the more expensive rings are now being made and collectors must be very careful.

Bamboo, Thistle Branch, White, Silver Rim, Fukagawa, 1950s	4
Figural, Bakelite, Bird, Open Beak, Yellow, c.1950, 1 ½ In.	98
Figural, Silver Plate, Buffalo, 2 x 3 In.	250
Figural, Silver Plate, California Seal, Poppies, El Camino, c.1900, 2 x 1 In.	75
Figural, Silver Plate, Dwarf, 3 ¾ In. .....*illus*	168
Figural, Silver Plate, Faun, Playing Cymbals, Goat Feet, Hammered, c.1888, 3 x 2 In.	268
Figural, Silver, Boy With Anchor & Rope, Leaf Feet, Reed & Barton, c.1900	450
Figural, Silver, Putti, Dancing, Roses, Marked, Spatterware, c.1930, 1 ½ In.	156
Ivory, Engraved Leaves, Scalloped & Perforated Flared Rim, c.1890, 1 ¾ In.	38
Silver Plate, Engraved, Bouquets, Meridian Silver Co., c.1870, 1 ½ x 1 ½ In.	12
Silver Plate, Engraved, Flowers, Pedestal, James Tufts, c.1880, 2 ¾ In.	80
Silver Plate, Peacock, Open Wings, Meriden, 1 ⅜ x 3 In. .....*illus*	157

Nanking, Platter, Armorial, Gilt,
Buildings, Landscape, 1700s, 12 x 14 ½ In.
$297

MBA Seattle Auction House

Napkin Ring, Figural, Silver Plate,
Dwarf, 3 ¾ In.
$168

Fox Auctions

N

Napkin Ring, Silver Plate, Peacock,
Open Wings, Meriden, 1 ⅜ x 3 In.
$157

Ruby Lane

Nash, Vase, Gold Iridescent, Stylized
Trumpet Form, Shaped Rim, 7½ In.
$399

Ruby Lane

Art Pottery Fakes
In 2011 art pottery fakes
were being sold online by a
United States company. They
are copies, some bad, of Pillin, Natzler, and Ohr pottery.
The Ohr pottery fakes have
stilt marks on the bottom,
something not seen on real
Ohr. The Pillin mark is just
enough wrong to be noticed.
Watch out for them.

Natzler, Bowl, Folded, Yellow, 1950s,
4 x 13 In.
$2,210

Treadway Toomey Auctions

Natzler, Bowl, Pompeian Glaze, Signed
GON, 329, 1939, 4 x 9 In.
$10,000

Los Angeles Modern Auctions

Silver, Applied Maltese Cross, c.1930, 1½ x 1¾ In.		195
Silver, Cherubs, Pierced, Reticulated, c.1901, 1½ x 1¾ In.		204

NASH glass was made in Corona, New York, from about 1928 to 1931. A. Douglas Nash bought the Corona glassworks from Louis C. Tiffany in 1928 and founded the A. Douglas Nash Corporation with support from his father, Arthur J. Nash. Arthur had worked at the Webb factory in England and for the Tiffany Glassworks in Corona.

Vase, Brown Feathers, Green Stripes, High Shoulders, Round Foot, Arthur Nash, 8½ x 4 In.		375
Vase, Gold Iridescent, Stylized Trumpet Form, Shaped Rim, 7½ In.	*illus*	399

NATZLER pottery was made by Gertrud Amon and Otto Natzler. They were born in Vienna, met in 1933, and established a studio in 1935. Gertrud threw thin-walled, simple, classical shapes on the wheel, while Otto developed glazes. A few months after Hitler's regime occupied Austria in 1938, they married and fled to the United States. The Natzlers set up a workshop in Los Angeles. After Gertrud's death in 1971, Otto continued creating pieces decorated with his distinctive glazes. Otto died in 2007.

Bottle, Gray Earth Crater, Glazed, Cylindrical, Signed, 1956, 16 x 3¾ In.		6250
Bottle, Ivory Crystalline Glaze, Teardrop, Squat, Ring Foot, Signed, 1965, 5 x 5 In.		2500
Bottle, Pale Gray, Melt Fissures, Teardrop, Bulbous, Pinched Roll Rim, 4 x 4 In.		1500
Bowl, Blue, Dimpled, Signed, 4¾ x 7¾ In.		1625
Bowl, Canary Yellow Glaze, Glossy, Flared, Signed, 3 x 8½ In.		1000
Bowl, Citron Yellow, Alkaline, Glazed, Signed, 1963, 2½ x 5½ In.		2000
Bowl, Crater Glazed, Signed, 1957, 5 x 9 In.		2000
Bowl, Folded, Yellow, 1950s, 4 x 13 In.	*illus*	2210
Bowl, Gray Earth Crater, Signed, 1951, 7¼ In.		4500
Bowl, Green, Black, Mottled, 2 x 7 In.		3200
Bowl, Green, Brown, Cone Shape, Signed, 1956, 7 In.		5000
Bowl, Ivory Glaze, Signed, 1962, 3¼ x 5¾ In.		2500
Bowl, Midnight Sky Blue & Gray Crystalline Glaze, Flared, c.1962, 9 In. Diam.		4688
Bowl, Moss Green & Pale Blue Glaze, Squat, Cylinder Foot, 1962, 3 x 6 In.		3000
Bowl, Pompeian Glaze, Signed GON, 329, 1939, 4 x 9 In.	*illus*	10000
Bowl, Red & Black Glaze, Flared, Cylindrical Foot, Signed, 1970, 2 x 6¼ In.		938
Bowl, Reduction Fired Glaze With Melt Fissures, Signed, 1961, 2½ x 4¾ In.		625
Bowl, Tan Glaze, Melt Fissures, Squat, Wide Rim, Cylinder Foot, 1963, 3 x 6 In.		2500
Bowl, Turquoise Volcanic Glass, Tapered, Flared Rim, Flat Edge, 4 x 8 In.		3250
Bowl, Velvet Chartreuse, Glazed, Signed, 1946, 3 x 6 In.		2813
Bowl, Yellow Volcanic Glaze, Flared, Signed, 2 x 4½ In.		1250
Chalice, Robin's Egg Blue Glaze, 9½ x 5 In.	*illus*	3570
Coupe, Orange & Brown Glaze, Cylindrical, Shouldered, Round Foot, 1958, 4 In.		2000
Plate, Brown, Ocher, Blue Hare's Fur Glaze, Streaky Circles, Flared, 1965, 8 In. Diam.		1500
Vase, Blue Frothy Glaze, Pink Highlights, Oval, Wide Rim, Ring Foot, 5 In.		2000
Vase, Blue, Oxblood, High Luster, Tapered, Signed, c.1960, 10 x 5¾ In.		6100
Vase, Chartreuse Glaze, Matte, Round, Wide Rim, Ring Foot, Signed, 5 x 5 In.		1875
Vase, Crystalline Glaze, Cylindrical, Saucer Top, Tapered Bottom, 6 In.		2125
Vase, Ocher & Brown Volcanic Glaze, Paneled, Signed, 4½ x 5 In.		1000

NAUTICAL antiques are listed in this category. Any of the many objects that were made or used by the seafaring trade, including ship parts, models, and tools, are included. Other pieces may be found listed under Scrimshaw.

Anchor, Brass, H.B. Nevins, City Island, Marked, 32 In.		350
Ashtray, Ship, Black, Round, Lid, 23 In.		117
Bell, Ship's, Yacht, Arched Mounting Bracket, 12 In.		192
Binnacle, Brass & Teak, Red Spheres, Kelvin Hughes, 53 x 35 In., 21 Diam.		488
Binnacle, Compass, Brass, Kelvin, Bottomley 7 Baird Ltd., 55 In.		600
Binnacle, Compass, Gimbaled, Brass, c.1920, 9½ In.		172
Binnacle, Hezzanith MKIII, Compass, Spheres, Brass, Teak, 59 x 30 In.	*illus*	1524
Binnacle, Liquid Magnetic Compass, Nunotani Seiki KK, Japan, 1940s, 14 x 30 In.		500
Binnacle, Yacht, Hexagonal Cover, Glass Panels, Inset Compass, Round Base, 17 In.		540

N

Boat Propeller, 2 Blades, Bronze, 1900s, 6 x 25 ½ In.	400
Box, Keepsake, Sailor's, Pine, Wire Hinges, Hex Pattern, Maine, 1800s, 4 x 11 In. .... *illus*	360
Buoy Light, Fresnel Lens, Brass, Copper, 35 In.	1800
Canoe, 2 Paddles, Arthur Levenseller, 12 Ft.	923
Canoe, Mahogany, Cedar, White & Green Paint, J.R. Robertson, c.1915, 16 Ft.	3250
Canoe, Wood, Ribbed, Green Paint, Canvas Seats, Old Town Label, 1956, 18 Ft.	600
Chronometer, 2-Day, Gimbaled, Brass, Silvered Dial, Craighead, London, c.1870	2289
Chronometer, 8-Day, Gimbaled, England, 1830, 8¾ x 8¼ In.	9000
Chronometer, Mahogany, Brass, Silver Dial, Engraved, Signed, J. Poole, 8 x 5 In.	4025
Chronometer, Metal Dial, Engraved, Jewels, Movement Only, Hamilton, 4 In.	863
Chronometer, Rosewood, Glass, Engraved Silver Dial, Thomas Mercer, 8 In.	5175
Clock, Ship's, Brass, Handle, 4-Footed Base, Waterbury Clock Co., 8 x 6 In.	500
Clock, Ship's, Chelsea, Brass, Bezel, c.1905, 6 x 6 In.	788
Clock, Ship's, Chelsea, Nickel Plated, Mahogany Stand, Key, Negus, 10 In.	475
Clock, Ship's, Seth Thomas, Brass, 8-Day, Wooden Base, 1900s, 10 x 6½ x 3 In.	240
Clock, Ship's, Seth Thomas, U.S. Navy, Deck, Gutta Percha, 1941, 7 In. Diam.	354
Clock, Ship's, Seth Thomas, Yacht, Brass, Nickel Plate Dial, Bell, c.1940, 10 In. Diam.	830
Clock, Ship's, Silvered Dial, Brass Ship's Wheel, Stand, 1952, 10 x 9 In.	442
Clock, Ship's, U.S. Navy, Black Dial, Gutta Percha Case, Chelsea, 8 In. Diam.	295
Compass, Brass, Case, Lionel Corporation, Early 1900s, 7 x 13¾ In.	183
Compass, Bronze, Round, Lionel Co., 1942, 4 In.	148
Compass, Ship's, Brass, John E. Hand & Sons, Early 1900s, 7½ In.	240
Deadeye, Carved Lignum, 6 In., Pair	180
Deadeye, Wanderer, Whaling Ship, Wood, Twisted Steel, Mounted, 1924, 35 In.	622
Desk, Sea Captain's, Walnut, Brass, Lift-Out Writing Surface, Handles, 1800s, 6 In.	800
Diorama, Garibaldi, Clipper Ship, Fully Rigged, Choppy Seas, c.1860, 30 x 39 In.	533
Diorama, Sailing Ship, Flag, Wood, Thread, Wire, Glass Case, c.1915, 19 x 27 In.	540
Figurehead, Bawdy Woman, Wood, Hat, Dutch, c.1820, 28 x 11 In.	18000
Figurehead, Bust, Mars, Roman God, Helmet, Plume, Pine, c.1782, 31 x 14 In.	9480
Figurehead, Eagle's Head, 18 In.	960
Figurehead, Eagle's Head, Scrollwork, 35½ In.	1800
Figurehead, Pine, Carved, Admiral Perry, S.W. Burgess, c.1900, 35 x 20 In. ....*illus*	5925
Foghorn, Buntline Hitch Balco, Red, Handle, 1900s, 15 x 20¾ In.	74
Grog Cask, Oak, Brass Bound, 1800s, 22¼ In.	6240
Half-Model, British Freighter, Raised Quarter Deck Coaster, 1914, 16 x 54 In.	1200
Half-Model, Laminated Wood, Lake Erie Schooner, Clyde, Oh., c.1850s, 5 x 42 In.	375
Half-Model, Yacht, Multicolor, 54 In.	250
Keg, Sailor's, Pine, Carved Whalebone, Inscribed, James Hale Maine, 1845, 7 x 7 In.	720
Ladder, Regency, Folding, 6 Rungs, 81 x 12½ In.	1062
Lamp, Silver Plate, Wood Mount, Pascall Atkey & Sons, c.1890, 8½ In.	650
Lantern, Anchor, Tin, Paint, Iron, Fresnel Lens, Cartouche, Rope, c.1890, 26 In.	474
Lantern, Beacon, Brass, Prism Lens, Caged, Vent Top, Handle, c.1900, 14 In.	593
Lantern, Boat, Canister Shape, 25 In.	375
Lantern, Copper, Seahorse, Corner Light, Oil Burner, 22½ x 15 In. ....*illus*	265
Lantern, Oil, Brass, 3 Lenses, Clark Bros., England, Mid 1800s, 20 In.	270
Lantern, Ship's, Globe, Onion, Blue Green Glass, Cage, Cylindrical Base, Fluted Vent, 15 In.	415
Lantern, Ship's, Brass, Glass Globe, Marked Anchor, Late 1800s, 14 In.	240
Lantern, Ship's, Standing, Oil, Brass Base. Cage, Handle, Perkins, 1916-31, 17 In.	660
Life Preserver, Great White Fleet Tours & Cruises, c.1907, 30 In.	300
Mailbag, USS Flagship Richmond, Sailcloth, Hand Sewn, c.1879, 16 x 17½ In.	540
Masthead Light, Brass, Triple Dome Lens, Hinged, Port & Starboard, 1910, 12 In.	770
Model, Arctic Whaling Ship, Hope, Fully Rigged, Glazed Case, 25 In.	5312
Model, Blockade Runner, Fergus, Wood, Metal, Alois Schmid, 1972, 41 x 15 In.	1440
Model, Boat Hull, Wood & Original Paint, c.1900, 8 x 28 In.	1560
Model, Canoe, Canvas & Wood, Green Paint, Closed Gunnels, c.1910, 48 x 10 In.	5925
Model, Coast Guard Cutter, Cayuga, Wood, Lifeboats, Col. R.E. Knie, 20 x 36 In.	540
Model, Colonial Schooner, 3-Masted, Bone, 1768, 32 In.	2750
Model, Continental Navy Brig, Cabot, Plank Frame, Glass Case, 28 x 37½ In.	2750
Model, Cruise Ship, c.1960, 15½ x 56¾ In.	200
Model, Friesland 1663, 32 x 36 In.	250
Model, Frigate, Metal, Gray, 5 x 15 In.	19

Natzler, Chalice, Robin's Egg Blue Glaze, 9½ x 5 In.
$3,570

MBA Seattle Auction House

Nautical, Binnacle, Hezzanith MKIII, Compass, Spheres, Brass, Teak, 59 x 30 In.
$1,524

DuMouchelles

Nautical, Box, Keepsake, Sailor's, Pine, Wire Hinges, Hex Pattern, Maine, 1800s, 4 x 11 In.
$360

Thomaston Place Auction Galleries

Nautical, Figurehead, Pine, Carved, Admiral Perry, S.W. Burgess, c.1900, 35 x 20 In.
$5,925

James D. Julia Auctioneers

TIP

Try the old-time recipe for cleaning copper. Mix lemon juice or vinegar with salt and use as a metal polish. Ketchup is a good emergency copper cleaner.

Nautical, Lantern, Copper, Seahorse, Corner Light, Oil Burner, 22 ½ x 15 In.
$265

Burchard Galleries

Model, HMS Pelorus, D-Day Invasion, Bronze Case, Mahogany Base, 33 x 67 In.	3750
Model, HMS Prince, 3-Masted, Billowing Sails, 38 x 48 In.	250
Model, HMS Victory, 3-Masted, 32 x 35 In.	281
Model, Hollandia, Carved, Wood, Holland, 17 ½ x 28 In.	500
Model, Packet Steamer, Wood, 3-Masted, Fully Rigged, Pine Base, 15 x 22 In.	600
Model, Ship In Bottle, 3-Masted, Lighthouse, Cork Closure, c.1910, 11 ¾ In. ......*illus*	98
Model, Ship In Bottle, Schooner, 5-Masted, Glass Bead, Stand, Germany, 12 In. ......*illus*	264
Model, Ship, 20-Gun Brig, Paint, Copper Hull, Mahogany Case, c.1980, 22 x 26 In.	711
Model, Ship, 3-Masted, Glass Dome, 21 ¼ x 21 ½ In.	767
Model, Ship, 3-Masted, Walnut & Glass Case, 19 x 26 In.	210
Model, Ship, Armed Brig, Tops & Sails, Gun Ports, Soldier, 1800s, 69 x 92 In.	2963
Model, Ship, Artic Whale, Hope, Fully Rigged, Glazed Case, 25 In.	5312
Model, Sovereign Of The Seas, 3-Masted, 32 x 35 In.	281
Model, Spanish Galleon, Metal, 28 x 28 In.	295
Model, Spanish Galleon, Wood, Paint & Cloth Sails, Late 1800s, 29 x 28 In.	90
Model, Spitfire, Canadian Gunship, Carved, Galleon Stern, Stand, 1900s, 26 x 33 In.	415
Model, Steam Yacht, 20 Portholes, Propeller, 22 x 31 In. ......*illus*	975
Model, Steam Yacht, Wintonia, Mahogany Case, Molded Baseplate, 23 ½ In.	2750
Model, Steamer, Minnie, Pilot House, Flags, Glass Case, c.1890, 13 x 26 In.	1778
Model, Steamship, Lackawanna, Wood, Juan Alva, Case, 10 x 16 In.	420
Model, Swedish 64-Gun Ship Of War, 37 In.	5312
Model, Warship, USS Essex, 32-Gun Sailing Frigate, 34 In.	3750
Model, Whaling Brig Wanderer, Case, 56 In.	1500
Model, Yacht, Defender, Nathanial Herrsehoff, Mahogany Case, 41 x 48 In.	3450
Model, Yacht, Endeavour, Wood, Copper, Paint, Rigging, Lannan, Boston, 69 In.	1180
Model, Yacht, North Wind, 2-Masted, Wood, Paint, Quincy, Mass., 24 x 19 In.	240
Motor, Inboard, 2 Cylinder, Brass Propeller, Arrow Motor & Machine Co., 32 In.	1132
Oar, Wood, Copper Tip, Rubber End, Label, Helmut Schoenbrod, c.1910, 118 In.	156
Octant, Mahogany, Brass, 19-In. Radius, Bone Plaque, G. Adams, London, 1767......*illus*	5885
Paddle Box, Lunette, Carved, Spread Wing Eagle, Shield, Globe, c.1850, 28 x 72 In.	11850
Pennant, Ship Owner's, Cloth, Red White & Blue, Stitched, c.1900, 97 x 184 In.	2091
Pilot House Eagle, Riverboat, Spread Wing, Sheet Zinc, c.1865, 15 x 44 In.	2370
Pilot House Eagle, Yellow Paint, Cast Iron, 10 x 30 ¼ In.	270
Plaque, Don't Give Up The Ship, Pine, Carved, Eagle, J.H. Bellamy, c.1870, 26 In. ......*illus*	2829
Pond Boat, Yacht, Wood, Rigging, Cloth Sails, Hand Stitched, c.1930s, 68 x 40 In.	375
Pressure Gauge, Submarine's, Brass, Howaldtswerke-Deusche Werft, c.1860, 8 In.	425
Propeller, Bronze, c.1915, 19 In.	198
Sailor's Valentine, Double, Shellwork, Heart, 8-Sided Case, Hinged, c.1900, 12 ½ In. ......*illus*	3328
Sailor's Valentine, Flower, Star, Octagonal, Mahogany Case, 14 In.	3750
Sailor's Valentine, Forget-Me-Not, Heart, Rose, Double, Hinge, 9 x 18 In.	3960
Sailor's Valentine, Hearts, Roses, Geometric Patterns, 14 ¾ In.	1680
Sailor's Valentine, Shells, Pine Box, Octagonal, Paper Lining, Early 1800s, 9 In.	1500
Sailor's Valentine, Star, Heart, Roses, Double, Hinge, 8 ½ x 16 ¾ In.	6480
Sea Chest, Blue, Sailing Ship On Lid, Whales, Dovetail, Rope Handles, 18 x 45 In.	450
Sea Chest, Blue, Stars, Rope Becket Handles, 13 ½ x 32 In.	240
Sea Chest, Brass Bound, Rope Handles, Dovetailed, 17 ½ x 36 In.	1020
Sea Chest, Pine, Blue, Black, Dovetailed, Rope Handles, 13 x 33 ½ In.	540
Sea Chest, Pine, Interior Ship Painting, Rope Becket Handles, 14 ½ x 45 In.	1000
Sea Chest, Pine, Paint, Monogram Plaque, Molded, Hinged Lid, c.1800, 18 x 44 In.	148
Sea Chest, Tilled, False Bottom, 1800s, 5 ¾ x 10 ¾ In.	540
Searchlight, Handle, Vesta, c.1920, 10 In.	37
Sextant, Black Metal, Brass Scale, 2 Lenses, Wood Case, Heath & Co., 9 x 9 In.	948
Sextant, Brass, Black Grip, Mahogany Case, 1942, 10 x 10 In.	1191
Sextant, Brass, Mahogany Case, Negretti & Lambia London, 4 ½ x 10 In.	250
Sextant, Brass, Wood Case, T.M. Moore, 10 x 9 In. ......*illus*	300
Sextant, Mahogany Case, Negretti & Zambra, England, 1800s, 5 x 11 x 11 In.	366
Ship's Wheel, 8 Spokes, Mahogany, Brass Hub, Oak Rim, 1800s, 48 In.	900
Ship's Wheel, 8 Spokes, Walnut, Iron Hub, 48 In.	240
Ship's Wheel, 8 Spokes, Wood, Brass, 49 In.	300
Ship's Wheel, 10 Spokes, Oak, Cast Iron Hub, 62 ½ In.	600
Ship's Wheel, Brass, Turned Wood Handles, Rosebank Ironworks, 36 In.	480

Nautical, Model, Ship In Bottle, 3-Masted, Lighthouse, Cork Closure, c.1910, 11¾ In.
$98

Skinner, Inc.

Nautical, Model, Ship In Bottle, Schooner, 5-Masted, Glass Bead, Stand, Germany, 12 In.
$264

Fox Auctions

Nautical, Model, Steam Yacht, 20 Portholes, Propeller, 22 x 31 In.
$975

Rago Arts and Auction Center

Nautical, Octant, Mahogany, Brass, 19-In. Radius, Bone Plaque, G. Adams, London, 1767
$5,885

Auction Team Breker

Nautical, Plaque, Don't Give Up The Ship, Pine, Carved, Eagle, J.H. Bellamy, c.1870, 26 In.
$2,829

Skinner, Inc.

Nautical, Sailor's Valentine, Double, Shellwork, Heart, 8-Sided Case, Hinged, c.1900, 12½ In.
$3,328

James D. Julia Auctioneers

Nautical, Sextant, Brass, Wood Case, T.M. Moore, 10 x 9 In.
$300

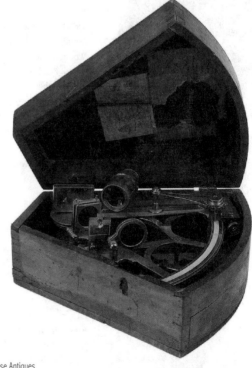

Case Antiques

TIP
Keep front hedges and fences under three feet high so prowlers can be seen from the street.

Netsuke, Wood, Hawk Pins Monkey, Signed Isihikawa, 2 ½ In.
$117

Ruby Lane

New Martinsville, Janice, Relish, 2 Sections, Ruby Red, 1 ¾ x 8 In.
$24

Ruby Lane

New Martinsville, Vase, Pink Rocket, Flower Brocade, Footed, c.1930, 8 x 7 ½ In.
$175

Ruby Lane

Ship's Wheel, Iron, Wood Grips, Wilcox Crittendon & Co., 1900s, 30 In.		240
Ship's Wheel, Oak & Brass, 37 x 2 In.		147
Ship's Wheel, Pilot, Maple, Block & Turned Spokes, Iron, Late 1800s, 34 In.		240
Ship's Wheel, Teak & Oak, 1900s, 48 ½ In.		384
Ship's Wheel, Iron, Yellow & Green Paint, Late 1800s, 40 In.		210
Sign, Brolite Z-Spar Marine Finishes, Tin Lithograph, Sailboats, Embossed, 1940s, 15 x 36 In.		545
Sign, SS Imperator, Hamberg-American Line, Steamship, Tin, 1911, 30 x 40 In.		237
Sign, Stella Anne Grisby, Thames River, Big Ben, 18 x 37 In.		178
Telegraph, Ship's, WWI Bendix Engine Order, Double Faced, 50 ½ In.		550
Tip Tray, Evinrude Motor Co., Girl In Motorboat, Tin Lithograph, 4 In. Diam.		575
Trailboard, Havanna, Carved Gold Letters, Black Ground, 91 ½ In., Pair		4080
Trailboard, Leaves, Gadrooned, Black, Cream, 14 ¾ In.		510
Trophy, Pitcher, Regatta, Transfer Print, Porcelain, England, 1800s, 10 In.		105
Winch, Engraved Fern 1906, American Ship Windlass Co., 19 ¾ In.		1920

 NETSUKES are small ivory, wood, metal, or porcelain pieces used as toggles on the end of the cord that held a Japanese money pouch or inro. The earliest date from the sixteenth century. Many are miniature carved works of art. This category also includes the ojime, the slide or string fastener that was used on the inro cord.

Bone, Man Lying Against A Treasure Sack, 3 In.		60
Bone, Man, Staff, Sign, 2 ¾ In.		84
Coral, Ojime, Seed Shape, Openings, ¾ In.		216
Silver, Ojime, Carp, Waves, ¾ In.		360
Silver, Ojime, Dragon, ¾ In.		360
Staghorn, Bat, Resting On Log, 2 ¾ In.		192
Stone, Silverwork, 1 ¾ In.		216
Wood, 2 Frogs, Lotus Leaves, Inlaid Eyes, Signed Masatsugu, 1 ½ In.		1680
Wood, 3 Rats, Inlaid Eyes, Signed Tomokazu, 2 In.		840
Wood, 15 Theatrical Masks, Signed Rakumin, 2 In.		1200
Wood, Hawk Pins Monkey, Signed Isihikawa, 2 ½ In.	*illus*	117
Wood, Hotei & Child, Playing, Hinged Treasure Sack, 1 ½ In.		540
Wood, Ojime, Ball Shape, Dragon, Clouds, ¾ In.		180
Wood, Pug Dog, Seated, 1 ½ In.		375
Wood, Rabbit, Mortar & Pestle, 2 In.		600

New Hall **NEW HALL** Porcelain Works was in business in Shelton, Hanley, Staffordshire, England, from 1781 to 1835. Simple decorated wares were made. Between 1810 and 1825, the factory made a glassy bone porcelain sometimes marked with the factory name. Do not confuse New Hall porcelain with the pieces made by the New Hall Pottery Company, Ltd., a twentieth-century firm working from 1899 to 1956 at the New Hall Works.

Creamer, Mother & Child, On Couch		125
Jug, Horses, Hunting Scene, White Bas Relief, Blue Ground, 3 In.		50
Tray, Sairey Gamp, Trunk, Coach, 4 x 4 In.		24

 NEW MARTINSVILLE Glass Manufacturing Company was established in 1901 in New Martinsville, West Virginia. It was bought and renamed the Viking Glass Company in 1944. In 1987 Kenneth Dalzell, former president of Fostoria Glass Company, purchased the factory and renamed it Dalzell-Viking. Production ceased in 1998.

Blossom Time, Bowl, Silver Overlay, 3-Footed, c.1950, 6 In.		35
Cornucopia, Candlestick, 3 ½ In.		20
Figurine, Hen, c.1948, 5 In., Pair		65
Figurine, Seal, Ball On Nose, 7 ½ In.		95
Janice, Candlestick, Ruby, c.1926, 5 ¼ In., Pair		80
Janice, Relish, 2 Sections, Ruby Red, 1 ¾ x 8 In.	*illus*	24
Janice, Tray, Emerald Green, 2 Cruets, 1940s, 3 Piece		110
Leaf & Star, c.1909, 5 ¼ x 5 In.		15
Marshall, Candlestick, 2-Light		20
Moondrops, Compote, Ruby, Ruffled Edge, 7 x 2 In.		44

N

Moondrops, Dish, Footed, Ruffled Edge, c.1935, 7 In.	44
New Frontier, Toothpick	45
Prelude, Bonbon, 5 x 2 ½ In.	40
Prelude, Torte Plate, 12 In.	9
Radiance, Bowl, Footed, 10 ¾ In.	10
Radiance, Butter, Cover, Round, 6 In.	187
Radiance, Creamer, Footed, 3 In.	14
Radiance, Punch Bowl, Ball Shape, Ice Blue, 8 In.	219
Radiance, Punch Bowl, Flared, 12 In.	37
Radiance, Punch Cup, Amber, 2 ¼ In.	5
Radiance, Punch Cup, Cutout Handle, 2 ½ In.	7
Radiance, Punch Cup, Wing Handle, Ice Blue, 2 ½ In.	10
Radiance, Torte Plate, 17 ¾ In.	30
Vase, Pink Rocket, Flower Brocade, Footed, c.1930, 8 x 7 ½ In. ....*illus*	175

NEWCOMB POTTERY was founded at Sophie Newcomb College, New Orleans, Louisiana, in 1895. The work continued through the 1940s. Pieces of this art pottery are marked with the printed letters *NC* and often have the incised initials of the artist and potter as well. A date letter code was printed on pieces made from 1901 to 1941. Most pieces have a matte glaze and incised decoration.

Biscuit Jar, Blue, Wild Roses, Sadie Irvine, 1925, 8 x 5 In.	1375
Biscuit Jar, Dome Lid, Wild Roses, Blue, Pink, Mushroom Knop, 1925, 8 In.	1375
Bowl, Cherokee Roses, White, Green, Blue, Matte Glaze, A. Simpson, 6 x 8 In.	3660
Bowl, Misty Landscape, Oak Trees, Spanish Moss, Impressed, c.1916, 6 x 7 In.	5250
Bowl, Roses, Blue, Yellow, Green, Striated Ground, Alma Mason, 1912, 3 x 8 In.	875
Bowl, White Narcissus, Blue, Green, Anna F. Simpson, c.1918, 1 ¾ x 4 In.	384
Candlestick, Oleander, Blue Matte, Dish Bobeche, Flared Base, 1923, 10 In.	2318
Candlestick, White Camellias, Blue Matte Glaze, Flared Base, Gasquet, 7 In.	610
Charger, 3 Carp, Pale & Dark Blue, White, Sabrina Wells, 9 ¼ In.	2625
Charger, Pale To Dark Blue, Fish Border, M.F. Baker, 1906, 9 ½ In.	2625
Jar, Dome Lid, Knop Finial, Pears, Leaves, Blue, Green, Bell Shape, 1907, 8 In.	5938
Jar, Lid, Roses, Blossom On Lid, Anna F. Simpson, 5 ½ x 5 ½ In.	3000
Jar, Lid, Spanish Moss, Moon, Blue, Bulbous, A.F. Simpson, 8 x 5 ½ In.	3750
Jardiniere, Stylized Oak Trees, Blue, Green, Leona Nicholson, 1906, 8 ¾ In. ....*illus*	14080
Mug, Blue Tulip Band, Green Ground, Bulbous, Folded-In Rim, 6 x 6 In.	1875
Pitcher, Buds, Banding, White, Speckled Blue & Green, Tapered, 7 In.	3125
Pitcher, Freesia, White, Blue, Anna F. Simpson, 6 x 6 In.	1375
Pitcher, Mint Green & Blue, Espanol Pattern, Anna F. Simpson, c.1929, 5 In.	488
Plaque, Cypress Trees, Landscape, Blue, A.F. Simpson, 1915, 6 x 10 In.	5000
Plate, Rabbit Border, Blue, Green, White, 1909, 8 ¼ In.	2750
Stand, Blue & Green Glaze, Anna F. Simpson, c.1913, 1 ¼ x 4 In.	610
Trivet, Fruiting Branch, Blue, Green, Square, Wood Frame, 1911, 6 In.	1625
Tyg, Stylized Iris, Cobalt Blue, Pale Green, Tubular Handles, 1901, 6 In.	7906
Vase, 4 Blue Handles, Gray Pink Body, Sadie Irvine, 6 ½ x 5 In.	1000
Vase, Arrowhead Blossoms, Marie De Hoa LeBlanc, 1906, 12 ½ x 5 In.	4063
Vase, Banana Plant, Blue, Green, Harriet Joor, Joseph Meyer, 1902, 11 In. ....*illus*	15860
Vase, Blooming Irises, Henrietta Bailey, 1918, 6 ¼ x 6 ¼ In.	9062
Vase, Blue Matte Glaze, Pale Pink Flowers, On Shoulder, S. Irvine, 3 x 5 In.	546
Vase, Blue Matte Glaze, Sadie Irvine, c.1932, 4 x 6 In.	976
Vase, Blue Over Turquoise Glaze, c.1941 3 In.	230
Vase, Blue, Green, White & Yellow, Henrietta Bailey, c.1918, 3 ½ x 4 In.	488
Vase, Calla Lily Buds, High Glaze, Ada Lonnegan, 1901, 9 x 4 In.	3500
Vase, Chrysanthemum, Anna F. Simpson, 9 In.	2750
Vase, Clematis, Blue, Sadie Irvine, 1930, 5 ½ x 5 In.	1125
Vase, Cotton Plants, Banding, Streaky Blue Glaze, Cylindrical, 1905, 6 In.	1375
Vase, Crocus Flowers, Green, Blue, Shouldered, Marked, c.1915, 7 x 4 In.	1750
Vase, Daffodils, Green, Corseted, A.F. Simpson, 1912, 8 ½ x 3 ½ In.	1750
Vase, Daisies, Blue, Tapered, E. Villere, 1903, 7 ½ x 4 In.	4063
Vase, Daylilies, Cobalt Blue, Harriet Joor, 1903, 9 x 10 In.	6875
Vase, Daylilies, Pink, Green Leaves, Blue Ground, A.F. Simpson, 1920, 5 x 4 In.	938

Newcomb, Jardiniere, Stylized Oak Trees, Blue, Green, Leona Nicholson, 1906, 8 ¾ In.
$14,080

Neal Auctions

Newcomb, Vase, Banana Plant, Blue, Green, Harriet Joor, Joseph Meyer, 1902, 11 In.
$15,860

Neal Auctions

Newcomb, Vase, Stylized Plant, Green, Blue, Roberta Kennon, 1902, 9 x 6 In.
$8,750

Rago Arts and Auction Center

N

Newcomb, Vase, Wild Rose, Blue,
Cynthia Pugh Littlejohn, 6½ x 8½ In.
$2,800

Ruby Lane

Niloak, Vase, Fluted, Melon Shape
Squat Base, Green Matte Glaze, Double
Handles, 6 x 5 In.
$26

Ruby Lane

Nippon, Dresser Jar, Gilt, Flowers,
Applied Gold Balls, Flowers, 3 Legs,
1920s, 3½ x 4 In.
$150

Ruby Lane

> **TIP**
> Bright sunlight will
> damage antiques by
> fading colors or drying
> wood. There are several
> brands of film that
> can be applied to your
> windows to cut UV rays,
> heat, and glare.

Vase, Dogwood, Blue, White, 3½ x 4 In.	1159
Vase, Flower Wreath, Pale Pink & Green Over Blue, H. Bailey, 3 x 5 In.	489
Vase, Flowers & Banding, Matte Glaze, May L. Dunn, 1911, 5 In.	2318
Vase, Flowers, Handles, Blue, Pink, Sadie Irvine, 4 x 5 In.	976
Vase, Flowers, Paperwhites, Blue, Green, White, Tapered Beaker, 1920, 10 In.	875
Vase, Lid, Pears, Elizabeth H. Pattison, 1907, 8 x 6 In.	5938
Vase, Live Oaks, Moon, Moss, Blue, Cylindrical, Flared, 1925, 14 In.	6250
Vase, Moon & Moss, Green, Blue, Shouldered, H.D. Bailey, 4½ In.	1500
Vase, Moon & Palms, Anna F. Simpson, 1920, 6½ x 4½ In.	7187
Vase, Moon & Pines, Dusk, Sadie Irvine, 1916, 6 x 3 In.	4500
Vase, Moon & Pines, Matte Glaze, Sadie Irvine, 1917, 10½ x 5 In.	4250
Vase, Mossy Trees, Bulbous, Anna F. Simpson, 1917, 3¼ In.	480
Vase, Oleander Band, Blue Ground, Squat, A.F. Simpson, 1925, 5 x 7 In.	313
Vase, Oleander, Blue, White, Swollen Shoulder, M. LeBlanc, 1911, 7 In.	1000
Vase, Palm Trees, At Dawn, Sadie Irvine, 1929, 5½ x 4 In.	4250
Vase, Pine Branch, Cones, Blue Glaze, Bulbous, J. Hunt, H. Bailey, 5 In.	1000
Vase, Pine Trees & Full Moon, Blue, Anna F. Simpson, 1916, 8 x 4 In.	5625
Vase, Pine Trees, Full Moon, Blue, Green, Cylindrical, Shouldered, 1916, 8 In.	5625
Vase, Spiderwort, Blue, White, Squat, Henrietta Bailey, 5½ In.	1750
Vase, Stylized Cherry Blossoms, Blue, Mauve, Swollen Shoulder, 1929, 6 In.	2875
Vase, Stylized Cotton, Blue, 1905, 6 x 3 In.	1375
Vase, Stylized Plant, Green, Blue, Roberta Kennon, 1902, 9 x 6 In......*illus*	8750
Vase, Twilight Scene, Pale Pink, Green & Blue Matte, c.1919, 3½ In.	1150
Vase, White Flowers, Green Leaves, Anna F. Simpson, 5 In.	1800
Vase, Wild Rose, Blue, Cynthia Pugh Littlejohn, 6½ x 8½ In......*illus*	2800

NILOAK POTTERY (*Kaolin* spelled backward) was made at the Hyten Brothers Pottery in Benton, Arkansas, between 1910 and 1947. Although the factory did make cast and molded wares, collectors are most interested in the marbleized art pottery line made of colored swirls of clay. It was called Mission Ware. By 1931 the company made castware, and many of these pieces were marked with the name Hywood.

Cordial Set, Marbleized, Streaky Blue, Beige, Cups, Bottle, Tray, 8 Piece	875
Figurine, Deer, Pink, 8 In.	22
Vase, Fluted, Melon Shape Squat Base, Green Matte Glaze, Double Handles, 6 x 5 In......*illus*	26
Vase, Green, Pink Interior, Footed, Flared, c.1950, 6½ In.	129
Vase, Marbleized, Brown, Tan, Blue, 7¼ In.	86

NIPPON porcelain was made in Japan from 1891 to 1921. *Nippon* is the Japanese word for "Japan." A few firms continued to use the word *Nippon* on ceramics after 1921 as a part of the company name more than as an identification of the country of origin. More pieces marked Nippon will be found in the Dragonware, Moriage, and Noritake categories.

Dresser Jar, Gilt, Flowers, Applied Gold Balls, Flowers, 3 Legs, 1920s, 3½ x 4 In......*illus*	150
Humidor, Dog Portrait, Pale Green, Yellow, Black & White, Jar, Lid, Finial, 7 In.	944
Salt, Open, Pink Flowers, Green Leaf Border, 3-Footed, ¾ In.	20
Tobacco Jar, Girl, Cards, 5 In.	112
Vase, Arts & Crafts Style, Pine Trees, Coralene, Cylindrical, 10 In.	944
Vase, Coralene, Lavender, Green Leaves, 10¾ In.	812
Vase, Diaper Pattern, Gold, Tan, Orange, Black Ground, Handles, 9½ In.	88
Vase, Flask Shape, Yellow Roses, Maroon Ground, 15 In.	440
Vase, Swan, Pond, Panels, Leaves, Handles, 10¼ x 7¾ In.	118

NODDERS, also called nodding figures or pagods, are figures with heads and hands that are attached to wires. Any slight movement causes the parts to move up and down. They were made in many countries during the eighteenth, nineteenth, and twentieth centuries. A few Art Deco designs are also known. Copies are being made. A more recent type of nodder is made of papier-mache or plastic. These often represent sports figures or comic characters. Sports nodders are listed in the Sports category.

Billy Goat, Papier-Mache, Platform, Wheels, 7½ x 6 In.	522

Cat, Chalkware, Tan, 1800s, 4 1/2 x 8 1/4 In. 381
Elephant, Papier-Mache, Red Blanket, Wheels, 18 x 18 In. 357
Pig, Chalkware, Old Gray & Red Paint, Pennsylvania, 1800s, 3 3/4 x 7 1/2 In. *illus* 270
Salt & Pepper Shakers are listed in the Salt & Pepper category.
Uncle Sam, Seated, Top Hat, Red, White & Blue, Chalkware, Germany, 3 In. *illus* 207

NORITAKE porcelain was made in Japan after 1904 by Nippon Toki Kaisha. A maple leaf mark was used from 1891 to 1911. The best-known Noritake pieces are marked with the *M* in a wreath for the Morimura Brothers, a New York City distributing company. This mark was used primarily from 1911 to 1921 but was last used in the early 1950s. The *N* mark was used from 1940 to the 1960s, and *N Japan* from 1953 to 1964. Noritake Azalea is listed in the Azalea category in this book.

Bowl, Cereal, Bright Side, 5 1/2 In. 8
Bowl, Cereal, Mardi Gras, 6 1/2 In. 10
Bowl, Fruit, Blue Lusterware Border, 1900s, 7 1/4 In. *illus* 70
Bowl, Fruit, Safari, 6 In. 10
Bowl, Fruit, Springfield, 5 3/4 In. 7
Bowl, Fruit, Tisdale, 5 1/2 In. 12
Bowl, Mountain Village, Shaped Edge, Multicolor, M In Wreath Mark, 1930s, 11 x 3 In. *illus* 49
Bowl, Vegetable, Blue Moon, 9 3/4 In. 26
Bowl, Vegetable, Lid, Palos Verde, 2 1/2 Qt. 75
Bowl, Vegetable, Lid, Round, Isabella, 8 1/4 In. 90
Bowl, Vegetable, Oval, Marguerite, 10 In. 14
Bowl, Vegetable, Oval, Shelby, 10 3/4 In. 35
Bowl, Vegetable, Round, Divided, Harley, 10 In. 21
Butter, Cover, Mardi Gras 21
Butter, Cover, Up-Sa Daisy 32
Candy Dish, Poppy Border, Pink, Green, Gold, Footed, M In Wreath Mark, 2 1/2 x 6 1/2 In. *illus* 39
Casserole, Lid, Melanie, 1 1/2 Qt., 9 In. 80
Creamer, Colburn 14
Creamer, Desert Flowers 5
Creamer, Milburn, 3 3/4 In. 14
Cup & Saucer, Angela 13
Cup & Saucer, Bamboo *illus* 15
Cup & Saucer, Blue Haven 7
Cup & Saucer, Golden Lily 25
Cup & Saucer, Sunny Side 7
Ferner, White Woodland, Square, Blue M In Wreath, 5 In. 484
Gravy Boat, Belda 40
Gravy Boat, Pacific 25
Gravy Boat, Palos Verde 20
Gravy Boat, Underplate, Dresdoll *illus* 45
Gravy Boat, Underplate, Dutch Treat 28
Jug, Wine, Portrait, Top Hat, Portly Man, Enamel Grapes & Leaves, M In Wreath, 9 1/2 In. 574
Plaque, Man Riding Camel, Molded, Tan, M In Wreath, 10 3/4 In. 272
Plaque, White Flowers, Black Trim, Moriage Border, M In Wreath, 10 In. 181
Plate, Bread & Butter, Arabesque, 6 1/4 In. 7
Plate, Bread & Butter, Safari, 6 1/2 In. 8
Plate, Dinner, Berries 'N Such, 10 In. 15
Plate, Dinner, Daisy, 10 In. 21
Plate, Dinner, Goldston, 10 1/2 In. 13
Plate, Dinner, Willowbrook, 10 3/4 In. 35
Plate, Salad, Daisy, 8 1/4 In. 8
Plate, Salad, Flower Time, 8 1/4 In. 10
Platter, Adrienne, 16 In. 65
Platter, Belda, 15 In. 45
Platter, Oval, Flower Time, 13 In. 21
Platter, Oval, Orange County, 13 1/4 In. 35

TIP
Lock doors and set security alerts even if you are just going for a short walk with the dog.

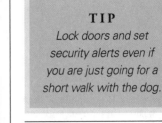

Nodder, Pig, Chalkware, Old Gray & Red Paint, Pennsylvania, 1800s, 3 3/4 x 7 1/2 In.
$270

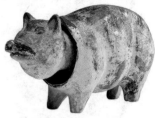

Cowan's Auctions

Nodder, Uncle Sam, Seated, Top Hat, Red, White & Blue, Chalkware, Germany, 3 In.
$207

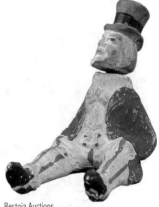

Bertoia Auctions

Noritake, Bowl, Fruit, Blue Lusterware Border, 1900s, 7 1/4 In.
$70

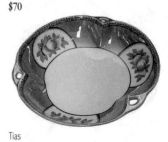

Tias

This is an edited listing of current prices. Visit **Kovels.com** to check thousands of prices from previous years and sign up for free information on trends, tips, reproductions, marks, and more.

Noritake, Bowl, Mountain Village, Shaped Edge, Multicolor, M In Wreath Mark, 1930s, 11 x 3 In.
$49

Ruby Lane

Noritake, Candy Dish, Poppy Border, Pink, Green, Gold, Footed, M In Wreath Mark, 2 1/2 x 6 1/2 In.
$39

Ruby Lane

Noritake, Cup & Saucer, Bamboo
$15

Tias

Noritake, Gravy Boat, Underplate, Dresdoll
$45

Tias

Noritake, Salt & Pepper, Women, Green Hats, Art Deco, 1900s, 1 7/8 In.
$81

Heritage Auctions

Noritake, Vase, Bird On Flower Stem, Green Luster, Handles, 10 In.
$200

Tias

Norse, Vase, Mottled Chocolate Brown, Molded Lizard, Smokestack, Trumpet Neck, 12 In.
$590

Humler & Nolan

North Dakota, Vase, Rabbits, Trees, Tapers, Alternating Square Panels, Matte Brown, U.N.D., 4 x 5 In.
$1,695

Ruby Lane

Northwood, Alaska, Celery Dish, Vaseline, 4-Footed, 1897, 2 1/2 x 9 1/2 In.
$112

Jeffrey S. Evans

N

Platter, Round, Melanie, 14 In.	30
Salt & Pepper, Blue Haven	30
Salt & Pepper, Homecoming	25
Salt & Pepper, Sunny Side	21
Salt & Pepper, Women, Green Hats, Art Deco, 1900s, 1⅞ In. ....*illus*	81
Soup, Dish, Daisy, 7½ In.	12
Soup, Dish, Goldston, 7½ In.	7
Soup, Dish, Laurel, 7 In.	10
Sugar & Creamer, Blue Moon	34
Sugar & Creamer, Homecoming	32
Sugar, Lid, Sunny Side	15
Teapot, Led, Blue Haven, 6 In.	76
Teapot, Lorenzo, 5 In.	60
Vase, Bird On Flower Stem, Green Luster, Handles, 10 In. ....*illus*	200
Vase, Bisque, Lavender, Horse, Rider, Pond, M In Wreath, 10 In.	968
Vase, Brick Red, Cobalt Blue, Moriage Decoration, M In Wreath, 9 In.	393
Vase, Ducks, Landscape, Pink & Cream Moriage Leaves, M In Wreath, 8 In.	363
Vase, Poppies, Pond, 12¼ In.	188
Vase, Vulture Scene, Molded-In-Relief, M In Wreath	2057

NORSE POTTERY COMPANY started in Edgerton, Wisconsin, in 1903. In 1904 the company moved to Rockford, Illinois. The company made a black pottery, which resembled early bronze relics of the Scandinavian countries. The firm went out of business in 1913.

Vase, Mottled Chocolate Brown, Molded Lizard, Smokestack, Trumpet Neck, 12 In. ....*illus*	590

NORTH DAKOTA SCHOOL OF MINES was established in 1898 at the University of North Dakota. A ceramics course was established in 1910. Students made pieces from the clays found in the region. Although very early pieces were marked *U.N.D.,* most pieces were stamped with the full name of the university. After 1963 pieces were only marked with students' names.

Charger, Fan, Red, Blue, Fawn, 7⅜ In.	275
Tumbler, Mattson, Abstract Patterns, Green, Brown, 4⅛ In.	118
Vase, Bentonite Glaze, Gold, Red, Rhonda Ford, 6¼ x 7 In.	500
Vase, Bison, Green, Panels, 5 In.	1353
Vase, Buffalo, Olive Green, Mustard, Margaret Cable, 5 In.	1118
Vase, Chevrons, Incised, Green, Elsa Grangaard, 2½ In.	100
Vase, Conestoga Wagon, Red, Yellow, Bell Shape, F. Huckfield, 1933, 3 x 5 In.	826
Vase, Landscape, Dark Green, c.1930, 11¼ In.	16500
Vase, Pasque Flowers, Light Blue, Mattson, 3⅜ x 5¾ In.	295
Vase, Ploughman, Horse, Dark Rose, Marked, 5 In.	800
Vase, Prairie Rose Design, Bulbous, Tapered, Rolled Rim, 1931, 6 In.	384
Vase, Rabbits, Trees, Tapers, Alternating Square Panels, Brown Matte, U.N.D., 4 x 5 In. ....*illus*	1695
Vase, Squat, Wide Shoulders, Blue, Flowers, Leaves, Band, 4¾ In.	780
Vase, Stylized Leaves, Cylindrical, Swollen, Flora Huckfield, 4 x 2½ In.	1063
Vase, Terra-Cotta, Red, Black, Tan, Swollen Waist, Marked, 1900s, 4½ In.	300
Vase, Wheat, Blue, Glossy, 2⅛ In.	325

NORTHWOOD glass was made by one of the glassmaking companies operated by Harry C. Northwood. His first company, Northwood Glass Co., was founded in Martins Ferry, Ohio, in 1887 and moved to Ellwood City, Pennsylvania, in 1892. The company closed in 1896. Later that same year, Harry Northwood opened the Northwood Co. in Indiana, Pennsylvania. Some pieces made at the Northwood Co. are marked "Northwood" in script. The Northwood Co. became part of a consortium called the National Glass Co. in 1899. Harry left National in 1901 to found the H. Northwood Co. in Wheeling, West Virginia. At the Wheeling factory, Harry Northwood and his brother Carl manufactured pressed and blown tableware and novelties in many colors that are collected today as custard, opalescent, goofus,

Nutcracker, Bird, Grackle, Raised Beak, Tail Lever, Wood, c.1875, 8¾ In.
$600

Heritage Auctions

Nutcracker, Clown, Head, Long Nose, White, Black Lips, c.1900, 7¼ In.
$1,342

Morphy Auctions

Nutcracker, Dwarf, Carved Wood, Switzerland
$132

Fox Auctions

Occupied Japan, Ashtray, Terrier, Looking Into Brown Bag, c.1950, 4 x 3 In.
$25

Ruby Lane

Office, Calculator, Addiator, Add, Subtract, Metal Sliders, Stylus, Case, Germany, 6 x 2 In.
$17

Ruby Lane

Office, Cash Recorder, Security, Metal Marquee, Cash Drawer, Houghs, 19 ½ x 18 ½ In.
$390

Milestone Auctions

carnival, and stretch glass. Pieces made between 1905 and about 1915 may have an underlined *N* trademark. Harry Northwood died in 1919, and the plant closed in 1925.

Alaska, Celery Dish, Vaseline, 4-Footed, 1897, 2 ½ x 9 ½ In. ....*illus*	112
Argonaut Shell, Candy Dish, Dome Lid, Ruffled, Carnival Glass, 6 In.	15
Cranberry & Amber, Bowl, Pull-Up, Cased Pink, 4-Footed, 8 x 10 In.	687
Cranberry, Sugar Castor, Opalescent, Lattice Striped, Brass Lid, 5 x 2 ½ In.	61
Cranberry, Syrup, Spatter Glass, 7 x 5 In.	121
Daisy & Fern, Cruet, Cranberry Opalescent, Ball Stopper, 1800s, 7 In.	375
Diamond Point, Vase, Iridescent Blue, Fuchsia, Beaker, Zigzag Rim, c.1920, 11 In.	75
Grape & Cable, Water Set, Iridescent Purple, 6 Glasses, Pitcher, 8 In., 7 Piece	165
Peacocks On Fence, Bowl, Ruffled Rim, Opalescent Blue, 3 x 8 ½ In.	177
Pitcher, Ruffled Mouth, Blue, White, 8 ¼ In.	72
Vaseline Glass, Syrup, Silver Plate Rim, Lid, 6 ½ x 5 In.	73

NUTCRACKERS of many types have been used through the centuries. At first the nutcracker was probably strong teeth or a hammer. But by the nineteenth century, many elaborate and ingenious types were made. Levers, screws, and hammer adaptations were the most popular. Because nutcrackers are still useful, they are still being made, some in the old styles.

Bird, Grackle, Raised Beak, Tail Lever, Wood, c.1875, 8 ¾ In. ....*illus*	600
Bird, Wood Grackle, 1800s, 8 ¾ In.	625
Chinaman, Iron, Yellow Face, Blue Jacket, 8 ½ In.	381
Clown, Head, Long Nose, White, Black Lips, c.1900, 7 ¼ In. ....*illus*	1342
Dog, Black, White, Iron, 5 ½ x 11 In.	185
Dog, Cast Iron, Wood, Battery Operated, Eyes Light Up, 5 ¼ x 9 In.	31
Dwarf, Carved Wood, Switzerland ....*illus*	132
Mariner, Cap, Hardwood, Continental, 1900s, 8 In., Pair	625
Squirrel, Cast Iron, Gray Paint, Walnut Base, Patent Date 1878, 9 ½ In.	502

NYMPHENBURG, *see Royal Nymphenburg.*

OCCUPIED JAPAN was printed on pottery, porcelain, toys, and other goods made during the American occupation of Japan after World War II, from 1947 to 1952. Collectors now search for these pieces. The items were made for export. Ceramic items are listed here. Toys are listed in the Toy category in this book.

Ashtray, Terrier, Looking Into Brown Bag, c.1950, 4 x 3 In. ....*illus*	25
Compote, Winged Cherub, Reticulated Bowl, Flowers, 12 ½ In.	72
Dish, Sweetmeat, Lounging Women, Flowers, 7 x 11 In., Pair	180
Figurine, Cowboy Hat, Red, Ceramic, 4 ½ x 5 In.	25
Figurine, Old Man, Colonial Clothes, Holding Up Hand, 5 ¼ In.	19
Lamp Base, Woman, Green Ruffled Skirt, Man, Blue Jacket, Column, 6 ½ In., Pair	22
Pencil Sharpener, Limousine, Tin, Red, Silver, 1930s	20
Salt & Pepper, Indians, Canoe, Multicolor, 6 ½ x 3 ½ In.	42

OFFICE TECHNOLOGY includes office equipment and related products, such as adding machines, calculators, and check-writing machines. Typewriters are in their own category in this book.

Adding Machine, Adix, 3-Digit, 9 Keys, Velvet Case, Pallweber & Bordt, 1903	248
Adding Machine, Comptometer, Model 1, 8-Digit, Mahogany, Felt & Tarrent, 1887	1683
Adding Machine, Curta, Type 1, Stepped Drum Form, 1948	757
Adding Machine, Gem, Chain, 7-Digit, Automatic Adding Machine Co., 1907	736
Adding Machine, Gordon's Addometer, Round, Nickel Plated, 9 ½ In.	676
Calculating Machine, Kuli, 4 Arithmetic Operations, Germany, 1909	1403
Calculator, Addiator, Add, Subtract, Metal Sliders, Stylus, Case, Germany, 6 x 2 In. ....*illus*	17
Cash Recorder, Security, Metal Marquee, Cash Drawer, Houghs, 19 ½ x 18 ½ In. ....*illus*	390
Computer, Mac 128K, Apple Macintosh, 1984	656
Pocket, Adder, Metal, Twin Discs, A.M. Stephenson, Joliet, Ill., 1910, 4 x 2 In.	348

Ohr, Bowl, Irregular Folds, Ocher, Gunmetal & Green Glaze, Stamped, c.1895, 4 x 4 In.
$1,188

Rago Arts and Auction Center

Ohr, Pitcher, Yellow Glaze, Brown Speckles, Bulbous, Flared Neck, Loop Handle, Marked, c.1890, 6 In.
$671

Neal Auctions

Ohr, Vase, Bisque, Folded, Cursive Signature, 5 x 9 x 8¾ In.
$3,660

Neal Auctions

Ohr, Vase, Bisque, Scroddled, Folded Rim, Script Signature, 1898, 4 x 6 In.
$20,000

Rago Arts and Auction Center

Ohr, Vase, Green, Gunmetal Glaze, Ruffled Rim, Pinched Sides, Stamped, 1897, 5 x 8 In.
$18,750

Rago Arts and Auction Center

Ohr, Vase, Indigo Glaze, Dimpled, Script Signature, c.1900, 9½ x 5 In.
$12,500

Rago Arts and Auction Center

Ohr, Vase, Twist Body, Ruffled Rim, Ribbon Handles, Feather Glaze, Stamped, 12 In.
$87,500

Rago Arts and Auction Center

Onion, Pitcher, Blue & White, Flared Rim, Marked, Meissen, 10¾ In.
$210

Cowan's Auctions

Onion, Serving Dish, Blue, Divided, Shaped Rim, Meissen, 13¾ In.
$495

Ruby Lane

O

335

Opalescent, Bubble Lattice, Sugar
Shaker, Lid, c.1875, 5 In.
$152

Jeffrey S. Evans

TIP
*Do not put wire-
stemmed artificial
flowers in a valuable
narrow neck glass vase.
The stems will scratch
and damage the vase.*

Opalescent, Opaline Brocade, Water
Set, Clear, 9-In. Pitcher, 7 Piece Set
$94

Hess Auction Group

Opaline, Vase, Clambroth, Ruffled
Cobalt Rim, Franco Bohemian, c.1880,
11 x 5¾ In., Pair
$562

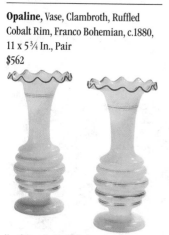

New Orleans Auction Galleries

OHR pottery was made in Biloxi, Mississippi, from 1883 to 1906 by George E. Ohr, a true eccentric. The pottery was made of very thin clay that was twisted, folded, and dented into odd, graceful shapes. Some pieces were lifelike models of hats, animal heads, or even a potato. Others were decorated with folded clay "snakes." Reproductions and reworked pieces are appearing on the market. These have been reglazed, or snakes and other embellishments have been added.

Bank, Potato, Figural, Light Brown Bisque, Molded, Slot, Marked, c.1890, 3 x 5 In.	1500
Bowl, Green & Brown, Speckled Glaze, Deeply Folded, c.1895, 2 x 6 In.	2125
Bowl, Green & Gunmetal Glaze, Squat, Folded Twist Rim, Ring Foot, c.1895, 3 x 7 In.	1188
Bowl, Gunmetal & Indigo Glaze, Mottled, Bulbous, Ring Foot, c.1900, 3 x 6 In.	1500
Bowl, Irregular Folds, Ocher, Gunmetal & Green Glaze, Stamped, c.1895, 4 x 4 In. ......*illus*	1188
Bowl, Spinach Green Glaze, Low, Incised Band, Folded-In Sides, 2 x 4 In.	610
Figurine, Cannon, Green & Gunmetal Glaze, c.1900, 4 x 7½ x 2 In.	1250
Jar, Lid, Brown Glaze, Bulbous, Dimpled, Peaked Lid, Applied Snake, Marked, 6 x 4 In.	610
Mug, Jefferson, Mahogany & Gunmetal Glaze, Signed, J. Jefferson, c.1900, 5 x 5 In.	1000
Pitcher, Brown, Ocher, Speckled Glaze, Dimpled, Twisted Ribbon Handle, Marked, 4 In.	4688
Pitcher, Ear Handle, Ocher, Gunmetal, Green Speckles, 2½ x 5½ In.	2000
Pitcher, Gunmetal & Gold Glaze, Squat, Trumpet Neck, Loop Handle, c.1898, 4 In.	1188
Pitcher, Gunmetal & Indigo Glaze, Wide Rim, Cutout Square Handle, c.1900, 3 x 5 In.	2625
Pitcher, Gunmetal Glaze, Folded, Crumpled Side, Incised Mark, 4½ x 6 In.	8125
Pitcher, Gunmetal, Ocher & Green, Bulbous, Cutout Handle, Fold-Out Spout, c.1900, 5 In.	5625
Pitcher, Gunmetal, Speckled, Bulbous, Ear Handle, Pinched Spout, c.1900, 3 x 5 In.	2000
Pitcher, Yellow Glaze, Brown Speckles, Bulbous, Flared Neck, Loop Handle, Marked, c.1890, 6 In.*illus*	671
Vase, Asymmetrical, 3-Lobed Rim, Black Matte, Brown Highlights, 3 In.	1150
Vase, Bisque, Folded, Cursive Signature, 5 x 9 x 8¾ In. ......*illus*	3660
Vase, Bisque, Scroddled, Folded Rim, Script Signature, 1898, 4 x 6 In. ......*illus*	20000
Vase, Bisque, Squat, Shouldered, Folded Body, Crimped Rim, Ring Foot, c.1900, 4 x 5 In.	1750
Vase, Bisque, Twisted & Pinched Body, Flattened Ruffled Rim, Signed, 6 x 6 In.	4375
Vase, Brown & Ocher, Speckled Glaze, Oval, Lobed Folded Rim, c.1900, 7 In.	1625
Vase, Brown Speckled Glaze, Spherical, Folded & Crimped Rim, c.1900, 5 In.	5000
Vase, Brown, Green & Gunmetal Glaze, Dimpled, Ruffled Rim, Stamped, 7 x 6 In.	12500
Vase, Brown, Gunmetal Speckled Glaze, Folded Rim, Ring Foot, c.1900, 5 x 6 In.	4375
Vase, Brown, Mottled Glaze, Squat, Saucer Foot, Pinched, Twist Waist, c.1895, 5 In.	2625
Vase, Green & Gunmetal, Sponge Glazed, Bulbous, Wide Crimped Rim, 5 x 5 In.	4063
Vase, Green & Indigo, Sponge Glazed, Pinched Waist, Bell Shape, c.1899, 6 x 4 In.	1875
Vase, Green & Purple, Sponge Glazed, Bulbous, Dimpled, Flared Rim, c.1900, 5 In.	5625
Vase, Green, Gunmetal Glaze, Ruffled Rim, Pinched Sides, Stamped, 1897, 5 x 8 In.......*illus*	18750
Vase, Gunmetal & Aventurine, Hare's Fur Glaze, Crumpled, Marked, 5 In.	16250
Vase, Gunmetal Glaze, Beaker, Scroll Ribbon Handles, Molded Band, c.1900, 7 In.	11250
Vase, Gunmetal Over Green Glaze, Ruffled Rim, c.1900, 4¼ x 5 In.	3750
Vase, Gunmetal, Amber, Mahogany, Sponge Glazed, Cylindrical, Bulbous Base, 9 In.	1750
Vase, Gunmetal, Green, Squat, Waisted, Cylinder Neck, Ruffled Rim, c.1899, 4 In.	3750
Vase, In-Body Twist, Blue & Yellow Glaze, c.1900, 5 x 4½ In.	5313
Vase, Indigo Glaze, Dimpled, Script Signature, c.1900, 9½ x 5 In.......*illus*	12500
Vase, Mahogany, Gunmetal & Aventurine Glaze, Ruffled Rim, c.1900, 5 x 5 In.	4688
Vase, Ocher & Brown, Speckled Glaze, Crumpled, Fold-Out Rim, 4 x 5 In.	11875
Vase, Ocher & Green Glaze, Folded Rim, Marked, 4¼ x 5 In.	5000
Vase, Ocher, Brown & Green, Speckled Glaze, Crimped Rim, c.1900, 4½ x 3 In.	5000
Vase, Ocher, Brown & Green, Speckled Glaze, Ruffled Rim, c.1900, 6 x 5 In.	4063
Vase, Raspberry & Green, Sponge Glazed, Dimpled, c.1900, 5¼ x 5½ In.	3625
Vase, Raspberry, Green & Gunmetal, Speckled Glaze, Cup, Rising Tubular Neck, c.1905, 3 In.	1875
Vase, Red & Gunmetal Glaze, Black Inside, Stepped Cup Shape, Marked, 3 x 3 In.	2074
Vase, Tan & Beige, Marbleized Glaze, Tapered, Stand-Up Ruffled Rim, 5 x 4 In.	2500
Vase, Twist Body, Ruffled Rim, Ribbon Handles, Feather Glaze, Stamped, 12 In.......*illus*	87500

OLD PARIS, *see Paris category.*

OLD SLEEPY EYE, *see Sleepy Eye category.*

O

Opaline, Vase, Gilt, Orange, Greek Youths, Maiden, France, c.1890, 10 x 4 In., Pair
$384

Neal Auctions

Orphan Annie, Book, Annie's Book About Dogs, Wander Co., 1936, 31 Pages
$65

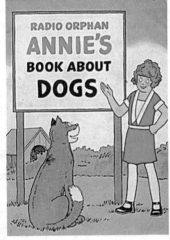

Tias

Orphan Annie, Doll, Marionette, Composition Head, Cloth Body, Box, 1930-40s, 9 In.
$84

Milestone Auctions

Orrefors, Vase, Clear & Smoky, Nils Landberg, 1950s, 5 ½ x 5 In.
$150

Ruby Lane

Overbeck, Figurine, Draft Horse, Glazed, Mary Frances, Incised, 6 ½ x 6 ½ In.
$1,063

Rago Arts and Auction Center

Overbeck, Vase, Dancing Figures, Incised, Elizabeth, Mary Frances, c.1920, 14 x 7 In.
$5,313

Rago Arts and Auction Center

Overbeck, Vase, Squirrels, Incised, Mary Frances, 4 x 4 In.
$2,500

Rago Arts and Auction Center

Owens, Vase, Red Drip Glaze Over Green, Oak Stand, Mission, c.1905, 11 In.
$354

Humler & Nolan

Oyster Plate, 6 Wells, Pink, Majolica, George Jones & Sons, 8 ¾ In.
$480

Strawser Auction Group

O

Painting, Miniature, On Wasli, Couple Embracing, Mat, India, Frame, c.1800, 7 x 4 In.
$1,353

Skinner, Inc.

Painting, Reverse On Glass, George Washington, Seated, Frame, c.1815, 12 x 9 In.
$308

Skinner, Inc.

Pairpoint, Lamp, Puffy, Rose Bouquet, Bonnet Shade, Gilt Base, Treebark Detail, 12 In.
$2,478

Humler & Nolan

ONION PATTERN, originally named bulb pattern, is a white ware decorated with cobalt blue or pink. Although it is commonly associated with Meissen, other companies made the pattern in the late nineteenth and the twentieth centuries. A rare type is called *red bud* because there are added red accents on the blue-and-white dishes.

Gravy Boat, Blue & White, Wavy Rim, Double Spout & Handles, Underplate, 6 In.	67
Nut Bowl, Blue & White, Leaf Shape, Open Square Upturned Handle, 3 x 3 In.	65
Pitcher, Blue & White, Flared Rim, Marked, Meissen, 10¾ In. ....*illus*	210
Platter, Blue & White, Oval, Wavy Rim, 21 In.	499
Relish, Cobalt Blue & White, Scalloped Oval, 10½ In.	60
Serving Bowl, Cobalt Blue & White, Square, Scrolling Flared Rim, 3 x 7 In.	105
Serving Dish, Blue, Divided, Shaped Rim, Meissen, 13¾ In. ....*illus*	495
Sugar & Creamer, Blue & White, Swirled, Gilt, Scalloped Rim, Lid, Flower Finial, 4 In.	86
Tray, Blue & White, Scalloped Square, Wavy Handles, 9 x 10 In.	75
Tureen, Soup, Blue & White, Bulbous, Fan Handles, Dome Lid, Finial, 10 x 13 In.	245

OPALESCENT GLASS is translucent glass that has the tones of the opal gemstone. It originated in England in the 1870s and is often found in pressed glassware made in Victorian times. Opalescent glass was first made in America in 1897 at the Northwood glassworks in Indiana, Pennsylvania. Some dealers use the terms *opaline* and *opalescent* for any of these translucent wares. More opalescent pieces may be listed in Hobnail, Pressed Glass, and other glass categories.

Bowl, 12 Paneled Sides, Fluted, Spiral, Pressed Glass, France, 13½ In.	354
Bowl, Cranberry To Opal, Pinched, Ruffled Rim, 2¼ x 5 In.	36
Bowl, Pheasants, Grass, c.1925, 14 In.	300
Bubble Lattice, Sugar Shaker, Lid, c.1875, 5 In. ....*illus*	152
Dish, Pink, Gilt Metal Feet, Duncan & Miller, 1900s, 3½ x 8 x 5 In.	51
Dish, Swan Shape, Pale Blue, Duncan & Miller, 6½ In.	18
Epergne, Green, 3 Stem Vases, 20½ x 12 In.	98
Opaline Brocade, Water Set, Clear, 9-In. Pitcher, 7 Piece Set ....*illus*	94
Vase, Aqua, Adventurine, Diamond Pattern, Elongated Pear Shape, 15 In.	266
Vase, Art Deco, Bands, Tapers, 9 In.	213
Vase, Gold, Pink, Fuchsia, Squat, Bumps & Furrows, Pinched, Ruffled Rim, 6 In.	154
Vase, Jack-In-The-Pulpit, Cranberry To Opal, Applied Glass, 8 x 4½ In.	36

OPALINE, or opal glass, was made in white, green, and other colors. The glass had a matte surface and a lack of transparency. It was often gilded or painted. It was a popular mid-nineteenth-century European glassware.

Compote, Blue, Gilt Decoration, Sterling Base, Acanthus, Birds, France, 7 In.	50
Dresser Box, Hinged Lid, Canted Corners, Twist Bail Handles, Leafy Feet, 5 x 6½ In.	714
Jardiniere, Urn Shape, Ormolu, Flowers, Butterflies, Pale Green Ground, 14 In.	144
Jewelry Box, Gilt Enamel, Flowerhead, Vine, Brass Band, 1920s, 5 x 9 In.	4000
Punch Bowl, Lid, Ladle, Undertray, Gilt Edges, Finial, 14 In., 4 Piece	180
Vase, Art Nouveau, Gilt Metal Mount, Leaves, Footed, 20 x 7½ In.	952
Vase, Black & White, Twisting Stripes, 17 In.	125
Vase, Clambroth, Ruffled Cobalt Rim, Franco Bohemian, c.1880, 11 x 5¾ In., Pair ....*illus*	562
Vase, Enamel, Gilt, Applied Green Snake, Bulbous, Stick Neck, Flared, c.1880, 11 In.	1680
Vase, Flowers, Pale Blue, Gold Bands, 1875, 22 In., Pair	1250
Vase, Gilt, Orange, Greek Youths, Maiden, France, c.1890, 10 x 4 In., Pair ....*illus*	384
Vase, Leaves, Gilt Metal Mount, Footed, Art Nouveau, 20 x 7½ In.	952

OPERA GLASSES are needed because the stage is a long way from some of the seats at a play or an opera. Mother-of-pearl was a popular decoration on many French glasses.

Aluminum, Incised, Flowers, Instrument Design, The Elite, France, 3 x 4 In.	100
Enameled, Flowers, Blue, Handle, France, 8¼ In.	200
Gold Plated, Filigree, Lamour Fab, France, 2½ x 4 In.	82
Gold, 14K, Leafy Openwork Handle, Twisted Rope Chain, 3 In.	360
Mother-Of-Pearl & Brass, Chevalier, France, 10¾ In.	360

O

Mother-Of-Pearl, Handle, France, 10 In. 94

ORPHAN ANNIE first appeared in the comics in 1924. The last strip ran in newspapers on June 13, 2010. The redheaded girl, her dog Sandy, and her friends were on the radio from 1930 to 1942. The first movie based on the strip was produced in 1932. A second movie was produced in 1938. A Broadway musical that opened in 1977, a movie based on the musical and produced in 1982, and a made-for-television movie based on the musical produced in 1999 made Annie popular again, and many toys, dishes, and other memorabilia have been made. A new adaptation of the movie based on the musical opened in 2014.

Book, Annie's Book About Dogs, Wander Co., 1936, 31 Pages ....*illus*   65
Comic Book, Annie In Circus, Lion, Pig, Cupples & Leon Pub., 1927   85
Doll, Annie, Celluloid, Paper Label, Japan, 7 In.   148
Doll, Annie, Vinyl, Red Hair, Blue Eyes, Tonner, 1997, 14 In.   89
Doll, Marionette, Composition Head, Cloth Body, Box, 1930-40s, 9 In. ....*illus*   84
Game, Rummy Cards, Annie, Sandy, Characters, Box, Full Set, 1935.................................   60
Medal, Bronze, Annie's Secret Society, Good Luck, Portrait, Clover, 1930s, 1 In.   45
Nodder, Daddy Warbucks, Hands In Pockets, Hertwig & Co., 3 ¼ In.   95
Plate, Annie, Lily & Rooster, Edwin Knowles, 1983, 8 ½ In..   38
Radio, Transistor, Annie & Sandy, Plastic, Battery, 1981, 7 x 6 ½ In.   22
Ring, Silver Plate, Crossed Keys, Silver Star Member, Secret Message, 1937   115
Shaker, Annie, Dog, Cream, Orange Top, Beetleware..   55
Toy, Car, Limousine, 1929 Model Duesenberg, Driver, Box, c.1980, 7 x 16 In.   62
Toy, Stove, Annie, Sandy, Green, Tin Litho, 3 Ovens, Electric, 1930s, 9 x 10 In.   105
Toy, Wind-Up, Annie, Jumps Rope, Tin Lithograph, Key, Box, 1930s   318

ORREFORS Glassworks, located in the Swedish province of Smaaland, was established in 1898. The company is still making glass for use on the table or as decorations. There is renewed interest in the glass made in the modern styles of the 1940s and 1950s. In 1990, the company merged with Kosta Boda. Most vases and decorative pieces are signed with the etched name *Orrefors*.

Bowl, Aquarium, Fish Circling, Seaweed, Edvard Hald, Signed, 2 ¼ x 7 In.   288
Bowl, Grail, Lavender, White, Straight-Sided, 1960, Marked, 8 ½ x 12 In.   188
Bowl, Tulip, Clear & Blue, Flower Petal Shape, Signed, 5 x 7 In..................................   124
Decanter, Engraved, Nude Dancer, Intaglio, Mushroom Stopper, 9 ½ In.......................   259
Vase, Apple, Ingeborg Lundin, 1959, 14 ½ x 12 In...   2250
Vase, Ariel, Green Heads, Clear, Cylindrical, Signed, c.1982, 7 ½ x 5 In.   1947
Vase, Clear & Smoky, Nils Landberg, 1950s, 5 ½ x 5 In. ....*illus*   150
Vase, Clear, Green Fish & Sea Plants, Etched, Teardrop Shape, c.1950, 8 x 5 In...........   295
Vase, Figural, Green Apple, Bulbous, Stem, Faceted Neck, 1957, 15 x 12 In.   5313
Vase, Fish, Seaweed, Internal Design, Edvard Hald, 5 x 4 ½ In.   406
Vase, Green Fish, Seaweed, Edvard Hald, Signed, 6 ½ In.   403
Vase, Internal Smoke, 8 ¼ x 4 In..   123
Vase, Internal Spiral, Amber, Black Round Foot, Signed, 13 ½ x 5 ½ In.   36
Vase, Woman, Seminude, Geese, Art Deco, Sven Palmquist, 5 ½ x 11 In........................   132

OTT & BREWER COMPANY operated the Etruria Pottery at Trenton, New Jersey, from 1871 to 1892. It started making belleek in 1882. The firm used a variety of marks that incorporated the initials *O & B.*

Chocolate Pot, Brown Band, Gold Clouds, Porcelain, 8 ¾ In.   145
Creamer, Belleek, Eggshell Glaze, Gold Trim, 2 ½ In..   56
Demitasse Set, Teacup & Saucer, Belleek, Eggshell Glaze, 1 ¾ In.   31

OVERBECK POTTERY was made by four sisters named Overbeck at a pottery in Cambridge City, Indiana. They started in 1911. They made all types of vases, each one of a kind. Small, hand-modeled figurines are the most popular pieces with today's collectors. The factory continued until 1955, when the last of the four sisters died.

Candleholder, Houses, Trees, Starry Sky, Brick Red, Cylindrical, c.1910, 5 In., Pair.................   10000

Paper, Fraktur, Bird, Cutwork, Esther Tonson, Watercolor, Frame, c.1800, 10 x 7 In.
$502

Hess Auction Group

Paper, Fraktur, Bookplate, Birds, Heart, Flowers, Watercolor, Penn., 1800s, 9 x 6 In.
$590

Hess Auction Group

Paper, Fraktur, Johannes Detweiler, 1834, Flower, Heart, Watercolor, Pa., Frame, 9 x 8 In.
$708

Hess Auction Group

Paper, Fraktur, Watercolor & Ink, Bird, Leafy Branch, Initialed F.H., Frame, 6 x 5⅝ In.
$1,770

Hess Auction Group

Paper, Silhouette, Couple, Flowers, Black On Ivory, Frame, 1930s, 8 x 6 In.
$40

Ruby Lane

Paper Doll, Dolly Dingle's Trip Around The World, G. Drayton, 1978, 12 x 9½ In.
$35

Ruby Lane

TIP
Never fold old paper.

Figurine, Draft Horse, Glazed, Mary Frances, Incised, 6½ x 6½ In......................*illus*	1063
Figurine, Sleeping Cat, Mottled Pink Glaze, Green Eyes, c.1900, 2 x 7 In.	1000
Figurine, Southern Belle, Pink, Blue, 2 In..	129
Vase, 3 Panels, Green Butterflies, Brown, Elizabeth & Hanna Overbeck, 5 In..................	3450
Vase, Butterfly, Matte Green, Brown, Cylindrical, Hannah, Elizabeth, 5⅜ In...............	3540
Vase, Cactus, Brown, Green, Hannah, Elizabeth, 6⅛ In..	3186
Vase, Cardinals, Circle Frames, Tan, Red, Pale Blue, Square, Flared Rim, c.1900, 5 In.............	5313
Vase, Cobalt Blue, Stick Neck, Geometric, 1900s, 6 In.	1250
Vase, Dancing Figures, Incised, Elizabeth, Mary Frances, c.1920, 14 x 7 In. ....*illus*	5313
Vase, Figures, Walking In Rain, Umbrellas, White Over Mint Green, 5 In......................	5938
Vase, Green, Blue Matte, Carved, 6¼ x 6 In.	7930
Vase, Pink Ground, Green & Yellow Design, c.1910, 5½ In..................................	875
Vase, Squirrels, Incised, Mary Frances, 4 x 4 In...*illus*	2500
Wall Pocket, Abstract Bird & Branch, Purple, Blue, Square Cutouts, c.1910, 8 In..................	2250

 OWENS POTTERY was made in Zanesville, Ohio, from 1891 to 1928. The first art pottery was made after 1896. Utopian Ware, Cyrano, Navarre, Feroza, and Henri Deux were made. Pieces were usually marked with a form of the name *Owens*. About 1907, the firm began to make tile and discontinued the art pottery wares.

Jardiniere, Green Matte, Storks & Cattails, Pedestal, Arts & Crafts, 43½ In.	2875
Tile, Purple Grapes, Green Grapevines, Matte Glaze, Frame, 6 x 6 In..........................	593
Vase, Red Drip Glaze Over Green, Oak Stand, Mission, c.1905, 11 In.................................*illus*	354

 OYSTER PLATES were popular from the 1880s. Each course at dinner was served in a special dish. The oyster plate had indentations shaped like oysters. Usually six oysters were held on a plate. There is no greater value to a plate with more oysters, although that myth continues to haunt antiques dealers. There are other plates for shellfish, including cockle plates and whelk plates. The appropriately shaped indentations are part of the design of these dishes.

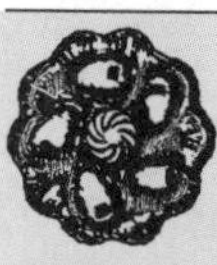

5 Wells, Cobalt Blue, Green Fish, Pinwheel, Majolica, Minton, 10¼ In.	1845
5 Wells, Diving Dolphin, Zebra Pattern, Majolica, Wedgwood, 9¼ In.........................	3600
5 Wells, Seashells, Gilt Seaweed, Tressermann & Vogt, 8 In., 6 Piece	336
6 Wells, Basket Weave, Longchamps, Ironstone, 9¾ In., 11 Piece	250
6 Wells, Brown, Green, Pink Flowers, Haviland, c.1880, 9 In.	250
6 Wells, Cobalt Blue, Seaweed, Turquoise, Shell Band, Minton, c.1875, 9 In.	369
6 Wells, Cream, Flowers, Purple & Gilt Rim, Limoges, 9 In., 12 Piece	188
6 Wells, Pale Blue, Seaweed, Dark Green, Conch Shell Band, c.1875, 9 In.	430
6 Wells, Pale Green, Seaweed, Dark Green, Conch Shell Band, c.1875, 9 In.	369
6 Wells, Pink, Majolica, George Jones & Sons, 8¾ In...................................*illus*	480
6 Wells, Pink, Seaweed, Turquoise, Conch Shell Band, Minton, c.1875, 9 In.	369
6 Wells, Shells, Center Circle, White & Pink, c.1890, 9 In., 9 Piece	540
6 Wells, Sunflower, Lavender, Samuel Lear, c.1880, 10 In.	246
7 Wells, Canary Yellow, Green, Minton, c.1875, 9 In..	1353
10 Wells, Alternating Pink & White, Gilt Border, Coalport, c.1890, 8¾ In.	232
12 Wells, Green Lime Slices, Cream, Tray, Majolica, 12 Plates, 13 Piece...........................	450

 PADEN CITY GLASS MANUFACTURING COMPANY was established in 1916 at Paden City, West Virginia. The company made over 20 different colors of glass. The firm closed in 1951. Paden City Pottery may be listed in Dinnerware.

Crow's Foot, Compote, Red, 6 In..	53
Gazebo, Sugar & Creamer, Etched	30
Penny, Cup & Saucer, Red..	13

 PAINTINGS listed in this book are not works by major artists but rather decorative paintings on ivory, board, or glass that would be of interest to the average collector. Watercolors on paper are listed under Picture. To learn the value of an oil painting by a listed artist, you must contact an expert in that area.

Miniature, Oil On Ivory, Boy In Blue Dress, Sprig Of Cotton, Oval Frame, 3 In. 677

Miniature, Oil On Ivory, Girl Holding Cat, Black Lacquer Frame, 2½ In.	1046
Miniature, Oil On Ivory, Girl In Blue Dress, Oval, Lock Of Hair, Gilt Frame, 2 In.	4305
Miniature, Oil On Ivory, Mother, Daughter, Giltwood Frame, c.1845, Each 2 In.	3690
Miniature, On Parchment, Grandmother, Grandfather Temmes, Frame, 1812, 5 In.	336
Miniature, On Wasli, Couple Embracing, Mat, India, Frame, c.1800, 7 x 4 In....illus	1353
Oil On Board, Autumn Landscape, Louis Kamp, 8 x 10 In.	90
Oil On Board, Brick Farmhouse, Buildings, Frame, c.1900, 17 x 24 In.	210
Oil On Board, Flowering Plum, Trees, A. Schulz, Frame, c.1900, 13 x 16 In.	1230
Oil On Board, Indians, Horseback, Adobe Building, Bells, Z. Zick, 1800s, 3 x 6 In.	390
Oil On Board, Still Life, Fruit, Marble Tabletop, Gilt Frame, 1800s, 16 x 22 In.	700
Oil On Bone, Woman, Smile, Gown, Ruffles, Oval, Brass & Ebony Frame, 5 In.	342
Oil On Canvas, 3 Chicks, Lobster, Oyster Shell, Gilt Frame, 1800s, 8 x 11 In.	117
Oil On Canvas, Barn, Sheep, Chickens, G. Marechal, Frame, 1800s, 26 x 31 In.	780
Oil On Canvas, Boy, Dog, White Dress, Red Sash, Giltwood Frame, 32 x 25 In.	237
Oil On Canvas, Cabin, Secluded, Countryside, Trees, Frame, c.1885, 10 x 12 In.	123
Oil On Canvas, Cattle In Stream, Thomas Corwin, c.1900, 17 x 22 In.	450
Oil On Canvas, Child With Grapes, Seated, Frame, c.1845, 32 x 25½ In.	360
Oil On Canvas, Covered Bridge, Church, Hills, Gilt Frame, c.1865, 12 x 18 In.	150
Oil On Canvas, Cows In Pasture, Stream, Brillet, Gilt Frame, 12 x 18 In.	260
Oil On Canvas, Dead Heat, Thoroughbreds, Carter Handicap, 1944, 30 x 36 In.	1200
Oil On Canvas, Figure By Stream, Camille Corot, Frame, c.1800, 23 x 29 In.	360
Oil On Canvas, Fortune-Teller Scene, 3 Women, Table, Frame, 1800s, 34 x 37 In.	180
Oil On Canvas, La Grande Marina Capri, Gesso Frame, 1868, 30 x 45 In.	1475
Oil On Canvas, Lion, Bird In Tree, Henri Maik, Frame, 1968, 6 x 8 In.	1080
Oil On Canvas, Lion, Reclining, Wood Cage Front, Molded Frame, 33 x 45 In.	5192
Oil On Canvas, Masonite, Twin Girls, Embracing, c.1830, 48 x 36 In.	1845
Oil On Canvas, Mountain Valley, Sheep, C. Leslie, Gilt Frame, c.1870, 12 x 24 In.	1638
Oil On Canvas, Old Farm, House, Laundry Line, Frame, 1924, 27 x 32 In.	120
Oil On Canvas, Oxbow, The Connecticut River, Landscape, Frame, 18 x 26 In.	3500
Oil On Canvas, Portrait Of Bride, Karl Kappes, Frame, 1924, 25 x 31 In.	240
Oil On Canvas, Portrait, Sea Captain, Coat, Scarf, Ship, Frame, c.1810, 34 x 29 In.	2963
Oil On Canvas, Portrait, Sea Captain, Telescope, Vervoort, 1825, 39 x 32 In.	1200
Oil On Canvas, Reclining Odalisque, Chinese, c.1940, 24 x 37 In.	1250
Oil On Canvas, Rocky Coast, Sidney Y. Johnson, Gilt Frame, c.1915, 12 x 23 In.	211
Oil On Canvas, Ships, Men In Rowboat, Waves, Gilt Frame, c.1850, 15 x 19 In.	531
Oil On Canvas, Sick Girl, Father & Doctor Watch Over, c.1885, 22 x 30 In.	250
Oil On Canvas, Still Life, Flowers, Stone Arch, Italy, Frame, 1900s, 39 x 27 In.	550
Oil On Canvas, Sunshine, Still Life, Pansies, A. Kinsey, Louisiana, 1933, 18 x 16 In.	576
Oil On Canvas, Village, Flowers, Jacques Eitel, Frame, 36 x 43 In.	570
Oil On Canvas, Warm Embrace, Mother & Child, B. Thomas, Frame, 47 x 35 In.	360
Oil On Canvas, Woman, Folk Dress, Head Scarf, Frame, c.1850, 35 x 27 In.	600
Oil On Canvas, Woman, Seated, Green Dress, Rose, Brooch, Frame, 21 x 18 In.	593
Oil On Masonite, Ballerina, Chalkboard, Richard J. Zolan, Frame, 27 x 23 In.	480
Oil On Masonite, Steam Ferry, Nantucket, Waves, Flag, Frame, 20 x 28 In.	830
Oil On Masonite, Stockyards, Street Scene, A. Uhrig, Frame, c.1931, 48 x 48 In.	600
Oil On Panel, 18th Century King Street, Folk Art, Oval, Cut Edge, 1985, 49 In.	142
Oil On Panel, Boy, Canary & Squirrel, Red Drapes, Frame, c.1810, 12 x 11 In.	1422
Oil On Panel, Rural Landscape, Bridge, Stream, France, Frame, 1800s, 7 x 9 In.	185
Oil On Panel, Ship In Rough Seas, Cliffs, Sailboats, Frame, c.1910, 11 x 17 In.	414
Reverse On Glass, George Washington, Seated, Frame, c.1815, 12 x 9 In....illus	308

PAIRPOINT Manufacturing Company started in 1880 in New Bedford, Massachusetts. It soon joined with the glassworks nearby and made glass, silver-plated pieces, and lamps. Reverse-painted glass shades and molded shades known as "puffies" were part of the production until the 1930s. The company reorganized and changed its name several times but is still working today. Items listed here are glass or glass and metal. Silver-plated pieces are listed under Silver Plate.

Biscuit Jar, Melon Ribbed, Pink Flowers, Metal Mount, 4¼ x 5 In.	147
Compote, Red Grapes, Leaves, Chipped Ice, Round Bowl, Pedestal Foot, 4 In.	354

Paperweight, Boston & Sandwich, Poinsettia, Red Flower, Blue Jasper Ground, 1852-88, 2⅞ In.
$269

Norman Heckler & Company

Paperweight, Glass Eye Studio, Octopus, Iridescent, Swirls, Sparkles, 4 x 4½ In.
$95

Ruby Lane

Paperweight, Lundberg, Underwater Scene, Tropical Fish, Coral, Seaweed, 3½ In.
$1,400

Ruby Lane

P

Paperweight, Perthshire, Flowers, Millefiori, Green, Blue, White, 2 x 2⁵⁄₈ In.
$300

Ruby Lane

Paperweight, Stankard, Paul, Root People, Jack-In-The-Pulpit, Lampwork, 1996, 2 In.
$2,625

Rago Arts and Auction Center

Paperweight, Sulphide, Sheep, Gold, Red & White Spirals, Germany, c.1900, 1⁷⁄₈ In.
$269

Norman Heckler & Company

Lamp, 3-Light, Sea Gulls, Boats, Vase Shaped Base, c.1900, 26 In.	2242
Lamp, Copley Shade, Landscape, Reverse Painted, Bulbous, Tapered, Bronze, 22 In.	1375
Lamp, Copley Shade, Sea Landscape, Reverse Painted, Sea Gulls, 25 In.	2125
Lamp, Landscape, Fall Harvest, Horses, c.1910, 8½ x 17 In.	944
Lamp, Puffy Flowers, Blue, Yellow, Pink, Silver Plate Artichoke Base, 14 In.	593
Lamp, Puffy Hollyhock, c.1910, 21 x 14 In.	1875
Lamp, Puffy Shade, Poppies, Orange, Grapevine Base, 3 Spider Arms, 21 In.	14220
Lamp, Puffy, Rose Bouquet, Bonnet Shade, Gilt Base, Treebark Detail, 12 In. *illus*	2478
Lamp, Reverse Painted Shade, Ships In Harbor, Village, Dolphin Base, 22 In.	1718
Lamp, Reverse Painted, Puffy, Flowers, Green, Purple, White, c.1900, 18 In.	5750
Lamp, Reverse Painted, Tulip, Puffy, Silvered Metal, c.1900, 15 In.	1250
Tankard, Copper, Pewter, Signed, 14½ In.	156
Vase, Puffy, Domed, Frosted, Molded Roses & Butterflies, 20 x 14½ In.	4500

PALMER COX, *Brownies, see Brownies category.*

PAPER collectibles, including almanacs, catalogs, children's books, some greeting cards, stock certificates, and other paper ephemera, are listed here. Paper calendars are listed separately in the Calendar category. Paper items may be found in many other sections, such as Christmas and Movie.

Birth Record, Watercolor, Children Birth Day, Glasser, Names, Dates, c.1910, 28 In.	923
Book Plate, Watercolor, Ink, Crossed Roses, J. Speicher, 1944, Frame, 7 x 4 In., Pair	177
Book, Big Little, Jack Armstrong & The Ivory Treasure, Whitman No. 1435, 1937	304
Book, Happy Little Whale, Little Golden Books, 1973, 8 x 6½ In.	11
Book, Tale Of Mrs. Tiggy-Winkle, Beatrix Potter, 1st Edition, Hardcopy, c.1905, 5 In.	1300
Broadside, California U.S. Mail Steamship Co., Monday, Sept. 5, 1859, 28 x 42 In.	10800
Broadside, Comet, Horse & Trainer, Michigan, 1846, 11½ x 16 In.	960
Broadside, Marshal's Sale, Cargo Of Blockade Runner Ariel, April 8, 1862, 9 x 12 In.	612
Broadside, Territorial Topic Extra, Purcell, Chickasaw Nation, Oklahoma, 1890, 8 x 11 In.	1255
Coloring Book, It's A Circus, Merrill Publishing, Copyright 1955, 40 Pgs., 10 x 14 In.	12
Comic Book, Captain America, Fighting Yank, No. 17, 1942	3131
Cutwork, Scherenschnitte, Jefferson Wigwam, Chalkley H. Baker, c.1812, 18 x 14 In.	576
Cutwork, Scherenschnitte, Rooster, Spread Tail, Inscription, Frame, 1809, 6 x 7 In.	240
Fraktur, Baptism, Ludwig Dauberman, Parrots, Watercolor, Pencil, 1817, 13 x 16 In.	7995
Fraktur, Bird, Cutwork, Esther Tonson, Watercolor, Frame, c.1800, 10 x 7 In. *illus*	502
Fraktur, Birth & Baptism, Printed, Hand Colored Mirror Image, 1811, 17 x 20 In.	295
Fraktur, Birth & Baptism, Printed, Hand Colored, Mirror Image, 1785, 18 x 21 In.	236
Fraktur, Birth & Baptism, Watercolor, Names, Angel, Christina, Penn., 1781, 7 x 12 In.	1476
Fraktur, Birth Record, Red & Green, Central Sunburst, 1814, 12½ x 15 In.	1180
Fraktur, Birth Record, Watercolor On Paper, Tulip Artist, 1809, Frame, 11 x 12 In.	1080
Fraktur, Birth, Birds, Tulips, Heart, Verse, Anna Showalter, Frame, c.1838, 11 x 8 In.	4305
Fraktur, Birth, Husband, Wife, Holding Hands, Wineglass, May 3, 1809, 10 x 8 In.	3690
Fraktur, Birth, Text, Vines & Stars, Bible Verse, Ephraim Herman, 1808, 13 x 12 In.	219
Fraktur, Birth, Watercolor & Ink, Flying Angel, Pennsylvania, 1779, 17 x 17 In.	219
Fraktur, Bookplate, Benjamin Bernn, May 24th, 1808, 6½ x 4 In.	295
Fraktur, Bookplate, Birds, Heart, Flowers, Watercolor, Penn., 1800s, 9 x 6 In. *illus*	590
Fraktur, Bookplate, Flower, Text, D. Kulp, Bucks Cty., Penn., c.1810, 5 x 3 In.	5843
Fraktur, Bookplate, Horizontal, Birds On Branches, Late 1700s, 4 x 6 In.	885
Fraktur, Hand Colored, Lebanon, Pennsylvania, 1814, 13 x 16 In.	381
Fraktur, Johannes Detweiler, 1834, Flower, Heart, Watercolor, Pa., Frame, 9 x 8 In. *illus*	708
Fraktur, Marriage Record, Heart, Berks County, Pa., Frame, 1804, 12 x 16 In.	180
Fraktur, Printed, Hand Colored, Heaven & Hell, G.A. Peters, Frame, 10 x 15 In.	780
Fraktur, Watercolor & Ink, Bird, Leafy Branch, Initialed F.H., Frame, 6 x 5⁵⁄₈ In. *illus*	1770
Fraktur, Watercolor On Paper, Maria Siegler, Lancaster, Frame, 1828, 9 x 6 In.	420
Fraktur, Watercolor, Eagle, Flowers, Frame, Signed, P. Godillor, 13 x 11 In.	118
Fraktur, Watercolor, Hymnal 139, Angels, Birds, Flowers, 1941, 12 x 16 In.	71
Fraktur, Watercolor, Potted Tulips, 1800s, 8½ x 6 In.	130
Fraktur, Women, Diamond Pattern Dresses, Flowers, Birds, Frame, Penn., 7 x 8 In.	7995
Land Grant, Signed, Thomas Jefferson, James Madison, Military Service, 1804	4428

Magazine, St. Nicholas, Illustrated, Stories, Puzzles, Vol. II, No. 1, 1874, 10 x 7 In.	15
Scroll, Hand, Ink On Paper, Calligraphy, Signed, Sealed, c.1940, 9 x 53 In.	461
Scroll, Hanging, Ink & Color On Paper, Chrysanthemums, Signed, 1969, 24 x 10 In.	308
Scroll, Ink On Paper, Hanging, Calligraphy, Pine Trees, Poem, 51 x 25 In.	2214
Silhouette, Couple, Flowers, Black On Ivory, Frame, 1930s, 8 x 6 In. *illus*	40

PAPER DOLLS were probably inspired by the pantins, or jumping jacks, made in eighteenth-century Europe. By the 1880s, sheets of printed paper dolls and clothes were being made. The first paper doll books were made in the 1920s. Collectors prefer uncut sheets or books or boxed sets of paper dolls. Prices are about half as much if the pages have been cut.

Dolly Dingle's Trip Around The World, G. Drayton, 1978, 12 x 9½ In. *illus*	35
Emma, Book, Interchangeable Heads, Augustin Legrand, c.1810, 5 x 4 In.	1254
La Corbeille, De La Mariee, Doll, Wedding Gown, Veil, 7 Trousseau Items, Box, 3 In.	1368
La Poupee Modele, Fashion, 6 Outfits, Card Stock, Mirror, Box, c.1850, 10 In.	1938
Toilette, 3 Dolls, 12 Outfits, 9 Hats, Card Stock, Envelope, France, c.1850, 12 In.	2850
Wee Patsy, 2 Dolls, 24 Outfits, Playhouse, Effanbee, 9 Pages, Uncut, 7 x 10 In.	15
Woman, Folded Arms, 12 Outfits, 2-Sided, Tempier, France, Box, c.1850	969

PAPERWEIGHTS must have first appeared along with paper in ancient Egypt. Today's collectors search for every type, from the very expensive French weights of the nineteenth century to the modern artist weights or advertising pieces. The glass tops of the paperweights sometimes have been nicked or scratched, and this type of damage can be removed by polishing. Some serious collectors think this type of repair is an alteration and will not buy a repolished weight; others think it is an acceptable technique of restoration that does not change the value. Baccarat paperweights are listed separately under Baccarat.

Advertising, Brown Wagons, Bug, Iron, Embossed, Yellow Paint, 4 x 4 In.	431
Advertising, Coates Clipper Co., Milk Glass Bottom, Barber Clippers, 2½ x 4 In.	130
Advertising, Danville Stove Co., Figural Beaver, Iron, 1898, 1¾ x 2¼ In.	130
Advertising, Eclipse Lawn Mowers, Figural, Hat, Iron, Embossed, 3¼ x 4 In.	83
Advertising, Greenduck Co., Cast Iron, Figural Duck, Green Paint, 3 x 3 In.	374
Advertising, Gurney & Overturf, Real Estate Insurance, Celluloid, Cast Iron, 2 x 1 In.	130
Advertising, Hazard Gunpowder, Smokeless, Keg Shape, Tin Litho, 3 x 2 In.	719
Advertising, Nassau Bank, Turtle, Hinged Lid, Cast Iron, Celluloid, 2 x 4 In.	115
Advertising, Packard Autos, Ask The Man, Embossed, Bronze, 4 x 4 In.	920
Advertising, Smith Brothers, Cough Drops, Iron, Embossed, 1 x 2¼ In.	35
Advertising, Winchester Ammo, Brass, Large Bullet On Stand, 3 x 6 In.	224
Ayotte, Bacchus, Grapes, Leaves, Green Ground, Signed, 3½ In.	1007
Ayotte, Daisies, Bellflowers, Translucent Blue Ground, Oval, Beveled, 6 In.	1067
Ayotte, Pink, Blue & Yellow Flowers, Ladybug On Leaf, 4¼ In.	711
Ayotte, Seascape, Setting Sun, Bird, Waves, Opaque Blue, Faceted, 4 In.	948
Ayotte, Secret Spot, Waterfall, Yellow Flowers, Hummingbird, 4 In.	948
Blues & Moons & Aurora Borealis, Signed, c.1971, 4 In.	259
Boston & Sandwich, Poinsettia, Red Flower, Blue Jasper Ground, 1852-88, 2⅞ In. *illus*	269
Buzzini, Ribbon Series, Amber Wall Flower, Purple Ribbons, 2 x 3 In.	2280
Buzzini, Wreath, Morning Glory, Buds, Multicolor, Signed, 1989, 2 x 3 In.	1800
Carnival Glass, Bell Shape, Interior Decoration, 6½ x 3½ In.	47
Clichy, Rose, Center Cane, Pink, White, 2¾ In.	1080
Deacons, John, Encased Overlay, Fuchsia, White, Flowers, 3 x 4 In.	330
Deacons, John, Green, White Double Overlay, Panda, Bamboo, 2 x 3 In.	192
Deacons, John, Triple Overlay, Black, White, Flower, Stem, 2¼ x 3 In.	192
D'Onofrio, Jim, Cactus, Pottery Shards, Rope, Sand, Signature, 3¼ In.	415
D'Onofrio, Jim, German Shorthaired Pointer, Tall Grass, Sky, 3¼ In.	474
Glass Eye Studio, Octopus, Iridescent, Swirls, Sparkles, 4 x 4½ In. *illus*	95
Glass, 5-Petal Flower, Fireworks, Multicolor, Stone Ground, 3¼ In.	100
Glass, Cube, Blue, Marbleized, Moths, Pate-De-Verre, France, 1900s, 3 x 2 In.	812
Glass, Figural Horseshoe, Teddy Roosevelt, Photo, Sepia, 5 x 5½ In.	115
Grubb, R., 2 Flowers, White, Yellow, Leaves, Buds, Clear Ground, 3 In.	474
Hunter, Mike, Twists, Lizard, Black, White, Gold, Silver Foil, 3 x 3 In.	204
Iron, Bug, Figural, Brown Cultivators, Mustard Paint Surface, 2½ x 4 In.	431

Papier-Mache, Tray, Scalloped, Flowers, Yellow Scroll, 1900s, 12 x 8½ In.
$100

Ruby Lane

Parian, Vase, Hand Holding Trumpet Shape Bloom, 1880s, 2 x 3 In.
$225

Ruby Lane

Paris, Tureen, Soup, Lid, Gilt Design, Melon Knob, Handles, 1800s, 12½ x 15 In.
$183

Neal Auctions

P

Paris, Urn, Bouquets, Swags, Blue Ground, Gilt Base, Classical Masks, 13 In., Pair
$500

New Orleans Auction Galleries

Paris, Vase, Gilt, Blue, Chinese Scenes, Swan Handles, 1800s, 18 x 9 In., Pair
$1,280

Neal Auctions

Iron, French Bulldog, Black & White Red Collar, Hubley, c.1910, 3 In.	60
Kazian, Blue Flower, Green Leaves, White & Blue Speckled Ground, 2 In.	240
Kazian, Rose Blossom, Leaves, Pedestal, 3 In.	450
Kuhn, J., Glass, Vase, Genie Bottle, Blue & Clear, Signed, 1980, 8 x 4 In.	812
Lewis, John, Blue Moons, Mountain, Lake, Swirls, Oval, Blue, Ivory, 1971, 5 In.	189
Lundberg, Map Of The World, 1991, 4 x 4 In.	87
Lundberg, Underwater Scene, Tropical Fish, Coral, Seaweed, 3 ½ In. .....*illus*	1400
Millefiori, Knob Shape, Cased With Clear, 1900s, 5 ½ x 4 In.	82
Millefiori, Multicolor, 3 ¼ In.	25
Murano, Glass, Aquarium, Fish, Italy, 5 ½ In.	110
Nishimura, John, Silver, Ram, Curly Hair, 1900s, 3 ½ In.	2750
Perthshire, Flowers, Millefiori, Green, Blue, White, 2 x 2 ⅝ In. .....*illus*	300
Perthshire, Multi-Cane, Animals, Multicolor, 1993, 3 In.	192
Satava, Rick, Anemone, Signed, 4 ½ x 4 ½ In.	281
Satava, Rick, Jellyfish, Coral, Sand, Red, Blue, Clear, Signed, 4 x 4 In.	375
Satava, Rick, Jellyfish, Orange, Signed, 6 ½ In.	312 to 468
Smith, G., Blue & Yellow Flowers, Leaves, Sandy Ground, Grass, 3 In.	1067
Smith, G., Dragonfly, Pink, White Flowers, Field, Signature Cane, 3 In.	1422
St. Louis, Acid Etched, Botticelli Pattern, Millefiori Flowers, 2 x 3 In.	338
St. Louis, Cane Rings, Blues, Whites, Pinks, Dancing Figure, 3 In.	2640
St. Louis, Crown, Red, Green, White, Twisted Ribbons, Blue Cane, 3 In.	1250
St. Louis, Double-Cut Overlay, Red & Blue Poinsettia, Leaves, 1975, 3 In.	156
St. Louis, Faceted, Pink & Green Snake, Broken White Cane, 3 In.	2280
St. Louis, Penholder, Twisted Ribbons, Red & Green, Flared Holder, 6 In.	711
St. Louis, Purple Flower, Yellow, 2 ¾ In.	144
St. Louis, Red Poinsettia, Green Leaves, Black Ground, 1970, 3 ¼ In.	168
St. Louis, White Overlay, Upright Bouquet, 3 In.	1875
Stankard, Paul, Blueberries, Purple Wildflowers, Knotweed, Moss, Orb, 3 In.	1778
Stankard, Paul, Blueberries, Tea Roses, Bee, Ant, Seeds In Cane, 3 In.	1481
Stankard, Paul, Honeycomb, 5 Floating Bees, Seedpods, Vines, Orb, 4 In.	3555
Stankard, Paul, Lampwork Glass, Trumpet Flowers, Clear, 1985, 2 x 3 In.	2000
Stankard, Paul, Root People, Jack-In-The-Pulpit, Lampwork, 1996, 2 In. .....*illus*	2625
Stankard, Paul, Spirit On Branch, Bee, Apple Blossoms, Blue Band, 3 In.	1718
Stankard, Paul, Tea Roses, Blueberries, Ant, Bee, Black Glass, Orb, 4 In.	3555
Stankard, Paul, White Mountain Laurels, Pink Buds, Leaves, Bee, Orb, 4 In.	2666
Sulphide, Sheep, Gold, Red & White Spirals, Germany, c.1900, 1 ⅞ In. .....*illus*	269
Tarsitano, Insect, Web, Blue Flowers, Leaves, Moss, 3 ½ In.	1500
Tarsitano, Snake, Coiled, Earthy Ground, Signed DT In Cane, 3 ¼ x 2 In.	474

PAPIER-MACHE is made from paper mixed with glue, chalk, and other ingredients, then molded and baked. It becomes very hard and can be painted. Boxes, trays, and furniture were made of papier-mache. Some of the nineteenth-century pieces were decorated with mother-of-pearl. Papier-mache is still being used to make small toys, figures, candy containers, boxes, and other giftwares. Furniture made of papier-mache is listed in the Furniture category.

Box, Chinoiserie, Cut Corners, Black Ground, 11 In.	125
Charger, Portrait, African American Boy, Brown, 21 ¾ In.	221
Cigar Case, American Fleet At Vera Cruz, 29 March 1847	1100
Coaster, Wine, Black, Gilt, Building, 6 In., Pair	163
Decoration, Easter Bunny, Basket, Cotton Batting, Glass Eyes, c.1900, 7 In.	160
Figurine, Bird, Perched, Sergio Bustamante, 53 ½ x 11 In.	468
Figurine, Dog, Greyhound, Losses & Repairs, 31 x 47 In.	236
Glove Box, Daisies, Blue Jay, Black Ground, c.1850, 12 x 4 In.	48
Lion's Head, Molded, Painted, Articulated Jaw & Tongue, 1800s, 10 x 7 In.	250
Mask, Bangkok Style, Gems, Mirrors, Bone Tusks, Tin Case, 25 x 11 In.	732
Parade Staff, Jester's Head, 42 In.	180
Tray, Black, Gilt, Sack Shape, Victorian, 23 x 31 In.	150
Tray, Church Interior, Shaped Rim, 27 In.	117
Tray, Flowers & Parrot, Black Lacquer, Inlaid Mother-Of-Pearl, 23 x 31 In.	180
Tray, Mother-Of-Pearl, Temples, Flowers, Gilt Willow Trees, 32 x 24 In.	106

P

Tray, Multicolor Flowers, Black Ground, 18 x 15 In.	245
Tray, Red, Parcel Gilt, Flowers, Leaves, Shaped Edge, 32 x 25 In.	200
Tray, Scalloped, Flowers, Yellow Scroll, 1900s, 12 x 8½ In. *illus*	100
Tray, Stand, Flower Spray, Black, 31 In.	500
Urn, Yellow, Faux Marble, Swirls, S-Scroll Handles, Italy, 19 x 17 In., Pair	296

PARASOL, *see Umbrella category.*

PARIAN is a fine-grained, hard-paste porcelain named for the marble it resembles. It was first made in England in 1846 and gained in favor in the United States about 1860. Figures, tea sets, vases, and other items were made of Parian at many English and American factories.

Bust, Sir Walter Scott, Bronze Socle, 1800s, 7¾ In.	125
Doll, Dancing Woman, Red Lace Dress, Revolves On Base, Pull String, 9 In.	235
Figurine, Dante, 20 In.	218
Figurine, Girl, Seated, Holding Open Book, Reading, c.1869, 13 In.	554
Figurine, Nude Woman, Holding Draped Cloth, Seated On Panther, 1845, 11 In.	1845
Figurine, Woman, Seated, Holding Nest, Birds, 14 In.	250
Group, Diana Of The Hunt, Dog & Putti, c.1850, 19 x 12 x 11 In.	2500
Vase, Hand Holding Trumpet Shape Bloom, 1880s, 2 x 3 In. *illus*	225
Vase, Pear Shape, Reeded, Blue Ribs, Grapevines, Pierced Leaf Rim, 17 x 7 In.	50

PARIS, Vieux Paris, or Old Paris, is porcelain ware that is known to have been made in Paris in the eighteenth or early nineteenth century. These porcelains have no identifying mark but can be recognized by the whiteness of the porcelain and the lines and decorations. Gold decoration is often used.

Basket, Gilt, Reticulated, Flared Rim, 10 x 14 In., Pair	875
Basket, Gilt, Reticulated, Square Foot, 8½ x 9 In., Pair	375
Bowl, Lid, Farmer, Tilling Field, Farmhouse, Child, Dog, 6 x 8 In.	165
Cachepot, Flowers, Cartouches, Birds, Royal Blue, Turquoise, Paneled, 6 x 6 In., Pair	1191
Cachepot, Gilded Dog Handle, Jasperware, Blue, Pelican, Crane, 11 x 9 In.	750
Compote, Pierced Basket, Kneeling Angel Stem, Paw Feet, c.1815, 12 x 9 In., Pair	2125
Garniture, Faux Cameo, Custard Ground, 3 Piece	2750
Plate, Ship Constitution, Hand Painted, 8½ In.	900
Platter, Blue, Dots, Flower Spray In Central Medallion, 17½ In.	156
Scent Bottle, Green, Cabochons, Style Of Jacob Petit, c.1850, 8 In.	325
Tea & Coffee Set, Coffee & Teapot, Sucrier, Cups, 7 Saucers, Gilt, Leaves, 21 Piece	384
Tureen, Sauce, Lid, Stand, Red, Gilt, Birds In Reserves, Finial, 1800s, 10 In., Pair	250
Tureen, Soup, Lid, Gilt Design, Melon Knob, Handles, 1800s, 12½ x 15 In. *illus*	183
Urn, Bouquets, Swags, Blue Ground, Gilt Base, Classical Masks, 13 In., Pair *illus*	500
Urn, Flowers, Portrait, Goddess Clio, Leaves, Curled Handles, Base, c.1815, 15 In.	875
Urn, Gilt, Handles, Square Base, 9½ In., Pair	88
Urn, Gilt, Lapis, Handles, Square Foot, 12 x 8½ In., Pair	812
Urn, Landscape, Mountains, Water, Gilt, Bearded Mask Handles, 10 x 7 In., Pair	354
Urn, Leafy Handles, Village Scene, Bouquet Of Flowers, 14 In.	750
Vase, Figures, White, Yellow & Orange Banding, Stylized Leaves, 14 In.	163
Vase, Flower Bouquets, Temple Bells, Paneled, Paint, France, c.1850, 20 In., Pair	375
Vase, Flower Reserves, Gilt Tracery, Flared, Flower & Branch Handles, 20 x 9 In.	150
Vase, Flowers, Blue, Parcel Gilt, 17 x 10½ In.	250
Vase, Flowers, Panels, Parcel Gilt, 20 x 11 In., Pair	1062
Vase, Flowers, Pierced Grape Handles, Flared, Undulating Rim, 14 x 6 In., Pair	300
Vase, Gilt, Blue, Chinese Scenes, Swan Handles, 1800s, 18 x 9 In., Pair *illus*	1280
Vase, Gilt, Roses, Flower Spray, Multicolor, 11 x 7¾ In., Pair	36
Vase, Multicolor Flowers, Gilt, White Ground, Curled Handles, Base, 16 In., Pair	960
Vase, Portrait, Woman, Classical, Yellow, Loop Handles, 9 In., Pair	98
Vase, Portrait, Woman, Looking Down, Gilt Brass, Chain Swag, c.1880, 13 x 7 In.	72
Vase, Rural Couple, Parcel Gilt, 14 x 9 In.	187
Vase, Trumpet, Gilt, Ruffled, Children Playing, 1800s, 14 x 8 In., Pair	250
Vase, Women, Cupid, Bulbous, Stick Neck, Flared Rim, Paint, c.1865, 19 In., Pair	687
Vase, Women, Gilt Decoration, Pink, 1800s, 10 In., Pair	126

Pate-De-Verre, Sculpture, Child, Seated, Toy, Wire, Wood, Ribbon, C. Bothwell, 22 x 10 In.
$3,900

Rago Arts and Auction Center

Patent Model, Brick Machine, Cherry, Brass, Edwin Andrews, c.1870, 8 x 12 In.
$375

Treadway Toomey Auctions

Pate-Sur-Pate, Plaque, Relief Nudes, Putti, Filigree, Black, Frame, 8 x 20 In.
$1,260

Fontaine's Auction Gallery

Paul Revere, Plate, Camels, Cuerda Seca, Signed, S.E.G., 1913, 8 In.
$2,250

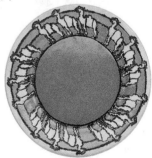

Rago Arts and Auction Center

P

Peanuts, Ornament, Christmas, Woodstock, Motorcycle, Presents, c.1965, 2½ x 2 In.

$21

Ruby Lane

Pearlware, Creamer, Oval, Rose Bouquet, Cartouche, 4⅛ x 4¼ In.

$98

Ruby Lane

Pearlware, Figurine, Andromache Mourning Hector's Ashes, 1790-1810, 9¼ In.

$795

Ruby Lane

PATE-DE-VERRE is an ancient technique in which glass is made by blending and refining powdered glass of different colors into molds. The process was revived by French glassmakers, especially Galle, around the end of the nineteenth century.

Sculpture, Child, Seated, Toy, Wire, Wood, Ribbon, C. Bothwell, 22 x 10 In......................*illus*	3900
Tray, Dark Red Moth, On Edge, Turquoise, Pale Green, Triangular, 7 In.....................................	885

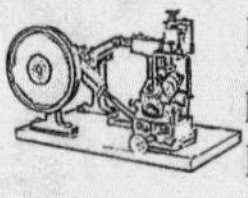

PATENT MODELS were required as part of a patent application for a United States patent until 1880. In 1926 the stored patent models were sold as a group by the U.S. Patent Office, and individual models are now appearing in the marketplace.

Brick Machine, Cherry, Brass, Edwin Andrews, c.1870, 8 x 12 In. ....*illus*	375

PATE-SUR-PATE means paste on paste. The design was made by painting layers of slip on the ceramic piece until a relief decoration was formed. The method was developed at the Sevres factory in France about 1850. It became even more famous at the English Minton factory about 1870. It has since been used by many potters to make both pottery and porcelain wares.

Plaque, Relief Nudes, Putti, Filigree, Black, Frame, 8 x 20 In. ....*illus*	1260
Plate, Classical Figures, Allegorical, Night, Scarves, G. Jones & Son, 7 In	593
Plate, Classical Women, Cobalt Blue Ground, Oval, 6 x 4 In., Pair..	406
Vase, Ormolu Mount, Blue, Martel En Tete, Louis Solon, c.1870, 18 In...................................	12500

PAUL REVERE POTTERY was made at several locations in and around Boston, Massachusetts, between 1906 and 1942. The pottery was operated as a settlement house program for teenage girls. Many pieces were signed *S.E.G.* for Saturday Evening Girls. The artists concentrated on children's dishes and tiles. Decorations were outlined in black and filled with color.

Bowl, Geese, Water, Blue, Green, Yellow, Wide Rim, 1926, 5 x 11½ In.........................	3375
Inkwell, Square, Semigloss Blue Glaze, Marked, 2 x 3 In..	92
Jar, Lid, Blue, Landscape, S.E.G., Signed, Esther, 1926, 10 x 7 In..............................	750
Pitcher, Band Of Trees, Cobalt Blue, Green, Loop Handle, Spout, 7 In........................	531
Plate, Camels, Cuerda Seca, Signed, S.E.G., 1913, 8 In............................*illus*	2250
Plate, Hen & Chick, O Don't Bother Me, F. Levine, S.E.G., 7 In., Pair........................	1063
Tea Caddy, Cuerda Seca, House, Trees & Lake, S.E.G., 1919, 4 x 3½ In.....................	4063
Tea Canister, Hexagonal, House, Trees, Lake, Brown, Blue, 1919, 5 In........................	4063
Teapot, Trivet, Band Of Trees, Green, Blue, Cuerda Seca, S. Galner, S.E.G.	2000
Tile, Dog In Landscape, Quote, Cuerda Seca, S.E.G., 1911, 4 x 6 In...........................	3125
Vase, Daffodil Band, Mustard Yellow, Cuerda Seca, F. Levine, S.E.G., 10 In................	1875
Vase, Landscape Shoulder Band, Navy Blue, Tapered, 1923, 9 In..............................	750
Vase, Landscape, Cuerda Seca, Black, S.E.G., Boston, Mass, 1923, 9 x 5 In.	750
Vase, Urn, Blue, Stylized Tulips At Shoulder, Marked, 5 In....................................	489

PEACHBLOW glass was made by several factories beginning in the 1880s. New England peachblow is a one-layer glass shading from red to white. Mt. Washington peachblow shades from pink to bluish-white. Hobbs, Brockunier and Company of Wheeling, West Virginia, made Coral glass that it marketed as Peachblow. It shades from yellow to peach and is lined with white glass. Reproductions of all types of peachblow have been made. Related pieces may be listed under Gundersen and Webb Peachblow.

Biscuit Barrel, Lid, Red To White, Gilt Peacock, Flowers, c.1900, 7 x 5 In.	650
Bowl, Square, Pink, Red, Ruffled Rim, Round Foot, 4¼ x 8 In.	73
Bride's Bowl, Amber, Ruffled Rim, Silver Plate Frame, Handles, Gilt, 11 x 7 In.	576
Ewer, Red To White, Pinched Neck, Folded Rim, Thorn Handle, c.1905, 6 In.	115
Pitcher, Cased, Red To Pink, Applied Glass Handle, 5½ x 5 In...............................	49
Vase, 2 Spouts On Lip, Double Handles, Mt. Washington, 4½ In..............................	861
Vase, Pink To Lavender, Ruffled Rim, Mt. Washington, 13 In..................................	132
Vase, Ruffled Mouth, Flowers, Butterflies, Applied Handles, 13½ In........................	108
Vase, Yellow Rose, Stem, Leaves, Gold Trim, Gourd, Mt. Washington, 8 In.	1067

P

PEANUTS is the title of a comic strip created by cartoonist Charles M. Schulz (1922–2000). The strip, drawn by Schulz from 1950 to 2000, features a group of children, including Charlie Brown and his sister Sally, Lucy Van Pelt and her brother Linus, Peppermint Patty, and Pig Pen, and an imaginative and independent beagle named Snoopy. The Peanuts gang has also been featured in books, television shows, and a Broadway musical.

Cookie Jar, Charlie Brown & Gang, Let's Celebrate, Chinese, 9 1/2 In.	95
Lunch Box, Woodstock, Snoopy, Metal, King-Seeley, c.1980	115
Ornament, Christmas, Woodstock, Motorcycle, Presents, c.1965, 2 1/2 x 2 In. ...*illus*	21
Print, SMAK!, Lucy, Snoopy, Limited Edition, 34 x 24 In.	400
Thermos, Baseball Game, American Thermos Company, Bottle No. 2868, 1959	25
Toy, Bus, Peanuts Special, Characters, Tin Litho, Batteries, Chein, 1966, 14 In.	280

PEARL items listed here are made of the natural mother-of-pearl from shells. Such natural pearl has been used to decorate furniture and small utilitarian objects for centuries. The glassware known as mother-of-pearl is listed by that name. Opera glasses made with natural pearl shell are listed under Opera Glasses.

Card Case, 18K Gold Escutcheon, 3 1/2 x 2 In.	30
Dish Set, 4 Plates, 2 Spoons With Pearl Tips, 6 Piece	168
Dish, Silver Handles, Filigree, 7 In.	96
Fish Service, 6 Knives, 6 Forks, Silver, Towle, 12 Piece	188
Napkin Ring, Turbo Shell, Silver Plate Rings, 2 1/2 x 2 In., 8 Piece	90
Tea Caddy, Regency, Coffin Shape, Key Escutcheon, Bun Feet, c.1820, 5 x 7 In.	1190
Tray, Figures, Boats, Carved, Chinese Export, 8 In.	780

PEARLWARE is an earthenware made by Josiah Wedgwood in 1779. It was copied by other potters in England. Pearlware is only slightly different in color from creamware and for many years collectors have confused the terms. Wedgwood pieces are listed in the Wedgwood category in this book. Most pearlware with mocha designs is listed under Mocha.

Pearl

Bowl, Amber Bands, Yellow Flower Sprays, 1800s, 5 x 10 In.	86
Cake Stand, Cream, Green, Gilt, Shells, Wavy Rim, Pedestal, c.1780, 13 x 12 In.	480
Charger, Blue Feather Edge, Peafowl, 12 In.	510
Coffeepot, Lid, Acorn Knop, Agate Design, Fluting, Banding, c.1795, 10 In.	923
Creamer, Oval, Rose Bouquet, Cartouche, 4 1/8 x 4 1/4 In. ...*illus*	98
Drainer, Embossed Edge, Green Outline, Staffordshire, c.1820, 11 x 7 In.	199
Figure, Rodent, Reclining, Oval Mound, Multicolor, c.1800, 3 In.	1230
Figurine, Andromache Mourning Hector's Ashes, 1790-1810, 9 1/4 In. ...*illus*	795
Figurine, Tithing, Tenth Child, Hay, Eggs, Pig, 5 3/4 x 7 In.	160
Jug, Brown & Blue Sponge, Staffordshire, c.1800, 9 In.	94
Jug, Brown Bear, Staffordshire, c.1798, 8 1/2 In.	2706
Mug, Blue & White Swirls, Mocha Splotches, Loop Handle, 1700s, 6 In.	500
Mug, Peafowl, Bird, Branch, Staffordshire, c.1810, 5 In.	164
Pepper Pot, Blue & White, Pedestal Base, Pierced Top, c.1780, 4 In.	263
Pitcher, Black Transfer, Hand Colored, Flowers, Birds, Landscape, c.1920, 6 In.	73
Pitcher, Hunters, Dog, Edward Jones Llanfitllin, Multicolor, 7 In. ...*illus*	149
Pitcher, Thomas & Ales Hardman, Success To All Flowerist, 1792, 8 1/2 In.	677
Plate, Blue Feather Edge, Peafowl, 9 In., Pair	480
Plate, Blue Transfer Flowers, Staffordshire, c.1815, 8 3/4 In.	293
Plate, Green Feather Edge, Peafowl, 9 In., Pair	450
Plate, Peafowl, Woman, Branches, Octagonal, Green Rim, c.1810, 7 1/2 In.	375
Plate, Swirling Flowers & Leafy Branches, Blue Feathery Rim, c.1810, 8 In.	650
Platter, Flowering Branches, Oval, Blue Wavy Rim, c.1810, 12 x 16 In.	325
Punch Bowl, Chinoiserie, Chinese Paintings, Staffordshire, c.1790, 4 x 11 In.	527
Punch Bowl, Figures, Landscape, Multicolor, Gilt Rim, 6 1/2 x 14 1/2 In.	1020
Salt, White, Green Band, Flower, Leaf Swags, Ribbed, Pedestal, 2 1/2 In., Pair	86
Teapot, Bear, Holding Hound Shape Spout, Bear's Head Lid, c.1810, 8 In.	1230
Teapot, Pink, Green, White, Swan Finial, 5 1/2 In.	74

Pearlware, Pitcher, Hunters, Dog, Edward Jones Llanfitllin, Multicolor, 7 In.
$149

Ruby Lane

Peloton, Vase, Electric Blue Threading Over Clear Glass, 4 In.
$125

Ruby Lane

> **TIP**
> *Remove pencil marks and other smudges with a Mr. Clean Magic Eraser or Scotch-Brite Easy Erasing Pad.*

Pen, Sheaffer Craftsman, Fountain, Black & Marbled Green Stripe, Chrome Trim, 1940s, 5 In.
$55

Ruby Lane

Pen & Pencil, Caran D'Ache, Hexagonal, Guilloche, Chevron, Switzerland, c.1940, 6 In.
$225

Ruby Lane

Pencil, Mechanical, Waterman, Lady Patricia, Celluloid, Marbled, c.1930, 4¼ In.
$88

Ruby Lane

Pencil Sharpener, U.S. Automatic, Keep Oil Cup Filled, 4½ x 5½ In.
$457

Showtime Auction Services

Tray, Oval, Molded, Farmers, Green, Blue, c.1790, 15 In.	4375
Tureen, Figural, Nesting Pigeon, Blue Bird Lid, Nest Bowl, c.1810, 5 x 8 In.	240

 PEKING GLASS is a Chinese cameo glass first made popular in the eighteenth century. The Chinese have continued to make this layered glass in the old manner, and many new pieces are now available that could confuse the average buyer.

Bowl, Flower Shape, Openwork Strands, Yellow Glaze, 1900s, 6 In., Pair	369
Bowl, Red, Green Overlay, Flared Rim, Geese, Mica Specks, c.1915, 5 In.	123
Bowl, Upturned Bell Shape, Ring Foot, Dark Purple, c.1800, 2 x 5 In., Pair	123
Brushpot, Cylindrical, Translucent Yellow, Incised, Goldfish, Lotus, 5 In.	215
Brushpot, Cylindrical, White, Scholar, Attendants, Ring Foot, c.1900, 6 In.	246
Brushpot, Yellow Snowflake Glaze, Red Overlay, Symbols, c.1910, 5 In.	123
Cup, Bell Shape, Raised Foot, Yellow, Openwork Wood Stand, 2 In.	369
Jar, Lid, Round, Butterflies, Flowers, 6½ In., Pair	232
Jar, Shouldered, Waisted, Cobalt Blue, Flat Neck, 1700s, 6 In.	185
Vase, Flared Neck, Opaque Red Orange, Swirls, Wood Stand, c.1900, 4 In.	369
Vase, Red, White, Relief Birds & Flowering Branches, c.1910, 12 In., Pair	278
Vase, White, Cobalt Blue Overlay, Birds, Branches, c.1900, 12 In., Pair	185

 PELOTON glass is a European glass with small threads of colored glass rolled onto the surface of clear or colored glass. It is sometimes called spaghetti, or shredded coconut, glass. Most pieces found today were made in the nineteenth century.

Pitcher, Amber, Reeded Handle, Kralik, 5½ In.	242
Sugar Shaker, Cylindrical, Green, Color Shards, Kralik, 6 In.	181
Vase, Electric Blue Threading Over Clear Glass, 4 In. ....*illus*	125

 PENS replaced hand-cut quills as writing instruments in 1780, when the first steel pen point was made in England. But it was 100 years before the commercial pen was a common item. The fountain pen was invented in the 1830s but was not made in quantity until the 1880s. All types of old pens are collected. Float pens that feature small objects floating in a liquid as part of the handle are popular with collectors. Advertising pens are listed in the Advertising section of this book.

Fountain, 14K, Namiki, Enameled, Black, Multicolor Flowers, Marked, Japan, 5 In.	112
Montblanc, Fountain, Catherine The Great, Aubergine Resin, Rose Gold Plate, 1997, 5½ In.	1375
Montegrappa, Roller Ball, Frank Sinatra Commemorative	750
Parker, Fountain, Gold Snake, 18K, Resin, Emerald, c.1997, 5¼ In.	3750
Sheaffer Craftsman, Fountain, Black & Marbled Green Stripe, Chrome Trim, 1940s, 5 In.*illus*	55

PEN & PENCIL

Caran D'Ache, Hexagonal, Guilloche, Chevron, Switzerland, c.1940, 6 In. ....*illus*	225
Cross, 14K Gold, Case, 1970s, 2 Piece	2160
Cross, Gold Filled, Case, 2 Piece	25
Montblanc, Mark Twain, Pencil, Roller Pen, Fountain, Rhodium, Box	1500
Parker, Sterling, Crosshatch, 2 Piece	36
Sheaffer, 14K Gold, Case, 6¼ In.	480
Sheaffer, Sterling Silver, Grapevine, Case, 2 Piece	72

PENCILS were invented, so it is said, in 1565. The eraser was not added to the pencil until 1858. The automatic pencil was invented in 1863. Collectors today want advertising pencils or automatic pencils of unusual design. Boxes and sharpeners for pencils are also collected. Advertising pencils are listed in the Advertising category. Pencil boxes are listed in the Box category.

Mechanical, 14K Gold, Cartier, 5 In.	265
Mechanical, Black, Silvertone Banding, Cartier, 5½ In.	58
Mechanical, Meisterstuck, Montblanc, 5½ In.	174
Mechanical, Waterman, Lady Patricia, Celluloid, Marbled, c.1930, 4¼ In. ....*illus*	88

P

PENCIL SHARPENER

6-Blade Cutting Wheel, Iron, 5 x 4 ½ In.	69
Automatic Pencil Sharpener Co., Climax, Feeder, Drawer, 1902, 5 x 8 In.	69
Automatic Pencil Sharpener Co., Steel, Oil Cup, Drawer, c.1906, 5 x 4 In.	185
Automatic Pencil Sharpener Co., Wizard, Drawer, 4 ½ x 5 In.	139
El Casco, Chrome, Black, Crank, 6 x 5 In.	230
Gould & Cook, Wheel, Crank, Iron, 1886, 8 x 9 In.	377
Happy, Dwarf, Figural, Hands On Hips, Celluloid, 1938, 2 ½ In.	205
Limousine, 1920s Style, Red, Silver, Tin, Japan, 2 ½ In.	24
Mechanical, Cast Iron, Jupiter, Germany, 1920s, 14 In.	131
Race Car, Plastic, Red, 2 In.	6
Roneo Company, Threaded Clamp Base, 8 ½ x 9 ½ In.	92
U.S. Automatic, Keep Oil Cup Filled, 4 ½ x 5 ½ In. ....*illus*	457

PENNSBURY POTTERY worked in Morrisville, Pennsylvania, from 1950 to 1971. Full sets of dinnerware as well as many decorative items were made. Pieces are marked with the name of the factory.

Pennsbury Pottery

Amish, Creamer, Man, In Heart, 4 In.	31
Bowl, Gay Ninety, 2 Couples, Mugs, Drinking, Here's Looking At You, 12 x 8 In. ....*illus*	55
Hex, Mug, 3 In.	21
Red Rooster, Cup & Saucer	27

PEPSI-COLA, the drink and the name, was invented in 1898 but was not trademarked until 1903. The logo was changed from an elaborate script to the modern block letters in 1963. Several different logos have been used. Until 1951, the words *Pepsi* and *Cola* were separated by two dashes. These bottles are called "double dash." In 1951 the modern logo with a single hyphen was introduced. All types of advertising memorabilia are collected, and reproductions are being made.

Clock, Say Pepsi Please, Gold Plastic, Glass Front, Light-Up, 1960s, 15 x 15 In.	245
Clock, Square, White Face, Pepsi Logo, Light-Up, 26 ½ x 35 ½ In.	80
Clock, Wall, Be Sociable Have A Pepsi, Electric, Light-Up, Double Bubble, 5 x 15 In.	546
Cooler, Blue, Metal, Bottle Opener, Progressive Refrigerator, 1940s, 16 x 17 In.	200
Cooler, Drink Pepsi-Cola, Blue, Handle, 19 x 13 In.	125
Cooler, Ice Chest, Drink Pepsi-Cola, Gray & Red, Handle, 1950s, 19 x 22 In.	335
Menu Board, Say Pepsi Please, Border, Bottle Cap, Stout Sign Co., 30 x 30 In	100
Radio, Cooler, Ice Cold, Cornflower Blue, 7 ½ x 6 ¼ In. ....*illus*	250
Radio, Pepsi Bottle Shape, 24 In.	700
Sign, Bottle Cap Shape, Drink, Ice Cold, 14 In.	250
Sign, Glass, Ice, Straw, Neon, 27 x 15 In.	130
Sign, The Light Refreshment, Woman, Yellow, Blue, 19 x 6 In.	175
Sign, Yellow, Say Pepsi Please, 53 x 17 In.	350
Thermometer, Any Weather's Pepsi Weather, Bottle Cap, White, 27 x 8 In.	180
Thermometer, Say Pepsi Please, Yellow, 28 x 7 In.	146
Thermometer, Say Pepsi Please, Yellow, Bottle Cap, 27 x 7 ¼ In.	85
Tray, Woman, Green Dress, Red, Green & Pink Border, Oval, 13 ½ x 11 In.	150

PERFUME BOTTLES are made of cut glass, pressed glass, art glass, silver, metal, enamel, and even plastic or porcelain. Although the small bottle to hold perfume was first made before the time of ancient Egypt, it is the nineteenth- and twentieth-century examples that interest today's collector. DeVilbiss Company has made atomizers of all types since 1888 but no longer makes the perfume bottle tops so popular with collectors. These were made from 1920 to 1968. The glass bottle may be by any of many manufacturers even if the atomizer is marked *DeVilbiss.* The word *factice,* which often appears in ads, refers to store display bottles. Glass or porcelain examples may be found under the appropriate name such as Lalique, Czechoslovakia, Glass-Bohemian, etc.

Amethyst Stopper, Nude Woman, Czechoslovakia Glass, 8 x 5 In.	172
Bracelet, Le Bracelet Miraculeux, 5 Scents, Art Deco, Parfums De Marcy, 1928	33000

PERFUME BOTTLE

Pennsbury, Bowl, Gay Ninety, 2 Couples, Mugs, Drinking, Here's Looking At You, 12 x 8 In.
$55

Pepsi-Cola, Radio, Cooler, Ice Cold, Cornflower Blue, 7 ½ x 6 ¼ In.
$250

TIP

To remove the remains of masking tape and labels from glass, rub the spot with WD-40 lubricating and penetrating oil.

P

Perfume Bottle, Cologne, Opalescent, Cameo, Fruit, Branches, Leaves, Bent Neck, 3 In.
$288

Peters & Reed, Vase, House On Hill, Lake Scene, 8 In. $403

American Antique Auctions

Peters & R eed, Wall Pocket, Green Matte, Trumpet Shape, Art Deco, 8 In. $123

Humler & Nolan

Pewabic, Vase, Green, 2 Square Handles, Glazed, Marked, c.1903, 13 x 6 In. $2,125

Rago Arts and Auction Center

Bronze, Enamel, Eros & Psyche Scenes, Multicolor, Austria, 1800s, 2 x 2 In.	562
Cologne, Opalescent, Cameo, Fruit, Branches, Leaves, Bent Neck, 3 In. ....*illus*	288
Cranberry Glass, Gilt Design, Rounded Shoulder, Ball Stopper, c.1890, 5 x 3 In.	280
Cut Glass, Strawberry Diamond, Cartouche, Thistle, 18K Granulated Gold Cap, 3 In.	2666
Glass, Clear, Enamel Design, Bird, Flowers, Leaves, Square, Rounded, 5 In.	325
Glass, Cranberry Stripes, Clear Stopper, Italy, 12 In.	75
Pink Glass, Gold Flecks, Green Trim, Bouquet Stopper, Murano, 8 In., Pair	126
Pompeian Swirl, Squat, Mother-Of-Pearl, Stevens & Williams, 1888, 6 In.	690
Porcelain, Figurine, Dog, Black Pug, Hinged Collar, c.1910, 3 In.	338
Porcelain, Transfer, Flowers, Ormolu Mount, France, 6 In., 3 Piece	92
Rock Crystal, Spiral Ribs, 18K Gold Lid, Topaz, Diamonds, 3 In.	2370
Short Neck, Petal Scalloped Rim, 9 x 4 In.	100

PETERS & REED POTTERY COMPANY of Zanesville, Ohio, was founded by John D. Peters and Adam Reed in 1897. Chromal, Landsun, Montene, Pereco, and Persian are some of the art lines that were made. The company, which became Zane Pottery in 1920 and Gonder Pottery in 1941, closed in 1957. Peters & Reed pottery was unmarked.

Umbrella Stand, Water Carrier, Terra-Cotta, c.1912, 20½ In.	187
Vase, House On Hill, Lake Scene, 8 In. ....*illus*	403
Vase, Twilight House Scene, Fences & Trees, 8 In.	805
Wall Pocket, Green Matte, Trumpet Shape, Art Deco, 8 In. ....*illus*	123

PEWABIC POTTERY was founded by Mary Chase Perry Stratton in 1903 in Detroit, Michigan. The company made many types of art pottery, including pieces with matte green glaze and an iridescent crystalline glaze. The company continued working until the death of Mary Stratton in 1961. It was reactivated by Michigan State University in 1968.

Tile, Little Blower, Girl, Red, 3½ x 6 In.	118
Tile, Round, Wayne State University, 6 In.	118
Vase, Blue Drip Glaze, Brown Metallic, 4 x 3½ In.	1062
Vase, Blue, 5 x 5½ In.	518
Vase, Blue, Luster, 5½ In.	531
Vase, Dimpled Iridescent Glaze, Green, Plum, Gold, Smokestack, Flared, 5 In.	1534
Vase, Drip Matte Glaze, Maple Leaf Mark, 6 x 10½ In.	1342
Vase, Green, 2 Square Handles, Glazed, Marked, c.1903, 13 x 6 In. ....*illus*	2125
Vase, Iridescent Cobalt Blue, Mottled Green Rim, Shouldered, Tapered, 10 In.	1003
Vase, Iridescent Glaze, Detroit, Mich., 8 x 5½ In.	563
Vase, Lily Of The Valley, Green Matte Glaze, Stamped, c.1905, 6 x 4 In. ....*illus*	13750
Vase, Metallic Blue Glaze, 4½ x 4 In.	518
Vase, Slate Gray, Pale Blue Iridescent, Mottled, Jug Shape, Rolled Rim, 8 x 6 In.	563
Vase, Urn, Blue & Green Luster Glaze, 5½ In.	518

PEWTER is a metal alloy of tin and lead. Some of the pewter made after 1840 has a slightly different composition and is called Britannia metal. This later type of pewter was worked by machine; the earlier pieces were made by hand. In the 1920s pewter came back into fashion and pieces were often marked Genuine Pewter. Eighteenth-, nineteenth-, and twentieth-century examples are listed here.

Basin, Robert Bonnynge, Touchmark, 1750, 2 x 6 In.	431
Beaker, Engraved Armorial, 1900s, 5 In., 9 Piece	86
Bowl, Hammered, Flower Shape Handle With Enamel Cabochons, c.1910, 4¼ x 22 In.......*illus*	50
Bowl, Handles, Oval, Italy, 12 x 6 In.	85
Bowl, Kayserzinn, Stingrays, Rounded Square Shape, 18 In.	188
Bowl, Lid, 2 Handles, Acorn Finial, John Trapp, England, c.1710, 6 x 9 In.	813
Box, Liberty & Co., Mountain Scene, Enamel, Foil, Hinged Lid, 2½ x 4 In..........*illus*	1180
Butter, Cover, Curved Flat Handles, Triangle Shape Handle, 1970, 2 x 8 In. ....*illus*	275
Candlestick, Conical Stem, Ring, Rolled Cup Rim, Flared Foot, 9 In., Pair	150
Candlestick, Stylized Openwork Figure, Dragons, Footed, 1900s, 19 In., Pair	1067

Charger, Edward Box, Touchmark, 1745, 16 ½ In.	168
Charger, Robert Garrett, Reeded Rim, Touchmark 16 In., 4 Piece	540
Coffeepot, Domed Lid, Loop Handle, Thumblift, Marked, Israel Trask, c.1835, 12 In. *illus*	150
Coffeepot, Lighthouse Shape, Dome Lid, Shaped Wood & Metal Handle, 10 In.	112
Dish, Joseph Danforth, Touchmark, c.1785, 13 In.	209
Dish, Townsend & Compton, 14 ⅝ In.	62
Flagon, Boardman & Co., Lighthouse, Dome Lid, Scroll Handle, c.1820, 11 In.	390
Flagon, Boardman & Co., Lighthouse, Spire Lid & Finial, Lion Mark, c.1820, 12 In.	300
Flagon, Touchmark Boardman & Co., c.1830, 11 ¼ In.	209
Flagon, Trophy, Yachting, Eastern Yacht Club, 12 ¼ In.	510
Jardiniere, Art Nouveau, Oval, Handles, Flowers, 25 In.	188
Kettle, Scroll Handle, Cartouches, Leaves, Mums, Lion, Beasts, Cranes, 19 x 20 In.	595
Kettle, Stand, Ribbed, Twist, Ebonized Handle, 13 ¼ In.	50
Lamp, Oil, Round Foot, 1800s	117
Lamp, Oil, Saucer Base, Blown Glass Font, Continental, c.1810, 14 In.	240
Measures, Austen & Son, Haystack, Graduated, ½ Gill To Gallon, Ireland, To 10 In.	861
Mold, Ice Cream, Rose, 3 ½ x 4 In. *illus*	38
Mold, Ice Cream, Santa Claus, Hat & Coat, Round Base, France, c.1905, 20 In.	5000
Mug, Thomas Danforth III, Scrolled Handle, Middletown, Connecticut, 4 ½ In.	308
Mug, William Clader, Touchmark, 6 In.	1440
Plate, Deep, Marked Jacob Eggleston, c.1800, 11 ¼ In.	1920
Plate, John Skinner, Beaded Rim, Marked, Rampant Lion, Pillars, c.1790, 8 ½ In.	123
Platter, Kayserzinn, Oval, Embossed, Boar, Relief, Pinecones, c.1905, 13 x 20 In.	900
Porringer, William Billings, Flower Handle, Rhode Island, c.1800, 5 ½ In.	360
Porringer, William Calder, Flower Handle, Marked, c.1830, 5 In.	995
Sconce, 2-Light, Lions, Stepped Disc, Removable Arms, England, 1700s, 11 In., Pair	860
Sculpture, A. Malinowski, Mother Mermaid, Children, Denmark, 1930s, 11 x 5 In.	531
Sculpture, Michael Boyett, Flat Out For Red River Station, 1984, 10 x 8 In.	343
Tablespoon, Peter Derr, Fiddleback, 1800s, 8 ¼ In.	266
Teapot, Samuel Hersey, Touchmark, c.1850, 7 In.	450
Tray, Art Nouveau, Flowers, Wave Tendrils, Germany, 10 In.	549
Tray, Rounded, Ripples, Openwork, 2 ½ x 12 ½ In.	366
Vase, Kayserzinn, 3 Antler Shape Handles, Germany, 14 ¼ In., Pair	500
Vase, Liberty & Co., 3 Open Buttresses, Bullet Shape, 7 ½ x 4 ½ In.	366
Vase, Liberty & Co., Petal Shape, Draping Tendrils, 10 x 6 In.	274
Vase, Turquoise Stones, c.1905, 13 ½ x 6 In.	2074

PHOENIX BIRD, or Flying Phoenix, is the name given to a blue-and-white dinnerware popular between 1900 and World War II. A variant is known as Flying Turkey. Most of this dinnerware was made in Japan for sale in dime stores in America. It is still being made.

Cup & Saucer, Birds, Flowers, Japan	16
Sugar & Creamer, Flying Birds, Scrolls, c.1900	82

PHOENIX GLASS Company was founded in 1880 in Pennsylvania. The firm made commercial products, such as lampshades, bottles, and glassware. Collectors today are interested in the "Sculptured Artware" made by the company from the 1930s until the mid-1950s. Some pieces of Phoenix glass are very similar to those made by the Consolidated Lamp and Glass Company. Phoenix made Reuben Blue, lavender, and yellow pieces. These colors were not used by Consolidated. In 1970 Phoenix became a division of Anchor Hocking, which was sold to the Newell Group in 1987. The factory is still working.

Pitcher, Spot Optic, Maroon, Opal, Lobed, Star Shape Rim, c.1883, 9 In.	96
Pitcher, Spot Optic, Yellow, Opal, c.1883, 8 ¾ In.	120
Shade, Amber Iridescent, Etched, Melon Lobed, Flared, 1920s, 5 In., Pair	900
Vase, Dancing Women, Blue, c.1930s, 11 ½ In.	93
Vase, Philodendron, White, Raised Leaves, Blue, c.1925, 11 ¼ In. *illus*	150

Pewabic, Vase, Lily Of The Valley, Green Matte Glaze, Stamped, c.1905, 6 x 4 In. $13,750

Rago Arts and Auction Center

TIP

Old pewter should not be washed in a dishwasher. It melts easily and also may tarnish. Wash pewter by hand.

Pewter, Bowl, Hammered, Flower Shape Handle With Enamel Cabochons, c.1910, 4 ¼ x 22 In. $50

Ruby Lane

Pewter, Box, Liberty & Co., Mountain Scene, Enamel, Foil, Hinged Lid, 2 ½ x 4 In. $1,180

Humler & Nolan

This is an edited listing of current prices. Visit **Kovels.com** to check thousands of prices from previous years and sign up for free information on trends, tips, reproductions, marks, and more.

PHONOGRAPH

Pewter, Butter, Cover, Curved Flat Handles, Triangle Shape Handle, 1970, 2 x 8 In.
$275

Ruby Lane

Pewter, Coffeepot, Domed Lid, Loop Handle, Thumblift, Marked, Israel Trask, c.1835, 12 In.
$150

Garth's Auctioneers & Appraisers

Pewter, Mold, Ice Cream, Rose, 3 ½ x 4 In.
$38

Ruby Lane

Archibald Knox

Although Knox's contract with Liberty & Co. ended in 1912 he never fell out of favor with the company. When founder Arthur Lasenby Liberty died in 1917, it was Knox who was commissioned to design his gravestone for the churchyard at The Lee, Buckinghamshire.

PHONOGRAPHS, invented by Thomas Edison in 1877, have been made by many firms. This category also includes other items associated with the phonograph. Jukeboxes and Records are listed in their own categories.

Bing, Pigmyphone, Green Case, Discs, Germany, 6 x 6 In., Child's	132
Capitol, Lamp, 8-Sided, Fringe, Metal Base, Burns Pollack Electric Mfg., 7 Records	2090
Columbia, Graphophone, Disc, Case, 8 ½ x 13 In., 24-In. Brass Horn	767
Colombia, Graphophone, Red Horn, Yellow Flowers, Oak, 30 x 13 In. *illus*	819
Dennet, Oak, 6 Openings, Lakeside Craftshops, 18 Records, 41 x 20 In.	976
Edison, Fireside, Model B, Cylinder, Cygnet Horn, Oak	773
Edison, Gem, Cylinder, Horn, Oak	328
Edison, Gem, Model B, Oak Base & Lid, Brass Horn, 2 Cylinders, c.1905	1053
Edison, Model C, Oak, Cylinder, Horn, Case	496
Edison, Oak Case & Lid, Box Shape, Brass Horn, 2-Minute Cylinders, 1895	2862
Edison, Oak, Windup, Sliding Volume Control, Gold Plate, 1916, 20 x 45 In.	895
Gramophone, Victor, Monarch Special, Oak, Turntable, Brass Horn, c.1905	1365
Sonora, Mahogany, Carved, Removable Crank, c.1915, 23 x 23 x 49 In.	895
Thorens, Silver Plate Case, Horn, Discs, 13 x 13 x 8 In.	234
Victor 6, Disc, SN2030, Exhibition Reproducer, Mahogany Spear Horn	2800
Victor, Model VV-IV, Oak, c.1914	325
Victor, Talking Machine, Tabletop, Model VVXA409141, Horn, 12 x 12 In.	650
Victrola, Nursery Model, Boy Blowing Bubbles, Cat, Inside Horn Speaker	44

PHONOGRAPH NEEDLE CASES of tin are collected today by music and phonograph enthusiasts and advertising addicts. The tins are very small, about 2 inches across, and often have attractive graphic designs lithographed on the top and sides.

Gramophone, His Master's Voice, Dog, Tin, c.1900, 1 ½ x 1 ¼ In.	58
Original Aeropoint Coin Machine Needle, Laurel Wreath, Black, 2 ¾ In. *illus*	10
Solo Needles, Record, Notes, Cream & Red, Tin, 1930s, 1 ½ x 2 In.	65
Songster, Bird, Branch, Yellow, Blue, Brown, Tin, 1930s, 1 ½ x 2 In.	65
Verona, Nude Woman, Red, Black, White, Tin, 1930s, 1 ½ x 1 ½ In.	65

PHOTOGRAPHY items are listed here. The first photograph was a view from a window in France taken in 1826. The commercially successful photograph started with the daguerreotype introduced in 1839. Today all sorts of photographs and photographic equipment are collected. Albums were popular in Victorian times. Cartes de visite, popular after 1854, were mounted on 2 ½-by-4-inch cardboard. Cabinet cards were introduced in 1866. These were mounted on 4 ¼-by-6 ½-inch cards. Stereo views are listed under Stereo Card. Stereoscopes are listed in their own section.

Album, Cowgirl, Multicolor, Embossed Border, Flowers, 10 ½ x 8 ½ In.	949
Album, Satin, Embroidered Flowers, Metal Clasp, Medallion, 1800s, 8 x 10 In.	310
Albumen, Abraham Lincoln, Anthony Berger, Mounted, 1864, 8 x 9 In.	4800
Albumen, Chatto, Chiricahua Apache, A. Randall, Boudoir Mount, 1884	2040
Albumen, Driving Last Spike, Canadian Pacific Railway, A. Ross, 7 x 9 In.	3024
Albumen, G. Custer In Buckskin, James A. Scholten, 1872, 6 x 10 In.	3000
Albumen, G. Custer, Russian Duke Alexis, D.F. Berry, 1872, 7 x 10 In.	2760
Albumen, Geronimo, Chiricahua Apache Chief, A. Randall, Mount, 1884	3600
Albumen, Palisades, Humboldt River, Salt Lake City, C. Savage, 10 x 8 In.	369
Albumen, Soldiers, Civilians, African Americans, Outside Home, 9 x 7 In.	660
Albumen, The Commodore Vanderbilt Locomotive, c.1870, 13 x 10 In.	360
Ambrotype, African American Woman, Child, 1800s, Half Case, ⅙ Plate	1320
Ambrotype, Allegorical Anchor Scene, ½ Plate	1792
Ambrotype, Confederate Soldier, Musket, Bowie Knife, ¼ Plate *illus*	8625
Ambrotype, Musician With Flute & Fife, Brown Leather Case, ⅙ Plate	960
Ambrotype, Pattern Maker In Shop, Tools, ¼ Plate, c.1860	4680
Ambrotype, Ruby, 2 Union Soldiers, With Pistols, Tinted, ⅙ Plate	480
Ambrotype, Ruby, Armed Private, Hat, Civil War, Thermoplastic Case, ⅙ Plate	720
Cabinet Card, African American Steward, J. Bell, USS Maine, 1885	360

Cabinet Card, Annie Oakley, Brisbois, Oakley's Signature, 14 x 12 In.	1080
Cabinet Card, Annie Oakley, Holding Dead Rabbit, J. Wood, 1800s	1080
Cabinet Card, Annie Oakley, Holding Shotgun, Baker's Gallery, Ohio..........................*illus*	1080
Cabinet Card, Annie Oakley, Little Sure Shot, Imprint, J. Wood, N.Y......................*illus*	1920
Cabinet Card, Armed White Man, Standing Over Dead Indian, 1800s	390
Cabinet Card, Buffalo Bill Cody, Portrait, Van Der Weyde, London, 1800s	840
Cabinet Card, Buffalo Bill Cody, Wearing Stetson & Fringed Jacket, 1887	523
Cabinet Card, Calamity Jane, C.E. Finn, Livingston, Montana, c.1870	3444
Cabinet Card, Composite View, Indian Chiefs, Indian Training School, c.1881	338
Cabinet Card, Curley, Custer's Scout, Survivor, Custer's Last Stand, c.1880	960
Cabinet Card, General George Crook, Mitchel & McGowan, c.1878	4305
Cabinet Card, Hanging, Gilbert & Rosengrants At Leadville, Luke, Wheeler, 1881	1046
Cabinet Card, May Lillie, Leaning Against Rifle, 1800s	800
Cabinet Card, Sioux Chief Last Horse, George Spencer	319
Cabinet Card, Sioux Indian & 2 Squaws, Zalmon Gilbert, c.1890	420
Cabinet Card, Sitting Bull, Notman & Son, Montreal	2304
Cabinet Card, Theodore Roosevelt, Pach Bros., New York, 1898	1728
Cabinet Card, Theodore Roosevelt, Rough Rider Uniform, 1898	1152
Cabinet Card, Western Mountain Man With Winchester Rifles, c.1874	720
Camera, Carl Zeiss, Planar, 135mm, Large Format, Box,	885
Camera, Daguerreotype, Brass Focus Knob, Double Lens, 4 1/2 x 5 In.	20160
Camera, Dry Plate, Oak, Brass, Iron & Glass, Plates & Lens, 73 x 31 In.	4500
Camera, Folmer & Schwing, Telescopic Graflex, 4x5 View, 1903, 6 x 9 In.	900
Camera, Fuji, GW690III, 6x9, Compact Format	236
Camera, Kodak Brownie 120, Box Film, Storage, Marked, 1910, 6 x 4 In.	20
Camera, Linhof, Master, Technika, 4x5, Large Format, 1980s	649
Camera, Ramlose, Model A, 4x5, Large Format, Press, c.1945	118
Camera, Rolleiflex, Manual Focus, Lens Caps, Zeiss Lens	1085
Camera, Rolleiflex, Manual Focus, Waist Level Viewer, Lens Hood	436
Camera, Rollicord, Synchro-Compur Lens, Leather Case, 6 In.	92
Camera, Spy, 12mm Lens, Petal, Occupied Japan, c.1949, 1 In.	336
Carte De Visite, 3 Men & Wagon Team, Front Of The Alamo, c.1860s	1680
Carte De Visite, 51 Confederate Officers & Leaders, Collage, 1863	250
Carte De Visite, Abraham Lincoln, Alexander Gardner, 1863	660
Carte De Visite, Abraham Lincoln, Warren, Last Pose Before Death, 1865	840
Carte De Visite, Abraham Lincoln's Horse, Old Robin, Ingmire, 1800s	1200
Carte De Visite, Alexander Gardner, Black Servant, To A Family, c.1866	1560
Carte De Visite, Armed Sioux Indian, Pistols, Mitchell & McGowan, 1800s	570
Carte De Visite, Brigadier General George A. Custer, Portrait, 1864..................*illus*	540
Carte De Visite, Colonel Samuel M. Hyams, Confederacy	984
Carte De Visite, Confederate Spy, John Yates Beall, c.1865	780
Carte De Visite, Gen. G. Pickett, Confederacy, Vannerson & Jones, 1865	540
Carte De Visite, Gen. J.E.B. Stuart, Confederacy, Vannerson & Jones, 1865	540
Carte De Visite, Gen. M. Thompson, Confederacy, POW, Gratiot Prison	180
Carte De Visite, Gen. Turner Ashby, Confederacy, Selby & Dulany, 1866	360
Carte De Visite, General Abner Doubleday, 2 1/2 x 4 In.	1000
Carte De Visite, General James Rains, Confederacy, Kia, Murfreesboro	840
Carte De Visite, General Robert E. Lee, 1863	437
Carte De Visite, J.B. Texas Jack Omohundro, 1874	600
Carte De Visite, James Garfield, 1862	875
Carte De Visite, Miner, Pipe, Tools	43
Carte De Visite, President Abraham Lincoln, Tintype, 1865	2500
Carte De Visite, President Andrew Johnson, 1860s	325
Carte De Visite, Robert E. Lee, Mathew Brady, Postwar Portrait, 1869	180
Carte De Visite, Samuel Colt, Inventor, Kellog Bros., Hartford, Conn., c.1860	1080
Carte De Visite, W.E. Dunlap, Co. G, 20th N.Y. Cavalry, Carbine & Sword	540
Carte De Visite, Washington Family	6
Daguerreotype, 3 Musicians, Brass Horns, Violin, Leather Case, 1/4 Plate	1599
Daguerreotype, Armed Man, Cincinnati, Leather Case, c.1845, 1/6 Plate	3000
Daguerreotype, Boy With A Squirrel, 1/6 Plate	2016

Phoenix Glass, Vase, Philodendron, White, Raised Leaves, Blue, c.1925, 11 1/4 In.

$150

Ruby Lane

Phonograph, Colombia, Graphophone, Red Horn, Yellow Flowers, Oak, 30 x 13 In.

$819

Fontaine's Auction Gallery

Phonograph Needle, Original Aeropoint Coin Machine Needle, Laurel Wreath, Black, 2 3/4 In.

$10

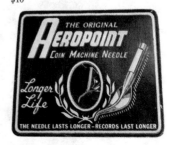

Ruby Lane

P

PHOTOGRAPHY

Photography, Ambrotype, Confederate Soldier, Musket, Bowie Knife, ¼ Plate
$8,625

James D. Julia Auctioneers

Photography, Cabinet Card, Annie Oakley, Holding Shotgun, Baker's Gallery, Ohio
$1,080

Cowan's Auctions

Photography, Cabinet Card, Annie Oakley, Little Sure Shot, Imprint, J. Wood, N.Y.
$1,920

Cowan's Auctions

Photography, Carte De Visite, Brigadier General George A. Custer, Portrait, 1864
$540

Cowan's Auctions

Photography, Photograph, Orotone, Chief Of The Desert, Portrait, Signed, Curtis, 10 x 8 in.
$9,000

Cowan's Auctions

Photography, Photogravure, Placating Spirit Of Slain Eagle, Curtis, E., Frame, 1926, 28 x 22 In.
$1,045

Cowan's Auctions

Daguerreotype, Daniel Webster, Secretary Of State, 1851	2016
Daguerreotype, Dionysos At The Met, ½ Plate	588
Daguerreotype, Eli Whitney Jr., Pressed Flower Case, c.1847, ¼ Plate	3000
Daguerreotype, First Presbyterian Church, Niagara Falls, N.Y., c.1880, ½ Plate	4320
Daguerreotype, Game Of Chess, ¼ Plate	3696
Daguerreotype, Greig Hall Mansion, Group, Urn, ½ Plate	2072
Daguerreotype, Lawrence S. Babbitt, Civil & Indian War Officer, ⅙ Plate	270
Daguerreotype, Military Band Musician, ¼ Plate	1568
Daguerreotype, Militiaman, Plumed Hat, Eagle Insignia, 1840s, ⅙ Plate	1152
Daguerreotype, Mother & Daughter, 1840s, ½ Plate	448
Daguerreotype, Musical Band, Guitar, 2 Fiddles, ¼ Plate	952
Daguerreotype, Mustached Man, Clenched Fist, Russia, ⅙ Plate	504
Daguerreotype, The Violinist, ⅙ Plate	616
Daguerreotype, Woman With Cat In Lap, c.1880, ⅙ Plate	886
Daguerreotype, Woman With Parrot, Late 1800s, ⅙ Plate	8280
Daguerreotype, Young Squirrel Hunter & His Dog, 1800s, ⅙ Plate	960
Photograph, Bettie Page & Tiger, Bikini, Signed, H. Sorayana, 17 x 24 In.	253
Photograph, Chief Crow, Sioux Crier, Custer Fight, Mount, D. Barry, 6 x 4 In.	432
Photograph, Civil War Union Soldiers, Tent, Sepia, c.1862, 4 x 7 In.	190
Photograph, Clark Gable, Portrait, Profile, Black & White, 10 x 13 In.	403
Photograph, Gary Cooper, Portrait, Black & White, c.1931, 8 x 10 In.	240
Photograph, Henry Hull, Werewolf Of London, Matt, 1935, 8 x 10 In.	306
Photograph, Nalte, San Carlos Apache Chief, Dude, Ben Wittick, N.M.	1402
Photograph, Orotone, Chief Of The Desert, Portrait, Signed, Curtis, 10 x 8 in. ....*illus*	9000
Photograph, Orotone, The Vanishing Race, Sheriff, Curtis, 1904, 11 x 14 In.	4250
Photograph, U.S.M.C. Infantry, Okinawa Battle, Black & White, 1945, 3 x 4 In.	475
Photograph, View Of Hostile Indian Camp, Wounded Knee, 1891, 9 x 6 In.	677
Photograph, Wild Men Of Borneo, Waino & Plutano, Sideshow, c.1880, 4 x 3 In.	185
Photogravure, Placating Spirit Of Slain Eagle, Curtis, E., Frame, 1926, 28 x 22 In. ....*illus*	1045
Photogravure, The Vanishing Race, E. Curtis, Velum, 1907, 15 x 18 In.	2880
Salt Print, B. McCulloch, Texas Ranger, Confederate General, c.1860, 6 x 8 In.	1920
Salt Print, Fireman Foreman, No. 2	364
Silver Gelatin Print, U. S. Airship, Frame, M. Bourke-White, 1931, 13 x 19 In. ....*illus*	2000
Silver Print, Buffalo Bill Cody, Studio Portrait, Gessford, 13 x 16 In.	1872
Silver Print, Custer's Scout, Curley Holding Rifle Outside, 6 x 8 In.	984
Silver Print, Ferry Landing, Baton Rouge, T.F. Winans, 1938, 16 x 20 In.	1750
Silver Print, Franklin D. Roosevelt, At Desk, Signed, c.1934, 18 x 20 In.	400
Silver Print, Geronimo & Other Apache Prisoners, c.1890, 6 ½ x 4 In.	2160
Silver Print, Juniper, Lake Tenaya, E. Weston, Print C. Weston, 1937, 9 x 7 In.	5000
Silver Print, Marilyn Monroe, At Circus, H. Leonard, 1953, 13 x 10 ½ In.	937
Silver Print, Prairie Gun Club Of Columbus, Nebraska, c.1900, 10 x 12 In.	270
Silver Print, Right Of Assembly, Cadillac Square, Detroit, 1939, Print 1977	9500
Silver Print, Rough Riders, Theodore Roosevelt, Gordon Johnston, 8 x 6 In.	960
Tintype, B. McCulloch, Confederate General, Paper Case, ⅑ Plate	3000
Tintype, Bar At Grey's Creek, 18 x 22 In.	616
Tintype, Civil War Drummer, Pemberton, c.1860, ¼ Plate	600
Tintype, Civil War, Zouave, 46th Indiana Infantry, Paper Case, ⅙ Plate	840
Tintype, Lieutenant J. Gardner, 101st Pennsylvania Volunteers, ⅙ Plate	330
Tintype, Sgt. John S. Jacobs, Armed, Volunteers, Gettysburg, ⅙ Plate	720

PIANO BABY is a collector's term. About 1880, the well-decorated home had a shawl on the piano. Bisque figures of babies were designed to help hold the shawl in place. They usually range in size from 6 to 18 inches. Most of the figures were made in Germany. Reproductions are being made. Other piano babies may be listed under manufacturers' names.

Baby, Grumpy, Pouting, Cracked Egg, Blond Hair, Fists, 6 In.	328
Baby, Holding Toe, Blue Hat, Bisque, Heubach, 11 In.	84
Baby, In Cradle, Holding Rattle, Blue Pillow, Blanket, Pink Bows, 6 In.	85
Baby, On Back, Holding Toes, Bonnet, Gebruder Heubach, 7 ½ x 11 In. ....*illus*	281
Boy, Chubby, Reclining, Pajamas, Ruffle Collar, Rabbit, Cat, Beading, 6 In.	255

Photography, Silver Gelatin Print, U. S. Airship, Frame, M. Bourke-White, 1931, 13 x 19 In.
$2,000

New Orleans Auction Galleries

Piano Baby, Baby, On Back, Holding Toes, Bonnet, Gebruder Heubach, 7 ½ x 11 In.
$281

Alderfer Auction Company

Pickard, Vase, Poinsettia, Hand Painted, Iridescent Ground, Porcelaingilber, 11 ½ In.
$118

Richard D. Hatch & Associates

Picture, Beadwork, Glass Beads, Silk, Sacrifice Of Isaac, Sword, Frame, c.1650, 16 x 20 In.
$6,250

Garth's Auctioneers & Appraisers

Picture, Immortal Group, Painted Faces, Kingfisher Feathers, Chinese, c.1890, 12 x 10 In.
$968

James D. Julia Auctioneers

Picture, Ink On Paper, Indian On The Move, Indian On Horseback, E. Borein, 8 x 10 in.
$338

Cowan's Auctions

Beadwork Roses
Victorian beadwork picturing roses is the highest priced. Other flowers are less popular with collectors.

Picture, Lithograph, Seneca Chief Red Jacket, Peace Medal, S.F. Bradford, Pa., Frame, 19 x 16 In.
$30

Hess Auction Group

Picture, Needlework, Memorial, Silk, Paint, Woman, 8 Year Old, Girl, Frame, c.1815, 20 x 15 In.
$720

Garth's Auctioneers & Appraisers

Picture, Scherenschnitte, Cut Paper, Men, Eagles, Flags, Frame, Pa., c.1800, 13 x 10 In.
$570

Cowan's Auctions

Picture, Scroll, Hanging, Ink & Color, On Paper, Scholars, Dragon, Chinese, 50 x 24 In.
$492

Skinner, Inc.

Picture, Silhouette, Music Room Scene, Family, Piano, Signed, P. Lord, 1839, 7 x 9 In.
$533

James D. Julia Auctioneers

Picture, Stumpwork, Silk, Metallic Braid, Couple, Field, Frame, c.1650, 13 x 17 In.
$7,920

Garth's Auctioneers & Appraisers

Boy, Playing Mandolin, French Dandy, Blue Hat, Pillar, Pedestal, 14 In.	300
Boy, Seated, Thumb In Mouth, Green Hat, Feather, Nightshirt, Beading, 6 In.	99
Boy, Sitting, Black Robe, Red Flowers, Japan, 10 x 6 In.	8
Boy, Sitting, Blue Collar, Apple, Hat, Bisque, 12 x 7 In., Pair	57
Girl, Crawling, Blond Hair, Blue Eyes, Pink Gown, 6 In.	65
Girl, Dancing, Blond Hair, Intaglio Eyes, Blue Pleated Dress, 10 In.	499
Girl, Seated, Removing Socks, Pink Sunbonnet, Blond Hair, Smiling, 6 In.	195
Girl, Sitting, Hat, Sucking On Finger, Red Ruffle, Bisque, c.1875, 11 ½ In.	36
Girl, Sitting, Hat, Sucking On Finger, Ruffle, Bisque, c.1875, 11 x 6 In., Pair	48
Girl, Sitting, Playing With Sock, Conta & Boehme, Germany, 11 In.	96

PICKARD China Company was started in 1893 by Wilder Pickard. Hand-painted designs were used on china purchased from other sources. In the 1930s, the company began to make its own china wares in Chicago, Illinois. The company now makes many types of porcelains, including a successful line of limited edition collector plates.

Bowl, Sprigs & Berries, Footed, Platinum, 24K Gold, Footed, Hiecke, c.1914, 7 In.	219
Dish, Lobed, Green, Gold, 1925-30, 8 ½ In.	86
Pitcher, Art Nouveau, Red Poppies, Gilt Handle, Signed Gasper, 6 In.	215
Pitcher, Gold Leaves, Vines & Grapes, Crimson Red, Black Ground, 11 In.	514
Tankard, Roses, Multicolor, Gold Trim, Signed, Burton, 11 In.	360
Vase, Gilt, Edgerton Pattern, Gold, Blue Bands, White Flowers, 7 x 2 In.	61
Vase, Poinsettia, Hand Painted, Iridescent Ground, Porcelaingilber, 11 ½ In. *illus*	118

PICTURES, silhouettes, and other small decorative objects framed to hang on the wall are listed here. Some other types of pictures are listed in the Print and Painting categories.

Beadwork, Glass Beads, Silk, Sacrifice Of Isaac, Sword, Frame, c.1650, 16 x 20 In. *illus*	6250
Engraving, 2 Men, Monk's Gravestone, Epitaph, England, c.1785, 9 x 7 In.	25
Engraving, Copper, Paper, Indian Warriors, Tattoos, Bow & Arrow, c.1828, 6 x 9 In.	150
Etching, On Paper, Springtime In Kentucky, Cottage, Signed, Frame, 8 x 10 In.	180
Etching, Woman, Walking Away, Hat, Dress, Holding Umbrella, c.1900, 12 x 5 In.	1230
Gold & Color On Paper, Sagittarius, Birds, Geometric Border, Frame, 10 x 12 In.	615
Gouache On Board, Covered Bridge, Frame, Signed, L. Cope, 1971, 18 x 24 In.	1020
Gouache On Paper, Abstract, Signed, R. Natkin, Frame, Under Glass, 24 x 19 In.	360
Gouache On Paper, Parrot, Frame, Signed, My Bird, Carrie W. Clark, 1852, 8 x 7 In.	480
Hairwork, Plaque, Wreath & Harp, Mother-Of-Pearl, Frame, c.1885, 14 x 12 In.	102
Immortal Group, Painted Faces, Kingfisher Feathers, Chinese, c.1890, 12 x 10 In. *illus*	968
Ink On Fabric, Geese & Reeds, Dry Brushwork, c.1800, 12 x 9 In.	861
Ink On Paper, Buddha, Lotus Throne, Inscription, Black, Gold, Frame, 51 x 23 In.	1353
Ink On Paper, Colors, Fan, Figures, Horse, Inscribed, Frame, 8 x 20 In.	677
Ink On Paper, His Move, Man & Woman, Kiss, Signed, 13 x 19 In.	240
Ink On Paper, Indian On The Move, Indian On Horseback, E. Borein, 8 x 10 In. *illus*	338
Ink On Paper, Rubbing, Landscape, Courtyard Scene, Houses & Lake, 33 x 72 In.	154
Ink On Silk, 2 Puppies, Playing, Field, Dandelions, Frame, c.1900, 16 x 19 In.	185
Ink On Silk, Blue Mountain, Pavilions & Pine Trees, Frame, 13 x 13 In.	1353
Lithograph, Automaton, Old Couple, Nod, Open Box, Cat, Germany, c.1910, 17 In.	819
Lithograph, Seneca Chief Red Jacket, Peace Medal, S.F. Bradford, Pa., Frame, 19 x 16 In. *illus*	30
Lithograph, Wall Hanging, Noah's Sacrifice Altar, For The Lord, c.1905, 16 x 19 In.	115
Miniature, On Bone, 18th Century Woman, Oval, Braided Hair, Frame, 1790s, 2 In.	560
Needlework, Cross-Stitch, Linen, Abstract Flowers, Morocco, c.1900, 17 x 87 In.	1125
Needlework, Cross-Stitch, Linen, Shapes, Red, Gold, Morocco, c.1900, 36 x 115 In.	1187
Needlework, Embroidery, Church, Trees, Landscape, Paint, Mat, Frame, 6 x 8 In.	312
Needlework, Embroidery, Eagle, American Flag & Shield, c.1900, 20 x 16 In.	420
Needlework, Embroidery, Farm, Applique, Figures, Sheep, Frame, c.1800, 12 x 14 In.	1107
Needlework, Embroidery, Flower Sprigs, Buds, Frame, c.1886, 12 x 10 In., Pair	356
Needlework, Embroidery, Silk, Dove, Burning Heart, Frame, c.1810, 7 x 5 In.	60
Needlework, Embroidery, Silk, Heron, Deities, Gold Thread, c.1890, 88 x 59 In.	3851
Needlework, Embroidery, Silk, Peacock, Fanned Tail, Frame, c.1900, 15 x 17 In.	185
Needlework, Embroidery, Wool, Ship, British & U.S. Flags, Frame, 1800s, 12 x 15 In.	154

TIP

Cover the nose of your hammer with a piece of felt to protect the wall when you are putting up picture hooks.

Picture, Theorem, Oil On Velvet, Fruit Basket, Gilt Frame, c.1835, 13 x 15 ½ In. **$360**

Garth's Auctioneers & Appraisers

Picture, Wall Sculpture, Metal, Paint, Arrow & Circle Shapes, Curtis Jere, Signed, 24 x 46 In. **$210**

Cowan's Auctions

Picture, Watercolor, Bird On Mound, Flowers, Heart, E.Y. Ellinger, Frame, 6 x 5 ¾ In. **$274**

Hess Auction Group

P

PICTURE

Picture, Watercolor, Woman, Blue Gown, Book & Bag, Rug, Frame, c.1840, 10 x 8 In.
$523

Skinner, Inc.

Picture, Watercolor, Woman, Wedding, Folk Art, Frame, J. Maentel, c.1840, 9 x 7 In.
$2,400

Cowan's Auctions

Picture, Wax, Portrait, Gen. George Washington, Gilt Molded Frame, Patience Wright, 15 x 13 In.
$708

Hess Auction Group

Needlework, Fisherman, Basket On Pole, Lantern, Japan, 16 x 13 In., Pair	812
Needlework, Maritime, Ship, Royal Crown, Flags, Frame, 1800s, 14 x 15 In.	308
Needlework, Memorial, Silk, Paint, Woman, 8 Year Old, Girl, Frame, c.1815, 20 x 15 In. ....*illus*	720
Needlework, Mermaid, Merman, Stumpwork, Velvet, Frame, c.1700, 8 x 11 In.	720
Needlework, Parrot, Tree, Leafy Branches, Silk, Blue, Frame, 1800s, 12 x 9 In.	2100
Needlework, Peacock, On Branch, Dog, Silk On Silk, Frame, 1800s, 12 x 9 In.	240
Needlework, Red House, No Place Like My Father's House, 1880, 9 x 12 In.	369
Needlework, Woman, Mourning, Grave, Willow Tree, S. Richmond, 1806, 20 x 17 In.	1476
Pastel, On Paper, Portrait, Child Holding Doll, Cane, Frame, 1800s, 23 x 18 In.	154
Pen & Ink, W.S. Trigg Saddlery Co., Paris, Texas, Frame, c.1880s, 16 x 20 In.	90
Scherenschnitte, Cut Paper, Men, Eagles, Flags, Frame, Pa., c.1800, 13 x 10 In. ....*illus*	570
Scroll, Hanging, Ink & Color, On Paper, Scholars, Dragon, Chinese, 50 x 24 In. ....*illus*	492
Silhouette, Ink On Paper, Girl, Doll, Caroline Stevenson, 6 Years, 1844, 8 x 6 In.	1200
Silhouette, Ink On Paper, Man, Woman In Rocker, Ashton Family, 1842, 11 x 14 In.	720
Silhouette, Music Room Scene, Family, Piano, Signed, P. Lord, 1839, 7 x 9 In. ....*illus*	533
Silhouette, Standing Man, Top Hat, Watercolor & Graphite, England, 12 x 8 In.	122
Stumpwork, Silk, Metallic Braid, Couple, Field, Frame, c.1650, 13 x 17 In. ....*illus*	7920
Thangka, Deity, Seated, In Dhyanasana, Palace, Red, Blue, Gold, Tibet, 49 x 37 In.	1185
Thangka, Padmasambhave, Seated, Lotus Throne, River, Frame, 31 x 23 In.	1778
Theorem, Fruit Basket, Flowers In Pitcher, Angel, Frame, 1812, 20 x 15 In.	2370
Theorem, Fruit Basket, On Greenery, Maine, c.1830, 14 x 16 In.	4920
Theorem, Oil, On Velvet, Fruit Basket, Gilt Frame, c.1835, 13 x 15 ½ In. ....*illus*	360
Theorem, Watercolor, Ink, On Velvet, Grieving Woman, Frame, c.1810, 17 x 19 In.	390
Wall Sculpture, Metal, Paint, Arrow & Circle Shapes, Curtis Jere, Signed, 24 x 46 In. ......*illus*	210
Watercolor & Gouache, Mississippi Steamboats, Frame, Signed, 1905, 20 x 29 In.	1187
Watercolor & Ink, Family Group, Military Man, Woman, Child, Verse, 8 x 7 In.	338
Watercolor & Oil, Baby In Crib, Flowered Gown, Frame, 1800s, 11 x 8 In.	1845
Watercolor, Bird On Mound, Flowers, Heart, E.Y. Ellinger, Frame, 6 x 5 ¾ In. ....*illus*	274
Watercolor, Courting Couple, Tree, Bench, Balustrade, Frame, c.1825, 13 x 17 In.	18450
Watercolor, Gouache, Villa Reale, Naples Coast, Boats, Italy, c.1820, 12 x 17 In.	246
Watercolor, Harvest Scene, Gilt Frame, Signed, Addison Millar, 14 x 18 In.	360
Watercolor, Miniature, Procession Scene, Elephants, Inscription, 1800s, 4 x 3 In.	90
Watercolor, Morgan County, Signed, William Forsyth, Frame, c.1900, 21 x 14 In.	720
Watercolor, Mourning, Grieving Parents, Monument, A. Stockwell, 11 x 12 In.	861
Watercolor, Needlework, Silk, Figures, Forest Scene, Fame, 1800s, 19 x 16 In.	180
Watercolor, Portrait, Girl, Holding Dog In Arms, Frame, c.1850, 6 x 5 In.	185
Watercolor, Portrait, Indian Chief, Headdress, Signed, c.1965, 19 x 14 In.	840
Watercolor, The Brulatour Courtyard, E. Loving, Frame, c.1950, 14 x 10 In.	120
Watercolor, Woman At Harbor, Ships, Dove, Olive Branch, c.1825, 16 x 14 In.	2091
Watercolor, Woman, Blue Gown, Book & Bag, Rug, Frame, c.1840, 10 x 8 In. ....*illus*	523
Watercolor, Woman, Mask, Masquerade Ball, Signed, 1893, 13 x 10 In.	1400
Watercolor, Woman, Wedding, Folk Art, Frame, J. Maentel, c.1840, 9 x 7 In. ....*illus*	2400
Wax, Portrait, Gen. George Washington, Gilt Molded Frame, Patience Wright, 15 x 13 In. .*illus*	708
Woolwork, Flower Wreath, Multicolor, Black Ground, Shadowbox Frame, 1800s, 19 x 15 In. .*illus*	160

PIERCE, *see Howard Pierce category.*

PIGEON FORGE POTTERY was started in Pigeon Forge, Tennessee, in 1946. Red clay found near the pottery was used to make the pieces. Molded or thrown pottery with matte glaze and slip decoration was made. The pottery closed in 2000.

Figurine, Racoon, Stylized, Cream, Brown Eyes, Signed, 6 x 8 ½ In.	265

PILKINGTON TILE AND POTTERY COMPANY was established in 1892 in England. The company made small pottery wares, like buttons and hatpins, but soon started decorating vases purchased from other potteries. By 1903, the company had discovered an opalescent glaze that became popular on the Lancastrian pottery line. The manufacture of pottery ended in 1937. Pilkington's Tiles Ltd. has worked from 1938 to the present.

Vase, Blue Chameleons, Royal Lancastrian, c.1905, 5 x 5 In.	2500

Vase, Lancastrian, Leaves, Red, Green, Blue, Copper Luster, 1927, 4 x 6 In.	1500
Vase, Leaves, Multicolor, Royal Lancastrian, William Mycock, 1927, 4 x 5 In.	1560
Vase, Lions, Apple Trees, Royal Lancastrian, Impressed, 1910, 14 x 9 In. ....*illus*	5000
Vase, Lions, Luster, Royal Lancastrian, Richard Joyce, 1926, 11 x 6 ½ In.	750
Vase, Lions, Roses, Turquoise, Lancastrian, Swollen Shoulder, 8 x 5 In.	1375
Vase, Lions, Royal Lancastrian, Gordon Forsyth, 1910, 14 x 9 ½ In.	5200
Vase, Red Flowers, Royal Lancastrian, Marked R, 8 x 7 In.	375

PILLIN pottery was made by Polia (1909–1992) and William (1910–1985) Pillin, who set up a pottery in Los Angeles in 1948. William shaped, glazed, and fired the clay, and Polia painted the pieces, often with elongated figures of women, children, flowers, birds, fish, and other animals. Pieces are marked with a stylized Pillin signature.

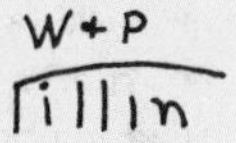

W + P
Pillin

Bowl, 2 Bulls, Blue, 2-Tone Ground, 7 x 3 In.	499
Bowl, 2 Bulls, Multicolor, Blue Ground, Signed, 2 x 6 ¾ In. ....*illus*	295
Bowl, 5 Horses, Tan, Orange, 6 ¼ In.	425
Bowl, Prancing Horses, Yellow, Red Interior, Round, Tapered, Square Rim, 5 In.	295
Box, Lid, Woman, Playing Lute, Green, Pink, Rounded Sides, 2 ½ x 5 ½ In.	295
Brushpot, Stylized Woman, Horse, Bird, Stippled Glaze, 4 ½ x 4 In.	1535
Plate, 2 Women, Horse, Damsel, Yellow Ground, 5 ¼ In.	365
Plate, Diamond Shape, Raised Rim, Seated Woman, Birds At Feet, Blue, 7 x 6 In.	450
Plate, Woman, White Dress, Holding Red Bird, Horses, Cobalt Blue, Square, 9 In.	177
Tray, Fish, Pale Blue Mottled Ground, Multicolor Glaze, Rim, 1 x 6 In.	130
Tray, Woman, Holding Flowers, Blue, Green, Red, Rounded Corners, 13 x 3 In.	295
Tray, Woman, Seated, Welcoming Friend, Tan, Cream, Maroon, 5 x 5 In.	245
Vase, 2 Women, Stylized White Horses, Tapered, Rectangular, 6 ½ x 4 ½ In.	1950
Vase, Black Luster Glaze, Rainbow Swirl Dip, 6 ¾ In.	324
Vase, Bottle, Gold Luster, Black Top, Rainbow Bottom, 6 ¾ In.	316
Vase, Boy Holding Fish, 2 Girls Dancing, Tricornered, Signed, 4 ½ In. ....*illus*	177
Vase, Fuchsia & Green Streak Glaze, Encircling Fish, Bulbous, Tubular Neck, 4 In.	384
Vase, Genie Style, Birds, 3 ¼ In.	328
Vase, Horse & Rider, Blue To Purple, Mottled Glaze, Red, Cobalt Blue, Square, 9 In.	384
Vase, Orange, 2 Female Faces, Pink Hair, Horse, Polia Pillin, 5 x 9 In.	389
Vase, Pale Green, Orange Speckles, Swirls, Shouldered, Pinched Neck, 3 In.	189
Vase, Portrait, Woman, Birds, Yellow, Square, Tapered Stick Neck, Flared Rim, 7 In.	325
Vase, Woman, Bird On Finger, Man, Outstretched Arms, Triangular Rim, 5 x 3 In.	325
Vase, Woman, Bird, Jockey, Horse, Blue, 12 In.	1003
Vase, Women, Netting Fish, Cylindrical, Blue, Tan, 9 In.	995

PINCUSHION DOLLS are not really dolls and often were not even pincushions. Some collectors use the term "half-doll." The top half of each doll was made of porcelain. The edge of the half-doll was made with several small holes for thread, and the doll was stitched to a fabric body with a voluminous skirt. The finished figure was used to cover a hot pot of tea, powder box, pincushion, whiskbroom, or lamp. They were made in sizes from less than an inch to over 9 inches high. Most date from the early 1900s to the 1950s. Collectors often find just the porcelain doll without the fabric skirt.

Bisque, Jointed Arms, Mohair Wig, Germany, c.1900, 6 x 3 In.	66
Woman, Dutch Hat, Pink Rose, Blue & Pink Dress, Heubach, 1920s, 5 In.	165
Woman, Flapper, Cloche Hat, Hand On Hip, Purple, 1920s, 4 ¼ In.	140
Woman, Gray Updo, Holding Fan, Full Skirt, 7 In.	110

PIPES have been popular since tobacco was introduced to Europe by Sir Walter Raleigh. Carved wood, porcelain, ivory, and glass pipes and accessories may be listed here.

Box, Wood, Stained, Backplate, Urn Crest, Dovetailed Drawer, 1800s, 19 ¼ In.	4200
Bronze, Bowl, Mythological Animal, 3 x 3 In.	70
Catlinite Stone, 2 Parts, Cylindrical, Carved Eagle, Seated, 18 In.	118

Fake Pillin
Fakes of Pillin Pottery are not uncommon. Experts say they are being made in Texas and sold online. The forgeries have the same scene on both sides of the vase. Pillin used different scenes. Fakes are heavy, the artwork crude. The mark is painted on the bottom, not incised.

Picture, Woolwork, Flower Wreath, Multicolor, Black Ground, Shadowbox Frame, 1800s, 19 x 15 In. $160

Neal Auctions

Pilkington, Vase, Lions, Apple Trees, Royal Lancastrian, Impressed, 1910, 14 x 9 In. $5,000

Rago Arts and Auction Center

P

Pillin, Bowl, 2 Bulls, Multicolor, Blue Ground, Signed, 2 x 6¾ In. $295

Humler & Nolan

Pillin, Vase, Boy Holding Fish, 2 Girls Dancing, Tricornered, Signed, 4½ In. $177

Humler & Nolan

Pipe, Folk Art, Bull Run, Laurel Root, Civil War, Young Woman's Face, Pewter, 2¾ In. $1,440

Cowan's Auctions

Folk Art, Bull Run, Laurel Root, Civil War, Young Woman's Face, Pewter, 2¾ In. ....*illus*	1440
Folk Art, Carved, Civil War Soldier, Beard, 3 Removable Sections, 7 x 4 In. ....*illus*	660
Meerschaum, Cheroot Holder, R.W. Tansil & Co., c.1875, 2 x 4½ In.	177
Meerschaum, Eagle Claw, 4 In.	35
Meerschaum, Native American, Wolf, Deer, Case, 1800s, 6 In.	212
Meerschaum, Skull In Hand, 1800s, Case, 13 In.	937
Meerschaum, Tattooed Moor, Woman, Case, 11½ In.	1875
Meerschaum, Union General Winfield Scott Hancock, 1800s, 8½ In.	937
Pipe Rack, Tiger Maple, Brass Pipe Support, Urn Stem, 5 Pipes, 1800s, 23 In.	225
Porcelain, Regimental, Garde Regt. Berlin, 1905-07, Helmet Cover, Tassel, 60 In.	168
Redware, Molded, President Franklin Pierce, 1800s, 2¼ In.	83

PIRKENHAMMER is a porcelain manufactory started in 1803 by Friedrich Holke and J. G. Lilst. It was located in Bohemia, now Brezova, Czech Republic. The company made tablewares usually decorated with views and flowers. Lithophanes were also made. The mark of the crossed hammers is easy to remember as the Pirkenhammer symbol.

Bowl, Basket Weave, Flowers, Open Handles, Gilt Trim, 10 x 8 x 2 In.	35
Figurine, Dog, English Setter, Pointing, 9 In.	199
Vase, Birds, Arts & Crafts, Sided, c.1910, 5½ x 3¼ In.	175
Vase, Gilt, Rosettes, Reticulated, Blue Bands, Flower Holders, 19¼ x 13 In. ....*illus*	1537

PISGAH FOREST POTTERY was made in North Carolina beginning in 1926. The pottery was started by Walter B. Stephen, who had been making pottery in that location since 1914. The pottery continued in operation after his death in 1961. The most famous kinds of Pisgah Forest ware are the cameo type with designs made of raised glaze and the turquoise crackle glaze wares.

Bowl, Cobalt Blue, Masonic, 2 x 5 In.	23
Pitcher, Covered Wagon, Horse, Man, Olive Green, Blue, 5½ In.	125
Pitcher, Turquoise Blue, Crackle Glaze, Pink Interior, 1942, 8½ x 5 In.	145
Vase, Blue Green, 9¼ In.	175
Vase, Turquoise Blue, Crackle Glaze, Pink Interior, 1939, 6 In.	85
Vase, Yellow Dip, Blue Crystals, Brown Glossy Glaze, 1945, 5½ In.	130

PLANTERS PEANUTS memorabilia are collected. Planters Nut and Chocolate Company was started in Wilkes-Barre, Pennsylvania, in 1906. The Mr. Peanut figure was adopted as a trademark in 1916. National advertising for Planters Peanuts started in 1918. The company was acquired by Standard Brands, Inc., in 1961. Standard Brands merged with Nabisco in 1981. Some of the Mr. Peanut jars and other memorabilia have been reproduced and, of course, new items are being made.

Costume, Mr. Peanut, Papier-Mache, Top Hat, Armholes, 44 In.	738
Display Bars, Planters, 5 Cent, Jumbo Block Candy Bars, 2 x 4½ In.	71
Figure, Mr. Peanut, Hard Plastic, Walks, Windup, 1950s, 8½ In.	190
Jar, 8 x 12 In.	146
Jar, Fish, Salted Peanuts, Glass Globe, Metal Lid, 1929, 6 x 5 In.	115
Jar, Glass, Molded Mr. Peanut, 5 Cents, Salted, Lid, Nut Finial, 1970s, 12 In.	65
Jar, Peanut Butter, Paper Label, Green & Red, c.1930s, 4¾ x 3 In.	1428
Peanut Butter Maker, Figural Mr. Peanut, Crank, Box, 1967, 8 x 11 In.	115
Stringholder, Planters Cocktail Peanuts, Mr. Peanut, Chalkware, 1950s	450
Tin, Pennant, Green, Red, 1906, 8¼ x 9 In. ....*illus*	145

PLASTIC objects of all types are being collected. Some pieces are listed in other categories; gutta-percha cases are listed in the Photography category. Celluloid is in its own category.

Canister, Flour, Red & White, Square, Rounded Corners, Lustroware, 1960s, 8 x 6 In.	32
Container, Swan Shape, Translucent Pink Lucite, Regaline, 6 x 8½ x 5½ In.	18
Ice Bucket, Blue, White, Faux Padded, Bail Handle, Lid, Lustroware, 1960s, 13 In.	28
Magazine Rack, G. Stoppino, Kartell, Italy, Mid 1900s, 14 x 15 x 7 In., Pair	98

Picnic Set, Plates, Teapot & Service, Red, Flowers, Wood Basket, Germany	62
Recipe Card Box, Tan, Gold, Rounded Flip Lid, 1950s	32
Salt & Pepper, Red & Black, Hexagonal, Dome Tops, 1930s, 2 ¼ In.	39
Sculpture, Dog, White, Seated, His Master's Voice, 36 In.	192
Serving Set, Acrylic, Tray, Spoon, Dip, Cloverware, Hungary, 14 x 14 In., 3 Piece	6000
Tray, Beverage, 6 Different Colored Recessed Slots For Glasses, 11 ¼ In.	12
Tray, Giltwood, Mod Orange Flower, Round, Japan, 1970s, 13 In., Pair	24
Vase, Injection Molded, Philippe Starck & Eugeni Quitlet, Italy, 24 x 64 In., Pair	300
Vase, Molded Basket Weave, 9 x 5 ¼ In.	12
Vase, Woven Plastic Over Glass, Green & Pink, Birds, c.1950s, 8 x 3 In.	29

PLATED AMBERINA was patented June 15, 1886, by Joseph Locke and made by the New England Glass Company. It is similar in color to amberina, but is characterized by a cream colored or chartreuse lining (never white) and small ridges or ribs on the outside.

Cruet, Ribbed, Tricorner Rim, Faceted Amber Stopper, Handle, 6 In.	*illus*	2950
Lemonade Cup, Ribbed, Straight-Sided, Low Amber Handle, 5 In.		1778
Punch Cup, Mahogany, Custard, Ribbed, Curling, Handle, 2 ½ In.	*illus*	2645

PLIQUE-A-JOUR is an enameling process. The enamel is laid between thin raised metal lines and heated. The finished piece has transparent enamel held between the thin metal wires. It is different from cloisonne because it is translucent.

Bowl, 6 Panels, Fish Scales, Flowers, Purple, Pink, Green, 4 x 7 In.		177
Bowl, Dragonflies, Cattails, 4 ¾ In.		125
Case, Green, Flowers, Red Berries, 9 ½ In.		625
Jar, Flower Petals, Multicolor, 5 ¼ In.		238
Salt, Spoon, Silver Gilt, Jacob Tostrup, Norway, 3 In., 2 Piece	*illus*	240
Spoon, Leaf Shape, Pale Blue, Gold Veins, Red Flowers On Handle, 4 In.		115

POLITICAL memorabilia of all types, from buttons to banners, are collected. Items related to presidential candidates are the most popular, but collectors also search for material related to state and local offices. Memorabilia related to social causes, minor political parties, and protest movements are also included here. Many reproductions have been made. A jugate is a button with photographs of both the presidential and vice presidential candidates. In this list a button is round, usually with a straight pin or metal tab to secure it to a shirt. A pin is brass, often figural, sometimes attached to a ribbon.

Armband, Votes For Women, Felt, Yellow, Brown, 1 ¼ x 24 In.		222
Badge, Campaign, Ben Butler, Workingman's Friend, Photo, Spoon Pin, 1884		2950
Badge, Company C, Blaine & Logan Club, Portrait, Tassels, c.1884, 3 x 8 In.		475
Badge, Harrison, Portrait, Engraved Brass, Diamond Shape, Flowers, c.1890, 1 In.		190
Badge, Jefferson, Portrait, Press, 1920 Democratic Convention, San Francisco		100
Badge, McKinley, Portrait, An Honest Dollar, Brass, Eagle, c.1896, 5 x 7 In.		115
Badge, McKinley, Portrait, Wisconsin Delegations, 1896 Convention, Celluloid		250
Badge, McKinley, Roosevelt, Bryan, Stevenson, Aluminum, Mechanical, 2 In.		224
Badge, Young Men's Republican Club, Baltimore, 1896 St. Louis Convention		300
Ballot Box, Mahogany, 1800s, 10 ½ x 13 In.		173
Bank, Do As Coolidge Does Save, Ceramic Bust, Bronze Finish, 4 ½ In.		128
Banner, Stamp Out Fascism, Mussolini Head, Snake Body, 1930s, 24 x 32 In.		190
Banner, Stop Lynching, Shame Of America, Hand Holding Sign, 22 x 35 In.		987
Book, J. Edgar Hoover, Story Of The F.B.I., Signed, Hardbound, 1959, 7 x 10 In.		165
Button, Bryan, Anti-Expansion, Portrait, Liberty Figures, Celluloid, 1 ½ In.	*illus*	2832
Button, Bryan, No Cross Of Gold, No Crown Of Thorns, 1896, 1 In.		403
Button, Debs, Hanford, Portraits, Torch, Handshake Drawing, Jugate, 1904, 1 In.		696
Button, Debs, Seidel, Socialist Candidates, Portraits, Torch, Jugate, 1912, 1 ½ In.		5762
Button, Dukakis, Glenn, Proposed Ticket By Labor Union, Celluloid, 1988, 2 ½ In.	*illus*	1103
Button, Equal-Rights Now, Handshake, Red, White & Blue, c.1963, 3 ½ In.		443
Button, For President, Robert M. La Follette, Portrait, Lion Heads, 1908, 1 In.		1297
Button, Free Gene Debs, Floating Head Portrait, Black & White, c.1920, 1 In.		1755
Button, Get Your (Ass) Off The Grass, It's Dewy, Donkey, Whitehouse, 1 ¾ In.		460

Pipe, Folk Art, Carved, Civil War Soldier, Beard, 3 Removable Sections, 7 x 4 In.
$660

Cowan's Auctions

Pirkenhammer, Vase, Gilt, Rosettes, Reticulated, Blue Bands, Flower Holders, 19 ¼ x 13 In.
$1,537

Fontaine's Auction Gallery

Planters Peanuts, Tin, Pennant, Green, Red, 1906, 8 ¼ x 9 In.
$145

Ruby Lane

P

Plated Amberina, Cruet, Ribbed, Tricorner Rim, Faceted Amber Stopper, Handle, 6 In.
$2,950

Humler & Nolan

TIP
Condition, size, and small details determine the value of political buttons. To be sure the description is accurate for buying, selling, or insurance, just put the buttons on the glass top of a photocopying machine. Make copies of both the front and the back.

Plated Amberina, Punch Cup, Mahogany, Custard, Ribbed, Curling, Handle, 2½ In.
$2,645

Early Auction Company

Plique-A-Jour, Salt, Spoon, Silver Gilt, Jacob Tostrup, Norway, 3 In., 2 Piece
$240

Cowan's Auctions

Political, Button, Bryan, Anti-Expansion, Portrait, Liberty Figures, Celluloid, 1½ In.
$2,832

Anderson Americana

Political, Button, Dukakis, Glenn, Proposed Ticket By Labor Union, Celluloid, 1988, 2½ In.
$1,103

Anderson Americana

Political, Button, Kennedy For President, Celluloid, Pinback, Photograph, 1960, 3 In.
$384

Anderson Americana

Political, Button, Wilson, Marshall, Liberty Cap, Jugate, 1912, ⅞ In.
$620

Hake's Americana & Collectibles

Political, Figure, George Washington, Paint, Cast Lead, J.E. Brubaker, Pa.,
37 x 12 In.
$7,110

James D. Julia Auctioneers

Political, Medal, Peace, John Adams, Silver, Brass Beads, 1797, c.1975, 27 x 3 In.
$402

Allard Auctions

Button, Hands Off Ethiopia, Young Ethiopian Defenders, Tin Litho, 1930s, 1 In.	166
Button, Harding, Coolidge, Eagle, Sunburst, Flag, Celluloid, Jugate, 1¼ In.	2296
Button, Harvey Milk, For Supervisor, Blue & White, Celluloid, 1975, 1½ In.	115
Button, Honest Days With Davis, Teapot Dome, Black & White, ⅞ In.	1202
Button, I Like Ike, Metal Easel Back, Red, White, Black, 1952, 9 In.	2070
Button, Join The Jury, Panther Demonstration, Black Panther Party, 1970, 2 In.	324
Button, Kennedy For President, Celluloid, Pinback, Photograph, 1960, 3 In. .... *illus*	384
Button, Landon For President, Sunflower, Tan & Yellow, 1936, 2 In.	339
Button, McKinley, Map, Pro-Expansion, Liberty Figures, Celluloid, 1900, 1½ In.	2077
Button, McKinley, Roosevelt, Full Dinner Pail, Jugate, Portraits, 1900, 1¼ In.	834
Button, Parker, Davis, Lady Liberty, Portraits, Stars, Jugate, 1904, 1¼ In.	127
Button, Parker, Davis, Portraits, Jugate, Star Shape, Flag, Celluloid, 1904, 1½ In.	1265
Button, Prosperity With Roosevelt, Portrait, Flag, Yellow, Red, 1933, 1 In.	506
Button, Roosevelt, America Demands Him, Portrait, Black & White, Stars, 2 In.	348
Button, Roosevelt, Fairbanks, Oval Portraits, Flag, Jugate, c.1904, 1¼ In.	177
Button, Roosevelt, Hat In The Ring, Hat, Black & White, Celluloid, 1912, ⁷⁄₁₆ In.	184
Button, Roosevelt, Photo, Rough Rider, Goldtone Twist Frame, c.1904, 1¼ In.	316
Button, Roosevelt, San Juan, Rough Rider, Horse, Saluting, Flag, 1904, 1¼ In.	569
Button, Roosevelt, Stark, Jugate, Celluloid, St. Louis Button Co., 1937, ⅝ In.	2714
Button, Roosevelt, Welcome, Sunrise, Portrait, Uncle Sam, c.1910, 1¼ In.	2783
Button, Save The Scottsboro Boys, Hands Pulling Open Jail Doors, 1 In.	308
Button, Taft On Steamroller, Bells, Roosevelt Driving, Cartoon, 1908, 1¼ In.	1725
Button, Theodore Roosevelt, Remember San Juan Hill, Celluloid, c.1898, 2 In.	1955
Button, Truman, Portrait, Camden, 70 Percent Truman, Celluloid, 1948, 4½ In.	462
Button, We Rose With Roosevelt, Portrait, Fabric Rose, 1936, ¾ In.	304
Button, Welcome Home Elba, Roosevelt, Uncle Sam, Africa Return, 1¼ In.	575
Button, Willkie McNary & Chemurgy, Airplane, Factory, Crops, 1940, 1¼ In.	509
Button, Wilson, Marshall, Liberty Cap, Jugate, 1912, ⅞ In. .... *illus*	620
Button, Wilson, Marshall, Portraits In Shields, Flags, Jugate, 1912, 1¼ In.	1518
Button, Wilson, Marshall, Portraits, Blue, Filigree, Jugate, c.1912, 1¼ In.	173
Button, Wilson, Portrait, Stand By The President, Flag, Celluloid, 1916, 1¼ In.	345
Button, Woodrow Wilson, Portrait, Black & White, Glossy, c.1912, 1½ In.	918
Button, Youth For Kennedy, Senate Campaign, Photo, 1958, 2¼ In.	345
Cane, Grover Cleveland, Wood, Nickel Plated Bust Handle, c.1885, 33 In.	174
Cigar Box, Harrison, Morton, 1888 Presidential Campaign, Wood, 2 x 8 x 5 In.	177
Decal, Harding, Coolidge, Portraits, Constructive Americans, Eagle, 1920, 5 x 9 In.	645
Doll, Roosevelt, Rough Rider, Plaster, Papier-Mache, Gun, Hat, c.1900, 6 In.	633
Envelope, Presidential, Free Frank, Z. Taylor, Postmarked Free, Feb. 4, 1850	3250
Figure, Elephant, Land-On Roosevelt, Yellow, Red, Cast Iron, 1936, 2 x 5 In.	345
Figure, George Washington, Paint, Cast Lead, J.E. Brubaker, Pa., 37 x 12 In. .... *illus*	7110
Lantern, Paper, Grant, Wilson, Metal Candleholder, Blue, White, c.1872, 9 x 16 In.	152
License Plate Attachment, Metal, Diecast, Roosevelt, Garner, Happy Days, 7 In.	400
License Plate, Commemorative, John F. Kennedy, D.C., 1961, 12 x 6 In, Pair.	432
Match Safe, Benjamin Harrison, Profile, Figural, Bronze Tone Metal, 2 In.	145
Medal, Irish Easter Rising, Sean Cullen, Lieutenant, 3rd Battalion, Dublin Brigade	6500
Medal, Peace, John Adams, Silver, Brass Beads, 1797, c.1975, 27 x 3 In. .... *illus*	402
Palm Card, Vote For Jimmy Carter, State Senator, Portrait, 1962, 16 x 4 In.	196
Parasol, Jackson, Decatur, War Of 1812, Silk, Black, Horn Handle, Eagle	1500
Pendant, Henry Clay, Brass, Embossed Portrait, Flower Border, c.1845, 1 In.	279
Photograph, Theodore Roosevelt, Silver, Signed, Frame, 1913, 16 x 18 In. .... *illus*	2760
Photograph, U.S. Presidents, Nixon, Ford, Carter, Reagan, 1981, 8 x 10 In.	1476
Pillowcase, Generals Washington & Lee, Images, Frame, 1912, 30 In.	420
Pin, Al Smith, Derby Hat Shape, Brass, Portrait, Photo, 2 In.	288
Pin, Gold Bug, McKinley, Hobart, Photos, Wings, Mechanical, Brass, 1896, 2 In.	158 to 190
Pin, Parker, Portrait, Figural Rooster Top, Celluloid, Metal, 1904, 1 x 2 In.	1740
Pitcher, Ulysses S. Grant, Portrait, Relief Ribbon, Wreath, Majolica, c.1872, 10 In.	230
Placard, Honor King, End Racism!, Memphis Sanitation Workers, 12 x 20 In.	1150
Plaque, Lenin, 4 Bolshevik Leaders, Portraits, Celluloid, Easel, c.1930, 6 x 8 In.	196
Plate, Eagle, Presidential, Benjamin Harrison, Gilt, Limoges, c.1892, 8½ In. .... *illus*	1187
Plate, President Garfield, Frosted, Profile, Glass, 6 In.	90
Plate, White House China, Abraham Lincoln, Haviland, Limoges, c.1861, 7 In. .... *illus*	8400

Political, Photograph, Theodore
Roosevelt, Silver, Signed, Frame, 1913,
16 x 18 In.
$2,760

Cowan's Auctions

Political, Plate, Eagle, Presidential,
Benjamin Harrison, Gilt, Limoges,
c.1892, 8½ In.
$1,187

New Orleans Auction Galleries

Political, Plate, White House China,
Abraham Lincoln, Haviland, Limoges,
c.1861, 7 In.
$8,400

Cowan's Auctions

P

Political, Poster, McKinley, Prosperity, Commerce, Civilization, Frame, 1900, 27 x 40 In.
$13,929

Hake's Americana & Collectibles

Pomona, Tumbler, Leaves & Berries, Frosted, Second Grind, 3¾ x 2½ In.
$225

Ruby Lane

Popeye, Toy, Popeye, Tumbling, Tin Lithograph, Windup, Linemar, Japan, 4½ In.
$826

Bertoia Auctions

Poster,	French Communist Party, Protest 1953, Rosenberg Executions, 31 x 46 In.	8750
Poster,	Landon Knox, Liberty, Prosperity, Ballot Box, Flower, 1936, 10 x 13 In.	190
Poster,	McKinley, Prosperity, Commerce, Civilization, Frame, 1900, 27 x 40 In. ....*illus*	13929
Poster,	Portrait, Kennedy, Garmatz, Congress, Cardboard, 1960, 11 x 14 In.	337
Poster,	Remember Brownsville, Anti-Roosevelt, Cartoon, c.1908, 10 x 13 In.	482
Poster,	Suffrage First, Vote Against Wilson, 10 x 13 In.	2736
Poster,	Tomorrow The World Today Spain, Civil War, Map, Children, 26 x 38 In.	562
Poster,	War Is Over, J. Lennon, Yoko Ono, World Peace, 1969, 19 x 25 In.	1082
Print,	Lincoln Campaign, Portrait, Seated In Chair, Beardless, 1860, 12 x 17 In.	791
Ribbon,	Delegate Communist Party, N.Y. State Convention, Silver, 1942, 5 In.	115
Ribbon,	Garfield, Photo Portrait, Silk, Fringe, Club Philadelphia, Brass, 10 In.	569
Ribbon,	George McClellan, Oval Portrait, Scrolling Vines, Silk, 1864, 2 x 6 In.	2088
Ribbon,	Henry Clay, For President, Portrait, Eagle, Flags, 1845, 2½ x 6 In.	371
Ribbon,	Lincoln, Austin Blair For Governor Of Michigan, 1860	2750
Ribbon,	McKinley, Hobart Campaign, Yellow, 1896, 6 Piece	58
Ribbon,	Winfield Scott, Vera Cruz Battle, Portrait, Silk, Scalloped, 1852, 3 x 7 In.	459
Ruler,	Roosevelt & Corliss, Portraits, Slogans, 2-Sided, Celluloid, 1902, 12 In.	380
Sewing Box,	John Adams, Portrait, Glass, Octagonal, Cardboard, 1828, 4 x 5 In.	1456
Sign,	Davis, Bryan, Teapot Dome, Cardboard, Jugate, 1924, 14 In.	2006
Skillet,	Franklin Roosevelt, Hoover Depression, Aluminum, 1932, 9 x 13 In.	418
Spice Shaker,	Silvered, Votes For Women, I'll Make It Hot For You, 4 In.	2500
Statue,	George Washington, Holding Sword, Carved, Painted, c.1910, 64 In.	2963
Statue,	Ku Klux Klan, Cloaked Member, Removable Arm, 1923, 15 In.	570
Stickpin,	Cleveland, Brass, Eagle, Spread Wings, Portrait, Flags, 1884, 1½ In.	302
Stickpin,	Gen. U.S. Grant, Brass, Eagle Hanger, Star, Portrait, 1868	380
Token,	Anti-Slavery, Am I Not A Woman & Sister, Liberty, Copper, 1838, 1 In.	285
Tray,	Serving, Bryan, Stevenson, Portraits, Capital, Eagle, Tin Litho, 1896, 13 x 16 In.	380
Tumbler,	Bryan, Free Silver, Glass, Flag, Rooster On Silver Coin, 1896, 3 x 4 In.	152
Umbrella,	McKinley, Hobart, Portraits, Jugate, Canvas, 1896, 33 In.	525

 POMONA glass is a clear glass with a soft amber border decorated with pale blue or rose-colored flowers and leaves. The colors are very, very pale. The background of the glass is covered with a network of fine lines. It was made from 1885 to 1888 by the New England Glass Company. First grind was made from April 1885 to June 1886. It was made by cutting a wax surface on the glass, then dipping it in acid. Second grind was a less expensive method of acid etching that was developed later.

Pitcher,	Blue & Purple, Flowers, Flared Mouth, Applied Rope Handle, 8 In.	36
Pitcher,	Frosted, Thumbprint, Squared Mouth, 6¼ In.	36
Pitcher,	Lemonade, Diamond Optic, Cornflower, c.1875, 6 In.	450
Pitcher,	Peach, Coin Dot, 8 In.	24
Spooner,	Gold Tint, Ruffled Rim, Petal Foot, 5 In.	60
Tumbler,	Leaves & Berries, Frosted, Second Grind, 3¾ x 2½ In. ....*illus*	225
Vase,	Cornflower Wreath, Pinched Rim, Petal Foot, 6¼ In.	156

PONTYPOOL, *see Tole category.*

 POOLE POTTERY was founded by Jesse Carter in 1873 in Poole, England, and has operated under various names since then. The pottery operated as Carter & Co. for several years and established Carter, Stabler & Adams as a subsidiary in 1921. The company specialized in tiles, architectural ceramics, and garden ornaments. Tableware, bookends, candelabra, figures, vases, and other items have also been made. The name *Poole Pottery Ltd.* was taken in 1963. The company went bankrupt in 2003 but is in business today with new owners.

Bowl,	Carter, Stabler & Adams, Attached Saucer, c.1930, 3 x 5½ In., Pair	45
Bowl,	Vegetable, Lid, Knob, Gray & Peach, Pebble, Sea Gull, c.1955, 3½ x 10 In.	3
Coffee Set,	Featherdrift, Ice Green & White, c.1955, 11 Piece	47
Plate,	Autumn, 6 In.	16
Plate,	Blue & Red Pattern, 5 In.	56

P

POPEYE was introduced to the Thimble Theatre comic strip in 1929. The character became a favorite of readers. In 1932, an animated cartoon featuring Popeye was made by Paramount Studios. The cartoon series continued and became even more popular when it was shown on television starting in the 1950s. The full-length movie with Robin Williams as Popeye was made in 1980. KFS stands for King Features Syndicate, the distributor of the comic strip.

Doll, Popeye, Wood, Paint, Composition Head, Jointed, Felt Shirt, Pipe, 1935, 14 In.	374
Figure, Popeye Express, Pushing Wheelbarrow, Parrot, Tin Litho, Clockwork, 9 In.	345
Game, Paper Board, Linen Mounted, Characters, Doe Mee, 1930s, 17 x 23 In.	338
Game, Puzzle, Popeye The Juggler, Metal Frame, Balls, Paint, Bar Zim Toys, 1920s	175
Statue, Carnival, Sea Hag, Standing, Crossed Eyes, Paint, Plaster, c.1930, 9 In.	230
Statue, Eugene The Jeep, Hollow Plaster, Paint, Yellow, Red, 1930s, 13 In.	1900
Statue, Popeye Dukes Up, Anchor Tattoo, Black Hair, Plaster, Paint, 1930s, 11 In.	437
Toy, Kazoo, Multicolored, Cartoon Scenes, Shape, Tin Lithograph, 1930s, 4 In.	20
Toy, Popeye, Heavy Hitter, Strength Game, Mallet, Windup, 1930s, 4 x 12 In.	1581
Toy, Popeye, Holding Spinach Can, Sailor Outfit, Moves, Vinyl, Metal, 1967, 11 In.	115
Toy, Popeye, Motorcycle Patrol, Cast Iron, Hubley, 8 In.	2250
Toy, Popeye, Tumbling, Tin Lithograph, Windup, Linemar, Japan, 4 ½ In. ....*illus*	826
Toy, Rowboat, Red, Tin Lithograph, Battery Operated, Linemar, Japan, 9 ¾ In.	1353

PORCELAIN factories that are well known are listed in this book under the factory name. This category lists pieces made by the less well-known factories. Additional pieces of porcelain are listed in this book in the categories Porcelain-Contemporary, Porcelain-Midcentury, and under the factory name.

Bonbon, Head Shape, Woman, Germany, 2 ¾ In.	437
Bonbonniere, Male & Female, Pair Of Baskets, Jacob Petit, 1800s, 6 x 6 In., Pair	500
Bowl, Blue, Ormolu, Pineapple Finial, 9 In.	240
Bowl, Elliptical, Coat Of Arms, Red 2-Headed Eagle, Russia, 10 In.	2812
Bowl, Famille Rose, Applied Scrolls, Vines, Insects & Flowers, 1700s, 4 x 9 In.	488
Bowl, Figures, Landscape, Gilt Bronze Mount, 6 ¼ In.	281
Bowl, Fin De Siecle, Gilt, Bronze Base, France, c.1880, 11 x 18 x 9 ½ In.	562
Bowl, Flowers, Red, Green, England, 12 In.	63
Bowl, Gilt Bronze, Putto, Dove, Sevres Style, 25 x 14 In.	1200
Bowl, Gilt, Flowers, Angels, Cherubs, Tapered Support, Paw Feet, 8 ½ x 14 In.	850
Bowl, Gilt, Flowers, Footed, Continental, 11 In.	38
Bowl, Thin Glaze, Crimped, Blue, White, 5 x 9 In.	50
Box, Scenes, Blue Ground, Hand Painted, France, 1900s, 3 ½ x 4 In.	812
Cachepot, Hunt Scenes, Double Handle, Blue, Gilt, 4 ½ In., Pair	1000
Cake Stand, Walnut, Green Shell, Flower Wreath, Turquoise Bands, 9 x 4 In.	35
Card Tray, Hand Painted, Gilt Bronze Supports, France, 1800s, 5 x 11 In.	343
Centerpiece, Courting Couple, Flowers, 22 In.	531
Charger, Gilt, Poseidon, Cherubs, Water, Prince, Red Border, 11 ½ In.	200
Coffee Set, Hand Painted, Paneled Scenes, Light Blue, France, c.1800s, 9 Piece	218
Coffeepot, Pear Shape, Dome Lid, Scroll Handle, Figures, Gilt, c.1724, 8 In.	14692
Compote, Reticulated, Dancing Figures, Tree Trunk Base, Von Schierholz, 15 In.	125
Compote, Sevres Style, Hand Painted, Gilt Bronze Mounts, 1800s, 11 x 12 In.	518
Cooler, Fruit, Flowers, Pink, Gilt, Russia, 13 In., Pair	2250
Cooler, Fruit, Lid, Flowers, Gilt Acorn Finial, Insert, France, 11 In., Pair ....*illus*	480
Corbeille, Cherubs, Basket, Caryatids, Jugs, Reticulated Border, Gilt, 20 x 16 In.	590
Cup & Saucer, Band Of Flowers, Painted, Gilt, Popov Factory, Russia, c.1815, 4 ¼ In. ....*illus*	600
Cup & Saucer, Lid, Blue Celeste, Gilt, Rose Finial, 5 ¼ In.	1000
Cup, Cabinet, Gilt Bird Head Handle, Armor & Helmet, Alexander I, 3 x 4 In.	1140
Dispenser, Gate City Stone Filter, Lemonade, White, 20 ½ x 10 ½ In.	125
Ewer, Basin, Shell Shape, Pink, White, Marked, Brevette Brianchon, 15 In., 2 Piece	750
Ewer, Fans, Bamboo, Butterflies, Grasshopper, Hungary, 9 ½ In.	240
Ewer, Gilt, Petal Opening, Pink, Yellow Flowers, Green, White Ground, 22 In.	88
Ewer, Light Green, Decoration, 7 ½ In.	188
Figurine, Bird, Orange Feathers, Green Feet, Brown Beak, 12 In., Pair	138

Porcelain, Cooler, Fruit, Lid, Flowers, Gilt Acorn Finial, Insert, France, 11 In., Pair
$480

Brunk Auctions

Porcelain, Cup & Saucer, Band Of Flowers, Painted, Gilt, Popov Factory, Russia, c.1815, 4 ¼ In.
$600

Brunk Auctions

TIP
Figurines are often damaged. Examine the fingers, toes, and other protruding parts for damage or repairs.

P

Porcelain, Figurine, Man, Woman, Period Multicolor Dress, Enamel, France, c.1875, 28 In., Pair
$1,125

New Orleans Auction Galleries

Porcelain, Jar, Lid, Chinese Jade, Silver
Lid & Base, Edward Farmer, c.1910,
4 x 4 In.
$2,125

Rago Arts and Auction Center

Porcelain, Pitcher, Portrait, Mother,
Father, 2-Sided, 2 Girls, Rudolph Lux,
1863, 8½ In.
$1,750

Selkirk Auctioneers & Appraisers

Porcelain, Vase, Obi Tie, Greek Key
Border, Turquoise, C. Dresser, c.1880,
6 In., Pair
$500

New Orleans Auction Galleries

Figurine, Boar, Leaping, Curved Branch Support, Gray, Base, c.1752, 4 In.	8921
Figurine, Bolognese Hound, Frankenthal, 6 In.	875
Figurine, Bulldog, Brown, White, 5¼ x 8 In.	88
Figurine, Circus Elephant, Gray, Blue Blanket, Marked, Bohne, 12 In.	228
Figurine, Cockatoo, White, Gilt, Hand Painted, c.1810, 12½ x 10 x 6 In.	687
Figurine, Gardener, Man Pushing Wheelbarrow, 6 x 8½ In.	625
Figurine, Gilt Metal, Ceres & Iris, Oval Portraits, Base, France, 1800s, 21 In., Pair	937
Figurine, Jaguar, Art Deco Style, White, 14 In.	531
Figurine, Man, Woman, Period Multicolor Dress, Enamel, France, c.1875, 28 In., Pair *illus*	1125
Figurine, Polar Bear, Open Mouth, Connoisseur Of Malvern, 17 In.	375
Figurine, Venus, Shells, Green, Purple, England, 14 x 6 In.	1321
Garniture, Bronze, Fin De Siecle, Late 1800s, 15 x 10 x 7½ In.	500
Garniture, Urn, Hand Painted, Blue, Lysel, France, 1900s, 24½ x 8 In., Pair	500
Group, Courting Couple, Flowered Skirt, Branch, Germany, 11½ In.	38
Group, Joker, Boys, White Shirt, Red Jacket, Russia, c.1850, 6 In.	4375
Group, Musician, Figures, Field, 21½ In.	2500
Group, Venus & Adonis, Seated Nymph, Dog, Ludwigsburg, c.1765, 12 In.	4353
Group, Woman & Seated Gentleman, Table, Grassy Base, Germany, c.1760	3305
Inkwell, Winged Monopodia With Headdress, England, c.1810, 3 x 4 In., Pair	750
Jar, Dog Head, Flower Garlands, Molded, Panels, Shouldered, Lid, c.1970, 20 In.	2750
Jar, Famille Rose, Armorial, Late 1800s, 21¼ In.	366
Jar, Lid, Chinese Jade, Silver Lid & Base, Edward Farmer, c.1910, 4 x 4 In. *illus*	2125
Jardiniere, Chinoiserie, Scalloped, Cabriole Legs, Painted, 23 x 32 In., Pair	2394
Jardiniere, Figures, Landscape, Ruins, Tendril Handle, 10 x 8½ In., Pair	937
Jardiniere, Gilt Bronze Mounts, Sevres Style, France, c.1910, 12½ In., Pair	687
Jardiniere, Stand, Oval, Black Panels, Gilt, France, 1900s, 9½ x 13 In.	937
Loving Cup, Blue To White, Dancing Woman, Kauffmann, c.1920, 8 x 5¼ In.	70
Moonpot, Dome Lid, Cream & Orange Glaze, Black Streak Design, 16 In.	5000
Paste Jar, Peachbloom, Circular, Unglazed Foot, 2 x ¾ In.	420
Pitcher, Green, Cream, Flowers, Silver Overlay, 8 In.	150
Pitcher, Portrait, Mother, Father, 2-Sided, 2 Girls, Rudolph Lux, 1863, 8½ In. *illus*	1750
Plaque, Giraffe Shape Rim, Nuzzling Mother & Child, Franz, 9 x 9 In.	62
Plaque, Landscape, Hills, Building, Stream, Continental, 7¾ x 4 In.	200
Plaque, Portrait, Ruth, Convex Oval, Paint, Gilt Frame, Germany, 1800s, 8 In.	390
Plaque, Sevres Style, Couples, Landscape, Blue Border, 22 In.	1625
Plate, Cherubs, Champleve Blue Rim, Gilt, Shaped, Handles, 14½ In.	750
Plate, Gilt, Courting Couple, Courtyard, Lavender Border, 9½ In.	344
Plate, Palace Of Prince Carl, Gilt Scroll Rim, Stars, Germany, c.1820, 8 In.	1625
Plate, Portrait, Girl, Curly Hair, Red Shrug, Cobalt Blue, Gilt, Continental, 11 In.	175
Plate, Portrait, Woman, Flowing Hair, Raised Gilt Border, Wagner, c.1900, 6 In.	540
Platter, Frolicking Group, Sevres Style, Hand Painted, France, 1800s, 31 x 32 In.	687
Platter, Rainbow Trout, Oval, Flared, Ribbed Edge, Signed, E. Dellavia, 27 In.	236
Platter, Westbourne, Scalloped Edge, Blue & White, England, 1800s, 12 x 15 In.	90
Punch Bowl, Cartouches, Grape Leaves, Green, Art Nouveau, 17 In.	236
Saucier, Peach & Gilt Banding, Lid, Fruit Finial, Underplate, 1800s, 7 x 10 In.	183
Sugar, Lid, Knob Finial, Stylized Flowers, White, Pink & Green, c.1900, 4 In.	1375
Tazza, Flowers, Mountain, Village, Lake, Scalloped, Peach Glaze, 7 x 10 In.	88
Tea & Coffee Set, Teapot, Coffeepot, Sugar, Creamer, Cups, Saucers, 26 Piece	156
Tea Set, Teapot, Sugar & Creamer, 2 Cups & Saucers, Tray, 8 Piece	531
Tea Set, Teapot, Tea Caddy Sugar & Creamer, Silver Overlay, 4 Piece	247
Teapot, Chinoiserie, Green, England, 6½ x 5½ In.	138
Teapot, Figural, Elephant Head, Monkey Body, 11 x 5¼ In., Pair	177
Teapot, White, Blue Flowers, Bird's Head Spout, Lid, Doccia, Italy, c.1770, 6 In.	1470
Tray, Gilt, Blue, Birds, Tree, Landscape, Handles, Sevres Style, 13¼ In.	312
Tray, Giraffe Shape, Mother & Child, Endless Beauty, J. Wood, Franz, 24 x 17 In.	93
Tray, Turquoise Ground, Pink Landscape, Gilt Scroll, Shaped, c.1755, 9½ In.	1672
Tureen, Lid, Boy & Girl Finial, Reserves, Carl Thieme, Germany, 13 x 10 In.	312
Tureen, Lid, Nut & Leaf Handle, Gilt, Blue Stripe, c.1850, 13 x 16 In.	450

Tureen, Pink Band, Delineres & Co., c.1885, 12 x 14 In.	90
Urn, Blue Bands, Roses, Gilt, 25 ¼ In.	1250
Urn, Blue Flowers, Green Leaves, Gilt, Bavaria Schumann, 14 In.	218
Urn, Courting Couple, Gilt, Bronze Mount, 43 In.	3000
Urn, Flower Sprays, Dolphins, White, Gilt Highlights, Triangle Base, 11 In., Pair	1375
Urn, Hunting, Gilt, Bronze, Cobalt Blue, Leaf Handles, Sevres Style, 30 In., Pair	9375
Urn, Lid, Bird Finial, Flowers, Pink, White Ground, Germany, 21 ½ In.	218
Urn, Lid, Finial, Cupid, Swans, Maidens, Pink, Vase Shape, c.1885, 26 In., Pair	1353
Urn, Lid, Napoleonic Scenes, 1800s, 13 x 13 ½ In.	4025
Urn, Lid, Reserves, Figures In Courtyard, Red, Blue, Handles, 21 In.	1000
Urn, Lid, Sevres Style, Cobalt Blue, 1800s, 25 x 14 In.	5175
Urn, Milkmaid, Hand Painted, France, Early 1900s, 17 x 8 In.	500
Urn, Mother & Children, Landscape, Blue Celeste, Gilt, Ram Handles, 8 In.	406
Urn, Portrait, Madame Sophie, Bronze Mounts, Sevres Style, France, 1800s, 30 In.	500
Urn, Putti, Garniture, Cobalt Blue, Bronze, Hand Painted, c.1880, 20 In., Pair	2125
Urn, Romantic Landscape, Celeste Blue, Sevres Style, M. Demonceaux, 21 x 10 In.	300
Urn, Swans, Landscape Panels, Gilt, Painted, France, 1900s, 25 ½ x 8 In.	1000
Urn, Warwick Vase, Pineapple Finial, 15 x 13 In.	1024
Urn, Women, Putti, Gilt, Bronze, Cobalt Blue, Lion Mask Handles, 32 In.	5250
Vase, Adelaide Robineau, Rotund, Blue Crystals, Blue Ground, c.1905, 4 In.	4600
Vase, Amphora, Peachbloom, With Stand, 6 ¼ In.	1020
Vase, Applied Fruit, Handles, c.1880, 25 ½ In.	3500
Vase, Blue, Courting Couple, Sevres Style, 16 ½ In., Pair	1000
Vase, Cartouche, Courting Couple, Creek, Green, 3-Footed, Polyet, 11 x 4 In.	153
Vase, Courting Couple, Landscape, Blue, Gilt, Sevres Style, 18 ¼ In., Pair	812
Vase, Courting Couples, Garniture, Rococo Revival, c.1880, 17 x 10 In., Pair	1187
Vase, Dragon, Blue & White, Bottle Shape, 18 In.	360
Vase, Flambe, Blue, Purple, Mottled, 7 In.	63
Vase, Flowers, Cartouche, Cobalt Blue & Gilt, 19 ¼ In., Pair	375
Vase, Garland, Gilt, Trumpet Shape, Continental, 1800s, 8 ½ In., Pair	219
Vase, Green, Teal, Raised Panels, Dragon Handles, 8 ½ In., Pair	750
Vase, Leaves & Buds, Mauve, Brown, Squat, Stick Neck, Mougin, c.1900, 8 In.	750
Vase, Leaves & Fish, Teal, Cobalt Blue & Gilt, 31 In.	5000
Vase, Lid, Potpourri, Gondola, Painted, Gilt, France, 1900s, 14 x 12 ½ In., Pair	562
Vase, Narrow Neck, Peachbloom, 8 ½ In.	25
Vase, Obi Tie, Greek Key Border, Turquoise, C. Dresser, c.1880, 6 In., Pair........*illus*	500
Vase, Pate-Sur-Pate, Classical Figures, Urn, Dove Gray, Footed, France, 17 In.	180
Vase, Pink Flowers, White Ground, Round Flared Foot, 29 In., Pair	250
Vase, Portrait, Woman, Head Scarf, Wreath, Pillow, Double Handles, 9 x 8 In.	177
Vase, Putto, Still Life, Gilt Reserves, Black, Pink, Flared, Base, 9 x 3 In., Pair	840
Vase, Ruby Red, Celadon Interior, Handles, 7 In.	63
Vase, Shield Shape, Pink, Purple, Flowers, Gilt, c.1820, 9 In., Pair	875
Water Cooler, Leaves & Scrolls, White, Gilt, 22 x 12 In.	267

PORCELAIN-ASIAN includes pieces made in Japan, Korea, and other Asian countries. Asian porcelain is also listed in Canton, Chinese Export, Imari, Japanese Coralene, Moriage, Nanking, Occupied Japan, Porcelain-Chinese, Satsuma, Sumida, and other categories.

Bottle, Figural Man, Seated, Poem, Blue, White, Lid, Leaf Finial, 1800s, 5 In.	123
Bowl, Blue Dragon, Green & Brown Glaze, Flared Rim, Marked, 3 x 6 In.	360
Bowl, Lid, Squat, Cobalt Blue Ground, Scrolling Flowers, c.1940, 8 In.	90
Bowl, Lotus Scrolls, Blue, White, Banded, Raised Foot, c.1900, 6 In., Pair	1230
Bowl, Rounded Walls, Inverted Foot, Yellow Glaze, 1900s, 5 In.	5925
Bowl, Stylized Flowers, Scrolling Leaves, Blue & White, 3 x 6 In., Pair	1845
Bowl, Yellow Glaze, Drainage Holes, 9 In.	1920
Brush Rest, Mountain Peaks, Arched, 4 Holders, Blue Glaze, 1900s, 6 In.	62
Brushpot, Roosters, Flowers, Cylindrical, Pierced, Scalloped, c.1935, 11 In.	120
Charger, Orange Peel Ground, Flowers, Red, Blue, Gilt, c.1890, 25 In.	400
Cup, Lotus Blossoms, Scrolling Vine Band, Blue, White, 1900s, 3 In., Pair	1067
Dish, 4 Cartouches, Characters, Yellow, 7 In.	132

PORCELAIN-ASIAN

Porcelain-Asian, Sculpture, Wall Hanging, Red Flowers, Matsuda Yuriko, Japan, 11 ½ x 6 ½ In.
$65

Rago Arts and Auction Center

Porcelain-Chinese, Basin, Famille Jaune, Egrets, Lotus Pond, Flowering Vines, c.1910, 13 x 4 In.
$1,037

Neal Auctions

Porcelain-Chinese, Bowl, 2 Dragons, Stylized Clouds, Yellow, Daoguang Seal, 2 x 4 In.
$5,700

Brunk Auctions

P

367

Porcelain-Chinese, Bowl, Lotus Leaf Shape, Flowers, Insects, Creatures, 1800s, 11 In.
$303

James D. Julia Auctioneers

Porcelain-Chinese, Bowl, Yellow, Green, Boys Playing, Fenced Garden, Flared Rim, Ring Foot, 1800s, 3 x 6 In.
$625

Neal Auctions

Porcelain-Chinese, Figurine, Guanyin, Jewels, Pearl Encrusted Base, Seal Mark, 19 In.
$7,200

Brunk Auctions

Ewer, Coiled Dragon, Tail Handle, Blue, Bulbous, Garlic Lid, 12 In.	118
Ewer, Globular, Ribbed, Handle, Octagonal Base & Lid, Finial, 6 In.	123
Figurine, Boar, Reclining, Looking Up, Orange Paint, 5 x 9 In.	1230
Figurine, Guanyin, Seated, Lotus Thrown, Robe, Holding Jar, 14 x 6 In.	59
Figurine, Ma Gu, Headdress, Deer, Blanc-De-Chine Glaze, c.1900, 16 In.	4018
Head Rest, Happy Boy, On Knees & Elbows, Ball, 9 x 13½ In.	224
Jar, Bamboo, Pine, Plum, Insects, Blue & White, c.1800, 10½ In.	523
Jardiniere, Mountains, Village, Painted, Signed, Japan, 11 x 15 In.	75
Plaque, Birds & Nest, Enamel, Rosewood Frame, 1900s, 19 x 14 In.	1363
Plaque, Immortal, Riding Deer, Symbols, Crane, Enamel, 1900s, 15 x 10 In.	308
Plate, Birds In Flight, Cherry Blossom Branches, 1900s, 10 In., Pair	3851
Plate, Dragon, 5 Claws, Blue & Yellow, 7¾ In.	1200
Plate, Medallion, Birds, Pond, Bamboo, Flared, Blue, White, c.1885, 10 In.	123
Plate, Mottled Copper Glaze, Green Specks, Peachbloom, c.1800, 9 In.	2460
Pot, Flowers, Vines, Relief, Globular, Bird Shape Handles, 1800s, 10 In.	1422
Sculpture, Wall Hanging, Red Flowers, Matsuda Yuriko, Japan, 11½ x 6½ In. ....*illus*	65
Teapot, Flowers, Vines, Tapered, Twist Handle, Lid, Berry Finial, 1700s, 10 In.	461
Temple Jar, Blue, White Plum Branches, Lid, Lotus Finial, 23 In., Pair	3567
Umbrella Stand, Landscape, Blue, White, Bands, Cylindrical, c.1900, 25 In.	474
Vase, Blue & White, Flowers, Scroll, Tapered Square, Flared Rim, 14 In.	250
Vase, Blue & White, Prunus Clusters, Cracked Ice Glaze, c.1900, 17 In.	923
Vase, Blue & White, Scrolling Lotus, Lozenge Shape, Handles, 11 In.	2583
Vase, Blue, White, Flowers, Emblems, Lions, Flared Rim, 1800s, 17 In.	123
Vase, Brown Crackle Glaze, Ribbed, Bottle Shape, Flared, c.1800, 10 In.	3321
Vase, Immortals, Red Glaze, Gilt, Bottle Shape, Garlic Mouth, c.1800, 5 In.	1353
Vase, Lid, Leaf, Animal With Spots, Bamboo, 24 In., Pair	375
Vase, Lotus Flowers, Vines, Ruyi, Double Gourd, Blue, White, 1900s, 10 In.	523
Vase, Mallet Shape, Flared Rim, Gray, Beige Crackle Glaze, 7 In.	3690
Vase, Mottled, Flambe Glaze, Flared Rim, c.1900, 14 In.	154
Vase, Mottled, Flambe Glaze, Lobed, Trumpet Neck, Flared, 8 In.	1968
Vase, Purple Flambe Glaze, Oval, Flared Rim, 1800s, 15 In.	474
Vase, Purple Irises, Gilt Rim, Urn Shape, Wood Stand, c.1880, 16 In.	2400
Vase, Qilins, Clouds, Branch Handles, Crackle Glaze, 1800s, 14 In.	923
Vase, Ruby Glaze, Round Panels, Landscapes, Tapered, c.1910, 8 In.	1067
Vase, Squat, White, Engraved Leaves, 7½ In.	330
Vase, Stick, Flowers, Fruit Tree, Blue, Carved Hardwood Stand, 11 x 5 In.	125
Vase, Teardrop Shape, Crackle Glaze, 9½ In.	204
Vase, Tiger, Rocky Landscape, Blue, White, Oval, Stick Neck	62
Vase, White, Cobalt Blue Splotches & Black, Lines, Square, 9 x 8 In.	2000
Water Dropper, Green, Crackle Glaze, Bottle Shape, Swollen Rim, 7 In.	123
Water Pot, Teadust Glaze, Squat, Bulbous, Flared Rim, 1900s, 2½ In.	267

PORCELAIN-CHINESE is listed here. See also Canton, Chinese Export, Imari, Moriage, Nanking, and other categories.

Basin, Famille Jaune, Egrets, Lotus Pond, Flowering Vines, c.1910, 13 x 4 In. ....*illus*	1037
Boat, Flying Fish, River, Blue, White, c.1910, 5 x 14 In.	97
Bowl, 2 Dragons, Stylized Clouds, Yellow, Daoguang Seal, 2 x 4 In. ....*illus*	5700
Bowl, Blue Leaves, Branches, White Ground, Peachbloom, 10 In.	3125
Bowl, Blue, Figures, Famile Rose, 7 In.	100
Bowl, Dragons, Chasing Pearls, Silver Wash, 1800s, 8 x 4½ In.	180
Bowl, Eggshell, Raised Enamel Flowers, 1900s, 2½ x 6 In., Pair	500
Bowl, Flowers, Scrolling Leaves, Lotus Shape, Blue, White, 7 In.	900
Bowl, Hundred Boys Pattern, 7¼ x 3 In.	265
Bowl, Iron Red, Gilt, Phoenix, Cloud Wisps, 4¼ In.	2500
Bowl, Lotus Leaf Shape, Flowers, Insects, Creatures, 1800s, 11 In. ....*illus*	303
Bowl, Lotus, Aqua Interior, Flared, Raised Foot, Marked, c.1770, 3 In., Pair	300
Bowl, Pair Of Dragons, White Glaze, Engraved, c.1880, 2 x 6 In.	2040
Bowl, Phoenixes, Scrollwork, Blue Underglaze, 9¼ x 2 In.	238
Bowl, Reserves, Birds, Butterflies, Flowers, Interior Scenes, 14 x 12 In.	200

P

Bowl, Yellow, Green, Boys Playing, Fenced Garden, Flared Rim, Ring Foot, 1800s, 3 x 6 In.*illus*	625
Bowl, Yellow, Stylized Flower Heads, Cloud Scrolls, 5 In., Pair	5625
Brush Washer, Ocean Figures, Cylindrical, Inscribed, c.1710, 6 x 4 In.	250
Brushpot, Dragon, Cloud, Sea, Flaming Pearl, 1700s, 5½ In.	350
Censer, Dragons, Flaming Pearl, Foo Dog, Lid, Jade Finial, 24 x 18 In.	2023
Censer, Robin's-Egg Blue, Handles, Ring Foot, 3½ x 7 In.	312
Charger, Center Medallion, Yellow, Blue Underglaze, 14½ In.	125
Charger, Horses, Flaming Pearl, Rocks, Waves, Green Border, 13 In.	1875
Charger, Women, Courtyard Scene, 17½ In., Pair	281
Compote, 5 Round Reserves, Blue Dragon, Yellow, 5½ In., Pair	281
Cup, Libation, Flaring Rim, Side Handle, 3-Footed, 2½ x 4 In.	93
Figurine, Child, Black Hair, Seated, Holding Pink Flower, 11 In., Pair	1250
Figurine, Foo Dog, Yellow, Faux Carpet, Stepped Base, 24 x 11 In., Pair	297
Figurine, Guanyin, Jewels, Pearl Encrusted Base, Seal Mark, 19 In. *illus*	7200
Figurine, Guanyin, Yellow, White, 9½ In.	343
Figurine, Guardian, Kneeling, Spear, Dragon, Enamel, c.1935, 27 In. *illus*	256
Figurine, Lu, Star God, Blue & Purple Robe, Standing, 18 x 7 In.	297
Figurine, Peacock, Green, Pink, Purple, 19 In., Pair	187
Ginger Jar, Blue & White, Lid, 1900s, 9 x 8½ In.	312
Ginger Jar, White, Lid, Metal Ring, 1900s, 12 x 8 In., Pair	343
Group, Water Buffalo, Boy Astride, 5 x 8 In.	900
Jar, Flowers, Blue, Light Gray, 11 x 13½ In.	595
Jar, Lid, Famille Rose, Hunt Scenes, 1900s, 7¾ In.	180
Jar, Lid, Oval, Red, Stand, 5 Legs, Early 1900s, 7½ In.	350
Jardiniere, Fish, Seaweed, Blue & White, 1900s, 18 x 17 In.	240
Jardiniere, Mountain Landscape, Palmettes, Blue, White, Flared, 7 In.	250
Jardiniere, Phoenixes & Flowers, Blue & White, 1800s, 17 x 12 In.	480
Planter, Faux Wood & Rope Decoration, 5¼ In., Pair	3570
Plaque, Flowers, Vase, Scroll, Censer, Wood Frame, 1900s, 16 x 12 In.	480
Platter, Scholars, Dragon & Bats, Blue & White, c.1880, 9½ x 12 In.	150
Potpourri, Serpent Handles, Foo Dog Finial, 11½ In.	250
Punch Bowl, Famille Rose, Ch'ien Lung, c.1780, 7½ x 9 In., Pair	2375
Punch Bowl, Figures, Landscape, 5 x 11 In.	500
Punch Bowl, Figures, Landscape, Gilt Tracery, Wood Stand, 4 x 10 In.	500
Punch Bowl, Flowers, Seated Figures, Gilt Trefoil Border, 4 x 10 In.	500
Soup, Dish, Pagodas, Figures, Leaves, Scrolls, Doves, 3-Footed, 10 In.	250
Tea Bowl, Group, Landscape, Fence, c.1900, 2 x 3¼ In.	129
Teapot, Blue, White, 3½ In.	625
Teapot, Blue, White, Double Wall, Honeycomb Openwork, Handle, c.1700, 5 In. *illus*	1303
Teapot, Landscape Reserves, Famille Jaune, 6½ In.	188
Teapot, Monkey & Baby Chimp, Yellow, 7¾ In.	250
Trivet, Trefoil, Figures, Green, 9 In.	156
Tureen, Underplate, Flowers & Leaves, 12 x 9 In.	250
Umbrella Stand, Blue, White, Bamboo, 18½ In.	438
Umbrella Stand, Flowers, Branches, Blue & White, 18 In.	500
Vase, 3 Flying Dragons, Turquoise, Hexagonal, 17¾ In.	600
Vase, 4 Loop Handles, Light Blue, c.1920, 12 In.	156
Vase, Bird & Tree, Pink Band At Shoulder, 16 In.	125
Vase, Birds, Flower Branches, Square, Trumpet Rim, 1900s, 26 In.	420
Vase, Buddhist Trigrams, Crackle Glaze, Cong Shape, 10¾ In.	1500
Vase, Cobalt Blue, Red Mums, Pear Shape, Flared Rim, 1900s	238
Vase, Court Scenes, Yellow, Reticulated, Square, Stand, 11 In., Pair	1187
Vase, Crayfish, Seaweed, Blue, White, Shouldered, 1900s, 5½ In.	250
Vase, Dehua, Incised Scrollwork, Oval, Trumpet Neck, 1700s, 11 In.	625
Vase, Double Gourd, Vines, Yellow, Pink Ribbon, Blue Rim, 10 x 5 In.	250
Vase, Dragon, Green Wave, Octagonal, 14 x 8 In.	297
Vase, Dragon, Landscape, 10 In.	625
Vase, Dragons, Flowers, Vines, Gilt, Sepia, 21½ In.	350
Vase, Famille Jaune, Pheasants, Mottled Yellow, c.1780, 15 x 8 In.	3120

Porcelain-Chinese, Figurine, Guardian, Kneeling, Spear, Dragon, Enamel, c.1935, 27 In.

$256

Neal Auctions

Porcelain-Chinese, Teapot, Blue, White, Double Wall, Honeycomb Openwork, Handle, c.1700, 5 In.

$1,303

James D. Julia Auctioneersa

Porcelain-Contemporary, Moonpot, Rattle, Cobalt Blue, Drip Glaze, Takaezu, 8 x 6 In.

$3,375

Rago Arts and Auction Center

P

Porcelain-Midcentury, Bowl, Flared, Bands, Vertical Lines, Lucie Rie, 28 In.
$18,000

Brunk Auctions

Postcard, St. George Hotel, Santa Cruz, California, Western Publishing, 1913, 3 x 5 In.
$6

Ruby Lane

TIP

If you want to preserve a poster, have it framed under glass with acid-free mounting, or roll and tie it loosely for safe storage. Plexiglas sheets filter out ultraviolet light and may be substituted for glass in a frame.

Poster, Bieres De La Meuse, Alphonse Mucha, Chromolitho, Signed, Frame, 1899, 15 x 12 In.
$1,800

Brunk Auctions

Vase, Famille Rose, Turquoise Interior, Bottle Shape, c.1880, 17 In.	5400
Vase, Famille Verte, Hundred Antiques, Diaper Pattern, 1800s, 28 In.	960
Vase, Figures, Blue Robes, Ocher, Pinched Mouth, 22 ½ In.	187
Vase, Figures, Room, Red & Green, Lid, Finial, 12 ½ In.	343
Vase, Flowers & Figures, Pink, Concave, 25 In.	125
Vase, Flowers & Scrolls, Tou Tsai, Tian Mark, 1900s, 3 ½ x 3 In.	1375
Vase, Flowers, Yellow Band On Shoulder, Trumpet Neck, 16 In.	156
Vase, Gilt, Blue, Flared, 12 x 6 In., Pair	300
Vase, Lavender, Flambe, Pear Shape, Flared Foot, 1800s, 15 In.	350
Vase, Lid, Tiger, Landscape, Scholar, Warrior, Red & Gilt, c.1900, 16 In.	120
Vase, Lid, White Lizard, 12 x 10 In.	406
Vase, Moon Flask, Blue, Red Sun Rising, Waves, 1900s, 12 x 9 In.	468
Vase, Oxblood Glaze, 1800s, 13 x 8 In.	275
Vase, Phoenix, Peonies, Leaves & Berries, Blue, Shouldered, 27 In., Pair	4760
Vase, Plum & Bats, Yellow, Bulbous, Trumpet Neck, 16 In.	180
Vase, Rouleau, Flambe, Oxblood Glaze, 1800s, 13 ½ In.	325
Vase, Stick, Flowers & Birds, 19 In.	100
Vase, Turquoise, Hexagonal Panels, Petal Rim, 1800s, 12 In.	4200
Vase, Warring States, Buddhist Trigrams, Crackle Glaze, 11 x 5 In.	1500
Water Dropper, Foo Dog, Reclining, Blue, Green, Amber Glaze, 4 In., Pair	300
Wine Cup, Rain, Branches, White Flowers, 1 ½ x 2 In.	562

PORCELAIN-CONTEMPORARY lists pieces made by artists working after 1975.

Coffee Set, Coffeepot, Cup, Wavy Lines, M. Graves, 1987, 2 Piece	215
Figurine, Balloon Dog, Reflective, J. Koons, Box, 1995, 10 In.	15000
Jardiniere, Inauguration Dinner, Eagle, Mottahedeh, 1981, 7 x 8 In.	425
Moonpot, Rattle, Cobalt Blue, Drip Glaze, Takaezu, 8 x 6 In. ....*illus*	3375
Plate, Home Sweet Home, Cigarette Butts, Damien Hirst, 8 In.	305
Teapot, Figural, Nude Woman Handle, Arms Form Spout, 9 x 8 In.	2500
Teapot, Freeform, Flattened, Pale Blue, Bridge, 1989, 7 x 16 In.	923
Vase, Oxblood, Silver Glaze, J. Takehara, 1982, 13 x 15 In.	1000
Vase, Piano Shape, Flattened, Bisected, R. Duckworth, 7 x 6 In.	2750

PORCELAIN-MIDCENTURY includes pieces made from the 1940s to about 1975.

Bowl, Flared, Bands, Vertical Lines, Lucie Rie, 28 In. ....*illus*	18000
Vase, Feelie, Brown, Yellow, Rose Cabat, c.1970, 5 ¾ In.	212
Vase, Leaf, Manganese & Black Glaze, Beaker Shape, c.1960, 6 In.	4613

POSTCARDS were first legally permitted in Austria on October 1, 1869. The United States passed postal regulations allowing the card in 1872. Most of the picture postcards collected today date after 1910. The amount of postage can help to date a card. The rates are: 1872 (1 cent), 1917 (2 cents), 1919 (1 cent), 1925 (2 cents), 1928 (1 cent), 1952 (2 cents), 1958 (3 cents), 1963 (4 cents), 1968 (5 cents), 1971 (6 cents), 1973 (8 cents), 1975 (7 cents), 1976 (9 cents), 1978 (10 cents), March 1981 (12 cents), November 1981 (13 cents), 1985 (14 cents), 1988 (15 cents), 1991 (19 cents), 1995 (20 cents), 2001 (21 cents), 2002 (23 cents), 2006 (24 cents), 2007 (26 cents), 2008 (27 cents), 2009 (28 cents), 2011 (29 cents), 2012 (32 cents), 2013 (33 cents), 2014 (34 cents), 2016 (35 cents beginning January 17 and back to 34 cents beginning April 10, 2016). While most postcards sell for low prices, a small number bring high prices. Some of these are listed here.

Andy Mouse IV, Woven Paper, Warhol, Homage, Signed, K. Haring, 1986, 8 x 4 In.	900
Andy Warhol & His Plastic Inevitable, Red, Black, Signed, c.1967, 8 x 5 In.	400
Arlette Dorgere, Photo, Reutlinger, French Writing, c.1910, 3 ½ x 5 ½ In.	22
Baseball, Ty Cobb, Detroit Tigers, Fielding, Dietsche, 1907-09	1920
Captain America, Sentinels Liberty Club, Handwritten, c.1941, 3 x 6 In.	4902
Carnation Bouquet, Decorated, Paul De Longpre, France, 1904	28
Cathedral, Watercolor, Signed, G. Besse, 1916	10
Easter, Bellboy Rabbit, Dachshund, Egg, Flowers, Winsch, 1909	15

Fighting In Juarez, Mex, Photo, D.W. Hoffman, Signed, 1911, 3 x 5 In.	200
First Communion, Girl, Adorned, Candle, France, 3 ½ x 5 ½ In.	18
Girl, Blue Dress, Posy, Pink Border, Embossed, Woolson Spice Co., Ohio, 3 x 5 In.	6
Girl, Carrying Daffodils, Paul Heckscher, 1934	12
Horse Drawn Rescue Hook & Ladder, Company No. 1, Black, White, 1901-07	30
Olympics, Photo, Jim Thorpe, Greatest Athlete Of All Time, Shot Put, 1912	1080
Paris, Eiffel Tower, Place De Concorde, Luigi Loir, c.1903, 3 ½ x 5 ½ In.	36
Pasadena Tournament Of Roses Parade, Damsel, Knight, Red, 1937, 6 x 4 In.	18
R.M.S. Aurania, Cunard Line, England	10
St. George Hotel, Santa Cruz, California, Western Publishing, 1913, 3 x 5 In. ....*illus*	6
Thanksgiving, Indian Maiden, Holding Turkey, Mechanical, Booklet, 1913	95
USS Wolverine, Public Dock, Erie, PA., H.H. Hamm, 1917	10
Valentine, Victorian Girls, Violets, Basket, Germany, 1900s, 3 ½ x 5 ½ In.	13
Yellowstone Park, Jackson Hole Country, Red Border, 8 ½ x 5 ¾ In.	12

POSTERS have informed the public about news and entertainment events since ancient times. Nineteenth-century advertising and theatrical posters and twentieth-century movie and war posters are of special interest today. The price is determined by the artist, the condition, and the rarity. Other posters may be listed under Movie, Political, and World War I and II.

100 Cans, Andy Warhol, 1978, 31 x 24 In.	2860
Bieres De La Meuse, Alphonse Mucha, Chromolitho, Signed, Frame, 1899, 15 x 12 In. ....*illus*	1800
Circus, Barnum & Bailey, Greatest Show On Earth, Photos, Frame, 1897, 23 x 17 In.	480
Circus, Buffalo Bill's Wild West, Sells Floto Circus, 34 x 21 ½ In.	497
Circus, Clyde Beatty & Cole, Coshocton, Clown, Acrobat, 1960s, 27 x 49 In. ......*illus*	225
Circus, Hagenback Wallace, Trained Wild Animals, Lion, Tiger, 1934, 49 x 27 In.	618
Circus, Ringling Bros., The Flying Vazquez, Frame, c.1947, 27 x 40 In.	148
Concert, Bo Diddley & Etta James, Rhythm & Blues, Cardboard, 1955, 22 x 28 In.	886
Concert, Bobby Darin & Count Basie Concert, Cardboard, Orchestra, 1962, 14 x 22 In.	472
Concert, Grateful Dead & Blues Brothers, New Year's Eve Concert, 1978, 19 x 28 In.	800
Concert, Jimi Hendrix Experience, Shrine Auditorium Concert, 1973, 14 x 22 In.	1360
Concert, Rat Pack, Civil Rights Benefit Concert, Stars For Freedom, 1963, 11 x 17 In.	2027
Concert, The Copa Proudly Presents Frank Sinatra, Copacabana, Photo, 15 x 11 In.	600
Show, Buffalo Bill, Still Holds The Reins, Russell-Morgan, c.1913, 41 x 28 In.	3900
Show, Buffalo Bill's Wild West Vaquero Show, 42 x 28 In.	2280
Show, Buffalo Bill's Wild West, This Indian Is Not A Bad Indian, 1910, 20 x 27 In.	2400
Show, Buffalo Ranch Real Wild West, c.1910, 20 ¼ x 56 In.	554
Show, Johnny Baker, Buffalo Bill's Wild West, Congress Of Rough Riders, 30 x 20 In.	4200
Show, Miller Bros. & Arlington, 101 Ranch Real Wild West, c.1910, 30 x 20 In.	1440
Show, Miller Bros. & Arlington, 101 Ranch Real Wild West, 1914, 13 x 17 In.	1680
Show, Miss Arizona & Sitting Bull, Wild West Act, c.1898, 29 x 38 ½ In.	1200
Show, S.F. Cody Contre Un Tandem, Horse Race, Cyclists, c.1892, 37 x 51 In.	1968
Travel, Airplane Rides, Inman Bros. Flying Circus, c.1929, 37 x 24 In.	3500
Travel, Bermuda, Beach, Lesnon, 38 x 23 In.	875
Travel, Cape Cod, The New Haven Railroad, Ben Nason, c.1945, 42 x 28 In.	2340
Travel, Holland America Line, Ship, W. Frederick, Ten Broek, 1936, 38 x 25 In.	3500
Travel, New York, Fifth Avenue, World's Greatest Shopping, 1932, 39 x 23 In.	6250
Travel, New Zealand, Sportsman's Paradise, Harry Rountree, c.1920, 36 x 26 In.	6750
Travel, Old Orchard Beach, Boston & Maine R.R., 44 x 29 In.	531
Travel, Orient Line To Australia, 20000 Ton Ships, W. Dobell, c.1938, 40 x 25 In.	4000
Travel, Palace Hotel, St. Moritz, Emil Cardinaux, Zurich, 1920, 50 x 35 In.	11875
Travel, Pan American, Fly To South Sea Isles, Paul G. Lawler, c.1938, 40 x 26 In.	20000
Travel, Play A Cool 18, Sun Valley, Idaho, Golf Course, Don B. Bennett, 32 x 23 In.	715
Travel, Santa Cruz, Southern Pacific Lines, 1926, 23 x 16 In.	4250
Travel, See More On The Vista Dome, California, Bern Hill, c.1950, 23 x 18 In.	4000
Travel, Ski The New Haven RR, Skier, Sascha Maurer, c.1940, 42 x 28 In.	938
Travel, Visit India, A.R. Acott, c.1920, 39 x 25 In.	5250
Travel, Washington, The City Beautiful, Pennsylvania Railroad, 1935, 40 x 25 In.	2500

Poster, Circus, Clyde Beatty & Cole, Coshocton, Clown, Acrobat, 1960s, 27 x 49 In.
$225

Ruby Lane

Potlid, Bear, Sitting In Chair, 2 People, The Ins, Multicolor Transfer, Pratt, 3 In.
$150

Glass Works Auctions

Potlid, Bear's Grease, Black Transfer, 2 Bears, Porcelain, England, 2 x 1 In.
$184

Glass Works Auctions

P

Potlid, Beef Marrow, Pomade, Black Transfer, Steer, H.P. & W.C. Taylor, 3 In. $978

Glass Works Auctions

Potlid, Carbolic, Tooth Paste, Art Nouveau, c.1890 $95

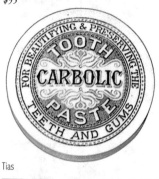

Tias

Pottery, Dish, Tulip, Blue Dashes, Yellow Lines, Tin Glaze, England, c.1695, 11 In. $2,706

Skinner, Inc.

Travel, Yosemite National Park, Southern Pacific, 1924, 23 x 16 In.	5750
United Air Lines, Pacific Northwest, Sailboat, Joseph Binder, 39 x 24 In.	563

POTLIDS are just that, lids for pots. Transfer-printed potlids had their heyday from the 1840s to the early 1900s. The English Staffordshire potteries made ceramic containers with decorative lids for bear's grease, shrimp or meat paste, cold cream, and toothpaste. Printed advertising and pictures of historical events, portraits of famous people, or scenic views were designed in black and white or color. Reproductions have been made.

Almond Shaving Cream, Army & Navy Co-Operative, Men In Uniform, 3 In.	150
Amandine, Chapped Hands, Black Transfer, 3 x 2 In.	431
American Eagle, Roussels Ambrosial Shaving Cream, Purple Transfer, 2 x 3 In.	403
Bazin's Ambrosial, Shaving Cream, Eagle, Cream, Purple Transfer, 3 In.	219
Bear, Sitting In Chair, 2 People, The Ins, Multicolor Transfer, Pratt, 3 In. *illus*	150
Bear's Grease, Black Transfer, 2 Bears, Porcelain, England, 2 x 1 In. *illus*	184
Beef Marrow, Pomade, Black Transfer, Steer, H.P. & W.C. Taylor, 3 In. *illus*	978
Ben Franklin Bust, Ambrosial Cream, Purple Transfer, 3 x 2 In.	374
Carbolic, Tooth Paste, Art Nouveau, c.1890 *illus*	95
Genuine Bear's Grease For The Hair, Bear, Cream, Black Transfer, 3¼ In.	1840
Genuine Beef Marrow, Pomatum, X. Bazin, Cow, Standing, Black Transfer, 3 In.	431
Jules Hauel Perfumer, Philadelphia, B. Franklin Bust, Cream, Red Transfer, 3½ In.	748
Jules Hauel Perfumer, Philadelphia, Benjamin Franklin Bust, Purple, 3½ In.	748
Man, Compound Extract, Black Transfer, C.E. Monell, 1½ x 3 In.	207
Odonto Oak Bark, Orris Tooth Paste, Under Revere House, Cream, Red, 3 In.	1495
Sitting Bear, Lion & Rooster, Pratt, Multicolor Transfer, 3¼ x 1½ In.	150
Superior Purified Bear'Grease, Bear Sitting, Black Transfer, 3 In.	489
Taylor's Saponaceous Compound, Man Looking In Mirror, Cream, Black, 3¼ In.	316
U.S. Capitol, Worsley Wholesale Perfumer, Purple Transfer, 4 x 2 In.	1380
Victoria White Rose Tooth Paste, Woman, Lion, Shield, Cream, Black, Square, 2 In.	81
Williams' Swiss Violet Shaving Cream, Violets, Multicolor Transfer, 3¾ In.	92
Worsley's Saponaceous Shaving Compound, Independence Hall, Black, 4 In.	978

POTTERY and porcelain are different. Pottery is opaque; you can't see through it. Porcelain is translucent. If you hold a porcelain dish in front of a strong light, you will see the light through the dish. Porcelain is colder to the touch. Pottery is softer and easier to break and will stain more easily because it is porous. Porcelain is thinner, lighter, and more durable. Majolica, faience, and stoneware are all pottery. Additional pieces of pottery are listed in this book in the categories Pottery-Art, Pottery-Contemporary, Pottery-Midcentury, and under the factory name. For information about pottery makers and marks, see *Kovels' Dictionary of Marks—Pottery & Porcelain: 1650–1850* and *Kovels' New Dictionary of Marks—Pottery & Porcelain: 1850 to the Present.*

Basin, Dragon Handles, Tripod Foot, Shaped Rim, Waves, Green, Chinese, 8 In.	601
Bean Pot, Brown Slip, Bulbous, Scroll Spout, Braided Handle, c.1900, 7 x 8 In.	370
Bird Whistle, James Seagreaves, Glazed & Molded, Signed, JCS, ½ In.	130
Bottle, Farmyard, Pond, Blue, White, Globular, Stick Neck, Flared, c.1760, 8 In.	3690
Bowl, Birds, Flowers, Molded Calligraphy Band, Green, Flared, Stem Foot, 5 In.	7995
Bowl, Coggled Rim, Yellow, Brown Slip, Trailing Lines, Combware, c.1810, 13 In.	6500
Bowl, Flower Arabesque, Pale Green, Bands, Conical, Stem Foot, 5 x 13 In.	123
Bowl, Geometric Bands, Cobalt Blue, Black, Raised Foot, Inscribed, Persia, 4 x 9 In.	123
Bowl, Hippopotamus, Scroll Band, Conical, Splay Foot, Tan Glaze, 4 x 11 In.	9225
Bowl, Horse, Rider, Leaf Band, Black & Yellow, Raised Foot, Persia, 3 x 8 In.	923
Bowl, Molded Dragons, Flower Sprays, Cone Shape, Yellow, 7 In.	505
Bowl, Molded, Crow, Blossoms, Leaves, Milled Rim, Banding, c.1755, 4½ In.	1968
Bowl, Opal, Purple Copper Glaze, Hexagonal, Benedictine Monks, 2 x 19 In.	1000
Bowl, Seated Child, Goat & Tree Border, Blue & Green, 9½ In.	900
Bowl, Swirls, Trellis, Panels, Bands, Turquoise, Black, Raised Foot, 5 x 11 In.	215
Bowl, Woman, Animals, Calligraphy Border, Turquoise, Raised Foot, 5 x 10 In.	1968

P

Brushpot, Globular, Mottled Green & Red, Peachbloom Glaze, c.1800, 5 In.	3444
Bust, Woman, Teal Hair, Pink Face, Franz Bergmann, German, 1931, 13 x 6 In.	562
Cake Plate, Fruit Tree In Garden, Pods, Fenced, Grass Border, c.1735, 9 In.	246
Cake Stand, Coastal Scene, Blue & White, Tin Glaze, Scroll Feet, c.1725, 5 In.	492
Censer, Bamboo Design, Crackle Glaze, Cylindrical, Bracket Feet, 2 x 3 In.	369
Censer, Stand, Squat, Blue Glaze, Wood Lid, Jade Finial, Handles, Splay Feet, 9 In.	593
Censer, Tripod, Green Blue Glaze, Lavender Splash, China, 1900s, 2 x 2 In.	500
Charger, Cartouche, Coronet, Griffin, Swags, Tassels, White, Blue, c.1693, 9 In.	1722
Charger, Coastal Landscape, Pagoda, White, Blue, Yellow, Tin Glaze, c.1755, 9 In.	1046
Charger, Pavilion, Cupola, Flowering Branch, Lattice Border, c.1752, 9 In.	1968
Charger, Portrait, Woman, Brown & Green Streaks, White Ground, 2 x 16 In.	2500
Charger, Swan Center, Tree, Column, Blue, Manganese, Tin Glaze, c.1750, 9 In.	1845
Charger, Wall Hanging, White, Black Splotches & Streaks, 26 x 22 In.	3375
Charger, Waterside Manor, White, Scallop Rim, Gilt, Tin Glaze, c.1755, 10 In.	492
Coupe, Globular, Green, Yellow & Cream Dot Design, Sancai Glaze, 3 In.	256
Creamer, Albany Slip, Flower, Leafy Branch, Spout, Loop Handle, Tanware, c.1850, 7 In.	875
Cup, Bulbous, Loop Handle, Pale Blue Ground, Cobalt Blue Figure, c.1690, 4 In.	4013
Cup, Copper Red Glaze, White Rim, Rounded Sides, Raised Foot, 1700s, 2 x 3 In.	1476
Cup, Fuddling, 3 Vases, Entwined Handles, Joined Center, Slipware, c.1650, 5 In.	3075
Dish, Entree, Taking Of Portobello, Warships, Blue, White, Tin Glaze, c.1740, 8 In.	2583
Dish, Flanged Rim, Turquoise, Black Glaze, Banding, Syria, 1600s, 10 In.	369
Dish, Pickle, Leaf Shape, Landscape, Blue, White, Tin Glaze, Curved Feet, c.1755, 5 In.	615
Dish, Tulip, Blue Dashes, Yellow Lines, Tin Glaze, England, c.1695, 11 In. *illus*	2706
Ewer, Black, Brown, Lobed, Strap Handle, 8 ¾ In.	390
Ewer, Lid, Shishi, Lion, Standing, Ball, Spout, Handle, c.1800, 4 In. *illus*	369
Figurine, Baby, Curled Up, Feet In Mouth, Sandstone, Signed, Ernest Reed, 11 In.	1200
Figurine, Dog, Spaniel Lying Down, White Clay, Late 1800s, 7 x 9 In.	375
Figurine, Dog, Spaniel Seated, Sewer Tile, George Bagnall, Ohio, c.1880, 9 In.	1800
Figurine, Dog, Spaniel Seated, Yellow Clay, Minor Flakes, Ohio, c.1950, 10 ½ In.	270
Figurine, Dog, Standing, Ears Pointed Up, Red, Earthenware, Chinese, 21 In.	185
Figurine, Horse & Rider, Equestrian, Holding Bird, Dog, Red, Base, Chinese, 17 In.	584
Figurine, Horse, Leg Raised, Saddle, Cloth, Bridle, Cream Glaze, Chinese, 23 In.	4018
Figurine, Magpie, Black & White, Stump, Ernst Bohne Sons, Germany, 1800s, 12 In.	70
Figurine, Rooster, Standing, Gray, Red Slip, Chinese, 12 In.	185
Figurine, Stylized Birds, On Branch, Openwork, Brown Glaze, c.1950, 14 In.	1375
Flower Brick, Fisherman, Bridge, Grass, Gilt, Pierced, Shaped Feet, c.1750, 5 In.	1476
Garniture, 2 Vases, 2 Jars, Lids, Figures, Architectural Landscape, Holland, 5 Piece	594
Group, Carp, Brown, Gilt, Tan, Japan, 11 ½ In.	344
Jar, Brushed Circles, Lines, Shouldered, Tubular Neck, Loop Handles, 13 In.	246
Jar, Bulbous, Rolled Rim, Iron Rust Glaze, Metal Sheen Sprinkled, 1700s, 8 In.	1597
Jar, Celadon Glaze, White Bands, Oval, Strap Handles, Edgefield, 6 Gal., 16 In.	1020
Jar, Dash & Eye Design, Blue, Manganese, Banding, Cylindrical, c.1670, 6 In.	3690
Jar, Dome Lid, Oval, Shouldered, Cobalt Blue Glaze, 1800s, 11 ½ In.	554
Jar, Globular, Flared, Rolled Rim, Incurved, Cream Glaze, Bisque Base, 7 In.	123
Jar, Lid, Lotus Knop, Globular, Green, Yellow Mottled, Scribble Design, 3 In.	369
Jardiniere, Green, Ocher, Dragon & Wave Band, Thailand, c.1900, 20 In. *illus*	94
Jug, Face, Brown & Frogskin, Albany Slip Glaze, J.O. Brown, S.C., 1920s, 6 In.	3900
Jug, Globular, Straight Spout, C-Shape Handle, White Glaze, Podium Base, 9 In.	1230
Jug, Oval, Handle, Ocher Mottled Glaze, Buff Clay, 10 ½ In.	94
Loving Cup, Flared Rim, Scalloped Handles, White Slip Initials, Black, 7 In.	8500
Marriage Plate, Garden, Flower & Berry Border, Blue, Yellow Border, c.1742, 9 In.	615
Pitcher & Bowl, Rooster, Adelaide Robineau, Threshold Pottery, 1924, 4 x 6 & 3 x 6 In. *illus*	1625
Pitcher, Bird, Leaves, Sgrafitto, Cream, 8 ½ In.	12
Pitcher, Fish & Seaweed, Fish Head Spout, Tail Handle, Green, Blue, 1896, 6 In.	118
Pitcher, Gypsy, Woods, Tent, Cauldron, Rockingham Glaze, Bennett, 1850, 8 ½ In. *illus*	738
Pitcher, Quatrefoil, Ribbed, Rooster Head Mouth, Brown Luster, Persia, 10 In.	7380
Pitcher, Rose, Bird, Black, Pear Shape, Scroll Handle, Saucer Foot, c.1770, 7 In.	677
Plaque, Landscape, Angry Mob, Pitchforks, Lipofsky, 35 ½ x 19 In.	125
Plaque, Nude Woman, Multicolor, Raku, 18 ½ x 13 In.	469

Pottery, Ewer, Lid, Shishi, Lion, Standing, Ball, Spout, Handle, c.1800, 4 In.
$369

Skinner, Inc.

Pottery, Jardiniere, Green, Ocher, Dragon & Wave Band, Thailand, c.1900, 20 In.
$94

Neal Auctions

Pottery, Pitcher & Bowl, Rooster, Adelaide Robineau, Threshold Pottery, 1924, 4 x 6 & 3 x 6 In.
$1,625

Rago Arts and Auction Center

P

Pottery, Pitcher, Gypsy, Woods, Tent, Cauldron, Rockingham Glaze, Bennett, 1850, 8 ½ In.
$738

Crocker Farm

Pottery, Plate, Mottled Brown, Green, Woven, Gadroon Edge, England, c.1765, 9 In.
$984

Skinner, Inc.

Pottery, Teapot, Cadogan, Teardrop Shape, Brown, Black Glaze, Handle, Chinese, 7 In.
$122

Neal Auctions

TIP

A dental mirror is useful when checking for damage or repairs inside a teapot or clock.

Plate, Boatman, Gazebo, Blue & White, Tin Glaze, Petal Rim, c.1755, 9 In.	400
Plate, Courtesan, Attendant, Flowering Trees, Blue, White, Tin Glaze, c.1755, 8 In.	308
Plate, Courtesan, Blue, Burnt Orange Rim, Diaper Border, Tin Glaze, c.1730, 9 In.	492
Plate, Flower Medallions, Blue & Brown, Slanted Sides, Splay Foot, 14 x 12 In.	923
Plate, Flowers, Leaves, Outcurved Rim, Raised Foot, Hanger, Turkey, 1600s, 12 In.	861
Plate, Flowers, Scroll, Bands, Incised Lines, Turquoise, Waisted Foot, 3 x 13 In.	123
Plate, Landscape, Seated Woman, Man, Trees, White, Blue & Pink, c.1755, 8 In.	431
Plate, Mottled Brown, Green, Woven, Gadroon Edge, England, c.1765, 9 In. *illus*	984
Plate, Pheasant, Trees, Rust & Blue Banded Rim, Tin Glaze, c.1720, 8 ½ In.	3075
Plate, Soup, Chinese Man, Landscape, Flower Border, Flanged, c.1765, 9 In.	1046
Plate, Squirrel, Scrollwork, Leafy Vines, Blue & White, Tin Glaze, c.1740, 8 In.	431
Plate, Star Medallion, Bands, Scrolls, Turquoise, Cobalt Blue, 1700s, 3 x 10 In.	369
Plate, Yellow, Coggled Rim, Brown Slip Design, Combware, c.1715, 8 In.	8000
Pouring Bowl, Incised Wave, Yellow Ash Deposit, Japan, 3 ½ x 7 In.	540
Prayer Brick, Buddha, Seated, Sanskrit Prayers, Painted, Tibet, 7 x 11 ½ In.	123
Punch Bowl, Landscape, Pagoda, Flowers, Blue, Manganese, Gilt, c.1760, 10 In.	7380
Serving Dish, Bird Catcher, Trees, Pale Blue, White, Iron Red Trim, c.1750, 13 In.	584
Serving Dish, Blue & Cream, Tin Glaze, Panels, Flowers, Songbird, c.1630, 8 In.	3075
Serving Dish, Waterside Scene, Fisherman, Bamboo, Tin Glaze, c.1755, 9 In.	1230
Spoon Tray, Water Landscape, Flower Border, Blue, Lattice Design, c.1760, 6 In.	1046
Sugar, Landscape, Cottages, Cylindrical, Dome Lid, Turnip Finial, c.1725, 6 In.	1845
Tea Bowl, Conical, Ring Foot, Hare's Fur Glazed, Black, Brown, 4 ½ In.	246
Tea Bowl, Mishima, Slip Inlaid, Eiraku, Cloth Bag & Box, 3 x 4 ¾ In.	360
Teapot, Cadogan, Teardrop Shape, Brown, Black Glaze, Handle, Chinese, 7 In. *illus*	122
Urn, Lid, Basket Weave, 14 ¼ In.	209
Vase, Austrian Heliosine, Flower Blossom Neck, Dragonflies & Leaves, 9 In.	345
Vase, Brown & Yellow Matte Glaze, Wavy Lines, Gourd, Stem Neck, 10 In.	255
Vase, Crane, Pine, Teal, c.1900, 10 ¾ In.	150
Vase, Cylinder, Banded, Cream, Leaves, 12 In.	96
Vase, Cylindrical, Shouldered, Neck Ridge, Cobalt Blue Glaze, White, 1800s, 14 In.	431
Vase, Double Phoenix, Head & Beak Handle, 8 ¾ x 7 In.	312
Vase, Exotic Flowers, M.M. Wendt, American Satsuma, c.1925, 7 In.	115
Vase, Flambe Glaze, Red, Purple Splashes, Handles, Chinese, 1800s, 12 In. *illus*	6150
Vase, Flared Foot, Cobalt Blue, Gilt Lotus Scrolls, Flowers, 1900s, 14 In.	369
Vase, Flowers, Leaves, Bands, Blue, White, 3 Trumpet Spouts, Flared, 1600s, 9 In.	246
Vase, Green Crackle Glaze, Bulbous, Flared Mouth, Rolled Rim, c.1800, 4 In.	1353
Vase, Green Luster Glaze, Blue, Gold, Dimpled, Tapered, Paul Katrich, 10 In.	885
Vase, Green, Enamel, Faceted, Hexagonal, Flared, Dragon Handles, c.1800, 8 In.	369
Vase, Hexagonal, Lobed, Raised Spine, Pinched Neck, Pale Blue Glaze, 7 In.	4018
Vase, Japanese Flowers, Blue, Red Glaze, Cylindrical, Swollen, 1890s, 19 In.	1000
Vase, Lions, Blue & White, Salt Glazed, Russell Crook, c.1910, 9 x 8 In. *illus*	6250
Vase, Marbleized, Mother Mar. 15 1844, Charles Stehm, Ozark, 6 x 3 In. *illus*	938
Vase, Mermaid, Fish, Turquoise, Gold Glaze, Shouldered, Tapered, 1940s, 15 In.	1875
Vase, Mistletoe, Carved, Green, White Berries, Flared Cylinder, c.1910, 6 In.	1875
Vase, Pale Blue Glaze, Purple, Squat, Flared Mouth, Chinese, c.1800, 5 In.	984
Vase, Pear Shape, Stick Neck, Garlic Mouth, Deep Blue Glaze, c.1885, 9 In.	1476
Vase, Peonies, Bronze Base, Pierced, Scroll Handles, Lid, Asia, c.1885, 22 In., Pair	1125
Vase, Phlox, White Ground, Saucer Foot, John Bennett, c.1880, 9 x 6 In.	4063
Vase, Pink, Blue & Purple Volcanic Glaze, Crock, Rolled Rim, Paul Katrich, 5 In.	142
Vase, Raspberry Glaze, Shouldered, Pinched Neck, Rolled Rim, 1700s, 3 In.	800
Vase, Rouleau, Blue, White, Mythical Animals, Scholars, Trellis, Chinese, 18 In. *illus*	2214
Vase, Squat, White, Orange, Green, Jervis, Rose Valley, Pa., 1904, 4 x 5 In. *illus*	1875
Vase, Stylized Waves, Plum Color, Blue, Bulbous, Squat, Flat Rim, 1912, 6 x 10 In.	625
Vase, Sugar Cane Design, Amber, Tan, Shouldered, Incurved Rim, c.1940, 10 In.	1625
Vase, Teadust Glaze, Ram Heads, Spherical, Stick Neck, Splay Foot, 1900s, 14 In.	593
Vase, Toffee Glaze, Mint Green Crystal Sprinkles, Bottle Shape, Flared Rim, 9 In.	165
Vase, Turquoise, Black, Flowers, Shouldered, Flat Rim, c.1800, 9 In.	210
Vase, Volcanic, Mottled Glaze, Multicolor, Louis Franchet, France, 5 ¾ In. *illus*	561
Water Filter, Jugendstil, Geometric Designs, Spigot, Cream Ground, 17 In.	93

POTTERY-ART. Art pottery was first made in America in Cincinnati, Ohio, during the 1870s. The pieces were hand thrown and hand decorated. The art pottery tradition continued until studio potters began making the more artistic wares. American, English, and Continental art pottery by less well-known makers is listed here. Most makers listed in *Kovels' American Art Pottery*, such as Arequipa, Ohr, Rookwood, Roseville, and Weller, are listed in their own categories in this book. More recent pottery is listed under the name of the maker or in another pottery category.

Bowl, Birmingham Rim, 1879, 5 x 8 In.	37
Bowl, Blue & Green Glaze, Cabat, Footed, 2 x 5 In.	184
Bowl, Brown, Turquoise & Yellow, Vivika & Otto Heino, 4 x 9 In.	3824
Bowl, Brown, White & Blue Glazes, Vivika & Otto Heino, 5 x 9 In.	230
Bowl, Figurehead Woman, Green, Red, Boat Shape, Art Nouveau, 22 In.	500
Bowl, Hand Molded, Thick Mottled Green Matte Glaze, Byrdcliffe, 3 x 6 In.	173
Box, Eggplant, Iron Leaves, Carabin, France, c.1897, 3 x 12 x 5 In.	2250
Charger, Blue & Black, Speckled Gray, Peter Voulkos, c.1870-1955, 14	1495
Egg Head, Orange, Black, Breasts, Arms Akimbo, Pol Chambost, 7 1/2 In.	688
Figurine, Cabin, Green, Brown & White Glaze, Chimney, c.1910, 7 x 8 In.	780
Figurine, Lion, Terra-Cotta, Carl Walters, Signed, 1953, 9 x 27 1/2 x 8 In.	2875
Figurine, Spaniel, Seated, Open Front Legs, Green, Brown, c.1910, 9 x 7 In.	3000
Group, 3 Female Figures, Art Deco, Glazed, K. Fulop, France, 1930s, 23 x 16 In.	2500
Humidor, Femme Et Poivre, Woman, Gourd, Carabin, c.1897, 5 x 6 In. ....*illus*	4063
Inkwell, Woman, Gourd, Femme A La Coloquinte, Carabin, c.1897, 5 x 6 In.	5625
Jar, Lid, Blue, Brown Drip Glaze, 6 Handles, 5 3/4 In.	72
Jardiniere, Lobed, Basket Weave, Ring Handles, Bretby, 14 3/4 In.	31
Jardiniere, Straight-Sided, Green Matte, 4-Footed, Decorations, 9 x 10 In.	308
Jug, Bronze & Pewter Mount, Revernay, G. Keller, France, 1896, 9 1/2 x 7 In.	625
Mug, Molded Frog Inside, Brown, Blue Glaze, Green Splashes, c.1875, 4 In.	840
Perfume Lamp, Old Man's Face, Molded, Nude Woman Looking In, 10 In.	443
Pilgrim Jar, Flowers, Leaves, Light Blue, Mary Louise McLaughlin, 12 In.	625
Pitcher, 3 Cranes, Blue, Black, Relief, W.P. Jervis, 4 In.	288
Pitcher, Brown & Blue Glaze, Stag, Doe, Branch Handle, Acorn Tip, c.1875, 9 In.	210
Pitcher, Carlton Ball & Aaron Bohrod, Green, Black Goose Front & Back, 7 In.	259
Pitcher, Charcoal Blue & Rose & Chocolate, Robinson-Ransbottom, 24 In.	345
Pitcher, Honey Glaze, Blue Streaks, Old Man Spout, Druid Snip, c.1870, 11 In.	420
Pitcher, Hunt Scene, Molded, Hound Handle, Rockingham Glaze, c.1870, 9 In.	688
Pitcher, Stoneware, Horse Handle, Dalpayrat, France, 1900, 6 1/2 x 6 x 4 In.	1188
Pitcher, Wood Carved Pattern, Black Handle, Bretby, English, 12 In.	123
Plate, Black, White Fish & Sun, Carlton Ball & Aaron Bohrod, 9 In.	518
Plate, Screws, Stripes, Blue & White, Mineo Mizuno, 1973, 18 In. ....*illus*	625
Roof Tile, Figural, Squirrel Holding Pinecone, Tin Glaze, c.1925, 16 x 14 In.	366
Statue, Pig, Glazed, Scratch Lines, Spots, Carl Walters, 1932, 8 1/2 x 18 In. ....*illus*	16250
Tray, Mermaid, Vide-Poche, Bronze, Stamped, Dalpayrat, c.1900, 4 x 7 In. ....*illus*	1188
Tray, Shell, Nude Rising From Waves, Crystalline Glaze, Mougin Nancy, 3 x 7 In.	431
Tumbler, Abstract, Green & Brown & Ivory On Pink Clay, Julia Mattson, 4 In.	115
Vase, 2 Handles, Sang De Boueuf Glaze, Dalpayrat, France, c.1900, 20 x 9 In.	7500
Vase, Azaleas, Lime Green, Tapered, Cylindrical Rim, J. Bennett, 1880, 6 In.	2500
Vase, Basket, Green Matte Glaze, Reticulated Handle, Paul Dachsel, 1905, 8 In.	1320
Vase, Blue Band, Flowers, Mosaic, France, Jean Gerbino, 11 In.	246
Vase, Boule, Red Glaze, Stick Neck, Signed, Georges Jouve, c.1957, 8 x 7 In. ....*illus*	20781
Vase, Brick Color, Green & Yellow Drip Glaze, E. Lion, c.1920, 15 In.	236
Vase, Brown Arching Branches, Blue Ground, Max Laeuger, Germany, c.1900, 9 In.	523
Vase, Brown, Cone Shape, Handles, Bretby, English, 8 3/4 In.	88
Vase, Brown, Spines, Short Neck, Sgraffito, Ring Foot, S. Carey, 9 x 6 In.	330
Vase, Burgundy With White Speckles & Pearl Luster, Paul Katrich, 9 In.	230
Vase, Canary Yellow, Gray Clouds, Green Raindrops, Paul Katrich, 4 In.	345
Vase, Carved Spiral Design, Oxblood Glaze, France, 1920s, 19 1/2 x 10 In.	1250
Vase, Cattails, Molded Frog, Trumpet, Zigzag Rim, Green Glaze, c.1910, 11 In.	1050
Vase, Chameleons, Royal Lancastrian, Blue, W.S. Mycock, England, c.1910, 5 x 5 In.	2500

Pottery, Vase, Flambe Glaze, Red, Purple Splashes, Handles, Chinese, 1800s, 12 In.
$6,150

Skinner, Inc.

Pottery, Vase, Lions, Blue & White, Salt Glazed, Russell Crook, c.1910, 9 x 8 In.
$6,250

Rago Arts and Auction Center

P

The Simpsons

The Simpsons animated TV series has spawned a quantity of collectibles, and because the series is thriving, more collectibles will appear. The show is now seen in more than sixty countries and is one of the most successful animated television series ever created. Looks like a promising collectibles field.

Pottery, Vase, Marbleized, Mother Mar. 15 1844, Charles Stehm, Ozark, 6 x 3 In. $938

Rago Arts and Auction Center

Pottery, Vase, Rouleau, Blue, White, Mythical Animals, Scholars, Trellis, Chinese, 18 In. $2,214

Skinner, Inc.

Pottery, Vase, Squat, White, Orange, Green, Jervis, Rose Valley, Pa., 1904, 4 x 5 In. $1,875

Rago Arts and Auction Center

Vase, Cherry Blossoms, Cobalt Blue Ground, John Bennett, c.1880, 10 x 6 In.....................*illus*	2875
Vase, Cobalt Blue, Crystalline, Round, Adelaide Robineau, 4 In.	4000
Vase, Crystalline Glaze, Red, 3 Sections, France, 10 In.	246
Vase, Curdled Russet, Green, Bulbous, Swollen Rim, W. Walley, 1900, 7 x 6 In.	2125
Vase, Diabolo, Enameled Stoneware, Roger Capron, 1957, 12 x 8 In. ....*illus*	1804
Vase, Dragon, Gilt, Iridescent Glaze, Charenton, France, c.1906, 20 x 10 In.	1875
Vase, Dragon, Green, 6½ x 13 In.	1000
Vase, Drip Glaze, Stamps, Olive, 3¼ x 6 In..................	625
Vase, Enameled & Glazed, Flowers, Gazo Foudji, France, 1890s, 19 x 7 In.	1000
Vase, Encircling Pattern, Purple Glaze, Incised, Paul Bellardo, c.1900, 3 In.	259
Vase, Feelie, White, Light Blue Glaze, Inscribed Cabat, A, Fine Crazing, 4 In.	431
Vase, Flowers, Panels, Green, Blue, Gold, Ernst Wahliss, Art Nouveau, 12 In.	920
Vase, Flowers, Red, Yellow, Tan To Pink Ground, A.D. England, c.1920, 7 In.	206
Vase, Geometric Pattern, Edouard Cazaux, Signed, 7½ x 4½ In.....................*illus*	375
Vase, Glazed Stoneware, Bronze Lily Pad Mount, Germany, c.1897, 20 x 11 In.	4375
Vase, Glazed Stoneware, Silver Mount, Eugene Baudin, Monaco, 1900s, 7 x 6 In............*illus*	1500
Vase, Green, Lizard, Squat, 4 Curled Feet, W.J. Walley, c.1900, 3 x 4 In.	2825
Vase, Herons In Flight & Standing, Bowl, Yellow, Arthur Baggs, 4 In.	374
Vase, Iridescent Blue, Dragonflies, Abdomen Handle, 9 In.	523
Vase, Mahogany Glaze, Oscar Bachelder, Omar Khayyam Pottery, 7 x 4 In.	938
Vase, Microcrystalline Glaze, Charles F. Binns, 1925, 12 x 5 In.	8750
Vase, Mottled Green, Impressed, Bretby, English, 12½ In.	246
Vase, Mottled Purple, Blue Matte Glaze, Tapered Urn, E. Lachenal, c.1900, 5 In.	767
Vase, Mottled Red, Flattened Sphere, Offcenter Hole, E. Lachenal, c.1900, 3 x 4 In.	443
Vase, Neptune, Mermaid, , Seaweed, Bubbles, Aqua, Art Nouveau, 17 In.	1481
Vase, Pear Shape, Swollen Collar, Elephant Heads, Brown Matte Glaze, Drip, 12 In.	590
Vase, Raised Coil, Gold & Copper Luster, Blue & White, Paul Katrich, 6 In.	575
Vase, Scarab, Crystalline Glaze, Blue, Adelaide Robineau, 3½ x 3 In................	9760
Vase, Stoneware, Reptile Lid, Celadon, Gensoli, France, 1900s, 8 x 11 In.	10000
Vase, Stylized Waves, Purple & Blue, 1912, 6 x 10 In...............	625
Vase, Tree, Landscape, Teal, Yellow, Almeric Walter, c.1890, 8¼ In.	687
Vase, Urn, Olive & Light Blue, Whimsical Design, Arthur Baggs, 6½ In.	345
Vase, Waisted, Reserves, Woman, Warrior, Blue, Brown, Yellow, 13 x 5½ In.	175
Vase, White With Metallic Brown Glazes, Vivika & Otto Heino, 5 In................	403
Vase, White, Purple Glaze, Pulled Pointy Tips, Mougin, France, c.1900, 7 x 7 In........	1125
Vase, Winter Scene, Blue, White, Faux Jewels, Tapered, Flat Rim, Wahliss, 14 In.	531
Vase, Yellow Sailboats, Avertine, Rhead For Wardle, 1899, 5¼ In.	375
Wall Pocket, Grapes & Grape Leaf, Buff Clay Green Highlights, Marked, 12 In..........	230

POTTERY-CONTEMPORARY lists pieces made by artists working about 1975 and later.

Bowl, 2 People In A Pickup Truck, Beige, Black, R. Nichols, 8 In.	480
Bowl, Drunk At Bar, Robert Nichols, 8¼ In......................	1080
Bowl, Enslavement Of Natives By Spanish Missionaries, 13 In.	960
Bowl, Faces, Volcanic Glaze, Pedestal, Beatrice Wood, 8 x 9 In.................*illus*	2500
Bowl, Stand, Celadon, Fluted, Wide Rim, Marked, Cliff Lee, 7 x 8 In.	1188
Bowl, Volcanic Glaze, Tan, Black, Green, Cylinder Foot, Wide Rim, Lovera, 5 x 14 In.	2375
Bust, Self-Portrait, Blue, White, Tongue Out, R. Arneson, 7 x 4 In.	8540
Bust, Self-Portrait, Pink, Blue, Robert Arneson, c.1972....................	9760
Bust, Self-Portrait, Pink, Robert Arneson, 1978, 7½ In.	9150
Chalice, Gold Luster, Spread Foot, Openwork, Beaded, 1980, 12 In.	5400
Charger, Brown, Piercing, Tan, Peter Voulkos, 1973, 17 In.	4687
Charger, Brown, Piercing, Tan, Peter Voulkos, 1979, 22 In.	6710
Cup, White, Hoshino & Kayoko Satoru, 4 Piece.........	62
Figurine, Minstrel, Glazed, Mulitcolor, Italy, c.1955, 25 x 10 In.	94
Figurine, Successful Business Man, Glazed, Beatrice Wood, 12 x 19 In.................*illus*	1500
Figurine, Taco, Frog Food Series, Glazed, D. Gilhooly, 1980, 2½ x 4 In. ....*illus*	875
Figurine, Warthog, Reclining, Paint, Gilhooly, c.1970, 11 x 17 In.	1560
Garden Seat, Stoneware, Glazed, T. Takaezu, 19 x 12 In..............*illus*	4375
Jar, Moonpot, Rattle, White, Green Drip Design, Takaezu, 7 x 6 In..........	2250
Mask, Brown, White, Cracked Earth, Michael A. Barnes, 15 x 8 In.	200

P

Pottery, Vase, Volcanic, Mottled Glaze, Multicolor, Louis Franchet, France, 5¾ In.
$561

Humler & Nolan

Pottery-Art, Humidor, Femme Et Poivre, Woman, Gourd, Carabin, c.1897, 5 x 6 In.
$4,063

Rago Arts and Auction Center

Pottery-Art, Plate, Screws, Stripes, Blue & White, Mineo Mizuno, 1973, 18 In.
$625

Los Angeles Modern Auctions

Pottery-Art, Statue, Pig, Glazed, Scratch Lines, Spots, Carl Walters, 1932, 8½ x 18 In.
$16,250

Rago Arts and Auction Center

Pottery-Art, Tray, Mermaid, Vide-Poche, Bronze, Stamped, Dalpayrat, c.1900, 4 x 7 In.
$1,188

Rago Arts and Auction Center

Pottery-Art, Vase, Boule, Red Glaze, Stick Neck, Signed, Georges Jouve, c.1957, 8 x 7 In.
$20,781

Sotheby's

Pottery-Art, Vase, Cherry Blossoms, Cobalt Blue Ground, John Bennett, c.1880, 10 x 6 In.
$2,875

Rago Arts and Auction Center

POTTERY-CONTEMPORARY

Pottery-Art, Vase, Diabolo, Enameled Stoneware, Roger Capron, 1957, 12 x 8 In.
$1,804

Pierre Berge & Associates

Pottery-Art, Vase, Geometric Pattern, Edouard Cazaux, Signed, 7½ x 4½ In.
$375

Rago Arts and Auction Center

TIP

Put ceramic saucers or glass or plastic plant holders under vases of flowers or potted plants. There are inexpensive throwaway plastic dishes that have a rim and are exactly the right size and shape for a plant.

P

POTTERY-CONTEMPORARY

Pottery-Art, Vase, Glazed Stoneware, Silver Mount, Eugene Baudin, Monaco, 1900s, 7 x 6 In.
$1,500

Rago Arts and Auction Center

Pottery-Contemporary, Bowl, Faces, Volcanic Glaze, Pedestal, Beatrice Wood, 8 x 9 In.
$2,500

Rago Arts and Auction Center

Pottery-Contemporary, Figurine, Successful Business Man, Glazed, Beatrice Wood, 12 x 19 In.
$1,500

Rago Arts and Auction Center

Pottery-Contemporary, Figurine, Taco, Frog Food Series, Glazed, D. Gilhooly, 1980, 2 ½ x 4 In.
$875

Rago Arts and Auction Center

Pottery-Contemporary, Garden Seat, Stoneware, Glazed, T. Takaezu, 19 x 12 In.
$4,375

Rago Arts and Auction Center

Pottery-Contemporary, Platter, Incised & Glazed, Long Arm Of The Law, RML, 16 x 9 In.
$150

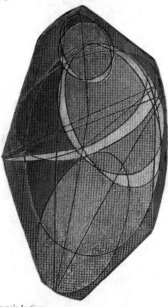

Cowan's Auctions

Pottery-Contemporary, Vase, Iron Oxide Glaze, Stoneware, Peter Voulkos, c.1956, 14 x 9 In.
$25,000

Los Angeles Modern Auctions

TIP

Plastic bubble wrap can ruin the glaze on old ceramics. If the wrap touches the piece for a long time in a hot storage area, it may discolor the glaze or adhere to the surface in an almost permanent glob.

Pottery-Contemporary, Vase, Scholar Owl, Blue Eyes, Mottled Brown Glaze, Ephraim, 2010, 11 In.
$325

Humler & Nolan

Pitcher, Pillow, Yellow, Green, Red, B. Woodman, c.1985, 20 x 23 In.	6875
Plaque, Nose, Round, Robert Arneson, 17 In.	5795
Plate, City Scene, Multicolor, Lidya Buzio, 16 In.	1375
Platter, Incised & Glazed, Long Arm Of The Law, RML, 16 x 9 In. ....*illus*	150
Sculpture, Abstract, Gray, Yellow, Red, Fred Stodder, 22 x 9 In.	165
Sculpture, Admonishment Of The Paint Take, P. Warashina, 17 x 13 In.	2500
Sculpture, El Hermoso Naufrago, Nudes, Flag, Cristina Cordova, 37 x 22 In.	3172
Sculpture, Geometric, Red, Yellow, Black Lines	62
Sculpture, Glazed & Painted, M. Lucero, N.Y., 1990s, 30 x 23 In.	3125
Sculpture, Horse With Swallows, Adrian Arleo, 24 x 21 In.	3416
Sculpture, Leatherlike Pouch, Marilyn Levine, 1982, 5 ½ x 5 In.	4270
Sculpture, Leroy & Bertha's, Streetscape, M. Garman, 1975, 24 x 31 In.	500
Sculpture, Man, Dog, Trashcan, Michael Garman, 1984, 13 x 13 In.	300
Sculpture, Mouth, Pink Lips, Teeth, Signed, Verne Funk, 3 x 5 In.	1000
Sculpture, Ohio Dog II, 1996, Jack Earl, 27 x 17 In.	1342
Sculpture, Place Setting XIII, Laslo Fekete, 4 x 9 ½ In.	579
Sculpture, Plate, Broken China, Round, Stephen Bowers, 14 ½ In.	500
Sculpture, Samothraki & Canicula, Viola Frey, 13 x 12 In.	2684
Sculpture, Smoker No. 1, Multicolor, Robert Charland, 16 x 16 In.	610
Sculpture, That's Bill Smokin, Jack Earl, 1981, 47 x 17 In.	3750
Sculpture, Untitled, Painted Building, Lidya Buzio, 18 x 16 In.	1220
Sculpture, Watching Evil Trying To Be Good, S. Bradford, 4 x 12 In.	312
Sphere, Gray Matte, Incised Striations, Ani Kasten, 11 x 12 In.	461
Teapot, Blue, Disc Handle, Rectangular, Peter Shire, 1981, 7 x 5 In.	1875
Teapot, Mother & Child, Blue, 11 x 17 ½ In.	854
Vase, 3 Blond Faces, Raku, 1980s, 7 ½ In.	71
Vase, Blue Luster, Cascading Flowers, Shouldered, P. Katrich, 6 In.	177
Vase, Blue, Green & Pink Iridescent, Bottle Shape, B. Wood, 10 x 9 In.	8750
Vase, Gilt, Zigzag, Brown, Rick Dillingham, 12 x 15 In.	3538
Vase, Human Shape, Modernist, Black, Purple, 1980s, 19 x 15 In.	708
Vase, Imperial Yellow, Prickly Melon, Cliff Lee, 10 In.	935
Vase, Iron Oxide Glaze, Stoneware, Peter Voulkos, c.1956, 14 x 9 In. ....*illus*	25000
Vase, Monumental, Multicolor, San Polo, Italy, c.1955, 24 x 12 In.	1875
Vase, Pinched, Iridescent Blue, Beato, 4 ½ In.	593
Vase, Puppy, White Glaze, Jeff Koons, Signed, 1998, 17 x 10 In.	10500
Vase, Purple, Oxblood Iridescent Glaze, Bulbous, C. Lee, 1990, 7 x 7 In.	1750
Vase, Rust Volcanic Glaze, Apple Shape, Top Hole, Lee, 1989, 6 x 5 In.	625
Vase, Scholar Owl, Blue Eyes, Mottled Brown Glaze, Ephraim, 2010, 11 In. ....*illus*	325
Vase, Teal, Brown, Bands, Beach Day, Julie Perry, 8 In.	64
Vase, Tide Pool Vessel, Anne Goldman, 9 x 15 In.	1708
Vase, Yellow, Fluted, Bulbous, Narrow Rim, Cliff Lee, c.1990, 8 x 6 In.	2500

POTTERY-MIDCENTURY includes pieces made from the 1940s to about 1975.

Bowl, Bird, Worm, Oxidized Paraffin, Picasso, 1952, 2 x 6 In. ....*illus*	1722
Bowl, Blue, Geometric, Wilhelm Kage, 1956, 11 ¾ In.	2500
Bowl, Deer, Grass, Green, Brown, Wayland Gregory, 5 In.	119
Bowl, Glazed, Brown, Tan, Lines, Laura Andreson, 1950, 4 ½ x 5 In.	500
Bowl, Yellow Interior, Green, Purple, 15 x 24 In.	354
Bowl, Yellow, Brown, Etched, Signed, c.1950, 8 ¼ In.	2750
Centerpiece, Blue, Crystalline, c.1947, 3 ½ x 12 ¼ In.	476
Chalice, Couple, Faces, Iridescent Glaze, Beatrice Wood, 11 x 9 In.	4688
Charger, Blue, Gray, Rust, Streaks Design, Wildenhain, c.1950, 16 In.	1063
Charger, Octopus, Crab, Multicolor, Pippo Garcia, 22 In.	86
Chicken Waterer, Grotesque Face, Green, Drip, B. Craig, N.C., 10 In.	1560
Coupe, Blue, White Circles, Bulbous, Pedestal, H. McIntosh, 5 x 7 In.	1188
Creamer, Figural Piglet, Pink Cheeks, Open Top, Tail Handle, 1950s, 3 x 5 In.	15
Dish, Brown, Blue, Smile, Sun, Pablo Picasso, 15 ½ x 12 In.	6875
Ewer, Face, White, Black, Brown, P. Picasso, 12 In.	7500
Figurine, Bullfrog, Base, Sandstone, Signed, E. Popey Reed, U.S.A., 9 In.	420

Pottery-Midcentury, Bowl, Bird, Worm, Oxidized Paraffin, Picasso, 1952, 2 x 6 In.
$1,722

Skinner, Inc.

Pottery-Midcentury, Figurine, Horse, Rearing, Black Matte, Glossy Gold, Signed, Waylande Gregory, 8 In.
$472

Humler & Nolan

Pottery-Midcentury, Jug, Face, Devil, Painted, China Teeth, Handle, Attrib. D. Brown, 21 In.
$3,600

Brunk Auctions

P

Pottery-Midcentury, Jug, Face, Runny
Mottled Green Alkaline Glaze, Lanier Meaders,
8 In.
$960

Brunk Auctions

Pottery-Midcentury, Jug, Face, Swirled Gray
& Cream Glaze, Applied Features, B. Craig,
16 In.
$1,140

Brunk Auctions

Pottery-Midcentury, Jug, Figural, Red
Brown Metallic Glaze, Strap Handle,
Attrib. N. Smith, 8 In.
$1,080

Brunk Auctions

Pottery-Midcentury, Pitcher,
Faces With Circles, White, Gray Patina,
Picasso, 1969, 11 In.
$5,750

New Orleans Auction Galleries

Pottery-Midcentury, Pitcher, Picador,
Partially Glazed, P. Picasso, Madoura, 1952,
5 In.
$2,750

Rago Arts and Auction Center

Pottery-Midcentury, Plate, Flute Player,
Embossed, Glazed, Picasso, Madoura, 1951,
10 In.
$7,500

New Orleans Auction Galleries

Pottery-Midcentury, Vase, Abstract Figure,
Buildings, Marcello Fantoni, 1950s,
19 x 9 In.
$750

Rago Arts and Auction Center

TIP
*Mayonnaise can be used to
remove old masking tape,
stickers, or labels from
glass or china.*

Pottery-Midcentury, Vase, Black, White,
Signed, Georges Jouve, c.1950, 20 x 8 In.
$27,709

Sotheby's

P

Figurine, Horse, Rearing, Black Matte, Glossy Gold, Signed, Waylande Gregory, 8 In........*illus*	472
Figurine, Toucan, Brown, Gilt, Head, Wayland Gregory, 12 x 4 In.	833
Figurine, Woman, Blue, White, Bjorn Wiinblad, 8 In.	126
Jug, Face, Bulging Eyes, Long Nose, Teeth, Green Over Brown, 11 In.	540
Jug, Face, Devil, Black, Bulging Eyes, Crooked Nose, Horns, D.P. Brown, 23 In......................	6000
Jug, Face, Devil, Mottled Black & Green, Broken Rock Teeth, L. Meaders, 9 In.	2160
Jug, Face, Devil, Painted, China Teeth, Handle, Attrib. D. Brown, 21 In. ....*illus*	3600
Jug, Face, Devil, Red Paint, Black Mustache, Goatee, Browns, N.C., 15 In.	660
Jug, Face, Exaggerated Nose & Ears, Black Paint, Arie Meaders, Ga., 8 In...........................	3360
Jug, Face, Idi Amin, Exaggerated, Runny Green Glaze, Lanier Meaders, 8 In.	780
Jug, Face, Runny Mottled Green Alkaline Glaze, Lanier Meaders, 8 In...................*illus*	960
Jug, Face, Swirled Gray & Cream Glaze, Applied Features, B. Craig, 16 In. ....*illus*	1140
Jug, Figural, Red Brown Metallic Glaze, Strap Handle, Attrib. N. Smith, 8 In. ....*illus*	1080
Pitcher, Centaur Au Vissages, Engobe & Paraffin Decoration, Picasso, 10 In.	10148
Pitcher, Green, Diamonds, Signed Wilhelm Kagel, 11 x 10 ½ In.	61
Pitcher, Faces With Circles, White, Gray Patina, Picasso, 1969, 11 In. ....*illus*	5750
Pitcher, Little-Headed Pitcher, Enamel, Picasso, Madoura, 5 x 6 In.	3750
Pitcher, Picador, Partially Glazed, P. Picasso, Madoura, 1952, 5 In. ....*illus*	2750
Pitcher, Quatre Visages, Face, White, Orange & Black Dots, Picasso, 9 In.	7800
Pitcher, Visage Aux Cercles, Stylized Face, Dated 1969, Picasso, Madoura, 11 In.	7308
Pitcher, Yan Barbu, Face, Red Earthenware, Black Paint, Picasso, Madoura, 10 In.	7080
Plaque, Abstract, Orange, Red, Harris Strong, Frame, 1960s, 30 x 6 In., Pair	187
Plaque, Luncheon On The Grass, Brown & Amber, P. Picasso, 1964, 20 x 24 In.	50000
Plaque, Square With Face, Red Earthenware, Picasso, Madoura, 6 In...............................	937
Plaque, Stoneware, Decorated, Brown, Round, Waylande Gregory, 17 In.	976
Plate, Apples, White, Flowerpot, Apple, P. Picasso, 1956, 10 In.	4063
Plate, Bird On Branch, White Enamel, Black Glaze, Picasso, Madoura, 6 ½ In........................	2016
Plate, Bird, Tufted Head Feathers, Black, White, Green, Pablo Picasso, 6 x 1 ½ In.	1740
Plate, Black Bull, Leaf Border, Orange Ground, Picasso, Madoura, 10 In.	2640
Plate, Bull Under The Tree, Oxidized Paraffin, Picasso, Madoura, 8 In.	1750
Plate, Flower Box, Blue, White, Madoura, Picasso, 9 ¾ In.	875
Plate, Flute Player, Embossed, Glazed, Picasso, Madoura, 1951, 10 In..................*illus*	7500
Plate, Joie De Vivre, White, Madoura, Picasso, 16 ½ In.	6490
Plate, Toros, Bulls, Stamped, Edition Picasso, Madoura, 7 ¾ In.	3250
Plate, Wide Rim, Mottled Brown, Olive, Sgraffito, Faces, 6 In.	338
Sculpture, Kimono Series, Pink, Arrow, P. Soldner, 1984, 20 x 16 In...............................	2375
Sculpture, Nudes, Garden, Blue, 4 Women, J. Greenberg, 22 x 12 In.	175
Teapot, Horse Finial, Iridescent Glaze, Beatrice Wood, 11 x 6 In.................................	5938
Tray, Black Cat, Smiling, White Ground, Rectangular, 13 ½ x 10 In.	369
Vase, Abstract Figure, Buildings, Marcello Fantoni, 1950s, 19 x 9 In..................*illus*	750
Vase, Batwing, White, Colin Pearson, 5 In...	431
Vase, Batwing, White, Red Smudges, Colin Pearson, 4 In.	443
Vase, Beige, Gray, Short, Narrow Neck, Raku, 15 x 4 ½ In.	1140
Vase, Bird, Glazed, Gambone, Signed, Italy, c.1960, 31 x 13 In.	6875
Vase, Black, White Swirls, 10 ½ x 14 In...	175
Vase, Black, White, Signed, Georges Jouve, c.1950, 20 x 8 In..................*illus*	27709
Vase, Blue, Flowers, Square, Flared, France, c.1960, 24 In., Pair	1500
Vase, Brown Glaze, Elephant Trunk Shape, Nude, Bampi, 1953, 36 In.	2875
Vase, Brown, Zebra Stripes, Basket Weave, C. Conover, 16 x 17 In.	47200
Vase, Cobalt Blue, Smudges, Wide Rim, Tapered, R. Staffel, 1950s, 7 In.	625
Vase, Double Gourd, Chevron Band, Gambone, Italy, c.1950, 6 In.	236
Vase, Feelie, Blue, White, Cabat, 4 In.	442
Vase, Feelie, Brown, Round, Rose Cabat, 5 ¾ In.	212
Vase, Feelie, Light Blue, Rose Cabat, 3 x 2 ½ In.	437
Vase, Feelie, Pink, White, Cabat, 3 In.	212
Vase, Female Figures, Glazed Ceramic, Beatrice Wood, 11 x 7 In.	3125
Vase, Flowers & Birds, Marked, Guido Gambone, 12 x 5 In.................*illus*	576
Vase, Geometrics, Symbols, Guido Gambone, Donkey Cipher, 1960s, 19 x 5 In. ....*illus*	3250
Vase, Glossy Brown, Black Drip, 3 Twisted Handles, A.R. Cole, 17 In.	300
Vase, Light Gatherer, Face, Tapered, Wavy Rim, R. Staffel, 5 x 4 In.	875
Vase, Mottled Green Blue & Brown, M. Fantoni, Signed, Italy, 24 x 8 In...........................	1875

Pottery-Midcentury, Vase, Flowers & Birds, Marked, Guido Gambone, 12 x 5 In.
$576

Neal Auctions

Pottery-Midcentury, Vase, Geometrics, Symbols, Guido Gambone, Donkey Cipher, 1960s, 19 x 5 In.
$3,250

Rago Arts and Auction Center

Pottery-Midcentury, Vase, Runny Mottled Green Malachite Glaze, J.B. Cole, 23 In.
$600

Brunk Auctions

P

Powder Flask, Copper, Raised Leaves, Pinched Waist, Hawksley, 8¼ x 3½ In. $225

Ruby Lane

Powder Horn, Half Moon Tavern, Men Dueling, Service Record, John Deen, 1758, 15 In. $15,525

James D. Julia Auctioneers

Pressed Glass, Atlanta, Syrup, Ruby Stain, Clear Cut, Tarentum Glass Co., c.1894, 5 In. $152

Jeffrey S. Evans

Pressed Glass, Currier & Ives, Syrup, Blue, Co-Operative Flint Glass Co., c.1887, 7 In. $70

Jeffrey S. Evans

Vase, Pear Shape, Applied Loops, Blue, Gray, Brown Matte, 6 x 3 In.	312
Vase, Runny Mottled Green Malachite Glaze, J.B. Cole, 23 In. ....*illus*	600

 POWDER FLASKS AND POWDER HORNS were made to hold the gunpowder used in antique firearms. The early examples were made of horn or wood; later ones were of copper or brass.

POWDER FLASK

Brass, American Eagle, Shield, Stars, Crossed Pistols, Colt	350
Brass, Clasped Hands, Eagle, 9 In.	212
Brass, Engraved, Concentric Circles, Spout, Lugs, Morocco, 5½ In.	31
Brass, Pear Shape, Engraved, Morocco, 9¼ In.	75
Brass, Pear Shape, Engraved, Morocco, c.1880, 8¾ In.	75
Brass, Pear Shape, Military Issue, Copper Fittings, 8¾ In.	100
Brass, Pierced, Engraved, Morocco, 9 In.	100
Coconut Shell, Central Cartouche, Flags, Cannon, Helmet, 5 x 3½ In.	480
Copper, Lacquered, Pear Shape, Brass Nozzle, 9¼ In.	300
Copper, Raised Leaves, Pinched Waist, Hawksley, 8¼ x 3½ In. ....*illus*	225
Damascus Steel, Figural, Jaguar, Gold Inlay, Arabesque Vines, 6½ In.	687
Hide, Tooled, Brass Cap, Chain, c.1880, 8¼ In.	25
Ivory, Figural, Parrot, India, 1700s, 9¾ In.	649
Ivory, Gunpowder, Oval, Hammered Metal, Handles, Beading, 1800s, 9 In.	395
Metal, Thumb Operated Opener, 9½ In.	31
Silver, Engraved, Round, Quadrants, Animals, Leaves, Tibet, 1700s, 6 In.	375
Wood, Metal, Leather Cover, c.1730, 8 x 4½ In.	1500

POWDER HORN

Chased Copper, Brass Mounts, Gilt, Cowboy Figures, Lasso, Bull, 18 In.	837
Engraved, Iron Staples, Wood Plug, Germany, Early 1800s, 10½ In.	720
Engraved, Jeremiah Eastman, Crosshatched Designs, c.1758, 17 In.	8118
Flowers, Relief Carved, Wooden Plug, Moon Face, L. Landry, c.1820, 11 In.	2806
French & Indian War, Engraved, British Great Seal, 15 In.	4600
Geometric Patterns, Scrollwork, 10½ In.	2400
Half Moon Tavern, Men Dueling, Service Record, John Deen, 1758, 15 In. .....*illus*	15525
Inscribed David Eaton Weare, c.1750, 11 In.	1020
Lion & Unicorn, Flowers, Cannon, Flags, Caleb Butters, c.1750, 13 In.	3690
Map, Upper Hudson, Mohawk River, 15⅝ In.	3840
Mountain Sheep, Flattened, 2 Pierced Holes, 16 In.	115
Owls, Relief Carved, Branch, Bird, Wooden Plug, Silver Mount, 13 In.	793
Peleg Beede Of Sandwich, 1756, 14¼ In.	2280
Relief Carved Pelican, 3 Figures, One Holding Rifle, Wooden Plug, 14 In.	488
Sailing Ships, Horse Isle, Wolff, Madison & Seneca, c.1813, 13 x 4 In.	3335
Samel Aken, Wooden Plug, 1827, 12¼ In.	2006
Scalloped Borders, Couple, Leaves, Birds, Inscribed James Wascot, 10 In.	2520
Scrimshaw, 2 Frigates Under Full Sail, Naval Cannons, Anchor, 11 In.	253
Siege Of Boston, Fleet, 8¼ In.	2160
Staghorn, Split, St. Michael, Brick Wall, Belt Hook, 9 In.	1013
Victoria Ship, 1869, 18½ In.	605
Wood Base, Indian Tacks, Tansel, c.1841, 10½ In.	1725

PRATT FENTON — **PRATT** ware means two different things. It was an early Staffordshire pottery, cream-colored with colored decorations, made by Felix Pratt during the late eighteenth century. There was also Pratt ware made with transfer designs during the mid-nineteenth century in Fenton, England. Reproductions of the transfer-printed Pratt are being made.

Creamer, Cow, White, Brown Spots, 6 x 6¼ In.	719
Figurine, Cow, Calf, Brown, Black Spots, Spongeware Base, c.1800, 5¾ x 6 In.	153
Figurine, Cow, Female Gardener, Spongeware Base, Multicolor, England, 6 x 6 In.	778
Figurine, Cow, Male Gardener, Spongeware Base, Multicolor, 6 x 6 In.	660
Figurine, Lion, Lying Down, Tan & Brown Sponge Design, Green Base, c.1800, 3 In.	201

P

PRESSED GLASS, or pattern glass, was first made in the United States in the 1820s after the invention of glass pressing machines. Hundreds of patterns of pressed glass were made in complete table settings. Although the Boston and Sandwich Works was the most famous of the pressed glass factories, there were about sixteen other factories making pressed glass from 1830 to 1850, and still more from 1850 to 1900, when pressed glass reached its greatest popularity. It is now being widely reproduced. The pattern names used in this listing are based on the information in the book *Pressed Glass in America* by John and Elizabeth Welker. There may be pieces of pressed glass listed in this book in other categories, such as Lamp, Ruby Glass, Sandwich Glass, and Souvenir.

Apple Blossom, Bowl, Crimped, Marigold, Dugan, 7 1/2 In.		42
Arched Fleur-De-Lis, Nappy, Finger Loop, Higbee, c.1898		7
Atlanta, Syrup, Ruby Stain, Clear Cut, Tarentum Glass Co., c.1894, 5 In.	*illus*	152
Cat's Eye & Block, Pitcher, Applied Handle, Higbee, c.1896, 12 In.		65
Currier & Ives, Syrup, Blue, Co-Operative Flint Glass Co., c.1887, 7 In.	*illus*	70
Dakota, Candy Jar, Globe, Ground Neck & Lid, 13 1/2 In.		93
Flamingo Habitat, Goblet, Hobbs, Brockunier, c.1880, 6 In.		12
Frosted Lion, Compote, Oval, Lid, Base, Gillinder, c.1877, 4 x 8 In.		95
Gibson Girl, Pitcher, Beaded Rim, National Glass Co., c.1903, 8 7/8 In.	*illus*	110
Honeycomb, Compote, Round Stepped Foot, 5 1/2 In.		183
Horseshoe, Bowl, Oval, Adams, c.1881, 9 x 5 x 2 In.		43
Horseshoe, Creamer, Adams, c.1881, 5 3/4 In.		38
Lacy Daisy, Relish, Handles, U.S. Glass, 1900s, 9 1/4 In.		10
Leaf & Dart, Goblet, c.1870, 6 1/2 In.		11
Liberty Bell, Butter, Cover, Round, Gillinder		95
Manhattan, Bowl, Scalloped Rim, U.S. Glass, c.1910, 8 In.		8
Overall Lattice, Pitcher, Water, Indiana Glass, 9 In.		13
Panama, Compote, Viking, 6 1/2 In.		14
Panama, Pitcher, Viking, Qt., 10 In.		14
Paneled Dewdrops, Pitcher, c.1878, 7 1/2 In.		24
Puffy Rose, Powder Jar		15
Queen Anne, Compote, 7 x 8 In.		15
Ruby Thumbprint, Compote, 7 1/2 In.		5
Snail, Syrup, Ruby Stain, Clear Cut, George Duncan, c.1890, 5 In.	*illus*	293
Sunburst & Star, Syrup, 6 In.		9
Tazza, Dolphin, Frosted, Paneled Bowl, Dome Base, 9 1/2 x 10 In.		153

PRINT, in this listing, means any of many printed images produced on paper by one of the more common methods, such as lithography. The prints listed here are of interest primarily to the antiques collector, not the fine arts collector. Many of these prints were originally part of books. Other prints will be found in the Advertising, Currier & Ives, Movie, and Poster categories.

Audubon bird prints were originally issued as part of books printed from 1826 to 1854. They were issued in two sheet sizes, 26 1/2 inches by 39 1/2 inches and 11 inches by 7 inches. The height of a picture is listed before the width. The quadrupeds were issued in 28-by-22-inch prints. Later editions of the Audubon books were done in many sizes, and reprints of the books in the original sizes were also made. The words *After John James Audubon* appear on all of the prints, including the originals, because the pictures were made as copies of Audubon's original oil paintings. The bird pictures have been so popular they have been copied in myriad sizes using both old and new printing methods. This list includes originals and later copies because Audubon prints of all ages are sold in antiques shops.

Audubon, American Elk, Wapiti Deer, Lithograph, Frame, 1840s, 20 x 26 In.		307
Audubon, Brown Pelican, Birds Of America, 39 x 26 In.		6405
Audubon, Cinereous Owl, Engraving, Frame, 1837, 36 x 24 In.		18450
Audubon, Great Northern Diver, Loons, Lake, Aquatint, Havell, 1836, c.1800, 26 x 39 In.		3000
Audubon, Great Tern, Aquatint Engraving, J. Whatman 1836, 38 x 25 In.	*illus*	1920
Audubon, Hare Indian Dog, Lithograph, Frame, c.1848, 26 x 20 In.		438

Pressed Glass, Gibson Girl, Pitcher, Beaded Rim, National Glass Co. c.1903, 8 7/8 In.
$110

Jeffrey S. Evans

Pressed Glass, Snail, Syrup, Ruby Stain, Clear Cut, George Duncan, c.1890, 5 In.
$293

Jeffrey S. Evans

P

Print, Audubon, Great Tern, Aquatint Engraving, J. Whatman 1836, 38 x 25 In.
$1,920

Neal Auctions

Print, Audubon, Maria's Woodpecker, Plate 417, Engraving, Havell, 1838, 37 x 25 In.

$900

Cowan's Auctions

Print, Audubon, Raven, Corvus Corax, Havell, Frame, 41 ½ x 29 In.

$1,210

James D. Julia Auctioneers

Print, Catesby, Ardea Alba, Egret, Engraving, Monogram, Frame, c.1730, 14 x 10 In.

$600

Cowan's Auctions

Print, Catesby, Mark, Hawksbill Sea Turtle, Engraving, Frame, 10 x 14 In.

$2,880

Brunk Auctions

Print, Jacoulet, Le Priere De Minuits, Lama Mongol, Woodblock, Frame, 18 x 14 In.

$562

New Orleans Auction Galleries

Print, Japanese, Hiroshige, Utagawa, Moon Pine On Temple, Frame, 1857, 14 x 10 In.

$984

Skinner, Inc.

Audubon, Labrador Falcon, Birds Of America, Aquatint, Havell, Frame, 1834, 36 x 23 In.	800
Audubon, Louisiana Heron, Colored, Ariel Press Edition, 25 x 38 In.................................	1159
Audubon, Maria's Woodpecker, Engraving, Havell, 1838, 37 x 25 In. ....*illus*	900
Audubon, Plumed & Thick Legged Partridge, Color, Engraving, Havell, 21 x 28 In....................	854
Audubon, Raven, Corvus Corax, Havell, Frame, 41 ½ x 29 In.................................*illus*	1210
Audubon, Say's Squirrel, Quadrupeds Of North America, Bowen, 1846, 25 x 20 In....................	154
Audubon, Sharp-Tailed Grouse, Colored, Engraving, Etched, Havell, 25 ½ x 34 In...................	1664
Audubon, Zenaida Dove, Colored, Engraving, Havell, 38 x 25 In.....................................	1708
Catesby, Ardea Alba, Egret, Engraving, Monogram, Frame, c.1730, 14 x 10 In..................*illus*	600
Catesby, Mark, Hawksbill Sea Turtle, Engraving, Frame, 10 x 14 In...............................*illus*	2880
Currier & Ives prints are listed in the Currier & Ives category.	

Icart prints were made by Louis Icart, who worked in Paris from 1907 as an employee of a postcard company. He then started printing magazines and fashion brochures. About 1910 he created a series of etchings of fashionably dressed women, and he continued to make similar etchings until he died in 1950. He is well known as a printmaker, painter, and illustrator. Original etchings are much more expensive than the later photographic copies.

Icart, Eve, Reclining, Holding Apple, Watercolor, Etching, Signed, 20 x 25 In.	600
Icart, Flower Seller, Arched Monument, c.1928, 36 x 30 In..	1500
Icart, Orange Seller, Signed, 1929, 18 ½ x 14 In.	960
Icart, Red Riding Hood, Trees, Drypoint Etching, 1927, 21 x 14 In...............................	1045
Icart, The Coach, Aquatint, On Paper, Color, Signed, Frame, c.1900, 23 x 18 In.	360
Icart, Woman With Dog, Window, 20 x 17 In.	1107
Icart, Woman, Cat, Carriage, Blue, Green, Drypoint Etching, 1850, 22 x 26 In.	492

Jacoulet prints were designed by Paul Jacoulet (1902–1960), a Frenchman who spent most of his life in Japan. He was a master of Japanese woodblock print technique. Subjects included life in Japan, the South Seas, Korea, and China. His prints were sold by subscription and issued in series. Each series had a distinctive seal, such as a sparrow or butterfly. Most Jacoulet prints are approximately 15 x 10 inches.

Jacoulet, Ebisu, Dieu Du Bonheur Personnifie, Woman, Fish, 1952, 19 x 14 In.	1210
Jacoulet, Le Priere De Minuit, Lama Mongol, Praying Man, 18 ½ x 14 In.	1125
Jacoulet, Le Priere De Minuits, Lama Mongol, Woodblock, Frame, 18 x 14 In. ....*illus*	562
Jacoulet, Mother & Child, Seated, Pink Robe, Signed, 15 x 11 In...................................	375
Jacoulet, Vieil Aino, Long Beard, Black & White Robe, Signed, 15 x 12 In.	250

Japanese woodblock prints are listed as follows: Print, Japanese, name of artist, title or description, type, and size. Dealers use the following terms: Tate-e is a vertical composition. Yoko-e is a horizontal composition. The words Aiban (13 by 9 inches), Chuban (10 by 7 ½ inches), Hosoban (13 by 6 inches), Koban (7 by 4 inches), Nagaban (20 by 9 inches), Oban (15 by 10 inches), Shikishiban (8 by 9 inches), and Tanzaku (15 by 5 inches) denote approximate size. Modern versions of some of these prints have been made. Other woodblock prints that are not Japanese are listed under Print, Woodblock.

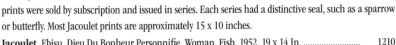

Japanese, Hiroshige, Utagawa, Moon Pine On Temple, Frame, 1857, 14 x 10 In. ....*illus*	984
Japanese, Hiroshige, Edono Meisho, Famous Places In Edo, 1853, 10 x 15 In.	277
Japanese, Hoshi, Joichi, Moon In The Forest, Color, Signed, 1970, 10 x 14 In........................	400
Japanese, Toyokuni, Kabuki Actor, Color, Artists Seal, Frame, c.1880, 13 x 9 In.	120
Japanese, Yoshida, Hiroshi, Barges On Waves, Color, Frame, c.1910, 10 x 15 In.	210
Lithograph, Color, Creekside Turbulence, Painted Glass, D. Kessler, Signed, 1985, 34 x 52 In..	1250
Lozowick, Louis, Subway Construction, Lithograph, Signed, Frame, c.1920, 7 x 13 In..............	2460

Nutting prints are popular with collectors. Wallace Nutting is known for his pictures, furniture, and books. Collectors call his pictures Nutting prints although they are actually hand-colored photographs issued from 1900 to 1941. There are over 10,000 different titles. Wallace Nutting furniture is listed in the Furniture category.

Nutting, Berkshire Brook, 1908, 15 ½ x 21 ½ In..	75
Nutting, Ivy & Rose Cloister, 1915-25, 16 x 14 In..	20
Nutting, The Great Wayside Oak, Mat, Frame, c.1915, 17 ½ x 15 In.	75

Print, Rockwell, Norman, Freedom Of
Speech, Four Freedom Series,
29 x 24 In., Pair
$1,250

Neal Auctions

Print, Tiger, Frame With Cage Bars,
Operational Door, Black & White,
37 x 41 In.
$384

Hess Auction Group

TIP
*Dust the backs of your
framed pictures once a
year.*

P

Purinton, Apple, Salt & Pepper, 3¾ In.
$40

Ruby Lane

Purse, Basket, Nantucket, Ivoryite, Mahogany Base, Signed, Farnum No. A-110 Naples, 12 In.
$189

Hess Auction Group

Minaudiere

A minaudiere is a jeweled box-purse often of gold that became popular in the 1930s. It is expensive, valuable for its gold and jewels and workmanship, and cleverly designed.

Purse, Crystals, Animal Print, Black, Gold, Drop-In Chain, Minaudiere, Judith Leiber, 7 x 2 In.
$1,125

New Orleans Auction Galleries

Parrish prints are wanted by collectors. Maxfield Frederick Parrish was an illustrator who lived from 1870 to 1966. He is best known as a designer of magazine covers, posters, calendars, and advertisements. His prints have been copied in recent years. Some Maxfield Parrish items may be listed in Advertising.

Parrish, Arabian Nights, De Luxe Edition, Mat, 1908, Set Of 12	515
Parrish, Cleopatra, Wood Frame, House Of Art, 1917, 19 x 21 In.	657
Parrish, Enchantment, Lithograph, Frame, c.1926, 41 x 27½ In.	615
Parrish, Stars, Frame, House Of Art, Label, 1927, 21½ x 33½ In.	1455
Parrish, The Page, Seated Figure, Balcony, Gesso Plaster Frame, c.1925, 16 x 12 In.	253
Rockwell, Norman, Freedom Of Speech, Four Freedom Series, 29 x 24 In., Pair .... *illus*	1250
Tiger, Frame With Cage Bars, Operational Door, Black & White, 37 x 41 In. .... *illus*	384

Woodblock prints that are not in the Japanese tradition are listed here. Most were made in England and the United States during the Arts and Crafts period. Japanese woodblock prints are listed under Print, Japanese.

Woodblock, Baumann, Gustave, Monterey Cypress, 8¼ In.	4200
Woodblock, Baumann, Gustave, Singing Woods, 13 In.	5600
Woodblock, Gorman, R.C., Yuyake, Seated Woman, 1981, 23 x 19 In.	400
Woodblock, Hyde, Helen, Senorita In Garden, Signed, 1912, c.1936, 10 x 12 In.	750
Woodblock, Soccer Game, Color, Signed, 1960s, 13½ x 18 In.	70
Woodblock, West, Kathleen, Winter Birds, 16 x 12½ In.	175

PURINTON POTTERY COMPANY was incorporated in Wellsville, Ohio, in 1936. The company moved to Shippenville, Pennsylvania, in 1941 and made a variety of hand-painted ceramic wares. By the 1950s Purinton was making dinnerware, souvenirs, cookie jars, and florist wares. The pottery closed in 1959.

Apple, Bowl, Vegetable, 8 In.	16
Apple, Casserole, Lid	40
Apple, Coffeepot, Lid, 6 In.	90
Apple, Drip Jar, Lid	37
Apple, Salt & Pepper, 3¾ In. ....*illus*	40
Apple, Tumbler, 12 Oz., 4¾ In.	18
Fruit, Salt & Pepper, Jug Shape	31
Heather Plaid, Cup & Saucer	10
Heather Plaid, Snack Set, 2 Piece	9
Heather Plaid, Sugar	18
Intaglio Brown, Casserole, Oval, 7⅜ In.	15
Intaglio Brown, Oil, Handle, Square	26
Ivy Red Blossom, Jug, Dutch, 32 Oz., 5 In.	22
Maywood, Cup & Saucer	11
Mountain Rose, Basket, Handle, Oval, 6¼ In.	12
Normandy Plaid, Jug, 14 Oz., 4 In.	24
Normandy Plaid, Plate, Salad, 6¾ In.	9
Shooting Star, Honey Jug	26
Shooting Star, Vase, Tab Handles, 5 In.	19

PURSES have been recognizable since the eighteenth century, when leather and needlework purses were preferred. Beaded purses became popular in the nineteenth century, went out of style, but are again in use. Mesh purses date from the 1880s and are still being made. How to carry a handkerchief and lipstick is a problem today for every woman, including the Queen of England.

Alligator, Box Style, Brown, Shoulder, 1940s, 10 x 3½ In.	155
Armour Mesh, Clark Gable, Portrait, Blue, Chain, Whiting & Davis, 1976, 4 x 6 In.	1200
Basket, Nantucket, Ivoryite, Mahogany Base, Signed, Farnum No. A-110 Naples, 12 In. ...... *illus*	189
Beaded, Baguette, Flap Top, Fendi Buckle, Leather Strap, Fendi, 9½ x 6 In.	306
Beaded, Black, Green, Red, Minaudiere, Jazzy, Push Closure, Judith Leiber, 4¼ x 6 In.	812
Beaded, Orange, Blue, Gray, Drawstring, Fringe, Wiener Werkstatte, Austria, 1920s	563
Calfskin, Black, Kelly Pochette, Silver Hardware, Hermes	1875
Calfskin, Havane Box, Retourne, Kelly, Hermes	3750

P

Canvas, Duffle, Brown, Monogram, Louis Vuitton, 24 x 12 In., Pair	438
Canvas, Leather, Toiletries Case, Travel Kit, Taupe, Brown, Signed, Hermes, 8 x 10 In.	183
Canvas, Pochette, Monogram, Canvas Illustre, Louis Vuitton, 4 x 6 In.	424
Canvas, Tote, Nova Check, Leather Trim, Burberry, 11 ½ x 7 ½ In.	359
Crocodile, Duffle, Light Brown, Double Handle, Tassels, 5-Footed, Gucci, 12 x 18 In.	4130
Crystals, Animal Print, Black, Gold, Drop-In Chain, Minaudiere, Judith Leiber, 7 x 2 In. *.illus*	1125
Crystals, Art Deco Design, Black, Red, Metal Frame, Chain, Dustbag, J. Leiber, 4 In.	732
Crystals, Minaudiere, Gold Twisted & Knotted Rope, Knot Closure, J. Leiber, 7 In.	937
Deerskin, Pleats, Ivory, Gold Logo, Padded & Chain Strap Handle, Prada, 7 x 14 In.	562
Embroidered, Clutch, Flame Stitch, Diamonds, Multicolor, John White, 1759, 7 In.	406
Fabric, Leather, Shoulder, Black Goldtone, Yves Saint Laurent, 1980s, 52-In. Strap	185
Faille, Black, Goldtone Frame, Lucite Handle, Lowy & Mund, c.1957, 12 x 9 In.	45
Gold Mesh, Ribbed Frame, Sapphire Thumbpieces, Chain Handle, Edwardian	1476
Jet Crystals, Minaudiere, Resting Lion, Metal, Cabochons, J. Leiber, c.1978, 6 In. *illus*	2000
Lambskin, Black, Quilted, Chanel, 10 x 14 ½ In.	740
Lambskin, Chocolate Brown, Cannage Stitching, Chain Handles, Dior, 9 x 15 In.	875
Lambskin, Navy, Lady Dior, Zipper Closure, Silvertone Hardware, 8 x 10 In. *illus*	2375
Leather, Backpack, Quilted, Bottega Veneta, 10 x 11 In.	344
Leather, Black, Intrecciato Weave, Snap Closure, Double Strap, Bottega Veneta, 11 x 10 In.	937
Leather, Briefcase, Sac A Depeces, Brown, Flip Closure, Hermes, 15 ½ x 11 ½ In.	1180
Leather, Clutch, Red, Black, Brown, Woven, Top Zip, Marni, 10 x 6 ½ In.	177
Leather, Clutch, Wrist Strap, Burgundy, Cartier, 9 ½ x 7 In.	350
Leather, Damier Ebene Brera, Double Handle, Louis Vuitton, 9 ½ x 8 In.	719
Leather, Flapbag, Black, Quilted, Chanel, 8 x 6 In.	2375
Leather, Handbag, Black, Goldtone Hardware, Rolled Handle, Gucci, 15 x 11 In.	241
Leather, Handbag, Brown, Trapezoid Shape, Arch Handle, Dust Bag, Judith Leiber	300
Leather, Hobo, Onatah PM, Mustard Yellow, Top Zip, Louis Vuitton, 10 x 6 In.	342
Leather, Piano Bag, Black, Arched Handle, Coin Purse, Box, Hermes, 10 x 11 In.	711
Leather, Python, Hobo, Rolled Handle, Lined, Byron, New York, 13 x 22 In. *illus*	1500
Leather, Rucksack, Brown, Prada, Italy, 11 x 13 In.	424
Leather, Shoulder, Caviar, Interlocking CC, Top Zip, Chanel, 7 ¼ x 6 In.	1121
Leather, Shoulder, Vitello Perl, Black, Salvatore Ferragamo, 6 ¼ x 9 In.	124
Leather, Shoulder, Woven, Zipper Pocket, Gold Color, Tassel, Ganson, 10 x 7 In.	35
Leather, Snake, Cluth, White, Chain Strap, Carlos Falchi, 5 ¼ x 12 In.	407
Leather, Tote, Black Caviar, Goldtone Hardware, Chanel, 10 ½ x 11 In.	1829
Leather, Tote, Brown, Rolled Handles, Louis Vuitton, 9 x 14 In.	483
Leather, Tote, Navy, Quilted, 12 x 8 In.	813
Leather, Trembled Blossoms, Nappa, Gathered, Straps, Lined, Prada, 6 x 11 In. *illus*	625
Lizard, Clutch, Black, Bottega Veneta, 6 x 4 In.	168
Lizard, Clutch, Black, Quilted, Chanel, Chain Strap, 6 ½ x 4 ½ In.	1188
Lizard, Clutch, Red, Bottega Veneta, 6 x 4 In.	375
Mesh, 14K Gold, Blue Stone Accents, Silk Lining, Chain Handle, Art Deco	6765
Mesh, Blue, Bakelite Handle, Italy, 12 x 14 ½ In.	94
Mesh, Chain Link, Silver, Beads, Finger Ring, Top Clasp, Chatelaine, c.1910, 4 x 2 In.	125
Mesh, Handbag, Pink & Yellow Flowers, Gold Trim, Whiting & Davis, 7 x 5 In.	141
Mesh, Handbag, Red & Purple Diamonds, Silver Trim, Whiting & Davis, 8 x 4 In.	200
Needlepoint, Wool Flame Stitch On Linen, Mid 1700s, 8 ½ In.	540
Needlework, Folds Over, Flame Stitch, Zigzags, Woven Edges, Linen Lining, 1766, 8 In.	3998
Nylon, Shoulder, Black, Gucci, 8 x 6 In.	63
Patent Leather, Handbag, Black, Goldtone Chain Strap, Gucci, 8 ½ x 6 ½ In.	188
Patent Leather, Mademoiselle Clasp, Tropical, 10 x 6 ½ In.	625
Patent Leather, Shoulder, Quilted, Blue, Tod's, 11 x 7 ½ In.	578
Python, Handbag, Metallic Gold, Beige Leather, Goldtone Hardware, Top Zip, Gucci, 15 x 9 In.	531
Silver, Engraved Countryside, Latvia, c.1930, 8 x 4 In.	371
Silver, Malachite, Clutch, Judith Leiber, 6 x 4 In.	281
Silver, Shaped Rectangle, Flowers, Shield Cartouche, Monogram, 1900s, 4 In.	138
Snakeskin, Wine, Garnet Cabochons, Beaded Clasp, Dust Bag, J. Leiber, c.1980, 6 x 9 In.	593
Suede, Handbag, Brown, Prada, 12 x 8 In.	281
Suede, Handbag, Chartreuse, Prada, 9 ½ x 5 ½ In.	281
Suede, Shoulder, Brown, Canvas, Ring Closure, Dolce & Gabbana, 11 x 8 In.	156
Velvet, Handbag, Purple, Square, Christian Dior, 6 ½ x 6 ¼ In.	375

Purse, Jet Crystals, Minaudiere, Resting Lion, Metal, Cabochons, J. Leiber, c.1978, 6 In.
$2,000

New Orleans Auction Galleries

Purse, Lambskin, Navy, Lady Dior, Zipper Closure, Silvertone Hardware, 8 x 10 In.
$2,375

New Orleans Auction Galleries

Purse, Leather, Python, Hobo, Rolled Handle, Lined, Byron, New York, 13 x 22 In.
$1,500

New Orleans Auction Galleries

TIP
Don't hang old purses. The weight of the purse puts too much strain on the handle.

P

PYREX

Purse, Leather, Trembled Blossoms, Nappa, Gathered, Straps, Lined, Prada, 6 x 11 In.
$625

New Orleans Auction Galleries

Pyrex, Mixing Bowl, Delphite, Blue, 5¾ In.
$29

Strawser Auction Group

Quezal, Vase, Trumpet, Ruffled, White Opal, Green Pulled Flowers, Iridescent, 7¾ x 2¾ In.
$1,850

Ruby Lane

PYREX glass baking dishes were first made in 1915 by the Corning Glass Works. Pyrex dishes are made of a heat-resistant glass that can go from refrigerator or freezer to oven or microwave and are nice enough to put on the table. Clear glass dishes were made first. Pyrex Flameware, for use over a stovetop burner, was made from 1936 to 1979. A set of mixing bowls in four colors (blue, red, green, and yellow) was made beginning in 1947. After Corning sold its Pyrex brand to World Kitchen LLC in 1998, changes were made to the formula for the glass.

Bowl, Delphite, Blue, 5¾ In.	25
Bowl, Opal White Milk Glass, 1950s, 4 Qt., 4 x 10½ In.	35
Bowl, Salad, Teal, White Vegetables, Promotional, 4¼ x 12¼ In.	48
Bowl, Vegetable, Divided, Delphite, Blue, Oval, 13¼ x 8 In.	35
Casserole, Lid, Snowflake, Blue Garland, Cornflower, White, 1½ Qt.	29
Double Boiler, Long Knob, 9½ x 6 In.	48
Mixing Bowl, Delphite, Blue, 5¾ In. ....*illus*	29
Teapot, Steel Band Around Middle, Round Finial, 6 Cup, 4½ x 9 In.	22

Quezal

QUEZAL glass was made from 1901 to 1924 at the Queens, New York, company started by Martin Bach. Other glassware by other firms, such as Loetz, Steuben, and Tiffany, resembles this gold-colored iridescent glass. Martin Bach died in 1921. His son-in-law, Conrad Vahlsing Jr., went to work at the Lustre Art Company about 1920. Bach's son, Martin Bach Jr., worked at the Durand Art Glass division of the Vineland Flint Glass Works after 1924.

Bowl, Blue Iridescent, Tapered, 6 In.	360
Bowl, Gold Iridescent, Green & White Pulled Feather, Ruffle Rim, c.1907, 4 x 9 In.	677
Chandelier, 3-Light, Art Glass Shades, Arts & Crafts, Early 1900s, 6 x 12 In.	1125
Compote, Iridescent, Gold Geometric, Lipped, 3½ x 3 In.	288
Lamp, Blown Glass, Patinated Metal, Single Socket, New York, 1920s, 6 x 5 In., Pair	815
Lamp, Desk, Bronze, Pawn Finial Above Bell Form Shade, Leaf Base, Early 1900s, 6½ In.	330
Sconce, 2-Light, Gold Iridescent, Brass, 11 x 11 In., Pair	488
Shade, Blue Iridescent, White Pulled Feathers, Blossom Shape, 6 x 4¼ In.	366
Shade, Green & Gold Vine, Gold Iridescent Interior, Ruffled Rim, 4½ x 2¼ In., Pair	230
Shade, Green Feathers, Gold Tips, Opal Ground, Gold Interior, Bullet Shape, 8 In.	502
Shade, Pale Green Feathers, Golden Coil Tips, Engraved, 4 In., Pair	259
Shade, Torchiere, Morning Glory, Blue & Green & Magenta, Engraved, 2¼ In.	2990
Vase, Green & Tan, Swirling, New York, 1900s, 6 x 6¾ In.	1875
Vase, Green, Beige, Pulled Feather, 8⅜ In.	1125
Vase, Iridescent Gold, Fuchsia, Green, Orange, Beaker Shape, Flared Rim, 10 x 5 In.	354
Vase, Iridescent, Feather Bands, Purple, Gold, Red Orange, 11½ x 5 In.	3000
Vase, Iridescent, Yellow To Green, Purple, Lobed, 12 In.	4000
Vase, Jack-In-The-Pulpit, Orange Iridescent, 7 x 6 In.	427
Vase, Pulled Feather, Green, White, Flower Bud Shape, 9 In.	375
Vase, Swirls, Green, Yellow, Pink Iridescent, Bulbous, Tapered, Rolled Rim, 1900s, 6 In.	1875
Vase, Trumpet, Green To Gold Feathers, Fluted Ruffled Rim, 8 x 4½ In.	937
Vase, Trumpet, Pink & Gold Plumes, Ivory Ground, Ribbed, Brass Stem, 14 In.	472
Vase, Trumpet, Ruffled, White Opal, Green Pulled Flowers, Iridescent, 7¾ x 2¾ In. ....*illus*	1850

QUILTS have been made since the seventeenth century. Early textiles were very precious and every scrap was saved to be reused. A quilt is a combination of fabrics joined to a filler and a backing by small stitched designs known as quilting. An appliqued quilt has pieces stitched to the top of a large piece of background fabric. A patchwork, or pieced, quilt is made of many small pieces stitched together. Embroidery can be added to either type.

Album, Hand Stitched, Appliqued, Squares, Birds, Flowers, Hand Quilted, c.1860, 68 x 88 In.	813
Amish, Diamond, Navy, Light Blue, Purple, 20 Blocks, 1900s, 76 x 89 In.	468
Amish, Patchwork, Diamond In Square, Blue, Red, Lancaster Co., Pa., 80 x 83 In. ....*illus*	767
Amish, Patchwork, Sunshine & Shadow, Dark Blue, Purple, Red, Green, c.1930, 82 x 84 In.	1200
Amish, Wool, Cotton, Diamonds, Green, Red & Black, Early 1900s, 69½ x 76½ In.	330
Appliqued, American Glory, Eagle, Flowers, Vines, White, Red, Teal Blue, 1950s, 80 x 90 In.	580
Appliqued, Axes & Liquor Jugs, Hand Stitched, Machine Binding, Early 1900s, 62 x 96 In.	240
Appliqued, Blocks Of Red Flowers, Hand Sewn, Late 1800s, 82 x 84 In.	600

Quilt, Amish, Patchwork, Diamond In Square, Blue, Red, Lancaster Co., Pa., 80 x 83 In.
$767

Hess Auction Group

Quilt, Crazy, Embroidered, Birds, Flowers, Fans, Advertising, Velvet Border, c.1910, 59 x 81 In.
$480

Garth's Auctioneers & Appraisers

Quilt, Crazy, Victorian, 20 Blocks, Various Materials, Ohio, c.1898, 69 x 83 In.
$351

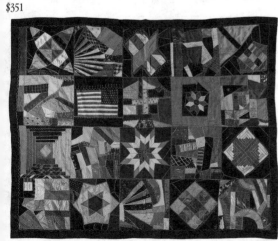

Jeffrey S. Evans

Quilt, Mennonite, Patchwork, Carpenter's Wheel, 12 Blocks, c.1900, 63 ½ x 91 In.
$117

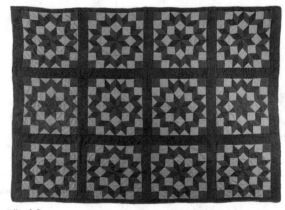

Jeffrey S. Evans

Quilt, Patchwork & Appliqued, Basket, 20 Blocks, Summer Spread, c.1930, 69 x 83 In.
$152

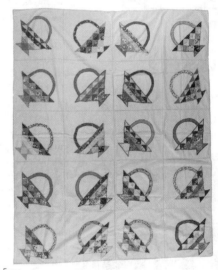

Jeffrey S. Evans

Quilt, Patchwork & Appliqued, Pieced, Lone Star, Chintz, Maryland, c.1840, 128 x 129 In.
$9,360

Jeffrey S. Evans

Quilt, Patchwork, Basket Of Flowers, Lehigh County, Pa., 77 x 78 In.
$177

Hess Auction Group

Quilt, Patchwork, Crazy Pattern, Multicolor, 70 x 84 In.
$130

Hess Auction Group

Quilt, Patchwork, Lantern Pattern, Blue, Red, White, 72 x 88 In.
$354

Hess Auction Group

Appliqued, Eagles, Spread Wings, Around Center Star, White, Tan, Red, c.1875, 74 x 75 In.	1125
Appliqued, Flower Baskets, Flower Vine Border, Cornucopias, c.1850, 88 x 88 In.	281
Appliqued, Flower Squares, Pots, Wreaths, Cornucopia, 1800s, 16 x 16 In.	3259
Appliqued, Flowers, Leaves, Red & Green, Sawtooth Sashing, c.1850, 108 x 108 In.	660
Appliqued, Grapes & Rose, 12 Blocks, Red, Green, Yellow, Virginia, c.1870, 78 x 94 In.	1755
Appliqued, Red Tulips, Green Leafy Rings, Red Border, Signed, 1893, 73 x 86 In.	415
Appliqued, Rose Pattern, Red, Green, Cream Ground, 1875-99, 89 x 75 In.	270
Appliqued, Tulips, Red, White Ground, 1900s, 62 x 80 In.	308
Appliqued, Wagon Wheels, Red & Brown, 4 Quadrants, c.1900, 72 x 72 In.	504
Appliqued, Whig Rose, 4 Blocks, Red, Tan, White, c.1890, 72 x 74 In.	152
Appliqued, Women Under Moon, Animals, Wreaths, White, Red, 1901, 73 x 80 In.	540
Appliqued, Xs & Os, Red, Green, Vine Border, c.1890, 75 x 76 In.	640
Crazy, Embroidered, Birds, Flowers, Fans, Advertising, Velvet Border, c.1910, 59 x 81 In....*illus*	480
Crazy, Victorian, 20 Blocks, Various Materials, Ohio, c.1898, 69 x 83 In....*illus*	351
Friendship, Red Print Flowers, Orange Ground, Green Border, 86 x 87 In.	295
Mennonite, Patchwork, Carpenter's Wheel, 12 Blocks, c.1900, 63 ½ x 91 In. ....*illus*	117
Patchwork & Appliqued, Basket, 20 Blocks, Summer Spread, c.1930, 69 x 83 In....*illus*	152
Patchwork & Appliqued, Buffalo Horns, Indian Head, Red, White, Blue, c.1940, 88 x 82 In.	1211
Patchwork & Appliqued, Pieced, Lone Star, Chintz, Maryland, c.1840, 128 x 129 In. ....*illus*	9360
Patchwork, 8-Point Star, Red, White, c.1900, 84 x 82 In.	600
Patchwork, Bars, Yellow, Red, Blue, Tan, White, c.1880, 76 x 80 In.	160
Patchwork, Basket Of Flowers, Lehigh County, Pa., 77 x 78 In. ....*illus*	177
Patchwork, Bay Leaf, Green, White, Virginia., 1890-1910, 78 x 78 In.	263
Patchwork, Crazy Pattern, Multicolor, 70 x 84 In. ....*illus*	130
Patchwork, Double Wedding Ring, Scalloped Edge, Multicolor, 52 x 38 In.	277
Patchwork, Flower Petals, Hearts, Yellow, Blue, Brown, c.1880, 73 x 82 In.	380
Patchwork, Flying Geese Variation, Multicolor, 1800s, 75 x 79 In.	234
Patchwork, Flying Geese, Green Ground, 1926, 62 x 75 In.	111
Patchwork, Irish Chain, Brown Flower Backing, 84 x 88 In.	142
Patchwork, Lantern Pattern, Blue, Red, White, 72 x 88 In. ....*illus*	354
Patchwork, LeMoyne Star, Taupe, Gray & Tan, c.1870, 74 x 74 In.	265
Patchwork, Lincoln Log Pattern, Zigzag Borders, Red, White, Blue, Yellow, 80 x 84 In.	502
Patchwork, Log Cabin, Barn Raising, 84 x 86 In. ....*illus*	236
Patchwork, Log Cabin, Multicolor, White Ground, c.1880, 89 x 78 In.	369
Patchwork, Log Cabin, Patriotic, 1876, 37 x 37 In.	369
Patchwork, Lone Star, Chintz Border, Reverse To Red & Yellow Print, c.1835, 100 x 100 In.	360
Patchwork, Lone Star, Pink, Blue, Yellow, 41 x 41 In.	60
Patchwork, New York Beauty, Chintz, 6 Full Blocks, 3 Half Blocks, c.1860, 83 x 93 In.....*illus*	3159
Patchwork, Pine Tree, Chain Stitch Embroidered Date, America, c.1886, 83 x 81 In.	344
Patchwork, Pinwheel Diamonds, Yellow, Green, White Ground, c.1890, 79 x 80 In.	135
Patchwork, Rainbow Fans, Red Ground, c.1925, 85 x 84 In.	111
Patchwork, Sawtooth Pattern, Blue & Pink, Hand Stitched, Early 1900s, 68 x 72 In.	240
Patchwork, Sawtooth, Diamond In Square, Green, Red, 81 x 80 In.	1080
Patchwork, Schoolhouse, Stitched Blocks, Wide Floral Print Border, Early 1900s, 80 x 86 In.	300
Patchwork, Silk, Velvet, Multicolor, 76 x 86 In.	625
Patchwork, Snowflake Pattern, Sawtooth Border, Cream, Red, Sage Green, 98 x 99 In.	201
Patchwork, Star In Grid, Green, Red, c.1875, 89 x 78 In.	172
Patchwork, String Star, Red, Yellow, Blue, 73 x 77 In.	523
Patchwork, Tumbling Block, Red, White, Blue, c.1875, 75 x 76 In.	111
Patchwork, Zigzag Diamond Pattern, Bar Backing, Geometric, Red & Green, 80 x 86 In.	236
Star Medallions, Red & Yellow Green, Early 1900s, 88 x 88 In.	210

QUIMPER pottery has a long history. Tin-glazed, hand-painted pottery has been made in Quimper, France, since the late seventeenth century. The earliest firm was founded in 1708 by Pierre Bousquet. In 1782, Antoine de la Hubaudiere became the manager of the factory and the factory became known as the HB Factory (for Hubaudiere-Bousquet), de la Hubaudiere, or Grande Maison. Another firm, founded in 1772 by Francois Eloury, was known as Porquier. The third firm, founded by Guillaume Dumaine in 1778, was known as HR or Henriot Quimper. All three firms made similar pottery decorated with designs of Breton peasants and sea and flower motifs. The Eloury (Porquier) and Dumaine (Henriot) firms merged in 1913.

Bousquet (HB) merged with the others in 1968. The group was sold to an American holding company in 1984. More changes followed, and in 2011 Jean-Pierre Le Goff became the owner and the name was changed to Henriot-Quimper.

Egg Server, Swan Shape, 6 Cups, Blue, Orange, 7 Piece	377
Letter Holder, Wood, 2 Inkwells, Carved Dividers, Ceramic Lids, c.1905, 8 x 8 In.	200
Planter, Duck, Yellow, Green, Flowers, Signed, 10 x 8 In. *illus*	55
Platter, Man With Children, Clock Tower, 17 x 12 In.	937
Platter, Musicians, Landscape, Octagonal, Blue, White, c.1895, 12 x 15 ½ In., Pair	750
Vase, Black, Man, Pipe, Incised, Multicolor, 9 ½ In.	62
Vase, Double, Horseshoe Shape, Blue, White, Yellow, c.1900, 9 ⅛ In.	500

RADIO broadcast receiving sets were first sold in New York City in 1910. They were used to pick up the experimental broadcasts of the day. The first commercial radios were made by Westinghouse Company for listeners of the experimental shows on KDKA Pittsburgh in 1920. Collectors today are interested in all early radios, especially those made of Bakelite plastic or decorated with blue mirrors. Figural advertising radios and transistor radios are also collected.

Bendix, Bakelite, Green Case, Black Grill, 11 x 6 In.	437
Call Box, Mackey Radio Co., Enameled Porcelain, c.1925, 6 ⅝ x 3 ⅜ x 2 ⅝ In.	47
Champion, 2 Wave Ranges, Wood, Bakelite Dials, Arched Telavox Junior Speaker, c.1928	172
Emerson, Catalin, EP-375, Red Plastic, White Louvers, Knobs, 1941, 7 x 10 In.	1999
Fada, Bakelite, Green, Yellow, 10 ½ x 5 ¾ In.	2000
Fada, Cloud, AM, Tube, Marbelized, Orange, Cream, Bakelite, Glass Dial, 1950s, 7 x 11 In.	650
Fada, Model 711, Catalin Case, Orange, 2 Knobs, Handle, Table Model	332
General Electric, AM, Plastic, Beige, White Tuner Dial, 6 ½ x 11 In. *illus*	55
Gilbert, Wireless Tube, Wooden Board, Loose Coupler, 1922, 9 x 15 In.	2811
Grundig, Majestic, Multi-Sonic, AM/FM, Wood Case, Feet, 15 ½ x 26 In.	80
Jackson Bell, Black Swan, Cathedral, Overlay, Wood Knobs & Base, 1930s, 15 x 12 In.	699
Motorola, Bullet, AM, Tube, Turquoise Blue, Bakelite, Gold Bullet Dial, c.1957, 6 x 12 In.	849
Motorola, Jetsons, AM, Clock, Sea Green, Bakelite, 1957, 6 x 14 In.	599
RCA Victor, Green, Built-In Cigarette Lighter, 6 ¾ x 12 ¾ In.	49
Sentinel, Bakelite, Red Case, Yellow Grill & Knobs, 10 ¾ x 6 ½ In.	1625
Siemens & Halske, Type RFE22, Oak, Sloping Ebonite Control Panel, 1927, 22 In.	1445
Sparton, Model 577, Art Deco, Blue, Black, c.1936, 8 ⅞ x 18 In.	1080
Sparton, Smitten, AM, Tube, Green Plastic, Mint Burlap Weave, 1950s, 6 x 14 In.	610
Tesla, Comet-9 Commodore, Transistor, Portable, Green, Leather, 1950s, 6 x 8 In.	85
Westinghouse, Refrigerator, Portable, Turquoise & Goldtone, Metal, 1950s, 10 x 6 In.	400
Zenith, Model 829, Mahogany, Lacquer, Chrome, Tombstone Shape, 1935, 19 x 15 In.	4000

RAILROAD enthusiasts collect any train memorabilia. Everything is wanted, from oilcans to whole train cars. The Chessie System has a store that sells many reproductions of its old dinnerware and uniforms.

Bell, Brooklyn City Railroad, 3 ½ x 3 ¼ In.	121
Car Lock, N.Y.N.H & Hartford Railroad Company, Embossed Padlock, Chain, 4 In.	92
Cuspidor, Pullman, Round, Nickeled Silver, 7 In.	119
Lantern, Glass Globe, B&O RR, 9 ½ x 7 In.	233
Lantern, Inspector, Dietz Acme, Metal, Round Foot, Square Top Handle, 1900s, 14 In.	185
Lantern, Mo. Pac. R.R., Metal, Black Paint, Tapered Handle, Wick, Marked, Eagle, 17 In.	62
Poster, MKT Railroad, San Antonio, Texas, Bern Hill, Art Deco, 1950s, 26 ⅝ x 20 ½ In.	575
Sign, Railroad Crossing, Porcelain, Glass Jewels, Black & White, X-Shape, 48 In.	677
Steam Engine, Labeled JF, 9 ½ x 5 In.	175
Steam Oiler, D & H Railway, Metal, Cylindrical, Tubular Neck, Handle, Marked, 27 In.	92
Steam Whistle, Brass, Cylindrical, Turned Pendant, 20 In.	185

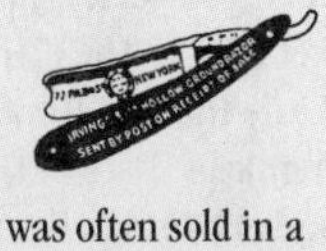

RAZORS were used in ancient Egypt and subsequently wherever shaving was in fashion. The metal razor used in America until about 1870 was made in Sheffield, England. After 1870, machine-made hollow-ground razors were made in Germany or America. Plastic or bone handles were popular. The razor was often sold in a

Quilt, Patchwork, Log Cabin, Barn Raising, 84 x 86 In.
$236

Hess Auction Group

Quilt, Patchwork, New York Beauty, Chintz, 6 Full Blocks, 3 Half Blocks, c.1860, 83 x 93 In.
$3,159

Jeffrey S. Evans

Quimper, Planter, Duck, Yellow, Green, Flowers, Signed, 10 x 8 In.
$55

Ruby Lane

R

This is an edited listing of current prices. Visit **Kovels.com** to check thousands of prices from previous years and sign up for free information on trends, tips, reproductions, marks, and more.

Radio, General Electric, AM, Plastic, Beige, White Tuner Dial, 6 ½ x 11 In.
$55

Ruby Lane

TIP

The playing surface of phonograph records should never be touched by a bare hand. The records should be stored vertically and packed to prevent warping. Keep away from extremes of heat or cold.

Reamer, Ceramic, Clown, Iridescent, Red Cheeks, Blue Rim, 3 ¼ x 3 ¾ In.
$36

Martin Auction Co.

Red Wing, Bob White, Cookie Jar, Quail, Cream Speckles, 11 x 6 ½ In.
$79

Ruby Lane

---

set of seven, one for each day of the week. The set was often kept by the barber who shaved the well-to-do man each day in the shop.

Ivory Handle, Declaration Of Independence, Train Yard, Wade & Butcher, 19 In.	3600
Straight, Buckeye B.S. Co., Bone Handle, Marked C.S. Wiggim, Early 1900s, 6 ½ In.	54
Strop, Leather, Brass Medallion Handle, Round Base, Mounting Holes, c.1900, 29 In.	195

 REAMERS, or juice squeezers, have been known since 1767, although most of those collected today date from the twentieth century. Figural reamers are among the most prized.

Ceramic, Clown, Iridescent, Red Cheeks, Blue Rim, 3 ¼ x 3 ¾ In. ....*illus*	36
Ceramic, Figural, Clown, 2 Parts, Juicer Head, Pitcher Body, Ruffle Collar, 1930s, 6 x 7 In.	43
Crisscross, Hazel Atlas, 5 ½ In.	27
Custard Glass, Embossed, Sunkist, Square Cutout Handle, Spout, 1930s	65
Glass, Pink Translucent, 6-Sided Center Cone, Side Handle, Spout, 1920s, 8 In. Diam.	165
Jadite Glass, Green, Embossed Sunkist, Molded Center, Handle, Spout, 1930s	75
Metal, Figural, Frying Pan, Handle, 1940s, 6 x 8 In.	38
Porcelain, Strawberry, Red, Bulbous, Dimpled, Green Leaf Handle, 2 Parts, 1930s, 5 In.	84
Vaseline Glass, Are, France, 5 ½ x 2 In.	18

 RECORDS have changed size and shape through the years. The cylinder-shaped phonograph record for use with the early Edison models was made about 1889. Disc records were first made by 1894, the double-sided disc by 1904. High-fidelity records were first issued in 1944, the first vinyl disc in 1946, the first stereo record in 1958. The 78 RPM became the standard in 1926 but was discontinued in 1957. In 1932, the first 33 ⅓ RPM was made but was not sold commercially until 1948. In 1949, the 45 RPM was introduced. Compact discs became available in the U.S. in 1982, and many companies began phasing out the production of phonograph records. Vinyl records are popular again. People claim the sound is better on a vinyl recording, and new recordings are being made. Some collectors want colored vinyl records. Vintage albums are collected for their cover art as well as for the fame of the artist and the music.

American Graffiti, Soundtrack, 41 Songs, MCA Records, 1973	10
Beach Boys, Spirit Of America, 2 Record Set, Capitol Records, 33 RPM, c.1975	20
Beatles, Hard Day's Night, United Artists, c.1964	69
Beatles, Help, Soundtrack, Capitol Records, 1965	69
Bee Gees, Best Of Bee Gees, Atco Records, 33 ⅓ RPM, 1969	6
Bee Gees, Spirits Having Flown, RSO Records, 33 ⅓ RPM, 1979	10
Bill Cosby, Wonderfulness, Warner Bros., c.1965	10
Bill Haley & His Comets, See You Later Alligator, 1950s, 45 RPM	15
Bing Crosby, Best Of Bing, 2 Record Set, MCA Records, 33 ⅓ RPM, 1973	9
Captain Kangaroo, I Love A Parade, I Went To The Animal Fair, Golden Records, 45 RPM, 1959 .	35
Cream, Eric Clapton, Jack Bruce, Ginger Baker, Signed, 1970s, 12 x 12 In.	1264
Dale Evans, Suzy Snowflake, 32 Feet, 8 Little Tails, RCA, 78 RPM, c.1950, 10 In.	10
Dolly Parton, Heartbreaker, RCA, 1978	19
Doris Day, I've Gotta Sing Away These Blues, Whatever Will Be, Columbia, 45 RPM, c.1950	5
Dr. Seuss, Green Eggs & Ham, Fox In Socks, RCA Corp., 1965, LP	12
Elvis Presley, Country Music, Time Life, Vinyl, 1981, LP	14
Elvis Presley, Elvis In Hollywood, 33 ⅓ RPM, c.1976	6
Evita, 2 Record Set, 33 ⅓ RPM, c.1979	15
Fats Domino, Here Comes Fats Vol. 1, Vinyl, EP, 1950s	18
Frank Sinatra, Stereophonics, Sinatra & Strings, Reprise, LP, 1961	9
Glen Campbell, New Place In The Sun, 33 ⅓ RPM, Capitol Records	5
I Am A Parrot, Die Cut, Parrot, Child's, Talking Book Corporation	33
John Denver, Rocky Mountain High, Signed, 1972, 12 x 12 In.	167
Johnny Cash, Sunday Morning Coming Down, Signed, 1972, 12 x 12 In.	275
Kenny Rogers, Kenny, 33 ⅓ RPM, 1979	4
Let's Go To The Circus, Peter Pan Records, 78 RPM, 1949	13
Little Hieland Mon, Die Cut, Scottish Boy, Child's	77
Monkees, More Of The Monkees, Colgems Records, 33 ⅓ RPM, c.1967	30
Robert Goulet, Don't Be Afraid Of Romance, Young At Love, Columbia, 45 RPM, 1963	4

R

Ronnie Milsap, Greatest Hits, Vol. 2, RCA Records, 1985	5
Sesame Street, Let Your Feelings Show, 16 Songs, 33⅓ RPM	2
Wizard Of Oz, Disneyland, c.1969, 78 RPM	12

RED WING POTTERY of Red Wing, Minnesota, was a firm started in 1878. The company first made utilitarian pottery, including stoneware jugs and canning jars. In the 1920s art pottery was introduced. Many dinner sets and vases were made before the company closed in 1967. Rumrill pottery made by the Red Wing Pottery for George Rumrill is listed in its own category. For more prices, go to kovels.com.

Beige Fleck, Meat Server, 12 In.	21
Beige Fleck, Relish, 5 Sections, 12½ In.	32
Blue Shadows, Cup & Saucer	15
Blue Shadows, Plate, Dinner, 10⅜ In.	12
Bob White, Bread Tray, 23 In.	99
Bob White, Butter, Cover, ¼ Lb.	81
Bob White, Casserole, Lid, 4 Qt.	100
Bob White, Casserole, Lid, Qt.	35
Bob White, Cookie Jar, Quail, Cream Speckles, 11 x 6½ In. ....*illus*	79
Brittany, Plate, Salad, 7¼ In.	12
Capistrano, Bowl, Cereal, 6¾ In.	18
Capistrano, Creamer	25
Capistrano, Salt & Pepper	35
Chrysanthemum, Plate, Dinner, Square, c.1950, 10¼ In. ....*illus*	20
Damask, Plate, Dinner, 10⅜ In.	10
Lute Song, Bowl, Vegetable, 8¼ In.	30
Lute Song, Cup & Saucer	9
Merrileaf, Cup & Saucer	12
Pepe, Creamer	12 to 18
Pepe, Gravy Boat	35
Provincial Oomph, Bean Pot, Lid.	55
Provincial Oomph, Mug, 4⅞ In.	25
Random Harvest, Butter, Cover, ¼ Lb.	20
Random Harvest, Cup & Saucer	8
Random Harvest, Relish, 2 Sections, 13 In.	16
Random Harvest, Teapot, 1955, 6½ x 8 In. ....*illus*	35
Tampico, Bowl, Vegetable, 9 In.	30
Tampico, Plate, Dinner, 10¾ In.	15
Tip Toe, Bowl, Fruit, 5¼ In.	8
Tip Toe, Gravy Boat	25
Turtle Dove, Creamer	12
Turtle Dove, Cup & Saucer	12
Turtle Dove, Gravy Boat, Underplate	35
Turtle Dove, Plate, Bread & Butter, 7 In.	7
Turtle Dove, Salt & Pepper	24 to 45

REDWARE is a hard, red stoneware that originated in the late 1600s and continues to be made. The term is also used to describe any common clay pottery that is reddish in color.

Bank, Apple, Red Paint, Minor Wear, 1800s, 3 In.	94
Bank, Dome Shape, Finial, Side Slot, Brown Mottled Glaze, 1800s, 5¼ In.	649
Bank, Gourd Shape, 3 Tiers, Finial, Speckled Mottled Glaze, England, 1800s, 7½ In.	190
Bank, Nest Of Birds, Molded, Mother & 3 Nestlings, Repairs On Beaks, 1800s, 5 In.	354
Basin, Flower, Pinched Rim, 2 Yellow Bands, Manganese, Extended Handles, 7 x 19 In.	240
Basin, Yellow Swag, 9½ x 25 In.	216
Bean Pot, Lid, Knob, Bulbous, Red, Manganese Spirals, Lug Handles, c.1810, 8 In.	2700
Bird Whistle, Molded, Glazed, New Jersey, 3½ In.	71
Bowl, Chicken Sgrafitto Design, Yellow, Red Flower & Border, Marked, JCS, 8 In.	107
Bowl, Flanged Rim, Yellow, Sine Wave, Lead Glaze, Beaded Edge, 1790-1830, 3⅛ In.	351
Bowl, Interior Decoration, Yellow Zigzag Band, Green Bands, 1800s, 2¾ x 8½ In.	234

Red Wing, Chrysanthemum, Plate, Dinner, Square, c.1950, 10¼ In.
$20

Tias

Red Wing, Random Harvest, Teapot, 1955, 6½ x 8 In.
$35

Tias

Redware, Charger, ABC Slipware, Coggled Edge, c.1825, 11 In.
$1,200

Ruby Lane

TIP

Lock your doors. There is a 12 percent chance that your home will be burglarized in the next 5 years. In the next 15 years, the odds are 33 percent; in 30 years, 50 percent. And that assumes there is no increase in the rate of burglaries nationwide.

R

Redware, Dish, Baking, Hollyhocks, Slip Decoration, Wavy Line Border, England, 13 x 17 In.
$899

Ruby Lane

Redware, Dish, Loaf, Slip Decorated, Coggle Wheel Edge, Oval, 1800s, 16½ In.
$767

Hess Auction Group

Redware, Figurine, Dog, Standing, Basket, Hollow Body, Incised Base, c.1875, 5¾ x 6 In.
$1,180

Hess Auction Group

TIP
Put foam or paper plates between the china plates stacked for storage.

Bowl, Lid, Rope Twist Handles, Convex Lid, Knob Handle, Early 1800s, 4¼ In.	175
Bowl, Pieced Decoration, Ear Handles, 4¼ In.	455
Bowl, Pumpkin Glaze, Yellow Slip Border, Wavy & Straight Line Design, 4 x 11 In.	154
Bowl, Round, Yellow Swirl, Norwalk, Ct., 1800s, 2½ x 13 In.	650
Bowl, Yellow Pine Tree, River, Pennsylvania, 1800s, 3 x 11½ In.	450
Candlestick, Swan Handle, 1800s, 4½ In.	295
Cann, Manganese Decoration, Strap Handle, Flared Base, Early 1800s, 6¼ In.	250
Charger, 2 Men, Horseback, Yellow Ground, Breininger, 1988, 12½ In. Diam.	142
Charger, ABC Slipware, Coggled Edge, c.1825, 11 In. ....*illus*	1200
Charger, Light Dragoon, Yellow, Soldier On Horse, Leafy Border, 1984, 14 In. Diam.	130
Charger, Marriage, Flower Vines, Yellow, Verse Border, Breininger, 1975, 16 In. Diam.	224
Charger, Yellow Wavy Lines, 1800s, 11¼ In.	135
Churn, Manganese Glaze, Pennsylvania, 1800s, 6 Gal., 19¼ In.	106
Colander, Handles, 3-Footed, 13 x 10 In.	58
Container, Cylindrical, Lid, Manganese Daubs, Mid 1800s, 14 In.	300
Creamer, Shouldered, Amber Glaze, Manganese, Loop Handle, Ring Foot, c.1850, 5 In.	240
Crock, Lead Glaze, Shoulder Ring, Emanuel Suter, 1870-90, ½ Gal., 7 x 6½ In.	176
Crock, Manganese Splash, 1800s, New England, 13 In.	308
Crock, Mug Shape, Apple Butter, Deep Red, Brown Mottled Glaze, Handle, 1800s, 5 In.	325
Cuspidor, Glazed, Solomon Miller Brush, 1864, 3½ x 7¼ In.	224
Cuspidor, Women, Glazed, Stamped Rosette, Henry Fair, 1800s, 2 x 3¾ In.	1062
Dish, Baking, Hollyhocks, Slip Decoration, Wavy Line Border, England, 13 x 17 In. ....*illus*	899
Dish, Loaf, Slip Decorated, Coggle Wheel Edge, Oval, 1800s, 16½ In. ....*illus*	767
Dish, Slip Decorated, Yellow Waves, Green Line, Coggled Rim, c.1830, 10¼ In.	3567
Dish, Slip Marbled, Brown, Green, Cream, Coggled Rim, 14¼ In.	4200
Dish, Strainer, Crimped Rim, Pierced Center, Coil Design, Slip Glaze, c.1770, 11 In.	6150
Figurine, Bear Holding Tree Stump, 1800s, 6 In.	750
Figurine, Dog, Spaniel, 5¾ In.	540
Figurine, Dog, Standing, Basket, Hollow Body, Incised Base, c.1875, 5¾ x 6 In. ....*illus*	1180
Figurine, Eagle, Feather Details, Spread Wings, 1800s, 11¼ x 9 In.	650
Figurine, Gentleman, Leaning, Stump, c.1875, 5¼ In.	330
Figurine, Lion, Reclining, Molded, Brown Glaze, 1800s, 4 x 9 In. ....*illus*	142
Figurine, Man, Hat, Broom, Manganese Glaze, c.1875, 3⅞ In. ....*illus*	450
Flask, Pocket, Round, Red Ground, Gold, Stars, Inscription, Slip Glaze, c.1799, 3 In.	1230
Flowerpot, Brushed Copper Feather, Saucer, Stamped, S. Bell & Son, c.1882, 8 In.	199
Flowerpot, Tapered, Molded Rim, Mottled Glaze, Coggle Wheel Band, Saucer, 5 x 5 In.	130
Jar, 2 Handles, Mottled Mustard & Green Glaze, Mid 1800s, 4½ In.	480
Jar, Angled Shoulder, Red, Sine Wave Band, Lead Glaze, Qt., Mid 1800s, 6¾ In.	527
Jar, Angular Shoulder, Wide Mouth, Green Glaze, Bristol County, Mass., 8¼ In.	1169
Jar, Canning, 2-Tone Glaze, Sponged Stripes, Mid 1800s, 6 In.	780
Jar, Canning, Green Glaze On Shoulder, Manganese Daubs, Mid 1800s, 6 In.	120
Jar, Coggled Rim, Mottled Green & Orange Glaze, Early 1800s, 7½ In.	480
Jar, Flower Decoration, Manganese, John Bell, Late 1800s, 12½ In.	720
Jar, Lid, Orange & Green Mottled Glaze, Top Knob, Oval, Lug Handles, c.1800, 7 In.	3000
Jar, Mottled Green Glaze, Mid 1800s, 6½ In.	540
Jar, Oval, Flared Rim, Recessed Lid, Orange Red & Black Speckled Glaze, Rings, 8¾ In.	480
Jar, Oyster, Rolled Rim, Pear Green, Glazed, Ocher Dots, Border, 1800s, 8 In.	500
Jar, Rounded Shoulder, Wide Squared Mouth, Green & Orange Splotchy Glaze, 8 In.	677
Jar, Shouldered, Gray, Green Splotch Design, Ring Foot, Lid, Finial, c.1800, 6 x 6 In.	7500
Jar, Storage, Coggled Rim, Mottled Green & Amber Glaze, Side Handles, c.1830, 8 In.	600
Jar, Storage, Cylindrical, Rolled Rim, Green & Manganese Mottled Glaze, 1800s, 10 In.	708
Jar, Storage, Round, Double Rolled Rim, Ring Foot, Mottled Streak Glaze, 1800s, 4 In.	385
Jar, Storage, Tapered, Rolled Rim & Foot, Brushed Glaze, 1800s, 6 In.	325
Jardiniere, Tray, Ruffled Rim, 1800s, 5¼ In.	394
Jug, Bulbous, Rolled Lip, Green Splotchy Glaze, Strap Handle, Bristol, Mass., 6¼ In.	4305
Jug, Bulbous, Rolled Rim, Green To Blue Glaze, Strap Handle, 1700s, 6 In.	2000
Jug, Bulbous, Rolled Rim, Orange, Manganese Splotches, Strap Handle, c.1800, 5 In.	3750
Jug, Cylindrical, Flat Band Collar, Applied Strap Handle, 1800s, 9½ In.	325
Jug, Glazed, Loop Handle, Fr. Smith, Catawissa, 1878, 10¼ In.	649
Jug, Harvest, Spout, Rolled Lip, Amber Spotted Glaze, Horizontal Top Handle, c.1850, 7 In.	420

R

Jug, Manganese Glaze, Pear Form, Applied Ribbed Handle, Pa., 4 In.	325
Jug, Oval, Pinched Neck, Loop Handle, Rolled Rim, Marked, Seagreaves, 12 In.	142
Jug, Rolled Rim, Green, Amber Spotted Glaze, Flat Loop Handle, Ring Foot, c.1860, 9 In.	960
Jug, Shouldered, Orange & Amber Running Glaze, Flat Strap Handle, c.1855, 7 In.	330
Jug, Strap Handle, Green Glaze, Mid 1800s, 9 ½ In.	1080
Jug, Tapered, Rolled Rim, Tan, Manganese Splotches, Strap Handle, c.1810, 5 In.	375
Loaf Pan, Coggled Rim, Yellow Slip, Chips, Mid 1800s, 3 ½ x 18 ¼ In.	330
Loaf Pan, Comb Decorated, 1800s, 13 ¼ x 17 In.	787
Loaf Pan, Rectangular, Sloping Sides, Yellow Squiggle Design, c.1850, 2 x 12 In.	474
Loaf Pan, Yellow Slip Design, Flared Rim, 1800s, 3 x 15 ½ In.	189
Loaf Pan, Yellow Slip Inscription, Hetty, Wavy Lines, Coggled Rim, c.1810, 10 x 12 In.	700
Mixing Bowl, Red, Yellow, Lead Glaze, Mid 1800s, 7 x 15 ¼ In.	129
Mug, Applied Strap Handle, Incised, Manganese Blotches, 1800s, 4 x 3 In. ....*illus*	275
Pie Plate, Coggled Rim & Yellow Slip Swirls, Mid 1800s, 11 In.	420
Pie Plate, Coggled Rim, Yellow Slip, ABC Decoration, Mid 1800s, 10 In.	469
Pie Plate, Coggled Rim, Yellow Slip, CB Initials, Mid 1800s, 9 In.	390
Pie Plate, Coggled Rim, Yellow Slip, Linear Decoration, Mid 1800s, 10 ½ In.	330
Pie Plate, Coggled Rim, Yellow Slip, Mary's Dish, c.1850, 10 In. Diam.	344
Pie Plate, Coggled Rim, Yellow Slip, Wavy Line, Mid 1800s, 9 ½ In.	150 to 390
Pie Plate, Green, Brown, Wavy Slip Lines, 1800s, 6 ¾ In.	600
Pie Plate, Yellow Wavy Lines, 1800s, 8 ⅛ In.	148
Pitcher, Beaded Shoulder, Lead, Copper, Manganese, Strap Handle, 1886-1903, 10 ¼ In.	380
Pitcher, Bulbous, Sage Green Glaze, Manganese, Loop Handle, c.1850, 8 In.	1920
Pitcher, Flared Rim, Spout, Manganese Splotches On Red, Strap Handle, c.1810, 10 In.	650
Pitcher, Gallery Rim, Dark Green Glaze, Oval, Applied Handle, c.1850, 7 ½ In.	270
Pitcher, Oval, Orange, Green, Manganese Splotches, Strap Handle, 8 In.	461
Pitcher, Pinched Spout, Flared Rim, Manganese Glaze, C-Scroll Handle, c.1865, 16 In.	474
Pitcher, Ribbed Strap Handle, Manganese Glaze, Green On Neck, Mid 1800s, 7 In.	540
Pitcher, Rolled Rim, Spout, Mottled Brown Glaze, Upright Strap Handle, 1800s, 7 In.	900
Pitcher, Sage Green Glaze, Manganese, Applied Handle, Mid 1800s, 7 ½ In.	875
Planter, Hanging, Bulbous, Mottled Glaze, Ruffled Rim, Saucer Base, Pa., 4 x 7 In.	18
Planter, Lion, Folksy Reclining Lion, Early 1900s, 15 x 23 In.	720
Planter, Tapered, Mottled Glaze, Coggle Wheel Design, Saucer Base, 1800s, 5 x 5 In.	142
Plate, Bread & Cheese, Coggled Rim, Yellow Slip Inscription, c.1810, 11 In.	4500
Plate, Octagonal, Yellow Slip Diagonal Bands, Green Splashes, 1800s, 6 In.	10800
Plate, Octagonal, Yellow Slip, Dot In Diamond, Green Splashes, 6 ⅛ In.	9000
Plate, Slipware, Yellow Tulips, Green Leaves, Black Lines & Dots, 1821, 7 ¼ In.	550
Plate, Wedding, Courting Couple, Flowers, Sgrafitto, Oley Valley, 1935, 11 In.	71
Pot, Bulbous, Wide Rim, Orange Glaze, Brown Shapes & Flowers, c.1850, 5 x 7 In.	950
Rundlet, Yellow & Green Slip Bands, 4 ½ In.	720
Rundlet, Yellow Glaze, Manganese Splotches, Initialed GW, 1800s, 5 ⅝ In.	240
Stew Pot, Oval, Orange, Green & Manganese Glaze, Strap Handle, c.1810, 9 In.	1800
Vase, Cylindrical, Green Glaze, Orange Spotting, Flared Foot, Ruffled Rim, c.1865, 7 In.	125
Vase, Wide Mouth, Green & Orange Glazed, Early 1800s, 8 ½ In.	400

RICHARD was the mark used on acid-etched cameo glass vases, bowls, nightlights, and lamps made by the Austrian company Loetz after 1918. The pieces were very similar to the French cameo glasswares made by Daum, Galle, and others.

Vase, Chartreuse, Blue Mottle, Burgundy Hops, Vine, Acorn Shape, Cameo, 5 In.	384
Vase, Dark Magenta Raised Flowers, Vines, Blue Ground, 7 ⅜ x 4 In. ....*illus*	495

RIDGWAY pottery has been made in the Staffordshire district in England since 1808 by a series of companies with the name Ridgway. Ridgway became part of Royal Doulton in the 1960s. The transfer-design dinner sets are the most widely known product. Other pieces of Ridgway may be listed under Flow Blue.

Bust, Man, Jacket, Waistcoat, Parian, 1857, 8 In.	59
Dresser Box, Blue, White, Landscape, Dividers, Transferware, c.1842, 7 ⅝ x 3 ½ In.	74
Meat Dish, India Temple, Blue, White, Transferware, c.1850, 20 ½ In.	123

Redware, Figurine, Lion, Reclining, Molded, Brown Glaze, 1800s, 4 x 9 In.
$142

Hess Auction Group

> **TIP**
>
> For best results, have your house sale on the 1st or 15th of the month (near payday), but not during holiday weekends.

Redware, Figurine, Man, Hat, Broom, Manganese Glaze, c.1875, 3 ⅞ In.
$450

Ruby Lane

R

Redware, Mug, Applied Strap Handle, Incised, Manganese Blotches, 1800s, 4 x 3 In.
$275

Ruby Lane

TIP

An unglazed rim on the bottom of a plate usually indicates it was made before 1850.

Richard, Vase, Dark Magenta Raised Flowers, Vines, Blue Ground, 7⅜ x 4 In.
$495

Ruby Lane

Ridgway, Platter, Agricultural, Vase, Cut Edges, Blue, c.1842, 21½ x 16 In.
$99

Jeffrey S. Evans

Riviera, Green, Jug, Batter, Lid
$66

Strawser Auction Group

Pitcher, Bamboo, Molded, Rope Bands, Twisted Rope Handle, Sage Green, 1800s, 8 In.	150
Pitcher, Tied Bamboo, Tan, 9 x 6¾ In.	129
Plate, Cornflower Blue, Flowers, Pink, Yellow, Scalloped Rim, Gilt Scroll, 1800s, 9 In.	180
Platter, Agricultural, Vase, Cut Edges, Blue, c.1842, 21½ x 16 In. ....*illus*	99
Platter, Canadian Scenery, Rectangular, Cut Edges, Blue, Transfer, c.1842, 21½ x 16⅛ In.	99
Platter, Eglinton Tournament, Medieval Arms, Blue & White, Scalloped, 1800s, 15 In.	499
Platter, Flowers, White, Blue, Purple, Gilt, Scroll Rim & Handles, 1800s, 12 In.	181
Platter, Water Lily, Green Flowers, Lavender Leaves, Paneled, Wavy, 1800s, 13 x 15 In.	450
Serving Dish, Oriental Pattern, Blue Transfer, Castles, Cartouche Border, 1800s, 10 In.	148
Teapot, Plum Transfer, Flag, Blue, Green, Flowers, Octagonal, Paneled, Lid, 1840s, 8 In.	265
Tureen, Blue, White, Asiatic Palaces, Hexagonal, 11¼ In.	120
Tureen, Flow Blue, Flowers, 8½ x 12½ In.	59
Tureen, Lid, Relief Merry Making Figures, 11¼ In.	31

RIFLES *that are firearms made after 1900 are not listed in this book. BB guns and air rifles are listed in the Toy category.*

RIVIERA dinnerware was made by the Homer Laughlin Co. of Newell, West Virginia, from 1938 to 1950. The pattern was similar in coloring and in mood to Fiesta and Harlequin. The Riviera plates and cup handles were square. For more prices, go to kovels.com.

Blue, Mug, 5 In.	86
Green, Jug, Batter, Lid ....*illus*	66
Green, Teapot, Lid, 3¾ In. ....*illus*	170
Mauve Blue, Butter, Cover, 3 x 6 In.	75
Mauve Blue, Teapot, Lid, 4 In.	280
Red, Plate, Dinner, c.1940, 10 In.	52
Red, Sugar, Lid, Footed, c.1935, 6 In.	75
Yellow, Creamer, 3 In.	25
Yellow, Cup & Saucer, 1940s	59

ROCKINGHAM, in the United States, is a pottery with a brown glaze that resembles tortoiseshell. It was made from 1840 to 1900 by many American potteries. Mottled brown Rockingham wares were first made in England at the Rockingham factory. Other types of ceramics were also made by the English firm. Related pieces may be listed in the Bennington category.

Cachepot, Gilt, Bronze, Pink, Flower Basket, White Reserve, Acorn Finial, Footed, 9 In., Pair..	875
Cuspidor, Mottled Brown Glaze, 8-Point Star, Ribbed, 1800s, 8 In. Diam.	100
Figurine, Bullfrog, Green Splashes, Mounded Base, c.1875, 3¾ In.	540
Pitcher, Acorn & Leaf Pattern, Yellow, Green Splotches, c.1875, 9 In.	188
Pitcher, Molded Flowers On Collar, Mottled Brown, Angled Handle, 1800s, 7 In.	125
Teapot, Octagonal, Molded Spout & Handle, Blue Splashes, c.1865, 8 x 11 In.	570
Tobacco Jar, Branch Handles, Cylindrical, Patterns, Embossed Eagle, c.1865, 6 In.	450

ROGERS, *see John Rogers category.*

ROOKWOOD pottery was made in Cincinnati, Ohio, beginning in 1880. All of this art pottery is marked, most with the famous flame mark. The *R* is reversed and placed back to back with the letter *P*. Flames surround the letters. After 1900, a Roman numeral was added to the mark to indicate the year. The company went bankrupt in 1941. It was bought and sold several times after that. For several years various owners tried to revive the pottery, but by 1967 it was out of business. The name and some of the molds were bought by a collector in Michigan in 1982. In 2004, a group of Cincinnati investors bought the company and 3,700 original molds, the name, and trademark. Pottery was made in Cincinnati again beginning in 2006. Today the company makes architectural tile, art pottery, and special commissions. New items and a few old items with slight redesigns are made. Contemporary pieces are being made to complement the dinnerware line designed by John D. Wareham in 1921. Pieces are marked with the *RP* mark and a Roman numeral for the four-digit date. Mold numbers on pieces made since 2006 begin with 10000.

Ashtray, Devil Mask, Dark Blue, 3 ½ x 5 ¾ In.	230
Bookends, Blue Gray Glaze, Readers, c.1916, 6 ¼ In., Pair	978
Bookends, Dutch Boy & Girl, Wall, Tulips, Matte Glaze, Sallie Toohey, 1943, 5 ¾ In. ....*illus*	100
Bookends, Hound Dog, Ivory Matte Glaze, Square Base, Marked, 1936, 5 x 6 In.	395
Bookends, Panthers, Tan High Glaze, Pair, c.1945, 5 ½ In.	196
Bookends, Water Lilies, Ivory Matte Glaze, 1948, 3 ¾ In., Pair	80
Bowl, Coromandel Glaze, c.1932, 8 ⅜ In.	207
Candleholder, Z-Line, Female Nude Draped Around Side, 2 ⅛ x 7 In.	431
Candlestick, Bronze, Seahorse, Arts & Crafts, 13 In., Pair	2070
Coffeepot, Lid, Knop, Daisies, Brown Glaze, Tapered, C-Scroll Handle, 1893, 7 In.	384
Ewer, Dull Finish, Flowers, Blue, White Bulbous Body, Matthew Daly, c.1887, 12 ½ In.	184
Ewer, Green To Brown Glaze, Flowers, High Loop Handle, Saucer Foot, 10 In.	711
Ewer, Red Clay, Dark & Yellow Glazes, Fish, Tiger Eye, Albert Valentien, c.1885, 8 ¼ In.	3450
Flask, Pilgrim, Light Blue High Glaze, Maria Longworth Nichols Storer, c.1896, 6 In.	173
Fountain, Nude Boy, Standing, Sphere, Wave, Water Nozzle In Mouth, 31 In.	948
Jar, Lid, Parrots, Flowers, Butterfat, Blue Ground, E.T. Hurley, 1927, 13 x 7 ¾ In.	3125
Lamp, Electrified Oil Lamp, Green Base, Purple Thistles, Yellow Shade, 24 In.	7188
Letter Opener, Bronze, Seahorse, Hurley, 9 In.	1093
Mug, Dog, Retriever, Standard Glaze, E.T. Hurley, 1933, 4 ¾ In. ....*illus*	450
Mug, Mustard Yellow, Black, Cherries, Branches, Swirled Handle, 1897, 6 In.	240
Paperweight, Penguin, Cast, Ivory Glaze, Shirayamadani, c.1934, 5 In.	460
Paperweight, Rook, Green & Brown Matte Glaze, Marked, 1936, 2 ⅞ In. ....*illus*	200
Paperweight, Rooster, Colorful Glazes, William McDonald, c.1946, 5 ⅛ In.	196
Pitcher, Cherries, Standard Glaze, Silver Overlay, Ruffled Rim, S. Markham, 7 In.	1375
Pitcher, Dogwood, Standard Glaze, Silver Overlay, Bulbous, Mary Perkins, 1892, 6 x 6 In.	1875
Pitcher, Flowers, Branch, Yellow, Brown Glaze Ground, Oval, Ruffled Rim, 1888, 9 In.	185
Pitcher, Kneeling Imp, Standard Glaze, Tiger Eye, Harriet Wilcox, c.1890, 8 In.	316
Planter, Rectangular, Tree-Lined Street Scene, Loretta Holtkamp, c.1940, 7 ⅝ In.	184
Plaque, Boats, Blue & White, Marked, Vellum, Frame, Label, c.1900, 15 x 13 In.	2880
Plaque, Landscape, Country Road, Vellum, Fred Rothenbusch, c.1925, 11 ¾ x 8 ¾ In.	4715
Plaque, Landscape, Mt. Rainier, Vellum Glaze, F. Rothenbusch, 1929, 11 ⅝ x 9 ⅝ In. ....*illus*	6785
Plaque, Scenic, Wooded Lake Scene, Vellum Glaze, F. Rothenbusch, 1923, 10 x 8 In.	2750
Tea Caddy, Limoges Style Glaze, Bat, Spider Decoration, Albert Valentien, c.1891, 6 ¾ In.	403
Tea Set, Blue Ship, Teapot, Lid, Creamer, Sugar, Lid, c.1930, 4 ⅛ In., 3 Piece	225
Teapot, Dome Lid, Goldfinch, Emerald To Moss Green, Double Gourd, 1894, 9 In.	649
Tile, Flower, Yellow, Teal, 3 ¾ In.	366
Tile, Lake Landscape, Faience, Frame, c.1910, 11 ¾ x 11 ¾ In.	1500
Tile, Raised Outline, Cottage In Wooded Landscape, Frame, 11 ¼ x 59 ½ In., 5 Piece	7500
Tile, Scottish Rose, Green, Pink, Spiral, Matte Glaze, 6 In.	244
Tile, Scottish Rose, Pink, Green, Blue, Wood Frame, 6 x 6 In.	2318
Vase, 5 Rooks, Light Blue, Matte Glaze, Marked, 1928, 5 ⅜ In. ....*illus*	266
Vase, Aventurine, Flowers, Sara Sax, Signed, c.1920, 6 ¼ In.	2070
Vase, Blue Matte, Cylindrical, Gourd Base, 1912, 12 In.	1225
Vase, Blue, Stylized Leaves, William Hentschel, c.1926, 8 ½ x 6 ½ In.	976
Vase, Blueberries, Blue Ground, Vellum Glaze, Lorinda Epply, 1921, 7 ¾ x 3 In.	2375
Vase, Brown Geometric Design, Pale Blue Matte, Ringed Neck, Flared Rim, 1931, 6 In.	266
Vase, Brown To Orange, Yellow Daffodils, Square, Pinched Neck, 1898, 7 In.	236
Vase, Calla Lily Leaves, Blue Glaze, 1913, 20 In.	415
Vase, Carved Flowers, Yellow High Glaze, Harriet Wenderoth, c.1884, 6 ¼ In.	150
Vase, Carved Matte, Incised Blue Leaves, William Hentschel, c.1913, 8 In.	546
Vase, Chickadees, Branch, Snow, Gold, Pale Green, Vellum Glaze, 1907, 9 In.	4248
Vase, Crocus, Standard Glaze, Silver Overlay, Elizabeth Lincoln, 1905, 7 x 3 In.	1625
Vase, Daffodils, Iris Glaze, Tapered, Charles Todd, 1910, 8 ¾ x 4 In.	1000
Vase, Dandelions, Iris Glaze, Cylindrical, Irene Bishop, 1903, 6 ¾ x 3 In.	313
Vase, Dark Blue, Glossy, Flaring Lip, Shouldered, Marked, 1932, 6 ¼ x 2 ¾ In.	95
Vase, Dogwood, Iris Glaze, Swollen Shoulder, Rolled Rim, Olga Reed, 1902, 9 ½ In.	1125
Vase, Dogwood, Sea Green, Bulbous, Squat, Sallie Toohey, 1901, 6 x 7 In.	1125
Vase, Exotic Flowers, Trees, Bird, Arthur Conant, c.1920, 6 ¾ In.	4255
Vase, Fish, Sang De Boeuf, Oval, 1929, 11 ½ x 7 ½ In.	938

Riviera, Green, Teapot, Lid, 3 ¾ In.
$170

Replacements, Ltd.

Rookwood, Bookends, Dutch Boy & Girl, Wall, Tulips, Matte Glaze, Sallie Toohey, 1943, 5 ¾ In.
$100

Humler & Nolan

Rookwood, Mug, Dog, Retriever, Standard Glaze, E.T. Hurley, 1933, 4 ¾ In.
$450

Cowan's Auctions

Revised Rookwood Mark
The Rookwood Pottery went out of business in the 1960s; the molds and name were purchased in 1984. A new version of the *RP* flame mark is used. The Roman numerals for the entire year are used instead of just the last numerals: 1908 is VIII, 2008 is MMVIII.

R

Rookwood Ink Stamp Mark
Henry Farny, who is now best-known for his western paintings, designed the ink stamp mark first used by Rookwood in 1881.

Rookwood, Paperweight, Rook, Green & Brown Matte Glaze, Marked, 1936, 2 7/8 In.
$200

Humler & Nolan

Rookwood, Plaque, Landscape, Mt. Rainier, Vellum Glaze, F. Rothenbusch, 1929, 11 5/8 x 9 5/8 In.
$6,785

Humler & Nolan

Rookwood, Vase, 5 Rooks, Light Blue, Matte Glaze, Marked, 1928, 5 3/8 In.
$266

Humler & Nolan

Vase, Flower Bands, Strapwork, Oval, c.1919, 13 1/2 In.	590
Vase, Flowers, Blue, Dusty Pink Matte Glaze, Tapered, Cylindrical Neck, 1926, 7 In.	236
Vase, Flowers, Curves, High Glaze, Marked, Jens Jensen, 1940s, 7 1/4 In. ....*illus*	215
Vase, Flowers, Dark Green, Citron Yellow, Streaks, Barrel, Rolled Rim, 1944, 5 In.	177
Vase, Flowers, Purple, Blue, Green, Ivory, Barrel Shape, Saucer Foot, 1926, 11 In.	472
Vase, Geometric Designs, Hand Incised, Yellow, Bert Munson, c.1931, 7 5/8 In.	230
Vase, Glossy, Burnt Sienna, Mum, Leaves, Clara C. Lindeman, 9 In.	369
Vase, Goldenrod, Standard Glaze, Oval, Olga Reed, 1899, 13 x 8 In.	875
Vase, Grape Filled Vines, Double Vellum, Lenore Asbury, c.1931, 7 3/8 In.	748
Vase, Green, 6 Fish, E.T. Hurley, 1901, 7 In. ....*illus*	649
Vase, Green, Amber, Carnations, Compressed Globular, Flared Rim, 1894, 7 In.	354
Vase, Horizontal Ribs, Green, Drip Glaze, W.E. Hentchel, Stamped, 7 1/2 In.	185
Vase, Intricate Pattern, Green Over Blue Glazes, 2 Handles, c.1925, 10 1/4 In.	230
Vase, Iris Glaze, Fish Swimming, Green, Cream, White, E.T. Hurley, c.1904, 6 1/4 In.	6900
Vase, Iris Glaze, Pansies, Leaves, Blue Black, Gray, Rolled Rim, 1903, 9 In.	1298
Vase, Iris Glaze, Poppies, White, Dark Green To Mint, Tapered, Rolled Rim, 1904, 8 In.	660
Vase, Iris Glaze, Water Lilies, Sara Sax, 10 x 4 3/4 In.	1375
Vase, Irises, Blue & Gray, Green Leaves, White Ground, 1906, 10 x 6 In.	1625
Vase, Irises, Flambe & Black Opal Glaze, Swollen Shoulder, Harriet Wilcox, 1920, 10 In.	750
Vase, Japonesque Scene, Ivory Jewel Porcelain, Arthur Conant, 1922, 6 x 3 In.	1063
Vase, Jonquils, Sea Green, White Blossoms, Shouldered, Tapered, 1902, 8 In.	523
Vase, Light Blue, Matte, Daisies, Kataro Shirayamadani, 4 1/2 In.	185
Vase, Lily Pads, Carved, Painted, Vellum Glaze, Mary Nourse, 1904, 5 1/4 In. ....*illus*	1416
Vase, Limoges Style Glaze, Pair Of Sparrows, Albert Humphreys, c.1882, 6 5/8 In.	863
Vase, Mahogany, Carp, Matthew Daley, 1885, 20 x 9 In.	5000
Vase, Melon Shape, Ribbed, Flowers, Matte Glaze, Kataro Shirayamadani, 1940, 8 In.	500
Vase, Multicolor, Cylindrical, Wax Matte, Sally Coyne, Marked, 1927, 6 In.	275
Vase, Peacock Feathers, Green Matte, Arts & Crafts, 7 In.	230
Vase, Pink Tulips, Gray Ground, Jens Jensen, 8 1/4 In.	861
Vase, Porcelain, 2 Prancing Horses, Jens Jensen, Signed, c.1945, 12 In.	1495
Vase, Porcelain, Oxblood, Tigers, John Dee Wareham, 1937, 19 1/2 x 9 1/2 In.	2750
Vase, Purple Irises On Soft Blue Ground, Vellum, Ed Diers, c.1931, 9 In.	2300
Vase, Rectangular Box, Cream, Red & Lavender Wisteria Branches, 1946, 8 x 6 In.	240
Vase, Sailing Ships, Light Blue, Vellum Glaze, Fred Rothenbusch, c.1931, 8 1/2 In.	3680
Vase, Salmon Matte Glaze, Irises, Pink, Green, Shouldered, Signed, c.1930, 6 In.	480
Vase, Scenic, Lake Landscape, Trees, Vellum Glaze, Oval, E.T. Hurley, 1920, 7 In.	2000
Vase, Scenic, Wooded Landscape, Vellum, Swollen Cylinder, Ed Diers, 1917, 12 In.	2125
Vase, Squat, Flowers, Blue, Yellow, Green, Matte Glaze, Lorinda Epply, 1918, 7 In.	250
Vase, Standard Glaze, Sunflowers, Bronze Mount, M. Daly, c.1890, 43 1/2 x 12 In.	5938
Vase, Standard Glaze, Tulips, Orange, Marianne Mitchell, c.1903, 9 7/8 In.	374
Vase, Stick, Gulls In Flight, Sea Green, Flared Lip, 1900, 9 1/4 In.	2006
Vase, Sweet Peas, Sea Green Glaze, Tapered, Elizabeth Lincoln, 1905, 6 3/4 x 3 In.	1188
Vase, Tiger Eye, Shouldered, Flared Neck, Rippled Rim, Marked, 1885, 26 In.	1845
Vase, Turtles, Dull Finish, Round, Rolled Rim, Albert Valentien, 1883, 9 x 7 In.	2000
Vase, Turtles, Sea Green Glaze, Swollen Cylinder, E.T. Hurley, 1897, 7 3/4 x 3 1/2 In.	3000
Vase, Water Lilies, Iris Glaze, Oval, Flame Mark, W. McDonald, 1903, 14 3/4 x 8 In.	8750
Vase, Wild Roses, Iris Glaze, Ed Diers, 1910, 9 1/4 x 4 3/4 In.	1000
Vase, Winged Sprite, Riding Fish, Kataro Shirayamadani, 1891, 14 1/2 In. ....*illus*	4248
Vase, Woodland Scene, Vellum Glaze, Lenore Asbury, Signed, c.1919, 7 In.	805
Vase, Yellow Matte Glaze, Pierced Greek Key Rim, Squat, 1911, 5 In.	325
Vases, Trio Of Conjoined Pointed Bottoms, Each Decorated With Flowers, 5 3/4 x 5 3/4 In.	288

Rörstrand **RORSTRAND** was established near Stockholm, Sweden, in 1726. By the nineteenth century Rorstrand was making English-style earthenware, bone china, porcelain, ironstone china, and majolica. The company is still working and is now owned by Fiskars Sweden. The three-crown mark has been used since 1884.

Bowl, Amber & Beige, Mottled Glaze, Boat Shape, Curved Design, 3 x 4 In.	135
Coffeepot, Lid, Blue Glaze, Feather Design, Upright Spout & Handle, Oval, 9 In.	83
Jar, Turquoise, Gloss Glaze, Incised Line Design, Flat Lid, 6 1/2 x 5 In.	200

R

Oyster Plate, 6 Wells, Green, Pink Trim, Bulrushes, Flowers, Majolica, 11 In. ....*illus*	360
Teapot, Lid, Brown Matte Glaze, Spherical, Bamboo Handle, Lid, Ball Finial, 1940s, 9 In.	399
Tureen, Rosita, Oval, Wavy Rim, Molded Handles, Gilt, Underplate, 1940s, 6 x 8 In.	118
Vase, Glossy White, Enamel, Hedgehog, Molded Bulky Texture, Nylund, 1940s, 6 In.	500
Vase, Mottled Gray & Rust, Matte Glaze, Boat Shape, Nylund, c.1940, 5 x 8 In.	549
Vase, Porcelain, Carved Cyclamen, Sweden, Signed, c.1900, 10¾ x 5 In.	625
Vase, Red & Brown Flambe Glaze, Bulbous Bottle Shape, Marked, 6 In.	177
Vase, Sheep's Head, Open Mouth, Alf Wallander, 3 Crowns, c.1900, 10 x 7¾ In. ....*illus*	2125

ROSALINE, *see Steuben category.*

ROSE BOWLS were popular during the 1880s. Rose petals were kept in the open bowl to add fragrance to a room, a popular idea in a time of limited personal hygiene. The glass bowls were made with crimped tops, which kept the petals inside. Many types of Victorian art glass were made into rose bowls.

Blue Spatter, Silver Mica, 5 x 5½ In. ....*illus*	89
Flowering Branch, Purple, Green, Translucent Pink, Ruffled Rim, Gilt, 1890s, 5 In.	115
Opalescent, Cranberry Speckled Rim, Spiral Optic, c.1900, 5 In.	79
Pine Branch, Translucent Green, Silvery Pinecones, 4 x 4 In.	95
Posy, Clear, Hand Painted, 1890, 6 x 6 In.	48
Satin Glass, Pink, White Roses & Bows Overlay, Gilt Accents, 1890s, 4 In.	87
Satin Glass, Yellow, Shaded, White Interior, Crimped, c.1890, 4 x 6 In.	51
Vaseline, Glass, Pinched, Opalescent, Applied Pink Glass Roses, 4½ x 5 In.	12
Wild Rose Glaze, Corn & Husks Pattern, Bulbous, Folded Rim, c.1960, 5 x 7 In.	99

ROSE CANTON china is similar to Rose Mandarin and Rose Medallion, except that no people or birds are pictured in the decoration. It was made in China during the nineteenth and twentieth centuries in greens, pinks, and other colors.

Bowl, Cabbage Leaf, 1800s, 5 x 12 In.	550
Dresser Box, Lid, Flowers, Plum Blossoms, Pink, Yellow, Gilt, Hexagonal, 2 x 4 In.	138
Garden Stool, Hand Painted, c.1900, 19 In.	2645
Jar, Lid, Vase Of Flowers, Leaves, Cartouche, Cylindrical, 14 x 9 In.	189
Pin Tray, Peony Flowers, Plum Blossoms, Vines, Canted Corners, c.1910, 4 x 5 In.	199
Platter, Peonies, Leaves & Buds, Panels, Oval, c.1910, 12 x 16 In.	285
Platter, Tree Peonies, Flowers, Butterflies, c.1925, 17¾ x 14 In. ....*illus*	750
Relish, Flowers, Pink, Green, Orange, Serpentine Rim, Disc Foot, 1800s, 4 x 7 In.	145
Trinket Box, Lift Lid, Peonies, Peaches, Leaves, Pale Green, Pink, Lift Lid, 1920s, 4 x 3 In.	82
Vase, Stick, Flowers, Clouds, Vines, Yellow, Pink, Flared, Stick, Saucer Foot, c.1920, 10 In.	169

ROSE MANDARIN china is similar to Rose Canton and Rose Medallion. If the panels in the design picture only people and not birds, it is Rose Mandarin.

Bough Pot, Lid, Gilded Twisted Handles, 5 Pierced Holes On Lid, 1800s, 8¾ In., Pair	2100
Bowl, Green & Pink, People, Tree Peonies, Cartouche, 1800s, 5 In. Diam.	115
Bowl, Women, Children, Garden, Shaped Cartouche, Blue, 1810-30, 4¼ x 10 In. ....*illus*	687
Charger, Peonies, Lotus, Leaves, People, Pink, Green, Gilt, 1800s, 10 In. Diam.	315
Cup & Saucer, Panels, People, Flowers, Gilt Accents, c.1890, 2 x 6 In.	240
Punch Bowl, Band Of Flowers & Butterflies, Late 1800s, 6 x 14½ In.	1300
Punch Bowl, Bands Of Flowers & Butterflies, Late 1800s, 9¼ x 20¾ In.	7000
Punch Bowl, Landscape, Court Scenes, Tall Foot, 1700s, 14 x 11 In.	3600
Soup Spoon, People, Flowers, Leaves, Pink, Green, 1800s, 6 x 2 In.	145
Sugar, Lid, People, Balcony, Pink, Green, Bulbous, Ear Handles, 1880s, 3 In.	195
Teapot, Lid, People, Flowers, Green, Pink, Gilt, Barrel Shape, c.1850, 6 In.	275
Vase, Applied Gilded Foo Dogs & Dragons, 23¼ In., Pair	1800
Vase, Bottle Shape, Gilded Elephant Trunk Handles, 1800s, 12½ In., Pair............................	650
Vase, Cartouches, Court Scenes, 10 x 3¾ In., Pair	297

Rookwood, Vase, Flowers, Curves, High Glaze, Marked, Jens Jensen, 1940s, 7¼ In.
$215

Cowan's Auctions

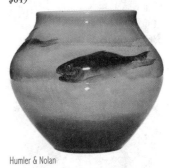

Rookwood, Vase, Green, 6 Fish, E.T. Hurley, 1901, 7 In.
$649

Humler & Nolan

Rookwood, Vase, Lily Pads, Carved, Painted, Vellum Glaze, Mary Nourse, 1904, 5¼ In.
$1,416

Humler & Nolan

R

Rookwood, Vase, Winged Sprite, Riding Fish, Kataro Shirayamadani, 1891, 14½ In.
$4,248

Humler & Nolan

Rorstrand, Oyster Plate, 6 Wells, Green, Pink Trim, Bulrushes, Flowers, Majolica, 11 In.
$360

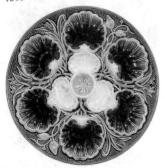

Strawser Auction Group

Rorstrand, Vase, Sheep's Head, Open Mouth, Alf Wallander, 3 Crowns, c.1900, 10 x 7¾ In.
$2,125

Rago Arts and Auction Center

R

ROSE MEDALLION china was made in China during the nineteenth and twentieth centuries. It is a distinctive design with four or more panels of decoration around a central medallion that includes a bird or a peony. The panels show birds and people. The background is a design of tree peonies and leaves. Pieces are colored in greens, pinks, and other colors. It is similar to Rose Canton and Rose Mandarin.

Back Plate, Rich Red Underside, 1700s, 1½ x 8 In.	3000
Basket, Fruit, Reticulated, Flared Rim, Mandarin, Peonies, c.1865, 4 x 11 In.	625
Basket, Fruit, Stand, Late 1800s, 3¾ In.	225
Bowl, Bell Shape, Flared, Pink Ground, Scroll, Birds, Boy, Ox, Raised Foot, 6 In.	615
Bowl, Figures, Gardens, Prunus Fruit, Lotus Blossoms, 23¾ x 9½ In.	2261
Bowl, Gilt, Medallions, People, Butterflies, Birds, Flowers, 23½ x 8¾ In.	4720
Bowl, Oval, Courtyard Scene, Women, Bird, Butterfly, Flowers, 11⅛ x 9⅛ In.	246
Bowl, People, Court, Birds, Branches, Medallions, 1800s, 14¾ In. ......*illus*	1230
Bowl, People, Flowers, Peonies, Butterflies, 5 x 11½ In.	178
Box, People, Birds, Butterflies, Flowers, Court, Square, 7 In. ......*illus*	320
Cup, Stand, People, Blue, Gold, 10¼ In.	1063
Dish, Wavy Edge, Gilt & Red Chain Border, c.1770, 8½ In.	400
Fishbowl, Figures, Garden, Fence, 21 x 18 In.	62
Pitcher, Flowers, Pear Shape, Wavy Rim & Spout, 1800s, 9 In.	475
Plate, Scalloped Rims, People, Flowers, Bird, Prunus Fruit, Butterflies, 8½ In., 12 Piece	208
Punch Bowl, Mandarin Panels, Pierced Gilt Discs, Birds, c.1835, 7 x 19 In.	3500
Punch Bowl, Panels, Flowers, People, Ring Foot, 1900s, 6 x 14 In.	120
Punch Bowl, People, Courtyard, Flowers, 6½ x 15¾ In.	1250
Punch Bowl, Reserves, People, Birds, Flowering Branches, 1800s, 16 In.	948
Tea Set, Teapot, Sugar, Lid, & Creamer, Lid, People, Flowers, 1900s, 3 Piece	192
Teapot, Rattan Handle, 6 In.	62
Tureen, Soup, Lid, Panels, Flowers, Birds, Butterflies, Gilt, Bombe, 15 In., Pair	875
Tureen, Soup, Mushroom Lid, Tray, Gilt Highlights, Mid 1800s, 1¾ x 12½ x 10½ In.	688
Tureen, Underplate, People, Flowers, Flowers, Birds, Butterflies, 9¼ x 12¾ In.	416
Umbrella Stand, People, Birds, Butterflies, 24¼ x 9½ In.	535
Urn, Lid, Frames, Figures, Peonies, Gilt Pistol Handles, Base, c.1835, 15 In., Pair	5750
Vase, Dome Lid, Gilt Foo Dog Knops & Handles, c.1850, 18 In., Pair	1875
Vase, Foo Dogs & Dragons On Neck, 1900s, 15 In., Pair	115
Vase, Gu Form, Late 1800s, 15½ x 10¼ In.	593
Vase, Mandarins, Molded Ground, Twist Handles, Pierced Lid, 9 x 7 In., Pair	2125
Vase, Waisted, Flared Foot & Mouth, Flowers, Figures, People, Peonies, 16 x 10 In.	330
Washbasin, 6 Figural Medallions, Birds, Butterflies, Flowers, c.1860, 16¼ x 4½ In.	324

ROSE O'NEILL, *see Kewpie category.*

ROSE TAPESTRY porcelain was made by the Royal Bayreuth factory of Tettau, Germany, during the late nineteenth century. The surface of the porcelain was pressed against a coarse fabric while it was still damp, and the impressions remained on the finished porcelain. It looks and feels like a textured cloth. Very skillful reproductions are being made that even include a variation of the Royal Bayreuth mark, so be careful when buying.

Basket, Flowers, Fan Shape, Upright Handle, Block Feet, Cutout Base, c.1890, 6 In.	265
Biscuit Jar, Woodland, Flowering Shrubs, 6½ In.	88
Bowl, Pink, Green, Yellow, 4 White Scalloped Lips, Royal Bayreuth	96
Creamer, Flowers, Gilt Trim, Ruffled Rim, Protruding Spout, 1880s, 4 In.	81
Creamer, Flowers, Shaped Handle, Folded Spout, c.1900, 5 In.	85
Hair Receiver, Pink Roses, Green, Yellow, Royal Bayreuth	30
Hatpin Holder, Flowers, Gilt Trim, Scalloped Rim, Scroll Base, 5 x 2 In.	125
Pitcher, Pink Roses, Gold Handle, Rim, Royal Bayreuth, c.1910, 7 x 8 In. ......*illus*	130
Planter, Flowers, Squat, Ruffled Rim, Gold Loop Handles, Insert, c.1890, 3 x 3 In.	125
Powder Jar, Flowers, Squat, Round Lid, Paw Feet, 2½ x 4 In.	85
Sugar & Creamer, Flowers, Squat, Oblong, Gold Upright Handles, Gilt Trim, 1920s	98

Rose Bowl, Blue Spatter, Silver Mica,
5 x 5 ½ In.
$89

Ruby Lane

Rose Canton, Platter, Tree Peonies, Flowers,
Butterflies, c.1925, 17 ¾ x 14 In.
$750

Ruby Lane

Rose Mandarin, Bowl, Women, Children,
Garden, Shaped Cartouche, Blue, 1810-30,
4 ¼ x 10 In.
$687

Kaminski Auctions

Rose Medallion, Bowl, People, Court, Birds,
Branches, Medallions, 1800s, 14 ¾ In.
$1,230

Leland Little Auctions

Rose Medallion, Box, People, Birds,
Butterflies, Flowers, Court, Square, 7 In.
$320

Brunk Auctions

Rose Tapestry, Pitcher, Pink Roses, Gold
Handle, Rim, Royal Bayreuth, c.1910, 7 x 8 In.
$130

Ruby Lane

Rosemeade, Vase, Bud, Yellow, Speckled,
Tapers, Diagonal Slant Mouth, 5 ¾ x 2 ½ In.
$33

Ruby Lane

Roseville, Carnelian II, Vase, Green Matte,
Art Deco, Zanesville, Ohio, c.1926, 16 x 11 In.
$1,375

Rago Arts and Auction Center

Roseville, Jardiniere, Pedestal, Landscape,
Squeezebag Slip, Sgraffito, Harry Rhead,
c.1900, 42 In.
$3,540

Humler & Nolan

R

Roseville, Peony, Vase, Yellow Flowers,
Handles, 8 ¼ In.
$472

Humler & Nolan

Roseville, Tourist, Planter, Window
Box, Horse Spooked By Jalopy, Liner,
8 ½ x 16 In.
$2,360

Humler & Nolan

Roseville, Wincraft, Vase, Blue, Yellow
Tulip, 18 ⅜ In.
$177

Humler & Nolan

Vase, Flowers, Oval, Flared Rim, Gilt Upright Cutout Handles & Trim, c.1900, 4 In. 95

 ROSEMEADE POTTERY of Wahpeton, North Dakota, worked from 1940 to 1961. The pottery was operated by Laura A. Taylor and her husband, R.I. Hughes. The company was also known as the Wahpeton Pottery Company. Art pottery and commercial wares were made.

Bell, Tulip Shaped, Pink & Green, 1940s, 4 In. 80
Figurine, Elephant, Seated, Trunk Up, Gray & Pink Glaze, Glossy, 1950s, 2 In. 73
Figurine, Raccoon, Paws In Air, Tan & Brown, 1950s, 2 In. 85
Flower Frog, Fish, Blue Glaze, 16 Holes, 1960s, 3 ½ In. 65
Planter, Elephant, Periwinkle Blue, Matte Glaze, Raised Trunk, 5 x 5 In. 568
Salt & Pepper, Swan, Pink, Glossy Glaze, 1940s, 2 ¼ x 3 In. 120
Vase, Bud, Yellow, Speckled, Tapers, Diagonal Slant Mouth, 5 ¾ x 2 ½ In. ....*illus* 33

 ROSENTHAL porcelain was made at the factory established in Selb, Bavaria, in 1891. The factory is still making fine-quality tablewares and figurines. A series of Christmas plates was made from 1910. Other limited edition plates have been made since 1971. Rosenthal became part of the Arcturus Group in 2009.

Bowl, Frosted, Masks, Octagonal, Versace, 5 ⅛ In. 212
Bowl, Silver Round Foot, 1950s, 4 ¼ x 9 In. 37
Cup & Saucer, Versace Le Jardin, Wing Handle, Gilt, Flowers, Bugs, Pink, 12 Piece 1000
Figurine, Horse, Dapple Gray, Standing, 16 In. 225
Figurine, Korean Dancer In Costume, Multicolor, C. Holzer-Defanti, Signed, 1919, 16 ¼ In. 1230
Figurine, Nude, Reclining Woman, Short Hair, 9 ½ x 13 In. 187
Figurine, Nude, Woman, Kneeling, Drinking, Signed Ernst Wenck, 7 x 6 ¾ In. 118
Figurine, Woman, Kneeling, Drying Ankle, 6 x 8 In. 218
Plate, Black & White, Stylized Zebra Print, Rounded Square, 1977, 12 x 14 In. 400
Vase, Birds, Leaves, Berries, Green Ground, 9 ½ In. 42
Vase, Cylindrical, Plate Like, 5 ½ x 8 ½ In. 120
Vase, Six Peacocks, Black & Gold & Blue & Orange & Green, 13 ¼ In. 575
Vase, Woman With Flowers, Bjorn Wiinblad, Denmark, 7 ⅛ In. 187

 ROSEVILLE POTTERY COMPANY was organized in Roseville, Ohio, in 1890. Another plant was opened in Zanesville, Ohio, in 1898. Many types of pottery were made until 1954. Early wares include Sgraffito, Olympic, and Rozane. Later lines were often made with molded decorations, especially flowers and fruit. Most pieces are marked *Roseville*. Many reproductions made in China have been offered for sale during the past few years.

Apple Blossom, Basket, Pink, White Flowers, 8 In. 130
Apple Blossom, Vase, Green, White Flowers, 7 ¼ In. 100
Baneda, Wall Pocket, Green, 1932, 8 ¼ In. 1325
Bird Of Paradise, Stylized, Vase, Brown To Cream Gradient Ground, c.1910, 8 In. 1320
Blackberry, Basket, Brown, Green, Upright Round Handle, Dome Foot, 7 In. 325
Blackberry, Bowl, 3 x 7 ½ In. 115
Blackberry, Candleholder, Green, Brown, 4 ¾ In. 215
Blackberry, Vase, Tapered, Closed Handles, Fine Crazing, 5 ⅛ In. 259
Cabbage Roses, Vase, Green Mottled, Jar, Molded Flowers, Band, Rolled Rim, 6 In. 944
Carnelian II, Vase, Green Matte, Art Deco, Zanesville, Ohio, c.1926, 16 x 11 In. ....*illus* 1375
Carnelian II, Vase, Pale Green Streak Glaze, Smokestack, Tapered, Saucer Foot, 14 In. 325
Clemana, Vase, Brown, Marked, 6 ½ In. 115
Clematis, Vase, Brown, Green, c.1940s, 6 In. 55
Creamware, Wall Pocket, Green & Yellow Flower, 17 In. 978
Della Robbia, Vase, Morning Glories, Gray, Blue, Green, Swirling, c.1910, 15 In. 7500
Della Robbia, Vase, Pinecones, Yellow, Green, Cylindrical, F. Rhead, c.1910, 7 x 2 In. 3129
Dogwood, Wall Pocket, Double Horn, 8 ¾ In. 127
Earlam, Vase, Tan & Blue Mottled, Bulbous, Arched Handles, Rolled Rim, 7 In. 177

Egypto, Oil Lamp, Green, 4¾ In.	395
Ferella, Bowl, Pink, Green, Glazed, Footed, c.1930s, 4 In.	600
Ferella, Vase, Fuchsia Mottled, Funnel, Cylinder Neck, Flared Cutout Rim, Handles, 9 In.	443
Ferella, Vase, Pink, Green, Glazed, Handles, 1930s, 9 In.	775
Freesia, Pitcher, Brown, Amber, Pedestal Foot, Wavy Spout, Pointed Handle, 15 In.	142
Fuchsia, Vase, Blue, Flowers & Leaves, Two Handles, Marked, 18¼ In.	518
Futura, Vase, Blue Triangle, 9⅛ In.	690
Futura, Vase, Cobalt Blue, Turquoise, Speckled, Elephant Leg Shape, Rings, 10 In.	354
Futura, Vase, Moss Green, Pink, Sunray Design, Flat Square, Ear Handles, Base, 5 In.	1770
Futura, Vase, Mottled Blue & Tan, Fan Shape, Rectangular Neck, Shaped Base, 6 In.	266
Futura, Vase, Tombstone, Orange, Yellow, 6¼ In.	215
Imperial II, Vase, Frothy Yellow Crystalline Glaze, Blue, Squat, Sloped Neck, 5 In.	236
Imperial, Wall Pocket, Triple, Verdigris Glaze, Mottled Brownish Orange, 6½ In.	184
Jardiniere, Pedestak, Art Nouveau, Female Bust Handles, Painted Cartouches, Irises, 43½ In.	625
Jardiniere, Pedestal, Landscape, Squeezebag Slip, Sgraffito, Harry Rhead, c.1900, 42 In..illus	3540
Morning Glory, Vase, White, Purple, Yellow, Brown, Bulbous, Square Handles, 6 In.	165
Pauleo, Vase, Mottled Gray & Brown Glaze, Tapered, Shouldered, Rolled Rim, 19 In.	354
Peony, Vase, Yellow Flowers, Handles, 8¼ In..illus	472
Peony, Wall Pocket, Yellow, Green, Brown, c.1942, 8½ x 5½ In.	300
Pine Cone, Tray, Brown, 8⅛ In.	288
Pine Cone, Vase, Amber & Gold, Smokestack, Tapered, Branch Handles, 12½ In.	384
Pine Cone, Vase, Pillow, Brown, Handles, Shaped Rim, Round Foot, 8 In.	177
Pine Cone, Vase, Triple Bud, Tubular, Cone Shape, Green, Handles, Dome Foot, 9 In.	142
Pine Cone, Wall Pocket, Brown, 9¼ In.	575
Poppy, Ewer, Pink, Yellow, Swollen, Tapered, Spread Foot, Handle, Wavy Spout, 19 In.	189
Poppy, Vase, Green Leaves, Brown, Yellow, 7 x 3 In.	265
Primrose, Umbrella Stand, Orange, Yellow, Spread Foot, Angled Handles, 21 In.	295
Rozane Mongol, Censer, Copper Red, Squat, Square Cutout Handles, Peg Feet, 5 x 11 In.	472
Rozane, Vase, Painted Flowers, Blanche Mallet, Signed, c.1910, 20½ x 14 x 7½ In.	562
Rozane, Vase, Peach, Turquoise, Smokestack, Tapered, Angled Handles, 8 In.	130
Rozane, Vase, Portrait, American Indian, Chief Josh, Green, Brown, Oval, Lid, c.1910, 23 In.	360
Sign, Roseville Pottery, White Script Against Blue Mat, Light Crazing, 4½ In.	748
Sunflower, Vase, 10¼ In.	1093
Teasel, Vase, Flowerheads, Stems, Yellow, Orange, Tapered, Swollen Collar, 9 In.	590
Tourist, Planter, Window Box, Horse Spooked By Jalopy, Liner, 8½ x 16 In. .....illus	2360
Tulip, Vase, Cobalt Blue, Amber, Green, Rounded Cylinder, Handles, Ring Foot, 9 In.	2242
Umbrella Stand, Matte Green, Footed, 2 Handles, 21¼ In.	978
Velmoss, Wall Pocket, Pink, Faint Overall Crazing, 8½ In.	431
Vista, Vase, Leaves, Cobalt Blue, Green, Pear Shape, Square Cutout Handles, 10 In.	885
Wincraft, Vase, Blue, Yellow Tulip, 18⅜ In..illus	177
Wisteria, Vase, Blue, 8¼ In.	403
Wisteria, Vase, Cobalt Blue, Mottled, Bell Shape, Rounded Bottom, Handles, 4 In.	354
Woodland, Vase, Ivory, Stippled, Hollyhocks, Green, Waisted, Shouldered, 11 In.	472
Woodland, Vase, Poppy Blossom, Stippled Tan Ground, Beaker, Swollen Rim, 8 In.	443
Woodland, Vase, Yellow Tulip, Buds, Green Leaves, Bottle, Swollen Neck, 11 In.	590

ROWLAND & MARSELLUS COMPANY is part of a mark that appears on historical Staffordshire dating from the late nineteenth and early twentieth centuries. *Rowland & Marsellus* is the mark used by an American importing company in New York City. The company worked from 1893 to about 1937. Some of the pieces may have been made by the British Anchor Pottery Co. of Longton, England, for export to a New York firm. Many American views were made. Of special interest to collectors are the plates with rolled edges, usually blue and white.

Bowl, Man & Woman, Sitting In Woods, Blue & White, c.1920, 8 In.	45
Pitcher, American Pilgrims, 8½ x 6⅛ In.	36
Pitcher, Declaration Of Independence, Green, Gilt Band, c.1908, 7 In.	192
Plate, Baltimore, Courthouse, Flow Blue, Rolled Edge, c.1910, 10 In.	108

Roy Rogers, Button, Roy Rogers Riders, Portrait, Roy & Trigger, Mt. Ephraim Theatre, 1¾ In.
$115

Hake's Americana & Collectibles

Royal Bayreuth, Creamer, Devil Playing Cards, 5¼ In.
$98

William H. Bunch Auctions

Royal Bonn, Vase, Woman, Orange Dress, Flowers, Germany, 1900, 12 In.
$825

DuMouchelles

TIP
Never buff a coin. It is worth more with the scratches than it would be if buffed.

Royal Copenhagen, Platter, Flora Danica, Notched Gilt Rim, Inscribed, Marked, 1900s, 18 In.
$984

Skinner, Inc.

Royal Copenhagen, Vase, Lid, St. George & Dragon, Oxblood Glaze, J. Nielsen, 1936, 13 x 12 In.
$1,500

Rago Arts and Auction Center

Royal Copenhagen, Vase, Man, Flute, Gazelles, Black Slip On Blue Ground, Kaj Lange, Marked, 7 3/4 In.
$354

Humler & Nolan

Plate, Brooklyn, N.Y., Flow Blue, c.1900, 6 In.	155
Plate, Nantucket Harbor, Old Windmill, Blue & White, c.1920, 10 In.	120
Plate, Niagara Falls, Blue & White, Rolled Edges, c.1910, 10 In.	105
Plate, Plymouth Rock, Blue & White, Rolled Edge, c.1940, 10 In.	99
Plate, Portland, Maine, City Hall, Brown & White, Rolled, c.1910, 10 In.	115
Plate, Theodore Roosevelt, Blue, White, 10 1/4 In.	61

ROY ROGERS was born in 1911 in Cincinnati, Ohio. His birth name was Leonard Slye. In the 1930s, he made a living as a singer; in 1935, his group started work at a Los Angeles radio station. He appeared in his first movie in 1937. He began using the name Roy Rogers in 1938. From 1952 to 1957, he made 101 television shows. The other stars in the show were his wife, Dale Evans, his horse, Trigger, and his dog, Bullet. Roy Rogers died in 1998. Roy Rogers memorabilia, including items from the Roy Rogers restaurants, are collected.

Button, Club, Roy Rogers Riders, Hiland's Corral, Roy & Horse, 1940s, 2 In.	127
Button, Owen's Corral, Roy Rogers Riders, Orange Ground, Roy & Trigger, 2 In.	171
Button, Roy Rogers Riders, Portrait, Roy & Trigger, Mt. Ephraim Theatre, 1 3/4 In. *illus*	115
Card, 3-D Pictures, Character Photos, Post Cereal, 1953, 3 x 4 In., 24 Cards	541
Card, Pop-Out, Color Art, Die Cut Design, Text, Post Cereal, 1952, 2 x 3 In., Set Of 36	288
Clock, Alarm, Roy, Trigger, Desert, Sun Face, Rope Numbers, Metal, 1950s, 4 x 4 In.	150
Cup, Figural, Bust, Roy Rogers Inscribed On Hat, Plastic, Quaker Oats, 1950s	75
Figure, Fringed Top, Hat, Pistol, Trigger, Chain Reins, Saddle, Box, c.1958, 9 x 9 In.	304
Flashlight, Signal Siren, Roy & Trigger, Tin Litho, Code Booklet, Box, 1950s, 7 In.	145
Holster, Leather Belt, Metal Buckle, Wood Bullets, Box, 1940s, 12 x 13 In.	286
Lamp, Figural Roy & Dale Evans, Clock, Metal, Copper Finish, Wood Base, 1940s	255
Lunch Box, Leather Handle, Riding Horse, 8 3/4 x 6 1/4 In.	244
Ring, Roy Rogers, Incised Signature, Saddle Shape, Nickel, Silver, 1948, Size 13	362
Saddle, Leather, Brown, Side Skirt & Stirrup, Embossed, Child's, 1950s, 13 x 19 In.	234
Toy, Guitar, Palomino Pony Design, Rope Border, Jefferson, 1950s, Child's	82
Toy, Truck & Trailer, Dodge, Roy & Trigger, Tin, Blue & Yellow Paint, 1950s, 16 In.	350
Wristwatch, Dale Evans, Queen Of The West, Leather Strap, Figure, Box, 1950s, 6 x 4 In.	115
Wristwatch, Roy & Trigger, Leather, Tooled Metal Clasp, Ingraham, 1950s, 8 In.	165

ROYAL BAYREUTH is the name of a factory that was founded in Tettau, Bavaria, in 1794. It has continued to modern times. The marks have changed through the years. A stylized crest, the name Royal Bayreuth, and the word *Bavaria* appear in slightly different forms from 1870 to about 1919. Later dishes may include the words *U.S. Zone* (1945–1949), the year of the issue, or the word *Germany* instead of *Bavaria*. Related pieces may be found listed in the Rose Tapestry, Sand Babies, Snow Babies, and Sunbonnet Babies categories.

Bowl, Portrait, Signed Wagner, 10 1/2 In.	575
Creamer, Devil Playing Cards, 5 1/4 In. *illus*	98
Creamer, Donkeys, Landscape, 3 1/2 In.	115
Creamer, Frog, Figural, Pink Nightcap, Tongue Out, c.1905, 4 1/2 In.	200
Creamer, Watermelon, Green, Pink, Ribbed, Leaf Border, Blue Mark, c.1930, 4 In.	199
Figurine, Lobster, Woman, Cherub, Flowered Dress, 12 In.	107
Hatpin Holder, Poppy, Red, Green Stem, Blue Mark, c.1900, 5 In.	399
Plate, Chinoiserie Scenes, Central Cartouche, 4 Molded Cartouches, Gilt, Black, 9 In.	1865
Relish, Roses, Gilt Trim, Scrolling Border, Cutout Handles, c.1900, 5 x 11 In.	80
Saucer, Devil & Cards, Cross Shape, c.1900, 3 1/2 x 3 1/2 In.	200
Sugar & Creamer, Fuchsia Flowers, Bulbous, Scalloped Rim, Gilt, 1890s, 4 In.	170

ROYAL BONN is the nineteenth- and twentieth-century trade name used by Franz Anton Mehlem, who had a pottery in Bonn, Germany, from 1836 to 1931. Porcelain and earthenware were made. Royal Bonn also made cases for Ansonia clocks. The factory was purchased by Villeroy & Boch in 1921 and closed in 1931. Many marks were used, most including the name Bonn, the initials FM, and a crown.

Cheese Keeper, Flowers, Wedge, Tray, Cover, Branch Handle, c.1900, 5 x 9 In.	175
Ewer, Poppies, Leaves, Ivory Matte, Gilt, Ribbed Swirl, c.1905, 12 In.	285

Jardiniere, Daisies, Leafy Stems, Gilded Upright Handles, Rim & Feet, c.1900, 9 In.	880
Letter Holder, Flower Sprays, Gilt, Serpentine Backs, Scroll Feet, c.1900, 8 x 14 In.	195
Tankard, Delft, Blue, White, 17 ½ In.	87
Vase, Art Nouveau, Woman, Blooming Mums, Misty, Sunny, Purple, 15 ¼ In.	312
Vase, Gilt, Flowers, Pink, White, Cream Ground, Ruffled Mouth, Germany, 13 In.	96
Vase, Multicolor Asters, Spiraling Reticulated Vine, Stick, Wavy Rim, 1800s, 17 In.	525
Vase, Thistle, Mounted As Lamp, 9 ¾ In.	132
Vase, Windmill, Double Handles, Blue, White, 15 In.	123
Vase, Woman, Orange Dress, Flowers, Germany, 1900, 12 In. *illus*	825

ROYAL COPENHAGEN porcelain and pottery have been made in Denmark since 1775. The Christmas plate series started in 1908. The figurines with pale blue and gray glazes have remained popular in this century and are still being made. Many other old and new style porcelains are made today.

Basket, Flora Danica, Pierced Sides, 3 ¼ x 8 ¼ In., Pair	2460
Basket, Fruit, Flora Danica, Vine Handles, Black Berries, Gilt, 3 ¼ x 10 In.	1073
Bottle Cooler, Flora Danica, c.1980, 6 ¼ x 9 ½ x 7 ¼ In., Pair	2750
Bowl, Oval, Flora Danica, c.1988, 6 ¼ x 14 ½ In.	1845
Cup & Saucer, Custard, Flora Danica, 3 ¼ In.	406
Cup & Saucer, Frijsenborg	60
Figurine, Boy With Umbrella, c.1977, 7 In.	140
Figurine, Elephant, Brown, Tan, Trunk Up, c.1955, 7 ¼ In.	325
Figurine, Falcon, 15 ¼ In.	1125
Figurine, Horse, Brown, Lying Down, Stoneware, 8 In.	88
Plaque, Daybreak, Nightfall, After Bertel Thorwaldsen, Round, 14 In., Pair	750
Plaque, White, Bisque, Mahogany, Angels, Round, 8 In.	69
Plate, Blue, Fluted, 9 ½ In.	115
Plate, Flora Danica, 10 In., 12 Piece	7500
Plate, Flora Danica, Oval, Blue Flower, Gilt Sawtooth Rim, 14 x 11 In.	649
Plate, Frijsenborg, 7 In.	35
Plate, Frijsenborg, 10 In.	65
Platter, Flora Danica, Notched Gilt Rim, Inscribed, Marked, 1900s, 18 In. *illus*	984
Serving Dish, Lid, Flora Danica, c.1982, 8 x 15 ¼ x 12 In., Pair	3998
Tray, Flora Danica, 20 ½ In.	2250
Tureen, Flora Danica, 15 In.	3000
Tureen, Lid, Flora Danica, Applied Flowers, Vines, Gilt, Handles, 9 x 12 In.	1888
Tureen, Lid, Stand, Flora Danica, Crabstock Handle, c.1972, 10 ¾ In.	4428
Vase, Blanc-De-Chine, Elongated Oval, Stylized Sea Life, Malinowski, 34 ¾ In.	2500
Vase, Cream, Brown, Triangular, Raised Budding, A. Salto, 1950s, 5 x 6 In.	2250
Vase, Glazed Porcelain, Bronze Base, G. Bogelund, K. Andersen, c.1950, 6 In.	1500
Vase, Glazed Porcelain, Bronze Lid, P. Nordstrom, K. Andersen, 1921, 6 ¾ x 5 ¾ In.	1625
Vase, Gold & Amber Glaze, Budding Gourd, Axel Salto, 1950s, 7 x 5 In.	3250
Vase, Lavender, Flamingos, Square, Round Neck, Footed, c.1900, 13 In.	2006
Vase, Lid, St. George & Dragon, Oxblood Glaze, J. Nielsen, 1936, 13 x 12 In. *illus*	1500
Vase, Man, Flute, Gazelles, Black Slip On Blue Ground, Kaj Lange, Marked, 7 ¾ In. *illus*	354
Vase, Mottled Gold Glaze, Oval Budding, Cylindrical, 1940s, 6 x 3 In.	2875
Vase, Stoneware, Bronze Lid & Base, Brown, C. Halier, K. Andersen, c.1930, 12 ½ x 9 In.	5000
Vase, Stoneware, Brown Glaze, Sampson & Lion, Jais Nielsen, 1930s, 31 x 19 In.	2500

ROYAL COPLEY china was made by the Spaulding China Company of Sebring, Ohio, from 1939 to 1960. The best known are the figural planters and the small figurines, especially those with Art Deco designs.

Figurine, Hen, Brown, Green Wing, c.1945, 8 In.	60
Planter, Bulldog, Standing, Head Turned To Side, Cream, Black, 1950s, 6 x 10 In.	58
Planter, Cocker Spaniel, Raised Paw, White, Orange, Black, 1940s, 9 In.	95
Planter, Finch, Branch, Red, Yellow, Teal, High Gloss, 5 x 5 ¼ In. *illus*	36
Planter, Mare With Colt, Tan, White, Black, Glossy Glaze, 1950s, 8 x 7 In.	85
Planter, Poodle, Off White, Prancing, 1940s, 6 x 8 In.	62
Wall Pocket, Asian Boy, Head, Round Woven Pattern Hat Brim, 1940s	55

Royal Copley, Planter, Finch, Branch, Red, Yellow, Teal, High Gloss, 5 x 5 ¼ In.
$36

Ruby Lane

Royal Crown Derby, Cup & Saucer, Mikado, Cobalt Blue, Chinoiserie, 2 Piece
$30

Ruby Lane

Royal Crown Derby, Urn, Gilt, Flowers, Out Swept Handles, Reticulated, 1877-90, 10 ½ In.
$615

Leland Little Auctions

S

Royal Doulton, Figurine, Monkey, Seated, Holding Open Book, HN 960, 4½ In.
$750

Bunte Auction Service

Royal Doulton, Lamp Base, Chang, Multicolor Glazes, White Crackle Glaze, Marked, 8⅞ In.
$2,124

Humler & Nolan

Royal Doulton, Plate, Shakespeare Country, Castles, Cottages, Gilt Rim, c.1925, 10 In., 12 Piece Set
$1,375

New Orleans Auction Galleries

ROYAL CROWN DERBY COMPANY, LTD., is a name used on porcelain beginning in 1890. There is a complex family tree that includes the Derby, Crown Derby, and Royal Crown Derby porcelains. The Royal Crown Derby mark includes the name and a crown. The words *Made in England* were used after 1921. The company became part of Allied English Potteries Group in 1964. It was bought in 2000 and is now privately owned.

Biscuit Jar, Imari Pattern, Octagonal, Lid, Square Handle, 1800s, 6 In.	560
Box, Lid, Cut Corners, Black, Orange, 2 x 6½ In.	156
Cake Stand, Imari Pattern, 24K Gold Trim, Marked, 1919, 4 x 9 In.	734
Cup & Saucer, Flowers & Leaves, Orange, Gold, Marked, 1800s	425
Cup & Saucer, Mikado, Cobalt Blue, Chinoiserie, 2 Piece......*illus*	30
Jug, Flowers, Fruit & Scrolls, Pink, Gilt, Bulbous, Ribbed, c.1890, 8 In.	880
Plate, Dinner, Imari, 10¼ In., 12 Piece	531
Plate, Salad, Red Aves, 8¼ In., 8 Piece	150
Platter, Imari, Scalloped, Ring Of Mums, 17 In.	178
Teapot, Roses & Pansies, Royal Blue, Gilt Scroll, Lid, Marked, c.1905	1818
Urn, Gilt, Flowers, Out Swept Handles, Reticulated, 1877-90, 10½ In.....*illus*	615
Vase, Imari Pattern, Jester Handles, c.1885, 6 In.	395

ROYAL DOULTON is the name used on Doulton and Company pottery made from 1902 to the present. Doulton and Company of England was founded in 1853. Pieces made before 1902 are listed in this book under Doulton. Royal Doulton collectors search for the out-of-production figurines, character jugs, vases, and series wares. Some vases and animal figurines were made with a special red glaze called flambe. Sung and Chang glazed pieces are rare. The multicolored glaze is very thick and looks as if it was dropped on the clay. Bunnykins figurines were first made by Royal Doulton in 1939. In 2005 Royal Doulton was acquired by the Waterford Wedgwood Group, which was bought by KPS Capital Partners of New York in 2009 and became part of WWRD Holdings. Beatrix Potter bunny figurines were made by Beswick and are listed in that category.

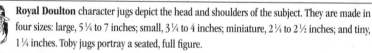

Royal Doulton character jugs depict the head and shoulders of the subject. They are made in four sizes: large, 5¼ to 7 inches; small, 3¼ to 4 inches; miniature, 2¼ to 2½ inches; and tiny, 1¼ inches. Toby jugs portray a seated, full figure.

Character Jug, Gunsmith, D 6573, 7 In.	50
Character Jug, Macbeth, D 6667, 7 In.	150
Character Jug, Poacher, D 6429, 1954, 7 In.	50
Character Jug, Sairey Gamp, D 5451, 6 In.	75
Character Jug, Santa Claus, D 6668, 7 In.	85
Character Jug, Veteran Motorist, D 6633, 1972, 7 In.	60
Figurine, Autumn Breezes, HN 1911, 7½ In.	125
Figurine, Blue Beard, HN 2105	50
Figurine, Christening Day, HN 3211, 7½ In.	57
Figurine, Daffy-Down-Dilly, H 1712, 8¼ In.	83
Figurine, Dog, English Setter, Black & White, HN 1050D, 5 x 8 In.	425
Figurine, Elaine, HN 2791, 7½ In.	72
Figurine, English Setter With Pheasant, HN 2529W, 10 x 8 In.	93
Figurine, Jack, HN 2016, 5½ In.	76
Figurine, Janet, HN 1537, 6½ In.	100
Figurine, Monkey, Seated, Holding Open Book, HN 960, 4½ In.....*illus*	750
Figurine, River Boy, HN 2128, 4 In.	45
Figurine, Thanksgiving, HN 2446, 8 In.	60
Figurine, Tracy, HN 2736	57
Jar, Holbein Ware, Brown With Yellow Top, Yellow Moths Near Top, 4½ In.	316
Lamp Base, Chang, Multicolor Glazes, White Crackle Glaze, Marked, 8⅞ In.....*illus*	2124
Pitcher, Milk, Green, Black Horses, Plow, 7½ In.	62
Pitcher, Rip Van Winkle, Dickens, Green, 7½ x 6½ In.	48
Plate, Castles, Landscapes, Gilt, Shaped Rims, 10 In., 12 Piece	540
Plate, Shakespeare Country, Castles, Cottages, Gilt Rim, c.1925, 10 In., 12 Piece Set.....*illus*	1375

Punch Bowl, Red Berries, Green Leaves, Andrew Wyeth, 1973, 5 1/2 x 13 In.	126
Vase, Apples, Leaves, Sparrows, Stoneware, Glazed, Pinched Rim, F. Butler, 14 In.	1875
Vase, Art Deco, Yellow With Green Stylized Flowers, Telescoping Top, 7 In.	81
Vase, Camels, Signed H. Fenton, 8 In.	156
Vase, Chang, Dragon, Flambe, C. Noke, H. Nixon, England, c.1920, 8 x 8 In.	6875
Vase, Chang, Drip Glaze, Crackled, Charles Noke, Harry Nixon, 1920s, 9 1/2 In. ...*illus*	1750
Vase, Chang, Pine Boughs, C. Noke, H. Nixon, England, c.1920, 17 1/2 x 7 1/2 In.	8125
Vase, Chang, Red, Blue & Mustard Yellow Flambe Glaze, Charles Noke, 9 In. ...*illus*	1020
Vase, Dragons, Stoneware, Blue & White, Oval, Matilda Adams, 1879, 11 In.	1063
Vase, Flambe, Sung Ware, Charles Noke & Fred Moore, Marked, 7 1/4 In.	403
Vase, Flambe, Sung Ware, Fred Moore, Incised, 10 3/8 In.	230
Vase, Flambe, Veined, Red, Ink Stamp, 8 3/4 In. ...*illus*	443
Vase, Lambeth, Art Nouveau, Flowers On Blue, c.1910, 10 1/4 x 5 1/4 In., Pair	500
Vase, Long Teardrop Cobalt Blue Neck, Round Brown Body, 1902-22, 16 x 8 In.	348
Vase, Red & Black, Flambe Glaze, Veined, Bulbous Bottle Shape, Marked, 10 In.	325
Vase, Trees Bordering Roadway, Hand Decorated, R. Holdcroft, 8 1/4 x 4 1/2 In.	345
Vase, Veined Flambe, Bottle Shape, 13 5/8 In.	177
Vase, Veined Flambe, Fred Moore, 10 3/8 In.	236

ROYAL DUX is the more common name for the Duxer Porzellanmanufaktur, which was founded by E. Eichler in Dux, Bohemia (now Duchcov, Czech Republic), in 1860. By the turn of the twentieth century, the firm specialized in porcelain statuary and busts of Art Nouveau–style maidens, large porcelain figures, and ornate vases with three-dimensional figures climbing on the sides. The firm is still in business. It is now part of Czesky Porcelan (Czech Porcelain).

Centerpiece, Women, Trumpet Shape Vase, Royal Dish, Irises, Leaves, 15 x 14 1/4 In.	875
Figurine, Apple Picker, Woman, Smock, Pitcher, 20 1/2 x 8 In.	118
Figurine, Man Kissing Woman, Pink, Green, c.1900, 22 In.	225
Figurine, Woman, Hiking, White Dog, Hat, Barefoot, Bag, Marked, c.1910, 9 In.	300
Figurine, Woman, Palm Tree, 1860-1914, 25 1/4 x 8 In.	295
Figurine, Woman, Shell, Purple Dress, Looks Down, 16 1/2 In.	187
Group, Boy, Bull, 10 3/4 x 15 In.	88
Group, Hounds, White, Sniffing, 9 1/2 In.	135
Vase, Ginko Leaves, Cream, Handles, 13 1/4 In.	94
Vase, Woman & Shell, 1900-18, 16 1/2 In.	187

ROYAL FLEMISH glass was made during the late 1880s in New Bedford, Massachusetts, by the Mt. Washington Glass Works. It is a colored satin glass decorated with dark colors and raised gold designs. The glass was patented in 1894. It was supposed to resemble stained glass windows.

Biscuit Jar, Lid, Cherub, Blue Panels, Gilt, Melon Ribbed, Handle, c.1890, 6 In.	2000
Biscuit Jar, Lid, Griffin, Dolphin, Pink, Gold, Gilt, Clover Loop Handle, 1890s, 7 In.	3750
Bottle, Bulbous, 2 Handles, Elaborate Gold Enameled, Finial Lid, 15 3/4 In.	17250
Bowl, Centerpiece, Chrysanthemum, Pairpoint Stand Putti Holding Bowl, 15 1/2 In.	3450
Ewer, Armorial Lion, Shield, Rope Twist Handle, 13 1/4 In. ...*illus*	3584
Rose Bowl, Roses, Blue Striated Panels, Gilt, Crimped, Mt. Washington, 6 In.	2050
Shade, Gold Enamel, Flowers, Green, Red, Stained Glass Collar, Flared, 1890s, 9 In.	910
Vase, Purple, Green, Gilt, Mt. Washington, 10 1/2 In.	2250
Vase, Roman Coins, Purple & Blue Panels, Gold, Bulbous, Handles, 1800s, 8 In.	1220

ROYAL HAEGER, *see Haeger category.*

ROYAL HICKMAN designed pottery, glass, silver, aluminum, furniture, lamps, and other items. From 1938 to 1944 and again from the 1950s to 1969, he worked for Haeger Potteries. Mr. Hickman operated his own pottery in Tampa, Florida, during the 1940s. He moved to California and worked for Vernon Potteries. During the last years of his life he lived in Guadalajara, Mexico, and continued designing for Royal Haeger. Pieces made in his pottery listed here are marked *Royal Hickman* or *Hickman.*

Royal Doulton, Vase, Chang, Drip Glaze, Crackled, Charles Noke, Harry Nixon, 1920s, 9 1/2 In. $1,750

Rago Arts and Auction Center

Royal Doulton, Vase, Chang, Red, Blue & Mustard Yellow Flambe Glaze, Charles Noke, 9 In. $1,020

Brunk Auctions

Royal Doulton, Vase, Flambe, Veined, Red, Ink Stamp, 8 3/4 In. $443

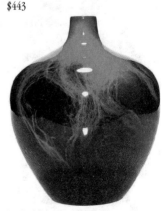

Humler & Nolan

Royal Flemish, Ewer, Armorial Lion, Shield, Rope Twist Handle, 13¼ In. $3,584

Jackson's International Auctioneers & Appraisers

Royal Hickman, Vase, Swan Form, Chartreuse, Florida, c.1950, 13½ x 12 In. $300

Ruby Lane

Royal Worcester, Figurine, Squirrelfish, R. Van Ruychevelt, Wood Base, Certificate, 1961, 9⅝ In. $549

Neal Auctions

Flower Frog, Nude Woman, Riding Fish, Pink, Blue, 10 x 12 In.	85
Planter, Gazelle, Moss Green, c.1950, 10 x 15 In.	150
Vase, Horse Head, Blue Purple Crystalline Glaze, 1914-44, 12 x 9¼ In.	175
Vase, Light Green, Forest Green, Tan, 1930s, 18 In.	90
Vase, Swan Form, Chartreuse, Florida, c.1950, 13½ x 12 In. *illus*	300

 ROYAL NYMPHENBURG is the modern name for the Nymphenburg porcelain factory, which was established at Neudeck-ob-der-Au, Germany, in 1753 and moved to Nymphenburg in 1761. The company is still in existence. Marks include a checkered shield topped by a crown, a crowned *CT* with the year, and a contemporary shield mark on reproductions of eighteenth-century porcelain.

Cane Handle, Man's Head, Wearing Cap, Beard, Gilt Trim, c.1765, 3 In.	9550
Creamer, Flower Spray, Yellow, Purple, Cream, 5 In.	13
Figurine, Putto, Holding Mask To Face, Draped, Gilt, c.1768, 4 In.	8363
Figurine, Seated Man, Asian, Blue Tunic, Yellow Pants, 1756, 5 In.	6218
Figurine, Seated Man, Pointy Cap, Robe, Chinoiserie, c.1760, 4 In.	6979
Figurine, Seated Woman Playing Xylophone, Sleeping Man, c.1700, 9¼ In.	10105
Pipe Bowl, Silver, Gilt Lid, Peasants, Rocailles, Scroll, 1765, 2¾ In.	1858
Pipe Bowl, Turk's Head, Young & Old Man's Face, c.1763, 2¾ In.	7062
Plate, Reticulated, Central Flower Bouquet, 9 In., 10 Piece	500

ROYAL RUDOLSTADT, *see Rudolstadt category.*

ROYAL VIENNA, *see Beehive category.*

 ROYAL WORCESTER is a name used by collectors. Worcester porcelains were made in Worcester, England, from about 1751. The firm went through many different periods and name changes. It became the Worcester Royal Porcelain Company, Ltd., in 1862. Today collectors call the porcelains made after 1862 "Royal Worcester." In 1976, the firm merged with W.T. Copeland to become Royal Worcester Spode. The company was bought by the Portmeirion Group in 2009. Some early products of the factory are listed under Worcester. Related pieces may be listed under Copeland, Copeland Spode, and Spode.

Bowl, Shell Shape, Gilt, Flowers, 10 In.	125
Candlestick, Square Capital, Column, Cream, 8 In., Pair	62
Cup & Saucer, Demitasse, Red, Gilt Decorated, 12 Piece	1062
Ewer, Gilt, Applied Dragon Handle, Flowers, Cream, 11½ In., Pair	625
Ewer, Patent Metallic, Gilt On Yellow Ground, Late 1800s, 16½ x 6 In.	625
Figurine, Samurai, Vase, Plant Stand, Multicolor, 15¾ x 6¼ In.	396
Figurine, Squirrelfish, R. Van Ruychevelt, Wood Base, Certificate, 1961, 9⅝ In. *illus*	549
Figurine, Uncle Sam, Standing, Hat, Multicolor, Base, Marked, 1891, 7 x 3 In.	95
Gravy Boat, Underplate, Deer Handles, Gilt, 8¼ x 5⅛ In.	218
Plate, Luncheon, Bessborough Green Pattern, 1900s, 9 In. Diam., 12 Piece	180
Potpourri, Leaf Handles, Pierced Neck, Ferns, Griffins, Swags, Lid, c.1890, 12 In.	510
Teapot, Blue Underglaze, Garden, Flowers, Leaves, Flower Finial, 5½ x 7½ In.	171
Urn, Lid, Thistle, Reticulated, 10¾ In.	250
Vase, Birds, Leaves, Blue, White, Matthew Smyth, c.1876, 12½ In.	187
Vase, Flowers, Gilt, 14 In., Pair	250
Vase, Pheasant, Game, Multicolor, 5½ In., Pair	156
Vase, Reticulated, Gilt Rim, Birds, Flying, Landscape, 3 Scenes, 6¼ x 5 In.	1722

 ROYCROFT products were made by the Roycrofter community of East Aurora, New York, in the late nineteenth and early twentieth centuries. The community was founded by Elbert Hubbard, famous philosopher, writer, and artist. The workshops owned by the community made furniture, metalware, leatherwork, embroidery, and jewelry. A printshop produced many signs, books, and the magazines that promoted the sayings of Elbert Hubbard. Furniture by the Roycroft community is listed in the Furniture category.

Bowl, Copper, Hammered, 2½ x 10½ In.	403

Bun Warmer, Copper, Tin, Brass, Hammered, Domed, 1920s, 6 x 11 In.	875
Candelabrum, 6-Light, Brass Finished, Hammered Copper, 4-Footed, 15 ½ x 4 ½ In.	396
Candelabrum, 8-Light, Brass Finished, Hammered Copper, 4-Footed, 20 ½ x 4 ¼ In.	213
Candlestick, Copper, Hammered, Twin Armed, 3 x 8 ¾ In., Pair	288
Dish, Copper, Hammered, Pale Green Specks, 8 In.	156
Jardiniere, Copper, Hammered, Squat, Cylinder Neck, Triangle Feet, c.1915, 11 In.	2750
Jug, Brown, Stopper, 4¾ In.	23
Lamp Base, Copper, Hammered, 3 Flattened Supports, Tripartite Base, 15 ½ In.	1000
Lamp, Copper, Hammered, Cylindrical Stem, Flattened Base, Mica Domed Shade, 15 In.	2250
Lamp, Copper, Hammered, Mica Shade, Single Socket, Orb & Cross, 1920s, 17 ½ In. .... *illus*	3250
Lamp, Copper, Hammered, Spread Foot, Jade Green Slag Glass Shade, c.1910, 19 In.	6250
Lamp, Copper, Hammered, Spread Foot, Steuben Gold Iridescent Bell Shade, 14 In.	5938
Vase, American Beauty, Copper, Hammered, Squat Base, Orb & Cross Mark, 19 x 8 In.	1750
Vase, Copper, Brass Wash, Hammered, Dogwood, Cylindrical, c.1915, 7 x 3 In.	594
Vase, Copper, Hammered, Cupped Foot, 10 x 4 ½ In.	460
Vase, Copper, Hammered, Smokestack, Beaded Banding, c.1910, 22 In.	2125
Vase, Metal, Hammered, Patina, 8 ½ In.	46

ROZANE, *see Roseville category.*

ROZENBURG worked at The Hague, Holland, from 1890 to 1914. The most important pieces were earthenware made in the early twentieth century with pale-colored Art Nouveau designs.

Cup & Saucer, Eggshell, Bird, Lavender Flowers, Paneled, Octagonal, c.1910	5000
Jug, Sunflowers, Blue, Yellow, Squat, Tapered Stick Neck, Handle, c.1910, 11 In.	513
Nut Bowl, Stylized Tulips, Orange, Yellow, Green, Purple, Oblong, 1909, 4 x 5 In.	350
Vase, Bird, Flowers, Stems, Paneled, Swollen, Square Rim, c.1910, 4 In.	3785
Vase, Lizards, Eggshell, Green, Red, Bottle Shape, Rectangle Handles, c.1900, 9 In.	3125
Vase, Lizards, Eggshell, Multicolor, Double Handles, 1900, 8 ½ x 4 ½ In. .... *illus*	3250
Vase, Stylized Butterflies & Leaves, Squat, Stick Neck, Arched Handles, c.1905, 6 In.	889
Vase, Stylized Flowers & Scroll, Brown, Curved Panels, Waisted Collar, 1900, 7 In.	190
Vase, Stylized Flowers, Green, Black, Blue, Red, Squat, Ring Foot, c.1899, 3 x 5 In.	620

RRP, or RRP Roseville, is the mark used by the firm of Robinson-Ransbottom. It is not a mark of the more famous Roseville Pottery. The Ransbottom brothers started a pottery in 1900 in Ironspot, Ohio. In 1920, they merged with the Robinson Clay Products Company of Akron, Ohio, to become Robinson-Ransbottom. The factory closed in 2005.

Ashtray, Dog, Standing, Round Tray, Black, Gold Iridescent Glaze, 1940s, 6 x 8 In.	75
Cookie Jar, Moon Girl, Red Hair, Red Lips, Pale Blue Lid, 1930s	195
Cookie Jar, Ned, Army Soldier, Standing, Brown Uniform, Smiling, 1940s	160
Cookie Jar, Yellow, Brown Sponge, Cookie In Script, c.1979, 10 x 6 ¼ In.	55
Dog Dish, Orange Rust, Embossed Dog, Ribbed, 1950s, 10 In. Diam.	95
Pitcher, Leaf, Stem, Cobalt Blue & Cream, Striped, Bands, Square Handle, 1940s, 6 x 7 In.	85
Planter, Sunburst, Raised Sun & Moon, Brown & Green Gloss, 1940s, 9 In.	100
Planter, White Matte, Raised Flowers, Drainage Hole, c.1939, 6 ½ x 7 ¾ In.	39
Vase, Burgundy, Stylized Flowers, c.1941, 8 x 4 In.	35
Vase, Victoria Glaze, Cornflower Blue, White Speckle, c.1939, 16 In.	145
Vase, Victoria Glaze, Red, White Speckle, Marked, c.1938, 6 In.	30

RS GERMANY is part of the wording in marks used by the Tillowitz, Germany, factory of Reinhold Schlegelmilch from 1914 until about 1945. The porcelain was sold decorated and undecorated. The Schlegelmilch families made porcelains marked in many ways. See also ES Germany, RS Poland, RS Prussia, RS Silesia, RS Suhl, and RS Tillowitz.

Bowl, Scallop, Forget-Me-Nots, Iridescent, Gilt, 1910, 8 In. .... *illus*	79
Cake Plate, Black Silhouette, Dancer, Yellow, 2 Handles, 9 ½ In.	47
Cake Plate, Green Iridescent, White Blossom Branch, Handles, c.1920, 10 In.	175
Pin Tray, Pink Roses, Gilt, Ormolu Swirls, Curved, Wavy Rim, Handles, 4 x 4 In.	52
Plate, Cream & Tan, Shaded, Pink & Peach Flowers, 1920s, 8 In.	84

Roycroft, Lamp, Copper, Hammered, Mica Shade, Single Socket, Orb & Cross, 1920s, 17 ½ In.
$3,250

Rago Arts and Auction Center

Rozenburg, Vase, Lizards, Eggshell, Multicolor, Double Handles, 1900, 8 ½ x 4 ½ In.
$3,250

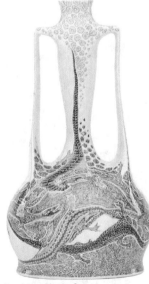

Rago Arts and Auction Center

RS Germany, Bowl, Scallop, Forget-Me-Nots, Iridescent, Gilt, 1910, 8 In.
$79

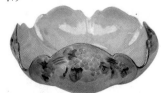

Ruby Lane

R

RS Prussia, Creamer, Swans, Lake, Flowers, Green, Gilt Red Mark, 3 7/8 x 2 3/4 In.
$95

Ruby Lane

RS Tillowitz, Tray, Tracery & Blue Luster, Gilt, 2 Handles, Pickard, c.1920, 12 3/4 x 5 3/4 In.
$123

Ruby Lane

RS Tillowitz, Vase, White Poppies, Green, Yellow, c.1925, 7 3/4 x 3 3/4 In.
$295

Ruby Lane

Ruby Glass
Remember the singer Kate Smith? She collected ruby stained glass—and started a collecting craze in the 1950s.

Relish, Pink Flowers, Branch, Double Oval, Tapered Strap Handles, 1920s, 6 x 9 In.	115
Serving Bowl, White, Green, Shaded, Flowers, Gilt, Square, Handles, c.1940, 6 x 7 In.	88
Snack Tray, White Roses, Green & Gold Border, Gilt Handles & Trim, c.1920, 11 In.	72
Sugar & Creamer, Roses, c.1890, 2 Piece	63
Sugar & Creamer, Shaded Green, Pink & White Roses, Gold Band, 1920s	149
Sugar, Green, Peach Flowers, Tapered, Angular Handles, Lid, Cutout, c.1930, 7 In.	128
Toothbrush Holder, Pink Roses, White Ground, Wall, 4 x 4 In.	75

 RS POLAND (German) is a mark used by the Reinhold Schlegelmilch factory at Tillowitz from about 1946 to 1956. After 1956, the factory made porcelain marked PT Poland. This is one of many of the RS marks used. See also ES Germany, RS Germany, RS Prussia, RS Silesia, RS Suhl, and RS Tillowitz.

Creamer, White, Pink Roses, Blush Interior, Ruffled Rim, Scroll Handle, Gilt, 1940s, 2 In.	54
Cup & Saucer, Peach Roses, Purple, Blue, Gilt, Shaped Rim, 3 x 5 In.	140
Dish, Hand Painted, Green, Flowers, 2 Handles, 12 1/8 x 6 1/4 In.	78
Hair Receiver, White, Peach Roses, Apricot Band, Gilt Leaves, Round, 1940s, 4 x 5 In.	67
Jar, Lid, Hydrangea, Leaves, 1939-45, 4 x 4 In.	60
Planter, Mottled Tan & White, Pheasants, Round, Pedestal Foot, c.1950, 7 x 7 In.	275
Plate, Hydrangea, Green, White, Marked, 1932-38, 7 1/2 In.	37
Plate, Shell Shape, Pink Roses, Spray, Pale Green, Scalloped Rim, Gilt, 9 In.	135
Rose Bowl, White, Molded Hearts, Peach Wild Roses, Gilt Trim, Scalloped, 3 x 10 In.	88
Tea Set, Pink Flowers, Teapot, 10 1/4 x 7 1/2 In., 6 Cups, 3 1/3 x 2 1/2 In.	77
Vase, Black Geese, 2 Handles, 5 3/4 In.	600

 RS PRUSSIA appears in several marks used on porcelain before 1917. Reinhold Schlegelmilch started his porcelain works in Suhl, Germany, in 1869. See also ES Germany, RS Germany, RS Poland, RS Silesia, RS Suhl, and RS Tillowitz.

Biscuit Jar, Roses, Gilt, Lavender, Teal, Leaf Feet, Paneled, Scallop Rim, Lid, 1800s, 6 In.	350
Bowl, 4 Seasons Women, Portraits, 10 1/4 In.	3304
Bowl, Iris Mold Variation, Wild Flower Center, Cobalt Blue Border, 10 In., Pair	354
Bowl, Pink Roses, White, Green, Scalloped Rim, Inturned Petals, 1800s, 11 In.	92
Bowl, Roses, Gilt, Iridescent Teal, Blue, Molded Scroll & Flower Rim, c.1885, 11 In.	175
Butter, Cover, Pink Tapestry, Blue Leaves, Octagonal, Strainer, c.1880, 7 In.	260
Celery Dish, Cobalt Blue, Flowers & Swirls, Gilt, Scalloped, Handles, 1800s, 12 In.	400
Chocolate Pot, Water Lilies, 9 In.	258
Chocolate Set, Chocolate Pot, 5 Cups & Saucers, Pink & Yellow Roses, 11 Piece	348
Creamer, Swans, Lake, Flowers, Green, Gilt Red Mark, 3 7/8 x 2 3/4 In. ....*illus*	95
Mustache Cup, Branches, Swallows, Pink Dogwood	100
Pitcher, Roses, Molded Flowers, Gilt, Crinkle Rim, Double Swirl Handle, c.1905, 9 In.	525
Plate, Pink Roses, Pale Green Center, Cobalt Blue Border, Gold Trim, 9 3/4 In.	324
Plate, Rust Leaves, White Flowers, Swallows, Scalloped, 8 1/2 In.	45
Serving Bowl, White, Pink Carnations, Caramel Border, c.1900, 2 x 10 In.	87
Sugar & Creamer, Pink Roses, Mother-Of-Pearl Finish, 2 Piece	165
Sugar & Creamer, Sheepherder, Landscape, 2 Piece	115
Tankard, Roses, Leaves, Beaker, Double Scroll Handle, Crimped Rim, c.1900, 11 In.	475
Toothbrush Holder, Leaf Border, Roses, Forget-Me-Nots, Wall, 9 1/4 In.	175
Tray, Medallion Mold, Lebrun I & II Portraits, Cream Center, Green Garland Border, 11 3/4 In.	206
Vase, Roses, Lavender Iridescent, Gilt, Beaded, Jewels, Beaker, Handles, c.1905, 11 In.	699

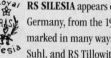 **RS SILESIA** appears on porcelain made at the Reinhold Schlegelmilch factory in Tillowitz, Germany, from the 1920s to the 1940s. The Schlegelmilch families made porcelains marked in many ways. See also ES Germany, RS Germany, RS Poland, RS Prussia, RS Suhl, and RS Tillowitz.

Bowl, Flowers, White Center, Shaped, Fluted, 4 1/2 x 9 1/4 In.	10
Bowl, Fretwork, Flowers, Gilt, 7 x 13 In.	327
Bowl, Leaf Shape, Flowers, Grapes, Signed	25
Bowl, Pink Peonies, Leaves, 3 x 9 In.	115

Candy Dish, Flower Sprays, Yellow, Pink, Blue, Shaped Rim, Gilt Trim & Ball Feet, 6 In.		123
Flower Frog, Green Luster, Roses, Gilt Swirl, Dome Cutout Lid, Marked, 4 x 4¼ In.		128
Gravy Boat, Underplate, Pink Peonies, 3 x 7 In.		138
Server, Handles, Crowned Cranes, 1930s, 8 In.		441
Vanity Tray, Orange Tulips, Boat Shaped, Cutouts, 5 x 11 In.		157
Vase, Red, Gold, 2 Handles, C.T. Altwasser, 6½ In.		36

RS SUHL is a mark used by the Reinhold Schlegelmilch factory in Suhl, Germany, between 1900 and 1917. The Schlegelmilch families made porcelains in many places. See also ES Germany, RS Germany, RS Poland, RS Prussia, RS Silesia, and RS Tillowitz.

Bowl, Fruit, Green Luster, White Blossoms, Gilt, Scalloped Rim, Ring Foot, c.1905, 10 In.		95
Bowl, Shaped Flower Rim, Blue Shading, Pink Flowers, Pentagon Reserve, c.1886, 10¾ In.		30
Candy Dish, White, Pink Rose Band, Gilt Trim, 2 Upright Looped Handles, c.1905, 8 In.		66
Plate, Yellow Roses, Green Leaves, Gilt Rim, 8½ In.		115
Relish, Pink & Yellow Roses, Green, Oblong, Shaped Edge, Cutout Handles, 6 x 12 In.		170
Shaker, White, Pink Peonies, Lavender, Green Leaves, Melon Ribbed, c.1910, 5 In.		55
Vase, Ivory & Olive, Shaded, Yellow Roses, Thorn Branches, Round, Gilt, c.1905, 5 In.		167
Vase, Women, Cherubs, Maroon Border, 4¾ In.		59

RS TILLOWITZ was marked on porcelain by the Reinhold Schlegelmilch factory at Tillowitz from the 1920s to the 1940s. Table services and ornamental pieces were made. See also ES Germany, RS Germany, RS Poland, RS Prussia, RS Silesia, and RS Suhl.

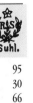

Bonbon, Butterflies, Roses On Exterior Rim, Hexagonal, Gilt Handles, 1929, 7 In.		48
Celery Dish, Yellow Poppies, Orange Iridescent, Cutout Handles, c.1930, 5 x 11 In.		55
Cheese & Cracker Set, Cream, Tan, Apricot Roses, Green Leaves, Gilt, 1930s, 3 x 9 In.		56
Chocolate Set, Chocolate Pot, 6 Cup & Saucer, White Roses, Green, 1914, 13 Piece		74
Gravy Boat, Saucer, Shaded Green, Pink & White Flowers, Leaves, Gilt Rim, 2 x 5 In.		59
Relish, White Flower Sprays, Leaves, Gilt Geometric Trim, Cutouts, 1920s, 4 x 9 In.		45
Serving Bowl, Sage Green, Orange Fuchsia Blossoms, Cutout Handles, 1930s, 9 In.		68
Serving Bowl, White & Blue, Gold Flowers, Boat Shape, Scalloped, Handles, 10 In.		54
Snack Tray, Cream & Tan, Shaded, Pink Flowers, Cutout Handles, Gilt, c.1940, 7 In.		44
Tidbit, Brown & Tan, Peach & White Roses, Gilded Loop Handles, c.1935, 9 In.		55
Tray, Dresser, Blue, Pink Flowers, Butterflies, Silver Border, Handles, c.1930, 16 In.		60
Tray, Tracery & Blue Luster, Gilt, 2 Handles, Pickard, c.1920, 12¾ x 5¾ In.	*illus*	123
Trinket Box, Melon Eater, Dog, Brown, 3¼ In.		206
Vase, White Poppies, Green, Yellow, c.1925, 7¾ x 3¾ In.	*illus*	295

RUBINA is a glassware that shades from red to clear. It was first made by George Duncan and Sons of Pittsburgh, Pennsylvania, in about 1885. This coloring was used on many types of glassware.

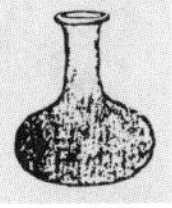

Bowl, Square, Rubina To Vaseline, Hobnail, 3 x 7½ In.		210
Dish, Sweetmeat, Block Pattern, Silver Plate Frame, 2¾ In.		36
Pitcher, Enamel, Daisy, Rubina To Clear, Applied Reeded Handle, 8½ In.		150
Pitcher, Overshot, Mold Blown, Swirled, Ribbed, Applied Handle, Harrach, c.1890, 8⅛ In.		84
Sugar Shaker, Spot Optic, Verde, Tapered, 5½ In.		390
Syrup, Coin Spot, Opalescent, Applied Handle, 7 In.		108
Vase, Hobnail, Dew Drop, Folded Over Rim, Frost Base, c.1880, 9 In.		168
Vase, Inverted Thumbprint, Ruby To Clear, Beaker, Rounded Base, c.1885, 7 In.		100

RUBINA VERDE is a Victorian glassware that was shaded from red to green. It was first made by Hobbs, Brockunier and Company of Wheeling, West Virginia, about 1890.

Cruet, Thumbprint, Inverted Funnel Shape, Citrus Faceted Stopper, 1800s, 7 In.		408
Pitcher, Opalescent Hobnails, Wide Wavy Rim, Loop Handle, c.1900, 8 In.		480
Punch Set, Ribbed Bowl, Ruffled Rim, Lid, Cut Finial, Circular Tray, 10 Cups, 12 x 17 In.		1323
Sugar Shaker, Spot Optic, Tapered, Shaded Red To Green, 1895-1910, 5½ In.	*illus*	380
Vase, Cylindrical, Daisies, Poppies, Ruffled Rim, Ribbed Interior, c.1900, 12 In.	*illus*	595

Rubina Verde, Sugar Shaker, Spot Optic, Tapered, Shaded Red To Green, 1895-1910, 5½ In.
$380

Jeffrey S. Evans

Rubina Verde, Vase, Cylindrical, Daisies, Poppies, Ruffled Rim, Ribbed Interior, c.1900, 12 In.
$595

Ruby Lane

Ruby Glass, Candy Dish, Ruffled, Crimped, Blown, 7½ In.
$50

Ruby Lane

This is an edited listing of current prices. Visit Kovels.com to check thousands of prices from previous years and sign up for free information on trends, tips, reproductions, marks, and more.

Rug, Agra, Sultanabad, Flowers, Pale Blue Gray Ground, 9 Ft. 2 In. x 6 Ft. 9 In. $3,000

New Orleans Auction Galleries

Rug, Contemporary, Flowers, Yellow, Brown, Green, Wool, Wm. Morris Style, 8 x 10 Ft. $688

Rago Arts and Auction Center

Rug, Hooked, Dog, Reclining, Leaf Border, 25¾ x 35 In. $118

Hess Auction Group

RUBY GLASS is the dark red color of a ruby, the precious gemstone. It was a popular Victorian color that never went completely out of style. The glass was shaped by many different processes to make many different types of ruby glass. There was a revival of interest in the 1940s when modern-shaped ruby table glassware became fashionable. Sometimes the red color is added to clear glass by a process called flashing or staining. Flashed glass is clear glass dipped in a colored glass, then pressed or cut. Stained glass has color painted on a clear glass. Then it is refired so the stain fuses with the glass. Pieces of glass colored in this way are indicated by the word *stained* in the description. Related items may be found in other categories, such as Cranberry Glass, Pressed Glass, and Souvenir.

Candy Dish, Ruffled, Crimped, Blown, 7½ In. ....*illus*	50
Centerpiece, Silver Plate, Footed, Hallmarked, 18¼ x 19½ In.	375
Compote, Lid, Gilt, Cut To Clear, Flowers, Lobed Foot, 10¼ x 5½ In.	184
Decanter, Bottle Shape, Faceted, Cut To Clear, Repeating Leaves, Egg Finial, 15⅝ In.	100
Epergne, Serpentine Rims, Deer, Landscape, Cut To Clear, 9 x 6⅛ In.	147
Jar, Ruby To Clear, Flowers, 4¾ In.	24
Sugar Shaker, Leaves, Cartouche, Scroll, Bulbous, Dome Foot, Metal Top, c.1880, 5 In.	198
Vase, Gilt, Coral Design, Wide Gilt Rim, Pair, 10¾ x 3½ In.	159
Vase, Trumpet, Octagonal, Engraved, Forest Scene, Rutting Stags, 12¼ In.	1243

RUDOLSTADT was a faience factory in the Thuringia region of Germany from 1720 to about 1791. In 1854, Ernst Bohne began working in the area. From about 1887 to 1918, the New York and Rudolstadt Pottery made decorated porcelain marked with the RW and crown familiar to collectors. This porcelain was imported by Lewis Straus and Sons of New York, which later became Nathan Straus and Sons. The word *Royal* was included in their import mark. Collectors often call it "Royal Rudolstadt." Most pieces found today were made in the late nineteenth or early twentieth century. Additional pieces may be listed in the Kewpie category.

Biscuit Jar, Cobalt Blue Flower Spray, Yellow, 7 In.	31
Compote, Gilt, Multicolor, Flowers, Figures, 6½ In.	161
Cup & Saucer, Kewpies Playing, 1915, Child's	80
Ewer, Gilt, Flowers, Swags, Scroll Handle, Shaped Mouth, Light Yellow, 12 In.	32
Vase, Double, Light Blue, Flower Spray, Pink, 8 x 6½ In.	82
Vase, Flowers, Purple, Cream, Gilt Handles, 12 x 6 In.	23
Vase, Gilt Reticulated Panel, Flowers, Leaves, Cream Ground, 8⅞ In.	61
Vase, Gilt, Figures, Reserve, Johannisbad, Leaves, Black Bands, c.1920, 14 x 8 In.	295
Vase, Tapestry, Leaves, Flowers, Pink Handle, 6 x 11 In.	177

RUGS have been used in the American home since the seventeenth century. The oriental rug of that time was often used on a table, not on the floor. Rag rugs, hooked rugs, and braided rugs were made by housewives from scraps of material. American Indian rugs are listed in the Indian category.

Abadeh, Persian, Flowers In Urns, Rows, Birds, Sprays, Lattice Border, c.1910, 5 Ft. x 6 Ft. 6 In..	948
Afghan, Central Medallion, Cross, Candlestick, Geometric Border, Red, c.1900, 3 Ft. 8 In. x 5 Ft. 2 In.	533
Agra, Sultanabad, Flowers, Pale Blue Gray Ground, 9 Ft. 2 In. x 6 Ft. 9 In..........*illus*	3000
Ardebil, Animals, Medallions, Guls, Ivory Panel, Blue & Red Accents, 5 Ft. 7 In. x 9 Ft.	480
Aubusson, Bird, Nest, Flowers, Vine Border, 10 Ft. x 7 Ft. 10 In.	200
Bakhshaish, Diamond Medallions On Red, 1900s, 9 Ft. 11 In. x 15 Ft.	5400
Bakhtiari, Floral, Geometric, Blue, Gold, Ivory, Red, Grid, 1900s, 4 Ft. 8 In. x 6 Ft. 8 In.	1000
Bakhtiari, Garden, Southwest Iran, c.1930, 9 Ft. 11 In. x 7 Ft.	308
Bakhtiari, Southwest Iran, c.1920, 17 x 12 Ft.	3998
Bamboo Silk, White Ground, Pale Blue & Gray, Doves, Flowers, 8 Ft. x 9 Ft. 10 In.	1875
Bidjar, Oriental, White Medallions, Orange & Red, Early 1900s, 6 Ft. 9 In. x 4 Ft. 7 In.	1955
Bidjar, Vases, Lanterns, Gold, Blue, Red, Border, Persia, Early 1900s, 8 Ft. 1 In. x 8 Ft. 3 In.	1700
Bokhara, Blue & Red Medallions, Geometric Design, 9 Ft. 9 In. x 8 Ft. 5 In.	380
Bokhara, Pakistani, Ivory Field Repeating Rows Of Guls, Border Stripes, 8 x 11 Ft..................	300
Bujar, Flowers On Central Panel, Red Field, Blue, Gold & Green Accents, 7 Ft. x 9 Ft. 6 In.	600
Caucasian, Geometric Medallions, Peacocks, Flowers, Zigzag Border, c.1950, 8 x 10 Ft.............	415
Caucasian, Medallions & Stars & Florets On Red Ground, 1900s, 4 Ft. 3 In. x 8 Ft. 3 In.	1200

Chichi, Stars, Octagons, Polygons, Blue, Brown Border, Late 1800s, 3 Ft. 8 In. x 5 Ft. 9 In........	1100
Chinese, Bamboo Pagoda, Flowers & Birds & Bat, Early 1900s, 17 Ft. 6 In. x 8 Ft. 11 In...........	3450
Chinese, Floral Orb, Spandrels, Greek Key, Blue, Ivory, Tan, 5 Ft. x 7 Ft. 8 In.	360
Contemporary, Flowers, Yellow, Brown, Green, Wool, Wm. Morris Style, 8 x 10 Ft. ....*illus*	688
Cuba, Oriental, Peacocks & Lions, Dark Blue & Red, Late 1800s, 5 Ft. 2 In. x 3 Ft. 7 In.	1380
Feraghan Sarouk, Urn & Flower Design, Floret Border, Turquoise, Blue, Olive, c.1900, 4 x 6 Ft.	472
Grenfell, 3 Polar Bears, Newfoundland & Labrador, Early 1900s, 2 Ft. 2 In. x 1 Ft. 8 In...........	3000
Hamadan, Center Panel, Serrated Edge, Repeating Designs, Sky Blue & Camel, 3 x 6 Ft.	240
Hamadan, Edge Medallions On Blue Ground, Runner, 1900s, 3 Ft. 5 In. x 10 Ft. 3 In.	420
Hamadan, Medallion, Ivory, Blue, Red, Rosettes, Serrated Leaves, 1900s, 6 Ft. 1 In. x 12 Ft. 2 In....	600
Hamadan, Oriental, Overall Design, Early 1900s, 6 Ft. 4 In. x 4 Ft. 3 In.	690
Hamadan, Pendant Medallion, Blue, Red, Gold, Serpent Border, 1900s, 3 Ft. 8 In. x 5 Ft. 11 In.	250
Hamadan, Red, Ivory, Sky Blue, Turtle Border, 1900s, 3 Ft. 9 In. x 6 Ft. 9 In........................	550
Hamadan, Runner, 7 Medallions, Cobalt Ground, c.1925, 3 x 11 Ft.	236
Heriz, Arabesque Medallion, Flowers, Leaves, Scrolling, c.1960, 7 Ft. 8 In. x 11 Ft. 6 In...........	2252
Heriz, Cobalt Blue Ground Medallion, Blue & Green Border, 1900s, 6 Ft. 8 In. x 10 Ft. 5 In.	1440
Heriz, Flowers, Stylized Leaves, Multicolor, Flowerhead Border, 8 Ft. 2 In. x 11 Ft. 3 In.	4750
Heriz, Gabled Medallion, Blue, Red, Ivory, Vines, Palmettes, 1900s, 8 Ft. x 10 Ft. 8 In.	2500
Heriz, Medallion, Cobalt Field, Red Ground, Ivory Spandrels, 7 Ft. 8 In. x 10 Ft. 5 In.	840
Heriz, Medallion, Salmon Field, Blue Border, Green & Ivory Accents, c.1940, 10 x 13 Ft.	5700
Heriz, Oriental, Browns & Dark Blue & Ivory, Early 1900s, 6 Ft. 8 In. x 4 Ft. 8 In.	1955
Heriz, Oriental, Medallion, Red & Light Blue, 1900s, 15 Ft. x 11 Ft. 4 In.	10925
Heriz, Pendant Medallions, Red Ground, Ivory & Olive Highlights, c.1925, 6 Ft. 8 In. x 9 Ft......	944
Heriz, Red Central, Blue Spandrels, Green & Ivory Highlights, 1900s, 9 Ft. 7 In. x 12 Ft. 7 In....	2160
Heriz, Red Ground, Dark Blue Border, Mid 1900s, 8 Ft. 10 In. x 10 Ft.	1680
Heriz, Runner, Iran, c.1930, 10 Ft. 1 In. x 2 Ft. 8 In.	425
Hooked, 16 Panels, Mittens, Easter Eggs, Sled, Flowers, 30 x 47 In.	210
Hooked, American, Hearts & Stars & Horseshoe & Dogs, Mounted, 27 x 64 In.	720
Hooked, Chicken On Path, House, Flagpole, Brown, Tan, c.1900, 32 x 38 In............................	375
Hooked, Conestoga Wagon & Mill Scene, Trees, Building, Wood Stretcher, 24 x 46 In.	325
Hooked, Deer, Standing, Red Ground, Multicolor Border, c.1920, 33 x 19 In.	308
Hooked, Demilune, Welcome, Poodle, Seated, Black, White, 36 x 20 In..................................	409
Hooked, Dog Sled Team, Tan, 39 x 65 In.	1920
Hooked, Dog, Reclining, Leaf Border, 25 ³⁄₄ x 35 In..*illus*	118
Hooked, Dog, Seated, Brown, 24 ¹⁄₂ x 39 In.	738
Hooked, Dogs, Birds, Flowers, Red, Blue, Brown, Cream, 35 x 46 In.......................................	3813
Hooked, Eagle, Spread Wings, Shield, Red Stripes, Stars, Blue & White, c.1910, 37 x 77 In........	3851
Hooked, Farmhouse, Winter Landscape, Striated Border, Brown, Black, Round, c.1825, 38 In.	355
Hooked, Floral Wreath, c.1900, 23 x 37 In...	120
Hooked, Flower Basket, Hand, Images, Diamond Grid, Stretcher, c.1915, 40 x 50 In.	270
Hooked, Flowers, Concentric Bands, Multicolor, 30 x 45 In...	23
Hooked, Girl, Blond, Landscape, Flowers, Hills, Oval Reserve, 35 ¹⁄₂ x 48 ¹⁄₂ In....................	132
Hooked, Graphic With Strong Colors, Repairs, Early 1900s, 29 x 52 In...................................	150
Hooked, Horse Head With Horseshoes, Mounted To Stretcher, c.1935, 20 x 40 In.....................	250
Hooked, Horse Smelling Flower, Oval Cartouche, Green & Red Scrollwork, 32 x 51 ¹⁄₂ In.	300
Hooked, Horse, Inscribed TOBE, c.1875, 25 x 40 In.	984
Hooked, House, Green, Riverbend, Yellow, Green, 24 ³⁄₄ x 39 In.	120
Hooked, House, Landscape, Trees, Multicolor, 39 x 24 In...	119
Hooked, Lighthouses, Ships, Water, Claire Murray, 72 x 102 In..	504
Hooked, Lion, Patchwork Floor, Twill Edge, Mounted To Stretcher, c.1925, 39 x 60 In.	400
Hooked, Mama, Papa & Baby Bear, Bowls, Multicolor, Wool, 1930s, 38 x 26 In.	540
Hooked, Map, Labrador & Newfoundland, Whale, Lighthouses, Kayaker, Teepees, 30 x 22 In. ..	1560
Hooked, Multicolor Center & Outer Border, Flower Middle Border, 1900s, 108 x 72 In.	492
Hooked, Pictorial, Flying Geese, Striated Sky, Silk, c.1935, 27 x 40 In.	1521
Hooked, Pictorial, Pond, Mallard, Cattails, c.1935, 34 x 46 In.	117
Hooked, Round, Crimson 5-Point Star Center, Leafy Border, Frame, c.1910, 51 In. Diam........	711
Hooked, Sailboat, Girl With Parasol, Gray Border With Red & Pink Diamonds, 112 x 35 In......	246
Hooked, Sailing Ship Blue Nose, 24 ¹⁄₂ x 39 ¹⁄₂ In...	270
Hooked, Spotted Dog, Puppies, Center Cartouche, C-Scroll Surround, c.1910, 32 x 60 In.	150

Rug, Hooked, Wool, Burlap, Ducks, Lake, Flowers On Stretcher, c.1910, 28 x 55 In.
$240

Garth's Auctioneers & Appraisers

Rug, Indo-Tabriz, Medallion, Scrolls, Red, Blue Border, c.1950, 12 Ft. 6 In. x 13 Ft. 6 In.
$360

Brunk Auctions

Rug, Turkish, Sampler, Oriental, Label, Azeri Yatak Carpet, 10 Ft. 8 In. x 16 Ft. 7 In.
$590

Hess Auction Group

R

Tongue Rugs

Some early rugs in America were made from fabric scraps. Tongue rugs were made from tongue-shaped pieces of cloth overlapped and sewn to the backing. The tongues completely covered the backing.

Ruskin, Vase, Sang-De-Boeuf & Rose Glaze, Porcelain, England, 1926, 9½ x 6 In.
$1,625

Rago Arts and Auction Center

Russel Wright, American Modern, Creamer, Coral, Steubenville
$12

Replacements, Ltd.

Russel Wright, Oceana, Tray, Olivewood, Klise Wood Working, 1935, 19½ x 4½ In.
$1,792

Wright

Hooked, Wagon, 6-Horse Team, Country Road, Fence, Tree, Grass, 31 x 68 In.	531
Hooked, Wool, Burlap, Ducks, Lake, Flowers On Stretcher, c.1910, 28 x 55 In. *illus*	240
Indo-Tabriz, Medallion, Scrolls, Red, Blue Border, c.1950, 12 Ft. 6 In. x 13 Ft. 6 In. *illus*	360
Isfahan, Central Shah Abbas Medallion, Flowers, Vines, Spandrels, c.1950, 5 x 7 Ft.	2074
Karabagh, Cloud Band, Southern Caucasus, Later 1800s, 9 Ft. 6 In. x 4 Ft.	350
Karabagh, Flowers, Rose Blossoms, Trellis Work Border, c.1900, 4 Ft. 11 In. x 7 Ft. 2 In.	1185
Karabagh, Red & Blue, Quadrupeds & Boteh, Runner, 1900s, 3 Ft. 5 In. x 9 Ft. 6 In.	480
Karastan, Heriz Pattern, Oval Center, Shapes, Flowers, Border, 8 Ft. 7 In. x 12 Ft.	826
Kashan, Flowers, Ivory Field, Green, Goldenrod, Beige, Red, 1900s, 3 Ft. 5 In. x 5 Ft. 8 In.	1200
Kashan, Green Lobed Circular Medallion, Vines, Flowers, West Central Persia, 2 x 3 Ft.	350
Kashan, Iran, Shah Abbas On Ivory Field, c.1960, 11 Ft. x 9 Ft. 4 In.	554
Kashan, Medallion, Floral, Blue, Red, Beige, Rust, 6 Ft. 6 In. x 9 Ft. 3 In.	1400
Kashan, Medallion, Matching Exterior Border, Red, Mid 1900s, 5 Ft. 1 In. x 3 Ft. 6 In.	480
Kashan, Oriental, Prayer, Red & Navy, Birds & Animals, Early 1900s, 4 Ft. 10 In. x 3 Ft. 7 In.	805
Kashan, Persia, Gold, Beige, Blue, Leaves, Field, c.1930, 8 Ft. 11 In. x 12 Ft. 9 In.	2250
Kashan, Prayer, Cypress Tree, Birds, Humans, Blue, Red, Ivory, 1900s, 4 Ft. x 6 Ft. 6 In.	2000
Kazak Kilim, Caucasus, c.1880, 8 Ft. 7 In. x 6 Ft. 6 In.	100
Kazak, Botehs, Geometric, Navy, Aubergine, Gold, Ivory, Red, c.1910, 4 Ft. 2 In. x 7 Ft. 2 In.	1600
Kazak, Center Cream Column, Diamond Medallions, Fringe, 1900s, 5 x 3 Ft.	35
Kazak, Hooked, Medallion, Gold, Red, Blue, Ivory, Serpent Border, 3 Ft. 10 In. x 4 Ft. 3 In.	400
Kazak, Oriental, Red & Light Blue, Geometric, Late 1800s, 6 Ft. 11 In. x 4 Ft. 5 In.	920
Kazak, Red, Tan, Blue, Stacked Diamond Pattern, Shaped, Border, c.1935, 8 Ft. 2 In. x 5 Ft. 1 In.	1440
Kazak, Runner, Medallions, Blue, Gold, Terra-Cotta, Ivory, Early 1900s, 3 Ft. 5 In. x 11 Ft.	1300
Kerman, Blue Field, Medallion, Palmettes, Vases, Persia, Strawbridge, 16 Ft. 3 In. x 11 Ft. 9 In.	1534
Kerman, Central Arabesque Medallion, Scrolling Flowers, c.1965, 11 Ft. 6 In. x 21 Ft. 3 In.	711
Kerman, Central Medallion, Cream, Blue, Scroll Corner Guards, Pink, Brown, 12 Ft. x 8 Ft. 8 In.	1298
Kerman, Flower Design, Oval Navy Ground Filed, Navy Border, Early 1900s, 15 x 11 Ft.	1800
Kerman, Medallion, Spandrels, Flowers, Yellow, Camel, Cobalt Ground, 4 Ft. 7 In. x 6 In.	360
Kerman, Tree Of Life, Khaki Ground, Fowl & Foxes & Deer, Late 1800s, 4 Ft. 6 In. x 7 Ft.	1080
Kerman, Urn & Flowers, Espalier Design, Ivory Ground, c.1900, 10 x 23 Ft.	5900
Kerman, Urn & Tree & Flowers On Ivory & Red, 1900s, 4 Ft. 3 In. x 6 Ft. 4 In.	480
Khamseh, Navy, Red, Tan, Medallion, Stylized Flowers & Shapes, Fringe, c.1935, 7 Ft. 7 In. x 4 Ft. 10 In.	390
Kilim, 3 Diamond Medallions, Blue, Red, Orange, Iran, c.1950, 5 Ft. 2 In. x 8 Ft. 8 In.	200
Kilim, Bands Of Red, Brown & Blue With Diamond Motives, 1900s, 5 Ft. 6 In. x 10 Ft. 11 In.	480
Kilim, Diamond Shapes, Alternating Bands, Rust, Blue, 11 Ft. 4 In. x 4 Ft. 8 In.	2135
Kilim, Medallions, Diamond Shapes, Tarantula Border, c.1900, 5 Ft. 2 In. x 10 Ft. 9 In.	415
Kilim, Repeating Diamonds, Ram Horn Border, Multicolor, Red Ground, 12 Ft. 3 In. x 4 Ft. 11 In.	365
Kilim, Yellow Geometric Border, Flower Border, 11 Ft. 7 In. x 8 Ft. 1 In.	271
Kurdish, Blue With White Border, c.1900, 6 Ft. x 2 Ft. 10 In.	1035
Kurdish, Burgundy & Dark Blue, Runner, c.1900, 12 Ft. 7 In. x 3 Ft. 4 In.	690
Kurdish, Medallion, Red, Rose, Gold, Blue Green, Early 1900s, 4 Ft. 3 In. x 6 Ft. 8 In.	375
Kurdish, Red & Brown, Early 1900s, 12 Ft. 2 In. x 5 Ft. 7 In.	2530
Lavar Kerman, Center Medallion, Ivory Field, Multiple Borders, Red, Blue, 11 x 15 Ft.	1920
Mahal, Ivory Field With Repeating, 1900s, 8 Ft. 10 In. x 11 Ft. 10 In.	2400
Mahal, Oval Flower Clusters, Rows, Triple Border, Cobalt Blue, Red, Gold, 4 Ft. 8 In. x 7 Ft.	750
Mahal, Vine, Flowers, Navy Ground, Teal, Ivory & Salmon Accents, 11 Ft. 10 In. x 18 Ft.	720
Malayer, Medallions On Red, Leaf & Calyx Border, 1900s, 3 Ft. 8 In. x 9 Ft. 8 In.	960
Malayer, Red, Black, Peaked Shapes, Flowers, Borders, Fringe, c.1935, 6 Ft. 9 In. x 3 Ft. 7 In.	390
Mazleghan, Linear Medallion, Spandrels, Flowers, Cobalt, Ivory, Sky Blue, 4 Ft. 6 In. x 7 Ft.	780
Modernist, Quarter Circle, Gray Ground, Figures, Green, Lavender, Scatter, 5 Ft. x 3 Ft. 8 In.	62
Naharand, Medallion, Flowers, Navy, Sky Blue, Gold & Red Highlights, 4 Ft. 9 In. x 6 Ft. 8 In.	480
Needlepoint, Runner, 6 Flower Medallions, Taupe Central Panel, c.1930, 2 Ft. 4 In. x 13 Ft.	354
Oriental, Center Medallion, Flowers, 3 Ft. 5 In. x 4 Ft. 10 In.	266
Oriental, Center Medallion, Flowers, 8 Ft. 7 In. x 13 Ft. 10 In.	1180
Oriental, Central Medallion, Corner Decoration, 12 Ft. 11 In. x 8 Ft. 9 In.	1600
Persian, 2 Stepped Edge Medallions, Stars & Hooks, Early 1900s, 3 Ft. 9 In. x 11 Ft. 6 In.	600
Persian, Arabesque Medallion, Ivory, Blue, Silk Thread, Flowers, 3 Ft. 8 In. x 5 Ft. 7 In.	948
Persian, Garden, Panels, Flowers, Yellow Ground, Lavender, Vines, c.1950, 4 Ft. x 6 Ft. 6 In.	593
Persian, Ivory Field, Repeating Flowers, Yellow & Green, 1900s, Runner, 2 Ft. 8 In. x 9 Ft. 7 In.	240
Persian, Mahal, Repeating Flowers & Leaves, Red, Blue Border, 9 Ft. 5 In. x 13 Ft. 9 In.	1020

Persian, Red Panel, Crosshatched Vine, Leaf & Flowers, c.1920, 10 Ft. 9 In. x 17 Ft. 7 In.	1200
Persian, Runner, Medallion, Navy, Rust Red, Ivory, Border, 1900s, 2 Ft. 9 In. x 17 Ft.	325
Persian, Silk, Starburst, Maroon, Gold, Ivory, Geometric Border, c.1950, 2 x 3 Ft.	1100
Persian, Wool, Geometric, Black On Red, 11 Ft. 10 In. x 8 Ft. 11 In.	300
Sarouk, Center Medallion, Cypress Trees, Peacocks, Blue, c.1865, 4 Ft. 10 In. x 6 Ft. 8 In.	2133
Sarouk, Flower Pattern, Red Ground, Navy & Olive Highlights, c.1900, 9 Ft. x 11 Ft. 5 In.	531
Sarouk, Flowering Branches, Red Field, Ivory Border, Mid 1900s, 4 Ft. 5 In. x 2 Ft. 2 In.	120
Sarouk, Vines, Flowerheads, Ivory, Blue, Western Persia, 1900s, 7 Ft. 8 In. x 8 Ft. 9 In.	1900
Savonnerie, Garnet Field, Urn & Fleur-De-Lis Border, 11 Ft. 11 In. x 20 Ft.	480
Serapi, Diamond Center, Flowers, Zigzag Border Edges, Red, Blue, Tan, 11 Ft. 4 In. x 15 Ft.	3750
Shag, Midcentury Modern, Bands Of Colors, Red, Pink, Orange, 10 Ft. 5 In. x 6 Ft.	615
Shirvan, Eastern Caucasus, Ivory Field With Perepedil, Late 1800s, 5 Ft. 3 In. x 3 Ft. 8 In.	400
Shirvan, Oriental, Brown & Navy Blue, c.1900, 3 Ft. 6 In. x 2 Ft. 6 In.	1438
Shirvan, Oriental, Navy With White Border, 1800s, 3 Ft. 6 In. x 3 Ft. 2 In.	403
Shirvan, Stylized Flowers, Red Ground, Blue Medallion, 8 Ft. 1 In. x 4 Ft. 6 In.	944
Soumak, Sunburst Medallion, Salmon, Ivory, Blue, Polygon Border, 1900s, 3 Ft. 10 In. x 6 Ft. 8 In.	300
Sultanabad, Cream Ground, Scroll, Blossoms, Stylized Flowerhead Border, 9 x 12 Ft.	1000
Sultanabad, Hand Woven, Red, White Border, Flowers, Leaves, 5 Ft. 1 In. x 6 Ft. 10 In.	413
Sumac, Navy, Orange, Red, Crosses & Diamonds, Hooked Edge, c.1925, 2 Ft. 6 In. x 3 Ft. 4 In.	420
Tabriz, Navy, Tan, Orange, Leaves, Shapes, 3 Borders, Fringe, c.1935, 7 Ft. 7 In. x 5 Ft.	420
Tabriz, Pairs Of Fowl, Florets, Vines, Medallion, Ivory Ground, c.1950, 5 Ft. 7 In. x 9 Ft.	472
Tabriz, Scalloped Diamond Medallion, Rose, Ivory, Leaves, Roses, Persia, 3 Ft. 1 In. x 5 Ft.	600
Tabriz, Shield Medallion, Ivory, Blue, Red Birds, Deer, Iran, c.1950, 10 Ft. x 14 Ft. 4 In.	1100
Tabriz, Tree Of Life, Flowers, Urns, Pale Green, Rust, Vine Border, c.1940, 4 Ft. 5 In. x 5 Ft. 8 In.	593
Tapestry, Yellow, Pink, Rows Of Blossom Circles, Flower & Leaf Border, 7 Ft. 3 In. x 9 Ft. 9 In.	118
Tekke, Guls, Columns, Blue, Apricot, Ivory, Brown, Octagon Border, 1800s, 4 Ft. 8 In. x 6 Ft. 7 In.	425
Tekke, Salor Guls, Western Turkestan, c.1900, 7 Ft. 3 In. x 4 Ft. 10 In.	500
Turkish, Angora Oushak, Cream, Sage Green, Tan, Flowers, Scrolls, Runner, 2 Ft. 6 In. x 25 Ft.	1375
Turkish, Columns Of Concentric Circles, White On Yellow, Flatweave, Wool, 9 x 12 Ft.	813
Turkish, Flowers, Swirls, Center Medallion Shapes, Cream, Gold, Gray, Angora, 8 x 10 Ft.	875
Turkish, Oriental, Prayer, Red With Blue & Red Borders, c.1900, 5 Ft. 11 In. x 3 Ft. 8 In.	230
Turkish, Prayer, Lamp & Pendant On Red, Late 1800s, 3 Ft. 10 In. x 5 Ft. 8 In.	240
Turkish, Sampler, Oriental, Label, Azeri Yatak Carpet, 10 Ft. 8 In. x 16 Ft. 7 In. ....*illus*	590
Turkish, Tight Spirals All Over, Hand Knotted, Tan, Black, Wool, 8 Ft. 9 In. x 12 Ft.	1625
Ushak, Medallion, Oval, Scalloped, Blue, Green, Ivory, Red, Border, 1900s, 3 Ft. 7 In. x 6 Ft. 6 In.	325

RUMRILL POTTERY was designed by George Rumrill of Little Rock, Arkansas. From 1933 to 1938, it was produced by the Red Wing Pottery of Red Wing, Minnesota. In January 1938, production was transferred to the Shawnee Pottery in Zanesville, Ohio. It was moved again in December of 1938 to Florence Pottery Company in Mt. Gilead, Ohio, where Rumrill ware continued to be manufactured until the pottery burned in 1941. It was then produced by Gonder Ceramic Arts in South Zanesville until early 1943.

RumRill

Bowl, Blue Interior, Nude Holding Vase, Red Wing, Athenian, c.1935, 5½ x 8¼ In.	165
Bowl, Trumpet Flower Handles, White, 5 x 9 x 8¼ In.	20
Flower Frog, Cream Glaze, Peach Interior, Spherical, Lobed Swirls, 3 Holes, 1933, 8 In.	48
Pitcher, Green & Orange, Goldenrod, c.1932, 6¾ x 7½ In.	21
Pitcher, Red Glaze, Brown Stain, Spherical, Square Handle, Tubular Spout, 1930s	115
Planter, Figural Swan, White, Mauve, Reeded Wings, Scalloped Rim, 1930s, 9 x 9 In.	55
Planter, Light Green, Brown Flecks, Lobed, 3¼ x 6¾ In.	32
Vase, 3 Nudes, Blue Interior, Red Wing, Athenian 10 x 8 In.	511
Vase, Art Deco, Cream, Spheres, Pale Green Interior, 15½ x 7½ In.	338
Vase, Desert Rose, Diamonds, Fanned, Marked, 1928, 6 x 9½ In.	32
Vase, Dutch Blue, Semimatte, Fluted, Marked, c.1930-38, 6 x 6 In.	29
Vase, Gypsy Orange Glaze, Speckled, Bulbous, Waisted, Serpentine Rim, 1930s, 6 In.	125
Vase, Ivory Matte, Brown Tint, Molded Leaves, Pedestal Foot, Scalloped Rim, 1930s, 10 In.	85
Vase, Ivory, Brown Tint, Swags, Ram's Heads, Square, Paneled, Shouldered, 1930s, 10 In.	60
Vase, Mottled Blue, Ribbed, Molded Bubble Rim, Scroll Handles, Squat, 1930s, 5 x 7 In.	65
Vase, Mottled Green Glaze, Squat, Arch Handles, 1930s, 8 x 9 In.	165
Vase, Urn Shape, Pink Speckle, Off White, Marked, 5½ x 9 In.	148

Sabino, Sculpture, Storks, Opalescent, France, c.1935, 6¼ In.
$275

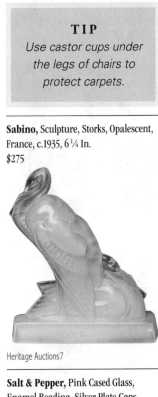

Heritage Auctions7

Salt & Pepper, Pink Cased Glass, Enamel Beading, Silver Plate Caps, 3¼ In.
$676

Forsythe's Auctions

Salt Glaze, Pitcher, Hunt, Hound Handle, Rabbits, Birds, Fox, High Relief, c.1850, 10¾ In.
$185

Ruby Lane

R

Sampler, Alphabet, Double Letters, Varied Stitch Bands, Multicolor, 1840-50, 12 x 11½ In.
$123

William H. Bunch Auctions

Sampler, Alphabet, Margret Glasier, Linen, Silk Thread, Frame, 1786, 11 x 7 In.
$984

Skinner, Inc.

Sampler, Alphabet, Verse, Leaf & Vine Border, Animals, House, 1700s, 21½ x 16 In.
$6,250

Fairfield Auction

RUSKIN is a British art pottery of the twentieth century. The Ruskin Pottery was started by William Howson Taylor, and his name was used as the mark until about 1899. The factory, at West Smethwick, Birmingham, England, stopped making new pieces in 1933 but continued to glaze and sell the remaining wares until 1935. The art pottery is noted for its exceptional glazes.

Ginger Jar, Mottled Orange Luster, Green Grapevine, Squat, Lid, Knob Finial, 1908		603
Ginger Jar, Oxblood, Cream & Blue, Flambe Glaze, Cutouts, Dome Lid, 1920s, 10 In.		4900
Vase, Blue, Green, Red, Spotted Glaze, Oval, Flared Foot, Rolled Rim, 1926, 10 In.		4876
Vase, Cobalt Blue & Silver Iridescent, Oil Slick Glaze, Squat, Trumpet Neck, 1916, 6 In.		1200
Vase, Frothy Aqua Luster Over Yellow, Crystalline Glaze, Bulbous, 1920s, 6 x 7 In.		429
Vase, Fuchsia Glaze, Lavender Speckled, Pale Green, Tubular, Rolled Rim, 1910, 6 In.		944
Vase, Mottled Crimson, Gray & Cream, Flambe Glaze, Squat, Trumpet Neck, 1927, 6 In.		1527
Vase, Mottled Green, Yellow, Cobalt Blue, Crystalline, Drip Glaze, 4 Handles, 1930, 10 In.		410
Vase, Mottled Red, Purple & Cream, Flambe Glaze, Oval, Pinched Neck, c.1928, 9 In.		1915
Vase, Mottled Turquoise, Sea Green, Rainbow Luster, Beaker, Swollen Rim, 1919, 9 In.		240
Vase, Mottled Yellow Luster, Green Vine, Shouldered, Tapered, Rolled Rim, 1911, 8 In.		518
Vase, Purple Mottled Flower, Cream, Red, Tapered, Shouldered, Flat Rim, 1933, 3¼ In.		649
Vase, Sang-De-Boeuf & Rose Glaze, Porcelain, England, 1926, 9½ x 6 In.	*illus*	1625

RUSSEL WRIGHT designed dinnerware in modern shapes for many companies. Iroquois China Company, Harker China Company, Steubenville Pottery, and Justin Tharaud and Sons made dishes marked *Russel Wright*. The Steubenville wares, first made in 1938, are the most common today. Wright was a designer of domestic and industrial wares, including furniture, aluminum, radios, interiors, and glassware. A new company, Bauer Pottery Company of Los Angeles, is making Russel Wright's American Modern dishes using molds made from original pieces. The pottery is made in Highland, California. Pieces are marked *Russel Wright by Bauer Pottery California USA*. Russel Wright Dinnerware and other original pieces by Wright are listed here. For more prices, go to kovels.com.

Aluminum, Cheese Tray, Lid, Walnut Board & Finial, 1930s, 16 In. Diam.		165
Aluminum, Cocktail Set, Spun, Rattan, Marked, 15-In. Shaker, 18-In. Tray, 9 Piece		2750
Aluminum, Pitcher, Wood Ball & Ring Handle, Upright Spout, c.1950, 10 In.		170
American Modern, Bean Pot, Seafoam Blue, Bulbous, Lid, Handle, 1940s, 5 x 12 In.		65
American Modern, Casserole, Lid, Chartreuse		35
American Modern, Clock, Straw Yellow, Plate Shape, Wall, Electric, 8 x 8 In.		84
American Modern, Creamer, Coral, Steubenville	*illus*	12
American Modern, Cup & Saucer, Coral, Steubenville		8
American Modern, Gravy Boat, Underplate, Coral, Steubenville		32
American Modern, Plate, Bread & Butter, Coral, Steubenville, 6⅛ In.		5
American Modern, Plate, Dinner, Coral, Steubenville, 10 In.		9
American Modern, Relish, Divided, Rosette, 1930s, 11 In. Diam.		70
American Modern, Serving Bowl, Oval, Divided, Coral, c.1940, 13 In.		95
American Modern, Sugar & Creamer, Black Chutney, Strap Handles, 1940s		45
American Modern, Teapot, Lid, Seafoam		95
Centerpiece, Birch Bowl, Copper Handles, Aluminum Base, c.1945, 5 x 24 In.		185
Chrome, Salt & Pepper, Orb, Cylindrical Foot, c.1935, 1 In. & 2 In.		75
Iroquois Casual, Bowl, Gumbo, Oval, Pink Sherbet, 2 x 8 In.		50
Iroquois Casual, Plate, Blue, 9¼ In.		20
Iroquois Casual, Teapot, Ripe Apricot, Bulbous, Lid, Strap Handle, 5 x 10 In.		60
Lamp, Torchiere, Aluminum Flared Shade, Carved Wood Post, 1930, 65 In.		2400
Lily Pad, Ashtray, Ivy Green, Folded, Shaped Rim, 1940s, 6 In. Diam.		90
Oceana, Tray, Olivewood, Klise Wood Working, 1935, 19½ x 4½ In.	*illus*	1792
Oceana, Tray, Wood, Almond Shape, Folded Out Handle, 1930s, 6 x 15 In.		1200

SABINO glass was made in the 1920s and 1930s in Paris, France. Founded by Marius-Ernest Sabino (1878–1961), the firm was noted for Art Deco lamps, vases, figurines, and animals in clear, colored, and opalescent glass. Production stopped during World War II but resumed in the 1960s with the manufacture of nude figurines and small opalescent glass animals. Pieces made in recent years are a slightly different color and can be recognized. Only vintage pieces are listed here.

Figurine, Butterflies, Opalescent, Blue, France, 1925, 5 ¾ In., Pair		187
Figurine, Elephant, Trunk Up, Opalescent, Signed, 2 ¼ In.		45
Figurine, Espangnole, Ruffled Skirt, Tambourine, Opalescent Blue, c.1935, 11 In.		625
Figurine, LeReveil, Nude, Woman, Standing, Long Hair, Opalescent, Aqua, 7 In.		443
Luminary, Leaping Fish, Waves, Aqua Opalescent, Nickel-Plated Stand, 10 x 9 In.		1888
Perfume Bottle, Petallia, Opalescent, France, 1935, 5 ¼ In.		175
Sculpture, Storks, Opalescent, France, c.1935, 6 ¼ In.	*illus*	275
Vase, Carangues, Blue, Layered Fish Heads, c.1935, 5 In.		350
Vase, Opalescent, Blue, White, Geometric, c.1935, 10 ¾ In.		687

SALOPIAN ware was made by the Caughley factory of England during the eighteenth century. The early pieces were blue and white with some colored decorations. Another ware referred to as Salopian is a late-nineteenth-century tableware decorated with color transfers.

Salopian

Coffeepot, Pagoda, Loop Handle, Dragon Spout, Inset Lid, Finial, c.1815, 9 x 8 In.		674
Cup Plate, Milkmaid, Gray, Yellow, Orange & Blue Flowers, 1800s, 5 In.		176
Pitcher, Willow, Blue & White, Gilt, Trees, Boat, Bulbous, Wavy Rim, c.1800, 10 In.		173
Teapot, Bird & Flower, Angular Handle, Saucer Foot, Lid, Finial, c.1820, 7 x 11 In.		311
Toddy Plate, Bird Of Paradise, Orange, Blue, Flowers, Beaded, 1800s, 6 In. Diam.		86
Waste Bowl, Cottage, Blue & Yellow Flowers, 3 x 5 In.		90

SALT AND PEPPER SHAKERS in matched sets were first used in the nineteenth century. Collectors are primarily interested in figural examples made after World War I. Huggers are pairs of shakers that appear to embrace each other. Many salt and pepper shakers are listed in other categories and can be located through the index at the back of this book.

Blue Cobalt Glass, Stainless Steel Cutout Frame, U.K., 2 ¾ In.		24
Conoco, Gas Pump Shape, Coyle, Oklahoma, 2 ¾ x 1 ⅛ In.		94
Faience, Enamel, Moorish Style, Flowers, Arabesques, Caddy, 3 Piece		265
Gingerbread Man & Woman, California Pottery, Brown, 5 ½ In.		38
Mammy, White & Green Apron, Bonnets, Pottery, 1950s, 6 ½ In.		85
Pachmayr Brand Shotgun Shells, Orange & Green, 2 ½ x ⅞ In.		47
Pink Cased Glass, Enamel Beading, Silver Plate Caps, 3 ¼ In.	*illus*	676
Rooster & Hen, Multicolor, Plastic Stopper, K & B, 4 ¾ In.		14
Rose & Daisy Pattern, Gold Embossed, Oval, 4 x 1 ¾ In.		15

SALT GLAZE has a grayish white surface with a texture like an orange peel. It is a method of decoration that has been used since the eighteenth century. Salt-glazed pieces are still being made.

Bowl, Yellow, Green Shaded, Basket Weave, Daisy, Cylindrical, 1930s, 4 In.		85
Garlic Jar, Tan, Hummingbird, Slash Cutouts, Blue Flared Rim, Crock, 4 In.		53
Jug, Whiskey, Green, Turquoise, Pink, Brown Mottle, Textured, Flared Rim, 1863, 8 In.		2350
Pitcher, Blue & White, Poinsettia, Embossed Burlap Pattern, Bulbous, c.1905, 7 In.		145
Pitcher, Hunt, Hound Handle, Rabbits, Birds, Fox, High Relief, c.1850, 10 ¾ In.	*illus*	185
Serving Dish, Dome Lid, Yellow Matte, Blue Leaves, Finial, 1930s, 5 x 10 In.		169
Vase, Indigo Blue, Bulbous, Cylindrical Neck, Banded Rim, c.1910, 9 In.		148

SAMPLERS were made in America from the early 1700s. The best examples were made from 1790 to 1840. Long, narrow samplers are usually older than square ones. Early samplers just had stitching or alphabets. The later examples had numerals, borders, and pictorial decorations. Those with mottoes are mid-Victorian. A revival of interest in the 1930s produced simpler samplers, usually with mottoes.

ABCDE

Alphabet & Verse, Silk On Linen, Frame, Early 1800s, 27 x 18 ½ In.		240
Alphabet, Adam & Eve, Martha Fawcett Wrought, Frame, c.1838, 21 x 16 In.		450
Alphabet, Checkered Triangle, Jean Deans, 1826, 17 ¼ x 10 In.		240

Sampler, Darning, Crosses, Cartouche, Anno 1792 Out 13 Iaar, Silk, Linen, Frame, 19 x 18 In.
$344

Garth's Auctioneers & Appraisers

TIP

Never store textiles on or in paper, cardboard, or unsealed wood. Store in unbleached muslin.

Sampler, Verse, Alphabet, Zigzag, Tree, Bouquets, Blue, Green, 1850, 16 ½ x 17 In.
$213

Copake Auction

Sampler, Verse, Biblical, House, Plants, Animals, Silk, Linen, Helen Samson, 1828, 25 x 26 In.
$21,240

Hess Auction Group

Sampler, Verse, Flowers, Baskets, Mayzie Taylor, Silk On Wool, Frame, 1761, 14 x 14 In.
$3,360

Garth's Auctioneers & Appraisers

Samson, Teapot, Drum Shape, Arms Of Honorable Dutch East India Company, 6 In.
$1,062

Alex Cooper Auctioneers

Sandwich Glass, Lamp, Triple Dolphin, Blue, Blown Glass, Brass, 17 ½ x 6 In.
$4,612

Cottone Auctions

Alphabet, Double Letters, Varied Stitch Bands, Multicolor, 1840-50, 12 x 11 ½ In. ....*illus*	123
Alphabet, Flowers & Deer, Silk On Linen, Mary Graham, 1814, 21 x 16 In.	420
Alphabet, Margret Glasier, Linen, Silk Thread, Frame, 1786, 11 x 7 In. ....*illus*	984
Alphabet, Mary Dick, 1826, 12 x 10 In..	246
Alphabet, Mary Wiltshire, 1792, 17 x 12 ½ In..	221
Alphabet, Numbers, Flowers, Eliza Scott, Silk On Linen, Frame, c.1851, 12 x 14 In...........	556
Alphabet, Numbers, House, Tree, Flowers, Julia A. Drake, Frame, c.1840, 17 x 7 In.	234
Alphabet, Numbers, Trees, Birds, Vine Border, Ruth Pellen, Frame, c.1802, 12 x 18 In.	222
Alphabet, Numbers, Verse, Susanah Fox, 12 Year Of Her Age, 1749, Frame, 14 x 7 In.	4920
Alphabet, Trees, Margaret Denton, 1810, 15 ½ x 12 In.	221
Alphabet, Verse, Bird, Flower Baskets, Silk On Linen, Frame, c.1830, 17 x 16 In.	380
Alphabet, Verse, Crowns, Ships, Lions, Geometric Patterns, 20 ½ x 12 In.	1560
Alphabet, Verse, Field, Sarah Dixon, Silk On Linen, Frame, c.1842, 12 x 10 In.	1053
Alphabet, Verse, House, Tree, Pink & Blue Leaves, Signature, 1793, 13 x 11 In.	3250
Alphabet, Verse, Ivy Border, Silk On Linen, Signed, Frame, 1800s, 16 In.	300
Alphabet, Verse, Leaf & Vine Border, Animals, House, 1700s, 21 ½ x 16 In......................*illus*	6250
Alphabet, Verse, Potted Plants, Sarah Fuller, Aged 12, 1824, 21 x 18 In.	156
Alphabet, Verse, Ruth B. Fletcher, Age 9, Silk On Linen, Frame, 1832, 17 x 15 In.	344
Alphabet, Verse, Silk On Linen, Margaret Barry, Frame, c.1830, 18 x 13 ½ In.	375
Alphabet, Verse, Silk On Linen, Mary Crissell, Frame, c.1799, 20 ½ x 16 In	219
Alphabet, Verse, Trees, Figures, Vines, Sally Ayer, Born 1780, Mass., 16 x 12 In.	6150
Alphabet, Verse, Trees, Mary E. Luce, Silk On Linen, c.1806, 17 x 17 ½ In.	468
Alphabet, Verse, Vine, Sawtooth, Sally Bodge Buzzell, 1808, 16 ½ x 13 In......................	300
Alphabet, Vines, Shepherd, Sheep, Tree, Linen, Sally Woodbery, 17 x 16 In.	1845
Alphabet, Wrought By Eliza Ann Symmes, Aged 13 Years, 1821, 17 x 16 In.	360
Darning, Crosses, Cartouche, Anno 1792 Out 13 Iaar, Silk, Linen, Frame, 19 x 18 In........*illus*	344
Family Record, Flower Border, Willow Tree, Butterflies, Frame, 1831, 26 x 24 In.	3259
Flowers & Geometrics, Amma Bechtelsin, 1794, Mennonite, Pa., Frame, 21 x 15 In.	1888
Flowers, Leaves, Vines, Rhoda Elizabeth Sage, 1852, 16 ⅝ x 13 In................................	94
House, Birds, Rosebushes, Lion, Initials, Silk On Linen, c.1830, 17 x 17 In.	1080
House, Border, Urns, Flowers, Jane Robinson, Baltimore, 1818, 17 x 17 In.	1625
Pictorial, 3-Story House, Flower Baskets, Butterfly, Lamb, Frame, c.1810, 17 x 17 In.	523
Pictorial, Alphabet, Numbers, Bible Verse, Emma Day, Aged 11, 1856, 11 x 12 In.	390
Pictorial, Bee, Birds, Stag, Flowers, Cross-Stitch, G Mirror Image, 21 x 19 In..................	295
Pictorial, Crowns, Birds, Flowers, Cross-Stitch, Barbara Brubaker, 1816, Frame, 14 x 15 In.	885
Pictorial, Flower Urn, Trees, Birds, Animals, Mary A. Longstroth, 1831, 21 x 20 In...................	210
Verse, 1838, Jane Lee, Solomon's Temple, 18 x 18 ½ In.	172
Verse, Adam & Eve, Apple Tree, Geometric Border, Ann Dobinson, 1810, 16 x 13 In.	1845
Verse, Advice To Young Ladies, Floral Border, Silk On Linen, Frame, 20 In.	1300
Verse, Alphabet, Birds, Squirrel, Flowering Vines, 1773, 14 x 11 In.	330
Verse, Alphabet, Zigzag, Tree, Bouquets, Blue, Green, 1850, 16 ½ x 17 In. ....*illus*	213
Verse, Biblical, House, Plants, Animals, Silk, Linen, Helen Samson, 1828, 25 x 26 In........*illus*	21240
Verse, Church, Flowers, Angels, Border, 1820, 20 x 16 In.	148
Verse, Flower Baskets, Lydia Corant, Age 11, Silk On Linen, Frame, 1795, 13 x 13 In.	570
Verse, Flowers, Baskets, Mayzie Taylor, Silk On Wool, Frame, 1761, 14 x 14 In. ....*illus*	3360
Verse, House, Trees, Border, Silk On Linen, 1841, 20 x 16 In.	394
Verse, Psalm 23, Birds, Baskets, Flower Border, Sarah Green, 1782, 13 x 11 In.	660
Verse, Sarah Richards, Aged 11, Wood Frame, 1860, 7 x 12 ½ In.................................	210
Verse, Silk Thread, Linen, Potted Flowers, England, c.1814, 13 x 13 In..........................	600
Verse, Strawberries, Wool On Linen, Jane Wood Fogg, Frame, 1800s, 13 x 17 In.	129
View Of Solomon's Temple, Mary Ann Maher, 1852, 25 x 26 In.	687
Yarnwork, Punched Paper, Bibles, Flowers, Elizabeth Keener, 1857, 13 x 12 In.	155

SAMSON and Company, a French firm specializing in the reproduction of collectible wares of many countries and periods, was founded in Paris in the early nineteenth century. Chelsea, Meissen, Famille Verte, and Chinese Export porcelain are some of the wares that have been reproduced by the company. The firm used a variety of marks on the reproductions. It closed in 1969.

Bowl, Armorial, Crest, Flower Sprays, Wide Rim, Ring Foot, 1800s, 10 In. Diam.	148

Bowl, Armorial, Famille Rose, Pink, White, 2¾ x 6 In.		200
Bowl, Square, Flared, Cut Corners, Rose Flower Sprays, Ship, Gilt Rim, 4 x 9 In.		60
Charger, Figures, Flower Border, Imari Style, Japan, c.1900, 18 In. Diam.		1250
Figurine, Touch, Emblem Of The Senses, Nymph, Parrot, Turtle, Nude, c.1870, 10 In.		1500
Figurine, Woman, Mallet, Chisel, Sculpting Vase, Pedestal, 9 x 4 In.		413
Flask, Armorial, Shield, Trefoil, Flowers, White, Red, Gold, Lug Handles, 1800s, 4 In.		175
Jewelry Box, Flower Sprays, Ivory, Orange, Raised Scrolls, Ormolu, c.1900, 3 x 8 In.		225
Teapot, Drum Shape, Arms Of Honorable Dutch East India Company, 6 In.	*illus*	1062
Trinket Box, Flowers, Pink, Green, Gilt, Bronze, Hinged, Bombay Shape, c.1870, 4 x 7 In.		500
Vase, Peony, Plum Blossom, Brocade, Orange, Blue, Jar Shape, Chinese, 1800s, 9 In.		490

SANDWICH GLASS is any of the myriad types of glass made by the Boston & Sandwich Glass Company of Sandwich, Massachusetts, between 1825 and 1888. It is often very difficult to be sure whether a piece was really made at the Sandwich factory because so many types were made there and similar pieces were made at other glass factories. Additional pieces may be listed under Pressed Glass and in other related categories.

Boat, Lacy, Salt, Lafayette, Opalescent Blue, Early 1800s, 3½ In.		375
Bowl, Chrysanthemum Leaf, 8 x 3 In.		16
Candlestick, Clam Broth, Columnar, Ruffled Rim, Square Base, 10 In., Pair		561
Candlestick, Dolphin Stem, Square Stepped Base, Ruffled Rim, 10 In., Pair		150
Candlestick, Electric Blue, Petal Sockets, Loop Bases, c.1850, 7 In., Pair		1200
Celery Vase, Loop Leaf Pattern, Paneled, Scalloped Rim, Spread Foot, 10 In., Pair		244
Cologne Bottle, Blue Translucent, Diamond Point, c.1840, 6½ In.		350
Jar, Pomade, Bear Shape, Amethyst, c.1860, 3¾ x 1¾ In.		70
Lamp, Fluid, Bull's Eye, Opaque Base, 10½ In.		84
Lamp, Oil, Cylindrical Glass, Blue To Milk Glass, Brass, Marble, 10 In.		439
Lamp, Overlay, White To Ruby, Cherries, Plume & Atwood, 1872, 12 In.		440
Lamp, Triple Dolphin, Blue, Blown Glass, Brass, 17½ x 6 In.	*illus*	4612
Salt, Oval, Lacy, Opalescent, Early 1800s, 3¼ In.		188
Vase, Canary Yellow, Loop, Ellipse, 7 In.		132
Vase, Tulip, Amethyst, Octagonal Base, c.1855, 9 In.		660
Vase, Tulip, Amethyst, Paneled, Octagonal Base, Mid 1800s, 10 In.		510
Vase, Tulip, Peacock Green, Paneled, Octagonal Base, c.1850, 10 In., Pair		1200

SARREGUEMINES is the name of a French town that is used as part of a china mark. Utzschneider and Company, a porcelain factory, made ceramics in Sarreguemines, Lorraine, France, from about 1775. Transfer-printed wares and majolica were made in the nineteenth century. The nineteenth-century pieces, most often found today, usually have colorful transfer-printed decorations showing peasants in local costumes.

Plate, Dessert, Cabbage Leaf Shape, Green, Folded Rim, 8 In., 6 Piece		350
Urn, Cobalt Blue, Yellow, Shoulders, 1800s, 26 In.		625
Urn, Square Handles, Leaves, Cobalt Blue, Gilt, 1800s, 12 x 15 In.		615
Vase, Art Deco, Zigzag, Crackle, Teal, Brown, White, Marked, c.1925, 10 In.	*illus*	187
Vase, Cobalt Blue, Molded Lace Frame Panels, Gilt Flowers, c.1880, 18 In.		308
Vase, Green, Gold Band, 11½ In., Pair		406
Vase, Majolica, Dark Blue, Ribbed, Leaf Garland, Pedestal, c.1880, 37 In.		800
Vase, Majolica, Lid, Dark Blue Ground, String Of Flowers, c.1880, 17 In.		338
Vase, Oval, Butterflies, Flowers, Lattice Banding, Gilt, 1800s, 17 In., Pair		1968
Vase, Sunflowers, Tan Shaded To Yellow, Tapered, Swollen Neck, 14 In.		125

SASCHA BRASTOFF made decorative accessories, ceramics, enamels on copper, and plastics of his own design. He headed a factory, Sascha Brastoff of California, Inc., in West Los Angeles, from 1953 until about 1973. He died in 1993. Pieces signed with the signature *Sascha Brastoff* were his work and are the most expensive. Other pieces marked *Sascha B.* or with a stamped mark were made by others in his company. Pieces made by Matt Adams after he left the factory are listed here with his name.

Ashtray, Lotus Blossom, Black Enamel, Gold & Violet, Oval, 1950s, 10 x 9 In.	120

Sarreguemines, Vase, Art Deco, Zigzag, Crackle, Teal, Brown, White, Marked, c.1925, 10 In.
$187

Heritage Auctions

Sascha Brastoff, Sculpture, Head, Blue Eyes, Openwork, Ceramic, Signed, 7¾ x 7 In.
$450

Ruby Lane

Satin Glass, Bowl, Open Flower On Stem Shape, Peach Serrated Rim, 7¾ x 6 In.
$24

Ruby Lane

S

Satsuma, Jar, Lid, Chrysanthemums, Butterflies, Gold Enamel, Signed, c.1900, 22 In.
$4,313

Cottone Auctions

Satsuma, Vase, Scenes, Scholars, Elders, Gilt, Wavy Rim, Dragon Handles, 1800s, 45 In.
$600

Brunk Auctions

Scale, Balance, Henry Troemner, Oak Case, Philadelphia, 1800s, 9 x 13 x 6 In.
$480

Brunk Auctions

Bowl, Smoke Tree, Black & Gray, Shaded, Serpentine Rim, 1960s, 2 x 10 In.	40
Bowl, Village, Green & Brown Houses, Crescent Shape, 10 ½ x 9 In.	106
Charger, Nature's Bounty, Fruits, Vegetables, Black Ground, Signed, 12 In.	73
Compote, Footed, Gold, Black Matte Interior, 10 x 12 ½ In.	153
Compote, Green Copper, Enamel, Red Berry Branch, Scroll Foot, 1960s, 3 x 8 In.	35
Creamer, Turquoise & Platinum, Surf Ballet, Squat, Wavy Spout, 1950s, 4 x 5 In.	69
Lighter, Tabletop, Orange Copper, Enamel, Leaves, 1960s, 5 In.	250
Pin Tray, Green Copper, Enamel, Flowers, White, Blue, Triangular, 1960s, 6 In.	20
Platter, Green Copper, Enameled Glass Circles, Gold Leaf, 1950s, 19 ½ In.	175
Sculpture, Head, Blue Eyes, Openwork, Ceramic, Signed, 7 ¾ x 7 In. ....*illus*	450
Tray, Gold Copper, Enamel, Sea Green Flowers, Kidney Shape, 1960s, 7 x 8 In.	125
Vase, Blue Flowers, Green Iridescent, Conical, Copper Foot, c.1855, 11 In.	275
Vase, Blue, Metallic Gold, Stylized Feathers, Crescent Shape, 1950s, 5 x 7 In.	45
Vase, Pagoda, 5 ½ x 4 In.	18

 SATIN GLASS is a late nineteenth-century art glass. It has a dull finish that is caused by hydrofluoric acid vapor treatment. Satin glass was made in many colors and sometimes has applied decorations. Satin glass is also listed by factory name, such as Webb, or in the Mother-of-Pearl category in this book.

Bowl, Blue, Mother-Of-Pearl, Diamond-Quilted, Applied Feet, 5 x 6 In.	86
Bowl, Diamond-Quilted, Pink, Ruffled, Gilt Rim, 11 ½ x 4 ½ In.	332
Bowl, Diamond-Quilted, Yellow, White, Round Foot, Ruffled Rim, 3 x 6 In.	96
Bowl, Open Flower On Stem Shape, Peach Serrated Rim, 7 ¾ x 6 In. ....*illus*	24
Bride's Bowl, Crimped Rim, Ribbed, Orange, Scrolls, Victorian, 6 x 15 In.	270
Ewer, Mother-Of-Pearl, Rainbow, Ruffled Rim, Applied Handle, 8 x 4 In.	184
Pitcher, Diamond-Quilted, Yellow, Green Stem, Ruffled Rim, c.1890, 9 In.	170
Vase, Blue, Flower Buds, Bottle Shape, Lobed, Ruffled Rim, c.1885, 10 In.	110
Vase, Diamond-Quilted, Peach To Pink, Stick Neck, Crimped Rim, 9 In.	190
Vase, Diamond-Quilted, Ruffled Rim, Etched, 10 x 11 In., Pair	86
Vase, Flower Shape, Fuchsia To White, Ruffled Rim, Round Foot, c.1900, 11 In.	126
Vase, Fluted Edges, Diamond-Quilted, 6 In., Pair	48
Vase, Opaque White, Molded, Layered Leaves, Folded-In Rim, c.1890, 5 In.	55
Vase, Pink & Blue, Splash Design, Cylindrical, Trumpet Neck, c.1895, 11 In.	63
Vase, Ruffled Rim, Blue, 10 In.	34
Vase, Stick, Diamond-Quilted, Mother-Of-Pearl, Pink, 8 x 4 In.	49
Vase, Yellow Custard, Bluebirds, Branches, Stick Neck, Ruffled Rim, 10 In.	112
Vase, Yellow To White, Ruffled Rim, Round Foot, 7 x 3 ½ In.	12

 SATSUMA is a Japanese pottery with a distinctive creamy beige crackled glaze. Most of the pieces were decorated with blue, red, green, orange, or gold. Almost all Satsuma found today was made after 1860, especially during the Meiji Period, 1868–1912. During World War I, Americans could not buy undecorated European porcelains. Women who liked to make hand-painted porcelains at home began to decorate plain Satsuma. These pieces are known today as "American Satsuma."

Bowl, Center Flower, Butterflies, Fluted Rim, 3 ½ x 11 In.	62
Bowl, Chrysanthemum, Relief Dragon, 4 In.	420
Bowl, Flowers, Grass, Birds, Stream, Flower Shape, Pinched Rim, 9 ½ In.	120
Bowl, Prunus Fruit, Court Figures, Gilt, 6 x 3 In.	535
Bowl, Red & Brown Carp, Blue Ground, Flower Shape, Scalloped Rim, 5 In.	281
Bowl, Thousand Faces, 2 Dragons, Figures, Lobed, 4 x 9 In.	457
Bowl, Thousand Flowers, 5 In.	132
Bowl, Thousand Flowers, Thousand Butterflies, 3 ½ x 6 In.	1560
Bowl, White Chrysanthemum, Flowers, Gold, Flower Shape, 8 In.	200
Censer, Flowers, Shishi, Boys, Handles, Lion's Head Feet, Dome Lid, c.1900, 24 In.	923
Compote, Irises, Scroll Handles, Silver Stem, Flared Foot, c.1900, 5 In., Pair	2963
Dish, Chrysanthemums, River, Fisherman, Crescent Panel, Banded, 1800s, 8 In.	1845
Figurine, Man With Staff, Scroll, 14 In.	660

Foo Dog, Earthenware, 12 x 9 In.		265
Foo Dog, Red, Pieced Ball, Gold Ribbon, 8 x 8 In.		383
Jar, Lid, Chrysanthemums, Butterflies, Gold Enamel, Signed, c.1900, 22 In.	*illus*	4313
Plate, Rooster, 2 Hens, Bamboo, 8 ½ In.		177
Tea Set, Teapot, Sugar, 5 Cups & Saucers, Rectangular Cartouche, 12 Piece		366
Tea Set, Teapot, Sugar, Creamer, 5 Cups & Saucers, Immortals, Dragons, 15 Piece		267
Teapot, Flowers & Vines, Gilt, Flaring Body, 5 In.		62
Urn, Flowers, Mother & Children, Gilt, Square, Scroll Handles, Shaped Feet, 3 In.		120
Urn, Lid, Foo Dog Finial, Figures, Landscape, Flared Rim, 12 x 5 In.		267
Vase, Bulbous, Waisted, Cylindrical Base, Moriage, Gilt Frog Handles, 13 In.		240
Vase, Carp, Red & Gray, Flower Border On Shoulder, 14 ½ x 8 ½ In.		450
Vase, Chrysanthemums, Moths, Gilt, Enamel, Bottle Shape, c.1910, 10 x 5 In., Pair		142
Vase, Dragons, Beige, Brown, Stick Neck, 4 ½ In., Pair		112
Vase, Figures & Landscape, Cream, Orange, Gilt, Rolled Rim, c.1875, 8 In.		308
Vase, Figures & Landscape, Lion Handles, Gilt, 12 In.		525
Vase, Figures & Landscape, Square, Gilded, Hand, Painted, c.1900, 6 x 3 In.		316
Vase, Figures, Gold, Hand Painted, Signed, c.1900, 5 In.		690
Vase, Immortals, Shouldered, Compressed Foot, Gold, 6 In.		138
Vase, Immortals, Trumpet Shape, Bulbous Base, Black Stand, 8 x 4 In.		1250
Vase, Mountains, Houses, Stream, Clouds, 24 x 11 In.		580
Vase, Samurai, Landscape, Trumpet Shape, Bamboo Shape Legs, 6 In.		900
Vase, Scenes, Scholars, Elders, Gilt, Wavy Rim, Dragon Handles, 1800s, 45 In.	*illus*	600
Wall Pocket, Cone Shape, Figures, Landscape, 13 x 4 In., Pair		59

SATURDAY EVENING GIRLS, *see Paul Revere Pottery category.*

SCALES have been made to weigh everything from babies to gold. Collectors search for all types. Most popular are small gold dust scales and special grocery scales.

Apothecary, Brass, Round Trays, Lantern Shape Stem, Marble Base, 1800s, 43 x 34 In.		895
Balance, Brass, Weights, 47 In.		875
Balance, Cast Iron, Paint, Brass Tray, 7 Weights, No. 250, R.H. Co., Reading, Pa., 9 x 14 In.		71
Balance, Henry Troemner, Oak Case, Philadelphia, 1800s, 9 x 13 x 6 In.	*illus*	480
Balance, Micrometer, Brass, Cast Iron, Marble, Dodge Mfg. Co., Yonkers, N.Y., 24 In.	*illus*	165
Candy, Dodge Mfg., Micrometer, Marble Base, 12 ¼ In.		615
Computing, White Porcelain, Meat, Counter		510
Jockey, Oak Slat Chair, Metal Rods, Hanging, 82 x 25 ½ In.		1200
Kitchen, Grand Union Tea Co., Black Metal, Silver Stencils, 1800s, 6 x 10 In.		100
Store, Cast Iron, Paint, Brass Tray, Shaped Legs, R H Company, No. 250, 8 x 14 In.		295
Weighing, Floor, Toledo, c.1925, 77 In.	*illus*	540
Weighing, Floor, Toledo, Green, 72 x 24 In.		117
Weighing, Hub Novelty Co., Green, Blue & White Face, 1 Cent, 69 In.		600
Weighing, Salter's Spring Balance, No. 50T, Brass Dial, Upholstered, c.1940, 20 In.		328
Weighing, Star-Kist, Sorry Charlie, Charlie The Tuna, Bubbles, Metal, 1972, 11 x 13 In.		105

SCHAFER & VATER, makers of small ceramic items, are best known for their amusing figurals. The factory was located in Volkstedt-Rudolstadt, Germany, from 1890 to 1962. Some pieces are marked with the crown and *R* mark, but many are unmarked.

Ashtray, Match Holder, Boy, Open Mouth, 4 In.		73
Ashtray, Match Holder, Boy, Open Mouth, Gray Nails, 3 ½ In.		61
Bottle, Woman, Robe, Hat, Blue, 6 ½ In.		50
Creamer, Bear, Robe, Handwarmer, 5 ½ In.		148
Figurine, Crybabies, 4 In.		43
Figurine, Nun, Bonnet, Holding Bottle, Blue, 8 In.		104
Figurine, Woman With Fan, Brown, 8 In.		61
Jar, Figural, Man Seated On Elephant, 8 In.		50
Pitcher, Girl With Keys, Pitcher, Basket On Back, Crown Mark, c.1910, 3 ½ In.	*illus*	125

Scale, Balance, Micrometer, Brass, Cast Iron, Marble, Dodge Mfg. Co., Yonkers, N.Y., 24 In.
$165

Hess Auction Group

Scale, Weighing, Floor, Toledo, c.1925, 77 In.
$540

Brunk Auctions

Schafer & Vater, Pitcher, Girl With Keys, Pitcher, Basket On Back, Crown Mark, c.1910, 3 ½ In.
$125

Ruby Lane

S

Scheier, Vase, Abstract Figures, Sgraffito, Brown, Peach, Blue Shaded, Marked, 15 In.

$2,829

Skinner, Inc.

Schneider, Candlestick, Striped, Mottled Candle Cup, Bronze Base, Signed, 12 In.

$690

Early Auction Company

Scientific Instrument, Level, Adjustable, Brass, Rosewood, Nesters, 12½ In.

$147

Myers Auction Gallery

Teapot, Face, Smile, Purple, 7 In.	123
Vase, Figural, Dutch Girl, Wooden Shoe, Frog, Pale Blue, Gilt, c.1905, 5 x 6 In.	150

SCHEIER POTTERY was made by Edwin Scheier (1910–2008) and his wife, Mary (1908–2007). They met while they both worked for the WPA, and married in 1937. In 1939, they established their studio, Hillcrock Pottery, in Glade Spring, Virginia. From 1940 to 1968, Edwin taught at the University of New Hampshire and Mary was artist-in-residence. They moved to Oaxaca, Mexico, in 1968 to study the arts and crafts of the Zapotec Indians. When the Scheiers moved to Green Valley, Arizona, in 1978, Ed returned to pottery, making some of his biggest and best-known pieces.

Bowl, Earthenware, Glossy, Brown, Mary & Edwin Scheier, 4½ In.	308
Bowl, Faces, Brown & Copper Glaze, Wide Rim, Ring Foot, c.1955, 6 x 9 In.	1063
Bowl, Incised Figures, Manganese Glaze, Marked, c.1950, 6 x 7 In.	938
Bowl, Line Drawn Faces, Pink, Earthenware, 6¾ In.	156
Bowl, Pale Green Matte, Interior Painted, Abstract Faces, 1 x 7 In.	207
Vase, Abstract Figures, Sgraffito, Brown, Peach, Blue Shaded, Marked, 15 In. .....*illus*	2829
Vase, Figures, Fish, Cream & Brown Glaze, Oval, Tapered, 1950s, 12 x 10 In.	2375
Vase, Pale Blue, Moss Green Glaze, Ribbed, Oval, Ring Foot, c.1950, 11 In.	1375

SCHNEIDER GLASSWORKS was founded in 1917 at Epinay-sur-Seine, France, by Charles and Ernest Schneider. Art glass was made between 1918 and 1933. The company still produces clear crystal glass. See also the Le Verre Francais category.

Candlestick, Striped, Mottled Candle Cup, Bronze Base, Signed, 12 In. .....*illus*	690
Compote, Frosted, Amber Rim, France, 4¾ x 8 In.	150
Compote, Orange, Cobalt Rim, Signed, 6 x 12 In.	531
Lamp, Campanules, Pink & Amber, c.1921, 23 x 11 In.	3125
Lamp, Lilac, Le Verre Francais, c.1925, 14 In.	2750
Lamp, Pheasant, Amber & Ruby, Leaded Glass, Bronze Base, 17 x 22 In.	2530
Vase, Glass, Red, Gold, Purple, 12 x 4 In.	468
Vase, Jades, Mottled Pink, Orange, Interior Flowers, Purple, Yellow, Oval, 9 In.	1778
Vase, Jades, Mottled Yellow, Stylized Orange Flowers, Shouldered, 11 In.	1600
Vase, Lobed, Mottled Orange, Acid Stamp, Iron Stand, 11 x 7½ In.	145
Vase, Mottled Cream, Interior Brown Pulled Design, Swollen Shoulder, 15 In.	1067
Vase, Orange To Yellow, Dots, Applied Ring, Round Foot, 1920s, 12 In.	1625
Vase, Orange, Black Applied Rim, 1920s, 11½ x 7½ In.	1625
Vase, Orange, Bulbous, Ribs, 3 Purple Prunts, Flared Purple Rim, Footed, 3 In.	711

SCIENTIFIC INSTRUMENTS of all kinds are included in this category. Other categories such as Barometer, Binoculars, Dental, Medical, Nautical, and Thermometer may also price scientific apparatus.

Calculator, Slide Rule, Stanley, Drum, Bakelite, Prof. G. Fuller, c.1900	602
Chronometer, Hamilton, Model 22, Brass, Mahogany Case, 6 x 6 In.	1003
Compass, C. Hurtin, Brass, Bar Limb, Sunray Star, Snake Needle, 1700s, 13 In.	2400
Compass, Plain, Harman & Saxe, 1850s, 13 In.	420
Compass, Plain, Lewis Michael, Star & Fleur-De-Lis, Box, 1800s, 15 In.	7200
Compass, Pocket, Silver, Magnifying Glass, 1880s, 1½ In. Diam.	715
Compass, Surveyor's, Bronze, Silver Face, Engraved, Mahogany, c.1810, 5 In.	350
Compass, Surveyor's, Walnut, Brass, Engraved Windrose, France, 1850, 9 In.	273
Compass, Telescope, Queen & Co. Railroad, c.1897, 11 In.	615
Compass, W. & L.E. Gurley, Brass, Case, Surveyor's, 4 In.	69
Galvanometer, Knott Universial, Wood, Glass Case, 14 x 16 In.	111
Induction Coil, 8 Volt, Switch For Alternating Poles, c.1920, 11 In.	191
Induction Coil, Mercury Interrupter, Metal, Glass, Wood Base, 1910, 19 In.	644
Lamp, Radiation, Ulvir, Bauhaus Style, Nickeled, Enameled, Case, c.1930	355
Level, Adjustable, Brass, Rosewood, Nesters, 12½ In. .....*illus*	147
Level, Surveyor's, Stanley, Brass, Adjustable, c.1910, 16 In.	246
Meter Stick, Otto Fennel, No. 46889, Brass, Germany, c.1930	191

Microscope, Bausch & Lomb, Brass, Iron, Walnut Case, 1915, 15 x 7 In.	177
Microscope, Brass, Monocular, Yoke Pivot, Horseshoe Base, 1800s, 10 In.	100
Microscope, C. Reichert, Brass, Case, Germany, c.1890, 11 In.	315
Microscope, Collapsible Mono, Tube, Marked Junior, c.1940, 6 In.	120
Microscope, Compound, Brass, Double Mirror, W. Ladd, England, c.1880	197
Microscope, Compound, Brass, Wood Base, Case, England, c.1860, 15 In.	669
Microscope, Compound, Case, Henry Crouch, London, c.1870, 11 In.	280
Microscope, Compound, Lacquered Brass, Box, Ed. Messter, Germany, 1899, 12 In.	308
Microscope, Monocular, 12 In.	148
Needle Galvanometer, Brass, Wood Case, Siemens & Halske, c.1910, 6 In.	328
Slide Rule, Calculating Tool, Cylindrical Mahogany, 6 x 22 In.	413
Slide Rule, Surveyor's, H. Morin, German Silver, Wood Box, c.1850, 20¾ In.	678
Slide Rule, Thacher's, Model 4012, Keuffel & Esser Co., Box, 1930s, 23 In. ....*illus*	660
Spyglass, Brass, Hide Case, 9 In.	138
Surveyor's Tool, Brass, Hexagonal, Angle Measuring Device, c.1820, 6 In.	270
Telegraph, L.M. Ericsson, Stockholm, Lacquered Brass, Walnut, c.1895, 17 In.	688
Telegraph, Morse Keys, Ink Writer, Wood Base, C. Lorenz, Germany, c.1890, 20 In.	631
Telegraph, Morse, Ink Writer, Motor, Spool, Bell, Wood Base, M. Kohl, 1910, 8 In.	348
Telescope, Brass, Collapsible, Leather Wrapped, Cloth Case, 1800s, 9 In.	120
Telescope, Brass, Single Draw, Tripod, Case, E. Vion, c.1850, 24 In.	450
Telescope, Brass, Wood Tripod Base, France, c.1880, 59 x 55 In.	510
Telescope, Mahogany, Brass, Tripod, Snake Feet, W&S Jones, London, 30 In.	1440
Telescope, Refracting, Tripod Base, A. Bardou, Paris, c.1870, 52 In.	757
Telescope, Ship's, Mahogany, Brass, 3 Draws, Troughton & Simms, c.1890, 30 In.	315
Telescope, Single Draw, Brass Tube, Mahogany Wrapped, Day, Night, 20½ In.	180
Theodolite, Brass, Breithaupt & Son, c.1900, 13½ In.	1125
Transit, Surveyor's, Black Walnut Box, Gurley, 15½ In. ....*illus*	354
Transit, Surveyor's, Brass, Isgard Warren Co., 1900, 15 In.	197
Transit, Surveyor's, Brass, Steel Dial, Tiensch & Stancliff, 16 x 9 In.	1534
Transit, Surveyor's, David White, Model 8202, Cased, 1900s, 14 In.	74
Western Ammeter, Cast Iron, Black, Cream, c.1920, 9 x 4 In.	49

SCRIMSHAW is bone or ivory or whale's teeth carved by sailors and others for entertainment during the sailing-ship days. Some scrimshaw was carved as early as 1800. There are modern scrimshanders making pieces today on bone, ivory, or plastic. Other pieces may be found in the Ivory and Nautical categories. Collectors should be aware of the recent laws limiting the buying and selling of scrimshaw and elephant ivory.

Boat, Clipper Ship, Stag, Hound In Flower Ring, Woman's Portrait, 1800s, 5 In.	300
Busk, Baleen, Corset, Geometrics, Nautical Designs, Inscribed, c.1862, 13 In.	185
Cribbage, Walrus Tusk, Carved, Northwest Coast, 19 In.	148
Hatpin Holder, Inked Sailing Ship, Union Jack, Flower Urn, Lizzie, 1800s, 4 In. ......*illus*	594
Knife Blade, Deer Antler, Signed Verrasjarvi, 13 In. ......*illus*	359
Parasol Handle, Flowers, Oval Cartouche, 5¼ In.	96
Picture Frame, Scrolled Edges, Openwork Stars, Heart, 6 x 4 In.	3600
Pie Crimper, Carved, Openwork Handles, Circle, Flowers, 5¾ In.	1920
Pie Crimper, Ebony Handle, Mother-Of-Pearl Heart Inlay, 5¼ In.	2160
Pie Crimper, Mother-Of-Pearl Inlay, 7 Wheels, 8¼ In.	4200
Pie Crimper, Unicorn Shape, Whalebone, Ivory, 6¼ In.	123
Pie Crimper, Whale, Ebony Bands, 2 Wheels, 6 In.	4500
Sculpture, Castle, Cannons, Prisoner Of War, France, c.1810, 12 x 12 In.	4800
Sculpture, Penis, Remember The Giver, Cream, Brown, Antler, 2 x 7 In.	1464
Sculpture, Sailor & Woman, Embracing, Holding Union Jack, England, 1800s, 6 In.	600
Seam Rubber, Geometric Incised Carving, 4 In.	450
Seam Rubber, Spiral, Ring Turned, Turk's Head, Inlaid Mahogany, 6 In.	4800
Tea Caddy, Scene, Chinese Figures, Copper, Brass, Handles, c.1900, 3½ x 7 In. ......*illus*	495
Whale's Tooth, Crossed Flags, Cannon, Masted Ship, Banding, 1800s, 6 In.	960
Whale's Tooth, Square-Rigged Ship, English Flag, Hull, Anchors, 1800s, 7 In.	800
Whale's Tooth, 2-Sided, Hermaphrodite Brig, Man Rowing, c.1930, 5 x 3 In.	700

Scientific Instrument, Slide Rule, Thacher's, Model 4012, Keuffel & Esser Co., Box, 1930s, 23 In.
$660

Cowan's Auctions

Scientific Instrument, Transit, Surveyor's, Black Walnut Box, Gurley, 15½ In.
$354

Myers Auction Gallery

Scrimshaw, Hatpin Holder, Inked Sailing Ship, Union Jack, Flower Urn, Lizzie, 1800s, 4 In.
$594

Garth's Auctioneers & Appraisers

Scrimshaw, Knife Blade, Deer Antler, Signed Verrasjarvi, 13 In. **$359**

Saco River Auction Co.

Scrimshaw, Tea Caddy, Scene, Chinese Figures, Copper, Brass, Handles, c.1900, 3½ x 7 In. **$495**

Ruby Lane

Sevres, Platter, Scene, People Eating, Drinking, Gold Leaf, Flower Border, 1800s, 15 x 22 In. **$575**

Cottone Auctions

Whale's Tooth, 3 Whaleboats, Weeping Willows, 7¼ In.	2520
Whale's Tooth, 4-Masted Coastal Schooner, Maine, c.1900, 5 In.	325
Whale's Tooth, British Jack Tar, Sword, British Flag, 7¼ In.	2640
Whale's Tooth, British Man-Of-War, Rigging, 8¾ In.	7200
Whale's Tooth, Long Boat, Harpoonist, Diving Whale, 5¼ In.	800
Whale's Tooth, Merchant Ship, Gunports, Flag, Masts, c.1850, 6½ In.	2900
Whale's Tooth, Presentation, Inscribed Shoal Of Sperm Whales, 6¼ In.	3600

SEG, *see Paul Revere Pottery category.*

SEVRES porcelain has been made in Sevres, France, since 1769. Many copies of the famous ware have been made. The name originally referred to the works of the Royal Porcelain factory. The name now includes any of the wares made in the town of Sevres, France. The entwined lines with a center letter used as the mark is one of the most forged marks in antiques. Be very careful to identify Sevres by quality, not just by mark.

Bowl, Gilt, Portrait, Teal Green, 9½ In.	250
Box, Classical Scene, Cobalt Blue, Gilt, Bronze Mount, Oval, 6 x 11 In.	275
Box, Cobalt Blue, Reserve, Raised Gilt Design, 4 x 6 In.	87
Centerpiece, Gilt Bronze Mounts, Winged Woman Handles, 1800s, 21 x 23 In.	4025
Charger, Battle Of Marseille, Hand Painted, C. Kollerl, Signed, 1800s, 15½ In.	805
Clock, Wall, Gilt Bronze, Jasper Mount, Flower Wreath, Thermometer, 38 In.	4305
Cup & Saucer, Bleu Celeste, Putto, Bow, Arrows, Clouds, 2 Piece	457
Cup & Saucer, Bleu Celeste, Sailors, Beach, 2 Piece	976
Cup & Saucer, Bleu Celeste, Still Life, Courting Couple, 2 Piece	1098
Dish, Bleu Celeste, Shell Shape, Gilt, Flowers, 8 x 6 In.	274
Dresser Box, Mother & Child, Portrait Of Father, Landscape, Gilt, 3 x 8 In.	1750
Garniture Set, Bowl, 2 Urns, Lid, Bronze Mount, Signed, M. Giloue, 3 Piece	2160
Group, Cupid & Psyche, Kissing, Terra-Cotta, Shaped Base, Marked, 18 x 16 In.	610
Group, Drunk Silenus, Seated, Rocks, 3 Nymphs & 2 Putti, White, c.1760, 8 In.	13939
Jardiniere, Beaded Ormolu, Lion Masks, Animal Shape Legs, Panels, 10 x 16 In.	1625
Plate, Courting Couple, Playing Board Game, Cobalt Blue Border, 9½ In.	125
Plate, Marli Rouge, Butterfly, Flowers, Leafy Scroll, Gilt, Red Border, 1809	5947
Plate, Napoleonic, Black Rim, Gold Flowers, 9½ In., 8 Piece	1500
Platter, Scene, People Eating, Drinking, Gold Leaf, Flower Border, 1800s, 15 x 22 In. *illus*	575
Table Casket, Domed, Cobalt Blue, Courting Couple, Landscape, 4 x 11 In.	750
Tea Set, Teapot, 2 Cups & Saucers, Sugar, Creamer, Pitcher, Tray, Case, 6 Piece	3600
Tea Set, Teapot, Underplate, Sugar, Creamer, 2 Cups, Bees, Coat Of Arms, 6 Piece	375
Tray, Birds, Swags, Shells, Flowers, Gilt Border, Scalloped Rim, Handles, c.1763	5947
Tray, Cobalt Blue & Gilt Scrolling Bands, Flower Sprays, Oval, c.1770, 10 In.	2044
Tray, Green Lattice, Flowers, Pieces Edge, Mathieu Foure, 1757, 6 In.	4250
Tray, Green, Diamond Reserves, Flower Sprays, 6 In.	500
Tray, Lobed, Serpentine Rim, Greek Key, Beasts, Cartouches, Starburst, 16 x 13 In.	507
Tray, White, Blue Trailing Flowers, Gilt Border, Block Feet, c.1758, 9½ In.	2230
Urn, Bleu Celeste, Berry Finial, Courting Couple, 1800s, 16½ In., Pair	1652
Urn, Bleu Celeste, Gilt, Leaf & Berry Finial, Gadroon, 21 x 8 In.	3900
Urn, Courting Couple, Landscape, Cobalt Blue, Gilt, Bronze Mount, 15 x 9½ In. *illus*	1499
Urn, Flower Spray, Figures, Cobalt Blue, Gilt, Egg & Dart, Bronze Foot, 25 x 35 In.	714
Urn, Gilt, Bronze, Courting Couple, Woman's Bust Handles, 29½ In.	3250
Urn, Gold Leaf, Gilt Bronze Mounts, 1800s, 28 x 15 In.	2185
Urn, Lid, Couple, Landscape, Cobalt Blue, Gilt Bronze, Openwork Base, 26 In.	2500
Urn, Lid, Tapering, Courting Couples, Pinecone Finial, 28 In., Pair	3000
Urn, Lid, Tulips, Arabesques, Rowing Party, Iridescent, France, 32 In.	4750
Urn, Lid, Woman & Gentleman, Hand Painted, Gilt Bronze Mounts, 1800s, 7 In.	690
Urn, Woman, Landscape, Ormolu Handles, Green, Gold, c.1890, 7 x 16½ In.	4995
Vase, Cobalt Blue, Bronze Dolphin Handles, Marked, c.1873, 17 In., Pair	4375
Vase, Crystalline Streaked, Purple, Green, Yellow, Paneled, Bottle, 1900, 9 In.	1500
Vase, Flambe Glaze, Striated Red, Black, Pear Shape, Stick Neck, 1892, 10 In.	2006
Vase, Gilt, Cobalt Blue, Stick Neck, Squat Body, Round Foot, 9 In.	125

Sevres, Urn, Courting Couple, Landscape, Cobalt Blue, Gilt, Bronze Mount, 15 x 9½ In.
$1,499

Ruby Lane

Sevres, Vase, Green, Blue & Yellow Speckles, Bronze Base, Paul Milet, 11 In., Pair
$1,121

Humler & Nolan

Sevres, Vase, Leafy Tendrils, Paper Label, Incised, Porcelain, 1908, 13 x 6 In.
$2,125

Rago Arts and Auction Center

Sevres, Vase, Stoneware, Peacock Feathers, Enamel, Anatole Fournier, 1918, 10 x 6 In.
$4,375

Rago Arts and Auction Center

Sevres, Vase, Stylized Chestnuts, Leaves, Celadon Green, France, Marked, 1949, 7 In.
$240

Brunk Auctions

Sewer Tile, Figure, Frog, Seated, Glazed, Ohio, 7 x 12 In.
$732

Norman Heckler & Company

Sewer Tile, Figure, Lion, Reclining, Oval Reeded Base, Cream & Orange, c.1900, 9 x 15 In.
$330

Garth's Auctioneers & Appraisers

Sewing, Bird, Brass, Embossed Flower Design, Pincushion, C Clamp, Victorian, 5 In.
$165

Hess Auction Group

Sewing, Box, Antler Veneer, Sandalwood, Lift-Out Tray, Brass Lock, Hobbs & Co., 9 x 15 In.
$590

Hess Auction Group

S

Sewing, Clamp, Thread Winder, Maple, Ebonized, Bone Spindles, 10 In. $142

TIP

If you have a book or other small item that smells peculiar, put it in a large plastic bag with kitty litter. Seal it and let it stand for about a week.

Sewing, Necessaire, Musical, Mother-Of-Pearl, Gold Tools, Palais Royale, France, c.1850, 9 In. $1,872

Vase, Green, Blue & Yellow Speckles, Bronze Base, Paul Milet, 11 In., Pair......................*illus*	1121
Vase, Leafy Tendrils, Paper Label, Incised, Porcelain, 1908, 13 x 6 In. ....*illus*	2125
Vase, Lid, Gilt Bronze, Pineapple Finial, Horned Satyr Mask, 1800s, 14 In., Pair	1230
Vase, Stoneware, Peacock Feathers, Enamel, Anatole Fournier, 1918, 10 x 6 In. ....*illus*	4375
Vase, Stylized Chestnuts, Leaves, Celadon Green, France, Marked, 1949, 7 In. ....*illus*	240

SEWER TILE figures were made by workers at the sewer tile and pipe factories in the Ohio area during the late nineteenth and early twentieth centuries. Figurines, small vases, and cemetery vases were favored. Often the finished vase was a piece of the original pipe with added decorations and markings. All types of sewer tile work are now considered folk art by collectors.

Doorstop, Dog, Spaniel, Seated, Collar, Locket, 10 ¼ In..	215
Figure, Dog, Mastiff, Lying Down, c.1940, 9 In.	240
Figure, Frog, Seated, Glazed, Ohio, 7 x 12 In...*illus*	732
Figure, Lion, Lying Down, Log Base, c.1940, 11 ½ In.	150
Figure, Lion, Lying Down, Oval Reeded Base, Cream & Orange, c.1900, 9 x 15 In..............*illus*	330
Figure, Lion, Lying Down, Scalloped Edge Base, c.1880, 7 x 10 In.	188
Figure, Lion, Relief, Early 1900s, 9 x 20 In., Pair..	390
Figure, Owl, Tree Stump, Tan, Amber, Inscribed EJE, c.1950, 15 In..................................	600
Figure, Spaniel, Doorstop, Combed Hair, Chain, Locket, 8 ½ In.	984
Pitcher, Stylized Cranes, Brown, White, c.1880, 9 In.	151

SEWING equipment of all types is collected, from sewing birds that held the cloth to tape measures, needle books, and old wooden spools. Sewing machines are included here. Needlework pictures are listed in the Picture category.

Bird, Brass, Embossed Flower Design, Pincushion, C Clamp, Victorian, 5 In......................*illus*	165
Bird, Steel, Brass Lid, Oval Box, Pincushion On Lid, Late 1800s, 6 In.	180
Bobbin Box, Oak, Ebonized, 6 Spindles, Drawer, Ogee Feet, 1800s, 9 x 6 In.	47
Box, Abalone Inlay, Black, 11 ½ In..	225
Box, Antler Veneer, Sandalwood, Lift-Out Tray, Brass Lock, Hobbs & Co., 9 x 15 In............*illus*	590
Box, Bed Shape, French Empire, Mahogany, Sleigh Ends, Drawers, Tools, 21 In.	2394
Box, Black Lacquer, Gilt, Octagonal, Drawer, Bail Handles, Paw Feet, 6 x 14 In.	1140
Box, Black Lacquer, Gilt, Paint, 2 Doors, Interior Drawers, Dogs, 1800s, 10 x 9 In..................	1560
Box, Burlwood, Octagonal, Peaked Lid, Inlaid Escutcheon, George III, 7 x 12 In......................	660
Box, Cigar Box Wood, Pincushion Top, Stepped Lid, Block Feet, c.1905, 7 x 11 In.	290
Box, Dome Lid, Parquetry, Inlay, England, 6 x 12 In..	325
Box, Mahogany, Bone Scroll Inlay, Fitted Interior, 18 Tools, c.1850, 14 x 10 In..................	1254
Box, Mahogany, Drawer, Pincushion Top, Ball Feet, 6 x 4 In..	129
Box, Mahogany, Ivory, Bone Pulls, Finials, 3 Tiers, Cushion Finial, c.1830, 8 x 9 In.	330
Box, Mahogany, Sailor Made Whalebone, Marquetry, Yarn Winder, 1800s, 7 x 11 x 10 In..........	1800
Box, Maple, Hinged Lid, Mother-Of-Pearl Design, Whalebone Fans, 5 x 13 In.	510
Box, Musical, Satinwood, Hinged, Serpentine Lid, Swing Handle, 1800s, 3 x 8 In..................	1020
Box, Octagonal, Marquetry, Parquetry, Flowers, Green Velvet, 1800s, 5 x 10 In.	125
Box, Pagoda Shape, Tortoiseshell, Pearl, Flowers, 7 x 11 In..	2124
Box, Prisoner-Of-War, Bone, Pincushion Top, 8 x 8 ½ In..	660
Box, Shaker, Maple, Hinged Top, Inset Bone Escutcheon, Trays, 5 x 8 In............................	4920
Box, Shaker, Pine, Stain, Brass Tacks, Hinged Lid, Spool Spindles, 4 x 11 In........................	3075
Box, Walnut, 2 Tiers, Drawer, Pincushion Top, c.1875, 7 x 6 In....................................	94
Box, Wood, Bone & Mosaic Inlay, Fitted Velvet Interior, Bone Tools, 11 x 6 In.	912
Box, Wood, Leather, Oil Painting, Shipwrecked Men, Gold Tools, c.1860, 5 x 3 In..................	456
Box, Yellow Paint, Lift-Out Tray, Bail Handle, Turned Feet, 1800s, 10 x 14 In....................	1230
Cabinet, Haberdashery, Wood, Gilt Stencil, Drawers, Metal Handles, 1920s, 13 x 14 In..........	195
Cabinet, Spool, see also the Advertising category under Cabinet, Spool.	
Cabinet, Wood, 2-Tier Drawers, Steeple Top, Sphere Pincushion, c.1890, 15 x 7 In..............	1298
Caddy, Pine, Nesting Duck, Multicolor, Drawer, Early 1900s, 8 x 9 In................................	1800
Case, Needle, Heart, Faceted Cube, Diamonds, Canada, 5 In..	3100
Clamp, Thread Winder, Maple, Ebonized, Bone Spindles, 10 In. ....*illus*	142

Companion, Doll, Bisque Shoulder Head, Curls, Silk Gown, Tools, 7 In.	1083
Companion, Doll, Porcelain, Muslin, Civil War Costume, Tools, 9 In.	1824
Compendium, Silver, Needle Holder, Thimble, Thread Spool, Late 1700s, 3 In.	1680
Darning Egg, Mushroom Shape, Wood, 4 ½ x 2 In.	14
Kit, Abalone Shell Case, Gold Thimble, Scissors, Bodkin, Needle Threader, 3 In.	603
Kit, Needlework, Wool, Diamond Pattern, Blue, Red, Green, Silk Interior, 3 x 4 In.	246
Machine, Frister & Rossmann, Mahogany Case	125
Machine, Gilt Design, Black, Crank, Cast Iron, France, c.1900, 10 x 15 In.	125
Machine, Singer, Black, Scroll, Gilt, Oak Folding Table Top, Foot Pedal, 1800s	900
Machine, Willcox & Gibbs, Metal, Gilt, Hand-Turned Crank, Wood Base, c.1872	429
Necessaire, Candy Box, Women In Park, Gilt, Tools, F. Marquis, France, 5 x 8 In.	513
Necessaire, Musical, Mother-Of-Pearl, Gold Tools, Palais Royale, France, c.1850, 9 In......*illus*	1872
Necessaire, Treasure Chest Shape, Plaid Silk, Brass, Gold Plate Accessories, 3 In.	798
Needle Case, Heart, Faceted Cube, Diamonds, Canada, 5 In.	3100
Pattern, Dress, McCall No. 7951, Size 13, Bust 31 In.	14
Pincushion Dolls are listed in their own category.	
Pincushion, Blue Fabric, On Round Box, Turquoise, Harrisburg, c.1870, 3 In.	369
Pincushion, Oval Box, 3-Finger, Lid, Domed Cushion Top, 1864, 3 x 4 In.	338
Spool Cabinets are listed here or in the Advertising category under Cabinet, Spool.	
Spool Cabinet, Victorian, Walnut, Canted, 7 Drawers, Molded Crest, 28 x 18 In.	356
Spool Cabinet, Wooden, 5 Drawers, Brainerd & Armstrong, 21 In.	1353
Spool Caddy, Walnut, Turned, Disc Shape, c.1880, 9 ½ In.	98
Spool Holder, Egg Shape, Tartanware Pattern, M'Gregor, 1800s, 3 x 1 ¾ In.	175
Spool Holder, Lazy Susan, 4 Tiers, Drawer, Heart Cutouts, c.1890, 21 x 9 In.	593
Stand, Gazebo, Domed Roof, Cupola, Twisted Pillars, Wood, Bone, Tools, 16 In.	342
Stand, Spool Pegs, Pincushion Top, Drawer, Oak, 1800s, 12 x 15 In.......................*illus*	232
Stringholder, Skater, On 1 Leg, Flowered Dress, Outstretched Arm, 8 In.	305
Stringholder, Victorian Woman, Red Cape, Iron, Cast, 7 ¼ In.	457
Stringholder, Woman Looking In Mirror, Tiered Dress, 8 ¼ In.	427
Table, Papier-Mache, Parcel Gilt, Black, Mother-Of-Pearl Sunburst, 28 x 21 In.	354
Tape Loom, Wood, Pale Blue Green Paint, 1800s, 15 ½ x 9 In.	984
Tape Measure, Silk Ribbon, Sewing Machine Case, Metal, Tortoise Shell, 3 In.	285
Thimble Case, Papier-Mache, Egg Shape, Cherry Blossoms, Gilt, Silk Lined, c.1905, 2 In.	25
Thimble, 14K Gold, Leaf & Grape Band, Engraved S.S.M.R., Septima Middlton	840
Wool Winder, Japanned, Red, Wheel, Hand Crank, Rectangular Base, 12 x 21 In.	1169
Wool Winder, Mixed Wood, Double Squirrel Cage, Adjustable Shaft, 1800s, 55 In.......*illus*	457
Wool Winder, Mixed Wood, Red, Sawtooth Wheel, Turned Gear, Legs, 38 x 28 In.......*illus*	153

Sewing, Stand, Spool Pegs, Pincushion Top, Drawer, Oak, 1800s, 12 x 15 In.
$232

Showtime Auction Services

Sewing, Wool Winder, Mixed Wood, Double Squirrel Cage, Adjustable Shaft, 1800s, 55 In.
$457

Norman Heckler & Company

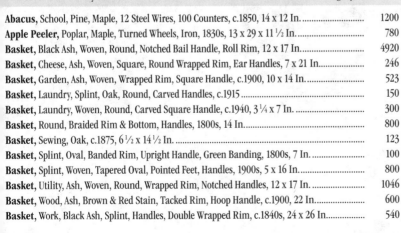

SHAKER items are characterized by simplicity, functionalism, and orderliness. There were many Shaker communities in America from the eighteenth century to the present day. The religious order made furniture, small wooden pieces, and packaged medicines, herbs, and jellies to sell to "outsiders." Other useful objects were made for use by members of the community. Shaker furniture is listed in this book in the Furniture category.

Abacus, School, Pine, Maple, 12 Steel Wires, 100 Counters, c.1850, 14 x 12 In.	1200
Apple Peeler, Poplar, Maple, Turned Wheels, Iron, 1830s, 13 x 29 x 11 ½ In.	780
Basket, Black Ash, Woven, Round, Notched Bail Handle, Roll Rim, 12 x 17 In.	4920
Basket, Cheese, Ash, Woven, Square, Round Wrapped Rim, Ear Handles, 7 x 21 In.	246
Basket, Garden, Ash, Woven, Wrapped Rim, Square Handle, c.1900, 10 x 14 In.	523
Basket, Laundry, Splint, Oak, Round, Carved Handles, c.1915	150
Basket, Laundry, Woven, Round, Carved Square Handle, c.1940, 3 ¼ x 7 In.	300
Basket, Round, Braided Rim & Bottom, Handles, 1800s, 14 In.	800
Basket, Sewing, Oak, c.1875, 6 ½ x 14 ½ In.	123
Basket, Splint, Oval, Banded Rim, Upright Handle, Green Banding, 1800s, 7 In.	100
Basket, Splint, Woven, Tapered Oval, Pointed Feet, Handles, 1900s, 5 x 16 In.	800
Basket, Utility, Ash, Woven, Round, Wrapped Rim, Notched Handles, 12 x 17 In.	1046
Basket, Wood, Ash, Brown & Red Stain, Tacked Rim, Hoop Handle, c.1900, 22 In.	600
Basket, Work, Black Ash, Splint, Handles, Double Wrapped Rim, c.1840s, 24 x 26 In.	540

S

Sewing, Wool Winder, Mixed Wood, Red, Sawtooth Wheel, Turned Gear, Legs, 38 x 28 In.
$153

Hess Auction Group

Shaker, Box, 3-Finger, Oval, 2 x 4¾ In.
$118

Myers Auction Gallery

Shaker, Carrier, 3-Finger, Lid, Handle, 11 x 13½ x 10 In.
$384

Hess Auction Group

Scuttle Mug

A scuttle shaving mug is shaped like an old coal scuttle. There is an opening to hold the brush.

Shaker, Carrier, 3-Finger, Sewing, Sister's, Maple, Pine, Satin Lined, Handle, 6 x 8 In.
$750

Willis Henry Auctions

Shaker, Spool Holder, Sister's, Maple, 2 Tiers, 12 Spools, Pincushion, 3-Footed, c.1850, 5 In.
$1,920

Willis Henry Auctions

Shaving Mug, Occupational, Volunteer Firefighter, E.A. Allworder, Limoges, 1900
$1,200

Ruby Lane

Shawnee, Planter, Bed, Green, White Quilt, Pink Canopy, Wood Posts, 7¾ x 6½ In.
$150

Ruby Lane

Shearwater, Bowl, Street Scene, People, Standing, Cast, Glazed, Peter Anderson, 1989, 5½ x 8 In.
$2,250

New Orleans Auction Galleries

Shearwater, Figurine, Horse, Stylized, Turquoise, Cast, Glazed, Peter Anderson, 1950s, 13 In.
$1,250

New Orleans Auction Galleries

S

Berry Bucket, Wood, Paint, Tin Bands, Bail Handle, Stave Construction, c.1900, 5 In.	390
Blanket, Shaker, Wool, White, Red Yarn Cross-Stitching, Blue & Red Stripes, 75 x 70 In.	461
Blanket, Wool, Blue & White Check, Jacquard, Initials, c.1840, 62 x 7 In.	1140
Blanket, Wool, White, Dark Red Edge, Cross-Stitched 17 In Corner, 87 x 69 In.	308
Box, 3-Finger, Oval, 2 x 4¾ In. *illus*	118
Box, 3-Finger, Oval, Gray, 1800s, 7½ x 5 In.	1521
Box, 3-Finger, Oval, Lid, Maple, Orange Stain, Copper Tacks, c.1885, 2 x 5 In.	1599
Box, 4-Finger, Lid, Maple, Pine, Oval, Bittersweet Stain, Copper Tacks, 4 x 11 In.	5228
Box, 4-Finger, Lid, Oval, Maple, Pine, Tacks, Yellow Paint, c.1840, 5 x 12 In.	1140
Box, 4-Finger, Maple, Pine, Lid, Copper Tacks, Steel Points, Oval, c.1830s, 4 x 10 In.	1680
Box, 4-Finger, Oval, Black Top, 10½ x 7½ In.	1404
Box, 4-Finger, Oval, Pine, Maple, Lid, Copper Tacks, Steel Points, c.1850, 2 x 5 In.	540
Box, Bible, Pine, Red Paint, Lift Top, Dovetailed, Hinged, Iron, c.1880, 5 x 19 In.	492
Box, Chip, Pine, Red Stain, 2-Board Lid, Arch Handle, Iron, 1800s, 10 x 19 In.	1353
Box, Document, Lid, Pine, Poplar, Brass Handles, Label, c.1840s, 5 x 12 x 10 In.	1200
Box, Letter, Pine, Poplar, Rectangular, 9 Drawers, 3 Rows, Ball Knobs, 1800s, 9 In.	1046
Box, Lid, Brown Paint Traces, Faneuil Hall, 1800s, 3 x 6½ In.	154
Box, Lid, Maple & Pine, Red Paint, Round, Copper Tacks, c.1850, 2 x 3 In.	11070
Box, Lift Lid, Pine, Red Stain, Brass Hardware, Hinges, Molded, 1800s, 5 x 14 In.	1845
Box, Medicine, Brass Lift Lid, Poplar & Pine, Shaker Tape, c.1850, 12 x 16 In.	1440
Box, Oak & Pine, Blue Paint, Round, Straight Lap, Iron Tacks, 6 x 10 In.	800
Box, Sewing, Swing Handle, Copper Tacks, Pink Silk Lining, c.1910, 11 In.	94
Box, Storage, Lift Lid, Pine, Yellow Paint, Brass Hinges, 1800s, 5 x 12 In.	1476
Box, Storage, Maple, 4 Drawers, Wood Knobs, Top Knop Handle, 8 x 13 In.	677
Box, Storage, Molded Lift Lid, Pine, Red Stain, Iron Hinges, 1800s, 12 x 24 In.	615
Box, Storage, Pine, Orange Paint, 3 Drawers, Walnut Pulls, c.1840, 8 x 14 In.	3720
Box, Utensil, Red Paint, Arched Divider, Pierced Handle, 1800s, 8 x 13 In.	1968
Brush, Dusting, Chrome, Yellow Paint, Horsehair, Turned Handle, 1800s, 10 In.	677
Bucket, Lid, Pine, Dark Blue Paint, Black Metal Bands, Stenciled 28, 16 x 12 In.	3840
Bucket, Pine, Ocher Paint, Iron Hoops, Wood Handle, Scribed, 1800s, 11 x 14 In.	1230
Bucket, Pine, Red Paint, Lid, Iron Hoops, Bail Handle, Scribed, c.1850, 10 x 8 In.	1475
Bucket, Pine, Red Paint, Steel Bands, Stenciled G, Swing Handle, c.1840, 19 x 13 In.	3300
Bucket, Sap, Blue, 1800s, 12 x 10½ In.	263
Bucket, Wood, Clothespins, Salmon Paint, Stave Construction, Iron Bands, 11 x 12 In.	492
Bucket, Yellow Paint, Pine Staves, Iron Plates, Wood Handle, 1800s, 6 In.	5535
Bucket, Yellow, Swing Handle, 1800s, 4 x 6 In.	1230
Caliper, Heart Shape, Iron, 1800s, 10½ x 21 In.	234
Candle Dryer, Pine, Lamb's Tongue Post, 8 Arms, Wire Loops, c.1840s, 40 x 35 In.	840
Carrier, 3-Finger, Lid, Handle, 11 x 13½ x 10 In. *illus*	384
Carrier, 3-Finger, Maple, Pine, Oval, Red Paint, Fixed Handle, c.1830s, 7 x 10 In.	1800
Carrier, 3-Finger, Maple, Red Stain, Copper Tacks, Fixed Handle, 1860, 7 x 11 In.	14760
Carrier, 3-Finger, Pine, Yellow Stain, Copper Tacks, Fixed Handle, c.1855, 7 x 9 In.	3075
Carrier, 3-Finger, Sewing, Sister's, Maple, Pine, Satin Lined, Handle, 6 x 8 In. *illus*	750
Carrier, 4-Finger, Maple, Red Paint, Fixed Handle, Copper Tacks, 1800s, 8 x 11 In.	923
Carrier, Butternut, Dovetailed, Riveted, Ash Swing Handle, 1800s, 6 x 6 In.	800
Cloak, Red Wool, Silk Ribbons, Silk Lined Hood, 2 Pockets, c.1910, 51 In.	420
Cloak, Wool, Rose Color, Head Cover, Shoulder Cape, 1900s, 62 In.	308
Dipper, Chestnut, Turned Bowl, Carved Handle, Hancock, Mass., c.1850, 4 x 6 In.	1260
Dipper, Maple, Iron Rivet, Copper Tacks, Yellow Paint, Handle, c.1840, 7 x 14 In.	3321
Duster, Maple, Turned Handle, Ebony Paint, Yellow Stain, c.1880s, 5 In.	240
Foot Warmer, Soapstone, Rectangular, Wool Pocket Cover, c.1900, 6 x 12 In.	185
Fruit Press, Tiger Maple, Oak & Cherry, Brass Hinge, c.1850, 18 x 8¾ In.	1440
Grinder, Pulverizing, Oak & Maple, Steel Chute, Hinged Box, 16 x 14 x 8 In.	240
Knife Box, Pine, Pale Salmon Paint, 2 Sliding Lids, Canted Sides, c.1875	420
Ladder, Fruit Tree, Folding, Pine, Turned Oak, Iron Spikes, c.1860, 97 x 12 In.	2400
Masher, Marked No. 2 L.S. Starretts, 1844, 20 x 8 In.	380
Peg Board, Pine, 11 Cherry Pegs, Finely Turned, c.1840, 92 In.	1200
Pincushion, Tabletop, Red Cloth, Blue Woven Tape, Maple Clamp, c.1870, 7 x 3 In.	540
Rack, Herb Drying, Oak & Pine, Iron Hanger, Hinged Slats, Twine, c.1880, 84 x 34 In.	780

Shearwater, Vase, Figural, Fish, Celadon, 4½ In.
$265

Ruby Lane

Sheet Music, When Dreams Come True, Philip Bartholomae, 1913, 10 x 14 In.
$10

Ruby Lane

Shelley, Coffeepot, Dainty Blue, Small Flowers At Rim, 8 In.
$104

Strawser Auction Group

Shelley, Vase, Butterfly On Each Side, Multicolor, Walter Slater, Lusterware, 6¾ In.
$295

Humler & Nolan

Shirley Temple, Doll, Composition, Socket Head, Sleep Eyes, Mohair Ringlets, Ideal, c.1935, 11 In.
$285

Theriault's

Rake, Wood, 12 Tines, 2 Arched Demilune Supports, Turned Handle, c.1900, 72 In.	246
Robe, Carriage, Wool, Black, Gray & Red, Plaid Panels, Label, 1884, 72 x 101 In.	5228
Rug, Cotton, Wool, Silver Dollar Circles, Multicolor, Mounted, Wired, 42 x 21 In.	1200
Rug, Shirred, Concentric Ovals, Various Fabrics, Late 1800s, 28 x 37 In.	188
Scoop, Carved Wood, Paint, Deep Bowl, Tapered Turned Handle, 1800s, 8 In.	4920
Scoop, Tin, 1800s, 9½ In.	351
Seed Box, Lid, Pine, Red Paint, Shakers Garden Seeds, Label, 1800s, 23 x 11 In.	1860
Seed Box, Shaker's Choice Vegetable Seeds, Yellow Paint, Label, c.1880, 5 x 22 In.	800
Sieve, Tin, Wood Handle, Brass Bar, Hand Crank, c.1850s, 14 x 8 In.	420
Spinning Wheel, Oak & Tiger Maple, Alfred, Maine, 35 x 36 x 24 In.	1200
Spool Holder, Sister's, Maple, 2 Tiers, 12 Spools, Pincushion, 3-Footed, c.1850, 5 In. *illus*	1920
Spool Holder, Wood, Brown Pincushion, Scissors Holder, Pins, c.1860, 8 In.	600
Spool, Yellow Paint, Apple Core Shape, Turned, Fitted With Awl, c.1885, 5 In.	554
Steps, Pine, 4 Rectangular Stairs, Arched Cutout Base, c.1840, 32 x 20 In.	3075
Stove, Iron, Removable Legs, 1800s, 15 x 30 In.	292
Stove, Retiring Room, Iron, Door, Wood Latch, 21 x 30 x 12½ In.	1560
Sweater Stretcher, Wood, Folding Frame, Outstretched Arms, c.1900, 16 x 29 In.	246
Swift, Maple & Pine, Yellow Stain, 1800s, 11 x 18 In.	369
Swift, Tabletop, Maple & Pine, Yellow Stain, Cup At Top, c.1870, 25 In.	360
Tailoring Table, Dropleaf, 2 Drawers, Pine, Red Wash, 52½ x 25 In.	5265
Tape Winder, New Lebanon, 1800s, 12 x 8 In.	672
Tub, Pine Staves, Red Paint, Iron Hoops, Lapped, Riveted, Earred Handles, 7 x 10 In.	861
Washstand, Butternut, 1800s, 18 x 18 In.	643

SHAVING MUGS were popular from 1860 to 1900. Many types were made, including occupational mugs featuring pictures of men's jobs. There were scuttle mugs, silver-plated mugs, glass-lined mugs, and others.

Automobile, Gilt, R.J. Garman, Stamped Royal China, 3½ In.	660
Fred Reidinger, Horse Drawn Bakery Wagon, C.A. Smith Barber Supplies, 3 In.	310
Hunter, Dog, Ducks, Marsh, Gilt, James C. Platt, Black Wrap, 3½ In.	240
Occupational, Blacksmith, Shop Interior, c.1890, 3½ In.	208
Occupational, Carpenter, H.E. Bowden, Gilt, Marked, Royal Austria, 4 In.	738
Occupational, Driver, Horse Drawn Cart, Gilt Inscribed, c.1910, 3½ In.	420
Occupational, Farmer, Horse In Field, Black Wrap, Gilt, c.1910, 4 In.	360
Occupational, Grocer, Woman Shopping, Gilt, S. Krish, Limoges, 3½ In.	593
Occupational, Hunter, M. Seiwell, Gilt, Marked, T&V France, 3¾ In.	677
Occupational, Livery Stable, Horse, Carriage, Gilt, Fred Benoit, 3½ In.	180
Occupational, Men, Fishing, Coming To Land, F.D. Bach, Gilt, 4 In.	522
Occupational, Railroad Engineer, Train, Gilt Inscribed, c.1910, 4 In., 3 Piece	210
Occupational, Volunteer Firefighter, E.A. Allworder, Limoges, 1900 *illus*	1200
Occupational, Weapon Dealer, J.S. Mitchell, Gilt, Crossed Shotguns, 4 In.	677
Pilots, Yellow Biplane, Gilt, Carl Dienstbach, 3½ In.	8400
Sailboat, Frank Jones, Gilt Banding, 3½ In.	215

Shawnee **SHAWNEE POTTERY** was started in Zanesville, Ohio, in 1937. The company made vases, novelty ware, flowerpots, planters, lamps, and cookie jars. Three dinnerware lines were made: Corn, Lobster Ware, and Valencia (a solid color line). White Corn pattern utility pieces were made in 1945. Corn King was made from 1946 to 1954; Corn Queen, with darker green leaves and lighter colored corn, from 1954 to 1961. Shawnee produced pottery for George Rumrill during the late 1930s. The company closed in 1961.

Cookie Jar, Smiley Pig, Blue Scarf, Flowers, Gold Trim & Buttons, Text, 1950s, 12 In.	180
Creamer, Elephant, Trunk Up, Red Accents, 4½ In.	18
Figurine, Tumbling Bear, Sticker, c.1950, 3 In.	32
Pie Bird, For Pillsbury Pie Co., 1950s, 5¼ In.	22
Planter, Baby Boy, Highchair, Blue Blanket, 6½ In.	15
Planter, Bed, Green, White Quilt, Pink Canopy, Wood Posts, 7¾ x 6½ In. *illus*	150
Planter, Pig, Wiping Brow, c.1940, 5¾ In.	12
Salt & Pepper, Jack & Jill, Gold Paint, Flower Decals, 5¼ In.	225

S

Salt & Pepper, King Corn, c.1960, 3¼ In.	22
Teapot, Peach, Flower On Handle, c.1943, 7 x 9 In.	15
Teapot, Tulips, Red, Yellow, Green, 1940s, 6½ x 8¾ In.	20
Vase, Flared, Handles, Ribbed, Scalloped Rim, c.1950, 5½ In.	23

SHEARWATER POTTERY is a family business started in 1928 by Peter Anderson, with the help of his parents, Mr. and Mrs. G.W. Anderson Sr. The local Ocean Springs, Mississippi, clays were used to make the wares in the 1930s. The company was damaged by Hurricane Katrina in 2005 but was rebuilt and is still in business, now owned by Peter's four children.

Ashtray, Alkaline Blue, Green Blended, Squat, Notched Rim, 1950s, 2 x 4 In.	199
Bowl, Blended Sage Green, Brown, Flat Rim, Ring Foot, 1930s, 12 In. Diam.	655
Bowl, Flying Fish, J. McConnell & Peter Anderson, 1900s, 3¾ x 4¾ In.	1375
Bowl, Street Scene, People, Standing, Cast, Glazed, Peter Anderson, 1989, 5½ x 8 In. *illus*	2250
Bowl, Street Scene, Peter & James McConnel Anderson, 1994, 4 x 6 In.	1500
Bowl, Stylized Mermaid, Oval & Triangle Border, Multicolor, 9 In. Diam.	712
Candlestick, Blended Cobalt Blue, Double Cup, Spread Foot, 1930s, 5 In.	166
Charger, Hurricane Katrina Design, Signed, Christopher I. Stebly, 16 In.	896
Figurine, Baseball Players, Batting, Running, Catching, Ink Stamp, 6 In., 6 Piece	384
Figurine, Cubist Cat, Blue, Peter & Walter Anderson, 1900s, 9 x 14 In.	937
Figurine, Horse, Stylized, Turquoise, Cast, Glazed, Peter Anderson, 1950s, 13 In. *illus*	1250
Figurine, Tern, Walter Inglis & Peter Anderson, 1900s, 5¾ x 10¾ In.	3750
Pitcher, Blended Green, Mottled, Pickle Texture, Bulbous, Droop Handle, 6 In.	345
Pitcher, Blue Rain & Antique Green Glaze, Peter Anderson, 8½ In.	313
Plate, 2 Giraffes, Blue Geometric Ground, Marked, 10⅝ In.	438
Rose Bowl, Reticulated, Flowers & Leaves, Peter Anderson, 1930s, 4 x 8 In.	1875
Vase, Calla Lily, Peter & Walter Inglis Anderson, 1900s, 8 x 5½ In.	3000
Vase, Duck, Peter Anderson, Walter Inglis Anderson, 1900s, 7½ x 7 In.	6000
Vase, Figural, Fish, Celadon, 4½ In. *illus*	265
Vase, Fish, Peter Anderson & J. McConnell Anderson, 1900s, 7½ x 7 In.	4250
Vase, Flying Birds & Waves, Walter Inglis Anderson, c.1955, 8 x 5½ In.	3250
Vase, Flying Ducks, Waves, Glazed, Marked, Peter Anderson, c.1950, 7 x 6 In.	2375
Vase, Gray & Tan, Mottled, Ringed Design, Beaker, Ring Foot, Marked, 8 In.	335
Vase, Multicolor Swirls, Peter & Walter Inglis Anderson, 1900s, 6 x 4 In.	1875
Vase, Oval, Lizards, Swirling Leaves, Peter Anderson, 1950s, 10 x 6½ In.	8125
Vase, Sea, Earth & Sky, Green Glaze, Round, Shouldered, Rolled Rim, c.1945, 12 In.	2625
Vase, Sea, Earth, Sky, Glazed, Blue Over Brown, Waves, c.1945, 11 x 7 In.	5000
Vase, Spirit, Walter Inglis Anderson & Peter Anderson, c.1950, 6 In.	1250
Vase, Tennis Player, Blue, Peter & Walter Anderson, 1900s, 9 x 7 In.	4750
Vase, Tennis Players, Shouldered, Green, Peter Anderson, c.1925, 9 x 7 In.	4750
Vase, Waves & Fish, Peter & J. McConnell Anderson, 1900s, 8 x 6 In.	2750

SHEET MUSIC from the past centuries is now collected. The favorites are examples with covers featuring artistic or historic pictures. Early sheet music covers were lithographed, but by the 1900s photographic reproductions were used. The early music was larger than more recent sheets, and you must watch out for examples that were trimmed to fit in a twentieth-century piano bench.

Grand March, Composed In Honor Of Grant & Colfax Inauguration, 1869, 12 x 9 In.	117
Rose Marie, Gypsy Woman, Gus Edwards, Music Pub. Co., 1908, 10 x 13 In.	12
Wanting You From The New Moon, Harms Inc., 1928, 9 x 12 In.	10
What D'ya Say?, George White, Scandals, 1928, 9 x 11 In.	8
When Dreams Come True, Philip Bartholomae, 1913, 10 x 14 In. *illus*	10

SHEFFIELD *items are listed in the Silver Plate and Silver-English categories.*

SHELLEY first appeared on English ceramics about 1912. The Foley China Works started in England in 1860. Joseph Ball Shelley joined the company in 1862 and became a partner in 1872. Percy Shelley joined the firm in 1881. The company

Shirley Temple, Ring, Molded Image, Sterling Silver, Gold Washed, 1930s, Size 3
$95

Ruby Lane

Silver Deposit, Decanter, Cobalt Glass, Flowers, Stopper, c.1900, 9 x 3¾ In.
$244

Neal Auctions

Silver Deposit, Decanter, Pierced, Birds, Fish, Green Glass, Hinged Lid, Putto, c.1920, 11 In.
$1,250

New Orleans Auction Galleries

Silver Flatware Plated, Heritage, Dinner Knife, International Silver, 9⅜ In.

$10

Ruby Lane

> **TIP**
> Never drain silver on a rubber mat. It will tarnish faster.

Silver Plate, Biscuit Box, Shell Shaped, Lobed, Scrolling Blossoms Frame, Arched Feet, 9 x 9 In.

$281

Neal Auctions

Silver Plate, Stand, Fruit, William IV, Laurel, Paw Feet, Glass, Old Sheffield, 10 In.

$562

New Orleans Auction Galleries

432

went through a series of name changes and in 1910 the then Foley China Company became Shelley China. In 1929 it became Shelley Potteries. The company was acquired in 1966 by Allied English Potteries, then merged with the Doulton group in 1971. Shelley is no longer being made. A trio is the name for a cup, saucer, and cake plate set.

Ashtray, Morning Glory, 5 In.	32
Bonbon, Forget-Me-Not, 7¾ In.	38
Bowl, Cereal, Coupe, Hedgerow, 6½ In.	37
Bowl, Vegetable, Oval, Pastoral, 9 In.	87
Butter, Cover, Round, Morning Glory	256
Cake Plate, Handles, Square, Old Mill, 9¾ In.	135
Coffeepot, Dainty Blue, Small Flowers At Rim, 8 In. ....*illus*	104
Coffeepot, Lid, Hedgerow, Cup, 6¼ In.	369
Creamer, Green & Turquoise Luster Glaze, Streaked, 1930s	28
Cup & Saucer, Brown, Dainty, Scalloped Rim, c.1940, 5 In.	299
Cup & Saucer, Duchess, Footed	60
Cup & Saucer, Ferndown, Footed	41
Cup & Saucer, Lilac Time	125
Cup & Saucer, Melody, Pale Green Ground, Gilt Accents, 1938	95
Cup & Saucer, Morning Glory	90
Cup & Saucer, Old Mill	64
Cup & Saucer, Red & White, Striped, Gilt Leafy Scrolls, Scalloped Rim, 1940s	99
Cup & Saucer, Summer Glory	76
Gravy Boat, Underplate, Pastoral	146
Jar, Striped, Apple Shape, Blue, Pale Green, Pink, Lid, Stem Finial, 1930s, 4 x 4 In.	35
Nut Dish, Primrose, Yellow, Chintz, 4¾ In.	23
Plate, Bread & Butter, Forget-Me-Not, 6 In.	10
Plate, Bread & Butter, Old Mill, 6 In.	44
Plate, Bread & Butter, Pompadour, 6 In.	21
Platter, Hedgerow, Oval, 12 In.	158
Platter, Oval, Pompadour, 14 In.	235
Sugar, Lid, Handles, Pastoral, 3¼ In.	74
Teapot, Dubarry Maroon Pattern, Gilt, Upright Spout, Dome Lid, 1950s, 7 In.	99
Vase, Butterfly On Each Side, Multicolor, Walter Slater, Lusterware, 6¾ In. ....*illus*	295

 SHIRLEY TEMPLE, the famous movie star, was born in 1928. She made her first movie in 1932. She died in 2014. Thousands of items picturing Shirley have been and still are being made. Shirley Temple dolls were first made in 1934 by Ideal Toy Company. Millions of Shirley Temple cobalt blue glass dishes were made by Hazel Atlas Glass Company and U.S. Glass Company from 1934 to 1942. They were given away as premiums for Wheaties and Bisquick. A bowl, mug, and pitcher were made as a breakfast set. Some pieces were decorated with the picture of a very young Shirley, others used a picture of Shirley in her 1936 *Captain January* costume. Although collectors refer to a cobalt creamer, it is actually the 4½-inch-high milk pitcher from the breakfast set. Many of these items are being reproduced today.

Book, Shirley Temple The Real Little Girl, Saalfield Pub., Co., 1938	45
Button, Little Princess Contest, Portrait, c.1939, 1¼ In. Diam.	115
Doll, Composition, Blond Curls, Box, Ideal, c.1934, 21 In.	812
Doll, Composition, Jointed Arms, Brown Sleep Eyes, Ideal, 15 In.	81
Doll, Composition, Mohair Ringlets, Cowgirl Outfit, Dimples, 1930s, 27 In.	2495
Doll, Composition, Sleep Eyes, Eyelashes, Teeth, Curls, c.1935, 20 In.	105
Doll, Composition, Sleep Eyes, Open Mouth, Lashes, Ideal, c.1934, 19 In.	300
Doll, Composition, Socket Head, Sleep Eyes, Mohair Ringlets, Ideal, c.1935, 11 In. ....*illus*	285
Doll, Vinyl, Box, 1957, 15 In.	45
Figure, Shirley, Curtsy Pose, Pleated Dress, Plaster, 1930s, 15 In.	252
Plate, Captain January, Danbury Mint, c.1980, 8½ In.	19
Ring, 14K Gold, Over Silver, Blue Enamel, Portrait, c.1935, 2½ In.	115
Ring, Molded Image, Sterling Silver, Gold Washed, 1930s, Size 3 ....*illus*	95

SHRINER, see Fraternal category.

SILVER, *Sheffield, see Silver Plate; Silver-English categories.*

SILVER DEPOSIT glass was first made during the late nineteenth century. Solid sterling silver is applied to the glass by a chemical method so that a cutout design of silver metal appears against a clear or colored glass. It is sometimes called silver overlay.

Basket, Handle, Flowers, Basket Weave, Green, c.1905, 13 1/2 x 4 x 8 In.	1995
Cake Plate, Flowers, Leaves, Four Raised Feet, Cambridge, 11 3/4 In.	65
Decanter, Cobalt Glass, Flowers, Stopper, c.1900, 9 x 3 3/4 In.....................................*illus*	244
Decanter, Glass, Concave Sides, Bamboo Design, Chinese, c.1900, 10 In............................	62
Decanter, Pierced, Birds, Fish, Green Glass, Hinged Lid, Putto, c.1920, 11 In. ....*illus*	1250
Flask, Glass, Leafy Scroll Overlay, Dog Show Trophy, c.1910, 11 In.	1625
Perfume Bottle, Geometric Designs, Cranberry Glass, Globular, 4 3/8 In.	419
Perfume Bottle, Steuben Shape, Flowers, Stopper, Marked, Alvin, 4 1/2 In.	279
Pitcher, Flowers, Green Blown Glass, 8 3/4 In..	275

SILVER FLATWARE includes many of the current and out-of-production silver and silver-plated flatware patterns made in the past eighty years. Other silver is listed under Silver-American, Silver-English, etc. Most silver flatware sets that are missing a few pieces can be completed through the help of a silver matching service.

SILVER FLATWARE PLATED

Abbey Rose, Butter Knife, Hollow, Wallace, 6 3/4 In.	5
Abbey Rose, Salad Fork, Wallace, 6 In.	7
Abbey Rose, Serving Spoon, Pierced, Wallace, 8 1/2 In.	10
Acanthus, Fish Server, Rogers & Hamilton, 1886, 12 In.	69
Ada, Cream Soup Spoon, Wm. Rogers, 1959, 7 In.	6
Ada, Pastry Server, Wm. Rogers, 1959	15
Adam, Asparagus Server, Oneida, 1917, 9 1/2 In.	49
Adam, Cake Server, Oneida, 1917, 10 1/4 In.	16
Adam, Cocktail Fork, Oneida, 1917, 6 In.	7
Adam, Fork, Oneida, 1917, 7 In.	10
Adoration, Gravy Ladle, Rogers International, 1930, 6 In..	25
Adoration, Salad Fork, Rogers International, 1930, 6 3/4 In...	10
Alden, Casserole Spoon, Reed & Barton, 1905, 9 In.	24
Aloutte, Dinner Knife, Oneida, 1978, 9 In.	10
Aloutte, Serving Spoon, Pierced, Oneida, 1978, 8 In.	12
Aloutte, Teaspoon, Oneida, 1978, 6 In.	5
Chippendale, Cheese Knife, Frank Cobb, c.1970s, 8 In.	50
Fairoaks, Baby Spoon, Rockford Silver, 1909, 3 3/4 In.	12
Fiddle, Cold Meat Fork, Reed & Barton, 8 In.	16
Fiddle, Serving Spoon, Reed & Barton, 1979, 8 1/2 In.	18
Fiddle, Sugar Spoon, Shell Bowl, Reed & Barton, 6 In.	16
Florida, Master Butter, Flat Handle, Twisted, Wm. Rogers, 7 In.	18
Heritage, Dinner Knife, International Silver, 9 3/8 In..*illus*	10
Old English, Caddy Spoon, John Turner, 1798, 2 3/4 In.	200
Paul Revere, Cold Meat Fork, Oneida, 8 1/2 In.	14
Paul Revere, Dinner Knife, Hollow Handle, Oneida, 1927, 9 1/2 In.	8
Paul Revere, Fruit Spoon, Oneida, 5 1/2 In.	6
Paul Revere, Gravy Ladle, Oneida, 1927, 7 In.	20
Providence, Cold Meat Fork, Gorham, 1920, 7 In.	18
Providence, Tomato Server, Gorham, 7 3/4 In.	28
Shell, Serving Spoon, Scalloped Bowl, Sheffield, 10 In.	28
Tudor, Dessert Server, 1904, 10 1/2 In.	30
York, Ladle, W. Rogers, 1900, 7 In.	15

SILVER FLATWARE STERLING

Acanthus, Cold Meat Fork, Jensen, 1917, 9 In..	279
Acanthus, Dinner Knife, Short Handle, Jensen, 1917, 9 In..	119
Acanthus, Teaspoon, Jensen, 1917, 6 In...	69
Acorn, Cream Ladle, Georg Jensen, 6 x 1 3/4 In...	175

Silver-American, Coffeepot, Dome Lid, Lobed, Chased Flowers, Gorham, 1892, 8 In.

$369

Skinner, Inc.5

Silver-American, Cup, Presentation, Grape & Leaf, Handle, Coin, Hyde & Goodrick, c.1855, 4 1/2 In.

$500

Neal Auctions

Silver-American, Epergne, Scrolls, 4 Baskets, Bailey, Banks & Biddle, c.1900, 14 In.

$3,900

Brunk Auctions

S

Silver-American, Pie Server, Ancestry, Flowers, Leaves, Scrolls, Stainless, c.1955, 9 ½ x 2 In.
$45

Ruby Lane

Silver-American, Pitcher, Blossom Repousse, Twig Handle & Border, Pedestal Foot, Coin, c.1852, 14 In.
$5,795

Neal Auctions

Silver-American, Pitcher, Flower Sprays, Hammered, Gorham Martele, c.1907, 9 In.
$7,995

Skinner, Inc.

Adam, Butter Knife, Shreve, 8 ½ In.	49
Adam, Teaspoon, Shreve, 6 In.	37
Albemarle, Butter Knife, Blunt, Gorham, 1894, 9 In.	219
Albemarle, Demitasse Spoon, Gorham, 1894, 4 In.	29
Albemarle, Fork, Gorham, 1894, 7 In.	69
Albemarle, Lemon Fork, Gorham, 1894, 4 In.	39
Albemarle, Salad Serving Set, Pierced, Gorham, 1894, 9 In., 2 Piece	279
Arlington, Ice Cream Spoon, Towle, 5 In., 12 Piece	356
Broom Corn, Tomato Server, Lion, Ball, Tiffany & Co., 1890, 8 In.	475
Chrysanthemum, Bonbon Spoon, Durgin, c.1900, 5 ¼ In.	95
Courtship, Butter Knife, Flowers, c.1936, 7 ⅛ In.	45
Daisy, Master Butter, Flat Handle, Brite Cut, Towle, 7 In.	73
Dancing Flowers, Butter Spreader, Paddle, Reed & Barton, 6 In.	29
Dancing Flowers, Dinner Knife, Reed & Barton, 9 ½ In.	42
Dancing Surf, Fish Fork, Kirk, 7 In.	95
Dancing Surf, Pie Server, Kirk, 1986, 10 ¾ In.	59
Demitasse Spoon, Pear Shape, Box, William Suckling, 4 In., 6 Piece	141
Dew Drop, Master Butter, Flat Handle, Twisted, Shiebler, 8 In.	149
Diamond Star, Butter Spreader, Hollow Handle, Stieff, 6 In.	26
Diamond Star, Cold Meat Fork, Stieff, 1958, 8 ½ In.	99
Diamond Star, Knife, Stieff, 1958, 9 In.	39
Florentine, Berry Fork, Alvin, 1900, 4 ½ In.	26
Georgian, Cream Soup Spoon, Towle, 6 In.	49
Georgian, Fork, Towle, 7 ½ In.	129
Georgian, Ladle, Flowers In Bowl, Towle, 7 ½ In.	249
Georgian, Tomato Server, Towle, 7 ¾ In.	379
Lily Of The Valley, Asparagus Fork, Hammered, Whiting, 8 In.	977
Lily Of The Valley, Butter Spreader, Flat Handle, Whiting, 6 In.	115
Lily Of The Valley, Knife, Whiting, 1885, 9 ¼ In.	195
Lily Of The Valley, Nut Spoon, Pierced, Whiting, 4 ¾ In.	143
Lily, Sugar Tongs, Whiting, 1902, 4 In.	110
Louvre, Bouillon Spoon, Wallace Silver Company, 1893, 5 In.	35
Marlborough, Fruit Spoon, 5 ¾ In., 8 Piece	137
New King, Salad Fork, 3-Tine, Dominick & Haff, 6 In.	121
Queens Pattern, Fork, Georgian, Armorial, W. Eley, 7 In., 6 Piece	431
Repousse, Relish Fork, Kirk & Son, 7 ½ x 1 ¼ In.	110
Rose, Punch Ladle, Double Spout, Stieff, 14 ¾ In.	512
St. George, Ladle, Wallace, 1890, 10 ¼ In.	525
Violet, Butter Pick, Twisted, Wallace, 1904, 6 In.	120
Violet, Cake Breaker, Wallace, 9 In.	68
Violet, Cocktail Fork, Wallace, 1904, 6 In.	40
Violet, Demitasse Spoon, Wallace, 1904, 4 ¼ In.	28
Violet, Teaspoon, Wallace, 1904, 6 In.	47
Wild Rose, Berry Spoon, Watson, c.1900, 9 In.	295
Wild Rose, Dinner Knife, Watson, c.1900, 10 In.	94
Wild Rose, Grapefruit Spoon, Fluted, Watson	119

Ⓔ Ⓟ Ⓢ Ⓝ Ⓢ **SILVER PLATE** is not solid silver. It is a ware made of a metal, such as nickel or copper, that is covered with a thin coating of silver. The letters *EPNS* are often found on American and English silver-plated wares. *Sheffield* is a term with two meanings. Sometimes it refers to sterling silver made in the town of Sheffield, England. Sometimes it refers to an old form of plated silver.

Basket, Flowers, Gold Wash, Serpentine Rim, Webster & Son, 23 x 11 In.	236
Biscuit Box, Shell Shaped, Lobed, Scrolling Blossoms Frame, Arched Feet, 9 x 9 In. ...*illus*	281
Bowl, Batteau Shape, Figure Of Diana, Continental, 1900s, 10 ¾ x 14 x 6 In.	687
Box, Concave Lid, Turned Handle, Bonwit Teller, Italy, 1960s, 14 In.	708
Box, Lid, Hammered, Herringbone Design, Jean Despres, France, 9 In.	1250
Brazier, Lid, Skyscraper, Square, Tapered, Handles, Apollo, 6 x 12 In.	5100
Centerpiece, 1 Center & 2 Side Bowls, Leaves, Art Nouveau, 12 x 21 In.	500

Centerpiece, Amber Glass, Bird Handles, 10 x 13 In.	160
Centerpiece, Candle Cups, Scroll, Repousse, 39 x 15 In.	300
Centerpiece, Oval, Scalloped Edge, Etched, Eagles, 5 x 17 In.	687
Centerpiece, Scrolling Leaf Design, Curled Handles, Christofle, 21 x 14 In.	2640
Centerpiece, Seminude Woman, Feeding Swans, Onyx Base, c.1925, 31 In.	4053
Centerpiece, Wreaths, Reticulated, Loop Handles, Plinth, Scroll Feet, 17 In.	554
Cocktail Set, Shaker, 6 Cordials, Tray, Golf Balls, Derby Plate, 1925, 8 Piece	1375
Cocktail Shaker, Lighthouse Shape, 14 In.	320
Compote, Gucci, Art Deco, Spherical Resin Knob, Shallow Bowl, 1900s, 11 ¾ In.	531
Decanter Set, Rams Horn, 4 Shot Glasses, 12 In.	1750
Egg Holder, Oval, Half Fluted Sides, Wood Handles, Sheffield, 7 x 11 In.	177
Egg Stand, 4 Fluted Cups, Charles James Allen, England, 1800s, 8 In.	687
Epergne, Center Bowl, 4 Surrounding Glass Bowls, 4-Footed, 13 x 22 In.	688
Epergne, Crystal Bowls, Griffin Supports, Elkington, 1800s, 17 In., Pair	1800
Epergne, Etched Crystal, Scroll Legs, 24 x 24 In.	1500
Epergne, Lion Mask, Paw Feet, Glass Inserts, Diamond Point, 19 x 14 In.	1770
Epergne, Palm Tree & Goat Base, Glass Dish Top, Grapes, 12 ½ In.	240
Figurine, Woman, Kneeling, Left Arm Draped Over Head, 14 In.	94
Frame, Staves Of Asclepius & Caduceus, Continental, 1900s, 20 ¾ x 14 ½ In.	531
Grapefruit Holder, Scroll Openwork Petals, Saucer Foot, Rockport Co., 1940s	130
Group, Pheasants, Continental, 1900s, 5 ¼ x 10 ½ In.	200
Hot Water Urn, Heating Sleeve, Turned Wood Handles, Eng., 1800s, 15 In.	448
Jewelry Box, Embossed Flowers, Leaves, Velvet, Marked, 1960s, 5 x 4 In.	18
Kettle Stand, Elkington, 15 ½ In.	156
Meat Dome, Oval, Ring Finial, Akin Brothers, England, 1900s, 11 ¼ x 19 x 14 In.	312
Meat Dome, Well & Tree, Hot Water Reserve, Maple & Co., 14 x 22 In.	562
Mug, Flower Cartouche, Footed, C-Scroll Handle, England, 5 In., 12 Piece	500
Ornament, Table, Cornucopia, 1900s, 24 In.	375
Pap Boat, Eoff & Phyfe, 5 In.	200
Pitcher, Ebonized Handle, Christofle, 9 ½ x 5 In.	112
Pitcher, Ericuis For The SS Normandie, 5 ¼ x 6 In.	812
Prayer Box, Copper, Gau, Buddha & Dragons, Tibet, 1900s, 13 x 12 In.	562
Punch Cup, Round Bakelite Handles, 1 ½ x 4 In., 6 Piece	187
Sauceboat, Footed, Elkington & Co., 2 Piece	75
Sauceboat, Ladle, Blue, Flat Rim, Round Foot, 2 ½ x 7 In.	86
Sculpture, Puzzle, Il Cofanetto, Miguel Berrocal, Italy, Art Deco, 1970s, 8 x 8 x 5 ¾ In.	3750
Server, Pastry, Gilt, Flat Scrolling Scoop, Flowers & Leaves, 5 In.	345
Spoon, Caviar, Plique-A-Jour, Coiled Finger Grip, Scroll, 4 ½ In.	173
Spoon, Plique-A-Jour, Serving, Multicolor Flowers, 10 x 2 In.	374
Spoon, Souvenir, see Souvenir category.	
Stand, Fruit, William IV, Laurel, Paw Feet, Glass, Old Sheffield, 10 In. *illus*	562
Supper Service, Revolving, Hot Water Reservoir, 1900s, 7 Piece	750
Tazza, Art Deco, Round, Stepped Foot, Jean Puiforcat, 2 x 5 ½ In.	343
Tea & Coffee Set, Teapot, Coffeepot, Sugar & Creamer, Tray, Gallery, 5 Piece	63
Tea & Coffee Set, Teapot, Coffeepot, Sugar, Creamer, Waste Bowl, Heritage, 6 Piece	156
Tea Set, Teapot, Sugar & Creamer, Berliner Elektroplate Warenfabrik, 8 x 9 In.	187
Tea Set, Teapot, Sugar & Creamer, Lobed, 5 In., 3 Piece	299
Tea Set, Teapot, Sugar & Creamer, Orange Bakelite, Meriden, c.1930, 3 Piece	300
Tea Set, Teapot, Sugar & Creamer, Tray, Puck Shape, Christofle, 4 Piece	1062
Tea Set, Teapot, Sugar & Creamer, Tray, Wood Handles, 1940, 4 Piece	325
Teapot, Immortals, Chased, Chinese, 3 ½ x 4 In.	125
Toast Rack, Triangles, Joseph Rodgers & Sons, 7 x 6 In.	671
Tray, Dresser, Cherubs, Ribbed Border, 10 ½ x 7 ¼ In.	68
Tray, Fan Shape, Argentor, Art Nouveau, Austria, 26 x 18 In.	50
Tray, Frog, Lily Pad, Bird, Flower, Branch Handles, 4 x 9 x 10 In.	178
Tray, Leaves, Lattice, Claw Feet, Gorham, 30 x 21 ½ In.	141
Tray, Oval, Flat Stamped Triangle Arabesques, Handles, 1800s, 29 x 18 ¾ In.	406
Tray, Plateau, Rococo, Scrolls, Flowers, c.1880, 3 x 16 In.	562
Tray, Scalloped, Reticulated Gallery, Etched Scroll, Lattice, 23 x 17 In.	395
Tureen, Lid, Ivory Knob, Fluted Legs, Paw Feet, Revolves, 1800s, 8 x 13 In.	120

Silver-American, Pitcher, Repousse, Flower Sprays, S. Kirk & Son Co., c.1910, 13 In.
$3,690

Skinner, Inc.

Silver-American, Pitcher, Repousse, Grapevines, Flowers Border, Samuel Kirk, c.1824, 12 In.
$2,706

Skinner, Inc.

Silver-American, Sugar & Creamer, Repousse, Coin, Mitchell & Tyler, Virginia, c.1860, 4 & 7 In.
$875

New Orleans Auction Galleries

S

Silver-American, Tablespoon, Downturned Handle Tip, Oval Bowl, Engraved, Revere, 8¾ In.

$3,840

Neal Auctions

Silver-American, Tankard, Dome Lid, S-Curve Handle, Coin, John Allen, John Edwards, c.1700, 8 In.

$14,520

James D. Julia Auctioneers

Silver-American, Tea Canister, Lid, Hammered, Copper, Lily, Pheasant, Gorham, 1880, 5 In.

$3,321

Skinner, Inc.

TIP

Never wash silver and stainless steel together, not even in a dishwasher.

Tureen, Lid, Loop Handles, JR & S, 16 In.	50
Urn, Neoclassical, Banding, Swags, Round Foot, 19½ In.	938
Urn, Tapered, Twisted Design, Henry Wilkinson & Co., 1800, 22 In., Pair	2500
Vase, Arts & Crafts, Turquoise Glass Cabochons, Handles, c.1910, 7 x 4 In.	976
Vase, Bean Shape, Lino Sabattini, 4 x 12½ In.	312
Vase, Glass Stand & Trumpet Vase, J. Deakin, England, 1800s, 22½ In.	625
Vase, Portland, Classical Figures, Relief, England, c.1900, 9 In.	861
Vase, Swans, Columns, Trumpet Shape, Paw Feet, 17 In., Pair	375
Wine Cooler, 4 Holders, Center Ice Well, Royal Castle, Sheffield, 10 In.	549
Wine Cooler, Swing Handle, 1900s, 28½ x 9¼ x 12¼ In.	687
Wine Cooler, Urn Shape, Fluted, Handles, Stepped Pedestal, Base, 9 In., Pair	510
Wine Trolley, Gun Carriage, Spoked Wheels, Beaded Rims, 1900s, 9 In.	562
Wine Trolley, Tilbury Carriage Shape, Leafy Scrolls, Bacchus Crest, 7 x 16 In.	2250

SILVER-AMERICAN. American silver is listed here. Coin and sterling silver are included. Most of the sterling silver listed in this book is subdivided by country. There are also other pieces of silver and silver plate listed under special categories, such as Candelabrum, Napkin Ring, Silver Flatware, Silver Plate, Silver-Sterling, and Tiffany Silver. The meltdown price determines the value of solid silver items. These prices are based on current silver values.

Basin, Wide Flat Rim, Stylized Family Crest, Coin, 1700, 2 x 13 In.	948
Berry Bowl, Francis I Pattern, Reed & Barton, c.1910, 8 In. Diam., Pair	562
Bezique Set, Embossed Flowers, William B. Durgin Co., c.1910, 4 x 7 In.	875
Bonbon, Grape Leaf Shape, Grape Cluster, Watson Co., 7¼ In.	201
Bonbon, Repousse, Flowers, Leaves, Schebler, c.1900, 7 In.	275
Bowl, Applied RH Monogram, Falick Novick, 2 x 9 In.	812
Bowl, Art Deco, Wheat, Orchid, Oval, 12¼ x 7½ In.	531
Bowl, Centerpiece, Flowers, Domed Foot, Galt & Brother, 5 x 10 In.	468
Bowl, Cow Handles, Footed, Gorham, c.1857, 3 x 7 x 5½ In.	413
Bowl, Flower Petals, Footed, Kalo Shop, 4½ x 12 In.	1830
Bowl, Francis I, Reed & Barton, Ernest Meyers, c.1907, 8 In.	2125
Bowl, Hammered, Copper Flowers & Insects, Footed, Whiting, 4 x 8 In.	3199
Bowl, Hammered, Undulating Rim, Raised Foot, Wallace, c.1880, 4 x 11 In.	500
Bowl, Lid, All Over Repousse, Leaf Rim, S. Kirk & Son, c.1930, 10 In.	2040
Bowl, Old Lace, Designs On Rim, Wallace, c.1950, 4 x 10 In.	300
Bowl, Openwork, Leaves, Flowers, Engraving, Octagonal, 14 In.	875
Bowl, Oval, Hammered, Arts & Crafts, Whiting, Mid 1900s, 12¼ In.	677
Bowl, Paul Revere Reproduction, Reed & Barton, 4 x 8 In., Pair	460
Bowl, Pierced Rocaille, Engraved A & B, 8 In.	175
Bowl, Rolled Rim, Elevated Corners, Flowers, Reed & Barton, 3 x 9 In.	281
Bowl, Shallow, Lobed, 1900s, 11½ In.	562
Bowl, Shaped, Reeded Rim, Stamped Arthur Stone, 7 In.	431
Bowl, Vegetable, Lid, Gorham, 11¾ In.	418
Bowl, Vegetable, Scalloped Rim, Monogram, Meriden Britannia, 9 x 6 In.	519
Bowl, Vegetable, Shaped Rim, Relief Border, Scroll, c.1910, 12 In., Pair	1625
Bowl, Wide Rim, Foot, Wallace, 17 In.	593
Bread Basket, Round Corners, Reticulated, Dominick & Haff, 12 x 9 In.	855
Bread Plate, Leaves, Openwork, Wyler, 7 In., 12 Piece	1250
Butter Pat, Repousse, Kirk & Son, 3¼ In., 12 Piece	656
Cake Basket, Footed, Flower & Shell Border, Coin, E. Lowne, c.1825, 11 x 11 In.	1220
Cake Basket, Pierced Leafy Panels, Lattice Ground, 12½ In.	2000
Cake Plate, Pierced Border, Tapered Foot, J.E. Caldwell & Co., 12 In.	501
Candelabra are listed in the Candelabrum category.	
Candlesticks are listed in their own category.	
Candy Dish, Scroll Leaves, Ribbed, Serpentine Rim, Gorham, 3 x 7 In., Pair	318
Carving Set, Fork & Knife, Reeded, Repousse, Flowers, Towle, 1898	310
Carving Set, Repousse Flower Handles, Stainless Steel Blades, 3 Piece	173
Centerpiece, Fruiting Grapevines, Satyr Heads, Wavy Rim, 13 x 19 In.	9000
Cigar Jar, Vignette, Enamel, 1900, 6¼ In.	625

S

Cigarette Case, Chevron Design, Leather Sleeve, Art Deco, Gorham, c.1930, 4 x 3 In.	308
Claret Jug, Putti, Grapevines, Cut Glass, Loop Handle, 14 In.	1000
Coffee & Tea Set, Coffeepot, Teapot, Sugar, Creamer, Tray, Rogers Co., 6 Piece	875
Coffee & Tea Set, Squat, C-Scroll Handle, Gorham, 1959, 5 Piece	900
Coffee Set, Coffeepot, Sugar, Creamer, Maintenon, International, 3 Piece	579
Coffeepot, Baltimore Rose, Allover Flowers, Schofield Co., 13 In.	1440
Coffeepot, Dome Lid, Lobed, Chased Flowers, Gorham, 1892, 8 In. ....*illus*	369
Coffeepot, Sugar, Creamer, Tray, Ivory, Monogram, F. Novick, 4 Piece	5795
Compact, Repousse, Mirror, Felt Bag, Wallace, Late 1800s, 3 In.	30
Compote, Birds & Grapevines, Neiman Marcus, Late 1900s, 6 ½ In.	738
Compote, Chased Rim, 6 ½ In., Pair	50
Compote, Fluted Panels, 3 Points, Flowers, 10 ½ In.	437
Compote, Francis I, Reed & Barton, 1900s, 5 x 8 In., Pair	593
Compote, Grapes & Grape Leaves, 7 x 10 ½ In.	541
Compote, Lion Mask, Leafy Rim, Handles, Wood & Hughes, 8 x 13 In.	1116
Compote, Repousse, Flowers, Handles, 1800s, 7 ¾ x 11 In.	1586
Compote, Ruby Glass, 4 Flower Sprays On Base, Early 1900s, 6 x 6 In.	60
Compote, Weighted, Watson Co., c.1940, 7 ½ x 5 In., Pair	312
Cordial, Flared Rim, Round Foot, Presentation Box, Towle, 3 In., 6 Piece	277
Cream Pail, Ladle, Cattails, Durgin, 1898, 2 Piece	162
Creamer, Classical, Helmet Shape, Lobed, Coin, S. Chaudron, c.1820, 6 In.	750
Cup, Family Crests, Shield, 3 Handles, Gorham, c.1880, 5 In.	250
Cup, Iris, Galmer Sterling, 3 In.	356
Cup, Mint Julep, Kentucky, William Kendrick, 3 ¾ x 3 In., Pair.	687
Cup, Presentation, Grape & Leaf, Handle, Coin, Hyde & Goodrick, c.1855, 4 ½ In. ....*illus*	500
Cup, Tapered, Inscribed, Touchmark, Coin, R. & W. Wilson, 4 In.	74
Dish, Entree, Chased Flowers, Oval, Shell Handles, Dominick & Haff, 12 In.	875
Dish, Entree, Lid, Handles, Gorham, 10 ½ In.	468
Dish, Lid, Repousse Flowers, Kirk & Son, c.1900, 4 x 10 x 7 In.	1680
Dish, Rope Handle, Sciarrotta, 13 In.	1500
Dish, Shell Shape, Winged Cupid, Gorham, Monogram, c.1872, 10 In.	1599
Dresser Box, Flower Sprays, Rocaille, Monogram, Gorham, c.1900, 7 In.	523
Entree Dish, Oval, Flower Scroll Rim, Gorham, 1906, 5 x 11 ¾ x 8 ¾ In.	437
Epergne, Scrolls, 4 Baskets, Bailey, Banks & Biddle, c.1900, 14 In. ....*illus*	3900
Ewer, Repousse Flower, Horses, Hayden Brothers & Co., c.1850, 16 In.	6600
Flask, Drinking Scene, Hinged Cap, Wallace & Sons, c.1875, 5 In.	472
Flask, Repousse Flowers, Mushroom Cap, Stieff, c.1925, 5 ½ In.	840
Goblet, Flared Rim, Stepped Foot, Kirk & Son, 6 x 3 In., 4 Piece.	271
Goblet, Flower Wreath, Flared Rim, Coin, J. Kitts, Kentucky, c.1860, 7 In.	660
Goblet, Inverted Bell Shape, Waisted Stem, Domed Foot, Fischer, 7 In., 8 Piece	937
Goblet, Rose Pattern, Chased, Leaves, Stieff, 1956, 9 In., 6 Piece	2478
Goblet, Wreath Cartouche, Cow, 5 In.	3068
Gravy Boat, Applied Monogram, ERH, Falick Novick, 4 ½ x 9 In.	218
Gravy Ladle, Coin, T.I Marsh, 6 ½ In.	472
Inkstand & Pen, Gorham, Rococo Style, Hinged, 1892, 8 x 6 In.	1500
Jug, Silver Mounted Cut Glass, Claret, Gorham, 1900s, 11 ½ x 4 In.	750
Julep Cup, Reeded Rim & Foot, Inscribed, Marked, Blanchard, c.1810, 3 In.	3000
Julep Cup, Wreath Cartouche, Molded Rim, Coin, c.1820, 3 ½ In.	501
Kettle Stand, Leaves, Shells, 10 ½ In.	529
Ladle, Tapered Handle, Monogram, Coin, C.L. Boehme, c.1800, 14 In.	478
Ladle, Tipt Fiddle Handle, Rounded Fins, John Campbell, 14 In.	4500
Loving Cup, Leaves, Flowers, Theodore B. Starr, 8 In.	562
Mug, Coat Of Arms, Scroll Handle, Molded Foot, Jacob Hurd, c.1735, 5 In.	4920
Mug, Paneled, Charleston, c.1850, 3 ¼ In.	472
Mug, Tapered, Bead Border, S. Carolina, Coin, Radcliffe & Guignard, 4 In.	660
Mug, Tapered, Reeded Rim, Scroll Handle, Hayden Bros., 1852, 3 ½ In.	780
Napkin Rings are listed in their own category.	
Pie Knife, Flowers & Leaves, 10 ¼ In.	49
Pie Server, Ancestry, Flowers, Leaves, Scrolls, Stainless, c.1955, 9 ½ x 2 In. ....*illus*	45
Pitcher, Band, Graff, Washbourne & Dunn, 10 ½ In.	812

Silver-American, Tray, Flower Sprays, Undulating Rim, Martele, Gorham, c.1909, 31 In.
$8,610

Skinner, Inc.

Silver-American, Tureen, Lid, Stag Finial, Beaded Rim, Ring Handles, Hyde & Goodrich, 12 x 11 In.
$18,910

Neal Auctions

Silver-American, Tureen, Lid, Urn Shape, Monogram, Loop Handles, Inscribed, Gorham, 1892, 15 In.
$1,845

Skinner, Inc.

S

Silver-Chinese, Dish, Reticulated, Dragons, Blossoms, Medallion, Shanghai, c.1900, 11 In.
$861

Skinner, Inc.

TIP
Rub silverware lengthwise when cleaning.

Silver-Chinese, Mirror, White Jade, Hardstone Cabochons, H.K. Silver, c.1900, 12 In.
$6,000

Brunk Auctions

Silver-Continental, Ice Trolley, Carriage Shape, Chased Flowers, Wheels, Tongs, c.1975, 12 In.
$1,125

New Orleans Auction Galleries

Pitcher, Band, Round Foot, Lebkuecher & Co., 10 ½ In.	625
Pitcher, Blossom Repousse, Twig Handle & Border, Pedestal Foot, Coin, c.1852, 14 In. ...... *illus*	5795
Pitcher, Crested Handle, Gorham 1900s, 8 ¾ x 9 x 6 In.	937
Pitcher, Engraved Cartouche, Bulbous, Meriden Britannia, 8 In.	660
Pitcher, Flower Sprays, Hammered, Gorham Martele, c.1907, 9 In. ...... *illus*	7995
Pitcher, Flowers, Leaves, Mauser, 9 ½ In.	812
Pitcher, Kalo Shop, c.1917, 6 ½ x 8 In.	1586
Pitcher, Leaves & Scrolls, Squat, Durgin, 7 ½ In.	437
Pitcher, Monogrammed, Gorham 1953, 8 ¾ x 8 ¾ x 5 ½ In.	375
Pitcher, Monogrammed, Schofield Co., 1900s, 9 ¼ x 8 ¾ x 5 ¾ In.	531
Pitcher, Presentation, Fruits & Tree, Scroll Handle, c.1850, 12 In.	1680
Pitcher, Repousse Flowers, Helmet Shape, Twig Handle, c.1900	1888
Pitcher, Repousse, Flower Sprays, S. Kirk & Son Co., c.1910, 13 In. ...... *illus*	3690
Pitcher, Repousse, Grapevines, Flowers Border, Samuel Kirk, c.1824, 12 In. ...... *illus*	2706
Pitcher, Repousse, Roses, Grapevine, Baltimore Silversmiths, c.1903, 9 In.	1736
Pitcher, Water, Melon Lobed, Footed, Dominick & Haff, 1938, 9 In.	780
Pitcher, Water, Repousse Flowers, Leafy Spout, Stieff, 9 ¼ In.	1680
Pitcher, Water, Swollen, Scroll Handle, J.E. Caldwell & Co., 12 In.	1440
Platter, Relief Pinecones, Round, Scroll Rim, T.B. Starr, N. York, 14 In.	948
Platter, Shells, Flowers, Rocaille, Monogram, Oval, Redlich & Co., 14 In., Pair	2074
Platter, Shells, Flowers, Rocaille, Monogram, Round, Redlich & Co., 17 In., Pair	2074
Platter, Shields, Laurel, Gadroon, Incised Rim, Oval, c.1915, 22 x 17 In.	1500
Platter, Turtleback Shape Rim, Reeded Edge, Gorham, 1925, 19 x 14 In.	1875
Porringer, Flat Rim, Reticulated Handle, Gorham, 7 x 5 In., Pair	171
Porringer, Keyhole Handle, Jacob Hurd, 1740, 7 ½ In.	4560
Porringer, Pierced Scroll Handle, S. Minott, Boston, c.1770, 8 x 5 In.	1845
Punch Bowl, Gold Wash Interior, 3 Handles, Ladle, Meriden Britannia, 1900s, 14 In.	1476
Punch Bowl, Leafy Rim, 13 In.	750
Punch Bowl, Stylized Leaves, Footed, Wilcox, 9 x 14 In.	192
Punch Bowl, Underplate, Ladle, Shreve, Crump & Low, c.1880, 10 x 10 x 13 In.	5250
Punch Ladle, Coffin Handle, Coin, Asa Blanchard, 14 In.	944
Salad Server, Colonial, Engraved O, 10 In., 2 Piece	92
Salt & Pepper, Ball Finial, Star, Kalo Shop, 3 ¼ x 1 ¾ In.	244
Salt, Chased Leaves, Shield, Footed, c.1895, 1 ¾ In.	94
Salver, Monogram, Flower Frame, Chased Leafy Scroll, c.1860, 7 In.	277
Scroll, Flower Swag, Gorham, 10 ¾ In., 12 Piece	6875
Sculpture, Eagle, Takeoff Pose, Wood Base, Plaque, G. Roberts, 15 In.	5333
Seafood Fork, Seashell, Gorham, c.1885, 5 ¾ In.	333
Serving Dish, Lid, Repousse Flowers, Handles, Splay Feet, c.1885, 14 In., Pair	5228
Serving Spoon, Elias Pelitreau, Southhampton, New York, c.1770, 8 In.	492
Stuffing Spoon, Hammered, Tapered Handle, Shaped End, Kalo, 12 In.	120
Sugar & Creamer, Lid, Tray, Rings, Engraved, Rogers, 1907, 3 Piece	535
Sugar & Creamer, Parcel Gilt, Repousse, Wood & Hughes, 2 Piece	207
Sugar & Creamer, Repousse, Coin, Mitchell & Tyler, Virginia, c.1860, 4 & 7 In. ...... *illus*	875
Sugar, Chased Scroll, Urn, Leaf Handles, Lid, Flower Finial, c.1850, 9 In.	554
Sugar, Lid, Repousse Flowers, Urn Shape, Scroll Handles, Stieff, 6 x 8 In.	240
Tablespoon, Downturned Handle Tip, Oval Bowl, Engraved, Revere, 8 ¾ In. ...... *illus*	3840
Tankard, Dome Lid, S-Curve Handle, Coin, John Allen, John Edwards, c.1700, 8 In. ...... *illus*	14520
Tea & Coffee Set, Chateau Rose, Teapot, Coffeepot, Sugar, Creamer, Alvin, 5 In.	1625
Tea & Coffee Set, Coffeepot, Teapot, Sugar & Creamer, Tray, 6 Piece	1062
Tea & Coffee Set, Coffeepot, Teapot, Sugar, Creamer, Fluted, Gorham, 4 Piece	395
Tea Canister, Lid, Hammered, Copper, Lily, Pheasant, Gorham, 1880, 5 In. ...... *illus*	3321
Tea Set, Bellflower, Tapered Sides, Meriden Britannia, 5 Piece	960
Tea Set, Kensington, Teapot, Sugar Bowl, Creamer & Waste Bowl, Gorham	875
Tea Set, Leaf Band, Lobed, Scroll Handle, Footed, Coin, P. Chitry, 3 Piece	1560
Tea Set, Melon Lobed, Footed, Virginia, Dominick & Haff, 5 Piece	3360
Tea Set, Teapot, Sugar, Creamer, Waste Bowl, Flowers, W. B. North & Co., 4 Piece	1298
Tea Set, Teapot, Sugar, Ebonized Handle, J.E. Floyd, 3 Piece	625
Teapot, Inverted Pear Shape, Flowers & Scroll, Lid, c.1760s, 6 x 5 In.	1845
Teaspoon, Architectural Design, Charles Robbins, 1898, 6 In., 12 Piece	159

Teaspoon, Paul Revere, PJP Monogram, Boston, Late 1700s, 5 In.	3198
Toasting Fork, La Pierre, c.1890, 6¾ x 2 In.	110
Tray, Carving, Oval, Rocaille Rim, Recessed Well, Splayed Feet, c.1910, 10 In.	1353
Tray, Chased, Repousse, Canted Corners, Stieff, 28 x 19 In.	4838
Tray, Cherry, Wallace, 11 x 7 In.	337
Tray, Ensko, 2 Handles, New York, 1900s, 21½ In.	1353
Tray, Flower Sprays, Undulating Rim, Martele, Gorham, c.1909, 31 In. ....*illus*	8610
Tray, Monogram, Repousse Rim, Ball & Claw Feet, S. Kirk & Son, 12 In.	1560
Tray, Plymouth Pattern, Oval, Handles, Gorham, c.1975, 25 In.	1970
Tray, Raised Orchids, Leafy Rim, 2 x 10 x 7 In.	173
Tray, Shell Shape, Scalloped Edge, Reeded, Gorham, 6 In.	213
Tray, Standish, Gorham, 1900s, 20 In.	800
Tureen, Lid, Crest, Cartouche, Wood & Hughes, c.1850, 15½ In.	3500
Tureen, Lid, Stag Finial, Beaded Rim, Ring Handles, Hyde & Goodrich, 12 x 11 In. ....*illus*	18910
Tureen, Lid, Urn Shape, Monogram, Loop Handles, Inscribed, Gorham, 1892, 15 In. ....*illus*	1845
Tureen, Louis XV, Oval, Footed, Flared Open Handles, Whiting, 1899, 12 In.	840
Vanity Set, Mirror, Brush, Comb, Button Hook, Nail Buffer, Shoehorn, c.1903, 9 Piece	805
Vase, 2 Swan's Head Handles, Fluted Rim, Tuttle, 9½ In.	1375
Vase, Flowers, Chased, Domed Foot, Martele, Gorham, 9 In.	8750
Vase, Plateau, Paneled, Shells & Scroll, Garland, Durgin, c.1910, 14 In.	1475
Vase, Trumpet, Arch Handle, Clarence Vanderbilt, America, c.1910, 10 In.	219
Waste Bowl, Beaded Rim, 5½ In.	1298

SILVER-ASIAN

Bowl, Repousse Design, Figures, Squat, Relief Rim, Footed, c.1900, 15 In.	948

SILVER-AUSTRIAN

Cigarette Box, Engine Turned, Central Oval, Tigers, 4 x 3 In.	375
Plaque, Open Scroll Rococo Shield, Late 1800s, 24 x 16 In.	1187
Salver, Repousse, Flower Swags, Ribbons, Pierced Feet, 9 In., Pair	300
Tazza, Birds, Flowering Branches, Stepped Base, Lion Mask, 12 x 10 In.	438
Tray, Leaves, Oval, Pierced Border, Beaded Rim, Handles, 1801, 12 x 7 In.	472

SILVER-CANADIAN

Berry Spoon, Wire Handle, Flower Blossom, Carl Pendersen, 8¼ In.	38

SILVER-CHINESE

Beaker, Peasants, Rocaille Cartouche, Chased, Engraved, 1851, 2 In., Pair	492
Bowl, Bamboo & Cherry Blossoms, Dragons & Scholars, 1800s, 8¼ In.	1968
Bowl, Flowers, Collet Foot, Threaded Rim, Cartouche, Late 1800s, 3¼ In.	400
Bowl, Flowers, Panels, Round, Beaded Rim, Leaf Handles, c.1900, 14 In.	1169
Bowl, Relief Irises, Monogram, Characters, c.1900, 4½ x 8½ In.	2160
Bowl, Scalloped Rim, Birds, Cherry Branches, Spread Feet, 3 x 6 In.	518
Box, Doorknob Shape, Domed, Beaded, Animal, Repousse, c.1925, 2 x 2 In.	125
Dish, Reticulated, Dragons, Blossoms, Medallion, Shanghai, c.1900, 11 In. ....*illus*	861
Figurine, Horse, Silver, Enamel, Coral, Turquoise & Gold Wash, 5 In.	173
Figurine, Warrior, Enamel, Gold, Coral & Turquoise, Su Hai, 6 In.	288
Jewelry Box, Jade, Velvet, Edward Farmer, c.1910, 3 x 7 In.	4375
Mirror, White Jade, Hardstone Cabochons, H.K. Silver, c.1900, 12 In. ....*illus*	6000
Plaque, Horse In Flight, Welcome To The Chinese Exhibition, 2⅞ x 2½ In.	687
Tea Service, Teapot, Creamer, Sugar, Hung Chong & Co., Late 1800s, Teapot 4⅛ In.	3198
Tea Strainer, Flowers, Reticulated Bamboo, 7 In.	138
Teapot, Chased, Chrysanthemums, Curved Spout, 8¼ In.	1125
Teapot, Shouldered, Twist Finial, 5¼ In.	258
Tray, Bamboo Edge, Engraved Birds, Insects & Flowers, Early 1900s, 14¾ In.	2091

SILVER-CONTINENTAL

Beaker, Flowers & Leaves, 3½ x 3 In.	281
Berry Set, Bowl, Sugar Sifter, Tongs, Repousse, Berries, Box, 3 Piece	265
Box, Coffin Shape, Flowers & Leaves, 1800s, 6 In.	281
Cigarette Case, Enamel, Gray, Rectangular, 1926, 3⅛ In.	344
Cigarette Case, Light Blue, 3⅛ In.	625
Creamer, Cow Shape, Horns, Loop Tail Handle, 5¼ In.	875

Silver-Continental, Pitcher, Engraved, Applied Bands, Crest Handle, Buccellati, Italy, 11 In.
$1,500

New Orleans Auction Galleries

Silver-Danish, Gravy Boat, Leaf, Loop Handle, G. Jensen, c.1950, 5 x 8 In.
$1,250

Rago Arts and Auction Center

TIP
Don't store silver in old newspapers. The ink will react with the metal and will slowly remove silver plating.

Silver-English, Chafing Dish, Reeded, Tripod Stand, Hoof Feet, Robert Sharp, 1792, 8 x 10 In.
$1,320

Cowan's Auctions

Silver-English, Condiment Set, Penguins, Glass Eyes, Comyns & Son, 1960s, 3 In., 3 Piece
$2,000

New Orleans Auction Galleries

Silver-English, Hot Water Urn, Wrigglework Bands, Beaded Spout, C. Wright, c.1755, 21 In.
$3,000

New Orleans Auction Galleries

Silver-English, Monteith, Repousse Flowers, Crenellated Rim, Coin, S. Kirk & Son, 6 x 9 In.
$2,337

Cowan's Auctions

Figurine, Pheasant, Etched Feathers, Spread Wings, c.1900, 21 In., Pair	2750
Ice Trolley, Carriage Shape, Chased Flowers, Wheels, Tongs, c.1975.12 In. *illus*	1125
Pitcher, Engraved, Applied Bands, Crest Handle, Buccellati, Italy, 11 In. *illus*	1500
Punch Ladle, Gold Wash Bowl, 13½ In.	50
Spice Tower, Castle, 3 Spires, Flags, Trumpet Base, 7½ In.	163
Tray, Chased, Cavalry Charge, Handles, Footed, 17¼ In.	531
Vase, Chased Lozenges, Stippled, Applied Gilt Flowers, Ruffled, 5 In.	244

SILVER-DANISH

Bowl, Harald Nielsen For Georg Jensen, 4 In., 12 Piece	2125
Bowl, Henning Kopel For Georg Jensen, c.1948, 15½ In.	8125
Bowl, Lid, Round, Sigvard Bernadette For Georg Jensen, 10 In., Pair	6250
Bowl, Shallow, Harald Nielsen, Georg Jensen, 1900s, 9½ In	687
Brandy Warmer, Hammered, Beading, Spout, Georg Jensen, 2 In.	738
Coffee & Teapot, Ivory Handle, Svend Weihrauch, 2 Piece	937
Compote, Shallow Bowl, Slender Stem, Georg Jensen, c.1910, 5 In., Pair	1046
Cup, Blue Enamel, Fluted, Bands, 3½ x 6½ In.	490
Dish, Lid, Tulip Finial, Pierced Tulip Foot, 5½ In.	600
Grape Shears, Figures, Grapevines, Georg Jensen	250
Gravy Boat, Leaf, Loop Handle, G. Jensen, c.1950, 5 x 8 In. *illus*	1250
Nutmeg Grater, Engraved Flowers, Hinged Lid, Side Panel, 2¾ In.	531
Pitcher, Figural Head On Base Of Handle, 10 In.	250
Pitcher, Hammered, Ribbed Bottom, Georg Jensen, c.1930, 9 In.	2242
Pitcher, Johann Rohde For Georg Jensen, 11¼ In.	3000
Salad Servers, Fork & Spoon, 8¼ In., 2 Piece	406
Salt & Pepper, Ove Brobeck, Georg Jensen, Late 1900s, 1½ In., 6 Piece	750
Samovar, Lobed, Ebony Handle, Beaded Stand, G. Jensen, 1930, 12 In.	3690
Sauceboat, Scroll Handle, Round Foot, Johann Rohde For Georg Jensen, 6½ In., Pair	2250
Sauceboat, Undertray & Ladle, Blossom Motif, George Jensen, 1900s, 4¾ x 8⅛ In.	2337
Sugar & Creamer, Lobed, Capped Handles, Georg Jensen, 2 Piece	1375
Tazza, Swirl Stem, Hanging Grape Clusters, Flared, G. Jensen, c.1930, 7 In., Pair	5000
Tea Set, Blossom Pattern, Lobed, Carved Ivory Handle, G. Jensen, 5 Piece	5333
Tray, Round, Gadroon Oval Ebony Handles, G. Jensen, c.1930, 21 In.	3750
Waiter, Lobed, Hammered, Round, G. Jensen, Late 1900s, 10 In.	937

SILVER-DUTCH

Condiment Jar, Swans, Cobalt Blue Glass Insert, 1800s, 6 In.	406

SILVER-EGYPTIAN

Tea & Coffee Set, Teapot, Coffeepot, 2 Creamers, Tray, 5 Piece	1750
Tray, Oval, Flower Border, Handles, 20½ x 13 In.	750
Tray, Rectangular, Beaded, 21 x 11 In.	750
Tray, Round, Elephants, Animals, 15½ In.	625
Tray, Round, Embossed Flowers, 16 In.	625
Tray, Round, Repousse, Flowers, Fruit, 24½ x 16 In.	1187

 SILVER-ENGLISH. English sterling silver is marked with a series of four or five small hallmarks. The standing lion mark is the most commonly seen sterling quality mark. The other marks indicate the city of origin, the maker, and the year of manufacture. These dates can be verified in many good books on silver. These prices are based on current silver values.

Basin, Oval, Scroll Handles, Engraved Horse Head Crest, c.1812, 10 In., Pair	1968
Basket, Repousse, Wheat, Flowers, Pierced Swing Handle, 6 x 5 In.	152
Basket, Reticulated Panels, Shaped Handle, W. Plummer, 14 x 11 In.	1680
Basket, Reticulated, Pierced, Martin, Hall & Co., c.1880, 5 x 14½ In.	84
Basket, Sweetmeat, Georgian, Gold Wash, Engraved, H. Chawner, 6 x 4 In.	241
Beaker, Ribbed Bands, Tapered, Peter, Ann & W. Bateman, 1799, 5 In.	1250
Bottle Collar, Stylized Leaves, Monogram, Crown, Gilt, c.1830, 4 In.	2091
Bowl, Calyx, Grapevines, Inverted Bell Shape, Pairpoint, 4 x 5 In., Pair	468
Bowl, Vegetable, Lid, Leaf Handle, Paul Storr, 1813, 5½ x 13 x 9 In.	2160
Cake Basket, George III, Ball Handle, Henry Chawner, c.1788, 13 In.	738

S

Candelabra are listed in the Candelabrum category.

Candlesticks are listed in their own category.

Castor, George III, Fluted, Garlands, Ribbons, Medallions, 7 In., Pair....................................	531
Chafing Dish, Reeded, Tripod Stand, Hoof Feet, Robert Sharp, 1792, 8 x 10 In.................*illus*	1320
Cheese Cradle, Beading, Robert Hennell II, 1812, 19 In.	5250
Cigarette Case, Paint, Bulldog Caricature, Smoking Cigar, c.1885, 3 In.	708
Cocktail Shaker, Bullet Form, 3 Piece, c.1960, 8 ¼ x 3 ¾ In.	875
Coffee & Tea Set, Egg Shape, Footed, S. Robert & C. Belk, 11-In. Pot, 4 Piece	1920
Coffeepot, Faceted Urn, Flared Base, Wood Handle, Monogram, c.1802, 12 In.	472
Coffeepot, George V, Coat Of Arms, Crichton Brothers, c.1916, 10 In.	554
Coffeepot, Lid, Wood Handle, London, 1764, 10 In.	438
Coffeepot, Lobed, Footed, Burwash & Sibley, 1810, 9 x 7 In.	660
Condiment Frame, Scrolling, 3 Red-Threaded Glass Jars, 9 ¼ x 9 ½ In.	437
Condiment Set, George II, Francis Crump, 1766, 3 Piece	2750
Condiment Set, Penguins, Glass Eyes, Comyns & Son, 1960s, 3 In., 3 Piece ....*illus*	2000
Creamer, Helmet Shape, Beaded Rim, Angular Handle, Bateman, 1789, 6 In.	720
Cruet Stand, George III, Upright Loop Handle, 7 Silver Mounted Bottles, 9 In.	246
Cruet Stand, Rococo Medallion, Armorial, Rings, Shell Feet, 1762, 9 x 9 In.	480
Cup, Christening, Grapevine Handle, Victorian, G. Adams, c.1865, 5 In.	923
Cup, George III, Campana Shape, Leaf Wreath, P. Storr, 1812, 9 x 7 In., Pair	7500
Decanter, Repousse, Figures, Flowers, Latticework, W. Comyns, 5 x 2 In., Pair	854
Dish, Feeding, Boat Shape, Elongated Pouring Lip, 1700s, 4 ½ In.	115
Dish, Lobed Bowl, Gadroon Rim, c.1810, 11 ½ In. Diam.	738
Dish, Spice, Clover Leaf Shape, Case, c.1906, 3 x 3 In., 12 Piece	112
Ear Wax Pick, Gilt, Turned Ivory Handle, Hester Bateman, 1783, 5 ½ In.	540
Epergne, Edward VII, Pierced, 4 Arms, Swing Baskets, Crichton Bros., 1909, 20 In.	7500
Figure, Dolphin, Around Anchor, Gilt, Stepped Plinth, c.1968, 7 In.	461
Fish Knife, Pierced, Leaves, Reeded Handle, H. Bateman, 1829, 12 In.	780
Fish Slice, Thread & Shell, Wallis & Hayne, 1814..	163
Hand Mirror, Enamel, Stamped, Liberty & Co., 11 x 5 ½ In.	610
Hot Water Urn, Coat Of Arms, Late 1700s, 21 In...	2760
Hot Water Urn, Lion & Ring Handles, Acorn Finial, c.1804...	2640
Hot Water Urn, Wreath Cartouche, Beaded, Handles, J. Carter, 1773, 13 In.	1320
Hot Water Urn, Wrigglework Bands, Beaded Spout, C. Wright, c.1755, 21 In..............*illus*	3000
Ladle, Shaped Bowl, Monogram HSE, Walnut Handle, London, 1754, 15 In.	90
Monteith, George V, Scalloped Rim, Monogram, Crichton Bros., 1927, 10 In.	4750
Monteith, Repousse Flowers, Crenellated Rim, Coin, S. Kirk & Son, 6 x 9 In.................*illus*	2337
Mug, George II, Bulbous, Scroll Handle, Flared Foot, R. Bailey, 1734, 4 In.	354
Mug, Scroll Leaf Handle, Splay Foot, Bateman, c.1776, 5 In.	1067
Mustard Pot, Glass Liner, Hester Bateman, 1788, 4 In...	469
Napkin Rings are listed in their own category.	
Nutmeg Grater, George III, Canister, Banded, Marked IT, 1 ¼ In.	138
Nutmeg Grater, George III, Canister, Banded, S. Pemberton, 1816, 1 ¼ In...........................	163
Nutmeg Grater, George III, Canister, Reeded Bands, Engraved Flowers, 1 ¼ In.	344
Nutmeg Grater, George III, Nut Shape, Reeded Banding, 1 ¾ In.	200
Pitcher, Lid, Hester Bateman, Late 1700s, 13 In.	2530
Pitcher, Milk, Georgian, Repousse, Cast Scroll Handle, 5 In...	552
Pitcher, Repousse, Gadroon Rim, Bateman, c.1800, 13 x 6 x 7 In.	1125
Pitcher, Washington Pattern, Paneled, Squat, Angular Handle, Wallace, 9 In.	780
Plate, Pierced Leafy Scroll Border, Elkington & Co., 1910, 9 In., 12 Piece...........................	3500
Punch Bowl, Leaves, Handles, Footed, Joseph Heming & Co., 1912, 14 In.	1625
Rattle, Flower Chasing, 4 Bells, 1800s, 3 ¾ In.	177
Salt & Pepper, Rabbits, Figural, William E. Hurcomb, Box, c.1905, 1 In.	738
Salt, Leaves, Shields, 4-Footed, Henry Matthers, c.1895, 1 ¾ In., Pair	94
Salt, Striped, Footed, Alexander Macrae, 1870, 1 ¼ x 2 ¼ In., 6 Piece..............................	218
Salver, Armorial, Gadroon Rim, Pierced Border, 13 In..	1250
Salver, Armorial, Piecrust Rim, Victorian, Charles S. Harris, c.1900, 12 In...........................	492
Salver, Armorial, S-Scroll, Rocaille Rim, Lattice Engraved, 13 ½ In.	1500
Salver, George III, John Parker & Edward Wakelin, c.1761, 9 In.	600
Salver, Laurel Garlands & Bows, Round, Gallery, 4-Footed, 20 In...	826

Silver-English, Stirrup Cup, Fox Head, Hester Bateman, George III, 1780, 5 ⅜ In.

$13,725

Neal Auctions

> **TIP**
> *Flatware that is used regularly should be polished just once or twice a year.*

Silver-English, Tankard, Dome Lid, George II, Handle, Engraved, Tearle, 1722, 7 In.

$1,353

Skinner, Inc.

Silver-English, Teapot, Engraved Band, Wood Handle, Finial, Hester Bateman, c.1790, 7 x 11 In.

$1,150

Cottone Auctions

S

Silver-English, Teapot, Repousse Flowers, Scroll, Wood Handle, Hester Bateman, 6 In.
$830

James D. Julia Auctioneers

Silver-English, Teapot, Stand, Engraved Swags, Wood Handle, Hester Bateman, c.1788, 8 In.
$6,875

New Orleans Auction Galleries

Silver-English, Teapot, Stand, George III, Chased Bands, Monogram, Wood Handle, Finial, 1797, 7 In.
$984

Cowan's Auctions

Salver, Leaves, Shell Border & Feet, Flowers, London, 1827, 2 x 9 In.	420
Salver, Scroll & Shell, Flowers, John Wellby, 1800s, 20 In.	2040
Salver, Shell Border, Scalloped Rim, Richard Rugg, c.1758, 15 In.	900
Salver, Shells, Coat Of Arms, Gadroon, Paw Feet, c.1815, 17 In. Diam.	2706
Scent Mull, Birds, Flowers, C-Scrolls, Horn Shape, 3 In.	344
Serving Dish, Engraved Basket Weave, c.1800, 2¼ x 15 In.	5500
Serving Dish, Gadroon Rim, Lid, Leafy Loop Finial, c.1822, 12 In., Pair	3444
Serving Spade, George III, Threaded Handle, Pierced Spatula, c.1800, 12 In.	562
Sorbet Service, Mappin & Webb, 8 Cups & Spoons, c.1955, 3 x 4½ In.	687
Soup, Dish, Gadroon Rim, R. Garrard II, c.1823, 9¾ In., Pair	687
Stirrup Cup, Fox Head, Hester Bateman, George III, 1780, 5⅜ In. *illus*	13725
Stuffing Spoon, Georgian, Touchmark George Smith, c.1785, 12 In.	135
Sugar Castor, George III, Urn Shape, Lid, Finial, c.1780, 9½ In.	338
Sugar, Basket Shape, Lobed, Footed, Swing Handle, H. Chawney, 1795	125
Sugar, Urn Shape, Dome Lid, Finial, Swag Handles, 9 In.	374
Tankard, Dome Lid, George II, Handle, Engraved, Tearle, 1722, 7 In. *illus*	1353
Tankard, George I, Tapered, Dome Lid, Philip Rollos II, 1714, 7 In.	2242
Tankard, George II, Leaves, Engraved Crest, R. Gurney & T. Cook, 1749, 7 In.	1300
Tea Set, Teapot, Sugar & Creamer, Tongs, 4 Piece	468
Teapot, Engraved Band, Wood Handle, Finial, Hester Bateman, c.1790, 7 x 11 In. *illus*	1150
Teapot, George III, Drum Shape, Beaded Rim, c.1784, 6 In.	738
Teapot, Repousse Flowers, Scroll, Wood Handle, Hester Bateman, 6 In. *illus*	830
Teapot, Repousse, Footed, c.1815	394
Teapot, Stand, Engraved Swags, Wood Handle, Hester Bateman, c.1788, 8 In. *illus*	6875
Teapot, Stand, Fluted, James Mince, 1796, 11 In.	687
Teapot, Stand, George III, Chased Bands, Monogram, Wood Handle, Finial, 1797, 7 In. *illus*	984
Teapot, Stand, Oval, Monograms, Reeded Rim, Engraved, c.1800, 7 In.	984
Teapot, Wood Handle & Finial, c.1792, 6 x 10½ x 4 In.	312
Tongs, Scalloped, Bone Handle, Rat, Bamboo Leaf, Atkins Bros., 10 In.	300
Tray, Canted Corners, Mappin & Webb, 1929, 28 In.	2500
Tray, George V, Lionel Alfred Chrichton, Engraved, c.1900, 18 x 10 In.	812
Tray, Shield, Wreath, Round, Ball & Claw Feet, Hester Bateman, 1781, 7 In.	840
Trophy, George II, Lobed, Flowers, Leaves, Charles Marsh, 1819	1500
Tureen, Soup, Lid, George III, John Wakelin & W. Taylor, c.1790, 17 In.	5228
Vase, Gilt, Ruby Glass, Cylindrical, Pierced Flared Rim, Ring Handles, 14 In.	3690
Vase, Repousse, Cobalt Blue Glass, Pierced, Trumpet, Edwardian, 13 In.	500
Vinaigrette, George III, Purse Shape, 1768, 1 In.	313
Vinaigrette, Leaves, Cartouche, William & Edward, 1845, 1¼ In.	163
Vinaigrette, Monogram Cartouche, Wriggle Work, 1 In.	138
Vinaigrette, Oval, Flower Design Rim, 1 In.	150
Vinaigrette, Stippled Flowers, Cartouche, William Withers, 1778, 1 In.	138
Waiter, George III, Crested, Scrollwork, John Carter, 1767, 7 In.	780
Wine Coaster, Squat, Cylindrical, Wood Base, c.1787, 1 x 5 In.	812
Wine Funnel, George III, Beaded Rim, Hester Bateman, 1786, 4½ In.	688
Wine Funnel, Hester Bateman, London, 5 x 3 In.	3120
Wine Funnel, Rubbed Marks, George III, 4 In. *illus*	122
Wine Funnel, Strainer, George III, John Chapman II, London, 1787, 5 In. *illus*	750

SILVER-FRENCH

Asparagus Tongs, Shaped, Reeded Border, Gustave Keller, Paris, c.1900	300
Bowl, Ecuelle, Empire 1st Standard, Scroll Banding, c.1800, 1¾ x 8 In.	750
Bowl, Lid, First Standard, Laurel Wreath Finial, Medard Fanot, 5 x 6 In.	1187
Castor, Octagonal, Tapered, Gilt Top, Cartier, 1½ In., 8 Piece	200
Castor, Salt, Pepper, Swag, Berry Finial, Reeded, 8 In., Pair	750
Centerpiece, Putti Supports, Debain, c.1875, 18 In.	3437
Centerpiece, Surtout De Table, Mirror, 4-Footed, Christofle & Cie, 50½ x 21 In.	4000
Cigarette Case, Art Deco, Rosettes, Sunburst, Engine Turned, 3⅝ In.	313
Cigarette Case, Leaves, Chinoserie Garden Scene, 3⅜ In.	200
Claret Jug, Arms Of The Farmer, Falcons, Gold Wash, c.1850, 13 In., Pair	2499
Coffee & Tea Set, Urn Shape, Beaded Borders, 19-In. Tray, 4 Piece	1200

S

Coffee Biggin, Pot, Stand, Burner, Die Stamped, Jean-Nicolas Boulanger, 11 In.	780
Creamer, Horse Head Spout, Wood Handles, c.1800, 8 x 5¼ In.	236
Epergne, Oval, Mirrored Plate, Shaped Containers, Gilt, c.1915, 15 In.	625
Goblet, Chrysanthemums, Gilt Interior, Art Nouveau, Galmer, 7 In.	720
Jar, Cobalt Blue Glass Insert, Van Conwenberghe, 1770, 4½ x 7 In.	500
Letter Seal, Etched Flowers, Garland, Spoon Shape, c.1905, 4 In.	165
Placecard Holder, Gilt, Ravine D'Enfert, Paris, Case, 12 x 7, 12 Piece	1250
Planter, Lily Pads, Swirls, Woman, Free-Form, Handles, c.1900, 13 x 8 In.	720
Platter, 10-Sided, Gadroon Rim, David Herbert, c.1757, 12 In.	937
Platter, Serpentine, Lobed, Repousse, Flower Sprays, Scroll Rim, c.1900, 14 In.	937
Salt Cellar, Shell Shape Bowls, Entwined Dolphins, Gold Wash, 4 x 5 In., Pair	5310
Salver, Lobed, Laurel Edge, Monogram JD, A. Cardeilhac, c.1915, 12 In. ....*illus*	875
Sauceboat, Roman Woman, Helmet, Acanthus, Gadrooned Rim, Bands, 3¾ x 9½ In. ....*illus*	522
Tea & Coffee Set, Coffeepot, Teapot, Sugar, Creamer, Rosewood, c.1930, 5 Piece	1375
Tea Set, Teapot, Sugar & Creamer, Cup, Tray, 7 In., 5 Piece	1625
Tea Set, Teapot, Sugar & Creamer, Wood Handles & Finials, 3 Piece	500
Tureen, Lid, Leaf Mounted, Openwork, Finial, 11½ x 10 In.	4750
Tureen, Lid, Pomegranate Finial, Maison Puiforcat, c.1900, 9 x 14 In.	2000
Urn, Gilt, Ram Heads, Swan Feet, 6¾ In., Pair	750
Wine Taster, Gadroon Design, Scroll Handle, Marked, Paris, c.1890, 4 In.	600

SILVER-GERMAN

Basket, Cup Shape, Hexagon, Putti, Openwork, 8¼ In.	531
Basket, Openwork Lattice, Leaves, Ribbon Festoons, 11 In.	438
Basket, Stand, Pierced, Fluted Square Foot, c.1900, 9½ x 10 In.	295
Bowl, Reticulated, 2 Handles, 5¼ In.	437
Box, Lid, Cupid & Flowers, Round, Gilt Interior, 4¾ x 9 In.	900
Box, Portraits, Leaves, Wreath, Oval, 6½ x 4 In.	332
Castor, Cherubs, Leaves, 6⅜ In.	425
Centerpiece, Pierced Sides, Profile Medallions, Rocaille, 1901, 17½ In.	2375
Citrus Spoon, Scroll, Lattice, Box, Gustav Memmert, 6 In., 6 Piece	64
Coffee & Tea Set, Coffeepot, Teapot, Pitcher, Sugar & Creamer, 5 Piece	2040
Coffee & Tea Set, Demi Teapot & Coffeepot, Sugar, Creamer, Tray, 6 Piece	3900
Condiment Basket, Openwork, Flowers, Stork & Sinsheimer, Hanau	562
Creamer, Cow, Lid, 7 In.	1098
Cup, Lid, Chased, Military Camp Scenes, Neresheimer, c.1900, 14 In.	1250
Cup, Lid, Leafy Cartouches, Flowers, Finial, Waisted, Hossauer, 13 In.	1250
Dish, Coquille, Seashell Scroll Crest, Wilkens & Sohne, 1900s, 14½ In.	562
Dish, Lily Of The Valley, Orchids, Repousse, Serpentine, Flared, 15 x 9 In.	365
Ewer, Rococo Style, Leaves, Serpentine Rim, Scroll Handle, c.1800s, 14 In.	1947
Figurine, Boy, Girl, On Sled, Silvered Lead, c.1920, 4 In. ....*illus*	244
Jar, Lid, Leaves, Berries, Ball Feet, Neresheimer & Sohne, 4 Piece	163
Jardiniere, Neoclassical, Oval, Panels, Flowers, Swags, Masks, 23 In.	1625
Music Box, Oval, Enamel Lid, Johann S. Kurtz & Co., c.1910, 2 x 4 In.	3000
Pitcher, Tankard, 28-Coin Inset, 1890, 16 In.	8125
Pitcher, Tankard, Applied Coat Of Arms, Crowned Eagle Finial, 13 In.	5000
Pitcher, Tankard, Armor Breastplate, Helmet Finial, Hossauer, 1846, 12 In.	10000
Pitcher, Tankard, Lobed, c.1850, 10½ x 23 In.	150
Pitcher, Tankard, Partial Gilt, Hunting Scene, Neresheimer, 1890, 20 In.	13750
Pitcher, Tankard, Partial Gilt, Maltese Iron Cross, Hossauer, 1885, 10 In.	5000
Plate, Beneath Coronet, 9¼ In., 6 Piece	2500
Salad Fork, Clipper Ship, Pierced, Scroll, Putti, Schleissner & Sohne, 2 Piece	354
Salt, Leaves, Gadroon, Seated Griffin, Pair	3660
Sauceboat, Medallion, Wavy Rim, Scroll Handle & Base, c.1910, 7 In., Pair	1125
Server, Pierced Bowl, Chased & Scrolling Leaves, Ebonized Handle, 12 In.	96
Spoon, Fairy, Reticulated Pedestal, Leaves, Cast, Georg Roth, 11 x 3 In.	342
Stirrup Cup, Bird, Open Beak, Gilt Interior, 6 x 2¾ In. ....*illus*	1638
Sugar & Creamer, Putti, Flower Swags, Panels, 6½ In.	625
Tea & Coffee Set, Coffeepot, Teapot & Sugar, Creamer, Tray, Bremen-Hemelingen, 5 Piece	1200
Tea & Coffee Set, Teapot, Coffeepot, Sugar & Creamer, Gebruder Kuhn, 4 Piece	1000

Silver-English, Wine Funnel, Rubbed Marks, George III, 4 In.

$122

Neal Auctions

Silver-English, Wine Funnel, Strainer, George III, John Chapman II, London, 1787, 5 In.

$750

Neal Auctions

Silver-French, Salver, Lobed, Laurel Edge, Monogram JD, A. Cardeilhac, c.1915, 12 In.

$875

New Orleans Auction Galleries

Silver-French, Sauceboat, Roman Woman, Helmet, Acanthus, Gadrooned Rim, Bands, 3¾ x 9½ In. $522

John McInnis Auctioneers

Silver-German, Figurine, Boy, Girl, On Sled, Silvered Lead, c.1920, 4 In. $244

RSL Auction

Silver-German, Stirrup Cup, Bird, Open Beak, Gilt Interior, 6 x 2¾ In. $1,638

Case Antiques

Tea & Coffee Set, Teapot, Coffeepot, Tray, Kettle, Stand, Creamer, Waste Bowl, 6 Piece	2375
Tray, Oval, Etched Center, Franz Mosgau, 11½ In.	156
Tray, Oval, Lobed Edge, Festoon Rim, Lazarus Pozen, 24 In.	813
Tray, Pierced, Repousse, Berries, Flowers, Leaves, George Roth & Co., 13 In.	531
Tray, Repousse, Flowers, Scroll Reserves, Serpentine Rim, 21 x 13½ In.	976
Vase, Etched Glass, Cherub, Swan, 10¾ x 6½ In.	737
Vase, Frankfurt Festival Scene, Medieval Clothing, 8¼ In.	300
Vase, Trumpet, Glass Mouth, 11¼ In.	125
Vinaigrette, Shoe, Chased, Flowers, Leaves, Animals, 2½ In.	500
Wedding Cup, Hanau, Repousse, Bearded Man In Skirt, c.1880, 11 In.	523
Wine Cooler, Round, Loop Supports, H. Meyer & Co., 10 In.	1062

SILVER-GREEK

Jug, Wine, Round, Hammered, Handle, Gilt Spout, 7 In.	281

SILVER-INDIAN

Ewer, Inverted Pear, Flowers, Leaves, Stippled, Hamilton & Co., Calcutta, 10⅜ In. ...*illus*	2583
Figure, Lion, Standing, Cast, 12½ x 19 In., Pair	6873
Tea Service, Teapot, Sugar & Creamer, Spherical, Scroll Feet, Elephant Finials, c.1900	750

SILVER-IRISH

Goblet, Repousse Leaves, Stop Fluting, Gold Washed Interior, 6¼ In.	540
Ladle, George IV, Rampant Griffin Crest, 1825	188
Stirrup Cup, Irish Wolfhound, Gold Wash, 4½ x 2½ In. ...*illus*	2625
Sugar Tongs, Grapes, Leaves, John Smyth, c.1950, 6¾ In.	312
Tray, Oval, Gadroon Rim, Monogram, Leaf Cartouch, 1775, 12 In.	1107

SILVER-ITALIAN

Bottle Basket, Pour, Wire, Grape Clusters, Grape Leaf Latch Handles, 7 x 9 In.	224
Bowl, Chased, Swirled, Fluted, 6½ x 2½ In.	153
Bowl, Figural, Swan, Embossed, Wings Up, Buccellati, c.1985, 4 x 8 In.	3750
Bowl, Shell Shape, Conch Shell Feet, Buccellati, 2½ x 9 In.	1187
Bowl, Square, Twist, Shaped, Fluted, 7½ x 2 In.	88
Centerpiece, Flowers, Footed, 5½ x 16 In.	625
Centerpiece, Woven Basket, Apple, Pears, Grapes, 9¼ In.	2375
Champagne Bucket, Medusa Head, Fluted, Swirl Handles, c.1940, 12 x 9 In.	2006
Coffee & Tea Set, Teapot, Coffeepot, Tray, Sugar & Creamer, 6 Piece	3000
Coffee Set, Coffeepot, Sugar & Creamer, Zigzag, Gilt, 4 Piece	2812
Decanter Set, Silver Mounted Glass, Coaster, Chained Cork, 1900s, 16 x 4 In.	812
Dish, Swan Shape, Buccellati, 7 In.	1750
Dresser Box, Rectangular, Undulating Sides, Buccellati, 2 x 4½ x 3 In.	500
Ewer, Art Deco, Ruffled Tapered Rim, Ebonized Handle, 12 In.	472
Ewer, Melon Shape, Ribbed, Leaf Scroll Handle, Buccellati, 14¼ In.	1375
Figurine, Elephant, Jewel Inset, Ida Hagenbeck, 8½ In.	875
Ice Bucket, Tongs, Hammered, 5 x 6 In.	271
Kettle Stand, Twisted, Leafy Handles, 17 In.	3750
Serving Dish, Lid, Scalloped Rim, Loop Finial, Buccellati, c.1970, 11 In.	1230
Sugar & Creamer, 3 Hoofed Feet, 6 x 4 In.	230
Tea & Coffee Set, Teapot, Coffeepot, Sugar & Creamer, Tray, 2 Vases, 7 Piece	3250
Tray, Buccellati, 27 x 21½ In.	4250
Urn, Lid, Trophy Shape, Square Base, Footed, c.1944, 7 In.	529
Vase, Chased, Scrolls, Acanthus Leaves, Footed, Buccellati Style, 20¾ In. ...*illus*	9500
Wine Cooler, Cylindrical, Banded Base & Collar, Late 1900s, 9 In.	875

SILVER-JAPANESE

Bowl, Flared Rim, Flowers, Leaves, Arthur & Bond, 4¾ In.	938
Bowl, Lotus Shape, Footed, Impressed, Art Deco, 7¼ In.	308
Box, Rosewood, Dragon, Stippled, 5 x 3½ In.	483
Cigarette Case, Bamboo, Leaves, 6½ x 3 In.	137
Spoon, Geisha, 6¼ In.	50
Vase, Incised Flowers, Mountains & Butterflies, c.1900, 14 In.	5750
Vase, Orchid, Lotus & Reeds, Enameled, 6 In.	1250

SILVER-MEXICAN

Bowl, Fluted, Scalloped, Impressed, Sanborns, 1925, 3¼ In.	369
Bowl, Fruit, Repousse, Grape Clusters, Pierced Lattice, 3 x 9 In.	387
Bowl, Oblong, Cast Scroll Feet, 3¾ x 19½ In.	661
Bowl, Oval, Lobed, Scroll Rim, Feet & Handles, c.1950, 4 x 10 In.	1125
Bowl, Swan, Gilt Interior & Rim, Marked Tane, c.1975, 10½ x 11 In.............*illus*	5100
Coffee Set, Coffeepot, Sugar & Creamer, Fluted, Leafy Feet, 8¼ In.	688
Dish, 3 Sections, Central Ball, 10¼ In.	295
Figure, Sombrero, Eagle & Snake, Juarez Mexico, 8½ x 17 In.	2250
Gravy Separator, Saucepan Shape, Side Spout, Eagle Mark, 3½ x 9 In.	240
Pitcher, Cavetto, Tapered, Flat Wide Spout, Arch Handle, c.1965, 11 In.	437
Pitcher, Flowers, Gadroon, Tobias, 1900s, 11 In.	531
Pitcher, Gem Set, Star Shape Medallions, Carmen Beckmann, 9 x 7 In.	900
Pitcher, Modern, Oval, Vertical Strap, 1960s, 8 x 5¾ In.	833
Pitcher, Modernist, Geometric Handle, Juventino Lopez Reyes, 7 In.	365
Pitcher, Oval, Vertical Strap, 1960s, 8 x 5¾ In.	833
Pitcher, Stone Inlay, Figural Parrot Handle, Brass Beak, c.1962, 10 In.	800
Platter, Chippendale Style Rim, Sanborn Hermanos, 1900s, 22¾ x 16 In.	1375
Platter, Round, Stepped Border, Hand Wrought, Hector Aguilar, c.1950, 17 In.	750
Platter, Serpentine Shape, Reeded Border, Early 1900s, 23 x 13 In.	1500
Serving Dish, Lid, Gadroon, Coat Of Arms, 22 In.	813
Spoon, Baby, Molded Duck, Oval Bowl, Shaped Handle, W. Spratling, c.1945, 5 In.............*illus*	512
Sugar & Creamer, Lid, Scrollwork Trim, 2 Piece	383
Tea Set, Kettle, Stand, Sugar & Creamer, Waste Bowl, Lobed, 4 Piece	2125
Tray, Leaf & Scroll Rim, Stirrup Handles, G.W. Moreno, 26 x 16 In.	1375
Tray, Shaped, Blue & Green Mosaic Upright Handle, c.1962, 3 x 8 In.	123
Trinket Box, Gourd Shape, Lid, Tane Orfebres, Mexico City, c.1975, 6 In.	750
Warming Pot, Tane Orfebres, 1900s, 3¾ x 6¾ In.............*illus*	47
Wine Coaster, Stone Inlay, Emilia Castillo, c.1980, 3¾ In.	200
Wine Cooler, Gadroon, Ring Handles, 11 In.	875

SILVER-MIDDLE EASTERN

Bucket, Flowers, Scrolls, Birds, Bail Handle, Scalloped Rim, 24 Oz.	602
Tazza, Footed, Interlocking Loop Design, Pierced Flower Rim, 10 In.	272

SILVER-NORWEGIAN

Pitcher, Hammered, Enamel, Carnelians, David Andersen, 1880s, 10 x 4 In.............*illus*	5000
Salt, Open, Viking Boat, Plique-A-Jour, Glass Insert, Marius Hammer, c.1900, 2¼ In.............*illus*	373

SILVER-PERSIAN

Charger, Genre Scene, Relief Flowers, 30¾ In.	247

SILVER-PERUVIAN

Bowl, Spanish Coin Center, Tapered Border, Serpentine Rim, 7 In.	365
Tea & Coffee Set, Teapot, Coffeepot, Sugar & Creamer, Tray, 5 Piece	1904

SILVER-PORTUGUESE

Pitcher, Basin, Chrysanthemums, Leaves, Banded, C-Scroll, 2 Piece	960

SILVER-PRUSSIAN

Box, Hinged Stepped Lid, Flowers & Shells, Paw Feet, c.1850, 3 x 6 In.	600

SILVER-RUSSIAN. Russian silver is marked with the Cyrillic, or Russian, alphabet. The numbers 84, 88, or 91 indicate the silver content. Russian silver may be higher 〔88〕 〔91〕 or lower than sterling standard. Other marks indicate maker, assayer, or city of manufacture. Many pieces of silver made in Russia are decorated with enamel. These prices are based on current silver values. Faberge pieces are listed in their own category.

Bowl, Hammered, Footed, 3½ In.	74
Box, Hammered, Applied Dragonflies, Silver Folded Tapestry Lid, Marked, 3 x 2 In..........*illus*	2400
Cigarette Box, Repousse, Bear Attacking Cossack, 4½ x 3¼ In.	2812
Cigarette Box, Royal Couple, Dancing, 4½ x 3 In.	687
Cigarette Case, Commemorative, Lyre, Blue Stone, 4¼ x 3 In.	271
Cigarette Case, Geometric Design, Applied Monogram, 5¼ In.	250

Silver-Indian, Ewer, Inverted Pear, Chased, Repousse, Flowers, Leaves, Stippled, Hamilton & Co., Calcutta, 10⅜ In.
$2,583

Leland Little Auctions

Silver-Irish, Stirrup Cup, Irish Wolfhound, Gold Wash, 4½ x 2½ In.
$2,625

Wiederseim Associates

Silver-Italian, Vase, Chased, Scrolls, Acanthus Leaves, Footed, Buccellati Style, 20¾ In.
$9,500

Ruby Lane

Silver-Mexican, Bowl, Swan, Gilt Interior & Rim, Marked Tane, c.1975, 10½ x 11 In.
$5,100

Brunk Auctions

Silver-Mexican, Spoon, Baby, Molded Duck, Oval Bowl, Shaped Handle, W. Spratling, c.1945, 5 In.
$512

Neal Auctions

Silver-Mexican, Warming Pot, Tane Orfebres, 1900s, 3¾ x 6¾ In.
$47

Heritage Auctions

TIP
Discovered some old silver in the attic? Wash it with a brush in warm soapy water before you polish it. Dirt can scratch the silver.

Cigarette Case, Gilt Wash, Enamel, Multicolor, 11th Artel, 4 In.	2250
Cigarette Case, Niello Inlay, Cartouch, Landscape, Scrollwork, c.1885, 5 In.	215
Cigarette Case, Repousse, Troika Scene, 4¾ In.	313
Cigarette Case, Troika Scene, Engraved NK, 4 x 2½ In.	206
Crucifix, Christ, Gilded, Niello, Shaped, Top Hanging, Loop, 1793, 6 x 5 In.	875
Egg, Hoof Feet, Tripod Base, 4 In.	998
Figurine, Bear, Lying Down, 6½ In.	423
Kovsh, Sapphire Cabochon, Scroll Handle, Strapwork, J. Tappoport, 2 x 6 In.	5227
Ladle, Oval, 1829, 14 x 4 In.	141
Salt Service, 12 Salts, 12 Spoons, Cobalt Blue, Cased, c.1890	2000
Salt, Master, Scroll & Flowers, Pierced, Hinged, Cutout Feet, 4 x 3 In.	384
Seal Stand, Grapevines, Frog, Garnet Eyes, Jade Handle, c.1910, 4 In.	1778
Sugar & Creamer, Silver Gilt, Cloisonne, Swing Handle, 2 Piece	4000
Tankard, Cartouche, Castle, Lid, Thumblift, Scroll Handle, 1858, 6 In.	3125
Tea Set, Teapot, Sugar & Creamer, Konstantine Petz, 1863, 3 Piece	1750
Teapot, Cloisonne, Flower, Blue, Red, Green, O. Kurliukov, c.1895, 6 In.	4000
Teapot, Lobed Pear Shape, Gooseneck Spout, Crested Handle, Moscow, 1856, 6 In.	343
Teapot, Squared Handle, 7½ In.	531

SILVER-SCOTTISH

Bowl, Buddhist Gods, Goddesses, Animals, Edward & Sons, c.1900, 3 x 4 In.	345
Ewer, Cartouche, Zodiac Designs, Tapered, Shaped Finial, c.1877, 10 In.	1476
Teapot, Bullet, George II, Oval, Gooseneck Spout, c.1780, 6 x 11 In.	875
Teapot, Ribbed Handle, 1848, 12 x 8 In.	967

SILVER-SPANISH

Candlestick Holder, Scrolled Handle, Applied Hardstones, 1900s, 15 In.	185
Figure, Fish, Articulated Body, Red Glass Eyes, 8 In., Pair	531
Salver, Seashells, Round, Fluted, Scalloped Border, Marked, 11 In.	201
Tea & Coffee Set, Coffeepot, Teapot, Strainer, Tray, Sugar & Creamer, 7 Piece	2214
Tray, Oval, Leaves, Flowers, Ribbon, Monogram, 13 x 10 In.	241

SILVER-STERLING. Sterling silver is made with 925 parts silver out of 1,000 parts of metal. The word *sterling* is a quality guarantee used in the United States after about 1860. The word was used much earlier in England and Ireland. Pieces listed here are not identified by country. These prices are based on current silver values. Other pieces of sterling quality silver are listed under Silver-American, Silver-English, etc.

Basket, Reticulated, Wavy Rim, Swags, Loop Bail Handle, 1774, 4 x 13 In.	1750
Bowl, Fruit, Openwork Bands, Columnar Legs, Swags, c.1877, 5 x 9 In.	2375
Bowl, Hammered, Applied Copper Berries, Spider, Dragonfly, c.1890, 9 x 3 In.	3894
Bowl, Oval, Gadroon, Pierced, Scroll Rim & Feet, Handles, c.1950, 17 In.	937
Bowl, Vegetable, Embossed Flowers, Shells & Scroll, Shaped, 1958, 12 In.	750
Cake Basket, Oval, Hinged Bail Handle, Openwork, Beaded Edge, 1782, 15 In.	1185
Candelabra are listed in the Candelabrum category.	
Candlesticks are listed in their own category.	
Card Case, Engraved, Chain Link Handle, Victorian, 4 x 3 In.	177
Coffeepot, Aladdin Lamp Shape, Dome Lid, Lobed, Flowers, 1892, 8 In.	369
Coffeepot, Hinged Lid, Repousse, Lake, Blossom Finial, Dome Foot, c.1900, 10 In.	600
Coffeepot, Leaf Handle, Chased Flowers, Crest, c.1760, 9 In.	1046
Coffeepot, Lid, George III, Ring Foot, Shaped Spout, 1768, 11 In.	600
Coffeepot, Lid, Tapered Cylinder, Slender Spout, Urn Finial, c.1737, 8 In.	1599
Coffeepot, Repousse Flowers, C-Scroll Handle, Pedestal, 1821, 10 In.	1080
Compote, Engraved Rim, Pedestal Foot, Arts & Crafts Style, c.1920, 9 In.	277
Compote, Flared Bowl, Drop Pendant, Grapes, Twist Stem, 1900s, 7 In., Pair	4200
Compote, Flared Bowl, Grape Clusters, Spiral Stem, Pedestal Foot, 1900s, 5 In.	840
Compote, Flared Bowl, Hanging Grapes, Twist Stem, Footed, c.1925, 7 In.	1845
Compote, Shell Shape Bowl, Dolphin Stem, Round Base, c.1910, 5 In., Pair	400
Console, Engraved Flag, Bear, Star, Governor Of California, c.1950, 5 In.	738
Cream Pail, Wrigglework, Beaded, Swing Handle, 1784, 4 x 4 In.	750

Dish, Oval, Gadroon Rim, Leaf Capped Shells, Engraved, c.1828, 15 In.	1845
Ewer, Urn Shape, Swags, Wreaths, Fluted Neck, Urn Finial, c.1775, 14 In.	1353
Flask, Hammered, Embossed Goat, Oval, Hinged Cap, c.1915, 6 In.	625
Goblet, Oval, Waisted Stem, Scalloped, Gadroon Foot, c.1886, 11 In.	810
Hot Water Urn, Beaded, Upswept Handles, Lid, Ball Feet, c.1778, 20 In.	6250
Ingots, 50 State Flags, Franklin Mint, Display Case, Book, 1973-74, 104 Troy Oz.	1512
Jug, Claret, Vermeil, Leaves, Flowers, Hinged Lid, 1885, 12 x 6 In.	1416
Loving Cup, 3 Handles, Engraved, 1906, 12 In.	800
Napkin Rings are listed in their own category.	
Pepper Pot, Embossed, Roses, Pineapple, Flared Foot, 1800s, 4 x 2 In.	475
Pin Tray, Repousse, Woman's Head, Long Wavy Hair, Art Nouveau, 5 In.	354
Pitcher, Bulbous, Loop Handle, Crimped Rim, Hoof Feet, c.1930, 4 In.	400
Pitcher, Hammered, Lobed Diamond, Scroll Handle, Flared Spout, 1900s, 8 In.	660
Pitcher, Helmet Shape, Scroll Handle, Flared Spout, Ring Foot, 1900s, 10 In.	540
Pitcher, Pear Shape, Repousse, Cartouche, Scroll Handle & Feet, c.1898, 10 In.	1625
Porringer, Hammered, Clover, Pierced Leaf Handle, c.1910, 1 x 5 In.	2214
Punch Bowl, Bacchus, Mask Handles, Pedestal Foot, 1886, 9 x 16 In.	12500
Salt & Pepper, Silver, Cone Top, Trumpet Body, Round Foot, 4 Piece	63
Salver, Engraved Crest, Scroll Feet, Scroll Leaf Border, 1824, 12 In.	1250
Salver, George III, Engraved Flowers, Gadroon, Paw Feet, 1803, 12 In.	338
Salver, Shell & Scroll Border, Rocaille Cartouche, Scroll Feet, 17 In.	1599
Sauceboat, Repousse Flowers, Scroll Rim, Paw Feet, c.1915, 6 x 9 In.	1000
Sauceboat, Shells, Gadroon, Scroll Handle, Hoof Feet, c.1915, 4 x 7 In., Pair	277
Serving Dish, Peacock, Spread Tail Forms Dish, c.1910, 10 In., Pair	984
Serving Spoon, Coffin End, Sawtooth Cartouche, Engraved, c.1808, 10 In.	200
Spoon, Repousse Rembrandt Portrait, Twist Stem, Dolphins, c.1850, 8 In.	71
Spoon, Souvenir, see Souvenir category.	
Sugar Castor, Acorn Finial, Gadroon, J.E. Caldwell & Co., 1800s, 9 In.	175
Sugar, Lid, Lobed, Flower Band, Scroll Handles, Basket Finial, c.1850, 10 In.	1000
Tazza, Dragonfly, Leaves, Scallop Rim, Pedestal Foot, 1882, 6 In. Diam.	708
Tea Caddy, Lily, Pheasant, Metal, Hammered, Cylindrical, 1880, 5 In.	3321
Teapot, Faceted Urn Shape, Wood Handle, Bears, Monogram, 1802, 12 In.	472
Teapot, George III, Oval, Lid, Beaded Edges, Footed, c.1782, 5 In.	861
Teapot, Hinged Lid, Fluted, Swan Neck Spout, Ebony Handle, 7 x 10 In.	354
Teapot, Hinged Lid, Repousse Leaves, Squat, Square Handle, c.1880, 4 x 6 In.	295
Teapot, Lid, Bullet Shape, Engraved Leaves, Coat Of Arms, c.1733, 4 In.	1353
Teapot, Trophy, Wood Handle, Finial, The Ballston Cup, Saratoga, c.1910, 7 In.	738
Tray, Oval, Leaf Scrolls, Shield Crest, Ribbed Handles, c.1797, 22 In.	2963
Tray, Serving, Lid, Top Loop Handle, Relief Flower Band, 1818, 14 In.	1481
Tureen, Lid, Oval, Beaded, Stepped Foot, Loop Handles, c.1781, 16 In.	2666
Tureen, Lid, Urn Shape, Beaded Loop Handles, Panel Foot, 1892, 15 In.	1845
Vase, Chevron Design, Flower Rim, Trumpet, Dome Foot, c.1910, 7 In.	4920
Vase, Daisies, Leaves, Hammered, Roll Down Collar, 10 x 11 In.	1534
Wine Cooler, Grapevines, Swags, Upright Handles, c.1814, 11 x 8 In.	3000
Wine Funnel, Domed Bowl, Gadroon Rim, Monogram, c.1783, 4 x 3 In.	625

SILVER-TIBETAN

Teapot, Zodiac Symbols, Dragon, Jade Rings, Lid, Monkey Finial, 1940s, 15 In.	485

SILVER-TURKISH

Charger, Crescent & Star, 4-Footed, 12 ½ In.	625
Vase, Village Scene, Cylindrical, Scrolls & Latticework, 1900s, 24 x 5 In.	405

SINCLAIRE cut glass was made by H.P. Sinclaire and Company of Corning, New York, between 1904 and 1929. He cut glass made at other factories until 1920. Pieces were made of crystal as well as amber, blue, green, or ruby glass. Only a small percentage of Sinclaire glass is marked with the *S* in a wreath.

Tankard, Bengal Pattern, 6 Matching Tumblers, 4 & 9 ½ In.	1380
Vase, Amethyst, Grapes, Leaves, 9 In.	121
Vase, Paneled, Egyptian Man, Hieroglyphs, Black, Acid Cut, 11 In.	698

Silver-Norwegian, Pitcher, Hammered, Enamel, Carnelians, David Andersen, 1880s, 10 x 4 In.
$5,000

Rago Arts and Auction Center

Silver-Norwegian, Salt, Open, Viking Boat, Plique-A-Jour, Glass Insert, Marius Hammer, c.1900, 2 ¼ In.
$373

Jeffrey S. Evans

Silver-Russian, Box, Hammered, Applied Dragonflies, Silver Folded Tapestry Lid, Marked, 3 x 2 In.
$2,400

Cowan's Auctions

S

Sleepy Eye, Pitcher, Cobalt Blue On Tan, Weir Pottery, 1899-1905, 9 x 7 In. $920

Allard Auctions

Sleepy Eye, Vase, Indian Chief, Cattails & Dragonfly, Embossed, Cobalt Blue, 9 In. $196

Wm Morford Auctions

Smith Brothers, Pitcher, Acorns & Leaves, 4 x 4 ½ In. $295

Ruby Lane

SKIING, *see Sports category.*

 SLAG GLASS resembles a marble cake. It can be streaked with different colors. There were many types made from about 1880. Caramel slag is the incorrect name for chocolate glass. Pink slag was an American product made by Harry Bastow and Thomas E.A. Dugan at Indiana, Pennsylvania, about 1900. Purple and blue slag were made in American and English factories in the 1880s. Red slag is a very late Victorian and twentieth-century glass. Other colors are known but are of less importance to the collector. New versions of chocolate glass and colored slag glass have been made.

Box, Green, Bronze Openwork, Green Patina, Apollo Studios, 11 x 7 In.	156
Caramel Slag is listed in the Imperial Glass category.	
Lamp, Electric, Lighted Base, Amber, Cream, 1910, 22 x 19 ½ In.	826
Shade, Spider Web Overlay, c.1920, 4 ½ x 8 In.	246

 SLEEPY EYE collectors look for anything bearing the image of the nineteenth-century Indian chief with the drooping eyelid. The Sleepy Eye Milling Co., Sleepy Eye, Minnesota, used his portrait in advertising from 1883 to 1921. It offered many premiums, including stoneware and pottery steins, crocks, bowls, mugs, and pitchers, all decorated with the famous profile of the Indian. The popular pottery was made by Weir Pottery Co. from c.1899 to 1905. Weir merged with six other potteries and became Western Stoneware in 1906. Western Stoneware Co. made blue and white Sleepy Eye from 1906 until 1937, long after the flour mill went out of business in 1921. Reproductions of the pitchers are being made today. The original pitchers came in only five sizes: 4 inches, 5 ¼ inches, 6 ½ inches, 8 inches, and 9 inches. The Sleepy Eye image was also used by companies unrelated to the flour mill.

Advertising Sign, Painted Sheet Metal, Cutouts, 58 In.	3600
Crock, Butter, Blue, Gray, Indian Head, Teepees, c.1905, 5 x 7 In.	495
Fan, Die Cut Indian Chief, Sleep Eye Milling Co., Flour & Cereals, 13 ¼ x 6 In.	307
Mug, Cobalt Blue, Indian Chief, Teepee, Molded Head Thumb Rest, 8 In.	733
Pitcher, Blue, White, 4 x 4 ¼ In.	74
Pitcher, Blue, White, Indian Chief, Teepees, 8 In.	375
Pitcher, Blue, Yellow, Weir Pottery, 1900s, 9 x 7 In.	860
Pitcher, Cobalt Blue On Tan, Weir Pottery, 1899-1905, 9 x 7 In. ....*illus*	920
Pitcher, Indian Chief Head, Teepees, Cobalt Blue, 6 ¼ In.	75
Pitcher, Indian Chief Head, Teepees, Cobalt Blue, 8 In.	295
Plaque, Brown Glaze, Indian Chief, Collectors Club, Oval, 1979, 6 x 5 In.	315
Stein, Blue, White, Indian Chief, Tree, Molded Head Thumb Rest, Marked, 1979, 8 In.	200
Stein, Brown, Tan, Indian Chief, Tree, Molded Head Thumb Rest, Marked, 1980, 7 In.	155
Vase, Cream, Cobalt Blue, Cattails, Cylindrical, Rolled Collar, 9 In.	181
Vase, Indian Chief Head, Stoneware, Weir Co., 1900s, 8 ½ In.	175
Vase, Indian Chief, Cattails & Dragonfly, Embossed, Cobalt Blue, 9 In. ....*illus*	196
Vase, White, Pale Blue, Indian Head, Cattails, Dragonfly, Frog, Cylindrical, 8 ½ In.	145

SLOT MACHINES *are included in the Coin-Operated Machine category.*

Smith Bros. Co. **SMITH BROTHERS** glass was made after 1878. Alfred and Harry Smith had worked for the Mt. Washington Glass Company in New Bedford, Massachusetts, for seven years before going into their own shop. They made many pieces with enamel decoration.

Biscuit Jar, What Stocks, Green Leaves, Marked SB, 9 In.	110
Bowl, Nut, Ribbed, Daisies, Silver Rim, 10 In.	92
Jar, Lid, Opal, Lobed, Brown, Green Ferns, 4 ¼ In.	61
Jar, Lid, Opal, Lobed, Pink & Blue Daisies, 6 In.	86
Pitcher, Acorns & Leaves, 4 x 4 ½ In. ....*illus*	295
Rose Bowl, Cream, Lobed, Brown, Green Leaves, 6 In., Pair	120
Vase, Cream, Molded Flowers, Blue Scrolls, Gilt Flowers, 9 In.	153
Vase, Opal, Birds, Leaves, Multicolor, Pale Blue Ground, 7 ¼ In., Pair	338
Vase, Opal, Ship, Santa Maria, Flattened, Oval Pedestal, 8 ½ In.	1495

SNOW BABIES, made from bisque and spattered with glitter sand, were first manufactured in 1864 by Hertwig and Company of Thuringia. Other German and Japanese companies copied the Hertwig designs. Originally, Snow Babies were made of candy and used as Christmas decorations. There are also Snow Babies tablewares made by Royal Bayreuth. Copies of the small Snow Babies figurines are being made today and a line called "Snowbabies" was introduced by Department 56 in 1987. Don't confuse these with the original Snow Babies.

Candleholder, Birthday, Baby, Standing, Outstretched Arms, Red Hat, 1 In.	104
Candy Container, Baby On Gift Box, Merry Christmas Tag, Germany, 3 ½ In.	595
Figurine, Baby On Skis, Knees Bent, c.1920, 1 ½ In.	93
Figurine, Baby, Holding Ski Upright, Waving, Snowsuit, 1920s, 1 ¾ In.	154
Figurine, Baby, Sliding Down Hill, Polar Bear, Hertwig & Co., c.1900, 2 x 2 In.	109
Figurine, Girl, On Sled, Red Skirt, Arms Raised, Germany, 1 ½ x 1 In.	181
Figurine, Girl, Standing, 4 ½ In.	108
Figurine, Kneeling Baby, Raised Arms, Snowsuit, 1 ½ In.	102
Figurine, Sitting Tumbler, Outstretched Arms, Snowsuit, Germany, 1930s, 2 In.	199
Figurine, Snow Santa, In Airplane, Hertwig & Co., c.1900, 2 ¼ x 2 In.	95
Ornament, Baby, Standing On Snowball, Waving, 1920s, 2 ¼ In.	89

SNUFF BOTTLES *are listed in the Bottle category.*

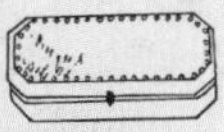

SNUFFBOXES held snuff. Taking snuff was popular long before cigarettes became available. The gentleman or lady would take a small pinch of the ground tobacco or snuff in the fingers, then sniff it and sneeze. Snuffboxes were made of many materials, including gold, silver, enameled metal, and wood. Most snuffboxes date from the late eighteenth or early nineteenth centuries.

18K Gold, Flowers, Leaves, France, 2 ¾ In.	2750
Architectural Scenes, Rectangular, Russia, c.1850, 3 ¼ In.	437
Bone, Relief Carved, Brass Plated, Nickel, Bust Portrait, Man, Leaves, 4 In.	156
Bone, Scrimshaw, Ball Joint, Figures & Verse, Continental, 1800s, 2 ½ In.	120
Burled Walnut, Portrait, General Lafayette, 1800s, 3 In.	875
Cowrie Shell, Engraved Lid, Federal Eagle & Flower Swag, 4 In.	3500
Gold Plate, Tiger's Eye, Carnelian Cabochons, Soapstone, 1930s, 1 x 2 In.	110
Gold, Bird, Red, Blue Cabochons, Paw Feet, Movement, Sound, Windup, Germany, 5 In.	1560
Gold, Bird, Red, Cream, Reserve, Courting Couple, Movement, 5 ¾ In.	1045
Gold, Painted Glass, Fisherman Scene, Enamel, St. Petersburg, Russia, c.1790, 3 In. ....*illus*	11070
Horn, Musical, Figured Lid, Silver Hinge, Plays Home Sweet Home, Swiss, c.1840, 4 In.	1229
Pewter, Pistol Shape, Double Barrel, Flint Lock, Hinged Lid, c.1815, 3 In., Pair	246
Porcelain, Gilt, White, Molded Flowers, Woman & Pug Interior Lid, c.1765, 3 In.	5877
Porcelain, Painted Deer, Bat, Coral Bead Stopper, 5 x 2 ¼ In.	4750
Silver Plate, Bird, Repousse, Multicolor, Movement, Windup, 4 In.	1845
Silver, Bird, Black, Openwork, Movement, Sound, Windup, 4 In.	1968
Silver, Chamfered, Repousse, Poseidon & Amphitrite, Chariot, 1842, 1 x 3 In.	369
Silver, Coi Fish, Reticulated Scales, Reeded Fins, Hinged Head, 14 ½ In.	502
Silver, Niello Design, 4 x 2 ½ In.	118
Silver, Rectangular, Leaves, Flowers, Cartouche, C-Scrolls, 3 In.	150

SOAPSTONE is a mineral that was used for foot warmers or griddles because of its heat-retaining properties. Soapstone was carved into figurines and bowls in many countries in the nineteenth and twentieth centuries. Most of the soapstone seen today is from China or Japan. It is still being carved in the old styles.

Brushpot, Globular, Wide Rim, Stylized Branches, Figures, Red, 1 x 4 In.	215
Carving, Ginseng Root, Boys Playing, Yellow, Mottled Green Glaze, 10 x 6 In.	3690
Carving, Horse, Standing, Tree Stump, Mottled Gray, Chinese, 10 x 11 In.	100

SOFT PASTE is a name for a type of pottery. Although it looks very much like porcelain, it is a chemically different material. Most of the soft-paste wares were made in the early nineteenth century. Other pieces may be listed under Gaudy Dutch or Leeds.

Snuffbox, Gold, Painted Glass, Fisherman Scene, Enamel, St. Petersburg, Russia, c.1790, 3 In. $11,070

Skinner, Inc.

TIP

Don't store fabrics in plastic bags. Use a well-washed white pillowcase. Plastic holds moisture, and the fabrics should "breathe."

Soft Paste, Bowl, Figural, Asian Boys Holding Bowl, Menecy Porcelain Factory, France, c.1750, 13 ½ In. $3,800

Ruby Lane

Souvenir, Scarf, Las Vegas, Casinos, Yellow, Green Highlights, Blue Skies, Rayon, 1960s, 36 In. $36

Ruby Lane

S

Spangle Glass, Jug, Cased, Green, Blue, Yellow, Cream, Mica, Applied Handle, c.1900, 4 1/2 In.

$275

Jeffrey S. Evans

Spatter Glass, Pitcher, Maroon, Opal, Applied Handle, Phoenix Glass, 1883-88, 8 In.

$136

Jeffrey S. Evans

Spatterware, Pepper Pot, Peafowl, Dome Top, Blue, Yellow, Black, Branch, 4 1/2 In.

$2,655

Hess Auction Group

Bowl, Egg & Spinach Glaze, Chinese, 6 3/4 In.	274
Bowl, Figural, Asian Boys Holding Bowl, Menecy Porcelain Factory, France, c.1750, 13 1/2 In....*illus*	3800
Coffeepot, Lid, Landscape, Ruins, Trees, Lake, Peasants, c.1780, 8 In.	1865
Creamer, Tent, Bushes, Red, Blue, c.1820, 4 x 6 In.	95
Cup & Saucer, Berries & Leaves, Pink Luster, Handleless, 1800s, 2 x 6 In.	77
Cup & Saucer, Sprig, Green, Pink, Paneled, c.1850, 2 x 4 In. & 4 x 6 In.	65
Cup, Tulip, White, Fuchsia, Green, Flared, Handleless, 1800s, 3 x 4 In.	45
Figurine, Falstaff, Derby c.1830, 15 x 8 1/2 In.	360
Inkwell, Flowers, 5 Paw Feet, c.1900, Italy, 4 1/2 x 12 In.	60
Plate, Brown Transferware, Signed Cologne, 10 In.	50
Plate, Feather, Red & Yellow Flowers, Teal Feathers, 1840s, 8 In.	32
Plate, King's Rose, Crosshatch Border, Purple Luster Bands, c.1824, 7 In.	88
Teapot, Sprigs, Leaves, Fuchsia Flowers, Paneled, C-Scroll Handle, 11 x 8 1/2 In.	190
Vase, Lid, Reticulated Band, C-Scroll Handles, Luss Straits, Loch Lomond, Locke & Co., 9 x 6 In.	275

SOUVENIRS of a trip—what could be more fun? Our ancestors enjoyed the same thing and souvenirs were made for almost every location. Most of the souvenir pottery and porcelain pieces of the nineteenth century were made in England or Germany, even if the picture showed a North American scene. In the twentieth century, the souvenir china business seems to have been dominated by the manufacturers in Japan, Taiwan, Hong Kong, England, and the United States. Another popular souvenir item is the souvenir spoon, made of sterling or silver plate. These are usually made in the country pictured on the spoon. Related pieces may be found in the Coronation and World's Fair categories.

Button, Atlantic City, Man & Woman, Swimsuits, Ocean, c.1896, 1 In.	115
Button, Armory Show, Modern Art Exhibition, Stylized Pine Tree, 1913, 1 In.	482
Button, Circus, Tiniest Man On Earth, Paul Del Rio, Portrait, 1930s, 1 3/4 In.	380
Button, Mid-West Championship, Omaha, Cartoon Tennis Player, 1904, 1 1/4 In.	115
Button, Oakland El Rey Burlesk, T.S. Club, Tempest Storm, Portrait, c.1945, 1 In.	115
Button, Waterloo Street Fair, Lady Liberty, Eagle, Horn, c.1900, 2 In.	115
Button, Yazoo Valley, Black Workers In Cotton Field, Land Promotion, 1 1/4 In.	115
Compact, Washington, D.C., Capitol, Berry Blossoms, Metal, Enamel, 1930s, 2 3/4 In.	35
Plate, Washington, D.C., Capitol Building, Porcelain, Landmark Bldg., 10 In.	25
Scarf, Las Vegas, Casinos, Yellow, Green Highlights, Blue Skies, Rayon, 1960s, 36 In.......*illus*	36
Statue, Hawaiian Hubba Hula Girl, Topless, String Skirt, Plaster, 1947, 14 In.	190
Token, Good Luck Horseshoe, Buffalo Bill Wild West Show, 1901, 1 1/2 In.	720

SPANGLE GLASS is multicolored glass made from odds and ends of colored glass rods. It includes metallic flakes of mica covered with gold, silver, nickel, or copper. Spangle glass is usually cased with a thin layer of clear glass over the multicolored layer. Similar glass is listed in the Vasa Murrhina category.

Bride's Bowl, Fuchsia To White, Mica Flecks, Ruffled Rim, c.1890s, 3 x 10 In.	79
Ewer, Cranberry, Pink, Silver Flecks, Ruffled Rim, Saucer Foot, 1800s, 7 In.	114
Jug, Cased, Green, Blue, Yellow, Cream, Mica, Applied Handle, c.1900, 4 1/2 In. ....*illus*	275
Pitcher, Coral, Silver Flakes, Crimped Rim, Reeded Handle, 1930s, 9 In.	118
Rose Bowl, Cased Opal, Pink, Cranberry, Clear, Scroll Trim, c.1905, 3 In.	124
Rose Bowl, Fuchsia, Mottled, Silver Flecks, Folded-In Rim, 1890s, 5 In.	105
Vase, Blue & Green Spatter, Mica, Ribbons, Squat, Ruffled Rim, c.1960, 4 In.	75
Vase, Cranberry, Silver Spangles, Melon, Crimped Rim, Saucer Foot, c.1890, 6 In.	89
Vase, Turquoise, White, Mica Flakes, Applied Vine, Globular, Stick Neck, 1800s, 9 In.	105

SPANISH LACE *is listed in the Opalescent category as Opaline Brocade.*

SPATTER GLASS is a multicolored glass made from many small pieces of different colored glass. It is sometimes called End-of-Day glass. It is still being made.

Basket, Orange, Fuchsia, Dimpled, Crimped Rim, Clear Wavy Handle, 1800s, 6 In.	126
Basket, Sky Blue, Red Spatters, Crimped, Rim, Twisted Handle, c.1890, 7 x 5 In.	149
Box, Gilt Flower Band, Cranberry, Opal, Blue, Oval, Ball Feet, 4 1/2 x 5 In.	240

Box, Yellow, Gilt Metal, Scrolling Gilt, Ball Feet, 4¼ x 5¼ In.	210
Finger Bowl, Green, Cream Spatters, Bulbous, Lobed, 1800s, 3 x 5 In.	95
Jar, Female Torso Shape, Red, Green, 12 In.	47
Lamp, Hobnail, Pink, 9¼ x 5 In.	59
Pitcher, Blue Opalescent Spatters, Spherical, Crimped Square Rim, c.1910, 9 In.	175
Pitcher, Clear, Yellow & Opalescent Spatters, Bulbous, Spill Over Rim, c.1925, 8 In.	99
Pitcher, Light Blue, Mold Blown, Fern Leaf, Reeded Handle, 7 x 7¾ In.	72
Pitcher, Maroon, Opal, Applied Handle, Phoenix Glass, 1883-88, 8 In. ....*illus*	136
Pitcher, Spot Optic, Pale Blue, Opal, Triangular Rim, Reeded Handle, 8 In.	36
Rose Bowl, Clear, White, Turquoise, Fuchsia Spatters, Folded-In Rim, c.1890, 3 In.	146
Vase, Cobalt Blue, Multicolor Spatters, Smokestack, Upright Handles, 1920s, 6 In.	180
Vase, Cranberry, White & Green Spatters, Ribbed, Oval, Flared Rim, c.1920, 9 In.	189
Vase, Flared, Green, White, 10 In.	54
Vase, Fuchsia, White, Blue Spatters, Lobed, Ruffled Rim, Round Foot, c.1960, 14 In.	290
Vase, Opaque White, Frost, Cobalt Blue, Turquoise Spatters, Trumpet, 1940s, 10 In.	164
Vase, Orange, Blue, Green, Threaded, Smokestack, Tulip Top, 1920s, 9 In.	99
Vase, Yellow To White, Basket Weave, Ruffled Rim, 7½ x 3½ In.	60

SPATTERWARE and spongeware are terms that have changed in meaning in recent years, causing much confusion for collectors. Some say that *spatterware* is the term used by Americans, *sponged ware* or *spongeware* by the English. The earliest pieces were made in the late eighteenth century, but most of the spatterware found today was made from about 1800 to 1850. Early spatterware was made in the Staffordshire district of England for sale in America. Collectors also use the word *spatterware* to refer to kitchen crockery with added spatter made in America during the late nineteenth and early twentieth centuries. Spongeware is very similar to spatterware in appearance. Designs were applied to ceramics by daubing the color on with a sponge or cloth. Many collectors do not differentiate between spongeware and spatterware and use the names interchangeably. Modern pottery is being made to resemble old spatterware and spongeware, but careful examination will show it is new.

Basin, Green, Blue Morning Glory, 13 x 4¼ In.	111
Basin, Red, Peafowl, 5 x 15 In.	240
Creamer, Peafowl, Leafy Branches, Shaped Spout, Saucer Foot, 1800s, 3 In.	425
Creamer, Tulip, Red Sponge, Swan Handle, 5¾ In.	49
Cup & Saucer, Blue, Purple, Rainbow, 2 Piece	2040
Cup & Saucer, Blue, Purple, Rainbow, Dahlia, 2 Piece	180
Cup & Saucer, Blue, Yellow, Tulip, 2 Piece	3120
Cup & Saucer, Red, Yellow, Bull's-Eye, 2 Piece	2040
Cup & Saucer, Red, Yellow, Thistle, 2 Piece	330
Cup & Saucer, Tree, Blue	187
Cup, Blue, White, Canada, c.1820, 4 In.	400
Entree, Lid, Blue, Holly Berry, 7½ x 10¼ In.	120
Jardiniere, Ritter, Blue Sponge, Cream Ground, 29 In.	320
Mug, Peafowl, Leafy Branch, Blue Banded Rim, Loop Handle, 1800s, 4 In.	800
Pepper Pot, Peafowl, Dome Top, Blue, Yellow, Black, Branch, 4½ In. ....*illus*	2655
Pitcher & Basin, Blue, Fort, 10¼ In., 2 Piece	74
Pitcher, 3 Blue Bands, Black, Blue Sponge, c.1850, 7¾ x 5½ In. ....*illus*	285
Pitcher, Basin, Purple, Black, Stripes, Rainbow, 2 Piece	390
Pitcher, Cobalt Blue, Sponge, 9½ In.	86
Pitcher, Yellow, Red Tulip In White Reserve, 7¾ In.	1140
Plate, Acorn Pattern, Blue Rim, England, Early 1800s, 9 In.	1020
Plate, Fort, Blue Sponge Border, 1800s, 7½ In.	185
Plate, Peafowl On Branch, Red, 1800s, 8 In.	83
Plate, Peafowl, Red, Blue, Ocher, Green, Ruffled Rim, c.1830, 9 In.	425
Plate, Red, Peafowl On Branch, Purple, Green & Yellow, 6½ In.	165
Plate, Tulip, Blue Rim, England, Early 1800s, 9½ In.	120
Platter, Rainbow, Octagonal, 1920s, 13 In.	1354
Platter, Red, Yellow, Flowers, Blue Sponge Border, 15 x 19 In.	74
Soup, Dish, Red, Blue & Green Bands, Wavy Rim, 10¾ In. Diam.	106
Sugar, Lid, Blue, Green, Sponge, 1800s, 4¾ In.	62

Spatterware, Pitcher, 3 Blue Bands, Black, Blue Sponge, c.1850, 7¾ x 5½ In. $285

Ruby Lane

Spinning Wheel, Shaker, Maple, Oak Table, Carved, Turned Handle, c.1830, 43 x 25 In. $1,200

Willis Henry Auctions

Sports, Baseball, Ball, Autographed, Yankees World Champions, Team Signed, Gehrig, c.1938 $2,700

Robert Edward Auctions

S

This is an edited listing of current prices. Visit **Kovels.com** to check thousands of prices from previous years and sign up for free information on trends, tips, reproductions, marks, and more.

Sports, Baseball, Box, Royal Desserts, Royal Stars Of Baseball No. 11, Rizzuto, Unopened, 1950
$540

Robert Edward Auctions

Sports, Baseball, Cigar Label, Honus Wagner, Inner Labels, Band, Frame, c.1909, 13 x 5 In., 2 Piece
$3,000

Robert Edward Auctions

Sports, Baseball, Felt, B18 Blanket, Red Infield, Variation Of Harry Coveleski, Square, 5 In.
$3,900

Robert Edward Auctions

TIP

A hair dryer set for cool can be used to blow the dust off very ornate pieces of porcelain.

Sugar, Lid, Red, Blue, Green, Drape Pattern, 1800s, 5 In.	390
Sugar, Red Cockscomb, Blue, 5 ¼ In.	49
Sugar, Thistle Pattern, Red & Yellow Rainbow, 5 In.	354
Teapot, Purple Star, 6 In.	120
Teapot, Purple, Dove, 5 ½ In.	49
Teapot, Red Shed, 1800s, 5 ¾ In.	1292
Teapot, Red, Peafowl, 7 x 9 ¾ In.	308
Toddy Plate, Peafowl, Blue & Green, Red Border	413
Waste Bowl, Red, Thistle, Footed, 1940s, 9 ½ In.	2298

SPELTER is a synonym for a zinc alloy. Figurines, candlesticks, and other pieces were made of spelter and given a bronze or painted finish. The metal has been used since about the 1860s to make statues, tablewares, and lamps that resemble bronze. Spelter is soft and breaks easily. To test for spelter, scratch the base of the piece. Bronze is solid; spelter will show a silvery scratch.

Sculpture, Bird, Wood Base, 15 x 14 In.	87
Sculpture, Dog, Labrador Retriever, Sitting, c.1890, 6 In.	100
Sculpture, Knight In Armor, Stepped Base, 1900s, 19 x 7 In.	125
Sculpture, Man, Catch Of Fish, 19 ¾ In.	135
Sculpture, Warrior On Horseback, Rearing Horse, Giltwood Base, 22 x 12 In., Pair	350
Sculpture, Warriors, Battle, Swords, Daggers, Chest Shields, Helmets, 25 x 11 In., Pair	283
Sculpture, Woman, Birds, Dog, c.1940, 10 x 17 ¾ In.	125

SPINNING WHEELS in the corner have been symbols of earlier times for the past 100 years. Although spinning wheels date back to medieval days, the ones found today are rarely more than 200 years old. Because the style of the spinning wheel changed very little, it is often impossible to place an exact date on a wheel.

Shaker, Maple, Oak Table, Carved, Turned Handle, c.1830, 43 x 25 In. *illus*	1200
Silk, Walnut, Wrought Iron, 1800s, 62 ½ x 38 In.	1562
Wood, Turned Legs, Spindles, Finials, Table Top, Castle, 49 In.	236

SPODE
Stone-China

SPODE pottery, porcelain, and bone china were made by the Stoke-on-Trent factory of England founded by Josiah Spode about 1770. The firm became Copeland and Garrett from 1833 to 1847, then W.T. Copeland or W.T. Copeland and Sons until 1976. It then became Royal Worcester Spode Ltd. The company was bought by the Portmeirion Group in 2009. The word *Spode* appears on many pieces made by the factories. Most collectors include all the wares under the more familiar name of Spode. Porcelains are listed in this book by the name that appears on the piece. Related pieces may be listed under Copeland, Copeland Spode, and Royal Worcester.

Cake Plate, Square, England, 9 ¼ In., Pair	88
Dish, Junket, Imari Pattern, Blue, Red, White, Gold Trim, Oval, c.1825, 17 x 14 In.	1680
Plate, Scalloped, Gadroon, Gilt, Leaves, Insects, 10 In., Pair	64
Plate, Songbird Series, Red, Black, Ray Harm, 9 In., 14 Piece	310

SPORTS equipment, sporting goods, brochures, and related items are listed here. Items are listed by sport. Other categories of interest are Bicycle, Card, Fishing, Sword, Toy, and Trap.

Badminton, Paddle, Painted, Woman, Starry Night, Terashima Tokushige, c.1930	3750
Baseball, Ashtray, Lighter, Brooklyn Dodgers, Stadium Shape, c.1950, 6 In.	226
Baseball, Ball, Autographed, Yankees World Champions, Team Signed, Gehrig, c.1938 *illus*	2700
Baseball, Ball, Lemon Peel, Single Piece Of Leather, 1850s	960
Baseball, Ball, Nellie Fox Single Signed, 15 Time All-Star, Blue Ink, c.1959	886
Baseball, Ball, Rawlings AL, Signed, Lefty Gomez, N.Y. Yankees, c.1935	221
Baseball, Banner, Dodgers, Autographs, 9 Players	600
Baseball, Base, Signed, Mickey Mantle, No. 7	1080
Baseball, Bat, Jackie Robinson Autograph, Hillerich & Bradsby, c.1970	1560
Baseball, Bat, Louisville Slugger, Signed By Ted Williams	600

S

Sports, Baseball, Felt, B18 Blanket, Ty Cobb, 1914, 5¼ In.
$360

Robert Edward Auctions

Sports, Baseball, Lithograph, Game In Progress, Color, L. Prang, Frame, 1887, 27 x 23 In.
$2,700

Robert Edward Auctions

Sports, Baseball, Pennant, Christy Mathewson, Giants, Cravats Series, Felt, 1913, 9 In.
$840

Robert Edward Auctions

Sports, Baseball, Pennant, New York Yankees, Uncle Sam, Wood Bat, 1950s, 28 In.
$2,700

Robert Edward Auctions

Sports, Billiards, Table, Pace, Steel, Burl Elm, Leather, Blatt Billiards, 1950s, 32 x 60 In.
$3,000

New Orleans Auction Galleries

TIP
For the best deal on a sports collectible, shop off-season.

Sports, Bowling, Stein, Tavern Bowling, Pewter Lid, Villeroy & Boch, c.1904, 3 Liter
$330

Cowan's Auctions

Sports, Hunting, Cartridge Board, Winchester Repeating Arms, Cardboard, Frame, 38 x 51 In.
$16,675

James D. Julia Auctioneers

Sports, Seats, Polo Grounds, 3-Seat Section, Double Figural, Freestanding Unit
$2,040

S

Robert Edward Auctions

Sports, Snowshoes, Indian, Bentwood, Laced Rawhide, Wool Tufts, c.1925, 43 x 31 In., Pair
$173

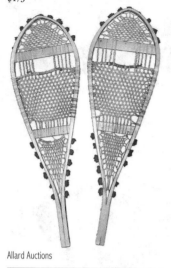

Allard Auctions

Staffordshire, Figurine, Dog, Poodle, Seated, Separate Front Feet, 9 x 6 In.
$140

Ruby Lane

Staffordshire, Mug, Agate, Cream & Brown, Blue Splashes, c.1755, 4 In.
$1,968

Skinner, Inc.

Baseball, Biography, Score Book, Champions, 1912, World's Series, Fenway Park, 10 In.	1560
Baseball, Box, Royal Desserts, Royal Stars Of Baseball No. 11, Rizzuto, Unopened, 1950...*illus*	540
Baseball, Button, Boston Red Sox, Ted Williams, Portrait, Tin Lithograph, 1956, 1 In.	115
Baseball, Button, Mantle & Maris, Photo Portraits, Baseball, 61 In '61 Or Bust, 4 In.	3102
Baseball, Button, Willie Mays, Green Duck, Portrait, Tin Litho, c.1972, 2 In.	267
Baseball, Charger, Lou Gehrig Memorial, Brass, Baseball Shape, Portrait, 1953, 9 In.	570
Baseball, Cigar Label, Honus Wagner, Inner Labels, Band, Frame, c.1909, 13 x 5 In., 2 Piece... *illus*	3000
Baseball, Clicker, Umpire's, Strike, Ball, Out, Stainless Steel, Wilson, 3 ¼ x 2 In.	24
Baseball, Drawing, Pencil, Babe Ruth, Signed, Sincerely, Babe Ruth, 1947, 7 In.	2400
Baseball, Felt, B18 Blanket, Red Infield, Variation Of Harry Coveleski, Square, 5 In.........*illus*	3900
Baseball, Felt, B18 Blanket, Ty Cobb, 1914, 5 ¼ In. *illus*	360
Baseball, Lemonade Set, Glass, Mary Gregory Style Players, 1880s, 6 Piece	600
Baseball, License Plate, 1939 New York World's Fair, Joe DiMaggio Signature	480
Baseball, Lithograph, Game In Progress, Color, L. Prang, Frame, 1887, 27 x 23 In. ....*illus*	2700
Baseball, Medallion, Brass, N.Y. Yankees, World Champion, 1961, 1 ½ In.	127
Baseball, Nodder, Player, New York Yankee, Composition, Painted, Label, c.1962, 6 ½ In.	255
Baseball, Pencil Case, Joe DiMaggio, Yankee Stadium, Snap Closure, 3 x 8 In.	192
Baseball, Pennant, Christy Mathewson, Giants, Cravats Series, Felt, 1913, 9 In. *illus*	840
Baseball, Pennant, Detroit Tigers, Felt, Black, Orange, Tiger's Head, Tassels, 1915, 29 In.	840
Baseball, Pennant, New York Yankees, Uncle Sam, Wood Bat, 1950s, 28 In. *illus*	2700
Baseball, Pennant, Phillies, Felt, Appliqued, Blue, White, 1915, 35 In.	7200
Baseball, Pennant, Red Sox, Red & White Felt, Tassels, 1912, 17 ½ In.	7200
Baseball, Photograph, Babe Ruth & Lou Gehrig, Yankee Stadium, c.1930, 7 In.	540
Baseball, Photograph, New York Yankees, Team, Panoramic, 1953, 15 x 32 In.	840
Baseball, Pillow Top, Leather, 1914 World Champion, Boston Braves, Frame, 26 x 33 In.	2450
Baseball, Postcard, Philadelphia Athletics, Champions, Panoramic, 1911, 11 x 3 In.	1200
Baseball, Poster, Coming!, Champion Young Lady Ball Players, 1890s, 32 x 15 In.	4200
Baseball, Presentation Tray, N.Y. Yankees, World Champions, Silver Plate, 1953, 13 In.	702
Baseball, Radio, Wood, Plastic, Batter, Autographs, M. Mantle & R. Maris, c.1962	2280
Baseball, Ring, Jack Armstrong, Centennial, Brass, Batter, Crossed Bats, 1938	115
Baseball, Ring, Scorer, Brass, Ball, Notched Wheels, Turn Numbers, 1950s	822
Baseball, Scorecard, 1919 World Series, Portraits, Cincinnati Reds, Pat Moran	3000
Baseball, Seat, Freestanding, Yankee Stadium	1440
Baseball, Scorer, M.H. Taggart, Liquor Dealer, Mitt Shape, Number Wheels, 3 In.	421
Baseball, Silver Pass, National League, Mr. & Mrs. M.J. Groh, Brooklyn, 1896	1950
Baseball, Stitching Vise On Bench, Wood, Metal, Spalding, 21 x 11 x 22 In.	540
Baseball, Tray, Detroit Tigers, Wood, Handles, Ball, Tiger, 1934 Champions, 7 x 16 In.	335
Basketball, Ball, Seamed With Laces, Sonnett Craft Built, 1900s, 9 In.	156
Basketball, Lighter, Tabletop, St. Louis Hawks, Mascot, Dribbling Ball, c.1958, 2 x 3 In.	127
Basketball, Shoes, Air Jordan I, Black, Red, Game Issued, Signed 1985	8962
Basketball, Shoes, Air Jordan IV, Black, Michael Jordan Worn, Signed, c.1988	8365
Billiards, Table, Pace, Steel, Burl Elm, Leather, Blatt Billiards, 1950s, 32 x 60 In..........*illus*	3000
Bowling, 10 Pins, 2 Balls, Table Top, Box, Cream, Red & Black Bands, 12 Piece	99
Bowling, Stein, Tavern Bowling, Pewter Lid, Villeroy & Boch, c.1904, 3 Liter ....*illus*	330
Boxing, Poster, Heavyweight Championship, Ali Vs. Foreman, Sept. 24, 1974.	300
Boxing, Poster, Muhammad Ali, Sonny Liston Vs. Cassius Clay, 1964, 14 x 22 In.	589
Boxing, Program, Heavyweight Championship, J. Braddock Vs. J. Louis, 1937, 24 Pages.	1440
Boxing, Ticket, Muhammad Ali Vs. Floyd Patterson, Press Box, Nov. 22, 1965.	300
Boxing, Ticket, Muhammad Ali Vs. Sonny Liston, Boston Garden, Nov. 16, 1964.	300
Boxing, Trophy, De Molay Boxing Championship, Silver Plate, Boxers, 1933, 13 x 11 In.	700
Football, Helmet, Black Leather, Dog Ear Style, Chin Strap, Padded, Wilson, 1920s	1005
Football, Helmet, Leather, Blue & Yellow, Hutch H-10, Early 1900s, 8 In.	250
Football, Program, Rose Bowl, Alabama Vs. Stanford, January 1st, 1927	600
Golf, Bag & Clubs, Canvas, Leather Trim, 10 Clubs, Early 1900s, 34 In.	156
Golf, Ball Marker, Stamping Machine, Cast Iron, Dial, Handle, Omnes, c.1910, 8 x 11 In.	1000
Golf, Figure, Penfold Golf, He Played A Penfold, Argyle Vest, Hat, Plaster, c.1930, 19 In.	1195
Hunting, Cartridge Board, Winchester Repeating Arms, Cardboard, Frame, 38 x 51 In.....*illus*	16675
Ice Skating, Skates, Wooden Platform, 11 ½ In.	36
Ice Skating, Skates, Wrought Iron, 1 Blade, Curled Tips, Flower, c.1840, 5 x 15 In.	1896
Juggling, Pins, Wood, Carved, Painted, Late 1800s, 2 Pair, 24 In. & 22 In.	850

Polo, Mallet, Wood, Paper Label, Ambercrombie & Fitch, Mid 1900s, 51 In.	94
Pool, Table, Ebonized Elephant Head Legs, Black, 31 x 104 In.	1070
Seats, Polo Grounds, 3-Seat Section, Double Figural, Freestanding Unit ....*illus*	2040
Snowshoes, Indian, Bentwood, Laced Rawhide, Wool Tufts, c.1925, 43 x 31 In., Pair........*illus*	173
Snowshoes, Wood Frames, Rawhide Lacing, Early 1900s, 39 In.	150
Snowshoes, Wood Frames, Rawhide Lacing, Leather Ties, c.1880, 42½ In.	150

STAFFORDSHIRE, England, has been a district making pottery and porcelain since the 1700s. Hundreds of kilns are still working in the area. Thousands of types of pottery and porcelain have been made in the many factories that worked and still work in the area. Some of the most famous factories have been listed separately, such as Adams, Davenport, Ridgway, Rowland & Marsellus, Royal Doulton, Royal Worcester, Spode, Wedgwood, and others. Some Staffordshire pieces are listed under categories like Fairing, Flow Blue, Mulberry, Shaving Mug, etc.

Bowl, Blue, Orange, Flowers, Royal Cauldon, 10 In.	25
Bowl, Vegetable, Tappan Zee From Greensburg, Blue Transfer, c.1836, 2 x 9 In.	1800
Bust, George Washington, Blue Coat, c.1920, 8 In.	271
Cake Stand, Capitol At Washington, Dark Blue, Footed, c.1820, 12 In.	2280
Coffeepot, Bald Eagle, Dark Blue, Transfer Print, 10 In.	2880
Coffeepot, Lafayette At Franklin's Tomb, Blue Transferware, c.1830, 11 In.	750
Creamer, Scroll Handle, Pineapples, Yellow, Green, c.1760, 3 In.	615
Creamer, Shaped Rim, Green & Yellow, Striped, c.1760, 4 In.	2460
Dish, Hen On Nest Lid, Red & White, 1800s, 4 In.	53
Ewer, Figural, Seated Man, Hat, Red Coat, Blue Pants, 9¾ In.	63
Figurine, Dog, Dalmatian, Rabbit In Mouth, Blue Base, 6 x 5 In., Pair	224
Figurine, Dog, Dalmation, Brown, Green Base, England, 6 x 6 In., Pair	106
Figurine, Dog, Poodle, Flower Basket, 1800s, 8 In., Pair	795
Figurine, Dog, Poodle, Seated, Separate Front Feet, 9 x 6 In..........*illus*	140
Figurine, Dog, Spaniel, Seated, Giltwood Base, c.1865, 21 x 9 In., Pair	1187
Figurine, Hawk, Spiral Turned Base, Mottled Green, Brown Glaze, 6 In.	1046
Figurine, Hen On Nest, Brown, Green & Yellow, Oval, c.1900, 4 x 4 In.	195
Figurine, Peacock, Multicolor, 12 In.	321
Group, Cow & Calf, White, Black Spots, Grassy Base, c.1900, 4 x 5 In., Pair	312
Jug, Handle, Checkerboard Design, Red, Cream, Slip Glaze, c.1760, 6 In.	4920
Jug, Milk, Lid, Agateware, Lion Finial, Paw Feet, 5½ In.	1625
Ladle, Soup, Royal Coburg Theatre, c.1825, 13 In.	720
Ladle, Soup, Upper Ferry Bridge Over River, Schuykill, c.1825, 10 In.	4080
Mug, Agate, Cream & Brown, Blue Splashes, c.1755, 4 In..........*illus*	1968
Nutmeg Grater, Nut Shape, White Enamel, Flowers, 1½ In., Pair	1000
Pitcher, Blue, White, Flowers, Transferware, 4½ In.	58
Pitcher, Dark Blue Transferware, Melon Shape, c.1830, 6½ In.	780
Pitcher, Lafayette At Franklin's Tomb, Blue Transferware, c.1836, 8 In.	475
Plate, Bank Of The United States, Philadelphia, Blue Transfer, 1800s, 10 In.	308
Plate, Biblical Scene, Scroll Banded Border, Shaped Rim, c.1800, 10 In.	246
Plate, City Hotel, New York, Blue Transfer, Ralph Stevenson & Williams, 8⅝ In. ....*illus*	94
Plate, Cupid Behind Bars, Dark Blue, Shaped Border, c.1826, 10 In..........*illus*	125
Plate, Dessert, Trellis Fretwork, Fruit Festoons, Scalloped Rim, c.1765, 9 In.	1353
Plate, Fall Of Montmorenci, Blue, White, Transferware, 1800, 9 In.	204
Plate, Historic, Views, Transfer, Brown, White, Black, Clews, 10½ In., 6 Piece	238
Plate, Landing Of Gen. Lafayette, Blue Transfer, Impressed Clews, 10 In..........*illus*	118
Plate, Landing Of General Lafayette, At Castle Garden, Blue Transfer, 10 In.	142
Plate, Landing Of General Lafayette, Blue, 9 In.	123
Plate, Portrait Medallion, President Washington, Erie Canal, 1825, 8 In.	1800
Plate, Portrait Medallions, Jefferson, Washington, Clinton, Lafayette, c.1825, 9 In.	2300
Plate, Salt Glaze, Basket Weave, Pierced Wavy Rim, c.1800, 10 In., Pair	270
Plate, Shelter'd Peasants, Blue & White Transfer, 1800s, 10 In.	250
Plate, Sunflower Pattern, Pink Petals, Leaves, Scalloped Rim, 9 In., Pair	142
Plate, Table Rock Niagara, Blue Transferware, Woods & Sons, c.1830, 10 In.	475
Plate, Winter View Of Pittsfield, Mass., Early 1800s, 8¾ In.	63

Staffordshire, Plate, City Hotel, New York, Blue Transfer, Ralph Stevenson & Williams, 8⅝ In.
$94

Hess Auction Group

Staffordshire, Plate, Cupid Behind Bars, Dark Blue, Shaped Border, c.1826, 10 In.
$125

Ruby Lane

TIP

Don't heat food on a cracked plate in either an oven or a microwave. The crack may widen.

Staffordshire, Plate, Landing Of Gen. Lafayette, Blue Transfer, Impressed Clews, 10 In.
$118

S

Hess Auction Group

Staffordshire, Teapot, Lid, Agate, Diamond Shape, Brown, Foo Dog Finial, c.1750, 6 In.
$9,840

Skinner, Inc.

Stangl, Bird, Cockatoo, Blue Crest, Green Tail, 12 ½ x 7 In.
$54

Martin Auction Co.

Stangl, Bird, Parakeets, Branch, Green, Yellow, Black, Brown, 7 ½ x 6 ½ In.
$170

Ruby Lane

Platter, Arms Of Georgia, Early 1800s, 2 ½ x 12 In.	3240
Platter, Boston State House, Rogers, Blue, Oval, Early 1800s, 13 x 16 In.	480
Platter, Brown, Picturesque View From Fishkill Hudson River, Clews, 15 ½ In.	357
Platter, Christiansburg, Danish Settlement On Gold Coast, Africa, 1800s, 14 In.	1476
Platter, Landing Of Columbus, Beach, Palm Trees, Red Transfer, 11 In.	118
Platter, Mendenhall Ferry, Dark Blue, c.1825, 17 In.	600
Platter, Mendenhall Ferry, Eagle & Flower Border, Transfer, c.1825, 16 x 13 In.	480
Platter, Pearl, Lockson London New York, 1800s, 14 x 17 In.	94
Platter, States Border, Wharf & Buildings, Late 1800s, 15 ½ x 18 ½ In.	813
Platter, Tyrolean, Brown Transfer, Castle, Trees, Wavy Border, 10 ½ x 13 In.	53
Platter, Upper Ferry Bridge Over River Schuylkill, Blue Transfer, c.1800, 19 x 16 In.	550
Platter, Upper Ferry Bridge Over River Schuylkill, Late 1800s, 14 x 19 In.	210
Pot, Tall, Washington Standing At His Tomb, Scroll, Beehive Finial, c.1810, 12 In.	375
Quill Holder, Parrot & Lamb, Perched On Branch, c.1850, 5 x 3 In., Pair	937
Tea & Coffee Set, Coffeepot, Teapot, Cups & Saucers, Plates, Ye Olde Willow, 33 Piece	192
Tea Canister, Hexagonal, Ribbed, Relief Shell Clusters, c.1770, 4 In.	923
Teapot, Agateware, Bird Spout, Chinoserie Figures, 7 In.	4687
Teapot, Agateware, Bird Spout, Dolphin Handle, Lion Finial, 1750, 7 In.	13750
Teapot, Agateware, Squat, Foo Dog Finial, c.1745, 7 In.	3125
Teapot, Lafayette At Franklin's Tomb, Blue Transfer, E. Wood & Sons, c.1836, 6 In.	400
Teapot, Lid, Agate, Diamond Shape, Brown, Foo Dog Finial, c.1750, 6 In. ....*illus*	9840
Teapot, Lid, Paneled Hexagonal, Cartouche, Red Glaze, Lion Finial, c.1740, 5 In.	738
Teapot, Lid, Pear Shape, Twig Handle, Stripes, Green, Yellow, c.1755, 5 In.	9840
Toby Jugs are listed in their own category.	
Tray, Landing Of General Lafayette At Castle Garden, Clews, c.1830, 10 x 6 In.	450
Tray, Spoon, Quatrefoil Shape, Flowers, Iron Red, Brown Slip, c.1740, 6 In.	2337
Tray, View Of La Grange, Blue Transfer, E. Wood & Sons, c.1840, 9 x 7 In.	700
Tureen, Sauce, Lid, Fulton Market, Masonic Hall, R. Stevenson, 1821, 5 In.	1440
Vase, Spill, Country Cottage, Dogs, Multicolor, 1800s, 8 x 5 ½ In.	100
Vase, Spill, Horse, China Leaves, Tree, c.1850, 6 In.	115
Vase, Spill, Molded Tree, Triple, Boy Chasing Bird, Leaves, Nest, 10 x 8 In.	153
Vase, Spill, Scottish Couple, Lamb, Flowers, Tree, c.1850, 7 In.	225
Waste Bowl, Arms Of The States, Dark Blue, Transfer 1800s, 7 In.	360
Watch Holder, Figures, Orange, Blue, Green, 8 ½ In.	800

STAINLESS STEEL became available to artists and manufacturers about 1920. They used it to make flatware, tableware, and many decorative items.

Cocktail Shaker, Double Handle, Urn Shape, 1950s, 9 x 3 ½ In.	54
Dessert Server, Rectangular, Dana, Denmark, Midcentury, 9 In.	8
Fish Platter & Strainer, Stelton, Denmark, 1970s, 22 x 10 In.	295
Salt & Pepper, Cylinda Line, Arne Jacobsen, Stelton, 1967, 2 In.	45
Scissors, Black Painted Handles, WISS Newark, USA, 1950s, 9 In.	28
Sculpture, Column, Rafe Affleck, 1970s, 96 x 9 In.	246
Sculpture, Modern, Bars, Circles, Yellow, Red, 1988, 21 ½ In.	492
Sculpture, Modern, Shaped U, c.1990, 25 ½ x 15 In.	461
Sculpture, Modern, Stylized Torch, 28 x 11 ½ In.	492
Sculpture, Pyramids, Rafe Affleck, 1970s	861
Sculpture, Space Churn With Cams II, Kinetic, 12 x 6 ¾ In.	12000
Spatula, Red Wood Handle, USA, 1950s, 11 ½ In.	5
Teakettle, Black Bakelite Handle & Knob, Farberware, 8 Cup, 2 Qt.	25
Tray, 3 Sections, Cromargan, Sweden, 12 x 9 ½ In.	35

STANGL POTTERY traces its history back to the Fulper Pottery of New Jersey. In 1910, Johann Martin Stangl started working at Fulper. He left to work at Haeger Pottery from 1915 to 1920. Stangl returned to Fulper Pottery in 1920, became president in 1926, and changed the company name to Stangl Pottery in 1929. Stangl acquired the firm in 1930. The pottery is known for dinnerware and a line of bird figurines. Martin Stangl died

S

in 1972 and the pottery was sold to Frank Wheaton Jr. of Wheaton Industries. Production continued until 1978, when Pfaltzgraff Pottery purchased the right to the Stangl trademark and the remaining inventory was liquidated. A single bird figurine is identified by a number. Figurines made up of two birds are identified by a number followed by the letter *D* indicating Double.

Amber Glo, Cup	6
Bamboo Green, Creamer	16
Bamboo Green, Cup & Saucer	9
Bird, Bluebird, 2 Birds On Branch, 8 In.	159
Bird, Cardinal, Red, 7 In.	84
Bird, Cerulean Warbler, Blue, 4¼ In.	36
Bird, Chickadee, 3 Birds On Branch, 8½ In.	156
Bird, Cockatoo, Blue Crest, Green Tail, 12½ x 7 In. ...... *illus*	54
Bird, Double Lovebirds, Yellow, 5⅛ In.	295
Bird, Double Parakeets, Blue, 7 In.	178
Bird, Hummingbird, 2 Birds On Flower, 9 In.	289
Bird, Indigo Bunting, 3¼ In.	50
Bird, Love Bird, Yellow, 4½ In.	84
Bird, Owl, On Perch, 4⅜ In.	399
Bird, Parakeets, Branch, Green, Yellow, Black, Brown, 7½ x 6½ In. ...... *illus*	170
Bird, Rivoli Hummingbird, Drinking From Flower, 6 In.	129
Bird, Rooster, Blue, 9 In.	199
Bird, Scissor Tailed Flycatcher, 11 In.	749
Bird, Western Bluebird, 7 In.	319
Bittersweet, Cup & Saucer	11
Blossom Ring, Cup & Saucer	8
Blossom Ring, Plate, Dinner, 10 In.	13
Blossom Ring, Salt & Pepper	19
Blue Daisy, Bowl, Fruit, 5⅝ In.	10 to 15
Blue Daisy, Chop Plate, 12⅜ In.	39
Blue Daisy, Cup & Saucer	7
Blue Daisy, Gravy Boat	52
Blue Daisy, Gravy Boat, Underplate	20
Blue Daisy, Plate, Dinner, 10 In.	22
Blue Daisy, Platter, Oval, 13 In.	43
Blueberry, Celery Vase, Footed, Tapered, 11¼ In.	55
Blueberry, Chop Plate, 12¼ In.	125
Blueberry, Cup & Saucer	23
Blueberry, Plate, Salad, 10 In.	36
Carnival, Bowl, Vegetable, Divided, Oval, 10 In.	33
Carnival, Pitcher, 20 Oz., 4⅝ In.	37
Caughley, Bowl, 6¼ In.	15
Caughley, Plate, Salad, 7½ In.	12
Chicory, Plate, Dinner, 10⅛ In.	28
Colonial Rose, Chop Plate, 12 In.	47
Colonial Rose, Cup & Saucer	8
Colonial Rose, Plate, Dinner, 10⅜ In.	21
Country Garden, Bowl, Fruit, 5½ In.	10
Country Garden, Creamer	14
Country Garden, Pitcher, 4⅝ In.	44
Country Garden, Plate, Dinner, 10⅛ In. ...... *illus*	26
Dahlia, Cup & Saucer	35
Dahlia, Plate, Dinner, 10 In.	35
Fairlawn, Plate, Dinner, 10⅛ In.	45
Field Daisy, Plate, Luncheon, 9 In.	13
Florentine, Bowl, Vegetable, 8 In.	16
Florentine, Plate, Dinner, 10 In.	8
Fruit & Flowers, Cup & Saucer	35
Fruit & Flowers, Plate, Dinner, 10 In.	33
Fruit & Flowers, Relish, 11¼ In.	32

Stangl, Country Garden, Plate, Dinner, 10⅛ In.
$26

Replacements, Ltd.

Star Trek, Belt Buckle, Starship Enterprise, Coppertone Metal, 1976, 1⅝ x 2 In.
$45

Ruby Lane

Star Wars, Cookie Jar, Darth Vader, C3PO, R2D2, Hexagon, White, 9 In.
$96

Milestone Auctions

TIP
Buy a paint-by-number kit to get an inexpensive assortment of paint colors to use for touch-ups and restorations for paintings and furniture.

S

Stein, Character, Alpine Man, Porcelain, Lithophane, ½ Liter
$780

The Stein Auction Company

Stein, Character, Barmaid, Holding Beer Steins, Hanke Pottery, No. 1571, ½ Liter
$216

Fox Auctions

Stein, Character, Hops Woman, Porcelain, Marked, Musterschutz, Schierholz, ½ Liter
$390

The Stein Auction Company

Fruit, Cup & Saucer	18
Fruit, Plate, Bread & Butter, 6¼ In.	11
Fruit, Plate, Dinner, 10 In.	35
Garden Flower, Creamer, 6 Oz., 3 In.	21
Garden Flower, Cup & Saucer	7
Garden Flower, Soup, Dish, Lugged, Yellow Trim, 6¼ In.	27
Golden Blossom, Plate, Bread & Butter, 6⅛ In.	4
Golden Grape, Bowl, Fruit, 5⅝ In.	9
Golden Grape, Chop Plate, 14¼ In.	19
Golden Grape, Creamer, 3 In.	12
Golden Grape, Creamer, 8 Oz., 3 In.	8
Golden Grape, Cup & Saucer	6
Golden Harvest, Plate, Dinner, 10⅛ In.	18
Golden Harvest, Plate, Salad, 8 In.	10
Hotpoint, Relish, 2 Sections, 7¾ In.	28
Jonquil, Plate, Dinner, 10⅛ In.	29
Magnolia, Bowl, Fruit, 5½ In.	14
Magnolia, Cup	15
Magnolia, Plate, Salad, 8 In.	14
Mediterranean, Pitcher, Blue & Green	42
Orchard Song, Cup & Saucer	6
Orchard Song, Plate, Bread & Butter, 6⅛ In.	5
Orchard Song, Salt & Pepper	23
Orchard Song, Sugar, Lid, 3 In.	16
Petite Flowers, Plate, Dinner, 10½ In.	25
Prelude, Bowl, Vegetable, Round, 9 In.	17
Prelude, Chop Plate, 12½ In.	20
Prelude, Cup & Saucer	10
Provincial, Casserole, Lid, Round, 1½ Qt.	67
Provincial, Cup & Saucer	11
Sculptured Fruit, Plate, Dinner, 10¼ In.	19
Sculptured Fruit, Platter, Oval, 15 In.	31
Sun Pebbles, Creamer, 6 Oz., 2¾ In.	15
Terra Rose, Bowl, Ruffled Edge, 4¾ In.	20
Terra Rose, Leaf Vase, Mauve, 6¼ In.	48
Town & Country, Casserole, Lid, 8½ In.	380
Town & Country, Chop Plate, 12 In.	10
Town & Country, Creamer	80
Town & Country, Gravy, Underplate	175
Town & Country, Platter, 15 In.	200
Tulip, Creamer	25
Wild Rose, Bowl, Fruit, 5 In.	12
Wild Rose, Chop Plate, Round, 12½ In.	18
Wild Rose, Cup & Saucer	8
Wild Rose, Gravy Boat	13
Wild Rose, Plate, Dinner, 10⅛ In.	27
Windfall, Plate, Bread & Butter, 6⅛ In.	8
Windfall, Plate, Dinner, 10 In.	15
Windfall, Saucer	4

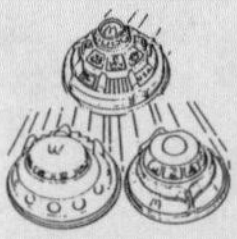

STAR TREK AND STAR WARS collectibles are included here. The original *Star Trek* television series ran from 1966 through 1969. The series spawned an animated TV series, three TV sequels, and a TV prequel. The first Star Trek movie was released in 1979 and twelve others followed, the most recent in 2016. The movie *Star Wars* opened in 1977. Sequels were released in 1980 and 1983; prequels in 1999, 2002, and 2005. *Star Wars: Episode VII* opened in 2015, which increased interest in Star Wars collectibles. The latest episode includes actors from the original cast. Other science fiction and fantasy collectibles can be found under Batman, Buck Rogers, Captain Marvel, Flash Gordon, Movie, Superman, and Toy.

STAR TREK

Belt Buckle, Starship Enterprise, Coppertone Metal, 1976, 1 5/8 x 2 In......................*illus*		45
Gum Card Set, Photos, Captain's Log Text, Wrapper, Stickers, 1976, 88 Cards		460
Paint By Numbers, Oil, 2 Pictures, Paintbrush, 10 Paints, Box, 1967, 10 x 11 In..............		410
Photograph, Main Cast, USS Enterprise, Black & White, Glossy, Signed, 8 x 10 In.		443
Toy, Activity Board, Chalk & Play, Alphabet, Numbers, Clock, 1967, 16 x 24 In.		1518
Toy, Astro-Buzz-Ray Gun, Buzzer, Flashing Light Beam, Box, 1967, 11 In...............		361
Toy, Probe, Metal Detection, Metal & Plastic, Handheld Controller, Box, 1976, 30 In.........		443

STAR WARS

Action Figure, Boba Fett, Empire Strikes Back, Blaster, Blister Card, 1980, 4 In.		1335
Action Figure, Chewbacca, Blaster Rifle, Blister Card, Kenner, 1980, 4 1/4 In.		237
Action Figure, Han Solo, Trench Coat, Posable, Pistol, Blister Card, 1985, 6 x 9 In.		405
Carrying Case, Action Figures, Vinyl, Character Insert, Labels, 1979, 9 x 12 In.		310
Comic Book, Star Wars, No. 1, 1st Issue, Main Characters Cover, Part 1, 1977		383
Cookie Jar, Darth Vader, C3PO, R2D2, Hexagon, White, 9 In...............................*illus*		96
Figure, Yoda, Robe, Cape, Star Wars The Phantom Menace, 34 In.		930

STEINS have been used by beer and ale drinkers for over 500 years. They have been made of ivory, porcelain, pottery, stoneware, faience, silver, pewter, wood, or glass in sizes up to nine gallons. Although some were made by Mettlach, Meissen, Capo-di-Monte, and other famous factories, most were made by less important German potteries. The words *Geschutz* or *Musterschutz* on a stein are the German words for "patented" or "registered design," not company names. Steins are still being made in the old styles. Lithophane steins may be found in the Lithophane category.

Character, Alpine Man, Porcelain, Lithophane, 1/2 Liter......................................*illus*		780
Character, Barmaid, Holding Beer Steins, Hanke Pottery, No. 1571, 1/2 Liter.................*illus*		216
Character, Bustle Woman, Purple & Green Salt Glaze, Stoneware, 1/2 Liter................		960
Character, Cat On Book, Porcelain, Bohne, 1/2 Liter		1140
Character, Frog Playing Banjo, Pottery, 1/2 Liter..		156
Character, Gnome, Mushroom, Porcelain, Marked, Musterschutz, Schierholz, 1/2 Liter		2760
Character, Hops Woman, Porcelain, Marked, Musterschutz, Schierholz, 1/2 Liter..............*illus*		390
Character, Lusty Barmaid, Porcelain, Schierholz, 1/2 Liter...............................		720
Character, Man With Pipe, Hanke Pottery, 1/2 Liter....................................*illus*		102
Character, Monkey With Top Hat, German Verse, Pottery, 1/2 Liter.....................*illus*		132
Character, Newspaper Woman, Musterschutz, Schierholz, Porcelain, 1/2 Liter................		2280
Character, Otto Von Bismarck, Bust, Hat, Finial, Mustache, Musterschutz, 1/2 Liter.............		215
Character, Rhinoceros, Sitting On Hind Legs, Porcelain, Schierholz, 1/2 Liter		840
Character, Roly Poly Woman, Lid, Marked 1579, Pottery, 1/2 Liter		312
Character, Sad Radish, Porcelain, Stem Finial, Musterschutz, Schierholz, 3 Liter		960
Character, Schwiegermama!, Inlaid Lid, Marked 680, Pottery, 1/2 Liter....................		240
Character, Singing Pig, Musterschutz, Schierholz, Porcelain, 1/2 Liter		336
Character, Singing Pig, Porcelain, Marked Musterschutz, By Schierholz, 1/2 Liter		144
Character, Skull On Book, Porcelain, Bohne, 1/2 Liter..		324
Character, Sparrow, Metal, Black, Marked Pour Paris A La Marquise, 1/2 Liter		300
Character, Target Girl, Porcelain, Marked Gesetzlich, Schierholz, 1/2 Liter ....*illus*		1560
Faience, Garden Scene, Pewter Lid & Footring, Crailsheimer Walzenkrug, c.1780, 9 In.		2400
Faience, Thuringer Walzenkrug, Pewter Lid & Foot Ring, Late 1700s, 9 1/4 In.		540
Faience, Wagon, Driver & Soldier, Pewter Lid & Foot Ring, Late 1700s, 9 In.		450
Faience, Woman, Fruit Basket, Austrian Birnkrug, Pewter Lid, Foot Ring, 1700s, 11 In.		660
Glass, Blown, Amber, Enameled, Pewter Lid, 3 Liter		156
Glass, Blown, Amber, Transfer, Hand Painted, Munchener Kindle, Pewter Base, 1/2 Liter..........		90
Glass, Blown, Blue On White On Clear Overlay, Cut, Silver Plated Lid, 1/2 Liter		228
Glass, Blown, Pale Orange, Faceted, Pewter Overlay, Pewter Lid, 1/2 Liter................		108
Glass, Blown, Transfer & Hand Painted, Turner 4F, Gut Heil!, Pewter Lid, 1/2 Liter		114
Glass, Ruby Stain & Clear, Cut Flowers & Animals, Clear Inlaid Lid, 1/2 Liter.................*illus*		180
Majolica, Heidelberg Castle Scene, Anniversary, 1 Liter		288
Mettlach Steins are listed in the Mettlach category.		

Stein, Character, Man With Pipe, Hanke Pottery, 1/2 Liter
$102

Fox Auctions

Stein, Character, Monkey With Top Hat, German Verse, Pottery, 1/2 Liter
$132

Fox Auctions

Stein, Character, Target Girl, Porcelain, Marked Gesetzlich, Schierholz, 1/2 Liter
$1,560

The Stein Auction Company

Stein, Glass, Ruby Stain & Clear, Cut Flowers & Animals, Clear Inlaid Lid, ½ Liter
$180

Fox Auctions

Stein, Porcelain, Card Playing Table Scene, Lithograph, Print Over Glaze, ½ Liter
$72

Fox Auctions

Military, 3rd Reich, Freiheit Und Brot, Heil Hitler!, Pewter Lid, Swastika, ½ Liter	630
Military, 3rd Reich, Labor Co., 6/131, Hasselsaar, Metal Lid, Pottery, ½ Liter	264
Military, 3rd Reich, Oberjager Vereinigung, Jager Batl. Inf. Regt. 15, Pottery, ½ Liter	420
Occupational, Bierbrauerei, Brewer, Lithophane, Porcelain, Transfer, Paint, ½ Liter	144
Pewter, Relief, Eagle, Footed, c.1880, 2 Liter	720
Porcelain, Blue & White, Bearded Face Spout, Bulbous, Pinched Neck, KPM, 3 Liter	288
Porcelain, Card Playing Table Scene, Lithograph, Print Over Glaze, ½ Liter ......*illus*	72
Porcelain, Munich Child, Robes, Arms Open, Pewter Lid & Base, ½ Liter	102
Porcelain, Nudes, Woman Handle, Goat Finial, Capo-Di-Monte, Crown Mark, 2 Liter.......*illus*	3000
Porcelain, Windmill, Transfer, Blue & White, Inlaid Lid, ½ Liter ......*illus*	192
Pottery, 3rd Reich, Kav. Regiment 17, Stab 1, 1937, Pewter Lid, ½ Liter......*illus*	690
Pottery, Cavalier & Verse, Print Over Glaze, Signed, Franz Ringer, ½ Liter ......*illus*	96
Pottery, College University, Junior, Discus Thrower, J.W. Remy, No. 1393, ½ Liter......*illus*	288
Pottery, Etched, Marked H.R., 427, Hauber & Reuther, Pewter Lid, ½ Liter	84
Pottery, Munich Child, Cat On Shoulder, Print Over Glaze, ½ Liter	144
Pottery, No. 3052, Tennis, Pewter Lid, Etched, M. & W. Gr., ½ Liter......*illus*	144
Pottery, Relief, Black Eagle, Relief Pewter Lid, Eagle Thumblift, 4 Liter, 17 In.	1050
Pottery, Relief, Jester & Bird, Threaded, Diesinger, ½ Liter	144
Pottery, Relief, Majolica, Capo-Di-Monte, Pewter Lid, Base Ring, 1 ½ Liter, 12 In.	240
Pottery, Relief, Marked D.R.G.M. 154927, Diesinger, Pewter Lid, Musicians, 2 Liter	192
Pottery, Shamrocks, Blue, White, Lid, Lever, Merkelback & Wick, c.1905, 6 In., Pair	165
Pottery, Suites Of Playing Cards, Etched, Squaresided, ½ Liter	96
Pottery, Tavern Scene, Etched, Pewter Lid, Ring Foot, Marked, Villeroy & Boch, 3 Liter	390
Pottery, Weight Lifters, Metal Dumbbell Lid, Thumblift, Merkelbach & Wick, ½ Liter	120
Regimental, 5. Comp., Bayr. Inft. Regt. Nr. 4, Roster, Lion, Thumblift, c.1912, ½ Liter	1800
Regimental, 5. Comp., Inft., Regt. Nr. 39, Dusseldorf, Porcelain, c.1897, ½ Liter, 10 In.	360
Regimental, 6. Comp., Inf. Regt. Nr. 13 Munster, H. Strickmann, Thumblift, ½ Liter...... *illus*	96
Regimental, Roster, 1 Battr. 4. Garde Feld Artl. Regt., Potsdam, c.1907, ½ Liter	420
Regimental, Roster, 2. Comp., Pionier Battln., Nr. 14, Kehl A. Rh, Porcelain, c.1895, ½ Liter...	276
Regimental, Roster, 3. Comp, Train Batl. Nr. 10, Hannover, c.1907, ½ Liter, 12 ½ In.	540
Regimental, Roster, 4. Komp., Pionier Bataillon Nr. 20, Metz, c.1907, ½ Liter, 12 In.	240
Regimental, Roster, L. Comp., Luftschiffer Bataillon, Tegel Berlin, c.1902, ½ Liter	3360
Regimental, Roster, Maschinengewehr Comp., Inft. Regt. Nr. 15, Minden, c.1912, ½ Liter	2220
Silver, Woman In Chariot, Parade, Hammered Relief, c.1900, 9 In.	1020
Stoneware, Applied Lion Faces, Relief, Westerwald, c.1700, 1 Liter	510
Stoneware, Applied Relief, Red On Orange, Altenburger Walzenkrug, 1700s, 10 In.	4560
Stoneware, Bird Wearing Vest & Shoes, Transfer, Hand Painted, F. Ringer, ½ Liter	156
Stoneware, Hunter & Dachshund, Eating In Woods, Print Over Glaze, ½ Liter	96
Stoneware, Hunter's Tools, Owl, Antlers, Print Over Glaze, Copper Inlaid Lid, ½ Liter	120
Stoneware, Incised, Birds & Flowers, Westerwalder Walzenkrug, Pewter Lid, 9 In.	264
Stoneware, Incised, Marked 671, Dumler & Breiden, Peter Dumler, Art Nouveau, ½ Liter	98
Stoneware, Incised, Marked Gerz, 572c, Salt Glaze, Art Nouveau, Pewter Lid, 1 Liter, 14 In.	121
Stoneware, Mary & Jesus, Wetterauer Walzenkrug, Pewter Lid & Footring, 1721, 10 In.	5880
Stoneware, Munich Child, Plate Of Food & Stein, Print Over Glaze, ½ Liter	108
Stoneware, Muskauer Birnkrug, Incised With Relief, Pewter Lid, Early 1800s, 8 In.	72
Stoneware, Relief, 2021, R. Merkelbach, R. Riemerschmid, Art Nouveau, ½ Liter	582
Stoneware, Relief, 2305, Marzi & Remy, Blue Salt Glaze, Art Nouveau, Pewter Lid, ½ Liter	30
Stoneware, Relief, Marked 2110, R. Merkelbach, Pewter Lid, P. Wynand, Art Nouveau, 2 Liter.	96
Stoneware, Relief, Marked 2110, Reinhold Merkelbach, Paul Wynand, Art Nouveau, ½ Liter...	144
Stoneware, Transfer, Hand Painted, Braeu-Rosl, Pewter Lid, 1 Liter	546
Stoneware, Transfer, Hand Painted, Brauerei Zum Munchener Kindle, Pewter Lid, ½ Liter.....	312
Stoneware, Transfer, Hand Painted, R. Merkelbach, T.O. Hahn, Gruss Aus Munchen, 1 Liter...	372
Stoneware, Transfer, Munchen Weihnachten, Pewter Lid, 1917, ½ Liter	44
Stoneware, Wild Boars & Stag, Westerwald, c.1760, 1 Liter	390
Tankard, Silver, Fruit & Designs, Putti Lid, Hanau, Germany, c.1880, 8 In.	780
Tankard, Wood, Burl, Carved Lion Lid & Thumblift, Norway, Late 1700s, 9 In.	480
Tankard, Wood, Burl, Carved Rosette On Lid, Norway, Early 1800s, 9 ½ In.	216
Wood, Daubenkrug, Pewter, Inlaid Stag, Walzenkrug, c.1840, 10 In.	780
Wood, Inlaid Checkerboard Design, Pewter Bands, Lid & Handle, ½ Liter	216

Stein, Porcelain, Nudes, Woman Handle, Goat Finial, Capo-Di-Monte, Crown Mark, 2 Liter
$3,000

The Stein Auction Company

Stein, Porcelain, Windmill, Transfer, Blue & White, Inlaid Lid, ½ Liter
$192

The Stein Auction Company

Stein, Pottery, 3rd Reich, Kav. Regiment 17, Stab 1, 1937, Pewter Lid, ½ Liter
$690

WEIHNACHTEN 1937

The Stein Auction Company

Stein, Pottery, Cavalier & Verse, Print Over Glaze, Signed, Franz Ringer, ½ Liter
$96

Fox Auctions

Stein, Pottery, College University, Junior, Discus Thrower, J.W. Remy, No. 1393, ½ Liter
$288

Fox Auctions

Stein, Pottery, No. 3052, Tennis, Pewter Lid, Etched, M. & W. Gr., ½ Liter
$144

The Stein Auction Company

Stein, Regimental, 6. Comp., Inft. Regt. Nr. 13 Munster, H. Strickmann, Thumblift, ½ Liter
$96

The Stein Auction Company

Stereo Card, Sitting Bull, Photographic Gems Of The Great Northwest, S.J. Morrow, 7 x 4 In.
$420

Robert Edward Auctions

Stereoscope, Jules Richard, Nickel Plated Viewer, Mahogany Case, Paris, c.1920, 6⅜ x 4¼ In.
$280

Ruby Lane

 STEREO CARDS that were made for stereoscope viewers became popular after 1840. Two almost identical pictures were mounted on a stiff cardboard backing so that, when viewed through a stereoscope, a three-dimensional picture could be seen. Value is determined by maker and by subject. These cards were made in quantity through the 1930s.

Acrobats, Paris, France, 1860s	24
American Indian, Battle Dress, Riding Steer, 7 x 3½ In.	30
Buffalo Bill With Rifle, Eaton, Omaha, Nebraska, c.1870	861
Buffalo Bones Ready For Shipment East, J.G. Evans, 1800s	1440
Captain Jack Crawford Surrounded By Furs & Buffalo Head, c.1870s	900
Conway Castle, Wales, 3⅜ x 7 In.	8
Noted Sioux Indian Chiefs, Standing Rock, F.J. Haynes, 1881	330
Panama Canal, Culebra Cut, Looking North, Keystone View Co., 1906	9
Pickers Grouped In Cotton Field, 1892, 7 x 3½ In.	50
Sitting Bull, Photographic Gems Of The Great Northwest, S.J. Morrow, 7 x 4 In. ....*illus*	420

 STEREOSCOPES were used for viewing stereo cards. The hand viewer was invented by Oliver Wendell Holmes, although more complicated table models were used before his was produced in 1859. Do not confuse the stereoscope with the stereopticon, a magic lantern that used glass slides.

Ernemann, Dove-Stereoscope, Geared Teakwood, Nickel Fittings, c.1902	1819
Graphoscope, French Burl, Ebonized, c.1890, 14 x 9 In.	394
Graphoscope, French Burl, Ebonized, c.1890, 16½ x 10¾ In.	394
Jules Richard, Nickel Plated Viewer, Mahogany Case, Paris, c.1920, 6⅜ x 4¼ In.........*illus*	280
London Stereoscopic Co., Walnut Venner, Rosewood Stand, c.1860, 3 x 6 In.	1100
Luxus, Verascope, Wood, Ebonized Trim, 1910, 16 In.	1884
Negretti & Zambra, Magic Stereoscope, Mahogany, Ivory Plaque, c.1880	4676
Smith, Beck & Beck, Rosewood, Inverted Top, Interior Latch, 12 x 8 In.	875

STERLING SILVER, *see Silver-Sterling category.*

 STEUBEN glass was made at the Steuben Glass Works of Corning, New York. The factory, founded by Frederick Carder and T.G. Hawkes Sr., was purchased by the Corning Glass Company. Corning continued to make glass called Steuben. Many types of art glass were made at Steuben. Aurene is an iridescent glass. Schottenstein Stores Inc. bought 80 percent of the business in 2008. The factory closed in 2011. In 2014 the Corning Museum of Glass took over the factory. It is reproducing some tableware, paperweights, and collectibles. Additional pieces may be found in the Cluthra and Perfume Bottle categories.

Bowl, Art Deco, Rosaline, Pink, Ball Feet, c.1925, 5¼ x 10 In.	1000
Bowl, Centerpiece, Calcite, Gold Iridescent Interior, Gold Lined Foot, 5 x 12 In.	144
Bowl, Centerpiece, Flemish Blue & Clear, Rigaree Foot	201
Bowl, Footed, Crystal, 7 x 11 In.	305
Bowl, Peonies, Scroll, White, Blue, Lavender, Acid Cut, Saucer Foot, 4 x 10 In.	767
Candlestick, Canary Candlecup & Foot, Clear Twist Stem, 8 In.	120
Candlestick, Jade Green Over White, Etched Chinoiserie Pattern, 10 In., Pair	2645
Candlestick, Peafowl & Grapevine, Rosa, Optic Ribbed Stem, Pair, 14 In.	863
Chandelier, 5-Light, Gold Iridescent Standard, Gold Aurene Shades, c.1910, 23 In.	615
Compote, Gold Aurene, Twisted Stem, c.1920, 6¾ x 6¼ In. ....*illus*	369
Compote, Rosaline, Flower Garlands, Swags, Baluster Stem, Flared Rim, 9 x 8 In.	472
Dish, Gold, Calcite, 12 Ribs, c.1925, 6¼ In.	82
Figurine, Dinosaur, Clear, 7¼ x 12¾ In. ....*illus*	738
Figurine, Elephant, Hand Cooler, 2½ In.	75
Figurine, Frog, Hand Cooler, 2¾ In.	60
Figurine, Owl, Hand Cooler, 2½ In.	60
Figurine, Pig, Hand Cooler, 3½ In.	125
Figurine, Puppy Love, Hand Cooler, 2 x 2¾ In.	125
Figurine, Sitting Hen, Hand Cooler, 3 In.	70

S

Goblet, Quatrefoil, Knopped Stem, Gilt Rim & Band, 5 In., 7 Piece		330
Lamp, Electric, Brass, Cobalt Blue Glass, Shell Shade, 9 1/2 x 6 In.		687
Lamp, Purple Acid Etched Flower, Gilt Bronze Base, c.1920, 20 x 5 x 2 3/4 In.		1625
Lamp, Tyrian, Gold Stick Base, Shade, Gilt Vines Design, Gold Border, 16 In.		2645
Mug, Green, Spiral Ribbed, Opalescent Handle, 5 3/4 In., 4 Piece		142
Pitcher, Water, Ivory, Mirror Black Handle, c.1925, 9 In.		152
Salt, Master, Amber, Squat, Iverted Scallop Rim, Gold Aurene, 1 x 3 In.		295
Salt, Opaque White, Gold Iridescent Interior, Circular Foot, 1 1/2 In.		82
Scent Bottle, Bulbous Ribbed Topper, Applied Green Threading, 4 1/2 In.		201
Scent Bottle, Bulbous, Cobalt Blue, Matching Flame Stopper, Signed, 5 In.		575
Scent Bottle, Purple, Opalescent Striping, Flower Stopper, 5 1/2 In.		1093
Sculpture, Castle Of Dreams, Frosted, Rock Walls, Diamond Base, 6 x 10 In.		1067
Sculpture, Cat, Isamu Noguchi, 16 In.		6100
Sculpture, Hippopotamus, Clear Crystal, Bulbous, Signed, 1980, 3 x 6 In.		431
Sculpture, Mephistopheles Face, Leaf Design Beard, Paneled, Matte, 3 x 7 In.		1150
Sculpture, Mushroom, Clear, Mottled Bubble Cap, Tapered Stem, 1971, 8 1/2 In.		861
Shade, Blue Pulled Feather, Gold Aurene, Calcite, Fleur-De-Lis Stamp, 6 In. ....*illus*		177
Shade, Feathered, Gold Aurene, c.1920, 4 1/2 In.		152
Shade, Morning Glory, Ribbed, Aurene, 5 x 6 In., 4 Piece		345
Shade, Red & Gold Leaves, Tangled Vines, Calcite, Deep Gold Aurene, 5 In.		944
Shade, Tulip, Calcite, Gold Leaves, Green & Gold Aurene Vines, Threaded, 5 In.		295
Urn, Aquamarine Frost, Dome Lid, Pear Finial, Ball & Spool Stem, Pedestal, 13 In.		708
Vase, Aurene, Yellow With Magenta On Shoulder, Engraved, 8 In.		460
Vase, Bat Pattern, Etched, Acid Cut, Rosaline Over Alabaster, 9 1/2 In.........*illus*		2530
Vase, Blue Aurene, Flared Rim, 2 Raised Double Handles, 10 In.		1320
Vase, Blue, Aurene, Incised, 8 1/4 In.		984
Vase, Calcite, Green, Gold Aurene, Feathering, Wavy Lines, Flared Rim, 9 In.		9440
Vase, Cut Back With Fish, Rose Over Alabaster, 1920s, 9 1/2 x 7 In.		1625
Vase, Fluted, Red To Orange, Wooden Base, c.1915, 34 In.		1031
Vase, Gold Aurene, Vine Pattern, Early 1900s, 10 x 4 1/2 In.		2125
Vase, Gold Ruby, Squat Foot, c.1925, 10 In.		468
Vase, Gold Stump, 3 Trunks Shape, Aurene, Sighed, 6 1/4 In.		431
Vase, Gold, Aurene, Trumpet Shape, Fluted Rim, 10 In.		523
Vase, Green, White Millefiori, Gold Iridescent Heart & Vine, Tapered, 4 In.		2963
Vase, Iridescent, Green Threading, Flared Neck, 8 3/4 x 6 In.		106
Vase, Iridescent, Pink Threading, Opaque, Verre De Soie, Signed, 9 x 6 In.		306
Vase, Jack-In-The-Pulpit, Aurene, 7 x 4 In.		649
Vase, Jade Green, Chrysanthemums, Leaves, Acid Cut, Cylinder Neck, 12 In.		472
Vase, Jade Green, Gold Aurene Threading, Iridescent Pearl, 9 In.		1888
Vase, Jade Green, Ribbed, Swirl, 10 x 7 1/2 In.		354
Vase, Plum Opalescent, Flowers, Leaves, 7 1/2 In.........*illus*		5715
Vase, Pomona Green, Bulbous Flattened Sides, Flared Top, 4 1/2 In.		259
Vase, Selenium Red, Flared Shape, Paneled, Ruffled Rim, 6 x 12 In.		1422
Vase, Selenium Red, Ribbed, Swirl, 10 x 7 1/2 In.		188
Vase, Verre De Soie, White, Ruffled Rim, Rainbow Luster, 10 x 6 1/2 In.		230

STEVENGRAPHS are woven pictures made like fancy ribbons. They were manufactured by Thomas Stevens of Coventry, England, and became popular in 1862. Most are marked *Woven in silk by Thomas Stevens* or were mounted on a cardboard that tells the story of the Stevengraph. Other similar ribbon pictures have been made in England and Germany.

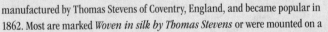

Baseball Scene, 1st Innings, Silk, Frame, Early 1890s, 9 1/2 x 7 In. ....*illus*		720
Betsy Ross Making First United States Flag, Anderson Brothers, c.1890, 5 x 8 In.		30
Carriage, Horses, The Good Old Days, 6 x 2 In.		73
Dinner Scene, 20 x 13 In.		24
Fire Engine, 4 Horses, 8 Firemen, Woven Silk, T. Stevens, London, Frame, 9 In.		171
Last Meeting Robert E. Lee & Stonewall Jackson, Horses, Trees, 9 x 5 1/2 In.		73
Old Couple, Baby, Smiling, Silk, Signed Massan, 9 x 7 1/2 In.		12
Signing Declaration Of Independence, Blue, Yellow, Green, 2 1/2 x 6 3/4 In.		36

Steuben Glassware

Steuben's glassware included Cluthra, Cintra, Verre de Soie, and other styles hand-made in a variety of colors. Aurene, an iridescent glass, remains the most popular of its early products.

Steuben, Compote, Gold Aurene, Twisted Stem, c.1920, 6 3/4 x 6 1/4 In. **$369**

Cottone Auctions

Steuben, Figurine, Dinosaur, Clear, 7 1/4 x 12 3/4 In. **$738**

Skinner, Inc.

Steuben, Shade, Blue Pulled Feather, Gold Aurene, Calcite, Fleur-De-Lis Stamp, 6 In. **$177**

Humler & Nolan

S

STEVENS & WILLIAMS of Stourbridge, England, made many types of glass, including layered, etched, cameo, and art glass, between the 1830s and 1930s. Some pieces are signed *S & W*. Many pieces are decorated with flowers, leaves, and other designs based on nature.

Basket, Opalescent, Quilted, Applied Pink Handle, 8½ x 5½ In.	24
Basket, Oval, Butterscotch, Crimson Pulls, Thorny Handles, 7½ In.	242
Cruet, Magenta, Molded Blue Flower, Amber Leaves, Stopper, 1940s, 10 In.	225
Vase, Aqua Blue, White Swags, Round, Cylindrical Neck, c.1890, 5 In.	715
Vase, Bud, Cranberry, Crimped Amber Feet, 8 In.	36
Vase, Olive Green, Amber, Applied Brown Flower, Ruffled Rim, 1890s, 8 In.	186
Vase, Pink To White, Molded Amber Branches, Flowers, c.1880, 10 In.	225
Vase, Stick, Intaglio, Green, Flowers, Butterflies, 13 In.	726
Vase, White, Pink, Molded Amber Leaves, Crimped Rim, c.1890, 7 In.	180
Vase, White, Wrapped Stem, Amber, Red Leaves, Trumpet Rim, 1800s, 5 In.	165

STONE includes those articles made of stones, coral, shells, and some other natural materials not listed elsewhere in this book. Micro mosaics (small decorative designs made by setting pieces of stone into a pattern), urns, vases, and other pieces made of natural stone are listed here. Stoneware is pottery and is listed in the Stoneware category. Alabaster, Jade, Malachite, Marble, and Soapstone are in their own categories.

Bowl, Fluted, Rock Crystal, Wood Stand, 1900s, 4½ x 7 In.	937
Bowl, Granite, Thick Wall Interior, Chisel Marks, 1800s, 5 x 13 In.	250
Box, Scene, Doves, Fountain, Mosaic, Gilt, Silver Lined, Italy, 1800s, 3 x 3 In. ....*illus*	5843
Censer, Agate, Lid, Carved Finial, Squat, Leaf Handles, Pierced, Pedestal, 12 In.	369
Centerpiece, Coral, White, Cast Iron Urn, 1900s, 27 x 13 In., Pair	750
Chimney, Hollow Blocks, Bonnet Top, Marietta, Ohio, 1800s, 52 In. ....*illus*	660
Cigarette Case, Gold Hinges & Clasp, Diamonds, Henrik Wigstrom, Russia, 4 In.	2460
Figure, Alabaster, Bust, Maiden, G.P. Cipriani, Signed, Italy, c.1880, 19 x 13 In.	812
Figure, American Indian, Portrait, Eagle, Bear Atop, c.1950, 12½ In.	188
Figure, Buddha, Purple Quartz, 5 In.	125
Figure, Double Gourd, Amber, Relief, Leaf Scroll, Chilong, Bat, Coins, 4 In.	1230
Figure, Elephant, Hardstone, Walking, Green Mottled, Chinese, 1900s, 12 x 13 In.	500
Figure, Foo Dog, Lying Down, Lapis Lazuli, Wood Stand, 2 x 2½ In.	188
Figure, Guanyin, Goddess, Lapis Lazuli, 3 x 2 In.	153
Figure, Horse, Running, Lapis Lazuli, 5½ x 7 In.	375
Figure, Jizo Bosatsu, Granite, Late 1940s, 12½ In.	720
Figure, Lion, Reclining, Rectangular Base, Cast, After A. Canova, 22 x 12 x 24 In., Pair....*illus*	1500
Figure, Lizard, Crawling, Rock, Turquoise, 2 x 4¼ In.	267
Figure, Stacked Stone, Frank McGuire, 29½ x 8 In.	589
Figure, Whispering, Rough Carved Faces, Eric Stanford, 1985, 9 x 12 In.	915
Figure, Woman, Basket, Coral, Wood Base, Chinese, 5¼ In.	1375
Figure, Woman, Fetal Position, Tony La Greca, 14½ In.	360
Figure, Woman, Meerschaum On Amber Specimen, Glass Dome, Wood Plinth, 1800s, 9½ In.	492
Group, Coral, Figures, Chinese, 12 In.	9375
Group, Crane & Lotus, Flowers, Rose Quartz, 10 In.	1000
Obelisk, Granite, Pyramid, Red, Green, 1900s, 33 x 7½ In.	1375
Obelisk, Malachite & Marble, Continental, c.1810, 22½ x 5 In.	1220
Obelisk, Malachite, Marble Base, 22 In., Pair	1750
Obelisk, Malachite, Raised Panels, Stepped Plinth Base, Neoclassical, 30 In., Pair ....*illus*	2500
Obelisk, Marble, Rouge, Gris De St. Anne, Continental, c.1900, 21 x 5 In., Pair	1375
Obelisk, Rock Crystal Pyramid, Malachite Base, 13 In.	1375
Obelisk, Rock Crystal, Blocked Trim, 1900s, 12¾ x 3 x 3 In., Pair	1000
Obelisk, Rock Crystal, Square Base, 31½ In., Pair	2750
Pedestal, Onyx, Bronze Mount, 43 In.	218
Pedestal, Onyx, Square Base, 30 In.	200
Saddlestone, 2 Parts, Mushroom Shape, Weathered Surface, 1800s, 26 In.	510
Salt, Banded Agate, Carved, German Silver Gilt Figural Stem, 3 Turtle Feet, 6 In.	1875
Sculpture, Black Granite, River Rock, Suspended Pool, Seiji Kunishima, 1985, 15 In.	2375

Steuben, Vase, Bat Pattern, Etched, Acid Cut, Rosaline Over Alabaster, 9½ In. $2,530

Early Auction Company

Steuben, Vase, Plum Opalescent, Flowers, Leaves, 7½ In. $5,715

DuMouchelles

S

Sculpture, Black Granite, River Rock, Untitled, Seiji Kunishima, 1986, 16 x 16 In.	3438
Sculpture, Boat, Hardstone, Flags & Chains, Dark Green, Chinese, 1900s, 58 x 82 In.	625
Sculpture, Buddhist Monk, Seated On Throne, Robes, Holding Animal, 31 In.	1481
Sculpture, Eagle, Pink Granite, Red Eyes, Ernest Tippletown, 1900s, 35 x 32 In.	4920
Sculpture, Guanyin, Limestone, Seated, Flowing Robes, Wood Stand, 39 x 22 In.	2489
Sculpture, Kwannon, Holding Rolled Scroll, Granite, 44 ½ In.	960
Sculpture, Seated Seal, Looking Upward, Dark Gray, Andy Miki, c.1960, 4 In.	615
Seal, Hardstone, Square, Dragons, Clouds, Relief, Mottled Brown, Russet, 1 x 2 In.	369
Sphere, Ocean Jasper, Pink, White, Green, Ocher, Tripod Stand, 10 ¼ In.	595
Urn, Malachite, Deer & Blossoms, Reticulated Flowers, 14 In.	1750
Vase, Malachite, Jug, Plants, 8 In.	188
Vase, Red Cabochon, Green Quartz, Carved, Gold Band, Chinese, 16 In.	113
Vase, Rose Quartz, Lid, Carved Flowers & Branches, Chinese, Early 1900s, 7 In.	360
Vase, Rose Quartz, Mask Handles, Phoenix, Carved, Foo Dog Finial, c.1900, 16 In.	415

STONEWARE is a coarse, glazed, and fired potter's ceramic that is used to make crocks, jugs, bowls, etc. It is often decorated with cobalt blue decorations. In the nineteenth and early twentieth centuries, potters often decorated crocks with blue numbers indicating the size of the container. A *2* meant 2 gallons. Stoneware is still being made. American stoneware is listed here.

Bank, Part Fish Part Pig, Green Glaze, Late 1800s, 6 ½ In.	600
Batter Jar, Cobalt Blue Leaf Design, Salt Glaze, 1800s, 11 x 8 In.	480
Batter Jar, Manganese, Incised Lines, Handle, Signed, 1800s, 7 In.	1020
Batter Jar, Tin Lid & Spout Cover, Bail Handle, Mid 1800s, 10 In.	330
Bottle, Frothy White Glaze, Candlestick Shape, Lucie Rie, c.1976, 10 In.	6875
Bottle, White, Gold Speckle, Linear Design, Square, Stick Neck, c.1950, 18 In.	1500
Bottle, Zoomorphic, Incised, Stopper, Cleveland, McVey, 1950s, 6 In. *illus*	2625
Bowl, Flutist, Flower Sprays, Interior Trellis Border, Salt Glaze, c.1760, 5 In.	523
Bowl, Lead Glazed Interior, Copper Slip, Wavy Rim, c.1810, 3 x 13 In.	439
Bowl, Yellow Glaze, Manganese Rim, Flared, Dame L. Rie, c.1970, 5 In.	2579
Bread Basket, White, Leaves, Honeycomb, Scallop Rim, Handles, c.1760, 12 In.	677
Butter Tub, Cobalt Blue, 1800s, 4 x 6 ½ In.	258
Butter, Cover, Oval, White, Basket Weave, Cow Finial, Salt Glaze, c.1755, 6 In.	1045
Candlestick, Tapered Stem, Round Base, Loop Handle, S. Routson, 6 In., Pair	690
Charger, Inset Porcelain Pellets, Punctures, Orange, Mottled, Fired, 1873, 20 In.	8400
Chicken Waterer, Brown Glaze, Pear Form, Saucer Base, c.1885, 11 ½ In.	325
Churn, Blue Squiggle Slip, Molded Rim, Ear Handles, 15 In.	325
Churn, Cobalt Blue Flower, 5, Hart Bros., Fulton, N.Y., Handles, c.1880, 18 In.	510
Churn, Cobalt Blue, 4, 1800s, 15 In.	111
Churn, Cobalt Blue, Bird, F.B. Norton, 1870, 4 Gal., 16 ½ In.	682
Churn, Cobalt Blue, Flowers, 1800s, 4 Gal., 16 ½ In.	148
Churn, Cobalt Blue, Hamilton & Jones, Greensboro, Pa., Handles, 19 In.	1320
Churn, Impressed, G. Benton & L. Stewart, 1800s, 14 In.	215
Cooler, Remmey, Cobalt Blue, Leaves, Ear Handles, 12 ½ x 8 In. *illus*	695
Creamer, Blue Flowers, Ruffled Rim, Scroll Handle, Paw Feet, c.1740, 3 In.	1230
Creamer, Fruiting Branches, Trellis Border, Salt Glaze, c.1760, 3 In.	738
Creamer, Pear Shape, White, Salt Glaze, Incised Emblems, Molded, c.1740, 4 In.	1107
Crock Lid, Round, Peach Glaze, Blue Wave Design, Finial Handle, 14 In. Diam.	142
Crock, Bird On Branch, Blue, Pfaltzgraff & Co., York, Pa., 10 ½ In.	443
Crock, Blue Flower, Leaves, Straight-Sided, Ear Handles, Shenfelder, 4 Gal., 9 In.	443
Crock, Blue Flower, Leaves, Tapered, Shenfelder, Reading, Pa., 3 Gal., 8 In.	130
Crock, Blue Flower, Rolled Rim, Ear Handles, Moyer, Harrisburg, Pa., 2 Gal.	826
Crock, Blue Peonies, Double Handles, J. Fisher & Co., c.1880, 10 In.	180
Crock, Blue Stencil, Grocer's Label, Wooden Lid, Metal Plaque, 1800s, 25 In.	1560
Crock, Blue Tulip, Bulbous, Ear Handles, Cowden & Wilcox, Harrisburg, Pa., 10 In.	106
Crock, Cake, Cobalt Blue Accents, Handles, c.1880s, 7 x 12 In.	330
Crock, Cake, Cobalt Blue Feather, Salt Glaze, c.1870, 5 ¾ In.	351
Crock, Cake, Cobalt Blue Flowers, Baltimore, 4 Gal., 8 x 14 In.	246

Stevengraph, Baseball Scene, 1st Innings, Silk, Frame, Early 1890s, 9 ½ x 7 In.
$720

Robert Edward Auctions

Stone, Box, Scene, Doves, Fountain, Mosaic, Gilt, Silver Lined, Italy, 1800s, 3 x 3 In.
$5,843

Skinner, Inc.

Stone, Chimney, Hollow Blocks, Bonnet Top, Marietta, Ohio, 1800s, 52 In.
$660

Garth's Auctioneers & Appraisers

Stone, Figure, Lion, Reclining, Rectangular Base, Cast, After A. Canova, 22 x 12 x 24 In., Pair
$1,500

S

New Orleans Auction Galleries

Stone, Obelisk, Malachite, Raised Panels, Stepped Plinth Base, Neoclassical, 30 In., Pair
$2,500

New Orleans Auction Galleries

TIP

Light your yard so that some of the lights face the garage door and light up the entrances to the house. Put the lights high enough to be out of easy reach.

Stoneware, Bottle, Zoomorphic, Incised, Stopper, Cleveland, McVey, 1950s, 6 In.
$2,625

Rago Arts and Auction Center

Crock, Cake, Cobalt Blue Tulips, 2 Handles, Late 1800s, 6 x 9 In.	240
Crock, Cake, Lid, Cobalt Blue Leaves, Knob Handle, Remmey, c.1880, 8 x 13 In.	923
Crock, Cobalt Blue Bird, 1800s, 3 Gal., 10 ½ In.	135
Crock, Cobalt Blue Bird, 1800s, 4 Gal., 12 In.	123
Crock, Cobalt Blue Bird, Flack & Van Arsdale, Cornwall, Ont., 3 Gal., 10 In.	380
Crock, Cobalt Blue Bird, Impressed, West Troy Pottery, 1800s, 6 Gal., 14 In.	344
Crock, Cobalt Blue Chicken, Corn, Straight-Sided, Ear Handles, 4 Gal., 11 In.	240
Crock, Cobalt Blue Feather, Flower, Handles, Miller & Fleet, c.1882, 4 Gal.	1755
Crock, Cobalt Blue Flower Band, Handles, Late 1800s, 12 ½ In.	120
Crock, Cobalt Blue Flower, 2, New York Stoneware Co., c.1880, 2 x 11 In.	150
Crock, Cobalt Blue Flower, 3 Gal., 11 In.	172
Crock, Cobalt Blue Flower, 3, J. Burger, Jr., Rochester, N.Y., c.1880, 10 In.	360
Crock, Cobalt Blue Flower, Leaves, Lug Handles, Rolled Rim, Cylindrical, 7 In.	140
Crock, Cobalt Blue Flowers, Impressed, F.B. Norton & Co., 1800s, 7 In.	172
Crock, Cobalt Blue Flowers, Impressed, Handles, Hamilton & Co., Pa., 16 In.	2160
Crock, Cobalt Blue Label, Eagles, Ear Handles, Lion Pottery, c.1880, 21 In.	4920
Crock, Cobalt Blue Label, Star, Ear Handles, Hamilton & Jones, c.1880, 20 In.	1080
Crock, Cobalt Blue Man In Moon, Cowden & Wilcox, Harrisburg, Pa., 11 In.	11800
Crock, Cobalt Blue Peacock, Rolled Rim, Harrington, c.1860, 3 Gal., 11 In.	3998
Crock, Cobalt Blue Roses, Handles, J. Hamilton & Co., Greensboro, Pa., 24 In.	2040
Crock, Cobalt Blue Roses, Handles, W.D. Cooper & Bro., No. 7 Diamond, 13 In.	570
Crock, Cobalt Blue Roses, James Hamilton & Co., Greensboro, Pa., 12 In.	570
Crock, Cobalt Blue Stencil, Tyler & Co. General Store, c.1880, 8 x 10 In.	688
Crock, Cobalt Blue Tulip, 4, Lug Handles, Wide Rim, c.1855, 14 In.	360
Crock, Cobalt Blue Tulips, 4, Double Handles, R.W. Russell, c.1850, 13 In.	300
Crock, Cobalt Blue, 3, Double Handles, Predman, Felicity, Ohio, c.1880, 13 In.	1680
Crock, Cobalt Blue, Bird, Flowers, F.B. Norton & Co., 6 Gal., 14 In.	192
Crock, Cobalt Blue, Diagonal Band, A.P. Donaghho, Parkersburg, W. Va., 15 In......*illus*	375
Crock, Cobalt Blue, Eagle Stencil, c.1875, 8 ½ x 5 In.	148
Crock, Cobalt Blue, Eagle, Handles, C. Miller, Matamoras, Ohio, 24 In.	4800
Crock, Cobalt Blue, Flower, N.A. White & Son, 3 Gal., 10 In.	160
Crock, Cobalt Blue, Flowers, 1800s, 4 Gal., 12 ½ In.	221
Crock, Cobalt Blue, Flowers, 1800s, 8 ¾ In.	172
Crock, Cobalt Blue, Laurel Wreath, 5, Ear Handles, Late 1800s, 12 ½ In.	120
Crock, Cobalt Blue, Stag, Edmands & Co., 1800, 9 ¼ In.	4560
Crock, G.A. Glass, Braddocksfield, Pa., Handles, 7 ½ x 11 In.	1560
Crock, Goodwin & Webster Hartford, 14 ½ In.	450
Crock, Gray, Brown, Blue Stencil, Eagle, Lug Handles, Roll Rim, 1800s, 15 In.	369
Crock, Gray, Cobalt Blue Eagle, J. Hamilton, Handles, c.1965, 20 Gal., 25 In.	2280
Crock, Lid, Cobalt Blue Flowers, Salt Glaze, 3 Gal., 1800s, 11 In.	660
Crock, Lid, Cobalt Blue Parrots, Branch, Norton & Co., Mass., c.1850, 12 In.	1500
Crock, Lid, Cobalt Blue, 2, Spotted Deer, T. Harrington Lyons, 1800s, 11 In.	3360
Crock, Lid, Cobalt Blue, Starin' Place Creamery, 6 ½ In.	185
Crock, Lid, Double Handles, I.M. Mead, Portage Co., Ohio, c.1850, 9 ½ In.	210
Crock, Lug Handles, Ottman Brothers & Co., c.1885, 3 Gal., 10 x 11 In.	250
Cup, Octagonal, White, Salt Glaze, Trelliswork, Dots & Stars, c.1745, 3 In.	1599
Cuspidor, Tan, Brown Glaze, Side Holes, E.R. Jones, Pittston, Pa., 5 x 10 In.	620
Dish, Lid, Speckled Beige, Brown, Leaves, G. Williams, c.1975, 14 In.	123
Figure, Songbird, Rocky Mound, White, Salt Glaze, Brown Slip, c.1725, 5 In.	1845
Flowerpot, Cobalt Blue Bird, Incised, Attached Saucer, c.1800s, 11 In.	600
Foot Warmer, Stencil, Henderson Foot Warmer, Dorchester Pottery Works, Boston, 11 In.*illus*	83
Jar, Brown Glaze, Terra-Cotta Color, Incised, Dome Lid, Finial, 8 x 7 In.	1625
Jar, Brown, 2 Handles, Loew Miles Stoneware Factory, c.1850, 15 In.	600
Jar, Bulbous, Rolled Rim, Ribbed Bands, Carved Designs, Chinese, 22 In.	119
Jar, Canning, Celadon Glaze, Cylindrical, Shouldered, J. Bell, c.1850, 7 In.	540
Jar, Canning, Cobalt Blue Label, Stars, Hamilton & Jones, Greensboro, Pa., 10 In.	510
Jar, Canning, Cobalt Blue, Groceries & Liquor, J.A. Franz, Pomeroy, Ohio, 8 In.	840
Jar, Canning, Olive Green Glaze, Streaked, Incised Bands, T. Ritchie, 12 In.	240
Jar, Cobalt Blue Band, Stenciled Kinnier & Co., Lynchburg, Va., 2 Gal., 12 In.	293

Jar, Cobalt Blue Bird, Trees, Gray, Albany Slip Glaze, Swollen, 2 Gal., 13 In.	1800
Jar, Cobalt Blue Flower, Incised, E.A. Fulcher, c.1860, ½ Gal., 7 In.	1404
Jar, Cobalt Blue Flower, Tooled Rim, Applied Lug Handles, 1800s, 2 In.	425
Jar, Cobalt Blue Heart, Fleur-De-Lis, Stencil, Salt Glaze, c.1875, 4 Gal., 15 In.	585
Jar, Cobalt Blue House, Salt Glaze, H. Nash Utica, c.1835, 2 Gal., 11 In.	129
Jar, Cobalt Blue Label, A & S Thistle, Sisterville, W.Va., 1800s, 10 In.	390
Jar, Cobalt Blue Roses, Hamilton & Jones, 10 In.	219
Jar, Cobalt Blue Stencil, Gray, Salt Glaze, E.J. Miller & Sons, Alexandria Va., 11 In.	600
Jar, Cobalt Blue Sunflower, Arch Handles, Stamped, c.1850, 1 ½ Gal., 12 In.	1404
Jar, Cobalt Blue, Horse Head, Lug Handles, Cowden & Wilcox, 3 Gal., 12 In.	2006
Jar, Diminutive Redware, New Erection Pottery, Va., c.1880, ½ Gal., 7 In.	497
Jar, Finger Swipe Design, Faceted, Handles, Copper, Gloss, Mackenzie, 12 In.	246
Jar, Gray & Green Salt Glaze, Cylindrical, Flared Rim, H. Fox, N.C., 9 In.	1140
Jar, Green Streaked Glaze, Globular, Everted Rim, Ring Foot, Chinese, 7 In.	2460
Jar, Lug Handles, Rim Impressed, Paul Cushman, New York, c.1810, 12 In.	425
Jar, Pale Green Glaze, Loop Design, Handles, Rolled Rim, c.1850, 15 In.	1920
Jar, Salt Glaze, Multicolor Neck, Square Rim, Stamped, c.1840, 1 Gal., 10 In.	94
Jar, Salt Glaze, Slip Wash, Stamped, Bell & Son, Strasburg, c.1890, 3 Gal., 14 In.	117
Jar, Tan, Cobalt Blue Feather, Lug Handles, Rolled Rim, c.1850, 3 Gal., 15 In.	1200
Jardiniere, Flowers, Bronze Base, Chaplet & Dammouse, c.1884, 5 x 5 In.	1375
Jug, 3 Egg Shape, Bird Claw Handle, Oxblood Glaze, Dalpayrat, c.1900, 5 In.	3760
Jug, Bellarmine, Angry Face On Neck, Pinwheels, Gray Salt Glaze, 8 In.	489
Jug, Bellarmine, Molded Face & Medallion, Germany, 1700s, 8 In.	510
Jug, Bellarmine, Smiling Face On Neck, 3 Belly Cartouches, Brown Glaze, 8 In.	316
Jug, Bellarmine, Smiling Face On Neck, Mottled Brown, Bulbous, 5 ½ In.	633
Jug, Blue Squiggled Lines, Tapered, 1895, 5 Gal., 19 In.	201
Jug, Brown & Black, Bearded Face Mask, 14 In.	228
Jug, Brown, Salt Glaze, Cylindrical, Pinch Spout, Loop Handle, T. Wyatt, 1767, 5 In.	738
Jug, Chas. D. Moul Pure Wines & Liquors, York, PA, 2-Tone, Bail Handle, 4 In. _illus_	354
Jug, Cobalt Blue American Flag, Joseph Silber, c.1870, Gal., 12 In.	527
Jug, Cobalt Blue Bird, Flower, Lug Handles, Rolled Rim, c.1870, 2 Gal., 15 In.	1020
Jug, Cobalt Blue Crescents & Tassels, Incised, 1800s, 14 In.	550
Jug, Cobalt Blue Daisy, Freehand, Oval, Garlic Mouth, c.1875, 2 Gal., 14 In.	510
Jug, Cobalt Blue Deer, Standing, S.W. Clifford, Boston, 3 Gal., 15 x 9 In.	4674
Jug, Cobalt Blue Design, John B. Caire & Co., Main St. Po'keepsie NY, 15 In.	123
Jug, Cobalt Blue Design, Tan, Oval, Wood Stopper, c.1850, 12 In.	360
Jug, Cobalt Blue Eagle & Star, Handle, Late 1800s, 14 ½ In.	1750
Jug, Cobalt Blue Flower Spray, C. Crolius, New York, 14 In.	431
Jug, Cobalt Blue Flower, 2, Handle, Cowden & Wilcox, Harrisburg, Pa., c.1880, 14 In.	360
Jug, Cobalt Blue Flowers, G. Lent Lansingburgh, c.1830, 14 ½ In.	1680
Jug, Cobalt Blue Flowers, Incised, Rolled Lip, Strap Handle, c.1810, 15 In.	350
Jug, Cobalt Blue Flowers, Salt Glaze, Applied Strap Handle, 1800s, 14 In.	240
Jug, Cobalt Blue Inverted Heart, Manganese, Salt Glaze, Westerwald, c.1710, 7 In.	960
Jug, Cobalt Blue Lamb, Strap Handle, N. Clark, Rochester N.Y., c.1850, 2 Gal., 15 In.	7380
Jug, Cobalt Blue Parrot, Perched, Freehand, Lug Handles, c.1870, 2 Gal., 14 In.	78
Jug, Cobalt Blue Roses, Eagle & Banner, Handle, Late 1800s, 16 In.	2040
Jug, Cobalt Blue Sunflower, Applied Handle, Late 1800s, 14 In.	150
Jug, Cobalt Blue Tulip & Bud, Cowden & Wilcox, Harrisburg, Pa., 13 In.	442
Jug, Cobalt Blue Tulip, 1800s, 11 ½ In.	123
Jug, Conjoined, Cobalt Blue Design, Oval, Reeded Strap Handle, c.1825, 3 In.	11000
Jug, Cream, Strap Handle, Impressed S. Routson, Wooster O, 12 In.	281
Jug, Dark Brown, Salt Glaze, 1800s, 3 ¼ In.	338
Jug, Drinking, Bearded Mask, Handle, Bulbous, Tapered Neck, 1607, 14 In.	47751
Jug, Face, 2 Faces, Olive Green Glaze, Meaders, Georgia Folk Pottery, 14 In.	253
Jug, Face, Alkaline Glaze, Lanier Meaders, c.1975, 10 In.	1062
Jug, Face, Brown, Double Handle, Joe Reinhardt, NC Folk Pottery, 8 In.	345
Jug, Face, Green Glossy Glaze, 2 Broken Teeth, Lanier Meaders, Ga., 10 In.	840
Jug, Face, Stacked Faces, Brown, Joe Reinhardt, NC Folk Pottery, 16 In.	184
Jug, Flowers, Leaves, Brown, Globular, Cutouts, Turned Neck, c.1700, 4 In.	7995

Stoneware, Cooler, Remmey, Cobalt Blue, Leaves, Ear Handles, 12 ½ x 8 In.
$695

Ruby Lane

Stoneware, Crock, Cobalt Blue, Diagonal Band, A.P. Donaghho, Parkersburg, W. Va., 15 In.
$375

Turner Auctions + Appraisals

Stoneware, Foot Warmer, Stencil, Henderson Foot Warmer, Dorchester Pottery Works, Boston, 11 In.
$83

Hess Auction Group

Stoneware, Jug, Chas. D. Moul Pure Wines & Liquors, York, PA, 2-Tone, Bail Handle, 4 In.
$354

Stoneware, Jug, Ribbed Neck, Coggle Wheel Bird, Vine, Cobalt Blue, Branch, 1800s, 2 Gal., 15 In.
$575

Stoneware, Jug, Salt Glaze, Yellow, Sand, 11¾ x 9½ In.
$110

Stoneware, Punch Bowl, Bardwell's Root Beer, Cobalt Blue, 3 Panels, Salt Glaze, 10¾ x 19 In.
$944

Stoneware, Teapot, Jiao Tai, Squat, Wave Pattern, Cream & Brown Glaze, Chinese, 5 In.
$242

Stoneware, Teapot, Lid, White, Salt Glaze, Bird, Trellis, Blossoms, England, c.1755, 4 In.
$1,599

Snow Domes

Snow domes were first made in the late nineteenth century in France. They almost always featured religious scenes with saints and churches. The first American patent for a dome was issued in 1927 for one that had a fish on a string floating in a seaweed patch.

Stoneware, Vase, Swirled, Gray, Pink, Volcanic Glaze, Long Neck, Flared Rim, Lucie Rie, 11¾ In.
$8,400

Stoneware, Vase, Swirled, Turquoise, Oxblood Glaze, Dalpayrat, France, c.1900, 7 In.
$4,375

Jug, Gemel, Albany Glaze, J.D. Richards, Impressed, Late 1800s, 8¾ In.	150
Jug, Heavy Drip Glaze, Southern, Mid 1800s, 14 In.	90
Jug, Impressed Marks On Neck, U. Kendall, 2 Gal., 1800s, 14½ In.	270
Jug, Red Poppies, Kronthaler, Germany, c.1875, 12 x 3½ In.	49
Jug, Ribbed Neck, Coggle Wheel Bird, Vine, Cobalt Blue, Branch, 1800s, 2 Gal., 15 In. ....*illus*	575
Jug, Salt Glaze, Yellow, Sand, 11¾ x 9½ In. ....*illus*	110
Jug, Temperance, Applied Snakes, c.1875, 5¼ In.	510
Ladle, Chrysanthemum Bowl, Rolled Stem, White, Salt Glaze, c.1755, 4 In.	1046
Loving Cup, Brown, Scored Band, Inscribed, Campana, Handles, c.1747, 9 In.	1353
Loving Cup, Red, Transferware, Wheat, Farm Tools, Leafy Handles, 7 x 12 In.	472
Muffineer, Cobalt Blue Stripes, Faceted, Round Foot, 1800s, 5 In.	9300
Oyster Jar, Glazed, Toad Brothers, New York, N.Y., 4¼ In.	47
Pillow, Cream Cat, Brown Spots, 10 In.	63
Pitcher, Bird, Abstract, Red Sun, Roger Capron, 1960s, 9½ x 9 In.	375
Pitcher, Cobalt Blue Bands, Salt Glaze, Tankard Shape, Pewter Lid, 7 In.	900
Pitcher, Cobalt Blue Feather, Joseph Silber, c.1880, ½ Gal., 9 In.	234
Pitcher, Cobalt Blue Flowers, Impressed, P. Herrmann, Baltimore, 11 In.	271
Pitcher, Cobalt Blue Tulip, Leaves, Strap Handle, c.1900, Pint, 5 x 3½ In.	1170
Pitcher, Cobalt Flowers, Impressed 2, Loop Handle, 13 In.	600
Pitcher, Flowers, Leaves, Clay Colored, Reeded Rim, Strap Handle, 1800s, 9 In.	384
Pitcher, Gourd, Paneled, Pale Blue, Brown Deer, Tan Ground, L. Lourioux, 7 In.	115
Pitcher, Green & Tan Glaze, Impressed 4, U.S. Stoneware Co., c.1900, 15 In.	240
Pitcher, Lid, Cobalt Blue, Spotted Deer, 2, Handles, Harrington, Lyons, 12 In.	900
Pitcher, Mottled Glaze, Wavy Rim, Shaped Spout, Signed, 8 In.	62
Pitcher, Presentation, Bust, George Washington, Molded, Relief, 13 In.	10148
Plate, Abstract Design, White, Gray, Brown Glaze, Voulkos, c.1950, 10 In.	3750
Plate, Fortune Teller, Diaper Pattern Border, Scalloped, Salt Glaze, c.1760, 9 In.	923
Plate, Swirl In Square, Squiggles, Molded, Brown, Mauve, c.1960, 21 In.	615
Pot, Spool Shape, White, Salt Glaze, Turned, Concave Well, c.1750, 2 In.	1046
Punch Bowl, Bardwell's Root Beer, Cobalt Blue, 3 Panels, Salt Glaze, 10¾ x 19 In. ....*illus*	944
Rolling Pin, Cobalt Blue Wild Flowers, Glazed, Turned Shaft & Handles, 15 In.	83
Rooster, Wrapped Rattle Snake, Cobalt Blue, Green Glaze, Meaders, 1990, 17 In.	600
Rundlet, Cobalt Blue, F.B., Bands, 8 In.	720
Sauceboat, Blue & White, Shells, 2 Spouts, Loop Handles, Salt Glaze, c.1755, 7 In.	615
Sauceboat, Swirling Leaves, Trellis Design, Scroll Rim, Salt Glaze, c.1755, 6 In.	1230
Tankard, Deer Hunters, Flowers, Salt Glaze, Tapered, Loop Handle, 1723, 8 In.	4013
Tea Canister, Square, Goddess Flora, Relief Molded, Salt Glaze, 1770, 6 In.	5940
Teapot, Flowers, Figures, Brown, Domed, 7 In.	683
Teapot, Jiao Tai, Squat, Wave Pattern, Cream & Brown Glaze, Chinese, 5 In. ....*illus*	242
Teapot, Lid, Blue, Roses, Globular, Crabstock Handle & Spout, c.1760, 5 In.	677
Teapot, Lid, Blue, Shells & Birds, Diamond Shape, Lizard Finial, c.1740, 6 In.	984
Teapot, Lid, King Of Prussia, Eagle, Globular, Salt Glaze, Enamel, c.1760, 4 In.	1968
Teapot, Lid, Leaves, Berries, Crabstock Handle & Spout, Salt Glaze, c.1750, 4 In.	923
Teapot, Lid, Red, Molded Flowering Branches, Ary De Milde, c.1700, 5 In.	5877
Teapot, Lid, Shell, Serpent Spout, Pear Shape, White, Salt Glaze, c.1750, 5 In.	861
Teapot, Lid, White, Salt Glaze, Bird, Trellis, Blossoms, England, c.1755, 4 In. ....*illus*	1599
Teapot, Melon Shape, Bud Finial, Brown, Chinese, 4¼ In.	625
Teapot, Melon Shape, Vine Handle, 5½ x 10 In.	125
Teapot, Mug Shape Lid, Tree Trunk, Branch Spout & Handle, c.1990, 17 In.	625
Teapot, Peach Shape, Branch Handle, 6 In.	125
Teapot, Water Lily, Frog Finial, 4¼ In.	94
Tobacco Jar, Figural, Comical Bird, Brown, Lid, Martin Bros., 1895, 8 In.	25795
Vase, Applied Leaves & Stamped Ornaments, Lead Glazed, 14½ In.	70
Vase, Black & Rust, Lines & Splotches, Swollen, Tapered, Flared Rim, 1958, 14 In.	3567
Vase, Black Paint, Ernie Kim, 1960s, 10 x 7½ In.	125
Vase, Blue, Medallions, Applied Fish Form Handles, Japan, c.1842, 14 In.	360
Vase, Bottle, Cobalt Blue, Salt Glaze, North State Pottery, 11¾ In.	138
Vase, Brown Glaze, Copper Speckles, Faceted, MacKenzie, c.1950, 12 x 11 In.	1500
Vase, Bulbous, Tapered, Incised Lines, Brown Speckles, Heino, 1970s, 10 In.	840

Store, Sign, Bootmaker, Figural, Boot, Black Paint, Gilt, Wood, Iron Hook, c.1880, 19 In.
$861

Skinner, Inc.

Old Stock Certificate Value
Tracing old stock certificates or historic stock quotes for tax reasons or for historic background? Many public libraries can help you find the information you need.

Store, Sign, Figural, Horse Head, Livery, Zinc, Molded, Wall Mount, Painted Gold, 1800s, 19 x 16 In.
$3,835

Hess Auction Group

S

Stoneware Face Jugs

Face jugs are dark jugs with distorted faces, crooked teeth, and big eyes. Older face jugs, pieces with alkaline glaze, and jars with cobalt decorations—animals, plants, or people—sell for the highest prices.

Store, Sign, Fishing Tackle & Ammunition, Fish Shape, Hollow, Wood, 2-Sided, Painted, 44½ In.
$4,720

Hess Auction Group

Stove, Heating, Conowingo Furnace, Cast Iron, 33 In.
$1,003

Hess Auction Group

Stove, Stove Plate, Cast Iron, Religious Scene, Embossed, 28 x 27 In.
$295

Hess Auction Group

Vase, Faceted, Paneled, Amber, Black Tenmoku Glaze, Hamade, c.1950, 10 In.	7500
Vase, Faceted, Square, Cream & Copper Glaze, MacKenzie, c.1950, 8 In.	625
Vase, Hu Shape, Square Base, Taotie Masks, Dome Square Lid, Holes, 14 In.	86
Vase, Ivory, Gold, Square, Free-Form, Jagged Rim, Marked, Kohyama, 8 x 6 In.	1000
Vase, Khaki Glaze, Round, Pinched Neck, Rolled Rim, Hamade, c.1955, 8 x 6 In.	750
Vase, Narrow Mouth, Rust, Green, Black Matte Glaze, G. Williams, 14 In.	800
Vase, Orange Peel Texture, C.R. Auman Pottery, 1920s, 5 In.,	230
Vase, Parakeets, Branches, Rust & White, Acid Etched, Flared Rim, 1885, 8 In.	826
Vase, Pinched Mouth, Incised P, 2 Gal., 14 In.	49
Vase, Purple & Red, Frothy Glaze, 4 Handles, Ruskin Pottery, c.1933, 9 In.	1187
Vase, Relief Figures, Masks, Shouldered, Rope Twist Handles, c.1795, 12 In.	1968
Vase, Shapes, Lines & Splotches, Wavy Cylinder, Multicolor, Bean, 1980, 9 In.	480
Vase, Shapes, Streaks & Splotches, Inset Glass, Flattened Oval, 1984, 17 In.	10000
Vase, Swirled, Gray, Pink, Volcanic Glaze, Long Neck, Flared Rim, Lucie Rie, 11¾ In. ......*illus*	8400
Vase, Swirled, Turquoise, Oxblood Glaze, Dalpayrat, France, c.1900, 7 In. ....*illus*	4375
Water Cooler, Blue Flowers, Slip Glaze, Ear Handles, Remmey, 2 Gal., 12 In.	1121
Water Cooler, Buff Glaze, Beehive Shape, Handles, Hole, c.1865, 28 x 17 In.	240
Water Cooler, Cobalt Blue, Flower Sprigs, Inscribed, R. Brown, 21 In.	1140
Water Cooler, Cobalt Blue, Swag, Clark & Fox Athens, c.1835, 16 In.	840
Water Cooler, Dome Lid, Barrel Shape, Blue Embossed Flowers, 19 In.	106
Water Cooler, Molded Flowers, Polar Bears, White's, Utica, c.1890, 5 x 18 In.	360

 STORE fixtures, cases, cutters, and other items that have no advertising as part of the decoration are listed here. Most items found in an old store are listed in the Advertising category in this book.

Bench, Shoe Sizing, Wood, Sloped Footrest, Inset Metal Ruler, c.1910, 15 x 24 In.	140
Bin, Flour, Poplar, Gray Paint, Scrub Top, Paneled, Bracket Feet, c.1855, 30 x 48 In.	570
Bin, Grain, Cherry, Red Paint, Slant Lid, Dovetailed, Divided, c.1900, 35 x 41 In.	330
Bin, Grain, Pine, Green Paint, Paneled, 3-Board Scrub Top, Footed, 1800s, 34 x 36 In.	630
Cabinet, 18 Drawers, White, Knobs, Grain Painted Finish, Locking Side Bars, 18½ x 14 In.	184
Cigar Cutter, Iron Shaped, Flat Iron Plug, 16 In.	676
Cigar Cutter, Match Holder, Brass, Dog, Tail Moves With Blade, 4 x 10 In.	602
Cigar Cutter, Standing Man, Oil Lamp, Cranberry Globe, 13½ In.	330
Coffee Grinders are listed in the Coffee Mill category.	
Display, Cheese, Red Arm, Glass Dome, 26 x 17 In.	1599
Mannequin, Pine, Carved, Papier-Mache, Baluster Stand, England, 49 x 18 x 11 In.	937
Mannequin, Wax Head, Glass Eyes, Jointed Arms, Canvas Body, 1900, 55 In.	1440
Mannequin, Wood Head, Cloth Body, Lanvin, 1921, 21 In.	950
Sign, Antiques, 2-Sided, Scalloped Top & Bottom, 1900s, 37¼ x 34¼ In.	240
Sign, Beauty Shop Globe, 2-Sided, Metal, Glass Lenses, Woman In Middle, 19 x 18 x 6 In.	1610
Sign, Boot Shape, Fitted, 3 Dollars, 50 Cents, Heavy Gauge Tin, Paint, 28 x 32 In.	266
Sign, Boot, Figural, Metal, Red Paint, Star Spur, Angle Rod, c.1900, 18 x 14 In.	770
Sign, Bootmaker, Figural, Boot, Black Paint, Gilt, Wood, Iron Hook, c.1880, 19 In. ....*illus*	861
Sign, Boy & Horse, Iron, Hanging, 20 x 18 In.	732
Sign, Butcher Shop, Long Horn Steer Head, Figural, Zinc, White Paint, 26 x 34 In.	4720
Sign, Butcher's Pig, Full Body, Carved Pine, Paint, England, 1800s, 16 x 33 In.	4148
Sign, Carpenter's Trade, Carved Relief With Tools, Black Paint, Wood, 59 x 19 In.	7800
Sign, Checkerboard, Red & White, Carved, Inscribed, 1782, 20 x 29 In.	70
Sign, Cigars, Wooden, Paint, White Letters, Black, Red, Blue Border, 15 x 57 In.	767
Sign, Dance To Your Favorite Old Tunes, Painted, Plywood, c.1940, 20 x 84 In.	325
Sign, Do Not Spit On The Sidewalk, Fine 20 Dollars, Porcelain, 2-Sided, 8 x 7 In.	1064
Sign, Do Not Spit On The Sidewalk, Porcelain, Enamel, 6 x 8 In.	661
Sign, Farm Stand, Double Gourd, 2-Sided, Wooden, Iron Hardware, 1800s, 27 In.	142
Sign, Figural, Horse Head, Livery, Zinc, Molded, Wall Mount, Painted Gold, 1800s, 19 x 16 In. . .*illus*	3835
Sign, Fishing Tackle & Ammunition, Fish Shape, Hollow, Wood, 2-Sided, Painted, 44½ In. .....*illus*	4720
Sign, French Wine, Yellow Text, Green, 18 In.	594
Sign, Green Ax Head, Gilt Edge & Spike, Pole, Visit The Sick, c.1880, 51 In.	1200
Sign, Hand-Painted Cards For All Occasions, Palette Shape, 21 x 35 In.	240

Sign, Horse Nameplate, Parade, Red On Black, Carved, Late 1800s, 4 x 18 In.	150
Sign, Horse, Tack Shop, Brass, 9 x 11 ½ In.	180
Sign, House & Sign Painting, 2-Sided, Black & Gilt, 1800s, 44 x 54 In.	3500
Sign, Ice Cream 5 Cents, Ice Cream Cone Shape, Copper, c.1920, 14 x 6 In.	160
Sign, Iron Sheet, Mrs. Burrell Dressmaker, 2-Sided, Gilt Lettering, 1800s, 14 x 20 In.	350
Sign, Iron, Haircutting & Shaving, Singing & Shampooing, c.1880, 13 x 21 In.	1900
Sign, Maine Lobster, Black, White, DSS, 14 x 50 In.	270
Sign, Meat Market, Wood, Paint, White, Black Shadowed Letters, 15 x 43 In.	2091
Sign, No Smoking In This Cellar, By Order J.L. Schwartz, c.1880, 12 x 22 In.	800
Sign, Raspberries, Red Text, White Ground, 6 x 42 In.	146
Sign, Repairing, Foil Gold Gilt, Black, 10 ½ x 30 In.	86
Sign, Roasting Chickens, Lb., Wood, 1900s, 16 x 36 ½ In.	234
Sign, Shoemaker, Woman's Shoe & Man's Boot, c.1910, 20 x 14 In.	330
Sign, Spectacles, Eyes, 1900s, 40 x 9 In.	234
Sign, Sperm Whale, Teeth, Carved, Gray Paint, Iron Rings, c.1910, 12 x 34 In.	2074
Sign, Stoneware The Best Food Container, Tin Lithograph, Late 1800s, 19 x 13 In.	875
Sign, Tailors, Copper, Window Screen, U.S. Seal, Scroll, Frame, c.1850, 37 x 25 In.	1778
Sign, Tourists, Black, White, 11 x 23 ½ In.	175
Sign, Trade, Chamberstick, Tin, Counter Display, Handle & Snuffer, 13 x 15 In.	1107
Sign, Trade, Furniture Repair, Cabinet Work, Star Shape Borders, Paint, 18 x 23 In.	960
Sign, Trade, Instrument Maker, Tin String Bass With Wooden Neck, 1800s, 69 In.	3120
Sign, Whale's Tale, Bait & Tackle, Whale Shape, 39 x 12 In.	380
Sign, Woman Holding Bottle, Cardboard, Hanging, 1902, 6 In.	4500
Tobacco Cutter, Curved Handle, Scroll, Figural Elf, Shaped Base, Cast Iron, 13 In.	266

STOVES have been used in America for heating since the eighteenth century and for cooking since the nineteenth century. Most types of wood, coal, gas, kerosene, and even some electric stoves are collected.

Cook, Cast Iron, 4-Burner, 2 Doors, Leaves, Charter Oak, Sample, 1880, 25 x 15 In.	178
Cook, Kenton Marvel, Cast Iron, Copper, Pipe, Scroll Apron, Footed, 17 x 13 In.	215
Cook, Qualified Range Co., Metal, Blue, Roll Hood, Salesman's Sample, 22 In.	738
Folding, Tin, 1700s, 18 x 11 In.	58
Heating, Conowingo Furnace, Cast Iron, 33 In. ....*illus*	1003
Heating, Shaker, Cast Iron, Arched Hearth Tray, Tapered Legs, 1800s, 20 x 33 In.	3444
Iron, Black, Decorated, Hooded, Quick Meal, Salesman Sample, 17 ½ x 16 In.	738
Iron, Black, Nickel, Scrolls, Removable Heat Exchange, Cylindrical, 28 x 68 In.	307
Iron, Enamel, Light Green, 4 Doors, Hooded	369
Parlor, Cast Iron, Floral Castings, J & S Schum-Wurzburg, 67 x 14 In.	625
Parlor, Majolica, Faience, Marble Top, 1800s, 42 x 20 In.	562
Stove Plate, Adam & Eve, 1741, 27 x 27 In.	3321
Stove Plate, Cast Iron, Religious Scene, Embossed, 28 x 27 In. ....*illus*	295
Stove Plate, Hearts, Tulips, Rock Forge Furnace, 1771, 20 x 22 In.	492
Stove Plate, Inscribed 1594, 30 x 18 In.	185
Stove Plate, Treasure Of Jahn Pot, Double Canopy, Flowers, Cast Iron, 24 x 25 In. ....*illus*	384

STRETCH GLASS is named for the strange stretch marks in the glass. It was made by many glass companies in the United States from about 1900 to the 1920s. It is iridescent. Most American stretch glass is molded; most European pieces are blown and may have a pontil mark.

Bowl, Console, Aquamarine, Ribbed, Flared, Fenton, 3 x 11 In. ....*illus*	125
Bowl, Fruit, Iridescent Yellow, Cupped Flare Rim, Pedestal, 1930s, 10 In. Diam.	82
Bowl, Triple Dolphin, Velva Rose, Fenton, 4 x 7 In. ....*illus*	9100
Bowl, Vaseline, Wavy Rim, 1920s, 3 x 10 In.	119
Candleholder, Blue Iridescent, Flared Foot, c.1910, 7 In., Pair	75
Compote, Blue, Cup Shaped, Square Foot, 1930s, 4 x 7 In.	76
Compote, Green Luster, Enameled Flowers, Iridescent, 1920s, 4 x 10 In.	85
Vase, Bud, Swung, Diamond, Cobalt Blue, 12 In. ....*illus*	150
Vase, Iridescent Amber, Crackle, Swollen Collar, 1930s, 6 In.	125

Stove, Stove Plate, Treasure Of Jahn Pot, Double Canopy, Flowers, Cast Iron, 24 x 25 In.
$384

Hess Auction Group

Stretch Glass, Bowl, Console, Aquamarine, Ribbed, Flared, Fenton, 3 x 11 In.
$125

Burns Auction Service (Tom Burns)

Stretch Glass, Bowl, Triple Dolphin, Velva Rose, Fenton, 4 x 7 In.
$9,100

Burns Auction Service (Tom Burns)

This is an edited listing of current prices. Visit **Kovels.com** to check thousands of prices from previous years and sign up for free information on trends, tips, reproductions, marks, and more.

Stretch Glass, Vase, Bud, Swung, Diamond, Cobalt Blue, 12 In.
$150

Burns Auction Service (Tom Burns)

Sumida, Vase, Moon Shape, Pagoda, Dozens Of Monkeys, Seal Mark, c.1890, 17 In.
$2,714

Humler & Nolan

Superman, Button, Supermen Of America, Image Of Superman, 1941, ⁷⁄₈ In.
$868

Hake's Americana & Collectibles

SULPHIDES are cameos of unglazed white porcelain encased in transparent glass. The technique was patented in 1819 in France and has been used ever since for paperweights, decanters, tumblers, marbles, and other type of glassware. Paperweights and Marbles are listed in their own categories.

Glass, Plaque, Lafayette, Within A Cut Glass Mount, France, 1800s, 3 ⅓ In.	500
Glass, Plaque, Thomas Jefferson, Beveled Circular Mount, 1800s, 3 ⅓ In.	2500

SUMIDA is a Japanese pottery that was made from about 1895 to 1941. Pieces are usually everyday objects—vases, jardinieres, bowls, teapots, and decorative tiles. Most pieces have a very heavy orange-red, blue, brown, black, green, purple, or off-white glaze, with raised three-dimensional figures as decorations. The unglazed part is painted red, green, black, or orange. Sumida is sometimes mistakenly called Sumida gawa, but true Sumida gawa is a softer pottery made in the early 1800s.

Figurine, Man, Frog On Back, Multicolor, 10 In.	168
Humidor, Figural, Boy On Waves, Boy Shape Knob, Red, Blue, 5 x 4 In.	147
Vase, Dragon, Stylized Waves, Brown, Red, White, 11 ½ x 4 ¼ In.	324
Vase, Figures, Exchanging Gifts, Multicolor, Mottled, Tapered, c.1880, 24 In.	1180
Vase, Moon Shape, Pagoda, Dozens Of Monkeys, Seal Mark, c.1890, 17 In. ......*illus*	2714

SUNBONNET BABIES were introduced in 1900 in the book *The Sunbonnet Babies*. The stories were by Eulalie Osgood Grover, illustrated by Bertha Corbett. The children's faces were completely hidden by the sunbonnets. The children had been pictured in black and white before this time, but the color pictures in the book were immediately successful. The Royal Bayreuth China Company made a full line of children's dishes decorated with the Sunbonnet Babies. Some Sunbonnet Babies plates have been reproduced, but they are clearly marked.

Bell, Ironing, Wood Clapper, Royal Bayreuth, c.1910, 3 ¼ In.	494
Bonbon, Scrubbing, Goldtone Center Handle, Triangular, 7 ¼ In. Diam.	82
Candleholder, Shieldback, Sweeping, 5 x 4 In.	118
Pin Dish, Ironing, Clover Shap, c.1920s, 5 In.	84
Plate, Playtime Series, Molly & May, 7 In., 4 Piece	160
Serving Bowl, Washing, Royal Bayreuth, c.1910, 3 x 10 In.	144

SUNDERLAND luster is a name given to a special type of pink luster made by Leeds, Newcastle, and other English firms during the nineteenth century. The luster glaze is metallic and glossy and appears to have bubbles in it. Other pieces of luster are listed in the Luster category.

Jug, Pink Luster, Maritime Scenes, Transfer, 8 In.	540
Jug, Pink Splotches, Black Transfer, Allegorical Figures, Pearlware, 9 In.	360
Pitcher, Pink Luster, Mariners Compass, 2 Ships, 8 In.	300
Pitcher, Pink Luster, Sailor's Farewell, Compass, Verse, Medallion, 7 ½ In.	143

SUPERMAN was created by two seventeen-year-olds in 1938. The first issue of *Action Comics* had the strip. Superman remains popular and became the hero of a radio show in 1940, cartoons in the 1940s, a television series, and several major movies.

Artwork, Patch Designs, Paper, Ink, Watercolor, 3 Pictures, 1 Sheet, 1946, 7 x 12 In.	1518
Badge, Strength Justice Courage, Brass, Enamel, Ogilvie Cereal, Canada, 1940, 1 In.	455
Badge, Supermen Of America, Action Comics, Felt, Cardboard, 1939, 6 In. Diam.	759
Binder, 3-Ring, Zippered, Textured Leatherette, Superman In Space, 1949, 11 x 13 In.	345
Book, Conoco Gasoline & Oil, Attendant, 10 Pgs., 1945, 14 x 19 In.	863
Book, Cutout, Superman, Lois, Lex Luther, Ultra, Stiff Paper, 4 Pgs., 1940, 11 x 15 In.	1684
Button, Arm Up, Fists Clenched, Blue Tights, Red Boots, 1 ¼ In.	60
Button, Supermen Of America, Image Of Superman, 1941, ⁷⁄₈ In. ......*illus*	868
Card Set, Gum, In The Jungle, Green Backs, Color, Story Text, 1968, 66 Cards	525
Card, Announcement, WOR 710 Radio, Superman, Full Body, Text, 4 x 7 In.	633

Card, Gum, Photos, TV Show Scenes, Black, White, 1950s, 3 x 4 In., 66 Cards	306
Card, Topps Complete Set, 1966, 66 Cards	2700
Comic Book, Adventure Comics, No. 247, Legion Of Superheroes, 1958	1058
Comic Book, Superman's Girlfriend, Lois Lane, No. 1, 1958	696
Cookie Jar, Telephone Booth, California Originals, 1978, 13 x 5 ½ In.	396
Doll, Wood & Composition, Jointed, Movable Head, Ideal, 1940, 13 In.	1742
Drawing, Concept Art, Superman Telephone, Flag, C. Swan, 1970s, 18 x 22 In.	727
Drawing, Pencil On Cardboard, Portrait, Joe Shuster, Signed, 1979, 11 x 14 In.	1113
Figure, Wood, Composition, Brown & Red, Hands On Hips, Base, c.1942	949
Figure, Wood, Composition, Paint, Hands On Hips, Base, 1942, 5 ½ In.	1898
Lighter, Superman Figure, Cast Metal, Bakelite Base, Batteries, c.1942, 3 x 5 In.	487
Magic Kit, Complete Pieces, Instructions, Inserts, Box, 1956, 12 x 15 In.	1085
Necklace, Pendant, Enamel, Painted Metal, Goldtone Chain, 1978, 18 In. Chain............*illus*	49
Paint Set, Pictures, Pallet, Paint Tablets, Dishes, Crayons, Box, c.1940, 12 x 16 In.	506
Patch, Supermen Of America, Club Members, Woven Fabric, c.1944, 2 x 3 In.	926
Patch, Tim Club, S-Shield, Superman, Tim Portrait, Felt, 1940s, 6 x 7 In.	239
Picture, Riding Rocket, Glow In The Dark, Wood Frame, c.1945, 8 x 10 In.	294
Pin, Brass, Figural, Full Body, Hands On Hips, Red, Yellow, No. 151, 1941, 1 In.	453
Poster, Movie, Chapter 12, Blast In The Depths, Film Scene, 1948, 27 x 41 In.	1670
Poster, Send Superman To War, Comics To Soldiers, WWII, 1944, 10 x 18 In.	978
Press Book, Promotion, 17 Color Cartoons, 16 Pgs., Paramount, 1941, 9 x 12 In.	4428
Puzzle Set, Gum Card, In The Jungle, Punch Out Pieces, Lion, 16 Cards	186
Puzzle, No. 1516, Superman Over The City, 500 Pieces, Box, 1940, 8 x 11 In.	311
Puzzle, Springs Into Action, Gangsters, Speedboat, Saalfield, Box, 16 x 20 In., 500 Piece	530
Puzzle, The Man Of Tomorrow, Saalfield, Box, 1940, 6 x 7 In., 300 Pcs.	1265
Ring, Supermen Of America, Lightning Bolts, Planets, Silvered Brass, 1940	2296
Sailor Cap, Silk Screen, Superman Flying, Shield Logo, 1950s, 8 ½ In.	321
Sign, War Stamps, Be A Superman To Your Family, Paper, 1943, 5 x 17 In.	581
Socks, Cartoon Images, Sportwear Hosiery, Box, Size 7, 1949, 8 x 10 In.	463
Statue, Plaster, Superman, Strength-Courage-Justice, Bronze Finish, 1940s, 7 In.	449
Target, Tin, Cardboard Back, Superman Flying, Villain's, 1950s, 8 In. Diam.	409
Telephone, Superman Figure, Rotary Dial, Red, Plastic, Paint, 1978, 10 x 17 In.	278
Toy, Krypto-Raygun, Steel, Film Viewer, 7 Filmstrips, Box, 1940, 8 x 10 In.	773
Travel Case, Superman In Flight, Plastic, Handle, Latches, 1960s, 11 x 14 In.	316
Wallet, Superman Flying, Brown Leather, Zipper, Snap Close, 1940s, 4 x 4 In.	115
Wristwatch, Supertime, Chrome Luster, Leather Band, Box, c.1955, 3 x 6 In.	411

SUSIE COOPER began as a designer in 1925 working for the English firm A.E. Gray & Company. In 1932 she formed Susie Cooper Pottery, Ltd. In 1950 it became Susie Cooper China, Ltd., and the company made china and earthenware. In 1966 it was acquired by Josiah Wedgwood & Sons, Ltd. The name *Susie Cooper* appears with the company names on many pieces of ceramics.

Cup & Saucer, Flower Spray	21
Platter, Wedding Ring Pattern, 16 x 12 ½ In.	30

SWANKYSWIGS are small drinking glasses. In 1933, the Kraft Food Company began to market cheese spreads in these decorated, reusable glass tumblers. They were discontinued from 1941 to 1946, then made again from 1947 to 1958. Then plain glasses were used for most of the cheese, although a few special decorated Swankyswigs have been made since that time. For more prices, go to kovels.com.

Archies, Sabrina Cleans Her Room, Yellow & Orange, 1971	10
Blue Violet, Purple Blue Flowers, Green Leaves, 3 ½ In.	12
Bustlin' Betty, Red, 1950s, 3 ¾ In.	10
Cherry, Red, 1950s, 3 ⅛ x 2 ½ x 1 ¾ In., 6 Piece	20
Crocus, Blue & Purple, 5 In., 2 Piece	24
Daffodil, 5 In., 4 Piece	26
Easter Lily, White Flowers, Yellow Center, Green Leaves, 5 In.	34 to 45

Superman, Necklace, Pendant, Enamel, Painted Metal, Goldtone Chain, 1978, 18 In. Chain
$49

Ruby Lane

Swastika Keramos, Ewer, Tapered Rim, Iridized, Green, Beaded White, Gold Tone, c.1907, 10 ¾ In.
$395

Ruby Lane

Sword, Belt Plate, Union Justice Confidence, Sand Cast, Louisiana Pelican, 1872
$923

Cowan's Auctions

S

Syracuse, Coronet, Plate, Dinner, 10¼ In.
$22

Replacements, Ltd.

Tea Caddy, Fruitwood, Apple Shape, Turned, Lid, Stem Finial, 1800s, 4½ In.
$826

Hess Auction Group

Tea Caddy, Mahogany, Inlay Flowers, Paper Lining, England, George III, c.1800, 5½ In.
$660

Brunk Auctions

Greyhound Racing Dogs, Red & White, 5¼ x 2¾ In.	8
Magnolia, Yellow Flowers, Black Center, Black Leaves, 5⅛ In.	17
Merliac Rose Water Lily, Red, 5 In.	30
Mexican Sunflower, Red, 5 In.	42
Oriental Poppy, Red, 5 In.	18
Red Roses, Green Leaves, Yellow Ribbon, 4½ In., 4 Piece	30
Trumpet Flower, Blue Flowers, Green Leaves, 3¾ In.	12
Tulip, Green, Red, Black, Blue, 2 x 3 In., 4 Piece	8
Tulip, Red Flowers, Green Leaves, 5 In.	14
Viola, Blue, 5 In.	36
Violet, Blue, White, Purple, Yellow, 5 In., 4 Piece	41
Water Lily, Blue, 5 In.	31

SWASTIKA KERAMOS is a line of art pottery made from 1906 to 1908 by the Owen China Company of Minerva, Ohio. Many pieces were made with an iridescent glaze.

Ewer, Tapered Rim, Iridized, Green, Beaded White, Gold Tone, c.1907, 10¾ In. ....*illus*	395
Vase, Coraline, White Beads, Green & Gold Squiggles, 3 Handles, 7 In.	121
Vase, Coraline, White Beads, Green & Gold Squiggles, Cylindrical, 6 In.	121
Vase, Coraline, White Beads, Green & Gold Squiggles, Handles, 8 In.	242
Vase, Iridescent, Forest Scene, Trees, Red Leaves, 11½ In.	242
Vase, Iridescent, Metallic Bronze, Panels Of Swastikas, 9 In.	393
Vase, Iridescent, Stylized Iris, Gold, Orange Luster, 2 Handles, 12 In.	290
Vase, Leafless Trees, Luster Glaze, c.1906, 8 x 3½ In.	605
Vase, Red Tulips, Green Leaves, Black Tracery, Gourd, 3 Handles, 7 In.	115
Vase, Tulips, Luster, Black Tracery, 3 Handles, 5½ x 7 In.	121

SWORDS of all types that are of interest to collectors are listed here. The military dress sword with elaborate handle is probably the most wanted. A tsuba is a hand guard fitted to a Japanese sword between the handle and the blade. Be sure to display swords in a safe way, out of reach of children.

Belt Plate, Union Justice Confidence, Sand Cast, Louisiana Pelican, 1872 ....*illus*	923
Brass Hilt, Molly Maguire, Ancient Order Of Hibernia, c.1876, 20 In.	650
Cavalry, Saber, Officer's, Engraved Blade, Captain Edward Godfrey, 1872, 32 In.	6221
Double Edge Blade, Scabbard, Austria, Silver Hilt, Winged Sphinx, 1800s, 31 In.	720
Fraternal, Staff, Odd Fellows, Heart-In-Hand, Wood, Figural Handle, 1800s, 63 In.	2760
Handle, Mixed Metal, Relief Design, Battle Ichi-No-Tani, Japan, c.1800, 8½ In.	948
Hanger, Ivory Chiseled Janus Head Hilt, Holland, c.1670, 18 In.	5500
Katana, Chrysanthemum, 3 Crabs	12500
Memphis Novelty, George Schwartz, Brass Knuckle Bow, Confederate, c.1861, 29 In.	5750
Officer's, Staff & Field, Non-Regulation, Horster, Scabbard, Germany, 33 In.	748
Officer's, Iron Hilt, France, c.1680, 27 In.	2600
Rapier, Pappenheimer, Cruciform Hilt, Fir Cone Pommel, Italy, c.1600, 39 In.	6700
Rapier, Steel Hilt, Solingen, Cornucopia Basket, Germany, c.1650, 37 In.	3450
Rapier, Swept Steel Hilt, Double Edge Blade, Continental, 1600s, 51 In.	1476
Saber, Iron 4-Slot Hilt, Heavy Knucklebow, Single Edge Blade, Eng., c.1770, 42 In.	2804
Saber, Iron Hilt, Pierced Guard, Curved Blade, Stars, Hearts, Continental, 1700s, 37 In.	738
Saber, Metal Hilt, Sharkskin Grip, Triple Wire Wrap, For Disabled, Eng., c.1822	445
Saber, Scabbard, Brass Hilt, Leather Grip, Steel Blade, U.S., c.1839, 39½ In.	1033
Saber, Scabbard, Napoleonic, 1st Empire, Crescent Moon, Arms Motif, 28½ In.	1035
Saber, Scabbard, Officer Of Light Cavalry, French, Blue & Gilt Blade, 34 In.	1680
Smallsword, Steel Hilt, Chiseled Flags, Military Trophies, Gilt, Italy, c.1720, 32 In.	3300
Swordfish Bill, Wood, Grip Handle, Painted, Lighthouse, Anchor, 1926, 36 In.	554
Tsuba, Copper, Brass, Cottage, Landscape, 2¾ In.	132
Tsuba, Inlaid Silver, Calligraphy, 2¾ In.	240
Tsuba, Iron, 2 Shells, 2¾ In.	180
Tsuba, Iron, Openwork Leaf, Brass Wire Inlay, Choshu Tomosato, 2¾ In.	240

SYRACUSE is a trademark used by the Onondaga Pottery of Syracuse, New York. The company was established in 1871. The name became the Syracuse China Company in 1966. Syracuse China closed in 2009. It was known for fine dinnerware and restaurant china.

Bombay, Plate, Dinner, 9¾ In.	25
Butter Chip, Union Pacific, Seal, Reserves, Historical, 3¼ In.	168
Coralbel, Bowl, Vegetable, Oval, 10 In.	40
Coralbel, Cup & Saucer	25
Coralbel, Plate, Dinner, 9¾ In.	23
Coralbel, Platter, 12¼ In.	45
Coronet, Cup & Saucer	24
Coronet, Gravy	110
Coronet, Plate, Bread & Butter, 6¼ In.	10
Coronet, Plate, Dinner, 10¼ In. .... *illus*	22
Midlothian, Bowl, Fruit, 6⅛ In.	14
Midlothian, Plate, Salad, 8 In.	14
Midlothian, Platter, 12 In.	45
Pink Carnation, Ashtray, Round, 4 In.	12
Rosalie, Cup & Saucer	35
Rosalie, Plate, Dinner, 10 In.	30
Rosalie, Platter, 14 In.	75
Rosalie, Sugar & Creamer	72
Suzanne, Bowl, Fruit	14
Suzanne, Bowl, Vegetable, Oval, 10¾ In.	50
Suzanne, Plate, Dinner, 10½ In.	35
Wayside, Creamer	25
Wayside, Cup & Saucer	20
Wayside, Platter, 11¼ In.	40
Wedding Ring, Cup & Saucer	50
Wedding Ring, Plate, Dinner, 10½ In.	10

TAPESTRY, *Porcelain, see Rose Tapestry category.*

TEA CADDY is the name for a small box made to hold tea leaves. In the eighteenth century, tea was very expensive and it was stored under lock and key. The first tea caddies were made with locks. By the nineteenth century, tea was more plentiful and the tea caddy was larger. Often there were two sections, one for green tea, one for black tea.

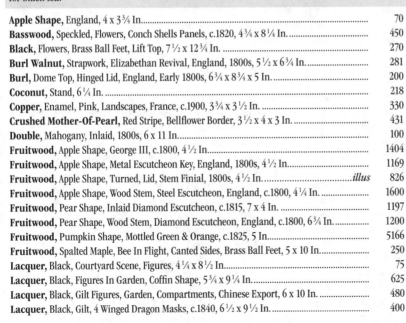

Apple Shape, England, 4 x 3¾ In.	70
Basswood, Speckled, Flowers, Conch Shells Panels, c.1820, 4¾ x 8¼ In.	450
Black, Flowers, Brass Ball Feet, Lift Top, 7½ x 12¾ In.	270
Burl Walnut, Strapwork, Elizabethan Revival, England, 1800s, 5½ x 6¾ In.	281
Burl, Dome Top, Hinged Lid, England, Early 1800s, 6¾ x 8¾ x 5 In.	200
Coconut, Stand, 6¼ In.	218
Copper, Enamel, Pink, Landscapes, France, c.1900, 3¾ x 3½ In.	330
Crushed Mother-Of-Pearl, Red Stripe, Bellflower Border, 3½ x 4 x 3 In.	431
Double, Mahogany, Inlaid, 1800s, 6 x 11 In.	100
Fruitwood, Apple Shape, George III, c.1800, 4½ In.	1404
Fruitwood, Apple Shape, Metal Escutcheon Key, England, 1800s, 4½ In.	1169
Fruitwood, Apple Shape, Turned, Lid, Stem Finial, 1800s, 4½ In. .... *illus*	826
Fruitwood, Apple Shape, Wood Stem, Steel Escutcheon, England, c.1800, 4¼ In.	1600
Fruitwood, Pear Shape, Inlaid Diamond Escutcheon, c.1815, 7 x 4 In.	1197
Fruitwood, Pear Shape, Wood Stem, Diamond Escutcheon, England, c.1800, 6¾ In.	1200
Fruitwood, Pumpkin Shape, Mottled Green & Orange, c.1825, 5 In.	5166
Fruitwood, Spalted Maple, Bee In Flight, Canted Sides, Brass Ball Feet, 5 x 10 In.	250
Lacquer, Black, Courtyard Scene, Figures, 4¼ x 8½ In.	75
Lacquer, Black, Figures In Garden, Coffin Shape, 5¾ x 9¼ In.	625
Lacquer, Black, Gilt Figures, Garden, Compartments, Chinese Export, 6 x 10 In.	480
Lacquer, Black, Gilt, 4 Winged Dragon Masks, c.1840, 6½ x 9½ In.	400

Tea Caddy, Quillwork, Crushed Abalone, 8-Sided, Medallion, Print, Lid, c.1800, 5 x 7 In.
$450

Garth's Auctioneers & Appraisers

Tea Caddy, Rosewood, Bird's Eye Maple, Bronze Banding, P. Milet, Sevres, c.1915, 14 In.
$1,560

Brunk Auctions

Tea Caddy, Tole, Lid, Red Flowers, Leaves, Black Ground, Pennsylvania, 1800s, 5¼ In.
$83

Hess Auction Group

T

TIP
Keep your keys on a pull-apart chain so the house keys and car keys can be separated when you leave the car in a parking lot.

Tea Caddy, Tortoiseshell, Metal Inlay, Compartments, Foil Lined, Regency, c.1815, 6 x 5 In.
$1,125

New Orleans Auction Galleries

Teco, Vase, Tulip, Avocado Green Matte Glaze, 11 ½ In.
$2,242

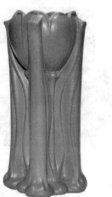

Humler & Nolan

Dating Teddy Bears
Early teddy bears had boot-button eyes before World War I, glass eyes beginning in the 1920s, and plastic eyes and noses since the 1950s.

Teddy Bear, Steiff, Mohair, Shoebutton Eyes, Felt Pads, Button In Ear, c.1915, 13 In.
$1,344

Theriault's

Lacquer, Black, Gilt, Figures, Flowers, Octagonal, Domed, 2 Pewter Jars, 5 ⅜ x 7 ¾ In.	350
Lacquer, Black, Gilt, Panoramic Landscape, Chinese Export, 5 x 7 In.	550
Mahogany, 2 Compartments, Conch Shell Inlay, English, 19th Century, 5 ¼ In.	350
Mahogany, Carved, Flowers, 4 Compartments, George III, c.1780, 7 ½ x 11 In.	5250
Mahogany, Coffin Shape, Canted Top, Ball Feet, 2 Compartments Inside, George III, 6 x 10 In.	180
Mahogany, Hinged, Trapezoidal, Brass Winged Paw Feet, Double, 7 x 12 In.	200
Mahogany, Inlaid Flowers, Tin Interior, George II, c.1760, 6 x 10 In.	344
Mahogany, Inlaid Starburst, Heart, Rectangular, Paper Lining, 4 x 9 In.	480
Mahogany, Inlaid, 2 Compartments, Copper Handle, Georgian, 4 ⅜ x 10 ½ In.	150
Mahogany, Inlay Flowers, Paper Lining, England, George III, c.1800, 5 ½ In. *illus*	660
Mahogany, Inlay, Zinc Lined, c.1800, 5 ⅛ In.	176
Mahogany, Ivory Inlay, Marquetry, Hinged Top, Ivory Bun Feet, c.1820, 7 x 13 In.	240
Mahogany, Plum Pudding, English Regency, Early 1800s, 5 ¼ x 8 x 4 ¾ In.	593
Mahogany, Rectangular, England, 12 In.	313
Mahogany, Shell Inlay, Basket Of Flowers, England, Late 1700s, 5 x 7 ⅝ x 5 In.	150
Mahogany, Sideboard, 2 Bins, Lion & Ring Faux Pulls, Regency, Early 1900s, 10 x 4 In.	360
Marquetry, 7 ½ In.	200
Mixed Wood, Triple Lidded, Regency, c.1835, 7 x 14 In.	175
Mother-Of-Pearl & Abalone, 2 Compartments, George III, c.1820, 5 ½ x 8 x 4 ½ In.	1464
Mother-Of-Pearl, 2 Compartments, Liverpool, England, c.1880, 5 x 6 x 3 In.	625
Mother-Of-Pearl, Canted Corners, Silver Escutcheon, Compartments, 5 ½ x 7 ¾ In.	900
Pear, Carved, Inlaid Escutcheon, Foil Lined, England, Early 1800s, 7 In.	960
Pear, Georgian, Walnut, Threaded Cover, Carved Leaf & Stem, 5 ½ In.	1140
Pear, Inlaid, Escutcheon, Key, 8 In.	1320
Penwork, Court Scenes, Regency, 6 ½ x 9 In.	687
Porcelain, Armorial, Crest, Fides Et Fortitud, Flower Finial, Chinese, 5 ⅜ In.	600
Porcelain, Colonial Harbor, Scrolls, Lid, Stand, Chinese, c.1800, 4 x 6 In.	270
Porcelain, Famille Noire, Garden Setting, Hexagonal, 1900s, 11 ¼ x 8 ⅜ In., Pair	732
Porcelain, Imari, Cobalt Blue & Orange Flowers, Silver Lid, China, 1700s, 4 ⅝ In.	225
Quillwork, Crushed Abalone, 8-Sided, Medallion, Print, Lid, c.1800, 5 x 7 In. *illus*	450
Quillwork, Hexagonal, Scrolled, Paper Flowers, Reserves, Georgian, 4 ½ x 7 In.	850
Rosewood, Bird's Eye Maple, Bronze Banding, P. Milet, Sevres, c.1915, 14 In. *illus*	1560
Rosewood, Coffin Shape, Lion's Mask Handles, Regency, c.1830, 8 x 12 x 6 In.	488
Rosewood, Hinged Lid, Coffin Shape, England, Early 1900s, 5 ½ x 8 x 5 In.	390
Rosewood, Inlay, Brass Lion Mask Handles, England, c.1810, 8 x 13 x 7 In.	125
Rosewood, Mother-Of-Pearl Plaque, Coffin Shape, 1840, 8 x 12 In.	150
Satinwood, Almond Reserve, Conch Shell, Ebony Banding, 2 Compartment, 4 ¾ x 7 In.	595
Satinwood, Flower Bouquet, Inlaid, Octagonal, 7 x 5 In.	643
Satinwood, Inlaid Shell, Potted Flowers, Hepplewhite, c.1800, 4 ½ x 5 In.	185
Satinwood, Inlaid, Conch Shell In Cartouche, Shield Escutcheon, 3 Compartment, 6 In.	600
Satinwood, Inlaid, Diamond Key Escutcheon, George III, 4 ¾ x 6 ⅜ In.	531
Shell, Wavy, Brown & Yellow, Red Velvet Interior, Early 1800s, 5 x 8 In.	805
Silver Plate, Copper, 4 Panels, Mill Houses, Farms, Rectangular, 5 ¾ x 5 In.	177
Silver Plate, Hinged Top, 5 In.	25
Silver, Bright Cut Engraving, Bead Border, Dome Lid, Urn Finial, H. Bateman, 5 x 5 In.	3360
Silver, Chased Leaves & Scrolls, Dome Lid, T.B. Starr, 5 x 3 ½ In.	254
Silver, Classical Figures, Eagle, Wreath Insignia, Swags, Continental, 7 ½ x 3 ½ In.	418
Silver, Enamel, Birds, Branches, Turquoise, Coral, Hexagonal, Lobed, 6 ¾ x 3 ⅞ In.	1875
Silver, Flowers, Decorated Neck, Vase Shape, Sweetser & Co., 5 In.	406
Silver, Repousse Flowers, Figures, Rococo Style, Paneled, Lid, Germany, 1800s, 7 In.	177
Silver, Repousse, Gold Washed, Splayed Feet, 5 ⅛ x 5 ⅛ In.	150
Silver, Scrolling Flowers, Cartouches, Lion, Oval, Hinged Lid, Urn Finial, 1738, 5 In.	1778
Tole, Lid, Red Flowers, Leaves, Black Ground, Pennsylvania, 1800s, 5 ¼ In. *illus*	83
Tole, Light Brown, Rose Spray, Boxy Apple Shape, 4-Footed, 1900s, 5 ¼ x 5 In.	111
Tortoiseshell Veneer, Silver Piping, Double, Pagoda Style Lid, Georgian, 5 ½ x 7 ¾ In.	1785
Tortoiseshell, 3 Compartments, Scrolled Feet, English Regency, c.1820, 12 x 6 In.	1755
Tortoiseshell, Ball Feet, 6 ½ x 7 In.	1080
Tortoiseshell, Ball Feet, Dome Lid, Regency, 6 ½ x 6 ¾ In.	1534
Tortoiseshell, Bombe Form, Ball Feet, Late 1800s, 6 x 7 ½ x 4 ½ In.	3000
Tortoiseshell, Bone, Mother-Of-Pearl, Regency, c.1820, 6 ½ x 7 ⅞ In.	2125

Tortoiseshell, Coffin Shape, 2 Lidded Compartments, Bun Feet, George III, 5 x 6 In.	1159
Tortoiseshell, Dome Lid, Silver Edges, Regency, 5 x 6 In.	1428
Tortoiseshell, Green, Silver Trim, 2 Compartments, George III, c.1800, 4 x 6⅝ x 3½ In.	1830
Tortoiseshell, Ivory Handle, Ivory Ball Feet, English Regency, c.1815, 7⅝ x 7 In.	1000
Tortoiseshell, Ivory Mounts, Engraved EF, Octagonal, 5 x 4¼ In.	1200
Tortoiseshell, Metal Inlay, Compartments, Foil Lined, Regency, c.1815, 6 x 5 In. _illus_	1125
Tortoiseshell, Name Plate, Ball Feet, George III, c.1810, 6½ x 4¼ In.	468
Tortoiseshell, Serpentine Front, Brass Ball Feet, Regency, Early 1800s, 6½ x 7 x 4½ In.	3000
Tortoiseshell, Serpentine Front, Stepped Hinged Lid, Bun Feet, c.1800, 6 x 8 In.	861
Walnut, Inlay, Coffin Shape, 2 Tea Boxes, Ebonized Disc Feet, 8 x 12½ In.	650
Walnut, Mahogany, Inlaid, Oval Conch, Turned Brass Knob, 4¾ x 4¾ In.	600
Wood, Inlaid Oak Leaves, Green Ground, Hardwood & String Banding, 6 x 12 x 6 In.	600
Wood, Reserve, Continental, 4⅜ x 6½ In.	63

TEA LEAF IRONSTONE dishes are named for their decorations. There was a superstition that it was lucky if a whole tea leaf unfolded at the bottom of your cup. This idea was translated into the pattern of dishes known as "tea leaf." By 1850 at least 12 English factories were making this pattern, and by the 1870s it was a popular pattern in many countries. The tea leaf was always a luster glaze on early wares, although now some pieces are made with a brown tea leaf. There are many variations of tea leaf designs, such as Teaberry, Pepper Leaf, and Gold Leaf. The designs were used on many different white ironstone shapes, such as Bamboo, Lily of the Valley, Empress, and Cumbow.

Bone Dish, Alfred Meakin, 6⅝ In.	37
Bone Dish, Red Cliff, 6⅞ In.	14
Bowl, Cereal, Adams, 6½ In.	18
Bowl, Vegetable, Lid, Oval, Alfred Meakin	249
Bowl, Vegetable, Round, Wedgwood, 9 In.	126
Butter Chip, Mellor Taylor, 2½ In.	8
Coffeepot, Lid, Wedgwood, 7 Cup, 7 In.	168
Cup & Saucer, Adams	9
Cup & Saucer, Alfred Meakin	42
Cup & Saucer, Footed, Royal Cauldon	37
Cup & Saucer, Red Cliff	17
Gravy Boat, Alfred Meakin	76
Gravy Boat, Furnivals	109
Gravy Boat, Grindley	111
Gravy Boat, Underplate, Wedgwood	179
Mug, Anthony Shaw, 3½ In.	40
Nappy, Wedgwood, 4 x 4 In.	17
Nut Dish, Square, Red Cliff, 4 In.	14
Pitcher, Adams, 32 Oz.	98
Pitcher, Red Cliff, 40 Oz., 7⅜ In.	55
Plate, Bread & Butter, Red Cliff, 6½ In.	7
Plate, Dinner, Adams, 10 In.	23
Plate, Dinner, Anthony Shaw, 9 In.	26
Plate, Dinner, Cumbow, 10 In.	30
Plate, Dinner, Grindley, 10 In.	52
Plate, Luncheon, Mellor Taylor, 9¼ In.	10
Plate, Luncheon, Wedgwood, 8¾ In.	14
Plate, Luncheon, Wilkinson, 9 In.	11
Plate, Salad, John Edwards, 7 In.	34
Platter, Anthony Shaw, 16 In.	169
Platter, Rectangular, Alfred Meakin, 15 In.	83
Platter, Rectangular, Furnivals, 13 In.	69
Platter, Rectangular, Mellor Taylor, 14 In.	138
Relish, Alfred Meakin, 8 x 4 In.	28
Salt & Pepper, Adams	97
Soup, Dish, Royal Cauldon, 7½ In.	23
Sugar & Creamer, Alfred Meakin,	220

Telephone, Western Electric, Quartersawn Oak, Model 250W, Wall Mount, 23 In.
$189

Hess Auction Group

Telephone, Western Electric, Rotary, Black, Ring Adjuster
$50

Ruby Lane

Teplitz, Vase, Heron, Grasses, 3 Frogs, Shaded Blue & White, Amphora, E. Wahliss, 21 In.
$4,148

James D. Julia Auctioneers

T

Teplitz, Vase, Symbolist, Nude Figures, Stamped, c.1900, 9 ½ x 8 ¾ In. $2,500

Rago Arts and Auction Center

Teplitz, Vase, Young Woman, Flower Headdress, Forest, Amphora, Stamped, RStK., 8 ⅜ In. $1,062

Humler & Nolan

Terra-Cotta, Bust, Father Jahn, White Hair & Long Beard, Base, 8 ½ In. $120

The Stein Auction Company

Sugar, Lid, Square, Wilkinson, 4 ¾ In.	117
Tureen, Lid, Handles, Adams	287
Vegetable, Oval, Adams, 9 In.	19

TECO is the mark used on the art pottery line made by the American Terra Cotta and Ceramic Company of Terra Cotta and Chicago, Illinois. The company was an offshoot of the firm founded by William D. Gates in 1881. The Teco line was first made in 1885 but was not sold commercially until 1902. It continued in production until 1922. Over 500 designs were made in a variety of colors, shapes, and glazes. The company closed in 1930.

Bowl, Flower, Brown Matte Glaze, Lobed, 2 ½ x 8 In.	396
Bowl, Pale Green Glaze, Molded Leaves & Berries Design, Disc Shape, Rolled Rim, 2 x 9 In.	472
Match Box, Green Matte Glaze, Tapered, Rectangular Lid, 2 x 3 ½ In.	671
Pitcher, Green Matte Glaze, Split Handle, W.D. Gates, 8 ½ x 5 In.	549
Pitcher, Green Matte Glaze, W.D. Gates, Whiplash Handle, 8 ¾ In.	529
Tray, Green Matte Glaze, Round, W.D. Gates, 10 ½ In.	976
Vase, Aventurine Glaze, Black, Orange, 3-Footed, W.D. Gates, 4 x 4 In.	793
Vase, Aventurine Glaze, Teardrop, Narrow Opening, 4 In.	460
Vase, Blue Matte Glaze, 12 In.	975
Vase, Bud, Green Matte Glaze, Impressed Signature, 6 x 5 In.	549
Vase, Bud, Green Matte Glaze, Round, W.D. Gates, 4 ½ x 4 ½ In.	457
Vase, Caramel Matte Glaze, Pointed Handles, W.B. Mundie, 11 x 5 In.	900
Vase, Deep Purple Matte Glaze, Buttressed, W.D. Gates, 6 ½ x 2 ½ In.	1037
Vase, Green Glaze, Tapered, 4 Buttress Handles At Top, 11 x 4 In.	1625
Vase, Green Matte Glaze, 2 Handles, 5 ½ In.	995
Vase, Green Matte Glaze, 4 Handles, Fritz Albert, c.1910, 15 x 9 ½ In.	9375
Vase, Green Matte Glaze, High Shoulders, V-Shape Petals, F. Moreau, 8 ½ x 4 In.	3965
Vase, Green Matte Glaze, Short Neck, Applied Metallic Decoration, Incised Lines, 7 x 8 In.	531
Vase, Green Matte Glaze, Small Mouth, 4 ½ x 4 In.	549
Vase, Green Matte Glaze, Tapered, Narrow Neck, W.D. Gates, 4 ½ x 3 ¾ In.	488
Vase, Holly & Berry, Green Matte Glaze, Impressed Signature, Fritz Albert, 10 In.	1037
Vase, Mint Green Matte Glaze, Bulbous, Swollen Stick, Buttress Handles, c.1910, 13 In.	5625
Vase, Mint Green Matte Glaze, Cylindrical, Buttress Handles, Cutouts, c.1910, 11 In.	2625
Vase, Mint Green Matte Glaze, Spherical, 4 Block Feet, Rolled Rim, c.1910, 12 x 10 In.	8750
Vase, Pale Green Glaze, Cylindrical, 4 Twisted Buttresses, 11 x 5 In.	938
Vase, Pale Green Glaze, Flattened Oval, 4 Cutout Handles, Pedestal Foot, c.1910, 15 x 10 In.	9375
Vase, Tulip, Avocado Green Matte Glaze, 11 ½ In. *illus*	2242
Vase, Tulip, Dark Green, c.1910, 12 In.	600
Wall Pocket, Green Glaze, F.R. Fuller, 6 ½ x 2 In.	793
Wall Pocket, Green Matte Glaze, Signed, Fritz Albert, 4 ¼ x 16 In.	1098
Wall Pocket, Green Matte Glaze, W.D. Gates, 5 ½ x 2 In.	610

TEDDY BEARS were named for a president of the United States. The first teddy bear was a cuddly toy said to be inspired by a hunting trip made by Teddy Roosevelt in 1902. Morris and Rose Michtom started selling their stuffed bears as "teddy bears" and the name stayed. The Michtoms founded the Ideal Novelty and Toy Company. The German version of the teddy bear was made about the same time by the Steiff Company. There are many types of teddy bears and all are collected. The old ones are being reproduced. Other bears are listed in the Toy section.

Bing, Skating, Brown Mohair, Button Eyes, Jointed, Jacket, Roller Skates, c.1912, 8 In.	336
Chiltern, Mohair, Swivel Head, Glass Eyes, Sewn Nose, Jointed, Felt Paw Pads, 17 ¾ In.	165
Ideal, Golden Mohair, Swivel Head, Embroidered Nose & Mouth, Shoebutton Eyes, 13 In.	336
Pink Mohair, Swivel Head, Embroidered Nose, Mouth, Amber Eyes, Jointed, 18 In.	280
Schuco, Yes No, Music, Curly Brown Mohair, Amber Glass Eyes, Key Wind, c.1950, 20 In.	448
Steiff, Blond Mohair, Bead Eyes, Embroidered Nose & Mouth, Jointed, 3 ¾ In.	305
Steiff, Blond Mohair, Shoebutton Eyes, Jointed, 1900s, 13 In.	900
Steiff, Cecil, Cinnamon Brown Mohair, Boot Button Eyes, 16 In.	1449
Steiff, Champagne Mohair, Felt Paw Pads, Stitched Ears, Silver Button, c.1910, 12 In.	896
Steiff, Mohair, Shoebutton Eyes, Felt Pads, Button In Ear, c.1915, 13 In. *illus*	1344

T

Steiff, Panda Bear, Black & White Mohair, Fully Jointed, 1951-61, 17 In.	660
Steiff, Ride-On, White, Red & White Wheels, 21 x 30 In.	192
Steiff, White Mohair, Rattle, Jointed 6 Ways, 1920s, 5 In.	900

TELEPHONES are wanted by collectors if the phones are old enough or unusual enough. The first telephone may have been made in Havana, Cuba, in 1849, but it was not patented. The first publicly demonstrated phone was used in Frankfurt, Germany, in 1860. The phone made by Alexander Graham Bell was shown at the Centennial Exhibition in Philadelphia in 1876, but it was not until 1877 that the first private phones were installed. Collectors today want all types of old phones, phone parts, and advertising. Even recent figural phones are popular.

American Telephone & Telegraph Co., Yellow Cab Taxi Box, Mid 1900s, 16 x 11 In.	469
ATEA, Rotary, Bakelite, White, Art Deco Style, Belgium, c.1930	309
Bell Telephone, Wall, Pay Phone, Token Slot, Key, For Belgian Market, 1966	252
Bell Type, Walnut Case, Butter Stamp Form, 2 Magnets, c.1880, 7¼ In.	2289
Dean Electric Co., 2 Bells, Earpiece On Left, 26 In.	210
Gamewell, Police Telegraph Call Box, Iron, Citizen's Key In Lock, 1900s, 25 In.	625
Julius Andrae & Sons Co., 2 Bells, Earpiece On Left, 32 In.	150
Kellogg, Oak, Cased, 18 x 10 In.	151
Mix & Genest, Wall, Wood Box, Double Bell, Leather-Covered Handset, Germany, 1899	468
Mix & Genest, Walnut Case & Stand, Bell On Back, Carbon Transmitter, c.1900	229
Pin, Hobson Electric Co., Jumbo Brand Wooden Wall Phone, Celluloid, 1⅝ x 1¼ In.	106
Pin, Pioneer Telephone Co., Image Of Woman On Candlestick Phone, 1¾ In.	130
Siemens & Halske, Wall, Shaped Wood Case, Movable Microphone, Spoon Handset, 1902	468
Sterling Electric Co., Wooden, Bells, Earpiece On Left, 33 In.	150
Western Electric, Quartersawn Oak, Model 250W, Wall Mount, 23 In. *illus*	189
Western Electric, Rotary, Black, 1900s	135
Western Electric, Rotary, Black, Ring Adjuster *illus*	50
Western Electric, U.S. Forest Service Box, Hand-Held Receiver, Mid 1900s, 19 In.	570

TELEVISION sets are twentieth-century collectibles. Although the first television transmission took place in England in 1925, collectors find few sets that pre-date 1946. The first sets had only five channels, but by 1949 the additional UHF channels were included. The first color television set became available in 1951.

Crosley, Model 10-401, Bakelite, Brown, Table Top, c.1950, 10 In.	349
Fada, Model TV-30, Mahogany, 1940s, 14 x 26 In.	70
Majestic, Model 12T6, 19 x 18 x 20 In.	200
Sony TV-750, Napoleon Dynamite Model, Portable, Black & White, c.1970, 7 In.	98

TEPLITZ refers to art pottery manufactured by a number of companies in the Teplitz-Turn area of Bohemia during the late nineteenth and early twentieth centuries. Two of these companies were the Alexandra Works founded by Ernst Wahliss, and the Amphora Porcelain Works, run by Riessner, Stellmacher, and Kessel.

Bowl, Fates, Women's Heads In Relief, Streaky Blue & Tan, Flared, RStK, 6 x 9 In.	1750
Bowl, Maiden, Figural, Flower On Shoulder, Gown Swirls To Bowl, Amphora, 27 In.	4148
Bust, Woman, Calla Lilies, Blond, Ernst Wahliss, 1900, 24 In.	1722
Ewer, Gold, Green Iridescent, Ribbon Handle, 10¾ In.	125
Figurine, Horse, Saddle, Bridle, Blanket, Stellmacher, 9 In.	75
Figurine, Water Bearer, Woman, Blue Gown, Eduard Stellmacher, 27½ x 19 In.	1952
Figurine, Woman, Hand On Hip, c.1905, Austria, 24¾ In.	525
Jug, Lotus Leaves, Embossed, Bud Spout, Amphora, Riessner, c.1905, 5⅞ In.	150
Pitcher, Brown, Wine, Geometric, Secessionist, Eduard Stellmacher, 9¼ In.	276
Pitcher, Leaves, Flower Spout, Blue Matte Ground, 1900, 19 In.	600
Plaque, Woman's Profile, Green, Brown, Ernst Wahliss, Austria, c.1900, 10½ In., Pair	687
Sculpture, Siren, Playing Her Harp, Ernst Wahliss, 1904, 13 In.	861
Tray, Mermaid, Seated, Oyster Shell, 2 Wells, 11 x 23 In.	750
Vase, Blue Iridescent, Beaker, Cylindrical Rim, Molded Putti, Amphora, 10 In.	354

Terra-Cotta, Sculpture, Nude, Kneeling, Glazed, Waylande Gregory, c.1934, 18 x 5 In.
$3,500

Rago Arts and Auction Center

Textile, Blanket, Hudson's Bay, White With Multicolor Bands, c.1995, 92 x 76 In.
$92

Allard Auctions

TIP

If your home has just been robbed, don't immediately give the police a list of the stolen items and damage. Sit down later and make a detailed list. This police copy is the one your insurance company will use to settle any claims. Take photographs of the damage as soon as possible.

Textile, Embroidery, Regimental, Remembrance, U.S.S. New Orleans, Silk, 22 x 25 In.
$216

Textile, Embroidery, Regimental, Silk, Eagle, E. Pluribus Unum, Frame, 25 x 22 ½ In.
$432

Textile, Embroidery, Regimental, Silk, Flags, Japan, China, Eagle, Dragon, c.1902, 26 x 32 In.
$600

Vase, Buzzard, Multicolor, 19 x 12 In.	500
Vase, Chestnut Leaf, Gilt, Green, White, Footed, 8 x 10 In.	200
Vase, Confetti, Art Nouveau Ormolu Mount, Amphora, Dachsel, c.1901, 23 x 13 In.	4375
Vase, English Ivy, Squat, Short Flared Neck, 6 ½ x 5 ¼ In.	330
Vase, Flowers, Faux Jewels, Figural Nude Woman, Gold, Blue, Squat, Amphora, 6 In.	1180
Vase, Flowers, Green Glaze, White, Gilt Twist Stem Handles, Scrolls Rim, c.1900, 10 In.	2500
Vase, Flowers, Swags, Wide Shoulder, Tapered, c.1920, 8 ⅝ x 8 ½ In.	212
Vase, Forest Sunrise, Gilt, Flowers, Wasps, 7 x 7 In.	531
Vase, Grapes & Leaves, Blue, Applied, Batwing Handles, 10 ¼ In.	123
Vase, Grapes & Leaves, Blue, Applied, Batwing Handles, Stippled, Mottled, Gilt, Blue, 15 In.	483
Vase, Grapes, Blue, Gold, Cream Rim, Amphora, 9 ¼ In.	406
Vase, Heron, Grasses, 3 Frogs, Shaded Blue & White, Amphora, E. Wahliss, 21 In. *illus*	4148
Vase, Iris, Green, Black, Dots, Swirls, Oval, Tapered, Double Loop Handles, c.1920, 8 x 5 In.	102
Vase, Peach Nasturtiums, Silver, Gold, Squat, Wide Rim, Stellmacher, 4 ½ In.	300
Vase, Poppy & Clover, Gold & White Outline, Amphora, Riessner, 9 ¼ In.	230
Vase, Shell, Beige Ground, Red, Green, Cabochon Decorations, Amphora, 1934, 6 In.	67
Vase, Shell, Drooping Vines, Art Deco, 1934, 6 In.	67
Vase, Stylized Pink Tulips, Applied, Green, Brown, Yellow, 11 ⅜ x 4 ½ In.	448
Vase, Summer Queen, Portrait, Crown, Amphora, RStK, c.1900, 5 ¾ x 5 In.	1495
Vase, Symbolist, Nude Figures, Stamped, c.1900, 9 ½ x 8 ¾ In. *illus*	2500
Vase, White Flowers, Gold Handles, Teal, Amphora, 7 ¾ In.	138
Vase, White Flowers, Yellow Hearts, Teal Handles, 15 ½ In.	250
Vase, Woman's Face, Gold, Flowers, Bulbous Top, Molded Swirl Rim, Amphora, 11 In.	1534
Vase, Woman's Profile, White Daisies, Amphora, 13 In.	1265
Vase, Young Woman, Flower Headdress, Forest, Amphora, Stamped, RStK., 8 ⅜ In. *illus*	1062

 TERRA-COTTA is a special type of pottery. It ranges from pale orange to dark reddish-brown in color. The color comes from the clay, which is fired but not always glazed in the finished piece.

Bust, Apollo Belvedere, Shoulder Drape, Turned Head, Socle Base, 30 In.	1187
Bust, Diana, Greek Goddess, Draped, Crown, Turned Head, Socle Base, 1900s, 30 In.	1250
Bust, Father Jahn, White Hair & Long Beard, Base, 8 ½ In. *illus*	120
Bust, Marie Antionette, Robe, Exposed Breast, 27 ¼ In.	812
Bust, Marquis Of Condorcet, France, 21 In.	750
Bust, Squint, Green, Tan, 17 x 13 In.	125
Bust, Turquoise, After Modigliani, 19 x 9 In.	281
Bust, Woman, Curly Hair, Draping, 30 In.	500
Candlestand, Tapered Column, Fluted Base, Octagonal Base, c.1880, 71 x 16 In., Pair	650
Figurine, 2 Persian Cats, Reclining On Pillow, Green Tassels, c.1915, 19 x 19 In.	750
Figurine, Bulldog, Seated, 23 In.	1875
Figurine, Reclining Cherub, Jug, 17 x 22 ½ In.	156
Ginger Jar, Lid, Red, Oval Panels, Landscapes, Moths, Chicken Finial, 29 In., Pair	937
Group, Bacchanalia, 16 ½ In.	250
Group, Panthers, Green, Walking, Nuzzling Back, After Andre Becquerel, 13 ¼ In.	500
Jardiniere, Bacchanal, Putti, Gadroon Neck, Socle Foot, 26 In.	416
Jardiniere, Dancing Putti, Relief Molded, 10 x 12 In., Pair	150
Medallion, Madonna & Child, Relief, c.1920, 3 ½ x 22 ⅞ In.	150
Plant Stand, Molded Tree Trunk, 2 Pigeons, Painted, 1900s, 18 In.	600
Planter, French Provincial, Black, 4 Ring Handles, 22 ¼ x 28 ½ In.	100
Plaque, Medallion, Benjamin Franklin, Jean Baptiste Nini, 4 ½ In.	1320
Plaque, Ram's Head, Butcher's Shop Emblem, White Glaze, Glass Eyes, 17 ½ In.	200
Sculpture, Blackamoor, Corsair Outfit, Turban, Tassel, 28 In.	177
Sculpture, Nude, Kneeling, Glazed, Waylande Gregory, c.1934, 18 x 5 In. *illus*	3500
Sculpture, Sphinx, Centaur, White, Base, 25 x 12 In.	225
Sculpture, Stylized Figure, Balls, Multicolor Geometric Shapes, 1986, 27 x 8 ¼ In.	595
Tile, Portrait, Relief, Cowboy Hat, Blue Shirt, 6 ½ x 10 In.	518
Tile, Roof, Warriors On Horses, China, c.1900, 15 ¼ x 5 ¼ x 13 ½ In., Pair	750
Tureen, Applied Decoration, Ribbons, Finial, 11 ½ In.	63
Umbrella Stand, Classical Woman, Carrying Urn, Frank Ferrel, c.1912, 20 ½ In.	187

Urn, Neoclassical, Nude, Busts, Angels, Swags, Plinth Base, 48 x 18 In., 2 Pieces	148
Vase, Applied Figures, Ibis, Hieroglyph Design, Austria, 1800s, 32 ½ In.	923
Vase, Hydra, Red Figure, Black Ground, Italy, 1900s, 15 ¼ In.	3250
Vase, Krater, Black Figure, 1900s, 17 ⅝ In.	2375
Vase, Nude Woman, Brown Glaze, Signed, Nakian, 19 ½ In.	750

TEXTILES listed here include many types of printed fabrics and table and household linens. Some other textiles will be found under Clothing, Coverlet, Rug, Quilt, etc.

Altar Hanging, Embroidery, Silk Brocade, Dragon, Flaming Pearl, c.1700, 34 x 55 In.	492
Apron, Cotton, Gathered Waist, Needlework, I.S. 1800, Frame, Penn., 25 x 32 In.	1121
Banner, Attached To American Flag, 25 Stars, Civil War Recruitment, 1863, 27 x 51 In.	4200
Banner, Silk, Civil War, The Union, Constitution & Flag Must Be Upheld, 32 x 30 In.	1560
Bedspread, Silk, Fleece, Ivory, Red, Green, Flowering Vines, Italy, c.1960, 98 x 82 In.	1085
Blanket, Homespun, 2 Panels, Blue & Yellow Stripes, Louisiana, c.1900, 61 x 80 In.	374
Blanket, Hudson's Bay, White With Multicolor Bands, c.1995, 92 x 76 In. ....*illus*	92
Blanket, Saddle, Wool, Mandala Center, Brown, Tan, Fringe, 1920s, 75 x 59 In.	425
Blanket, Wool, Woven, Tiger Skin, Red Ground, c.1965, 59 ½ x 46 In.	185
Embroidery, Medallions, Dragons, Wave Border, Black, Tan, 22 x 81 In.	313
Embroidery, Paddy's Courtship, Silk, c.1810, 7 x 5 ¾ In.	510
Embroidery, Regimental, Remembrance, U.S.S. New Orleans, Silk, 22 x 25 In. ....*illus*	216
Embroidery, Regimental, Silk, Eagle, E Pluribus Unum, Frame, 25 x 22 ½ In. ....*illus*	432
Embroidery, Regimental, Silk, Flags, Japan, China, Eagle, Dragon, c.1902, 26 x 32 In. .....*illus*	600
Embroidery, Serenity Prayer, Flowers, Linen, c.1955, 12 x 16 In.	30
Embroidery, Silk, Eagle, American Crest, Flag, Gilt Thread, Frame, 23 x 26 In.	531
Flag, American, 12 Stars, Confederate Exclusionary, P. Whittington, Frame, 23 x 42 In. ...*illus*	11193
Flag, American, 33 Stars, Canvas, Hand Painted, Charles Gilman, Union POW, 12 x 6 ½ In.	3360
Flag, American, 34 Stars, Medallion Form, Haloed Center Star, Cotton, c.1861, 15 x 21 ½ In.	2000
Flag, American, 35 Stars, Wool Bunting	690
Flag, American, 36 Stars, Frame, 20 ½ x 26 In.	2106
Flag, American, 36 Stars, Pole, 90 x 52 In.	594
Flag, American, 36 Stars, Wool, Appliqued Stars, 1865-1867, 41 x 64 In.	1328
Flag, American, 37 Stars, Red Wool, White Cotton, Blue Wool & Silk Mix, c.1870, 57 x 78	10800
Flag, American, 38 Stars, Cotton Muslin, Stars In Medallion Form, c.1876, 6 x 9 In.	840
Flag, American, 39 Stars, Centennial, 1776-1876, 12 x 16 In.	1755
Flag, American, 40 Stars, Glazed Cotton, Parade, c.1889, 17 ¾ x 12 In.	1440
Flag, American, 40 Stars, Wool, c.1889, 48 x 80 In.	660
Flag, American, 42 Stars, 13 Stripes, U.S. Navy, Wool, Cotton, 1890, 108 x 78 In.	425
Flag, American, 45 Stars, Frame, 19 x 34 In.	409
Flag, American, 45 Stars, Worsted Wool, Double Applique Cotton Stars, Pole, 1869, 48 x 96 In.	720
Flag, American, 48 Stars, 56 x 121 In.	58
Flag, American, Wool, Remember The Maine, Stitched, Frame, c.1900, 32 In.	700
Flag, British Navy, Red Ensign, Silk, Red, Union Jack, c.1825, 40 x 31 In.	5100
Flag, Confederate, 1st National, 7 Sequin & Bullion Stars, Silk, c.1861, 21 x 40 In. ....*illus*	31250
Flag, Confederate, Battle, Letcher Artillery, Marked T.A. Brander, c.1860, 60 x 60 In.	5333
Flag, Guidon, Civil War, Silk, 35 Gold Stars, Frame, c.1863, 14 ½ x 16 In. ....*illus*	13800
Flag, Imperial Dragon, Cobalt Blue, Silk, Stitched Scales, Cream Color Ground, c.1890, 52 x 35 In. *illus*	2118
Flag, Mississippi, Stars & Bars, Red, White, Blue, 1900-25, Frame, 11 x 17 ⅛ In.	325
Flag, Presidential Seal, Presentation, Frame, 45 x 45 In.	2375
Flag, World War I, Blue Star, Red Rectangle, 12 x 17 In.	23
Handkerchief, Cotton, G. Washington Commemorative, Printed, 1800s, 11 ¼ x 11 ¼ In.	780
Handkerchief, Cross-Stitched Sampler, Flowers, Freni Wohlgmuth, 1795, 21, In.	767
Handkerchief, Pink & Yellow Flowers, Happy Birthday, Cotton, Scalloped Edge, 1950s, 14 x 14 In.	30
Handkerchief, White Batiste Cotton, Pink Organdy Trim, Zigzag Edge, 1920s, 14 x 14 In.	15
Hanging, Appliqued, Birds & Flowers, Leafy Vines, Sequins, Felt, Glitter, Frame, 30 x 16 In.	50
Kerchief, Commemorative, Landing Of Lafayette At New York, c.1824, 26 ½ x 29 In.	4750
Mattress Cover, Cotton, Homespun, Brown Check Pattern, c.1815, 61 x 68 In.	1062
Needlepoint, Panel, 2 Couples In Forest, Flower Wreath Border, Octagonal, Frame, 37 In.	2880
Needlepoint, Panel, Shepherd & Shepherdess, Wool On Canvas, Oval, Frame, 16 x 15 In.	4800

Grand Old Flag

If your American flag is tattered and can no longer be used be sure to dispose of it in the official way. Give it to a Boy Scout, Girl Scout, American Legion post or the U.S. military. They can do the official ceremony that includes burning the old flag

Textile, Flag, American, 12 Stars, Confederate Exclusionary, P. Whittington, Frame, 23 x 42 In. **$11,193**

James D. Julia Auctioneers

Textile, Flag, Confederate, 1st National, 7 Sequin & Bullion Stars, Silk, c.1861, 21 x 40 In. **$31,250**

Neal Auctions

TIP

Flags have been made of many different fabrics, so cleaning requires testing. A wool flag should be tested with a drop of water and blotting paper. If no color is removed, you can wash it in warm water with a wool washing product. It can be dry-cleaned with care. Store a wool flag in an insect-proof container.

Textile, Flag, Guidon, Civil War, Silk, 35 Gold Stars, Frame, c.1863, 14½ x 16 In.
$13,800

James D. Julia Auctioneers

Textile, Flag, Imperial Dragon, Cobalt Blue, Silk, Stitched Scales, Cream Color Ground, c.1890, 52 x 35 In.
$2,118

James D. Julia Auctioneers

Textile, Sculpture, Cube, Jute Fiber, The Ball You Blow, Naoko Serino, Japan, 2003, 8 x 8 In.
$938

Rago Arts and Auction Center

Textile, Tapestry, Sun, Maguey Fiber, After Alexander Calder, 1974, 48 x 72 In.
$16,250

Rago Arts and Auction Center

Textile, Tapestry, Wool, Rosalia, Signed In Weave, Bjorn Wiinblad, 58 x 54 In.
$563

Rago Arts and Auction Center

Textile, Towel, Cross-Stitch, Eagle, Flowers, Franey Kulp, 1861, 47 x 14 In.
$561

Hess Auction Group

T

Panel, Door, Woven, Shaped, Dragons, Pearls, Clouds, Yellow, Chinese, c.1800, 32 x 39 In........	7380
Panel, Embroidery, Couched Silk, Landscape, Temple, Pond, Gold Cord, Japan, 71 x 63 In.......	437
Panel, Embroidery, Figures In Landscape, Sequin, Blue, Gold, 1800s, 57 x 40 In.	47
Panel, Embroidery, Man, Woman, Child, Roses, Multicolor, 24 x 17¾ In................................	344
Panel, Embroidery, Silver Thread, Mounted Knights, Cross Of Jerusalem, Brown, 38 x 17 In. ..	306
Panel, Needlepoint, Chinoiserie, Wool, Flowers, Trees, Birds, Multicolor, France, 56 x 25½ In.	687
Panel, Red, Gold, Flowers, Vines, Columns, Silk, Egypt, 91 x 60 In................................	578
Pillow Case, Embroidered, Medallion, Surrounded By Tulips, 1814, 21 x 24 In.	480
Pocket, Embroidery, Crewel, Flowers, Scrolling Vines, Cream, Pink, 1700s, 15 x 11 In.........	3000
Pouch, Drawstring, Silk, Embroidery, Landscape, England, Early 1600s, 6¼ x 7¼ In.............	1107
Roundel, Robe, Embroidered Silk, Crane, Waves, Buddhist Symbols, 1800s, 12 In. Diam........	185
Sculpture, Cube, Jute Fiber, The Ball You Blow, Naoko Serino, Japan, 2003, 8 x 8 In........illus	938
Table Mat, Embroidery Applique, Flower Basket, Birds, Frame, 1800s, 45 x 37 In.	4920
Tablecloth, Linen, Green & White, Damask, c.1920, 52 x 52 In.	25
Tapestry, Abstract City Scape, Wool, Jette Thyssen, Denmark, 1959, 58 x 40 In.	3500
Tapestry, Abstract, Blue, White, Pink, Handwoven, Martha Heine, 52 x 53 In.	270
Tapestry, Aubsson, Floral Shield, 24 x 20 In.	531
Tapestry, Aubusson, Birds, Pond, Woods, 86 x 50 In..	2500
Tapestry, Aubusson, Esther, King Ahasuerus Of Persia, Scepter, c.1700, 120 x 101 In.	10625
Tapestry, Aubusson, Rose Pink, Beige, Brown, Egg & Dart, Border, 61 x 34 In.	354
Tapestry, Aubusson, Verdant Landscape, 2 Birds, Trees, Garland, Border, 112 x 92 In............	2337
Tapestry, Birds, Forest, Castle, City, 71 x 65 In.	1920
Tapestry, Birds, Perched Among Flowers, Leafy Border, Continental, 63 x 50 In.	188
Tapestry, Boar Hunt, Mounted Spearman, Roman Attire, Hound, 46 x 62 In.	1000
Tapestry, Coat Of Arms, Mantled Still Life, War, Trophies, Chariot, Louis XVI Style, 110 x 71 In.	2500
Tapestry, Cranes, Forest, Green, Olive, Tan, Handwoven, Brussels, 1600s, 96 x 72 In.	6875
Tapestry, Diana, Hunt, France, c.1725, 89 x 112 In.	4750
Tapestry, Figures, Landscape, Pink, Green, France, 42 x 54 In.	94
Tapestry, Flags, Lavender Blue, Black, Tan Ground, After Miro, 77 x 61 In.	984
Tapestry, Grapes, Flowers, Ribbons, Multicolor, 79 x 18 In......................................	125
Tapestry, Landscape, Green, Blue, Gold, Rod, 37 x 36½ In.	129
Tapestry, Landscape, Shepherd, Sheep, Dogs, Trees, c.1705, 98 x 129 In.	2500
Tapestry, Medieval Scene, Belgium, 71 x 76 In..	593
Tapestry, Musical Ensemble, Dog, Pillars, Multicolor, 72 x 59 In...............................	625
Tapestry, Musicians & Maidens In Park, Handwoven, Netherlands, c.1900, 54 x 74 In.	1187
Tapestry, Mythical Figures, Wool, Multicolor, France, c.1800, 60 x 66 In	1875
Tapestry, Needlepoint, Petit Point, Multicolor, 79 x 147 In.....................................	625
Tapestry, Peasants At Work, Woods, Leafy Border, Multicolor, 96 x 106 In.	2000
Tapestry, Pink, Multicolor, Red Border, Wool, Aubusson Style, c.1930, 70 x 109 In.	500
Tapestry, Prairial, Flowers, Butterflies, Yellow Ground, Dom Robert, France, 1963, 94 x 114 In.	11875
Tapestry, Pressing Of The Grapes, Machine Made, France, 1900s, 48 x 41 In.	625
Tapestry, Royal Hunt, Machine Made, 1900s, France, 79 x 82 In.	468
Tapestry, Royal Procession, Machine Made, France, 1900s, 58 x 60 In.	812
Tapestry, Sheep, Woods, Flower Border, Flemish, 1700s, 118 x 75 In...........................	2125
Tapestry, Sun, Maguey Fiber, After Alexander Calder, 1974, 48 x 72 In. ....illus	16250
Tapestry, Tan, Red Splotch, Textured, Josep Grau-Garriga, 64 x 42 In.	2312
Tapestry, Village Gate, France, 1900s, 56½ x 75½ In..	500
Tapestry, Wool, Rosalia, Signed In Weave, Bjorn Wiinblad, 58 x 54 In.........................illus	563
Towel, Cross-Stitch, Eagle, Flowers, Franey Kulp, 1861, 47 x 14 In...........................illus	561
Towel, Cross-Stitch, Flowers, Birds, Mary Nissley, January 2, 1841, 59 x 16 In.	1652
Towel, Cross-Stitch, Parrot, Flowers, Catharina Balmer, May 6, 1833, 71 x 17 In..................	325
Towel, Needlework, Horses, Stag, Geese, Birds, c.1855, 58 x 16 In.	354
Towel, Yarn Work, Taufschein, Birds, Flowers, Hearts, B. Leaman, 1846, 62 x 17 In..............	531

THERMOMETER is a name that comes from the Greek word for heat. The thermometer was invented in 1731 to measure the temperature of either water or air. All kinds of thermometers are collected, but those with advertising messages are the most popular.

Bubble Up Soda, Deliciously Lighter, Bubble Logos, Tin, Paint, 1950s, 5 x 17 In.	168
Craine Silos, Enamel, Dilapidated Silos Rebuilt The Crainelox Way, 27 x 7 x¾ In..................	403

Thermometer, Moxie, Good At Any Temperature, Frank Archer, Tin Lithograph, 25½ x 9⅝ In.
$1,323

Wm Morford Auctions

Tiffany, Chandelier, Turtleback Tiles, Leaded Glass, Favrile, Bronze, Metal Tag, 1900s, 45 In.
$31,250

Rago Arts and Auction Center

Tiffany, Desk Set, Zodiac, Medallions, Bronze, Gold Dore, Marked, 12-In. Paper Rack, 12 Piece
$7,110

T

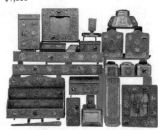

James D. Julia Auctioneers

Tiffany, Lamp, Desk, Damascene Shade, Iridescent Waves, Bronze Counterbalance Base, 12 In. $5,925

James D. Julia Auctioneers

Tiffany, Lamp, Lily, 12-Light, Iridescent Glass Shades, Brown Patina, Mark, c.1910, 19 In. $18,400

Cottone Auctions

Tiffany, Lamp, Pendant, Dragonfly, Dichroic Glass, Green Cabochons, Bronze Chains, 9¾ In. $4,740

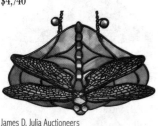

James D. Julia Auctioneers

TIP	
Have an inventory of your collections and adequate insurance.	

Dairy Queen, Country Fresh Flavor, Ice Cream Cone, Tin Litho, 1950s, 6 x 16 In.	335
Esso, Atlas Anti-Freeze, Service Station, Square, Blue & Red, 17¼ x 17¼ x ⅞ In.	345
Ex-Lax, Enameled Tin, Mid 1900s, 39¼ In.	330
Ex-Lax, The Chocolated Laxative, Porcelain, Blue, Red, Black, 36 In.	369
Gilman's Garage, Theresa, N.Y., Esso Station Sign & Ford Dealership, 16 x 6⅜ In.	604
Headquarters, Bowes, Cooling System Service, Tin, 38½ x 7½ In.	146
Hires Root Beer, 29 x 8 In.	105
Jack & Jill, Carrying Pails, Chalkware, c.1950, 5 x 5¼ In.	30
Jacquin's Cordials, Man, Liquor Bottles, Round, Aluminum, Glass, Dome, 1940s, 10 In.	115
L & M, Liggett & Myers, Embossed, 11¾ x 5 x 1 In.	153
Moxie, Good At Any Temperature, Frank Archer, Tin Lithograph, 25½ x 9⅝ In. *illus*	1323
National Barber School, Wood Plank, Black & White, 1920s, 5 x 21 In.	115
Native American, Seated, Globe Shape, Thermo-Dial, Black, 6½ In.	123
Orange Crush, Naturally, It Tastes Better, Orange, White, Tin, Arched, 16 x 6 In.	300
Pillsbury Flour, Wood, Painted, 21 x 5 x ⅞ In.	83
Red Marble, Columnar, Bust, Female Looking Down, 19 x 4¾ In.	640
Thermo Denatured Alcohol, Non-Rusting, Protect Your Radiator, 8 x 39 In.	146
Valvoline Motor Oil, Domed Glass, Aluminum, 1950s, 12 In.	420
Wall, Walnut, Carved, Fahrenheit & Centigrade, c.1910, 33 In.	350
Weather Station, Outdoor, Galvanized, Ets Maxant, 1970, 11 x 5 In.	105
Wood, Turned Shaft, Inset Glass Tube, Shaped Handle, Strap, 1800s, 12 In.	125

Louis C. Tiffany **TIFFANY** is a name that appears on items made by Louis Comfort Tiffany, the American glass designer who worked from about 1879 to 1933. His work included iridescent glass, Art Nouveau styles of design, and original contemporary styles. He was also noted for stained glass windows, unusual lamps, bronze work, pottery, and silver. Tiffany & Company, often called "Tiffany," is also listed in this section. The company was started by Charles Lewis Tiffany and Teddy Young in 1837 in New York City. In 1853 the name was changed to Tiffany & Company. Louis Tiffany (1848–1933), Charles Tiffany's son, started his own business in 1879. It was named Louis Comfort Tiffany and Associated American Artists. In 1902 the name was changed to Tiffany Studios. Tiffany & Company is still working today and is best known for silver and fine jewelry. Louis worked for his father's company as a decorator in 1900 but at the same time was working for his Tiffany Studios. Other types of Tiffany are listed under Tiffany Glass, Tiffany Gold, Tiffany Pottery, or Tiffany Silver. The famous Tiffany lamps are listed in this section. Tiffany jewelry is listed in the Jewelry and Wristwatch categories. Some Tiffany Studio desk sets have matching clocks. They are listed here. Clocks made by Tiffany & Co. are listed in the Clock category. Reproductions of some types of Tiffany are being made.

Ashtray Stand, Neo Grec, Bronze, Adjustable, Early 1900s, 27¾ x 9¾ In.	812
Bookends, Buddha, Bronze, Gold Dore, Figural, Marked, c.1925, 6 x 4¾ In.	468
Box, Pinecone, Bronze, Slag Glass, Bun Feet, 4 x 2¼ In.	277
Candelabrum, 8-Light, Bronze, Reticulated Cup, Blown Out Glass Inserts, Center Handle, 15 In.	6518
Candlestick, Bronze, 3 Flared Legs, Large Ball Feet, Favrile Glass Cup, Bobeche, 8 In.	2903
Candlestick, Bronze, Reticulated Cup, Blown Out Glass Insert, Saucer Foot, 18 In.	2548
Candlestick, Bronze, Round, Gimbal Style, Suspended From Frame, Attached Snuffer, 7 In.	4740
Chandelier, Turtleback Tiles, Leaded Glass, Favrile, Bronze, Metal Tag, 1900s, 45 In. *illus*	31250
Charger, Bronze, Gold Dore, Abalone Insets, Flower Head Border, 1728, 14 In. Diam.	325
Clock, Carriage, Bronze Dore, Flowers In Corners, Handle, 6¾ In.	406
Clock, Desk, Graduate, Bronze, Gold Dore, Red Ground, 1900s, 2¾ x 3½ x 4¼ In.	875
Clock, Mantel, Bronze, Glass Regulator, Porcelain Dial, Enamel Numbers, Blue Steel Hands	288
Desk Set, Zodiac, Bronze, Verdigris Patina, Marked, Early 1800s	840
Desk Set, Zodiac, Medallions, Bronze, Gold Dore, Marked, 12-In. Paper Rack, 12 Piece *illus*	7110
Frame, Double, Pine Needle, Bronze, Green Slag Glass, Center Hinge, 7½ x 12⅝ In.	1896
Frame, Grapevine, Bronze, Slag Glass, 1900s, 7¼ x 10¼ In.	2875
Frame, Grapevine, Green Slag Glass, 2 Openings, Easel Back, 7½ x 10 In.	2370
Frame, Sailing Ships, Bronze, Scroll Crest, Rope Twist Trim, Easel Back, 1848, 6 x 7 In.	2832
Inkwell, Bronze, Modeled Pattern, Hammered Panels, Hinged Cover, 3 x 5¼ In.	518
Inkwell, Sterling, Trout Fish, Camp Albany 1894, Hinged Cover, Monogram, 2¼ x 2 In.	2760
Inkwell, Zodiac, Bronze, Green Patina, Hinged Lid, Glass Insert, Impressed, 3¾ x 6⅜ In.	633

Lamp Base, Roman, 6-Light, Bronze, Original Patina, 1900s, 28 ½ x 11 ½ In.	7500
Lamp, Apple Blossom Shade, Original Patina On Base, Signed, Early 1900s, 22 x 16 In.	35650
Lamp, Arabian Shade, Platinum & Gold Iridescent Zipper, Bronze Organic Base, 19 In.	3555
Lamp, Counterbalance, Bronze, Domed Shade, Stamped, 15 In.	2091
Lamp, Desk, Blown Out Shade, Grapevine Overlay, Bronze Harp, Fluted Base, 12 x 9 In.	2250
Lamp, Desk, Damascene Shade, Iridescent Waves, Bronze Counterbalance Base, 12 In.....*illus*	5925
Lamp, Desk, Scarab Shade, Bronze Base, 2 Arm Supports, Ribbed Platform Foot, 8 In.	10665
Lamp, Favrile Glass Shade, Pulled Feather, Base, Vase Shape, Mushroom Cap, c.1910, 17 In.	3600
Lamp, Geranium, Leaded Glass, 3-Light, Bronze & Art Glass Base, Mark, 20 x 14 In.	52325
Lamp, Green Damascene Shade, Orange Zigzag, Bronze Urn Base, c.1900, 21 x 16 In.	2583
Lamp, Lily, 3-Light, Iridescent Shades, Bronze, Gooseneck Arms, Ribbed Platform Foot, 13 In.	3555
Lamp, Lily, 12-Light, Iridescent Glass Shades, Brown Patina, Mark, c.1910, 19 In.............*illus*	18400
Lamp, Linenfold Shade, 8 Panels, Striated Blue Glass, Bronze, Tapered, Base, 19 In.	9184
Lamp, Linenfold Shade, Green Glass, Bronze, Swivel Light, Lily Pad Feet, 1936, 56 In.	10620
Lamp, Linenfold Shade, Green, 8 Panels, Bronze Harp Base, Ribbed Foot, c.1940, 18 In.	6518
Lamp, Oil, Bee Design, Squat, Coin Handle, Pouch, c.1901, 4 x 3 In.	378
Lamp, Pendant, Dragonfly, Dichroic Glass, Green Cabochons, Bronze Chains, 9 ¾ In.......*illus*	4740
Lamp, Peony Shade, Leaded Glass, Bronze Stick Base, Etched Heat Cap, 30 In. ....*illus*	71100
Lamp, Tulip Shade, Leaded Glass, Bronze Art Nouveau Base, Organic Foot, 18 In.	38513
Lamp, Turtleback Shade, Bronze Base, Beaded, Leaves, Green Cabochons, Ball Feet, 14 In.	8889
Lamp, Turtleback Tile Shade, Striated Amber, Turtleback Band, Bronze Paneled Base, 23 In.	21330
Lampshade, Acorn, Green, Yellow Acorn Band, c.1910, 12 ½ In.	4250
Letter Holder, Pinecone, Bronze, Green Glass, Stamped, 6 ¼ x 10 In.	800
Letter Opener, Grapevine, Bronze, Glass, Teardrop Handle, Marked, 9 In.	260
Letter Opener, Nautilus Pattern, Bronze, Molded Fish On Handle, Rope Trim, 1844, 10 In.	649
Letter Rack, Bookmark Pattern, Bronze, 2 Tiers, Marked, c.1910, 6 x 9 In.	400
Letter Rack, Nautical, Bronze, Dolphins, Shell Crest, 2 Sections, Wave Edges, 1849, 7 x 11 In.	1888
Match Holder, Pine Needle Pattern, Bronze, Green Shapes, Bulbous, Flared Rim, 3 In.	885
Note Pad Holder, Grapevine, Bronze, Green Slag Glass, 7 ⅝ x 4 ⅝ In.	518
Panel, Moorish, Opalescent Slag Glass, Patinated Metal Frames & Links, 30 x 25 In.	8750
Paperweight, Bronze, Lion, Reclining, c.1920, 5 In.	740
Pen Tray, Nautical, Bronze, Shell, Nautical, Wide Rim, Marked, 1843, 3 x 10 In.	708
Tazza, Bronze Dore, Repousse Swag Border, Blue Enamel Cabochons, Footed, 10 In.	384
Teapot, Mixed Metal, Incised Vines, Copper & Gold Leaves, Butterflies, Dragonfly, 5 In.....*illus*	17775
Thermometer, Pine Needle, Bronze, Slag Glass, 1900s, 8 ¾ x 4 In.	1125

TIFFANY GLASS

Bowl, Blue Iridescent, Pulled Swirls, Squat, c.1902, 6 ½ x 11 In.	2750
Bowl, Blue, Gilted Metal Stand, Favrile, 7 x 12 ¾ In.	563
Bowl, Cobalt Blue, Turquoise Iridescent, Gold Flecks, Favrile, c.1910, 4 x 10 In.	800
Bowl, Dessert, Aqua, Tiered, Opalescent, Spread Foot, Scallop Rim, Favrile, 2 x 5 In.	384
Bowl, Gold Iridescent, Ribbed Sides, Undulating Rim, Favrile, 9 ¾ In.	593
Bowl, Morning Glory, Green, Purple Blue Inside, Greenish Blue, Engraved, 3 x 6 In.	489
Bowl, Wisteria, Lavender Border Opalescent Pinwheels, Signed, 1 ⅝ x 7 ⅝ In.	920
Candlestick, Mauve, Original Patina Base, Art Nouveau, Favrile, c.1890, 19 x 5 ½ In.	937
Candlestick, Pink & White, Feathered, Swollen Stem, Favrile, c.1900, 11 In.	625
Compote, Iridescent Foot & Bowl, Translucent Gold Stamp, Favrile, Signed, 6 In.	230
Compote, Laurel Leaf, Opalescent & Pink, Flared Clear Stem, Spread Foot, 5 x 6 In.	354
Decanter, Gold & Magenta, Lily Pad, Double Gourd, Engraved, Stopper, Favrile, 9 ¼ In.	1265
Dish, Sherbet, Blue Iridescent, c.1920, 3 ⅜ In.	152
Finger Bowl, Gold Iridescent, Scalloped Rim, Signed, c.1920, 2 ¼ In.	222
Flower Frog, Gold, Hearts & Vines, Favrile, c.1917, 4 x 10 In.	1000
Lamp, Arabian, Platinum Iridescent Zipper, Gold Iridescent Prunts, Boudoir, 14 In.	8295
Lamp, Pendant, Dragonfly, Blue Wings, Green & Cream Ground, Cabochons, 6 x 10 In.	8295
Lamp, Turtleback Tiles, Emerald Green, Bronze Urn Base, Green Tiles, 22 ½ In.	34500
Perfume Bottle, Cut Glass, Harvard Pattern, 18K Gold Cap, Lay Down, 9 In.	212
Seal, Scarab, Gold Iridescent, Rainbow Highlights, 1 ⅝ In.	127
Shade, Damascene, Gold & Pink, Dome Shape, Marked, Favrile, c.1912, 5 In.	6765
Shade, Red Iridescent, Flower Shape, Opal Stretch Ruffled Border, 4 x 7 In.	2006
Tazza, Gold Iridescent, Flared Out & Ruffled Rim, Flattened Foot, Favrile, 4 x 8 In.	354

Tiffany, Lamp, Peony Shade, Leaded Glass, Bronze Stick Base, Etched Heat Cap, 30 In.
$71,100

James D. Julia Auctioneers

Tiffany, Teapot, Mixed Metal, Incised Vines, Copper & Gold Leaves, Butterflies, Dragonfly, 5 In.
$17,775

James D. Julia Auctioneers

Tiffany Glass, Vase, Blue, Iridescent, Hearts & Vines, Signed, 2 ¾ In.
$2,070

T

Early Auction Company

Tiffany Glass, Vase, Flower Form, Green Pulled Feather, Cream Ground, Ruffled Rim, 9 ½ In.
$2,963

James D. Julia Auctioneers

What's a Tiffany?

The description "Tiffany lamp" is often used today for any old or new lamp with a stained glass shade or even a colored glass shade. True Tiffany lamps have stained glass or other art glass shades and are almost all marked "Tiffany Studios" or, on the iridescent glass shades, "Favrile." Tiffany made over 500 lampshade designs.

Tiffany Glass, Vase, Gold Iridescent, Intaglio Leaves, Vine, Favrile, Louis C. Tiffany, c.1910, 9 In.
$2,300

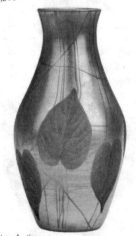

Cottone Auctions

Toothpick Holder, Gold Iridescent, Pinched Sides, Signed, 1 ⅞ In.	105
Toothpick Holder, Gold Iridescent, Purple, Pink, Blue, Prunts, Favrile, c.1910, 2 In.	350
Vase, Blue, Iridescent, Hearts & Vines, Signed, 2 ¾ In. ....*illus*	2070
Vase, Blue, Yellow & Amber, Splotches, Swollen Shoulder, Favrile, 1919, 6 In.	7500
Vase, Cypriote, Blue & Orange, Favrile, c.1919, 6 ¼ x 3 ½ In.	7500
Vase, Flower Form, Blue Iridescent, Shaded To Amethyst On Base, Ribbed, 6 ¾ In.	805
Vase, Flower Form, Green & White, Pulled Leaves, Teardrop, Favrile, 1905, 12 In.	4063
Vase, Flower Form, Green Pulled Feather, Cream Ground, Ruffled Rim, 9 ½ In. ....*illus*	2963
Vase, Gold Iridescent, Blue & Turquoise Accents, Pulled Feather, Bottle, c.1910, 6 In.	5313
Vase, Gold Iridescent, Fuchsia, Copper, Gourd Shape, Lobed, Scalloped Rim, 6 In.	590
Vase, Gold Iridescent, Green Hearts & Vines, Opal Blossoms, Signed, Favrile, 2 ½ In.	863
Vase, Gold Iridescent, Green Vines, Trumpet Shape, Knop, Dome Foot, Favrile, 1916, 14 In.	1500
Vase, Gold Iridescent, Hearts & Vines & Millefiori Blossoms, Barrel Shape, 4 In.	1783
Vase, Gold Iridescent, Intaglio Leaves, Vine, Favrile, Louis C. Tiffany, c.1910, 9 In. ...*illus*	2300
Vase, Gold Iridescent, Lavender, Turquoise, Pulled Feather, Favrile, c.1900, 15 In.	4688
Vase, Gold Iridescent, Pink, Blue, Opalescent, Pulled Feathers, Favrile, 1902, 6 In.	1353
Vase, Gold Iridescent, Pulled Feather, Bulbous Bottom, Footed, 8 In.	1067
Vase, Gold Iridescent, Pulled Feather, Gourd Shape, Swollen Collar, c.1900, 8 In.	738
Vase, Gold Iridescent, White Flower Band, Green Heart Shape Leaves, 6 In.	9480
Vase, Gold, Ribbed, Flower Form, Favrile, Signed, c.1909, 18 In. ....*illus*	1000
Vase, Golden Iridescent, Bulbous, 10 Vertical Ribs, Signed, 1915, 4 In.	351
Vase, Golden Iridescent, Green Leaves, Vines, Signed, 1919, 7 In.	497
Vase, Green & Blue Iridescent, Pulled Feather, Genie Bottle, Favrile, c.1905, 5 In.	1250
Vase, Green & White Feather Pulled, Favrile, New York, c.1905, 4 ¼ x 3 In.	1250
Vase, Green, Dogwood Blossoms, Paperweight, c.1906, 5 x 5 ¾ In.	10000
Vase, Jack-In-The-Pulpit, Gold & Pink Iridescent, Ruffled Rim, Favrile, 1906, 19 In.	8750
Vase, Jack-In-The-Pulpit, Gold Iridescent, Favrile, L.C. Tiffany, c.1909, 19 x 11 In. ....*illus*	3750
Vase, Jack-In-The-Pulpit, Gold Iridescent, Flaring Stem, Stretched Rim, 15 In.	3851
Vase, Jack-In-The-Pulpit, Gold, Favrile, c.1906, 19 ¼ x 9 ½ In.	8750
Vase, Jack-In-The-Pulpit, Gold, Pink, Iridescent, Dome Foot, Favrile, c.1905, 14 In.	6875
Vase, Pale Gold, Six Iridescent Feathers, Pulled, Gooseneck, Signed, 15 In.	11500
Vase, Parfait Shape, Pastel Green, Yellow Opalescent Fern, Signed, 6 ½ In.	316
Vase, Pink & Green, Leaves, Swollen Collar, Dome Foot, Favrile, 1904, 14 In.	3250
Vase, Red, Genie Bottle Shape, Ring Foot, Favrile, c.1918, 10 x 6 ½ In.	4688
Vase, Red, Pulled Gold Iridescent Drip From Rim, Bulbous, Squat, 2 ¾ In.	4148
Vase, Stick, Blue, Squat Base, Elongated Neck, Favrile, 6 ½ In.	546
Vase, Tulip, Gold Iridescent, Ribbed, Ruffle Rim, Round Foot, Marked, c.1910, 11 In.	738
Vase, Yellow Flowers, Green & Brown Leaves, Colorless Iridescent, 5 In.	7999
Window, Leaded, Slag, 3 Layers, Wood Frame, Tiffany Studios, 1900s, 57 x 25 In., Pair ....*illus*	3000

TIFFANY GOLD

Flask, 18K Gold, Oval, Fluted, Stepped Shoulder, Hinged Screw Top, 4 In.	3894
Lorgnette, 14K Gold, Hinged Spring, Leaves, Art Deco, Marked, 6 In.	767

TIFFANY POTTERY

Vase, Figural, Artichoke, Leaves, Pale Green Glaze, Favrile, c.1910, 6 In.	5313
Vase, Organic Leaves, Opal, Iridescent Tones, Incised Signature, 5 ¼ In. ....*illus*	1725
Vase, Plants, Brown Matte Glaze, Favrile, Incised LCT, 1904-19, 6 x 7 In. ....*illus*	6875
Vase, Wisteria Pods, Moss Green Glaze, Swollen Bottle, Favrile, c.1908, 9 In.	8125

TIFFANY SILVER

Basket, Reticulated Ferns, Swirls, Flared Fan Shape, Scroll Handle, c.1920, 16 In.	4013
Berry Bowl, Reticulated Strawberry Rim, Monogram, c.1925, 8 In. Diam., Pair	431
Berry Spoon, Strawberry, Kidney Shape Bowl, 9 ¾ In.	450
Bonbon, Embossed, Wide Reeded Rim, Outcurved Legs, Pad Feet, 1910, 4 x 6 In.	531
Bonbon, Lift Lid, Swan Finial, Oval, Footed, Mark, 4 x 5 In.	390
Bowl, Center, Lobed, Octagonal, Openwork Clover Rim, c.1900, 3 x 12 In.	1375
Bowl, Console, Lobed, Presentation Engraving, Names, c.1930, 9 In.	492
Bowl, Flowers In Classical Pattern, Sloping Sides, Flattened Rim, Early 1900s, 2 x 10 In.	344
Bowl, Flowers, Draping Rim, 12 In.	875
Bowl, Flowers, Scroll Mantels, Shaped Rim, Early 1900s, 3 x 17 In.	1187

T

Bowl, Fruit, Clover, Round, Repousse Rim, Monogram, c.1900, 10 1/4 In.		437
Bowl, Fruit, Clover, Tiffany & Co., 1902, 11 1/4 In.		1125
Bowl, Fruit, Scalloped Rim, Shell & Scroll Feet, 7 1/4 In. Diam.		413
Bowl, Lobed, Winged Griffin Legs, 1854-1869, 3 5/8 x 6 1/2 In.		600
Bowl, Monogram, C-Scroll & Flower Border, Marked, c.1892, 2 x 10 In.		300
Bowl, Monogram, Reeded Sides, Molded Wave Rim, Marked, c.1900, 9 In.		201
Bowl, Nut, Double Shell, Stylized Dolphin Center Handle, Ball Feet, 3 x 10 In.		502
Bowl, Repousse Flowers, Bulbous, 4-Lobed Rim, 4 Flower Feet, c.1900, 5 x 11 In.		1680
Bowl, Scalloped Pattern, Gilt, Mid 1900s, 8 In., Pair		1046
Bowl, Scrollwork, Reticulated, Hexagonal, Marked, c.1925, 3 x 9 In.		415
Bowl, Trumpet, Footed, Monogram, c.1947, 9 In.		615
Bowl, Vegetable, Flowers, Leaves, Heron, 2 Handles, Folded Feet, c.1880, 6 1/2 In.		3000
Bread Tray, Oval, Reticulated Lattice Rim, Shell & Scroll Edge, c.1900, 11 x 9 In.		593
Bread Tray, Oval, Scalloped Edge, Flowers, Early 1900s, 12 1/2 x 10 1/4 In., Pair		1187
Candlestick, Urn Shape Sconce, Fluted Tapered Stem, Square Foot, c.1947, 12 In., Pair		1599
Carafe, Teardrop, Indented, Handles, Swirls, Italy, c.1980, 11 In.		1500
Centerpiece, Round, Flared Rim, Early 1900s, 13 In.		615
Check Cutter, Scrolls, Urns, Raised Monogram, Marked, c.1880, 11 In.		649
Christening Cup, Gilt, Engraved Cartouche, Figures, Cylindrical, c.1885, 4 In.		3075
Cigarette Box, Fluted, Hinged, Marked, Mid 1900s, 4 x 3 1/2 x 2 In.		390
Cigarette Box, Shells, 6 1/2 In.		750
Cocktail Shaker, Gilt, Tapered, Shouldered, c.1920, 10 1/2 In.		1476
Cocktail Shaker, Tapered Sides, Marked, Tiffany & Co., 9 In., 3 Piece	*illus*	660
Cocktail Shaker, Tapered Sides, Rounded Strap Handle, Chained Stopper Cap, c.1930s, 9 In.		1000
Coffeepot, Monogram, Bulbous, Cylindrical Neck, Loop Handle, c.1860, 9 In.		496
Compote, Persian Rim, Stylized Flowerheads & Scrolls, Footed, c.1880, 5 In.		523
Console, Gilt, Reticulated, Center Monogram, c.1925, 8 1/2 In.		308
Demitasse Spoon, Bamboo, 4 1/4 In., 6 Piece		262
Dresser Box, Lid, Gilt, Applied Monogram, Velvet Lined, c.1940, 4 In.		431
Flask, Battle Scene, Acid Etched, Engraved Inscription, c.1880, 9 In.		615
Flask, Engraved, Monogram, Flattened Sphere, Threaded Cap, c.1880, 5 x 3 In.		177
Glove Stretcher, 1892-1902, 7 5/8 In.		100
Gravy Boat, Flowers, Leaves, Folded Feet, Engraved, c.1880, 5 In., Pair		2500
Kettle Stand, Ebonized Wood Swing Handle, Paw Feet, 7 1/2 In.		3000
Kettle Stand, Ribbed, Burner, Lion Paw Feet, c.1905, 15 In.		1968
Kettle Stand, Urn, Scrolls, Flowers, Leaves, Handles, Pedestal, c.1860, 15 x 10 In.		4375
Lettuce Fork, Japanese Pattern, 2 Splayed Prongs, 1871, 8 In.		200
Muffineer, 8 Panels, Pierced Top, 8-Sided Foot, 1907-47, 7 In.		142
Pie Server, Sinuous Blade, Ruffled Tip, English King Handle, c.1880, 12 In.		800
Pitcher, Flower Medallions, Monogram, Engraved, Early 1900s, 9 1/4 In.		1169
Pitcher, Pussy Willow Design, Gilt, Slender Tapering Shape, c.1980, 9 1/2 In.		800
Pitcher, Scrolled Handle, c.1970, 7 1/2 In.		1230
Pitcher, Stylized Handle, Sleek, Early 1900s, 8 1/2 In.		1375
Pitcher, Water, Paneled, Heraldic Shield, Angular Handle, 1907-1947, 8 In.		1440
Placecard Holder, Pineapple, Round Base, c.1950, 1 In., 12 Piece		800
Plateau, Mirror, Round, Gadroon, Frame, c.1910, 11 In. Diam.		308
Platter, Drainage Tree, Flowers, Foliage, Claw Feet, Engraved, c.1880, 22 In.		2800
Platter, Round, Molded Rim, 1900s, 14 In.		1000
Platter, Tree & Well, Oval, Reeded Rim, Early 1900s, 20 x 14 1/4 In.		2250
Platter, Wave Edge Pattern, Oval, c.1902, 20 x 14 In.		1875
Punch Bowl, Scroll & Key, Engraved, c.1942, 6 1/2 In.		2100
Salad Server, Dolphin, 10 1/4 In., 2 Piece		5900
Salver, George IV, Piecrust Rim, 3-Footed, Comyns & Sons Ltd., c.1952, 12 In.		677
Salver, Merlions, Leaf & Scroll, Band, Beaded Rim, Plinth Feet, c.1865, 12 In. Diam.		1500
Soup, Dish, Lid, Gilt, Round, 2 Handles, Scrolled Shell Knob Finial, c.1905, 10 In.		923
Soup, Dish, Lid, Pierced Handles, Knob Finial, c.1905, 10 In.		738
Spoon, Vine & Peapod, Marked, c.1880, 9 3/4 In.		480
Tazza, Chased Shells & Scrolls, Flower Sprays, Flared Rim, c.1900, 3 x 8 In.		738
Tea Caddy, Lid, Trailing Vines, c.1905, 5 In.		461
Tea Caddy, Oak Leaf Wreath, Tied Ribbon, c.1896, 3 1/2 In.		555

Tiffany Glass, Vase, Gold, Ribbed, Flower Form, Favrile, Signed, c.1909, 18 In.
$1,000

New Orleans Auction Galleries

Tiffany Glass, Vase, Jack-In-The-Pulpit, Gold Iridescent, Favrile, L.C. Tiffany, c.1909, 19 x 11 In.
$3,750

Rago Arts and Auction Center

Tiffany Glass, Window, Leaded, Slag, 3 Layers, Wood Frame, Tiffany Studios, 1900s, 57 x 25 In., Pair
$3,000

Rago Arts and Auction Center

T

Tiffany Pottery, Vase, Organic Leaves, Opal, Iridescent Tones, Incised Signature, 5 ¼ In.
$1,725

Early Auction Company

Tiffany Pottery, Vase, Plants, Brown Matte Glaze, Favrile, Incised LCT, 1904-19, 6 x 7 In.
$6,875

Rago Arts and Auction Center

Tiffany Silver, Cocktail Shaker, Tapered Sides, Marked, Tiffany & Co., 9 In., 3 Piece
$660

Brunk Auctions

Tea Set, Teapot, Coffeepot, Sugar & Creamer, Bowl, 5 Piece	1287
Teapot, Engraved Leaves, Scroll, Dedication, c.1864, 11 ¼ In.	700
Toasted Cheese Dish, Gadrooned Rim, Removable Wood Handle, c.1920, 9 In.	1169
Tray, Flower & Shell, Rectangular, Footed, Ball Feet, Liner, c.1890, 12 In.	2000
Tray, Monogram, Scalloped Edge, c.1947, 20 In.	1230
Tray, Pierced Gallery, Latticework, Geometric Decoration, Round Foot, 3 x 7 ½ In.	330
Tumbler, Straight-Sided, Slightly Flared, Monogram, Date 12-25-69, 4 ½ In.	660
Tureen, Flowers, Leaves, Rooster Heads, Rolled Feet, Engraved, c.1880s, 9 In.	5500
Urn, Federal, Covered, Round Foot, Finial, Leaf, Olive Wreath, 1907-47, 14 In.	3000
Vase, Bud, Trailing Leafy Tendril, Louis Comfort Tiffany Collection, c.1980, 5 In.	431
Vase, Stylized Iris, 12 ½ In.	2300
Vase, Trumpet Shape, c.1970, 16 ¼ In.	431

TIFFIN Glass Company of Tiffin, Ohio, was a subsidiary of the United States Glass Co. of Pittsburgh, Pennsylvania, in 1892. The U.S. Glass Co. went bankrupt in 1963, and the Tiffin plant employees purchased the building and the inventory. They continued running it from 1963 to 1966, when it was sold to Continental Can Company. In 1969, it was sold to Interpace, and in 1980, it was closed. The black satin glass, made from 1923 to 1926, and the stemware of the last 20 years are the best-known products.

Plate, Gold Encrusted, Roses, 8 In., 12 Piece	92
Vase, Green, Blue, Silver Overlay, Phoenix, Spread Foot, 6 ½ In., Pair	215

TILES have been used in most countries of the world as a sturdy building material for floors, roofs, fireplace surrounds, and surface toppings. The cuerda seca (dry cord) technique of decoration uses a greasy pigment to separate different glaze colors during firing. In cuenca (raised line) decorated tiles, the design is impressed, leaving ridges that separate the glaze colors. Many of the American tiles are listed in this book under the factory name.

Animal, Antlers, Landscape, Tin Glaze, 6 Tiles, 20 x 26 In.	146
Beetle & Winged Insect, Woven Ground, Iridescent Green Glaze, Square, c.1890, 8 In.	75
Birds & Flowers, Square, Turquoise, Cobalt Blue, Purple, Black, Syria, 1600s, 9 x 9 In.	923
Cherubs, Children, Fishing, Boat, Cattails, Green, 12 In., 4 Piece	50
Cottage, Thatch Roof, Stone Fence, Flowers, Claycraft, 1921-39, 5 ¾ x 5 ¾ In. ....*illus*	135
Flowers, Leaves, Entwined, Octagonal, Turquoise, Blue, Brown, Iznik, c.1800, 10 In.	431
Flowers, Leaves, Purple, Yellow, Art Nouveau, Germany, 6 In.	488
Flowers, Vase, Multicolor, Wood Frame, Claycraft Potteries, 3 ¼ In.	305
Frieze, Crow In Snowy Landscape, 2 Tiles, Flint Faience, Wood Frame, 18 x 9 In.	3750
Garden, Woman, Johan Van Schwarz, 10 ¾ x 6 ½ In.	826
Hacienda, Couple, Spanish Dress, Relief, Multicolor, California Art Tile, 8 x 12 In...........*illus*	369
Landscape, Blue & White, Holland, 6 x 6 In., 6 Piece	31
Lion, Wearing Crown, Flowers, Donkey, Rut Bryk, Finland, 1960s, 15 x 22 In. ....*illus*	15000
Mirror, Woman, Johan Van Schwarz, 6 ½ x 11 In.	708
Mission Church, Round, Multicolor, California Faience, 5 ⅜ In.	354
Moose, Landscape, Green, 12 In., 4 Piece	125
Nudes, Relief, Blue Ground, Volara, Marla, Sara, Marsha, Surving Studio, 6 x 6 In., 4 Piece	186
Panel, Cherubs, Climbing Hanging Oil Lamps, Brown, 6 Tiles, 36 In., Pair	125
Panel, Flamingoes, Irises, Tree, Cattails, Shaped Tiles, Mueller Mosaic Co., 80 x 48 In.	8750
Panel, Peasants Cutting Wheat, Blue & White, Wheat Sheaf Border, 30 Tiles, 31 x 38 In.	1375
Panel, Warriors, 56 Tiles, Wood Frame, Leon Solon, c.1920, 84 x 24 In.	1500
Portrait, Elaborate Leaf, Flower, Brown, Glossy, 6 x 6 In., 14 Piece	50
Portrait, Profiles, Skin Tone, 6 ½ x 6 ½ In., 10 Piece	63
Portrait, Seasonal Themes, Square, Teal Glaze, Marked, J.G. & J.F., 1885, 6 x 4 In.	400
Rider On Horseback, Multicolor, Persia, 12 ⅜ x 10 ⅛ In.	182
Roof, Immortal Riding A Deer, Chinese, 1900s, 13 ½ In.	98
Southwestern Scene, Man, Boat, Marked, San Jose, Frame, 8-In. Tile...........*illus*	443
Southwestern Scene, Man Riding Donkey, Wood Frame, San Jose Pottery, 17 In.	531
Star Shape, Flowers, Fish, Calligraphy Band, Cobalt Blue, Tan, Luster Glaze, Persia, 7 In.	923
Water Lilies, Green, C. Pardee, Perth Amboy, N.J., c.1920, 6 x 6 In.	688

Woman, Classical, Standing, Arm Up, 5¾ x 18 In., 3 Piece	63
Woman, Garden Landscape, Johann Von Schwarz, Gold Frame, 10¾ x 6¼ In.	748
Woman, Playing Harp, Multicolor, Persia, 13¼ x 9⅝ In.	135
Woman, Reclining, String Instrument, 18¼ In., 3 Piece	63

TINWARE containers for household use have been made in America since the seventeenth century. The first tin utensils were brought from Europe, but by 1798, tin plate was imported and local tinsmiths made the wares. Painted tin is called tole and is listed separately. Some tin kitchen items may be found listed under Kitchen. The lithographed tin containers used to hold food and tobacco are listed in the Advertising category under Tin.

Cage, Squirrel, House Shape, Mounted On Plank Base, 12 In. ....*illus*	118
Canister, Gray Smoke Decorated, 8 In.	74
Chestnut Roaster, Cylindrical, Wood Handle, 1700s, 35 In.	234
Coffeepot, Wrigglework, Eagle, Conical, Scroll Handle, Porcelain Finial, c.1810, 13 In.	3068
Coffeepot, Wrigglework, Tulip, 10¾ In.	615
Coffeepot, Wrigglework, Tulips, Flared Body, Dome Lid, Gooseneck Spout, c.1900, 11 In.	105
Coin Box, Peter Rabbit, Thorton Burgess, Squirrel, Storing Nuts, Round, Slot, 1920s, 3 x 5 In.	80
Eagle On Ball, Post, 27 In.	750
Foot Warmer, Punched Heart, Mortised & Pegged, Wire Bail Handle, Pa., 1800s, 6 x 9 In.*illus*	236
Foot Warmer, Punched Hearts, Wooden Frame, 1800s, 5¾ x 9 In.	160
Mold, Candle, 18 Tubes, Wood, 19th Century, 15 x 20 x 8 In. ....*illus*	561
Mold, Candle, 24 Tubes, Wood Frame, 19th Century, 11 x 12 x 6¾ In.	767
Mold, Candle, 36 Tubes, 2 Handles On Sides, 10½ x 17½ x 4¾ In.	210
Mold, Candle, 43 Tubes, 1 Pewter Tube, Wood Stand, 4 Legs, 5 x 22 x 7½ In.	800

TOBACCO JAR collectors search for those made in odd shapes and colors. Because tobacco needs special conditions of humidity and air, it has been stored in special containers since the eighteenth century.

4 Faces, Cobalt Blue, Green, Teplitz, Amphora, 10½ In.	63
Animal Trophy, Ram's Head, Silver Plate, Humidor, 16½ In.	4250
Burled Walnut, 2 Doors, 2 Drawers, Drawers, Recessed Brass Handles, Humidor, 11 x 12 In.	660
Burlwood, Inlaid, Benson & Hedges, Humidor, Edwardian, 12½ In.	312
Cylindrical, Brown, Mottled, Sunken Knob, Leaves, Birds, Bennington, 5 x 6 In. ....*illus*	62
Gilt Bronze, Neoclassical Scene, Humidor, c.1920, 3¾ x 11¼ In.	126
Glass, Reverse Painted, Yellow, Banner, Rhubarb, Cylindrical, Gold Lid, 24 In.	780
Hinged Sterling Silver Lid, Monogram, Humidor, 6¾ In.	228
Inlaid, Briarwood & Mother-Of-Pearl, Humidor, c.1870, 5½ x 9½ x 7 In.	122
Jasper Dip, Light Blue, Classical Figures, Cover, Adams & Bromley, England, c.1880, 7 In.	154
Kaiser Shape, Beige, Porcelain, Germany, 7⅜ In.	125
Pilgrim Hat, Whalebone, 1840-70, 4 x 4½ In.	1800
Pottery, 8-Sided, Basket Weave, Pipe, Dog Head Finial, Flower, Japan, 7½ x 5 In. ....*illus*	45
Rosewood, Brass Bound, Humidor, Dunhill, 5½ x 15¾ In.	531
There Is No Herb Like It Under The Sun, Canopy Of Heaven, c.1900, 4½ x 4½ In.	427
Underplate, Lid, Copper, Rivets, Handles, Humidor, 5 x 8 In.	488
Wood Skull, Snakes Crawling Though Eyes, c.1900, 7 In. ....*illus*	343

TOBY JUG is the name of a very special form of pitcher. It is shaped like the full figure of a man or woman. A pitcher that shows just the top half of a person is not correctly called a toby. More examples of toby jugs can be found under Royal Doulton and other factory names.

Jester, Seated, Red & White, Ruffled Rim, c.1860, 10 In.	365
Man, Seated, Blue Willow Jacket, Tricorn Hat, c.1900, 7 In.	561
Man, Seated, Holding Jug, Hat, Blue & White, Faience, 10 In.	975
Man, Seated, Smiling, Willow Pattern Waistcoat, Blue, White, c.1800, 6 In.	495
Man, Sitting, Spongeware Base, Green, 9¼ x 4½ In.	837
Older Man, White Wig, 6½ In.	25
Vincent Van Gogh, Seated, Painter's Palette, Hand On Chin, Flower Handle, 8¾ In.	231

Tile, Cottage, Thatch Roof, Stone Fence, Flowers, Claycraft, 1921-39, 5¾ x 5¾ In. $135

Leland Little Auctions

Tile, Hacienda, Couple, Spanish Dress, Relief, Multicolor, California Art Tile, 8 x 12 In. $369

Leland Little Auctions

Tile, Lion, Wearing Crown, Flowers, Donkey, Rut Bryk, Finland, 1960s, 15 x 22 In. $15,000

Rago Arts and Auction Center

Tile, Southwestern Scene, Man, Boat, Marked, San Jose, Frame, 8-In. Tile $443

Humler & Nolan

Tinware, Cage, Squirrel, House Shape, Mounted On Plank Base, 12 In.
$118

Hess Auction Group

Tinware, Foot Warmer, Punched Heart, Mortised & Pegged, Wire Bail Handle, Pa., 1800s, 6 x 9 In.
$236

Hess Auction Group

Tinware, Mold, Candle, 18 Tubes, Wood, 19th Century, 15 x 20 x 8 In.
$561

Hess Auction Group

Tobacco Jar, Cylindrical, Brown, Mottled, Sunken Knob, Leaves, Birds, Bennington, 5 x 6 In.
$62

Turner Auctions + Appraisals

TOLE is painted tin. It is sometimes called japanned ware, pontypool, or toleware. Most nineteenth-century tole is painted with an orange-red or black background and multicolored decorations. Many recent versions of toleware are made and sold. Related items may be listed in the Tinware category.

Apple Tray, Cutout Handles, Pa., 1800s, 11¾ In. ....*illus*	153
Basket, Pilgrim Girl, Pumpkins & Turkeys, Orange & Black, Round, Lid, 1920s, 2 x 4 In.	125
Bin, Lid, No. 8, Green Ground, 1800s, 17½ In.	246
Box, Document, Black Ground, Birds & Flowers, c.1835, 7 x 10 In.	180
Box, Flower Basket, Black, Coffered, Ball Feet, 7 x 10 In.	70
Box, Hat, Officer's Dress Helmet, 13½ x 18 In., Pair	593
Box, Ice, Brass Button, Paw Feet, 13 x 21 In.	200
Box, Painted, Flowers, Red, Yellow, Green, Dotted Wavy Lines On Sides, Oval, 3 In., Pair	738
Box, Swags, Handle, 9 x 4½ In.	234
Box, Travel, Oval, Drop Handle, Travel Sticker, 12¼ x 16½ In.	150
Bread Basket, Black, Gold Crystalline Center, Flower Border, H. Filley, c.1830, 13 x 8 In.	3321
Bread Pan, Paint, Red Apples, Green Leaves, Lobed Rim, 3 x 12 In.	1500
Bread Tray, Flowers, 1800s, 3¼ x 14 In.	25
Canister, Black Ground, Red & Yellow Fruit, 1800s, 5 x 6½ In.	266
Canister, Green, Reserves, Chinoserie Scenes, 17½ In., Pair	938
Canister, Painted, Red Flowers, Yellow Leaves, 1825-35, 4 In.	861
Canister, Tea, Black, Red Flowers, Yellow Leaves, Squared Knob, 1825-35, 4 In.	861
Canister, Tea, Red Flowers, Green & Yellow Leaves, Conical Top, 6½ In.	1000
Cann, Black, Green & Yellow Flowers, Yellow Leaf Circle, Flat Handle, c.1830, 6 In.	1476
Chandelier, 6-Light, Pineapple Knob, Bronze Masks, Brass Gallery, c.1835, 28 x 31 In.	1500
Cheese Wheel, Gilt, Tracery, Scrolls, Georgian, c.1800, 4 x 11⅝ In.	225
Church, White, Colored Glass Windows, Steeple, 2 Story, 16 x 16 In.	420
Coal Box, Burgundy, Flowers, Japanned, Handles, Benjamin Walton & Co., c.1850, 25 In.	1250
Coal Scuttle, Bowfront, Cottage, Black Ground, 23 x 20 In.	500
Coffeepot, Black, Red, Yellow & Blue Flowers, Yellow Leaf Border, 8½ In.	3075
Coffeepot, Dome Lid, Red, Yellow & Green Flowers, Gooseneck Spout, 1800s, 10¼ In.	900
Coffeepot, Flowers, Lime Green Band, 1800s, 10½ In.	369
Coffeepot, Flowers, Red, Orange, Gray, Gooseneck Spout, 10¼ In.	172
Coffeepot, Lighthouse Shape, Fruit, Flowers, C-Scroll Handle, Shaped Spout, 11 In.	384
Coffeepot, Punched, Basket Of Flowers, Banded Oval Neck, 1800s, 11 In.	1353
Coffeepot, Red Flowers, 1800s, 8½ In.	600
Cup, Red, Yellow & Green Leaves, Penn., c.1825, Child's, 2 In.	800
Fire Screen, Shaped Panel, Birds On Branches, Scroll Brass Feet, 39½ x 29 In.	531
Flower Spray, Leaves, Tied With Bow, 24 In.	75
Garniture, Flowers, Leaves, Wood Base, Gold Trim, Italian Baroque, 29 In., Pair.............*illus*	625
Jardiniere, Green, Flower Bouquet, 4¾ In., Pair...	100
Jardiniere, Yellow, Landscape Vignettes, Oval, Pierced Rim, Lion Ring Handles, 6 x 10 In.	390
Mug, Black, Band Of Flowers, Red, Yellow, Green, Flattened Handle, Penn., c.1830, 4⅜ In.	492
Mug, Pink Rose, Yellow & Green Leaves, Tapered, Loop Strap Handle, 6 x 4 In.	500
Rattle, Embossed, Eagle, For A Good Boy, 1800s, 5½ In.	37
Shield, Union, American Flag, Red, White & Blue Paint, 1800s, 30 x 24 In.	510
Sign, La Bourgogne, Map, Multicolor, 51 x 19⅞ In.	438
Sugar, Cover, Black, Red & Green Flowers, Leaves, c.1830, 4 x 4 In.	1353
Sugar, Red Flowers, Green & Yellow Leaves, Lid, Looped Handle, 4 x 4 In.	1400
Syrup, Hinged Lid, Black Ground, Flowers, Leaves, 4 x 3 In.	550
Teapot, Urn, Boat On Water In Reserve, Green, 1800s, 17½ x 10¼ In.	175
Topiary, Green, Box, 1950s, 16 In., Pair	875
Tray, 2 Lions, Jungle, Black, Gilt, Cutout Handles, 22 x 30½ In.	100
Tray, Black, Pale Yellow, Compote Of Grapes, 16½ x 23¼ In.	96
Tray, Black, Red, White, Blue Flowers, Exotic Bird, Flower, Serpentine, Doris Smith, 27¼ In. ..	132
Tray, Brown, Flowers, Serpentine, Bird, Flower, Doris Smith, 25 In.	96
Tray, Center Vignette, Boy, 3 Dogs, 26 In.	360
Tray, Elephant, Flowers, Palms, Flowered Border, 15 x 20 In.	156
Tray, Figures, Landscape, Gilt, Rectangular, 19½ x 24 In.	171
Tray, Flowers, Red Ground, Crystalline Center, 13 x 8 In.	1320

T

Tray, Genre Scene, Soldier Saying Goodbye, Vines, Leaves, Cutout Handle, 30 x 24 In.	177
Tray, Hunter, Red Outfit, Gun, 1800s, 20 ½ x 28 In.	123
Tray, Orange Fruit, Green Leaves, Black Ground, Octagonal, 8 ¾ In.	2706
Tray, Orange Hot Air Balloons, Yellow Gallery, Italy, 24 ½ x 18 In.	177
Tray, Painted, Red, Blue Flowers, Yellow & Green Feathery Leaves, 8-Sided, 12 x 8 In.	2460
Tray, Sailing Ship, Iris Of Saem, Flag, Painting On Paper, Flared Rim, 1806, 22 x 30 In.	2370
Tray, Wine Goddess, Oval, Open Handles, Label, Fornasetti, Milano, Italy, 18 x 14 In. ....*illus*	531
Tureen, Peacocks, Flowers, Gilt, Brass Knop, Scroll Handles, c.1835, 10 In., Pair	625
Urn, Flowers, Multicolor, 1800s, 30 ¾ In.	125
Urn, Red, Gold Reserve, Round Foot, Continental, 12 ¼ In., Pair	750
Vase, Cranes, Bronze Mount, 11 ½ In., Pair	750

TOM MIX was born in 1880 and died in 1940. He was the hero of over 100 silent movies from 1910 to 1929, and 25 sound films from 1929 to 1935. There was a Ralston Tom Mix radio show from 1933 to 1950, but the original Tom Mix was not in the show. Tom Mix comics were published from 1942 to 1953.

Badge, Wrangler, Cowboy Bust, Checkerboard, Brass, Enamel, 1970s, 2 In.	230
Button, Tom Mix & Tony, Toledo Paramount Theatre, 1900s, 1 ½ In. Diam.	380
Pitcher, Portrait, Glass, Cobalt Blue, 4 x 4 In. ....*illus*	30
Ring, Deputy, Shield & Star, White & Yellow Gold, Brass, 1933	507
Window Card, King Cowboy, Cardboard, Original Release, 1938, 14 x 22 In.	150

TOOLS of all sorts are listed here, but most are related to industry. Other tools may be found listed under Iron, Kitchen, Tinware, and Wooden.

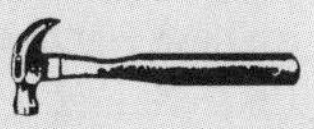

Backsaw, Double Eagle, Brass, Applewood, Henry Disston, 12 In.	1582
Bark Spud, Turned Wood Handle, Iron Scrolled Blade, Doorknob Finial, 1800s, 16 In.	83
Beer Tap, Portable, Hardwood, Brass, 4 Taps, Cooler, c.1905, 39 x 26 In.	3600
Book Press, Cast Iron, Fluted Base, Molded Dolphin Supports, Late 1800s, 17 x 18 x 11 In.	531
Book Press, Oak, Screw Form, 2 Drawers, Bun Feet, Late 1800s, 56 ½ x 37 x 19 In.	812
Box, Farmer's, Softwood, Open Crate, Compartments, Arched Feet, Square Handle, 15 x 20 In.	83
Box, Wood, Lift Lid, Interior Compartments, Steel Handles, Riser Base, c.1940, 15 x 28 In.	675
Brace, Beech, William Marples & Sons, Brass, Ebony, Ivory, Hibernia Works, England ..... *illus*	186
Cabinet, Hardware, Oak, 54 Cubbyholes, Hobart Brothers Co., Troy, Oh., 64 x 38 In. ....*illus*	354
Candle Dipper, Wood, Cylindrical Top Handle, Round Hook Base, Wire Hooks, 10 In. Diam. ..	266
Clothes Brush, Wood, Penguin Shape Handle, Green, Yellow Beak, Bristles, 1920s, 7 In.	25
Cultivator, Metal, Wood Handles, Salesman's Sample, 17 ½ In.	1200
Drill, Hand, Stanley, No. 624A, Wood Handle, 13 In.	25
Grain Cleaner, Salesman's Sample, 26 In.	1320
Grain Shovel, Wood, Hand Carved, Paddle Shape, Cylindrical Handle, 1800s, 51 x 10 In.	182
Hand Oil Pump, Mobiloil, Red, Salesman's Sample, 11 ½ In.	1680
Hatchel, Punched Tin, Notched Wood, Pennsylvania, 1800s ....*illus*	47
Hay Rake, Salesman's Sample, Horse Drawn, 6 ¾ x 13 ½ x 13 In.	6900
Honey Extractor, AI Root Co., Centrifuge, Top Hand Crank, Spout, c.1905, 27 x 18 In.	275
Incubator, Chicken, Buckeye, Burner, Fuel Tank, Red Paint, Decal, c.1915, 15 x 23 In.	185
Plane, Jack, Stanley No. 605-1/4, Type 6, Bed Rock Series, Decal, Japanning, 1925, 11 ½ In.	250
Plane, Plow, Type 3, Adjustable Face, Double-Ended Cutters, Edwin Walker, Box	5424
Plane, Stanley, No. 50, Cast Iron, Copper Wash, Rosewood Knobs, Charles Miller, 1872	7232
Press, Figural, Stylized Ram, Oak, Turned Handle, 1800s, 11 x 11 In. ....*illus*	125
Scraper, Steel, Hand Forged, Wide Flat Blade, Short Handle, 1800s, 4 x 3 In.	431
Seed Sorting Cart, French Provencial, Pine, Iron, Wheels, 44 ½ x 33 In.	200
Stove Tongs, Shovel, Scissors Design, Square Tapered Handle, Disc Ends, c.1850, 18 In.	1230
Tape Loom, Chestnut, New England, 1700s, 22 ¼ In. ....*illus*	531
Tape Measure, Stanley, Bakelite Case, Red, Steel Tape, c.1935, 72 In.	9
Tape Measure, Stanley, Bundles For Britain, Brass, 1939-41, 72 In. ....*illus*	181
Thresher, Salesman's Sample, Moving Parts, Late 1800s, 16 In.	720
Tool Chest, Cypress, Removable Tray, Folding Iron Handles, 12 ¼ x 36 In.	325
Tool Chest, Oak, Steel, Brass Hardware, Lift Lid, Side Handles, Lock, 1897, 38 x 19 In.	1500
Try Square, Ebony, German Silver Trim, Level Vial, Unruled Blade, 15 x 9 ½ In. ....*illus*	689
Wagon Jack, For Conestoga Wagon, Iron, Wood, 1852, Closed, 22 In. ....*illus*	177

Tobacco Jar, Pottery, 8-Sided, Basket Weave, Pipe, Dog Head Finial, Flower, Japan, 7 ½ x 5 In.
$45

Ruby Lane

Tobacco Jar, Wood Skull, Snakes Crawling Though Eyes, c.1900, 7 In.
$343

Turner Auctions + Appraisals

Tole, Apple Tray, Cutout Handles, Pa., 1800s, 11 ¾ In.
$153

Hess Auction Group

This is an edited listing of current prices. Visit **Kovels.com** to check thousands of prices from previous years and sign up for free information on trends, tips, reproductions, marks, and more.

Tole, Garniture, Flowers, Leaves, Wood Base, Gold Trim, Italian Baroque, 29 In., Pair
$625

New Orleans Auction Galleries

Tole, Tray, Wine Goddess, Oval, Open Handles, Label, Fornasetti, Milano, Italy, 18 x 14 In.
$531

New Orleans Auction Galleries

Tom Mix, Pitcher, Portrait, Glass, Cobalt Blue, 4 x 4 In.
$30

Ruby Lane

Wantage Rod, Folding, Boxwood, Brass Tips, 4-Fold, Firkins, Kilderkins, J. Buck, 1850, 24 In.		181
Water Pump, Wood Case, Iron Spout, Hand Crank, Early 1900s, 37 x 23 ½ x 14 In.		420
Welding, Soldering Iron, Copper Head, 4-Sided Point, Wood Handle, c.1910, 13 x 2 In.		20
Wine Press, Oak, Cast Iron, Tabletop, Barrel, Square Base, Bar Handle, c.1900, 9 x 12 x 12 In.		275
Wool Carder, Iron, Pine, Integral Bench Seat, Trestle Base, Multicolor, 44 x 15 ½ In.		150
Workbench, Cabinet Maker's, Plank Top, Trestle Base, Integral Vise, 30 x 90 In.		650

 TOOTHBRUSH HOLDERS were part of every bowl and pitcher set in the late nineteenth century. Most were oblong covered dishes. About 1920, manufacturers started to make children's toothbrush holders shaped like animals or cartoon characters. A few modern toothbrush holders are still being made.

3 Little Pigs, Bisque, Playing Instruments, Japan, c.1945, 4 In.		87
Blue Flowers, Ruffled Edge & Foot, Porcelain, 5 x 4 In.		45
Chrome Plated, Copper, Marble Base, 6 In.		10
Dog, Blue, Paw Up, Chalkware, 5 ¼ In.		13
Elephant, Tree Stump, California Pottery, c.1940, 3 ½ In.		25
Little Boy, Hands In Pocket, Green Hat, Porcelain, 4 ½ In.		18
Peacocks, Flowers, Gilt Trim, Pottery, Satsuma, Japan, 1960s, 3 ⅝ In.		8
Porcelain, Man, Candlestick Maker, Blue Striped Apron, Orange Tie, 5 In.	*illus*	75
Pottery, Drip Plate, Blue Flowers, c.1980, 4 In.		15
Soldier Boy, Uniform, Black, Orange, Porcelain, Japan, 6 ¾ In.		65
Swirled Luster, Oval, Silver Trim, Steven Rhoades Designs, c.1990, 4 ¼ In.		10
Tea Rose, Pfaltzgraff, 3 In.		15

 TOOTHPICK HOLDERS are sometimes called *toothpicks* by collectors. The variously shaped containers used to hold small wooden toothpicks are made of glass, china, or metal. Most of the toothpick holders are made of Victorian pressed glass. Additional items may be found in other categories, such as Bisque, Silver Plate, Slag Glass, etc.

Applied Rigaree On Neck, Scalloped Rim, New England Glass Co., c.1885, 2 In.		108
Children Playing, Acanthus, Glass, Acid Etched, Silver Base, Schleissner Sohne, c.1880, 5 In.		937
Donkey, Silver, 3 x 4 ½ In., 6 Piece		100
Millefiori, Gourd Base, Flared Rim, Multicolor, Glass, 2 ¾ In.		48
Millefiori, Multicolor, Glass, Italy, 2 ½ x 2 ¾ In.		86
Ruby Stained, Cut Glass, Red Rim, c.1900, 2 ½ In.	*illus*	591
Wicker Basket, Pink, Green, Porcelain, Germany, c.1900, 2 x 2 ½ In.		89

TORQUAY

TORQUAY is the name given to ceramics by several potteries working near Torquay, England, from 1870 until 1962. Until about 1900, the potteries used local red clay to make classical-style art pottery vases and figurines. Then they turned to making souvenir wares. Items were dipped in colored slip and decorated with painted slip and sgraffito designs. They often had mottoes or proverbs, and scenes of cottages, ships, birds, or flowers. The Scandy design was a symmetrical arrangement of brushstrokes and spots done in colored slips. Potteries included Watcombe Pottery (1870–1962), Torquay Terra-Cotta Company (1875–1905), Aller Vale (1881–1924), Torquay Pottery (1908–1940), and Longpark (1883–1957).

Cup & Saucer, Help Yourself To A Cup Of Tea		35
Egg Cup, Pedestal, Cottage, Rolling Stone Gathers No Moss, 2 ¾ In.		48
Match Holder, Ships, Sunset, Striker, 2 ½ In.		59
Perfume Bottle, Motto Ware, Purple Flower, Heart Shape Leaves, 2 ¾ In.	*illus*	17
Vase, Peacock, Blue Green Red, 3 Curved Handles, 6 ½ In.		450
Vase, Pinch, King Fisher Design, Tree Branch, Lilies, Reeds, Blue, 6 In.		60

 TORTOISESHELL is the shell of the tortoise. It has been used as inlay and to make small decorative objects since the seventeenth century. Some species of tortoise are now on the endangered species list, and old or new objects made from these shells cannot be sold legally.

Blotter, George V, Silver Mount, Acanthus Scrolls, 1923		148
Box, Silver Mounts, Hinged, Fluted Lid, 8 x 5 In.		743

Tool, Brace, Beech, William Marples & Sons, Brass, Ebony, Ivory, Hibernia Works, England
$186

Brown Tool Auctions

Tool, Cabinet, Hardware, Oak, 54 Cubbyholes, Hobart Brothers Co., Troy, Oh., 64 x 38 In.
$354

Hess Auction Group

Tool, Hatchel, Punched Tin, Notched Wood, Pennsylvania, 1800s
$47

Hess Auction Group

Tool, Press, Figural, Stylized Ram, Oak, Turned Handle, 1800s, 11 x 11 In.
$125

Garth's Auctioneers & Appraisers

Tool, Tape Loom, Chestnut, New England, 1700s, 22 ¼ In.
$531

Hess Auction Group

Tool, Tape Measure, Stanley, Bundles For Britain, Brass, 1939-41, 72 In.
$181

Brown Tool Auctions

Tool, Try Square, Ebony, German Silver Trim, Level Vial, Unruled Blade, 15 x 9 ½ In.
$689

Brown Tool Auctions

Tool, Wagon Jack, For Conestoga Wagon, Iron, Wood, 1852, Closed 22 In.
$177

Hess Auction Group

Toothbrush Holder, Porcelain, Man, Candlestick Maker, Blue Striped Apron, Orange Tie, 5 In.
$75

Ruby Lane

Toothpick, Ruby Stained, Cut Glass, Red Rim, c.1900, 2½ In.
$591

Jeffrey S. Evans

Torquay, Perfume Bottle, Motto Ware, Purple Flower, Heart Shape Leaves, 2¾ In.
$17

Martin Auction Co.

Box, Silver Repousse Hinged Lid, Cylindrical, Swag Overlay, c.1895, 3 x 3 In.	177
Cigar Case, Carved Post, Bail Handle, Edwardian, 2 x 8 x 6 In.	500
Coin Purse, Key Wind Clock, Mother-Of-Pearl Ornaments	271
Trinket Box, Lid, Round, Carved, Pierced, Figures, Leaves, 1800s, 4 In.	1265

 TORTOISESHELL GLASS was made during the 1800s and after by the Sandwich Glass Works of Massachusetts and some firms in Germany. Tortoiseshell glass is, of course, named for its resemblance to real shell from a tortoise. It has been reproduced.

Vase, Fired-On Gold Scrolls & Flowers, Ball, Cone Foot, Flared Stick Neck, 15 In.	177

 TOY collectors have special clubs, magazines, and shows. Toys are designed to entice children, and today they have attracted new interest among adults who are still children at heart. All types of toys are collected. Tin toys, iron toys, battery-operated toys, and many others are collected by specialists. Dolls, Games, Teddy Bears, and Bicycles are listed in their own categories. Other toys may be found under company or celebrity names.

Action Figure, Captain America, Fly Away Action, Shield, Window Box, 1979, 12½ In.	870
Action Figure, Captain America, Posable, Cloth Star, Shield, Sealed, Blister Card, 1979, 8 In.	664
Action Figure, Conan, Posable, Tan Loincloth, Scabbard, Throwing Ax, Card, 1979, 8 In.	1835
Action Figure, Green Arrow, Posable, Polyester Outfit, Window Box, Mego, 1973, 8 In.	422
Action Figure, Invincible Iron Man, Posable, Cutout Picture Card, Box, 1974, 8 In.	380
Action Figure, Isis, Posable, Jointed Arms, Actress Photo On Blister Card, 1976, 8 In.	211
Action Figure, Matt Dillon, Gunsmoke, Hat, Gun, Buckskin Horse, Box, c.1958, 9 x 10 In.	317
Action Figure, Stinger, Thundercats, Movable Wings, Trigger, Blister Card, 9 x 12 In.	291
Action Figure, Thor, Posable, Long Hair, Cape, Helmet, Hammer, Blister Card, 1979, 8 In.	618
Action Figure, Wonder Woman, Posable, Painted Top, Alter Ego Outfit, Box, 1976, 12 In.	279
Airplane, 3 Pilots, Gun Turret, Propellers, Windup, Camouflage, Masudaya, Prewar, 16 In.	11590
Airplane, Flying Dutchman, Tin Litho, Plastic, Remote Control, KLM, Box, 1950s, 11 x 14 In.	173
Airplane, Sea Gull, Amphibian, Blue Fuselage, Embossed Wings, Kilgore, c.1930, 8 In.	530
Airplane, Silver Eagle, Windup, American, 1930s, 13 In.	145
Airplane, Sirius, Pressed Steel, 2 Seats, Lockheed Decal, c.1931, 21½ In. *illus*	944
Airplane, Sports, Tin Litho, Red, D-2934 On Wings, Clockwork, Tippco, c.1936, 15 In.	1228
Amos, Taxi Driver, Walker, Amos 'n' Andy, Rocks, Walks, Tin Litho, Windup, 1930, 12 In.	316
Archie Sparkler, Smile, Multicolor, Metal, Ronson, c.1920, 9 x 5 In.	95
Armchair, Doll's, Bent Twig, Slat Seat, c.1920, 13 In.	47
Automobile Sisters, 2 Women In Car, Driver, Dog, Tin Litho, Clockwork, Lehmann, 1903, 5 In.	930
Barn, 2 Story, Sliding Front Door, Hinged Side Door, Cupola, 39½ x 33¼ In.	295
Barney Google & Sparkplug, Tin Litho, Windup, Built-In Key, Nifty Copyright, 1924, 7 In.	385
Bears are also listed in the Teddy Bear category.	
Bicycles that are large enough to ride are listed in the Bicycle category.	
Bingola, I, Germany, Child's, Original Box, 8 x 5 In.	275
Black Tap Dancer, Blue Coat, Tin Litho, Clockwork, Lehmann, Box, 10 In.	1431
Blocks, Alphabet, Noah's Ark, Animals, Ark Storage Box, Wheels, 1900s, 7 x 12 In.	123
Blocks, Alphabet, Wood, Printed Animal Figures, Red & Light Blue, 1¾ In., 20 Piece	106
Boat, Ocean Liner, 2 Masts, Stack, Airplane, Windup, Tin Litho, Lindstrom, 10¾ In. *illus*	266
Boat, Ocean Liner, Gold, Black Bands, 3 Decks, 3 Stacks, Series IV, Bing, c.1930, 16 In.	2950
Boat, Red & Yellow Hull, Green Deck, Lifeboat, People, Jackie N.Y.C.	217
Boat, Yacht, Racing, Tin Litho, Embossed, Painted, Battery Operated, Anfoe, c.1920, 17 In.	197
Bucking Bronco, Tin Lithograph, Windup, Lehmann, Germany, 7 In.	518
Bus, Blue, White Roof, Greyhound Lines, New York's World Fair, Cast Iron, Arcade, 8½ In.	148
Bus, Cast Iron, Orange & Black Paint, Rubber Tires, Arcade, c.1920, 13 In.	5605
Bus, Circus, Tin Friction, Germany, 9 In.	175
Bus, City Of Detroit, Automotive Div., Rubber Tires, Cast Iron, Arcade, 13 In. *illus*	1416
Bus, Coast To Coast, Green, Rubber Tires, GMC, 11 In.	649
Bus, Double-Decker, Green & Red Paint, Passengers, Kenton Hardware *illus*	1180
Bus, Fageol Coach, Promotional, Nickel Wheels, Cast Iron, Arcade, c.1928, 8 In. *illus*	531
Bus, Jitney, Green, Windup, Tin, Strauss, 9½ In.	272
Bus, Pressed Steel, Blue & White Paint, Battery Tail Light, Windup, Buddy L, 16 In.	649

T

Toy, Airplane, Sirius, Pressed Steel, 2 Seats, Lockheed Decal, c.1931, 21½ In.
$944

Bertoia Auctions

Toy, Boat, Ocean Liner, 2 Masts, Stack, Airplane, Windup, Tin Litho, Lindstrom, 10¾ In.
$266

Bertoia Auctions

Toy, Bus, City Of Detroit, Automotive Div., Rubber Tires, Cast Iron, Arcade, 13 In.
$1,416

Bertoia Auctions

Toy, Bus, Double-Decker, Green & Red Paint, Passengers, Kenton Hardware
$1,180

Bertoia Auctions

Popular Brands
Some brands are more popular with collectors than others. Coca-Cola, McDonald's, and M&Ms are tops. Others are Planters Peanuts, Anheuser-Busch, Budweiser, Kentucky Fried Chicken, and soft drinks like Pepsi-Cola, Moxie, and Hires Root Beer.

Toy, Bus, Fageol Coach, Promotional, Nickel Wheels, Cast Iron, Arcade, c.1928, 8 In.
$531

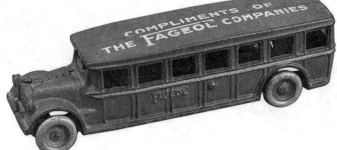

Bertoia Auctions

Toy, Camel, Rider, Bell, 3 Ringers, Tin, Platform, Lead Wheels, Althof Bergmann, 9 In.
$1,534

Bertoia Auctions

Toy, Cap Gun, Chinese Must Go, Man Kicking, Trigger Releases Foot, Cast Iron, Patd. 1879, 5 x 4 In.
$522

Showtime Auction Services

Toy, Car, Chevrolet, Coupe, 2 Door, Nickel, Friction, Marusan, Linemar, Japan, 11½ In.
$944

Bertoia Auctions

Toy, Car, Limousine, Driver, Doors Open, Lights, Tin, Clockwork, Karl Bub, Germany, c.1930, 13 In.
$1,020

Bertoia Auctions

Toy, Car, Sedan, Trailer, Mullins Red Cap, Red Paint, Rubber Tires, Cast Iron, Arcade, 9 In.
$472

Bertoia Auctions

Toy, Cat, Walking, Balanced On Long Tail, Painted, Tin, Clockwork, Japan, 5 In.
$177

Bertoia Auctions

Toy, Chest, Doll's, Fruitwood, Inlay, Flowers, Claw Feet, c.1850, 11 x 14 In.
$1,083

Theriault's

Toy, Cradle, Doll's, Mahogany, Carved, Gilt Stencil Annie, 1902, 16 x 13 In.
$342

Theriault's

Toy, Cradle, Doll's, Painted Tulips, Scalloped Ends, Wood, Jacob Weber, Pa., c.1850, 5 x 9 In.
$1,416

Hess Auction Group

Toy, Cradle, Doll's, Softwood, Cutouts, Red Paint, Pennsylvania, 1800s, 20 In.
$53

Hess Auction Group

Toy, Desk, Doll's, Slant Front, Chippendale, Cherry, c.1820, 6 x 6 In.
$285

Theriault's

Toy, Dog, Bulldog, Papier-Mache, Barks, Growls, Mohair, Wheels, France, c.1920, 27 In.
$1,337

Auction Team Breker

Toy, Dollhouse, 2 Story, 2 Rooms, Wooden, Front Door, Porch Pillars, Balcony, Bliss, c.1890, 12 In.
$855

Theriault's

TIP

Old metal toy trucks were made of iron or tin, not brass or aluminum, the metals favored by some reproductions.

Bus, Tin Litho, Brown & Yellow, Upper Deck Seating, Driver, Key, Ferdinand Strauss, 10 In.	472
Bus, Tin Litho, Vinyl Tires, Grendizer Robot Lithography, Friction, Popy, Box, 1970s, 11 In.......	917
Bus, Tour, Cast Iron, Paint, Light Blue, Orange, Metal Wheels & Driver, Upper Deck, 4 x 6 In...	489
Cabinet, Doll's, Mirrored, Porcelain, Wavy Shelves, Pillars, c.1880, 15 x 17 In..........................	513
Camel, Rider, Bell, 3 Ringers, Tin, Platform, Lead Wheels, Althof Bergmann, 9 In.............*illus*	1534
Cap Gun, Chinese Must Go, Man Kicking, Trigger Releases Foot, Cast Iron, Patd. 1879, 5 x 4 In. *illus*	522
Car, Amazing Spider, Red Plastic, Black Spider, Web Trap, Box, 1976, 7 x 11 In.	173
Car, Aston Martin, James Bond 007, Plastic, Figure, Ejector Seat, Corgi, Box, 1977, 5 In.	146
Car, Cadillac, Gold, Tin Litho, Plastic, Hood Emblem, Friction, Bandai, Box, 1959, 11 In.	253
Car, Chevrolet, Coupe, 2 Door, Nickel, Friction, Marusan, Linemar, Japan, 11½ In...........*illus*	944
Car, Convertible, 2 Door, Tin, Chrome Plated, Copper Plate Bumpers, Italy, 1948, 10 In.	460
Car, Cunningham, Tin, Red, Cream, Japan, Box, 1950s, 8½ In...	375
Car, Fire Chief, Pressed Steel, Red, Yellow Paint, Battery Head & Taillights, Windup, 15 In.	891
Car, Ford, Convertible, Battery Operated, Tin, Japan, 1950s, 7½ In.	95
Car, Ford, Mustang, Red, Tin Litho, Rubber Tires, Plated Bumper & Grille, Box, 1965, 11 In.	279
Car, Highway Patrol, Battery Operated, Japan, 1960s, 10 In.	175
Car, Limousine, Driver, Doors Open, Lights, Tin, Clockwork, Karl Bub, Germany, c.1930, 13 In..*illus*	1020
Car, Mercedes-Benz, C-111, Magenta, Black, Doors Open & Close, Hot Wheels, 1972	115
Car, Mercedes-Benz, Metal Friction, Asahi Toys, Japan, 8½ In.	195
Car, Open Wheel Racer, Red, Tires, No. 5, Cast Iron, Arcade, 7 In..	425
Car, Porsche 917, Salmon, Grand Prix Series, Hot Wheels, On Card, Mattel, c.1970	140
Car, Racing Set, Sprint, Slot Cars, Mercedes, Ferrari, Track, Remote, Marklin, 1/32 Scale	210
Car, Racing, Cast Iron, Rubber Tires, Wood Wheels, Driver, Hubley No. 1877, 1930s, 7 In.	225
Car, Racing, Ferocious Ferrari, Die Cast, Plastic Head, Tootsietoy, On Card, 1965, 5 In.	197
Car, Racing, Open Top, Woman Driver, Orange, Black, Tin Litho, Windup, Gundka, 6 In..........	242
Car, Roadster, Sonny & Cher, Red, Plastic, Windshield, Duesenberg Style, Box, 1976, 17 In.......	518
Car, Romance, Driver, Lights, Battery, Red, Japan, Box, 1950s	225
Car, Sedan, Trailer, Mullins Red Cap, Red Paint, Rubber Tires, Cast Iron, Arcade, 9 In. .....*illus*	472
Car, Soap Box Derby, Plywood, Rubber Tires, Vinyl Seat, Late 1900s, 39 In.	150
Car, Touring, Hessmobile, Driver, Open Top, Red, Black, Tin Litho, JHL Works, Germany, 8 In.	518
Car, Triumph, Roadster, Convertible, Metal, Paint, Rubber Tires, Tootsietoy, 1950s, 1 x 3 In. ...	15
Car, Uncle Wiggily, Tin Lithograph, Clockwork Drive, Marx, 7¼ In.	354
Car, Volkswagen, Brown, Hot Wheels, On Card, Mattel, 1968, 3¼ x 2¼ In..............................	185
Car, Yellow Cab, Seated Driver, Cast Iron, Orange & Black Paint, Marked, Arcade, 8 In.	215
Carousel, 3 Seats, 3 Bisque Doll Riders, Lattice Pedestal, Revolving, Tin Litho, 17 In...............	1140
Carousel, Wood, Fabric, Metal, 2 Tiers, 16 Horses, 7 Coaches, Celluloid Dolls, Electric, 38 In...	478
Carriage, Bisque Doll, Pressed Tin, 3 Wheels, Silk, Mechanical, Pull String, c.1890, 7 In.........	969
Carriage, Horse Drawn, 3 Wheels, Squared Push Handle, 38 x 55 In.	236
Cart, Horse Drawn, Woven, Upholstered Seat, Spoke Wheels, Hide Covered, c.1880, 49 In.	1254
Cat, Felix, On Cart, 2 Mice, All Move Up & Down, Tin Litho, Pull String, 1920s, 4 x 8 In.	612
Cat, Felix, On Scooter, Circles, Moves Back & Forth, Paint, Tin Litho, Windup, 1922, 8 In.	241
Cat, Walking, Balanced On Long Tail, Painted, Tin, Clockwork, Japan, 5 In......................*illus*	177
Chair, Doll's, Chippendale, Fruitwood, Claw Feet, Petit Point Seat, Braid Edging, 4 In.	112
Chair, Doll's, Salon, Giltwood, Tufted Silk Seat, Carved, Faux Bamboo Design, c.1885, 11 In. ..	1368
Chest, Doll's, Fruitwood, Inlay, Flowers, Claw Feet, c.1850, 11 x 14 In................................*illus*	1083
Circus, Humpty Dumpty Circus, Wood, Painted, Cage, 12 Jointed Figures, Schoenhut	1476
Circus, Humpty Dumpty, Tent, Performers, Animals, Wood, Cloth, Schoenhut, 30 Piece	2240
Clock, Doll's, Tall Case, Mahogany, Shaped, Gilt Scrolls, Sunburst Pendulum, 19 In.	969
Clock, Doll's, Tall Case, Walnut, Steeple, Finials, Carved, c.1880, 12 In.	342
Clown, Inside Double Hoop, Arms Revolves, Tin Lithograph, Bells, 6½ In. Diam	255
Clown, Papier-Mache Head, Glass Eyes, Painted Face, Wood, Jointed, Jester, c.1890, 18 In.	1710
Comical Cart, Clown Driver, Horn, Lantern, Tin Litho, Clockwork, Lehmann, 1927, 5 In.........	644
Cradle, Doll's, Mahogany, Carved, Gilt Stencil Annie, 1902, 16 x 13 In.............................*illus*	342
Cradle, Doll's, Painted Tulips, Scalloped Ends, Wood, Jacob Weber, Pa., c.1850, 5 x 9 In....*illus*	1416
Cradle, Doll's, Painted, Lancaster, Pa., 1800s, 8¼ x 15 x 8¾ In.	590
Cradle, Doll's, Softwood, Cutouts, Red Paint, Pennsylvania, 1800s, 20 In.........................*illus*	53
Cradle, Doll's, Softwood, Old Yellow Paint, Side Peg Handles, 24½ In.	30
Creeping Crawling Hand, Rubber Over Tin Litho, Battery, Frankenstein Box, 1960s, 9 In......	2785
Desk, Doll's, Maitrise, Drop Front, Black, Red, Gilt Chinoiserie, Cubicles, 16 In.........................	3420
Desk, Doll's, Maple, Slant Front, Marquetry, Flowers, c.1885, 25 x 16 In.	1938

Toy, Dollhouse, 2 Story, Wood, Paper, Elevator, Steeple, Tower, Gottschalk, c.1890, 30 x 16 In.
$1,710

Theriault's

Toy, Fawn, Curled Up, Plush, Stuffed, Steiff, 8½ In.
$59

Hess Auction Group

TIP
Rusted toys have very low value.

T

Toy, Garden Gazebo, Simulated Wood Sides, Faux Greenery, Table, Painted, Bing, 6 In.
$480

Bertoia Auctions

Toy, Goose, Long Neck Moves, Wheeled Platform, Penny, Distler, Germany, 3 In.
$177

Bertoia Auctions

Toy, Happy Violinist, Wooden Box, Glass, Man, Marquis Costume, Sand Toy, c.1850, 6 In.
$456

Theriault's

Desk, Doll's, Slant Front, Chippendale, Cherry, c.1820, 6 x 6 In. ....*illus*	285
Desk, Doll's, Walnut, Mirror, Slant Front, Bombe Shape, c.1815, 32 x 17 In.	627
Desk, Doll's, Woman's, Mahogany, Slant Top, Painted, Drawer, 10 x 8 In.	342
Dinosaur, Robot, Steel Man, Daitarn, 3 Play Modes, Robot, Ship, Tank, Box, 1978, 11 x 14 In.	259
Dog, Bulldog, Papier-Mache, Barks, Growls, Mohair, Wheels, France, c.1920, 27 In. ....*illus*	1337
Dog, Bulldog, Papier-Mache, Wheels, Mouth Moves, Teeth, Growls, Pull Chain, c.1885, 16 In...	1938
Dog, Curly Mohair, Stuffing, Shoebutton Eyes, Metal Wheels, Germany, c.1910, 9 In.	112
Dog, Dachshund, Kidskin, Hinged Legs, Wheels, Collar & Chain, Windup, c.1890, 11 In...........	1368
Dog, German Shepherd, Mohair, Upright Ears, Shuco, 6 In.	71
Dog, Papier-Mache, Fluffy White Fur, Glass Eyes, Leather Collar, Bells, France, c.1885, 5 In.....	570
Dog, Poodle, On Wheels, Teeth, Brown Spots, Steiff, 11 ½ In.	305
Dog, Sitting, Flannel, Stuffed, Glass Eyes, Ears, Leather Collar, Bell, Opens Mouth, 9 In.	252
Dog, St. Bernard, Ride On, Plastic, Steel Frame & Wheels, Handle Bar, c.1905, 19 x 24 In.	325
Dog, Standing, Cream Wool Plush, Felt, Muzzle, Silver Collar, Knickerbocker, 1930s, 10 In.....	112
Dolls are listed in the Doll category.	
Dollhouse Furniture, Candy Dispenser, Tin Litho, Glass Windows, Stollwerck, c.1890, 12 In.	342
Dollhouse, 1 Room, Open Front, Crown Roof, Chandelier, Furnishings, c.1890, 23 x 22 In......	6270
Dollhouse, 2 Story, 2 Rooms, Wooden, Front Door, Porch Pillars, Balcony, Bliss, c.1890, 12 In... *illus*	855
Dollhouse, 2 Story, Tara, Gone With The Wind, 1987, 35 x 65 In.	147
Dollhouse, 2 Story, Wood, Paper, Elevator, Steeple, Tower, Gottschalk, c.1890, 30 x 16 In. *illus*	1710
Dollhouse, 3 Story, Victorian, Blue, 43 x 24 In.	125
Dollhouse, Colonial, White, Awnings, Clapboard, Electrified, 36 x 43 ½ In.	590
Dollhouse, Wood, Paint, Wallpaper Roof & Interior, Attic, Lift-Off Roof, 1900s, 10 x 15 In.	60
Dressing Table, Doll's, Mirror & Salon Chair, Gilt, Painted Silk, c.1875, 8 In.	1026
Drum, Tin Lithograph, Boat, House, Ball, Sticks, Ohio Art, 6 x 4 In., Pair.	36
Drummer Boy, Walks, Beats Drum, Wheel, Tin Litho, Windup, Marx, Box, 1930s, 9 x 8 In......	425
Eagle, Carved, Push Toy, Painted Eagle On Iron Cart, 1900s, 21 In.	1200
Elephant, Circus, Celluloid, Jacket, Holding Bell, Moves, Rings Bell, Windup, 1930s, 10 In.......	417
Elephant, Gray Mohair, Felt Tusks, Jointed, Steiff, 9 ½ In.	396
Erector Set, Locomotive & Tender, Track, Black, Painted, A.C. Gilbert, 1933, 8 x 29 In.............	1857
Erector Set, Mysterious Walking Robot, Metal Case, A.C. Gilbert, 1959, 14 x 25 In....................	1107
Erector Set, Zeppelin, Silver & Red, A.C. Gilbert, Cardboard Box, 1932, 13 x 21 In.	6289
Fawn, Curled Up, Plush, Stuffed, Steiff, 8 ½ In. ....*illus*	59
Ferris Wheel, Airships, Crank Movement, Ernst Planck, Germany, 16 ½ In.	1220
Ferris Wheel, Hercules, Tin Lithograph, Windup, J. Chein, 16 ½ In.	41
Ferris Wheel, Red & Yellow Tin Litho, Clown Face, Basket Seats, Windup, Box, c.1905	325
Fighting Knights, Tin Lithograph, Jousting, Wheels, Multicolor, Germany, 10 In.	1464
Figure, Alien, Plastic, Posable, Spring Loaded, Brain Glows In Dark, Box, 1979, 18 In..............	765
Figure, Busy Lizzie, Sweeper, Pushes Broom, Tin Lithograph, Windup, 1930s, 7 In.	209
Figure, General Robert E. Lee, Horse Traveler, Saddle, Flag, Sword, Box, c.1958, 9 x 9 In.........	266
Figure, Pee Wee Herman, Cloth, Vinyl Head, Suit, Shipping Container, Box, 1989, 40 In..........	328
Fingerprint Kit, Man From U.N.C.L.E., Roller, Ink, Pressure Plate, Box, 1965, 11 x 14 In........	466
Fire Truck, Brigade Crew Wagon, Men, Hose, Ladders, Tin Litho, Clockwork, Karl Bub, 16 In.	1431
Fire Truck, Ladder, Driver, Cast Iron, Fleur-De-Lis, Red Paint, Kenton, c.1920, 5 ½ x 3 In.	265
Fire Truck, Pumper, Cast Iron, Red & Silver, Rubber Tires, Wood Rim, Hubley, 1930s, 5 In.....	150
Fire Wagon, Ladder, 3-Horse Team, 2 Drivers, Bell, Red & White Paint, Cast Iron, 30 In.........	189
Fireplace Set, Doll's, Brass, Cast Iron, Andirons, Scuttle, Tools, 8-In. Mantel, 12 Piece	399
Flamingo, Standing, Unjointed, Mohair, Synthetic Leather, Felt, Steiff, 65 In.	2160
Flower Peddler, Bisque Doll, Basket, Tin Base, Wheels, Moves, Windup, c.1860, 10 In.	1140
Games are listed in the Game category.	
Garden Gazebo, Simulated Wood Sides, Faux Greenery, Table, Painted, Bing, 6 In. ....*illus*	480
Goat & Cart, Red & Yellow Paint, Spike Wheels, Tinned Sheet Iron, c.1890, 9 x 4 In.	200
Goose, Long Neck Moves, Wheeled Platform, Penny, Distler, Germany, 3 In. ....*illus*	177
Grasshopper, Articulated, Iron, Hubley, Front Wheels, Movable Rear Wheels, Pull Toy, 11 In..	510
Grasshopper, Cast Iron & Alloy, Green, Wheels, Pull String, Hubley, 9 ¼ In.............................	649
Gravity Sand, Man, Rocking Chair, Child On Knee, Paper Litho, Die Cut, Frame, 8 x 10 In.	120
Grocery Store, Wood, Open Front, Cashier Desk, Shelves, Furnishings, 1880s, 20 x 28 In.	8550
Gun, Sixfinger, Hard Plastic, Finger Shape, Attachments, Blister Card, Topper, 1965, 4 In.	255
Hansom Cab, Horse, Brown, Black, Tin Lithograph, 1920-30s, 9 In.	183

Toy, Harold Lloyd, Face, Squeeze, Expressions Change, Bell Rings, Tin, Germany, 1920s, 6 In.
$118

Bertoia Auctions

> **TIP**
> *Reproduction cast-iron toys and banks are heavier and thicker than the originals.*

Toy, Horse & Wagon, 4 Figures, 2 Horses, Cast Iron, Nickel Plated, Shimer, 15 ½ In.
$767

Bertoia Auctions

Toy, Krazy Car, Gran Circo Pipo, Tin, Windup, Argentina, 7 In.
$148

Bertoia Auctions

Toy, Krazy Kat, Mice, 4-Wheel Platform, Tin Litho, Squeak, Pull Toy, Chein, 1934, 7 ½ In.
$720

Bertoia Auctions

Toy, Lab Set, Nuclear Physics Atomic Energy Lab, Gilbert, 1952, 16 ½ x 25 In.
$8,696

Hake's Americana & Collectibles

Toy, Madelon The Maid, Carrying Dishes, Dutch Girl, Clockwork, Bonnet, France, 6 ¾ In.
$2,700

Bertoia Auctions

Toy, Motorcycle, Big Red, Sidecar, Tin Lithograph, Windup, Marked J.M.L., France, 1950s, 12 In.
$1,320

Potter & Potter Auctions

Toy, Motorcycle, Mac 700 Daredevil, Rider, Tin Lithograph, Windup, Arnold, Germany, 1950s, 8 In.
$570

Potter & Potter Auctions

Toy, Motorcycle, Police Officer, Siren, Tin Litho, Windup, Louis Marx, Pats Pendg., 1950s
$180

Potter & Potter Auctions

Toy, Motorcycle, Police, Rollover, Clockwork, Tin Lithograph, Marx, 1930s, 8 ½ In.
$270

Bertoia Auctions

Toy, Parrot, On Stump, Squeaks, Flaps Wings, Multicolor, Germany, 5 In.
$502

Bertoia Auctions

Toy, Pedal Car, Tractor, McCormick Farmall, International Harvester, Eska, c.1980, 22 x 32 In.
$344

Garth's Auctioneers & Appraisers

Toy, Pig Merchant, Man Walks, Strikes Pigs, Clockwork, Ferdinand Martin, France, c.1910, 7 In.
$3,540

Bertoia Auctions

Toy, Sewing Machine, Metal, Brass Plaque, Singer Man'f. Co., Italy, c.1900, 6 In.
$224

Theriault's

Toy, Sewing Machine, Muller, Metal, Windup, Lithograph Box, France, 4 In.
$420

Theriault's

Toy, Sewing Machine, Tin, Stencils, Gold & Red Garland & Flowers, Box, c.1900, 7 In.
$224

Theriault's

The First Roller Skates
The four-wheel roller skate was made in 1863. It was invented by James L. Plimpton, a Massachusetts inventor.

Toy Trains
The easiest trains to sell are the O gauge trains of the 1950s, not the larger trains of earlier years.

Toy, Smitty Scooter, Comic Strip Office Boy, On Scooter, Tin Litho, Windup, Marx, c.1925, 8 In.
$1,140

Bertoia Auctions

Toy, Station, Durchgang, Telegraph, Wartesaal, Doors, Roofs, Candles, Marklin, 17 ½ In.
$3,540

Bertoia Auctions

Toy, Stove, Marklin, Metal, Spirit Burner, 4 Pots, Lids, 2 Ladles, c.1925, 12 x 9 In.
$358

Auction Team Breker

Happy Violinist, Wooden Box, Glass, Man, Marquis Costume, Sand Toy, c.1850, 6 In. ......*illus*	456
Harold Lloyd, Face, Squeeze, Expressions Change, Bell Rings, Tin, Germany, 1920s, 6 In.*illus*	118
Helicopter, Airport, Tin Litho, Vinyl, Rubber, Folding Rotor, Yonezowa, Box, 1960s, 13 In........	190
Helicopter, Sikorsky, Red & White Metal Body, Blue Plastic, Tootsietoy, 3 In.	100
Hobbyhorse, Carved, Glass Eyes, Leather Tack, Horsehair Mane & Tail, 1800s, 20½ x 43 In....	1080
Hobbyhorse, Wood Stand, Dappled Gray, Hair Mane & Tail, Glass Eyes, c.1890, 35 x 47 In.......	474
Horse & Rider, Carved & Painted, Plank Platform, Spoke Wheels, Pull Cord, c.1900	1788
Horse & Wagon, 4 Figures, 2 Horses, Cast Iron, Nickel Plated, Shimer, 15½ In................*illus*	767
Horse & Wagon, Ladder, Blue, 2 Figures, c.1900, 21 In.	240
Horse & Wagon, Milk, Borden's, Yellow Wheels, Wood, Metal, 1900-25, 9 x 19½ In................	168
Horse, Rearing, Horsehair Covering, Windup, Early 1900s, 11½ In...	210
Horse, Rocking, Carved Wood, Paint, Hair Mane, Leather, Stand, c.1900, 29 x 34 In.	240
Horse, Rocking, Cutout Solid Rockers, Dapple Paint, Late 1800s, 24½ x 42½ In.	780
Horse, Rocking, Wood, Paint, Saddle, Stirrups, Cast Iron Wheels, 1960s, 22 x 31 In.	635
Jeep, Circus, Clown Driver, Elephant On Back, Tin Lithograph, Friction, Box, 1950s, 6 In.	127
Jerry Mahoney, Ventriloquist's Dummy, Box, 11¼ x 18½ In.	147
Jester, Polichinelle, Hunchback, Waves Baton, Painted Tin, Windup, c.1900, 9 In.	3534
Jetter Mars, Figure, Tin Litho, Plastic Head, Vinyl Cape, Windup, Popy, Japan, 1970s, 9 In.	259
Jigger, Tombo, Alabama Coon, Dances A Jig, Tin Litho, Windup, Cardboard Box, 1918, 8 In.	443
Jouncing Jeep, Tin Lithograph, Slogans, Windup, Unique Art, Box, c.1950, 7½ In....................	295
Kiddy Cyclist, Boy On Tricycle, Circles, Tin Litho, Windup, Unique Art, Box, 1940s, 9 In.	190
Kiddyphone, Round, Horn, Bomgwerle, Child's..	303
Kite Rope Winder, Spool, Wood, Cylindrical Handle, 2 Center Dowels, c.1905, 18 x 13 In.	55
Krazy Car, Gran Circo Pipo, Tin, Windup, Argentina, 7 In......................................*illus*	148
Krazy Kat, Mice, 4-Wheel Platform, Tin Litho., Squeak, Pull Toy, Chein, 1934, 7½ In.....*illus*	720
Lab Set, Nuclear Physics Atomic Energy Lab, Gilbert, 1952, 16½ x 25 In. ....*illus*	8696
Little Wonder, Disc, Cast Iron Base, Horn	303
Machine Gun, Gang Busters, Revolving Chamber, Tin Lithograph, Windup, 1930s, 24 In........	204
Madelon The Maid, Carrying Dishes, Dutch Girl, Clockwork, Bonnet, France, 6¾ In......*illus*	2700
Magic Space Dog, Spinning Flying Saucer, Tin Litho, Remote Control, Box, 1950s, 5 x 7 In.....	4217
Marble Roller, Painted Wood, Tin, Multicolor Slide, Slatted Supports, 12 x 27 In.	106
Mirrorman, Tin Litho, Plastic, Removable Vinyl Mask, Windup, Japan, Box, 1972, 10 In.	403
Model Kit, Creature From The Black Lagoon, Glow In Dark Parts, Aurora, Box, 1975, 8 In.......	291
Model Kit, Dracula, No. 427-98, Bela Lugosi As Count Dracula, Box, 1962.............................	627
Model Kit, Godzilla, No. 469-149, Aurora, Color Illustrated Box, 1964.............................	557
Model Kit, Haunted House, Addams Family, No. 805-198, Instructions, Box, 1964..................	633
Model Kit, Incredible Hulk, No. 421-100, Color Illustrated Box, Marvel, 1966.......................	765
Model Kit, James Bond 007, Instruction Sheet, Aurora, Factory Sealed Box, 1966.....................	327
Model Kit, Spartacus, Instruction Sheet, Aurora, Glossy Sealed Box, 1964	177
Model Kit, Wolf Man, No. 425-98, Universal Pictures Co., Color Illustrated Box, 1964..............	1486
Model Kit, Wonder Woman, Aurora, Factory Sealed Box, 1965	633
Model, Train, Steam Engine, Metal, Painted Flywheel, Wood Base, Late 1800s, 11¾ In.	510
Monkey, Record Peter, Brown Mohair, Felt Face, Amber Eyes, Wheeled Base, Steiff, c.1949, 9 In.	224
Mother Goose, Walker, Riding On Goose, Cat, Tin Litho, Windup, Marx, 1930s, 9 In.	335
Motorcycle, Auto Cycle, Harley-Davidson, Tin Litho, Red, Friction, Japan, 9 In......................	150
Motorcycle, Big Red, Sidecar, Tin Lithograph, Windup, Marked J.M.L., France, 1950s, 12 In...*illus*	1320
Motorcycle, Fire Patrol, Tin Litho, Rubber, Fireman Rider, Masudaya, Box, 1960s, 5 x 12 In...	1265
Motorcycle, Mac 700 Daredevil, Rider, Tin Lithograph, Windup, Arnold, Germany, 1950s, 8 In. *illus*	570
Motorcycle, Police Officer, Siren, Tin Litho, Windup, Louis Marx, Pats Pendg., 1950s........*illus*	180
Motorcycle, Police Rider, Tin Litho, Unique Art Mfg. Co., Windup, 1930s, 8½ In.	230
Motorcycle, Police, Rollover, Clockwork, Tin Lithograph, Marx, 1930s, 8½ In.................*illus*	270
Motorcycle, Sidecar, Sunbeam, Tin Litho, Spoke Wheels, Marusan, Box, 1950s, 6 x 10 In.	1342
Motorcycle, Speed Boy 4, Delivery, Open Cart, Lights, Tin Litho, Marx, 1930s, 9½ In..............	390
Movie Viewer, Horrorscope, Plastic, 4 Monster Films, Hand Crank, Box, 1960s, 12 x 20 In.	1392
Musicians, Platform, Carved Figures, Play Music, March, Mechanical, c.1810, 8 x 5 In.	1482
Nesting Dolls, My Pet Shmoo, White Hard Plastic, Removable Top, 1948, 6 Piece.....................	190
Noah's Ark, House Boat, Hinged Roof, Wood, 26 Animal Pairs, 5 People, 1880s, 18 In.............	798
Noisemaker, Dancing Woman, Multicolor Tin Litho, Wood Handle, Twirls, 1930s, 5 In............	15
Omnibus, Clockwork Motor, Yellow, 2 White Horses, George Brown, 1860-70s, 13 In.................	9150
Paint Set, The Munsters, Stardust, Velvet Art By Numbers, Box, 1965, 11 x 15 In.	337

Toy, Stove, Marklin, Tin, Chrome Trim, Claw Feet, Pots, Coffeepot, Lids, c.1900, 18 In.
$672

Theriault's

Toy, Taxi, Black & White, Running Boards, Disc Wheels, Cast Iron, Hubley, 8½ In.
$443

Bertoia Auctions

Toy, Taxi, Yell-O-Taxi, Driver, Orange & Black, Windup, Tin Litho, Disc Wheels, 8½ In.
$236

Bertoia Auctions

Fisher-Price

Fisher-Price toys were made of wood from 1931 to 1950. Some plastic was used in the 1950s. By 1964 the toys were almost entirely plastic.

Toy, Tea Set, Mother, Children, Adam Buck Series, Ceramic, England, c.1825, 16 Piece
$556

Jeffrey S. Evans

Toy, Tea Set, Porcelain, Tete-A-Tete, Tray, Flowers, Scrolls, France, c.1875, 5½-In. Tray
$952

Theriault's

Toy, Train Accessory, Bing, Guard House, Water Pump, Semaphore, Bell, Tin Lithograph, 8 x 6 In.
$1,800

Bertoia Auctions

Parrot, On Stump, Squeaks, Flaps Wings, Multicolor, Germany, 5 In...............................*illus*	502
Pedal Car, Fire Truck, City Of Beverly Hills, Bell On Hood, c.1960, 17 x 41 x 15 In.	150
Pedal Car, Gendron Packard Six, Red & Black Paint, Early 1900s, 27 x 48 x 24 In.	7800
Pedal Car, Hydraulic Dump Truck, Metal, Vinyl Seat, Late 1900s, 20 x 39 In.	300
Pedal Car, International Harvester Farm Crawler, c.1960, 26 x 30 x 28 In..............................	1188
Pedal Car, Tractor, Ford 8000, Cast Metal, Wagon Pull, Late 1900s, 25 x 35 x 28 In.	250 to 406
Pedal Car, Tractor, McCormick Farmall, International Harvester, Eska, c.1980, 22 x 32 In...*illus*	344
Phonograph, Records, Mahogany Finish, Lift Lid, c.1910, 17 In.	855
Piano Player, Woman, Moves, Hand Crank, Plink-Plink Music, Germany, 5 In.	579
Pig Merchant, Man Walks, Strikes Pigs, Clockwork, Ferdinand Martin, France, c.1910, 7 In...*illus*	3540
Pistol Cane, Man From U.N.C.L.E., Aluminum, Fires Plastic Bullets, Card, 1966, 25 In.	2214
Play Set, Chemistry Outfit, Glass Vials, Canisters, Manuals, Metal Case, 1933, 15 x 25 In.	506
Play Set, Cher's Dressing Room, 2 Dolls, Outfits, Magic Mirror Cards, Box, 1976, 12 In.	115
Play Set, Man From U.N.C.L.E., Briefcase, Gun, Passport, I.D., Grenade, 1965, 11 x 15 In.........	4744
Play Set, Man From U.N.C.L.E., Walkie Talkie, Transmitter, Box, 1966, 8 x 12 In.....................	645
Play Set, Mysto Magic, Tricks & Supplies, Directions, Cardboard Box, 1910, 7 x 13 In.	1619
Play Set, Six Million Dollar Man, Headquarters, Filmstrip, Viewer, Box, 1977, 15 x 15 In.	222
Play Set, T. Corbett Space Academy, Tin Litho, Doors, Gate, Figures, Box, 1950s, 15 x 23 In......	369
Play Set, Zorro, Figures, Flag, Pole, Hitching Post, Palm Trees, Cave, Box, c.1958, 15 x 24 In. ...	253
Pop Eye Pete, Body Shakes, Eyes Pop In & Out, Tin Litho, Windup, Box, 1960s, 5 In.................	234
Powerful Katrinka, Pushes Wheelbarrow, Rider Jimmy, Tin Litho, Windup, 1923, 4 x 7 In.	638
Rabbit, On Wheels, Mohair, Felt, Amber Glass Eyes, Ribbon & Bell, Steiff, 8 In.	168
Railroad, Town, Paper Litho Mat, Cardboard Buildings, Locomotive, Parker Bros., Box, 1907, 15 In.	560
Ray Gun, Satellite Launcher, Tin Litho, Images, Rocket Shape, Friction, Japan, 1950s, 8 In.....	173
Rifle, Mirrorman Jet Launcher, Plastic, Telescopic Sight, Saucer Discs, Box, 1970s, 17 In.	230
Rifle, Sparking, Atomic, Astro Boy, Plastic Barrel, Tin Litho, Paint, Japan, 1960s, 18 In.	209
Robot, Big Loo Giant Moon, Light Bulb Eyes, Hands Open, Voice Box, Marx, 1963, 37 In.	2531
Robot, Combattra, Transforms, 5 Vehicles Or Space Tank, Godaikin, Box, 1982, 14 x 22 In.	1720
Robot, Daimos, Transforms Into Tranzer Vehicle, Swords, Fires Missiles, Box, 1984, 10 In.......	477
Robot, Grendizer, UFO Robot, Tin Lithograph, Plastic, Windup, Japan, Popy, 1970s, 9 In.........	221
Robot, Lost In Space, Motorized, Red & Blue, Plastic, Light-Up Chest, Remco, Box, 1966, 12 In.	385
Robot, Magne Robo Gakeen, Die Cast, Metal, Plastic, Japan, Window Box, 1976, 6¼ In............	772
Robot, Mazinga, Shogun Warriors, Plastic, Firing, Spaceship Brain Hand, Box, 1976, 24 In. ...	201
Robot, Sparky, Atomic Symbol, Piston Design, Antenna, Walks, Tin, Windup, c.1958, 8 In.	173
Robot, Sparky, Tin Lithograph, Walks, Eyes Light Up, Yoshiya, Box, 1950s, 7¾ In....................	230
Robot, Tetsujin 28, Gigantor, Metal, Missile Launcher, Carrying Case Box, 1982, 16 In............	3795
Robot, Thunder, Tin, Plastic, Moves, Arms Raise, Blinking, Light-Up, Guns, Box, 1957, 12 In. .	3922
Robot, Tin, Plastic, Walks Forward, Pistons & Lights, Mechanical, Box, c.1957, 13 In................	1267
Robot, UFO Grendizer, Spaceship, Die Cast Metal & Plastic, Popy, Japan, Box, 1976, 9 In........	682
Robot, Ultra Seven, Superhero, Tin Litho, Plastic, Windup, Bullmark, Japan, 1960s, 9 In.........	455
Rocket Ship, Kamen Rider, Pilot, Scarf, Tin Litho, Rolls, Sounds, Friction, Box, 1970s, 13 In..	1335
Rocket Ship, Space Captain, Pilot, Spins, Lights, Sounds, Metal, Plastic, Box, 1960s, 10 In.......	173
Rocket, Moon Traveler, Apollo-Z, Astronauts, Sounds, Plastic Cone, Tin Litho, Box, 1969, 12 In.	173
Rocking Horse, Platform, Wood, 34 x 44 In...	153
Salon Chair, Doll's, Faux Bamboo, Carved, Gilt, Spindles, Silk, c.1885, 11 In.	1083
Screen, Doll's, 3 Panels, Clock, Porcelain, Brass Scroll Frame, 1800s, 8 In.............................	855
Sewing Machine, Brass Frame, Mahogany, France, c.1885, 9 x 7 In.	2166
Sewing Machine, Metal, Brass Plaque, Singer Man'f. Co., Italy, c.1900, 6 In. ....*illus*	224
Sewing Machine, Muller, Metal, Windup, Lithograph Box, France, 4 In. ....*illus*	420
Sewing Machine, Tin, Stencils, Gold & Red Garland & Flowers, Box, c.1900, 7 In............*illus*	224
Shmoo, Utility Bag, Stuffed Figure, Vinyl, Zipper, Handle, Box, c.1948, 16½ x 24 In.	230
Skating Bears, Three Bears, Multicolor, T.P.S., Japan, 9¼ In..	366
Skyzel, Space Ironman, Firing Fists, Missiles, Removable Head, Metal, Box, 1976, 6 In............	185
Slate, Writing, Reeded Wood Frame, Zoar, Mid 1800s, 16 x 12 In...	180
Sled, Wood, Iron Runners & Red Paint, Ohio, c.1896, 36½ In..	281
Sled, Wood, Iron Runners, Red Paint, Flowers, 36 In...	165
Sled, Wood, Metal Edged Runners, Early 1900s, 62 x 14 In..	78
Sleigh, Wood, Lightning Scooter, Shaped Seat, Curved Blade, Upright Handle, 33 x 39 In........	95
Smitty Scooter, Comic Strip Office Boy, On Scooter, Tin Litho, Windup, Marx, c.1925, 8 In...*illus*	1140

Smokey Sam The Wild Fireman, Tin Litho, Plastic, Windup, Marx, Box, 1950, 5 ½ In...........	325
Space Pistol, Planet Gun, Plastic, Trigger Launcher, Saucers, Toho, Box, 1950s, 6 x 10 In......	539
Space Pistol, Tom Corbett Space Cadet, Tin Lithograph, Clicker, Marx, Box, 1950s, 10 In.......	362
Spaceship, Bio Dragon, Plastic Missiles, Doubles As Aircraft Carrier, Box, 1984, 14 In........	211
Spaceship, Captain Future, Metal, Plastic, Pilot, Firing Ports, Japan, Box, c.1978, 6 In..........	209
Spaceship, Explorer, Dome, Astronaut Moves, Lights, Tin Litho, Plastic, Box, 1960s, 5 x 8 In...	165
Spaceship, Jupiter, Tin Litho, Disc Shape, Plastic Dome, Sparks, Windup, Box, 1960s, 3 x 5 In.	115
Spaceship, Message From Space, Metal, Plastic, Missiles, Pilot, Box, 1978, 3 x 4 In..................	171
Spaceship, Space 1999, Space Eagle, Metal, Plastic, Pilots, Fires Missiles, Box, 1970s, 5 In.......	232
Spaceship, X8, Dome Cockpit, Spaceman, Blinks, Beeps, Tin Litho, Plastic, Box, 1960s, 8 In...	380
Spider-Man, Pink Scooter, Plastic, Friction, Cardboard Box, 1960s, 4 ¼ In.........................	3163
Spy Kit, Secret Sam, Briefcase, Plastic, Gun, Scope, Launcher, Sleeve, 1965, 12 x 16 In............	209
Station, Durchgang, Telegraph, Wartesaal, Doors, Roofs, Candles, Marklin, 17 ½ In........*illus*	3540
Stereo Viewer, Marvel Super Hereos, No. 103-T, Display Box, Kenner, 1966, 6 x 11 In..............	635
Stove, Doll's, Empire Metal Ware, Black Painted, 2 Pans, c.1930, 16 ½ In.	35
Stove, Marklin, Metal, Spirit Burner, 4 Pots, Lids, 2 Ladles, c.1925, 12 x 9 In.....................*illus*	358
Stove, Marklin, Tin, Chrome Trim, Claw Feet, Pots, Coffeepot, Lids, c.1900, 18 In.............*illus*	672
Stove, Parlor, Metal & Brass, Bulbous, Chimney, Door, 1904, 19 In..	1596
Submarine, Nautilus, 20,000 Leagues Under The Sea, Metal Periscope, Box, 1954, 10 In........	253
Tank, Missile Launcher, Track, Darts, Targets, Hard Plastic, Japan, Box, 1970s, 6 x 9 In...........	139
Tap Dancer, Fred Astaire, Jointed Metal Body, Celluloid, Dances, Windup, Box, 1940s, 7 In.	190
Taxi, Black & White, Running Boards, Disc Wheels, Cast Iron, Hubley, 8 ½ In.................*illus*	443
Taxi, Yell-O-Taxi, Driver, Orange & Black, Windup, Tin Litho, Disc Wheels, 8 ½ In. ....*illus*	236
Tea Party, Moving Dolls On Platform, Music, Flower Arbor, Windup, c.1890, 12 x 11 In............	3876
Tea Set, Mother, Children, Adam Buck Series, Ceramic, England, c.1825, 16 Piece............*illus*	556
Tea Set, Porcelain De Paris, Blue, Red Flowers, Gold Trim, c.1860, 15 Piece, Fitted Box	399
Tea Set, Porcelain, Tete-A-Tete, Tray, Flowers, Scrolls, France, c.1875, 5 ½-In. Tray..........*illus*	952
Tea Set, Silver, Fluted, Shaped Handles, Oval Tray, Ball Feet, c.1885, 4-In. Tray, 5 Piece	912
Teddy Bears are also listed in the Teddy Bear category.	
Telephone, Flintstones, Hard Vinyl, Animal Horn Receiver, Relief Images, c.1962, 5 In.	290
Toonerville Trolley, Cracker Jack, Tin Lithograph, Penny Toy, 1 ¾ In.	201
Tractor, John Deere, Iron, Fixed Iron Wheels, Late 1900s, 7 x 12 In.	30
Tractor, John Deere, Iron, Movable Axles, Rubber Wheels, Late 1900s, 15 x 16 In.	125
Train Accessory, Bing, Guard House, Water Pump, Semaphore, Bell, Tin Lithograph, 8 x 6 In...*illus*	1800
Train Accessory, Lionel, Corner Tunnel, Mountain, Trees, Box	120
Train Accessory, Marklin, Central Station, Painted, English Signs, Etched Glass, 13 x 9 In.*illus*	6600
Train Accessory, Marklin, Railway Crossing, Guard House, Halt Sign, 11 x 9 In. ....*illus*	1440
Train Accessory, Marklin, Station, Passenger, Walkway, Windows, 1920s, 14 In. ....*illus*	472
Train Car, Buddy L, Clam Shovel, Pressed Steel, Boiler, 1920s, 18 In..................................*illus*	3245
Train Car, Cor-Cor, Pullman, Corcoran Mfg., Early 1900s, 4 Piece..	480
Train Car, Lionel, 217, Caboose, Orange, Red..	300
Train Car, Lionel, 219, Crane, Green, Cream, Red Roof, Standard Gauge	335
Train Car, Lionel, 219, Crane, Green, Yellow, Red Roof, Standard Gauge	244
Train Car, Lionel, 318, Locomotive, Gray, Strap Headlights, Box...	152
Train Car, Locomotive, Passenger, Santa Fe, Steel Gray, Red, Yellow, O Gauge, 13 In.	130
Train Car, Locomotive, Steam, Wood, Metal Wheels, 13 ½ x 26 In.	120
Train Car, Marklin, Locomotive, Model 01, Tender, Steam, O Gauge, Tin, c.1938, 20 In.	1638
Train Car, Marklin, PRR Boxcar, Simulated Wood, Sliding Doors, O Gauge, 7 ½ In. ....*illus*	531
Train Car, Marklin, Summer Car, Painted Curtains On Windows, O Gauge, 5 In..............*illus*	3600
Train Set, Obake No Q-Taro, Locomotive, Cars, Tin Litho, Images, Japan, Box, 1960s, 9 In.......	704
Train, Leo Express, Ultraman, Track, Tin Litho, Wire, Revolving Ship, Box, c.1975, 6 x 6 In.....	115
Transformer, Battle Fortress, Die Cast, Plastic, Matchbox Robotech, Box, 1985, 9 x 17 In.	215
Travelchiks, Train Car, 4 Chickens, Multicolored, Tin Litho, Windup, Box, 1920s, 5 x 8 In.	460
Tricycle, Figural Horse, Leather Saddle, Wood & Metal Spokes, 1890s, 22 x 35 In.	480
Truck, Aerial Ladder, Driver, Red, Keystone, 1930s, 24 In..	175
Truck, Army, Searchlight, Driver, Passenger, Battery Operated, Hausser, Germany, 10 In...*illus*	270
Truck, Cab, Open Slatted Trailer, Blue Paint, Cast Iron, 1900s, 9 x 4 In.	90
Truck, Dump, Blue Cab, Red Bucket, Painted Cast Iron, 1900s, 7 x 3 In.	225
Truck, Heinz, Pressed Steel, Decals, Rubber Tires, Electric Lights, Metalcraft, 12 In.........*illus*	177

Toy, Train Accessory, Marklin, Central Station, Painted, English Signs, Etched Glass, 13 x 9 In.
$6,600

Toy, Train Accessory, Marklin, Railway Crossing, Guard House, Halt Sign, 11 x 9 In.
$1,440

Toy, Train Accessory, Marklin, Station, Passenger, Walkway, Windows, 1920s, 14 In.
$472

TIP
When repairing a table or toy take digital pictures at each step. Even photograph the screws and nails so you can put everything back in the same place. The photos in reverse order are a step-by-step guide to what to do.

T

503

Truck, Hunter, Lion & Hunter, Painted Tin, Plastic, Cage, Litho Lion, Friction, Box, 1950s, 9 In.	127
Truck, Sheffield Farms, Red, Pressed Steel, Sealect Milk, 6¾ x 22½ x 5⅝ In.	920
Truck, Stake, Pressed Steel, Rubber Tires, Red, Wyandotte, 6½ In.	135
Truck, Straddle, Die Cast Metal, Rubber Tires, Wood Lumber, Hyster, Box, c.1955, 6 In.	390
Truck, Tanker, Gasoline, Cast Iron, Paint, Dispensing Faucets, Orange, A.C. Williams, 5 In.	158
Truck, Tanker, Gasoline, Pressed Steel, Red, Louis Marx & Co., Box, 3 x 14 In.	690
Truck, Tow, Mack, Red, Nickel Lever & Driver, Disc Wheel, Iron, Arcade, c.1930, 12½ In. *illus*	1416
Trunk, Doll's, Brass, Wood, Interior Divided Tray, Lock Plate, c.1880, 10 In.	94
Turkey, Tan & Black Mohair, Tags, Steiff, 30 x 30 In.	5100
Turkey, Tin, Painted, Windup, Gunthermann, 4½ In.	825
Van, CBS-TV, Navy, White Stripe, Tin Litho, Camera, Light, Marusan, Japan, 9½ In.	854
Wagon, Transfer, Cast Iron, Ives Manufacturing Co., c.1885, 7 In.	263
Wagon, Wood, Green Paint, Spoke Wheels, Acme Wagon Co., 1885, 27 x 42 In.	1005
Wagon, Wood, Red Trim, Spoke Wheels, Auto Wheel Coaster, Upright Handle, 34 In.	225
Washstand, Doll's, Wood, Wicker Frame, White Paint, Oval Ceramic Basin, c.1950, 24 In.	59
Wheelbarrow, Green, Black, c.1880, 8¾ In.	82
Wheelbarrow, Wood, Paint, Wire Banded Spoke Wheel, Curved Handles, 39 In.	142
Zeppelin, Macon, Propeller, 15½ In.	1320
Zeppelin, Yellow, Windup, 10 In.	390

TRAMP ART is a form of folk art made since the Civil War. It is usually made from chip-carved cigar boxes. Examples range from small boxes and picture frames to full-sized pieces of furniture.

Birdcage, Wood, Wire, House Shape, 5 Doors, Relief Carved, Green Paint, 35 In. *illus*	615
Box, Heart Keyhole, Red Embroidery, Signed Zum Andenken, 1913, 8¼ x 9 In.	179
Box, Lid, Pedestal, 1800s, 8 x 10½ x 7½ In. *illus*	95
Box, Lift Top, Geometric Chi Carving, 5¼ x 11 In.	96
Box, Lift Top, Horseshoe Mount, Double Pedestal Foot, 18 x 11¼ In.	672
Box, Lift Top, Mirror, Diamonds, Red Velvet Trim, 6¼ x 13½ In.	70
Box, Lift Top, Tiered Geometric Carvings, 1905, 7¼ x 12¾ In.	60
Box, Pedestal, Triangular Shapes, Velvet Interior, c.1890, 7 x 10 In.	680
Box, Ridges, Footed, 8 x 13 In.	563
Box, Wood, Tooled, 2 Geometric Shape Tiers, Carved Head Finial, c.1900, 15 x 9 In.	615
Bureau, Wood, Carved Panels, Notched, Layered, 4 Drawers, Mirror, 56 x 28 In.	984
Cabinet, Carved Wood, Gallery Top, Mirrored Cabinet Doors, 1921, 68 x 42 In.	5228
Cabinet, Starburst Crest, 3 Sections, Cathedral Architecture, 16½ x 16 In.	780
Chest, 3 Story Mill, Hinge, Platform Base, 12 x 12 In. *illus*	732
Chest, 4 Drawers, Mirror, c.1925, 30¼ x 17½ In.	137
Chest, Mirror, Green X, Hinged Lid, 17 x 10 In.	272
Church, Wood, Gothic Style, Arched, Side Steeple, Fleur-De-Lis Glass, Plinth Base, 24 In.	584
Cupboard, Hanging, Raised Pyramids & Rectangles, Chipwork, Painted, 20 x 16 In.	148
Diorama, Tugboat, Carved Maple, Pebbles, Chip-Carved Frame, 1910, 9 x 15 In.	1067
Frame, Crown Of Thorns, Extended Corners, 24¼ In.	240
Frame, Wood, 15 Openings, Presidents, Generals, Made By Pen Knife, W. Harris, 34 In.	800
Jewelry Box, Cigar Box Wood, Stepped Shape, c.1910, 10 x 11½ In.	55
Lamp, 2-Light, Clock, Heart, 1930s, 13½ x 9 In.	360
Mirror, Chip Carved, Circles, Hearts, Stars, Crescents, 34 x 37 In.	1260
Mirror, Shaped Crest, Carved Geometrics, Heart Piercing, Scalloped Edges, 31 In.	1169
Picture Frame, Diamonds At Corners, 23½ x 27½ In.	125
Picture Frame, Diamonds, 13 x 17 In.	94
Picture Frame, Repeating Stars, c.1925, 16 In.	125
Picture Frame, Repeating Stepped Rectangles, 13 x 11 In. *illus*	96
Sewing Box, Cigar Box Wood, Tax Stamps, Pincushion Top, Drawer, Pedestal, 9 x 12 In.	400
Sewing Box, Wood, Hinged Lid, Tacks, Heart Pincushion, Velvet Lined, 7 x 13 In.	62
Shelf, Corner, Wood, Scrollwork Sides, Applied Heart, Star, Bird, 23½ In. *illus*	738
Shrine, Green Trim, Gold Highlights, Triple Peaked Roof, 25½ x 10 In.	108
Tower, 5 Sections, Wood, Tooled Molding, Yellow Paint, Red Lens In Top, c.1910, 57 In. *illus*	984
Tower, Wood, Yellow Paint, 5 Open Tiers, Pitched Roof, Urn Finial, c.1915, 57 x 11 In.	984
Trinket Box, Raised Geometrics, Chip Work, Purple Felt Lining, 7 x 13 x 11 In.	189
Vanity, Carved, Decoupage, Cutout Crest, Slant Mirror, 4 Drawers, Gilt, 40 x 30 In.	1599

TIP

Remove the batteries from a stored toy.

Toy, Train Car, Buddy L, Clam Shovel, Pressed Steel, Boiler, 1920s, 18 In. $3,245

Bertoia Auctions

Toy, Train Car, Marklin, PRR Boxcar, Simulated Wood, Sliding Doors, O Gauge, 7½ In. $531

Bertoia Auctions

Toy, Train Car, Marklin, Summer Car, Painted Curtains On Windows, O Gauge, 5 In. $3,600

Bertoia Auctions

Rules for Dating Most Cars by the Wheels

Before World War II, toy car wheels were open-spoked metal wheels, solid metal disc wheels, solid metal disc wheels with embossed spokes, white rubber tires with metal rims, or solid white rubber tires mounted directly on the axles. The rule is that white rubber tires were used before World War II, black tires after. Since the 1960s, black plastic wheels have been used.

T

Toy, Truck, Army, Searchlight, Driver, Passenger, Battery Operated, Hausser, Germany, 10 In.
$270

Bertoia Auctions

Toy, Truck, Heinz, Pressed Steel, Decals, Rubber Tires, Electric Lights, Metalcraft, 12 In.
$177

Bertoia Auctions

Toy, Truck, Tow, Mack, Red, Nickel Lever & Driver, Disc Wheel, Iron, Arcade, c.1930, 12 ½ In.
$1,416

Bertoia Auctions

Tramp Art, Birdcage, Wood, Wire, House Shape, 5 Doors, Relief Carved, Green Paint, 35 In.
$615

Skinner, Inc.

Tramp Art, Box, Lid, Pedestal, 1800s, 8 x 10 ½ x 7 ½ In.
$95

Hess Auction Group

Tramp Art, Chest, 3 Story Mill, Hinge, Platform Base, 12 x 12 In.
$732

Hess Auction Group

T

TIP
If your heavy cast-iron toy has rubber tires, display it on a partial stand so there is no pressure on the tires.

Tramp Art, Picture Frame, Repeating Stepped Rectangles, 13 x 11 In. $96

Milestone Auctions

Tramp Art, Shelf, Corner, Wood, Scrollwork Sides, Applied Heart, Star, Bird, 23 ½ In. $738

Skinner, Inc.

Tramp Art, Tower, 5 Sections, Wood, Tooled Molding, Yellow Paint, Red Lens In Top, c.1910, 57 In. $984

Skinner, Inc.

Trap, Fish, Basketry, Fish Shape, Split Oak, Woven, E. Brown, South Carolina, 62 In. $420

Brunk Auctions

Trench Art, Stein, Brass, Pattern, Wood Handle, Propeller Design, 10 ½ In. $276

The Stein Auction Company

Trivet, Brass, Hearts, House, Wheel, Spade Shaped, 9 ½ In. $18

Ruby Lane

Trunk, E. Goyard, Steamer, Canvas, V Monogram, Brass, Inscribed, Paris, c.1915, 23 x 43 In. $7,995

Skinner, Inc.

Trunk, Louis Vuitton, Wardrobe, Canvas, 6 Drawers, Hangers, Handles, c.1937, 26 x 44 In. $10,937

New Orleans Auction Galleries

Typewriter, Hammond, No. 1, 2-Row Split Piano Keyboard, Mahogany Cover, 1880 $2,140

Auction Team Breker

TRAPS for animals may be handmade. One of the most unusual is the mousetrap made so that when the mouse entered the trap, it was hit on the head with a mallet. Other traps were commercially manufactured and often are marked with the name of the manufacturer. Many traps were designed to be as humane as possible, and they would trap the live animal so it could be released in the woods.

Fish, Basketry, Fish Shape, Split Oak, Woven, E. Brown, South Carolina, 62 In. ....*illus*	420
Gun, Gopher, Moles, Log, Bait Hook, 8½ x 6¾ In.	374
Minnow, Glass, Wire, 10 In.	93
Squirrel, Cage, House Shape, Steeple & Flag, Tin, 1800s, 28 x 27 In.	443

TREEN, *see Wooden category.*

TRENCH ART is a form of folk art made by soldiers. Metal casings from bullets and mortar shells were cut and decorated to form useful objects, such as vases.

Desk Set, Shell Casing, Airplane Shapes, World War II, 11½ x 11¼ In.	318
Stein, Brass, Pattern, Wood Handle, Propeller Design, 10½ In. ....*illus*	276
Vase, Art Nouveau, Repousse, Flowers, 1917, 3 Piece.	200
Vase, Brass, Scalloped Neck, Pokerwork, Repousse Leaf, 13¾ x 3⅜ In., Pair	100
Vase, Brass, Scalloped Rims, Crimped Sides, 13⅛ x 3⅜ In., Pair	100
Vase, Flared, Pierced Rim, Souvenir De La Campagne, 1914-15, 11 x 6 In., Pair	175
Vase, Rooster, Crushing German Eagle, 1918, 11½ In.	115

TRIVETS are now used to hold hot dishes. Most trivets of the late nineteenth and early twentieth centuries were made to hold hot irons. Iron or brass reproductions are being made of many of the old styles.

Aluminum, Open Design, Tab Feet, Elpo, Japan, 1960s, 9 x 6 In.	6
Brass, 3-Footed, 1800s, 11¾ x 14½ In.	49
Brass, Hearts, House, Wheel, Spade Shaped, 9½ In. ....*illus*	18
Brass, Iron, 3-Footed, U-Shape Stretcher, 1800s, 11½ x 15 In.	58
Brass, Ships, Open Cut Sails, Waves, 7¼ In.	12
Brass, Virginia Metalcrafters, Tassel & Grain, c.1930, 8¾ x 5 In.	30
Cast Iron, Enameled, White, Brown, Green, Pheasants In Flight, Handle, c.1950, 6 In.	48
Iron, 3-Leaf Clover Shape, Tall Round Legs, Penny Feet, c.1800, 5 x 10 In.	150
Iron, Circle, Revolving, 25¼ In.	146
Iron, Hanging, Rectangular, 18 x 12 In.	146
Iron, Heart Shape, 3-Footed, 6½ In.	321
Iron, Round, Footed, 18½ In.	263
Lucite & Abalone Shell, Clear Ball Feet, USA, 6½ In.	12
Pottery, Fleur-De-Lis, Frankoma, 6 x 6 In.	29
Pottery, Hermosa Tea Tile, Dutch Woman, Gladding McBean, Octagonal, 6¼ In.	50
Pottery, Royal Ivory, Mexico Pattern, Adams, England, c.1900, 7¼ In.	32
Pottery, Shelley China, Daisy Design, Queen Anne Shape, c.1928, 7 x 6 In.	48
Pottery, Tile, Hen, Checkered Border, Oak Frame, 9 x 9 In.	15
Silverplate, Teapot Shape, Godinger, c.1990	10

TRUNKS of many types were made. The nineteenth-century sea chest was often handmade of unpainted wood. Brass-fitted camphorwood chests were brought back from the Orient. Leather-covered trunks were popular from the late eighteenth to mid-nineteenth centuries. By 1895, trunks were covered with canvas or decorated sheet metal. Embossed metal coverings were used from 1870 to 1910. By 1925, trunks were covered with vulcanized fiber or undecorated metal. Suitcases are listed here.

Campaign, Camphorwood, Brass, Hinged Lid, Drop Handles, 1800s, 16 x 34¾ In.	416
Camphorwood, Blue, Leather, Flowers, 12¼ x 15½ In.	360
Camphorwood, Brassbound Bail Handles, Cut Corners, 11¾ In.	132
Camphorwood, Red, Leather, Flowers, 25½ x 12¾ In.	360

Typewriter, Smith, Premier No. 1, Upstroke, Type Cleaning Brush, 1889
$631

Auction Team Breker

Typewriter Tin, Hercules Brand, M.S. Apter, Red, White, Pink, Stylized Border, 2½ In.
$15

Ruby Lane

Umbrella, Masters Golf Logo, North America Silhouette, Foldout Seat, Green, White
$125

Ruby Lane

TIP
Store parasols and umbrellas closed.

Union Porcelain Works, Oyster Plate, 4 Wells, Clamshell Shape, Black, Multicolor, 8½ In.
$570

Strawser Auction Group

Union Porcelain Works, Oyster Plate, 6 Wells, Seaweed, Light Blue, Round, c.1879, 9½ In.
$625

Ruby Lane

University City, Vase, Brown Crystalline Glaze, Aztec Style Feet, Porcelain, A. Robineau, 1910, 5¾ In.
$46,875

Rago Arts and Auction Center

TIP

If you are storing a large closed container like a trunk for a long time, put a piece of charcoal in it to absorb odors.

Dome Top, Hide Covered, Black Leather Edges, Brass Tacks, c.1825, 8 x 15 In.	308
Dome Top, Hinged, Handles, Carved Apron, Cabriole Feet, Flowers, 1700s, 30 x 51 In.	625
Dome Top, Oak, c.1975, 26½ x 38½ In.	92
Dome Top, Pine, Painted, Flowers, Bands, Wavy Lines, Red, Yellow, Green, 13 x 24 In.	24600
Dome Top, Pine, Sponge Painted, Repeating Fan Designs, Blue, Red Brown, 14 x 32 In.	1968
Dome Top, Softwood, Paint Design, Crisscross Banding, Metal Latch, c.1830, 8 x 18 In.	1298
Dome Top, Walnut, Molded Banding, Brass Nail, 19 x 41¾ In.	595
E. Goyard, Steamer, Canvas, V Monogram, Brass, Inscribed, Paris, c.1915, 23 x 43 In......*illus*	7995
James Boyd & Sons, Leather, Nailhead Trim, Monogram, Label, c.1850, 13 x 36 x 18 In.	550
Jones Bros. & Co., Steel, Ribbed Lid, Iron Ball Handles, Yellow, 19½ x 27½ In.	480
Leather, Chinese Export, Bronze Mount, Green, 15½ x 36¼ In.	600
Leather, Handles, Latches, 23 x 18½ In., Pair	812
Leather, Studded, Black, 24¾ x 42½ In.	1875
Louis Vuitton, Canvas, Monogram, Leather Handles, Early 1900s, 16 x 45 x 22 In.	2944
Louis Vuitton, Case, Canvas, Monogram, Leather, Lock, Handle, c.1920, 13 x 24 In.	1476
Louis Vuitton, Leather, Canvas, Fabric Lined, Monogram, 23 x 20½ In.	8540
Louis Vuitton, Monogram, Wood, Latch, Handles, 23 x 40 In.	7500
Louis Vuitton, Shoe, Suitcase, 9 x 27 In.	1250
Louis Vuitton, Suitcase, 8½ x 32 In.	1187
Louis Vuitton, Suitcase, Canvas, Leather & Brass Bound, Early 1900s, 9¼ x 24 x 7 In.	1107
Louis Vuitton, Suitcase, Soft-Sided, Leather, 16 x 23 In.	246
Louis Vuitton, Suitcase, Soft-Sided, Leather, 18 x 27 In.	215
Louis Vuitton, Suitcase, Soft-Sided, Leather, 21 x 31 In.	215
Louis Vuitton, Wardrobe, Canvas, 6 Drawers, Hangers, Handles, c.1937, 26 x 44 In.......*illus*	10937
Louis Vuitton, Yellow Canvas, Wood Slats, Brass Trim, Rivets, Lock, c.1935, 22 x 44 In.	5500
Marine, Camphorwood, Leather, Black, Brass Banding, Chinese, 1800s, 16 In.	375
Officer's, Camphorwood, China Trade, Lock, Early 1800s, 19 x 41 In.	2500
Pine, Front Panel, 3 Arches, Rectangular, 47¼ In.	250
Steamer, Wood, Staves, Iron, 29 x 18 In.	81
Valise, Leather, Brown, Round, Brass Tacks, Iron Lock, 1816, 22 x 11½ In.	360
Wood, Brass Inlay, Brass Joining Straps, 21 x 33¾ In.	118
Wood, Drawer, Lift Top, 16¼ x 36 In.	188
Wood, Iron Corner Mounts & Front Lock, Side Handles, Silk Lined, Key, 1900s, 15 x 8 In.	119
Wood, Shellac, Latches, Line Drawing, Japan, 15 x 25 In.	60

TYPEWRITER collectors divide typewriters into two main classifications: the index machine, which has a pointer and a dial for letter selection, and the keyboard machine, most commonly seen today. The first successful typewriter was made by Sholes and Glidden in 1874.

Anderson & Sorenson, Braille, Ribbonless, Metal Case, Base, 1950s, 6 x 15 In.	455
Blickensderfer, No. 6, Aluminum, Featherweight, 1893	491
Columbia, No. 2, Large Typewheel, C. Spiro, 1884	4767
Corona, Model 3, Portable, Folding, Case, c.1920, 11 x 10 x 4 In.	190
Draper, Chicago, Munson, Wood Case, c.1898	1402
Empire, Portable, Wood Base, Canada, c.1892, 11 x 15 x 7 In.	295
Hammond Multiplex Universal, Folding Keyboard, c.1913	145
Hammond, No. 1, 2-Row Split Piano Keyboard, Mahogany Cover, 1880......*illus*	2140
Olivetti, Lettera, 32, Blue	150
Pittsburg, Visible, No. 10, Interchangeable Typebar, 2 Levers, 1902	619
Polyphone Musikwerke, Polygraph, Art Nouveau Design, Tin Cover, Germany, c.1905	7852
Remington, Model 17, Rubber Keys, Rubber Cover, 15 x 14½ x 9 In.	119
Royal Quiet De Luxe Portable, Case, c.1950, 13 x 12 x 6 In.	150
Royal Standard, No. 1, Black, Gold, c.1911, 14¾ x 7⅜ x 14 In.	1580
Smith, Premier No. 1, Upstroke, Type Cleaning Brush, 1889 ......*illus*	631
Smith-Corona, Portable, Model 4, 1920s	225
Smith-Corona, Skyriter, Portable, Case, c.1950, 10 x 11 x 2 In.	45
Smith-Corona, Super Speed, 1930s, 16 x 10½ In.	104
Underwood, Portable, Hunter Green, Black Case, 12 x 12 x 6 In.	350

TYPEWRITER RIBBON TINS are now being collected. The lithographed tin containers have been used since the 1870s. Most popular with collectors are tins with pictorial graphics.

Bellaire, Burroughs Corp., White, Gold & Black Design, 2⅝ In.	10
Carter's Stylewriter, Green, White Wreath, 2⁹⁄₁₆ x 15 x 16 In.	15
Elk, Silhouette, Yellow, Miller Bryant Co., 2½ In.	16
Gibraltar Brand, Rock, Sunset, 2½ In.	42
Hercules Brand, M.S. Apter, Red, White, Pink, Stylized Border, 2½ In.............*illus*	15
Kee Lox, Dri Kleen, Remington 17-J, 2½ x ¾ In.	12
Oriental Motif, Codo Mfg. Bonsai Trees, Butterfly, 2⁹⁄₁₆ In.	20
Park Avenue, Roytype, Silk Ribbon, Dark Blue, Silver, 2½ In. Diam.	15
Perm-O-Rite, Old Dutch Carbon & Ribbon Co., Red, Blue, White, 2¼ Diam.	10
Preferred, The Aristocrat, Baby Blue, Crest, Slip On Lid, 2½ In.	19
Silver Medal, Silver, Blue, Hand Holding Torch, Stenno Ribbon Co., 2½ In.	12
Star Brand, F.S. Webster Co., Hinged, Geometric Design, Black, Gold, 2 x 2 In.	24
Thorobred, Underwood Corp., 2½ In.	14

UHL POTTERY was made in Evansville, Indiana, in 1854. The pottery moved to Huntingburg, Indiana, in 1908. Stoneware and glazed pottery were made until the mid-1940s.

Cookie Jar, Light Blue, White Flowers, 8½ In.	60
Cookie Jar, Red, White Flowers, 8½ In.	55
Crock, Cobalt Blue, Huntingburg Indiana Corn Wares, 3 Gal., 13½ x 9½ In.	108
Jug, Foil Liquor Sticker, Gallo California Sherry, Turquoise, 3 In.	50
Jug, Tapered Neck, Flush Handle, High Gloss Rose, 3⅞ In.	25

UMBRELLA collectors like rain or shine. The first known umbrella was owned by King Louis XIII of France in 1637. The earliest umbrellas were sunshades, not designed to be used in the rain. The umbrella was embellished and redesigned many times. In 1852, the fluted steel rib style was developed and it has remained the most useful style.

Advertising, Peter Max Funbrella, Metal Shaft, Right Guard Promo, 1970s, 35 In.	143
Advertising, Red, White, Alternating Panels, Blankets, Horses, 41 In.	369
Handle, Mother-Of-Pearl, Antique Gold, Monogram AMC	61
Horn Handle, Black, Gold Collar, S. Fox, Paragon, 36½ In.	86
Masters Golf Logo, North America Silhouette, Foldout Seat, Green, White........*illus*	125
Silver Handle, Gorham, Snake, Salamander, Jeweled Eyes, 1890, 35 In.	522

UNION PORCELAIN WORKS was originally William Boch & Brothers, located in Greenpoint, New York. Thomas C. Smith bought the company in 1861 and renamed it Union Porcelain Works. The company went through a series of ownership changes and finally closed about 1922. The company made a fine quality white porcelain that was often decorated in clear, bright colors. Don't confuse this company with its competitor, Charles Cartlidge and Company, also in Greenpoint.

Oyster Plate, 4 Wells, Clamshell Shape, Black, Multicolor, 8½ In.........*illus*	570
Oyster Plate, 6 Wells, Gold Rim, Multicolor, 9½ In.	393
Oyster Plate, 6 Wells, Seaweed, Light Blue, Round, c.1879, 9½ In.........*illus*	625
Oyster Plate, 6 Wells, Shell, Crab, Green, Brown, Light Green Rim, 9½ In.	246
Oyster Plate, 6 Wells, Shell, Seaweed, Frog, 10 In.	307
Soap Dish, White, Green Transfer Emblem, Oval, Marked, c.1905, 4 x 5 In.	25
Water Cooler, Light Green, Red & Yellow Decoration, 17¼ In.	358

UNIVERSITY CITY POTTERY, of University, Missouri, worked from 1909 to 1915. Well-known artists, including Taxile Doat, Adelaide Alsop Robineau, and Frederick Hurten Rhead, worked there.

Vase, Brown Crystalline Glaze, Aztec Style Feet, Porcelain, A. Robineau, 1910, 5¾ In.........*illus*	46875
Vase, Brown Crystalline Glaze, White Speckle Shading, Tapered, c.1910, 7 In.	6250
Vase, Carved, Brown, Tan, Crystalline Drip, Smokestack, c.1905, 7 In.	32500

University City, Vase, Gourd Shape, Ivory, Green, Blue, Crystalline Drip Glaze, T. Doat, 1913, 8½ In.
$33,750

Rago Arts and Auction Center

TIP

A vase that has been drilled for a lamp, even if the hole for the wiring is original, is worth 30% to 50% of the value of the same vase without a hole.

University City, Vase, Gourd Shape, Lumpy Surface, Crystalline Glaze, Porcelain, 1913, 7½ In.
$21,250

Rago Arts and Auction Center

U V

UNIVERSITY CITY

University City, Vase, Russet Crystalline Glaze, Porcelain, A. Robineau, 1910, 6 ¼ In.
$11,875

Rago Arts and Auction Center

Van Briggle, Candlestick, Pottery, Tulip, Mulberry, 1920-40, 3 ½ x 3 In.
$40

Ruby Lane

Van Briggle, Vase, Flowers, Purple & Green Glaze, Incised, 1905, 7 x 3 In.
$313

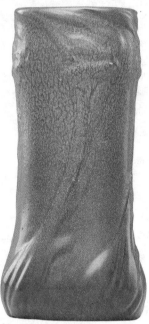

Rago Arts and Auction Center

Van Briggle, Vase, Persian Rose, Tulip, Pink, Purple Highlights, 1940-60, 3 ½ x 2 ¾ In.
$60

Ruby Lane

Vaseline Glass, Pitcher, Queen Pattern, 8 ¾ x 5 ½ In.
$42

Martin Auction Co.

Vernon Kilns, Organdie, Plate, Yellow, Brown, Cream Ground, 13 ¾ In
$28

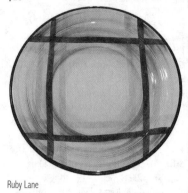

Ruby Lane

Villeroy & Boch, Tray, Dresden, 1888, 14 x 22 ½ In.
$1,380

The Stein Auction Company

Volkmar, Tile, Windmill, Squeezebag Decoration, Frame, Incised HJ, 1915, 7 ¾ In.
$1,063

Rago Arts and Auction Center

Vaseline Glass
Vaseline glass was made using natural uranium until World War II broke out and uranium was needed for military purposes. Depleted uranium has been used since 1959.

U
V

Vase, Celadon, Peach, Crystalline Glaze, Spherical, Pierced Base, c.1910, 5 In.		8750
Vase, Gourd Shape, Green Crystalline Glaze, Green, Incised, 1913, 8 x 3 In.	*illus*	33750
Vase, Gourd Shape, Lumpy Surface, Crystalline Glaze, Porcelain, 1913, 7½ In.	*illus*	21250
Vase, Moss Green, Ivory, Crystalline Glaze, Streaked, Cylindrical, 1910, 8 In.		11875
Vase, Mottled Green & Brown, Crystalline Glaze, Bottle Shape, c.1912, 8 In.		9375
Vase, Opalescent White, Stick Neck, Flared Rim, Pierced Stand, c.1910, 4 In.		10625
Vase, Russet Crystalline Glaze, Porcelain, A. Robineau, 1910, 6¼ In.	*illus*	11875

UNIVERSITY OF NORTH DAKOTA, *see North Dakota School of Mines category.*

VAL ST. LAMBERT Cristalleries of Belgium was founded by Messieurs Kemlin and Lelievre in 1825. The company is still in operation. All types of table glassware and decorative glassware have been made. Pieces are often decorated with cut designs.

Vase, Acid Cut, Flowers, Belgium, 11½ x 4½ In.		1098
Vase, Brass, Glass, Copper, Gustave Serrurier-Bovy, Belgium, c.1904, 16 x 6¼ In.		8750

VALLERYSTHAL GLASSWORKS was founded in 1836 in Lorraine, France. In 1854, the firm became Klenglin et Cie. It made table and decorative glass, opaline, cameo, and art glass. A line of covered, pressed glass animal dishes was made in the nineteenth century. The firm is still working.

Box, Squirrel On Acorn, White Opaque, 6 x 5 x 3 In.	225
Candlestick, Diving Dolphin & Snake, Cattails, Lily Pad, 9 In.	125
Candy Dish, Lid, Pineapple Shape, Blue Milk Glass, Scrolled Leaf Feet, 7½ In.	42
Dish, Lid, Fish Shape, Blue Milk Glass, 7½ In.	230
Vase, Globular, Green, Frosted Flower Heads, 6½ In.	325

VAN BRIGGLE POTTERY was started by Artus Van Briggle in Colorado Springs, Colorado, after 1901. Van Briggle had been a decorator at Rookwood Pottery of Cincinnati, Ohio. He died in 1904 and his wife took over managing the pottery. One of the employees, Kenneth Stevenson, took over the company in 1969. He died in 1990 and his wife, Bertha, and son, Craig, ran the pottery. She died in 2010. Craig, who is the chief designer, continues to run the pottery. Some of the old pieces are still being made and new designs are also being made. The wares usually have modeled relief decorations and a soft, matte glaze.

Ashtray, Rose, 1940s, 7 In.		40
Basket, Handled, Green, Brown, Glaze, 1920s, 3 In.		70
Bowl, Flower Frogs, Dark Over Light Blue, c.1915, 1⅞ x 8⅛ In.		115
Bowl, Gold, Glaze, Scalloped Rim, 1956, 3 In.		75
Candlestick, Pottery, Tulip, Mulberry, 1920-40, 3½ x 3 In.	*illus*	40
Figurine, Shell Maiden, Teal, Seated, Holding Lap-Size Shell, 7¾ x 6¼ In.		182
Tile, Tree In Landscape, Green Grass, Blue Sky, Square, Wood Frame, 12½ In.		3375
Urn, Mulberry Glaze, Incised, Leaves, Spear Stems, Handles, Flared Rim, 1917, 11 In.		531
Vase, Daisies, Celadon Shaded To Pink Glaze, Tapered, 6 In.		2500
Vase, Dos Cabezas, Purple Matte Glaze, Draping, 1917, 7½ x 5 In.		3172
Vase, Embossed Flowers, Mulberry Glaze, Black, Beaker, Swollen Collar, 21 In.		189
Vase, Flower, Molded Brown Glaze, Squat, Swollen Stick Neck, c.1920, 8 In.		201
Vase, Flowers, Green Matte Glaze, 1904, 3½ x 4½ In.		813
Vase, Flowers, Purple & Green Glaze, Incised, 1905, 7 x 3 In.	*illus*	313
Vase, Leaves, Leathery Green Glaze, Swollen Shoulder, Tapered, 1905, 5 In.		2125
Vase, Lorelei, Blue, Woman's Head, Arms At Rim, Hair Flows To Base, 1960s, 10¾ In.		312
Vase, Lorelei, Turquoise, 1910s, 7½ In.		795
Vase, Ombre Green To Brown, Tapered, 11 x 13½ In.		1200
Vase, Persian Rose, Tulip, Pink, Purple Highlights, 1940-60, 3½ x 2¾ In.	*illus*	60
Vase, Poppy, Green Matte Glaze, Black Speckled, Cylindrical, Swollen, 1902, 8 In.		1298
Vase, Stylized Flowers, Celadon & Green Glaze, Oval, 1904, 3¾ x 4 In.		938
Vase, Stylized Geese, Variegated Green Glaze, Bulbous, Swollen, 1902, 6 x 5 In.		3500
Vase, Stylized Leaves, Leathery Green Glaze, c.1905, 5 x 5¼ In.		2125
Vase, Stylized Poppies, Purple & Green Glaze, Cylindrical, c.1903, 10 In.		3150

VAN BRIGGLE

Pattern Numbers
The pattern numbers on Van Briggle pottery can help date a piece. Numbers below 899 were used before 1912. AA alone was used before 1920, AA-USA was used from 1922 to 1929.

Volkstedt, Figurine, Royal Coach, Dapple Gray Horses, Courtiers, Germany, c.1910, 12 x 21 In.
$240

Garth's Auctioneers & Appraisers

TIP
Sculptures should be dusted with a clean, dry paintbrush. Never use water.

Walrath, Vase, Roses, Green Matte Glaze, Incised, c.1910, 8½ In.
$5,938

Rago Arts and Auction Center

U
V

This is an edited listing of current prices. Visit **Kovels.com** to check thousands of prices from previous years and sign up for free information on trends, tips, reproductions, marks, and more.

Watch, F. Samuel, 3-Color Dial, Key Wind, Gold, Leaves, Flowers, 1800s, Pocket
$2,550

Ruby Lane

Watch, Holder, English Bobbie, Eyes Light Up, Metal, Painted, 6 1/4 In.
$350

Tom Harris Auctions

Watch, Holder, Lamp Pole, Devilish Figure, White Metal, 7 1/8 In.
$110

Tom Harris Auctions

VASA MURRHINA is the name of a glassware made by the Vasa Murrhina Art Glass Company of Sandwich, Massachusetts, about 1884. The glassware was transparent and was embedded with small pieces of colored glass and metallic flakes. The mica flakes were coated with silver, gold, copper, or nickel. Some of the pieces were cased. The same type of glass was made in England. Collectors often confuse Vasa Murrhina glass with aventurine, spatter, or spangle glass. There is uncertainty about what actually was made by the Vasa Murrhina factory. Related pieces may be listed under Spangle Glass.

Basket, Blue, White, Silver Flecks, Clear Crimped Rim, Square Thorn Handle, 5 In.	96
Basket, Turquoise, White, Silver Flecks, Twisted Handle, Crimped, c.1890, 9 In.	92
Basket, White, Yellow, Gold Flecks, Twisted Handle, Crimped, 1880s, 7 In.	102
Pitcher, Pink Mica, Silver & Gold Flecks, Lobed, Reeded Handle, 1880s, 9 In.	188
Vase, Ewer, Blue, White, Silver Flecks, Thorn Handle, Ruffled Rim, c.1880, 7 In.	198
Vase, Fuchsia, Green Spangles, Mica Flecks, Dimpled, Ruffled Rim, 9 In.	129

VASELINE GLASS is a greenish-yellow glassware resembling petroleum jelly. Pressed glass of the 1870s was often made of vaseline-colored glass. Some vaseline glass is still being made in old and new styles. Additional pieces of vaseline glass may also be listed under Pressed Glass in this book.

Compote, Pedestal, Lid, Daisy & Button, Scalloped Edge, 12 1/2 x 9 In.	390
Glass, Ewer, Twist, Applied Handle, 6 1/2 x 4 In.	60
Parfait Cup, Green To Clear, Etched Vines, Trumpet, Round Foot, 1920s, 5 In., Pair	25
Pitcher, Queen Pattern, 8 3/4 x 5 1/2 In.	*illus* 42
Rose Bowl, Dot Design, Wide Pinched Rim, 1940s, 4 In.	124
Vase, Fluted, 11 x 11 In.	12

VENETIAN GLASS, *see Glass-Venetian category.*

VENINI GLASS, *see Glass-Venetian category.*

VERLYS glass was made in Rouen, France, by the Societe Holophane Français, a company that started in 1920. It was made in Newark, Ohio, from 1935 to 1951. The art glass is either blown or molded. The American glass is signed with a diamond-point-scratched name, but the French pieces are marked with a molded signature. The designs resemble those used by Lalique.

Bowl, Fish, Oval, Mold Blown, Blue, c.1925, 18 1/2 x 7 In.	687
Bowl, Frosted, 3 Birds In Flight Above 2 Fish Swimming, 2 3/4 x 13 1/2 In.	115
Bowl, Frosted, Molded, Water Lilies, Signed, 2 1/2 x 13 3/4 In.	61
Bowl, Vaseline Glass, Molded, Blue, Brass, 16 1/2 In.	375
Ice Bucket, Half Circle Handles, Blue, France, c.1925, 8 x 13 In.	343
Vase, Mermaid, Etched, Frosted Lower Half, 10 x 8 In.	103
Vase, Molded, Chinese Man With Parasol In Garden, Engraved, 9 1/4 In.	127

VERNON KILNS was the name used by Vernon Potteries, Ltd. The company, which started in 1931 in Vernon, California, made dinnerware and figurines until it went out of business in 1958. The molds were bought by Metlox, which continued to make some patterns. Collectors search for the brightly colored dinnerware and the pieces designed by Rockwell Kent, Walt Disney, and Don Blanding. For more prices, go to kovels.com.

Anytime, Bowl, Vegetable, Divided, Round, 9 3/4 In.	35
Anytime, Plate, Dinner, 10 In.	14
Anytime, Platter, 10 7/8 In.	25
Brown Eyed Susan, Bowl, Vegetable, Round, 9 In.	23
Brown Eyed Susan, Coffeepot, Cup	55
Brown Eyed Susan, Creamer	20
Brown Eyed Susan, Cup & Saucer	16
Brown Eyed Susan, Plate, Luncheon, 9 1/2 In.	12

U
V

Desert Bloom,	Plate, Bread & Butter, Scalloped Edge, 6 ½ In.	5
Fruit Basket,	Sugar, Lid, c.1970, 5 x 4 ½ In.	16
Hawaiian Flowers,	Salt & Pepper, 2 ¼ x 2 ½ In.	85
Lotus,	Bowl, Cereal, 6 ⅞ In.	20
Lotus,	Cup & Saucer	22
Lotus,	Plate, Dinner, 11 In.	22
May Flower,	Coffee Cup, 1942-53, 2 ½ In.	7
Organdie,	Chop Plate, 12 In.	14
Organdie,	Cup & Saucer	10
Organdie,	Gravy	30
Organdie,	Mug	25
Organdie,	Plate, Bread & Butter, 6 ½ In.	4
Organdie,	Plate, Yellow, Brown, Cream Ground, 13 ¾ In ....*illus*	28
Organdie,	Platter, 12 ¾ In.	22

VERRE DE SOIE glass was first made by Frederick Carder at the Steuben Glass Works from about 1905 to 1930. It is an iridescent glass of soft white or very, very pale green. The name means "glass of silk," and it does resemble silk. Other factories have made verre de soie, and some of the English examples were made of different colors. Verre de soie is an art glass and is not related to the iridescent, pressed, white carnival glass mistakenly called by its name. Related pieces may be found in the Steuben category.

Bowl,	Cut Ribbons, Flower Swags, Stretch Border, Red Lip, Steuben, 4 ¾ x 12 ¾ In.	270
Bowl,	Rounded, Steuben, 4 x 6 In.	25
Sculpture,	Round, Orange & White Orchids, Blue Leaf Blades, John Lotton, 10 ⅜ In.	3600
Vase,	Applied Green Threading, Steuben, 7 ¼ In.	84
Vase,	Opalescent Peach, Aurene Blue & Green Tangled Vines, Bulbous, 5 x 6 In.	354

VIENNA, *see Beehive category.*

VIENNA ART plates are round metal serving trays produced at the turn of the century. The designs, copied from Royal Vienna porcelain plates, usually featured a portrait of a woman encircled by a wide, ornate border. Many were used as advertising or promotional items and were produced in Coshocton, Ohio, by J. F. Meeks Tuscarora Advertising Co. and H.D. Beach's Standard Advertising Co.

Plate,	Square, Rococo Style, Green Border, Woman, Wavy Brown Hair, Red Flower, 1905, 10 In.	123
Plate,	Topless Woman, Sitting, Tin Lithograph Tray, Frame, 15 x 15 In.	184
Plate,	Woman, Candle, Red Skirt, Red Border, White Flowers, 10 In.	24

VILLEROY & BOCH POTTERY of Mettlach was founded in 1836. The firm made many types of wares, including the famous Mettlach steins. Collectors can be confused because although Villeroy & Boch made most of its pieces in the city of Mettlach, Germany, the company also had factories in other locations. The dating code impressed on the bottom of most pieces makes it possible to determine the age of the piece. Additional items, including steins and earthenware pieces marked with the famous castle mark or the word *Mettlach*, may be found in the Mettlach category.

Charger,	Drinking Men, Keys, Multicolor, 17 ¼ In.	125
Charger,	Scenic, Chalet, Mountains, Chickens, Marked, 17 In.	118
Lazy Susan,	Blue Onion, Saxony, Black Ink Stamp, c.1885, 9 ½ x 14 In.	140
Tankard,	Portrait Medallions, Relief, Teapot Shape, Saucer Foot, c.1900, 16 In.	561
Tray,	Dresden, 1888, 14 x 22 ½ In. ....*illus*	1380
Tray,	Dresden, Man, Stein, Scrolling Vines, Text, Transfer, Frame, 17 x 11 In.	420
Tureen,	Underplate, Rust Red, Figural Handles, Relief Decoration, Stoneware, 15 In.	200
Vase,	Drip Glaze, Blue, Gray, Bulbous, Tapered Bottom, 11 x 8 ½ In., Pair	750
Vase,	Flambe Oxblood, Drip Glaze, Multicolor, 11 x 9 ½ In.	312
Vase,	Mottled Green Glaze, Blue, Shouldered, Slight Pinched Waist, 10 In.	118
Vase,	Striped, Red, Black, Mettlach, c.1920, 14 ½ In.	187

Waterford, Centerpiece, Diamond, Thumbprint, Vertical, 8 ½ x 6 ½ In., 4 ¾-In. Base
$225

Ruby Lane

Watt, Apple, Bowl, No. 73, 1952-62, 4 ¼ x 9 ½ In.
$75

Ruby Lane

Watt, Apple, Pitcher, No. 15, Yellowware, 5 ½ In.
$29

Ruby Lane

Watt Giveaways
Watt bowls were made as "giveaways" in big stores. Some pieces had printed words inside with the name of a company and phrases like "To a Good Cook."

U
V

Watt, Autumn Foliage, Bowl, Spaghetti, No. 39, 13 In.
$80

Ruby Lane

Watt, Starflower, Creamer, No. 15, 1951, 5 ½ In.
$32

Ruby Lane

Weather Vane, Arrow, Banner, Sheet Iron, Red Paint, Openwork, Mounted, c.1890, 26 x 54 In.
$390

U
V

Garth's Auctioneers & Appraisers

514

VOLKMAR
Corona N.Y

VOLKMAR POTTERY was made by Charles Volkmar of New York from 1879 to about 1911. He was associated with several firms, including the Volkmar Ceramic Company, Volkmar and Cory, and Charles Volkmar and Son. He was hired by Durant Kilns of Bedford Village, New York, in 1910 to oversee production. Volkmar bought the business and after 1930 only the Volkmar name was used as a mark. Volkmar had been a painter, and his designs often look like oil paintings drawn on pottery.

Mug, Charles Volkmar, White Ducks On Water, Dark Blue Background, Signed, 6 In.	1495
Mug, Ducks, Landscape, Blue, Gray, 1901, 6 In.	1300
Mug, Sailboats, Lake, Blue, White, 5 ⅞ In.	177
Tile, Windmill, Squeezebag Decoration, Frame, Incised HJ, 1915, 7 ¾ In. ....*illus*	1063

VOLKSTEDT was a soft-paste porcelain factory started in 1760 by Georg Heinrich Macheleid at Volkstedt, Thuringia. Volkstedt-Rudolstadt was a porcelain factory started at Volkstedt-Rudolstadt by Beyer and Bock in 1890. Most pieces seen in shops today are from the later factory.

Ewer, Putti, Playing Around Orb, 14 ¾ x 9 In.	115
Figurine, Courting Couple, Cupid Whispering In Woman's Ear, 7 x 8 In.	413
Figurine, Courting Couple, Yellow Jacket, Hat, Flowered Skirt, 6 x 5 In.	177
Figurine, Royal Coach, Dapple Gray Horses, Courtiers, Germany, c.1910, 12 x 21 In. ....*illus*	240
Figurine, Ruth, Parian, Knee Out, 1800s, 18 In.	281
Figurine, Woman, Angel, Floral Dress, Scarf, Clouds, Branches, Gilt, 12 x 5 ¼ In.	47

WADE
Figures
c. 1936+

WADE pottery is made by the Wade Group of Potteries started in 1810 near Burslem, England. Several potteries merged to become George Wade & Son, Ltd., early in the twentieth century, and other potteries have been added through the years. The best-known Wade pieces are the small figurines called Whimsies. They were first were made in 1954. Special Whimsies were given away with Red Rose Tea beginning in 1967. The Disney figures are listed in this book in the Disneyana category.

Box, Figural, Crab, 3 ¾ x 3 x 1 ¼ In.	14
Box, Figural, Hedgehog, 2 ⅜ x 4 In.	17
Figurine, Collie Dog, Red Rose, Brown	19
Figurine, Corgi, Red Rose, Brown, c.1971	3
Figurine, Gnome, Bed Of Flowers, 2 ½ x 2 ¾ In.	159
Figurine, Gnome, Bed Of Flowers, 3 ¼ x 3 ¾ In.	194
Figurine, Mermaid, Red Rose, Turquoise	1
Figurine, Raccoon, Red Rose, Brown, c.1985, 1 x 1 ¾ x ⅞ In.	5
Figurine, Sailor Child, 3 ¼ In.	53
Figurine, Tinker Child, 2 ¼ In.	63
Nativity Set, White With Gold Trim, Original Boxes, 6 Piece	16
Vase, Fantasia, Sky Blue, Gilt Rim, Milkweed Ballet Images, 1940s, 9 In.	253

WAHPETON POTTERY, *see Rosemeade category.*

WALL POCKETS were popular in the 1930s. They were made by many American and European factories. Glass, pottery, porcelain, majolica, chalkware, and metal wall pockets can be found in many fanciful shapes.

Flower Frog, Faience, Pink Roses, France, 5 ½ x 9 In., Pair	59
Majolica, Basket Weave, Blue, George Jones, c.1875, 11 In.	307
Majolica, Butterfly, Griffen Smith & Hill, c.1880, 7 ½ In.	2767
Majolica, Carnation, White, Purple Tips, Mont Chevalier, c.1890, 7 ½ In.	172
Majolica, Iris, Pink, 12 ½ In.	276
Majolica, Monkey, Climbing Palm Tree, Coconut, Jose Cunha, c.1880, 8 In., Pair	615
Majolica, Pansy, Pink, c.1880, 11 ½ In.	209
Majolica, Parrot, Blue To Yellow To Green, 8 ¼ In.	233
Majolica, Rose, Yellow, Rose Tips, Pierre Perret, c.1880, 8 In.	307
Majolica, Wicker Basket, Ivy, Brown Shield, c.1875, 10 ½ In., Pair	369

Salamander, Blue, Light Blue, 10 In. 2006

WALLACE NUTTING *photographs are listed under Print, Nutting. His reproduction furniture is listed under Furniture.*

WALRATH was a potter who worked in New York City; Rochester, New York; and at the Newcomb Pottery in New Orleans, Louisiana. Frederick Walrath died in 1920. Pieces listed here are from his Rochester period.

Vase, Putty, 4¾ x 3¼ In. 400
Vase, Roses, Green Matte Glaze, Incised, c.1910, 8½ In. ....*illus* 5938
Vase, Roses, Green, c.1910, 8½ x 4½ In. 5842
Vase, Scenic, Trees, Blue, Red & Amber, Cylindrical, Smokestack, c.1910, 6 x 4 In. 8125
Vase, Scenic, Trees, c.1910, 5½ x 3¾ In. 7995
Vase, Stylized Roses, Green & Mauve Matte, Shouldered, Beaker, c.1910, 14 In. 23750
Vase, Stylized Roses, Pink, Tan, Green Ground, Corseted, Squat Base, 11¾ x 6 In. 10625

WALT DISNEY, *see Disneyana category.*

WALTER, *see A. Walter category.*

WARWICK china was made in Wheeling, West Virginia, in a pottery working from 1887 to 1951. Many pieces were made with hand painted or decal decorations. The most familiar Warwick has a shaded brown background. The name *Warwick* is part of the mark and sometimes the mysterious word *IOGA* is also included.

Pitcher, Flowers, Red, Orange, Tan Glaze, 9½ x 6½ In. 54
Urn, Bronze, Heads, Round Foot, Signed A.D. Delafontaine, 9¾ x 14 In. 531
Vase, Portrait, Brown, 10½ In. 23
Vase, Portrait, Woman, Flower, Tan, Brown Glaze, Twig Handles, c.1890, 12 x 6¼ In. 85

WATCH pockets held the pocket watch that was important in Victorian times because it was not until World War I that the wristwatch was used. All types of watches are collected: silver, gold, or plated. Watches are listed here by company name or by style. Wristwatches are a separate category.

Audemars Piguet & Co., Open Face, Repeater, 31 Jewel, Gold Matte Dial, Pocket, 2 In. 4750
Bergner & Fils, Hunter Case, For Colonel Audenried, U.S. Army, 18K, c.1870, 15 In. 2645
Cartier, Platinum & 18K Gold, Open Face, White Dial, Roman Numerals, Art Deco, 1⅞ In. 1968
E. Howard, Hunting Case, Silver, Key Wind, Porcelain Dial, c.1959, Pocket 1755
Elgin, Platinum, Textured Dial, 19 Jewel, 8 Position, Art Deco, Pocket, 1¾ In. 944
Erismann & Sons, 14K Gold, Blue Enamel, Rose Cut Diamond, Woman's, Pocket, 3 In. 1250
F. Samuel, 3-Color Dial, Key Wind, Gold, Leaves, Flowers, 1800s, Pocket ....*illus* 2550
Holder, English Bobbie, Eyes Light Up, Metal, Painted, 6¼ In. ....*illus* 350
Holder, Lamp Pole, Devilish Figure, White Metal, 7⅛ In. ....*illus* 110
Hunter Case, Silver, Moon Phase, Swiss Bern Bear, Pocket, 2⅛ x 2¾ In. 813
Hunting Case, J. Picard, 18K Gold, Swiss Landscape, Gazebo, Rope Twist Chain, Garnet 1230
Invicta, 14K Gold, Diamond Clover, Pearls, Chain, Opal Slide, Case, 1897, Pocket, 1 In. 2185
Longines, 18K Gold, Grand Prix 1900, Guilloche Blue & White, Enamel, Pocket 1840
Omega, Silver Case, Engraved Design, Enameled 24-Hour Dial, Seconds Dial, c.1920 546
Paul Flato, Travel, Silvertone Metal, Black Enamel, Diamond Monogram, Art Deco, 2 In. 523
Paul Matthey, Hunting Case, 14K Gold, Porcelain Dial, c.1880, Pocket 1989
Pendant, 14K Gold, Diamond Encrusted, Woman's, ¾ In. 3500
Pendant, 14K Yellow Gold, Green Guilloche, Seed Pearls, Central Fleur, Woman's, 1¼ In. 800
Pin, Woman With Poppy, 14K Gold, Enamel, Art Nouveau, Krementz, 1 In. 1230
Pin, Woman, Mucha Style Headdress, Gold & Pearl Frame, Alling & Co., 1 In. 1046
Royce, Platinum, Diamond, Black Enamel Trim, Brushed Dial, 1¾ In., Lapel 738
Swiss, 18K Gold, Open Face, Key Wind, Engraved Dial, c.1850, 1⅝ In., Pocket 351
Tracy & Co., Silver, 16 Jewel, Key Wind, Hunter Case, 1857-59, Pocket 585
Ulysse Nardin, Silver, Open Face, Porcelain Dial, Early 1900s, 2 In., Pocket 410

Weather Vane, Heron, Frog, Grass, Sheet Metal, c.1810, 23 x 9 In. $2,950

Ruby Lane

Weather Vane, Horse & Sulky, Trotting, Copper, Cast Metal, c.1890, 17¾ x 32 In. $3,075

Cowan's Auctions

Weather Vane, Horse, Jockey, Copper, Primer, Gold Leaf, Cushing & White Waltham, c.1885, 16 x 29 In. $4,840

James D. Julia Auctioneers

The Howard Johnson Company Weather Vanes
The Howard Johnson weather vanes used on top of the company's orange-roofed buildings sent a message. The silhouette of the pieman and the boy meant the building was a restaurant. A lantern indicated an inn. A combination of pieman, boy, and lantern advertised an inn with a typical full-service restaurant, with clam rolls, its specialty, and 28 flavors of ice cream. The last orange-roofed building is in Maine.

W

Weather Vane, Sailboat, Copper, Verdigris, Directionals, 59 x 30 In. $130

Kamelot Auction House

Weather Vane, Sturgeon, Brass, 1900s, 17 x 35½ In. $218

Roland Auctioneers & Valuers

TIP
American postcards from long-gone towns have extra value to collectors.

Webb Burmese, Epergne, 3 Fairy Lamp Shades, 4 Vases, Crimped Rim, Clarke's Patent, 10½ In. $1,093

Early Auction Company

Vacheron & Constantin, 14K Gold, Slim Case, Open Face, Matte Dial, 1¼ In., Pocket	900
Waltham, 14K Tricolor Gold, Carved Hunting Case, Diamond, Ferns, Woman's, 1½ In.	508
Waltham, Gold Filled, 23 Jewel, Open Face, Screw Back, c.1948, Size 16, Pocket	129
Waltham, Hunting Case, 14K Gold, 17 Jewel, Porcelain Dial, c.1903, Pocket	1112

WATCH FOBS were worn on watch chains. They were popular during Victorian times and after. Many styles, especially advertising designs, are still made today.

American Watch Co., Coin Silver, Open Face Case, Chain	87
Corby Canadian Whiskey, Celluloid, Topless Girl, 1⅞ x 1⅝ In.	47
Gold Plated Pocket Knife, 14K Gold Chain, 13 In.	125
John Deere, Brass Logo, Mother-Of-Pearl Backing, 1⅝ x 1⅜ In.	118
Sir John Carling, 14K Gold, Blue, 1¼ x 1 In.	236
Star Case Company, Gold Plated, Open Face, Pocket Knife	31
The International Brotherhood Of Magicians, Logo, Brass, c.1930, 2 In.	115

WATERFORD type glass resembles the famous glass made from 1783 to 1851 in the Waterford Glass Works in Ireland. It is a clear glass that was often decorated by cutting. Modern glass is being made again in Waterford, Ireland, and is marketed under the name Waterford. Waterford merged with Wedgwood in 1986 to form the Waterford Wedgwood Group. Most Waterford Wedgwood assets were bought by KPS Capital Partners of New York in 2009 and became part of WWRD Holdings. WWRD was bought by Fiskars in 2015.

Centerpiece, Diamond, Thumbprint, Vertical, 8½ x 6½ In., 4¾-In. Base......*illus*	225
Compote, Lismore, 4⅜ x 6¼ In.	53
Punch Bowl, Cut Glass, Fan Cut Rim, 7⅜ x 14⅜ In.	305
Ring Holder, Cut Reeded Sides, Star Cut Base, 3 In., 3 Piece	97
Vase, Marquis, Shell Shape, Germany, 6⅛ x 5¼ In.	40
Wine, Lismore, Claret, Diamond & Wedge Cuts, 5⅞ x 3 In.	35

WATT family members bought the Globe pottery of Crooksville, Ohio, in 1922. They made pottery mixing bowls and tableware of the type made by Globe. In 1935 they changed the production and made the pieces with the freehand decorations that are popular with collectors today. Apple, Starflower, Rooster, Tulip, and Autumn Foliage are the best-known patterns. Pansy, also called Rio Rose, was the earliest pattern. Apple, the most popular pattern, can be dated from the leaves. Originally, the apples had three leaves; after 1958 two leaves were used. The plant closed in 1965. For more prices, go to kovels.com.

Apple, Bowl, No. 6, 3-Leaf, Ribbed, 6 In.	72
Apple, Bowl, No. 73, 1952-62, 4¼ x 9½ In.......*illus*	75
Apple, Bowl, No. 73, 9½ In.	25
Apple, Creamer, No. 62, 3-Leaf, 4¼ In.	65
Apple, Mixing Bowl, No. 65, 8⅞ In.	95
Apple, Pitcher, No. 15, Yellowware, 5½ In.......*illus*	29
Apple, Pitcher, No. 16, 2-Leaf, 6½ In.	95
Autumn Foliage, Bean Pot, Peshtigo Feed Mill	37
Autumn Foliage, Bowl, Cereal, No. 94, Ovenware, 6 In.	10
Autumn Foliage, Bowl, No. 7, Ribbed, 7 In.	29
Autumn Foliage, Bowl, Spaghetti, No. 39, 13 In.......*illus*	80
Autumn Foliage, Creamer, No. 62, 4¼ In.	64
Autumn Foliage, Cruet, Vinegar, No. 126, 7 In.	35
Autumn Foliage, Mixing Bowl, No. 5, 5 In.	74
Double Apple, Casserole, Lid, No. 73, 9½ In.	45
Double Apple, Mixing Bowl, No. 63, 6½ In.	25
Pansy, Bowl, Spaghetti, No. 39, 13 In.	26
Pansy, Cookie Jar, Lid, No. 503, 8¼ In.	200
Pansy, Mixing Bowl, No. 5, 5 In.	24
Pansy, Pitcher, No. 16, 6¾ In.	36

Pansy, Plate, Dinner, Bull's-Eye	20
Pansy, Platter, Cut-Leaf	75
Petal Starflower, Pitcher, 5¼ In.	80
Rooster, Bean Pot, No. 76, 6½ x 7½ In.	75
Rooster, Bowl, No. 39, 13 In.	43
Rooster, Creamer, No. 62, 4¼ In.	32
Rooster, Pitcher, No. 15, 5½ In.	115
Rooster, Pitcher, No. 16, 6¾ In.	28
Starflower, Bowl, No. 55, 11¾ In.	30
Starflower, Casserole, Lid, No. 73, 4-Petal, 9½ In.	57
Starflower, Creamer, No. 15, 1951, 5½ In. ....*illus*	32
Starflower, Mixing Bowl, No. 9, 5-Petal, 9 In.	20
Starflower, Nesting Bowls, 4-Petal, 4 Piece	50
Starflower, Pitcher, No. 15, 5-Petal, 5½ In.	49
Starflower, Pitcher, No. 15, Ovenware, 5½ In.	15
Starflower, Pitcher, No. 16, 5-Petal, 6½ In.	30
Starflower, Pitcher, No. 17, 4-Petal, 8 In.	85
Starflower, Salt & Pepper, 4¼ In.	21
Tulip, Ashtray	15
Tulip, Cookie Jar, Lid, No. 503, 8¼ In.	100
Tulip, Mug, Commemorative	140
Tulip, Pitcher, No. 16, 6¾ In.	85

WATT, *Rio Rose, see Pansy*

WAVE CREST glass is an opaque white glassware manufactured by the Pairpoint Manufacturing Company of New Bedford, Massachusetts, and some French factories. It was decorated by the C.F. Monroe Company of Meriden, Connecticut. The glass was painted in pastel colors and decorated with flowers. The name Wave Crest was used starting in 1892.

WAVE CREST WARE

Dresser Box, Enamel, Blue Daisies, Brass Trim, 3½ x 7½ In.	86
Dresser Box, Enamel, Pink Roses, Blue Green, Brass Trim, 2½ x 4½ In.	24
Vase, Cherry Blossoms, Light Green, White, Gilt Metal Mounts, Handles, 11¼ x 9½ In.	342
Vase, Molded, Painted, White, Pink Flowers, Diagonal Band, 9¾ x 3 In.	86

WEAPONS listed here include instruments of combat other than guns, knives, rifles, or swords, and clothing worn in combat. Firearms made after 1900 are not listed in this book. Knives and Swords are listed in their own categories.

Armor, Full Suit, Sheet Metal, Black Paint, Metal Shield, Late 1900s, 70 In.	780
Armor, Pikeman, Breastplate, Backplates, Faulds, Helmet, England, Mid 1600s, 28 In.	4428
Breast Strap, Dragoon, Brass Scale, Brass Heart Center, c.1810	1495
Breastplate, Iron, Triplex, Suspension Studs, England, c.1640, 11½ In.	4250
Bullet & Shot Mold, Isaac Maynard, Brass, c.1777, 11¾ In.	11070
Bullet Pouch, Leather, Flintlock Musket, Red Wool, Ottoman, c.1700-1800, 4¼ x 5¼ In.	375
Cannon, Naval, Cast Iron, Carriage, Shell, Rack, Raised Crown Stamp, 1840, 55 In.	1481
Cap, Militia Rifleman, Leather, Bugle Cap Badge, False Feathers, c.1813-20, 7¾ In.	4798
Cartridge Box, Sling, Carrying Strap, Stamped U.S., Brass Eagle, c.1865	570
Flail, Iron Spiked Wooden Ball, Hardwood Handle, Europe, c.1650, 46¼ In.	2066
Halberd, Piedmontese, Waldensian Militia, Italy, c.1600s, 96½ In.	2250
Helmet, Morian, Iron, Brim Points In Front & Back, Continental, 1600s, 7 x 10¼ x 11⅝ In.	517
Helmet, Morion, Crescent Shape, Germany, c.1570-80	5850
Helmet, Pickelhaube, Prussian, Black Hard Leather Shell, Brass Fittings, c.1912, 9 In.	480
Helmet, Rolled Steel, Blued, Lobster Tail, England, c.1630-50	5950
Helmet, Samurai Or Kabuto, Red Lacquer, Iron, Japan, 1600s, 11 x 13 In.	812
Helmet, Sapper's, England, c.1625	3450
Polearm, O Naginata, Edo Period, Brass Habaki, Wood Cover, Japan, 24 In.	1840
Polearm, Partisan, Iron Head, Fleur-De-Lis, Napoleonic, Italy, c.1790, 87¼ In.	4500
Reloading Tools, Marlin Ballard, For 20-Gauge Shotgun Shell	1265

Wedgwood
The real Wedgwood company run by Josiah Wedgwood is spelled WEDGWOOD. Another English company took advantage of the name by using the mark WEDGEWOOD.

Wedgwood, Barber Bottle, Lid, Jasper Dip, 4-Color, Medallions, Bacchus Heads, c.1890, 11 In.
$2,337

Skinner, Inc.

Wedgwood, Bough Pot, Lid, Jasperware, Blue, 4 Seasons, Figures, Marked, c.1790, 6 In., Pair
$1,599

Skinner, Inc.

Wedgwood, Bulb Pot, Lid, Terra-Cotta, Brown Slip, Festoons, Handled Bowl, c.1790, 9 In., Pair
$3,567

Skinner, Inc.

W

Wedgwood, Compote, Nautilus Shell, Dolphin Supports, Mottled Glazes, Majolica, c.1866, 16 In.
$1,599

Skinner, Inc.

Trash to Treasure
Pierced-tin wall shrines for saints were made from tin cans left behind by soldiers in New Mexico and nearby areas during the 1840s and 1850s.

Wedgwood, Figurine, Kangaroo, Caneware, John Skeaping, Impressed, c.1930, 9 In.
$400

Skinner, Inc.

Wedgwood, Figurine, Taurus The Bull, Black Glaze, Gold Zodiac Signs, Marked, 1966, 14½ In.
$246

Skinner, Inc.

Shako, Yeoman's Crown, Visor, Plume Pocket, England, Early 1800s, 8¼ x 7¾ In.	2804
Staff & Club, Combined, Tapered To Tip, Tubular Hide Grip, c.1879, 37½ In.	325

WEATHER VANES were used in seventeenth-century Boston. The direction of the wind was an indication of coming weather, important to the seafaring and farming communities. By the mid-nineteenth century, commercial weather vanes were made of metal. Many were shaped like animals. Ethan Allen, Dexter, and St. Julian are famous horses that were depicted. Today's collectors often consider weather vanes to be examples of folk art, even though they may not have been handmade.

American Eagle, Full Body Copper, Zinc Head, Verdigris Patina, Pa., 1880s, 15 In.	2280
Apple, Horizontal Branch, Metal, Paint, Mounted, Stand, 1900s, 45 x 38 In.	738
Arrow, Banner, Sheet Iron, Red Paint, Openwork, Mounted, c.1890, 26 x 54 In. ....*illus*	390
Banner, Iron, Cutout Date, C-Scrolls, Turned Finials, Wood Base, c.1898, 42 In.	593
Banner, With Hand, Copper, Zinc, Cushing & White, 36 x 17 In.	4972
Bannerette, Arrow, Copper, Scalloped Design, Cutouts, Verdigris, c.1900, 50 In.	652
Bannerette, Copper, Directionals, Iron Stand, 53 In.	197
Billy Goat, Standing, Horns, Tail Up, 21 x 19 In.	7605
Blacksmith, Copper, Anvil, Folk Art, 1900s, 39 In.	175
Bull, Copper, Cast Metal Head, Old Worn Gold Leaf Surface, Early 1900s, 16¾ x 26 In.	3000
Bull, Gilt Copper, Zinc, Stand, Late 1800s, 18 x 26 In.	14000
Cow, Full Body, Gilt Copper, Zinc Head, Deep Chest, Stand, c.1900, 20 x 26 In.	3555
Cow, Full Body, Molded, Sheet Copper, Cast Iron Head, Horn & Ears, 28 In.	3998
Cow, Sheet Copper, Gilded, Custom Stand, Late 1800s, 10 x 14½ In.	1400
Cricket, Sheet Copper, Old Gilt Surface, Textured Legs & Features, c.1910, 31 In.	1353
Dolphin, Copper, On Arrow, Old Regilt Surface, Early 1900s, 26 x 27 In.	720
Eagle, Copper, Gilt, Verdigris, c.1880, 8¾ In.	1320
Eagle, In Flight, Directionals, Copper, c.1890, 44¾ In.	467
Eagle, Spread Wings, Molded Copper & Cast Zinc, Verdigris, Late 1800s, 16½ x 24 x 13 In.	2640
Eagle, Spread Wings, Perched On Ball, Copper, Green Patina, Stand, 1900s, 58 In.	180
Eagle, Spread Wings, Sheet Copper, On Sphere, Arrow Directional, 42 x 64 In.	3998
Eagle, Spread Wings, Zinc, Old Paint & Gilt, 14 x 16½ In.	708
Fish, Copper, Old Gold Painted Surface, Late 1800s, 25¾ In.	1920
Gabriel, Blowing Horn, Full Body, Copper, Gold Leaf, Stand, c.1950, 22 x 39 In.	4148
Grasshopper, Copper, Verdigris, L.W. Cushing, Waltham, Mass., 1850s	4720
Grasshopper, Sheet Copper, Black Paint, Weathered Gilt, Wire Antennae, 42 In.	615
Heron, Frog, Grass, Sheet Metal, c.1810, 23 x 9 In. ....*illus*	2950
Horse & Sulky, Rider, Copper, Cast Lead Horse's Ears & Rider's Head, 32 x 20 In.	4613
Horse & Sulky, Trotting, Copper, Cast Metal, c.1890, 17¾ x 32 In. ....*illus*	3075
Horse, Blackhawk, Copper, Cast Metal Ears, Verdigris, Late 1800s, 18½ x 26½ In.	2640
Horse, Full Body, Sheet Copper, Copper Rod, Late 1800s, 15 x 25½ In.	1200
Horse, Jockey, Copper, Primer, Gold Leaf, Cushing & White Waltham, c.1885, 16 x 29 In...*illus*	4840
Horse, Running, Black Hawk Stallion, Copper, Ocher Paint, Stand, 21 x 28 In.	1900
Horse, Running, Copper, Zinc, 19½ x 34 In.	944
Horse, Running, Copper, Zinc, Stand, Mount Hanger, 20½ x 34 In.	500
Horse, Running, Flattened Body, Sheet Copper, Cast Zinc Head, Stand, 29 x 18 In.	2337
Horse, Running, Full Body, Cast Zinc Head, Verdigris Patina, Pole, c.1890, 30 In.	840
Horse, Running, Full Body, Copper, Cast Iron, Molded, Stand, c.1890, 21 x 49 In.	5925
Horse, Running, Full Body, Copper, Flat, Zinc Head, Gilt, Stand, c.1890, 18 x 29 In.	2074
Horse, Running, Full Body, Copper, Zinc, Molded, Jewell, c.1880, 18 x 31 In.	2074
Horse, Running, Full Body, Gilt Copper, Molded, Stand, c.1875, 22 x 31 In.	7000
Horse, Running, Hackney, Copper, Gilt & Verdigris, E.G. Washburne & Co., 22 x 30 In.	7200
Horse, Running, Sheet Copper, Verdigris, Stand, c.1900, 15 x 26 In.	1353
Horse, Running, Sheet Metal, Cutout, White, Early 1900s, 28 x 50 In.	688
Horse, Sheet Iron, Standing, Original Ball & Spike, 1800s, 55½ In.	375
Horse, Sulky, Copper, 1900s, 15½ x 32½ In.	418
Horse, Trotting, Full Body, Copper, Metal Stand, 1900s, 20 x 31 In.	1020
Horse, Trotting, Pine, Cutout, White Paint, Iron Bridle & Strapping, 31 x 18 In.	1968
Horse, Zinc Head, Verdigris Patina, 22 x 33 In.	2520

Index Horse, Prancing, Copper, Zinc, Crimped Tail, J. Howard, Mass., c.1855, 18 In.	13530
Indian, Drawing Bow, Headdress, Arrow, Copper, Full Body, c.1910, 21 x 21 In.	3851
Indian, On Horse, Full Gallop, Shooting Arrow, Sheet Iron, Paint, Stand, 33 x 24 In.	554
Indian, Shooting Bow, 2 Dogs In Weight, Late 1800s, 71 ½ In.	2760
Indian, Silhouette, Bow & Tomahawk, Rust, Tin, Early 1900s, 24 In.	688
Locomotive, Turned Smokestack, Bell, Pine, Carved, Painted, White, Black, 40 In.	861
Mermaid, Horn, Full Body, Forked Tail, Sheet Copper, Pole, c.1940, 37 x 32 In.	1481
Mermaid, Mirror In Hand, Combwood, 18 ½ x 39 In.	300
Pig, Copper, Cast Metal Ears & Tail, Worn Gold Leaf Surface, Early 1900s, 15 ¼ In.	10800
Pig, Full Body, Molded Curled Tail, Copper, Gilt, Flat, Stand, c.1940, 22 x 37 In.	5925
Pig, Leaping, Full Body, Copper, Directionals & Stand, 1900s, 30 x 24 In.	431
Pig, Sheet Copper, Flattened, Verdigris, Stand, c.1890, 20 x 33 In.	3198
Quill, Copper, Verdigris, Rod Mounted, Ball Finial, Stand, c.1885, 25 x 52 In.	6518
Rooster, 3 Spheres, Directional, Copper, Gilt, Harris & Co., Boston, c.1880, 34 In.	7380
Rooster, Crowing, Ball, Arrow, Molded Copper, Fiske & Co., 28 x 26 In.	4740
Rooster, Fluted Tail, Stylized, Sheet Metal, Rivets, Weathered Yellow Paint, 25 In.	2583
Rooster, Full Body, Cylindrical Neck, Curved Tail, Stylized, Copper, c.1840, 28 In.	1778
Rooster, Full Body, Gold Paint, Sheet Metal, 19 x 17 In.	180
Rooster, Full Body, Hollow, Copper, Gilt, Metal, Rod & Stand, c.1890, 36 x 32 In.	2963
Rooster, Full Body, Lead, Gilded, Iron Stand, 1800s, 16 x 18 In.	120
Rooster, Full Body, Zinc, Speckle Gray Patina, Red, France, c.1890, 65 x 20 In.	1100
Rooster, Hamburg, Full Body, Copper, Verdigris, Stand, c.1890, 28 x 30 In.	5925
Rooster, On Arrow, Copper, Verdigris, Mid 1900s, 21 ¾ In.	840
Rooster, Sheet Metal, c.1900, 20 x 31 In.	449
Rooster, Silhouette, Sheet Iron, Painted, Wood Base, 29-In. Rooster	885
Sailboat, Copper, Schooner, Old Gold Leaf & Painted Surface, Mid 1900s, 33 ½ x 35 In.	200
Sailboat, Copper, Verdigris, Directionals, 59 x 30 In. *illus*	130
Sailor, Peg Leg, Spy Glass, Copper, 26 In.	1599
Sheep, Full Body, Copper, Verdigris Patina, Late 1800s, 24 x 30 In.	2760
Ship, Wood, Painted, 18 x 13 In.	263
Squirrel, Holding Nut, Copper, Cast Metal Ears, Worn Gold Leaf Surface, 1900s, 23 In.	3240
Stag, Leaping, Copper, Zinc Head & Antlers, Verdigris Patina, Late 1800s, 23 x 30 In.	2400
Stag, Leaping, Molded Copper, Cast Zinc Head, Gilt, 1870-90, 27 ¾ In.	3360
Stag, Sheet Metal, Folk Art, 1900s, 38 ½ x 30 In.	660
Steer, Copper, Cushing & White, Waltham, M.A. Late 1800s, 12 ¾ x 24 In.	5700
Sturgeon, Brass, 1900s, 17 x 35 ½ In. *illus*	218
Swan, Full Body, Hissing, Scrolling Neck, Curved Tail, Pine, c.1900, 17 x 34 In.	2963
Whale, Copper, Green Patina, Directionals, 13 x 19 In.	180
Windmill, Copper, Brown, Verdigris, 1900s, 73 In.	1062

WEBB glass was made by Thomas Webb & Sons of Ambelcot, England. Many types of art and cameo glass were made by them during the Victorian era. Production ceased by 1991 and the factory was demolished in 1995. Webb Burmese and Webb Peachblow are special colored glasswares of the Victorian era. They are listed at the end of this section. Glassware that is not Burmese or Peachblow is included here.

Webb

Biscuit Jar, Enamel, Red To Pink, Gold Blossom Branch, Silver Plate Handle & Lid, 6 ½ In.	489
Bowl, Queen's Burmese, Blue Birds, Flowers, Ruffled Rim, c.1887, 2 ¾ x 7 ¾ In.	495
Bowl, White Over Red, Flowers, Silver Rim, Cameo, c.1900, 5 x 9 In.	1750
Centerpiece, Cranberry Glass, Flower Petal Cups, Fern Shape Arms, 8 ½ x 12 In.	687
Lamp, Yellow, Raised Red & White Flowers, Cameo, Matching Shade, Oil, 9 ½ In.	4485
Serving Set, Yellow, Morning Glories, Silver Mount, Serving Spoons, c.1880, 3 Piece	812
Vase, Blue, Flowers, Cameo, 13 In.	2500
Vase, Gilt, Dragon, Orange Ground, 7 ½ x 7 ½ In.	600
Vase, Overlay Glass, Flowers, Brown Ground, c.1890, 5 In.	500
Vase, Red Satin Ground, Silvery White Flower Vines, Bottle Shape, c.1910, 9 In.	1845
Vase, Shouldered Urn, White Flowers, Vines, Cameo, Banding At Foot, Neck & Rim, 8 ½ In.	518
Vase, Stick, Prunus, Flowers, Leaves, 6 x 2 In.	153
Vase, White Morning Glories, Fuchsia Stippled Ground, Oval, Trumpet Neck, 8 In.	1416

Wedgwood, Lustres, Amber Glass Prisms, Jasperware Base, Brass Mount, 13 ½ In., Pair
$360

Cowan's Auctions

Wedgwood, Platter, Cherubs, Flute, Drums, Black & Green Border, Creamware, 11 x 8 ⅛ In.
$1,600

Ruby Lane

Wedgwood, Urn, Black Basalt, Leaves, Berries, Greek Key, Mask Head Handles, c.1863, 11 In.
$1,722

Skinner, Inc.

W

Wedgwood, Vase, Jasper Dip, Green, Portland, White Figures, Handles, Marked, c.1890, 10 In. $1,599

Skinner, Inc.

Wedgwood, Vase, Jasper, Black, Applied Classical Figures, Handles, Thomas Lovatt, c.1880, 10 In. $5,843

Skinner, Inc.

Wedgwood, Vase, Potpourri, Moonlight Luster, Footed, 1800s, 13 In., Pair $1,020

Cowan's Auctions

WEBB BURMESE is a shaded Victorian glass made by Thomas Webb & Sons of Stourbridge, England, from 1886. Pieces are shades of pink to yellow.

Compote, Pink To Yellow, Ruffle Rim, Swollen Top Stick Stem, Round Foot, 6 In.	195
Epergne, 3 Fairy Lamp Shades, 4 Vases, Crimped Rim, Clarke's Patent, 10 ½ In. ....*illus*	1093
Pitcher, Pink To Yellow, Ruffled Rim, Reeded Handle, c.1900, 9 In.	100
Vase, Pink To Yellow, Squat, Cylinder Neck, 2 Handles, c.1890, 5 In.	162

WEBB PEACHBLOW is a shaded Victorian glass made by Thomas Webb & Sons of Stourbridge, England, from 1885.

Vase, Cranberry To Pink To White, Inverted Tulip Rim, c.1885, 4 In.	335
Vase, Fuchsia Shaded To Pink, Gilt Branches, Bottle Shape, 9 In.	580

WEDGWOOD

WEDGWOOD, one of the world's most successful potteries, was founded by Josiah Wedgwood, who was considered a cripple by his brother and was forbidden to work at the family business. The pottery was established in England in 1759. The company used a variety of marks, including Wedgwood, Wedgwood & Bentley, Wedgwood & Sons, and Wedgwood's Stone China. A large variety of wares has been made, including the well-known jasperware, basalt, creamware, and even a limited amount of porcelain. There are two kinds of jasperware. One is made from two colors of clay; the other is made from one color of clay with a color dip to create the contrast in design. In 1986 Wedgwood and Waterford Crystal merged to form the Waterford Wedgwood Group. Most Waterford Wedgwood assets were bought by KPS Capital Partners of New York in 2009 and became part of WWRD Holdings. Some manufacturing will be transferred to Germany, Indonesia, and Slovakia. Other Wedgwood pieces may be listed under Flow Blue, Majolica, Tea Leaf Ironstone, or in other porcelain categories. WWRD was bought by Fiskars in 2015.

Baptismal Font, Black Basalt, Banded Rim, Crisscross Ribbons, Late 1700s, 17 ⅝ In.	6765
Barber Bottle, Lid, Jasper Dip, 4-Color, Medallions, Bacchus Heads, c.1890, 11 In. ....*illus*	2337
Bough Pot, Lid, Jasperware, Blue, 4 Seasons, Figures, Marked, c.1790, 6 In., Pair..........*illus*	1599
Bowl, Fairyland Luster, Elves & Bell, Branch, Poplar Trees, 4 x 9 In.	3000
Bowl, Fairyland Luster, Orange, Green, 1920, 8 ½ x 4 In.	413
Bowl, Fairyland Luster, Woodland Elves VII Pattern, Fairy In Cage Inside, 9 In.	8295
Bowl, Fairyland Luster, Zodiac Signs, Early 1900s, 2 x 4 In., Pair	300
Bowl, Fruit, Black Basalt, Bellflowers, Oak Leaf Border, c.1850, 12 In.	923
Bowl, Hummingbird Luster, Octagonal, 1920, 8 ½ x 4 In.	495
Bulb Pot, Lid, Terra-Cotta, Brown Slip, Festoons, Handled Bowl, c.1790, 9 In., Pair..........*illus*	3567
Bust, Black Basalt, Mercury, Mounted On Waisted Circular Socle, 1800s, 17 ⅝ In.	3936
Bust, Carrara, Mercury, Winged Helmet, Waisted Circular Socle, c.1860, 18 In.	5535
Candlestick, Black Basalt, Egyptian Revival, Sphinx, 1800, 6 ¼ x 4 In., Pair	1000
Candlestick, Pale Blue Jasper, Figural, White Cherub Against Tree Trunk, Late 1700s, 10 In...	1107
Censer, Jasper Dip, Blue, Flower Festoons, 3 Dolphin Supports, Base, c.1805, 4 In.	585
Charger, Earthenware, Birds & Fruit Border, Women & Cherubs, Lessore, c.1860, 25 In.	3690
Charger, Enamel, Earthenware, Landscape, Man & Woman & Putti, Lessore, c.1860, 19 In.	1107
Charger, Majolica, Nymph Riding Sea Serpent, Birds, Dolphins, Flowers, c.1876, 15 In.	308
Charger, Queen's Ware, Footed, Religious Scene, Lessore, c.1861, 15 In.	1230
Compote, Nautilus Shell, Dolphin Supports, Mottled Glazes, Majolica, c.1866, 16 In.........*illus*	1599
Compote, Queen's Ware, Aesop's Fable, Lessore, c.1864, 9 ⅛ In.	615
Cup, Teardrop Shape, Lattice, Burslem, c.1785-90, 1 ½ x 2 ½ In.	275
Dip Jar, Lid, Light Blue Jasper, Foot Rim, White Flower Border, Late 1700s, 4 In.	1169
Dish, Game, Caneware, 7 ½ In.	125
Dish, Game, Lid, Dry Finish, Oval, Molded, Garland, Animals, Hare Finial, 7 x 11 In.	480
Dish, Game, Majolica, Signed, Late 1800s, 7 x 12 In.	288
Dish, Queen's Ware, Oval, Compartmented Interior, Lessore, c.1861, 7 ½ In.	400
Figurine, Antelope, Standing, Tan & Gray Glazed, Square Base, c.1959, 8 In.	431
Figurine, Child, Black Basalt, Reclining, Holding Fruit In Hands, Early 1900s, 4 ⅜ In.	554
Figurine, Kangaroo, Caneware, John Skeaping, Impressed, c.1930, 9 In..........*illus*	400
Figurine, Polar Bear, Seated, Moonstone, White, Square Base, c.1950, 7 In.	492
Figurine, Sphinx, Seated, Rectangular Base, 1800s, 9 In., Pair	2952
Figurine, Syren, Creamware, Seated Woman, R. Garbe, c.1941, 12 ⅛ In.	312

Figurine, Taurus The Bull, Black Glaze, Gold Zodiac Signs, Marked, 1966, 14½ In.........*illus*	246
Goblet, Sterling, Embossed Banding, Gilt Interior, Dome Foot, 1925, 6 In., 6 Piece	2750
Incense Burner, Lid, Black Basalt, Dolphin Supports, 1800s, 15¾ In.	2091
Incense Burner, Lid, Caneware, Dolphin Supports, Early 1800s, 5¼ In.	2583
Jar, Fairyland Luster, Pheasant, Peonies, Fuchsia, Gilt, Dome Lid, Marked, 10 In.....................	2950
Jardiniere, Jasperware, Green, Swags, Round Foot, 7⅛ x 8 In.	125
Jardiniere, Majolica, Argenta, Paneled Sides, Blossom Branches, c.1862, 16 x 14⅝ In.	400
Jardiniere, Majolica, Argenta, Paneled Sides, Flowers, 1891, 17 x 24½ In.	431
Jardiniere, Majolica, Leo With Wreath, Red, Yellow & Brown, Scalloped Rim, 1862, 13 In.	182
Jardiniere, Majolica, Openwork, Green Leaf Swags, Flowers, c.1872, 4⅜ x 14⅜ In.	212
Jug, Jasper Dip, Crimson & White, Rope Twist Handles, Figures, Vines, c.1920, 4 In.	431
Jug, Rosso Antico, Applied Black Basalt Relief, Bacchanalian Boys, Early 1800s, 4½ In.	338
Lamp, Oil, Black Basalt, Gilt, Bronzed, Genie, Maiden Atop, 1800s, 8¾ In., Pair.......................	3321
Lustres, Amber Glass Prisms, Jasperware Base, Brass Mount, 13½ In., Pair.....................*illus*	360
Malfrey Pot, Lid, Fairyland Luster, Bubbles Pattern, Gray Fairies, Pond, Spider On Lid, 6 In....	2666
Pap Boat, Creamware, Scalloped, Brown Edge Decoration, 3¾ x 1⅞ In.	75
Plaque, Black Basalt, Death Of Roman Warrior, High Relief, c.1900, 11 x 19 In.	1046
Plaque, Black Basalt, Dr. Johnstone, Oval, 4¾ x 3¾ In.	187
Plaque, Black Basalt, Hercules & Erymanthian Boar, Oval, 1800s, 5¼ x 7¼ In.	615
Plaque, Earthenware, Landscape, Trees, Figures By Fountain, Lessore, c.1860, 7 x 8¼ In...........	615
Plaque, Earthenware, Maidens Bathing By Fountain, Signed, Lessore, c.1860, 13 x 16½ In.....	2583
Plaque, Jasper Dip, Blue, Mythological Scene, Frame, 6¾ x 9¼ In....................................	437
Plaque, Jasper Dip, Blue, Mythological Scene, Frame, 8½ x 13½ In....................................	625
Plaque, Jasperware, Blue, Dancing Hours, White Figures, Frame, 1800s, 8 x 20 In.	677
Plaque, Jasperware, Blue, High Relief, Perseus & Andromeda, E.W. Wyon, 1848, 7 In...............	7380
Plaque, Majolica, Classical Maiden, Molded, Brown Glazed, c.1862, 5½ x 13¾ In., Pair..........	800
Plate, Ventnor, Raised Fruit Swags, Grapes, Leaves, 10¾ In.	354
Plate, White, Blue Transfer, Duke University Scenes, 10 In., 1938, 12 Piece................................	480
Platter, Cherubs, Flute, Drums, Black & Green Border, Creamware, 11 x 8⅛ In................. *illus*	1600
Platter, Majolica, Salacia Wrestling Sea Serpent, Burslem, 15 In.	200
Platter, Stoneware, Center Urn, Yellow Flowers, Blue Decorated Rim, 14⅝ In.	75
Pot, Lid, Jasperware, Black, Square, Flat Pierced Disk Lid, Late 1700s, 8½ In.	2583
Tea Set, Teapot, Cream & Sugar, 2 Cup & Saucer, Blue Fans, Branches, 8 Piece	275
Teapot, Lid & Stand, Jasperware, Solid Blue, Neale & Co., c.1800, 9¼ In.	369
Umbrella Stand, Majolica, Hexagonal, Multicolor, Alternating Flowers, c.1864, 21½ In.	615
Urn, Black Basalt, Leaves, Berries, Greek Key, Mask Head Handles, c.1863, 11 In.................*illus*	1722
Vase, Black Basalt, Amphora, Encaustic, Red Maiden, Loop Handles, Early 1800s, 8¾ In.........	1169
Vase, Black Basalt, Urn Shape, Handles, Scrolling Wave Band, 1800s, 37 In., Pair	10455
Vase, Dome Lid, Black Basalt, Ball Finial, 4 Handles, c.1770, 15½ In.	3690
Vase, Earthenware, Portland, Green, Classical Figures, 1800s, 10⅝ In.	984
Vase, Fairyland Luster, Candlemas Pattern, 3 Panels, Candles, Fairies, Bell Pull, 9 In...............	5036
Vase, Fairyland Luster, Firbolgs, Maroon, Green Luster Interior With Dolphins, 8⅝ In.............	748
Vase, Green Jasper Dip Portland, White Classical Figures In Relief, 1800s, 10½ In.................	984
Vase, Hummingbird, Blue Mottled Luster Ground, Gilt, c.1910, 9 In.	470
Vase, Jasper Dip, Black Portland, Classical Figures, 1800s, 10⅛ In.........................	1599
Vase, Jasper Dip, Green, Portland, White Figures, Handles, Marked, c.1890, 10 In. ....*illus*	1599
Vase, Jasper Dip, Moonflask, Lilac, Green Medallions, Prunus Branches, 1800s, 6 In.	1968
Vase, Jasper Dip, Tricolor, Pilgrim, Flat Circular Form, Medallions, 1800s, 5¾ In.	1169
Vase, Jasper Dip, Tricolor, White, Applied Lilac, Green Relief, Early 1900s, 13⅝ In., Pair..........	2583
Vase, Jasper, Black, Applied Classical Figures, Handles, Thomas Lovatt, c.1880, 10 In........*illus*	5843
Vase, Jasperware, Blue, Neoclassical Roman Motifs, 10 In.	875
Vase, Jasperware, Dark Blue, Drum Base, Classical Muses, Flower Frames, Late 1800s, 9½ In. ...	2091
Vase, Jasperware, White, Blue Figures, Shouldered, Handles, Flared, c.1980, 10 In.....................	1599
Vase, Jasperware, White, Portland, 1800s, 6⅝ In.........................	200
Vase, Lid, Black Basalt, Leaf & Palm Design, Classical Figures, Relief, c.1850, 22 In.	9840
Vase, Lid, Jasper Dip, Tricolor, Engine-Turned Black Center, Yellow Border, c.1880, 12 In.	2706
Vase, Lid, Light Blue Jasper, Loop Handles, Urn Finial, Muses, Apollo, Early 1800s, 18 In.........	1845
Vase, Lid, Victoria Ware, White Relief, Deep Teal, Gold, c.1880, 11¼ In.	3321
Vase, Majolica, Teal With Green, Brown, Gray, Flower Handles, Goat Heads, c.1863, 31 In.	492
Vase, Potpourri, Moonlight Luster, Footed, 1800s, 13 In., Pair..........................*illus*	1020

Weller, Ardsley, Bowl, Kingfisher Flower Frog, Bowl 16½ In., Kingfisher 8⅝ In. $236

Humler & Nolan

Weller, Baldwin Apple, Umbrella Stand, Marked, 22 In. $677

Cowan's Auctions

Weller, Frosted Matte, Cigar Holder, Mottled Blue Glaze, 2 x 6¼ In. $236

Humler & Nolan

TIP

Don't store ceramic dishes or figurines for long periods of time in old newspaper wrappings. The ink can make indelible stains on china.

W

Weller, Gardenware, Sprinkler, Frog, Coppertone Glaze, Blade, Hose Fitting, 7¾ In.
$1,770

Humler & Nolan

Weller, Muskota, Flower Frog, 4 Blue Flowers, Impressed Mark, 1¾ x 4½ In.
$106

Humler & Nolan

Weller, Muskota, Flower Frog, Pagoda, Impressed Mark, 6¼ In.
$213

Humler & Nolan

Weller, Sicard, Vase, Morning Glory, Blue, Green, Purple, Impressed Mark, Signed, 10¼ In.
$944

Humler & Nolan

Weller, Sicard, Vase, Poppies, Lobed, Signed, Stamped, 1903, 11 x 6½ In.
$2,125

Rago Arts and Auction Center

Westmoreland, Candy Dish, Lid, Blue Milk Glass, Shell Finial, Argonaut Dolphin Feet, 6 x 5 In.
$68

Ruby Lane

Vase, Tricolor Jasper, Dancing Hours, Lid, Bacchus Mask Handles, c.1900, 8 3/8 In. 1107
Vase, Urn Shape, Portland, Double Handles, White On Blue, Stamped, c.1850, 10 In. 875
Vase, Victoria Ware, Dark Teal Blue, Gilded Trim, Bacchus Head Handles, c.1880, 6 3/4 In. 431

WELLER pottery was first made in 1872 in Fultonham, Ohio. The firm moved to Zanesville, Ohio, in 1882. Artwares were introduced in 1893. Hundreds of lines of pottery were produced, including Louwelsa, Eocean, Dickens Ware, and Sicardo, before the pottery closed in 1948.

LOUWELSA WELLER

Ardsley, Bowl, Kingfisher Flower Frog, Bowl 16 1/2 In., Kingfisher 8 5/8 In........................*illus* 236
Baldwin Apple, Umbrella Stand, Marked, 22 In. ....*illus* 677
Bowl, Mottled Pale Blue, Brown, 5 1/2 In.. 120
Coppertone, Tray, Frog & Lily, Marked, 2 3/8 x 6 3/8 In... 288
Coppertone, Vase, Blue, Brown, Crystalline, Tapered Oval, Pedestal Foot, c.1910, 8 In............. 1500
Coppertone, Vase, Frog, Lily Pad, c.1925, 4 In.. 106
Dickens Ware, Vase, Little Bo Peep & Her Sheep, Marked, 17 7/8 In. 1495
Dickens Ware, Vase, Squirrel, Tree Branch, Black, Cylindrical, Ring Neck, Flared Rim, 11 In. 590
Eocean Rose, Vase, Pale Green, Purple Thistle, Tubular, 3 Square Cutout Handles, 16 In........ 3235
Eocean, Vase, Mushrooms, Jar, Shouldered, Flared Collar, Ringed Neck, Pink, Green, 6 In. 266
Etched Matte, Vase, Pale Orange, Yellow Leaves, Berries, Tapered, Round Bottom, 9 In. 590
Figurine, Dog, Pop-Eye, White, Painted Features, Marked, c.1910, 4 x 4 In., Pair..................... 688
Figurine, Rabbit, Garden Ornament, Brown, 7 3/4 x 12 In., Pair 1625
Forest, Jardiniere, Base, Woodland, Brown, Green, Blue, 19 1/4 In., Pair.............................. 1476
Frosted Matte, Cigar Holder, Mottled Blue Glaze, 2 x 6 1/4 In. ....*illus* 236
Fru Russet, Vase, Molded Wheat, Mottled Green Glaze, Elongated Oval, 12 In. 2006
Gardenware, Figure, Squirrel, Seated, Eating Nut, Cream & Rust Matte, 11 3/4 In.................... 354
Gardenware, Sprinkler, Frog, Coppertone Glaze, Blade, Hose Fitting, 7 3/4 In.....................*illus* 1770
Glendale, Vase, 2 Parakeets, Perched, Green, Pink, Blue, Tapered, Shouldered, 9 In................. 266
Hudson, Vase, Peacock, Perched, Cascading Feathers, Pale Blue, Pink, 16 In.......................... 1180
Hudson, Vase, Wild Roses, Red On Red, Deep Plum Color, Bulbous, 6 1/4 In................................ 767
Hunter, Vase, Flying Duck, Green, Yellow, Round, Pinched Neck, Square Rim, 6 In. 118
Jap Birdimal, Vase, 4-Sided, Trees & Goose, Marked, 4 1/4 In.. 403
Jap Birdimal, Vase, Pale Blue, White Geese, Flying, Shouldered, Pinched Neck, 4 In................ 177
Knifewood, Bowl, Hunting Dog, Marked, 11 1/2 In... 863
Knifewood, Vase, Goldfinches & Wisteria, 5 1/8 In.. 403
Louwelsa, Vase, Pillow, Clover, c.1900, 3 7/8 x 3 3/4 In.. 95
Matte Ware, Vase, Green, Squat, Ribbed Neck, Flat Rim, Scrolling Square Handles, 5 In......... 177
Matte Ware, Vase, Purple, Yellow, Molded Thistle, Waisted, Twist Handle, 12 In...................... 1180
Mistletoe, Bowl, Lid, Iridescent, 4 Lobes, Quatrefoil Lid, Sicard, 6 x 8 1/2 In...................... 1000
Muskota, Flower Frog, 4 Blue Flowers, Impressed Mark, 1 3/4 x 4 1/2 In................*illus* 106
Muskota, Flower Frog, Figural Fish, Curled Up, Green & Yellow, 2 x 3 In.................................... 236
Muskota, Flower Frog, Pagoda, Impressed Mark, 6 1/4 In. ....*illus* 213
Perfecto, Vase, Portrait, Gypsy Woman, Pale Green, Cream, Flared Rim, 13 In......................... 826
Rhead Faience, Humidor, Lid, Curdled Red Glaze, Incised Band, Cutout Handle, 4 x 6 In. 1298
Rhead Faience, Humidor, Lid, Green, Verse, Bell Shape, Ring Foot, Loop Handles, 4 In........... 354
Sicard, Vase, Chrysanthemums, Iridescent, Tapered, Tubular Neck, c.1910, 15 In. 2750
Sicard, Vase, Chrysanthemums, Stylized, Gold Iridescent, Swollen, 18 x 5 In........................... 2000
Sicard, Vase, Clover, Blue Iridescent, Ruffled Fan Form, 2 Wavy Handles, 6 x 10 In. 1125
Sicard, Vase, Clover, Iridescent Drapery, Tapered, Raised Ear Handles, 6 1/2 x 6 In.................. 1063
Sicard, Vase, Mistletoe, Turquoise, Green, Saucer Shape, Short Cylindrical Neck, 3 In. 295
Sicard, Vase, Morning Glory, Blue, Green, Purple, Impressed Mark, Signed, 10 1/4 In.........*illus* 944
Sicard, Vase, Pink, Green, Gold Iridescent, Leaves, Bulbous, Tube Neck, Flare Rim, 15 In........ 2950
Sicard, Vase, Poppies, Lobed, Signed, Stamped, 1903, 11 x 6 1/2 In. ....*illus* 2125
Sicard, Vase, Poppy, Pink, Gold, Crystalline, Freeform, Double Loop Wavy Handles, 5 In......... 826
Silvertone, Vase, Fruit Blossoms, Stem, Mottled Blue, Arched Handles, 8 In. 266
Umbrella Stand, Classical Figures, Octagonal, Relief, 22 1/4 In... 156
Umbrella Stand, Square, Panels, Scalloped Rim, Brown Glaze, Palm Leaves, 1900s, 24 In..... 180
Vase, Cherry Blossom, c.1925, 9 3/4 In. 275
Vase, Frog & Lily Pad, Green, Yellow, 1925, 4 In. 106
Vase, Green Matte, Twist, Glazed With Crystallization, 5 1/8 In.. 230

Westmoreland, Scales, Bowl, Aqua, Opalescent, 8 1/2 In.
$81

Strawser Auction Group

Wheatley, Vase, Canteen, Wild Roses, Daisy, Blue Ground, Marked, 1880, 11 3/4 In.
$354

Humler & Nolan

Wheatley, Vase, Seashells, Seaweed, Palissy, Incised, 1882, 12 x 6 In.
$1,188

Rago Arts and Auction Center

W

Willets, Vase, Pink Roses, Leaves, Belleek, 15 ½ In.
$1,795

Ruby Lane

Willow, Biscuit Jar, Bridge, Birds, Willow Tree, Brass Mount, Ye Olde, c.1950, 6 ¾ In.
$61

Leland Little Auctions

Window, Stained, Munich Child Design, Hand Painted, Colored Panel Border, 13 In. Diam.
$780

The Stein Auction Company

WEMYSS ware was first made in 1882 by Robert Heron, the owner of Fife Pottery in Kirkaldy, Scotland. Large colorful flowers, hearts, and other symbols were hand painted on figurines, inkstands, jardinieres, candlesticks, buttons, pots, and other items. Fife Pottery closed in 1932. The molds and designs were used by a series of potteries until 1957. In 1985 the Wemyss name and designs were obtained by Griselda Hill. The Wemyss Ware trademark was registered in 1994. Modern Wemyss Ware in old styles is still being made.

Bowl, Plums, Purple Fruit, Green Leaves, Plum Border, c.1910, 8 ¾ In.	225
Figurine, Cat, Seated, Cabbage Roses, White Ground, Brian Adams Exon, 13 In.	591
Figurine, French Bulldog, Cabbage Roses, Brian Adams Exon, 15 ¾ In.	1332
Figurine, Pig, Ears Up, Clover, 17 ½ In.	400
Figurine, Pig, Seated, Red Clover, Red Flowers, Green Leaves, c.1900, 4 x 7 In.	312
Figurine, Pig, Sleeping, Green Plums, Pale Pink Ground, 6 ½ In.	221
Inkwell, Dog Roses, Red Flowers, Green Leaves, Heart Shaped, c.1900, 2 x 7 In.	352
Jug & Basin, Cabbage Roses, Pink, Green Leaves, c.1890, 9 In.	1680
Pitcher, Canterbury Bells, Purple Flowers, Green Leaves, c.1900, 6 In.	656
Saltshaker, Pig, Posies, White, Pink Flowers & Green Leaves, Plump Porker, 3 x 5 In.	128
Tray, Comb, Jazzy, Pink Roses, Multicolor Ground, 10 x 8 In.	29
Tray, Vanity, Cabbage Roses, Ivory, Pink, Green, Canted Corners, 1899, 10 x 8 In.	505
Vase, Thistle, Purple Blooms, Green Stems & Leaves, Beaker, 6 In.	467

WESTMORELAND GLASS was made by the Westmoreland Glass Company of Grapeville, Pennsylvania, from 1889 to 1984. The company made clear and colored glass of many varieties, such as milk glass, pressed glass, and slag glass.

Argonaut Shell, Sugar, Lid, Milk Glass, Dolphin Feet, Finial, 6 x 6 In.	31
Ashburton, Goblet, Golden Sunset, 6 ¼ In.	15
Ashburton, Wine, Golden Sunset, 5 ¼ In.	12
Ashburton, Wine, Yellow, 5 In.	21
Beaded Swirl & Ball, Cruet, Stopper, 5 ¼ In.	35
Beaded Swirl, Sugar & Creamer	62
Candy Dish, Lid, Blue Milk Glass, Shell Finial, Argonaut Dolphin Feet, 6 x 5 In. ....*illus*	68
Cherry, Sugar & Creamer	57
Della Robbia, Sugar & Creamer, Flashed, Apples, Grapes, Pears	48
Della Robbia, Sugar & Creamer, Milk Glass	22
Doric, Compote, Cream, Ruffle Rim, Scroll Feet, Round Base, c.1955, 5 In.	18
Doric, Dish, Sweetmeat, Compote, Ruffled Edge, 5 x 5 In.	35
Eggcup, Whimsical Chick, Milk Glass, Painted Feet, Eyes, Beak & Tail Feather, 3 In., Pair	17
English Hobnail, Goblet, 6 ⅛ In.	10
English Hobnail, Salt Dip, 3 In.	12
English Hobnail, Sherbet, 3 ½ In.	5
Fruits, Punch Bowl Set, Bowl, Stand, Cups, Milk Glass, 9 Piece	189
Lily Of The Valley, Vase, Milk Glass, Flared, 7 In.	17
Old Quilt, Dish, Sweetmeat, Milk Glass, 4 ⅛ In.	12
Old Quilt, Honey, Lid, Milk Glass	12
Old Quilt, Juice, Milk Glass, 5 Oz.	28
Old Quilt, Punch Cup, Milk Glass, 2 ⅜ In.	11
Old Quilt, Sugar & Creamer, Milk Glass	35
Paneled Grape, Basket, Ruby Iridescent, Ruffled Rim, c.1980, 12 In.	120
Paneled Grape, Candlestick, Milk Glass, 4 In.	10
Paneled Grape, Pitcher, Pt.	21
Paneled Grape, Salt & Pepper, Milk Glass	48
Paneled Grape, Vase, Scalloped, Footed, Milk Glass, 9 ½ In.	26
Pearly Dots, Bowl, Marigold, Iridescent, 9 ¼ In.	38
Princess Feather, Bonbon, Amber, Crimped Rim, c.1960, 8 In. Diam.	26
Scales, Bowl, Aqua, Opalescent, 8 ½ In. ....*illus*	81
Shell & Jewel, Bowl, Footed, 8 ½ In.	53
Swan, Sugar, Milk Glass, Lid	23
Thousand Eye, Cup & Saucer, Footed	28

Thousand Eye, Rose Bowl, c.1934, 7 ½ x 5 ¾ In.	55
Three Ball, Cake Plate, 14 In.	39

WHEATLEY POTTERY was founded by Thomas J. Wheatley in Cincinnati, Ohio. He had worked with the founders of the art pottery movement, including M. Louise McLaughlin of the Rookwood Pottery. He started T.J. Wheatley & Co. in 1880. That company was closed by 1884. Thomas Wheatley worked for Weller Pottery in Zanesville, Ohio, from 1897 to 1900. In 1903 he founded Wheatley Pottery Company in Cincinnati. Wheatley Pottery was purchased by the Cambridge Tile Manufacturing Company in 1927.

Tile, Tree Of Life, Brown, Green, White Ground, Round, 6 In.	488
Vase, Black & Green Streaked, Molded Cherry Blossoms, Tapered, 1880, 18 In.	1000
Vase, Canteen, Wild Roses, Daisy, Blue Ground, Marked, 1880, 11 ¾ In. ....*illus*	354
Vase, Frog, Molded, Green Mottled Glaze, Spherical, Rolled Rim, c.1905, 9 x 7 In.	3000
Vase, Leaves & Buds, Golden Yellow Glaze, Speckles, Angular Feet, c.1905, 12 In.	1875
Vase, Leaves & Buds, Green Glaze, Mottled, Squat, Cylindrical Neck, c.1905, 10 In.	1875
Vase, Olive Green, Celadon Streak, Molded Blue Iris, Squat, Cylinder Neck, 1880, 9 In.	750
Vase, Peonies, Gray To Black Heavy Slip Glaze, 1879, 13 In.	531
Vase, Seashells, Seaweed, Palissy, Incised, 1882, 12 x 6 In. ....*illus*	1188

WHIELDON was an English potter who worked alone and with Josiah Wedgwood in eighteenth-century England. Whieldon made many pieces in natural shapes, like cauliflowers or cabbages, and they are almost always unmarked. Do not confuse it with F. Winkle & Co., which made a dinnerware pattern marked *Whieldon Ware*.

Figurine, Turk, Hands On Hips, Cloak, Turban, c.1760, 5 ⅜ In.	676
Pitcher, Tortoiseware, Creamware, England, c.1750, 3 ½ In.	360

WILLETS MANUFACTURING COMPANY of Trenton, New Jersey, began work in 1879. The company made belleek in the late 1880s and 1890s in shapes similar to those used by the Irish Belleek factory. It stopped working about 1912. A variety of marks were used, most including the name *Willets*.

Pitcher, Brown, Tavern Scene, Serving Woman, Patron, Multicolor, 15 In.	156
Pitcher, Cider, Blackberries, Flowers, Leaves, Scalloped Rim, Belleek, 1880-1909, 7 In.	84
Pitcher, Grapes, Leaves, Belleek, Signed J.B. Greene, 9 x 7 In.	287
Tankard, Grapes, Belleek, 5 ¾ In., Pair	48
Vase, Leaves, Light Green, Brown, Belleek, 13 ½ In.	120
Vase, Pink Roses, Leaves, Belleek, 15 ½ In. ....*illus*	1795

WILLOW pattern has been made in England since 1780. The pattern has been copied by factories in many countries, including Germany, Japan, and the United States. It is still being made. Willow was named for a pattern that pictures a bridge, birds, willow trees, and a Chinese landscape. Most pieces are blue and white. Some made after 1900 are pink and white.

Biscuit Jar, Bridge, Birds, Willow Tree, Brass Mount, Ye Olde, c.1950, 6 ¾ In. ....*illus*	61
Bowl, Vegetable, Peaked Lid, Finial, Square, Shaped Handles, Ironstone, c.1880	125
Creamer, Georgian Shape, Churchill Of England, 3 ⅝ In.	17
Pitcher, Lobed, Cylindrical, Angled Stick-Shape Handle, Gilt Trim, 1881, 6 x 7 In.	155
Platter, Oval, Shaped Rim, 1800s, 22 x 17 In.	395
Teacup, Bulbous, Spherical Handle, Interior Image, c.1908, 3 x 4 In.	65
Teapot, Bulbous, S Spout, Loop Handle, Lid, Round Finial, 1907, 5 x 9 In.	205

WINDOW glass that was stained and beveled was popular for houses during the late nineteenth and early twentieth centuries. The old windows became popular with collectors in the 1970s; today, old and new examples are seen.

Awning, Beveled Glass, Half Hemisphere, 2 Side Lights, 18 x 48 In.	649
Flower Specimens, 12 Panels, 46 x 45 In.	875
Leaded, Alternating Yellow Daisies & Leaves, Portrait Medallions, 59 ¾ x 14 ¼ In., Pair	49

Wood Carving, Bed, Single, Pine, Plywood, Stain, Spindle Head & Footboard, Inscribed, F. Adams, 38 x 77 In.
$500

Neal Auctions

Wood Carving, Eagle, Spread Wings, On Scroll Design, Gold & Black Paint, c.1886, 21 x 43 In.
$3,198

Skinner, Inc.

Wood Carving, Indian Maiden, From Circus Wagon, Samuel Robb, N.Y., 1880s, 57 x 75 In.
$22,420

Hess Auction Group

TIP

When you go away on a driving trip, be sure to cover the window in your garage door so the missing car won't be noticed. New garage doors usually have no window at all, for security reasons.

W

WINDOW

Wood Carving, Madonna & Child, Carved, Painted, Italy, 22½ x 11 x 7 In.
$1,840

Cottone Auctions

Wood Carving, Mask, Hotei, Cutout Eyes, Open Smiling Mouth, Painted, Chinese, c.1900, 15½ In.
$180

Brunk Auctions

Wood Carving, Mirror, Bear, Turned Head, Leg Handle, Black Forest, c.1910, 13 x 6 In.
$510

The Stein Auction Company

Wood Carving, Paperweight, Eagle Head, 1900, 4¼ In.
$216

Ruby Lane

Wood Carving, Plaque, Eagle, Banner, Don't Give Up The Ship, Gold Paint, John Haley Bellamy, 26 In.
$16,335

James D. Julia Auctioneers

Wood Carving, Putto, Painted, Gilt Shawl, Italy, 32 x 15 In.
$1,375

New Orleans Auction Galleries

Wood Carving, Robin, Carved, Painted, A.E. Crowell, Life Size, 6½ x 8½ In.
$3,933

James D. Julia Auctioneers

Wood Carving, San Raphael, Staff With Cross, Painted, New Mexico, Anita R. Jones, 21 In.
$122

Neal Auctions

Leaded, Arched, Jesus's Ascension, Multicolor, 65 In.		1845
Leaded, Arched, Resurrection, Multicolor, 65 In.		2091
Leaded, Art Deco, Geometric, Beveled, Green Frame, 29 x 26¼ In., Pair		324
Leaded, Arts & Crafts, Triangles, Beige, Yellow, 27¼ In.		63
Leaded, Birds, Branches, Leaves, Clear Ground, 60¾ x 35 In.		42
Leaded, Blue, Green, Geometric, Checks, Wood Frame, 72 x 91 In.		437
Leaded, Chevron & Arrow, Frank Lloyd Wright, c.1909, 54 x 16 In., Pair		11599
Leaded, Demilune, Dark Green, Blue, 44 x 24 In.		146
Leaded, Demilune, Flower, Blue, Red, Green, 37 x 20 In.		146
Leaded, Demilune, Flower, Circles, Band, Multicolor, 44 x 23 In.		93
Leaded, Flowers, Braids, Ribbons, Multicolor, Frosted, Frame, 39½ x 19¼ In., Pair		138
Leaded, Flowers, Window Box, Red, Green, 36¾ x 26 In.		163
Leaded, Leaded, Multicolor, Geometric Design, Arched, Frame, 88½ x 30 In., Pair		1875
Leaded, Leaded, Orange, Green, Metal Cage Front, Frame, 1930s, 94 x 48 In., Pair		3970
Leaded, Mountains, Red Roof Church, Animals, 15½ x 34¼ In.		531
Leaded, Poppy, Yellow, Green, Geometric, Prairie School, Frame, 61 x 23 In.		2806
Leaded, Portraits, Head, Shoulders, Multicolor, Oval, 17 x 13 In., 10 Piece		200
Leaded, Prairie School, Yellow, Green, 17¼ x 21 In.		93
Leaded, Prairie Style, Green Slag Glass, Panels, Brown Border, 3 Parts, 18 x 46 In.		228
Leaded, Roundel, Green, Yellow, Pink, Clover Shape, 20½ In.		125
Leaded, Tree, Church, Landscape, Arch, c.1920, 40 x 21 In.		2196
Leaded, Violet Slag Glass, Green Dragonflies, Ruby, Opal Swirl, Metalwork, 14 x 14 In.		472
Neoclassical Scenes, 12 Panes, 45 x 46 In.		295
Stained, Demilune, Cross, 39 x 20 In.		117
Stained, Hollyhocks, Irises, Lily Pads, Bigelow Kennard & Co., c.1920, 29½ x 19½ In.		11250
Stained, Jeweled Kokomo Glass, Flowers, Frame, 1800, 21½ x 36 In.		3894
Stained, Lady Of Shalott, Enid, 36½ x 18½ In., 2 Piece		5000
Stained, Munich Child Design, Hand Painted, Colored Panel Border, 13 In. Diam....illus		780
Stained, Roses & Leaves, Striping, Red, Green, Frame, 1900s, 50 x 15 In., 4 Piece		2625
Stained, Roses, Line Pattern, Prairie Style, Wood Frame, c.1910, 18½ x 28 In., Pair		875
Stained, Slag Glass, Gothic Design, Roundels, Frame, c.1880, 51 x 29 In.		360

WOOD CARVINGS and wooden pieces are listed separately in this book. There are also wooden pieces found in other categories, such as Folk Art, Kitchen, and Tool.

Altar Figure, St. John The Baptist, Carved, Painted, Gilt Loin Cloth, Cross, 1700s, 25 x 12 In.		687
Artist's Figure, Pine, Articulated Arms & Torso, 1900s, 15 x 3 In.		437
Baby, Nude, Hairless, Walking, Painted, Continental, 23 In.		625
Bear, Clothing Hook, Black Forest, Linden, Glass Eyes, Swiss, Early 1900s, 14 In.		1680
Bed, Single, Pine, Plywood, Stain, Spindle Head & Footboard, Inscribed, F. Adams, 38 x 77 In....illus		500
Birds In Cage, Folk Art, Painted, Yellow & Green, Signed, William J. Gottshall, 14 In.		71
Bison, Rosewood, Hand Carved, 11½ x 14¼ In.		271
Bluebird, Carved, Painted, Standing, Gazing Upward, U.S.A., 1800s, 3 x 6 In.		2000
Boy, Mama's Boy, Standing, Geometric, Multicolor, Mary Spain, 15½ x 7½ In.		354
Bust, Man, Trade Figure, Open Mouth, Tongue Out, Turban, Paint, 19 x 10 In.		1185
Bust, Pine, Michelangelo's David, Metal Pole, Bronze Base, Late 1700s, 9 x 7 x 7½ In.		750
Bust, Saint, Cone Hat, Beard, 1900s, 33 x 22 In.		1190
Cactus, Cowboy, Hounds, Relief, Sculptural Panel, Ogden, c.1945, 60 x 44 In.		1230
Canoe, Grooved Gunwales & Prow, Nuu-Chah-Nulth, c.1885, 24 In.		1920
Cherub, Head, Painted, Gilt Open Wings, Stand, Mexico, c.1800, 16 x 13 In.		800
Cleric, Standing, Stern Face, Finely Combed Hair, Walnut, c.1800, 22 In.		300
Cow, Holstein, Folk Art, Painted Wood, Signed, William J. Gottshall, 1984, 6 x 7¾ In.		325
Crane, Flying, Neck Curved, Japan, 1800s, 37 In.		2000
Cutout, Indian Maiden, Pine, Paint, 2-Sided, Silhouette, c.1915, 66 x 14 In.		1680
Dewi Sri, Fertility Goddess, Bust, Nude, Reticulated Crown, 1930s, 15 In.		945
Dolphin, Clark Voorhees, Jr., 18 In.		3600
Duck, Paint & Canvas, Green, White, Red, Signed, W.M. Mosley, 12 In.		118
Eagle, Perched, Closed Wings, Yellow Glass Eyes, Plinth, c.1980, 20 In.		356
Eagle, Pine, Posed For Takeoff, Detachable Wings, c.1900, 19 x 28 In.		593

Wood Carving, Statue, Infant Of Prague, Standing, Gesso, Paint, Glass Eyes, Continental, 1800s, 18 In.
$780

Garth's Auctioneers & Appraisers

Wood Carving, Tankard, Burlwood, Raised Design, Man On Horseback, Lion Thumbpiece, 1800s, 8 In.
$885

Hess Auction Group

Wood Carving, Uncle Sam, Full Body Silhouette, Painted, 70 In.
$153

Hess Auction Group

W

Wood Carving, Valet, Andy Gump, Holding Tray, Cutout Silhouette, Painted, Marked, c.1935, 37 In. $60

Garth's Auctioneers & Appraisers

Wooden, Artist's Model, Woman, Walnut, Brass Ball Joints, Stamped, Paris, 20 x 6 In. $1,250

New Orleans Auction Galleries

Eagle, Spread Wings, On Scroll Design, Gold & Black Paint, c.1886, 21 x 43 In. ....*illus*	3198
Eagle, Spread Wings, Pine, Carved, Brown Stain, 1800s, 12 x 29 In.	400
Eagle, Spread Wings, Walnut, Rocks, Pedestal, X Base, c.1865, 62 x 36 In.	5925
Eaglet, Orange, Green, Blue, Carl Snavely, 4¾ In., Pair	984
Elephant, Walnut, Crass Mount, Raymor, 13 x 14 In.	236
Falconer, Arm Raised, Falcon, Wings Outstretched, 59¾ x 18½ In.	1440
Fish, Butternut, Peaked Fin, Teeth, Beaded, Plinth, E. Offner, 1972, 27 x 29 In.	1722
Heron, White Paint, Standing, Driftwood Base, R. Koeditz, Signed, 16 In.	148
Horse, Leather Tack, Glass Eyes, Child Size, c.1910, 25 x 30 In.	840
Indian Maiden, From Circus Wagon, Samuel Robb, N.Y., 1880s, 57 x 75 In. ....*illus*	22420
Madonna & Child, Carved, Painted, Italy, 22½ x 11 x 7 In. ....*illus*	1840
Mask, 2-Man Mask, John Buck, Signed, 1994, 16½ x 5⅝ x 6⅛ In.	1625
Mask, Bearded Man, 11½ In.	75
Mask, Hotei, Cutout Eyes, Open Smiling Mouth, Painted, Chinese, c.1900, 15½ In. ...*illus*	180
Mask, Shiva, Hindu God, Growling, Teeth, Hand Carved, Painted, 1800s, 19 x 13 In.	3000
Michael, Archangel, Wood, Paint, Metal Sword, Tin Scales, Plinth, 1700s, 26 In.	780
Milliner's Head, Fruitwood, Incised Features, 1900s, 9 x 5½ x 7 In.	406
Mirror, Bear, Turned Head, Leg Handle, Black Forest, c.1910, 13 x 6 In. ....*illus*	510
Model, Cow & Suckling Calf, Boxwood, c.1900, 7 x 3 x 6 In.	950
Monkey, Seated On Cat Creature, Tombat Obat, Medicine Container, 20 In.	201
Monkey, Sitting, Joseph Constant, Ukraine, 1892-1969, 13 In.	750
Motorcycle, Stained, Movable Steering Column & Wheel, Stand, 17 x 27 In.	593
Mountain Grouse, Paint, Glass Eyes, Base, Okey J. Canfield, 11 x 18 In.	156
Night Watchman, Black Forest, Linden, Lantern Light, Germany, Mid 1900s, 32½ In.	450
Night Watchman, Black Forest, Linden, Working Lantern, Germany, Late 1900s, 16½ In.	156
Nude Torso In Motion, Benson Whittle, 30 x 19 In.	472
Nude Woman With Wide Eyes, Folk Art, Early 1900s, 18½ In.	180
Nude, Kneeling, Hand On Head, 18 In.	360
Owl, Modernist, E. Volterrani, 16 In.	531
Panel, Capitol, Flag, Flower, 34 x 48 In.	3660
Panel, Crouching Tiger, Bamboo Groove, 9 x 21 In.	54
Panel, Neoclassical, Mahogany, Arched Top, Urn, Fruit, Acanthus, 14½ x 4½ In., Pair	236
Panel, Relief, Oak, Rubenesque Woman, 33 In.	238
Paperweight, Eagle Head, 1900, 4¼ In. ....*illus*	216
Parrot, Paint, Glass Eyes, Perched, Newel Post Base, Okey J. Canfield, 21 In.	375
Pieta, Virgin Mary, Holding Christ, 24 In.	3000
Plaque, Eagle With Shield, Spread Wings, Gilt Paint, c.1890, 6 x 26 In.	2667
Plaque, Eagle, Banner, Don't Give Up The Ship, Gold Paint, John Haley Bellamy, 26 In. ...*illus*	16335
Plaque, Eagle, Bellamy Style, White, Don't Give Up The Ship, 16½ In.	780
Plaque, Eagle, Clutching Crossed Arrows, Shield, Pine, c.1850, 10 x 26 In.	1659
Plaque, Eagle, Live & Let Live, Artistic Carving Co., 25 x 73 In.	3900
Plaque, Eagle, Live Free Or Die, Multicolor, 48½ In.	1680
Plaque, Eagle, Pine, Arrow, 23¾ In.	660
Plaque, Eagle, Spread Wings, Banner In Beak, Flag, Gilt, Paint, c.1910, 25 x 72 In.	1778
Plaque, Lion, Relief, Andrew Langone, Signed, New England, 1909, 10¾ x 5¾ In.	90
Plaque, Pine, Paint, Geometric Star Carvings, Cross, Multicolor, 1900s, 9 x 10 In.	219
Plaque, Walnut, Grotesque Mask, Sea Serpents, 12½ x 36 In.	369
Putto, Painted, Gilt Shawl, Italy, 32 x 15 In. ....*illus*	1375
Rainbow Trout, Multicolor, Hook, Driftwood, Marked Anthony, 23¾ x 23 In.	250
Robin, Carved, Painted, A.E. Crowell, Life Size, 6½ x 8½ In. ....*illus*	3933
San Raphael, Staff With Cross, Painted, New Mexico, Anita R. Jones, 21 In. ....*illus*	122
Santo, St. Dominic, Glass Eyes, Multicolor, 34 In.	570
Screech Owl, Paint, Perched On Curved Branch, Oval Base, Artist Plaque, 11 In.	237
Sculpture, Hollow Sphere, Silver Maple, Signed, John Jordan, c.1988, 6¾ x 9 In.	460
Sculpture, Interlocking, 2 Links, Signed Marie Clark, 16 x 10 In.	554
Shaman, Transforms Into Winged Being, Round Base, c.1900, 6 x 9 In.	480
Shelf, Castle, Black Forest, Linden, Germany, Mid 1900s, 21 x 13 x 6 In.	168
Songbird, Folk Art, Signed, Joseph Moyer, Berks County, Pa., 1889, 3½ In.	295
Songbird, Perched On Finial Pedestal, Painted, 8 In.	649
Songbirds, Fungus Base, Multicolor, 15 In.	295

W

Sphinx, Reclining, Spheres In Hands, Red & Green Paint, 1900s, 18 x 29 In.	405
St. John The Baptist Holding Shell, Fruitwood, Late 1800s, 20 ½ In.	738
Statue, Infant Of Prague, Standing, Gesso, Paint, Glass Eyes, Continental, 1800s, 18 In. ...*illus*	780
Statue, Jesus, Paint, Penitente Gown, Cross, Crown, Mexico, c.1865, 43 In.	1230
Statue, Madonna, Carved Wood, Paint, Glass Eyes, Round Pedestal, Spain, 1700s, 27 In.	984
Statue, St. Joseph, Painted, Standing, Square Base, Turned Feet, 1700s, 32 In.	600
Tankard, Burlwood, Raised Design, Man On Horseback, Lion Thumbpiece, 1800s, 8 In. ...*illus*	885
Temple Guard, Scroll, Paintbrush, Stepped Base, Japan, 25 ⅝ x 20 ⅜ In.	3660
Temple Guard, Standing, Arm Out, Rocky Base, Japan, 20 x 15 ½ In.	3050
Thunderbird, Spread Wing, Multicolor Paint, C. James, c.1900, 6 x 10 In.	360
Tiger, Mouth Open & Teeth Bared, Rocky Incline, Folk Art, 1900s, 32 x 29 In.	123
Totem Pole, Eagle On Top, Wings Outstretched, 70 x 31 In.	555
Uncle Sam, Full Body Silhouette, Painted, 70 In. ......*illus*	153
Valet, Andy Gump, Holding Tray, Cutout Silhouette, Painted, Marked, c.1935, 37 In. ....*illus*	60
Walnut, Ash, Walnut, 2 Pieces, Signed, Jon Brooks, 1973, 17 x 21 In.	2250
Whale, Clark Voorhees, Jr., 17 In.	3000
Woman, Allegorical, Primavera, Milton Hebald, 1974, 74 x 25 In.	826
Woman, Supplicant, Kneeling Red Draping, Continental, 9 ½ In.	281
Woman's Head, Spalted Maple, Ward, Signed, Late 1900s, 26 x 15 ½ x 11 ½ In.	1000

WOODEN wares were used in all parts of the home. Wood was used for many containers and tools. Small wooden pieces are called *treenware* in England, but the term *woodenware* is more common in the United States. Additional pieces may be found in the Advertising, Kitchen, and Tool categories.

Apple Tray, Red Paint, Flared Sides Rectangle, Molded Rim & Base, 1800s, 3 x 12 In.	295
Artist's Model, Woman, Walnut, Brass Ball Joints, Stamped, Paris, 20 x 6 In. ....*illus*	1250
Artist's Model, Bakelite Limbs, Steel Joints, Atsco Oscar, 1930s, 32 x 8 In.	2375
Artist's Model, Fruitwood, Woman, Articulated, Ball Joints, 1800s, 26 x 7 In.	593
Artist's Model, Horse, Articulated, Carved Walnut, France, Late 1800s, 20 x 26 x 8 In.	7500
Artist's Model, Pine, 1 Bone Leg Prosthetic, England, 1800s, 25 ½ x 6 ½ In.	812
Artist's Model, Pine, Ball Joints, Incised Features, England, 38 ½ In. ....*illus*	7500
Artist's Model, Pine, Facial Features, Articulated, Ball Joints, Early 1800s, 19 x 5 ½ In.	1250
Artist's Model, Woman, Geometric, Articulated, Ball Joints, 22 ¼ In.	593
Barrel, Rundlet, Oak, Inscribed E.G., 1807, 5 x 6 ¼ In.	420
Bowl, American Treen, Dark Blue Paint On Exterior, 1800s, 4 ½ x 16 ½ In.	406
Bowl, American Treen, Green Paint On Exterior, 1800s, 5 x 16 In.	360
Bowl, Ash, Round, Carved Handles, 20 In.	2460
Bowl, Ashleaf Maple, Edward Moulthrop, c.1985, 9 ½ x 10 ½ In.	5000
Bowl, Burl Walnut, Carved, Footed, Overhung Rim, Early 1900s, 8 ½ x 22 ½ In.	1920
Bowl, Burl, Carved, Oval, Upswelled Ends, 1800s, 7 ¼ x 17 ⅞ x 13 ½ In.	1600
Bowl, Burl, Carved, Wide Rim, Curved Faceted Handle, 1800s, 10 x 19 In.	16000
Bowl, Burl, Flared, Turned, Collared Rim, Low Foot, 2 ¼ x 7 In.	338
Bowl, Burl, Petal Shape, Alligatored Varnish, Late 1800s, 2 ¼ x 7 ½ In.	780
Bowl, Burl, Plugged Center Hole, 1800s, 2 x 5 In.	240
Bowl, Burl, Turned, 2 Rectangular Handles, 10 x 20 ½ In.	2280
Bowl, Burl, Turned, Incised Rings, Wide Rim, 1800s, 4 x 9 In.	840
Bowl, Burlwood, Turned, Molded Rim, c.1810, 5 ¾ x 16 In. ....*illus*	1888
Bowl, Cherry, Edward Moulthrop, c.1975, 5 ¾ x 10 ½ In. ....*illus*	3438
Bowl, Double Incised Lines, Raised Lip, Patina, 18 x 7 In. ....*illus*	2,091
Bowl, Loblolly Pine, Round, Matt Moulthrop, 12 ¾ In.	600
Bowl, Mother-Of-Pearl, Bird Shape Handles, 17 ½ In.	420
Bowl, Pine, Trencher, Single Handle, Original Surface, Early 1800s, 5 ¾ x 27 ½ In.	330
Bowl, Pine, Turned, 1800s, 5 ½ x 14 In.	351
Bowl, Treen, White Paint On Exterior, Late 1800s, 25 In.	720
Bowl, Tulipwood, Figured, Edward Moulthrop, c.1975, 8 ¾ x 15 ¼ In.	3438
Bowl, Turned Maple, Original Red Paint On Exterior, 1800s, 16 ½ x 4 ¼ In.	240
Bowl, Turned Painted, Salmon, American, Early 1800s, 10 ¾ x 27 ½ In.	1955
Bowl, Wild Cherry Burl, Shallow & Flared, Philip Moulthrop, 10 ¾ In.	660
Brushpot, Bamboo, Relief, Landscape, Figures, Animals, Cylindrical, 6 In.	8888

Wooden, Artist's Model, Pine, Ball Joints, Incised Features, England, 38 ½ In.
$7,500

New Orleans Auction Galleries

Wooden, Bowl, Burlwood, Turned, Molded Rim, c.1810, 5 ¾ x 16 In.
$1,888

Hess Auction Group

Wooden, Bowl, Cherry, Edward Moulthrop, c.1975, 5 ¾ x 10 ½ In.
$3,438

Los Angeles Modern Auctions

W

This is an edited listing of current prices. Visit **Kovels.com** to check thousands of prices from previous years and sign up for free information on trends, tips, reproductions, marks, and more.

Wooden, Bowl, Double Incised Lines, Raised Lip, Patina, 18 x 7 In.
$2,091

Cowan's Auctions

Wooden, Candle Dipper, Round, Hooks, Handle, Pennsylvania, 1800s, 10¼ In.
$248

Hess Auction Group

Wooden, Carrier, Utensil, Brown Paint, Softwood, Curved Wood Handle, 6 x 13½ In.
$36

Hess Auction Group

Wooden, Carrier, Utensil, Softwood, Red Paint, Center Handle, 12½ In.
$71

Hess Auction Group

W

Brushpot, Figures, Flowering Trees, Cylindrical, Chinese, 5 x 3 In.	154
Brushpot, Relief Carved Dragons, Clouds, Temple, Incised & Punched, 9½ In.	185
Bucket, George III, Mahogany, Brass Bound, Swing Handle, 12 In.	468
Bucket, Mahogany & Brass Accents, Brass Handle, George III, Late 1700s, 17 In.	1438
Butter Stamp, Pinwheel, Concentric Circles, Canada, 1800s	200
Candle Dipper, Round, Hooks, Handle, Pennsylvania, 1800s, 10¼ In. ....*illus*	248
Canister, Maple, Treen, Cut Sponge Decoration, Rounded Lid, Bone Finial, 3 x 4 In.	354
Canister, Poplar, Finial, 1800s, 4½ In.	600
Canteen, Blue Paint, Cylindrical, 4 Splint Bands, c.1800, 5 x 7 In.	4500
Canteen, Red Paint, Round, Stave Construction, Ash Bands, Iron Straps, 11 In.	492
Carrier, Utensil, Brown Paint, Softwood, Curved Wood Handle, 6 x 13½ In. ....*illus*	36
Carrier, Utensil, Softwood, Red Paint, Center Handle, 12½ In. ....*illus*	71
Chalice, Lid, Mulberry, Carved Shakespeare Bust, Momento Mori, 1800s, 6¾ In.	594
Child Minder, Barrel Shape, Staves, Iron Bands, Chinese, c.1910, 31 x 26 In. ....*illus*	545
Container, Peaseware, Lid, Knob Finial, Late 1800s, 4½ In.	250
Container, Peaseware, Lid, Missing Bail Handle, Late 1800s, 4 x 3½ In.	120
Container, Peaseware, Lid, Urn Finial, Bail Handle, Late 1800s, 8½ In.	360
Container, Peaseware, Lid, Urn Finial, Bail Handle, Ohio, Late 1800s, 7½ In.	531
Cup, Saffron, Lehnware, Painted, Pomegranate Flowers, Salmon Ground, 3 In.	1476
Cup, Saffron, Lid, Blue Ground, Painted Designs, Pedestal Base, Lehnware, 4⅜ In. ....*illus*	1003
Cup, Saffron, Lid, Poplar, Painted, Strawberry & Thistle Flower, Lehnware, c.1875, 4 In. ....*illus*	189
Dipper, Ladle, Burl, Carved, Round Bowl, Tapered Slight Curve Handle, 1800s, 38 In.	1600
Dish, Red Leopard Maple, Flared, Rounded Rim, Philip Moulthrop, 12½ In.	840
Easel, Mahogany, Carved Laurel Swags & Dolphins, Late 1800s, 83 x 26 x 24 In.	3000
Eggcup, Lehnware, Painted, Strawberries, Blue Ground, Footed, 3 In.	1230
Hand Brush, Folk Carved Face Handle, Wooden Bristles, 1700s, 9 x 4 In.	2100
Hand Mirror, Carved Pine, Square, Shaped Handle, U.S.A., 4 x 10 In.	375
Hibachi, Keyaki Wood, 2 Drawers, Copper Lined, Japan, 1800s, 12¼ x 18¾ x 30¼ In.	240
Lazy Susan, Bubinga Wood, Free-Form Edge, Mira Nakashima, 1997, 29¾ In.	625
Lazy Susan, Mahogany, Round, Fluted Pedestal Base, 6 x 24 In.	270
Loom Board, Mahogany, Heart Cutout, Arched Handle, 23 In.	153
Panel, Carved Giltwood, Pierced, Scholars, Warriors, Lacquer, 17 x 12 In., Pair	366
Pitcher, Oak Barrel Shape, Brass Staves, 20¾ In.	281
Planter, Portrait, Leaves, 1800s, 10¾ x 22 In.	375
Plaque, Shield, Stars & Stripes, Painted, Red, White, Blue, Carved Stars, 31 x 24 In.	472
Plate, J.B. Blunk, c.1975, 11¼ x 11⅞ In.	2500
Salt, Master, Turned, Painted, Flowers, Rolled Rim, Pedestal Dome Foot, Lehnware, 3 In.	944
Salt, Master, Turned, Painted, Pussy Willow, Cup, Pedestal Foot, Lehnware, 4 In.	531
Salt, Turned, Painted, Blue, Short Stem, Wide Turned Foot, c.1810, 2¼ In.	1600
Saucer, Lehnware, Poplar, Turned & Painted, 1888, 3 In.	384
Scepter, Ruyi, Double Gourd Vines, Relief Carved Head & Handle, Zitan, 13 In.	492
Spice Canister, Stacking, Locking Channels On Rims, Banner Labels, 8 In. ....*illus*	212
Sugar Bucket, Lid, Trailing Vines, Iron Bands, Staves, Lehnware, 1800s, 9 x 7 In. ....*illus*	325
Tankard, Carved, Swastika Motif, Plank Design, Tapered, Lid, c.1910, 1 Liter	420
Teapot, Peaseware, Bail Handle, Ohio, Late 1800s, 2½ In.	1320
Tray, George III, Mahogany, Inlay, Round, Ruffled Gallery, 18¼ In.	75
Tray, Mahogany, Brass Bound, Handles, 1950-70, 4 x 22 In.	150
Tray, Mahogany, Georgian, Handles, 20 In.	50
Tray, Maple, Oblong, Carved, 1800s, 20¾ x 11¼ In.	140
Tray, Relief Carved, Palace, Figures, Arabic Writing, Bird & Flower Border, 22 x 16 In.	356
Tray, Walnut, Beaded, Lobed Shape, Flowers, Scrolls, Magenta, 4-Footed, 23¼ x 13⅜ In.	125
Trencher, Softwood, Rectangular, Red Paint, 1800s, 32 In. ....*illus*	189
Tub, Pine, Blue Paint, Steel Hoops, Oval, Stave Constructed, c.1885, 4 x 11 In.	840
Union Shield, Painted, 13 Stars, 13 Stripes, Red, White & Blue, c.1880, 33 x 26 In. ....*illus*	1599
Urn, Flared, Squat Base, Turned Foot, Marked, T.A.D., England, 8½ In., Pair	540
Urn, Lid, Peaseware, Footed, Finial, Signed, Hiram Pease, Late 1800s, 2½ In.	688
Vase, Doughnut Shape, Turning, Figured Tulipwood, Ed Moulthrop, Marked, 6 x 7 In. ......*illus*	2000
Vase, Redwood Burl, Lacy, Swollen, Tapered, Rude Osolnik, 7½ In.	480
Vase, Tulipwood, High Shine, Ed Moulthrop, 4¼ x 8½ In.	1500

Wooden, Child Minder, Barrel Shape, Staves, Iron Bands, Chinese, c.1910, 31 x 26 In.
$545

James D. Julia Auctioneers

Wooden, Cup, Saffron, Lid, Blue Ground, Painted Designs, Pedestal Base, Lehnware, 4 3/8 In.
$1,003

Hess Auction Group

Wooden, Cup, Saffron, Lid, Poplar, Painted, Strawberry & Thistle Flower, Lehnware, c.1875, 4 In.
$189

Hess Auction Group

Wooden, Spice Canister, Stacking, Locking Channels On Rims, Banner Labels, 8 In.
$212

Hess Auction Group

Wooden, Sugar Bucket, Lid, Trailing Vines, Iron Bands, Staves, Lehnware, 1800s, 9 x 7 In.
$325

Hess Auction Group

Wooden, Trencher, Softwood, Rectangular, Red Paint, 1800s, 32 In.
$189

Hess Auction Group

Aviator Goggles
Amelia Earhart's goggles with a cracked lens from a plane crash sold for $17,775 at a 2011 auction.

Wooden, Union Shield, Painted, 13 Stars, 13 Stripes, Red, White & Blue, c.1880, 33 x 26 In.
$1,599

Skinner, Inc.

Wooden, Vase, Doughnut Shape, Turning, Figured Tulipwood, Ed Moulthrop, Marked, 6 x 7 In.
$2,000

Rago Arts and Auction Center

Felix Flies
Did you know Charles Lindbergh took his Felix the Cat toy with him on his solo flight across the Atlantic?

W

WOODEN

Worcester, Teapot, Lid, Globular, Flower Knop, Chinese Figures, 1700s, 5 ½ In.
$215

Skinner, Inc.

Worcester, Vase, Fancy Bird In A Tree, Vines, Birds, Blue Underglaze, 6-Sided, 11 ½ In.
$480

Brunk Auctions

World War II, Airplane Propeller, Black, Marked, Curtis Forg, No. 49112 DWG, 67 x 11 In.
$600

The Stein Auction Company

World War II, Artillery Shell, Wood, Metal, Dummy Cartridge, Marked 329486 B-6BFT, 1943, 35 In.
$192

The Stein Auction Company

World War II, Canteen, Leather Strap, Japan, 8 ½ x 12 In.
$150

Ruby Lane

World War II, Patch, Marine Corps, 1st MAC Raiders, Skull, Red Diamond, Blue, Stars, 3 x 3 In.
$495

Ruby Lane

War Souvenirs

War souvenirs can be dangerous, so if you find or are given a bullet casing, grenade, or any other supposedly safe bit of memorabilia from an armed conflict, have it checked by your local police or fire department. Souvenirs of past wars that have been stored in a hot attic are very unstable and could blow up.

World War II, Sign, Anti-Axis, Blame Them, 3 Dictators, Cardboard, Easel Back, 1940s, 15 x 18 In.
$575

Hake's Americana & Collectibles

World's Fair, Bracelet, 1933, Chicago, Century Of Progress, Cuff, Etched Roundels, Buildings, 1 In.
$75

Ruby Lane

World's Fair, License Plate Topper, 1939, New York, Trylon & Perisphere, 3 x 4 In.
$120

Ruby Lane

Vase, Turned Wood, Mulberry, Signed, Philip Moulthrop, 6 ½ x 13 ½ In.	1500
Vase, Walnut, Black Forest, Banana Tree, Birds, Flowers, Round Base, 14 In., Pair	812
Wastepaper Basket, Rosewood, Tapered, 12 In.	88
Water Pot, Buddha's Hand, Citron, Pomegranates, Chinese, 1800s, 8 In.	62

WORCESTER porcelains were made in Worcester, England, from 1751. The firm went through many name changes and eventually, in 1862, became The Royal Worcester Porcelain Company Ltd. Collectors often refer to Dr. Wall, Barr, Flight, and other names that indicate time periods or artists at the factory. It became part of Royal Worcester Spode Ltd. in 1976. The company was bought by the Portmeirion Group in 2009. Related pieces may be found in the Royal Worcester category.

Basket, Blue, Flowers, Oval, Reticulated, Applied Handle & Flowers, c.1770, 3 x 7 In.	180
Bowl, Fluted, Dragon In Compartments, Flight & Barr, 13 ¾ In.	813
Chalice, Gilt, Blue, Green, Footed, 8 ¾ In.	138
Coffeepot, Double Ogee Lid, Blue, Grasses, Branches, Paneled, Flower Finial, 10 In.	480
Cooler, Lid, Fruit, Fan Designs, Stars, Gilt, Leaf Handles, Twig Finial, 11 In., Pair	1046
Ewer, Cream, Gilt, Flowers, Round Foot, 7 ¾ In.	88
Ink Stand, Blue, Flowers, Rectangular, 4 Sections, Candle Cup, Tab Handles, 3 x 9 In.	420
Jug, Transferware, Blue & White, Cabbage Leaf, England, 1700s, 8 ¾ In.	175
Pitcher, Molded Cabbage Leaf, Mask Spout, Crescent Mark, c.1790, 11 ¾ In.	710
Plate, Oriental Theme, Birds, Leaves, Blue & White, 1900, 8 ½ In., 11 Piece	241
Plate, Sir Joshua Reynolds, Ho Ho Bird, Butterflies, Branches, 1770, 8 In.	780
Platter, Flower Spray, Multicolor, FBB, 23 x 18 In.	225
Teapot, Blue & White, Fence Pattern, 1780-85, 4 ½ x 7 In.	300
Teapot, Lid, Globular, Flower Knop, Chinese Figures, 1700s, 5 ½ In. ....*illus*	215
Tureen, Lid, Flowers, Lobed, Gadrooned Rim, Artichoke Finial, Shell Handles, 7 x 11 In.	360
Vase, Fancy Bird In A Tree, Vines, Birds, Blue Underglaze, 6-Sided, 11 ½ In. ....*illus*	480
Wall Pocket, Cornucopia, Prunus Root Pattern, Dr. Wall, 1758-60, 11 x 6 In., Pair	1080

WORLD WAR I and World War II souvenirs are collected today. Be careful not to store anything that includes live ammunition. Your local police will tell you how to dispose of the explosives. See also Sword and Trench Art.

WORLD WAR I

Bugle, Brass, Wurlitzer, Philadelphia, 9 ½ In.	90
Flag, Blue Star, Red Border, White Ground, Frame, 17 x 22 In.	105
Game, Target, Hunting The Hun, Base, Soldiers, Targets, Box, c.1915, 11 x 16 In.	484
Poster, Army Recruiting, Color Lithograph, Frame, c.1915, 40 ½ In.	129
Poster, Be A U.S. Marine, Soldier Standing, J.M. Flagg, c.1918, 41 x 27 In.	1235
Poster, Bonds, Color Lithograph, Frame, c.1920, 39 ½ In.	152
Poster, Call To Duty, Join The Army, Soldier Playing Trumpet, 1917, 40 x 30 In.	845
Poster, Destroy This Mad Brute, Enlist, King Kong, Woman, 1917, 27 x 42 In.	6958
Poster, Follow The Flag, Enlist In The Navy, James H. Daugherty, 1917, 41 x 28 In.	531
Poster, I Want You For The U.S. Army, Uncle Sam, J.M. Flagg, 1917, 39 x 29 In.	6760
Poster, I Want You For The U.S. Navy, Howard Chandler Christy, 1917, 41 x 27 In.	910
Poster, Join The Navy, Richard Fayerweather Babcock, 1917, 38 x 27 In.	688
Poster, Miss Liberty Sewing Seeds, James Montgomery Flagg, 1918, 34 x 22 ½ In.	437
Poster, Wake Up America Day, J.M. Flagg, 1917, 39 x 27 In.	8750
Ring, Uncle Sam Strangling Kaiser, I Got Him, Shield Design, Silver Luster, c.1916	115
Shovel, German, Wood Handle, Steel Blade, Canvas Case, 19 ½ In.	35
Stickpin, Photos, Leaders Of Central Powers, Celluloid, Tin, Round, c.1916, 1 x 2 In.	239
Trench Lighter, Brass, Pocket Watch Case, Eagle, Spread Wings, Arrows, Shield, c.1910	145

WORLD WAR II

Airplane Propeller, Black, Marked, Curtis Forg, No. 49112 DWG, 67 x 11 In. ....*illus*	600
Artillery Shell, Wood, Metal, Dummy Cartridge, Marked 329486 B-6BFT, 1943, 35 In. ...*illus*	192
Ashtray, Figural Boy, Urinating, Hitler's Face, Octagonal, Brass, 2 In.	127
Ashtray, RAF Squadron, No. 88, Brass, Copper, Match Box Holder, c.1942	115
Binoculars, No. 183, Metal, Swinging Post, Fixed On Tripod, Japan, 18 x 9 In.	1067

> **TIP**
> *Chrome should be cleaned with a mild chrome cleaner, not an abrasive.*

World's Fair, Match Safe, 1892, Chicago, Uncle Sam, Reverse Side American Eagle, 2 ½ In.
$300

Pook & Pook

World's Fair, Vase, 1904, St. Louis, Palace Of Electricity, Blown Milk Glass, Transfer, 14 ½ In.
$162

The Stein Auction Company

Wristwatch, Boucheron, 18K White Gold, Vertical Grooves, Eaglehead Hallmark, Woman's, 6 In.
$687

New Orleans Auction Galleries

W

Wristwatch, Cartier, Tank, Gold
Over Silver, Burgundy Dial, Quartz
Movement, Marked, Box
$2,000

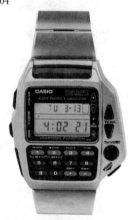

New Orleans Auction Galleries

> **TIP**
> *Replace a broken watch crystal immediately to avoid letting dust or moisture into the watch works.*

Wristwatch, Casio, CMD-40, Digital,
Calculator, c.1994
$104

Auction Team Breker

Wristwatch, Hamilton, 14K Yellow
Gold, Subdial, Manual, 19 Jewel,
Alligator Strap, c.1937
$344

Leslie Hindman Auctioneers

W

534

Bugle, Brass, Red Artillery Cord, Tanabe, Japan, 12½ In.	120
Button, America Wants To Get Hitler, Hanging From Gallows, c.1943, 1 In.	327
Button, Uncle Sam Hanging Hitler, Mechanical, Tin Lithograph, c.1945, 1⅝ In.	152
Cane, Carved Snake Shaft, Painted, 36½ In.	60
Canteen, Leather Strap, Japan, 8½ x 12 In. *illus*	150
Cap, Garrison, Red Piping, Signed By General George S. Patton, Jr., 10¾ x 5 In.	1080
Cigarette Case, Olive Wood, Air Force Wings & Spinning Propeller, 8 Slots	345
Cuspidor, Figural, Hitler, Open Mouth, Arrows To Head, Ceramic, 1940s, 9 x 9 In.	253
Figure, Sailor Baby, Remember Pearl Harbor, Plaster, Paint, 1942, 13 In.	115
Flag, Nazi, Swastika Cross, Wool, Red, White, Black, 20 x 35½ In.	300
Helmet, Africa Corps, Pith, Leather Strap, Liner, 11 x 14 In.	258
Helmet, Leather Chin Strap, Germany, Size 66	240
Helmet, U.S. Marine Corps, Eagle, Globe, Anchor, Leather Lining, Soldier's Name, Chin Strap	225
License Plate, Hit Hitler, Boycott Germany, Embossed Tin, c.1940, 5 x 12 In.	139
Patch, Marine Corps, 1st MAC Raiders, Skull, Red Diamond, Blue, Stars, 3 x 3 In. *illus*	495
Pin, Officer, Hilborn & Hamburger, Sterling Silver, Submarine, Dolphins, 1940s, 3 x 1 In.	68
Poster, Avenge December 7, Sailor, Raised Fist, Pearl Harbor, 1942, 22 x 28 In.	562
Poster, Bombs Away, AAF, C.C. Beall, 1944, 37 x 25 In.	1500
Poster, Build & Fight In The Navy Seabees, John Philip Falter, c.1940, 36 x 25 In.	531
Poster, Give It Your Best, American Flag, Charles Coiner, 1942, 42 x 57 In.	1875
Poster, Keep Em Shooting, Tank, Mead Schaeffer, 1943, 39 x 28 In.	1125
Poster, Keep Him Flying, Buy War Bonds, Georges Schreiber, 1943, 39 x 28 In.	650
Poster, Liberty Lives On, Howard Chandler Christy, 1942, 40 x 26 In.	1000
Poster, Serve In Silence, C.H., c.1940, 22 x 17 In.	293
Poster, We're Moving Up, Keep Those Supplies Coming, Albert Dorne, 1943, 39 x 28 In.	293
Punchboard, Artillery Crew, Shooting German Bomber, 1940s, 11 x 16 In.	127
Sign, Anti-Axis, Blame Them, 3 Dictators, Cardboard, Easel Back, 1940s, 15 x 18 In. *illus*	575
Telephone, Field, Signal Corps, Hand Cranked Generator, Leather Case, c.1940	84
Telescope, U.S. Navy BU Ships, 1942, 30¾ In.	177
Transmitter, U.S Army Signal Corps, Used On Aircraft, Farnsworth, No. 764, 1944	869

WORLD'S FAIR souvenirs from all of the fairs are collected. The first fair was the Great Exhibition of 1851 in London. Some other important exhibitions and fairs include Philadelphia, 1876 (Centennial); Chicago, 1893 (World's Columbian); Buffalo, 1901 (Pan-American); St. Louis, 1904 (Louisiana Purchase); Portland, 1905 (Lewis & Clark Centennial Exposition); San Francisco, 1915 (Panama-Pacific); Philadelphia, 1926 (Sesquicentennial); Chicago, 1933 (Century of Progress); Cleveland, 1936 (Great Lakes); San Francisco, 1939 (Golden Gate International); New York, 1939 (World of Tomorrow); Seattle, 1962 (Century 21); New York, 1964; Montreal, 1967; Knoxville, 1982 (Energy Turns the World); New Orleans, 1984; Tsukuba, Japan, 1985; Vancouver, Canada, 1986; Brisbane, Australia, 1988; Seville, Spain, 1992; Genoa, Italy, 1992; Seoul, South Korea, 1993; Lisbon, Portugal, 1998; Hanover, Germany, 2000; and Aichi, Japan, 2005. Memorabilia of fairs include directories, pictures, fabrics, ceramics, etc. Memorabilia from other similar celebrations may be listed in the Souvenir category.

Ashtray, 1933, Chicago, Firestone Tires, Pink Glass Insert, Rubber Tire, 1¾ x 5¾ In.	153
Ashtray, 1934, Chicago, Copper, Center Of Progress, 3 x 3 In.	14
Bottle, 1939, New York, Milk Glass, Raised Map Of World, Ribbed Neck, Metal Cap, 9 In.	35
Bracelet, 1933, Chicago, Century Of Progress, Cuff, Etched Roundels, Buildings, 1 In. *illus*	75
Button, 1898 Trans-Mississippi Expo, Fatima The Dancing Bear, Circus, 2 In.	403
Charm, 1964, New York, 14K Gold, ⅞ x ¾ In.	130
Glass, 1939, New York, Aviation Building, 4½ In.	40
Lamp, 1904, Louisiana Purchase Exposition, Man, Lighthouse, Metal, 58 In.	2625
License Plate Topper, 1939, New York, Trylon & Perisphere, 3 x 4 In. *illus*	120
License Plate, 1939, San Francisco, Treasure Island	40
Match Safe, 1892, Chicago, Uncle Sam, Reverse Side American Eagle, 2½ In. *illus*	300
Match Striker, 1893, Chicago, Horticultural Building, Silver, Flip Lid, 2⅞ In.	95
Penny, Elongated, 1964, New York,	18
Photo Album, 1962, Seattle, Gold Tone Metal, Century 21, Monorail, Accordion Style, 4 x 3 In.	28

Ring, 1964, New York, Gold Tone Metal, Unisphere, Red & Blue		8
Spoon, 1892, Chicago, White City Building, Sterling Silver, 3 ^{15}/₁₆ In.		48
Textile, 1876, Philadelphia, Skyline, Frame, 21 x 27 ½ In.		175
Vase, 1904, St. Louis, Palace Of Electricity, Blown Milk Glass, Transfer, 14 ½ In.	*illus*	162

WPA is the abbreviation for Works Progress Administration, a program created by executive order in 1935 to provide jobs for millions of unemployed Americans. Artists were hired to create murals, paintings, drawings, and sculptures for public buildings. Pieces are marked *WPA* and may have the artist's name on them.

Sculpture, Head, Man, Wooden, 8 x 16 In. 492

WRISTWATCHES came into use during World War I. Wristwatches are listed here by manufacturer or as advertising or character watches. Wristwatches may also be listed in other categories. Pocket watches are listed in the Watch category.

Baume & Mercier, Hampton, 18K Gold Rectangular Dial, Quartz, Leather, Woman's		375
Boucheron, 18K White Gold, Vertical Grooves, Eaglehead Hallmark, Woman's	*illus*	687
Bulova, 14K White Gold, Hexagon Face, Encrusted Diamonds, Speidel Band, Woman's		84
Cartier, 18K Gold, Stainless Steel, 2-Tone, Octagonal, Burgundy Dial		1062
Cartier, 18K Yellow Gold, White Dial, Crocodile Strap, Signed, Box, Woman's		1875
Cartier, Panthere, 18K Gold, Ivory Dial, Roman Numerals, Date, Quartz		6150
Cartier, Tank Quartz, 18K Gold, White Dial, Black Strap, Marked, Woman's		1375
Cartier, Tank, Gold Over Silver, Burgundy Dial, Quartz Movement, Marked, Box	*illus*	2000
Casio, CMD-40, Digital, Calculator, c.1994	*illus*	104
Hamilton, 14K White Gold, Diamonds, Bracelet, Square, Art Deco, Woman's		797
Hamilton, 14K Yellow Gold, Subdial, Manual, 19 Jewel, Alligator Strap, c.1937	*illus*	344
Hermes, Kelly, Gold Plated Steel, White Dial, Quartz Movement, Leather Strap		554
J. Jurgensen, Silvertone Dial, Dot & Stick Indicators, 14K Gold, Brickwork Band		1046
Longines, 18K White Gold, Diamond, Sapphire, Blue Steel Hands, Woman's		649
Omega, 14K Gold, Oval Face, Brushed Gold Band, Felt Case, Swiss, Woman's, Late 1900s		375
Patek Philippe, 18K Gold, Subdial, 18 Jewel, Leather Strap	*illus*	3500
Patek Philippe, 18K Rose Gold, White Dial, Seconds Dial, Roman Numerals, Leather		10200
Patek Philippe, Calatrava Gold, Ivory Tone Dial, Arabic Numerals, Seconds, Box		7380
Piaget, Gold Tone Dial, Dot Indicators, Diamond Bezel, 18K Gold, Flexible Mesh Band		3321
Piaget, Goldtone Dial, Dot Indicators, Diamond Melee, 18K Gold, Link Band, 1990s		3075
Piaget, Rectangular Dial, 18K Gold, Brickwork Bezel, Leather Strap, Woman's		984
Rolex, Aviator, Stainless Steel, Shockproof, Manual Wind, c.1936		980
Rolex, Cellini, 18K Gold, Gold Dial, Baton Numerals & Hands, Woven Band, Woman's, 1971		2198
Rolex, GMT Master, Stainless Steel, Luminous, 24-Hour, Oyster Bracelet		8303
Rolex, GMT-Master II, Stainless Steel, Screw Case, 31 Jewel, c.1999	*illus*	5500
Rolex, Oyster Perpetual Datejust, 18K Gold, Date Window, Woman's, Box	*illus*	3851
Rolex, Oyster Perpetual, 18K Gold, Gold Dial, Diamond Numerals, Day, Date		7995
Rolex, Oyster, Datejust, 18K Yellow Gold, Diamonds, Signed	*illus*	1125
Rolex, Oyster, Perpetual Datejust, Screw Case, 30 Jewel, Self-Winding, c.1982	*illus*	3750
Rolex, Perpetual Datejust, Diamonds, 18K Gold, Goldtone Dial, Stick Indicators		4920
Tiffany & Co., Rectangular Dial, 15 Jewel, 14K White Gold Mesh Band, Art Deco		1968
Tissot, T-Touch, Stainless Steel, Hands, Digital, Quartz, Fold Clasp	*illus*	113

YELLOWWARE is a heavy earthenware made of a yellowish clay. It varies in color from light yellow to orange-yellow. Many nineteenth- and twentieth-century kitchen bowls and jugs were made of yellowware. It was made in England and in the United States. Another form of pottery that is sometimes classed as yellowware is listed in this book in the Mocha category.

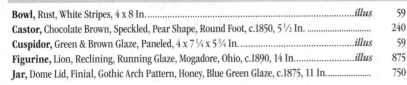

Bowl, Rust, White Stripes, 4 x 8 In.	*illus*	59
Castor, Chocolate Brown, Speckled, Pear Shape, Round Foot, c.1850, 5 ½ In.		240
Cuspidor, Green & Brown Glaze, Paneled, 4 x 7 ¼ x 5 ¾ In.	*illus*	59
Figurine, Lion, Reclining, Running Glaze, Mogadore, Ohio, c.1890, 14 In.	*illus*	875
Jar, Dome Lid, Finial, Gothic Arch Pattern, Honey, Blue Green Glaze, c.1875, 11 In.		750

Wristwatch, Patek Philippe, 18K Gold, Subdial, 18 Jewel, Leather Strap
$3,500

Leslie Hindman Auctioneers

Wristwatches

Early wristwatches were hand-wound. In the early 1950s miniature batteries were invented. The first electric wristwatches were sold in 1957. Miniaturization made the first quartz watches possible in the late 1960s.

Wristwatch, Rolex, GMT-Master II, Stainless Steel, Screw Case, 31 Jewel, c.1999
$5,500

Leslie Hindman Auctioneers

TIP
Wind your watch clockwise. Don't wind it while it is on your wrist.

Wristwatch, Rolex, Oyster Perpetual Datejust, 18K Gold, Date Window, Woman's, Box
$3,851

James D. Julia Auctioneers

Wristwatch, Rolex, Oyster, Datejust, 18K Yellow Gold, Diamonds, Signed
$1,125

New Orleans Auction Galleries

Wristwatch, Rolex, Oyster, Perpetual Datejust, Screw Case, 30 Jewel, Self-Winding, c.1982
$3,750

Leslie Hindman Auctioneers

Mixing Bowl, Blue Mocha Seaweed Band, Rolled Rim, 5 ¾ x 12 In.	153
Mixing Bowl, Blue Mocha Seaweed Band, Rolled Rim, 6 ½ x 13 ¼ In.	130
Mixing Bowl, Wide Rounded Rim, Saucer Foot, Flower Band, 5 x 11 In.	30
Mold, Food, Impressed Rabbit, Oval, 4 x 9 ½ x 6 In.	106
Mug, Blue Mocha Seaweed Band, Cylindrical, Loop Handle, Child's, 3 In.	165
Pitcher, Green, Black, Brown Roses, R. Web & Co., c.1890, 10 ½ In.	575
Platter, 8-Sided, Flat Rim, Marked, Bennett & Brothers, c.1840, 9 ½ In.	1156
Platter, Kendall, Cincinnati, 1800s, 14 x 10 In., Pair	1140
Soap Dish, Rockingham Glaze, Molded Rim, 2 ¼ x 5 ½ In. ....*illus*	59
Teapot, Mottled Glaze, Molded, Rebecca At The Well, Palm Tree, c.1865, 9 In.	630
Teapot, Rockingham Glaze, Beavers, Maple Leaves, Beaver Finial, 6 ½ In.	800

LA MORO   **ZANESVILLE** Art Pottery was founded in 1900 by David Schmidt in Zanesville, Ohio. The firm made faience umbrella stands, jardinieres, and pedestals. The company closed in 1920 and Weller bought the factory. Many pieces are marked with just the words *La Moro.*

Tankard, Grapes Decoration, La Moro, 15 ⅜ In.	460
Vase, Drip Glaze, Dark Green, Brown, Black, Soft Gray Ground, 1920s, 4 x 5 In. ....*illus*	35
Vase, Green Matte Glaze, 6-Sided, Molded, Lyre Scrolls & Leaves, 3 x 5 In.	115
Vase, Tan, Dripping Cobalt Blue Glaze From Rim, Over Shoulder, 27 In.	1416

 ZSOLNAY pottery was made in Hungary after 1853 and was characterized by Persian, Art Nouveau, or Hungarian motifs. A series of new Zsolnay figurines with green-gold luster finish is available in many shops today. Early Zsolnay was not marked, but by 1878 the tower trademark was used.

Bowl, Flowers, Gold Swirls, 2 Maidens On Rim, Eosin Glaze, 6 x 13 In.	7500
Bowl, Red, Speckled, Pedestal, 4 x 6 In.	250
Bowl, Reticulated, Handles, Applied Sides, 4-Footed, 7 x 12 In.	1003
Box, Red Eosin Glaze, Streaked, Lid, Ball Finial, Block Feet, c.1914, 5 x 7 In.	938
Butter Chip, Prince & Princess, Courting Couple, Flowers, 1930s, 3 In., Pair	42
Centerpiece, Bees, Flowers, Reticulated, Multicolor, 1800s, 12 x 19 ¼ In. ....*illus*	708
Ewer, Anthemion & Flowers, Iridescent Gold, 11 ¾ In.	59
Figurine, Bedouin Woman, Eosin Glaze, 1910s, 15 ½ x 6 ½ In.	938
Figurine, Meditazione, Eosin Glaze, c.1930, 15 x 4 ½ x 4 ¾ In.	875
Figurine, Rabbit, Bunnies, Green Iridescent, 3 In.	38
Figurine, Spaniel, Iridescent, Green, Blue, 4 ¾ In.	49
Figurine, Stylized Cat, Marked, 9 ¼ In.	325
Group, Ducks, Green Iridescent, 7 In.	50
Jar, Lid, Stylized Coral Flowers, Beading, Gold Sinewy Stems Form Feet, 10 x 7 x 3 In.	8125
Pitcher, Green, Eosin Glaze, Applied Dragon Handle, 10 x 8 In.	5625
Pitcher, Red Eosin Glaze, c.1887, 15 ½ x 8 In.	1188
Pitcher, Yellowware, Flowers, Double Spout, Handle, 1880, 11 x 8 In. ....*illus*	295
Planter, Teal, Green Swag, Red, 1900s, 17 ⅞ x 17 In.	812
Plaque, Nude Maidens, Satyr, Green, Orange, L. Mack, c.1900, 13 In.	2125
Vase, 3 Lobes, Labrador Glaze, Blue Green, 2 ½ In.	288
Vase, Blue Flowers, Tapered Neck, Twisted Handle, 16 ¾ x 7 ½ In.	654
Vase, Boar Hunting, Green, Brown, Eosin Glaze, Barrel Shape, c.1900, 20 x 16 In.	11250
Vase, Creation Of Adam, Red Ground, Eosin Glaze, Tapered, 5 Churches Mark, 7 x 6 In.	3125
Vase, Gold, Cream, Purple, Green, Leaves, 1880s, 20 In.	1500
Vase, Iridescent Green, Gold, Squat, Tubular Neck, Molded Figure Of Woman, 18 In.	354
Vase, Landscape, Boats, Trees, Eosin Glaze, Marked, 5 Churches, 12 x 5 In.	10625
Vase, Landscape, Classical Buildings, Eosin Glaze, Swollen, 5 Churches Mark, 12 ½ In.	9375
Vase, Landscape, Sunrise, Trees, Eosin Glaze, Purple Sky, Rays, 5 Churches Mark, 9 x 3 In.	16250
Vase, Luster, Marbled, Green, Purple, Gold Ground, c.1900, 7 In.	687
Vase, Stylized Birds, Green, Gold, Tapered, 3 Ribbon Handles Stretched From Rim, 13 In.	9375
Vase, Tulip, Red, Green, 11 x 4 In.	261
Vase, Tulips, Slender Neck, Eosin Glaze, 5 Churches Mark, c.1899, 9 x 4 In. ....*illus*	5625
Vase, Urn, Flower Medallions, c.1920, 10 ½ x 6 In.	1625

Wristwatch, Tissot, T-Touch, Stainless Steel, Hands, Digital, Quartz, Fold Clasp
$113

Yellowware, Bowl, Rust, White Stripes, 4 x 8 In.
$59

Yellowware, Cuspidor, Green & Brown Glaze, Paneled, 4 x 7 ¼ x 5 ¾ In.
$59

Yellowware, Figurine, Lion, Reclining, Running Glaze, Mogadore, Ohio, c.1890, 14 In.
$875

Yellowware, Soap Dish, Rockingham Glaze, Molded Rim, 2 ¼ x 5 ½ In.
$59

Zanesville, Vase, Drip Glaze, Dark Green, Brown, Black, Soft Gray Ground, 1920s, 4 x 5 In.
$35

Zsolnay, Centerpiece, Bees, Flowers, Reticulated, Multicolor, 1800s, 12 x 19 ¼ In.
$708

Zsolnay, Pitcher, Yellowware, Flowers, Double Spout, Handle, 1880, 11 x 8 In.
$295

Zsolnay, Vase, Tulips, Slender Neck, Eosin Glaze, 5 Churches Mark, c.1899, 9 x 4 In.
$5,625

X
Y
Z

INDEX

This index is computer-generated, making it as complete and accurate as possible. References in uppercase type are category listings. Those in lowercase letters refer to additional pages where pieces can be found. There is also an internal cross-referencing system used in the main part of the book, so if you look for a Kewpie doll in the Doll category, you will be told it is in its own category. There is additional information at the end of many paragraphs about where to find prices of pieces similar to yours.

PHOTO CREDITS

We have included the name of the auction house or photographer with each pictured object. This is a list of the addresses of those who have contributed photographs and information for this book. Every dealer or auction has to buy antiques to have items to sell. Call or email a dealer or auction house if you want to discuss buying or selling. If you need an appraisal or advice, remember that appraising is part of their business and fees may be charged.

Accurate Auctions
2900 Jackson Highway
Sheffield, AL 34654
401-390-3139

Alderfer Auction
501 Fairgrounds Rd.
Hatfield, PA 19440
alderferauction.com
215-393-3000

Ahlers & Ogletree Auction Gallery
715 Miami Circle
Suite 210
Atlanta, GA 30324
aandoauctions.com
404-869-2478

Alex Cooper Auctioneers
908 York Rd.
Towson, MD 21204
Alexcooper.com
800-272-3145

Allard Auctions
P.O. Box 1030
St. Ignatius, MT 59865
allardauctions.com
406-745-0500

American Antique Auctions
P.O. Box 344
Palmyra, NJ 08065
americanantiqueauctions.net
856-547-5521

Anderson Americana
P.O. Box 644
Troy, OH 45373
anderson-auction.com
937-339-0850

Antique Reader
41-20B College Point Blvd., 2nd Floor
Flushing, NY 11355
antiquereader.com
718-661-2400

AntiqueAdvertising.com
P.O. Box 247
Cazenovia, NY 13035
antiqueadvertising.com
315-662-7625

Auction Team Breker
P.O. Box 50 11 19
50971 Koeln, Germany
breker.com
207-485-8343

Bertoia Auctions
2141 DeMarco Dr.
Vineland, NJ 08360
bertoiaauctions.com
856-692-1881

Brown Tool Auctions
P.O. Box 737
Watervliet, MI 49098
finetoolj.com
800-248-8114

Brunk Auctions
P.O. Box 2135
Asheville, NC 28802
brunkauctions.com
825-254-6846

Bunte Auction Services, Inc.
755 Church Rd.
Elgin, IL 60123
bunteauction.com
847-214-8423

Burchard Galleries
2528 30th Ave. North
St. Petersburg, FL 33713
burchardgalleries.com
727-821-1167

Burns Auction Service
183 Sunnyside Dr.
Clermont, FL 34711
tomburnsauctions.com
407-592-6552

Case Antiques
2240 Sutherland Ave.
Knoxville, TN 37919
caseantiques.com
865-558-3033

Copake Auction Inc.
P.O. Box 47
Copake, NY 12516
copake.com
518-329-1142

Cottone Auctions
120 Court St.
Geneseo, NY 14454
cottoneauctions.com
585-243-1000

Cowan's Auctions
6270 Este Ave.
Cincinnati, OH 45232
cowanauctions.com
513-871-1670

Crocker Farm
15900 York Rd.
Sparks, MD 21152
crockerfarm.com
410-472-2016

DuMouchelles
409 East Jefferson Ave.
Detroit, MI 48226
dumouchelles.com
313-963-6255

Early American History Auctions
P.O. Box 3507
Rancho Santa Fe, CA 92067
earlyamerican.com
858-759-3290

Early Auction Company
123 Main St.
Milford, OH 45150
earlyauctionco.com
513-831-4833

Fairfield Auction
707 Main St.
Monroe, CT 06468
fairfieldauction.com
203-880-5200

Fenton Art Glass Collectors of America
P.O. Box 384
Williamstown, WV 26187
fentonartglass.com
304-375-6196

Fontaine's Auction Gallery
1485 West Housatonic St.
Pittsfield, MA 01201
fontainesauction.com
413-448-8922

Forsythe's Auctions
206 West Main St.
Russellville, OH 45168
forsythesauctions.com
937-377-3700

Fox Auctions
P.O. Box 4069
Vallejo, CA 94590
foxauctionsonline.com
631-553-3841

Garth's Auctioneers & Appraisers
P.O. Box 369
Delaware, OH 43015
garths.com
740-362-4771

Glass Works Auctions
P.O. Box 38
Lambertville, NJ 08530
glswrk-auction.com
609-483-2683

Hake's Americana & Collectibles
P.O. Box 12001
York, PA 17402
hakes.com
717-434-1600

Heritage Auctions
3500 Maple Ave., 17th Floor
Dallas, TX 75219
ha.com
214-528-3500

Hess Auction Group
768 Graystone Rd.
Manheim, PA 17545
hessauctiongroup.com
717-898-7284

Hudson Valley Auctions
270 Breunig Rd.
New Windsor, NY 12553
hudsonvalleyauctions.com
914-213-0425

Humler & Nolan
225 East Sixth St., 4th Floor
Cincinnati, OH 45202
humlernolan.com
513-381-2041

Jackson's International Auctioneers
2229 Lincoln St.
Cedar Falls, IA 50613
jacksonsauction.com
319-277-2256

James D. Julia Auctioneers
203 Skowhegan Rd.
Fairfield, ME 04937
jamesdjulia.com
207-453-7125

Jeffrey S. Evans & Associates
P.O. Box 2638
Harrisonburg, VA 22801
jefffreyevans.com
540-434-3939

John McInnis Auctioneers
76 Main St.
Amesbury, MA 01913
mcinnisauctions.com
978-388-0400

Kamelot Auction House
4700 Wissahickon Ave.
Philadelphia, PA 19144
kamelotauctions.com
215-438-6990

Kaminski Auctions
117 Elliott St.
Beverly, MA 01915
978-927-2223

Kimballs Auction & Estate Services
169 Meadow St.
Amherst, MA 01002
kimballsauction.com
413-549-8300

Leighton Galleries
112 Franklin Turnpike
Waldwick, NJ 07463
leightongalleries.com
201-327-8800

Leland Little Auctions
620 Cornerstone Ct.
Hillsborough, NC 27278
lelandlittle.com
919-644-1243

Leonard Auction
1765 Cortland Ct., Suite D
Addison, IL 60101
leonardauction.com
630-495-0229

Leslie Hindman Auctioneers
1338 West Lake St.
Chicago, IL 60607
lesliehindman.com
312-280-1212

Los Angeles Modern Auctions (LAMA)
16145 Hart St.
Van Nuys, CA 91406
lamodern.com
323-904-1950

Martin Auction Co.
P.O. Box 2
Anna, IL 62906
martinauctionco.com
864-520-2208

MBA Seattle Auction House
717 South Third St.
P.O. Box 1617
Renton, WA 98057
mbaauction.com
425-235-6345

McMasters Harris Auction Co.
1625 West Church St.
Newark, OH 43055
mcmastersharris.com
800-842-3526

Milestone Auctions
3860 Ben Hur Ave.
Unit 8
Willoughby, OH 44094
milestonesuctions.com
440-527-8060

Morphy Auctions
2000 North Reading Rd.
Denver, PA 17517
morphyauctions.com
717-335-3435

Myers Auction Gallery
1600 4th St. North
St. Petersburg, FL 33704
myersfineart.com
727-823-3249

Neal Auction Co.
4038 Magazine St.
New Orleans, LA 70115
nealauction.com
800-467-5329

New Orleans Auction Galleries
333 St. Joseph St.
New Orleans, LA 70130
neworleansauction.com
504-566-1849

Norman C. Heckler & Co.
79 Bradford Corner Rd.
Woodstock Valley, CT 06282
hecklerauction.com
860-974-1634

North American Auction Co.
34156 East Frontage Rd.
Bozeman, MT 59715
northamericanauctioncompany.com
800-686-4216

Pierre Bergé & Associates
92, Avenue d'Iéna
75116 Paris, France
pba-auctions.com

Pook & Pook
463 East Lancaster Ave.
Downingtown, PA 19335
pookandpook.com
610-269–4040

Potter & Potter Auctions
3759 North Ravenswood Ave., #121
Chicago, IL 60613
potterauctions.com
773-472-1442

Rachel Davis Fine Arts
1301 West 79th St.
Cleveland, OH 44102
racheldavisfinearts.com
216-939-1190

Rago Arts and Auction Center
333 North Main St.
Lambertville, NJ 08530
ragoarts.com
609-397-9374

Replacements, Ltd.
P.O. Box 26029
Greensboro, NC 27420-6029
replacements.com
800-737-5223

Rich Penn Auctions
P.O. Box 1355
Waterloo, IA 50704
richpennauctions.com
319-291-6688

Richard D. Hatch & Associates
913 Upward Rd.
Flat Rock, NC 28731
richardhatchauctions.com
828-696-3440

Robert Edward Auctions
P.O. Box 430
Chester, NJ 07930
robertedwardauctions.com
908-888-2555

Roland Auctioneers & Valuers
80 East 11th St.
New York, NY 10003
rolandsantiques.com
212-260-2000

RSL Auction
P.O. Box 635
Oldwick, NJ 08858
rslauctions.com
908-823-4049

Ruby Lane
381 Bush St., Suite 400
San Francisco, CA 94104
rubylane.com
415-362-7611

Saco River Auction Co.
2 Main St.
Biddeford, ME 04005
sacoriverauction.net
207-602-1504

Selkirk Auctioneers & Appraisers
4739 McPherson Ave.
St. Louis, MO 63108
selkirkauctions.com
314-696-9041

Showtime Auction Services
22619 Monterey Dr.
Woodhaven, MI 48183
showtimeauctions.com
951-453-2415

Skinner Auctioneers & Appraisers
274 Cedar Hill St.
Marlborough, MA 01752
skinnerinc.com
508-970-3000

Sotheby's
1334 York Ave.
New York, NY 10021
sothebys.com
212-606-7000

Stevens Auction Co.
P.O. Box 58
Aberdeen, MS 39730
stevensauction.com
662-369-2200

Strawser Auction Group
200 North Main St.
P.O. Box 332
Wolcottville, IN 46795
strawserauctions.com
260-854-2859

Susanin's Auctioneers & Appraisers
900 South Clinton St.
Chicago, IL 60607
susanins.com
312-832-9800

The Stein Auction Co.
P.O. Box 136
Palatine, IL 60078
TSACO.com
847-991-5927

Theriault's
P.O. Box 151
Annapolis, MD 21404
theriaults.com
800-638-0422

Thomaston Place Auction Galleries
P.O. Box 300
Thomaston, ME 04861
thomastonauction.com
207-354-8141

Tias: The Internet Antique Shop
tias.com
88-653-7883

Time & Again Auction Galleries
1416 East Linden Ave.
Linden, NJ 07036
timeandagaingalleries.com
908-862-0200

Tom Harris Auctions
203 South 18th Ave.
Marshalltown, IA 50158
tomharrisauctions.com
641-754-4890

Treadway Toomey Auctions
c/o Treadway Gallery
2029 Madison Rd.
Cincinnati, OH 45208
treadwaygallery.com
513-321-6742

Treasureseeker Auctions
123 West Bellevue Dr., Suite #2
Pasadena, CA 91105
treasureseekerauction.com
626-529-5775

Turner Auctions + Appraisals
461 Littlefield Ave.
South San Francisco, CA 94080
turnerauctionsonline.com
415-964-5250

Weiss Auctions
74 Merrick Rd.
Lynbrook, NY 11563
516-594-0731
weissauctions.com

Wickliff Auctioneers
12232 Hancock St.
Carmel, IN 46032
Wickliffauctioneers.com
317-844-7253

Wiederseim Associates
P.O. Box 470
Chester Springs, PA 19425
wiederseim.com
610-827-1910

William H. Bunch Auctions & Appraisals
1 Hillman Dr.
Chadds Ford, PA 19317
bunchauctions.com
610-558-1800

Willis Henry Auctions
22 Main St.
Marshfield, MA 02050
willishenry.com
781-834-7774

Wilton Gallery
1444 NE 26th St.
Fort Lauderdale, FL 33305
wiltonauctions.com
954-530-4396

Wm Morford Auctions
RD #2 Cobb Hill Rd.
Cazenovia, NY 13035
morfauction.com
315-662-7625

Woody Auction
P.O. Box 618
317 South Forrest
Douglass, KS 67039
woodyauction.com
316-747-2694

Wright
1440 West Hubbard St.
Chicago, IL 60642
wright20.com
312-563-0020